INDUSTRIAL/ORGANIZATIONAL PSYCHOLOGY
An Applied Approach

7e

MICHAEL G. AAMODT
DCI Consulting and Radford University

WADSWORTH
CENGAGE Learning™

Australia • Brazil • Japan • Korea • Mexico • Singapore • Spain • United Kingdom • United States

WADSWORTH
CENGAGE Learning™

Industrial/Organizational Psychology: An Applied Approach, Seventh Edition
Michael G. Aamodt

Publisher: Jon-David Hague

Senior Acquisitions Editor: Timothy Matray

Editorial Assistant: Lauren K. Moody

Media Editor: Lauren Keyes

Program Manager: Sean Foy

Marketing Communications Manager: Laura Localio

Production Management and Composition: PreMediaGlobal

Art Director: Pamela Galbreath

Manufacturing Buyer: Judy Inouye

Rights Acquisition Specialist: Thomas McDonough

Cover Designer: Chris Miller

Cover Image: © Chris Ryan/Getty Images

For product information and technology assistance, contact us at **Cengage Learning Customer & Sales Support, 1-800-354-9706.**

For permission to use material from this text or product, submit all requests online at **www.cengage.com/permissions.**
Further permissions questions can be e-mailed to **permissionrequest@cengage.com.**

Library of Congress Control Number: 2011934199

ISBN-13: 978-1-111-83997-0

ISBN-10: 1-111-83997-2

Wadsworth
20 Davis Drive
Belmont, CA 94002-3098
USA

Cengage Learning is a leading provider of customized learning solutions with office locations around the globe, including Singapore, the United Kingdom, Australia, Mexico, Brazil, and Japan. Locate your local office at **www.cengage.com/global.**

Cengage Learning products are represented in Canada by Nelson Education, Ltd.

To learn more about wadsworth visit **www.cengage.com/wadsworth.**

Purchase any of our products at your local college store or at our preferred online store **www.cengagebrain.com.**

Printed in the United States of America
1 2 3 4 5 6 7 15 14 13 12 11

This edition is dedicated to my good friend Larry Amy, who put up a valiant fight against throat cancer. His caring manner, great sense of humor, and crazy personality will be missed—as will the dollars he lost every other week with the Charlton Lane poker group.

BRIEF CONTENTS

CONTENTS

Chapter 4   Employee Selection: Recruiting and Interviewing   117

Chapter 7   Evaluating Employee Performance   233

Chapter 10   Employee Satisfaction and Commitment   357

Chapter 11   Organizational Communication   395

Chapter 12   Leadership   429

Chapter 13   Group Behavior, Teams, and Conflict   463

Chapter 14   Organization Development   503

Chapter 15   Stress Management: Dealing with the Demands of Life and Work   541

Appendix   **Working Conditions and Human Factors**   **583**

PREFACE

I can't imagine a career better than industrial/organizational psychology; it has something for everyone. You can be a scientist, a detective, a lawyer, an adviser, a statistician, an inventor, a writer, a teacher, a mentor, a trainer, a high-stakes gambler, a motivator, a humanitarian, and an engineer—all at the same time. In no other field can you experience such challenging opportunities, earn an excellent salary, and derive the satisfaction of bettering the lives of others.

I wrote this book because there was a strong need for a text that would appeal directly to undergraduates without sacrificing scholarship. Our field is so exciting, yet the existing texts do not reflect that excitement. This book contains many real-world examples that illustrate important points; employment profiles that demonstrate the wide variety of I/O career paths; humor to make your reading more enjoyable; and charts and tables that integrate and simplify such complicated issues as employment law, job satisfaction, work motivation, and leadership.

In writing this book, I tried to strike a balance between research, theory, and application. In addition to the fundamental theories and research in I/O psychology, you will find such practical applications as how to write a résumé, survive an employment interview, write a job description, create a performance appraisal instrument, and motivate employees.

For the Student

Two Books in One!

At the request of your instructor, a workbook (ISBN 978-1-133-42343-0) or a statistics primer (ISBN 978-1-133-42344-7) will accompany each new textbook at no additional cost. Each chapter comes with exercises to help you apply what you have learned. Thus, not only will you read about I/O psychology, you will get the opportunity to experience it as well. You will take psychological tests, conduct the critical incident technique, solve case studies, analyze situations, write a résumé, prepare for an interview, and create a structured interview. The text website includes additional materials to help you study: a complete chapter outline, a list of key terms that you can use as flash cards, and a practice exam. Making good grades was never easier!

Student Friendly!

To make your reading easier, humor, stories, and real-world examples are used. The text is written at a level designed to help you understand the material rather than at a level designed to show off the author's vocabulary. The feedback I have received indicates that students actually *enjoy* reading this text!

To help you learn, *innovative charts* such as those found in Chapters 3, 8, 9, 10, and 13 integrate the main points of the chapter. At the beginning of each chapter, a list of *learning objectives* helps organize your thinking for what you are about to read.

On each page, *key terms* are defined in the margins. At the end of each chapter, a *chapter summary* reminds you of the important points you learned, and *critical thinking questions* test the depth of your new knowledge.

To help you apply the material to whatever career you choose, each chapter contains an employment profile and some advice from a professional, a Career Workshop Box that provides tips on how to use the chapter information to help your career, a case study of an actual situation experienced by a real organization, and a Focus on Ethics Box that presents an ethical dilemma related to the chapter material.

For the Instructor

An Instructor's Manual to Make Teaching Easier!

The instructor's manual will make teaching I/O Psychology easier by providing help in three areas: constructing tests, grading student exercises, and delivering classroom lectures. To help in constructing tests, the instructor's manual contains multiple-choice and short-answer test questions for each chapter. Multiple-choice items are also included in an *electronic test bank*.

To help in grading student exercises, the instructor's manual contains the answers to exercises for which there are objective answers. This section also contains information to help interpret the psychological tests in the text. Psychological tests in the textbook section include the following:

- Personality
- Leadership style (self-monitoring; LPC; task orientation; and needs for achievement, power, and affiliation)
- Predisposition to job satisfaction (core evaluation, life satisfaction, vocational interest)
- Predisposition to work motivation (self-esteem, intrinsic versus extrinsic motivation)
- Communication style (listening skills, listening style)
- Predisposition to stress (Type A, optimism, lifestyle)

To help make lectures more interesting, I have provided the most useful instructor's manual in the field. The manual contains the following:

- *PowerPoint slides* for each topic (these PowerPoint slides are also included on a CD-ROM)
- *Lecture outlines* for each topic
- Suggestions for *demonstrations* and *examples*
- Information to tie *video segments* to text material
- *Humorous examples* to lighten up material (for example, Top 10 Stupid Interviewer Tricks, Strange Cover Letters)

New to This Edition

- More examples of diversity efforts spread throughout the text
- Increased discussion of test fairness issues
- Chapters 8, 14, and 15 were restructured to provide a better flow of material

- New section on monitoring the legality and fairness of performance appraisal systems
- Increased coverage of organizational justice and fairness issues
- Increased discussion of personality spread throughout the text
- New section on authentic leadership
- Updated use of technology examples
- Updated references and examples in every chapter
- Key terms in the margins on each page
- Photos more directly connected to chapter topics

Acknowledgments

I am grateful to the excellent staff at Wadsworth, including Senior Acquisitions Editor Tim Matray and editorial assistant Lauren Moody. I am especially grateful to Ann Francis of PreMediaGlobal for working so diligently and patiently in getting the text through production. The quality of this edition was greatly enhanced by the thoughtful responses of reviewers, including: Robert Bubb, Auburn University; Mary Fox, University of Maryland; Christopher Nave, University of California; Steven Scher, Eastern Illinois University; Ross Steinman, Widener University; and Tiffani Tribble, University of Mount Union.

I would also like to thank the reviewers of the previous edition, whose comments and suggestions continue to make the text stronger: Sheree Barron, Georgia College and State University; Jay Brand, Haworth Inc.; Linda Butzin, Owens Community College; Maureen Conard, Sacred Heart University; George Cook, University of Rochester; Daniel DeNeui, University of Southern Oregon; Elizabeth Erffmeyer, Western Kentucky University; Armando Estrada, Washington State University; Donald Fisher, Southwest Missouri State; Mark Frame, University of Texas at Arlington; Alisha Francis, Northwest Missouri State University; Dean Frost, Portland State University; William Gaeddert, SUNY-Plattsburgh; David Gilmore, University of North Carolina at Charlotte; Matthew Grawitch, St. Louis University; George Hampton, University of Houston; Paul Hanges, University of Maryland; Kathy Hanish, Iowa State University; Donald Hantula, Temple University; Steven Hurwitz, Tiffin University; Brian Johnson, University of Tennessee at Martin; Scott Johnson, John Wood Community College; Harold Kiess, Framingham State College; Jean Powell Kirnan, The College of New Jersey; Janet Kottke, California State University at San Bernardino; Charles Lance, University of Georgia; Laurie Lankin, Mercer University; Paul Lloyd, Southwest Missouri State University; Janine Miller Lund, Tarrant County College; James Mitchel, LIMRA International; Paul Nail, Southwestern Oklahoma Sate University; Craig Parks, Washington State University; Charles Pierce, University of Memphis; Marc Pratarelli, University of Southern Colorado; Juan Sanchez, Florida International University; Eugene Sheehan, University of Northern Colorado; Ken Schultz, California State University, San Bernardino; William Siegfried, University of North Carolina at Charlotte; Sharmin Spencer, University of Illinois; Keith Syrja, Owens Community College; and Todd Thorsteinson, University of Idaho.

I would also like to thank my family, friends, and students for accommodating my time spent writing and for all their ideas and support. I appreciate my colleagues Eric Dunleavy, Mark Nagy, Michael Surrette, and David Cohen, who patiently allowed me to bounce ideas off them, vent, and ask dumb questions. Thanks also to my SIOP,

IPMA, IPAC, and SHRM colleagues for their insight and stories. There is no way I can properly express my gratitude to my mentor, Dr. Wilson W. Kimbrough, who taught me much more than facts and theories, and to Dr. Al Harris and Dr. Daniel Johnson, who have been so supportive throughout my career.

Finally, I thank my wife, Bobbie, and son, Josh, for their love and emotional support. Most of the time, writing a book is an enjoyable process. However, during the times I was stressed or confused (an increasingly common occurrence), my family was always patient and understanding. I could not have done this, or much of anything, without them. I would also like to thank Bobbie for her contributions in helping write the stress chapter, the section on organizational culture, several of the Career Workshop Boxes, and all of the Focus on Ethics Boxes.

Michael G. Aamodt

ABOUT THE AUTHOR

Mike is a professor emeritus of industrial/organizational psychology at Radford University in Radford, Virginia. In 2009, after 26 years of teaching at RU, Mike took advantage of an early retirement option and joined DCI Consulting Group as a principal consultant. He continues to teach a course each semester to fulfill his love of teaching.

Mike received his B.A. in psychology from Pepperdine University in Malibu, California, and both his M.A. and Ph.D. from the University of Arkansas. Over the years, Mike has taught courses in employee selection, job analysis, compensation, employee training and development, organizational psychology, organizational influence, organizational politics, and forensic psychology. Mike has received teaching awards as a graduate student at the University of Arkansas and as a professor at Radford University.

As a researcher, Mike has published over 50 articles in professional journals and presented many papers at professional conferences. He is the author of *Applied Industrial/Organizational Psychology*, now in its seventh edition, *Research in Law Enforcement Selection*, *I/O Psychology in Action*, *Understanding Statistics in I/O Psychology*, and *Human Relations in Business*. Mike is on the editorial boards of the *Journal of Police and Criminal Psychology*, *Applied H.R.M. Research*, and *Criminal Justice and Behavior*.

In over 28 years as a trainer and consultant, Mike has helped a wide variety of organizations deal with such issues as employee selection, performance evaluation, downsizing, organizational change, compensation, and motivation. He is considered one of the nation's experts in police psychology. Mike's fast-paced and humorous presentation style makes him a frequently requested speaker throughout the region.

Mike is an active member in many organizations, including SIOP, SHRM, IPAC, and the Society for Police and Criminal Psychology.

In his spare time, Mike likes to make lame attempts at being athletic, cook what at times turn out to be edible meals, travel, and SCUBA dive. He lives in Pulaski, Virginia, with his wife, Bobbie, and two neurotic dogs (Gretchen and Sydney). Mike and Bobbie have a son, Josh, who is an attorney in northern Virginia, but they continue to love him anyway.

Chapter

1

INTRODUCTION TO I/O PSYCHOLOGY

© Chris Ryan/OJO Images/Getty Images

Learning Objectives

➡ Be able to describe I/O psychology and what I/O psychologists do

➡ Learn about the history of I/O psychology

➡ Know the admissions requirements for graduate programs in I/O psychology

➡ Understand the importance of conducting research

➡ Understand how to conduct research

➡ Be able to differentiate the various research methods

The Field of I/O Psychology
Differences Between I/O and Business Programs
Major Fields of I/O Psychology
Brief History of I/O Psychology
Employment of I/O Psychologists
Educational Requirements and Types of Programs

Research in I/O Psychology
Why Conduct Research?
Considerations in Conducting Research

Ethics in Industrial/Organizational Psychology

On the Job: Applied Case Study: Conducting Research at the Vancouver (British Columbia) International Airport Authority, Canada

Wouldn't it be wonderful if all employees loved their jobs so much that they couldn't wait to get to work and were so well suited and trained that their performances were outstanding? Well, this is the ultimate goal of industrial psychology. Unfortunately, not every employee will enjoy his or her job, and not every employee will do well on a job. In this book, you will learn the techniques developed by industrial/organizational (I/O) psychologists that show the way toward the goal of a happy and productive workforce.

Before we can talk about these techniques, several areas must be discussed so that you will have the basics to help you better understand the rest of the book. This chapter has two distinct sections. The first section provides a brief overview of the field of I/O psychology, and the second section discusses the research methods that will be mentioned throughout the text.

The Field of I/O Psychology

Differences Between I/O and Business Programs

Industrial/organizational (I/O) psychology A branch of psychology that applies the principles of psychology to the workplace.

Perhaps the best place to begin a textbook on I/O psychology is to look at the field itself. **Industrial/organizational psychology** is a branch of psychology that applies the principles of psychology to the workplace. The purpose of I/O psychology is "to enhance the dignity and performance of human beings, and the organizations they work in, by advancing the science and knowledge of human behavior" (Rucci, 2008).

For example, principles of learning are used to develop training programs and incentive plans; principles of social psychology are used to form work groups and understand employee conflict; and principles of motivation and emotion are used to motivate and satisfy employees. The application of psychological principles is what best distinguishes I/O psychology from related fields typically taught in business colleges. Although many of the topics covered in this text are similar to those found in a human resource management (HRM) or organizational behavior text, the techniques and the reasons behind them are often different. For example, many HRM texts advocate the unstructured interview as an excellent solution for selecting the best employees. I/O psychologists, however, consider unstructured interviews to be of less value than more suitable alternatives such as psychological tests, behavioral interviews, work samples, biodata, and assessment centers (Berry, 2003).

A second difference between I/O psychology and business fields is that I/O psychology examines factors that affect the *people* in an organization as opposed to the broader aspects of running an organization such as marketing channels, transportation networks, and cost accounting (Kimbrough, Durley, & Muñoz, 2005). As you can see from the typical graduate courses listed in Table 1.1, business (MBA) programs examine such areas as accounting, economics, and marketing, whereas I/O programs focus almost exclusively on issues involving the people in an organization (Moberg & Moore, 2011).

I/O psychology relies extensively on research, quantitative methods, and testing techniques. I/O psychologists are trained to use empirical data and statistics rather than intuition to make decisions. I/O psychologists are not clinical psychologists who happen to be in industry, and they do not conduct therapy for workers. There are psychologists who work for organizations and help employees with such problems as drug and alcohol abuse, but these are counselors rather than I/O psychologists. A factor that helps differentiate I/O psychology from other branches of psychology is the reliance

Table 1.1 Comparison of commonly required courses in I/O psychology and MBA programs

	Program Type	
Course	**I/O**	**MBA**
Research methods	90%	6%
Quantitative methods	82%	50%
Employee selection	80%	0%
Organizational psychology/behavior	80%	48%
Psychometrics/test construction	62%	0%
Training & development	60%	2%
Performance appraisal	38%	2%
Finance	0%	94%
Marketing	0%	90%
Corporate strategies and policies	4%	82%
Accounting	0%	78%
Information systems	0%	68%
Economics	0%	66%
Operations management	0%	56%
Culture/global/international business	12%	42%
Ethics	20%	36%

Source: Adapted from Moberg & Moore (2011).

on the scientist-practitioner model. That is, I/O psychologists act as scientists when they conduct research and as practitioners when they work with actual organizations. In addition, I/O psychologists act as scientist-practitioners when they apply research findings so that the work they perform with organizations will be of high quality and enhance an organization's effectiveness.

One reason that I/O psychology continually increases in popularity is that, perhaps more than in any other field, professionals in the field can have a positive impact on the lives of other people. To support this last statement, let us look at a typical day in the life of a typical person:

Work	8 hours
Commute to work	1 hour
Watch TV	3 hours
Sleep	8 hours
Prepare and eat meals	2 hours
Other	2 hours

With the possible exception of sleeping, people spend more time at their jobs than at any other activity in life (and sometimes these two activities overlap!). Thus, it makes sense that people who are happy with and productive at their jobs will lead more fulfilling lives than people unhappy with their jobs. If a person is unhappy at work for 8 hours a day, the residual effects of this unhappiness will affect the quality of that person's family and leisure life as well.

From a societal perspective, I/O psychologists can also improve the quality of life by increasing employee effectiveness, which reduces the cost of goods sold by improving product quality. This in turn reduces repair and replacement costs by improving organizational efficiency, which can result in decreases in inefficient activities such as waiting in line.

Thus, I/O psychology can improve the quality of life at levels equal to, and often exceeding, those of fields such as counseling psychology and medicine. So, even though I/O psychologists earn a good salary, the real benefits to the field involve the positive impacts on the lives of others.

Major Fields of I/O Psychology

Though the goal of I/O psychology is to increase the productivity and well-being of employees, there are two approaches as to how this can be accomplished. The industrial approach (the "I" in I/O psychology) focuses on determining the competencies needed to perform a job, staffing the organization with employees who have those competencies, and increasing those competencies through training. The organizational approach (the "O" in I/O psychology) creates an organizational structure and culture that will motivate employees to perform well, give them the necessary information to do their jobs, and provide working conditions that are safe and result in an enjoyable and satisfying work/life environment.

Personnel Psychology

Personnel psychology The field of study that concentrates on the selection and evaluation of employees.

I/O psychologists and HRM professionals involved in **personnel psychology** study and practice in such areas as analyzing jobs, recruiting applicants, selecting employees, determining salary levels, training employees, and evaluating employee performance. Professionals working in these areas choose existing tests or create new ones that can be used to select and promote employees. These tests are then constantly evaluated to ensure that they are both fair and valid.

Personnel psychologists also analyze jobs to obtain a complete picture of what each employee does, often assigning monetary values to each position. After obtaining complete job descriptions, professionals in personnel psychology construct performance-appraisal instruments to evaluate employee performance.

Psychologists in this area also examine various methods that can be used to train and develop employees. People within this subfield usually work in a training department of an organization and are involved in such activities as identifying the organization's training needs, developing training programs, and evaluating training success.

Organizational Psychology

Organizational psychology The field of study that investigates the behavior of employees within the context of an organization.

Psychologists involved in **organizational psychology** are concerned with the issues of leadership, job satisfaction, employee motivation, organizational communication, conflict management, organizational change, and group processes within an organization. Organizational psychologists often conduct surveys of employee attitudes to get ideas about what employees believe are an organization's strengths and weaknesses. Usually serving in the role of a consultant, an organizational psychologist makes recommendations on ways problem areas can be improved. For example, low job satisfaction might be improved by allowing employees to participate in making certain company decisions, and poor communication might be improved by implementing an employee suggestion system.

Professionals in organization development implement organization-wide programs designed to improve employee performance. Such programs might include team building, restructuring, and employee empowerment.

Human Factors/Ergonomics

Psychologists in the area of **human factors** concentrate on workplace design, human-machine interaction, ergonomics, and physical fatigue and stress. These psychologists frequently work with engineers and other technical professionals to make the workplace safer and more efficient. Sample activities in this subfield have included designing the optimal way to draw a map, designing the most comfortable chair, and investigating the optimal work schedule.

Brief History of I/O Psychology

Considering that the field of psychology itself has been around for only a relatively short time (since 1879), it is not surprising that I/O psychology has a correspondingly short history. Although various experts disagree about the precise beginning of I/O psychology (Table 1.2), it is generally thought to have started either in 1903 when Walter Dill Scott wrote *The Theory of Advertising*, in which psychology was first applied to business; in 1910 when Hugo Münsterberg wrote *Psychology and Industrial Efficiency*, which was first published in English in 1913; or in 1911 when Scott wrote the book *Increasing Human Efficiency in Business* (Koppes & Pickren, 2007). Regardless of the official starting date, I/O psychology was born in the early 1900s. In addition to Scott and Münsterberg, pioneers in the field include James Cattell, Walter Bingham, John Watson, Marion Bills, and Lillian Gilbreth (DiClemente & Hantula, 2000). Interestingly, the term "industrial psychology" was seldom used prior to World War I. Instead, the common terms for the field were "economic psychology," "business psychology," and "employment psychology" (Koppes & Pickren, 2007).

I/O psychology made its first big impact during World War I. Because of the large number of soldiers who had to be assigned to various units within the armed forces, I/O psychologists were employed to test recruits and then place them in appropriate positions. The testing was accomplished mainly through the **Army Alpha** and **Army Beta** tests of mental ability. The Alpha test was used for recruits who could read and the Beta test for recruits who could not read. The more intelligent recruits were assigned to officer training, and the less intelligent to the infantry. Interestingly, John Watson, who is better known as a pioneer in behaviorism, served as a major in the U.S. Army in World War I and developed perceptual and motor tests for potential pilots (DiClemente & Hantula, 2000). I/O psychologists, along with engineers such as Henry Gantt, were responsible for increasing the efficiency with which cargo ships were built, repaired, and loaded (Van De Water, 1997).

Though certainly not an I/O psychologist, inventor Thomas A. Edison understood the importance of selecting the right employees. In 1920, Edison created a 163-item knowledge test that he administered to over 900 applicants. The test and passing score were so difficult that only 5% of the applicants passed! You will learn more about Edison's test in the Applied Case Study at the end of Chapter 6.

Two of the most interesting figures in the early years of I/O psychology were the husband and wife team of Frank Gilbreth and Lillian Moller Gilbreth. The Gilbreths were among the first, if not the first, scientists to improve productivity and reduce fatigue by studying the motions used by workers. Frank began his career as a

Table 1.2 Important Events in I/O Psychology

Year	Event
1903	Walter Dill Scott publishes *The Theory of Advertising*
1911	Walter Dill Scott publishes *Increasing Human Efficiency in Business*
1913	Hugo Münsterberg publishes *Psychology and Industrial Efficiency* (German version published in 1910)
1917	*Journal of Applied Psychology* first published
1918	World War I provides I/O psychologists with first opportunity for large-scale employee testing and selection
1921	First Ph.D. in I/O psychology awarded to Bruce Moore and Merrill Ream at Carnegie Tech
1932	First I/O text written by Morris Viteles
1933	Hawthorne studies published
1937	American Association for Applied Psychology established
1945	Society for Industrial and Business Psychology established as Division 14 of APA with 130 members
1951	Marion Bills elected as first woman president of Division 14
1960	Division 14 renamed as Society for Industrial Psychology, membership exceeds 700
1963	Equal Pay Act passed
1964	Civil Rights Act passed
	First issue of *The Industrial-Organizational Psychologist* (TIP) published
1970	Division 14 membership exceeds 1,100
1971	B. F. Skinner publishes *Beyond Freedom and Dignity*
1980	Division 14 membership exceeds 1,800
1982	Division 14 renamed Society for Industrial and Organizational Psychology (SIOP)
1986	Society for Industrial and Organizational Psychology (SIOP) holds first annual national conference separate from APA meeting
1989	Supreme Court sets conservative trend and becomes more "employer friendly"
1990	Americans with Disabilities Act passed
	SIOP membership exceeds 2,500
1991	Civil Rights Act of 1991 passed to overcome 1989 conservative Supreme Court decisions
1995	SIOP membership exceeds 4,500
1997	SIOP celebrates golden anniversary at its annual conference in St. Louis
2000	SIOP membership exceeds 5,700
2005	OFCCP and EEOC become more aggressive in fighting systemic discrimination
2008	The journal *Industrial and Organizational Psychology: Perspectives on Science and Practice* begins publication as an official journal of SIOP
2009	Lilly Ledbetter Fair Pay Act and Americans with Disabilities Act Amendment (ADAAA) passed
2010	SIOP membership exceeds 8,000; SIOP members narrowly vote to keep the name Society for Industrial Organizational Psychology rather than change the name to the Society for Organizational Psychology

contractor and became famous for developing improvements in bricklaying that reduced from 18 to 4½ the number of motions needed to lay a brick. Lillian, the much more educated of the two, received her Ph.D. from Brown University in 1915—a rare achievement for a woman at that time. As a couple, they had 12 children, and the efficiency methods they used to raise their children while having busy careers were the inspiration for the book and the movie *Cheaper by the Dozen* (the 1950 version of the movie). After Frank's death in 1924 at the age of 55, Lillian continued her consulting with industry, as the Great Depression forced companies to find ways to reduce costs and be more productive. In 1935, she became a professor of management and engineering at Purdue University, the first woman to hold such a position.

During these early years, I/O psychology thrived outside of the United States. Prominent psychologists who applied psychology to problems in industry outside the United States included Jules Suter in Switzerland; Bernard Muscio in Australia; Franziska Baumgarten-Tramer, Walter Moede, William Stern, Otto Lipmann, and Emil Kraepelin in Germany; Jean-Marie Lahy in France; Edward Webster in Canada; and Cyril Burt, Charles Myers, and Sir Frederick Bartlett in Great Britain (Vinchur & Koppes, 2007; Warr, 2007).

In the 1930s, I/O psychology greatly expanded its scope. Until then, it had been involved primarily in personnel issues such as the selection and placement of

Frank and Lillian Gilbreth were two pioneers in I/O psychology.

© Courtesy of Purdue University Libraries, Archives and Special Collections

Hawthorne studies A series of studies, conducted at the Western Electric plant in Hawthorne, Illinois, that have come to represent any change in behavior when people react to a change in the environment.

employees. However, in the 1930s, when the findings from the famous **Hawthorne studies** were published, psychologists became more involved in the quality of the work environment, as well as the attitudes of employees. The Hawthorne studies, conducted at the Hawthorne plant of the Western Electric Company in the Chicago area, demonstrated that employee behavior was complex and that the interpersonal interactions between managers and employees played a tremendous role in employee behavior. The Hawthorne studies were initially designed to investigate such issues as the effects of lighting levels, work schedules, wages, temperature, and rest breaks on employee performance.

Much to the surprise of the researchers, the actual work conditions did not affect productivity in the predicted manner. That is, there were times when productivity improved after work conditions were made worse, and times when productivity decreased after work conditions were made better. After interviewing employees and studying the matter further, the researchers realized that employees changed their behavior and became more productive *because* they were being studied and received attention from their managers, a condition that is now commonly referred to as the **Hawthorne effect**. Perhaps the major contribution of the Hawthorne studies was that it inspired psychologists to increase their focus on human relations in the workplace and to explore the effects of employee attitudes (Olson, Verley, Santos, & Salas, 2004).

Hawthorne effect When employees change their behavior due solely to the fact that they are receiving attention or are being observed.

The 1960s were characterized by the passage of several major pieces of civil rights legislation, which are discussed in Chapter 3. These laws focused the attention of HR professionals on developing fair selection techniques. As a result, the need for I/O psychologists greatly increased. The 1960s were also characterized by the use of sensitivity training and T-groups (laboratory training groups) for managers (Carson, Lanier, Carson, & Guidry, 2000).

The 1970s brought great strides in the understanding of many organizational psychology issues that involved employee satisfaction and motivation. The decade also saw the development of many theories about employee behavior in organizations. B. F. Skinner's (1971) *Beyond Freedom and Dignity* resulted in the increased use of behavior-modification techniques in organizations.

The 1980s and 1990s brought four major changes to I/O psychology. The first involved an increased use of fairly sophisticated statistical techniques and methods of analysis. This change is evident if one compares journal articles written in the 1960s with those written since 1980. More recent articles use such complex statistical techniques as path analysis, structural equation modeling, meta-analysis, multivariate analysis of variance (MANOVA), and causal modeling. Prior to the 1970s, simpler statistical techniques such as *t*-tests and analysis of variance (ANOVA) were used (unless you are wearing a pocket protector or have taken a statistics course, these methods probably are not familiar to you). This reliance on statistics explains why students enrolled in an I/O psychology doctoral program take at least five statistics courses as part of their education.

A second change concerned a new interest in the application of cognitive psychology to industry. For example, articles written about performance appraisal in the 1970s primarily described and tested new methods for evaluating employee performance. In the 1980s and early 1990s, however, many articles approached the performance appraisal issue by examining the thought process used by managers when they conduct such appraisals.

The third change was the increased interest in the effects of work on family life and leisure activities (McCarthy, 1998). Though stress had long been of interest to psychologists, it was during the last two decades of the twentieth century that employee stress—especially stress resulting in workplace violence—received attention.

The final major change in the 1980s and 1990s came about when I/O psychologists took a renewed interest in developing methods to select employees. In the 1960s and 1970s, the courts were still interpreting the major civil rights acts of the early 1960s, with the result that I/O psychologists took a cautious approach in selecting employees. By the mid-1980s, however, the courts became less strict, and a wider variety of selection instruments was developed and used. Examples of these instruments include cognitive ability tests, personality inventories, biodata, and structured interviews. Other changes during the 1980s and 1990s that had significant effects on I/O psychology included massive organizational downsizing, greater concern for diversity and gender issues, an aging workforce, increased concern about the effects of stress, and the increased emphasis on such organizational development interventions as total quality management (TQM), reengineering, and employee empowerment.

In the 2000s, perhaps the greatest influence on I/O psychology is the rapid advances in technology. Many tests and surveys are now administered on the Internet, employers recruit and screen applicants online; job seekers use such social media outlets as Twitter, LinkedIn, and Facebook to find jobs; employees are being trained using e-learning and distance education; and managers are holding meetings in cyberspace rather than in person.

Another important factor impacting I/O psychology is the changing demographic makeup of the workforce. Women are increasingly entering the workforce and taking on managerial roles; Hispanics and Latinos are now the largest minority group in the United States; Asian Americans are the fastest-growing segment of the U.S. population; and an increasing number of workers, vendors, and customers have English as their second language. Thus, diversity issues will continue to be an important factor in the workplace.

The global economy is also affecting the role of I/O psychology. As many manufacturing jobs are shifted to developing countries with lower wages, there will be an increased emphasis on service jobs requiring human relations skills. As an increasing number of employees work in other countries (as expatriates) and as rates of immigration (both legal and illegal) increase, efforts must keep pace to understand various cultures, and training must be conducted so that employees and managers can successfully work not only in other countries, but at home with expatriates from other countries.

Other factors that are currently impacting I/O psychology include high unemployment rates, movements toward flexible work schedules, family-friendly work policies, accommodation of an increasing number of employees with child-care and elder-care responsibilities, flatter organizational structures with fewer management levels, population shifts from urban to suburban locations, and increasing costs of health-care benefits. In addition, potential changes in the retirement age for Social Security may result in employees working into their late sixties.

Employment of I/O Psychologists

Throughout this text, you will find Employment Profiles, which look at specific jobs done by people with degrees in I/O psychology. However, it is useful to examine some of the broad areas in which I/O psychologists work as well. As shown in Table 1.3, I/O psychologists typically work in one of four settings: colleges and universities, consulting firms, the private sector, and the public sector. As one would expect, I/O

Table 1.3 Employment Settings of I/O Psychologists

Employment Setting	Highest Degree Obtained	
	M.A.	Ph.D.
Education	0.8%	40.0%
Private sector	44.0	23.3
Public sector	10.5	8.2
Consulting	37.3	25.0
Other	7.4	3.5

Source: Medsker, Katkowski, & Furr (2005).

psychologists who work at colleges and universities typically teach and conduct research, although some work as administrators (e.g., deans, provosts, vice presidents).

I/O psychologists who work in consulting firms help a wide variety of organizations become more productive by helping them select a high-quality and diverse workforce, designing systems that will motivate employees while treating them fairly, training employees, and ensuring that organizations treat applicants and employees in a legal and ethical manner. Consulting firms range in size from one-person organizations to large consulting firms employing hundreds of consultants. Some consulting firms specialize in one area of I/O psychology (e.g., employee selection, diversity, attitude surveys), whereas others offer a range of services.

I/O psychologists who work in the private and public sectors perform similar duties as consultants, but they do so in very different environments. I/O psychologists who work in the private sector work for a single company such as IBM, Microsoft, and FedEx, whereas consultants work with many companies. I/O psychologists in the public sector work for a local, state, or federal government agency. Though the private sector historically paid more than the public sector, many employees believe the higher job stability of the public sector offsets the potential for lower pay. Though master's- and doctoral-level graduates can be found in all employment areas, Ph.D.s are much more likely to be employed in an academic setting; master's-level graduates are more often employed as HR generalists, data analysts, trainers, and compensation analysts.

As you can see by the job titles listed in Table 1.4, there are many careers in I/O psychology, ranging from entry-level jobs to presidents and CEOs of large companies. Whether one wants to work in the public or private sector, work with data or work with people, spend the day talking, writing, or analyzing, there is some job or other in I/O psychology that fits everyone.

As of 2009 the median salary was $74,500 for master's-level positions and $105,000 for doctoral-level positions (Khanna & Medsker, 2010); the top 10% of I/O psychologists with doctoral degrees earned more than $200,000! Current information about I/O salaries can be found at the website of the Society for Industrial and Organizational Psychology [SIOP] at www.siop.org.

Educational Requirements and Types of Programs

Although people with bachelor's degrees can find employment in the HRM field, having a master's or doctoral degree certainly increases employment and career opportunities. Obtaining a master's in I/O psychology takes between one and two years after the completion of a bachelor's degree. Admission requirements vary greatly from

Table 1.4 Job Titles of I/O Psychologists

Chairman and CEO	Industrial-organizational psychologist
City manager	Manager of leadership and development
Compensation analyst	Personnel manager
Compensation manager	President
Consultant	Professor
Director of assessment and selection	Recruiter
Director of organizational effectiveness	Research analyst
Director of training and development	Research scientist
Director of workforce planning	Research psychologist
EEO/Diversity specialist	Senior partner
Employee relations manager	Staffing manager
HR director	Trainer
HR generalist	Training coordinator
HR representative	Training manager
HR specialist	Vice president for human resources
HR supervisor	Vice president for organizational development

Graduate Record Exam (GRE) A standardized admission test required by most psychology graduate schools.

school to school, but an undergraduate grade point average (GPA) of at least 3.0 and a score of 1,000 on the **Graduate Record Exam (GRE)**—the graduate school version of the Scholastic Aptitude Test, or SAT, that you took after high school—are not uncommon prerequisites (Nagy, Schrader, & Aamodt, 2005). Advice for getting into graduate school can be found in the Career Workshop Box.

Types of Graduate Programs

Master's degree programs come in two varieties: those that are part of a Ph.D. program and those that terminate at the master's degree. Schools with **terminal master's degree programs** do not have Ph.D. programs, and a master's degree is the highest that can be earned at such schools. Schools with doctoral programs offer both master's degrees and Ph.D.s. Terminal programs are best suited for students wanting an applied HR position in an organization (although many students in terminal degree programs go on to earn their doctorates at other universities). These programs usually have less stringent entrance requirements and provide more financial aid and individual attention to master's students than do Ph.D. programs. Doctoral programs, on the other hand, usually have more well-known faculty members and better facilities and research funding. Doctoral programs are best suited for students who eventually want to teach, do research, or consult.

Terminal master's degree programs Graduate programs that offer a master's degree but not a Ph.D.

Master's Programs. Completion of most master's programs requires about 40 hours of graduate coursework (Nagy et al., 2005). Although 15 to 18 hours is considered a full undergraduate semester load, 9 to 12 hours is considered a full graduate load. In addition to coursework, many programs require a student to complete a thesis, which is usually an original research work created and conducted by the student. The thesis is completed in the second year of graduate school.

Internship A situation in which a student works for an organization, either for pay or as a volunteer, to receive practical work experience.

Practicum A paid or unpaid position with an organization that gives a student practical work experience.

Most programs also allow the student to complete an **internship**, or **practicum**, with a local organization. The internship requirements vary by program. Depending on the university, students may work 10 hours per week at an organization during their last semester of graduate school, or do their internships in the summer between their first and second years, or take a semester off to work full time with an organization.

Finally, most programs require a student to pass a comprehensive oral and/or written examination before graduation. These exams usually are taken during the final semester and cover material from all of the courses taken during the graduate program. As you can see, completing a master's degree program in I/O psychology is tough, but it can lead to excellent employment and professional benefits.

Doctoral Programs. Obtaining a Ph.D. is more difficult than obtaining a master's, with the typical doctoral program taking five years to complete (Rentsch, Lowenberg, Barnes-Farrell, & Menard, 1997). Common entrance requirements are a 3.5 GPA and a GRE score of 1,200. The first two years of a doctoral program involve taking a wide variety of courses in psychology. In most programs, the student does not concentrate on I/O courses until the third and fourth years. In addition to a thesis, a student working toward a Ph.D. must complete a **dissertation**. No formal definition distinguishes a thesis from a dissertation, but the major differences are that the dissertation is broader in scope, longer, and requires more original and independent effort than the thesis (Riddle & Foster, 1997). Doctoral programs also involve a series of

Dissertation A formal research paper required of most doctoral students in order to graduate.

Career Workshop **Getting into Graduate School**

Although different graduate programs often emphasize different entrance requirements, most place some weight on GRE scores, GPA, letters of recommendation, and previous research or professional experience. With this in mind, following the advice below should increase your chances of being selected for a graduate program.

➡ Take extra mathematics and English courses. The GRE consists of four sections: quantitative, verbal, writing, and psychology. The quantitative portion requires knowledge of algebra, geometry, and some trigonometry. Thus, often the only way to do well on this section is to take extra courses in these subjects. Taking English courses in reading comprehension, writing, and vocabulary will help your score on the verbal and writing sections. It is important to understand that the GRE is a test of knowledge, not intelligence. Thus, with extra coursework, you can improve your scores. Remember, it will have been a long time since you took these courses in high school.

➡ Study for your GRE and get a good night's sleep before you take the test. You may not be able to learn much new material by studying, but you can at least refresh your memory about material that you have already learned but may have forgotten. Remember that the GRE will help

determine your future and is probably the most important test that you will ever take. Treat it as such and prepare.

➡ Take at least one psychology course in each of the areas of statistics, experimental methods, abnormal psychology, personality, social psychology, physiological psychology, learning, and cognitive psychology; each area is covered in the GRE's psychology portion. Although courses in sex and group dynamics are interesting and will help you in the future, they will not help you to score well on the GRE.

➡ Make sure that you have at least three people who can write positive letters of recommendation for you. Getting an A in a professor's class is not enough to expect a good letter that will carry weight with an admissions committee. Let the professors get to know you as both student and person. Talk with different professors and become involved with their research; this not only will allow you to have research of your own to show prospective graduate programs, but will result in better and more complete letters of recommendation.

➡ Get involved! Conduct independent research projects, join professional clubs, get a summer job or an internship related to your field—anything to demonstrate your desire to be a professional.

comprehensive exams that are similar to, but more extensive than, the exams taken in a master's program. A complete list of I/O psychology graduate programs can be found on the text webpage. (Information on programs is available from the SIOP at www.siop.org).

Research in I/O Psychology

Now that you have a good idea about the field of I/O psychology, it is time to learn the essentials of one of the foundations of the upcoming chapters: research. This section does not provide an in-depth discussion of research techniques and procedures, but it gives you enough information so that you can understand the method that was used when a study is mentioned in the text.

Why Conduct Research?

Though most of you will probably not go on to careers as researchers, understanding research and statistics is important for several reasons.

Answering Questions and Making Decisions

As mentioned earlier in the chapter, one of the characteristics of I/O psychology is its extensive use of research and statistics. Although there are many reasons for this reliance on research, the most important is that research ultimately saves organizations money. To many of you, this last statement may seem a bit insensitive. Keep in mind, however, that for most organizations, the most important thing is the bottom line. If I/O psychologists are not able to save the company considerably more money than it pays for their salary and expenses, they will be without a job.

These monetary savings can result from many factors, including increased employee satisfaction, increased productivity, and fewer accidents. Perhaps an excellent example of how research can save organizations money involves the employment interview. For years, many organizations relied on the employment interview as the main method for selecting employees (most still do). But researchers have shown that the unstructured employment interview is not the best predictor of future behavior on the job (Schmidt & Hunter, 1998). Thus, without research, an organization might still be spending money on a method that actually lowers its profits rather than raises them.

Research and Everyday Life

Research confronts us on an almost daily basis, both at home and on the job. As a student, you will encounter research throughout this and other courses. As a professional, you will receive advertisements and sales pitches containing references to research supporting a particular product. At home, you read the results of political polls in the newspaper and are bombarded with TV commercials trumpeting the fat-burning wonders of the AbMaster or claiming that "nine out of ten dentists" recommend a product. Understanding research helps you to critically listen and analyze results of these studies to make more intelligent decisions. After all, you would hate to buy a fitness product based on the results of poorly conducted research!

When I was an undergraduate at Pepperdine University in Malibu, California (yes, the surf was always up), the students attempted to hold the first dance ever at the university. Until this point, dancing was prohibited, and the students wanted the prohibition removed. The dance proposal came under heavy attack by the church sponsoring the university as well as by several administrators. An opponent of the dance proposal wrote a letter to the school newspaper citing research "that in a study of Catholic confessionals, nine out of ten fallen women had their downfall on the dance floor." When confronted with this devastating piece of research, we pulled out our trusty experimental psychology books and, using our finely honed research skills, challenged the validity of the study on such grounds as the poorly defined dependent variable (what is a fallen woman?), the sample size (how many women fell?), and the question of whether the study actually existed (there is no way the Catholic Church would allow a study of confessionals). After our impressive critique, the administration gave in, and we were allowed to hold our dance off campus but advertise it on campus. If you consider allowing 200 students with no rhythm to dance as a victory, then our superior knowledge of research made us victors.

A crazy story? Sure. But the fact that intelligent people actually used such research to support their point underscores the importance of understanding research.

Common Sense Is Often Wrong

Often, there is a temptation not to conduct research because the answer to a question is "common sense." Unfortunately, common sense is not so common and is often wrong. Until the end of the fifteenth century, it was common sense that the world was flat and that a person sailing toward the horizon would fall off the Earth. Until late in the twentieth century, common sense said that women employees could not perform as well as men. In other words, many of our commonsense policies have been, and continue to be, wrong.

As a good example, imagine taking a multiple-choice test. After finishing the test, you go back and read question 32 but can't decide if you should stick with your original response of "b" or change it to "c." What would you do? Most students respond with what they have always been told: *Stick with your first answer.* If you stuck with this piece of common advice, you probably would miss the question. Thirty-three studies investigating this question concluded that contrary to common sense, the majority of the time, an answer will be changed from wrong to right (Kruger, Wirtz, & Miller, 2005). Another victory for research over common sense!

Considerations in Conducting Research

Ideas, Hypotheses, and Theories

The first step in conducting research is to decide *what to research.* Though the majority of I/O psychology research is conducted to test the accuracy of theories, many research ideas stem from a person starting a sentence with "I wonder …" For example, a manager might say, "I wonder why some of my employees can't get to work on time"; an employee might say, "I wonder if I could assemble more parts if my chair were higher"; or a supervisor might say, "I wonder which of my employees is the best to promote." All three seem to be ordinary questions, but each is just as valid and important in research as those asked by a professor in a university. Thus, everyone is a researcher at heart, and conducting some form of research to answer a question will undoubtedly lead to a better answer than could be obtained by guesswork alone.

	Idea or question	Hypothesis or prediction	Theory or explanation
	Does all this noise affect my employees' performance?	High levels of noise will increase the number of errors made in assembling electronic components.	Noise causes a distraction, making it difficult to concentrate.
		What will happen	**Why it will happen**

Figure 1.1

Hypothesis Example 1

Hypothesis An educated prediction about the answer to a research question.

Theory A systematic set of assumptions regarding the cause and nature of behavior.

Once a question has been asked, the next step is to form a **hypothesis**—an educated prediction about the answer to a question. This prediction is usually based on a **theory**, previous research, or logic. For example, as shown in Figure 1.1, a researcher is curious about the effect of noise on employee performance (the question) and believes that high levels of noise will result in decreased performance (the hypothesis). The prediction is based on the theory that distracting events reduce the ability to concentrate. To see if the hypothesis is correct, the researcher would need to conduct a study.

If the results support the hypothesis, it becomes important to test the theory. In psychology, there are often competing theories that predict the same outcome, but for different reasons. Take the situation depicted in Figure 1.2 as an example. An I/O psychologist wants to know which method of recruiting employees is best. She predicts that employee referrals will result in longer employee tenure (employees staying with the company) than will the other recruitment methods.

Though she is sure about her hypothesis, she is not sure about the reason, as there are four possible theories or explanations for her hypothesis:

1. Applicants referred by a current employee will stay with the company longer because they were given an accurate picture of the job and the company by the person telling them about the job (realistic job preview theory).
2. The personalities of applicants using employee referrals are different than the personalities of applicants using other methods to find jobs (differential recruitment-source theory).

Figure 1.2

Hypothesis Example 2

	Idea or question	Hypothesis or prediction	Theory or explanation
	What employee recruitment source is best?	Employee referrals will result in employees who stay with the company longer than will the other recruitment methods.	1. Realistic job preview theory 2. Differential recruitment-source theory 3. Personality similarity theory 4. Socialization theory
		What will happen	**Why it will happen**

3. Friends have similar personalities; thus, if one person has the type of personality that makes her want to stay with her current job, her friend should also like the job in question (personality similarity theory).
4. Employees who know someone in a workplace are more quickly absorbed into the informal system, receive coaching, and have their social needs met (socialization theory).

Thus, even though a study might support a hypothesis, it is still important to determine *why* the hypothesis is true. In this example, it would be necessary to conduct further studies to determine which of the four theories, if any, best explains the results. This is important because our ability to understand and use the best theory allows us to develop new methods to improve productivity in the workplace. In this example, if the first theory were true, we would give every applicant a realistic job preview. If the third theory were true, we would encourage current successful employees to recruit their friends.

At times, forming a hypothesis can be difficult. In some cases, no previous research has been conducted or theory proposed that would suggest a clear hypothesis about the answer to a question. For example, a student of mine wanted to see if personality was related to handwriting neatness. She couldn't find any research on handwriting neatness, much less on the relationship between personality and handwriting. There were also no theories or logical reason to predict what types of personalities would write a particular way. So, she conducted an *exploratory study* without a hypothesis—a practice that is not uncommon but is generally frowned on by scientists. If exploratory studies are used, follow-up studies should then be conducted to confirm the results of the exploratory study.

In other cases, it is difficult to form a hypothesis because a prediction could go either way. For example, another of my students was curious about whether a recommendation letter written by an important person (such as a senator) would be more influential than one written by a professor (Hey, I thought professors were important!). She had trouble forming a hypothesis because there were as many reasons that a reference by an important person would be more influential as there were reasons that such a reference would be less influential.

At times, a hypothesis may not be supported by a study even though the logic and theory behind it is correct. Often, a poor research design is the culprit. Other times, it is because the topic is more complicated than originally thought. When studying a topic, psychologists wish for simple answers. Unfortunately, most situations in life are not simple. For example, psychologists have been trying for years to understand aggression and violence. They have postulated many theories for why people are violent: genetics, brain abnormalities, learning, and frustration, to name a few. Some studies support these reasons, but others don't. Why the lack of consistency? Because no one theory by itself is the answer. Each of the theories is partially true in that each explains violence in certain people under certain circumstances. Furthermore, violent behavior may be the result of a combination of several factors, each of which by itself will not result in violence.

Confused? I hope not. The purpose of the preceding discussion is to show you the complexity of research. At times many theories may explain a particular behavior. At other times, behavior can be predicted, but the reason for the behavior may not be known. At still other times, we have questions but can't predict what the answer will be. This complexity of life is what makes research fun.

Literature Reviews

Once a research idea has been created, the next step is to search the literature for similar research. This search is important because if the question you are interested in answering has already been researched in 20 studies, it is probably not necessary for you to conduct a new study. As a graduate student, it took me a while to realize that most of my research ideas that were "so brilliant, no one else could have thought of them" had already been conducted several times over. I guess the moral of this story is, don't forget about your university library, even after you have finished school. I would venture to say that most of the questions you will have can be answered by a quick trip to the library or a thorough Internet search; it is not necessary, or smart, to constantly reinvent the wheel.

Even if your specific question has not been researched before, the probability is high that similar research has been conducted. This research is useful even though it does not directly answer your question, because it can provide some good ideas on how to conduct your study.

Literature reviews can be conducted in many ways, the most common of which are using such electronic databases as *PsycINFO* and *Academic Search Complete*, browsing through journals, searching the reference sections of related articles, and asking other researchers (Tubré, Bly, Edwards, Pritchard, & Simoneaux, 2001).

When reviewing the literature, you are likely to encounter four types of periodicals: journals, bridge publications, trade magazines (listed in Table 1.5), and magazines. **Journals** consist of articles written by researchers directly reporting the results of a study. Journals can be difficult to read (and boring) but are the best source of unbiased and accurate information about a topic. The leading journals in I/O psychology are the *Journal of Applied Psychology, Personnel Psychology, Academy of Management Journal, Academy of Management Review,* and *Organizational Behavior and*

Journals A written collection of articles describing the methods and results of new research.

Popular reading in I/O psychology.

Courtesy of the author

Table 1.5 List of I/O Psychology Periodicals

Journals	
Academy of Management Journal	*Journal of Management*
Academy of Management Review	*Journal of Occupational and Organizational Psychology*
Administrative Science Quarterly	*Journal of Organizational Behavior*
Applied Ergonomics	*Journal of Vocational Behavior*
Applied H.R.M. Research	*Organizational Behavior and Human Decision Processes*
Applied Psychological Measurement	*Personnel Psychology*
Applied Psychology: An International Review	*Public Personnel Management*
Ergonomics	**Bridge Publications**
Human Factors	*Academy of Management Executive*
Human Performance	*Harvard Business Review*
Industrial and Organizational Psychology: Perspectives on Science and Practice	*Organizational Dynamics*
	The Psychologist Manager Journal
International Journal of Selection and Assessment	**Trade Magazines**
International Journal of Training and Development	*HR Magazine*
Journal of Applied Psychology	*Personnel*
Journal of Applied Social Psychology	*Personnel Journal*
Journal of Business and Psychology	*Staffing Management*
	Training
Journal of Consulting Psychology: Practice & Research	*T+D Magazine (Training plus Development Magazine)*

Human Decision Processes (Zickar & Highhouse, 2001). Fortunately, most journals are available online, making them much easier to obtain.

Bridge publications are designed to "bridge the gap" between academia and the applied world. Articles in these publications are usually written by professors about a topic of interest to practitioners, but they are not as formal or statistically complex as articles in journals. Examples of bridge publications relevant to I/O psychology are *Academy of Management Executive, Harvard Business Review,* and *Organizational Dynamics.*

Trade magazines contain articles usually written by professional writers who have developed expertise in a given field. The main audience for trade magazines is practitioners in the field. Trade magazines present the research on a topic in an easy-to-understand format; however, the articles in these publications do not cover all the research on a topic and can be somewhat biased. *HR Magazine* and *Training* are examples of I/O-related trade magazines.

You are already familiar with **magazines** such as *People, Time,* and *Cat Fancy.* These periodicals are designed to entertain as well as inform. Magazines are good sources of ideas but terrible sources to use in support of a scientific hypothesis. Magazine articles are often written by professional writers who do not have training in the topic and thus little expertise in what they are writing about. As a result, the "scientific" information in magazines is often wrong.

An increasingly popular source of information is the Internet. As most of you have already discovered, the Internet contains a wealth of information on just about

Trade magazines A collection of articles for those "in the biz," about related professional topics, seldom directly reporting the methods and results of new research.

Magazines An unscientific collection of articles about a wide range of topics.

every topic. As useful as the Internet is, a word of caution is in order. There is no review of information placed on the Internet to ensure that it is accurate. For example, I was once involved with a project in which we were trying to profile the people who were setting off church fires. Because our first step was to get a list of church fires, we searched the Internet and found three webpages on church burnings. One was from *USA Today* and had a rather complete listing of church burnings, one was from a left-wing group, and the other was from a right-wing group. As you can imagine, the left- and right-wing pages listed only churches that confirmed their hypotheses about why the churches were burned. Had we used only one of these webpages, we would have made an inaccurate profile.

A problem with relying on secondary sources such as the Internet is that one cannot be sure if the information in a secondary source accurately reflects the information in the primary source. In the field of psychology, two excellent examples of this lack of accuracy are the use of the "little Albert" story to demonstrate the role of classical conditioning in learning phobias and the use of the Kitty Genovese story to demonstrate the lack of bystander intervention. In reviews of the accuracy of textbook information, Harris (1979) found many errors in the secondary accounts of little Albert, as did Manning, Levine, and Collins (2007) with what really happened to Kitty Genovese. For example, whereas Harris (1979) found that two texts indicated little Albert was conditioned to fear a rabbit rather than a rat, many texts incorrectly included such postconditioning stimuli as a teddy bear, a white furry glove, a fur pelt, a cat, and Albert's aunt and three texts described how Watson removed little Albert's fear of the rat, although no such reconditioning was actually done.

Manning and her colleagues (2007) compared the myth of the attack on Genovese to what actually happened and found numerous discrepancies between the story and reality. For example, most textbooks as well as an early newspaper article mention the 38 witnesses who saw the attack yet did nothing to help. Not only is there no evidence that there were 38 eyewitnesses, but there is evidence that at least two of the witnesses took action and called the police.

The Location of the Study

Once a research idea has been created and a hypothesis formed, you must decide whether to conduct the study in the laboratory or in the field.

Laboratory Research. Often when one hears the word *research,* the first thing that comes to mind is an experimenter in a white coat running subjects in a basement laboratory. Few experimenters actually wear white coats, but 32% of I/O psychology research is conducted in a laboratory (Roch, 2008). Usually, this is done at a university, but research is also conducted in such organizations as AT&T, the U.S. Office of Personnel Management, and Microsoft.

One disadvantage of laboratory research is **external validity**, or **generalizability** of results to organizations in the "real world." An example of this issue involves research about employee selection methods. It is not uncommon in such research for subjects to view a résumé or a videotape of an interview and make a judgment about a hypothetical applicant. The problem: Is the situation similar enough to actual employment decisions made in the real world, or is the laboratory environment so controlled and hypothetical that the results will not generalize? Although the answers to these questions have not been resolved, research is often conducted in laboratories because researchers can control many variables that are not of interest in the study.

External validity The extent to which research results can be expected to hold true outside the specific setting in which they were obtained.

Generalizability Like external validity, the extent to which research results hold true outside the specific setting in which they were obtained.

Field research Research conducted in a natural setting as opposed to a laboratory.

Field Research. Another location for research is away from the laboratory and out in the "field," which could be the assembly line of an automotive plant, the secretarial pool of a large insurance company, or the interviewing room at a personnel agency. **Field research** has a problem opposite to that of laboratory research. What field research obviously gains in external validity it loses in control of extraneous variables that are not of interest to the researcher (*internal validity*).

Does the location of a study make a difference? It can. A meta-analysis by Reichard and Avolio (2005) found that leadership training was more effective in laboratory studies than in field studies, and Gordon and Arvey (2004) found that age bias was stronger in laboratory settings than in field settings. However, in studies of teams, group cohesion (Mullen & Copper, 1994) and group personality composition (Bell, 2007) were related to performance more in field studies of real groups than in laboratory studies of groups created for the experiment.

Informed consent The formal process by which subjects give permission to be included in a study.

Field research also provides researchers with an ethical dilemma. Psychologists require that subjects participate in studies of their own free will—a concept called **informed consent**. In laboratory studies, informed consent is seldom an issue because potential subjects are told the nature and purpose of a study, their right to decline participation or withdraw from participation, the risks and benefits of participating, limits of confidentiality, and whom they can contact with questions (Salkind, 2006). They are then asked to sign an informed consent form indicating that they understand their rights as subjects and have chosen to voluntarily participate. In field studies, however, obtaining informed consent can not only be difficult but change the way people behave.

For example, suppose we think that making a supervisor's office more pleasant looking will increase the number of employees who visit the supervisor's office. After decorating five supervisors' offices with plants and paintings and making five other supervisors' offices look messy and cold, we use a video camera to record the number of office visitors. Would the results of our study be affected if we told our employees that they were going to be part of a study? Probably so.

On the basis of our ethical guidelines, informed consent can be waived only when the research involves minimal risk to the participants, the waiver will not adversely affect the rights of the participants, and the research could not be carried out without the waiver (Ilgen & Bell, 2001a).

Institutional review boards A committee designated to ensure the ethical treatment of research subjects.

When studies involve negative consequences for a subject, as would be the case if we subjected employees to intense heat to study the effects of temperature, informed consent can be waived only if the importance of the study outweighs the negative consequences. Universities have **institutional review boards** to monitor research to ensure ethical treatment of research participants. One area to which these review boards pay close attention is *confidentiality*. Because the data collected in research can be of a sensitive nature (e.g., performance ratings, salaries, test scores), researchers ensure confidentiality by using subject ID numbers rather than names and avoiding discussion of individual participants. Interestingly, authors of studies conducted in organizations submitted their research plans to institutional review boards only 44% of the time (Ilgen & Bell, 2001b).

The Research Method to Be Used

After deciding the location for the research, the researcher must determine which type of research method to use. The choices include experiments, quasi-experiments, archival research, observations, surveys, and meta-analyses.

Experiments. As you might recall from your general psychology course, the experimental method is the most powerful of all research methods because it is the only one that can determine **cause-and-effect relationships**. Thus, if it is important to know whether one variable produces or causes another variable to change, then the **experiment** is the only method that should be used.

Two characteristics define an experiment: (1) **manipulation** of one or more independent variables and (2) random assignment of subjects to experimental and control conditions. If either of these characteristics is missing, a research project cannot be called an experiment; instead, it is called a *quasi-experiment*, a *study*, a *survey*, or an *investigation*.

In an experiment, the researcher intentionally manipulates one or more aspects of the question of interest, called the **independent variable**, and measures the changes that occur as a result of that manipulation, called the **dependent variable**. For example, as shown in Table 1.6, a researcher might randomly assign 100 employees to receive customer service training and 100 employees to receive no training. Following the training program, the researcher looks at the change in customer spending. In this example, training is the independent variable (what was manipulated), and customer spending is the dependent variable (what was expected to change as a result of the independent variable). The employees who received the training are collectively called the **experimental group**, and the employees who did not receive the training are collectively called the **control group**.

Suppose we were interested in finding out whether wearing a suit to an interview is better for men than wearing a coat and slacks. We could study this issue by observing job applicants at a specific company and comparing the interview scores of people with suits with those of people wearing coats and slacks. We might find that the better-dressed applicants received higher scores, but we could not conclude that wearing a suit *caused* the higher scores; something other than the suit may be at work. Perhaps applicants who own suits are more socially skilled than other applicants; it then might have been social skill and not dress style that led to the higher interview scores.

If we want to determine that dress style affects interview scores, we have to manipulate the variable of interest and hold all other variables as constant as possible. How could we turn this into an experiment? Let us take 100 people and randomly assign 50 of them to wear suits and assign the other 50 to wear sport coats and slacks. Each subject then goes through an interview with an HR director. Afterward, we compare the interview scores of our two groups. In this case, the independent variable is the type of dress and the dependent variable is the interview score.

Even though this particular research design is not very sophisticated and has some problems (see if you can spot them), the fact that we manipulated the applicant's dress style gives us greater confidence that dress style was the cause of higher

Cause-and-effect relationships The result of a well-controlled experiment about which the researcher can confidently state that the independent variable caused the change in the dependent variable.

Experiment A type of research study in which the independent variable is manipulated by the experimenter.

Manipulation The alteration of a variable by an experimenter in expectation that the alteration will result in a change in the dependent variable.

Independent variable The manipulated variable in an experiment.

Dependent variable The measure of behavior that is expected to change as a result of changes in the independent variable.

Experimental group In an experiment, the group of subjects that receives the experimental treatment of interest to the experimenter.

Control group A group of employees who do not receive a particular type of training so that their performance can be compared with that of employees who do receive training.

Table 1.6   Example of an Experimental Design

Received Customer-Service Training in September	Average Customer Sales Per Employee		
	August	October	Change
Yes	$3,200	$4,700	$1,500
No	$3,100	$3,500	$ 400

interview scores. Even though the results of experiments provide more confidence regarding cause-and-effect relationships, ethical and practical considerations do not always make experimental designs possible.

Suppose we wish to study the effect of loud noise on worker performance. To make this an experimental design, we could have 50 subjects work on an assembly line while being subjected to very loud noise and 50 subjects work on an assembly line with no noise. Two months later, we compare the productivity of the two groups. But what is wrong with this study? In addition to having lower productivity, the high-noise group now has poorer hearing—not a very ethical-sounding experiment (yes, the pun *was* intended).

Quasi-experiments. Even though researchers prefer to use experiments, it is not always possible. **Quasi-experiments** are then used. As an example, let's go back to our noise study. Because we cannot manipulate the level of noise, we will instead test the noise level of 100 manufacturing plants and compare the average productivity of plants with lower noise levels with that of plants with higher noise levels. As you can easily see, this is not as good a research design as the unethical experiment that we created earlier. There are too many variables other than noise that could account for any differences found in productivity; however, given the circumstances, it still provides us with more information than we had before the study.

Quasi-experiments Research method in which the experimenter either does not manipulate the independent variable or in which subjects are not randomly assigned to conditions.

Quasi-experiments are often used to evaluate the results of a new program implemented by an organization. For example, an organization that had instituted a child-care center wanted to see whether the center had any effect on employee absenteeism. To find the answer, the organization compared absenteeism levels from the year before the center was introduced with the absenteeism levels for the year following the implementation; the organization found that both absenteeism and turnover had decreased.

Although it is tempting to conclude that the child-care center was a success, such a conclusion would not be prudent. Many other variables might have caused the reduction. As shown in Table 1.7, the organization implemented several other progressive programs during the same period. Thus, the decrease in absenteeism and turnover could have been the result of other programs or some combination of programs. Furthermore, the economy changed and jobs became more difficult to obtain. Workers may have reduced their absentee rates out of fear of being fired, and turnover may have been reduced because employees realized that few jobs were available. In addition, the weather improved in the second year, which meant workers were rarely unable to get to work.

Taken by itself, we would certainly not want to bet the mortgage on the results of our quasi-experiment. But if 10 other researchers conduct separate quasi-experiments to study the same question and find similar results, we might feel confident enough to make changes or reach conclusions based on the available research evidence.

Archival Research. Another research method that is commonly used in I/O psychology is **archival research**. Archival research involves using previously collected data or records to answer a research question. For example, if we want to know what distinguishes good workers from poor workers, we could look in the personnel files to see whether the backgrounds of good workers have common characteristics not shared by poor workers. Or, if we want to see if people on the night shift had more turnover than people on the day shift, we could get information on shift and turnover from the company records. Archival research has many desirable features, such as not

Archival research Research that involves the use of previously collected data.

Table 1.7   Why Nonexperimental Studies Are Difficult to Interpret: The Child-Care Center

Date	Absenteeism %	External Factor	Internal Factor
1/10	2.8		
2/10	3.1		
3/10	4.7	Unemployment rate at 4.1%	
4/10	4.7		
5/10	4.8		
6/10	6.7	Main highway closed	
7/10	6.5		
8/10	4.9	Highway reopens	
9/10	4.5		
10/10	4.4		
11/10	8.7	Terrible snowstorm	
12/10	5.3		
1/11	5.3		Child care center started
2/11	5.2		
3/11	5.1		Flextime program started
4/11	2.0	Local unemployment rate hits 9.3%	
5/11	2.0		
6/11	2.0		
7/11	1.8		Wellness program started
8/11	1.8		
9/11	2.0		New attendance policy
10/11	2.1		
11/11	4.0	Mild weather	
12/11	4.2	Mild weather	

Note: Absenteeism rate in 2010 before child care center = 5.09%; rate in 2011 after child care center = 3.01%.

being obtrusive or expensive, but it also has severe drawbacks (Shultz, Hoffman, & Reiter-Palmon, 2005). Records in files are not always accurate and are not always kept up-to-date. Furthermore, the type of data needed by a researcher may not be in the archives because the data were never recorded in the first place.

As an undergraduate (this was before the big dance), I was involved with an archival study designed to determine why some students in an executive Master of Business Administration (MBA) program dropped out while others completed their coursework. What was supposed to be an easy job of getting records from a few files turned into a nightmare. The records of more than 300 students were scattered in storage rooms in three locations in Southern California and were not filed in any order. Furthermore, almost every student had at least one important item missing from his or her file. Needless to say, these problems kept the results of the study from being as accurate as desired. Now, however, the computerization of information has greatly increased the potential for archival research.

Surveys. Another method of conducting research is to *ask* people their opinion on some topic. Surveys might ask employees about their attitudes toward the organization, HR directors about their opinions regarding the best recruitment method, or managers about the success of their child-care centers.

Surveys can be conducted by mail, personal interviews, phone, fax, email, Internet, or magazines. The method chosen depends on such factors as sample size, budget, amount of time available to conduct the study, and need for a representative sample. For example, mail surveys are less expensive and time-consuming than personal interviews but result in lower response rates and, at times, lower-quality answers. Email surveys are inexpensive but are limited to people who have email (not a representative sample), are more subject to size and format restrictions, and result in lower response rates than mail surveys (Czaja & Blair, 2005). Internet surveys are also inexpensive, but as with email, are limited to people who have access to a computer. A comparison of people responding to Internet surveys and those responding to more traditional methods indicates that Internet surveys more accurately reflect the population in terms of gender and social class but less accurately reflect the population in terms of race (Gosling, Vazire, Srivastava, & John, 2004).

The importance of the survey method used cannot be overstated. For example, in 1998 the *Roanoke Times and World News* conducted a survey of the top motion pictures in history. People who mailed in their votes chose *Gone with the Wind, The Sound of Music, The Wizard of Oz, It's a Wonderful Life,* and *To Kill a Mockingbird* as their top five; people who responded by email chose *Gone with the Wind, Star Wars, Schindler's List, The Wizard of Oz,* and *The Shawshank Redemption.*

Another example of differences in survey samples occurred in February 1998. Nykesha Sales was one point short of setting the University of Connecticut career-scoring record in women's basketball when she ruptured an Achilles tendon, an injury that ended her season. Her coach arranged a deal with their next opponent (Villanova) to allow Sales to score an uncontested basket so that she could break the record. In the days after the Villanova game, the media debated whether allowing Sales to score was a class act designed to honor a great player or a strike at the integrity of the game. In separate surveys, 60% of respondents to ESPN's website thought the gesture was a class act compared with only 47% of the respondents to *USA Today*'s website (Patrick, 1998).

A multinational study by Church (2001) found some interesting results regarding survey methods. Employees from the United States, Japan, and France preferred automated phone response technology, whereas employees in Germany, Italy, and the United Kingdom preferred the traditional paper-and-pencil method. Employees completing the survey online were more likely to leave items blank than were employees using a paper-and-pencil format.

Although a high response rate is essential for trust to be placed in survey results, survey response rates have been on the decline (Anseel, Lievens, Schollaert, & Choragwicka, 2010). Based on the meta-analysis results of Anseel et al. (2010), response rates can be increased by doing the following:

- Notifying participants in advance that they will be receiving a survey
- Personalizing the survey through such means as an original signature or addressing the participant in a cover letter

- Ensuring that survey responses will be anonymous by using identification numbers
- Having a university sponsor the survey
- Distributing the survey in person rather than through the mail

Contrary to popular belief, providing incentives and sending reminders do not increase survey responses (Anseel et al., 2010).

Well-designed survey questions are easy to understand, use simple language, do not ask about hypothetical situations, and are relatively short in length. Care must be taken in choosing the words used in each question. An excellent example of this comes from the polls conducted during the impeachment of former president Bill Clinton. First, accurate poll results were hindered by the fact that nearly one-third of adults didn't understand the word *impeachment* (Morin, 1999). Second, the wording of the different polls resulted in substantially different results. Consider the following examples provided by Morin (1999):

Should Clinton resign if he is impeached or should he *fight the charges* in the Senate?

Should Clinton resign if he is impeached or should he *remain in office to stand trial* in the Senate?

For the first question, 59% said that Clinton should resign. For the second question, only 43% said he should resign.

A final issue involving surveys is the extent to which responses to the survey questions are accurate. This issue is especially important when asking about sensitive or controversial issues. That is, if I ask whether you believe that men and women are equally qualified to be managers, would you tell the truth if you thought men were better qualified? Would people honestly respond to questions about their former drug use, poor performance at work, or unethical behavior? Probably not. But they do seem to be accurate when reporting such things as height and body weight (Imrhan, Imrhan, & Hart, 1996). A good example of people not being truthful in surveys occurred when researchers asked 1,000 adults if they regularly washed their hands after using a public restroom; 94% said yes. However, when researchers observed people in restrooms, less than 70% washed their hands (Mattox, 1997).

Inaccurately responding to survey questions is not always an intentional attempt to be dishonest. Instead, inaccurate responses can be the result of a person not actually knowing the correct answer to a question. For example, an employee might respond to a question about attendance by stating she has missed three days of work in the past year when in fact she missed five. Was she lying, or just mistaken about her attendance record?

An interesting investigation into the accuracy of survey responses was a meta-analysis of studies comparing self-reported grade point averages and SAT scores with the actual scores (Kuncel, Credé, & Thomas, 2005). The meta-analysis indicated that the self-reported GPAs and SAT scores correlated highly with actual scores (.90 for college GPA and .82 for SAT scores). Although the scores were highly correlated, there was a tendency for the self-reported GPAs and SAT scores to be higher than the actual scores.

Meta-Analysis. Meta-analysis is a statistical method of reaching conclusions based on previous research. Prior to meta-analysis, a researcher interested in reviewing the

Effect size Used in meta-analysis, a statistic that indicates the amount of change caused by an experimental manipulation.

Mean effect size Used in meta-analysis, a statistic that is the average of the effect sizes for all studies included in the analysis.

Correlation coefficients A statistic, resulting from performing a correlation, that indicates the magnitude and direction of a relationship.

Difference score A type of effect size used in meta-analysis that is signified by the letter *d* and indicates how many standard deviations separate the mean score for the experimental group from the control group.

Practical significance The extent to which the results of a study have actual impact on human behavior.

literature on a topic would read all of the available research and then make a rather subjective conclusion based on the articles. With meta-analysis, the researcher goes through each article, determines the **effect size** for each article, and then finds a statistical average of effect sizes across all articles. A meta-analysis results in one number, called the **mean effect size**, which indicates the effectiveness of some variable.

Correlation coefficients (r) are used as the effect size when researchers are interested in the *relationship* between two variables, and the majority of studies use correlation as their statistical test. Examples include studies looking at the relationship between personality and job performance, integrity test scores and employee theft, and the relationship between job satisfaction and performance.

A **difference score** (d) is used as the effect size when researchers are looking at the *difference* between two groups. Examples are studies looking at the effectiveness of a training method, the effect of goal setting, and the effects of shift work. Effect sizes can be interpreted in two ways: by comparing them to norms or directly applying them to a particular situation. Effect sizes (d) less than .40 are considered to be small; those between .40 and .80 are moderate, and those higher than .80 are considered large (Cohen, 1988). Of course, these numbers are "rules of thumb"; the actual **practical significance** of an effect size depends on many factors—formulas are available to be more precise. The average effect size for an organizational intervention is .44 (Guzzo, Jette, & Katzell, 1985).

When directly applying an effect size to a particular situation, you need to know the standard deviation of the variable in question. This standard deviation is then multiplied by the effect size from the meta-analysis to yield a meaningful score. Confused? Perhaps an example would help.

Suppose employees at a John Deere manufacturing plant miss an average of 9.5 days of work per year with a standard deviation of 3.6 days. John Deere is considering a new incentive system to improve attendance that a meta-analysis indicates has an effect size of .32 in reducing absenteeism. What can John Deere expect to gain from this incentive system? By multiplying their absenteeism standard deviation (3.6 days) by the effect size from the meta-analysis (.32), John Deere can expect the incentive system to reduce absenteeism by an average of 1.15 days per employee (3.6 × .32 = 1.15). If the attendance data for General Motors were an average of 10.4 days per year missed with a standard deviation of 5.6, it could expect an annual reduction in absenteeism of 1.79 days per employee (5.6 × .32 = 1.79). John Deere and General Motors would each have to decide if the predicted reduction in savings is worth the cost of the incentive system.

A complete discussion of meta-analysis is beyond the scope of this book and probably beyond your interest as well. It is important, however, that you be able to interpret the outcomes of meta-analyses because they are used in this text and are the current standard when reviewing previous research. Points to keep in mind as you read the text:

- Because meta-analyses summarize all of the available studies on a topic, a reference to a meta-analysis should carry more weight than a reference to only one or two studies.
- When describing meta-analysis results, I will often include the effect size at the end of a sentence. For example, I might write, "References are not good predictors of performance, $r = .18$, $p = .27$." The symbol r indicates the actual correlation from the meta-analysis. The symbol p, known as *rho*, is the correlation after it has been corrected for factors that can reduce the size of a

correlation. These factors are called artifacts, and you can learn more about them in the meta-analysis chapter of the statistics primer that was written to accompany this text (Aamodt, Cohen, & Surrette, 2010). Rho is often referred to as the *corrected* correlation or the *true* correlation.

To help you understand the various research designs you just learned about, complete Exercise 1.1 in your workbook.

Subject Samples

Decisions also must be made regarding the size, composition, and method of selecting the subjects who will serve as the sample in a study. Although it is nice to have a large sample for any research study, a large sample size is not necessary if the experimenter can choose a random sample and control for many of the extraneous variables. In fact, properly conducted surveys need only about 1,000 participants to generalize survey results to the entire U.S. population (Deane, 1999).

The method of selecting the sample is certainly dependent on the nature of the organization. A small organization will probably be forced to use all of its employees, which means that the sample will be small but highly representative of the intended population. For economical and practical reasons, a large organization will select only certain employees to participate in a study rather than use the entire workforce. The problem then becomes one of which employees will participate.

If the study involves a questionnaire, it is no problem to randomly select a desired number of employees and have them complete the survey. If, however, the study is more elaborate, such as investigating the effects of lighting on performance, it would be difficult to randomly select employees. That is, it would not be practical to have one employee work under high levels of light while the person next to her is uninvolved with the experiment. If we decide to have one plant work with high levels of light and another with lower levels, what we gain in practicality we lose in randomness and control. So we try to strike a balance between practicality and experimental rigor.

To increase experimental rigor and decrease the costs of conducting research, many studies are conducted at universities using students as subjects rather than employees. In fact, college students served as subjects in 46% of research studies published in four leading I/O journals (Roch, 2008). This use of students has led to considerable debate regarding the generalizability of university research; that is, do students behave in the same fashion as employees? Some authors (e.g., Sears, 1986) point out that compared with adults, college students are younger, more educated, and more egocentric; possess a less formulated sense of self; and have a stronger need for peer approval. Because of these differences, it makes sense that students would behave differently from adults who are in the working world.

Research on this issue, however, is mixed. Some researchers have found differences between student subjects and professional subjects, but others have not (Bordens & Abbott, 2011). For example, in a meta-analysis investigating the relationship between personality and team performance, the personality traits of agreeableness and conscientiousness predicted team performance when professionals were used as subjects but not when students were used as subjects (Peeters, Van Tuijl, Rutte, & Reymen, 2006). Likewise, Gordon and Arvey (2004) found that students and professionals differed in research on age bias. However, in a meta-analysis of the relationship between locus of control (the extent to which a person believes she has control over her life) and work outcome, Ng, Sorensen, and Eby (2006) found that the relationship was similar whether the subjects were employees or students. Because students and professionals do not always respond the same way in studies, it is important to keep in mind that studies using students as research subjects may not generalize to the real world.

A final important issue concerns the method used to recruit subjects. To obtain the best research results, it is essential to use a **random sample** so that the sample will be as representative as possible. This means that if a survey is randomly sent to 100 employees, the research will be most accurate only if all employees return the survey. The problem is that researchers are unlikely to get a 100% return rate if study participation is voluntary. The ethics of the American Psychological Association (APA) require voluntary participation, but accurate research often requires compulsory participation. How do researchers resolve this dilemma? In some organizations, employees are required to sign a statement when they are hired agreeing to participate in any organizational research studies. To underscore this agreement, research participation is listed in each employee's job description.

Proponents of this method argue that participation in research is still voluntary because the individual had the choice of either not taking the job or taking it with the advance knowledge of research requirements. Opponents argue that taking a job or not taking a job in order to make a living does not constitute a proper and completely free choice. Similarly, in some universities, students have the option of participating in a few research studies or writing a term paper. Even though the students are given an alternative to research participation, some psychologists argue that the choice between writing a term paper that will take several days and participating in two or three experiments that will take a few hours is not a legitimate choice (Sieber & Saks, 1989).

Because obtaining random samples is very difficult, especially in industry, many studies use a **convenience sample** and then randomly assign subjects to the various experimental conditions. A convenience sample, such as students in a psychology class, is easily available to a researcher. With **random assignment**, each subject in a nonrandom sample is randomly *assigned* to a particular experimental condition. For example, in a study designed to test the effectiveness of a training method, 60 subjects agree to participate in the study. Thirty of the subjects are randomly assigned to the group receiving training, and another 30 are randomly assigned to the control group that does not receive training. Random assignment is important when using convenience samples, as research indicates that random and nonrandom assignment result in different outcomes (Shadish & Ragsdale, 1996). If random assignment is a better method than nonrandom assignment, why would a researcher not randomly assign participants? Usually because of limitations placed on the researcher. For example, if a union contract stipulated that employees with longer tenure had first choice in the shift they worked, a researcher studying the effects of shift work could not randomly assign employees to various shifts.

Running the Study

When all of these decisions have been made, it is finally time to run the study and collect data. To ensure that data are collected in an unbiased fashion, it is important that all instructions to the subjects be stated in a standardized fashion and at a level that is understandable. Once the subject is finished with her participation, she should be **debriefed**, or told the purpose of the experiment and be given a chance to ask questions about her participation.

Random sample A sample in which every member of the relevant population had an equal chance of being chosen to participate in the study.

Convenience sample A nonrandom research sample that is used because it is easily available.

Random assignment The random, unbiased assignment of subjects in a research sample to the various experimental and control conditions.

Debriefed Informing the subject in an experiment about the purpose of the study in which he or she was a participant and providing any other relevant information.

Statistical Analysis

After all data have been collected, the results are statistically analyzed. A discussion of statistics is beyond the scope of this book, but it is important to understand why statistics are used. Statistical analysis helps us determine how confident we are that our results are real and did not occur by chance alone. For example, if we conducted a study in your classroom in which we compared the average age of students on the left side of the room with that of students on the right side of the room, we would no doubt get a difference. That is, the average age of the students on the right would not be exactly the same as that for students on the left. If we did not conduct a statistical analysis of our data, we would conclude that people on the right side are older than people on the left side. Perhaps we could even develop a theory about our results.

Does this sound ridiculous? Of course it does. But it points out the idea that any set of numbers we collect will in all probability be different. The question is, are they *significantly* different? Statistical analysis provides the answer by determining the probability that our data were the result of chance. In psychology, we use the .05 level of significance: If our analysis indicates that the probability that our data resulted from chance is 5% or less, we consider our results to be statistically significant. Although the .05 level of significance is the most commonly used, some researchers have suggested that we should be more flexible and use either more conservative or more liberal levels, depending upon the situation (Bordens & Abbott, 2011).

At this point, a caution must be made about the interpretation of significance levels. Significance levels indicate only the level of confidence we can place on a result being the product of chance. They say nothing about the strength of the results. Thus, a study with results significant at the .01 level does not necessarily show a stronger effect than a study with results significant at the .05 level of confidence.

To determine the strength of a finding, we use the effect size, discussed earlier in the section on meta-analysis. Significance levels tell us the *statistical significance* of a study, and effect sizes (combined with logic) tell us the *practical significance* of a study.

For example, suppose we conduct a study comparing the SAT scores of male and female high school students. Based on a sample of 5 million students, we find that males average 1,502 and females 1,501. With such a huge sample size, we will probably find that the two means are statistically different. However, with only a 1-point difference between the two groups on a test with a maximum score of 2,400, we would probably not place much practical significance in the difference.

Correlation A statistical procedure used to measure the relationship between two variables.

Correlation. It is necessary to discuss one particular statistic—correlation—because it is so widely used in I/O psychology and throughout this book. **Correlation** is a statistical procedure that enables a researcher to determine the *relationship* between two variables—for example, the relationships found between an employment test and future employee performance; job satisfaction and job attendance; or performance ratings made by workers and supervisors. It is important to understand that correlational analysis does not necessarily say anything about causality.

Intervening variable A third variable that can often explain the relationship between two other variables.

Why does a correlation coefficient not indicate a cause-and-effect relationship? Because a third variable, an **intervening variable**, often accounts for the relationship between two variables. Take the example often used by psychologist David Schroeder. Suppose there is a correlation of +.80 between the number of ice cream cones sold in New York during August and the number of babies that die during August in India.

Does eating ice cream kill babies in another nation? No, that would not make sense. Instead, we look for that third variable that would explain our high correlation. In this case, the answer is clearly the summer heat.

Another interesting example was provided by Mullins (1986) in a presentation about the incorrect interpretation of correlation coefficients. Mullins pointed out that data show a strong negative correlation between the number of cows per square mile and the crime rate. With his tongue firmly planted in his cheek, Mullins suggested that New York City could rid itself of crime by importing millions of heads of cattle. Of course, the real interpretation for the negative correlation is that crime is greater in urban areas than in rural areas.

A good researcher should always be cautious about variables that seem related. Several years ago, *People* magazine reported on a minister who conducted a "study" of 500 pregnant teenage girls and found that rock music was being played when 450 of them became pregnant. The minister concluded that because the two are related (i.e., they occurred at the same time), rock music must cause pregnancy. His solution? Outlaw rock music, and teenage pregnancy would disappear. In my own "imaginary study," however, I found that in all 500 cases of teenage pregnancy, a pillow also was present. To use the same logic as that used by the minister, the real solution would be to outlaw pillows, not rock music. Although both "solutions" are certainly strange, the point should be clear: Just because two events occur at the same time or seem to be related does not mean that one event or variable causes another.

The result of correlational analysis is a number called a correlation coefficient. The values of this coefficient range from -1 to $+1$; the further the coefficient is from zero, the greater the relationship between two variables. That is, a correlation of .40 shows a stronger relationship between two variables than a correlation of .20. Likewise, a correlation of $-.39$ shows a stronger relationship than a correlation of $+.30$. The $(+)$ and $(-)$ signs indicate the *direction* of the correlation. A positive $(+)$ correlation means that as the values of one variable increase, so do the values of a second variable. For example, we might find a positive correlation between intelligence and scores on a classroom exam. This would mean that the more intelligent the student, the higher her score on the exam.

A negative $(-)$ correlation means that as the values of one variable increase, the values of a second variable decrease. For example, we would probably find a negative correlation between the number of beers that you drink the night before a test and your score on that test. In I/O psychology, we find negative correlations between job satisfaction and absenteeism, age and reaction time, and nervousness and interview success.

To put together everything you have learned about research in Chapter 1, complete Exercises 1.2 and 1.3 in your workbook.

Ethics in Industrial/Organizational Psychology

Organizations and employees are faced with ethical dilemmas every day. Ethical dilemmas are ambiguous situations that require a personal judgment of what is right or wrong because there are no rules, policies, or laws guiding such decisions.

Individuals often rely on their morals and personal values, which often leads to different decisions by different people in similar situations. Because people have different backgrounds that impact their personal values and how they define a particular situation, the decision one person makes may be very different than what another one makes.

For example, suppose you want to sell your car. You know that your car has been in several accidents and has had a lot of work done on it. Do you share that information with a prospective buyer? There is no law or policy that says you must. In fact, most people would say that unless the buyer specifically asks you that question you shouldn't bring it up at all. Is it morally wrong or unfair not to share this information? Based on an individual's value system, the answer may be "yes," it is morally wrong, or "no," it's not morally wrong.

In life, we often encounter two types of ethical dilemmas: Type A and Type B.

In a Type A dilemma, there is a high level of uncertainty as to what is right or wrong, there appears to be no best solution, and there are both positive and negative consequences to a decision. For example, many people would say that drug research that uses animals to test new drugs is unethical, because it is morally wrong to hurt any living creature. Others would say that new drugs could save millions of lives and that it would be morally wrong *not* to make and test drugs that could potentially save human lives. As you can see, there seems to be no one best answer, as there are both negative and positive consequences in making this decision.

In a Type B dilemma, also called rationalizing dilemmas, the difference between right and wrong is much clearer than in a Type A dilemma. Usually, individuals know what is right but choose the solution that is most advantageous to themselves. For example, choosing not to tell a prospective buyer about any past damage that occurred with a car for sale would have the most advantages for the seller. Type B dilemmas are called rationalizing dilemmas because individuals "rationalize" they are right because "everyone else does it." For example, many students will say that they have cheated at least one time on a test. Most of those students would agree that it is morally wrong to cheat. So why have so many done it? They rationalize that "for just this one time" it is okay and that it is not hurting anyone. And they convince themselves that because everyone else is doing it, it must be okay. This ability to rationalize is why unethical behavior is at an all-time high in organizations. In a survey done by Careerbuilder.com (2005) of 2,050 workers, 19% of them reported participating in the unethical act of lying in the workplace at some point in their professional career. In a survey by the Ethics Resource Center in 2007, 56% of workers surveyed reported witnessing unethical behavior from others, including such things as "borrowing" work supplies and taking them home, stealing pencils and other equipment, using sick leave when they weren't sick, abuse of employees by management, and coming in late and leaving early.

At the end of each successive chapter in this textbook, you will be presented with some ethical dilemmas for which you are asked to discuss and answer questions. Using the information from this section, decide whether you think those situations are ethical or unethical. There is no right or wrong answer. Compare your thoughts and ideas with other classmates to get a clear perspective of how difficult it is to get everyone to make the same decision when faced with an ethical dilemma as opposed to a decision that is guided by law or policy.

Applied Case Study

The Vancouver International Airport, located in Richmond, British Columbia, is Canada's second busiest airport, having served over 16.8 million passengers in 2010. It has twice been named the top airport in North America for overall customer satisfaction. Thus, it takes great pride in its employees and their performance.

The Airport Authority oversees more than 300 employees in such areas as project management, finance, human resources, engineering, communications, and emergency preparedness. Employees working for the airlines, stores, and restaurants are not part of the Airport Authority, as they are employees of private companies.

To reduce costs and increase productivity, the Vancouver Airport Authority designed a wellness program for its employees. The program, called *Fitness and Balance*, comprises many components, including seminars on such topics as smoking cessation and stress management; health-related newsletters and announcements; outdoor-activity days in which employees and their families could hike, skate, or walk; and discounts at fitness facilities. To determine the effectiveness of this program, the Airport Authority collected data and found that absenteeism dropped from 4.07% to 2.55% and that the number of annual injuries dropped from 22 to 6.

■ How would you have designed the study to determine the effectiveness of the wellness program?

■ What outcome measures other than absenteeism and injuries might you use?

■ What ethical or practical considerations need to be considered when collecting and reporting data in a study such as this one?

More information on this case can be found at http://www.phac-aspc.gc.ca/pau-uap/fitness/work/study_vancouver_e.html

Chapter Summary

In this chapter you learned:

■ The field of I/O psychology consists of three major subfields: personnel psychology, organizational psychology, and human factors. Industrial psychologists work in a variety of settings including industry, government, education, and consulting firms.

■ The field of I/O psychology began in the early 1900s and has grown rapidly since then: Division 14 of the APA began in 1945 with 130 members and now has over 8,000 members.

■ World War I, World War II, the Hawthorne studies, civil rights legislation, new technology, and changing demographics have had important impacts on I/O psychology.

■ At least a master's degree is required to find employment in the field, and median salaries currently are around $74,500 at the master's level and $105,000 at the Ph.D. level.

■ Research is important so that I/O psychologists can make the best decisions.

■ Decisions must be made regarding what to research, the location of the research (laboratory or field), the research method that will be used (experimental method, nonexperimental method, survey, archival research, meta-analysis), the sample that will be used, and the statistics that will be selected to analyze the research data.

Questions for Review

1. What were the important events that shaped the field of I/O psychology?
2. What role will changes in demographics play in how we hire and manage employees?
3. If you wanted to pursue a career in I/O psychology, what would you need to do between now and graduation to make this career possible?
4. How are theories and hypotheses different?
5. Is a random sample really better than a convenience sample? Why or why not?
6. When would you use a quasi-experiment rather than an experiment?
7. Why don't correlations between two variables indicate that one caused the other?

Media Resources and Learning Tools

- Visit our website. Go to www.cengage.com/psychology/aamodt, where you will find online resources directly linked to your book, including chapter-by-chapter quizzing, flashcards, crossword puzzles, application activities, and more.
- Want more practice applying industrial/organizational psychology? Check out the *I/O Applications Workbook.* This workbook (keyed to your textbook) offers engaging, high-interest activities to help you reinforce the important concepts presented in the text.

© Chris Ryan/OJO Images/Getty Images

Learning Objectives

➡ Understand the definition and uses of job analysis

➡ Know how to write a job description

➡ Know how to conduct a job analysis

➡ Learn when to use the various job analysis methods

➡ Understand the concept of job evaluation

➡ Understand the concept of pay equity

In 1585, 15 English settlers established a colony on Roanoke Island near what is now the Outer Banks of the North Carolina coast. When John White arrived at Roanoke Island in 1590, he found no trace of the colony and only the word *Croatan* carved on a tree. To this day, it is not known what happened to the settlers of the Lost Colony of Roanoke.

Many theories have been put forth to explain the fate of the lost colony—killed by Indians, moved to another location, and so on. One theory is that the members of the colony were not prepared to survive in the new continent; that is, the group consisted of politicians, soldiers, and sailors. Although worthy individuals were sent to the New World, few had the necessary training and skills to survive. In fact, the colony might have survived if settlers with more appropriate skills, such as farmers, had been sent instead of the traditional explorer types. Thus, a better match between job requirements and personnel might have saved the colony.

Does this sound far-fetched? Perhaps so, but the story does underscore the importance of a process called *job analysis*—gathering, analyzing, and structuring information about a job's components, characteristics, and requirements (Sanchez & Levine, 2000).

Job Analysis

Importance of Job Analysis

A thorough job analysis is the foundation for almost all human resources activities. It is difficult to imagine how one could write a job description, select employees, evaluate performance, or conduct training programs without knowing the tasks an employee performs, the conditions under which they are performed, and the competencies needed to perform the tasks. A thorough job analysis provides such information.

Writing Job Descriptions

One of the written products of a job analysis is a job description—a brief, two- to five-page summary of the tasks and job requirements found in the job analysis. In other words, the job analysis is the *process* of determining the work activities and requirements, and the job description is the written *result* of the job analysis. Job analyses and job descriptions serve as the basis for many HR activities, including employee selection, evaluation, training, and work design.

Employee Selection

It is difficult to imagine how an employee can be selected unless there is a clear understanding of the tasks to be performed and the competencies needed to perform those tasks. By identifying such requirements, it is possible to select tests or develop interview questions that will determine whether a particular applicant possesses the necessary knowledge, skills, and abilities to carry out the requirements of the job. Although this seems like common sense, the discussion of the unstructured employment interview in Chapter 4 demonstrates that many non-job-related variables are often used to select employees. Examples are height requirements for police officers, firm handshakes for most jobs, and physical attractiveness for airline flight attendants.

Training

Again, it is difficult to see how employees can be trained unless the requirements of the job are known. Job analyses yield lists of job activities that can be systematically used to create training programs.

Personpower Planning

One important but seldom employed use of job analysis is to determine *worker mobility* within an organization. That is, if individuals are hired for a particular job, to what other jobs can they expect to eventually be promoted and become successful? Many organizations have a policy of promoting the person who performs the best in the job immediately below the one in question. Although this approach has its advantages, it can result in the so-called **Peter Principle**: promoting employees until they eventually reach their highest level of incompetence (Peter & Hull, 1969). For example, consider an employee who is the best salesperson in the company. Even though this person is known to be excellent in sales, it is not known what type of supervisor he or she will be. Promotion solely on the basis of sales performance does not guarantee that the individual will do well as a supervisor. Suppose, however, that job analysis results are used to compare all jobs in the company to the supervisor's job. Instead of promoting the person in the job immediately below the supervisor, we promote the best employee from the most similar job—that is, a job that already involves much of the same knowledge, skills, and abilities as the supervisor's job. With this approach, there is a better match between the person being promoted and the requirements of the job.

Peter Principle The idea that organizations tend to promote good employees until they reach the level at which they are not competent—in other words, their highest level of incompetence.

Performance Appraisal

Another important use of job analysis is the construction of a performance appraisal instrument. As in employee selection, the evaluation of employee performance must be job related. Employees are often evaluated with forms that use such vague categories as "dependability," "knowledge," and "initiative." The use of specific, job-related categories leads to more accurate performance appraisals that are better accepted not only by employees but also by the courts (Werner & Bolino, 1997). In addition, when properly administered and utilized, job-related performance appraisals can serve as an excellent source of employee training and counseling.

Job Classification

Job analysis enables a human resources professional to classify jobs into groups based on similarities in requirements and duties. Job classification is useful for determining pay levels, transfers, and promotions.

Job Evaluation

Job analysis information can also be used to determine the *worth* of a job. Job evaluation will be discussed in greater detail later in this chapter.

Job Design

Job analysis information can be used to determine the optimal way in which a job should be performed. That is, what would be the best way for an employee to sit at her computer or what would be the best way for a warehouse person to lift boxes? By analyzing a job, wasted and unsafe motions can be eliminated, resulting in higher productivity and reduced numbers of job injuries. A job design was mentioned in Chapter 1 with the example of Frank Gilbreth, who, after studying the inconsistency with which brick masons did their work, was able to reduce from 18 to 4½ the number of motions needed to lay a brick.

Compliance with Legal Guidelines

As will be discussed in greater detail in Chapter 3, any employment decision must be based on job-related information. One legally acceptable way to directly determine job relatedness is by job analysis. No law specifically requires a job analysis, but several important guidelines and court cases mandate job analysis for all practical purposes.

First, the *Uniform Guidelines on Employee Selection Procedures* (UGESP, 1978)—the HR principles designed to ensure compliance with federal standards—contain several direct references to the necessity of job analysis. Even though the *Uniform Guidelines* are not law, courts have granted them "great deference" (Brannick, Levine, & Morgeson, 2007).

Second, several court cases have discussed the concept of job relatedness. For example, in *Griggs v. Duke Power* (1971), employment decisions were based in part upon applicants' possession of a high school diploma. Because a higher percentage of blacks than whites did not meet this requirement, smaller percentages of blacks were hired and promoted. Thus, a suit was filed against the Duke Power Company charging that a high school diploma was not necessary to carry out the demands of the job. The court agreed with Griggs, the plaintiff, stating that the company had indeed not established the job relatedness of the high school diploma requirement.

Although not specifically mentioning the term "job analysis," the decision in *Griggs* was the first to address the issue of job relatedness. Subsequent cases such as *Albermarle v. Moody* (1975) and *Chance v. Board of Examiners* (1971) further established the necessity of job relatedness and the link between it and job analysis.

Organizational Analysis

During the course of their work, job analysts often become aware of certain problems within an organization. For example, during a **job analysis interview**, an employee may indicate that she does not know how she is evaluated or to whom she is supposed to report. The discovery of such lapses in organizational communication can then be used to correct problems and help an organization function better. For example, while conducting job analysis interviews of credit union positions, job analyst Deborah Peggans discovered that none of the workers knew how their job performances were evaluated. This let the organization know it had not done an adequate job of communicating performance standards to its employees.

Writing a Good Job Description

As mentioned earlier, one of the most useful results of a job analysis is the job description. A job description is a relatively short summary of a job and should be about two to five pages in length. This suggested length is not really typical of most job descriptions used in industry; they tend to be only one page. But for a job description to be of value, it must describe a job in enough detail that decisions about activities such as selection and training can be made. Such decisions probably cannot be made if the description is only one page long.

Though I/O psychologists believe that job descriptions should be detailed and lengthy, many professionals in organizations resist such efforts. These professionals worry that listing each activity will limit their ability to direct employees to perform tasks not listed on the job description. The concern is that an employee, referring to

My company conducts research to develop and validate physical performance and cognitive tests and medical guidelines. To provide our clients with valid, defensible selection, evaluation, and promotion instruments, we conduct detailed job analyses to determine job requirements. Job analysis provides the foundation for establishing the validity of selection and promotion procedures. To develop valid, defensive procedures that reflect the essential job functions, the job tasks, knowledge, skills, and abilities must be defined. Conducting the job analysis can be one of the most rewarding aspects of a project because the job analyst is exposed to new environments and new people.

To become an effective job analyst, one must be able to learn the details involved in another person's job. This is a highlight of the process because it affords us the opportunity to visit job sites and interview incumbents. These site visits have provided us with some exciting and interesting experiences. For example, our work in the natural gas industry involved observing work performed on a drilling platform 100 miles out in the Gulf of Mexico to learn how to repair engines with 5-foot-long pistons. Similarly, interviewing workers in a manhole while they repair telephone cable provides a true understanding of why there may be occasional static on your home phone line.

Each project provides new challenges to the job analyst in capturing the purpose and details associated with the job tasks. In many instances, this information is best obtained by accompanying the worker on a shift and participating in the work. To understand the work of public safety personnel, we rode with paramedics in New York

**Deborah
L. Gebhardt, Ph.D.**
*President, Human
Performance Systems, Inc.*

Courtesy of the author

City, followed firefighters into a burning building, and answered domestic dispute calls with police officers.

When developing physical performance assessment procedures and medical guidelines, it is important to gather information about the ergonomic parameters that affect the workplace and the worker. Ergonomics applies knowledge of human capabilities and requirements to the design of work devices, systems, and the physical work setting. Ergonomic evaluations can involve specific analysis of working postures and their effect on muscle fatigue or general gathering of data such as heights, weights, and forces involved in task performance. This again involves on-site measurements and observations. For instance, we obtained measurements of the force required to open the hatches and doors on navy destroyers and in nuclear power plants. In another study, learning to climb telephone poles was necessary to obtain the ergonomic data needed to determine whether men and women used different climbing techniques.

Conducting a job analysis provides an appreciation and understanding of the ingenuity of the American workforce. We observed firsthand the advances in mechanized and electronic control systems and administrative procedures that have increased productivity, made work environments more pleasant, and decreased work-related injuries.

If you are conducting a job analysis, the best advice I can offer is to get involved in the process by learning as much as possible about the job. All jobs are not exciting, but for a job analyst it is important to be interested in the job and allow the incumbent to provide relevant information. This requires asking many questions about the work to obtain detailed information. To do this effectively, the job analyst must be fully and genuinely engaged in the process.

---

the job description as support, might respond, "It's not my job." This fear, however, can be countered with two arguments. The first is that duties can always be added to a job description, which can, and should, be updated on a regular basis. The second is that the phrase "and performs other job-related duties as assigned" should be included in the job description. In fact, Virginia Tech has a policy stating that the university can require employees to perform any duties not on the employees' job descriptions for a period not to exceed three months. After three months, the duty must either be eliminated or permanently added to the employee's job description, at which time a review will also be made to determine if the addition is significant enough to merit a salary increase.

Job descriptions can be written in many ways, but the format discussed here has been used successfully for many jobs and is a combination of methods used by many organizations and suggested by several researchers. A job description should contain the following eight sections: job title, brief summary, work activities, tools and equipment used, work context, performance standards, compensation information, and personal requirements.

Job Title

A job title is important for several reasons. An accurate title describes the nature of the job, its power and status level, and the competencies needed to perform the job (Martinez, Laird, Martin, & Ferris, 2008). When industrial psychologist David Faloona started a new job at Washington National Insurance in Chicago, his official title was "psychometric technician." Unfortunately, none of the other workers knew what he did. To correct that problem, his title was changed to "personnel assistant," and supervisors then began consulting with him on human resources related problems. A job analysis that I conducted provides another example. After analyzing the position of "secretary" for one credit union, I found that her duties were actually those of a position that other credit unions labeled "loan officer." This change in title resulted in the employee's receiving a higher salary as well as vindication that she was indeed "more than a secretary."

An accurate title also aids in employee selection and recruitment. If the job title indicates the true nature of the job, potential applicants for a position will be better able to determine whether their skills and experience match those required for the job. In the example given in the previous paragraph, applicants for a secretary's job in the usual sense might not possess the lending and decision-making skills needed by a loan officer.

When conducting a job analysis, it is not unusual for an analyst to discover that some workers do not have job titles. Job titles provide workers with some form of identity. Instead of just saying that she is a "worker at the foundry," a woman can say that she is a "welder" or a "machinist." At most universities, students receiving financial aid are called "work-study students" rather than "clerks," "computer operators," or "mail sorters." This inaccurate title causes many students to think that they are supposed to study as they work rather than sort mail or operate a computer.

Job titles can also affect perceptions of the status and worth of a job. For example, job descriptions containing gender-neutral titles such as "administrative assistant" are evaluated as being worth more money than ones containing titles with a female sex linkage such as "executive secretary" (Naughton, 1988). As another example, Smith, Hornsby, Benson, and Wesolowski (1989) had subjects read identical job descriptions that differed only in the status of the title. Jobs with higher-status titles were evaluated as being worth more money than jobs with lower-status titles. Some authors, however, have questioned the gender effects associated with titles (Mount & Ellis, 1989; Rynes, Weber, & Milkovich, 1989).

Though some organizations allow their employees to create their own titles, it is important that employees who are doing the same job have the same title and that the title accurately reflect the nature of the job (Garvey, 2000).

Brief Summary

The summary need be only a paragraph in length but should briefly describe the nature and purpose of the job. This summary can be used in help-wanted advertisements, internal job postings, and company brochures.

Work Activities

The work activities section lists the tasks and activities in which the worker is involved. These tasks and activities should be organized into meaningful categories to make the job description easy to read and understand. The category labels are also convenient to use in the brief summary. As you can see in the sample job description in Table 2.1, the 72 work activities performed by the bookkeeper are divided into seven main areas: accounting, clerical, teller, share draft, collections, payroll and data processing, and financial operations.

Tools and Equipment Used

A section should be included that lists all the tools and equipment used to perform the work activities in the previous section. Even though tools and equipment may have been mentioned in the activities section, placing them in a separate section makes their identification simpler. Information in this section is used primarily for employee selection and training. That is, an applicant can be asked if she can operate an adding machine, a computer, and a credit history machine.

Job Context

This section should describe the environment in which the employee works and should mention stress level, work schedule, physical demands, level of responsibility, temperature, number of coworkers, degree of danger, and any other relevant information. This information is especially important in providing applicants with disabilities with information they can use to determine their ability to perform a job under a particular set of circumstances.

Work Performance

The job description should outline standards of performance. This section contains a relatively brief description of how an employee's performance is evaluated and what work standards are expected of the employee.

Compensation Information

Grade A cluster of jobs of similar worth.

This section of the job description should contain information on the salary **grade**, whether the position is exempt, and the compensable factors used to determine salary. These concepts will be described later in the chapter. The employee's actual salary or salary range should *not* be listed on the job description.

Job Competencies

Job specifications A relatively dated term that refers to the knowledge, skills, and abilities needed to successfully perform a job. *Competencies* is the more common term used today.

Competencies The knowledge, skills, abilities, and other characteristics needed to perform a job.

This section contains what are commonly called **job specifications** or **competencies**. These are the knowledge, skills, abilities, and other characteristics (KSAOs) (such as interest, personality, and training) that are necessary to be successful on the job. Competencies are determined by deciding what types of KSAOs are needed to perform the tasks identified in the job analysis. These KSAOs can be determined through a combination of logic, research, and use of specific job analysis techniques discussed later in this chapter.

The competencies section should be divided into two subsections. The first contains KSAOs that an employee must have at the time of hiring. The second subsection contains the KSAOs that are an important part of the job but can be obtained after being hired. The first set of KSAOs is used for employee selection and the second for training purposes (Wooten, 1993).

Table 2.1 Example of a Job Description

Bookkeeper
True Value Credit Union

Job Summary

Under the general supervision of the office manager, the bookkeeper is responsible for all of the accounting duties of the office. Specifically, the bookkeeper is responsible for keeping all financial records accurate and up-to-date; processing loans; and preparing and posting statements, reports, and bonds.

Work Activities

The work activities of the bookkeeper are divided into seven main functional areas:

Accounting Activities

- Prepares quarterly income statements
- Maintains and posts all transactions in general ledger book
- Pays credit union bills
- Prepares statistical reports
- Updates undivided earnings account
- Prepares and files tax returns and statements
- Completes IRA forms and reports in cooperation with CUNA
- Annually computes Cumis Bond
- Balances journal and cash records

Clerical Activities

- Looks up members' account information when requested
- Answers phone
- Makes copies of transactions for members
- Drafts statements of account to members
- Types certificates of deposit
- Makes copies of letters that are sent to members
- Picks up, sorts, and disperses credit union mail
- Folds monthly and quarterly statements and places into an envelope to be mailed to members
- Processes and mails savings and share draft statements
- Sorts checks or copies of checks in numerical order
- Orders supplies
- Types reports and minutes from board meetings
- Maintains and updates files for members
- Prepares, types, and files correspondence
- Enters change-of-address information into the computer

Teller Activities

- Enrolls new members and opens and closes accounts
- Reconciles accounts
- Issues money orders and traveler's checks
- Conducts history of accounts
- Processes and issues receipts for transactions
- Asks for identification if person making transaction is not known
- Daily enters transaction totals onto a list sent to the bank
- Orders new or replacement checks for members
- Prints and issues checks
- Makes proper referrals

Share Draft Activities

- Deducts fee from member's account when a share is returned
- Processes statements for share draft accounts
- Issues stop payments and sends copy of form to member
- Deducts fee in form of an overdraft when more than three transfers have occurred for any one member in a month
- Checks and records share drafts or additions from previous day
- Receives share draft totals for each member from CUNA data
- Decides on an individual basis whether overdrafts will be covered by credit union
- Determines if overdrafts on account have been paid
- Checks to see if share drafts have cleared
- Telephones Chase-Manhattan Bank when a member does not have enough money to cover a share draft

Collections Activities

- Withholds money from member's check in order to meet loan payments
- Decides if a member who has a delinquent loan will be able to take money out of account
- Locates and communicates with members having delinquent loans
- Completes garnishee form to send to courts on delinquent loans
- Resubmits garnishee form once every 3 months until delinquent loan has been paid in full by member
- Makes collection on delinquent loans
- Checks on previous member's address and current job to see if loan payments can be made
- Determines number and length of time of delinquent loans
- Sends judgment form to court, which sends it to delinquent member
- If a member is delinquent, finds out if he or she is sick or on vacation

Payroll and Data-Processing Activities

- Checks and verifies payroll run for all necessary deductions
- Reads and interprets computer printouts
- Computes and subtracts deductions from payroll
- Sets up and changes deduction amounts for payroll savings plan
- Runs payroll on computer
- Annually sends out backup disk to outside vendor who transfers information to a magnetic tape that is sent to IRS
- Computes payroll
- Runs daily trial balances and transaction registers
- Loads paper into printer
- Makes backup copies of all daily computer transactions
- Runs quarterly and/or monthly statements on computer

Financial Operations Activities

- Scans business/financial environment to identify potential threats and opportunities
- Makes recommendations to the board regarding investments
- Invests all excess money into accounts that will earn interest
- Computes profits and amounts to be used for investments
- Prepares statements of financial condition and federal operating fee report
- Obtains enough funds for day-to-day operation of branch
- Notifies and makes available investment funds to the NCUA

Tools and Equipment Used

- Adding machine
- Computer
- Computer printer
- Credit history machine
- Motor vehicle

Continued

Table 2.1   Example of a Job Description (*Continued*)

- Photocopy machine
- Folding machine
- Microfiche reader
- Safe
- Telephone
- Security check writer

Job Context

The bookkeeper spends the majority of time making entries in and balancing journals and ledgers. The work day is spent in a climate-controlled office with four coworkers. Physical demands are minimal and sitting is required for most of the day. Work hours are Monday-Friday from 8:00 a.m. to 5:00 p.m., with an unpaid hour for lunch. No weekend or holiday work is required and overtime seldom occurs. Psychological stress is usually low but becomes moderate when dealing with an angry customer.

Work Performance

The bookkeeper is evaluated annually by the office manager using the credit union's standard performance appraisal system. To receive an excellent performance appraisal, the bookkeeper should do the following:

- Maintain neat and accurate records
- Meet all deadlines
- Maintain an orderly office
- Make sure all ledgers and journals balance
- Perform duties of other jobs when the need arises
- Have a good attendance record

Compensation Information

Grade: 6

FLSA Status: Not exempt

Job Competencies

Upon hire, the bookkeeper must do the following:

- Have a high school diploma and a basic knowledge of math and English
- Understand financial documents
- Be able to make limited financial decisions
- Have completed advanced coursework in accounting and finance
- Be skilled in using Microsoft Excel and Word

After hire, the bookkeeper must do the following:

- Learn general office procedures
- Learn the style of credit union accounting procedures and regulations
- Learn how to complete the various forms

Preparing for a Job Analysis

Prior to conducting a job analysis, several decisions must be made that will influence how it is conducted.

Who Will Conduct the Analysis?

Typically, a job analysis is conducted by a trained individual in the Human Resources department, but it can also be conducted by job incumbents, supervisors, or outside consultants. If job incumbents or supervisors are used, it is essential that they be thoroughly trained in job analysis procedures. The *Uniform Guidelines* state that a job analysis must be "professionally conducted," and a job analyst certainly cannot be called a professional unless she has been trained. In addition, research indicates that analysts who have been trained produce slightly different results from those produced by untrained analysts (Cellar, Curtis, Kohlepp, Poczapski, & Mohiuddin, 1989; Surrette, Aamodt, & Johnson, 1990).

Time is always an issue when using supervisors or incumbents. Telling a supervisor to "write job descriptions in your spare time" is not likely to go over well. Thus, supervisors and employees will need to be released from other duties—a situation that is seldom possible.

The state of Virginia developed a system in which all employees were asked to follow set guidelines and write their own job descriptions. The system itself was well conceived, but employees were not given enough job analysis training, which resulted in substantial confusion and, in some cases, inaccurate job descriptions.

Consultants are a good choice for conducting a job analysis because they are well trained and have extensive experience. The main drawback, though, is their expense. Consultants typically charge between $100 and $500 per hour based on their degree, experience, and reputation. Given that 10 hours is probably the least amount of time that will be spent analyzing the simplest job, and the most complex jobs can take weeks of analysis, an organization must carefully weigh the benefits of consultants against their cost.

An interesting alternative to consultants is the use of college interns. Graduate students from I/O psychology programs tend to have job analysis training and experience and can be employed for a relatively small cost (often, at no cost). In fact, Radford University operates the Community Human Resource Center in which graduate students obtain job analysis experience by conducting job analyses free of charge to such local nonprofit agencies as school systems, towns, and hospitals. In this way, graduate students obtain experience, and the nonprofit organizations receive professional-quality job analyses and job descriptions at no cost. Similar programs can be found at the University of Tulsa, Minnesota State University at Mankato, Middle Tennessee State University, and the University of Southern Mississippi.

How Often Should a Job Description Be Updated?

The typical answer to this tough question is that a job description should be updated if a job changes significantly. With high-tech jobs, this is probably fairly often. With jobs such as package handling, the job might not change substantially for 20 years. An interesting study by Vincent, Rainey, Faulkner, Mascio, and Zinda (2007) compared the stability of job descriptions at intervals of 1, 6, 10, 12, and 20 years. After one year, 92% of the tasks listed in the old and updated job descriptions were the same, dropping to 54% after 10 years. As one would expect, the stability of tasks performed, the tools and equipment used, and KSAOs needed to perform the job varied by the complexity of the job.

Job crafting A process in which employees unofficially change their job duties to better fit their interests and skills.

An interesting reason that job descriptions change across time is **job crafting**—the informal changes that employees make in their jobs (Wrzesniewski & Dutton, 2001). That is, it is common for employees to quietly expand the scope of their jobs to add tasks they want to perform and to remove tasks that they don't want to perform. In a study of sales representatives, 75% engaged in job crafting in just one year (Lyons, 2008)!

Which Employees Should Participate?

For organizations with relatively few people in each job, it is advisable to have all employees participate in the job analysis. In organizations in which many people perform the same job (e.g., teachers at a university, assemblers in a factory), every person need not participate. If every incumbent is not going to participate, the question becomes, "How many people need to be included in the job analysis?" This is a difficult question, one that I normally answer by advising job analysts to keep interviewing incumbents until they do not hear anything new. Anecdotally, this seems to be after the third or fourth incumbent for a particular job.

The answer to this question to some extent depends on whether the job analysis will be committee based or field based. In a committee-based job analysis, a group of subject-matter experts (people who are knowledgeable about the job and include job incumbents, supervisors, customers, and upper-level management) meet to generate the tasks performed, the conditions under which they are performed, and the KSAOs needed to perform them. In a field-based job analysis, the job analyst individually interviews/observes a number of incumbents out in the field. Taken together, the results of four studies (Ash, Levine, Higbee, & Sistrunk, 1982; Maurer & Tross, 2000; O'Leary, Rheinstein, & McCauley, 1990; Tannenbaum & Wesley, 1993) suggest that committee-based job analyses yield similar results to field-based job analyses.

Rouleau and Krain (1975) developed a table to estimate how many incumbents should be included in a job analysis; their recommendation is that a committee-based approach should have one session of 4 to 6 incumbents for jobs having fewer than 30 incumbents and two to three sessions for jobs with higher numbers of incumbents. Green and Stutzman (1986) have suggested a minimum of 3 incumbents, and Gael (1988) has suggested 6 to 10. Unfortunately, no research is available to verify the accuracy of these estimates.

Beatty (1996) compared the results of job analysis samples of 10, 15, 20, and 212 incumbents in a federal law enforcement position. His results indicated that the job tasks and job requirements resulting from the use of 10 versus 212 incumbents were nearly identical. These results support and extend those found by Fletcher, Friedman, McCarthy, McIntyre, O' Leary, and Rheinstein (1993) and Pass and Robertson (1980), who found that job analysis samples of 10 and 20 yielded comparable results.

Mullins (1983) had 97 campus police officers at 13 universities generate critical incidents as part of a job analysis. The results indicated that no new incidents appeared after examining the incidents from the first three universities. Furthermore, after examining the incidents supplied by the first 19 incumbents, no new incidents or categories appeared.

After the number of participants has been determined, a decision needs to be made about which *particular employees* will participate. If every employee will not participate, the same sampling rules used in research should be used in job analysis. That is, as discussed in Chapter 1, participants should be selected in as random a way as practical yet still be representative. The reason for this, according to research, is that employee differences in gender, race, job performance level, experience, job enjoyment, and personality can at times result in slightly different job analysis outcomes.

Job Competence. Sanchez, Prager, Wilson, and Viswesvaran (1998) and Mullins and Kimbrough (1988) found that high-performing employees generated different job analysis outcomes than did low-performing employees; Ansoorian and Shultz (1997) found moderate differences in physical effort made by employees with varying levels of expertise; and both Landy and Vasey (1991) and Prien, Prien, and Wooten (2003) found that more experienced employees rated tasks differently than less experienced employees. However, Mailhot (1996) did not find any differences in job analysis ratings made by employees of different performance levels.

If higher-performing employees generate different job analysis results than lower-performing employees, a tough decision must be made regarding which employees to include in the job analysis. On the one hand, it would be nice to include a representative sample of employees. On the other hand, do we really want to write a job description and select future employees on the basis of how poorly performing employees do their jobs?

Race. Aamodt, Kimbrough, Keller, and Crawford (1982); Schmitt and Cohen (1989); Veres, Green, and Boyles (1991); and Landy and Vasey (1991) report small but significant differences in the ways in which white and African American incumbents viewed their jobs. For example, Landy and Vasey found that white police officers administered first aid more often and African American officers were more involved in sweeps and raids related to widespread narcotics use. Veres et al. (1991) found that job analysis ratings were related not only to the race of the incumbent but to the race of the incumbent's coworkers.

Gender. Landy and Vasey (1991) found possible differences in the ways men and women viewed their jobs. Because gender was confounded with experience, they were not able to draw any definite conclusions. Schmitt and Cohen (1989) found that male middle-level managers were more often involved in budgetary or finance-related tasks than were their female counterparts. Ansoorian and Schultz (1997) found no differences in the physical-effort ratings assigned by male and female incumbents.

Education Level. Landy and Vasey (1991) found that police officers with only a high school diploma were less involved in court activities than were their more educated counterparts.

Personality. Cucina, Vasilopoulos, and Sehgal (2005) found that the personality of the incumbent was related to the personality traits rated by the incumbent to be important to the job. That is, extroverted incumbents rated such traits as friendliness, leadership ability, and ambition as being important for the job whereas conscientious incumbents rated such traits as work ethic and attention to detail as being important. Similarly, Ford, Truxillo, Wang, & Bauer (2008) found that extroverts and people high in agreeableness were likely to inflate task and KSAO ratings.

Viewpoint. It should be no surprise that people with different perspectives on the job (e.g., incumbent, supervisor, customer) produce different job analysis results. For example, Mueller and Belcher (2000) found that incumbents (fire captains) and their supervisors (fire chief, deputy fire chiefs, and division chiefs) produced different task ratings during a job analysis of the fire captain position. Truxillo, Paronto, Collins, and Sulzer (2004) found differences in ratings provided by police officers and district attorneys of the criticality of different aspects of report writing for reports written by police officers. Wagner (1950) conducted a job analysis of dentists and found that patients generated more incidents where patient–dentist relationship was critical, whereas dentists reported more technical-proficiency incidents. Likewise, Fisher and Greenis (1996) and Andersson and Nilsson (1964) found differences in the critical incidents generated by managers, incumbents, and customers.

The consideration of which employees are chosen to participate is an important issue because a job can often be performed in several ways. If males and females perform equally well on a job, yet perform the job in different ways, the job analyses must contain information about both styles. For example, suppose research indicates that male supervisors lead by setting goals and being directive and female supervisors use more of a participative approach. Consequently, a job analysis conducted only on male supervisors would result in a different set of KSAOs than a job analysis using both male and female supervisors. Because job analysis is the basis for every personnel decision, it can be seen that equal opportunity efforts begin as early as the job analysis.

The issue of using the best employees or the typical employees is also important. During a job analysis at a large printing factory, it was discovered that one employee performed his job differently from the employees on the other two shifts. Further investigation revealed that the one employee was also rated much higher in job performance than the other two. Thus, it appeared that the logical thing to do was write the job analysis results based on the way the best employee performed the job and then retrain the other two.

What Types of Information Should Be Obtained?

An important decision concerns the *level of specificity*. That is, should the job analysis break a job down into very minute, specific behaviors (e.g., "tilts arm at a 90-degree angle" or "moves foot forward three inches"), or should the job be analyzed at a more general level ("makes financial decisions," "speaks to clients")? Although most jobs are analyzed at levels somewhere between these two extremes, there are times when the level of analysis will be closer to one end of the spectrum than the other.

For some jobs that involve intricate work, extensive and expensive efforts have been undertaken to identify the optimal way in which tasks should be performed. For example, in a window manufacturing plant, job analysis determined that many more windows could be mounted in frames by lifting the glass just six inches and then sliding it into place, than by lifting the glass higher and placing it in the frame. In such a situation, the work obviously must be performed in a specific manner for the greatest financial savings. Thus, the job analysis is more effective at a more detailed level.

A related decision addresses the issue of *formal versus informal* requirements. Formal requirements for a secretary might include typing letters or filing memos. Informal requirements might involve making coffee or picking up the boss's children from school. Including informal requirements has the advantages of identifying and eliminating duties that may be illegal or unnecessary. For example, suppose a job analysis reveals that a secretary in one department picks up the boss's children from school and takes them to a day-care center. This is an important finding because the company may not want this to occur. However, because the manager makes $200,000 per year, the company may prefer that the lower-paid secretary rather than the higher-paid executive take an hour a day to pick up the children. If this task is in the job description, an applicant will know about this duty in advance and can decide at the time of hire whether it is acceptable.

In addition, informal requirements (e.g., picking up mail) may need to be made more formal to reduce potential confusion regarding who is responsible for the task. At one credit union, a continued source of bickering involved whose job or whose turn it was to pick up the mail, especially when the weather was bad and post office

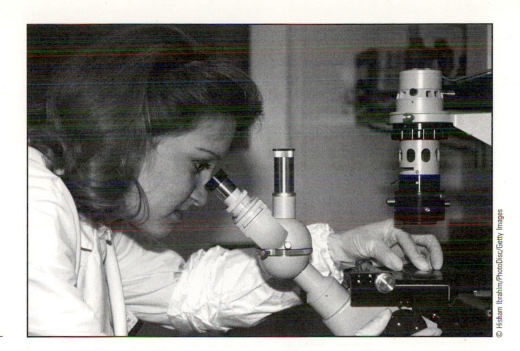

Some jobs require tremendous attention to detail.

parking became limited. This problem could have been eliminated if the task were assigned to one individual.

Conducting a Job Analysis

Although there are many ways to conduct a job analysis, the goal of most job analyses is to identify the tasks performed in a job, the conditions under which the tasks are performed, and the KSAOs needed to perform the tasks under the conditions identified. This section will begin with a commonly used strategy for conducting a job analysis and conclude with descriptions of alternative methods.

Step 1: Identify Tasks Performed

The first step in conducting a job analysis is to identify the major job dimensions and the tasks performed for each dimension, the tools and equipment used to perform the tasks, and the conditions under which the tasks are performed. This information is usually gathered by obtaining previous information on the job, interviewing job incumbents, observing performance, or actually performing the job itself.

Gathering Existing Information. Prior to interviewing incumbents, it is always a good idea to gather information that has already been obtained. For example, one might gather existing job descriptions, task inventories, and training manuals. This information might come from the organization with which you are working, other organizations, trade publications, and journal articles.

Subject-matter experts (SMEs) Sources such as supervisors and incumbents who are knowledgeable about a job.

Interviewing Subject-Matter Experts. The most common method of conducting a job analysis is to interview **subject-matter experts (SMEs)**. SMEs are people who are knowledgeable about the job and include job incumbents, supervisors, customers, and upper-level management. Job analysis interviews differ greatly from employment

Interviews are a common job analysis technique.

© PhotoDisc/Getty Images

Job analyst The person conducting the job analysis.

SME conference A group job analysis interview consisting of subject-matter experts (SMEs).

interviews in that the purpose of the job analysis interview is to obtain information about the job itself rather than about the person doing the job. Job analysis interviews come in two main forms: individual and group. In the individual interview, the **job analyst** interviews only one employee at a time. In the group interview, or **SME conference**, a larger number of employees are interviewed together. As mentioned earlier in the chapter, individual interviews tend to yield similar results to group interviews.

Regardless of whether individual or group interviews are used, certain guidelines should be followed that will make the interview go more smoothly.

1. *Prepare* for the interview by announcing the job analysis to the employees well in advance by selecting a quiet and private interview location.
2. *Open* the interview by establishing rapport, putting the worker at ease, and explaining the purpose of the interview.
3. *Conduct* the interview by asking open-ended questions, using easy-to-understand vocabulary, and allowing sufficient time for the employee to talk and answer questions. Avoid being condescending and disagreeing with the incumbent.

Most workers are proud of their jobs and are willing to talk about them in great detail. Once the initial apprehensions and jitters are over, most job analysis interviews go well. A good way to start the actual interview is by asking the employee to describe what she does from the moment she first enters the parking lot at work to the moment she arrives back home. A question such as this provides some structure for the employee in recalling the various aspects of her job and also provides the interviewer with many follow-up questions and areas that will provide additional information.

With a committee-based approach, a committee of SMEs meets to brainstorm the *major duties* involved in a job. Once this has been done, the committee identifies the tasks (work-related activities) that must be completed for each of the duties. The results are then summarized in job descriptions or a job analysis report.

An excellent job analysis interview technique was developed by Ammerman (1965) and reported by Robinson (1981). The basic steps for the **Ammerman technique** are as follows:

1. Convene a panel of experts that includes representatives from all levels of the organization.
2. Have the panel identify the objectives and standards that are to be met by the ideal incumbent.
3. Have the panel list the specific behaviors necessary for each objective or standard to be attained.
4. Have the panel identify which of the behaviors from step 3 are "critical" to reaching the objective.
5. Have the panel rank-order the objectives on the basis of importance.

The results of these procedures will yield a set of important objectives and the behaviors necessary to meet them. These behaviors can be used to create employee selection tests, develop training programs, or evaluate the performance of current employees. An example of Ammerman-style objectives and behaviors is shown in Figure 2.1.

Observing Incumbents. Observations are useful job analysis methods, especially when used in conjunction with other methods such as interviews. During a job analysis observation, the job analyst observes incumbents performing their jobs in the work

Ammerman technique A job analysis method in which a group of job experts identifies the objectives and standards to be met by the ideal worker.

Observations A job analysis method in which the job analyst watches job incumbents perform their jobs.

Figure 2.1

Example of Ammerman Technique Objectives and Tasks for a Bank Teller

Cross-sell bank products.
• Study daily rate charts.
• Explain new products to customers.

Balance drawer within 30 minutes at end of day.
• Accurately count money.
• Trial balance drawer during downtimes.

Comply with federal and state regulations.
• Notify federal government of cash transactions in excess of $10,000.
• Treat customers equally regardless of age, race, gender, or national origin.

Accurately complete paperwork.
• Obtain all necessary information from customers.
• Obtain all necessary signatures.

Make each customer feel a "part of the family."
• Know each customer's name.
• Refer to customers by their first names.
• Smile and greet each customer.

setting. The advantage to this method is that it lets the job analyst actually see the worker do her job and thus obtain information that the worker may have forgotten to mention during the interview. This is especially important because many employees have difficulty describing exactly what they do; to them, performing their job is second nature and takes little thought. A good demonstration of this point is people's difficulty in naming the location of keys on a typewriter or the location of gears when they drive. We all type and shift gears without thinking (well, most of us do), but quickly describing to another person the location of the V key on our keyboard or "Reverse" on our manual transmission console is difficult.

The method's disadvantage is that it is very obtrusive. Observing someone without their knowing is difficult. Think of the jobs at which you have worked; there is seldom anyplace from which an analyst could observe without being seen by employees. This is a problem because once employees know they are being watched, their behavior changes, which keeps an analyst from obtaining an accurate picture of the way jobs are done. When I was in college and working third shift at a bookbinding factory, the company hired an "efficiency expert" to analyze our performance. The expert arrived in a three-piece suit, armed with a stopwatch and clipboard. He stuck out like a sore thumb! You can bet that for the two weeks the efficiency expert observed us, we were ideal employees (I can even remember calling my supervisor "sir") because we knew he was watching. Once he left, we went back to being our normal time-wasting, soda-drinking, wise-cracking selves.

Job Participation. One can analyze a job by actually performing it. This technique, called **job participation**, is especially effective because it is easier to understand every aspect of a job once you have done it yourself. The technique is easily used when the analyst has previously performed the job. An excellent example would be a supervisor who has worked her way up through the ranks. As mentioned earlier, the problem with using a supervisor or an incumbent is that neither has been trained in job analysis techniques.

A professional job analyst can also perform an unfamiliar job for a short period of time, although this, of course, is limited to certain occupations that involve quick training and minimal consequences from an error. Brain surgery would probably not be good to analyze using this method.

The analyst should spend enough time on the job to properly sample work behavior in addition to job difficulty. Yet spending long periods of time can be very expensive and still not guarantee that all aspects of behavior will be covered. Psychologist Wayman Mullins used job participation techniques to analyze the job of a firefighter. Mullins spent two weeks living at the fire station and performing all the duties of a firefighter. The only problem during this two-week period—no fires. If Mullins had not already had a good idea of what a firefighter did, he would have concluded that the most important duties were sleeping, cleaning, cooking, and playing cards!

Step 2: Write Task Statements

Once the tasks have been identified, the next step is to write the task statements that will be used in the **task inventory** and included in the job description. As shown in Table 2.2, at the minimum, a properly written task statement must contain an *action* (what is done) and an *object* (to which the action is done). Often, task statements will also include such components as *where* the task is done, *how* it is done, *why* it is done, and *when* it is done.

Job participation A job analysis method in which the job analyst actually performs the job being analyzed.

Task inventory A questionnaire containing a list of tasks each of which the job incumbent rates on a series of scales such as importance and time spent.

Table 2.2 Writing Effective Task Statements

Poorly Written Task Statement	Properly Written Task Statement
Sends purchase requests	Sends purchase requests to the purchasing department using campus mail
Drives	Drives a five-speed truck to make food deliveries within the city of Toledo
Locks hall doors	Uses master key to lock hall doors at midnight so that nonresidents cannot enter the residence hall

Here are some characteristics of well-written task statements:

- One action should be done to one object. If the statement includes the word *and*, it may have more than one action or object. For example, the statement "Types correspondence to be sent to vendors" has one action and one object. However, "Types, files, and sends correspondence to vendors" contains three very different actions (types, files, sends).
- Task statements should be written at a level that can be read and understood by a person with the same reading ability as the typical job incumbent.
- All task statements should be written in the same tense.
- The task statement should include the tools and equipment used to complete the task.
- Task statements should not be competencies (e.g., "Be a good writer").
- Task statements should not be a policy (e.g., "Treats people nicely").
- The statement should make sense by itself. That is, "Makes photocopies" does not provide as much detail as "Makes photocopies of transactions for credit union members," which indicates what types of materials are photocopied and for whom they are copied.
- For those activities that involve decision making, the level of authority should be indicated. This level lets the incumbent know which decisions she is allowed to make on her own and which she needs approval for from a higher level.

It has also been suggested that a few tasks not part of a job be placed into the task inventory; data from incumbents who rate these irrelevant tasks as part of their job are removed from the job analysis due to their carelessness (Green & Stutzman, 1986). Including "bogus tasks" is probably a good idea. Pine (1995) included five such items in a 68-item task inventory for corrections officers and found that 45% reported performing at least one of the bogus tasks. For example, a task inventory might include "operates a Gonkulator" or "uses PARTH program to analyze data" even though no such machine or computer program actually exists. A study by Dierdorff and Rubin (2007) found that incumbents who are low in cognitive ability and are confused about their work role (role ambiguity) are the most likely to endorse the bogus tasks on a task inventory.

Step 3: Rate Task Statements

Task analysis The process of identifying the tasks for which employees need to be trained.

Once the task statements have been written (usually including some 200 tasks), the next step is to conduct a **task analysis**—using a group of SMEs to rate each task statement on the frequency and the importance or criticality of the task being

Table 2.3   Example of Task Inventory Scales

Frequency

0	Task is not performed as part of this job
1	Task is seldom performed
2	Task is occasionally performed
3	Task is frequently performed

Importance

0	Unimportant: There would be no negative consequences if the task was not performed or if the task was not performed properly
1	Important: Job performance would be diminished if the task was not completed properly
2	Essential: The job could not be performed effectively if the incumbent did not properly complete this task

performed. For example, consider the task *accurately shoots a gun.* For a police officer, this task occurs infrequently, but when it does, its importance is paramount. If a frequency scale alone were used, shooting a gun might not be covered in training. Although many types of scales can be used, research suggests that many of the scales tap similar types of information (Sanchez & Fraser, 1992); thus, using the two scales of frequency of occurrence and importance shown in Table 2.3 should be sufficient. In fact, rather than asking for ratings of frequency of occurrence or relative time spent on a task, some researchers advise that the task inventory should simply ask, "Do you perform this task?" (Wilson & Harvey, 1990). Raters tend to agree on ratings of task importance but not on time spent (Lindell, Clause, Brandt, & Landis, 1998).

After a representative sample of SMEs rates each task, the ratings are organized into a format similar to that shown in Table 2.4. Tasks will not be included in the *job description* if their average frequency rating is 0.5 or below. Tasks will not be included in the final *task inventory* if they have either an average rating of 0.5 or less on *either* the frequency (F) or importance (I) scales or an average combined rating (CR) of less than 2. Using these criteria, tasks 1, 2, and 4 in Table 2.4 would be included in the job description, and tasks 2 and 4 would be included in the final task inventory used in the next step of the job analysis.

Table 2.4   Example of Task Analysis Ratings

	Raters						Combined Average		
	Scully			Mulder					
Task #	F	+ I	= CR	F	+ I	= CR	F	+ I	= CR
1	2	0	2	3	0	3	2.5	0.0	2.5
2	2	2	4	2	1	3	2.0	1.5	3.5
3	0	0	0	0	0	0	0.0	0.0	0.0
4	3	2	5	3	2	5	3.0	2.0	5.0

F = frequency; I = importance; CR = combined rating.

Step 4: Determine Essential KSAOs

Once the task analysis is completed and a job analyst has a list of tasks that are essential for the proper performance of a job, the next step is to identify the KSAOs needed to perform the tasks.

- A **knowledge** is a body of information needed to perform a task.
- A **skill** is the proficiency to perform a learned task.
- An **ability** is a basic capacity for performing a wide range of different tasks, acquiring a knowledge, or developing a skill.
- **Other characteristics** include such personal factors as personality, willingness, interest, and motivation and such tangible factors as licenses, degrees, and years of experience.

Currently, KSAOs are commonly referred to as *competencies* (Campion et al., 2011). In the old days, KSAOs were called job specifications (job specs). Though there may be some disagreement among I/O psychologists, the terms "KSAOs," "competencies," and "job specs" can be used interchangeably and there is no real difference among the three (other than which term is in vogue). When competencies are tied to an organization's strategic initiatives and plans rather than to specific tasks, the process is called *competency modeling*.

To refer back to our example of a police officer accurately shooting a gun (skill), the police officer would need to hold the gun properly and allow for such external conditions as the target distance and wind conditions (knowledge), and have the hand strength, steadiness, and vision necessary to hold the gun, pull the trigger, and aim properly (abilities). To carry the gun, the officer would need to have a weapons certification (other characteristic). Determining important KSAOs can be done in one of two ways: logically linking tasks to KSAOs or using prepackaged questionnaires.

To logically link KSAOs to tasks, a group of SMEs brainstorm the KSAOs needed to perform each task. For example, a group of police officers might consider the task of "writing accident reports" and determine that grammar skills, spelling skills, legible handwriting, and knowledge of accidents are the KSAOs needed for a police officer to perform this task.

Once the list of essential KSAOs has been developed, another group of SMEs is given the list and asked to rate the extent to which each of the KSAOs is essential for performing the job. If a scale such as that shown in Table 2.5 is used, KSAOs with an average score of .5 or less are eliminated from further consideration.

As you can see in Table 2.5, it is also important for the SMEs to determine when each KSAO is needed. Using data from the table, KSAOs that receive average ratings of 2.5 or higher will be part of the employee selection process, KSAOs with average ratings between 1.5 and 2.49 will be taught at the police academy, and KSAOs with average ratings between .5 and 1.49 will be learned on the job during the officer's probationary period.

Rather than using the previously discussed process, KSAOs, or competencies, can be identified using such structured methods as the Job Components Inventory (JCI), Threshold Traits Analysis (TTA), Fleishman Job Analysis Survey (F-JAS), Critical Incident Technique (CIT), and the Personality-Related Position Requirements Form (PPRF). Each of these will be discussed in detail later in the chapter.

Step 5: Selecting Tests to Tap KSAOs

Once the important KSAOs have been identified, the next step is to determine the best methods to tap the KSAOs needed at the time of hire. These methods will be used to select new employees and include such methods as interviews, work samples,

Table 2.5 Scales Used to Rate KSAOs for Law Enforcement

Importance of KSAO

0	KSAO is **not needed** for satisfactory completion of the academy or satisfactory job performance
1	KSAO is **helpful** for satisfactory completion of the academy or satisfactory job performance
2	KSAO is **important/essential** for satisfactory completion of the academy or satisfactory job performance

When KSAO Is Needed

0	KSAO is not needed
1	KSAO is needed after completion of field training
2	KSAO is needed after completion of the academy
3	KSAO is needed at the time of hire

KSAO = knowledge, skill, ability, other characteristics.

ability tests, personality tests, reference checks, integrity tests, biodata, and assessment centers. These methods, and how to choose them, will be discussed in great detail in Chapters 4, 5, and 6.

The average ratings obtained from step 4 will be used to weight test scores. That is, a test tapping a KSAO with a rating of 2.9 should receive more weight than a test tapping a KSAO with a rating of 2.5.

Using Other Job Analysis Methods

In the previous pages, the most common method for conducting a job analysis was discussed. Though this method provides great information, it can be rather lengthy and unstructured. To save time, increase structure, or supplement information obtained from interviews, observations, and task analysis, other job analysis methods are available. These methods tend to provide information on one of four specific factors that are commonly included in a job description: worker activities, tools and equipment used, work environment, and competencies.

Methods Providing General Information About Worker Activities

Using the strategy discussed previously yields *specific* information about the tasks and activities performed by an incumbent in a *particular job.* Though such detailed information is ideal, obtaining it can be both time-consuming and expensive. As an alternative, several questionnaires have been developed to analyze jobs at a more general level. This general analysis saves time and money and allows jobs to be more easily compared with one another than is the case if interviews, observations, job participation, or task analysis is used.

**Position Analysis
Questionnaire (PAQ)** A
structured job analysis method
developed by McCormick.

Position Analysis Questionnaire. The **Position Analysis Questionnaire (PAQ)** is a structured instrument developed at Purdue University by McCormick, Jeanneret, and Mecham (1972), and is now available from PAQ Services in Bellingham, Washington. The PAQ contains 194 items organized into six main dimensions: information input, mental processes, work output, relationships with other persons, job context, and other job-related variables such as work schedule, pay, and responsibility. In the sample PAQ page shown in Figure 2.2, notice that the level of analysis is fairly

RELATIONSHIPS WITH OTHER PERSONS

Code Importance to This Job (I)
N Does not apply
1 Very minor
2 Low
3 Average
4 High
5 Extreme

4 Relationships with Other Persons

This section deals with different aspects of interaction between people involved in various kinds of work.

4.1 Communications

Rate the following in terms of how important the activity is to the completion of the job. Some jobs may involve several or all of the items in this section.

4.1.1 Oral (communicating by speaking)

99 I Advising (dealing with individuals in order to counsel and/or guide them with regard to problems that may be resolved by legal, financial, scientific, technical, clinical, spiritual, and/or other professional principles)

100 I Negotiating (dealing with others in order to reach an agreement or solution, for example, labor bargaining, diplomatic relations, etc.)

101 I Persuading (dealing with others in order to influence them toward some action or point of view, for example, selling, political campaigning, etc.)

102 I Instructing (the teaching of knowledge or skills, in either an informal or a formal manner, to others, for example, a public school teacher, a machinist teaching an apprentice, etc.)

103 I Interviewing (conducting interviews directed toward some specific objective, for example, interviewing job applicants, census taking, etc.)

104 I Routine information exchange: job related (the giving and/or receiving of job-related information of a routine nature, for example, ticket agent, taxicab dispatcher, receptionist, etc.)

105 I Nonroutine information exchange (the giving and/or receiving of job-related information of a nonroutine or unusual nature, for example, professional committee meetings, engineers discussing new product design, etc.)

106 I Public speaking (making speeches or formal presentations before relatively large audiences, for example, political addresses, radio/TV broadcasting, delivering a sermon, etc.)

4.1.2 Written (communicating by written/printed material)

107 I Writing (for example, writing or dictating letters, reports, etc., writing copy for ads, writing newspaper articles, etc.: do not include transcribing activities described in item 43, but only activities in which the incumbent creates the written material)

4.1.3 Other Communications

108 I Signaling (communicating by some type of signal, for example, hand signals, semaphore, whistles, horns, bells, lights, etc.)

109 I Code communications (telegraph, cryptography, etc.)

E. J. McCormick, P. R. Jeannert, and R. C. Mecham, *Position Analysis Questionnaire,* Copyright © 1969 by Purdue Research Foundation, West Lafayette, Indiana 47907. Reprinted with permission of the publisher.

Figure 2.2
Example of PAQ Questions

general. That is, the PAQ tells us if a job involves interviewing but does not indicate the type of interviewing that is performed (interviewing job applicants versus interviewing a witness to a crime) or how the interview is conducted. Thus, the results would be difficult to use for functions such as training or performance appraisal.

The PAQ offers many advantages. It is inexpensive and takes relatively little time to use. It is one of the most standardized job analysis methods, has acceptable levels of reliability, and its results for a particular position can be compared through computer analysis with thousands of other positions.

Although the PAQ has considerable support, research indicates its strengths are also the source of its weaknesses. The PAQ's instructions suggest that incumbents using the questionnaire have education levels between grades 10 and 12. Research has found, however, that the PAQ questions and directions are written at the college graduate level (Ash & Edgell, 1975); thus, many workers may not be able to understand the PAQ. This is one reason developers of the PAQ recommend that trained job analysts complete the PAQ rather than the employees themselves.

In addition, the PAQ was designed to cover all jobs; but limited to 194 questions and six dimensions, it has not proven very sensitive. For example, a homemaker and a police officer have similar PAQ profiles (Arvey & Begalla, 1975). Similar profiles also are obtained regardless of whether an analyst actually observes the job or just looks at a job title or a job description (Brannick, Levine, & Morgeson, 2007).

Finally, having a large amount of information about a job yields the same results as having little information (Surrette et al., 1990). Although these studies speak favorably about the reliability of the PAQ, they also provide cause for worry because the PAQ appears to yield the same results regardless of how familiar the analyst is with a job.

Job Structure Profile. A revised version of the PAQ was developed by Patrick and Moore (1985). The major changes in the revision, which is called the **Job Structure Profile (JSP)**, include item content and style, new items to increase the discriminatory power of the intellectual and decision-making dimensions, and an emphasis on having a job analyst, rather than the incumbent, use the JSP. Research by JSP's developers indicates that the instrument is reliable, but little research has been conducted on the JSP since 1985.

Job Elements Inventory. Another instrument designed as an alternative to the PAQ is the **Job Elements Inventory (JEI)**, developed by Cornelius and Hakel (1978). The JEI contains 153 items and has a readability level appropriate for an employee with only a tenth-grade education (Cornelius, Hakel, & Sackett, 1979). Research comparing the JEI with the PAQ indicates that the scores from each method are very similar (Harvey, Friedman, Hakel, & Cornelius, 1988); thus, the JEI may be a better replacement for the difficult-to-read PAQ. But as mentioned with the JSP, much more research is needed before conclusions can be confidently drawn.

Functional Job Analysis. **Functional Job Analysis (FJA)** was designed by Fine (1955) as a quick method that could be used by the federal government to analyze and compare thousands of jobs. Jobs analyzed by FJA are broken down into the percentage of time the incumbent spends on three functions: data (information and ideas), people (clients, customers, and coworkers), and things (machines, tools, and equipment). An analyst is given 100 points to allot to the three functions. The points are usually assigned in multiples of 5, with each function receiving a minimum of 5 points. Once the points have been assigned, the highest level at which the job incumbent functions is then chosen from the chart shown in Table 2.6.

Job Structure Profile (JSP) A revised version of the Position Analysis Questionnaire (PAQ) designed to be used more by the job analyst than by the job incumbent.

Job Elements Inventory (JEI) A structured job analysis technique developed by Cornelius and Hakel that is similar to the Position Analysis Questionnaire (PAQ) but easier to read.

Functional Job Analysis (FJA) A job analysis method developed by Fine that rates the extent to which a job incumbent is involved with functions in the categories of data, people, and things.

Table 2.6   Data, People, and Things Levels

Data	People	Things
0 Synthesizing	0 Mentoring	0 Setting up
1 Coordinating	1 Negotiating	1 Precision working
2 Analyzing	2 Instructing	2 Operating-Controlling
3 Compiling	3 Supervising	3 Driving-Operating
4 Computing	4 Diverting	4 Manipulating
5 Copying	5 Persuading	5 Tending
6 Comparing	6 Speaking	6 Feeding-Offbearing
	7 Serving	7 Handling
	8 Taking instructions	
	9 Helping	

Methods Providing Information About Tools and Equipment

Job Components Inventory (JCI) A structured job analysis technique that concentrates on worker requirements for performing a job rather than on specific tasks.

Job Components Inventory. To take advantage of the PAQ's strengths while avoiding some of its problems, Banks, Jackson, Stafford, and Warr (1983) developed the **Job Components Inventory (JCI)** for use in England. The JCI consists of more than 400 questions covering five major categories: tools and equipment, perceptual and physical requirements, mathematical requirements, communication requirements, and decision making and responsibility. It is the only job analysis method containing a detailed section on tools and equipment.

Published research on the JCI is not abundant. But it does appear to be a promising technique, with research indicating that it is reliable (Banks & Miller, 1984), can differentiate between jobs (Banks et al., 1983), can cluster jobs based on their similarity to one another (Stafford, Jackson, & Banks, 1984), and, unlike the PAQ, is affected by the amount of information available to the analyst (Surrette et al., 1990).

Methods Providing Information About the Work Environment

AET An ergonomic job analysis method developed in Germany (*Arbeitswissenschaftliches Erhebungsverfahren zur Tätigkeitsanalyse*).

The techniques discussed so far provide information about the activities that are performed and the equipment used to perform them. The job analyst still needs information about the conditions under which the activities are performed. For example, two employees might perform the task "delivers mail," yet one might do it by carrying 50-pound mail bags in very hot weather while the other delivers mail by driving a golf cart through an air-conditioned warehouse. To obtain information about the work environment, a job analyst might use the **AET**, an acronym for "Arbeitswissenschaftliches Erhebungsverfahren zur Tätigkeitsanalyse" (try saying this three times!), which means "ergonomic job analysis procedure." By *ergonomic*, we mean that the instrument is primarily concerned with the relationship between the worker and work objects. Developed in Germany by Rohmert and Landau (1983), the AET is a 216-item, standardized questionnaire that analyzes a job along the dimensions shown in Table 2.7. Sample items from the AET can be found in Table 2.8. Although the AET appears to be a promising method for obtaining certain types of job analysis information, there has not been enough published research to draw any real conclusions.

Table 2.7 AET Dimensions

Part A Work System Analysis

1 Work objects
  1.1 material work objects (physical condition, special properties of the material, quality of surfaces, manipulation delicacy, form, size, weight, dangerousness)
  1.2 energy as work object
  1.3 information as work object
  1.4 man, animals, plants as work objects
2 Equipment
  2.1 working equipment
    2.1.1 equipment, tools, machinery to change the properties of the work objects
    2.1.2 means of transport
    2.1.3 controls
  2.2 other equipment
    2.2.1 displays, measuring instruments
    2.2.2 technical aids to support human sense organs information
    2.2.3 work chair, table, room
3 Work environment
  3.1 Physical environment
    3.1.1 environmental influences
    3.1.2 dangerousness of work and risk of occupational diseases
  3.2 Organizational and social environment
    3.2.1 temporal organization of work
    3.2.2 position in the organization of work sequence
    3.2.3 hierarchical position in the organization
    3.2.4 position in the communication system

  3.3 Principles and methods of remuneration
    3.3.1 principles of remuneration
    3.3.2 methods of remuneration

Part B Task Analysis

1 Tasks relating to material work objects
2 Tasks relating to abstract work objects
3 Man-related tasks
4 Number and repetitiveness of tasks

Part C Demand Analysis

1 Demands on perception
  1.1 mode of perception
    1.1.1 visual
    1.1.2 auditory
    1.1.3 tactile
    1.1.4 olfactory
    1.1.5 proprioceptive
  1.2 absolute/relative evaluation of perceived information
  1.3 accuracy of perception
2 Demands for decision
  2.1 complexity of decision
  2.2 pressure on time
  2.3 required knowledge
3 Demands for response/activity
  3.1 body postures
  3.2 static work
  3.3 heavy muscular work
  3.4 light muscular work
  3.5 strenuousness and frequency of movements

AET = Arbeitswissenschaftliches Erhebungsverfahren zur Tätigkeitsanalyse = ergonomic job analysis procedure.
Rohmert, W., and Landau, K. (1983). *A new technique for job analysis*. New York: Taylor & Francis. Reprinted with permission of the publisher.

Methods Providing Information About Competencies

Occupational Information Network (O*NET) The job analysis system used by the federal government that has replaced the Dictionary of Occupational Titles (DOT).

Occupational Information Network. The **Occupational Information Network (O*NET)** is a national job analysis system created by the federal government to replace the *Dictionary of Occupational Titles* (DOT) which had been in use since the 1930s (Peterson et al., 2001). O*NET is a major advancement in understanding the nature of work, in large part because its developers understood that jobs can be viewed at four levels: economic, organizational, occupational, and individual. As a result, O*NET has incorporated the types of information obtained in many job analysis techniques. A chart comparing O*NET with other job analysis methods is located on this text's webpage.

O*NET includes information about the occupation (generalized work activities, work context, organizational context) and the worker characteristics (ability, work style, occupational values and interests, knowledge, skills, education) needed for success in the occupation. The O*NET also includes information about such economic factors as labor demand, labor supply, salaries, and occupational trends. This information can be used by employers to select new employees and by applicants who are

Table 2.8 Sample AET Items

CNO	CC
1.1.7	Weight
		Answer questions 22–24 indicating the individual proportions of *time* during which the incumbent performs tasks involving work materials of *different* weights.
22	D	*Low* weight
		objects weighing up to 1 kg can normally be manipulated with fingers or hands
23	D	*Medium* weight
		1–10 kg can normally be manipulated with hands
24		*Heavy* weight
		more than 10 kg can partly be manipulated by one person without using additional auxiliaries, partly including the use of handling equipment and hoisting machines
1.1.8	Danger
		Answer questions 25–30 indicating the individual proportions of *time* during which the incumbent performs tasks involving *dangerous work materials*
25	D	Work materials that are *explosive*
		e.g., explosives and igniting mixtures, ammunition, fireworks
26	D	Work materials that are *conductive to fire or inflammable*
		e.g., petrol, technical oils, lacquers, and varnishes
27	D	Work materials that are *poisonous or caustic*
		e.g., basic chemicals, chemical-technical materials, plant protectives, cleaning materials
28	D	Work materials that are *radioactive*
		e.g., uranium concentrate, nuclear materials
29	D	Work materials *irritating skin or mucous membrane*
		e.g., quartz, asbestos, Thomas meal, flax, raw cotton
30	D	Work materials *causing other health hazards*
		If characteristic I is rated D=5, continue with characteristic 34.

AET = Arbeitswissenschaftliches Erhebungsverfahren zur Tätigkeitsanalyse = ergonomic job analysis procedure.
Rohmert, W., and Landau, K. (1983). *A new technique for job analysis.* New York: Taylor & Francis. Reprinted with permission of the publisher

searching for careers that match their skills, interests, and economic needs. O*NET-based information can be obtained at http://online.onetcenter.org.

Critical Incident Technique (CIT) The job analysis method developed by John Flanagan that uses written reports of good and bad employee behavior.

Critical Incident Technique. The **Critical Incident Technique (CIT)** was developed and first used by John Flanagan and his students at the University of Pittsburgh in the late 1940s and early 1950s. The CIT is used to discover actual incidents of job behavior that make the difference between a job's successful or unsuccessful performance (Flanagan, 1954). This technique can be conducted in many ways, but the basic procedure is as follows:

1. Job incumbents each generate between one and five incidents of both excellent and poor performance that they have seen on the job. These incidents can be obtained using logbooks, questionnaires, or interviews; research has shown that the method used makes little difference (Campion,

Table 2.9 Critical Incident Examples

1. About a year ago, I was driving home from school and had a flat tire. I was having trouble changing the tire when the police officer stopped and helped me. He then followed me to the nearest gas station to make sure that I didn't have any more trouble. Most cops probably wouldn't have done a darn thing to help.

2. I got pulled over for doing 45 in a 25 mph zone. Instead of just writing me up, the cop told me what a jerk I was for speeding and that if he ever saw me speed again, I would get more than a ticket. He was the one who was the jerk!

Greener, & Wernli, 1973), although questionnaires are usually used because they are the easiest. A convenient way to word requests for critical incidents is by asking incumbents to think of times they saw workers perform in an especially outstanding way and then to write down exactly what occurred. Incumbents are then asked to do the same for times they saw workers perform poorly. This process is repeated as needed. Two examples of critical incidents are shown in Table 2.9.

2. Job experts examine each incident and decide whether it is an example of excellent or poor behavior. This step is necessary because approximately 5% of incidents initially cited as poor examples by employees are actually good examples and vice versa (Aamodt, Reardon, & Kimbrough, 1986). For example, in a recent job analysis of the position of university instructor, a few students described their worst teachers as those who lectured from material not included in their textbooks. A committee of faculty members and students who reviewed the incidents determined that lecturing from nontext material actually was excellent. Thus, the incidents were counted as examples of excellent rather than poor performance.

3. The incidents generated in the first stage are then given to three or four incumbents to sort into an unspecified number of categories. The incidents in each category are then read by the job analyst, who combines, names, and defines the categories.

4. To verify the judgments made by the job analyst in procedure 3, three other incumbents are given the incidents and category names and are asked to sort the incidents into the newly created categories. If two of the three incumbents sort an incident into the same category, the incident is considered part of that category. Any incident that is not agreed upon by two sorters is either thrown out or placed in a new category.

5. The numbers of both types of incidents sorted into each category are then tallied and used to create a table similar to Table 2.10. The categories provide the important dimensions of a job, and the numbers provide the relative importance of these dimensions.

The CIT is an excellent addition to a job analysis because the actual critical incidents can be used for future activities such as performance appraisal and training. The CIT's greatest drawback is that its emphasis on the difference between excellent and poor performance ignores routine duties. Thus, the CIT cannot be used as the sole method of job analysis.

Job Components Inventory. In addition to information about tools and equipment used on the job, which were discussed earlier, the JCI also provides information about the perceptual, physical, mathematical, communication, decision making, and responsibility skills needed to perform the job.

Table 2.10 CIT Categories and Frequencies for Excellent and Poor Resident Assistants

Category	Excellent	Poor	Total
Interest in residents	31	19	50
Availability	14	27	41
Responsibility	12	20	32
Fairness	18	10	28
Self-adherence to the rules	0	28	28
Social skills	19	7	26
Programming	13	7	20
Self-confidence	12	8	20
Rule enforcement	4	14	18
Authoritarianism	1	16	17
Counseling skills	12	4	16
Self-control	5	2	7
Confidentiality	1	2	3

CIT = Critical Incident Technique.

Threshold Traits Analysis (TTA) A 33-item questionnaire developed by Lopez that identifies traits necessary to successfully perform a job.

Threshold Traits Analysis. An approach similar to the JCI is the **Threshold Traits Analysis (TTA)**, which was developed by Lopez, Kesselman, and Lopez (1981). This method is available only by hiring a particular consulting firm (Lopez and Associates), but its unique style makes it worthy of mentioning. The TTA questionnaire's 33 items identify the traits that are necessary for the successful performance of a job. The 33 items cover five trait categories: physical, mental, learned, motivational, and social. An example of an item from the TTA can be found in Figure 2.3. The TTA's greatest advantages are that it is short and reliable and can correctly identify important traits (Lopez et al., 1981). The TTA's greatest disadvantage is that it is not available commercially. Because the TTA also focuses on traits, its main uses are in the development of an employee selection system or a career plan (Lopez, Rockmore, & Kesselman, 1980).

Fleishman Job Analysis Survey (F-JAS) A job analysis method in which jobs are rated on the basis of the abilities needed to perform them.

Fleishman Job Analysis Survey. Based on more than 30 years of research (Fleishman & Reilly, 1992a), the **Fleishman Job Analysis Survey (F-JAS)** requires incumbents or job analysts to view a series of abilities such as the one shown in Figure 2.4 and to rate the level of ability needed to perform the job. These ratings are performed for each of the 73 abilities and knowledge. The F-JAS is easy to use by incumbents or trained analysts, and is supported by years of research. Its advantages over TTA are that it is more detailed, is commercially available, and can be completed online.

Job Adaptability Inventory (JAI) A job analysis method that taps the extent to which a job involves eight types of adaptability.

Job Adaptability Inventory. The **Job Adaptability Inventory (JAI)** is a 132-item inventory developed by Pulakos, Arad, Donovan, and Plamondon (2000) that taps the extent to which a job incumbent needs to adapt to situations on the job. The JAI has eight dimensions:

1. Handling emergencies or crisis situations
2. Handling work stress
3. Solving problems creatively
4. Dealing with uncertain and unpredictable work situations

Problem Solving

Job Functions Include	Incumbent Must
Processing information to reach specific conclusions, answering problems, adapting and assessing ideas of others, and revising into workable form.	Analyze information and, by inductive reasoning, arrive at a specific conclusion or solution (trait also known as *convergent thinking, reasoning*).

Level	Job Activities That Require Solving	Level	Incumbent Must Solve
0	Very minor problems with fairly simple solutions (running out of supplies or giving directions).	0	Very minor problems with fairly simple solutions.
1	Problems with known and limited variables (diagnosing mechanical disorders or customer complaints).	1	Problems with known and limited variables.
2	More complex problems with many known variables (programming or investment analysis).	2	Problems with many known and complex variables.
3	Very complex and abstract problems with many unknown variables (advanced systems design or research).	3	Very complex and abstract problems with many unknown variables.

Adapted from Lopez, F. M., Kesselman, G. A., and Lopez, F. E. (1981). An empirical test of a trait-oriented job analysis technique. *Personnel Psychology,* 34, 479–502. Reprinted with permission of the authors.

Figure 2.3

Sample from Threshold Traits Analysis Questionnaire

5. Learning work tasks, technologies, and procedures
6. Demonstrating interpersonal adaptability
7. Demonstrating cultural adaptability
8. Demonstrating physically oriented adaptability

Though the JAI is relatively new, it has excellent reliability and has been shown to distinguish among jobs (Pulakos, Arad, Donovan, & Plamondon, 2000).

Personality-Related Position Requirements Form (PPRF). The **Personality-Related Position Requirements Form (PPRF)** was developed by Raymark, Schmit, and Guion (1997) to identify the personality types needed to perform job-related tasks. The PPRF consists of 107 items tapping 12 personality dimensions that fall under the "Big 5" personality dimensions (openness to experience, conscientiousness, extroversion, agreeableness, and emotional stability). Though more research is needed, the PPRF is reliable and shows promise as a useful job analysis instrument for identifying the personality traits necessary to perform a job.

Personality-Related Position Requirements Form (PPRF) A job analysis instrument that helps determine the personality requirements for a job.

Evaluation of Methods

In the previous pages, many job analysis methods were presented. To help compare the methods, Table 2.11 summarizes the potential uses for each method. Any time there are multiple methods for something, a logical question is, "Which one is best?" Unfortunately, there is no clear answer to this question in job analysis. The best method to use in analyzing a job appears to be related to the end use of the job analysis information.

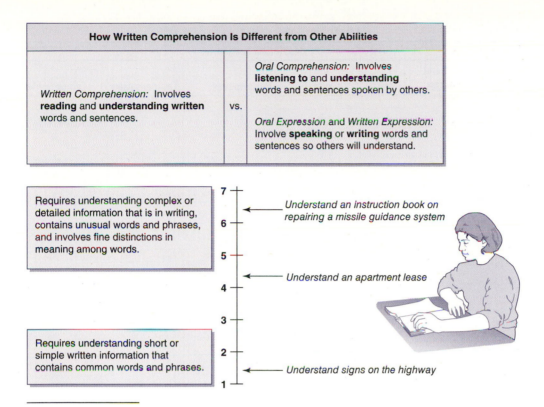

How Written Comprehension Is Different from Other Abilities		
Written Comprehension: Involves **reading** and **understanding written** words and sentences.	vs.	*Oral Comprehension:* Involves **listening to** and **understanding** words and sentences spoken by others. *Oral Expression* and *Written Expression:* Involve **speaking** or **writing** words and sentences so others will understand.

Requires understanding complex or detailed information that is in writing, contains unusual words and phrases, and involves fine distinctions in meaning among words.

7

6

5

4

3

2

1

← Understand an instruction book on repairing a missile guidance system

← Understand an apartment lease

Requires understanding short or simple written information that contains common words and phrases.

← Understand signs on the highway

Figure 2.4

Fleishman Job Analysis Survey Example

That is, different methods are best for different uses—*worker-oriented methods*, such as the CIT, JCI, and TTA, are the best for employee selection and performance appraisal; *job-oriented methods*, such as task analysis, are best for work design and writing job descriptions. To get the most out of a job analysis, several techniques should be used so that information on each of the job description sections can be obtained.

From a legal perspective, courts have ruled that job analysis is necessary (Sparks, 1988) and that acceptable job analyses should (1) use several up-to-date sources, (2) be conducted by experts, (3) use a large number of job incumbents, and (4) cover the entire range of worker activities and qualifications (Thompson & Thompson, 1982).

Other than a meta-analysis demonstrating that job analysis ratings of specific tasks are more reliable than ratings of general work activities (Dierdorff & Wilson, 2003), little research directly comparing job analysis methods has been conducted. This lack of research is primarily because direct comparison of methods is virtually impossible: Each method yields results that differ in both the number and type of dimensions. Thus, the comparative research that has been conducted has focused on opinions of job analysts.

Survey research by Levine, Ash, and their colleagues (Levine, Ash, & Bennett, 1980; Levine, Ash, Hall, & Sistrunk, 1983) has found the following:

1. The PAQ is seen as the most standardized technique and the CIT the least standardized.
2. The CIT takes the least amount of job analyst training and task analysis the most.

Table 2.11 Comparison of the Output of the Types of Information Gained from Various Job Analysis Methods

Job Analysis Method	Job Description Section						
	Specific Tasks	**General Duties**	**Tools**	**Job Context**	**Performance**	**Compensation**	**Competencies**
Interview	X	X	X	X	X	X	X
Observation	X	X	X	X			X
Job participation	X	X	X	X			X
PAQ		X		X			X
JSP		X		X			X
JEI		X		X			X
FJA		X					
JCI			X				X
AET				X			
O*NET		X					X
CIT		X					X
TTA							X
F-JAS							X
JAI							X
PPRF							X

PAQ = Position Analysis Questionnaire; JSP = Job Structure Profile; JEI = Job Elements Inventory; FJA = Functional Job Analysis; JCI = Job Components Inventory; AET = Arbeitswissenschaftliches Erhebungsverfahren zur Tätigkeitsanalyse = ergonomic job analysis procedure; O*NET = Occupational Information Network; CIT = Critical Incident Technique; TTA = Threshold Traits Analysis; F-JAS = Fleishman Job Analysis Survey; JAI = Job Adaptability Inventory; PPRF = Personality-Related Position Requirements Form.

3. The PAQ is the least costly method and the CIT the most.
4. The PAQ takes the least amount of time to complete and task analysis the most.
5. Task analysis has the highest-quality results and TTA the lowest.
6. Task analysis reports are the longest and job-elements reports the shortest.
7. The CIT has been rated the most useful and the PAQ the least.
8. Task analysis gives the best overall job picture and the PAQ the worst.

Keep in mind, however, that these findings were based on users' opinions rather than on actual empirical comparison and that many of the newer (post-1980) job analysis methods were not included in the Levine and Ash studies.

Job Evaluation

Job evaluation The process of determining the monetary worth of a job.

Once a job analysis has been completed and a thorough job description written, it is important to determine how much employees in a position should be paid. This process of determining a job's *worth* is called **job evaluation**. A job evaluation is typically done in two stages: determining internal pay equity and determining external pay equity.

Should employees in dangerous jobs be compensated for the increased risk?

Determining Internal Pay Equity

Internal pay equity involves comparing jobs within an organization to ensure that the people in jobs worth the most money are paid accordingly. The difficulty in this process, of course, is determining the worth of each job. Because a complete discussion of all job evaluation methods is beyond the scope of this text, we will stick to a discussion of the most commonly used method.

Step 1: Determining Compensable Job Factors

The first step in evaluating a job is to decide what factors differentiate the relative worth of jobs. Possible **compensable job factors** include the following:

Compensable job factors
Factors, such as responsibility and education requirements, that differentiate the relative worth of jobs.

- Level of responsibility
- Physical demands
- Mental demands
- Education requirements
- Training and experience requirements
- Working conditions

The philosophical perspectives of the job evaluator can affect these factors. Some evaluators argue that the most important compensable factor is responsibility and that physical demands are unimportant. Others argue that education is the most important. The choice of compensable factors thus is often more philosophical than empirical.

Step 2: Determining the Levels for Each Compensable Factor

Once the compensable factors have been selected, the next step is to determine the levels for each factor. For a factor such as education, the levels are easy to determine (e.g., high school diploma, associate's degree, bachelor's degree). For factors such as responsibility, a considerable amount of time and discussion may be required to determine the levels.

Step 3: Determining the Factor Weights

Because some factors are more important than others, weights must be assigned to each factor and to each level within a factor. Here is the process for doing this:

1. A job evaluation committee determines the total number of points that will be distributed among the factors. Usually, the number is some multiple of 100 (for example, 100, 500, 1,000) and is based on the number of compensable factors. The greater the number of factors, the greater the number of points.
2. Each factor is weighted by assigning a number of points. The more important the factor, the greater the number of points that will be assigned.
3. The number of points assigned to a factor is then divided into each of the levels. If 100 points had been assigned to the factor of education, then 20 points (100 points/5 degrees) would be assigned to each level. An example of this procedure is shown in Table 2.12. The job evaluation committee takes the job descriptions for each job and assigns points based on the factors and degrees created in the previous steps.

Table 2.12   Example of Completed Job Evaluation Results

Factors	Points
Education (200 points possible)	
High school education or less	40
Two years of college	80
Bachelor's degree	120
Master's degree	160
Ph.D.	200
Responsibility (300 points possible)	
Makes no decisions	75
Makes decisions for self	150
Makes decisions for 1–5 employees	225
Makes decisions for more than 5 employees	300
Physical demands (90 points possible)	
Lifts no heavy objects	30
Lifts objects between 25 and 100 pounds	60
Lifts objects more than 100 pounds	90

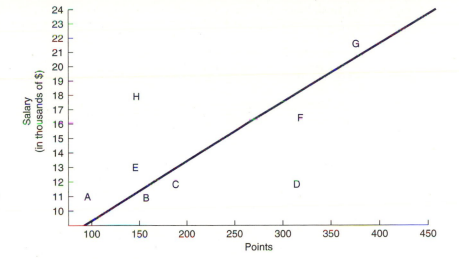

4. The total number of points for a job is compared with the salary currently being paid for the job. This comparison is typically graphed in a fashion similar to the **wage trend line** shown in Figure 2.5. Wage trend lines are drawn based on the results of a regression formula in which salary is predicted by the number of job analysis points. Jobs whose point values fall well below the line (as with Job D in Figure 2.5) are considered underpaid ("green circled") and are immediately assigned higher salary levels. Jobs with point values well above the line (as with Job H) are considered overpaid ("red circled") and the salary level is decreased once current jobholders leave. To better understand this process, complete Exercise 2.6 in your workbook.

Determining External Pay Equity

With external equity, the worth of a job is determined by comparing the job to the external market (other organizations). External equity is important if an organization is to attract and retain employees. In other words, it must be competitive with the compensation plans of other organizations. That is, a fast-food restaurant that pays cooks $8 an hour will probably have trouble hiring and keeping high-caliber employees if other fast-food restaurants in the area pay $10 an hour.

To determine external equity, organizations use **salary surveys**. Sent to other organizations, these surveys ask how much an organization pays its employees in various positions. An organization can either construct and send out its own survey or use the results of surveys conducted by trade groups, an option that many organizations choose. On the basis of the survey results such as those shown in Table 2.13, an organization can decide where it wants to be in relation to the compensation policies of other organizations (often called *market position*). That is, an organization might choose to offer compensation at higher levels to attract the best applicants as well as keep current employees from going to other organizations. Other organizations might choose to pay at the "going rate" so that they have a reasonable chance of competing for applicants, even though they will often lose the best applicants to higher-paying organizations. Market position is most important in a good economy where jobs are plentiful and applicants have several job options. It may seem surprising that

Table 2.13 Example of Salary Survey Results

Position	# orgs with position	Number of employees	Weighted average	Salary Range				
				Low	Q1	Median	Q3	High
Assembly/Production								
Foreperson	18	286	$22.21	11.67	18.96	21.67	27.69	36.44
Machinist	9	419	$19.83	9.28	16.79	18.63	21.09	25.80
Production control planner	9	36	$18.73	16.64	18.68	20.63	23.59	36.44
Production worker	15	3,487	$17.91	8.49	12.24	15.05	15.62	23.27
Quality control inspector	10	45	$14.23	10.00	12.84	14.01	20.31	23.18
Maintenance								
Janitor	10	322	$11.00	7.85	9.02	10.15	11.04	19.81
Maintenance person A	17	112	$14.90	9.65	12.54	14.97	19.40	26.78
Mechanic	11	382	$18.80	11.99	17.10	18.30	20.27	24.98

Q1 = first quartile; Q3 = third quartile.

competing organizations would supply salary information to each other, but because every organization needs salary data from other organizations, compensation analysts tend to cooperate well with one another.

Roanoke County, Virginia, provides an excellent example of the importance of market position. The county was concerned about the high turnover rate of its police dispatchers and undertook a study to determine the reason for the problem. Possible reasons were thought to be working conditions, location, reputation, and pay. The study revealed that most of the turnover was due to a neighboring city paying its dispatchers $2,500 more per year. This resulted in Roanoke County dispatchers resigning after a year of experience to take a higher-paying job only five miles away. Adjusting the salary greatly reduced the turnover rate.

Keep in mind that job evaluation concerns the worth of the *job itself*, not the worth of a *person* in the job. For example, suppose a salary survey reveals that the going rate for a job falls within the range of $20,000 to $30,000, and an organization, deciding to be at the upper end of the market, sets its range for the position at $27,000 to $32,000. Decisions must then be made regarding where in the $5,000 range each particular employee will be paid. This decision is based on such factors as years of experience, years with the company, special skills, education, local cost of living, and performance level.

We have earlier discussed the amount of money a job is worth: this amount is called **direct compensation**. Employees are also compensated in other ways, such as pay for time not worked (e.g., holidays, vacation, sick days), deferred income (e.g., Social Security and pension plans), health protection such as medical and dental insurance, and perquisites ("perks") such as a company car (Martocchio, 2009). Consequently, a job with a direct compensation of $30,000 might actually be worth more than one at $35,000 because of the indirect compensation package. In fact, anytime your author complains to his neighbors about low faculty salaries, they shed few tears as they mention such benefits as three-week Christmas vacations and three-month summer holidays.

Direct compensation The amount of money paid to an employee (does not count benefits, time off, and so forth).

Determining Sex and Race Equity

In addition to analyses of internal and external equity, pay audits should also be conducted to ensure that employees are not paid differently on the basis of gender or race. For organizations with 50 or more employees and federal contracts in excess of $50,000, compensation analyses are mandatory each year. The Office of Federal Contract Compliance Programs (OFCCP) monitors these analyses to ensure that they are conducted and that contractors are not discriminating on the basis of pay. Two types of audits should be conducted: one that looks at pay rates of employees within positions with *identical duties* (equal pay for equal work) and a second that looks at pay rates of employees in jobs of *similar worth and responsibility* (comparable worth).

This second type of analysis is normally conducted by comparing jobs with similar worth (salary grade) and responsibility (job family). The OFCCP calls such groups *similarly situated employee groups* (SSEGs).

Comparable worth is an issue very much related to the discussion of job evaluation. Comparable worth is often in the news because some groups claim that female workers are paid less than male workers. This perception of pay inequity stems from the statistic that, on average, female workers in 2010 made only 81.2% of what male workers were paid. On average, African American workers and Hispanics made less than Asian Americans and whites. As shown in Table 2.14, the pay

Comparable worth The idea that jobs requiring the same level of skill and responsibility should be paid the same regardless of supply and demand.

Table 2.14 Trends of Salary Level of Women as a Percentage of Men's Salaries and Minorities as a Percentage of White's Salaries

	Sex Comparison	Race Comparison		
Year	Women to Men	Blacks to Whites	Hispanics to Whites	Asians to Whites
2010	81.2	79.9	69.9	111.8
2009	80.2	79.4	71.5	116.2
2008	79.9	79.4	71.3	116.0
2007	80.2	79.5	70.3	115.9
2006	80.8	80.3	70.4	113.6
2005	81.0	77.3	70.1	112.1
2004	80.4	79.9	71.7	107.8
2003	79.4	80.8	72.3	109.0
2002	77.9	79.9	72.6	105.6
2001	76.4	80.5	74.3	104.8
2000	76.9	80.3	72.9	104.2
1995	75.5	77.5	73.5	
1990	71.9	77.6	71.7	
1985	68.1	77.8	75.8	
1980	64.2	78.8	78.2	

U.S. Department of Labor.

gap, which was narrowing for many years, seems to have stagnated at approximately 80% for women and African Americans and 70% for Hispanics. It should be noted that Asians make more money than do the other ethnic and racial groups, a gap that is widening each year.

Research indicates that all but 6.2% of the gap between men and women can be explained by such factors as men being in the workforce longer, having a higher percentage of full-time jobs, and working more hours in a year (Wall, 2000). Thus, sex differences in pay are often less an issue of pay discrimination by organizations than one of vocational choice and educational opportunity discrimination. To alleviate gender differences in pay, it is essential that young women be encouraged to enter historically male-dominated fields (assembly lines, management, police) and that young men be encouraged to enter historically female-dominated fields (nursing, clerical, elementary education). Furthermore, because men are more inclined to negotiate such things as starting salaries than are women (Babcock & Laschever, 2008; Stuhlmacher & Walters, 1999), some of the pay gap can be narrowed either by not allowing applicants to negotiate salaries or by teaching all applicants how to negotiate salaries. Although a complete discussion on this topic goes beyond the scope of this text, an excellent assortment of articles and links on this issue can be found at http://www.swcollege.com/bef/policy_debates/gender.html.

For some advice on salary negotiation, see the Career Workshop Box.

Conducting a Sex and Race Equity Study

The first step in conducting a salary equity analysis for an organization is to place jobs into the SSEGs mentioned previously. This task takes considerable time, as one needs to use salary grades to determine similarity of worth and use job descriptions to determine similarity of duties and responsibilities. The goal of these analyses is to determine if the average salary for men differs significantly from the average salary for women, and whether the average salary for whites differs from the average salary for minorities (in salary analyses, all minorities are initially lumped into one group). This analysis is conducted for each SSEG, rather than the organization as a whole.

Two types of statistical analyses are typically used: hierarchical regression and Fisher's exact tests. For smaller SSEGs (fewer than 30 total employees), a Fisher's exact test is used to compare median salaries. If there are at least 30 employees in the SSEG and at least 5 employees in each sex or race group (i.e., 5 men and 5 women), this can be done through a statistical technique called *hierarchical regression.*

With hierarchical regression, the first step is to enter your merit variables into the equation to determine what percentage of individual differences in pay they explain. The second step in the equation is to enter sex (coded 0 for males, 1 for females) to determine whether, after controlling for the merit variables, an employee's sex is still related to pay. That is, suppose the average salary for men in grade 8 is $27,000 and for women $24,000. It may be that this $3,000 difference can be explained by the fact that the average man in the grade has been with the organization five years longer than the average woman in the SSEG. The results of the regression will determine if the $3,000 salary difference can be fully explained, partially explained, or not explained by differences in the merit variables.

Negotiating Salary

Toward the end of this chapter you learned that one of the main causes of salary inequity between men and women is that men are more likely to negotiate salaries than are women. It is important for a job applicant to understand that most salary offers are negotiable. Most organizations have a pay range in which employee salaries must fall for each job. For example, the range for an accountant at IBM might be $30,000 to $40,000. An applicant will never get less than the $30,000 or more than the $40,000. The negotiation determines where in that $10,000 range you will fall. Here are some thoughts for negotiating:

➡ Know what the job is worth. All public organizations and some private organizations will make their salary ranges available to applicants. If they don't, you can use information from salary surveys and your university career placement office to help you find information about salary ranges for a type of job. Good Internet sources include www.jobstar.org, www.salary.com, and www.salaryexpert.com.

➡ Ask your career placement center about the typical starting salaries for graduates in your field from your university.

➡ Know what you need to earn. Think about the cost of living and your expenses (e.g., rent, utilities, student loans, car payment). That will give you an idea about the minimum salary you will accept. There are times when the offer you get is not negotiable and is below what you need to survive. In such cases, you must turn down the offer.

➡ Know what you are worth. If you have experience, graduated from a top school, were a top student in your university, or have unusual skills, you are worth more than the typical applicant. If you are asked in an interview about your expected starting salary, you might use this information to respond, "The typical salary for accounting majors at our university is $28,000. Because I have done an internship and was one of the top students in our department, my expectation is to start above $30,000."

➡ Don't be afraid to negotiate. When the organization makes an offer, counter with a higher amount. In doing so, be realistic and base your offer on logic and facts. Explain why you think an increased starting salary is justifiable. If you graduated with no experience and a 2.01 GPA, you probably have little room to negotiate above the bottom of the range.

➡ When the job market is tight and employers are having trouble finding good applicants, your value is higher.

➡ In addition to salary, there are times when you can negotiate such things as vacation time, starting dates, and other benefits.

If the results of the regression analysis indicate that the merit variables do not explain sex or race differences in salary, one still cannot conclude that discrimination has occurred. It could be that there are valid factors involved in the differences (e.g., the economy at the time of hire) that were not entered into the regression. However, in the absence of a valid explanation, salary adjustments may be in order.

Salary adjustments are determined by entering the merit variables for each employee into a regression equation to estimate what the employees "should" be making. For this approach to be reliable, the merit variables should account for a statistically significant percentage of the individual differences in salary. An employee whose actual salary is two standard errors below his or her predicted salary is a potential candidate for a salary adjustment. I realize that this process is complicated and highly statistical, but that is the nature of salary equity analysis, and salary equity analyses are becoming an important function performed by Human Resources departments. The process can be made substantially easier by using software such as *HR Equator* or *COMPARE*, which are designed for such purposes.

Applied Case Study

To become a veterinarian, a person must pass the North American Veterinary Licensing Exam (NAVLE), a national exam typically taken after graduation from veterinary school. This exam has 360 items and is offered twice a year. Examples of questions on the exam include the following:

1. Which of the following is the most common cause of maxillary sinusitis in the horse?
   (A) Bacterial lower respiratory tract disease extending into the sinus
   (B) Infection and abscessation of a tooth root extending into the sinus
   (C) Inhaled foreign bodies lodging in the sinus
   (D) Puncture wounds extending into the maxillary sinus
2. An African gray parrot that is presented for necropsy is suspected to have psittacosis. Which of the following findings is most likely to confirm the diagnosis?
   (A) Hepatomegaly and splenomegaly on gross examination
   (B) Identification of the causative organism by Gram's stain
   (C) Isolation and identification of Chlamydia psittaci
   (D) Presence of acid-fast organisms in the liver

To ensure that this national exam covers the important information needed to be a veterinarian, the National Board of Veterinary Medical Examiners decided to conduct a job analysis of the position of entry-level veterinary practitioner. Given that there are over 60,000 veterinarians throughout the country, this was indeed a daunting task. This number is compounded by the fact that veterinarians work in a variety of settings such as private practice, governmental agencies, veterinary medicine colleges, pharmaceutical companies, zoos, and research laboratories. Furthermore, major job duties can range from direct health care to research to disease control.

1. How would you conduct such a large-scale job analysis?
2. In determining the sample of veterinarians that would participate in the job analysis, what factors (e.g., region of the country) would you need to consider?
3. How many veterinarians would you include in your job analysis?

More information about this case can be found by following the link on the text website.

FOCUS ON ETHICS | **Compensating CEOs and Executives**

There is no question that executives are compensated well. And there has always been a gap between executives and workers. But this gap is widening. In 1973, the top CEOs in the nation made about 45 times the wage of the average worker. As of August 29, 2007, according to Daniel Lubien of Interpress Service, CEOs were being paid approximately 364 times that of an average worker.

The top five CEOs in 2010 earned the following amounts through salaries and stock options:

- Philippe Dauman, CEO, Viacom: $84.5 million ($13.9 in cash, $55.7 in stock and options)

- Ray Irani, CEO, Occidental Petroleum: $76.1 million ($34.2 in cash, $40.25 in stock)

- Larry Ellison, CEO, Oracle: $70.14 million ($6.7 in cash, $61.95 in stock and options)

- John Hammergren, CEO, McKesson: $54.58 million ($14.41 in cash, $18.7 in stock and options)

- David Zaslav, CEO, Discovery Communications: $42.59 million ($6.4 in cash, $35.74 in stock and options)

CEOs and other executives say that high compensation buys better performance from them, which includes their ability to create new jobs for workers in communities that might otherwise have high unemployment. The job factors usually used to decide such compensation include the level of responsibility, education requirements, experience, and sometimes working conditions.

There are advocates and opponents for these high compensation packages. On the one hand, the level of education, experience, and responsibility greatly differentiates CEOs and executives from the average worker. Publicly traded companies are accountable to their stockholders. So, these executives are being paid to make money for the company and its stockholders. And to make money, the company has to significantly compensate its executives for high performance.

On the other hand, these high compensation packages could come at the expense of the workers who actually make the product or deliver a service to consumers. As executives continue to be compensated at higher and higher levels for their performance, the focus of increasing wages and salaries for the average worker may decline if the company does not have some set standards of values and ethics. And, as your textbook says, the choice of compensable factors is often more philosophical than empirical—which means this level of compensation may not be necessary to motivate executives to perform well.

What Do You Think?

- Are CEOs being paid too much or are they worth the high compensation packages they receive?

- Is it ethical or fair that a CEO receives a bonus when employees are being laid off or having their benefits reduced?

- Does high compensation for CEOs actually increase company performance?

- Should a company's number one focus be on making money for its shareholders?

- What might be other ethical factors surrounding this issue?

Chapter Summary

In this chapter you learned:

- Job analysis provides the foundation for such areas as performance appraisal, employee selection, training, and job design.
- A properly written job description contains a job title, a brief summary, an extensive list of work activities, a list of tools and equipment, information about the work context, compensation information, performance standards, and personal requirements.
- Before a job analysis is begun, decisions must be made about the type of information that will be obtained, who will conduct the job analysis, and who will participate in it.
- The typical job analysis involves interviewing and observing subject-matter experts (SMEs) to determine tasks that are performed, the conditions under which they are performed, the tools and equipment needed to perform them, and the knowledge, skills, abilities, and other characteristics (KSAOs) needed to perform them.
- Although no job analysis method is always better than others, each is better for certain purposes. For example, the Position Analysis Questionnaire (PAQ) is an excellent method for compensation uses, and the Critical Incident Technique (CIT) is an excellent method for performance appraisal.
- Job evaluation is the process of assigning a monetary value to a job.
- Internal equity, external equity, and comparable worth are important pay issues that must be addressed during any job evaluation.

Questions for Review

1. Why is job analysis so important?
2. What are the main sections of a job description?
3. Would a job analyst expect to find gender and race differences in the way employees perform the duties of their jobs? Why or why not?
4. How should a task statement be written?
5. Why are there so many job analysis methods?
6. Research indicates that the average salary for women in the United States is about 80% of the average salary for men. Why is this?
7. Is external pay equity more important than internal pay equity? Why or why not?

Media Resources and Learning Tools

- Visit our website. Go to www.cengage.com/psychology/aamodt, where you will find online resources directly linked to your book, including chapter-by-chapter quizzing, flashcards, crossword puzzles, application activities, and more.
- Want more practice applying industrial/organizational psychology? Check out the *I/O Applications Workbook*. This workbook (keyed to your textbook) offers engaging, high-interest activities to help you reinforce the important concepts presented in the text.

© Chris Ryan/OJO Images/Getty Images

Learning Objectives

➡ Understand the legal process involving employment law

➡ Know what classes of people are protected by federal law

➡ Be able to determine the legality of an employment practice

➡ Understand the concept of adverse impact

➡ Understand affirmative action

➡ Know the important issues involving employee privacy rights

Equal Employment Opportunity Commission (EEOC) A branch of the Department of Labor charged with investigating and prosecuting complaints of employment discrimination.

I n the field of human resources (HR), it is not a question of *whether* you will get sued by an applicant or former employee but *when* and *how often*. In 2010 alone, 99,222 discrimination complaints were filed with the **Equal Employment Opportunity Commission (EEOC)**, resulting in more than $319 million in awards and settlements. These statistics should convince anyone entering the HR field that knowledge of employment law is essential (updated statistics can be obtained on the web at www.eeoc.gov/eeoc/statistics/enforcement/index.cfm).

The Legal Process

To know whether a given employment practice is legal, it is important to understand the legal process as it relates to employment law. The first step in the legal process is for some legislative body, such as the U.S. Congress or a state legislature, to pass a law. If a law is passed at the federal level, states may pass laws that *expand* the rights granted in the federal law; states may not, however, pass laws that will *diminish* the rights granted in federal legislation. For example, if Congress passed a law that gave women six months of maternity leave, a state or local government could pass a law extending the leave to eight months, but it could not reduce the amount of maternity leave to less than the mandated six months. Thus, to be on firm legal ground, it is important to be aware of state and local laws as well as federal legislation.

Once a law has been passed, situations occur in which the intent of the law is not clear. For example, a law might be passed to protect disabled employees. Two years later, an employee is denied promotion because he has high blood pressure. The employee may file a charge against the employer claiming discrimination based on a disability. He may claim that high blood pressure is a disability but that he can still work in spite of the disability and consequently deserves the promotion. The organization, on the other hand, might claim that high blood pressure is not a disability and that even if it were, an employee with high blood pressure could not perform the job. It would then be up to the courts to decide.

Resolving the Complaint Internally

Grievance system A process in which an employee files a complaint with the organization and a person or committee within the organization makes a decision regarding the complaint.

Mediation A method of resolving conflict in which a neutral third party is asked to help the two parties reach an agreement.

Before a complaint can be filed with the EEOC, an employee must utilize whatever internal resolution process is available within the organization. As a result, most organizations have formal policies regarding how discrimination complaints will be handled internally. Typically, these policies involve such forms of alternative dispute resolution (ADR) as a grievance process, mediation, and arbitration. ADR will be discussed in greater detail in Chapter 13, but a brief description is provided here. With a **grievance system**, employees take their complaints to an internal committee that makes a decision regarding the complaints. If employees do not like the decision, they can then take their complaints to the EEOC. With **mediation**, employees and the organization meet with a neutral third party who tries to help the two sides reach a mutually agreed upon solution. If they cannot reach a solution, the complaint can be taken to arbitration or to the EEOC. The EEOC has begun to strongly recommend mediation as a solution to discrimination complaints, in part because 96% of employers who tried mediation said they would try it again, and data indicate that the time taken to resolve a dispute through mediation is less than half that of going through more formal channels (Tyler, 2007).

What to Do If You Feel You Are Being Discriminated Against at Work

There may be times during your career when you believe you are being treated unfairly on the basis of your sex, race, age, religion, or national origin. If you feel you have been discriminated against or are being harassed in the workplace, consider the following advice provided by consultant Bobbie Raynes:

➤ Most organizations have policies explaining how employees should handle situations in which they have been harassed or discriminated against. Refer to your organization's policy manual for guidance.

➤ Document what occurred, when it occurred, and who was involved.

➤ Report the situation to your supervisor or the HR director. (If it is your supervisor who has harassed or discriminated against you, take your concerns directly to the HR director.)

➤ Some employees have gone directly to the person who did the harassing or discriminating to see if they can work out the situation without getting others involved. However, this step works only if you feel comfortable with it. You are under no obligation to go directly to that person.

➤ Remember that there are time limits involved in reporting discrimination or harassment situations.

➤ Consider mediation to resolve the situation. This process includes a neutral third party who meets with all parties involved in the incident, as well as the HR director, to discuss how best to resolve the situation. The mediator will not decide who is right or wrong. The mediator's goal is to help all parties consider options, other than legal options, for resolving past and future problems. Research shows that 90% of all workplace disputes that go through mediation are amicably resolved without help from the courts. This process can be less stressful than going to court and will often preserve workplace relationships.

➤ If mediation is not an option and/or the organization seems unwilling to address the situation, another option is to file a complaint with the EEOC.

➤ Being discriminated against or harassed is a very upsetting experience and can cause anger, anxiety, depression, or other feelings. Even if the matter is handled amicably, you may still have some of these feelings. Consider using the organization's employee assistance program (EAP) to talk to a counselor about your feelings. If the organization does not have an EAP, seek a counselor outside of the organization.

Arbitration A method of resolving conflicts in which a neutral third party is asked to choose which side is correct.

Binding arbitration A method of resolving conflicts in which a neutral third party is asked to choose which side is correct and in which neither party is allowed to appeal the decision.

Nonbinding arbitration A method of resolving conflicts in which a neutral third party is asked to choose which side is correct but in which either party may appeal the decision.

With **arbitration**, the two sides present their case to a neutral third party who then makes a decision as to which side is right. Arbitration and mediation differ in that the neutral third party *helps* the two sides reach an agreement in mediation, whereas in arbitration, the neutral third party *makes* the decision. If **binding arbitration** is used, neither side can appeal the decision. If **nonbinding arbitration** is used, the parties can either accept the decision or take the case to court. The U.S. Supreme Court has ruled (*Circuit City Stores v. Adams*, 2001) that the applicant or employee is not allowed to take the complaint to the EEOC or to court if an organization has a policy of mandatory arbitration.

Filing a Discrimination Charge

As shown in Figure 3.1, a charge of discrimination is usually filed with a government agency. A state agency is used if the alleged violation involves a state law; a federal agency, usually the EEOC, handles alleged violations of federal law. An EEOC complaint must be filed within 180 days of the discriminatory act, but within 300 days if the complainant has already filed a complaint with a state or local fair-employment practice agency. The government agency will try to notify the employer within 10 days about the complaint, obtain further information from both parties if necessary, and review the charge to determine whether it has merit.

© William Fritsch/Jupiter Images

Discrimination suits
are common in
organizations.

It is important to note that the Lilly Ledbetter Fair Pay Act, signed into law by President Barack Obama in 2009, clarified that the 180-day period for filing a lawsuit alleging pay discrimination begins at the time of the last paycheck rather than when the employee's salary was determined. Take for example a situation in which two equally qualified applicants, Mary and John, were both hired on January 1, 2010. Mary's starting salary was $60,000 and John's was $80,000. On January 1, 2011, Mary discovers that she is making less than John and considers filing a discrimination lawsuit. Prior to the Ledbetter Act, she would not be able to do so because the decision regarding her salary was made 360 days ago, outside of the 180-day statute of limitations. However, because the Ledbetter Act changed the focus from the date of the decision to the date of the last paycheck, she would not be time-barred from filing her lawsuit.

Outcomes of an EEOC Investigation

Charge Does Not Have Merit

If, after reviewing a complaint, the governmental agency does not find merit, one of two things can happen based on whether the person filing the complaint accepts the

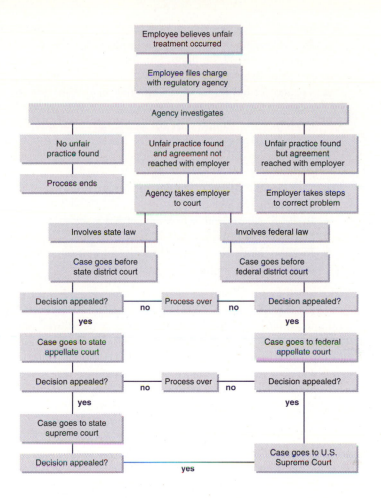

Figure 3.1
Legal Process in Employment Law

decision. If the complainant accepts the decision, the process ends. If the complainant does not accept the decision, he is issued a "right to sue" letter that entitles him to hire a private attorney and file the case himself.

Charge Has Merit

If the EEOC believes that the discrimination charge has merit, it will try to work out a settlement between the claimant and employer without taking the case to court. These settlements might include an employer offering a job or promotion to the person filing the complaint, the payment of back wages, and the payment of compensatory or punitive damages. These settlements can range in size from a few dollars to more than $100 million:

- In 2000, Coca-Cola settled a racial discrimination case for a record $192.5 million.
- In 1993, the Shoney's restaurant chain settled a racial discrimination case for $132.5 million. Most of the money went to approximately 10,000 African Americans who either worked for or were denied employment with Shoney's over a 7-year period. The size of the settlement was based not only on the high number of victims but also on the severity of the discrimination. For example, the number of African American employees in each restaurant was

limited to the percentage of African American customers. When African Americans were hired, they were placed in low-paying kitchen jobs. In addition to the $132.5 million, Shoney's agreed to institute an affirmative action program over the next 10 years.

- Texaco settled its racial discrimination suit in 1996 by agreeing to pay $176 million to 1,400 current and former African American employees. The settlement was prompted by the public airing of a tape recording of a Texaco executive using a racial slur.
- In 2000, Nextel settled its gender, race, and age discrimination suit for $176 million.
- In 2004, the Morgan Stanley brokerage house settled a sex discrimination complaint for $54 million.
- In 2005, Abercrombie & Fitch settled a sex and race discrimination complaint for $40 million.
- In 2010, Novartis settled a sex discrimination suit involving pay and promotions for $175 million.

Case law The interpretation of a law by a court through a verdict in a trial, setting precedent for subsequent court decisions.

If a settlement cannot be reached, however, the case goes to a federal district court, with the EEOC representing (physically and financially) the person filing the complaint. When the district court makes a decision, the decision becomes **case law**. Case law is a judicial interpretation of a law and is important because it establishes a precedent for future cases. If one side does not like the decision rendered in a lower court, it may take the case to the circuit court of appeal. A ruling by one of the 12 circuit courts of appeal serves as binding case law only for that particular circuit. That is why, in this chapter, the circuit is identified along with most of the court cases.

If either side does not agree with the appeals court decision, it can ask the U.S. Supreme Court to review it. The Supreme Court will consider a case only if the decision is legally important or if the rulings on an issue are inconsistent across the circuit courts. Obviously, a ruling by the U.S. Supreme Court carries the most weight, followed by appeals court rulings, and then district court rulings.

Determining Whether an Employment Decision Is Legal

At first glance, the legal aspects of making employment decisions seem complicated. After all, there are many laws and court cases that apply to employment decisions. The basic legal aspects, however, are not that complicated. Use the flowchart in Figure 3.2 to make the process easier to understand as each stage is discussed.

Does the Employment Practice Directly Refer to a Member of a Federally Protected Class?

An employment practice is any decision that affects an employee. Employment practices include hiring, training, firing, promoting, assigning employees to shifts, determining pay, disciplining, and scheduling vacations. Thus, *any* decision made by an employer has the potential for legal challenge.

The first step in determining the legality of an employment practice is to decide whether the practice directly refers to a member of a protected class.

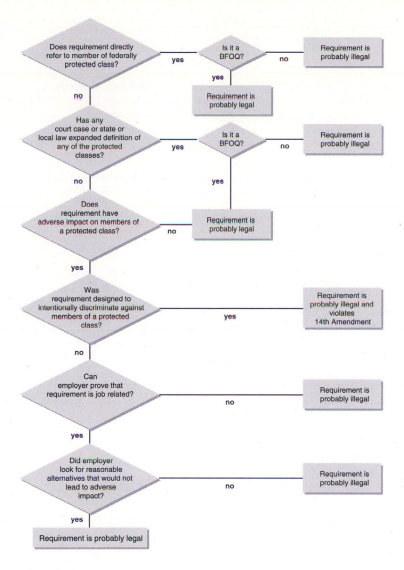

Figure 3.2

Determining Whether an Employment Practice Is Legal

A **protected class** is any group of people for which protective legislation has been passed. A federally protected class is any group of individuals specifically protected by *federal* law. A list of U.S. federally protected classes is shown in Figure 3.3. Table 3.1 shows the similarity of protected classes in the United States and in selected other countries. In Canada, there are no federally protected classes; each province makes its own employment law. Thus, the protected classes listed for Canada in Table 3.1 are those protected by law in *all* provinces and territories. A complete list of provincially protected classes can be found in the appendix at the end of this chapter.

Though one would assume that few employers in the twenty-first century would intentionally make employment decisions on the basis of a person's sex, race, national origin, color, age, religion, or disability, there are hundreds of organizations each year that do exactly that. For example, in 2001, Rent-A-Center settled a sex discrimination

Protected Class	Federal Law
Age (over 40)	Age Discrimination in Employment Act
Disability	Americans with Disabilities Act
	Americans with Disabilities Amendments Act
	Vocational Rehabilitation Act of 1973
Race	Civil Rights Acts of 1964, 1991
National origin	Civil Rights Acts of 1964, 1991
Religion	Civil Rights Acts of 1964, 1991
Sex	Civil Rights Acts of 1964, 1991
	Equal Pay Act of 1963
Pregnancy	Pregnancy Discrimination Act
Qualified military veterans	Vietnam-Era Veterans Readjustment Act of 1974
	Jobs for Veterans Act of 2002

Figure 3.3

Federally Protected Classes in the United States

case for $47 million after its chief executive officer and other managers discriminated against women. Some of their quotes included, "Get rid of women any way you can," "In case you didn't notice, we do not employ women," and "The day I hire a woman will be a cold day in hell."

Table 3.1   International Comparison of Federally Protected Classes

Protected Class	US	Canada	Australia	UK	EU	Mexico	Japan
Race	yes	yes	yes	yes	yes	yes	
National origin	yes	yes		yes	yes	yes	yes
Sex	yes	yes	yes	yes	yes	yes	yes
Age	yes	yes	yes	yes	yes		yes
Disability	yes	yes	yes	yes	yes		yes
Color	yes	yes		yes			
Religion	yes		yes		yes	yes	yes
Pregnancy	yes	yes	yes			yes	
Vietnam veteran	yes						
Marital status		yes	yes	yes			
Sexual orientation		yes	yes		yes		
Political beliefs			yes			yes	yes
Family status			yes				
Transgender status				yes			
Criminal conviction			yes				
National extraction			yes				
Social origin			yes				
Medical record			yes				
Trade union activity			yes				
Social status							yes

Race

Fifth Amendment The amendment to the U.S. Constitution that mandates that the federal government may not deny a person equal protection under the law.

Fourteenth Amendments The amendment to the U.S. Constitution that mandates that no state may deny a person equal protection under the law.

Race According to Congress, the four races are African American, European American, Asian American, and Native American Indian.

On the basis of the Civil Rights Acts of 1866, 1964, and 1991, as well as the **Fifth** and **Fourteenth Amendments** to the U.S. Constitution, it is illegal to discriminate against a person based on **race**. According to Congress, the four races are African American, White, Asian American, and Native American Indian.

The *equal protection clauses* of the Fifth and Fourteenth Amendments mandate that no federal or state agency may deny a person equal protection under the law. This implies that a government may not *intentionally* discriminate or allow intentional discrimination to take place. Because any suit filed under the Fifth or Fourteenth Amendment must demonstrate intent, they are not often invoked.

The Civil Rights Acts of 1964 (known as Title VII) and 1991 extended the scope of the Fifth and Fourteenth Amendments to the private sector and to local governments. Title VII, Section 703, makes it illegal for employers with more than 15 employees and for labor unions, employment agencies, state and local governmental agencies, and educational institutions to

- fail or refuse to hire or to discharge any individual, or otherwise to discriminate against any individual with respect to his compensation, terms, conditions, or privileges of employment, because of such individual's race, color, religion, sex, or national origin; or
- limit, segregate, or classify his employees in any way which would deprive or tend to deprive any individual of employment opportunities or otherwise adversely affect his status as an employee because of an individual's race, color, religion, sex, or national origin.

Unlike the Fifth and Fourteenth Amendments, the Civil Rights Acts do not require that the employment practice discriminate intentionally to be deemed as potentially illegal. Instead, proof of discrimination is determined through statistical analysis of selection rates and by the presence or absence of adverse impact, which will be discussed in detail later in the chapter.

The Civil Rights Acts have also been interpreted by the courts to cover the "atmosphere" of an organization, which includes such behavior as sexual harassment (*Broderick v. Ruder*, 1988; *Brundy v. Jackson*, 1971); age harassment (*Louis v. Federal Prison Industries*, 1986); race harassment (*Hunter v. Allis-Chalmers*, 1986); and religious harassment (*Abramson v. William Paterson College of New Jersey*, 2001).

An interesting example of courts considering the atmosphere of the organization is the case of *Forbes v. ABM Industries* (2005). Cheryl Forbes was a top-producing manager who accused the company of using subtle political ploys to create an atmosphere in which women could not be successful. Some of these ploys included area managers going to dinner with male managers but not with female managers, employees being encouraged to bypass female managers and go directly to their subordinates, and rumors being started about female managers. The jury found in favor of Forbes, and a Washington State appeals court upheld the jury award of over $4 million for sexual discrimination and harassment.

Color

Also protected by the Civil Rights Acts is color. Though commonly used as a synonym for race, the reference to color protects individuals against discrimination based specifically on variations in skin color. For example, in the 1989 case of *Walker v. Secretary of the Treasury*, a district court found that a darker-skinned African American supervisor at the Internal Revenue Service illegally fired a lighter-skinned African American employee. In a similar case, Applebee's Neighborhood Bar and Grill paid a $40,000 settlement to a dark-skinned African American employee who complained that his lighter-skinned African American manager made disparaging remarks about his skin color (Mirza, 2003).

Sex

The Civil Rights Acts, as well as the Equal Pay Act of 1963, prohibit discrimination based on sex. The courts have ruled that intentional discrimination against either women or men is illegal (*Diaz v. Pan American Airways, 1991*). Included in the definition of sex are sexual stereotypes. That is, it would be illegal to not hire a female applicant because she looks or dresses too masculine (*Lewis v. Heartland Inns of America*, 2010). The courts are split on the legality of discrimination against transsexuals, as the Seventh (*Ulane v. Eastern Airlines*, 1984), Eighth (*Sommers v. Budget Marketing*, 1982), and Ninth (*Voyles v. Ralph Davies Medical Center*, 1975) Circuits have ruled such discrimination legal, whereas the Sixth Circuit Court of Appeals has ruled it illegal (*Barnes v. City of Cincinnati*, 2005; *Jimmie L. Smith v. City of Salem, Ohio*, 2004).

National Origin

National origin is protected under the Civil Rights Acts. Note that Hispanics are protected under national origin, not race. Claims of discrimination based on national origin have increased greatly over the past few years. One of the most common complaints is about "English only" or "understandable English" speaking requirements. The courts have generally ruled that language requirements are legal if they are job related (Quinn & Petrick, 1993) and limited to communication during "company time" rather than on breaks.

A good example of an illegal "English only" language requirement was in the case that resulted in a $1.5 million settlement between the EEOC and Colorado Central Station Casino in 2003. The casino required employees to always speak English, even during private conversations between two employees. To "encourage" employees to speak English, managers and other employees would yell, "English, English, English" at any employee speaking Spanish. Such harassment caused great embarrassment to the employees.

Religion

Also protected under the Civil Rights Acts is religion. It is illegal to use an individual's religion as a factor in an employment decision unless the nature of the job is religious. For example, the Catholic Church can require its priests to be Catholic but cannot require this of its clerical staff. The Civil Rights Acts also require organizations to make accommodations for religious beliefs unless to do so would be an undue hardship. The accommodation failures most cited in the 3,000 complaints of religious discrimination filed annually with the EEOC are those involving days of worship, worship practices, and religious attire.

Days of Worship. Many religions forbid their members from working on particular days. For example, Seventh-day Adventists and Orthodox Jews cannot work from sundown Friday to sundown Saturday, and members of the Greek Orthodox Church cannot work on Sunday. Such nonwork *requirements* should not be confused with *preferences* for nonwork on days of worship (e.g., Protestants working on Sunday or Christmas;

attending a morning rather than an evening worship service), as the courts have ruled that an employee's preference does not need to be accommodated (*Dachman v. Shalala*, 2001; *Tiano v. Dillard Department Stores*, 1998).

Days of worship are often easily accommodated by scheduling employees without religious restrictions to work on those days. When there are only a few employees, scheduling rotations or "shift swapping" can be used to reduce, but not eliminate, the number of days of worship that an employee might have to miss. Accommodations become legally unreasonable when there are no coworkers available, overtime will have to be paid to cover an employee's day of worship, or another employee's seniority or collective bargaining rights have been violated. However, with a little ingenuity and proper explanations of an employee's religious requirements, reasonable accommodations can usually be made.

The case of Eddie Kilgore provides an example of a poorly handled case of religious accommodation. Kilgore had been employed for 18 years by Sparks Regional Medical Center in Arkansas when he was suddenly ordered to be on call on Saturdays. As a Seventh-day Adventist, he was forbidden to work on Saturdays, a requirement long known by his employer. When Kilgore refused the Saturday work, he was fired. Kilgore filed a suit for religious discrimination and a jury awarded him $100,000 and his former job back.

Worship Practices. Two practices in particular can cause potential problems: prayer and fasting. Some religions require members to pray at certain times. For example, followers of Islam perform the Salat ritual prayer five times daily: at sunrise, noon, afternoon, sunset, and night. Because each prayer can take 15 minutes (including preparation such as hand washing), organizations such as fast-food restaurants and retail stores often have difficulty accommodating every prayer request. Fasting requirements can also pose problems. For example, followers of Islam must refrain from food and drink from sunrise to sunset during the 30-day period of Ramadan. Though Islamic employees are available to work, their endurance and performance may be most affected during the latter part of the day. Thus, fasting can be accommodated by having dangerous, strenuous, or complicated work performed earlier in the day or scheduling Islamic employees for earlier hours. A good example of this practice occurred in 2010 when Ramadan fell during the period in which "two-a-day" football practices were held at most U.S. high schools. Fordson High School in Dearborn, Michigan, whose student body is predominantly Muslim, moved its football practices from daytime to 11:00 p.m. so that players could drink water while they practiced.

Though fasts and prayer are the most common worship practices that need accommodation, they are certainly not the only ones. For example, because Jehovah's Witnesses cannot celebrate birthdays or nonreligious holidays, their lack of participation in an office birthday party or celebration is often viewed by uninformed coworkers as an "attitude problem." The traditional office Christmas party in which Christmas decorations are hung, a tree is decorated, inexpensive presents are exchanged among employees, and alcohol and food are served provides a great example of potential religious diversity issues. Would such a party offend people who don't celebrate Christmas? Are there employees whose religion would prohibit them from attending the party? Is the food served consistent with the dietary restrictions of groups such as Muslims, Hindus, Buddhists, and Jews?

Religious Attire. Because many religions require their members to wear certain attire, potential conflicts can occur when an organization wants employees to have a

I am one of 11 attorneys and 1 paralegal specializing in labor and employment law in a law firm of approximately 70 attorneys in southwestern Virginia. Due to the nature of labor and employment law, my practice encompasses a wide range of legal issues that are addressed in a variety of ways to best serve the needs of my clients. One day I may be advising clients on steps to help them remain union free; the next day I may find myself training supervisors in avoiding harassment lawsuits; and the next, I may be in court litigating these matters.

The majority of our clients consist of medium-size to large businesses; therefore, I work solely on the management side of legal issues. In this context, I work directly with representatives from human resources departments to offer advice in such areas as establishing company policies, determining appropriate employee discipline, and developing employee training. I enjoy the diversified nature of labor and employment law and the day-to-day involvement in my clients' operations.

As a labor and employment attorney, I perform many of the tasks people usually think of when they think of lawyers. For example, upon receipt of a new case file involving a harassment or discrimination lawsuit, I first interview the company's human resources director to get an overall idea of what has happened to instigate the lawsuit. It is imperative that I understand all of the facts involved in the case, so I next conduct witness interviews in an effort to fully comprehend the situation.

After I thoroughly understand what has taken place, it then becomes my job to apply relevant labor and employment laws accordingly and present the circumstances of the case in the best possible light for my client. Admittedly, there are times when clients have not conducted themselves in a manner that will allow for the summary dismissal of a case, and the clients are advised to settle the claims. The settlements of claims are also a simple function of the cost of

**Victor O. Cardwell,
Attorney**
Labor and Employment Law

© Jill Mooney

pursuing the defense of a lawsuit, i.e., it is cheaper to pay a little to get out of the situation and get back to the business of the client. Such settlements require negotiation on the part of the clients and attorneys involved. Fortunately, these situations are not common, especially when I have been working on an ongoing basis with the company's human resources director or participating in employee training in an effort to minimize the types of issues that can turn into lawsuits.

An aspect of my profession that I particularly enjoy is training my clients' employees. Being in front of a group requires good communication skills and the ability to understand the audience in order to give the trainees what they need. My particular training style works best when I have a lot of feedback and audience participation. Clients request training in all areas of employment, including performance evaluations, discipline and discharge, diversity, and workplace violence, to name a few. Once again, I assess with my clients exactly what they are seeking from the training. Next, I meticulously research a myriad of labor and employment laws and current events that could conceivably apply to the training. Finally, I develop written materials so that the trainees, who may include front-line supervisors, will have something to take with them to use as a reference when the training is over.

In addition to training our corporate clients, I am frequently asked to speak to groups, including schools, churches, and nonprofit organizations, on various topics. The firm supports and encourages community involvement, and it allows me the opportunity to become actively involved not only in my work, but in my community as well.

The part of my chosen profession that makes it all worthwhile to me is that it allows a great deal of interaction with a diverse group of people. My advice to students is to get to know your clients well to understand how they work and the working environment from which they come. The better you understand your clients and their organizations, the better the advice you will be able to provide.

uniform appearance, either to promote a company image or to keep customers happy. Because of this desire for employees to look alike, several complaints of religious discrimination regarding religious attire have been made by Sikhs. Sikh males are required to wear turbans—head apparel that often conflicts with required job uniforms—and many Sikhs wear a religious bracelet on their right wrists. The courts have also supported face-piercing for members of the Church of Body Modification (*Cloutier v. Costco Wholesale*, 2004).

If, however, the religious apparel creates the potential of danger to the employee or others (for example, a bracelet getting caught in a piece of machinery or a turban preventing the wearing of a safety helmet), the courts have been clear that banning such apparel is legal. For example, in *EEOC v. GEO Group, Inc.* (2010), the court upheld the prison's zero-tolerance policy for employees wearing nonissued headgear (e.g., hats, scarves). The policy was challenged by three female Muslim employees who claimed that their religion required that they wear a *khimar* (religious head scarf). The prison responded by stating that such headgear posed a safety risk, as it made it easier to smuggle contraband, made it more difficult to visually identify a prison employee, and the *khimar* could be used by inmates to strangle the employee. Consistent with its ruling in a similar case (*Webb v. City of Philadelphia*, 2009), the U.S. Court of Appeals for the Third Circuit ruled that the prison's safety concerns took precedence over the employee's religious rights.

Age

Age Discrimination in Employment Act (ADEA) A federal law that, with its amendments, forbids discrimination against an individual who is over the age of 40.

The **Age Discrimination in Employment Act (ADEA)** and its later amendments forbid an employer or union from discriminating against an individual over the age of 40. In part, this act was designed to protect older workers from employment practices aimed at reducing costs by firing older workers with higher salaries and replacing them with lower-paid younger workers. Such legislation is important because, despite evidence to the contrary, people often view older workers as being less competent and less economically worthwhile than younger workers (Finkelstein, Burke, & Raju, 1995; Letvak, 2005). To file suit under this act, an individual must demonstrate that he or she is in the specified age bracket, has been discharged or demoted, was performing the job adequately at the time of discharge or demotion, and has been replaced by a younger worker, even if the younger worker is older than 40 (*O'Connor v. Consolidated Coin Caterers*, 1996). Though mandatory retirement ages are allowed in certain circumstances (e.g., 70 years for college professors), they are usually illegal because, as research indicates, in general, work performance does not decline with age.

Age discrimination is also a factor in countries outside the United States. As shown in Table 3.1, many countries have age discrimination laws. In the European Union, practices that have an adverse impact on older workers may be illegal. For example, the common practice of hiring younger workers by recruiting at colleges and universities (called "milk runs" in the UK) may no longer be allowed (Gomm, 2005).

Disability

Vocational Rehabilitation Act of 1973 Federal act passed in 1973 that prohibits federal government contractors or subcontractors from discriminating against the physically or mentally handicapped.

Americans with Disabilities Act (ADA) A federal law, passed in 1990, that forbids discrimination against the physically and mentally disabled.

Discrimination against people with disabilities by the federal government is forbidden by the **Vocational Rehabilitation Act of 1973**, and discrimination against the disabled by any other employer with 15 or more employees is forbidden by the **Americans with Disabilities Act (ADA)**.

The ADA, signed into law by President George H. W. Bush in 1990, is the most important piece of employment legislation since the 1964 Civil Rights Act. An amendment to the ADA, the ADA Amendments Act (ADAAA), was signed into law by President George W. Bush in 2008. The ADA requires organizations with 15 or more employees to make "reasonable accommodation for the physically and mentally disabled, unless to do so would impose an undue hardship." Though Congress did not provide a list of disabilities, it did define disability as

1. a physical or mental impairment that substantially limits one or more of the major life activities of an individual;
2. a record of such impairment; or
3. being regarded as having such an impairment.

For the first part of the definition, *major life activities* include such things as walking, hearing, and speaking. The ADAAA expanded the list of major life activities to include the operation of major bodily functions (e.g., digestive, bowel, bladder). A condition that keeps a person from working a *particular* job, as opposed to all jobs or a class of jobs, is not a disability (*Toyota v. Williams*, 2002). Examples of conditions considered disabilities by case law or the U.S. Department of Labor are blindness, paralysis, asthma, muscular dystrophy, and various learning disabilities such as dyslexia. Conditions not considered by the courts to be disabilities have included fear of heights, color blindness, hypertension, depression, temporary illnesses such as pneumonia, sprained ankles, being 20 pounds overweight, carpal tunnel syndrome, and wearing glasses.

The second part of the definition was designed to protect people who were once disabled but no longer are. Examples include recovering alcoholics, cancer patients in remission, people who spent time in a mental health facility, and drug addicts who have successfully completed treatment.

The final part of the definition protects individuals who don't have a disability but are regarded or treated as if they do. Examples of people protected under this clause are those with facial scarring or severe burns. In an interesting case (*Johnson v. Apland & Associates*, 1997), the U.S. Court of Appeals for the Seventh Circuit ruled that a man missing 18 teeth had a right to file an ADA suit on the grounds that he was regarded as having a disability. The case was sent back to the lower court to

Accommodations, such as providing Braille versions of tests, are sometimes necessary.

© PhotoDisc/Getty Images

determine whether this perception actually "substantially" limited "one or more major life activit[ies]."

The ADAA expanded this part of the definition, clarified that if an impairment was expected to last less than six months, it would not be considered a disability, and clarified that employers do not need to provide reasonable accommodation to employees who are regarded as being disabled. The ADA does not require an organization to hire or give preference to the disabled, only that the disabled be given an equal chance and that reasonable attempts be made to accommodate their disabilities. Although there are no guidelines regarding what is "reasonable," accommodations can include providing readers or interpreters, modifying work schedules or equipment, and making facilities more accessible. In spite of the fact that two-thirds of accommodations cost less than $500 (Cohen, 2002), many employees are reluctant to ask for, and many organizations are reluctant to provide, accommodations (Baldridge & Veiga, 2001).

In an interesting case demonstrating that many organizations do not comply with the spirit of the ADA, in 2005 a jury awarded $8 million to Dale Alton, an applicant for a customer service position who asked EchoStar Communications to accommodate his blindness by providing him with a computer program, Job Access with Speech (JAWS), that translates text into speech. When Alton first applied for the job, EchoStar told him not to bother because the company was "not set up to handle blind people."

If a disability keeps a person from performing the "essential functions" of a job identified during a job analysis or poses a direct threat to her own or others' safety, the person does not have to be hired or retained (Zink, 2002). Furthermore, the Seventh Circuit Court of Appeals ruled that an organization is not required to make significant changes in the essential functions of a job to accommodate a disabled employee (*Ammons v. Aramark Uniform Services*, 2004). For example, in *Caston v. Trigon Engineering* (1993), a district court ruled that a woman with 44 personalities was unable to perform her job as an environmental engineer. In another case (*DiPompo v. West Point*, 1991), a district court ruled that a dyslexic applicant, though considered disabled, was not able to perform essential job functions such as inspecting vehicles and buildings for the presence of dangerous materials and recording information such as work schedules and emergency calls. In *Calef v. Gillette Company* (2003), the First Circuit Court of Appeals ruled that although Fred Calef had attention deficit/hyperactivity disorder, his threatening behavior and inability to handle his anger was not protected. In *Ethridge v. State of Alabama* (1994), a district court ruled that a police applicant with restricted use of his right hand could not perform the essential job functions because he was unable to shoot in a two-handed position (Weaver stance).

An interesting and well-publicized ADA case was that of golfer Casey Martin (*Martin v. PGA Tour*, 2000). Martin suffered from Klippel-Trènaunay-Weber syndrome in his right leg. Because this syndrome made it difficult for Martin to walk on the golf course, he requested an accommodation that he be allowed to use a golf cart. The Professional Golfers Association (PGA) denied the request, arguing that walking is an "essential function" of golf, and thus, using a cart would not be a reasonable accommodation. The U.S. Supreme Court ruled in favor of Martin's contention that walking was not an essential function of golf and that allowing Martin to use a cart was not an unreasonable accommodation.

Pregnancy

Pregnancy Discrimination Act A 1978 federal law protecting the rights of pregnant women.

The **Pregnancy Discrimination Act** states that "women affected by pregnancy, childbirth, or related medical conditions shall be treated the same for all employment related purposes, including receipt of benefit programs, as other persons not so affected but similar in their ability or inability to work." Simply put, this act requires pregnancy to be treated as any other short-term disability. For example, in *Adams v. North Little Rock Police Department* (1992), the U.S. Court of Appeals ruled that a police department discriminated against a pregnant police officer when the department denied her "light duty," yet granted light duty to male officers with temporary disabilities such as strained backs.

In the case of *California Federal Savings and Loan Association v. Guerra* (1987), the U.S. Supreme Court expanded the scope of the law. Pregnant women may receive better treatment than other persons with disabilities and cannot receive worse treatment. In 2010, 6,119 charges of pregnancy discrimination were filed with the EEOC. Many of the rights provided in the Pregnancy Discrimination Act have been greatly expanded by the Family Medical Leave Act (FMLA), which will be discussed later in this chapter.

Military Veteran Status

Vietnam-Era Veterans Readjustment Act (VEVRA) A 1974 federal law that mandates that federal government contractors and subcontractors take affirmative action to employ and promote Vietnam-era veterans.

Jobs for Veterans Act A law passed in 2002 that increased the coverage of VEVRA to include disabled veterans, veterans who have recently left the service, and veterans who participated in a U.S. military operation for which an Armed Forces Service Medal was awarded.

Bona fide occupational qualification (BFOQ) A selection requirement that is necessary for the performance of job-related duties and for which there is no substitute.

Due to the large-scale discrimination in the 1960s and 1970s against soldiers returning from duty in Vietnam, Congress passed the **Vietnam-Era Veterans Readjustment Act (VEVRA)** in 1974. This act mandates any contractor or subcontractor with more than $100,000 in federal government contracts to take affirmative action to employ and promote Vietnam-era veterans. VEVRA was amended by the 2002 **Jobs for Veterans Act** to increase the coverage of VEVRA to include disabled veterans, veterans who have recently left the service (within three years), and veterans who participated in a U.S. military operation for which an Armed Forces Service Medal was awarded. This law is one reason that veterans applying for civil service jobs often receive credit for their military service as well as for their qualifications.

To test your knowledge of the federally protected classes, complete Exercise 3.1 in your workbook.

Is the Requirement a BFOQ?

Employment decisions based on membership in a protected class (e.g., "We will not hire females because they are not strong enough to do the job") are illegal unless the employer can demonstrate that the requirement is a **bona fide occupational qualification (BFOQ)**.

If a job can be performed only by a person in a particular class, the requirement is considered a BFOQ. Actually, some jobs can be performed only by a person of a particular gender; for instance, only a female can be a wet nurse (a woman who breast-feeds another woman's baby), and only a male can be a sperm donor. However, there are very few jobs in our society that can be performed only by a person of a particular race, gender, or national origin. Take for example a job that involves lifting 150-pound crates. Although it is true that on average, males are stronger than females, a company cannot set a male-only requirement. The real BFOQ in this example is strength, not gender. Thus, restricting employment to males would be illegal.

The courts have clearly stated that a BFOQ must involve the ability to perform the job, not satisfy a customer's or client's preferences. For example:

- In *Geraldine Fuhr v. School District of Hazel Park, Michigan* (2004), the Sixth Circuit Court of Appeals ruled that the *preference* that a man rather than a woman coach a boy's basketball team was not a BFOQ.
- In *Diaz v. Pan American Airways* (1991), the court ruled that even though airline passengers prefer female flight attendants, the nature of the business is

to transport passengers safely, and males can perform the essential job functions as well as females.

- In 1989, Caesar's Casino in Atlantic City was fined $250,000 for removing African American and female card dealers from a table to appease a high-stakes gambler who preferred White male dealers.

One of the few exceptions to the BFOQ requirement seems to be grooming standards. It is not unusual for an organization to have separate dress codes and grooming standards for males and females. Though different standards based on sex would appear to violate the law, the courts have generally upheld them (Fowler-Hermes, 2001; *Jespersen v. Harrah's Casino*, 2005).

Perhaps the most interesting of the BFOQ cases was the EEOC complaint against Hooters, the restaurant chain famous for its chicken wings and scantily clad waitresses. Hooters allowed only women to be servers and claimed that it was a BFOQ due to the restaurant's unique atmosphere. In fact, a Hooters spokesman was quoted as saying that the restaurant doesn't sell food, it sells (female) sex appeal, and to have female sex appeal, you have to be female. The EEOC disagreed; and in an unusual settlement, Hooters agreed to pay $3.75 million to a group of men who were not hired, and the EEOC agreed to let Hooters continue to hire only women for the server positions.

Has Case Law, State Law, or Local Law Expanded the Definition of Any of the Protected Classes?

An employment decision may not violate a federal law, but it may violate one of the many state and local laws that have been passed to protect additional groups of people. For example, at the state level:

- Two states (California, New York) and the District of Columbia forbid discrimination on the basis of a person's political affiliation.
- Nineteen states (California, Colorado, Connecticut, Hawaii, Illinois, Iowa, Maine, Maryland, Massachusetts, Minnesota, Nevada, New Hampshire, New Jersey, New Mexico, New York, Oregon, Rhode Island, Vermont, and Wisconsin) and the District of Columbia prohibit discrimination by private and public employers based on sexual orientation; and nine states (Alaska, Delaware, Indiana, Louisiana, Michigan, Montana, Nevada, Ohio, Pennsylvania) only prohibit discrimination by public employers (updated information can be found at www.lambdalegal.org/our-work/states).
- Twenty-one states (Alaska, California, Connecticut, Delaware, Florida, Hawaii, Illinois, Maryland, Michigan, Minnesota, Montana, Nebraska, New Hampshire, New Jersey, New Mexico, New York, North Dakota, Oregon, Virginia, Washington, and Wisconsin) and the District of Columbia forbid discrimination based on marital status.

At the local level:

- Santa Cruz, California, outlaws discrimination based on height and physical appearance.
- Discrimination based on sexual orientation is prohibited in 124 cities and counties.
- Cincinnati, Ohio, prohibits discrimination against people of Appalachian heritage.

In addition to state and local laws, the definitions of protected classes can be expanded or narrowed by court decisions. As discussed previously, these decisions become case law. For example, in a variety of cases, the courts have ruled that the definition of disability should be expanded to include obesity but not former drug use, and that transsexuals are not protected as a gender.

Does the Requirement Have Adverse Impact on Members of a Protected Class?

Adverse impact An employment practice that results in members of a protected class being negatively affected at a higher rate than members of the majority class. Adverse impact is usually determined by the four-fifths rule.

If the employment practice does not refer directly to a member of a protected class, the next step is to determine whether the requirement *adversely affects* members of a protected class. **Adverse impact** means that a particular employment decision results in negative consequences more often for members of one race, sex, or national origin than for members of another race, sex, or national origin. For example, an employee-selection requirement of a college degree would lead to a lower percentage of African American applicants being hired compared with White applicants. Thus, even though such a requirement does not mention African Americans (a protected class), it does adversely impact them because according to U.S. Census data, in 2009, 29.9% of Whites have bachelor's degrees or higher compared with 19.3% of African Americans. Though adverse impact analyses have traditionally been limited to groups protected by the 1964 Civil Rights Act, the U.S. Supreme Court ruled in 2005 that employees could file adverse impact charges on the basis of age, which is protected under the ADEA (*Roderick Jackson v. Birmingham Board of Education*, 2005).

The courts use two standards to determine adverse impact: statistical significance and practical significance. Experts believe that both standards should be met for a finding of adverse impact (Cohen, Aamodt, & Dunleavy, 2010). The statistical significance burden is met if a plaintiff can demonstrate that the differences in selection rates for two groups (e.g., men and women) would not have occurred by chance alone. Statistics used to make this determination include the standard deviation test, chi-square, and Fisher's exact test.

If the statistical test suggests that the selection rate differences would probably not have occurred by chance, the next step is to use a test of practical significance. That is, is the difference between the two groups at a level high enough to suggest potential discrimination? Although there are several methods of determining practical significance, by far the most common is the **four-fifths rule**. With the four-fifths rule, the percentage of applicants hired from one group (e.g., women, Hispanics) is compared to the percentage of applicants hired in the most favored group (e.g., men, Whites). If the percentage of applicants hired in the disadvantaged group is less than 80% of the percentage for the advantaged group, adverse impact is said to have occurred.

Four-fifths rule When the selection ratio for one group (for example, females) is less than 80% (four-fifths) of the selection ratio for another group (for example, males), adverse impact is said to exist.

It is important to keep in mind that adverse impact refers to *percentages* rather than raw numbers. For example, as shown in Table 3.2, if 25 of 50 male applicants are hired, the hiring percentage is 50%. If 10 females applied, at least four would need to be hired to avoid adverse impact. Why 4? Because the hiring percentage for women must be at least 80% of the hiring percentage for men. Because the male-hiring percentage in this case is 50%, the hiring percentage for females must be at least four-fifths (80%) of 50%. Thus, $.50 \times .80 = .40$, indicating that at least 40% of all female applicants need to be hired to avoid adverse impact and a potential charge of unfair discrimination. With 10 applicants, this results in hiring at least 4.

Table 3.2 Adverse Impact Example

	Sex	
	Male	**Female**
Applicants	50	10
Hires	25	4
Selection ratio	.50	.40

Adverse impact is computed separately for race and gender. That is, an organization would not compute hiring rates for White males or African American females. Instead, hiring rates would be computed for males and for females and then be computed separately for Whites and for African Americans.

It is illegal to *intentionally* discriminate against Whites and males, but employment practices that result in adverse impact against White males, although technically illegal, are probably not illegal in practice. No court has upheld an adverse impact claim by a White applicant. For example, it was mentioned previously that requiring a college degree adversely impacts African Americans because 29.9% of Whites have bachelor's degrees compared with 19.3% of African Americans and 13.2% of Hispanics. Though 52.3% of Asian Americans have college degrees, a White applicant could not realistically win a discrimination charge based on adverse impact.

Though determining the adverse impact of a test seems simple—which is done by comparing the hiring rates (hires ÷ applicants) of two groups—the actual nuts and bolts of the calculations can get complicated, and it is common that plaintiffs and defendants disagree on who is considered an "applicant" and who is considered a "hire." For example, as shown in Table 3.3, if a person applying for a job does not meet the minimum qualifications, he is not considered as an applicant in adverse impact calculations. For example, if a plumber applies for a job as a brain surgeon, he clearly lacks the minimum qualifications for the job—a medical degree.

There are three criteria for a minimum qualification: it must be needed to perform the job, and not merely be a preference; it must be formally identified and communicated prior to the start of the selection process; and it must be consistently applied. As you can imagine, with such criteria, there is much room for disagreement. Your CD-ROM contains data that you can use to compute adverse impact and determine who is an applicant and who should be counted as a hire/offer.

To see if you grasp how to determine if adverse impact exists, complete Exercise 3.2 in your workbook.

Was the Requirement Designed to Intentionally Discriminate Against a Protected Class?

If an employment practice does not refer directly to a member of a protected class but adversely affects a protected class, the courts will look closely at whether the practice was initiated to intentionally reduce the pool of qualified minority applicants. For example, suppose a city requires all of its employees to live within the city limits. The city believes that this is a justifiable requirement because salaries are paid by tax dollars, and town employees should contribute to that tax base. Though such a requirement is not illegal, the court might look deeper to see if the tax base was in fact the reason for the residency requirement. That is, if the city population was 99% White and the

Table 3.3   Who Is an Applicant and Who Is a Hire?

Who is an Applicant?

   Count as an applicant

      Those meeting minimum qualifications

   Remove from calculation

      Those who did not meet minimum qualifications

      Those who are not eligible to apply

         Former employees who were terminated (if this is company policy)

         Former employees who did not wait the required time to apply (if this is company policy)

         Duplicate applications within a specified period of time

      Those who are no longer interested

         Found another job

         No longer interested in the job

         Declined or did not show up for the interview

Who is a Hire?

   Both hires and offers count

   Hires

      Hired and reported to work

      Hired but did not report to work

      Hired but failed drug test or background test

   Offers

      Offered job but declined

---

population of the surrounding area was 90% African American, the court might argue that the residency requirement was a subtle way of discriminating against minorities.

Though such subtle requirements are probably no longer common in the employment sector, they have been used throughout history. For example, before the 1970s, some states required voters to pass a "literacy test" to be eligible to vote. Though the stated purpose of the test was to ensure that voters would make intelligent and educated decisions, the real purpose was to reduce the number of minority voters.

Can the Employer Prove That the Requirement Is Job Related?

As shown in the flowchart in Figure 3.2, if our employment practice does not result in adverse impact, it is probably legal. If adverse impact does result, then the burden of proof shifts to the employer to demonstrate that the employment practice is either **job related** or exempt from adverse impact. Before discussing these two strategies, two points need to be made. First, adverse impact is a fact of life in personnel selection. Almost any hiring test is going to have adverse impact on some protected class, though some may have less adverse impact than others.

Second, the burden of proof in employment law is different than in criminal law. In criminal law, a defendant is innocent until proven guilty. In employment law, both the 1991 Civil Rights Act and the court's ruling in *Griggs v. Duke Power* (1972) shift

Job related The extent to which a test or measure taps a knowledge, skill, ability, behavior, or other characteristic needed to successfully perform a job.

the burden of proof: Once adverse impact is established, an employer (the defendant) is considered guilty unless it can prove its innocence by establishing the job relatedness of the test.

Valid Testing Procedures

An employment practice resulting in adverse impact may still be legal as long as the test is job related (valid) and as long as reasonable attempts have been made to find other tests that might be just as valid but have less adverse impact (refer to the flowchart in Figure 3.2). For example, if an employer uses a cognitive ability test to select employees, there is a strong possibility that adverse impact will occur. If the employer can demonstrate, however, that the cognitive ability test predicts performance on the job and that no other available test with less adverse impact will predict performance as well, the use of the test is probably justified. A more in-depth discussion of validity strategies is found in Chapter 6.

An interesting example of adverse impact and job relatedness comes from the town of North Miami, Florida. For 30 years, North Miami required that police recruits be able to swim. Although the requirement seemed logical given that the town is located next to the ocean, it had adverse impact against African Americans. When the town looked further at the job relatedness of the requirement, it discovered that North Miami officers seldom entered the water for rescues: only eight times from 1986 to 2004. Because swimming was an infrequent activity and the swimming requirement resulted in adverse impact, in 2004 North Miami eliminated the swimming ability as a requirement for the job of police officer.

Exceptions

Bona Fide Seniority System. An organization that has a long-standing policy of promoting employees with the greatest seniority or laying off employees with the least seniority can continue to do so even though adverse impact occurs. For a seniority system to be considered bona fide, the *purpose* of the system must be to reward seniority; not to discriminate (Twomey, 2010). That is, if an organization established a seniority system to protect male employees, it would not be considered bona fide.

National Security. In certain circumstances, it is legal for an employer to discriminate against a member of a particular national origin or other protected class when it is in the best interest of the nation's security to do so. For example, for years Russian citizens living in the United States were prohibited from working in any defense-related industry.

Veteran's Preference Rights. Most civil service jobs provide extra points on tests for veterans of the armed forces. For example, in Fort Worth, Texas, veterans who apply for city jobs get five points added to their exam score. Because most people in the military are male, awarding these extra points for military service results in adverse impact against females. However, according to the Civil Rights Act of 1964, such practices are exempt from legal action. To test your knowledge of these exceptions, complete Exercise 3.3 in your workbook.

Did the Employer Look for Reasonable Alternatives That Would Result in Lesser Adverse Impact?

As shown in Figure 3.2, if an employer proves a test is job related, the final factor looked at by the courts is the extent to which the employer looked for other valid selection tests that would have less adverse impact. For example, if an organization wanted to use a particular cognitive ability test, did it explore such alternatives as education level or other cognitive ability tests that would be just as valid but would have less adverse impact? To get experience using the flowchart in Figure 3.2, complete Exercise 3.4 in your workbook.

Harassment

An issue of growing concern in the workplace is sexual harassment. In 2010, 30,989 complaints of harassment were filed with the EEOC; 11,717 of these were for sexual harassment. Of these 11,717, 16.4% were filed by males. Of harassment claims filed with the EEOC, approximately 27% involve racial harassment, 38% sexual harassment, and 35% harassment of other protected classes. Research indicates that as many as 44% of women and 19% of men have been victims of sexual harassment (U.S. Merit Systems Board, 1995). These percentages increase when employees are the sole representative of their gender (called *gender pioneers*) or consist of a small minority of the employees in a particular work setting (called *gender isolates*) (Niebuhr & Oswald, 1992).

Harassment is not an issue limited to the United States. Though the United States has taken the lead in preventing and punishing harassment, Canada, the United Kingdom, Australia, New Zealand, Ireland, and the European Union also have laws prohibiting sexual harassment (Gutman, 2005).

Though the following discussion focuses on sexual harassment, the courts have ruled that racial, religious, disability, and age harassment are also illegal (e.g., *Crawford v. Medina General Hospital*, 1996; *Lanman v. Johnson County, Kansas*, 2004). For example:

- In 2010, Austin Foam Plastics, Inc. in Texas settled an EEOC charge of race harassment for $600,000. The harassment included racially offensive jokes and cartoons, racially motivated insults, and racist comments such as, "You don't mess with Whitey around here."
- In 2004, Fairfield Toyota in California settled an EEOC charge of religion (Muslim), color (dark-skinned), and national origin (Afghani) harassment for $550,000. Supervisors and other employees commonly referred to seven Afghani Muslim employees as "the bin Laden gang," "sand niggers," and "camel jockeys."
- In 2003, Lexus of Kendall in Miami, Florida, reached an agreement to pay $700,000 for race, national origin, and religious harassment by a senior manager who made comments such as, "America is for Whites only" and calling employees terms such as "spic" and "nigger."

Types of Harassment

Legally, sexual harassment can take one of two forms: *quid pro quo* or *hostile environment*.

Quid Pro Quo

Quid pro quo A type of sexual harassment in which the granting of sexual favors is tied to an employment decision.

With **quid pro quo**, the granting of sexual favors is tied to such employment decisions as promotions and salary increases. An example of a quid pro quo case of harassment is a supervisor who tells his secretary that she must sleep with him to keep her job. In quid pro quo cases, a *single* incident is enough to constitute sexual harassment and result in the organization being liable for legal damages (Gutman, 2005).

Hostile Environment

In a **hostile environment** case, sexual harassment occurs when an unwanted *pattern* of conduct related to *gender* unreasonably interferes with an individual's work performance. Though men and women differ in their perceptions of what constitutes harassment (Rotundo, Nguyen, & Sackett, 2001), the courts have ruled that such conduct can include comments, unwanted sexual or romantic advances, or the display of demeaning posters, signs, or cartoons (*Jenson v. Eveleth Taconite Co.*, 1993).

Pattern of Behavior. For conduct to be considered sexual harassment based on a hostile environment, the U. S. Supreme Court has ruled that the conduct must be a *pattern* of behavior rather than an isolated incident (*Clark County School District v. Breeden*, 2001). It would not be harassment to ask a coworker for a date, even if the coworker does not agree to the date. It becomes harassment if the coworker *continually* makes unwanted romantic or sexual overtures or repeatedly makes inappropriate remarks.

Based on Gender. To be considered sexual harassment, conduct must be due to the *sex* of the employee. That is, but for the sex of the employee, would the conduct have occurred? For example, in *Christopher Lack v. Wal-Mart* (2001), the Fourth Circuit Court of Appeals ruled that a supervisor's lewd and vulgar language and jokes were not sexual harassment because they were made both to males and to females. The Courts of Appeal for the Seventh (*Holman v. Indiana Department of Transportation*, 2000) and Eighth (*Jenkins v. Southern Farm Bureau Casualty*, 2002) Circuits have made similar rulings. Members of a police department consistently referring to female officers as "babes" or "honey" would be an example of sexual harassment because the comments are based on gender and are demeaning to the female officers. A male officer calling a female officer "stupid" would be an example of rude behavior, but not sexual harassment because the nature of the comment was not based on gender.

In 1998, the U.S. Supreme Court considered whether an employee can sexually harass a member of the same gender. That is, if a male makes sexual comments or improperly touches another male, is this a case of sexual harassment? In the case of *Oncale v. Sundowner Offshore Services* (1998), the Supreme Court said yes. As a roustabout on an oil platform, Joseph Oncale was subjected to sexual threats and battery by other male roustabouts. After getting no help from his supervisor, Oncale quit his job and filed suit, eventually reaching the Supreme Court. The key to the *Oncale* ruling was that the harassment was due to Oncale's *sex* (he was harassed because he was a *male*), not his *sexual orientation*. It should be noted that in states that have not added sexual orientation as a protected class, harassment on the basis of sexual orientation is probably not illegal because sexual orientation is not a *federally* protected class (*Bibby v. Coca Cola*, 2001; *Rene v. MGM Grand Hotel*, 2001; *Spearman v. Ford*, 2000).

It should be pointed out that employers should not tolerate harassment of any type. Protected classes are a legal concept rather than a moral one, and few HR professionals would argue against the idea that employers have a moral obligation to provide a workplace free of harassment.

Hostile environment A type of harassment characterized by a pattern of unwanted conduct related to gender that interferes with an individual's work performance.

Negative to the Reasonable Person. Any pattern of behavior based on gender that causes an employee discomfort might constitute sexual harassment. In *Harris v. Forklift Systems* (1993), the U.S. Supreme Court found that a male supervisor's comments such as, "Let's go to the Holiday Inn and negotiate your raise" and "You're just a dumb-ass woman" constituted harassment, even though the female employee did not suffer any great psychological damage or "have a nervous breakdown."

Organizational Liability for Sexual Harassment

In cases of quid pro quo harassment of its employees, an organization will always be liable. In hostile environment cases, however, the U.S. Supreme Court has ruled that an organization can avoid liability by showing that it "exercised reasonable care to prevent and correct promptly any sexually harassing behavior" or that the complainant did not take reasonable advantage of the corrective opportunities provided by the organization (*Burlington Industries v. Ellerth*, 1998; *Faragher v. City of Boca Raton*, 1998).

Preventing Sexual Harassment

In determining an organization's liability for the sexual harassment of its employees, the courts look first at the organization's attempts to prevent this behavior. To avoid liability, the organization must have a well-conceived policy regarding sexual harassment, must have communicated that policy to its employees (*Frederick v. Sprint*, 2001), and must have enforced that policy (*MacGregor v. Mallinckrodt, Inc.*, 2004). The policy must explain the types of harassment (*Smith v. First Union National Bank*, 2000) and include a list of the *names* of the company officials to whom an employee should report any harassment (*Gentry v. Export Packaging*, 2001). It is important to note that organizations are also responsible for harassment committed by vendors, customers, and other third parties.

Correcting Sexually Harassing Behavior

If an employee complains of sexual harassment, it is essential that the organization investigate the complaint quickly and then promptly take any necessary action to rectify the situation and punish the offender. To reduce an organization's liability for sexual harassment, Jacobs and Kearns (2001) advise the following:

- All complaints, no matter how trivial or far-fetched they appear, must be investigated.
- The organization's policy must encourage victims to come forward and afford them multiple channels or sources through which to file their complaint.
- Complaints must be kept confidential to protect both the accused and the accuser. Information from the investigation should be kept in a file separate from the employee's personnel file.
- Action must be taken to protect the accuser during the time the complaint is being investigated. Actions might include physically separating the two parties or limiting the amount of contact between them.
- Both the accused and the accuser must be given due process, and care must be taken to avoid an initial assumption of guilt.
- The results of the investigation must be communicated in writing to both parties.
- The severity of the punishment (if any) must match the severity of the violation.

As mentioned previously, the proper handling of a sexual harassment complaint can protect an employer from legal liability. In such cases as *Linda Roebuck v. Odie Washington* (2005) and *Rheineck v. Hutchinson Technology* (2001), courts of appeal ruled that the organization was not liable for sexual harassment because it investigated the complaint in a timely manner and then took prompt corrective action against the harasser. In contrast, in *Intlekofer v. Turnage* (1992), the court of appeals found the Veterans Administration liable for harassment because it ignored nearly two dozen complaints by a female employee and refused to take corrective action against the harasser.

However, the concern for prompt action should not deny the accused due process. In 1997, a jury awarded a man accused of sexual harassment $26.6 million. He was fired by Miller Brewing Company for discussing an episode of the TV show *Seinfeld* in which Jerry Seinfeld forgot the name of a date (Delores) but remembered that it rhymed with a female body part. The jury ruled that a reasonable person would not have been offended by the discussion, and thus Miller Brewing went too far in firing the accused employee.

Rather than being *reactive* to sexual harassment complaints, it is in the best interests of an organization to be *proactive*, and prevent harassment. Proactive steps include having a strong organizational policy against harassment (*Frederick v. Sprint*, 2001) and training employees about behavior that constitutes harassment.

In addition to the obvious legal costs, sexual harassment has other financial ramifications for an organization. Sexual harassment results in higher levels of turnover, greater absenteeism, and lower levels of productivity (Munson, Hulin, & Drasgow, 2000; Pratt, Burnazi, LePla, Boyce, & Baltes, 2003; Willness, Steel, & Lee, 2007). To test your knowledge of sexual harassment, complete Exercise 3.5 in your workbook.

Family Medical Leave Act

In 1993, Congress passed the Family Medical Leave act, or FMLA, which entitles eligible employees (both male and female) to a minimum of 12 weeks of unpaid leave each year to deal with the following family matters:

- Births, adoptions, or placement for foster care
- To care for a child, parent, or spouse with a serious health condition
- For employee's own serious health condition that makes him or her unable to perform the job

In 2008, President George W. Bush signed the National Defense Authorization Act that amended the FMLA to provide 26 weeks of unpaid leave for a spouse, son, daughter, parent, or next of kin to care for a member of the military.

All public agencies and private organizations with 50 or more employees physically employed within a 70-mile radius of one another are covered by the act. Employers can decide if they want to define the eligibility period as a calendar year (i.e., January through December) or as a rolling 12-month period measured backward from the date an employee uses any FMLA leave. If the employer does not define its eligibility period in the employee handbook, the method most favorable to the employee will be in force (*Dodaro v. Village of Glendale Heights*, 2003).

Employees are eligible if they

1. work for a covered employer,
2. have worked for the organization for at least one year, and
3. have worked at least 1,250 hours over the previous 12 months.

Because the FMLA allows employees to take leave for the *serious illness* of a child, parent, spouse, or themselves, there has been some debate about how serious an illness has to be to qualify. The Department of Labor defines a serious health condition this way:

■ Any period of incapacity of more than 3 consecutive calendar days *and* at least 2 visits to a health-care provider *or* one visit and issuance of prescription medicine (or)
■ Any period of incapacity due to a chronic serious health condition requiring periodic treatment covering an extended period of time (or)
■ Any period of absence to receive multiple treatments for a condition that would result in a 3 or more day period of incapacity if left untreated.

On the basis of this definition, the courts have ruled such conditions as an ear infection (*Juanita Caldwell v. Kentucky Fried Chicken*, 2000) or a cold/flu (*Miller v. AT&T*, 2001; *Rose Rankin v. Seagate Technologies*, 2001) to be serious.

If employees take advantage of family or medical leave, the organization must continue the employees' health-care coverage and guarantee them that when they return they will either have the same or an equivalent position. In return, employees must provide a doctor's certification and give 30 days notice if the leave is foreseeable (e.g., birth or adoption). Employees on FMLA leave from one company cannot work at another job (moonlight) during that period (*Pharakhone v. Nissan North America, Inc., and Rodney Baggett*, 2003).

To protect employers from potential problems in complying with the FMLA, Congress allows them to exempt their key employees from using it. "Key employees" are the highest-paid 10% in the organization. Other than record-keeping headaches, however, the FMLA has not resulted in many hardships for most organizations.

The extent of family leave in the United States is similar to that in many countries. For example, laws in other countries mandate *unpaid* leave of 15 weeks in Belgium, 120 days in Brazil, and, depending on the province, 17 to 70 weeks in Canada. Mexico mandates 12 weeks and the European Union 14 weeks of *paid* leave. In England, employees who have been with an organization less than 26 weeks are entitled to 18 weeks of unpaid leave, employees with 26 weeks to one year of service are entitled to 18 weeks of paid leave, and employees with more than one year of service are entitled to 40 weeks of paid leave.

Affirmative Action

Reasons for Affirmative Action Plans

Organizations have affirmative action plans for one of four reasons, two of which are involuntary and two voluntary (Robinson, Allen, & Abraham, 1992).

Involuntary: Government Regulation

Most affirmative action requirements are the result of Presidential Executive Order 11246. This order, as well as sections of several laws, requires federal contractors and subcontractors with more than 50 employees to submit an annual EEO-1 Report and requires federal contractors and subcontractors with at least one federal contract in excess of $50,000 to have formal affirmative action plans. Most state and local governments also have such requirements, although the number of employees and dollar amounts of contracts will differ. These mandatory affirmative action plans typically involve analyses of all major job groups (e.g., managers, professionals) and indicate which job groups have underrepresentations of the protected classes, as well as goals and plans for overcoming such underrepresentations.

Involuntary: Court Order

When a court finds a public agency such as a police or fire department guilty of not hiring or promoting enough members of a protected class, it can order the agency to begin an affirmative action program. As previously discussed, this program may involve increased recruitment efforts or may entail specific hiring or promotion goals.

Voluntary: Consent Decree

If a discrimination complaint has been filed with a court, a public agency can "voluntarily" agree to an affirmative action plan rather than have a plan forced on it by the court. With a consent decree, the agency agrees that it has not hired or promoted enough members of a protected class and is willing to make changes. The specific nature of these changes is agreed upon by the group filing the complaint and the agency that is the subject of the complaint. This agreement is then approved and monitored by the court.

Voluntary: Desire to Be a Good Citizen

Rather than wait for a discrimination complaint, many organizations develop affirmative action and diversity programs out of a desire to be good citizens. That is, they want to voluntarily ensure that their employment practices are fair to all groups of people.

Affirmative Action Strategies

Although most people associate affirmative action with hiring goals or quotas, there are actually four main affirmative action strategies.

Monitoring Hiring and Promotion Statistics

One of the primary affirmative action strategies is for organizations to monitor their hiring, placement, and promotion rates for men and women and minorities and nonminorities. Though such monitoring is a good idea for all organizations, it is mandatory for federal contractors, for banks, and for educational institutions that receive federal funds. Such organizations must write affirmative action plans in which they monitor adverse impact as well as compare the percentages of women and minorities in the organization with the percentages of women and minorities in the qualified workforce.

Intentional Recruitment of Minority Applicants

A common affirmative action strategy is to target underrepresented groups for more extensive recruitment. Such efforts might include advertising in magazines and newspapers with a minority readership, recruiting at predominantly minority or female universities, visiting minority communities, or paying current employees a bonus for recruiting a member of a protected class.

A related technique is to establish training programs designed to teach minorities the skills needed to obtain employment with the organization. For example, Hogan and Quigley (1994) found that providing a six-week exercise program would result in fewer female applicants failing physical ability tests for positions such as firefighter.

Identification and Removal of Employment Practices Working Against Minority Applicants and Employees

A third affirmative action strategy, and the heart of most diversity initiatives, is to identify and remove practices that might discourage minority applicants from applying to an organization, being promoted within an organization, or remaining with an organization. Such practices might involve company policy, supervisor attitudes, training opportunities, availability of mentors and role models, or the way in which an organization is decorated. For example, an African American employee in a southern city filed a lawsuit alleging race as the reason he wasn't promoted. As evidence, he cited the embroidered Confederate flag hanging in his supervisor's office. The city's affirmative action officer suggested that the flag be removed because, even though the supervisor was a Civil War enthusiast rather than a racist, a Confederate flag in a supervisor's office might give the perception of institutional acceptance of racism.

As another example, it is a common practice for police applicants to receive information and obtain employment applications from the police department itself. However, many minorities are uncomfortable with the idea of going to a police station and asking White police officers for information and application materials. As a result, an easy affirmative action strategy would be to have employment applications available only at the city's personnel office.

When your author presented the above example to a meeting of police chiefs, the overwhelming response was, "How can someone be a cop if they don't feel comfortable going to a police station?" I responded that it is uncomfortable for anyone to go into a new environment, much less one with the stigma associated with a police station. I then told the group a story of how scared I was when, back in high school, I had to go to a police station to register a car rally that our school group was having. I still recall the icy stare and gruff voice of the desk sergeant, which quickly turned my legs to jelly. When a few others in the crowd joined in with similar stories, it drove home the point that there are many things, seemingly trivial, that deter others from applying for jobs.

Preferential Hiring and Promotion of Minorities

This is certainly the most controversial and misunderstood of the affirmative action strategies. Under this strategy, minority applicants will be given preference over an equally qualified nonminority applicant. It is important to note that in no way does affirmative action require an employer to hire an unqualified minority over a qualified nonminority. Instead, affirmative action requires employers to monitor their employment records to determine whether minority groups are underrepresented. If they are, affirmative action requires that an organization do the best it can to remedy the situation. One such remedy might be preferential hiring and promotion.

Legality of Preferential Hiring and Promotion Plans

Recently, the courts have indicated that any form of preferential hiring or promotion must undergo a "strict scrutiny analysis," in which the plan must be narrowly tailored and meet a compelling government interest (Gutman, 2004). The various courts have ruled that achieving diversity in such settings as a university (*Grutter v. Bollinger*, 2003) and a police department (*Petit v. City of Chicago*, 2003) are compelling government interests.

If the plan does not meet a compelling government interest, it is illegal. If it does meet a compelling government interest, as shown in Figure 3.4, the courts use five criteria to "strictly scrutinize" the extent to which an affirmative action plan involving preferential hiring is narrowly tailored. It is always legal to monitor employment statistics, actively recruit minorities, and remove barriers discouraging women and minorities from being hired or staying with an organization.

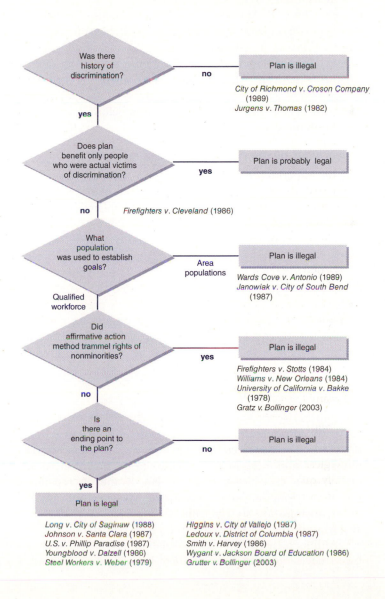

Figure 3.4

Determining the Legality of an Affirmative Action Plan

The five criteria used to assess an affirmative action plan are history of the organization, beneficiaries of the plan, population to be considered, impact on the nonminority group, and the end point of the plan.

A History of Discrimination

The first criterion examined is whether there has been a history of discrimination by a particular organization (*Western States Paving v. Washington State Department of Transportation*, 2005). If there is no strong basis in evidence to indicate that discrimination has recently occurred, then preferential hiring is neither necessary nor legal. For example, if 30% of the qualified workforce is African American, as is 30% of a police department's officers, it would be illegal to engage in preferential hiring based on race. However, if 25% of the qualified workforce is African American and there are no African American state troopers (as was the case in Alabama in 1980), preferential hiring could be justified (*U.S. v. Phillip Paradise*, 1987).

In *Taxman v. Board of Education of the Township of Piscataway* (1996), the Third Circuit Court of Appeals ruled against the use of race as a factor to break a tie between two equally qualified applicants. Sharon Taxman, a White teacher, and Debra Williams, an African American teacher, were tied in seniority. When the Piscataway School Board decided to lay off a teacher, it kept Williams because she was African American. The appeals court ruled the decision to be unconstitutional because there was no racial disparity between the faculty and the qualified workforce. This case was settled in 1997, a few days before it was scheduled to be heard by the U.S. Supreme Court.

Beneficiaries of the Plan

The second criterion concerns the extent to which the plan benefits people who were not actual victims of discrimination. If the plan benefits only actual victims, it will probably be considered legal, but if it benefits people not directly discriminated against by the organization, other criteria will be considered.

For example, imagine an organization consisting of 100 male but no female managers. Twenty female assistant managers, after being denied promotions for several years, file suit charging discrimination. The organization agrees to hire ten of the females to fill the next ten openings. Because the beneficiaries of this plan were themselves the actual victims of the organization's previous discrimination, the plan would be legal. If the plan, however, involved promoting females who had not previously applied for the management positions, the courts, before determining the legality of the plan, would consider three factors: the population used to set the goals, the impact on nonminorities, and the end point of the plan.

Population Used to Set Goals

The third criterion concerns which of two types of populations was used to statistically determine discrimination and to set affirmative action goals. With area populations, an organization compares the number of minorities in the general area with the number of minorities in each position in the organization. If a discrepancy occurs, the organization sets hiring goals to remedy the discrepancy. For example, if 80% of the area surrounding an organization is Hispanic but only 20% of the salaried workers in the organization are Hispanic, the organization might set hiring goals for Hispanics at 90% until the workforce becomes 80% Hispanic.

Although the use of area population figures has been traditional, recent Supreme Court decisions have declared them inappropriate. Instead, the population that must

Qualified workforce The percentage of people in a given geographic area who have the qualifications (skills, education, and so forth) to perform a certain job.

be used in goal setting is that of the **qualified workforce** in the area rather than the area population as a whole.

For example, several southern states are under court supervision to increase the number of minority faculty in their public universities. Rather than a goal consistent with the percentage of African Americans in the United States (roughly 12%), the goal of 7% is based on the qualified workforce—African Americans with doctoral degrees. This example is important because it illustrates that the courts are not unreasonable when it comes to setting affirmative action goals. They realize that a university cannot hire minorities in numbers equal to the national population because a lower percentage of minorities than nonminorities have doctorates.

Another example is the case of *City of Richmond v. Croson* (1989). Because 50% of the Richmond population is minority, the city required that contractors receiving city funds subcontract at least 30% of their work to minority-owned businesses. The J. A. Croson Company received a contract with the city but was unable to subcontract the required 30% because there were not enough minority-owned businesses in the city. The U.S. Supreme Court found Richmond's plan illegal because the goal of 30% was based on the area population rather than the percentage of relevant qualified minority-owned businesses (less than 5%). The U.S. Supreme Court ruled similarly in *Adarand v. Pena* (1995).

Impact on Nonminorities

The fourth criterion used by courts to determine the legality of an affirmative action program is whether the remedy designed to help minorities is narrowly tailored: Does the plan "unnecessarily trammel" the rights of nonminorities? That is, a plan that helps women cannot deny the rights of men. Preference can be given to a qualified minority over a qualified nonminority, but an unqualified minority can never be hired over a qualified nonminority.

Affirmative action becomes controversial when an organization realizes it has discriminated against a particular protected group. For example, police and fire departments have long been staffed by White men. In some cases, this composition has been accidental; in others it has been intentional. To remedy such situations, police and fire departments often set goals for minority hiring. These goals are objectives and are not to be confused with quotas, which *require* a certain percentage of minorities to be hired. This is an important distinction, as the 1991 Civil Rights Act forbids the use of quotas.

Should only a small number of minority applicants test highly enough to be considered qualified, the organization is under no obligation to hire unqualified applicants. In fact, if an organization hires unqualified minorities over qualified nonminorities, hires a lesser-qualified minority over a more qualified nonminority, or sets unreasonable goals, it can be found guilty of reverse discrimination. For example, in *Bishop v. District of Columbia* (1986), the U.S. Court of Appeals ruled that reverse discrimination occurred when an African American battalion chief was promoted ahead of five higher-ranking White deputy chiefs. The court ruled the promotion to be illegal because it was the result of political pressure rather than qualifications and previous job performance. A similar decision was reached in *Black Firefighters Association v. City of Dallas* (1994), when the U.S. Court of Appeals ruled that "skip promotions" were not legal.

In *Higgins v. City of Vallejo* (1987), however, the U.S. Court of Appeals ruled that promotion of a minority applicant with the third-highest score over a nonminority applicant with the highest score was legal. The court's decision was based on the idea that even though the two applicants had different scores, they were close enough to be considered "equally qualified." When two candidates are equally qualified, affirmative action needs can be taken into consideration to decide which of the candidates will be chosen. As one can imagine, the question of how close different qualifications need to be before two candidates are no longer considered equal is difficult to answer. In Chapter 6, methods to answer this question, such as banding and passing scores, will be discussed.

The two most recent U.S. Supreme Court cases involving affirmative action confirm what you have learned in the previous discussion. Both cases involved preferential treatment of minorities in the admission practices at the University of Michigan: *Grutter v. Bollinger* (2003) involved law school admissions, and *Gratz v. Bollinger* (2003) involved undergraduate admissions. In both cases, the Supreme Court ruled that increasing diversity was a compelling government interest. In the *Grutter* case, the court ruled that using race as one of many factors in admissions decisions was narrowly tailored and did not trammel the rights of nonminorities. In the *Gratz* case, however, the Court ruled that automatically giving points to an applicant because of his or her race was not narrowly tailored and thus was illegal. Taken together, the two cases reinforce previous case law that the legality of preferential hiring will be determined on a case-by-case basis and that the plan must be narrowly tailored and not trammel the rights of nonminorities.

End Point of the Plan

The fifth and final criterion concerns setting an end point for the plan. That is, an affirmative action plan cannot continue indefinitely; it must end when certain goals have been obtained. For example, in *Detroit Police Officers Association v. Coleman Young* (1993), the U.S. Court of Appeals ruled that an affirmative action plan that had been utilized for 19 years had resulted in its intended goal: 50% of the Detroit police department was minority. Continuing the plan would be illegal, reasoned the court, because it would now result in a substantial hardship on non-minority-group applicants. The court also reasoned that should the percentage of minorities in the department drop in the future, the preferential hiring plan could be reinstated. To test your knowledge of affirmative action, complete Exercise 3.6 in your workbook.

Unintended Consequences of Affirmative Action Plans

Though affirmative action and diversity programs are an important tool in ensuring equal opportunity, they can result in some unintended negative consequences for people hired or promoted as the result of affirmative action (Kravitz et al., 1997). Research indicates that employees hired due to affirmative action programs are perceived by coworkers as less competent (Heilman, Block, & Lucas, 1992; Heilman, Block, & Stathatos, 1997), have a tendency to devalue their own performance (Heilman & Alcott, 2001; Heilman, Lucas, & Kaplow, 1990), and behave negatively toward others who are hired based on affirmative action programs (Heilman, Kaplow, Amato, & Stathatos, 1993). These effects can be reduced when applicants are given positive information about their abilities (Heilman et al., 1993; Kravitz et al., 1997). Not surprisingly, women and ethnic minorities hold more positive views toward affirmative action than do males and nonminorities (Harrison, Kravitz, Mayer, Leslie, & Lev-Arey, 2006). With these studies in mind, it is essential that an organization be sensitive about how it promotes and implements its diversity and affirmative action efforts.

Privacy Issues

Fourth Amendment The amendment to the U.S. Constitution that protects against unreasonable search or seizure; the amendment has been ruled to cover such privacy issues as drug testing, locker and office searches, psychological testing, and electronic surveillance.

As discussed previously in the chapter, an employment practice is illegal if it results in adverse impact and is not job related. An employment practice can also be illegal if it unnecessarily violates an individual's right to privacy.

The **Fourth Amendment** to the U.S. Constitution protects citizens against unreasonable search or seizure by the government. Its importance to I/O psychology is in the area of drug testing and locker searches. Several courts have ruled that drug testing is considered a "search" and that therefore, to be legal in the public sector, drug testing programs must be reasonable and with cause. It is important to understand that the Fourth Amendment is limited to public agencies such as state and local governments. Private industry is not restricted from drug testing by the Fourth Amendment but government regulation may require drug testing (for example, for trucking companies and railroads), but drug testing and searches by a private organization must be conducted in "good faith and with fair dealing."

Drug-Free Workplace Act Requires federal contractors to maintain a drug-free workplace.

Generally, employers are free (even encouraged by the government) to test job applicants for current drug use. In fact, the federal **Drug-Free Workplace Act** requires employers with federal contracts of $100,000 or more to maintain a drug-free workplace. Furthermore, such states as Alabama, Arkansas, Florida, and Georgia provide discounts on workers' compensation rates to employers with a drug-free workplace program (Steingold, 2011).

Drug Testing

There are few legal problems associated with testing *job applicants* for drug use. However, drug testing of *current employees* by a *public agency* must be based on "reasonable suspicion" and with "just cause." On the basis of prior cases, reasonable suspicion means that there is reason to suspect that employees are using drugs at work (Goldstein, 2000). Such suspicion can be produced from a variety of sources, including "tips" that employees are using drugs (*Copeland v. Philadelphia Police Department*, 1989; *Feliciano v. Cleveland*, 1987; *Garrison v. Justice*, 1995), accidents or discipline problems (*Allen v. City of Marietta*, 1985; *Burnley v. Railway*, 1988), actual observation of drug usage (*Everett v. Napper*, 1987), or physical symptoms of being under the influence (*Connelly v. Newman*, 1990).

The legality of random drug testing in the public sector is a murky area. When considering it, the courts consider the extent to which the special needs of the employer outweigh the employees' right to privacy. For example, in *Local 6000 v. Janine Winters* (2004), the Sixth Circuit Court of Appeals ruled that random drug testing of probation and parole officers was justified, and in *National Treasury Employers Union v. Von Rabb* (1989), the U.S. Supreme Court ruled that random testing of customs officials involved in drug interdiction efforts was legal.

Traditionally, the courts consider the degree to which an employee's behavior affects the safety and trust of the public as a factor in deciding whether the needs of the employer outweigh the employee's right to privacy. For example, air traffic controllers (*Government Employees v. Dole*, 1987) and teachers (*Knox County Education Association v. Knox County Board of Education*, 1998) have been deemed to be responsible for the safety of the public, but school bus attendants have not (*Jones v. McKenzie*, 1987).

Other factors taken into consideration by the courts include the accuracy of the drug tests and the care and privacy taken during the testing (*Hester v. City of Milledgeville*, 1986; *Triblo v. Quality Clinical Laboratories*, 1982). The issue of privacy is an especially interesting one because employees who use drugs often try to "cheat" on their drug tests (Cadrain, 2003a). Attempts at cheating include bringing in "clean" urine that has been taken or purchased from a friend, or diluting the urine sample with soap, toilet water, or other chemicals. Strangely enough, to help applicants cheat on their drug tests, one company markets a product called "The Original Whizzinator," a prosthetic penis containing a 4-ounce bag of dehydrated drug-free urine and an organic heating pad to keep the urine at body temperature (Cadrain, 2003a). You might recall seeing on TV in May 2005 that Onterrio Smith, the former Minnesota Vikings running back who had failed previous drug tests, was caught at the Minneapolis airport with a Whizzinator.

To stop such attempts, some organizations have required those to be tested to strip so that they cannot bring anything into the test area; they also may require that the employee be observed while he provides the urine specimen. Testing conditions such as these would be allowed only under the most serious situations involving national security.

Two other important issues are the appeal process (*Harvey v. Chicago Transit Authority*, 1984) and the confidentiality of test results (*Ivy v. Damon Clinical Laboratory*, 1984). Employees must be given the opportunity to have their specimens retested and to explain why their tests were positive even though they may not have taken illegal drugs.

Thus, for a drug testing program to be legal, the organization must have reason to suspect drug usage, the job must involve the safety or trust of the public, the testing process must be accurate and reasonably private, the results should be handled in a confidential manner, and employees who test positive must be given opportunities to appeal and undergo rehabilitation. A detailed discussion of the use and validity of drug testing for employee selection can be found in Chapter 5.

Office and Locker Searches

Office and locker searches are allowed under the law as long as they are reasonable and with cause (*O'Conner v. Ortega*, 1987). Allowing employees to place their own locks on lockers, however, removes the right of the organization to search the locker.

Psychological Tests

An employment test may be illegal if its questions unnecessarily invade the privacy of an applicant. At most risk are psychological tests originally developed to measure psychopathology. These tests often include questions about such topics as religion and sexual preference that some applicants feel uncomfortable answering. In *Soroka v. Dayton Hudson* (1991), three applicants for store security guard positions with Target Stores filed a class action suit after taking a 704-item psychological test (Psychscreen). The applicants believed some of the questions, a few of which are shown in Table 3.4, violated their right to privacy guaranteed by the California constitution.

Though the two sides reached a settlement prior to the case being decided by the U.S. Supreme Court, the case focused attention on the questions used in psychological

Table 3.4 Do These True-False Questions Violate an Applicant's Right to Privacy?

I go to church almost every week.

I am very religious.

I believe there is a God.

My sex life is satisfactory.

I like to talk about sex.

I have never indulged in any unusual sex practices.

testing. Of particular concern to I/O psychologists was that the tests were scored by a consulting firm, and Target Stores never saw the individual answers to the questions. Instead, it received only overall scores indicating the applicant's level of emotional stability, interpersonal style, addiction potential, dependability, and socialization. The finding by courts that use of the test was an invasion of privacy was troubling to psychologists, who routinely make decisions based on overall test scores rather than the answers to any one particular question (Brown, 1993).

Electronic Surveillance

Almost 80% of organizations in the United States use electronic surveillance or monitor their employees' behavior, email, Internet usage, or telephone conversations. The idea behind this electronic monitoring is that unproductive behavior can be tracked and potential legal problems (e.g., inappropriate email, insider trading) or theft of trade secrets can be prevented (Leonard & France, 2003).

A 2007 survey by the American Management Association (AMA, 2007) found that

- 66% of large organizations monitor the Internet sites viewed by their employees,
- 65% use software to block connections to certain Internet sites,
- 43% monitor email, and
- 28% have fired employees in the past year for violation of an email policy.

The First Circuit Court of Appeals has ruled that video surveillance is not an invasion of privacy because employees do not have an expectation of privacy while working in open areas (*Vega-Rodriguez v. Puerto Rico Telephone*, 1997). Furthermore, several district courts have ruled that organizations can monitor their employees' email or search their computer files (*Gary Leventhal v. Lawrence Knapek*, 2001), especially when the employees have been told that monitoring is part of organizational policy (Leonard & France, 2003; Raynes, 1997). To be on safe legal ground, organizations should tell employees that they are being monitored and at the time of hire, get new employees to sign consent forms agreeing to be monitored. To test your knowledge of employee privacy issues, complete Exercise 3.7 in your workbook. To practice what you have learned in this chapter, complete Exercise 3.8.

Protected Class	Province											
	Alb	**BC**	**Man**	**Ont**	**NB**	**NF**	**NS**	**NWT**	**PEI**	**Queb**	**SAS**	**Yukon**
Race	yes	yes	yes	yes	yes	yes	yes	yes	yes	yes	yes	yes
Sex	yes	yes	yes	yes	yes	yes	yes	yes	yes	yes	yes	yes
Disability	yes	yes	yes	yes	yes	yes	yes	yes	yes	yes	yes	yes
Color	yes	yes	yes	yes	yes	yes	yes	yes	yes	yes	yes	yes
Religion	yes	yes	yes	yes	yes	yes	yes	yes	yes	yes	yes	yes
Marital status	yes	yes	yes	yes	yes	yes	yes	yes	yes	yes	yes	yes
Pregnancy	yes	yes	yes	yes	yes	yes	yes	yes	yes	yes	yes	yes
National origin	no	no	yes	yes	yes	yes	yes	yes	yes	yes	yes	yes
Age	18+	19–65	all	18–65	all	19–65	all	all	all	all	18–64	all
Sexual orientation	yes	yes	yes	yes	yes	yes	yes	no	yes	yes	yes	yes
Drug/alcohol dependence	yes	yes	yes	yes	yes	yes	yes	no	yes	yes	yes	no
Ancestry/place of origin	yes	yes	yes	yes	no	no	no	yes	no	no	yes	yes
Political beliefs	no	yes	yes	no	no	yes	yes	no	yes	yes	no	yes
Family status	yes	yes	yes	yes	no	no	yes	yes	yes	yes	yes	yes
Association	No	no	yes	yes	yes	no	yes	no	yes	no	no	yes
Criminal conviction	No	yes	no	no	no	no	no	no	yes	yes	no	yes
Language	No	no	no	yes	no	no	no	no	no	yes	no	yes
Social condition	No	no	no	no	no	yes	no	no	no	yes	no	no
Source of income	No	no	no	no	no	no	no	no	yes	no	no	no
Citizenship	No	no	no	yes	no	yes	no	no	no	no	no	no
Receipt of public assistance	No	no	no	no	no	no	no	no	no	no	yes	no

ON THE JOB   Applied Case Study

Keystone RV Company, Goshen, Indiana

For safety reasons, Keystone RV in Goshen, Indiana, has a zero-tolerance policy regarding drug abuse at its manufacturing plant. In 2005, the company received complaints from police that its employees were using drugs during breaks. To deal with the problem, Keystone closed the plant for a day to test its 125 employees and then fired the 28 who tested positive for drugs and the 6 who refused to be tested. Keystone transferred 20 employees from another facility to handle the new shortage of employees while it quickly filled the open positions from nearly 2,000 applicants who heard the news about the firings and wanted to work there.

- On the basis of what you learned in this chapter, do you think Keystone handled the situation properly? Why or why not?

- What legal considerations would come into play when randomly testing and then firing employees in a private company?

- What could Keystone have done to prevent its employees from using drugs at work in the first place?

More information on this case can be found by following the links on your text website: www.shrm.org/hrnews_published/archives/CMS_012433.asp and www.etruth.com/News/Content.

The Ethics Behind Workplace Privacy

You read in this chapter that drug testing, office and locker searches, psychological testing, and electronic surveillance are legal, with few restrictions. Genetic screening checks for genetic abnormalities in healthy people at risk for developing certain diseases in the future. This type of screening can be used to screen job applicants and employees who may be likely to develop disease if exposed to certain worksite substances such as chemicals or radiation. And even though President George W. Bush signed the Genetic Information Nondiscrimination Act on May 21, 2008, that prohibits employers from firing, refusing to hire or otherwise discriminating against workers on the basis of genetic information, there is still fear that it will be used for just that reason.

Proponents for such practices in the workplace say that these types of practices can protect and help employees, consumers and/or companies. Electronic surveillance such as email, Internet, and telephone monitoring, and use of video cameras is a proactive step toward catching potentially harmful or illegal behaviors by employees. For example, by monitoring Internal emails, management can learn about inappropriate emails of a sexual or discriminatory nature directed toward a specific employee or employees and can take immediate action to stop this behavior. And this type of monitoring can help employers more fairly evaluate employee performance, because managers are able to track both good and bad behaviors throughout the day by monitoring emails, Internet usage, and telephone conversations. For example, there is software that can be used to view an employee's screen while they are working, count keystrokes of data entry personnel to track speed and reliability, and track the amount of time an employee's computer remains idle. This type of software is beneficial to both employees and employers.

And genetic screening, according to its supporters, can keep both employee and employer safe. Research has identified about fifty genetic disorders that could increase a person's susceptibility to toxins or chemicals. For example, people with sickle cell trait could be at risk for sickle cell anemia if exposed to carbon monoxide or cyanide. Genetic screening could reduce certain people's chances of getting such diseases, which would spare them from spending thousands of dollars in medical bills and from premature death. Employers would benefit from the savings incurred from less workers'

compensation payments, health-care premiums, low productivity, and high absenteeism and turnover. And job applicants don't have to agree to the screening. According to defenders of this practice, those applicants have the right to seek employment elsewhere.

Many opponents of such practices in the workplace say that there are many issues involved with these practices, one of which is employee privacy. Critics state that there are certain aspects of an employee's personal life, both at work and at home, that should not be available to employers, such as personal phone conversations or personal emails. Although making personal phone conversations or personal emails may cut into company time, it is unrealistic to think that there are never times when it is necessary for an employee to do such personal things during work hours.

Although some amount of employee monitoring, if used properly, may be useful to evaluate employees' performance, critics say there should be a limit to how much monitoring can be done. Information that is gathered can be stored and used against the employee many years later, which could impact an employees' potential promotion within the company or his/her references when applying to other companies. And it is not necessary that managers watch everything employees do to be able to fairly evaluate their performance. Some limits should be imposed, by law, including some mechanism that can warn employees when they are being monitored so that they will not be engaging in activities of a private matter.

As for genetic testing, this will remain an ongoing debate. Opponents state that such screening violates the Fourteenth Amendment to the Constitution, which provides equal protection to all people (not just healthy ones) and states that all people should be treated fairly. They state that a person's health is a private matter and should not be under scrutiny of potential or actual employers. If companies find out that applicants or employees are at risk for certain diseases, these applicants and employees will be treated differently from those who aren't at risk. Not only is that breaking the law, according to critics, it is unfair, and therefore, unethical treatment of a certain class of people. Other objections to genetic testing include the fact that the validity and reliability of such tests have not been established, and the fear that the information gained from the genetic tests could fall into the hands of health-care providers, who can then reject some people who may never actually end up with a disease from adequate health-care coverage.

What Do You Think?

- Do you think the legal reasons for these workplace practices outweigh the ethical responsibilities of organizations?

- Are companies being unfair, and therefore, unethical by engaging in such activities?

- What are the ethical responsibilities to employees from companies who chose to use such practices?

- What are some other ethical dilemmas that you think could arise from such practices?

- Conduct an Internet search on the Genetic Information Nondiscrimination Act signed by President Bush. Do you think that act is fair to employers and employees? Why or why not?

Chapter Summary

In this chapter you learned:

- Discrimination complaints are filed with the EEOC.
- A variety of federal laws forbid discrimination based on sex (male, female), race (African American, European American, Asian American, Native American), national origin, color, religion, disability, age (over 40), pregnancy, and qualified veteran status.
- The legality of an employment practice is determined by such factors as the presence of adverse impact and the job relatedness of the employment practice.
- Adverse impact is usually determined by the four-fifths rule.
- Affirmative action consists of a variety of strategies, such as intentional recruitment of minority applicants, identification and removal of employment practices working against minority applicants and employees, and preferential hiring and promotion.
- Employers need to be cautious about violating employee privacy rights regarding drug testing, office and locker searches, psychological testing, and electronic surveillance.
- Organizations can be held liable for the sexual harassment of their employees. This harassment can take the form of quid pro quo or a hostile environment.

Questions for Review

1. What would make an employment practice a BFOQ?
2. Is affirmative action still needed? Why or why not?
3. Why do public employees have more privacy rights than private employees?
4. If a male employee asks out a female coworker, is this sexual harassment? Would your answer be different if the male were a supervisor rather than a coworker? Why or why not?
5. Would a color-blind person be considered disabled under the ADA? Why or why not?

Media Resources and Learning Tools

- Visit our website. Go to www.cengage.com/psychology/aamodt, where you will find online resources directly linked to your book, including chapter-by-chapter quizzing, flashcards, crossword puzzles, application activities, and more.
- Want more practice applying industrial/organizational psychology? Check out the *I/O Applications Workbook*. This workbook (keyed to your textbook) offers engaging, high-interest activities to help you reinforce the important concepts presented in the text.

Chapter 4

EMPLOYEE SELECTION: RECRUITING AND INTERVIEWING

© Chris Ryan/OJO Images/Getty Images

Learning Objectives

➡ Know how to recruit applicants

➡ Learn how to recruit employees and be able to use this information when applying for jobs

➡ Understand why the traditional, unstructured interview doesn't work

➡ Learn how to construct a valid, structured interview

➡ Know how to perform well when being interviewed

➡ Learn how to write a résumé and a cover letter

In the television version of the motion picture *The Enforcer*, Clint Eastwood, as detective Harry Callahan, upon learning that he has been transferred from homicide to personnel, replies, "Personnel—only idiots work in personnel!" Although this statement is a bit strong, it represents the attitude many people hold about the field of human resources. That is, if you can't do anything else, you can always work in human resources.

The image of the human resources (HR) field has been greatly enhanced in recent years, however, for the most part by its application of modern, scientific principles in employee selection and by the realization that properly designed employee selection procedures can save organizations a lot of money.

In this chapter, we will first explore ways to recruit employees and explain job hunting methods, and then discuss interviewing techniques as well as offer some tips that you can use to help find and obtain a desired job.

As shown in Figure 4.1, certain steps can be taken to successfully choose employees. Some of the steps are designed to attract excellent applicants to the organization, others are designed to select the best applicants, and still others are designed to give applicants a good image not only of the organization but of the job search process in general. Keep in mind that for most job openings, many more people will apply than will be hired. If you multiply the number of people who are not hired by the number of job openings each year, it is clear that a lot of people will be in contact with a particular organization. Those people not hired are potential customers, with friends who are also potential customers. Furthermore, applicants not hired for one position may turn out to be well qualified for future positions with the organization. Leaving them with a positive image of the company should be a priority.

Job Analysis

As discussed in Chapter 2, job analysis is the cornerstone of personnel selection. Remember, unless a complete and accurate picture of a job is obtained, it is virtually impossible to select excellent employees. Thus, during the job analysis process, in addition to identifying the important tasks and duties, it is essential to identify the knowledge, skills, and abilities needed to perform the job.

Therefore, the methods used to select employees should tie in directly with the results of the job analysis. In other words, every essential knowledge, skill, and ability identified in the job analysis that is needed on the first day of the job should be tested, and every test must somehow relate to the job analysis. For example, if a job analysis reveals that an office manager types correspondence and proofreads reports to ensure that the reports are grammatically correct, then the battery of selection tests might include a typing test and a grammar test.

Recruitment

Recruitment The process of attracting employees to an organization.

An important step in selecting employees is **recruitment**: attracting people with the right qualifications (as determined in the job analysis) to apply for the job. The first decision is whether to promote someone from within the organization

Internal recruitment
Recruiting employees already employed by the organization.

External recruitment
Recruiting employees from outside the organization.

(**internal recruitment**) or to hire someone from outside the organization (**external recruitment**). Many organizations first advertise employment openings for two weeks to current employees. If no qualified applicants are found, the organizations then advertise outside.

To enhance employee morale and motivation, it is often good to give current employees an advantage in obtaining new internal positions. In fact, an examination of the 2005 rankings of the 25 Best Small Companies to Work for in America and the 25 Best Medium Companies to Work for in America indicates that these companies fill more than 20% of their openings with internal promotions rather than external hires (Pomeroy, 2005).

Internal promotions can be a great source of motivation, but if an organization always promotes employees from within, it runs the risk of having a stale workforce that is devoid of the many ideas that new employees bring with them from their previous employment settings. Heavy reliance on internal sources is thought to perpetuate the racial, gender, and age composition of the workforce. Thus, a balance between promoting current employees and hiring outside applicants is needed.

Media Advertisements

Newspaper Ads

Running ads in periodicals such as local newspapers or professional journals is a common method of recruiting employees. Although many organizations use newspaper ads, especially for local positions, in 2007 recruiters considered print advertising as one of the least effective recruitment methods (SHRM, 2007). This finding demonstrates the huge change in recruiting that has occurred in the past decade: In 2002, recruiters rated newspaper advertising as one of the most effective avenues of applicant recruitment (Gere, Scarborough, & Collison, 2002)!

As shown in Figure 4.2, newspaper advertisements typically ask the applicant to respond in one of four ways: calling, applying in person, sending a résumé directly to the organization, or sending a résumé to a blind box. Applicants are asked to **respond by calling** when an organization wants to either quickly screen applicants or hear an applicant's phone voice (e.g., for telemarketing or receptionist positions). Organizations use **apply-in-person ads** when they don't want their phones tied up by applicants calling (e.g., a travel agency or pizza delivery restaurant), want the applicants to fill out a specific job application, or want to get a physical look at the applicant. Applicants are asked to send a résumé directly to the company (**send-résumé ads**) when the organization expects a large response and does not have the resources to speak with thousands of applicants.

The fourth type of ad directs applicants to send a résumé to a **blind box**. Organizations use blind boxes for three main reasons. First, the organization doesn't want its name in public. This might be the case when a well-known company such as AT&T or IBM has a very specific job opening and is concerned that rumors will spread that there are many openings for a variety of positions. This could result in an avalanche of résumés, many from unqualified applicants.

Respond by calling ads
Recruitment ads in which applicants are instructed to call rather than to apply in person or send résumés.

Apply-in-person ads
Recruitment ads that instruct applicants to apply in person rather than to call or send résumés.

Send-résumé ads Recruitment ads in which applicants are instructed to send their résumé to the company rather than call or apply in person.

Blind box ads Recruitment ads that instruct applicants to send their résumé to a box at the newspaper; neither the name nor the address of the company is provided.

Figure 4.1
Steps in Selecting Employees

(Flowchart, top to bottom: Job analysis → Selection of testing methods → Test validation → Recruitment → Screening → Testing → Selecting → Hiring/ rejecting)

Figure 4.2

Examples of Help-Wanted Ads

PLUMBER needed immediately in Rocky Mount area. Top pay for experienced person. Call 712-483-2315

LEGAL ASSISTANT

TITLE AGENCY ADMINISTRATOR

Downtown law firm seeking experienced real estate legal assistant/title agency administrator with working knowledge of WordPerfect 5.1. All benefits and parking provided. Send résumé in confidence to: Box M262. c/o Poncha Springs Times & World News, P.O. Box 2491, Poncha Springs, Va. 24010

HOTEL DESK CLERK

Afternoon & night shift available. Apply in person at Comfort Inn, Bassville.

Engineering Manager

Highly motivated and professional individual with 10 years performance track record to successfully lead a large engineering department. Must have clear conceptual understanding of the telephone industry including PABX and Key telephone systems. Engineering abilities including analog circuit design, digital logic design, microprocessor, and infrared design. Familiarity with regulatory agencies is necessary. Ability to maintain productivity and quality schedules for timely work completion. Most desirable credentials include BSEE degree plus MBA.

Respond by sending résumé to:

Volcan, Inc.
Attn: Human Resources
2222 Industry Ave.
Sweed, VA 24013

EOE
No agencies or phone calls please.

Second, the company might fear that people wouldn't apply if they knew the name of the company. For example, an ad for sales positions would probably not draw a large response if applicants were asked to send their résumés to a funeral home (even though selling burial plots can be a lucrative job). Third, on rare occasions, a company needs to terminate an employee but wants first to find a replacement. As you can imagine, running an ad containing the name of the company would not be smart if the current employee were not aware that he or she was about to be fired.

Advice on how to respond to various kinds of ads is shown in the Career Workshop Box. To help you identify the types of help-wanted ads, complete Exercise 4.1 in your workbook.

Writing Recruitment Ads. Although little research is available, there is plenty of expert advice on the best way for an employer to write recruitment advertisements. Research on recruitment ads indicates the following findings:

- Ads displaying the company emblem and using creative illustrations attract the greatest *number* of applicants, but ads that include the salary range and a company phone number attract the *highest-quality* applicants (Kaplan, Aamodt, & Wilk, 1991).
- Ads containing realistic information about the job, rather than information that is "too good to be true," increase applicant attraction to the organization (Thorsteinson, Palmer, Wulff, & Anderson, 2004).

- Ads containing detailed descriptions of the job and organization provide applicants with an idea of how well they would fit into an organization and result in positive thoughts about it (Roberson, Collins, & Oreg, 2005).
- Ads containing information about the selection process affect the probability that applicants will apply for a job. For example, ads stating that an in-person interview will be used to select employees result in applicants being more likely to apply for a job than ads indicating that grade point average (GPA) will be a factor (Reeve & Schultz, 2004).

In recent years, a trend in help-wanted advertising has been the use of creative, high-energy ads (Levit, 2008). By using innovative advertising, On-Line Software tripled the number of applicants who responded to its help-wanted ad for secretarial positions. Hyundai's innovative ad cost only $5,000 and had almost 2,000 responses to advertised positions. Some organizations have tried to recruit employees by making fun of the job openings. Here are some examples:

- FH Company, a Norwegian importer and distributor, ran a help-wanted advertisement reading, "Tiresome and boring wholesale company seeks indolent people with a total lack of service mindedness for a job that is completely without challenge."
- C. Rinker Paving, a Virginia asphalt company, ran a help-wanted advertisement asking for applicants who "have hair short enough to see and hear, are able to gulp down a sandwich in 30 minutes and be able to work at least 30 minutes without going to the restroom or drinking something, and have nose and earrings light enough not to interfere with their work."
- A national sales company advertised that they were "interested in hiring five semi-obnoxious pushy sales pros for a very boring repetitive job of selling. Our current sales staff is the laziest group of individuals that you'll ever see drag themselves to work 5 days a week to decide whether to complain about the weather, coffee, thermostat or the manager."
- The New York City Administration for Children's Services ran an advertisement stating "Wanted: men and women willing to walk into strange buildings in dangerous neighborhoods, be screamed at by unhinged individuals—perhaps in a language you do not understand—and, on occasion, forcibly remove a child from the custody of a parent because the alternative could have tragic consequences."

Thus, the same techniques and imagination used in product advertisements may increase the recruitment yield from help-wanted ads. That is one reason major advertising firms such as Bernard Hodes and Austin-Knight are increasingly involved in the development of recruitment ads and campaigns. To practice what you have learned about writing help-wanted advertisements, complete Exercise 4.2 in your workbook.

Electronic Media

Whereas 96% of organizations run recruitment advertisements in newspapers, only 26% use television and radio to advertise job openings (SHRM, 2001b). Perhaps the best use of television recruitment in the private sector has been by McDonald's, whose television commercials show the fast-food chain to be the ideal place for retirees to work part-time. In addition to generating applicants, the commercials are an excellent public relations vehicle.

The potential advantage to using electronic media for recruitment is that, according to a 2008 Ipsos OTX study, Americans spend 3.4 hours per day watching TV and 1.6 hours a day listening to the radio. Furthermore, different types of radio stations (e.g., rock, rap, classical, country, oldies, news) reach different types of audiences, and thus radio ads can be easily targeted to the desired audience. For example, Harris Trucking often advertises

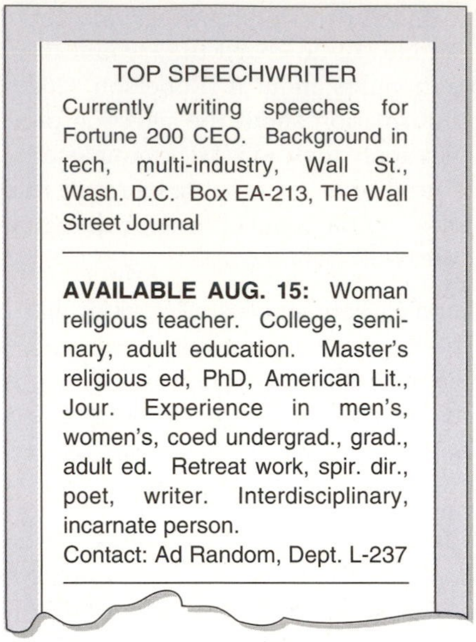

Figure 4.3

Examples of
Situation-Wanted Ads

> **TOP SPEECHWRITER**
> Currently writing speeches for Fortune 200 CEO. Background in tech, multi-industry, Wall St., Wash. D.C. Box EA-213, The Wall Street Journal
>
> ---
>
> **AVAILABLE AUG. 15:** Woman religious teacher. College, seminary, adult education. Master's religious ed, PhD, American Lit., Jour. Experience in men's, women's, coed undergrad., grad., adult ed. Retreat work, spir. dir., poet, writer. Interdisciplinary, incarnate person.
> Contact: Ad Random, Dept. L-237

its openings for drivers on radio stations playing country music. The radio ads are used not only to recruit new drivers but to thank current drivers for doing such a good job.

Situation-Wanted Ads

Situation-wanted ads (also called jobs-wanted or positions-wanted ads) are placed by the applicant rather than by organizations. As shown in Figure 4.3, these ads take a variety of forms: some list extensive qualifications, some give applicants' names, and some are generally more creative than others. Two studies (Williams & Garris, 1991; Willis, Miller, & Huff, 1991) investigated the effectiveness of these ads by contacting applicants for white-collar jobs who had placed situation-wanted ads in a variety of daily and professional publications. The results of the two studies are encouraging: 69.4% of those applicants placing ads were contacted. However, not all contacts were from employers. Instead, some were from employment agencies and resume-writing services. Of the applicants who placed the ads, 21.5% did receive actual job offers. Situation-wanted ads appear to be a useful way of looking for a job, and given that they don't cost an organization any money, they may be a beneficial method of recruitment. Modern versions of situation-wanted ads are social networking sites such as LinkedIn, Facebook, and Twitter which will be discussed later in the chapter.

Point-of-Purchase Methods

The point-of-purchase method of recruitment is based on the same "POP" (point-of-purchase) advertising principles used to market products to consumers. For example, consider shopping at a local grocery store. As you push your cart through one aisle, you see a special display for potato chips, in the next aisle a display for cookies. When you get to the checkout stand, items such as the *National Enquirer*, candy, and batteries are conveniently placed so you can examine them while you wait in line. The idea is to get you to buy more items once you are already in the store.

In employee recruitment, job vacancy notices are posted in places where customers or current employees are likely to see them: store windows, bulletin boards,

Respond-by-Calling Ads

➤ Practice your first few sentences, such as "I saw your help-wanted advertisement in the local newspaper and would like to get more information." Don't count on being able to ad-lib or you might sound as inarticulate as the typical person leaving a message on an answering machine.

➤ Be prepared for a short interview by making sure you have time to talk, having your résumé handy to answer questions, and having paper and pencil close by. GeGe Beall, a human resources manager, once received a phone call just as she was stepping out of the shower and before she had time to get dressed. The caller turned out to be an employer, who interviewed Beall for the next hour. The employer told Beall that she liked phone interviews because the applicant "didn't have to worry about putting on her interview suit." In this case, she didn't realize just how accurate her statement was!

Apply-in-Person Ads

➤ Be prepared to interview on the spot. The organization may simply take your résumé and call at a later date to schedule an interview. However, it is not unusual for an organization to interview applicants as they drop off their résumés.

➤ Dress as if you were going to an interview. It might be convenient to drop off your résumé on your way to the beach, but dressing poorly will leave a bad impression, whether you receive an immediate interview or not.

➤ Bring copies of your résumé and leave one even if you are asked to complete a job application.

➤ Bring a pen. Many organizations automatically eliminate applicants who do not do this.

➤ Be nice to the receptionist or any other person with whom you come in contact. The organization's first look at you is probably the most important, and you can be sure that word of a rude or poorly dressed applicant will quickly get back to the person making the actual hiring decision.

Send-Résumé Ads

➤ Always include a cover letter (a concept that will be discussed later in the chapter).

➤ Type the envelope if possible.

Blind Box Ads

➤ Don't be afraid to respond to these types of ads. Most of the time, they will result in good jobs with respectable organizations.

➤ Respond promptly, as these boxes are assigned to advertisers only for the period in which they run their ad.

restaurant placemats, and the sides of trucks. The advantages to this method are that it is inexpensive and it is targeted toward people who frequent the business. The disadvantage is that only a limited number of people are exposed to the sign.

Cabela's, a retail chain specializing in hunting and fishing goods, is an excellent example of an organization that recruits current customers for job openings. Because Cabela's needs employees with extensive knowledge of hunting and fishing, they find it much easier to hire customers who already have that interest and knowledge than to train new employees from scratch. In addition to targeting current customers, Cabela's also lures hunting and fishing clubs whose members are not only potential employees, but potential customers as well. A perk that also helps recruit avid hunters and fishermen is product discounts and a policy that allows sales staff to take a product home for 60 days so that they can provide customers with accurate opinions about the product (Taylor, 2007).

Because of the difficulty in obtaining employees, many fast-food restaurants are using unusual point-of-purchase techniques. McDonald's, Arby's, Burger King, and Carl's Jr. have all printed help-wanted ads with application blanks on their paper placemats. To apply for a job, customers (can we now call them McApplicants?) simply wipe the spilled ketchup off the placemat, fill in their name and address, and give the placemat to the manager.

Wendy's has printed announcements of job openings on its cash-register receipts ("Now hiring smiling faces"), as do Target and Home Depot; Domino's Pizza placed help-wanted ads on its pizza boxes; and Kentucky Fried Chicken placed signs on vans that stopped at student gathering places to distribute free sodas and application materials. Because Store 24 had difficulty recruiting manager trainees, it took the unique approach of placing a help-wanted advertisement on one side of its milk cartons. The cost of the recruitment campaign was minimal, as the company already bore the expense of creating and printing the milk cartons. Other examples of innovative recruitment methods include Lauriat's Books placing a job posting and mini-résumé on a bookmark; the clothing store Rugged Wearhouse putting help-wanted signs in its dressing rooms; and both SmithKline and Prudential Insurance posting help-wanted ads on billboards in the Philadelphia area. To record point-of-purchase methods you have seen, complete Exercise 4.3 in your workbook.

Recruiters

Campus Recruiters

Many organizations send recruiters to college campuses to answer questions about themselves and interview students for available positions. Not surprisingly, the behavior and attitude of recruiters can greatly influence applicants' decisions to accept jobs that are offered (Chapman, Uggerslev, Carroll, Piasentin, & Jones, 2005; Rynes, Bretz, & Gerhart, 1991).

Due to cost considerations, many employers have cut back on the use of on-campus recruiting. As a result, an increasing number of colleges are organizing **virtual job fairs**, in which their students and alumni can use the web to "visit" with recruiters from hundreds of organizations at one time. In a virtual job fair, applicants can talk to or instant message a recruiter, learn more about the company, and submit résumés.

Outside Recruiters

More than 75% of organizations use such outside recruiting sources as private employment agencies, public employment agencies, and **executive search firms** (SHRM, 2001b). Private employment agencies and executive search firms are designed to make a profit from recruitment activities, whereas public employment agencies are operated by state and local public agencies and are strictly nonprofit.

Employment Agencies and Search Firms

Employment Agencies

Employment agencies operate in one of two ways. They charge either the company or the applicant when the applicant takes the job. The amount charged usually ranges from 10% to 30% of the applicant's first-year salary.

From an organization's perspective, there are few risks in using an employment agency that charges the applicant for its services. That is, if the employment agency cannot find an appropriate candidate, the organization has not wasted money. But if the employment agency is successful, the organization gets a qualified employee at no cost.

Employment agencies are especially useful if an HR department is overloaded with work or if an organization does not have an individual with the skills and experience needed to select employees properly. The disadvantage of employment agencies is that a company loses some control over its recruitment process and may end up with undesirable applicants. Remember, most "counselors" at employment agencies are hired because of their skill in sales, not because of their solid background in the area of personnel selection. In fact, one employment agency turned down one of its own job applicants because the applicant had earned a degree in personnel management. During the interview the head of the agency told the applicant, "We are not really looking for a personnel professional. What we want is the type of person who could sell aluminum siding to the owner of a brick home."

Virtual job fair A job fair held on campus in which students can "tour" a company online, ask questions of recruiters, and electronically send résumés.

Executive search firms Employment agencies, often also called headhunters, that specialize in placing applicants in high-paying jobs.

Employment agency An organization that specializes in finding jobs for applicants and finding applicants for organizations looking for employees.

The applicant can seldom go wrong using an employment agency. If the fee is charged to the company, the applicant gets a job at no cost. However, even if the fee is charged to the applicant, the applicant may still benefit. For example, suppose you are having difficulty finding a job, and an employment agency finds you a good job paying $36,000 per year. Spending $3,600 to obtain a good job might be worthwhile because every month of unemployment is costing you $3,000 in lost income. So, the fee is essentially one month's salary that you would not have earned anyway without the job.

Executive Search Firms

Executive search firms, better known as "head hunters," differ from employment agencies in several ways. First, the jobs they represent tend to be higher-paying, non-entry-level positions such as executives, engineers, and computer programmers. Second, reputable executive search firms always charge their fees to organizations rather than to applicants. Third, fees charged by executive search firms tend to be about 30% of the applicant's first-year salary.

A word of caution about both employment agencies and executive search firms: Because they make their money on the number of applicants they place, they tend to exert tremendous pressure on applicants to take jobs that are offered. But applicants are not obligated to take jobs and should not be intimidated about turning down a position that appears to be a poor match.

Public Employment Agencies

Public employment agency An employment service operated by a state or local government, designed to match applicants with job openings.

The third type of outside recruitment organization is state and local employment agencies. These **public employment agencies** are designed primarily to help the unemployed find work, but they often offer services such as career advisement and résumé preparation. From the organization's perspective, public employment agencies can be of great value in filling blue-collar and clerical positions. Not only is there no cost involved in hiring the applicants, but often government programs are also available that will help pay training costs. In addition, with the advent of standardized testing programs (which will be discussed in Chapter 5), the quality of employees hired through public agencies is now much higher than in the past.

Many public employment agencies have made finding jobs easier by placing kiosks in locations such as shopping malls and public buildings. Applicants can use the kiosks to search for local job openings and get information on how they can apply for the jobs. Recruiting kiosks are increasingly being used by employers that receive large numbers of walk-in applicants. Rather than speaking to a receptionist, potential job applicants can use the kiosk located in the company lobby to search for current job openings and then apply to jobs for which they are qualified.

Employee Referrals

Employee referral A method of recruitment in which a current employee refers a friend or family member for a job.

Another way to recruit is by **employee referral**, in which current employees recommend family members and friends for specific job openings. Surveys investigating this referral method indicate that about 50% of private organizations have formal referral programs and 66% use employee referrals in some way (Burke, 2005b). Of the 50 best small and medium organizations to work for in America discussed previously, 92% use employee referrals and over 30% of all hires were referred by a current employee (Pomeroy, 2005). Only 1% of public organizations such as state and city governments have such programs, and the few that do, use them to encourage minority recruitment of police officers and firefighters (Trice, 1997).

© Lee Raynes

Many organizations provide kiosks for applicants to apply for jobs

In a survey of 450 HR professionals, employee referrals were rated as the most effective recruitment method (SHRM, 2007). Some organizations are so convinced of the attractiveness of this method that they provide financial incentives to employees who recommend applicants who are hired. For example, Integrated Systems Consulting Group gave $3,000 and a chance to win a vacation in Hawaii to employees referring successful applicants. Transaction Information Systems gave $1,000 to employees recommending applicants for a World Wide Web programming position; Temporary Associates in Illinois gave $250 college scholarships to students who recommended applicants for seasonal positions; 7-Eleven offered employees $1,000 for recommending potential field consultants; Sybase ran a referral campaign in which employees whose referrals resulted in an interview were entered in a raffle for such prizes as a TV, five cases of beer, 36 Baby Ruth bars, and a hammock; and White Memorial Medical Center provided

I am a Human Resources Representative for an ammunition and propellant manufacturer in southwestern Virginia. Our company operates a government-owned facility and manufactures a number of propellants and ammunition components for the United States armed forces. My responsibilities include compensation, benefits administration, and workers' compensation. I am also involved in employee recruitment and selection. Recruiting and hiring highly qualified applicants is a critical component in the success of our operation, particularly in light of the volatile nature of the materials our employees are exposed to in their work environment.

Whether a position is a new or an existing one, the first step in recruiting is to ensure that an accurate job description exists for the position. Information from this job description is utilized for development of the internal personnel requisition and in advertisements for the position. The appropriate market for advertising the position is determined by the type of position to be filled.

Entry-level production positions are generally filled in partnership with the local employment commission, in addition to newspaper advertisements as needed. Recruiting for technical or management-level positions requires a broader focus. Recruiting for professional, scientific, and managerial positions often includes a national search. In national searches, it is essential to use a variety of recruitment methods to reach more potential applicants. All open positions are posted on the

Rhonda Duffie, MS, PHR
Human Resources Representative
Alliant Techsystems, Inc.

company's website, which includes a database searchable by location, facility, or job category.

Candidates may complete an online application and attach a résumé file to their online application. For critical or difficult-to-fill positions, Alliant Techsystems offers an incentive to employees to encourage referrals of candidates for these positions. In addition to the company website, a variety of other advertising resources are used, including local and national newspapers, trade and professional organizations, and online job search services. Another important aspect of our recruiting involves participation in on-campus recruiting efforts and hosting information booths at professional association meetings. The participation in these events is generally a team-based approach involving recruiting staff from several company locations.

As with most organizations, an important part of the selection process is the employment interview. To increase the effectiveness of the interview as a selection tool, a structured interview is used for all open positions. For each position, a set of essential competencies is identified. Questions for each competency are developed and may be either technical or situational in nature. A panel whose members are selected by the hiring manager interviews the applicants. Each interviewer takes notes during the interview and completes a standard rating sheet on each of the applicants. The ratings are utilized to identify the successful candidate for the position. Using a structured interview and a panel of interviewers reduces the bias involved in typical interviews.

recommenders of successful employees free maid service for a full year. The average amount of such bonuses offered by organizations is less than $1,000 (SHRM, 2001a). The typical time period that a new employee must stay with the company before the referring employee is eligible for a bonus is three months (Stewart, Ellenburg, Hicks, Kremen, & Daniel, 1990). Stewart and his colleagues (1990) found no relationship between the size of the bonus and the number of referrals, nor did they find that organizations offering referral bonuses received more referrals than did organizations not offering bonuses. Though such a finding might be surprising, 42% of employees said they made a referral to help a friend, and another 24% said they made the referral to help their employer. Only 24% reported making the referral for the incentive (Lachnit, 2001).

Although the idea of employee referrals sounds good, not all referrals are the same. Aamodt and Carr (1988) and Rupert (1989) compared the success of employees who had been referred by current successful and unsuccessful employees and found that employees referred by successful employees had longer tenure than did employees who had been referred by unsuccessful employees. Thus, only those referrals made by successful employees should be considered. This finding, explained by social psychology research, indicates that our friends tend to be similar to us in characteristics such as personality, values, and interests. If a particular employee is a good employee, then the same characteristics that make her a good employee are probably shared by her friends and family. The same would be true of an unsuccessful employee.

Even though referrals by successful employees are a good recruitment avenue, the similarity of friends can also pose some problems. The biggest is that our friends also tend to be the same gender, race, and national origin as we are. For example, Mouw (2002) found that 88% of the friends of White employees and 92% of the friends of African American employees are of the same race, and 50% of job applicants used their social networks to help find a job.

Thus, if an organization uses employee referrals and the organization consists predominantly of White male Protestants, it will seldom hire African Americans or females. Thus, even though the organization didn't intend to discriminate, the consequences of its recruitment policy may have that effect. However, organizations such as Alpine Banks of Colorado have used this similarity bias to their advantage by asking its bilingual employees to refer bilingual applicants. Similarly, Wegmans Food Markets encourages employees to refer family members—so much so that as of 2009, 7,000 of the organization's 37,000 employees were related to at least one person on the company payroll (Owens, 2009).

Direct Mail

Direct mail A method of recruitment in which an organization sends out mass mailings of information about job openings to potential applicants.

Because **direct mail** has been successful in product advertising, several organizations have used it to recruit applicants, especially those who are not actively job hunting. With direct-mail recruitment, an employer typically obtains a mailing list and sends help-wanted letters or brochures to people through the mail.

One California branch of Allstate Insurance had been using newspaper advertisements and getting limited response. However, from a single mailing of 64,000 letters that explained the career opportunities available at Allstate to current policyholders, the company received more than 500 calls and was able to hire 20 new employees. Union Special, an Illinois manufacturer of sewing machines, had difficulty filling 10 engineering positions, so they direct-mailed 3,300 cards to Chicago-area engineers at a cost of about $5,000. As a result, the company received 100 responses and conducted 30 interviews. A third company that successfully used direct-mail recruitment is the Bank of America. To save money, Bank of America did something different from Allstate and Union Special. Instead of sending a special recruitment mailing, Bank of America included recruitment literature in the regular monthly mailing of bank statements to its customers.

Direct-mail recruiting is especially useful for positions involving specialized skills. For example, Minor's Landscape Services in Texas had difficulty finding licensed irrigators, so the company located a list of people in Texas who had irrigation licenses and sent letters to each person on the list. The company found 20 qualified candidates and was able to fill both of its openings. An example of direct-mail recruiting can be found in Figure 4.4.

Internet

The Internet continues to be a fast-growing source of recruitment. Internet recruiting efforts usually take one of two forms: employer-based websites and Internet recruiting sites.

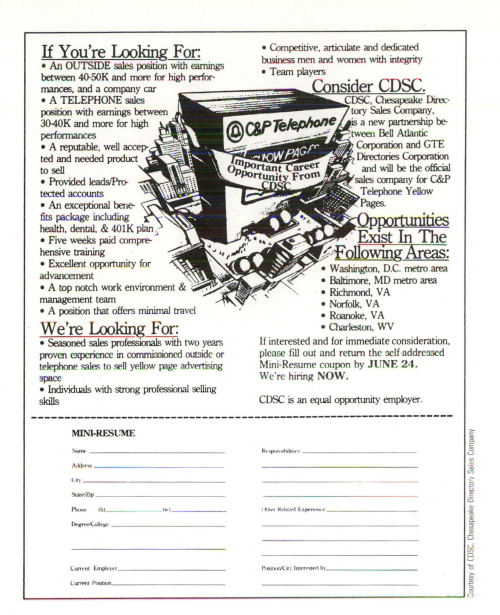

If You're Looking For:
- An OUTSIDE sales position with earnings between 40-50K and more for high performances, and a company car
- A TELEPHONE sales position with earnings between 30-40K and more for high performances
- A reputable, well accepted and needed product to sell
- Provided leads/Protected accounts
- An exceptional benefits package including health, dental, & 401K plan
- Five weeks paid comprehensive training
- Excellent opportunity for advancement
- A top notch work environment & management team
- A position that offers minimal travel

We're Looking For:
- Seasoned sales professionals with two years proven experience in commissioned outside or telephone sales to sell yellow page advertising space
- Individuals with strong professional selling skills

- Competitive, articulate and dedicated business men and women with integrity
- Team players

Consider CDSC.

CDSC, Chesapeake Directory Sales Company, is a new partnership between Bell Atlantic Corporation and GTE Directories Corporation and will be the official sales company for C&P Telephone Yellow Pages.

Opportunities Exist In The Following Areas:
- Washington, D.C. metro area
- Baltimore, MD metro area
- Richmond, VA
- Norfolk, VA
- Roanoke, VA
- Charleston, WV

If interested and for immediate consideration, please fill out and return the self-addressed Mini-Resume coupon by **JUNE 24**. We're hiring **NOW.**

CDSC is an equal opportunity employer.

MINI-RESUME

Name _____
Address _____
City _____
State/Zip _____
Phone (h)_____ (w)_____
Degree/College _____

_____

Current Employer_____
Current Position_____

Responsibilities _____
_____
_____
_____
Other Related Experience_____
_____
_____
_____
_____
Position/City Interested In_____
_____

Courtesy of CDSC, Chesapeake Directory Sales Company

Figure 4.4

Example of a Direct Mail Recruitment Advertisement

Employer-Based Websites

With employer-based websites, an organization lists available job openings and provides information about itself and the minimum requirements needed to apply to a particular job. Though the level of sophistication varies across organization websites, on most, applicants can upload their résumés, answer questions designed to screen out unqualified applicants, and then actually take employment tests. On many sites, the tests are instantly scored, and if the applicant is deemed qualified, interviews are scheduled electronically.

A change in employer-based websites has been the use of the .jobs domain (SHRM, 2007). Previously, an applicant interested in a job at a company such as All-state Insurance would need to go to the Allstate website and then find the link to the jobs section. As of 2008, most major employers have added the .jobs domain to make this process easier; a person interested in a job at Allstate or Raytheon, for example, could directly access jobs at that company by typing the URL www.allstate.jobs or www.raytheon.jobs.

Rock Bottom restaurants (Rock Bottom Brewery, Old Chicago pizza, Chop House, Walnut Brewery, and Sing Sing nightclub) provide an excellent example of an employer using an automated hiring system. Applicants can apply for jobs and complete personality inventories online at home, at a Rock Bottom restaurant, or at a career fair. The system automatically screens for work eligibility, scores the tests, and sends messages to restaurant managers letting them know when a high-quality applicant has applied. The system even suggests interview questions the manager should ask a particular applicant (e.g., Why did you have a three-month gap between jobs in 2009?). Since using the new online system, turnover has gone down.

Research indicates that the effective employer-based websites contain information that is detailed and credible, are easy to navigate, are aesthetically pleasing, are interactive, and contain videos of employee testimonials regarding the company (Allen, Mahto, & Otondo, 2007; Breaugh, 2008). Including employee testimonials from racially and ethnically diverse employees can enhance an organization's diversity efforts (Walker, Feild, Giles, Armenakis, & Bernerth, 2009).

Internet Recruiters

Internet recruiters continue to grow and have an impact on hiring: A 2009 survey of more than 1,000 large employers indicated that 90% of employers planned to invest significantly in Internet recruiting in 2010 (Arbita, 2009). An Internet recruiter is a private company whose website lists job openings for hundreds of organizations and résumés for thousands of applicants. The largest Internet recruiter, CareerBuilder, had more than 21 million unique visitors per month in 2010. Although small organizations are as likely as larger ones to recruit employees through their webpages, larger organizations are more likely to use Internet recruiters (Hausdorf & Duncan, 2004).

Employers are finding that there are many advantages to using Internet recruiting compared with traditional newspaper help-wanted ads. Perhaps the biggest advantage is the cost; depending on the geographic location, advertisement size, and length of the ad run, advertising in a major city newspaper can be 10 times more expensive than Internet recruiting. Internet recruiting reaches more people over a larger geographic area than do newspaper ads, and whereas the Sunday edition is the main newspaper recruitment tool, "every day is Sunday" on the Internet. Though the Internet changes every day, these were the leading recruitment websites in 2011:

www.monster.com

www.CareerBuilder.com

www.hotjobs.com

www.craigslist.org

www.career.com

www.job.com

Though the use of online recruiting and screening has certainly increased, there is little research investigating whether the Internet is an effective recruitment source (Hausdorf & Duncan, 2004). There seems to be little doubt that the Internet generates monster

Back to Job Search Results

HR Generalist

Company:	Fitzgerald Industries	**Location:**	Los Angeles, CA
Status:	Full Time, Employee	**Job Category:**	Human Resources/Recruiting
Relevant Work Experience:	2 to 5 Years	**Career Level:**	Experienced (Non-Manager)
Education Level:	Bachelor's Degree		

Save to File

Job Description

Due to increased growth, we have an immediate need for a **Human Resource Generalist** to support the organization through administration of HR policies, procedures, benefits and compliance issues. This position reports to the human resource manager and offers much potential for career advancement and growth. Qualified candidates will have worked in a human resource department and will have experience with OFCCP and EEOC compliance issues.

Specific areas of responsibility include:

- Ensure compliance with employment laws and OFCCP regulations
- Complete Fitzgerald Industries' affirmative action report
- Monitor fairness in selection and promotion decisions
- Coordinate immigration documentation
- Assist with benefits analysis and implementation
- Collect, maintain, and analyze employee data

Essential Skills and Experience Required:

- At least three years human resource experience
- Experience in OFCCP and EEOC compliance
- High level of discretion required for sensitive information

Fitzgerald Industries offers a competitive salary, an excellent benefits package including health, dental, vision, life, and disability insurances, as well as a 401(k) plan with 5% company match, up to 25 days of paid time off, and a professional and growth oriented environment.

Figure 4.5
Example of a Monster.com job posting

more applications than more traditional recruiting methods, but the relative quality of those applicants is not known. In the only study to date addressing this issue, McManus and Ferguson (2003) found that Internet sources produced better-quality applicants than did newspaper ads and career fairs and produced similar quality to school placement offices.

As is the case with print media, the look and content of a web recruitment page or advertisement greatly influences applicant reactions. A study by Dineen, Ling, Ash, and Del Vecchio (2007) found that web-based job postings were most effective when the posting was aesthetically pleasing *and* contained customized information about the job and the company. Aesthetics or content by themselves were not enough to influence applicant reactions.

Many organizations are expanding the traditional web approach by blogging (Hasson, 2007). Blogging allows recruiters to more informally discuss an organization's career opportunities and corporate culture with potential applicants. The blog will usually include links to the organization's official employment website. An example of a blog for T-Mobile can be found at www.wirelessjobs.com and the blog for Honeywell Corp. at www.honeywellblogs.com. Note the vast difference in the style and tone of the two blogs.

Job Fairs

Job fair A recruitment method in which several employers are available at one location so that many applicants can obtain information at one time.

Job fairs are used by 70% of organizations (SHRM, 2001b) and are designed to provide information in a personal fashion to as many applicants as possible. Job fairs are typically conducted in one of three ways. In the first, many types of organizations have booths at the same location. For example, a multiemployer job fair sponsored by the Detroit NAACP Branch in 2011 drew over 3,000 applicants and 36 employers (Meyer, 2011). Your college probably has one or two of these job fairs each year, in which dozens of organizations send representatives to discuss employment opportunities with students and to collect résumés. In addition, representatives usually hand out company literature and souvenirs such as T-shirts, yardsticks, and cups. If you haven't been to a campus job fair, contact your career services center to see when they are scheduled on your campus.

Job fairs are also held when an event or disaster occurs that affects local employment. Following the September 11, 2001, attack on the World Trade Center, a job fair for displaced workers attracted more than 25,000 job seekers. Similar fairs were held for airline workers in Philadelphia and Pittsburgh (Gelbart, 2001). Similarly, in the rebuilding process in the aftermath of Hurricane Katrina, a multiemployer job fair called "West of the Connection" was held in the New Orleans area.

The second type of job fair has many organizations in the same field in one location. For example, an education job fair in Honolulu, Hawaii, in 2011 had 50 private and public schools attend to recruit new teachers. The advantage to this type of job fair is that with a single employment field represented, each visitor is a potential applicant for every organization. The drawback, of course, is that each organization must compete directly with the other organizations at the fair.

The third approach to a job fair is for an organization to hold its own. Here are some examples:

- Gaylord Palms in Kissimmee, Florida, held a job fair attended by more than 12,000 people interested in the resort's 1,400 job openings. The job fair began with an overnight "pajama party" attended by 3,000 applicants.
- LG Chem in Holland, Michigan, had more than 800 job seekers attend its job fair held to fill 100 production positions at its new plant.
- Microsoft held a job fair in Atlanta that attracted 3,000 people, and Concentra Corporation held an "open house" that attracted more than 100 applicants and resulted in four job openings being filled.

Although this approach is certainly more expensive, it has the advantage of focusing the attention of the applicants on only one company.

Incentives

When unemployment rates are low, organizations have to take extra measures to recruit employees. One of these measures is to offer incentives for employees to accept jobs with an organization. Though these incentives often come in the form of a financial signing bonus, other types of incentives are increasing in popularity. For example, such organizations as Sears and Starwood Hotels offer employee discounts on company products and services, and 6% of organizations offer mortgage assistance to lure employees (Tyler, 2001).

Increasing Applicant Diversity

Many organizations make special efforts to recruit underrepresented groups such as women and minorities. Efforts include recruiting at historically black colleges (HBCs), developing targeted intern positions, and highlighting the organization's openness to diversity in recruitment materials (e.g., including affirmative action statements, displaying pictures of minority employees, and using minority recruiters). Research by Avery and McKay (2006) and McKay and Avery (2006) indicates that a key to recruiting minority applicants is how they perceive the diversity of the organization during a site visit. That is, minority applicants look at how may minorities they see, what positions the minorities are in, and how well they perceive the quality of the interaction between minority and nonminority employees.

Nontraditional Populations

When traditional recruitment methods are unsuccessful, many organizations look for potential applicants from nontraditional populations. Here are a few examples:

- Manpower Incorporated, in Chandler, Arizona; the Chicago Police Department; and the Hackensack, New Jersey, Police Department formed partnerships with local churches that resulted in successful hires (Tyler, 2000).
- Borders teams with AARP to actively recruit older, retired applicants to work at its bookstores.
- IBM, Google, Morgan Stanley, and Cisco Systems developed recruitment strategies and such gay-friendly benefits as domestic partner benefits to recruit and retain gay and lesbian employees.
- Seventy percent of organizations have reported that hiring welfare recipients has been a successful source of recruitment (Minton-Eversole, 2001).
- Due to low wage-and-benefit costs, Jostens Incorporated and Escod Industries are using prison inmates to perform work. In addition to the financial savings to the employer and the work skills learned by the inmates, 20 cents of every dollar earned by inmates is used to pay the cost of incarceration, and another 10 cents goes for victim compensation and support of the inmate's family (Workplace Visions, 1999).
- In 2011, The Ridge House and Safe Harbors in Reno, Nevada, sponsored a job fair attended by 15 employers and 500 ex-convicts who were seeking employment.
- Cub Foods in Illinois hires people with intellectual disabilities to serve as baggers in their grocery stores, and at rug maker Habitat International in Tennessee, over 80% of the employees have a physical or intellectual disability (Andrews, 2005).
- To solve the driver-shortage problem, many trucking companies are trying to hire married couples to be team drivers. To better entice them, trucks are enhanced to include larger sleeping berths and appliances such as microwave ovens (Taylor, 2007b).

Recruiting "Passive" Applicants

With the exception of the direct-mail approach, and at times, the use of executive recruiters, most of the recruiting methods previously discussed in this chapter deal with applicants who are actively seeking work. Because "the best" employees are already employed, recruiters try to find ways to identify this hidden talent and then convince the person to apply for a job with their company.

One such approach is for recruiters to build relationships with professional associations for each of the fields in which they recruit. For example, SIOP would be the professional association for I/O psychologists, the Society for Human Resource Management (SHRM) for HR professionals, and the American Compensation Association (ACA) for compensation professionals. Recruiters would then attend the association's conferences, read their newsletters and magazines, and scan the association's website to identify the "cream of the crop" and then approach those people about applying for a job (Overman, 2007).

An increasingly common method to find these passive applicants is to surf the web, especially blogs and social networking sites such as Facebook and Myspace. A 2010 survey of 600 companies by Jobvite found that the most common social networking sites used by recruiters are LinkedIn (78%), Facebook (54%), Twitter (45%), and YouTube (4%). Only 14% of organizations did not use social networks! As will be discussed in Chapter 5, many employers examine social networking sites to gather information about applicants, but because people put so much information about their lives and careers, recruiters also examine these sites to see if there are people they want to contact about applying for jobs.

Evaluating the Effectiveness of Recruitment Strategies

Considering the number of potential recruitment sources, it is important to determine which source is the best to use. Such an evaluation can be conducted in several ways. As shown in Figure 4.6, one method is to examine the *number of applicants* each recruitment source yields. That is, if a newspaper ad results in 100 applicants and an in-store sign results in 20 applicants, newspaper ads could be considered the better method.

Cost per applicant The amount of money spent on a recruitment campaign divided by the number of people that subsequently apply for jobs as a result of the recruitment campaign.

Using the number of applicants as the measure of success may be appropriate when the emphasis is simply getting enough bodies to fill the job openings, but looking only at the number of applicants does not take into account the cost of the recruitment campaign. Thus, a second method for evaluating the success of a recruitment campaign is to consider the **cost per applicant**, which is determined by dividing the number of applicants by the amount spent for each strategy. Continuing with the previous example, suppose our newspaper ad cost $200 and yielded 10 applicants and

Figure 4.6

Evaluating the Effectiveness of Recruitment Strategies

	Recruitment Sources		
Criterion	Advertisements	Referrals	Walk-ins
Number of applicants	40	30	10
Number qualified	10	15	5
Number hired	2	7	1
Number successful	0	4	1

our in-store sign cost $5 and yielded 2 applicants. The cost per applicant for the newspaper ad would be $20, whereas the cost per applicant for the in-store sign would be just $2.50. Using this method of evaluation, the in-store sign would be best as long as it generated the number of applicants needed by the organization. But if the organization needs to hire 10 new employees and there are only 2 applicants for jobs, this recruitment strategy by itself is not effective.

Although the cost-per-applicant evaluation method is an improvement on the applicant-yield method, it too has a serious drawback. An organization might receive a large number of applicants at a relatively low cost per applicant, but none may be qualified for the job. Therefore, the third and fourth strategies would be to look at either the *number of qualified applicants* or the **cost per qualified applicant**.

Another method for evaluating the effectiveness of various recruitment sources, and perhaps the best one, looks at the number of successful employees generated by each recruitment source. This is an effective method because, as shown in Figure 4.6, every applicant will not be qualified, nor will every qualified applicant become a successful employee.

A final method for evaluating recruitment source effectiveness is to look at the number of minorities and women that applied for the job and were hired. It is not uncommon for large organizations to hold recruiters accountable for their efforts in attracting a diverse applicant pool. Though there has not been much research on this topic, Kirnan, Farley, and Geisinger (1989) found that women and African Americans were more likely to use formal sources of recruitment (e.g., newspaper ads, job fairs) than were men and nonminorities.

To determine differences in recruitment-source effectiveness, a meta-analysis conducted by Zottoli and Wanous (2000) first categorized recruitment methods as being from either an inside source (employee referrals, rehires) or an outside source (advertisements, employment agencies, school placement offices, recruiters). They found that employees recruited through inside sources stayed with the organization longer (higher tenure) and performed better than employees recruited through outside sources. Several theories might explain the superiority of inside sources.

The first theory suggests that rehires or applicants who are referred by other employees receive more accurate information about the job than do employees recruited by other methods (Wanous, 1980). This theory has been supported in research by McManus and Baratta (1992), Conard and Ashworth (1986), and Breaugh and Mann (1984), who found that applicants referred by current employees received not only more information but also more accurate information about the job than did applicants recruited through other channels.

The second theory postulates that differences in recruitment-source effectiveness are the result of different recruitment sources reaching and being used by different types of applicants (Schwab, 1982). Although some research has supported this theory of individual differences (Breaugh & Mann, 1984; Swaroff, Barclay, & Bass, 1985; Taylor & Schmidt, 1983), other research has not (Breaugh, 1981). In fact, no variables have *consistently* distinguished users of one recruitment method from users of another method. Furthermore, the typical person looking for a job uses a wide variety of job search strategies. To underscore this point, think of the part-time jobs you have held. How did you find out about each one? Was it the same method each time? As you can see, it is unlikely that a certain type of person responds only to newspaper ads, while another type goes only to employment agencies.

A third theory might better explain the finding that employee referrals result in greater tenure than do other recruitment strategies. This theory, cited earlier in the

---

Cost per qualified applicant The amount of money spent on a recruitment campaign divided by the number of qualified people that subsequently apply for jobs as a result of the recruitment campaign.

discussion on employee referral programs, has its roots in the literature on interpersonal attraction, which indicates that people tend to be attracted to those who are similar to themselves (Baron & Byrne, 2006). If true—and research strongly suggests it is—then an employee recommending a friend for a job will more than likely recommend one similar to herself. Thus, it would make sense that a person who is happy with her job would recommend a person who, because of her similarity to the incumbent, should also be happy with the job. Likewise, an unhappy employee would recommend similar friends who would also be unhappy and would probably have short tenure with the organization.

This theory has not been heavily researched, but it has been supported by two studies. As discussed earlier, both Aamodt and Carr (1988) and Rupert (1989) found that long-tenured employees referred applicants who, after being hired, stayed on their jobs longer than applicants who were referred by short-tenured employees. No significant differences were found when job performance was examined instead of tenure.

Realistic Job Previews

Realistic job preview (RJP) A method of recruitment in which job applicants are told both the positive and the negative aspects of a job.

Because recruitment sources have only a slight effect on tenure of future employees, using other methods during the recruitment process may be helpful in recruiting applicants who will be successful. One such method is the **realistic job preview (RJP)**. RJPs involve giving an applicant an honest assessment of a job. For example, instead of telling the applicant how much fun she will have working on the assembly line, the recruiter honestly tells her that although the pay is well above average, the work is often boring and there is little chance for advancement.

The logic behind RJPs is that even though telling the truth scares away many applicants (Saks, Wiesner, & Summers, 1996), especially the most qualified ones (Bretz & Judge, 1998), the ones who stay will not be surprised about the job. Because they know what to expect, informed applicants will tend to stay on the job longer than applicants who did not understand the nature of the job. As one would imagine, RJPs have the greatest impact on applicants who have little knowledge or unrealistic expectations about a job or company and who are also in a financial position that they can actually decline a job offer (Breaugh, 2008).

In a meta-analysis of 40 RJP studies, Phillips (1998) found that although RJPs result in lower turnover, higher job satisfaction, and better performance, the size of the effect is rather small. The meta-analysis also suggested that RJPs will be most effective if they are given in an oral rather than a written format, and if they are given to the applicant at the time of the job offer rather than earlier in the recruitment process or after the job offer has been accepted.

In another meta-analysis, Shetzer and Stackman (1991) found that RJPs discussing opportunities for career advancement ($d=.19$) were more effective than ones without a career component ($d=.05$). These two meta-analyses indicate that RJPs, especially if they are conducted orally and contain a career component, may be useful in the recruitment process. To practice developing a recruitment campaign, complete Exercise 4.4 in your workbook.

expectation-lowering procedure (ELP) A form of RJP that lowers an applicant's expectations about the various aspects of the job.

A variation of the RJP is a technique called an **expectation-lowering procedure (ELP)**. Unlike an RJP, which focuses on a particular job, an ELP lowers an applicant's expectations about work and expectations in general (Buckley, Mobbs, Mendoza, Novicevic, Carraher, & Beu, 2002). For example, an RJP might include a statement such as,

"This job is performed in a very small space, in high levels of heat, with few opportunities for social interaction," whereas an ELP might include a statement such as:

"We often start a new job with high expectations, thinking the job will be perfect. As you will discover, no job is perfect and there will be times when you become frustrated by your supervisor or your coworkers. Prior to accepting this job, be sure to give some thought regarding whether this job and our organization will meet the expectations that you have. Also, give some thought to whether your expectations about work are realistic."

Effective Employee Selection Techniques

If the recruitment process was successful, an organization will have several applicants from which to choose. At this point, many techniques can be used to select the best person from this pool of applicants. In the remainder of this chapter, we will discuss the employment interview. In Chapter 5, such methods as reference checks, assessment centers, biodata, psychological tests, and physical ability tests will be discussed.

Effective employee selection systems share three characteristics: They are valid, they reduce the chance of a legal challenge, and they are cost-effective. A valid selection test is one that is based on a job analysis (content validity), predicts work-related behavior (criterion validity), and measures the construct it purports to measure (construct validity). As you will recall from Chapters 2 and 3, selection tests will reduce the chance of a legal challenge if their content appears to be job related (face validity), the questions don't invade an applicant's privacy, and adverse impact is minimized. Ideal selection tests are also cost-effective in terms of the costs to purchase or create, to administer, and to score. With these characteristics in mind, let's begin our discussion of selection techniques with the employment interview.

Employment Interviews

Employment interview A method of selecting employees in which an interviewer asks questions of an applicant and then makes an employment decision based on the answers to the questions as well as the way in which the questions were answered.

Undoubtedly, the most commonly used method to select employees is the **employment interview**. In fact, if you think back to all of the part-time and summer jobs to which you applied, most of those jobs were obtained after you went through an interview process. You might even remember the sweaty palms that went along with the interview. In all likelihood, the interviews you have been through could be labeled "traditional" or "unstructured" and must be distinguished from the structured interviews that will be discussed in this chapter.

Types of Interviews

Perhaps a good place to start a discussion on interviews is to define the various types. Interviews vary on three main factors: structure, style, and medium.

Structure

The structure of an interview is determined by the source of the questions, the extent to which all applicants are asked the same questions, and the structure of the system

Structured interviews Interviews in which questions are based on a job analysis, every applicant is asked the same questions, and there is a standardized scoring system so that identical answers are given identical scores.

Unstructured interview An interview in which applicants are not asked the same questions and in which there is no standard scoring system to score applicant answers.

used to score the answers. A **structured interview** is one in which (1) the source of the questions is a job analysis (job-related questions), (2) all applicants are asked the same questions, and (3) there is a standardized scoring key to evaluate each answer. An **unstructured interview** is one in which interviewers are free to ask anything they want (e.g., Where do you want to be in five years? What was the last book you read?), are not required to have consistency in what they ask of each applicant, and may assign numbers of points at their own discretion. Interviews vary in their structure, and rather than calling interviews structured or unstructured, it might make more sense to use terms such as *highly structured* (all three criteria are met), *moderately structured* (two criteria are met), *slightly structured* (one criterion is met), and *unstructured* (none of the three criteria are met). The research is clear that highly structured interviews are more reliable and valid than interviews with less structure (Huffcutt & Arthur, 1994).

Style

The style of an interview is determined by the number of interviewees and number of interviewers. *One-on-one interviews* involve one interviewer interviewing one applicant. *Serial interviews* involve a series of single interviews. For example, the HR manager might interview an applicant at 9:00 a.m., the department supervisor interviews the applicant at 10:00 a.m., and the vice-president interviews the applicant at 11:00 a.m. *Return* interviews are similar to serial interviews with the difference being a passing of time between the first and subsequent interview. For example, an applicant might be interviewed by the HR manager and then brought back a week later to interview with the vice president. *Panel interviews* have multiple interviewers asking questions and evaluating answers of the same applicant at the same time, and *group interviews* have multiple applicants answering questions during the same interview. Of course one could put together several combinations such as a *serial-panel-group interview*, but life is too short for such nonsense.

Medium

Interviews also differ in the extent to which they are done in person. In *face-to-face interviews*, both the interviewer and the applicant are in the same room. Face-to-face interviews provide a personal setting and allow the participants to use both visual and vocal cues to evaluate information. *Telephone interviews* are often used to screen applicants but do not allow the use of visual cues (not always a bad thing). *Videoconference interviews* are conducted at remote sites. The applicant and the interviewer can hear and see each other, but the setting is not as personal, nor is the image and vocal quality of the interview as sharp as in face-to-face interviews. *Written interviews* involve the applicant answering a series of written questions and then sending the answers back through regular mail or through email.

Advantages of Structured Interviews

Though some HR professionals think they are using a structured interview because they ask the same questions of everyone, it is the job relatedness and standardized scoring that most distinguish the structured from the unstructured interview. The distinction is an important one because meta-analyses (Huffcutt & Arthur, 1994; McDaniel, Whetzel, Schmidt, & Maurer, 1994) clearly indicate that interviews high in structure are more valid than unstructured interviews. This is true even when the interview is conducted over the phone (Schmidt & Rader, 1999). Furthermore, research (Campion, Campion, & Hudson, 1994; Cortina, Goldstein, Payne, Davison, & Gilliland, 2000) indicates that structured interviews can add predictive power (called *incremental validity*) to the use of cognitive ability tests.

From a legal standpoint, structured interviews are viewed more favorably by the courts than are unstructured interviews (Williamson, Campion, Malos, Roehling, & Campion, 1997). There are two probable reasons for this. One, structured interviews are based on a job analysis. A review of interview research by Campion, Palmer, and Campion (1997) concluded that interviews based on a job analysis will be more valid and legally defensible than ones not based on a job analysis. Two, structured interviews result in substantially lower adverse impact than do unstructured interviews (Huffcutt & Roth, 1998). In part, this is because unstructured interviews concentrate on general intelligence, education, and training, whereas structured interviews tap job knowledge, job skills, applied mental skills, and interpersonal skills (Huffcutt, Conway, Roth, & Stone, 2001). A further advantage to structured interviews is that the racial and gender similarity issues mentioned previously as a problem with unstructured interviews do not appear to greatly affect structured interviews (Buckley, Jackson, Bolino, Veres, & Feild, 2007; McCarthy, Van Iddekinge, & Campion, 2010).

Although structured interviews are considered superior to unstructured ones, applicants perceive structured interviews to be more difficult (Gilmore, 1989). Furthermore, because the interview is so structured, applicants may feel that they did not have the chance to tell the interviewer everything they wanted to (Gilliland & Steiner, 1997).

Problems with Unstructured Interviews

Why does the unstructured interview seem *not* to predict future employee performance? Researchers have investigated this question for several years and have identified eight factors that contribute to the poor reliability and validity of the unstructured interview: poor intuitive ability, lack of job relatedness, primacy effects, contrast effects, negative-information bias, interviewer-interviewee similarity, interviewee appearance, and nonverbal cues.

Poor Intuitive Ability

Interviewers often base their hiring decisions on "gut reactions," or intuition. However, people are not good at using intuition to predict behavior: research indicates that human intuition and judgment are inaccurate predictors of a variety of factors ranging from future employee success to the detection of deception (Aamodt, 2008). And contrary to what many HR professionals think, there are no individual differences in interviewers' ability to predict future performance (Pulakos, Schmitt, Whitney, & Smith, 1996). That is, research does not support the idea that some interviewers are able to predict behavior, whereas others are not. Divorce rates provide an excellent example of this poor predictive ability. Couples involved in romantic relationships spend, on average, two years together before getting married. In spite of this time together, 50% of all marriages fail—an important reason for which is lack of compatibility. So, if after two years of "interviewing" a prospective spouse, we make the wrong choice 50% of the time, is it logical to assume that after spending only 15 minutes interviewing an applicant we can predict how well she will get along with the varied members of an organization?

1. Why should I hire you?
2. What do you see yourself doing five years from now?
3. What do you consider your greatest strengths and weaknesses?
4. How would you describe yourself?
5. What college subjects did you like best? Least?
6. What do you know about our company?
7. Why did you decide to seek a position with the company?
8. Why did you leave your last job?
9. What do you want to earn five years from now?
10. What do you really want to do in life?

Figure 4.7

Commonly Asked Unstructured Employment Interview Questions

Lack of Job Relatedness

Research by Bolles (2011) has identified the most common questions asked by interviewers. As you can see in Figure 4.7, these questions are not related to any particular job. Furthermore, the proper answers to these questions have not been empirically determined. Research has shown which answers personnel managers prefer (Bolles, 2011), but preference for an answer does not imply that it will actually predict future performance on the job. As discussed earlier in this and preceding chapters, information that is used to select employees *must* be job related if it is to have any chance of predicting future employee performance. In addition to not being job related, many questions asked by interviewers are illegal (e.g., "Are you married?" or "Do you have any health problems?"). Interestingly, most interviewers who ask illegal questions know that they are illegal (Dew & Steiner, 1997).

Primacy Effects

Primacy effect The fact that information presented early in an interview carries more weight than information presented later.

The research on the importance of **primacy effects** or "first impressions" in the interview is mixed. Some research indicates that information presented prior to the interview (Dougherty, Turban, & Callender, 1994) or early in the interview carries more weight than does information presented later in the interview (Farr, 1973). Furthermore, it has been suggested that interviewers decide about a candidate within the first few minutes of an interview (Dessler, 2002; Otting, 2004). In fact, of a group of personnel professionals, 74% said they can make a decision within the first five minutes of an interview (Buckley & Eder, 1989), and three studies (Barrick, Swider, & Stewart, 2010; Giluk, Stewart, & Shaffer; 2008; Stewart, Dustin, Shaffer, & Giluk, 2008) found significant correlations between interviewer ratings made after a few minutes of rapport building and the final interview rating.

However, more recent research (Raymark, Keith, Odle-Dusseau, Giumetti, Brown, & Van Iddekinge, 2008) found that only 5% of interviewers made up their mind in the first minute and only 31% within the first five minutes. Thus, most interviewers take at least five minutes to make their decisions. As one would imagine, the time taken by interviewers to make a decision was influenced by several factors, such as the degree to which the interview is structured, the behavior of the interviewee, and the interview dimensions being tapped.

To reduce potential primacy effects, interviewers are advised to make repeated judgments throughout the interview rather than one overall judgment at the end of the interview. That is, the interviewer might rate the applicant's response after each question or series of questions rather than waiting until the end of the interview to make a single rating or judgment.

Contrast Effects

Contrast effect When the performance of one applicant affects the perception of the performance of the next applicant.

With the **contrast effect**, the interview performance of one applicant may affect the interview score given to the next applicant (Oduwole, Morgan, & Bernardo, 2000; Wexley, Sanders, & Yukl, 1973). If a terrible applicant precedes an average applicant, the interview score for the average applicant will be higher than if no applicant or a very qualified applicant preceded her. In other words, an applicant's performance is judged in relation to the performance of previous interviewees. Thus, it may be advantageous to be interviewed immediately after someone who has done poorly.

Research by Wexley, Yukl, Kovacs, and Sanders (1972) found that interviewers who were trained to be aware of the occurrence of contrast effects were able to reduce them. Other researchers (Landy & Bates, 1973), however, have questioned whether the contrast effect actually plays a significant role in the interview process.

Negative-Information Bias

Negative information bias The fact that negative information receives more weight in an employment decision than does positive information.

Negative information apparently weighs more heavily than positive information (Bocketti, Hamilton, & Maser, 2000; Rowe, 1989). **Negative-information bias** seems to occur only when interviewers aren't aware of job requirements (Langdale & Weitz, 1973). It seems to support the observation that most job applicants are afraid of being honest in interviews for fear that one negative response will cost them their job opportunities.

This lack of honesty may be especially evident in the interview, where the face-to-face nature of the process increases the odds that an applicant would respond in such a way as to look better to the interviewer. In a study conducted to increase the honesty of applicants during the interview process, Martin and Nagao (1989) had applicants interview for a job in one of four conditions. In the first, applicants read written interview questions and then wrote their responses to the questions. In the second condition, applicants were "interviewed" by a computer. In the third condition, applicants were interviewed face-to-face by an interviewer who behaved warmly; and in the fourth condition, applicants were interviewed by an interviewer who seemed cold. As expected, Martin and Nagao found that applicants were more honest in reporting their GPAs and their SAT scores under the nonsocial conditions that involved paper-and-pencil and computer interviewing. Thus, one might increase the accuracy of information obtained in the interview by reducing social pressure and using written or computerized interviews.

Interviewer-Interviewee Similarity

In general, research suggests that an interviewee will receive a higher score (Howard & Ferris, 1996) if he or she is similar to the interviewer in terms of personality (Foster, 1990), attitude (Frank & Hackman, 1975), gender (Foster, Dingman, Muscolino, & Jankowski, 1996), or race (McFarland, Ryan, Sacco, & Kriska, 2004; Prewett-Livingston et al., 1996). However, a study by Sacco, Scheu, Ryan, and Schmitt (2003) found that the method used to analyze interview data is a factor in whether similarity matters. Sacco et al. found that when using a traditional approach (d scores) to analyze their findings, interviewers gave higher ratings to same-race interviewees. When a more sophisticated method was used (hierarchical linear models), neither racial nor sex similarity affected interview scores. Thus, further research is needed to accurately determine the importance of similarity in unstructured interview decisions.

Interviewee Appearance

Meta-analyses (Barrick, Shaffer, & DeGrassi, 2009; Hosada, Stone-Romero, & Coats, 2003; Steggert, Chrisman, & Haap, 2006) indicate that, in general, physically attractive applicants have an advantage in interviews over less attractive applicants, and applicants who dress professionally receive higher interview scores than do more poorly dressed applicants. This attractiveness bias occurred for men and women and for traditionally masculine and feminine job types.

The appearance bias extends to weight, as research (Kutcher & Bragger, 2004; Pingitore, Dugoni, Tindale, & Spring, 1994) indicates that obese applicants receive lower interview scores than their leaner counterparts. Interviewee appearance, it seems, is a potent hiring factor (Posthuma, Morgeson, & Campion, 2002).

Nonverbal Cues

A meta-analysis by Barrick et al. (2009) found that the use of appropriate **nonverbal communication** is highly correlated with interview scores. Appropriate nonverbal cues include such things as smiling and making appropriate eye contact (Levine & Feldman, 2002). Howard and Ferris (1996) found a significant relationship between use of appropriate nonverbal behaviors and interviewer perceptions of interviewee competence. Not surprisingly, meta-analysis results indicate that structured interviews are not as affected by nonverbal cues as are unstructured interviews (Barrick et al., 2008). Meta-analysis results also indicate that the appropriate use of such verbal cues as tone, pitch, speech rate, and pauses is also related to higher interview scores (Barrick et al., 2008).

Although many more studies and variables could be listed, this discussion shows that the interview contains many sources of bias that are not job related. Remember that one of the major purposes of the employment interview is to determine which applicant will be the most successful in performing a job. To determine this, decisions must be based on ability to do the job and not on such variables as physical attractiveness and eye contact.

Creating a Structured Interview

To create a structured interview, information about the job is obtained (job analysis) and questions are created that are designed to find out the extent to which applicants' skills and experiences match those needed to successfully perform the job. These questions are incorporated into an interview form used by all interviewers for all applicants. Examples of good and bad answers are located next to the questions to help an interviewer score the answers given by applicants.

Determining the KSAOs to Tap in the Interview

The first step in creating a structured interview is to conduct a thorough job analysis and write a detailed job description. As discussed in Chapter 2, the job analysis should identify the tasks performed, the conditions under which they are performed, and the competencies needed to perform the tasks. The second step is to determine the best way to measure an applicant's ability to perform each of the tasks identified in the job analysis. Some of the competencies can be appropriately measured in an interview; others will need to be tapped through such methods as psychological tests, job samples, assessment centers, references, background checks, and training and experience ratings (these other methods will be thoroughly discussed in Chapter 5). For example, suppose a job description for a receptionist indicated that the primary tasks included typing reports, filing correspondence, answering the phone, and dealing with people visiting the organization. Typing ability might best be measured with a typing test, filing correspondence with a filing test, answering the phone with a job sample, and customer service with an interview question. The important point here is that not every competency can or should be tapped in an interview. To practice this process, use the job description in Chapter 2 (Table 2.1) to complete Exercise 4.5 in your workbook and determine the competencies you would tap in an interview.

Creating Interview Questions

As shown in Figure 4.8, there are six types of interview questions: clarifiers, disqualifiers, skill-level determiners, past-focused, future-focused, and organizational fit. **Clarifiers** allow the interviewer to clarify information in the résumé, cover letter, and application, fill in gaps, and obtain other necessary information. Because each applicant's résumé and cover letter are unique, specific clarifiers are not standard across applicants. For example, an interviewer may need to ask one applicant to explain what she won the McArthur Award for and another applicant what she was doing during a two-year gap between jobs. **Disqualifiers** are questions that must be answered a particular way or the applicant is disqualified. For example, if a job requires that employees work on weekends, a disqualifier might be, "Are you available to work on weekends?" If the answer is no, the applicant will not get the job.

Skill-level determiners tap an interviewee's level of expertise. For example, if an applicant says she is proficient in Microsoft Word, an interviewer might ask some questions about the word processing program. If an applicant claims to be fluent in Spanish, the interviewer might want to ask her a few questions in Spanish.

Future-focused questions, also called **situational questions**, ask an applicant what she would do in a particular situation. As shown in Table 4.1, the first step in creating situational questions is to collect critical incidents, a technique you learned in Chapter 2. These incidents are then rewritten into questions that will be used during the interview. It is important that these questions can be answered with the applicant's current knowledge. That is, asking police applicants situational questions in which they would need knowledge of police procedures would not be appropriate

Clarifier A type of structured interview question that clarifies information on the résumé or application.

Disqualifier A type of structured interview question in which a wrong answer will disqualify the applicant from further consideration.

Skill-level determiner A type of structured-interview question designed to tap an applicant's knowledge or skill.

Future-focused question A type of structured interview question in which applicants are given a situation and asked how they would handle it.

Situational question A structured-interview technique in which applicants are presented with a series of situations and asked how they would handle each one.

Question Type	Example
Clarifier	I noticed a three-year gap between two of your jobs. Could you tell me about that? You were a bench hand at AT&T. What is that?
Disqualifier	Can you work overtime without notice? Do you have a valid driver's license?
Skill-level determiner	Several months after installing a computer network, the client calls and says that nothing will print on the printer. What could be going wrong?
Past-focused (behavioral)	When you are dealing with customers, it is inevitable that you are going to get someone angry. Tell us about a time when a customer was angry with you. What did you do to fix the situation?
Future-focused (situational)	Imagine that you told a client that you would be there at 10:00 a.m. It is now 10:30 and there is no way you will be finished with your current job until 11:30. You are supposed to meet with another client for lunch at noon and then be at another job at 1:15 p.m. How would you handle this situation?
Organizational fit	What type of work pace is best for you? Describe your experience working with a culturally diverse group of people.

Figure 4.8

Types of Structured Interview Questions

Table 4.1   Creating Situational Interview Questions

The Critical Incident

A customer entered a bank and began yelling about how the bank had messed up his account. He became so angry that he began to swear, saying that he would not leave the bank until the problem was solved. Unfortunately, the computer was down and the teller could not access the needed information.

The Question

You are working as a teller and have a long line of waiting customers. One customer runs to the front of the line and yells that he bounced a check and was charged $20, which caused other checks to bounce. He then swears at you and tells you that he will not leave until the problem is solved. You are unable to check on his account because the information is at another branch. What would you do?

The Benchmark Answers

5   Because I do not have the information and the line is long, I would call my supervisor and have her talk to the customer in her office away from everyone else.

4   While trying to calm him down, I would call my supervisor.

3   I would try to calm him down and explain to him that the computer is down.

2   I would explain that I cannot help him because the computer is down, and ask him to come back later.

1   I would tell him to get to the end of the line and wait his turn.

---

because they won't learn this information until they graduate from the police academy. After creating the questions, the next step is to create a scoring key. This step will be discussed later in the chapter.

Past-focused question A type of structured-interview question that taps an applicant's experience.

Past-focused questions, sometimes referred to as **patterned behavior description interviews (PBDIs)**, differ from situational interview questions by focusing on *previous* behavior rather than future intended behavior. That is, applicants are asked to provide specific examples of how they demonstrated job-related skills in previous jobs (Janz, Hellervik, & Gilmore, 1986). Although future-focused and past-focused interview questions have different orientations, interviewees who do well on one type typically do well on the other (Campion et al., 1994; Cohen & Scott, 1996). However, scores on past-focused questions are better predictors of performance in higher-level positions than are future-focused questions (Huffcutt, Roth, Conway, & Klehe, 2004; Huffcutt, Weekley, Wiesner, DeGroot, & Jones, 2001; Pulakos & Schmitt, 1995).

Patterned-behavior description interview (PBDI) A structured interview in which the questions focus on behavior in previous jobs.

Rather than trying to predict future performance, **organizational-fit questions** tap the extent to which an applicant will fit into the culture of an organization or with the leadership style of a particular supervisor. For example, some organizations are very policy oriented, whereas others encourage employees to use their initiative. Some supervisors are very task oriented, whereas others are more person oriented. The idea behind organizational-fit questions is to make sure that the applicant's personality and goals are consistent with those of the organization. To practice creating interview questions, complete Exercise 4.6 in your workbook.

Organizational-fit questions A type of structured-interview question that taps how well an applicant's personality and values will fit with the organizational culture.

Creating a Scoring Key for Interview Answers

Once interview questions are created, the next step is to create a key to score applicants' answers to the questions. Though answers to some questions can be scored as being right or wrong (e.g., "Do you have to pay an employee overtime for working over 8 hours in a day?"), as shown in Table 4.2, there are two main methods of scoring most answers: typical-answer approach and key-issues approach.

Table 4.2   Scoring Examples

Typical-Answer Approach

1   I would tell him to get to the end of the line and wait his turn.

2   I would explain to him that I cannot help him because the computer is down, and ask him to come back later.

3   I would try to calm him down and explain to him that the computer is down.

4   I would call my supervisor.

5   Because I do not have the information and the line is long, I would call my supervisor and have her talk to the customer in her office away from everyone else.

Key-Issues Approach

_____   Acknowledged the long line and the concern for other customers

_____   Recognized the need to calm the customer

_____   Recognized the need to get the customer away from the other customers

_____   Recognized that help could not be immediately given because the computer was down

_____   Was not confrontational with the customer

Right/Wrong Approach. Some interview questions, especially skill-level determiners, can be scored simply on the basis of whether the answer given was correct or incorrect. For example, consider the question "As a server, can you give a glass of wine to a 16-year-old if his parents are present and give permission?" If the interviewee answers no, she would get a point for a correct answer. If she answers yes, she would not get a point. If the question type being asked was a disqualifier (e.g., Can you work weekends?), the wrong answer would actually disqualify the individual from further consideration rather than merely result in no points being awarded.

Typical-answer approach A method of scoring interview answers that compares an applicant's answer with benchmark answers.

Benchmark answers Standard answers to interview questions, the quality of which has been agreed on by job experts.

Typical-Answer Approach. The idea behind the **typical-answer approach** is to create a list of all possible answers to each question, have subject-matter experts (SMEs) rate the favorableness of each answer, and then use these ratings to serve as benchmarks for each point on a five-point scale. Though some scoring keys have only one benchmark answer for each point on the scale, research by Buchner (1990) indicates that increasing the number of **benchmark answers** will greatly increase the scoring reliability. Because the number of possible answers to any question is probably finite, it might be a good idea at this stage to brainstorm all possible answers to a question and then benchmark each of the answers. This approach would result in 10 or so benchmarked answers per question rather than the traditional 5.

Key-issues approach A method of scoring interview answers that provides points for each part of an answer that matches the scoring key.

Key-Issues Approach. A problem with the typical-answer approach is that there are many possible answers to a question, and applicants often provide answers that could fit parts of several different benchmarks. To correct this problem, the **key-issues approach** can be used. In this approach, SMEs create a list of key issues they think should be included in the perfect answer. For each key issue that is included, the interviewee gets a point. The key issues can also be weighted so that the most important issues get more points than the less important issues.

Psychologist Pete DiVasto uses the key-issues approach when he interviews applicants for law enforcement positions. In one of his questions, he asks applicants to imagine that they are a police officer and have received a call about a possible break-in at a store. Upon arrival, the officer notices the following: a police car in the parking lot with its lights flashing, an officer on the ground next to the police car, an alarm going off in the store, and a person running from the store. DiVasto then asks the applicant what he or she would do in that situation. The key issues in a good answer include indicating that a cop is hurt and needs help, an understanding that the person running could be dangerous but could also be a victim, the realization that backup is needed, and articulation of a good rationale for choosing to either help the cop first or attend to the person running.

When scoring interviews, it is appropriate to have a system to evaluate an applicant's nonverbal cues, especially when the job involves interpersonal skills. Such scoring is supported by research demonstrating that an applicant's nonverbal cues in interviews can predict job performance (Barrick et al., 2008; Burnett & Motowidlo, 1998; DeGroot & Motowidlo, 1999). To practice scoring interviews, complete Exercise 4.7 in your workbook.

Conducting the Structured Interview

Though it is common to use a panel interview, research suggests that interviews will best predict performance when one trained interviewer is used for all applicants (Huffcutt & Woehr, 1999). The first step in conducting the interview is to build rapport; do not begin asking questions until applicants have had time to "settle their nerves." Building rapport is an important step, as it results in the applicant feeling more positive about the interview (Chapman & Zweig, 2005).

Once an applicant feels at ease, set the agenda for the interview by explaining the process. Most applicants have not been through a structured interview, so it is important to explain the types of questions that will be asked and point out that each interviewer will be taking notes and scoring the answers immediately after the interviewee has responded. After the agenda has been established, ask the interview questions. You may want to have only one person ask all of the questions or have each panel member ask some questions. It is important to score each answer after it has been given. Once the questions have been asked, provide information about the job and the organization. Such information might include salary and benefits, the job duties, opportunities for advancement, a history of the organization, and so on. Then, answer any questions the applicant might have. It is a good idea at this point to say something like, "We have asked you a lot of questions but may not have asked you about things you want to tell us. Is there any information you would like to tell us that we did not ask about?" End the interview on a pleasant note by complimenting the interviewee ("It was a pleasure meeting you") and letting her know when you will be contacting the applicant about job offers. At the conclusion of the interview, the scores from the questions are summed and the resulting figure is the applicant's interview score.

Job Search Skills

Though the orientation of this and the next chapter is on selecting employees, it is important that you master the skills necessary to obtain a job. The following three sections provide advice on how to interview, write a cover letter, and write a résumé.

Successfully Surviving the Interview Process

Even though the unstructured employment interview has many problems, the odds are high that a person being considered for a job will undergo such an interview. Research and experience both indicate that applicants can take several steps to increase their interview scores. One of the most important of these steps is to obtain training on how to interview. Research by Maurer and his colleagues (Maurer, Solamon, Andrews, & Troxtel, 2001; Maurer, Solamon, & Troxtel, 1998) has shown that such training can increase an applicant's score on structured interviews. Receiving interview training and practicing interviewing skills are good ways to reduce interview anxiety. Reducing anxiety is important, as research indicates that there is a negative correlation between interviewee anxiety and interview performance (McCarthy & Goffin, 2004; McCarthy & Saks, 2008).

Scheduling the Interview

Contrary to advice given in popular magazines, neither day of week nor time of day affect interview scores (Aamodt, 1986; Willihnganz & Myers, 1993). What will affect the score, however, is *when* applicants arrive for the interview. If they arrive late, the score will be drastically lower (Lantz, 2001). In fact, in a study I conducted (Aamodt, 1986), no applicant who arrived late was hired. No differences, however, have been found in interview scores based on whether an applicant arrives on time or five or ten minutes early. Therefore, the interview can be scheduled for any time of the day or week, but the applicant must not be late!

Before the Interview

Learn about the company (Williams, 2005). Recall from Figure 4.7 that one of the most commonly asked unstructured interview questions ("What do you know about our company?") is used to determine the applicant's knowledge of the organization. Not only does this advice make sense, but research has found that an applicant's knowledge significantly correlates (.32) with the interview rating (Aamodt, 1986) and that interview preparation significantly correlates with being asked back for a second interview (Caldwell & Burger, 1998). Organizations are especially impressed if an applicant knows its products and services, future needs, major problems faced, and philosophy or mission. Statistics such as market share and sales volume are not as valuable (Gardner, 1994).

A former student of mine tells the story of an interview for a managerial position that she had with Allstate Insurance. The night before the interview, she read all the available information on Allstate on the Internet. During the interview, she was asked why she wanted to work for Allstate. She replied that she was active in the community and was attracted to Allstate because of its "Helping Hands" community program—which she had read about the night before. The interviewer was greatly impressed and spent the next 10 minutes describing the program and its importance. The interview was a success in part because the applicant had done her homework. To see how the Career Services Center at your university can help you prepare for interviews, complete the Finding Career Resources Exercise (4.8) in your workbook.

On the day of the interview, dress neatly and professionally, and adjust your style as necessary to fit the situation (Williams, 2005). Avoid wearing accessories such as flashy large earrings and brightly colored ties. Hair should be worn conservatively— avoid "big hair" and colors such as purple and green (impersonating a member of MTV's Jersey Shore is not a good interview strategy).

During the Interview

Most suggestions about how best to behave in an interview take advantage of the interviewer biases discussed in this chapter. Nonverbal behaviors should include a firm handshake, eye contact, smiling, and head nodding. Desired verbal behaviors include asking questions, subtly pointing out how you are similar to the interviewer, not asking about the salary, not speaking slowly, and not hesitating before answering questions (DeGroot & Motowidlo, 1999). Keep in mind that first impressions are the most important.

As a method of saving travel expenses associated with face-to-face interviews, many organizations interview applicants through a videoconference in which an applicant goes to a local FedEx Office (or similar location) or gets onto Skype from their own home and is interviewed by employers hundreds or thousands of miles away. Although the previous interview advice still holds for videoconference interviews, some additional advice includes speaking loudly, keeping hand and arm movements to a minimum, looking directly at the camera, and dressing in conservative, solid colors.

After the Interview

Immediately following the interview, write a brief letter thanking the interviewer for her time. Although research evidence supports all of the suggestions offered in this section, no research has been done on the effects of thank-you letters. Still, this nice touch certainly cannot hurt. To help you prepare for the employment interview, complete the Surviving the Employment Interview Exercise (4.9) in your workbook.

Writing Cover Letters

Cover letter A letter that accompanies a résumé or job application.

Cover letters tell an employer that you are enclosing your résumé and would like to apply for a job. Cover letters should never be longer than one page. As shown in the sample cover letters in Figures 4.9 and 4.10, cover letters contain a salutation, four basic paragraphs, and a closing signature.

Salutation

If possible, get the name of the person to whom you want to direct the letter. If you aren't sure of the person's name, call the company and simply ask for the name of the person (have it spelled) to whom you should send your résumé. If the first name leaves doubt about the person's gender (e.g., Kim, Robin, Paige), ask if the person is male or female so that you can properly address the letter to Mr. Smith or Ms. Smith. Do not refer to the person by his or her first name (e.g., Dear Sarah). If you can't get the person's name, a safe salutation is "Dear Human Resource Director." Avoid phrases such as "Dear Sir or Madam" (unless the company is a "house of ill repute") or "To Whom It May Concern" (it doesn't concern me).

Paragraphs

The opening paragraph should be one or two sentences long and communicate three pieces of information: the fact that your résumé is enclosed, the name of the job you are applying for, and how you know about the job opening (such as a newspaper ad or from a friend). The second paragraph states that you are qualified for the job and provides about three reasons why. This paragraph should be only four or five sentences in length and should not rehash the content of your résumé. The third paragraph

April 18, 2012

Mr. John Smith
Alco, Inc.
217 West Street
Johnson, VA 24132

Dear Mr. Smith:

Enclosed is a copy of my résumé. Please consider me for the position of welder that was advertised in the *Roanoke Times and World News*.

For several reasons, I believe that I am qualified for your position. First, I have six years of welding experience in an industrial setting. Second, I am a very dependable worker, as shown by the fact that I have missed only two days of work in the last five years. Finally, I am available to work any shift at any of your three plants.

I look forward to hearing from you. I can best be reached after 3:00 p.m. on weekdays and anytime on weekends.

Sincerely,

Andrew S. Jones

Figure 4.9

Example of a Cover Letter

explains why you are interested in the particular company to which you are applying. The final paragraph closes your letter and provides information on how you can best be reached. Though your phone number will be on your résumé, this paragraph is a good place to tell the employer the best days and times to reach you.

Signature

Above your signature, use words such as "cordially" or "sincerely." "Yours truly" is not advised, and words such as "Love," "Peace," or "Hugs and snuggles" are strongly discouraged. Personally sign each cover letter; and type your name, address, and phone number below your signature.

HR professional GeGe Beall provides job applicants with the following tips about cover letters:

- Avoid sounding desperate and don't beg (I really need a job bad! Please, please, please hire me!).
- Avoid grammar and spelling errors. Employers view cover letters and résumés as examples of the best work applicants can produce. If your cover letter contains errors, an employer will be concerned about the quality of your regular work.
- Avoid officious words or phrases. Don't use a 25-cent word when a nickel word will do. Not only will employers be unimpressed by a large vocabulary, but applicants using "big words" often misuse them. As an example, one applicant tried to describe his work productivity by saying that his

July 15, 2012

Ms. Maria Duffie, Director
Human Resource Department
Raynes Cosmetics, Inc.
69 Beall Avenue
Amityville, NY 00312

Dear Ms. Duffie:

Enclosed is a copy of my résumé. Please consider me for the position of sales representative that was adver-tised this past Sunday in the *Washington Post.* As you can see below, my qualifications are a good match for the requirements stated in your advertisement.

Your Requirements	My Qualifications
Bachelor's degree	B.A. in marketing from Radford University
Two years of sales experience	Five years of sales experience
History of success in sales	Received three sales awards at L.L. Bean
Strong clerical skills	A.A.S. in secretarial science
	Three years of clerical experience
	55 words per minute typing speed

I am especially interested in working for your company because I have used your products for over ten years and thus am familiar with both your product line and the high quality of your cosmetics.

I am looking forward to hearing from you. Please feel free to call me at home after 6:00 p.m. or at work from 8:00 a.m. until 5:00 p.m. Because L.L. Bean is downsizing, my employer will not mind your calling me at work.

Sincerely,

Mable Leane

Mable Leane
2345 Revlon Blvd.
Avon, VA 24132
Home: (540) 555–5678
Work: (540) 555–7676
mimi@aol.com

Figure 4.10

Example of a
Customized Cover
Letter

writings were "voluptuous," rather than "voluminous," as we think he meant to say.

- Don't discuss personal circumstances such as "I find myself looking for a job because I am recently divorced." Employers are interested in only your qualifications.
- If possible, tailor your letter to each company. Standard cover letters are efficient but not as effective as those written specifically for each job you are applying for.
- Don't write your cover letter on the stationery of your current employer. Ensure that you have used the correct name of the organization throughout the letter. It is not uncommon when sending out large numbers of cover let-ters to change the company name in the address but forget to change it in the body of the letter.

Writing a Résumé

Résumés are summaries of an applicant's professional and educational background. Although résumés are commonly requested by employers, little is known about their value in predicting employee performance. Some studies have found that when an interviewer reads a résumé before interviewing an applicant, the validity of the employment interview may actually be *reduced* (Dipboye, Stramler, & Fontenelle, 1984; Phillips & Dipboye, 1989). Beyond these studies, however, it is unclear how much predictive value, if any, résumés have.

Résumés may not predict performance partly because they are intended to be advertisements for an applicant. Companies that specialize in résumé design openly brag about their ability to "make your strengths more obvious and your weaknesses hard to find." As a result, many résumés contain inaccurate information. In a review of surveys on résumé fraud, Aamodt and Williams (2005) found that the median estimate was that 25% of résumés contained inaccurate information.

Contrary to popular belief, there is no one best way to write a résumé. Because people have such different backgrounds, a format that works for one individual may not work for another. Therefore, this section will provide only general advice about writing a résumé; the rest is up to you.

Views of Résumés

Résumés can be viewed in one of two ways: as a history of your life or as an advertisement of your skills. Résumés written as a history of one's life tend to be long and to list every job ever worked, as well as personal information such as hobbies, marital status, and personal health. Résumés written as an advertisement of skills tend to be shorter and contain only information that is both positive and relevant to a job seeker's desired career. This latter view of résumés is the most commonly held today.

Characteristics of Effective Résumés

One of the most frustrating aspects of writing a résumé is that asking 100 people for advice results in 100 different opinions. However, though there are many *preferences*, there are really only three *rules* that must be followed in writing résumés:

1. *The résumé must be attractive and easy to read.* To achieve this, try to leave at least a 1-inch margin on all sides, and allow plenty of white space; that is, do not "pack" information into the résumé. An undergraduate student of mine came to me with the "great idea" of typing his résumé onto a legal-sized sheet and then using a photocopy machine to reduce the size to regular paper with a 1-inch margin. Although this technique may look nice, it is probably not advisable because you are still "packing" information into a small space, and personnel directors do not spend much time reading résumés. A résumé can have great content, but if the "package" is not attractive, few employers will want to read it. This rule is hardly surprising, as physical attractiveness provides a first impression for many activities, such as interviewing, dating, and purchasing products. White is probably the best paper color, as it scans, copies, and faxes more clearly than other colors.

2. *The résumé cannot contain typing, spelling, grammatical, or factual mistakes.* When Walter Pierce, Jr., was a personnel officer for Norfolk Southern Corporation, his boss received a résumé from an excellent applicant who was applying for a job as a computer programmer. Even though the applicant had

outstanding credentials, the personnel director would not even offer him an interview, because the applicant had misspelled two words on his résumé. A similar story is told by Dick Williams, general manager of N & W Credit Union. He once received two cover letters stapled together—both referring to the résumé that wasn't there. To make matters worse, four words were misspelled. I could tell you more horror stories, but the point should be clear: Do not make any careless mistakes!

3. *The résumé should make the applicant look as qualified as possible—without lying.* This is an important rule in determining what information should be included. If including hobbies, summer jobs, and lists of courses will make you look more qualified for *this particular job*, then by all means, include them.

If a résumé follows the above three rules—it looks nice, it doesn't contain mistakes, and it makes the applicant look as good as possible—then it is an effective résumé. Opinions to the contrary (such as "use boldface type instead of underlining" or "outline your duties instead of putting them in a paragraph") probably represent differences in individual preferences rather than any major problem with the résumé.

Types of Résumé

There are three main types of résumé: chronological, functional, and psychological. As shown in Figure 4.11, **chronological résumés** list previous jobs in order from the most to the least recent. This type of résumé is useful for applicants whose previous jobs were related to their future plans and whose work histories do not contain gaps.

The **functional résumé**, as shown in Figure 4.12, organizes jobs based on the skills required to perform them rather than the order in which they were worked. Functional résumés are especially useful for applicants who are either changing careers or have gaps in their work histories. The problem with this type of résumé is that it takes employers longer to read and comprehend than the other résumé types—this problem makes functional résumés the least popular with employers (Toth, 1993).

The **psychological résumé** is the style I prefer, as it contains the strengths of both the chronological and functional styles and is based on sound psychological theory and research. As shown in Figure 4.13, the résumé should begin with a short summary of your strengths. This section takes advantage of the impression-formation principles of *priming* (preparing the reader for what is to come), *primacy* (early impressions are most important), and *short-term memory limits* (the list should not be longer than seven items).

The next section of the résumé should contain information about either your education or your experience—whichever is strongest for you. The design of the education section is intended to provide an organizational framework that will make it easier for the reader to remember the contents. In deciding which information to put into these two sections, three impression-management rules should be used: relevance, unusualness, and positivity. If information is *relevant* to your desired career, it probably should be included. For example, you might mention that you have two children if you are applying for a position in day care or elementary school teaching, but not if you are applying for a job involving a lot of travel. How far back should one go in listing jobs? Using the principle of relevance, the answer would be far enough back to include all relevant jobs. It is certainly acceptable to list hobbies if they are relevant.

Unusual information should be included when possible, as people pay more attention to it than to typical information. A problem for college seniors is that their

CHRISTOPHER R. MILLER

812 Main Street, Gainesville, FL 32789   (904) 645–1001
s8281@mgamail.net

Objective	Entry-level management position in financial services.
Education	B.S., University of Florida, May 2009
	Major: Business Administration
	GPA: 3.43/4.0
	Minor: Information Systems
	Business-Related Courses: Accounting, Money & Banking, Principles of Marketing, Economics, Statistics
Professional Experience	July 2013–Present
	Assistant Manager. TCBY Yogurt, Gainesville, FL
	Responsible for posting daily receipts and making bank deposits. Further responsible for supervising and scheduling counter personnel, writing progress reports, and handling employee disputes.
	August 2012–July 2013
	Cashier/Customer Service, TCBY Yogurt, Gainesville, FL
	Responsible for assisting customers promptly and courteously, maintaining a balanced cash drawer, and cleaning work station.
	May 2011–August 2012
	Bank Teller: Barnett Bank, Gainesville, FL
	Responsible for assisting and advising customers with financial transactions. Cash drawer balanced 99% of the time. Received excellent performance ratings.
	August 2010–May 2011
	Waiter, Shakers Restaurant, Gainesville, FL
	Responsible for taking food and drink orders from customers and serving them courteously and efficiently. Worked in a high-volume, fast-paced environment.
Activities	Member of Phi Kappa Phi Honor Society
	Member of Phi Beta Lambda Business Organization
	Vice President, Kappa Alpha Pi Social Fraternity
	Member of Circle K Service Organization
	Participated in Intramural Football

Figure 4.11
Chronological Résumé

résumés look identical to those of their classmates. That is, most business majors take the same classes, belong to the same clubs, and have had similar part-time jobs. To stand out from other graduates, an applicant needs something unusual, such as an internship, an interesting hobby, or an unusual life experience (e.g., spent a year in Europe, rode a bike across the country).

Though it is advisable to have unusual information, the information must also be *positive*. It probably would not be a good idea to list unusual information such as "I've been arrested more times than anyone in my class" or "I enjoy bungee jumping without cords." The unacceptability of these two examples is obvious, and few applicants would make the mistake of actually placing such information on their résumés; however, more subtle items can have the same effect. For example, suppose you enjoy hunting and are

MATTHEW F. JOHNSON

818 Broadway Road, Lexington, KY 63189
(508) 814-7282
s8281@mgamail.net

Career Objective   Management-level position in banking services.

Banking & Management Experience

Posted receipts and made bank deposits daily for Dunkin' Donuts coffee shop in Lexington, Kentucky. July 2008–present.

Supervised and scheduled cashier personnel for Dunkin' Donuts coffee shop in Lexington, Kentucky. July 2008–present.

Bank teller for Citizen's Fidelity Bank in Lexington, Kentucky. Maintained balanced cash drawer 99% of the time. Trained in various financial transactions of the banking field. May 2009–August 2009.

Customer Service Experience

Customer service/cashier for Dunkin' Donuts coffee shop in Lexington, Kentucky. Assisted customers with placing orders and was responsible for maintaining a balanced cash drawer.

Assisted customers promptly and courteously with financial transactions at Citizen's Fidelity Bank in Lexington, Kentucky. Received excellent performance ratings. May 2009–August 2009.

Waited on customers at EL Torito Mexican Restaurant in Lexington, Kentucky. After taking customers' orders, served customers promptly and courteously. August 2007–May 2008.

Leadership Experience

Vice President of Sigma Epsilon Phi Social Fraternity. Was responsible for assisting pledges with the transition into the fraternity and for raising money for the fraternity philanthropy through various fundraisers.

Coordinated and participated in the actual intramural team for the fraternity.

Community Service and Campus Activities

Member of Key Club Service Organization on campus.

Member of Management Association.

Member of Phi Kappa Phi Honor Society.

Education   B.A., Management University of Kentucky. May 2009.
GPA: 3.44/4.0   Minor: Information Systems
Courses: Accounting, Economics, Marketing, Money & Banking, Principles of Management.

Figure 4.12
Functional Résumé

ALEXANDER G. BELL
1421 Watson Drive • Ringem, Virginia 24147
(540) 555–5555 • *abell@runet.edu*

PROFESSIONAL STRENGTHS
- Bachelor's degree in business
- Two years of supervisory and leadership experience
- Three years of customer service experience
- Skilled in using spreadsheets (Excel) and presentation software (PowerPoint)
- Conversational in Spanish
- Excellent accounting and statistical skills

EDUCATION
B.S., Business Administration (May, 2013)
Radford University, Radford, VA

Highlights:
– 3.33 G.P.A.
– Extensive coursework in human resource management
– Minored in psychology
– President, Society for the Advancement of Management (SAM)
– Received two academic scholarships
– Worked to finance 50% of own education
– Participated in a variety of college activities including intramurals, two professional organizations, and a fraternity

PART-TIME AND SUMMER EMPLOYMENT
Student Manager (August 2011–present)
Radford University Dining Services, Radford, VA
  Responsible for supervising 30 students working in the dining hall. Specific responsibilities include scheduling employees, solving customer complaints, balancing the cash drawers, promoting high levels of customer service, and ensuring health regulations are being followed.

Food Server (August 2010–May 2011)
Radford University Dining Services, Radford, VA
  Responsible for serving food to students, keeping work area clean, and following health regulations.

Server (Summers 2009, 2010, 2011)
Whale's Tail Restaurant, Redondo Beach, CA

Figure 4.13
Psychological Résumé

Averaging versus adding model A model proposed by Anderson that postulates that our impressions are based more on the average value of each impression than on the sum of the values for each impression.

a member of the Young Democrats on campus. Including these items might make a negative impression on Republicans and those who oppose hunting. Include only information that most people will find positive (such as Red Cross volunteer, worked to help finance education, and so on), and avoid information that may be viewed negatively, such as political affiliation, religion, and dangerous hobbies (Bonner, 1993).

Of the many positive activities and accomplishments that you could list, list only your best. Do not list everything you have done; research by Spock and Stevens (1985) found that it is better to list a few great things, rather than a few great things and many good things. This finding is based on Anderson's (1965) **averaging versus adding model** of impression formation, which implies that activity quality is more important than quantity. It is neither necessary nor desirable to list all of your coursework. To practice writing a psychological résumé, complete the Résumé Writing Exercise (4.10) in your workbook.

Recruitment at the Borgata Hotel Casino and Spa

The Borgata Hotel Casino and Spa was about to open the first new resort in Atlantic City in 13 years. The 2,000-room casino and resort needed to hire 5,000 employees across hundreds of positions. To find enough high-quality employees, the Borgata engaged in a creative recruitment campaign that resulted in 30,000 well-qualified job applicants.

■ How would you have conducted such an extensive recruitment campaign?

■ What factors would affect not only the number of available applicants but the quality as well?

■ How would you handle the practical aspects of receiving and screening the 30,000 applications?

To see how the hotel handled this situation, follow the Web links on your text website.

FOCUS ON ETHICS # The Ethics of Recruiting and Hiring Based on Physical Appearance

Harvard economics professor Robert Barro believes that physical appearance is always a bona fide worker qualification as long as customers and coworkers think that it is. That is, if customers want to be served by beautiful people and coworkers prefer working with beautiful people, then it should be okay for companies to recruit and hire based on an individual's looks.

When people refer to someone's "looks" or "physical appearance," they are generally referring to that person's height, weight, and facial symmetry (i.e., high cheekbones vs. no visible cheekbones; small nose vs. big or bulbous nose). Because looks are subjective, beauty really is in the eyes of the beholder. In the United States, as well as other countries, beautiful people are often judged based on their external characteristics, rather than such internal characteristics as personality and ability. And it appears that many employers want employees who are tall and strong (for men), small/petite (for women), with no visible body fat, and a handsome or pretty face. Even those HR professionals who know better can often fall into the "looks" trap when recruiting and hiring.

Although some cities have laws against discrimination of applicants based on their height, weight, and/or physical appearance (e.g., San Francisco, CA; Santa Cruz, CA; Washington, D.C.), basically, there is no real protection from appearance-based discrimination unless it singles out applicants based on race, gender, or age. That is, you don't have to hire ugly people so long as you aren't hiring them because of their race, gender, or age.

The hiring professionals at the Borgata Hotel Casino and Spa in Atlantic City, New Jersey, embrace this philosophy.

Applicants for positions of waiters and waitresses are told that once hired, their weight cannot increase by more than 7% This means that a 125-pound woman cannot gain more than eight pounds over her tenure at the company. Of course, if you are a little too heavy to begin with (not obese, though), you won't even get an interview.

Defenders of the right to hire based on looks say that physically attractive people are perceived as smarter, more successful, more sociable, more dominant, and as having higher self-esteem. And customers would rather be helped by those types of employees instead of by the less attractive ones. The assumption is that the more beautiful employees a company has, the more clients or customers that business will attract. This, of course, means more money for the company. And, the more money the company brings in, the higher the salaries employees can earn. So, according to the defenders, it's a win-win situation. Well, win-win for the beautiful people, anyway.

And speaking of salaries: In 2005, the Federal Reserve Bank of St. Louis reviewed the correlation between looks and wages. The research showed that workers with below average looks earned, on average, 9% less per hour than above average looking workers. Above average looking employees earn 5% more than their average looking coworkers. And Fortune 500 companies seem to hire male CEOs that are about 6 feet tall, which is 3" taller than the average man.

Competency and the ability to do the job are often overlooked when emphasis is placed on looks. Although these beautiful people may be able to do the job, there may be less attractive people denied a position who could do the job more successfully.

So, like Professor Barro implies, as long as we, the customer, prefer looks over highly skilled professionals, companies should have the right to refuse employment to unattractive, short, and overweight applicants.

What Do You Think?

■ Do you see any potential ethical dilemmas of recruiting and hiring based on looks? If so, what are they?

■ Is it ethical to take a less skilled applicant over a more skilled one just because one is more attractive than the other?

■ Is it fair or ethical for places like Borgata Casino and Spa to refuse employment to less than average looking employees?

■ Is there a more ethical way to balance the rights of companies to have attractive people and the rights of people who are perceived as unattractive?

■ Do you think that more states and cities should make laws against discrimination of people based on their looks?

Chapter Summary

In this chapter you learned:

■ Employees can be recruited by a variety of methods, including help-wanted and situation-wanted advertisements, employee referrals, employment agencies, point-of-purchase methods, direct mail, and job fairs.

■ The traditional, unstructured interview isn't valid, because of such factors as lack of job relatedness, poor interviewer intuition, contrast effects, negative-information bias, use of nonverbal cues, interviewer-interviewee similarity, and primacy effects.

■ The structured interview is a valid predictor of employee performance because it is based on a job analysis, all applicants are asked the same questions, and applicant answers are scored with a standardized scoring procedure.

■ To perform well when being interviewed, you need to be on time, learn about the company, dress neatly, and use appropriate nonverbal behavior.

■ There are three main types of résumé: functional, chronological, and psychological.

Questions for Review

1. Why are employee referrals an effective means of recruitment?
2. Describe the principles one should follow to write an effective help-wanted ad.
3. If the unstructured interview is so bad, why is it still used so often?
4. Is the key-issues approach to scoring interview questions better than the typical-answer approach? Why or why not?
5. What psychological principles of impression formation are important to consider when writing a résumé?

Media Resources and Learning Tools

■ Visit our website. Go to www.cengage.com/psychology/aamodt, where you will find online resources directly linked to your book, including chapter-by-chapter quizzing, flashcards, crossword puzzles, application activities, and more.

■ Want more practice applying industrial/organizational psychology? Check out the *I/O Applications Workbook*. This workbook (keyed to your textbook) offers engaging, high-interest activities to help you reinforce the important concepts presented in the text.

Chapter 5

EMPLOYEE SELECTION: REFERENCES AND TESTING

© Chris Ryan/OJO Images/Getty Images

Learning Objectives

➥ Understand why references typically don't predict performance

➥ Learn how to use the trait approach to score letters of recommendation

➥ Understand how to choose the right type of employment test for a particular situation

➥ Be able to describe the different types of tests used to select employees

➥ Be able to create and score a biodata instrument

➥ Know how to write a well-designed rejection letter

In Chapter 4, interviews and résumés were described as the most commonly used methods to screen and select employees. Although these methods are the most commonly used, they are certainly not the best. In this chapter, we discuss several other techniques that are preferred by industrial psychologists to select employees.

Predicting Performance Using References and Letters of Recommendation

In psychology, a common belief is that the best predictor of future performance is past performance. Thus, if an organization wants to hire a salesperson, the best applicant might be a successful salesperson who held jobs that were similar to the one for which he is now applying.

Verifying previous employment is not difficult, but it can be difficult to verify the *quality* of previous performance. I recently watched the National Football League's draft of college players on television (ESPN, of course) and was envious of the fact that professional football teams can assess a player's previous performance by watching game films. That is, they do not have to rely on the opinions of other coaches. Instead, the scouts can watch literally every minute a player has spent on the field while in college.

Unfortunately, few applicants bring "game films" of their previous employment performances. Instead, an employer must obtain information about the quality of previous performance by relying on an applicant's references, either by calling those references directly or asking for letters of recommendation from previous employers. The Career Workshop Box tells how to ask for a letter of recommendation.

Before discussing this topic further, it might be a good idea to differentiate among *reference checks, references,* and *letters of recommendation.* A **reference check** is the process of confirming the accuracy of information provided by an applicant. A **reference** is the expression of an opinion, either orally or through a written checklist, regarding an applicant's ability, previous performance, work habits, character, or potential for future success. The content and format of a reference are determined by the person or organization asking for the reference. A **letter of recommendation** is a letter expressing an opinion regarding an applicant's ability, previous performance, work habits, character, or potential for future success. The content and format of a letter of recommendation are determined by the letter writer.

Reasons for Using References and Recommendations

Confirming Details on a Résumé

As mentioned in Chapter 4 it is not uncommon for applicants to engage in **résumé fraud**—lying on their résumés about what experience or education they actually have. Thus, one reason to check references or ask for letters of recommendation is simply to confirm the truthfulness of information provided by the applicant. An excellent example of résumé fraud is the bizarre 1994 assault against figure skater Nancy Kerrigan arranged by the late Shawn Eckardt, the bodyguard of Kerrigan's skating rival Tonya Harding. Harding hired Eckardt as her bodyguard because his résumé indicated he

Reference check The process of confirming the accuracy of résumé and job application information.

Reference The expression of an opinion, either orally or through a written checklist, regarding an applicant's ability, previous performance, work habits, character, or potential for future success.

Letter of recommendation A letter expressing an opinion regarding an applicant's ability, previous performance, work habits, character, or potential for success.

Résumé fraud The intentional placement of untrue information on a résumé.

Whether you will be going on to graduate school or applying for jobs, at some point you will need to ask for references or letters of recommendation. Here is some advice on the topic by Professor Mark Nagy at Xavier University in Ohio (Nagy, 2005).

➤ Provide your reference with a copy of your résumé and any other information you think might be useful to him or her. This person may know you from the classroom but may not know about your other experiences.

➤ Be sure to give your reference enough time to write a good letter. Asking two days prior to the deadline or asking that the letter be written over Thanksgiving break is probably not a good idea.

➤ Ask whether the reference feels that he or she can write you a *positive* letter.

➤ Choose references who can provide information from multiple perspectives. For example, a professor who can talk about how you performed in the classroom, a professor who can talk about your research experience, or an employer who can talk about your work ethic.

➤ If there are certain types of information you need the reference to include, don't be shy about speaking up. For example, if you are applying to a manager training program, you might mention that the prospective employer is interested in hearing about your leadership skills. If you are applying to a doctoral program, mention that the program is interested in hearing about your research.

Don't be shy about asking a reference if they sent the letter; people do tend to forget and they won't think you are pestering them if you give a friendly reminder.

---

was an expert in counterintelligence and international terrorism, had graduated from an elite executive protection school, and had spent four years "tracking terrorist cells" and "conducting a successful hostage retrieval operation" (Meehan, 1994). After the attack against Kerrigan, however, a private investigator discovered that Eckardt never graduated from a security school and would have been 16 during the time he claimed he was in Europe saving the world from terrorists. The president of a school he did attend stated that he "wouldn't hire Eckardt as a bodyguard in a lifetime"—an opinion that would have been discovered had Harding checked Eckardt's references.

Résumé fraud may not initially seem like a great problem, but consider these examples:

■ In 2009, Patrick Avery, the president of Intrepid Potash, Inc., was fired when it was discovered that he had lied on his résumé about having a master's degree from Loyola Marymount University and a bachelor's degree from the University of Colorado.

■ In 2008, *Dinner: Impossible* host Robert Irvine was fired from the Food Network after a newspaper reported that Irvine's claims of designing Princess Diana's wedding cake and being a chef at the White House were not true. Apparently the Food Network didn't think such a falsehood was too serious, as they rehired Irvine later that same year.

■ In 2007, Marilee Jones, the dean of admissions at the Massachusetts Institute of Technology, resigned after admitting that she had lied about having college degrees from three different universities.

■ In April of 2005, Federiqkoe DiBritto was fired from his $100,000 job as a fund-raiser at UCLA after it was discovered that his résumé listed phony credentials. This was not the first time DiBritto had engaged in résumé fraud; he had also doctored his credentials so that he could obtain previous jobs as a Catholic priest, a youth counselor, and the executive director of the Southern California chapter of the National Kidney Foundation.

- In October of 2002, Kenneth Lonchar was forced to resign after serving as the chief financial officer of Veritas Software Corp. for five years when the company discovered he had lied about having an MBA from Stanford.
- In May of 2002, Sandra Baldwin was forced to resign as chair of the U.S. Olympic committee when it was discovered she had lied on her résumé about having a Ph.D.
- In December of 2001, George O'Leary resigned after only a few days as the head football coach at Notre Dame University after it was discovered that he had lied about lettering in high school football and about receiving a master's degree from New York University.

These stories are tragic and may not be typical of résumé-fraud cases, but 98% of employers believe that it is enough of a problem to merit reference checks (Meinert, 2011). In a survey of employers in the United Kingdom, 25% said that they had withdrawn job offers in the past year after discovering that applicants had lied on their applications, and another 23% said they had fired current employees after discovering résumé fraud (Reade, 2005). In 2006, legislators in the state of Washington thought résumé fraud was so much of a problem that they passed a law making résumé fraud illegal, a misdemeanor punishable by up to $5,000 in fines or one year in jail.

Checking for Discipline Problems

A second reason to check references or obtain letters of recommendation is to determine whether the applicant has a history of such discipline problems as poor attendance, sexual harassment, and violence. Such a history is important for an organization to discover to avoid future problems as well as to protect itself from a potential charge of **negligent hiring**. If an organization hires an applicant without checking his references and background and he later commits a crime while in the employ of the organization, the organization may be found liable for negligent hiring if the employee has a criminal background that would have been detected had a background check been conducted.

Negligent-hiring cases are typically filed in court as common-law cases, or torts. These cases are based on the premise that an employer has the duty to protect its employees and customers from harm caused by its employees or products. In determining negligent hiring, courts look at the nature of the job. Organizations involved with the safety of the public, such as police departments and day-care centers, must conduct more thorough background and reference checks than organizations like retail stores. Such checks are important, as demonstrated by a study done by a reference-checking firm, which found that 12.6% of applicants had undisclosed criminal backgrounds (Mayer, 2002).

For example, a child-care center in California hired an employee without checking his references. A few months later, the employee molested a child at the center. The employee had a criminal record of child abuse that would have been discovered with a simple call to his previous employer. As one would expect, the court found the employer guilty of negligent hiring because the employer had not taken "reasonable care" in ensuring the well-being of its customers.

In Virginia, an employee of a grocery store copied the address of a female customer from a check she had written to the store. The employee later went to the customer's home and raped her. In this example, a case for negligent hiring could not be made because the company had contacted the employee's previous employment references and had found no reason not to hire him. Because there was nothing to discover and because the store had taken reasonable care to check its employees, it was not guilty of negligent hiring.

Discovering New Information About the Applicant

Employers use a variety of methods to understand the personality and skills of job applicants; references and letters of recommendation certainly can be two of these methods. Former employers and professors can provide information about an applicant's work habits, character, personality, and skills. Care must be taken, however, when using these methods because the opinion provided by any particular reference may be inaccurate or purposefully untrue. For example, a reference might describe a former employee as "difficult to work with," implying that everyone has trouble working with the applicant. It may be, however, that only the person providing the reference had trouble working with the applicant. This is an important point because every one of us knows people we don't get along with, even though, all things considered, we are basically good people. Thus, reference checkers should always obtain specific behavioral examples and try to get consensus from several references.

A relatively recent trend in reference checking is for employers to "Google" an applicant's name to find more information about the applicant. A CareerBuilder.com survey of 2,600 employers found that in 2009, 45% of them used social networking sites to discover applicant information. Potential job applicants should carefully monitor what is on their blogs or social network sites, as 70% of organizations reported that they eliminated a job candidate on the basis of information that was found on the web (Meinert, 2011).

Predicting Future Performance

In psychology, a common belief is that the best predictor of future performance is past performance. References and letters of recommendation are ways to try to predict future performance by looking at past performance.

Even though references are commonly used to screen and select employees, they have not been successful in predicting future employee success. In fact, a meta-analysis found that the average uncorrected **validity coefficient** for references/letters of recommendation and performance is only .18, with a **corrected validity** of .29 (Aamodt & Williams, 2005). This low validity is largely due to four main problems with references and letters of recommendation: leniency, knowledge of the applicant, low reliability, and extraneous factors involved in writing and reading such letters.

Leniency. Research is clear that most letters of recommendation are positive: Fewer than 1% of references rate applicants as below average or poor (Aamodt & Williams, 2005). Because we have all worked with terrible employees at some point in our lives, it would at first seem surprising that references typically are so positive. But keep in mind that *applicants choose their own references!* Even Adolf Hitler, serial killer Ted Bundy, and terrorist Osama bin Laden would have been able to find three people who could provide them with favorable references.

Figure 5.1 shows how coworkers' attitudes toward an employee affect the references they give that person. In the first situation, all of the applicant's eight coworkers have positive feelings about the applicant. Thus, if we ask for references from two coworkers, both would be positive *and* representative of the other six coworkers. In situation 2, most coworkers have neutral regard for the applicant, with two having positive feelings and two having negative feelings. In this situation, however, both references chosen by the applicant would be positive and *more favorable* than most coworkers'

Validity coefficient The correlation between scores on a selection method (e.g., interview, cognitive ability test) and a measure of job performance (e.g., supervisor rating, absenteeism).

Corrected validity A term usually found with meta-analysis, referring to a correlation coefficient that has been corrected for predictor and criterion reliability and for range restriction. Corrected validity is sometimes called "true validity."

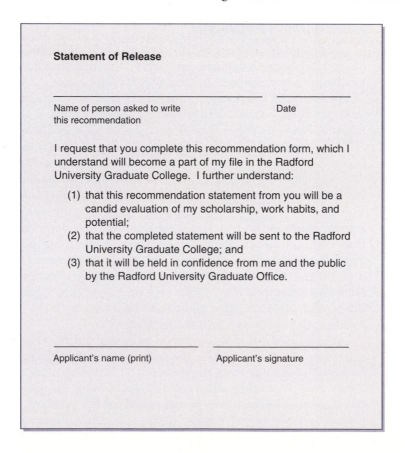

Situation	Positive	Neutral	Negative
1	👤👤👤👤👤👤👤👤		
2	👤👤	👤👤👤	👤👤
3	👤👤		👤👤👤👤👤👤
4			👤👤👤👤👤👤👤👤

Figure 5.1

Coworkers' Attitudes Toward Employee

attitudes. In situation 3, only two of eight people like the applicant—yet the two reference letters will be the same as in the first and second situations, even though most coworkers have negative feelings about our applicant. In situation 4, no one likes our applicant. In this case, our request for references would either keep the person from applying for our job or force the applicant to find references from somewhere else. But if we *require* work-related references, they probably, but not necessarily, would be negative because research has shown that coworkers *are* willing to say negative things about unsatisfactory employees (Grote, Robiner, & Haut, 2001).

Although coworkers are willing to say negative things about unsatisfactory employees, *confidentiality concerns* can hold them back. By law, students have a right to see their reference letters, but most sign waivers such as that shown in Figure 5.2 to

---

Statement of Release

_____   _____

Name of person asked to write   Date
this recommendation

I request that you complete this recommendation form, which I understand will become a part of my file in the Radford University Graduate College. I further understand:

(1) that this recommendation statement from you will be a candid evaluation of my scholarship, work habits, and potential;

(2) that the completed statement will be sent to the Radford University Graduate College; and

(3) that it will be held in confidence from me and the public by the Radford University Graduate Office.

_____   _____

Applicant's name (print)   Applicant's signature

Figure 5.2

A Typical Reference Waiver

encourage reference providers to be more candid. This increased candidness was demonstrated in research that found that people providing references tend to be less lenient when an applicant waives his right to see a reference letter (Ceci & Peters, 1984; Shaffer & Tomarelli, 1981). That is, when a person writing a reference letter knows that the applicant is allowed to see the letter, the writer is more inclined to provide a favorable evaluation. With this in mind, a colleague of mine almost completely discounts any recommendation letters for which the waiver is not signed.

A third cause of leniency stems from the *fear of legal ramifications*. A person providing references can be charged with defamation of character (slander if the reference is oral, libel if written) if the content of the reference is both untrue and made with malicious intent. This fear keeps many organizations from providing references at all (Kleiman & White, 1991). However, people providing references are granted what is called a *conditional privilege*, which means that they have the right to express their opinion provided they believe what they say is true and have reasonable grounds for this belief (Ryan & Lasek, 1991; Zink & Gutman, 2005). Furthermore, many states have passed laws strengthening this conditional privilege. One way to avoid losing a defamation suit is to provide only behavioral information in a reference. That is, rather than saying "This employee is a jerk," you might say "He was warned three times about yelling at other employees and four employees requested that they not have to work with him." To reduce the possibility of a lawsuit, 72% of organizations have applicants sign a waiver stating that they will not sue the company for checking references nor the people providing references (Burke, 2005b).

In recent years, several companies have emerged that make their living by contacting companies to see what they will say about former employees. These firms are hired by applicants who are concerned that their former employer might be providing a negative reference. These "reference detectives" contact the former employer under the guise of being a company considering hiring the former employee. The reference information is then passed on to the client, who has the option of filing a defamation suit if he or she doesn't like what is being said (Cadrain, 2004).

Negligent reference An organization's failure to meet its legal duty to supply relevant information to a prospective employer about a former employee's potential for legal trouble.

Because an employer can be guilty of negligent hiring for not contacting references, a former employer also can be guilty of **negligent reference** if it does not provide relevant information to an organization that requests it. For example, if Dinero Bank fires John Smith for theft and fails to divulge that fact to a bank that is thinking of hiring Smith, Dinero Bank may be found liable if Smith steals money at his new bank.

Many years ago, on the basis of several letters of recommendation, our department hired a part-time instructor. Two weeks after he started the job, we discovered that he had to return to his home in another state to face charges of stealing drugs from his former employer, a psychology department at another university. We were upset because neither of the references from his former job mentioned the charges. After a rather heated conversation with one of the references, we learned that the applicant was the son of the department chairman and that the faculty were afraid to say anything that would anger their boss.

These last examples show why providing references and letters of recommendations can be so difficult. On the one hand, a former employer can be charged with slander or libel if it says something bad about an applicant that cannot be proven. On the other hand, an employer can be held liable if it does not provide information about a potentially dangerous applicant. Because of these competing responsibilities, many organizations will confirm only employment dates and salary information unless a former employee has been convicted of a criminal offense that resulted in termination. The use of professional reference-checking companies can help alleviate this problem.

Knowledge of the Applicant. A second problem with letters of recommendation is that the person writing the letter often does not know the applicant well, has not observed all aspects of an applicant's behavior, or both. Professors are often asked to provide recommendations for students whom they know only from one or two classes. Such recommendations are not likely to be as accurate and complete as those provided by professors who have had students in several classes and perhaps worked with them outside the classroom setting.

Even in a work setting in which a supervisor provides the recommendation, he often does not see all aspects of an employee's behavior (Figure 5.3). Employees often act very differently around their supervisors than they do around coworkers and customers. Furthermore, as Figure 5.3 shows and as will be discussed in greater detail in Chapter 7, those behaviors that a reference writer actually recalls are only a fraction of the behaviors actually occurring in the presence of the person writing the recommendation.

Reliability. The third problem with references and letters of recommendation involves the *lack of agreement* between two people who provide references for the same person. Research reveals that reference **reliability** is only .22 (Aamodt & Williams, 2005). The problem with reliability is so severe that there is more agreement between recommendations written *by the same person* for two different applicants than between two people writing recommendations *for the same person* (Aamodt &

Reliability The extent to which a score from a test or from an evaluation is consistent and free from error.

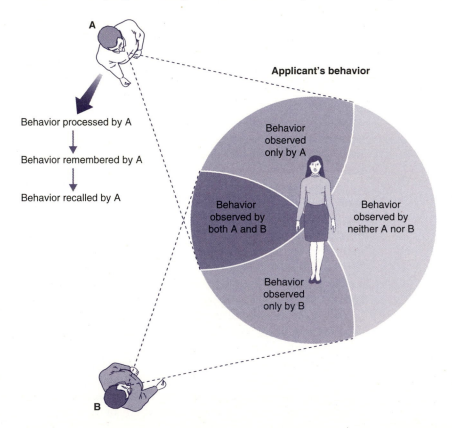

Figure 5.3

A Reference Writer Often Lacks Competent Knowledge of an Employee's Behavior

Williams, 2005). Thus, letters of recommendation may say more about the person writing the letter than about the person for whom it is being written.

This low level of reliability probably results from the point cited earlier that a reference writer has not seen all aspects of an applicant's behavior. Thus, a reference provided by a professor who has observed an applicant in a classroom may not agree with a reference provided by a supervisor who has observed the same applicant in a work setting. Although there may be good reasons for the low levels of reliability in reference letters that limit their validity, research has yet to answer this question: If two references do not agree, which one should be taken the most seriously?

Extraneous Factors. The fourth problem with letters of recommendation concerns extraneous factors that affect their writing and evaluation. Research has indicated that the method used by the letter writer is often more important than the actual content. For example, Knouse (1983), but not Loher, Hazer, Tsai, Tilton, and James (1997), found that letters that contained specific examples were rated higher than letters that contained generalities. Mehrabian (1965) and Weins, Jackson, Manaugh, and Matarazzo (1969) found that even though most letters of recommendation are positive, letters written by references who like applicants are longer than those written by references who do not. This is important because Loher and colleagues (1997) found that the longer the recommendation letter, the more positively the letter was perceived.

A promising approach to increasing the validity of references is to increase the structure of the reference check. This can be done by conducting a job analysis and then creating a reference checklist that is tied directly to the job analysis results. When such a process is used, research has demonstrated higher levels of predictability (McCarthy & Goffin, 2001; Taylor, Pajo, Cheung, & Stringfield, 2004; Zimmerman, Triana, & Barrick, 2010).

As this discussion illustrates, references and letters of recommendation often are not great predictors of performance. But with further refinement and research, techniques such as the trait approach or increased structure may increase the predictive abilities of references.

Ethical Issues

Because providing references and letters of recommendation is a rather subjective process, several ethical problems can arise involving their use. Raynes (2005) lists three ethical guidelines that reference providers should follow.

First, *explicitly state your relationship* with the person you are recommending. That is, are you the applicant's professor, boss, coworker, friend, relative, or some combination of the five? This is important because people often have dual roles: A person may be a supervisor as well as a good friend. Without understanding the exact nature of the referee–referent relationship, making judgments about the content of a reference can be difficult. For example, I was told of a situation in which an applicant received a glowing letter of recommendation from a coworker and in which the applicant was hired in part due to the strength of that letter. Within a few months, the new employee was engaged in discipline problems, and it was only then that the organization discovered that the person who had written the glowing letter was the applicant's daughter. Because the mother's and daughter's last names were different and because the exact relationship between the two was not stated in the letter, the organization never suspected that they were related.

Second, *be honest* in providing details. A referee has both an ethical and a legal obligation to provide relevant information about an applicant. A good rule of thumb is to ask, "If I were in the reference seeker's shoes, what would I need to know?" Of course, deciding what information to provide can often be a difficult process. I was once contacted by a Secret Service agent conducting a reference check on an applicant for a position in a Human Resources (HR) department. My reservations about the student concerned his excessive use of alcohol in social situations and his negative attitude toward women. After some soul searching (as much as can be done with a federal agent staring at you), I decided to provide information about the student's attitude toward women, as I thought it was relevant to an HR job, but not to mention the social drinking problem. Had the student been an applicant for a position as an agent, I would have mentioned the drinking. I'm not sure that my decision was correct, but the example demonstrates the dilemma of balancing the duty to provide information to the reference seeker with a duty to treat an applicant fairly.

Finally, let the *applicant see your reference* before sending it, and give him the chance to decline to use it. Such a procedure is fair to the applicant and reduces the referee's liability for any defamation charge. Though this last piece of advice seems wise, it can result in some uncomfortable discussions about the content of references that are not positive.

Predicting Performance Using Applicant Training and Education

For many jobs, it is common that applicants must have a minimum level of education or training to be considered. That is, an organization might require that managerial applicants have a bachelor's degree to pass the initial applicant screening process. A meta-analysis by Ng and Feldman (2009) found that better educated employees had higher performance, were more likely to engage in organizational citizenship behaviors, less likely to be absent, and less likely to engage in on-the-job substance abuse than were employees with lower levels of education. A meta-analysis of the relationship between education and police performance found that education was a valid predictor of performance in the police academy ($r = .26$, $\rho = .38$) and performance on the job ($r = .17$, $\rho = .28$) and added incremental validity to cognitive ability tests (Aamodt, 2004).

Meta-analyses indicate that a student's GPA can predict job performance (Roth, BeVier, Switzer, & Schippmann, 1996), training performance (Dye & Reck, 1989), promotions (Cohen, 1984), salary (Roth & Clarke, 1998), and graduate school performance (Kuncel, Hezlett, & Ones, 2001). GPA is most predictive in the first few years after graduation (Roth et al., 1996). As with many measures of cognitive ability, the use of GPA will result in high levels of adverse impact (Roth & Bobko, 2000). Another factor complicating the use of education and GPA to select employees is the increased use of homeschooling; more than 1.5 million children are currently being homeschooled in the United States (Lloyd, 2009).

Predicting Performance Using Applicant Knowledge

Job knowledge test A test that measures the amount of job-related knowledge an applicant possesses.

Used primarily in the public sector, especially for promotions, **job knowledge tests** are designed to measure how much a person knows about a job. For example, applicants for a bartender position might be asked how to make a martini or a White Russian, and applicants for an HR position might be asked how to conduct a job analysis. These tests are similar to the exams given several times a semester in a college class.

They are typically given in multiple-choice fashion for ease of scoring, but they also can be written in essay format or given orally in a job interview. Common examples of job knowledge tests include tests of computer programming knowledge, knowledge of electronics, and knowledge of mechanical principles. Standardized job knowledge tests are commonly used by state licensing boards for such occupations as lawyers and psychologists.

Job knowledge tests have excellent content and criterion validity (Schmidt & Hunter, 1998), and because of their high face validity, they are positively accepted by applicants (Robertson & Kandola, 1982). Even though job knowledge tests do a good job of predicting performance, they often result in adverse impact and can be used only for jobs in which applicants are expected to have job knowledge at the time of hire or promotion.

Predicting Performance Using Applicant Ability

Ability tests tap the extent to which an applicant can learn or perform a job-related skill. Ability tests are used primarily for occupations in which applicants are not expected to know how to perform the job at the time of hire. Instead, new employees will be taught the necessary job skills and knowledge. Examples of such occupations include police officers, firefighters, and military personnel. For example, cognitive ability would enable a police cadet to obtain knowledge of search-and-seizure laws; psychomotor ability (dexterity) would enable a secretary to type fast or an assembler to rapidly assemble electronic components; perceptual ability would enable a mail clerk to distinguish zip codes or a textile worker to distinguish colors; and physical ability would enable a firefighter to learn how to climb a ladder or carry a victim from a burning building.

Cognitive Ability

Cognitive ability Abilities involving the knowledge and use of information such as math and grammar.

Cognitive ability includes such dimensions as oral and written comprehension, oral and written expression, numerical facility, originality, memorization, reasoning (mathematical, deductive, inductive), and general learning. Cognitive ability is important for professional, clerical, and supervisory jobs, including such occupations as supervisor, accountant, and secretary.

Cognitive ability test Tests designed to measure the level of intelligence or the amount of knowledge possessed by an applicant.

Cognitive ability tests are commonly used because they are excellent predictors of employee performance in the United States (Schmidt & Hunter, 1998) and in Europe (Salgado, Anderson, Moscoso, Bertua, & DeFruyt, 2003), are easy to administer, and are relatively inexpensive. Cognitive ability is thought to predict work performance in two ways: by allowing employees to quickly learn job-related knowledge and by processing information resulting in better decision making. Though cognitive ability tests are thought by many to be the most valid method of employee selection, especially for complex jobs, they certainly have some drawbacks. Perhaps the most crucial of these is that they result in high levels of adverse impact (Roth, BeVier, Bobko, Switzer, & Tyler, 2001) and often lack face validity. Because cognitive ability tests have the highest level of adverse impact of any employee selection method, it is not surprising that they also are frequently challenged in court. As you learned in Chapter 3, an organization can still use a test with adverse impact if it can show that it is related to performance, and cognitive ability tests that have been

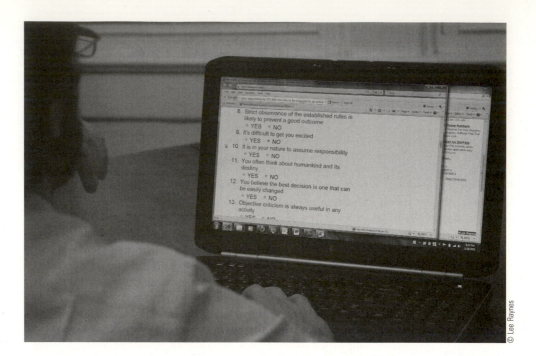

Many employment tests are now administered on-line.

© Lee Raynes

properly developed and validated usually survive legal challenges (Shoenfelt & Pedigo, 2005). However, defending lawsuits, even if the company wins, can be expensive.

Another drawback to cognitive ability tests is the difficulty of setting a passing score. That is, how much cognitive ability do you need to perform well in a particular job? Should we always give preference to the smartest applicant or is there a point at which increased cognitive ability doesn't help? The On the Job case study at the end of this chapter will give you a good opportunity to explore this question further.

Though meta-analyses suggest that cognitive ability is one of the best predictors of performance across all jobs (Salgado et al., 2003; Schmidt & Hunter, 1998), the results of job-specific meta-analyses raise some doubt about this assumption. For example, in a meta-analysis of predictors of law enforcement performance, Aamodt (2004) found cognitive ability to be significantly related to performance, but the corrected validity ($\rho = .27$) was not nearly as high as that reported in the meta-analysis by Schmidt and Hunter ($\rho = .51$). Similar results were found by Vinchur, Schippmann, Switzer, and Roth (1998) in their meta-analysis of predictors of performance for salespeople: Cognitive ability was significantly related to supervisor ratings ($\rho = .31$) but not to actual sales performance ($\rho = -.03$). Thus, further meta-analyses on specific occupations are still needed before we can conclude that cognitive ability is one of the best predictors for all jobs.

Wonderlic Personnel Test

The cognitive ability test that is most commonly used in industry.

One of the most widely used cognitive ability tests in industry is the **Wonderlic Personnel Test**. The short amount of time (12 minutes) necessary to take the test, as well as the fact that it can be administered in a group setting, makes it popular. Sample items from the Wonderlic are shown in Figure 5.4. Other popular cognitive tests are the Miller Analogies Test, the Quick Test, and Raven Progressive Matrices. To better understand cognitive ability tests, complete the short form of the Basic Cognitive Ability Test (BCAT) found in Exercise 5.1 in your workbook.

PERSONNEL TEST
FORM II

NAME _____ (Please Print)   Date _____

**READ THIS PAGE CAREFULLY. DO EXACTLY AS YOU ARE TOLD.
DO NOT TURN OVER THIS PAGE UNTIL YOU ARE
INSTRUCTED TO DO SO.**

**PROBLEMS MUST BE WORKED WITHOUT THE AID OF A CALCULATOR
OR OTHER PROBLEM-SOLVING DEVICE.**

This is a test of problem-solving ability. It contains various types of questions. Below is a sample question correctly filled in.

PLACE
ANSWERS
HERE

REAP is the opposite of
    1 obtain.   2 cheer.   3 continue.   4 exist.   5 <u>sow.</u>

[_5_]

The correct answer is "sow." (It is helpful to underline the correct word.) The correct word is numbered 5. Then write the figure 5 in the brackets at the end of the line.

Answer the next sample question yourself.

Paper sells for 23 cents per pad. What will 4 pads cost?

[___]

The correct answer is 92¢. There is nothing to underline so just place "92¢" in the brackets.

Here is another example:

MINER   MINOR — Do these words
    1 have similar meanings?   2 have contradictory meanings?   3 mean neither the same nor opposite?

[___]

The correct answer is "mean neither the same nor opposite," which is number 3, so all you have to do is place a figure "3" in the brackets at the end of the line.

When the answer to a question is a letter or a number, put the letter or number in the brackets.
All letters should be printed.

This test contains 50 questions. It is unlikely that you will finish all of them, but do your best. After the examiner tells you to begin, you will be given exactly 12 minutes to work as many as you can. Do not go so fast that you make mistakes since you must try to get as many right as possible. The questions become increasingly difficult, so do not skip about. Do not spend too much time on any one problem. The examiner will not answer any questions after the test begins.

Now, lay down your pencil and wait for the examiner to tell you to begin!

Do not turn the page until you are told to do so.

Source: E. F. Wonderlic Personnel Test, Inc., Northfield, IL. Reprinted by permission.

Figure 5.4
Wonderlic Personnel
Test

A potential breakthrough in cognitive ability tests is the Siena Reasoning Test (SRT). The developers of this test theorized that the large race differences in scores on traditional cognitive ability tests were due to the knowledge needed to understand the questions rather than the actual ability to learn or process information (intelligence). Take, for example, the analogy, *Colt is to horse as _____ is to dog.* To correctly answer this question, one must have prior knowledge of animals as well as the ability to do analogies. To reduce the reliance on previous knowledge, the SRT items contain nonsense words and words that are commonly known (e.g., lamp, couch). A study comparing the SRT with other cognitive ability tests found that not only did the SRT predict college grades and work performance at least as well as traditional cognitive ability tests, but almost eliminated the racial differences in test scores (Ferreter, Goldstein, Scherbaum, Yusko, & Jun, 2008).

A type of test related to cognitive ability is the situational judgment test. In this test, applicants are given a series of situations and asked how they would handle each one. These situations cover such topics (constructs) as leadership skills, interpersonal skills, personality tendencies, teamwork, and job knowledge (Christian, Edwards, & Bradley, 2010). A meta-analysis by McDaniel, Morgeson, Finnegan, Campion, and Braverman (2001) found that situational judgment tests correlated highly with cognitive ability tests ($r = .46$) and with job performance ($r = .34$). Though situational judgment tests are correlated with cognitive ability, the combination of the two is more valid than either test alone (Clevenger, Pereira, Wiechmann, Schmitt, & Harvey, 2001).

Perceptual Ability

Perceptual ability Measure of facility with such processes as spatial relations and form perception.

Perceptual ability consists of vision (near, far, night, peripheral), color discrimination, depth perception, glare sensitivity, speech (clarity, recognition), and hearing (sensitivity, auditory attention, sound localization) (Fleishman & Reilly, 1992b). Abilities from this dimension are useful for such occupations as machinist, cabinet maker, die setter, and tool and die maker. An example of a perceptual ability test is shown in Figure 5.5.

Psychomotor Ability

Psychomotor ability Measure of facility with such processes as finger dexterity and motor coordination.

Psychomotor ability includes finger dexterity, manual dexterity, control precision, multilimb coordination, response control, reaction time, arm-hand steadiness, wrist-finger speed, and speed-of-limb movement (Fleishman & Reilly, 1992b). Psychomotor abilities are useful for such jobs as carpenter, police officer, sewing-machine operator, post office clerk, and truck driver. An example of a psychomotor test is shown in Figure 5.6.

Physical Ability

Physical ability tests Tests that measure an applicant's level of physical ability required for a job.

Physical ability tests are often used for jobs that require physical strength and stamina, such as police officer, firefighter, and lifeguard. Physical ability is measured in one of two ways: job simulations and physical agility tests. With a job simulation, applicants actually demonstrate job-related physical behaviors. For example, firefighter applicants might climb a ladder and drag a 48-pound hose 75 feet across a street, police applicants might fire a gun and chase down a suspect, and lifeguard applicants might swim 100 yards and drag a drowning victim back to shore. Though job simulations are highly content valid, from a financial or safety perspective they are often impractical (Hoover, 1992).

CAREER ABILITY PLACEMENT SURVEY

2. SPATIAL RELATIONS (SR)

This is a test of Spatial Relations. Following are patterns which can be folded into figures. You are to choose which figure can be correctly made by folding the pattern and then darken the answer space above it. Only one of the four figures is correct for each pattern shown. Practice on these examples.

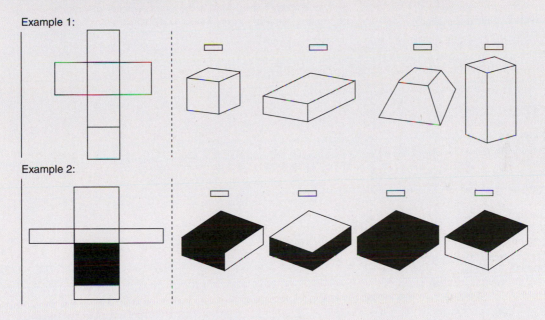

Example 1:

Example 2:

In Example 1, the first figure, the cube, is correct. You should have darkened the answer space above the first figure. In Example 2, all of the figures are correct in shape, but only one of them is shaded correctly. The last figure is correct.

Remember the surfaces you are shown in the pattern must always be the outside of the folded figure.

When the signal is given turn the page over and begin. Work as quickly and as carefully as you can.

NOTE: If you change an answer, mark a heavy "X" on the answer you wish to change, then darken the correct answer.

You will have 5 minutes to complete this section.

DO NOT TURN THIS PAGE UNTIL YOU ARE TOLD TO DO SO.

Figure 5.5
Perceptual Ability Test

8. MANUAL SPEED AND DEXTERITY (MSD)

This is a test of Manual Speed and Dexterity. Following is a series of arrows arranged in columns. You are to draw straight vertical lines connecting the tips of the adjacent arrows.

Start each line at the tip of the top arrow and draw to the tip of the bottom arrow. Make sure that you touch both arrow tips without crossing the tips into the shaded area. Start at the top of each column and work down making sure the lines you draw are straight, heavy and dark. Practice on the following examples:

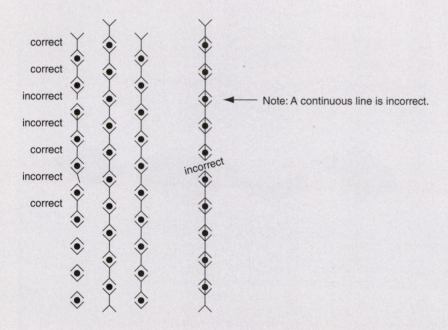

When the signal is given turn the page over and begin. Work as quickly and as accurately as you can. Your score will depend on both speed and accuracy. You will have 5 minutes to complete this section.

DO NOT TURN THIS PAGE UNTIL YOU ARE TOLD TO DO SO.

Figure 5.6
Psychomotor Ability
Test

Testing the physical ability of police applicants is an excellent example of this impracticality. Job analyses consistently indicate that the physical requirements of police officers can be divided into two categories: athletic and defensive. *Athletic requirements* are easy to simulate because they involve such behaviors as running, crawling, and pulling. *Defensive requirements*, however, are difficult to safely and accurately simulate because they involve such behaviors as applying restraining holds, kicking, and fending off attackers. One can imagine the liability and safety problems of physically attacking applicants to see if they could defend themselves.

Because of the difficulty in using simulations to measure these last types of behaviors, physical ability tests are used. Instead of simulating defensive behaviors, tests are developed that measure the basic abilities needed to perform these behaviors. Tests commonly used to measure the abilities needed to perform defensive behaviors include push-ups, sit-ups, and grip strength. Research has shown that there are nine basic physical abilities (Fleishman & Reilly, 1992b):

- dynamic strength (strength requiring repetitions)
- trunk strength (stooping or bending over)
- explosive strength (jumping or throwing objects)
- static strength (strength not requiring repetitions)
- dynamic flexibility (speed of bending, stretching, twisting)
- extent flexibility (degree of bending, stretching, twisting)
- gross body equilibrium (balance)
- gross body coordination (coordination when body is in motion)
- stamina (ability to exert effort over long periods of time)

Because physical ability tests have tremendous adverse impact against women (Hough, Oswald, & Ployhart, 2001), they have been criticized on three major points: job relatedness, passing scores, and the time at which they should be required.

Job Relatedness

Though few people would disagree that it is *better* for a police officer to be strong and fit than weak and out of shape, many argue whether it is *necessary* to be physically fit. Critics of physical agility testing cite two reasons for questioning the necessity of physical agility: current out-of-shape cops and technological alternatives. Currently, many police officers are overweight, slow, and out of shape, yet they perform safely and at high levels. Furthermore, there is research to suggest that physical size is not related to police safety (Griffiths & McDaniel, 1993). Thus, critics argue that physical agility is not an essential part of the job. This is especially true due to technological advances in policing. As an example, Sollie and Sollie (1993) presented data showing that the use of pepper spray in Meridian, Mississippi, almost completely reduced the need for officers to physically restrain drunk or physically aggressive suspects. However, supporters of physical ability testing cite studies demonstrating significant relationships between isometric strength tests and supervisor ratings of employee physical ability (Blakley, Quiñones, Crawford, & Jago, 1994). Such discrepancies in research findings demonstrate the importance of conducting studies to determine the importance of physical ability for any particular job.

Passing Scores

A second problem with physical ability tests is determining passing scores; that is, how fast must an applicant run or how much weight must be lifted to pass a physical ability test? Passing scores for physical ability tests are set based on one of two types of standards: relative or absolute. Relative standards indicate how well an individual scores compared with others in a group such as women, police applicants, or current police officers. The advantage to using relative standards is that adverse impact is eliminated because men are compared with men and women with women. The problem with relative scales, however, is that a female applicant might be strong compared with other women, yet not strong enough to perform the job. Furthermore, relative standards based on protected classes (e.g., sex, race) were made illegal by the 1991 Civil Rights Act (although technically illegal, the Justice Department has not enforced the ban against gender-specific physical standards). In contrast, absolute passing scores are set at the minimum level needed to perform a job. For example, if a police officer needs to be able to drag a 170-pound person from a burning car, 170 pounds becomes the passing score. As one can imagine, the problem comes in determining the minimum amounts. That is, how fast does an officer *need* to run to adequately perform the job? Because people come in all sizes, how many pounds does an officer *need* to be able to drag?

When the Ability Must Be Present

A third problem with physical ability requirements is the point at which the ability must be present. Most police departments require applicants to pass physical ability tests on the same day other tests are being completed. However, the applicant doesn't need the strength or speed until he is actually in the academy or on the job. Furthermore, applicants going through an academy show significant increases in physical ability and fitness by the end of the academy (Henderson, Berry, & Matic, 2007). Showing awareness of this problem, cities such as San Francisco and Philadelphia provide applicants with a list of physical abilities that will be required of them once they arrive at the academy. Applicants are then given suggestions on how they can get themselves into the proper condition. Some cities even hold conditioning programs for applicants! Such policies greatly reduce adverse impact by increasing the physical ability of female applicants.

An interesting example of the importance of monitoring ability testing is provided in a study by Padgett (1989), who was hired to determine vision requirements for a municipal fire department. Prior to Padgett's study, national vision standards for firefighters had been set without any empirical research. The standards stipulated that firefighters needed a minimum uncorrected vision of 20/40 and could not wear contact lenses because they might be "blown out of their eyes."

After conducting his study of actual job-related duties, however, Padgett discovered that the minimum vision needed to perform firefighting tasks was 20/100 if the person wore glasses and that there was no minimum if the person wore contacts. The difference in requirements for contacts and glasses was because certain duties might result in a loss of glasses, but it was very unlikely a firefighter would lose contacts while performing a task requiring acute vision. As a result of this study, many qualified applicants who had been turned away because of the archaic vision requirements were allowed the chance to become firefighters.

Predicting Performance Using Applicant Skill

Rather than measuring an applicant's current knowledge or potential to perform a job (ability), some selection techniques measure the extent to which an applicant already has a job-related skill. The two most common methods for doing this are the work sample and the assessment center.

The Vinson Institute of Government is one of several service units of the University of Georgia. The Governmental Services division provides technical assistance to municipal, county, and state government agencies. Within this division, assistance is provided primarily in human resource management.

My position is primarily as a consultant. My clients are law enforcement agencies. Typical projects range from helping a small city choose a new police chief to helping a state law enforcement agency develop new promotion procedures.

I develop and administer written job knowledge tests and assessment centers. Much of my time is spent ensuring that these testing instruments are valid predictors of future job performance. The primary strategy I use is content validity. The basis of this approach is ensuring that the questions on the job knowledge tests and the assessment center exercises measure actual duties and responsibilities that are required by the individual who performs the job.

The content validation approach relies heavily on conducting a thorough job analysis. This is a lengthy process in which I will spend time with job incumbents while they perform their jobs. For example, if we are developing test materials for police sergeants, I will ride with a representative sample of police sergeants and observe them while they perform their jobs. During this time, I ask questions

Mark Foster, Ph.D.

Senior Public Service Associate, Carl Vinson Institute of Government, The University of Georgia

and take extensive notes on exactly what they are doing and why. From this information, a task list of necessary knowledge and skills are developed. From these two lists, we know which knowledge to test for on the written examination and which skills to test for during the assessment center.

Examples of job knowledge might include basic laws, departmental policy and procedures, and proper collection and handling of evidence. Examples of skills might include recognizing and handling performance problems of a subordinate, making decisions, communicating orally and in writing, and organizing and planning.

The development of written examinations is relatively straightforward; the development of assessment centers is much more involved. The assessment center is a series of job simulations, or exercises, that require the candidate to perform skills necessary for the job. These job simulations can take many forms. I typically use three or four different exercises, which might include a role-play, an oral presentation, and a written problem exercise.

If what I do sounds like an interesting career for you, my advice is to talk extensively with someone in the profession. Ask them about academic preparation, what type of previous work experience would be helpful, what they like and dislike about their career, and how they see the future of the profession.

Work Samples

With a work sample, the applicant performs actual job-related tasks. For example, an applicant for a job as automotive mechanic might be asked to fix a torn fan belt; a secretarial applicant might be asked to type a letter; and a truck-driver applicant might be asked to back a truck up to a loading dock.

Work samples are excellent selection tools for several reasons. First, because they are directly related to job tasks, they have excellent content validity. Second, scores from work samples tend to predict actual work performance and thus have excellent criterion validity (Callinan & Robertson, 2001; Roth, Bobko, & McFarland, 2005). Third, because job applicants are able to see the connection between the job sample and the work performed on the job, the samples have excellent face validity and thus are challenged less often in civil service appeals or in court cases (Whelchel, 1985). Finally, work samples have lower racial differences in test scores than do written cognitive ability tests (Roth, Bobko, McFarland, & Buster, 2008), although the actual extent of the difference is still under debate (Bobko, Roth, & Buster, 2005). The main reason for not using work samples is that they can be expensive to both construct and administer. For this reason, work samples are best used for well-paying jobs for which many employees will be hired.

Assessment Centers

An **assessment center** is a selection technique characterized by the use of multiple assessment methods that allow multiple assessors to actually *observe* applicants perform simulated job tasks (Joiner, 2002). Its major advantages are that assessment methods are all job related and multiple trained assessors help to guard against many (but not all) types of selection bias. For a selection technique to be considered an assessment center, it must meet the following requirements (Joiner, 2000):

- The assessment center activities must be based on the results of a thorough job analysis.
- Multiple assessment techniques must be used, at least one of which must be a simulation.
- Multiple trained assessors must be used.
- Behavioral observations must be documented at the time the applicant behavior is observed.
- Assessors must prepare a report of their observations.
- The overall judgment of an applicant must be based on a combination of information from the multiple assessors and multiple techniques.
- The overall evaluation of an applicant cannot be made until all assessment center tasks have been completed.

Development and Component

Although many different techniques may be used in assessment centers, the basic development and types of exercises are fairly standard. The first step in creating an assessment center is, of course, to do a job analysis (Caldwell, Thornton, & Gruys, 2003). From this analysis, exercises are developed that measure different aspects of the job. Common exercises include the in-basket technique, simulations, work samples, leaderless group discussions, structured interviews, personality and ability tests, and business games. Each of these techniques can be used by itself, but only when several are used in combination do they become part of an assessment center. The typical assessment center has four or five exercises, takes two to three days to complete, and costs about $2,000 per applicant. Once the exercises have been developed, assessors are chosen to rate the applicants going through the assessment center. These assessors typically hold positions two levels higher than the assessees and spend one day being trained (Eurich, Krause, Cigularov, & Thornton, 2010; Spychalski, Quiñones, Gaugler, & Pohley, 1997).

The In-Basket Technique. The **in-basket technique** is designed to simulate the types of daily information that appear on a manager's or employee's desk. The technique takes its name from the wire baskets typically seen on office desks. Usually these baskets have two levels: the "in" level, which holds paperwork that must be handled, and the "out" level, which contains completed paperwork.

During the assessment center, examples of job-related paperwork are placed in a basket, and the job applicant is asked to go through the basket and respond to the paperwork as if he were actually on the job. Examples of such paperwork might include a phone message from an employee who cannot get his car started and does not know how to get to work or a memo from the accounting department stating that an expense voucher is missing.

The applicant is observed by a group of assessors, who score him on several dimensions, such as the quality of the decision, the manner in which the decision was carried out, and the order in which the applicant handled the paperwork—that is, did he start at the top of the pile or did he start with the most important papers? Research on the reliability and validity of the in-basket technique provides only modest support for its usefulness (Schippmann, Prien, & Katz, 1990).

Simulations. Simulation exercises are the real backbone of the assessment center because they enable assessors to see an applicant "in action." **Simulations**, which can include such diverse activities as role-plays and work samples, place an applicant in a situation that is as similar as possible to one that will be encountered on the job. To be effective, simulations must be based on job-related behaviors and should be reasonably realistic.

A good example of a role-playing simulation is an assessment center used by a large city to select emergency telephone operators. The applicant sits before a switchboard to handle a distressed caller who is describing an emergency situation. The applicant must properly answer the call, calm the caller, and obtain the necessary information in as little time as possible. Other examples include a police applicant writing a traffic citation for an angry citizen, and an applicant for a resident assistant position breaking up an argument between two roommates.

To reduce the high costs associated with actual simulations, many public organizations such as the New York State Civil Service Commission and the City of Fairfax, Virginia, have developed situational exercises on videotape. Organizations using video simulations administer them to a group of applicants, who view the situations in the tape and then write down what they would do in each situation. The written responses are scored by personnel analysts in a fashion similar to that used with situational interviews. In a series of simulations called a B-PAD (Behavioral Police [or Personnel] Assessment Device), police applicants respond orally as they view tapes of situations encountered by police officers.

The development of simulation exercises can be expensive, but prepackaged exercises can be purchased at a much lower price. Though simulation exercises can be expensive, the cost may be money well spent, as simulations result in lower adverse impact than do traditional paper-and-pencil tests (Schmitt & Mills, 2001).

Work Samples. Usually, when a simulation does not involve a situational exercise, it is called a **work sample**. Work samples were discussed earlier in this section but are listed again here because they are common assessment center exercises.

Leaderless Group Discussions. In this exercise, applicants meet in small groups and are given a job-related problem to solve or a job-related issue to discuss. For example, supervisory applicants might be asked to discuss ways to motivate employees, or resident assistant applicants might be asked to discuss ways to reduce noise in residence halls. No leader is appointed, hence the term leaderless group discussion. As the applicants discuss the problem or issue, they are individually rated on such dimensions as cooperativeness, leadership, and analytical skills. To better understand leaderless group discussions, complete Exercise 5.2 in your workbook.

Business Games. **Business games** are exercises that allow the applicant to demonstrate such attributes as creativity, decision making, and ability to work with others. A business game in one assessment center used a series of Tinkertoy models. Four individuals

---

Simulation An exercise designed to place an applicant in a situation that is similar to the one that will be encountered on the job.

Work sample A method of selecting employees in which an applicant is asked to perform samples of actual job-related tasks.

Business game An exercise, usually found in assessment centers, that is designed to simulate the business and marketing activities that take place in an organization.

joined a group and were told that they were part of a company that manufactured goods. The goods ranged from Tinkertoy tables to Tinkertoy scuba divers, and the group's task was to buy the parts, manufacture the products, and then sell the products at the highest profit in an environment in which prices constantly changed.

Evaluation of Assessment Centers

Research indicates that assessment centers have been successful in predicting a wide range of employee behavior (Arthur, Day, McNelly, & Edens, 2003; Gaugler, Rosenthal, Thornton, & Bentson, 1987). Though assessment center scores are good predictors of performance, it has been argued that other methods can predict the same criteria better and less expensively than assessment centers (Schmidt & Hunter, 1998). Thus, even though an assessment center may be excellent in predicting certain aspects of employee behavior, other, less expensive methods may be as good if not better. Furthermore, there is some question regarding the ability of an assessment center developed at one location to predict performance in similar jobs at other locations (Schmitt, Schneider, & Cohen, 1990).

Though assessment centers were once thought to result in low levels of adverse impact, meta-analysis results (Dean, Roth, & Bobko, 2008) indicate that African Americans score substantially lower ($d = .52$) and Hispanics slightly lower ($d = .28$) on assessment centers than do whites. Women score higher than men ($d = .19$).

Predicting Performance Using Prior Experience

Applicant experience is typically measured in one of four ways: experience ratings of application/résumé information, biodata, reference checks, and interviews. Because interviews were discussed extensively in Chapter 4 and reference checking was discussed earlier in this chapter, only experience ratings and biodata will be discussed here.

Experience Ratings

The basis for experience ratings is the idea that past experience will predict future experience. Support for this notion comes from a meta-analysis by Quiñones, Ford, and Teachout (1995) that found a significant relationship between experience and future job performance ($r = .27$). In giving credit for experience, one must consider the amount of experience, the level of performance demonstrated during the previous experience, and how related the experience is to the current job. That is, experience by itself is not enough. Having 10 years of low-quality unrelated experience is not the same as 10 years of high-quality related experience. Sullivan (2000) suggests that there be a cap on credit for experience (e.g., no credit for more than five years of experience) because knowledge obtained through experience has a shelf life, and paying for experience is expensive. For example, given the rapid changes in technology, would a computer programmer with 20 years of experience actually have more relevant knowledge than one with 5 years of experience?

Biodata A method of selection involving application blanks that contain questions that research has shown will predict job performance.

Biodata

Biodata is a selection method that considers an applicant's life, school, military, community, and work experience. Meta-analyses have shown that biodata is a good predictor of job performance, as well as the best predictor of future employee tenure (Beall, 1991; Schmidt & Hunter, 1998).

In a nutshell, a biodata instrument is an application blank or questionnaire containing questions that research has shown measure the difference between successful and unsuccessful performers on a job. Each question receives a weight that indicates how well it differentiates poor from good performers. The better the differentiation, the higher the weight. Biodata instruments have several advantages:

- Research has shown that they can predict work behavior in many jobs, including sales, management, clerical, mental health counseling, hourly work in processing plants, grocery clerking, fast-food work, and supervising.
- They have been able to predict criteria as varied as supervisor ratings, absenteeism, accidents, employee theft, loan defaults, sales, and tenure.
- Biodata instruments result in higher organizational profit and growth (Terpstra & Rozell, 1993).
- Biodata instruments are easy to use, quickly administered, inexpensive, and not as subject to individual bias as interviews, references, and résumé evaluation.

Development of a Biodata Instrument

In the first step, information about employees is obtained in one of two ways: the file approach or the questionnaire approach. With the **file approach**, we obtain information from personnel files on employees' previous employment, education, interests, and demographics. As mentioned in the discussion of archival research in Chapter 1, the major disadvantage of the file approach is that information is often missing or incomplete.

Second, we can create a biographical questionnaire that is administered to all employees and applicants. An example is shown in Figure 5.7. The major drawback to the **questionnaire approach** is that information cannot be obtained from employees who have quit or been fired.

After the necessary information has been obtained, an appropriate criterion is chosen. As will be discussed in detail in Chapter 7, a criterion is a measure of work behavior such as quantity, absenteeism, or tenure. It is essential that a chosen criterion be relevant, reliable, and fairly objective. To give an example of developing a biodata instrument with a poor criterion, I was once asked to help reduce absenteeism in an organization by selecting applicants who had a high probability of superior future attendance. When initial data were gathered, it was realized that absenteeism was not an actual problem for this company. Less than half of the workforce had missed more than one day in six months; but the company perceived a problem because a few key workers had missed many days of work. Thus, using biodata (or any other selection device) to predict a nonrelevant criterion would not have saved the organization any money.

Once a criterion has been chosen, employees are split into two **criterion groups** based on their criterion scores. For example, if tenure is selected as the criterion measure, employees who have worked for the company for at least one year might be placed in the "long tenure" group, whereas workers who quit or were fired in less than one year would be placed in the "short tenure" group. If enough employees are available, the upper and lower 27% of performers can be used to establish the two groups (Hogan, 1994).

Once employee data have been obtained and the criterion and criterion groups chosen, each piece of employee information is compared with criterion group

File approach The gathering of biodata from employee files rather than by questionnaire.

Questionnaire approach The method of obtaining biodata from questionnaires rather than from employee files.

Criterion group Division of employees into groups based on high and low scores on a particular criterion.

Figure 5.7
Biodata Questionnaire

1. Member of high school student government?
   ☐ No   ☐ Yes

2. Number of jobs in past 5 years?
   ☐ 1   ☐ 2   ☐ 3–5   ☐ More than 5

3. Length of time at present address?
   ☐ Less than 1 year   ☐ 1–3 years
   ☐ 4–5 years   ☐ More than 5 years

4. Transportation to work:
   ☐ Walk   ☐ Bike   ☐ Own car
   ☐ Bus   ☐ Ride with a friend   ☐ Other

5. Education:
   ☐ Some high school
   ☐ High school diploma or GED
   ☐ Some college
   ☐ Associate's degree
   ☐ Bachelor's degree
   ☐ Master's degree
   ☐ Doctoral degree

Table 5.1   Biodata Weighting Process

Variable	Long Tenure (%)	Short Tenure (%)	Differences in Percentages	Unit Weight
Education				
High school	40	80	−40	−1
Bachelor's	59	15	+44	+1
Master's	1	5	−4	0

Vertical percentage method For scoring biodata in which the percentage of unsuccessful employees responding in a particular way is subtracted from the percentage of successful employees responding in the same way.

membership. The purpose of this stage is to determine which pieces of information will distinguish the members of the high criterion group from those in the low criterion group. Traditionally, the **vertical percentage method** has been used to do this. Percentages are calculated for each group on each item. The percentage of a particular response for the low group is subtracted from the percentage of the same response in the high group to obtain a weight for that item. An example of this weighting process is shown in Table 5.1. It is important to ensure that the weights make rational sense. Items that make sense are more face valid and thus easier to defend in court than items that are empirically valid but don't make rational sense (Stokes & Toth, 1996).

Once weights have been assigned to the items, the information is weighted and then summed to form a composite score for each employee. Composite scores are then correlated with the criterion to determine whether the newly created biodata instrument will significantly predict the criterion. Although this procedure sounds complicated, it actually is fairly easy, although time-consuming.

A problem with creating a biodata instrument is *sample size.* To create a reliable and valid biodata instrument, it is desirable to have data from hundreds of employees. For most organizations, however, such large sample sizes are difficult if not impossible to obtain. In creating a biodata instrument with a small sample, the risk of using items that do not really predict the criterion increases. This issue is important because most industrial psychologists advise that employees should be split into two samples when a biodata instrument is created: One sample, the **derivation sample**, is used to form the weights; the other sample, the **hold-out sample**, is used to double-check the selected items and weights. Although this sample splitting sounds like a great idea, it is not practical when dealing with a small or moderate sample size.

Research by Schmitt, Coyle, and Rauschenberger (1977) suggests that there is less chance of error when a sample is not split. Discussion on whether to split samples is bound to continue in the years ahead, but because many HR professionals will be dealing with relatively small numbers of employees, it might be best to create and validate a biodata instrument without splitting employees into derivation and hold-out samples.

A final issue to consider is the sample used to create the biodata instrument. Responses of current employees can be used to select the items and create the weights that will be applied to applicants. Stokes, Hogan, and Snell (1993) found that incumbents and applicants respond in very different ways, indicating that the use of incumbents to create and scale items may reduce validity.

Criticisms of Biodata

Even though biodata does a good job of predicting future employee behavior, it has been criticized on two major points. The first holds that the validity of biodata may not be stable—that is, its ability to predict employee behavior decreases with time. For example, Wernimont (1962) found that only three questions retained their predictive validity over the five-year period from 1954 to 1959. Similar results were reported by Hughes, Dunn, and Baxter (1956).

Other research (Brown, 1978), however, suggests that declines in validity found in earlier studies may have resulted from small samples in the initial development of the biodata instrument. Brown used data from more than 10,000 life insurance agents to develop his biodata instrument, but data from only 85 agents were used to develop the biodata instrument that was earlier criticized by Wernimont (1962). Brown compared the validity of his original sample (1933) with those from samples taken 6 years later (1939) and 38 years later (1971). The results indicated that the same items that significantly predicted the criterion in 1933 predicted at similar levels in 1971.

A study of the use of a biodata instrument created in one organization and used in 24 others found that the validity generalized across all organizations (Carlson, Scullen, Schmidt, Rothstein, & Erwin, 1999). Thus, biodata may be more stable across time and locations than was earlier thought (Rothstein, Schmidt, Erwin, Owens, & Sparks, 1990; Schmidt & Rothstein, 1994).

The second criticism is that some biodata items may not meet the legal requirements stated in the federal Uniform Guidelines, which establish fair hiring methods. Of greatest concern is that certain biodata items might lead to racial or sexual discrimination. For example, consider the selection item "distance from work." Applicants who live close to work might get more points than applicants who live farther away. The item may lead to racial discrimination if the organization is located in a predominantly White area. Removal of such discriminatory items, however, should eliminate most legal problems while still allowing for significant predictive validity (Reilly & Chao, 1982).

To make biodata instruments less disagreeable to critics, Gandy and Dye (1989) developed four standards to consider for each potential item:

1. The item must deal with events under a person's control (e.g., a person would have no control over birth order but would have control over the number of speeding tickets she received).
2. The item must be job related.
3. The answer to the item must be verifiable (e.g., a question about how many jobs an applicant has had is verifiable, but a question about the applicant's favorite type of book is not).
4. The item must not invade an applicant's privacy (asking why an applicant quit a job is permissible; asking about an applicant's sex life is usually not).

Even though these four standards eliminated many potential items, Gandy and Dye (1989) still obtained a validity coefficient of .33. Just as impressive as the high validity coefficient was that the biodata instrument showed good prediction for African Americans, Whites, and Hispanics.

The third criticism is that biodata can be faked, a charge that has been made against every selection method except work samples and ability tests. Research indicates that applicants do in fact respond to items in socially desirable ways (Stokes et al., 1993). To reduce faking, several steps can be taken, including:

- warning applicants of the presence of a lie scale (Kluger & Colella, 1993),
- using objective, verifiable items (Becker & Colquitt, 1992; Shaffer, Saunders, & Owens, 1986), and
- asking applicants to elaborate on their answers or to provide examples (Schmitt & Kunce, 2002). For example, if the biodata question asked, "How many leadership positions did you have in high school?" the next part of the item would be, "List the position titles and dates of those leadership positions."

By including bogus items—items that include an experience that does not actually exist (e.g., Conducted a Feldspar analysis to analyze data)—attempts to fake biodata can be detected (Kim, 2008). When including bogus items in a biodata instrument, it is important that the items be carefully researched to ensure that they don't represent activities that might actually exist (Levashina, Morgeson, & Campion, 2008). For example, a bogus item of "Have you ever conducted a Paradox analysis of a computer system?" might be interpreted by an applicant as, "Have you ever used the computer program, Paradox?"

A study by Ramsay, Kim, Oswald, Schmitt, and Gillespie (2008) provides an excellent example of how endorsing a bogus item might be due more to confusion than to actual lying. In their study, Ramsay et al. found that only 3 out of 361 subjects said they had operated a rhetaguard (this machine doesn't exist), yet 151 of the 361 said they had resolved disputes by isometric analysis. Why the difference? It may be that most people know the word *isometric* and most people have resolved disputes. They may not be sure if they ever used an isometric analysis to resolve their dispute, so many indicated that they had. With the rhetaguard, no applicant would have heard of it so they were probably sure they had not used it.

Interestingly, bright applicants tend not to fake biodata items as often as applicants lower in cognitive ability. But when they do choose to fake, they are better at doing it (Lavashina et al., 2008). Not surprisingly, applicants who fake biodata instruments are also likely to fake personality inventories and integrity tests (Carroll, 2008).

Predicting Performance Using Personality, Interest, and Character

Personality Inventories

Personality inventory A psychological assessment designed to measure various aspects of an applicant's personality.

Personality inventories are becoming increasingly popular as an employee selection method, in part because they predict performance better than was once thought, and in part because they result in less adverse impact than do ability tests. Personality inventories fall into one of two categories based on their intended purpose: measurement of types of normal personality or measurement of psychopathology (abnormal personality).

Tests of Normal Personality

Tests of normal personality measure the traits exhibited by normal individuals in everyday life. Examples of such traits are extraversion, shyness, assertiveness, and friendliness.

Determination of the number and type of personality dimensions measured by an inventory can usually be (1) based on a theory, (2) statistically based, or (3) empirically based. The number of dimensions in a *theory-based* test is identical to the number postulated by a well-known theorist. For example, the Myers-Briggs Type Indicator has four scales and is based on the personality theory of Carl Jung, whereas the Edwards Personal Preference Schedule, with 15 dimensions, is based on a theory by Henry Murray. The number of dimensions in a *statistically based* test is determined through a statistical process called factor analysis. The most well-known test of this type, the 16PF (Personality Factor), was created by Raymond Cattell and, as its name implies, contains 16 dimensions. The number and location of dimensions under which items fall in an *empirically based* test is determined by grouping answers given by people known to possess a certain characteristic. For example, in developing the **Minnesota Multiphasic Personality Inventory - 2 (MMPI-2)**, hundreds of items were administered to groups of psychologically healthy people and to people known to have certain psychological problems such as paranoia. Items that were endorsed more often by paranoid patients than healthy individuals were keyed under the paranoia dimension of the MMPI-2.

Minnesota Multiphasic Personality Inventory - 2 (MMPI-2) The most widely used objective test of psychopathology.

Although there are hundreds of personality inventories that measure hundreds of traits, there is general agreement that most personality traits can be placed into one of five main personality dimensions. Popularly known as the "Big Five" or the *five-factor model*, these dimensions are

- openness to experience (bright, inquisitive),
- conscientiousness (reliable, dependable),
- extraversion (outgoing, friendly),
- agreeableness (works well with others, a team player), and
- emotional stability (not anxious, tense).

Examples of common measures of normal personality used in employee selection include the Hogan Personality Inventory, the California Psychological Inventory, the NEO-PI (Neuroticism Extraversion Openness Personality Inventory), and the 16PF. To better understand personality inventories, complete the Employee Personality Inventory found in Exercise 5.3 in your workbook.

That objective personality inventories are useful in predicting performance in the United States and Europe is indicated in meta-analyses by Tett, Jackson, and Rothstein (1991), Barrick and Mount (1991), Tett, Jackson, Rothstein, and Reddon (1994), Salgado (1997), and Hurtz and Donovan (2000). Though there is some disagreement across the various meta-analyses, probably the best interpretation is that

- personality can predict performance at low but statistically significant levels;
- personality inventories can add incremental validity to the use of other selection tests;
- conscientiousness is the best predictor in most occupations and for most criteria; and
- the validity of the other four personality dimensions is dependent on the type of job and criterion for which the test is being validated. For example, a meta-analysis of predictors of police performance found that openness was the best personality predictor of academy performance; conscientiousness was the best predictor of supervisor ratings of performance; and emotional stability was the best predictor of disciplinary problems (Aamodt, 2004). In contrast, a meta-analysis of predictors of sales performance found that conscientiousness was the best predictor of both supervisor ratings and actual sales performance (Vinchur, Schippmann, Switzer, & Roth, 1998).

One of the concerns about using personality inventories for employee selection is that, because they are self-reports, they are relatively easy to fake. Research indicates that applicants can fake personality inventories, but do so less often than thought. When they do fake, it has minimal effect on the validity of the test results (Morgeson et al., 2007).

Though personality inventories aren't the best predictors of employee performance, they are useful in training and development programs in which employees and managers attempt to get insight into the ways in which they have related to others. In such contexts, personality inventories such as the Myers-Briggs Type Indicator are commonly used. It is important to understand that the personality inventories used in training and self-development programs were not designed for employee selection and should never be used for that purpose.

Tests of Psychopathology

Tests of psychopathology (abnormal behavior) determine whether individuals have serious psychological problems such as depression, bipolar disorder, and schizophrenia. Though used extensively by clinical psychologists, these tests are seldom used by industrial-organizational (I/O) psychologists except in the selection of law enforcement officers. Because the courts consider tests of psychopathology to be "medical exams," they can be administered only after a conditional offer of employment has been made to an applicant.

Tests of psychopathology are generally scored in one of two ways: objectively or projectively. **Projective tests** provide the respondent with unstructured tasks such as describing ink blots and drawing pictures. Because projective tests are of questionable reliability and validity (Lilienfeld, Wood, & Garb, 2001) and are time-consuming and expensive, they are rarely used in employee selection. Common tests in this category also include the **Rorschach Inkblot Test** and the **Thematic Apperception Test (TAT)**.

Projective tests A subjective test in which a subject is asked to perform relatively unstructured tasks, such as drawing pictures, and in which a psychologist analyzes his or her responses.

Rorschach Ink Blot Test A projective personality test.

Thematic Apperception Test (TAT) A projective personality test in which test-takers are shown pictures and asked to tell stories. It is designed to measure various need levels.

Objective tests are structured so that the respondent is limited to a few answers that will be scored by standardized keys. By far the most popular and heavily studied test of this type is the MMPI-2. Other tests in this category are the Millon Clinical Multiaxial Inventory (MCMI-III) and the Personality Assessment Inventory (PAI).

Interest Inventories

As the name implies, these tests are designed to tap vocational interests. The most commonly used **interest inventory** is the **Strong Interest Inventory (SII)** , which asks individuals to indicate whether they like or dislike 325 items such as bargaining, repairing electrical wiring, and taking responsibility. The answers to these questions provide a profile that shows how similar a person is to people already employed in 89 occupations that have been classified into 23 basic interest scales and 6 general occupational themes. The theory behind these tests is that an individual with interests similar to those of people in a particular field will more likely be satisfied in that field than in a field composed of people whose interests are dissimilar. Other popular interest inventories include the Minnesota Vocational Interest Inventory, the Occupational Preference Inventory, the Kuder Occupational Interest Survey, the Kuder Preference Record, and the California Occupational Preference System.

Although meta-analyses indicate that scores on interest inventories have poor validity in selecting employees (Aamodt, 2004; Schmidt & Hunter, 1998), meta-analyses by Morris and Campion (2003) and Nye, Su, Rounds, and Drasgow (2011) found that employees whose interests are congruent with those of the job are more satisfied and perform at higher levels than employees whose interests are not congruent with the job. Interest inventories are useful in **vocational counseling** (helping people find the careers for which they are best suited). Conducted properly, vocational counseling uses a battery of tests that, at a minimum, should include an interest inventory and a series of ability tests. The interest inventory scores suggest careers for which the individual's interests are compatible; the ability tests will tell him if he has the necessary abilities to enter those careers. If interest scores are high in a particular occupational area but ability scores are low, the individual is advised about the type of training that would best prepare him for a career in that particular area. To get a better feel for interest inventories, complete the short form of the Aamodt Vocational Interest Inventory (AVIS) found in Exercise 5.4 in your workbook.

Integrity Tests

Integrity tests (also called *honesty tests*) tell an employer the probability that an applicant would steal money or merchandise. Approximately 19% of employers use integrity tests to select employees for at least some jobs (Seitz, 2004). Such extensive use is due to the fact that 42% of retail employees, 62% of fast-food employees, and 32% of hospital employees have admitted stealing from their employers (Jones & Terris, 1989). One study estimates that 50% of employees with access to cash steal from their employers (Wimbush & Dalton, 1997). The 2010 National Retail Security Survey found that 43% of retail shrinkage is due to employee theft, 35% to shoplifting, and 18.3% to administrative error or vendor fraud. With increases in employee theft and identify theft, it is not surprising that integrity tests are commonly used.

Prior to the 1990s, employers used both electronic and paper-and-pencil integrity tests to screen applicants. In 1988, however, the U.S. Congress passed the Employee

Polygraph Protection Act making general use of electronic integrity tests, such as the **polygraph** and the **voice stress analyzer**, illegal except in a few situations involving law enforcement agencies and national security.

The law did, however, allow the use of paper-and-pencil integrity tests, which are either (1) overt or (2) personality based. **Overt integrity tests** are based on the premise that a person's attitudes about theft as well as his previous theft behavior will accurately predict his future honesty. They measure attitudes by asking the test taker to estimate the frequency of theft in society, how harsh penalties against thieves should be, how easy it is to steal, how often he has personally been tempted to steal, how often his friends have stolen, and how often he personally has stolen. **Personality-based integrity tests** are more general in that they tap a variety of personality traits thought to be related to a wide range of counterproductive behavior such as theft, absenteeism, and violence.

Overt tests are more reliable and valid in predicting theft and other counterproductive behaviors than are personality-based tests (Ones, Viswesvaran, & Schmidt, 1993). In addition to predicting counterproductive behavior, both overt and personality-based integrity tests have been shown to predict job performance (Ones et al., 1993) and have low levels of adverse impact against minorities (Ones & Viswesvaran, 1998). To see how integrity tests work, complete Exercise 5.5 in your workbook.

There are many integrity tests on the market, several of which do a decent job of predicting either polygraph results or admissions of theft (Ones et al., 1993). Unfortunately, few studies have attempted to correlate test scores with actual theft. Of course, these would be difficult to conduct. Instead, the validity of integrity tests has been determined by comparing test scores with

- polygraph test results,
- self-admissions of theft,
- shrinkage (the amount of goods lost by a store),
- known groups (e.g., priests vs. convicts), and
- future theft.

Unfortunately, all of these measures have problems. If polygraph results are used, the researcher is essentially comparing integrity test scores with the scores of a test— the polygraph—that has been made illegal partly because of questions about its accuracy. If self-admissions are used, the researcher is relying on dishonest people to be honest about their criminal history. If **shrinkage** is used, the researcher does not know which of the employees is responsible for the theft or, for that matter, what percentage of the shrinkage can be attributed to employee theft as opposed to customer theft or incidental breakage. Even if actual employee theft is used, the test may predict only employees who *get caught* stealing, as opposed to those who steal and do not get caught. The problems with known-group comparisons will be discussed in great detail in Chapter 6.

Predicting actual theft from an integrity test can be difficult because not all theft is caused by a *personal tendency* to steal (Bassett, 2008). Normally honest people might steal from an employer due to *economic pressure* caused by factors such as high debts or financial emergencies or by an organizational culture in which it is considered *normal to steal* (e.g., "It's OK because everyone takes food home with them"). Employee theft can also be the result of a *reaction to organizational policy* such as layoffs or a change in rules that employees perceive as unfair. To reduce theft caused by situational factors, nontesting methods such as increased security, explicit policy, and availability of appeal and suggestion systems are needed.

Polygraph An electronic test intended to determine honesty by measuring an individual's physiological changes after being asked questions.

Voice stress analyzer An electronic test to determine honesty by measuring an individual's voice changes after being asked questions.

Overt integrity test A type of honesty test that asks questions about applicants' attitudes toward theft and their previous theft history.

Personality-based integrity test A type of honesty test that measures personality traits thought to be related to antisocial behavior

Shrinkage The amount of goods lost by an organization as a result of theft, breakage, or other loss.

Although paper-and-pencil integrity tests are inexpensive and may be useful in predicting theft, they also have serious drawbacks. The most important disadvantage might be that males have higher failure rates than do females, and younger people have higher failure rates than do older people. Adverse impacts on these two groups pose little legal threat, but telling the parents of a 17-year-old boy that their son has just failed an honesty test is not the best way to foster good public relations. Failing an integrity test has a much more deleterious psychological impact than failing a spatial relations test. Another drawback to integrity tests is that, not surprisingly, applicants don't think highly of them (Anderson, Salgado, & Hülsheger, 2010).

Conditional Reasoning Tests

A problem with self-report measures such as personality inventories and integrity tests is that applicants may not provide accurate responses. This inaccuracy could be due to either the applicant *faking* responses to appear to be honest or to have a "better" personality or the applicant not actually being *aware* of his or her own personality or values. **Conditional reasoning tests** were initially developed by James (1998) to reduce these inaccurate responses and get a more accurate picture of a person's tendency to engage in aggressive or counterproductive behavior.

Conditional reasoning tests provide test takers with a series of statements and then ask the respondent to select the reason that best justifies or explains each of the statements. The type of reason selected by the individual is thought to indicate his or her aggressive biases or beliefs. Aggressive individuals tend to believe (LeBreton, Barksdale, Robin, & James, 2007) that

- most people have harmful intentions behind their behavior (hostile attribution bias);
- it is important to show strength or dominance in social interactions (potency bias);
- it is important to retaliate when wronged rather than try to maintain a relationship (retribution bias);
- powerful people will victimize less powerful individuals (victimization bias);
- evil people deserve to have bad things happen to them (derogation of target bias); and
- social customs restrict free will and should be ignored (social discounting bias).

As a result of these biases, aggressive individuals will answer conditional reasoning questions differently than less aggressive individuals. For example, a test taker might be given the following statement, "A senior employee asks a new employee if he would like to go to lunch." The test taker would then be asked to select which of the following statements best explains why the senior employee asked the new employee to lunch: (a) The senior employee was trying to make the new employee feel more comfortable or (b) The senior employee was trying to get the new employee on her side before the other employees had a chance to do the same thing. Selecting the first option would suggest an altruistic tendency whereas selecting the second option represents hostile attribution bias and would suggest a more aggressive tendency.

A meta-analysis by Berry, Sackett, and Tobares (2010) indicates that conditional reasoning tests of aggression predict counterproductive behaviors (r = .16) and job performance (r = .14) at statistically significant, yet low levels. Even more promising is that conditional reasoning tests are more difficult to fake than are integrity tests (LeBreton et al., 2007).

Though more research is needed, a study by Bing, Stewart, Davison, Green, McIntyre, and James (2007) found that counterproductive behavior is best predicted when conditional reasoning tests (implicit aggression) are combined with self-reports of aggressive tendencies (explicit aggression). That is, people who hold the six beliefs discussed previously and report that they have aggressive personalities tend to engage in counterproductive behavior to a much greater extent than those who score highly in only implicit or explicit aggression.

Credit History

According to a survey by the Society for Human Resource Management, 60% of employers conduct credit checks for at least some jobs (SHRM, 2010). These credit checks are conducted for two reasons: (1) Employers believe that people who owe money might be more likely to steal or accept bribes, and (2) employees with good credit are more responsible and conscientious and thus will be better employees. On the basis of limited research, it appears that the use of credit histories may result in adverse impact against Hispanic and African American applicants as well as low validity coefficients in predicting supervisor ratings (r = .07) and counterproductive work behaviors (r = .13; Aamodt, 2010). Several states have enacted legislation limiting the use of credit histories for employment purposes and the U.S. Congress is considering doing the same.

Graphology

Graphology Also called handwriting analysis, a method of measuring personality by looking at the way in which a person writes.

An interesting method to select employees is handwriting analysis, or **graphology**. The idea behind handwriting analysis is that the way people write reveals their personality, which in turn should indicate work performance. Contrary to popular belief, graphology is not a commonly used selection method in Europe (Bangerter, König, Blatti, & Salvisberg, 2009) and European employees react as poorly to it as do their American counterparts (Anderson & Witvliet, 2008).

To analyze a person's handwriting, a graphologist looks at the size, slant, width, regularity, and pressure of a writing sample. From these writing characteristics, information about temperament and mental, social, work, and moral traits is obtained.

Research on graphology has revealed interesting findings. First, graphologists are consistent in their judgments about script features but not in their interpretation about what these features mean (Keinan & Barak, 1984; Rafaeli & Klimoski, 1983). Second, trained graphologists are no more accurate or reliable at interpreting handwriting samples than are untrained undergraduates (Rafaeli & Klimoski, 1983) or psychologists (Ben-Shakhar, Bar-Hillel, Bilu, Ben-Abba, & Flug, 1986). Most importantly, the small body of scientific literature on the topic concludes that graphology is not a useful technique in employee selection (Simner & Goffin, 2003). Graphology predicts best when the writing sample is autobiographical (the writer writes an essay about himself), which means that graphologists are making their predictions more on the *content* of the writing than on the quality of the *handwriting* (Simner & Goffin, 2003).

Predicting Performance Limitations Due to Medical and Psychological Problems

As mentioned in Chapter 3, the Americans with Disabilities Act (ADA) limits the consideration of medical and psychological problems to those that keep the employee from performing essential job functions.

Drug Testing

Drug Testing Tests that indicate whether an applicant has recently used a drug.

Drug testing certainly is one of the most controversial testing methods used by HR professionals. The reason for its high usage is that 8.2% of employees admit to using drugs in the past month (Larson, Eyerman, Foster, & Gfroerer, 2007) and HR professionals believe not only that illegal drug use is dangerous but also that many employees are under the influence of drugs at work. Their beliefs are supported by research indicating that compared with non–drug users, illegal drug users are more likely to miss work (Bahls, 1998; Larson et al., 2007; Normand, Salyards, & Mahoney, 1990), are 16 times as likely to use health-care benefits (Bahls, 1998), are more likely to be fired and quit their jobs (Larson et al., 2007; Normand et al., 1990), and have 3.6 times as many accidents on the job (Cadrain, 2003a). One consulting firm estimates that a substance-abusing employee costs the employer $7,000 per year in lost productivity, absenteeism, and medical costs (Payne, 1997). Though the few available studies conclude that applicants testing positive for drugs will engage in some counterproductive behaviors, some authors (e.g., Morgan, 1990) believe that these studies are terribly flawed.

Because of such statistics, organizations are increasing their drug testing before applicants are hired. The increase in drug testing has resulted in fewer applicants testing positive for drugs; 4.6% in 2003 compared to 11% in 1990 (OHS, Inc., n.d.).

According to a survey of 143,565 adults by the Substance Abuse and Mental Health Services Administration (Larson et al. 2007; SAMHSA, 2010),

- 42.9% of employers test applicants for drug use;
- 8.0% of full-time employees admitted to using drugs in the previous month and 8.5% reported to recent alcohol abuse;
- men, people without college degrees, the unemployed, and employees with low-paying jobs were the most likely to have recently used drugs; and
- food preparation workers (17.4%), restaurant servers (15.4%), construction workers (15.1%), and writers, athletes, and designers (12.4%) are the most common drug users, whereas protective services (3.4%), social services (4.0%), and people working in education (4.1%) were the least common users of drugs.

Ninety-eight percent of the time, when applicants test positive for drugs, their job offers are withdrawn. When current employees test positive, 25% of organizations fire them and 66% refer them for counseling and treatment (Greenberg, 1996).

In general, applicants seem to accept drug testing as being reasonably fair (Mastrangelo, 1997; Truxillo, Normandy, & Bauer, 2001). Not surprisingly, compared with people who have never tried drugs, current drug users think drug testing is less fair, and previous drug users think drug testing is less fair if it results in termination but not when the consequence for being caught is rehabilitation (Truxillo et al., 2001).

Regardless of their popularity, drug testing programs appear to reduce employee drug use (French, Roebuck, & Alexandre, 2004).

Drug testing usually is done in two stages. In the first, an employee or applicant provides a urine or hair sample that is subjected to an initial screening test. The most common initial drug screens for urine are the **enzyme multiplied immunoassay technique (EMIT)** and **radioimmunoassay (RIA)**. EMIT uses enzymes as reagents, while RIA uses radioactive tagging. Both cost approximately $50 per sample. Hair-follicle testing costs two to three times as much per sample.

If the initial test for drugs is positive, then second-stage testing is done. The urine sample undergoes a more expensive confirmation test, such as **thin-layer chromatography** or **gas chromatography/mass spectrometry analysis**.

When both stages are used, testing is very accurate in detecting the presence of drugs. But drug tests are not able to determine whether an individual is impaired by drug use. An employee smoking marijuana on Saturday night will test positive for the drug on Monday, even though the effects of the drug have long since gone away. Most drugs can be detected 2 to 3 days after they have been used. The exceptions are the benzodiazepines, which can be detected for 4 to 6 weeks after use; PCP, which can be detected for 2 to 4 weeks; and marijuana, which can be detected up to 8 days for the casual user and up to 60 days for the frequent user. Testing conducted on hair follicles rather than urine samples can detect drug usage over longer periods, whereas testing using blood, saliva, or perspiration samples detect drug usage over shorter periods of time. A disadvantage to testing hair follicles is that it takes a few days before drugs will be detected in the hair; thus it is not a good method to determine whether an employee is currently under the influence.

Because positive drug tests have a certain degree of uncertainty, if applicants fail a preemployment drug test, they can usually reapply 6 months later. With such a policy, there are few legal pitfalls.

In the public sector or in the union environment, however, drug testing becomes complicated when it occurs after applicants are hired. Testing of employees usually takes one of three forms:

1. All employees or randomly selected employees are tested at predetermined times.
2. All employees or randomly selected employees are tested at random times.
3. Employees who have been involved in an accident or disciplinary action are tested following the incident.

The second form is probably the most effective in terms of punishing or preventing drug usage, but the third form of testing is legally the most defensible.

Psychological Exams

In jobs involving public safety (e.g., law enforcement, nuclear power, transportation), it is common for employers to give psychological exams to applicants after a conditional offer of hire has been made. If the applicant fails the exam, the offer is rescinded. Psychological exams usually consist of an interview by a clinical psychologist, an examination of the applicant's life history, and the administration of one or more of the psychological tests discussed earlier in this chapter. It is important to keep in mind that psychological exams are not designed to predict employee performance. Therefore, they should only be used to determine if a potential employee is a danger to himself or others.

Enzyme multiplied immunoassay technique (EMIT) A method of drug testing that uses enzymes to detect the presence of drugs in a urine sample.

Radioimmunoassay (RIA) A method of drug testing that uses radioactive tagging to determine the presence of drugs in a urine sample.

Thin-layer chromatography A method of analyzing urine specimens for drugs that is performed by hand and requires a great deal of analyst skill.

Gas chromatography/ mass spectrometry analysis A means of analyzing urine samples for the presence of drugs in which the urine sample is vaporized and then bombarded with electrons.

Medical Exams

In jobs requiring physical exertion, many employers require that a medical exam be taken after a conditional offer of hire has been made. In these exams, the physician is given a copy of the job description and asked to determine if there are any medical conditions that will keep the employee from safely performing the job.

Comparison of Techniques

After reading this chapter, you are probably asking the same question that industrial psychologists have been asking for years: Which method of selecting employees is best?

Validity

As shown in Table 5.2, it is clear that the unstructured interview, education, interest inventories, and some personality traits are not good predictors of future employee performance for most jobs. It is also clear that ability, work samples, biodata, and structured interviews do a fairly good job of predicting future employee performance. Over the past few years, researchers have been interested in determining which *combination* of selection tests is best. Though much more research is needed on this topic, it appears that the most valid selection battery includes a cognitive ability test and either a work sample, an integrity test, or a structured interview (Schmidt & Hunter, 1998).

Even though some selection techniques are better than others, *all* are potentially useful methods for selecting employees. In fact, a properly constructed selection battery usually contains a variety of tests that tap different dimensions of a job. Take, for example, the job of police officer. We might use a physical ability test to make sure the applicant has the strength and speed necessary to chase suspects and defend himself, a situational interview to tap his decision-making ability, a personality test to ensure that he has the traits needed for the job, and a background check to determine whether he has a history of antisocial behavior.

The late industrial psychologist Dan Johnson likened the selection process to a fishing trip. During our trip, we can try to catch one huge fish to make our meal or we can catch several small fish that, when cooked and placed on a plate, make the same size meal as one large fish. With selection tests, we try for one or two tests that will predict performance at a high level. But by combining several tests with smaller validities, we can predict performance just as well as with one test with a very high validity.

Legal Issues

As you might recall from Chapter 3, methods used to select employees are most prone to legal challenge when they result in adverse impact, invade an applicant's privacy, and do not appear to be job related (lack face validity). As shown in Table 5.3, cognitive ability and GPA will result in the highest levels of adverse impact, whereas integrity tests, references, and personality inventories will result in the lowest levels (in viewing this table, you might want to review the concept of *d* scores and effect

Table 5.2 Validity of Selection Techniques

Criterion/Selection Technique	Validity Observed	Validity Corrected	K	N	Meta-analysis
Performance					
Cognitive ability (US)	.39	.51			Schmidt & Hunter (1998)
Job knowledge		.48			Hunter & Hunter (1984)
Biodata	.36	.51	22	20,905	Beall (1991)
Structured interviews	.34	.57	60	6,723	Huffcutt & Arthur (1994)
Work samples (verbal)	.34	.48	58	4,220	Hardison, Kim, & Sackett (2005)
Work samples (motor)	.31	.43	32	2,256	Hardison, Kim, & Sackett (2005)
Behavioral description interviews	.31	.51	22	2,721	Huffcutt et al. (2003)
Cognitive ability (Europe)	.29	.62	93	9,554	Salgado et al. (2003)
Assessment centers	.28	.38	258	83,761	Arthur et al. (2003)
Situational interviews	.26	.43	32	2,815	Huffcutt et al. (2003)
Work samples	.26	.39	54	10,469	Roth et al. (2005)
Spatial-mechanical ability (Europe)	.23	.51	40	3,750	Salgado et al. (2003)
Experience	.22	.27	44	25,911	Quiñones et al. (1995)
Integrity tests	.21	.34	222	68,722	Ones et al. (1993)
Situational judgment tests	.20	.26	118	24,756	McDaniel et al. (2007)
Personality (self-efficacy)	.19	.23	10	1,122	Judge & Bono (2001)
References	.18	.29	30	7,419	Aamodt & Williams (2005)
Personality (self-esteem)	.18	.26	40	5,145	Judge & Bono (2001)
Grades	.16	.32	71	13,984	Roth et al. (1996)
Graphology (autobiographical)	.16	.22	17	1,084	Simner & Goffin (2003)
Personality (conscientiousness)	.15	.24	42	7,342	Hurtz & Donovan (2003)
Personality (locus of control)	.14	.22	35	4,310	Judge & Bono (2001)
Personality (overall)	.12	.17	97	13,521	Tett et al. (1994)
Unstructured interview	.11	.20	15	7,308	Huffcutt & Arthur (1994)
Interest inventories	.10	.13			Hunter & Hunter (1984)
Personality (emotional stability)	.09	.15	35	5,027	Hurtz & Donovan (2003)
Graphology (nonautobiographical)	.09	.12	6	442	Simner & Goffin (2003)
Personality (agreeableness)	.07	.12	38	5,803	Hurtz & Donovan (2003)
Education	.13	.18	7	1,562	Ng & Feldman (2009)
Personality (extraversion)	.06	.09	37	5,809	Hurtz & Donovan (2003)
Personality (openness)	.03	.06	33	4,881	Hurtz & Donovan (2003)
Tenure					
Biodata	.28		27	70,737	Beall (1991)
References	.08		3	2,131	Aamodt & Williams (2005)

Table 5.2   Validity of Selection Techniques *(Continued)*

Criterion/Selection Technique	Validity		K	N	Meta-analysis
	Observed	**Corrected**			
Training Proficiency					
Cognitive ability (US)		.56			Hunter & Hunter (1984)
Work samples (verbal)	.39	.44	50	3,161	Hardison, Kim, & Sackett (2005)
Work samples (motor)	.36	.41	38	7,086	Hardison, Kim, & Sackett (2005)
Cognitive ability (Europe)	.28	.54	97	16,065	Salgado et al. (2003)
Spatial-mechanical ability (Europe)	.20	.40	84	15,834	Salgado et al. (2003)
Integrity tests		.38			Schmidt et al. (1994)
Biodata		.30			Hunter & Hunter (1984)
Personality (extraversion)	.15	.26	17	3,101	Barrick & Mount (1991)
Personality (openness)	.14	.25	14	2,700	Barrick & Mount (1991)
Personality (conscientiousness)	.13	.23	17	3,585	Barrick & Mount (1991)
References		.23			Hunter & Hunter (1984)
Education		.20			Hunter & Hunter (1984)
Vocational interest		.18			Hunter & Hunter (1984)
Personality (emotional stability)	.04	.07	19	3,283	Barrick & Mount (1991)
Personality (agreeableness)	.04	.06	19	3,685	Barrick & Mount (1991)

Note: Observed = mean observed validity; Corrected = observed validity corrected for study artifacts; k = number of studies in the meta-analysis; N = total number of subjects in the meta-analysis

sizes discussed in Chapter 1). In terms of face validity, applicants perceive interviews, work samples/simulations, and résumés as being the most job-related/fair, and they view graphology, integrity tests, and personality tests as being the least job related/ fair (Anderson, Salgado, & Hülsheger, 2010).

Rejecting Applicants

Once a decision has been made regarding which applicants will be hired, those who will not be hired must be notified. Rejected applicants should be treated well because they are potential customers and potential applicants for other positions that might become available in the organization (Koprowski, 2004; Waung & Brice, 2003). In fact, Aamodt and Peggans (1988) found that applicants who were rejected "properly" were more likely to continue to be a customer at the organization and to apply for future job openings.

A good example of this was provided in a letter to the editor of *HR Magazine* by HR professional Jim Reitz, who was treated poorly on two different occasions when applying for a job with an employment agency. When he became an HR manager

Table 5.3 Racial and Ethnic Differences in Scores of Selection Techniques

Selection Technique	d Score			Meta-analysis
	White-Black	White-Hispanic	Male-Female	
Cognitive ability	1.10	.72		Roth et al (2001)
GPA	.78			Roth & Bobko (2000)
Work samples				
Applicants	.73			Roth, Bobko, McFarland, & Buster (2008)
Incumbents—civilian	.53			Roth, Bobko, McFarland, & Buster (2008)
Incumbents—military	.03			Roth, Bobko, McFarland, & Buster (2008)
Assessment centers	.52	.28	−.19	Dean, Roth, & Bobko (2008)
Job sample/job knowledge	.48	.47		Roth, Huffcutt, & Bobko (2003)
Situational judgment tests	.38	.24	−.11	Whetzel, McDaniel, & Nguyen (2008)
Biodata	.33			Bobko, Roth, & Potosky (1999)
Structured interview	.23			Huffcutt & Roth (1998)
Personality—extraversion	.16	.02		Foldes, Duehr, & Ones (2008)
Personality—openness	.10	.02		Foldes, Duehr, & Ones (2008)
Personality—emotional stability	.09	−.03		Foldes, Duehr, & Ones (2008)
References	.08		−.01	Aamodt & Williams (2005)
Integrity tests	.07	−.05		Ones & Viswesvaran (1998)
Personality—agreeableness	.03	.05		Foldes, Duehr, & Ones (2008)
Personality—conscientiousness	.07	−.08		Foldes, Duehr, & Ones (2008)

Rejection letter A letter from an organization to an applicant informing the applicant that he or she will not receive a job offer.

with a large company, one of the first things he did was contact the employment agency to notify it that his company would not be doing business with it due to the way in which he had been treated as an applicant. Reitz pointed out that his new company spends over a million dollars on temps and the employment agency would get none of it.

What is the best way to reject an applicant? The most interesting **rejection letter** I have seen came from Circuit City about 20 years ago. At the bottom of the letter was a sentence stating that you could take the rejection letter to any Circuit City store within the next 30 days and get a 10% discount. Imagine the clerk calling for assistance over the store intercom; "We have a rejected applicant on register four, could a manager please come and approve the discount?"

I remember getting a rejection letter from a graduate school back in 1978 stating that they had 400 people apply and that my application lacked the quality to get past the department clerk! They were kind enough to wish me success in my career.

Clearly the above two examples are not best practices. So, what is? Aamodt and Peggans (1988) found that rejection letters differ to the extent that they contain the following types of responses:

- A personally addressed and signed letter
- The company's appreciation to the applicant for applying for a position with the company

- A compliment about the applicant's qualifications
- A comment about the high qualifications possessed by the other applicants
- Information about the individual who was actually hired
- A wish of good luck in future endeavors
- A promise to keep the applicant's résumé on file

Though research has not clearly identified the best way to write a rejection letter, the following guidelines are probably a good place to start.

- Send rejection letters to applicants. Though most organizations do not do this (Brice & Waung, 1995), failure to send a letter results in applicants feeling negatively toward an organization (Waung & Brice, 2000). Excuses about not having the funds to notify applicants are probably not justified when one considers the ill feelings that may result from not contacting applicants.
- Don't send the rejection letter immediately. The surprising results of a study by Waung and Brice (2000) suggest that applicants react more positively if there is a delay in receiving the letter. Though these findings seem to go against the thought that applicants can better manage their job searches if they know they have been rejected, it may be that too quick a rejection makes applicants feel as if they are such a loser that the organization quickly discarded them (e.g., the graduate school whose clerk rejected my application).
- Be as personable and as specific as possible in the letter. With the use of automated applicant tracking systems, it is fairly easy to individually address each letter, express the company's appreciation for applying, and perhaps explain who was hired and what their qualifications were. In general, "friendly" letters result in better applicant attitudes (Aamodt & Peggans, 1988; Feinberg, Meoli-Stanton, & Gable, 1996).
- Including a statement about the individual who received the job can increase applicant satisfaction with both the selection process and the organization (Aamodt & Peggans, 1988; Gilliland et al., 2001).
- Do not include the name of a contact person. Surprisingly, research has shown that including such a contact decreases the probability that a person will reapply for future jobs or use the company's products (Waung & Brice, 2000).

Perhaps the most important thing to consider when writing a letter of rejection is to be honest. Do not tell applicants that their résumés will be kept on file if the files for each job opening will not be used. Adair and Pollen (1985) think rejection letters treat job applicants like unwanted lovers; they either beat around the bush ("There were many qualified applicants") or stall for time ("We'll keep your résumé on file"). A study by Brice and Waung (1995) supports these ideas, as most organizations either never formally reject applicants, or when they do, take an average of almost a month to do so.

Applied Case Study
City of New London, Connecticut, Police Department

The City of New London, Connecticut, was developing a system to select police officers. One of the tests it selected was the Wonderlic Personnel Test, a cognitive ability test that was mentioned in this chapter. For each occupation, the Wonderlic provides a minimum score and a maximum score. For police officers, the minimum score is 20 and the maximum is 27. Robert J. Jordan applied for a job as a police officer but was not given an interview because his score of 33 (equivalent to an IQ of 125) made him "too bright" to be a cop. New London's reasoning was that highly intelligent officers would get bored with their jobs and would either cause trouble or would quit. The New London deputy police chief was quoted as saying, "Bob Jordan is exactly the type of guy we would want to screen out. Police work is kind of mundane. We don't deal in gunfights every night. There's a personality that can take that." Turnover was a great concern, as the city spent about $25,000 sending each officer through the academy.

The police department in neighboring Groton, Connecticut, also uses the Wonderlic but tries to hire the highest scorers possible—a policy with which most I/O psychologists would agree.

When New London's policy received national publicity, the city became the butt of many jokes and the policy became a source of embarrassment to many of the residents. According to one resident, "I'd rather have them hire the right man or woman for the job and keep replacing them than have the same moron for twenty years." Another commented, "Your average dunderhead is not the person you want to try to solve a fight between a man and his wife at two a.m." The ridicule got so bad that another city ran an ad asking, "Too smart to work for New London? Apply with us"; San Francisco police chief Fred Lau encouraged Jordan to apply to the San Francisco Police Department; and host Jay Leno rewrote the theme song for the television show to include, "Dumb cops, dumb cops, whatcha gonna do with a low IQ?"

Jordan filed a lawsuit but lost. The judge ruled, "Plaintiff may have been disqualified unwisely but he was not denied equal protection."

- Do you agree with New London's reasoning about being "too bright"?

- Do you agree with the judge's decision that it was not discriminatory to not hire people who are highly intelligent? Why or why not?

- How would you have determined the cognitive ability requirements for this job?

Information about this case can be found by following the web links in the text website.

The Ethics of Tests of Normal Personality in Employee Selection

In this chapter you learned that personality testing for selection purposes has become increasingly popular, particularly those which are given for normal personality. And, as with any other selection test (i.e., cognitive ability, physical agility), an applicant has no choice but to complete the test or otherwise risk not being considered for a position. So, applicants are asked to share a bit of who they are, rather than what they can do and how well they can do it.

As long as these tests aren't used to discriminate against protected classes, they are not illegal to use in the selection process. But opponents of personality inventories wonder just how ethical these tests are. First, the personality inventories can be considered a violation of privacy: many of these inventories ask questions about how a person feels or thinks about a particular concept or situation. For example: the online Jung Typology test (www.humanmetrics.com) asks a test taker to answer yes or no to such questions as: You often think about humankind and its destiny; You trust reason more than feelings; You feel involved when you watch TV soap operas. If these questions don't pertain to the actual job a person will be doing, what business is it of a company to know that information? Supporters of personality inventories will say,

"It might show us whether a candidate is an introvert or extrovert." But what right do employees have to know whether a candidate is an introvert or extrovert as long as the applicant can do the job well?

Second, just how well do these tests predict work performance in a particular job? That is, if your personality score shows you are low in creativity, is it saying that you will be a poor performer in a position that requires a certain level of creativity?

And, third, the results of some of these tests can be impacted by how the test taker is feeling that day. If the test taker is feeling sad or tired, how she rates herself on a question that asks about how much she likes to be around other people may be different than how the test taker really feels on a normal or usual day. So, rather than using these tests to make crucial hiring decisions based on test results, critics believe they should only be used as icebreakers, as exercises in employee training programs, or for counseling purposes.

The testing industry is basically unregulated, although there have been some attempts to introduce legislation preventing or better regulating these, as well as any other employment tests. The Association of Test Publishers continues to fight off such legislative challenges preventing the use of these tests for selection purposes. The Association contends, as do companies that use personality inventories, that using personality inventories in conjunction with other selection methods increases the validity of the selection process.

Interviews and other types of tests show the skill and knowledge of an applicant. Personality inventories will show how well an applicant might fit into the organizational culture and get along with others, which is just as important as the applicant's other competencies. So, why shouldn't the personality inventory be part of the selection process?

What Do You Think?

- In your class, your professor will probably ask you to take the Employee Personality Inventory in your workbook. After you do, consider whether or not you want your job performance to be judged based on the results of such a test. Would you say that this test would fairly predict your ability to perform in certain jobs?

- Does it accurately portray how you would fit into an organization's culture or how you would get along with others? If it doesn't accurately portray you, would you then say such a test is unethical?

- Should the tests be better regulated? Are companies right in using them in their selection process?

- Do you see any other ethical concerns related to using personality tests?

- Is there a fairer and more ethical way for companies to determine if applicants will fit into the organizational culture and get along with others?

Chapter Summary

In this chapter you learned:

- References typically are not good predictors of performance due to such factors as leniency, poor reliability, fear of legal ramifications, and a variety of extraneous factors.
- The trait approach to scoring letters of recommendation is a valid method of predicting future performance.
- Reliability, validity, cost, and potential for legal problems should be considered when choosing the right type of employment test for a particular situation.
- Cognitive ability tests, job knowledge tests, biodata, work samples, and assessment centers are some of the better techniques in predicting future performance.
- Personality inventories, interest inventories, references, and graphology are not highly related to employee performance.
- Drug testing and medical exams are commonly used to screen employees prior to their starting a job.
- Writing a well-designed rejection letter can have important organizational consequences.

Questions for Review

1. Should an organization provide reference information for former employees? Why or why not?
2. What should be the most important factors in choosing a selection method? Explain your answers.
3. What selection methods are most valid?
4. Should employers test employees for drugs? Why or why not?
5. Are integrity tests fair and accurate? Explain your answer.

Media Resources and Learning Tools

- Visit our website. Go to www.cengage.com/psychology/aamodt, where you will find online resources directly linked to your book, including chapter-by-chapter quizzing, flashcards, crossword puzzles, application activities, and more.
- Want more practice applying industrial/organizational psychology? Check out the *I/O Applications Workbook*. This workbook (keyed to your textbook) offers engaging, high-interest activities to help you reinforce the important concepts presented in the text.

© Chris Ryan/OJO Images/Getty Images

Learning Objectives

➡ Understand how to determine the reliability of a test and the factors that affect test reliability

➡ Understand the five ways to validate a test

➡ Learn how to find information about tests

➡ Understand how to determine the utility of a selection test

➡ Be able to evaluate a test for potential legal problems

➡ Understand how to use test scores to make personnel selection decisions

n Chapter 3, you learned that many laws and regulations affect employee selection methods. In Chapters 4 and 5, you learned about the ways in which to recruit and select employees. In this chapter, you will learn how to evaluate whether a particular selection method is useful and how to use test scores to make a hiring decision. Throughout this chapter, you will encounter the word *test*. Though this word often conjures up an image of a paper-and-pencil test, in industrial/organizational (I/O) psychology, *test* refers to any technique used to evaluate someone. Thus, employment tests include such methods as references, interviews, and assessment centers.

Characteristics of Effective Selection Techniques

Effective selection techniques have four characteristics. They are reliable, valid, cost-efficient, fair, and legally defensible.

Reliability

Reliability The extent to which a score from a test or from an evaluation is consistent and free from error.

Reliability is the extent to which a score from a selection measure is stable and free from error. If a score from a measure is not stable or error-free, it is not useful. For example, suppose we are using a ruler to measure the lengths of boards that will be used to build a doghouse. We want each board to be 4 feet long, but each time we measure a board, we get a different number. If the ruler does not yield the same number each time the same board is measured, the ruler cannot be considered reliable and thus is of no use. The same is true of selection methods. If applicants score differently each time they take a test, we are unsure of their actual scores. Consequently, the scores from the selection measure are of little value. Therefore, reliability is an essential characteristic of an effective measure. Test reliability is determined in four ways: test-retest reliability, alternate-forms reliability, internal reliability, and scorer reliability.

Test-Retest Reliability

Test-retest reliability The extent to which repeated administration of the same test will achieve similar results.

Temporal stability The consistency of test scores across time.

With the **test-retest reliability** method, each one of several people take the same test twice. The scores from the first administration of the test are correlated with scores from the second to determine whether they are similar. If they are, the test is said to have **temporal stability**: The test scores are stable across time and not highly susceptible to such random daily conditions as illness, fatigue, stress, or uncomfortable testing conditions. There is no standard amount of time that should elapse between the two administrations of the test. However, the time interval should be long enough so that the specific test answers have not been memorized, but short enough so that the person has not changed significantly.

For example, if 3 years have elapsed between administrations of a personality inventory, there may be a very low correlation between the two sets of scores; but the low correlation may not be the result of low test reliability. Instead, it could be caused by personality changes of the people in the sample over time (Kaplan & Saccuzzo, 2009). Likewise, if only 10 minutes separate the two administrations, a very high correlation between the two sets of scores might occur. This high correlation may represent only what the people remembered from the first testing rather than what they actually believe. Typical time intervals between test administrations range from 3 days to 3 months. Usually, the longer the time interval, the lower the reliability coefficient. The typical test-retest reliability coefficient for tests used in industry is .86 (Hood, 2001).

Test-retest reliability is not appropriate for all kinds of tests. It would not make sense to measure the test-retest reliability of a test designed to measure short-term moods or feelings. For example, the State–Trait Anxiety Inventory measures two types of anxiety. *Trait anxiety* refers to the amount of anxiety that an individual normally has all the time, and *state anxiety* is the amount of anxiety an individual has at any given moment. For the test to be useful, it is important for the measure of trait anxiety, but not the measure of state anxiety, to have temporal stability.

Alternate-Forms Reliability

With the **alternate-forms reliability** method, two forms of the same test are constructed. As shown in Table 6.1, a sample of 100 people are administered both forms of the test; half of the sample first receive Form A and the other half Form B. This **counterbalancing** of test-taking order is designed to eliminate any effects that taking one form of the test first may have on scores on the second form.

The scores on the two forms are then correlated to determine whether they are similar. If they are, the test is said to have **form stability**. Why would anyone use this method? If there is a high probability that people will take a test more than once, two forms of the test are needed to reduce the potential advantage to individuals who take the test a second time. This situation might occur in police department examinations. To be promoted in most police departments, an officer must pass a promotion exam. If the officer fails the exam one year, the officer can retake the exam the next year. If only one form of the test were available, the officer retaking the test for the seventh time could remember many of the questions and possibly score higher than an officer taking the test for the first time. Likewise, applicants who fail a credentialing exam (e.g., the Bar Exam for attorneys or the Professional in Human Resources (PHR) certification for human resources professionals) would be likely to retake the exam.

Will retaking an exam actually result in higher test scores? A meta-analysis by Hausknecht, Halpert, Di Paolo, and Moriarty Gerard (2007) found that applicants retaking the same cognitive ability test will increase their scores about twice as much ($d = .46$) as applicants taking an alternate form of the cognitive ability test ($d = .24$). Not surprisingly, the longer the interval between the two test administrations, the lower the gain in test scores. It should be noted that the Hausknecht et al. meta-analysis was limited to cognitive ability tests. It appears that with knowledge tests, retaking the test will still increase tests scores, but the increase is at the same level whether the second test is the same test or an alternate form of the same test (Raymond, Neustel, & Anderson, 2007).

Multiple forms also might be used in large groups of test takers where there is a possibility of cheating. Perhaps one of your professors has used more than one form

Table 6.1 Design for Typical Alternate Forms Reliability Study

Subjects	Administration Order	
	First	**Second**
1–50	Form A	Form B
51–100	Form B	Form A

of the same test to discourage cheating. The last time you took your written driver's test, multiple forms probably were used, just as they were when you took the SAT or ACT to be admitted to college. As you can see, multiple forms of a test are common.

Recall that with test-retest reliability, the time interval between administrations usually ranges from 3 days to 3 months. With alternate-forms reliability, however, the time interval should be as short as possible. If the two forms are administered 3 weeks apart and a low correlation results, the cause of the low reliability is difficult to determine. That is, the test could lack either form stability or temporal stability. Thus, to determine the cause of the unreliability, the interval needs to be short. The average correlation between alternate forms of tests used in industry is .89 (Hood, 2001).

In addition to being correlated, two forms of a test should also have the same mean and standard deviation (Clause, Mullins, Nee, Pulakos, & Schmitt, 1998). The test in Table 6.2, for example, shows a perfect correlation between the two forms. People who scored well on Form A also scored well on Form B. But the average score on Form B is two points higher than on Form A. Thus, even though the perfect correlation shows that the scores on the two forms are parallel, the difference in mean scores indicates that the two forms are not equivalent. In such a case, either the forms must be revised or different standards (norms) must be used to interpret the results of the test.

Any changes in a test potentially change its reliability, validity, difficulty, or all three. Such changes might include the order of the items, examples used in the questions, method of administration, and time limits. Though alternate-form differences potentially affect test outcomes, most research indicates that these effects are either nonexistent or rather small. For example, meta-analyses suggest that computer administration (Dwight & Feigelson, 2000; Kingston, 2009) or PowerPoint administration (Larson, 2001) of cognitive ability or knowledge tests results in scores equivalent to paper-and-pencil administration. However, a quasi-experimental study by Ployhart, Weekley, Holtz, and Kemp (2003) found that personality inventories and situational judgment tests administered on the Web resulted in lower scores and better internal reliability than the same test administered in the traditional

Table 6.2 Example of Two Parallel but Nonequivalent Forms

Subjects	Test Scores	
	Form A	Form B
1	6	8
2	9	11
3	11	13
4	12	14
5	12	14
6	17	19
7	18	20
8	19	21
9	21	23
10	24	26
Average Score	14.9	16.9

paper-and-pencil format. Interestingly, research suggests that African Americans, but not Whites, score higher on video-based tests than on traditional paper-and-pencil tests (Chan & Schmitt, 1997).

Internal Reliability

A third way to determine the reliability of a test or inventory is to look at the consistency with which an applicant responds to items measuring a similar dimension or construct (e.g., personality trait, ability, area of knowledge). The extent to which similar items are answered in similar ways is referred to as *internal consistency* and measures **item stability**.

In general, the longer the test, the higher its internal consistency—that is, the agreement among responses to the various test items. To illustrate this point, let us look at the final exam for this course. If the final were based on three chapters, would you want a test consisting of only three multiple-choice items? Probably not. If you made a careless mistake in marking your answer or fell asleep during part of the lecture from which a question was taken, your score would be low. But if the test had 100 items, one careless mistake or one missed part of a lecture would not severely affect your total score.

Another factor that can affect the internal reliability of a test is **item homogeneity**. That is, do all of the items measure the same thing, or do they measure different constructs? The more homogeneous the items, the higher the internal consistency. To illustrate this concept, let us again look at your final exam based on three chapters.

If we computed the reliability of the entire exam, it would probably be relatively low. Why? Because the material assessed by the test questions is not homogeneous. They are measuring knowledge from three topic areas (three chapters), two sources (lecture and text), and two knowledge types (factual and conceptual). If we broke the test down by chapter, source, and item type, the reliability of the separate test components would be higher, because we would be looking at groups of homogeneous items.

When reading information about internal consistency in a journal article or a test manual, you will encounter three terms that refer to the method used to determine internal consistency: split-half, coefficient alpha, and **K-R 20 (Kuder-Richardson formula 20)**. The **split-half method** is the easiest to use, as items on a test are split into two groups. Usually, all of the odd-numbered items are in one group and all the even-numbered items are in the other group. The scores on the two groups of items are then correlated. Because the number of items in the test has been reduced, researchers have to use a formula called the **Spearman-Brown prophecy** to adjust the correlation.

Cronbach's **coefficient alpha** (Cronbach, 1951) and the K-R 20 (Kuder & Richardson, 1937) are more popular and accurate methods of determining internal reliability, although they are more complicated to use and thus are calculated by computer program rather than by hand. Essentially, both the coefficient alpha and the K-R 20 represent the reliability coefficient that would be obtained from all possible combinations of split halves. The difference between the two is that the K-R 20 is used for tests containing dichotomous items (e.g., yes-no, true-false), whereas the coefficient alpha can be used not only for dichotomous items but for tests containing interval and ratio items such as five-point rating scales. The median internal reliability coefficient found in the research literature is .81, and coefficient alpha is by far the most commonly reported measure of internal reliability (Hogan, Benjamin, & Brezinski, 2003).

Item stability The extent to which responses to the same test items are consistent.

Item homogeneity The extent to which test items measure the same construct.

Kuder-Richardson Formula 20 (K-R 20) A statistic used to determine internal reliability of tests that use items with dichotomous answers (yes/no, true/false).

Split-half method A form of internal reliability in which the consistency of item responses is determined by comparing scores on half of the items with scores on the other half of the items.

Spearman-Brown prophecy formula Used to correct reliability coefficients resulting from the split-half method.

Coefficient alpha A statistic used to determine internal reliability of tests that use interval or ratio scales.

Scorer Reliability

A fourth way of assessing reliability is **scorer reliability**. A test or inventory can have homogeneous items and yield heterogeneous scores and still not be reliable if the person scoring the test makes mistakes. Scorer reliability is an issue in projective or subjective tests in which there is no one correct answer, but even tests scored with the use of keys suffer from scorer mistakes. For example, Allard, Butler, Faust, and Shea (1995) found that 53% of hand-scored personality tests contained at least one scoring error, and 19% contained enough errors to alter a clinical diagnosis. Goddard, Simons, Patton, and Sullivan (2004) found that 12% of hand-scored interest inventories contained scoring or plotting errors, and of that percentage, 64% would have changed the career advice offered.

When human judgment of performance is involved, scorer reliability is discussed in terms of *interrater reliability*. That is, will two interviewers give an applicant similar ratings, or will two supervisors give an employee similar performance ratings? If you are a fan of *American Idol*, how would you rate the interrater reliability among Steven, Jennifer, and Randy?

Evaluating the Reliability of a Test

In the previous pages, you learned that it is important that scores on a test be reliable and that there are four common methods for determining reliability. When deciding whether a test demonstrates sufficient reliability, two factors must be considered: the magnitude of the reliability coefficient and the people who will be taking the test.

The reliability coefficient for a test can be obtained from your own data, the test manual, journal articles using the test, or test compendia that will be discussed later in the chapter. To evaluate the coefficient, you can compare it with reliability coefficients typically obtained for similar types of tests. For example, if you were considering purchasing a personality inventory and saw in the test manual that the test-retest reliability was .60, a comparison with the coefficients shown in Table 6.3 would show that the reliability for the test you are considering is lower than what is normally found for that *type* of test.

The second factor to consider is the people who will be taking your test. For example, if you will be using the test for managers, but the reliability coefficient in the test manual was established with high school students, you would have less confidence that the reliability coefficient would generalize well to your organization. A good example of this was the meta-analysis of the reliability of the NEO personality scales. In that meta-analysis, Caruso (2003) found that the reliability was lower on samples of men and students than on samples of women and adults. The Career Workshop Box gives a summary of evaluating tests.

Validity

Validity is the degree to which inferences from scores on tests or assessments are justified by the evidence. As with reliability, a test must be valid to be useful. But just because a test is reliable does not mean it is valid. For example, suppose that we want to use height requirements to hire typists. Our measure of height (a ruler) would certainly be a reliable measure; most adults will get no taller, and two people measuring an applicant's height will probably get very similar measurements. It is doubtful, however, that height is related to typing performance. Thus, a ruler would be a reliable measure of height, but height would not be a valid measure of typing performance.

Table 6.3 Comparison of Typical Test Reliability Coefficients

| Test Type | Reliability Type | | | Meta-analysis |
	Combined	Internal	Test-retest	
Cognitive ability			.83	Salgado et al. (2003)
Grade Point Average				
First year		.86		Beatty et al. (2011)
Overall		.93		Beatty et al. (2011)
Integrity tests		.81	.85	Ones, Viswesvaran, & Schmidt (1993)
Overt		.83		
Personality based		.72		
Interest inventories		.92		Barrick, Mount, & Gupta (2003)
Personality inventories	.76			Barrick & Mount (1991)
Openness		.80	.73	Viswesvaran & Ones (2003)
Conscientiousness		.83	.76	Viswesvaran & Ones (2003)
Extraversion		.81	.78	Viswesvaran & Ones (2003)
Agreeableness		.74	.75	Viswesvaran & Ones (2003)
Stability		.82	.73	Viswesvaran & Ones (2003)
Situational judgment tests	.80			McDaniel et al. (2001)

Even though reliability and validity are not the same, they are related. The potential validity of a test is limited by its reliability. Thus, if a test has poor reliability, it cannot have high validity. But as we saw in the example above, a test's reliability does not imply validity. Instead, we think of reliability as having a *necessary but not sufficient relationship* with validity.

There are five common strategies to investigate the validity of scores on a test: content, criterion, construct, face, and known-group.

Content Validity

Content validity The extent to which tests or test items sample the content that they are supposed to measure.

One way to determine a test's validity is to look at its degree of **content validity**—the extent to which test items sample the content that they are supposed to measure. Again, let us use your final exam as an example. Your instructor tells you that the final exam will measure your knowledge of Chapters 8, 9, and 10. Each chapter is the same length, and your instructor spent three class periods on each chapter. The test will have 60 questions. For the test to be content valid, the items must constitute a representative sample of the material contained in the three chapters; therefore, there should be some 20 questions from each chapter. If there are 30 questions each from Chapters 8 and 9, the test will not be content valid because it left out Chapter 10. Likewise, if there are questions from Chapter 4, the test will not be content valid because it requires knowledge that is outside of the appropriate domain.

In industry, the appropriate content for a test or test battery is determined by the job analysis. A job analysis should first determine the tasks and the conditions under which they are performed. Next the KSAOs (knowledge, skills, abilities, and other characteristics) needed to perform the tasks under those particular circumstances are determined. All of the important dimensions identified in the job analysis should be covered somewhere in the selection process, at least to the extent that the dimensions (constructs) can be accurately and realistically measured. Anything that was not identified in the job analysis should be left out.

One way to test the content validity of a test is to have subject matter experts (e.g., experienced employees, supervisors) rate test items on the extent to which the content and level of difficulty for each item are related to the job in question. These subject matter experts should also be asked to indicate if there are important aspects of the job that are not being tapped by test items.

The readability of a test is a good example of how tricky content validity can be. Suppose we determine that conscientiousness is an important aspect of a job. We find a personality inventory that measures conscientiousness, and we are confident that our test is content valid because it measures a dimension identified in the job analysis. But the personality inventory is very difficult to read (e.g., containing such words as *meticulous, extraverted, gregarious*) and most of our applicants are only high school graduates. Is our test content valid? No, because it requires a high level of reading ability, and reading ability was not identified as an important dimension for our job.

Criterion Validity

Criterion validity The extent to which a test score is related to some measure of job performance.

Criterion A measure of job performance, such as attendance, productivity, or a supervisor rating.

Concurrent validity A form of criterion validity that correlates test scores with measures of job performance for employees currently working for an organization.

Predictive validity A form of criterion validity in which test scores of applicants are compared at a later date with a measure of job performance.

Another measure of validity is **criterion validity**, which refers to the extent to which a test score is related to some measure of job performance called a **criterion** (criteria will be discussed more thoroughly in Chapter 7). Commonly used criteria include supervisor ratings of performance, objective measures of performance (e.g., sales, number of complaints, number of arrests made), attendance (tardiness, absenteeism), tenure, training performance (e.g., police academy grades), and discipline problems.

Criterion validity is established using one of two research designs: concurrent or predictive. With a **concurrent validity** design, a test is given to a group of employees who are already on the job. The scores on the test are then correlated with a measure of the employees' current performance.

With a **predictive validity** design, the test is administered to a group of job applicants who are going to be hired. The test scores are then compared with a future measure of job performance. In the ideal predictive validity situation, every applicant (or a random sample of applicants) is hired, and the test scores are hidden from the people who will later make performance evaluations. If every applicant is hired, a wide range of both test scores and employee performance is likely to be found, and the wider the range of scores, the higher the validity coefficient. But because it is rarely practical to hire every applicant, the ideal predictive design is not often used. Instead, most criterion validity studies use a concurrent design.

Why is a concurrent design weaker than a predictive design? The answer lies in the homogeneity of performance scores. In a given employment situation, very few employees are at the extremes of a performance scale. Employees who would be at the bottom of the performance scale either were never hired or have since been terminated. Employees who would be at the upper end of the performance scale often get promoted. Thus, the **restricted range** of performance scores makes obtaining a significant validity coefficient more difficult.

A major issue concerning the criterion validity of tests focuses on a concept known as **validity generalization**, or **VG**—the extent to which a test found valid for a job in one location is valid for the same job in a different location. It was previously thought that the job of typist in one company was not the same as that in another company, the job of police officer in one small town was not the same as that in another small town, and the job of retail store supervisor was not the same as that of supervisor in a fast-food restaurant.

In the past three decades, research has indicated that a test valid for a job in one organization is also valid for the same job in another organization (e.g., Schmidt, Gast-Rosenberg, & Hunter, 1980; Schmidt & Hunter, 1998; Schmidt, Hunter, Pearlman, & Hirsh, 1985). Schmidt, Hunter, and their associates have tested hundreds of thousands of employees to arrive at their conclusions. They suggest that previous thinking resulted from studies with small sample sizes, and test validity in one location but not another was the product primarily of sampling error. With large sample sizes, a test found valid in one location probably will be valid in another, providing that the jobs actually are similar and are not merely two separate jobs sharing the same job title.

The two building blocks for validity generalization are meta-analysis, discussed in Chapter 1, and job analysis, discussed in Chapter 2. Meta-analysis can be used to determine the average validity of specific types of tests for a variety of jobs. For example, several studies have shown that cognitive ability is an excellent predictor of police performance. If we were to conduct a meta-analysis of all the studies looking at this relationship, we would be able to determine the average validity of cognitive ability in predicting police performance. If this validity coefficient is significant, then police departments similar to those used in the meta-analysis could adopt the test without conducting criterion validity studies of their own. This would be especially useful for small departments that have neither the number of officers necessary to properly conduct criterion validity studies nor the financial resources necessary to hire professionals to conduct such studies. Validity generalization should be used only if a job analysis has been conducted, the results of which show that the job in question is similar to those used in the meta-analysis. Though validity generalization is generally accepted by the scientific community, federal enforcement agencies such as the Office of Federal Contract Compliance Programs (OFCCP) seldom accept validity generalization as a substitute for a local validation study if a test is shown to have adverse impact.

A technique related to validity generalization is **synthetic validity**. Synthetic validity is based on the assumption that tests that predict a particular component (e.g., customer service) of one job (e.g., a call center for a bank) should predict performance on the same job component for a different job (e.g., a receptionist at a law office). Thus, if studies show that a particular test predicts customer service performance, it follows

Restricted range A narrow range of performance scores that makes it difficult to obtain a significant validity coefficient.

Validity generalization (VG) The extent to which inferences from test scores from one organization can be applied to another organization.

Synthetic validity A form of validity generalization in which validity is inferred on the basis of a match between job components and tests previously found valid for those job components.

logically that a company should be able to use that test if its own job analyses indicate that customer service is important to the job in question. The key difference between validity generalization and synthetic validity is that with validity generalization we are trying to generalize the results of studies conducted on a particular job to the same job at another organization, whereas with synthetic validity, we are trying to generalize the results of studies of different jobs to a job that shares a common component (e.g., problem solving, customer service skills, mechanical ability).

Construct Validity

Construct validity The extent to which a test actually measures the construct that it purports to measure.

Construct validity is the most theoretical of the validity types. Basically, it is defined as the extent to which a test actually measures the construct that it purports to measure. Construct validity is concerned with inferences about test scores, in contrast to content validity, which is concerned with inferences about test construction.

Perhaps a good example of the importance of construct validity is a situation I encountered during graduate school. We had just completed a job analysis of the entry-level police officer position for a small town. One of the important dimensions (constructs) that emerged was honesty. Almost every officer insisted that a good police officer was honest, so we searched for tests that measured honesty and quickly discovered that there were many types of honesty—a conclusion also reached by Rieke and Guastello (1995). Some honesty tests measured theft, some cheating, and others moral judgment. None measured the honesty construct as it was defined by these police officers: not taking bribes and not letting friends get away with crimes. No test measured that particular construct, even though all of the tests measured "honesty."

Construct validity is usually determined by correlating scores on a test with scores from other tests. Some of the other tests measure the same construct (convergent validity), whereas others do not (discriminant validity). For example, suppose we have a test that measures knowledge of psychology. One hundred people are administered our Knowledge of Psychology Test as well as another psychology knowledge test, a test of reading ability, and a test of general intelligence. If our test really measures the construct we say it does—knowledge of psychology—it should correlate highest with the other test of psychology knowledge but not very highly with the other two tests. If our test correlates highest with the reading ability test, our test may be content valid (it contained psychology items), but not construct valid because scores on our test are based more on reading ability than on knowledge of psychology.

Known-group validity A form of validity in which test scores from two contrasting groups "known" to differ on a construct are compared.

Another method of measuring construct validity is **known-group validity** (Hattie & Cooksey, 1984). This method is not common and should be used only when other methods for measuring construct validity are not practical. With known-group validity, a test is given to two groups of people who are "known" to be different on the trait in question.

For example, suppose we wanted to determine the validity of our new honesty test. The best approach might be a criterion validity study in which we would correlate our employees' test scores with their dishonest behavior, such as stealing or lying. The problem is, how would we know who stole or who lied? We could ask them, but would dishonest people tell the truth? Probably not. Instead, we decide to validate our test by administering it to a group known as honest (priests) and to another group known as dishonest (criminals).

After administering the test to both groups, we find that, sure enough, the priests score higher on honesty than do the convicts. Does this mean our test is valid? Not necessarily. It means that the test has known-group validity but not necessarily other types of validity. We do not know whether the test will predict employee theft (criterion validity), nor do we know whether it is even measuring honesty (construct validity). It is possible that the test is actually measuring another construct on which the two groups differ (e.g., intelligence). Because of these problems, the best approach to take with known-group validity is this: If the known groups do not differ on test scores, consider the test invalid. If scores do differ, one still cannot be sure of its validity.

Even though known-group validity usually should not be used to establish test validity, it is important to understand because some test companies use known-group validity studies to sell their tests, claiming that the tests are valid. Personnel analyst Jeff Rodgers once was asked to evaluate a test his company was considering for selecting bank tellers. The test literature sounded impressive, mentioning that the test was "backed by over 100 validity studies." Rodgers was suspicious and requested copies of the studies. After several months of "phone calls and teeth pulling," he obtained reports of the validity studies. Most of the studies used known-group methodology and compared the scores of groups such as monks and priests. Not one study involved a test of criterion validity to demonstrate that the test could actually predict bank teller performance. Thus, if you hear that a test is valid, it is important to obtain copies of the research reports.

Choosing a Way to Measure Validity

With three common ways of measuring validity, one might logically ask which of the methods is the "best" to use. As with most questions in psychology, the answer is that "it depends." In this case, it depends on the situation as well as what the person conducting the validity study is trying to accomplish. If it is to decide whether the test will be a useful predictor of employee performance, then content validity will usually be used, and a criterion validity study also will be conducted if there are enough employees and if a good measure of job performance is available.

In deciding whether content validity is enough, I advise organizations to use the "next-door-neighbor rule." That is, ask yourself, "If my next-door neighbor were on a jury and I had to justify the use of my test, would content validity be enough?" For example, suppose you conducted a job analysis of a clerical position and find that typing, filing, and answering the phone are the primary duties. So you purchase a standard typing test and a filing test. The link between these tests and the duties performed by our clerical worker is so obvious that a criterion validity study is probably not essential to convince a jury of the validity of the two tests. However, suppose your job analysis of a police officer indicates that making decisions under pressure is an important part of the job. To tap this dimension, you choose the Gandy Critical Thinking Test. Because the link between your test and the ability to make decisions under pressure is not so obvious, you may need a criterion validity study.

Why not always conduct a criterion validity study? After all, isn't a significant validity coefficient better than sex? Having the significant validity coefficient is great. But the danger is in conducting the validity study. If you conduct a criterion validity study and do not get significance, that failure could be deadly if you are taken to court. To get a significant validity coefficient, many things have to go right. You need a good test, a good measure of performance, and a decent sample size. Furthermore, most validity coefficients are small (in the .20 to .35 range). Though assessment experts understand the utility of such small correlations, it can be difficult to convince a jury or governmental agencies to share your excitement after you explain that the range for a correlation coefficient is 0 to 1, you got a correlation of .20, and your test explains 4% of the variance.

Finally, a test itself can never be valid. When we speak of validity, we are speaking about the validity of the *test scores* as they relate to a particular job. A test may be a valid predictor of tenure for counselors but not of performance for shoe salespeople. Thus, when we say that a test is valid, we mean that it is valid for a particular job and a particular criterion. No test will ever be valid for all jobs and all criteria.

Face Validity

Although face validity is not one of the three major methods of determining test validity cited in the federal *Uniform Guidelines on Employee Selection Procedures*, it is still important. **Face validity** is the extent to which a test appears to be job related. This perception is important because if a test or its items do not appear valid, the test takers and administrators will not have confidence in the results. If job applicants do not think a test is job related, their perceptions of its fairness decrease, as does their motivation to do well on the test (Hausknecht, Day, & Thomas, 2004). Likewise, if employees involved in a training session on interpersonal skills take a personality inventory and are given the results, they will not be motivated to change or to use the results of the inventory unless the personality profile given to them seems accurate.

The importance of face validity has been demonstrated in a variety of research studies. For example, Chan, Schmitt, DeShon, Clause, and Delbridge (1997) found that face-valid tests resulted in high levels of test-taking motivation, which in turn resulted in higher levels of test performance. Thus, face validity motivates applicants to do well on tests. Face-valid tests that are accepted by applicants decrease the chance of lawsuits (Rynes & Connerley, 1993), reduce the number of applicants dropping out of the employment process (Thornton, 1993), and increase the chance that an applicant will accept a job offer (Hoff Macan, Avedon, & Paese, 1994). The one downside to a face-valid test, however, is that applicants might be tempted to fake the test because the correct answers are obvious. For example, if you are applying to graduate school and you are asked to take a test that clearly measures academic motivation, it would be very tempting to appear highly motivated in your responses.

The face validity and acceptance of test results can be increased by informing the applicants about how a test relates to job performance (Lounsbury, Bobrow, & Jensen, 1989) and by administering the test in a multimedia format (Richman-Hirsch, Olson-Buchanan, & Drasgow, 2000). Acceptance of test results also increases when applicants receive honest feedback about their test performance and are treated with respect by the test administrator (Gilliland, 1993).

But just because a test has face validity does not mean it is valid (Jackson, O'Dell, & Olson, 1982). For example, have you ever read a personality description based on your astrological sign and found the description to be quite accurate? Does this mean astrological forecasts are accurate? Not at all. If you also have read a personality description based on a different astrological sign, you probably found it to be as accurate as the one based on your own sign. Why is this? Because of something called **Barnum statements** (Dickson & Kelly, 1985)—statements so general that they can be true of almost everyone. For example, if I described you as "sometimes being sad, sometimes being successful, and at times not getting along with your best friend," I would probably be very accurate. However, these statements describe almost anyone. So, face validity by itself is not enough.

Finding Reliability and Validity Information

Over the previous pages, we have discussed different ways to measure reliability and validity. But even though most of you will eventually be involved with some form of employee testing, few of you will actually conduct a study on a test's reliability and validity. Consequently, where do you get information about these? There are many excellent sources containing reliability and validity information in the reference section of most university libraries.

Mental Measurements Yearbook (MMY) A book containing information about the reliability and validity of various psychological tests.

Perhaps the most common source of test information is the *Eighteenth Mental Measurements Yearbook (MMY)* (Spies, Carlson, & Geisinger, 2010), which contains information on over 2,700 psychological tests as well as reviews by test experts. Your library probably has online access to the *MMY*. Another excellent source of information is a compendium entitled *Tests in Print VIII* (Murphy, Geisinger, Carlson, & Spies, 2010). To help you use these test compendia, complete Exercise 6.1 in your workbook.

Cost-efficiency

If two or more tests have similar validities, then cost should be considered. For example, in selecting police officers, it is common to use a test of cognitive ability such as the Wonderlic Personnel Test or the Wechsler Adult Intelligence Scale (WAIS). Both tests have similar reliabilities and validities, yet the Wonderlic costs only a few dollars per applicant and can be administered to groups of people in only 12 minutes. The WAIS must be administered individually at a time cost of at least an hour per applicant and a financial cost of more than $100 per applicant. Given the similar validities, it doesn't take a rocket scientist (or an I/O psychologist) to figure out which is the better deal. In situations that are not so clear, the utility formula discussed later in this chapter can be used to determine the best test.

A particular test is usually designed to be administered either to individual applicants or to a group of applicants. Certainly, group testing is usually less expensive and more efficient than individual testing, although important information may be lost in group testing. For example, one reason for administering an individual intelligence test is to observe the *way* in which a person solves a problem or answers a question. With group tests, only the answer can be scored.

An increasing number of organizations are administering their tests over the Internet or at remote testing locations. With computer-assisted testing, an applicant takes a test at a computer terminal, the computer scores the test, and the test's results and interpretation are immediately available. Because computer-assisted testing can lower testing costs, decrease feedback time, and yield results in which the test takers can have great confidence, many public and private employers are switching to this method. Many state governments have found considerable cost savings in allowing applicants to take a computerized test near where they live rather than having them travel great distances to take a test at a central location. This increase in efficiency does not come at the cost of decreased validity because, as mentioned previously, tests administered electronically seem to yield results similar to those administered through the traditional paper-and-pencil format.

Computer-adaptive testing (CAT) A type of test taken on a computer in which the computer adapts the difficulty level of questions asked to the test-taker's success in answering previous questions.

An increasingly common use of computer testing is **computer-adaptive testing (CAT)**. In fact, you probably took the SAT in a computer-adaptive format. With CAT, the computer "adapts" the next question to be asked on the basis of how the test taker responded to the previous question or questions. For example, if the test taker successfully answered three multiplication questions in a row, the computer would move to another type of math rather than wasting time by asking seven more multiplication questions. When taking a CAT, the computer starts by asking questions of average difficulty. If the test-taker answers these correctly, the computer asks more difficult questions. If the test-taker answers these questions incorrectly, the computer asks easier questions. The logic behind CAT is that if a test taker can't answer easy questions (e.g., addition and subtraction), it doesn't make sense to ask questions about algebra and geometry. The advantages to CAT is that fewer test items are required, tests take less time to complete, finer distinctions in applicant ability can be made, test takers can receive immediate feedback, and test scores can be interpreted not only on the number of questions answered correctly, but on which questions were correctly answered.

Establishing the Usefulness of a Selection Device

Even when a test is both reliable and valid, it is not necessarily useful. At first, this may not make much sense, but consider a test that has been shown to be valid for selecting employees for a fast-food restaurant chain. Suppose there are 100 job openings and 100 job seekers apply for those openings. Even though the test is valid, it will have no impact because the restaurant chain must hire every applicant.

As another example, imagine an organization that already has a test that does a good job of predicting performance. Even though a new test being considered may be valid, the old test may have worked so well that the current employees are all successful. Or the organization may have such a good training program that current employees are all successful. Thus, a new test (even though it is valid) may not provide any improvement.

To determine how useful a test would be in any given situation, several formulas and tables have been designed. Each formula and table provides slightly different information to an employer. The *Taylor-Russell tables* provide an estimate of the percentage of total new hires who will be successful employees if a test is adopted (organizational success); both *expectancy charts* and the *Lawshe tables* provide a probability of success for a particular applicant based on test scores (individual success); and the *utility formula* provides an estimate of the amount of money an organization will save if it adopts a new testing procedure.

Taylor-Russell Tables

Taylor-Russell tables

A series of tables based on the selection ratio, base rate, and test validity that yield information about the percentage of future employees who will be successful if a particular test is used.

Taylor-Russell tables (Taylor & Russell, 1939) are designed to estimate the percentage of future employees who will be successful on the job if an organization uses a particular test. The philosophy behind the Taylor-Russell tables is that a test will be useful to an organization if (1) the test is valid, (2) the organization can be selective in its hiring because it has more applicants than openings, and (3) there are plenty of current employees who are not performing well, thus there is room for improvement. To use the Taylor-Russell tables, three pieces of information must be obtained.

The first information needed is the test's *criterion validity coefficient*. There are two ways to obtain this coefficient. The best would be to actually conduct a criterion validity study with test scores correlated with some measure of job performance. Often, however, an organization wants to know whether testing is useful before investing time and money in a criterion validity study. This is where validity

Preventing mistakes by hiring the right people can save an organization money

© Michael Okoniewski/THE IMAGE WORKS

generalization comes into play. On the basis of findings by researchers such as Schmidt and Hunter (1998), we have a good idea of the typical validity coefficients that will result from various methods of selection. To estimate the validity coefficient that an organization might obtain, one of the coefficients from Table 5.2 in the previous chapter is used. The higher the validity coefficient, the greater the possibility the test will be useful.

Selection ratio The percentage of applicants an organization hires.

The second piece of information that must be obtained is the **selection ratio**, which is simply the percentage of people an organization must hire. The ratio is determined by the formula

$$\text{Selection ratio} = \frac{\text{number hired}}{\text{number of applications}}$$

The lower the selection ratio, the greater the potential usefulness of the test.

Base rate Percentage of current employees who are considered successful.

The final piece of information needed is the **base rate** of current performance—the percentage of employees currently on the job who are considered successful. This figure is usually obtained in one of two ways. The first method is the most simple but the least accurate. Employees are split into two equal groups based on their scores on some criterion such as tenure or performance. The base rate using this method is always .50 because one half of the employees are considered satisfactory.

The second and more meaningful method is to choose a criterion measure score above which all employees are considered successful. For example, at one real estate agency, any agent who sells more than $700,000 of properties makes a profit for the agency after training and operating expenses have been deducted. In this case, agents selling more than $700,000 of properties would be considered successes because they made money for the company. Agents selling less than $700,000 of properties would be considered failures because they cost the company more money than they brought in. In this example, there is a clear point at which an employee can be considered a success. Most of the time, however, there are no such clear points. In these cases, managers will subjectively choose a point on the criterion that they feel separates successful from unsuccessful employees.

After the validity, selection ratio, and base rate figures have been obtained, the Taylor-Russell tables are consulted (Table 6.4). To understand how they are used, let us take the following example. Suppose we have a test validity of .40, a selection ratio of .30, and a base rate of .50. Locating the table corresponding to the .50 base

Table 6.4 Taylor-Russell Tables

Employees Considered Satisfactory	r	Selection Ratio										
		.05	.10	.20	.30	.40	.50	.60	.70	.80	.90	.95
10%	.00	.10	.10	.10	.10	.10	.10	.10	.10	.10	.10	.10
	.10	.14	.13	.13	.12	.12	.11	.11	.11	.11	.10	.10
	.20	.19	.17	.15	.14	.14	.13	.12	.12	.11	.11	.10
	.30	.25	.22	.19	.17	.15	.14	.13	.12	.12	.11	.10
	.40	.31	.27	.22	.19	.17	.16	.14	.13	.12	.11	.10
	.50	.39	.32	.26	.22	.19	.17	.15	.13	.12	.11	.11
	.60	.48	.39	.30	.25	.21	.18	.16	.14	.12	.11	.11
	.70	.58	.47	.35	.27	.22	.19	.16	.14	.12	.11	.11
	.80	.71	.56	.40	.30	.24	.20	.17	.14	.12	.11	.11
	.90	.86	.69	.46	.33	.25	.20	.17	.14	.12	.11	.11
20%	.00	.20	.20	.20	.20	.20	.20	.20	.20	.20	.20	.20
	.10	.26	.25	.24	.23	.23	.22	.22	.21	.21	.21	.20
	.20	.33	.31	.28	.27	.26	.25	.24	.23	.22	.21	.21
	.30	.41	.37	.33	.30	.28	.27	.25	.24	.23	.21	.21
	.40	.49	.44	.38	.34	.31	.29	.27	.25	.23	.22	.21
	.50	.59	.52	.44	.38	.35	.31	.29	.26	.24	.22	.21
	.60	.68	.60	.50	.43	.38	.34	.30	.27	.24	.22	.21
	.70	.79	.69	.56	.48	.41	.36	.31	.28	.25	.22	.21
	.80	.89	.79	.64	.53	.45	.38	.33	.28	.25	.22	.21
	.90	.98	.91	.75	.60	.48	.40	.33	.29	.25	.22	.21
30%	.00	.30	.30	.30	.30	.30	.30	.30	.30	.30	.30	.30
	.10	.38	.36	.35	.34	.33	.33	.32	.32	.31	.31	.30
	.20	.46	.43	.40	.38	.37	.36	.34	.33	.32	.31	.31
	.30	.54	.50	.46	.43	.40	.38	.37	.35	.33	.32	.31
	.40	.63	.58	.51	.47	.44	.41	.39	.37	.34	.32	.31
	.50	.72	.65	.58	.52	.48	.44	.41	.38	.35	.33	.31
	.60	.81	.74	.64	.58	.52	.47	.43	.40	.36	.33	.31
	.70	.89	.62	.72	.63	.57	.51	.46	.41	.37	.33	.32
	.80	.96	.90	.80	.70	.62	.54	.48	.42	.37	.33	.32
	.90	1.00	.98	.90	.79	.68	.58	.49	.43	.37	.33	.32
40%	.00	.40	.40	.40	.40	.40	.40	.40	.40	.40	.40	.40
	.10	.48	.47	.46	.45	.44	.43	.42	.42	.41	.41	.40
	.20	.57	.54	.51	.49	.48	.46	.45	.44	.43	.41	.41
	.30	.65	.61	.57	.54	.51	.49	.47	.46	.44	.42	.41
	.40	.73	.69	.63	.59	.56	.53	.50	.48	.45	.43	.41
	.50	.81	.76	.69	.64	.60	.56	.53	.49	.46	.43	.42
	.60	.89	.83	.75	.69	.64	.60	.55	.51	.48	.44	.42
	.70	.95	.90	.82	.76	.69	.64	.58	.53	.49	.44	.42
	.80	.99	.96	.89	.82	.75	.68	.61	.55	.49	.44	.42
	.90	1.00	1.00	.97	.91	.82	.74	.65	.57	.50	.44	.42
50%	.00	.50	.50	.50	.50	.50	.50	.50	.50	.50	.50	.50
	.10	.58	.57	.56	.55	.54	.53	.53	.52	.51	.51	.50
	.20	.67	.64	.61	.59	.58	.56	.55	.54	.53	.52	.51
	.30	.74	.71	.67	.64	.62	.60	.58	.56	.54	.52	.51
	.40	.82	.78	.73	.69	.66	.63	.61	.58	.56	.53	.52
	.50	.88	.84	.76	.74	.70	.67	.63	.60	.57	.54	.52
	.60	.94	.90	.84	.79	.75	.70	.66	.62	.59	.54	.52

Table 6.4 Taylor-Russell Tables (*Continued*)

Employees Considered Satisfactory	r	.05	.10	.20	.30	.40	.50	.60	.70	.80	.90	.95
									Selection Ratio			
	.70	.98	.95	.90	.85	.80	.75	.70	.65	.60	.55	.53
	.80	1.00	.99	.95	.90	.85	.80	.73	.67	.61	.55	.53
	.90	1.00	1.00	.99	.97	.92	.86	.78	.70	.62	.56	.53
60%	.00	.60	.60	.60	.60	.60	.60	.60	.60	.60	.60	.60
	.10	.68	.67	.65	.64	.64	.63	.63	.62	.61	.61	.60
	.20	.75	.73	.71	.69	.67	.66	.65	.64	.63	.62	.61
	.30	.82	.79	.76	.73	.71	.69	.68	.66	.64	.62	.61
	.40	.88	.85	.81	.78	.75	.73	.70	.68	.66	.63	.62
	.50	.93	.90	.86	.82	.79	.76	.73	.70	.67	.64	.62
	.60	.96	.94	.90	.87	.83	.80	.76	.73	.69	.65	.63
	.70	.99	.97	.94	.91	.87	.84	.80	.75	.71	.66	.63
	.80	1.00	.99	.98	.95	.92	.88	.83	.78	.72	.66	.63
	.90	1.00	1.00	1.00	.99	.97	.94	.88	.82	.74	.67	.63
70%.	.00	.70	.70	.70	.70	.70	.70	.70	.70	.70	.70	.70
	.10	.77	.76	.75	.74	.73	.73	.72	.72	.71	.71	.70
	.20	.83	.81	.79	.78	.77	.76	.75	.74	.73	.71	.71
	.30	.88	.86	.84	.82	.80	.78	.77	.75	.74	.72	.71
	.40	.93	.91	.88	.85	.83	.81	.79	.77	.75	.73	.72
	.50	.96	.94	.91	.89	.87	.84	.82	.80	.77	.74	.72
	.60	.98	.97	.95	.92	.90	.87	.85	.82	.79	.75	.73
	.70	1.00	.99	.97	.96	.93	.91	.88	.84	.80	.76	.73
	.80	1.00	1.00	.99	.98	.97	.94	.91	.87	.82	.77	.73
	.90	1.00	1.00	1.00	1.00	.99	.98	.95	.91	.85	.78	.74
80%	.00	.80	.80	.80	.80	.80	.80	.80	.80	.80	.80	.80
	.10	.85	.85	.84	.83	.83	.82	.82	.81	.81	.81	.80
	.20	.90	.89	.87	.86	.85	.84	.84	.83	.82	.81	.81
	.30	.94	.92	.90	.89	.88	.87	.86	.84	.83	.82	.81
	.40	.96	.95	.93	.92	.90	.89	.88	.86	.85	.83	.82
	.50	.98	.97	.96	.94	.93	.91	.90	.88	.86	.84	.82
	.60	.99	.99	.98	.96	.95	.94	.92	.90	.87	.84	.83
	.70	1.00	1.00	.99	.98	.97	.96	.94	.92	.89	.85	.83
	.80	1.00	1.00	1.00	1.00	.99	.98	.96	.94	.91	.87	.84
	.90	1.00	1.00	1.00	1.00	1.00	1.00	.99	.97	.94	.88	.84
90%	.00	.90	.90	.90	.90	.90	.90	.90	.90	.90	.90	.90
	.10	.93	.93	.92	.92	.92	.91	.91	.91	.91	.90	.90
	.20	.96	.95	.94	.94	.93	.93	.92	.92	.91	.91	.90
	.30	.98	.97	.96	.95	.95	.94	.94	.93	.92	.91	.91
	.40	.99	.98	.98	.97	.96	.95	.95	.94	.93	.92	.91
	.50	1.00	.99	.99	.98	.97	.97	.96	.95	.94	.92	.92
	.60	1.00	1.00	.99	.99	.99	.98	.97	.96	.95	.93	.92
	.70	1.00	1.00	1.00	1.00	.99	.99	.98	.97	.96	.94	.93
	.80	1.00	1.00	1.00	1.00	1.00	1.00	.99	.99	.97	.95	.93
	.90	1.00	1.00	1.00	1.00	1.00	1.00	1.00	1.00	.99	.97	.94

Source: "The relationship of validity coefficients to the practical effectiveness of tests in selection: Discussion and tables," by H. C. Taylor and J. T. Russell, 1939, *Journal of Applied Psychology*, 23, 565–578.

rate, we look along the top of the chart until we find the .30 selection ratio. Next, we locate the validity of .40 on the left side of the table. We then trace across the table until we locate the intersection of the selection ratio column and the validity row; we have found .69. If the organization uses that particular selection test, 69% of future employees are likely to be considered successful. This figure is compared with the previous base rate of .50, indicating a 38% increase in successful employees (.19 ÷ 50 = .38).

Proportion of Correct Decisions

Proportion of correct decisions A utility method that compares the percentage of times a selection decision was accurate with the percentage of successful employees.

Determining the **proportion of correct decisions** is easier to do but less accurate than the Taylor-Russell tables. The only information needed to determine the proportion of correct decisions is employee test scores and the scores on the criterion. The two scores from each employee are graphed on a chart similar to that in Figure 6.1. Lines are drawn from the point on the y-axis (criterion score) that represents a successful applicant, and from the point on the x-axis that represents the lowest test score of a hired applicant. As you can see, these lines divide the scores into four quadrants. The points located in quadrant I represent employees who scored poorly on the test but performed well on the job. Points located in quadrant II represent employees who scored well on the test and were successful on the job. Points in quadrant III represent employees who scored high on the test, yet did poorly on the job, and points in quadrant IV represent employees who scored low on the test and did poorly on the job.

If a test is a good predictor of performance, there should be more points in quadrants II and IV because the points in the other two quadrants represent "predictive failures." That is, in quadrants I and III no correspondence is seen between test scores and criterion scores.

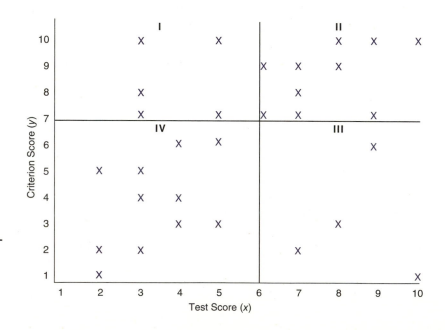

Figure 6.1

Determining the Proportion of Correct Decisions

To estimate the test's effectiveness, the number of points in each quadrant is totaled, and the following formula is used:

Points in quadrants II and IV ÷ Total points in all quadrants

The resulting number represents the percentage of time that we expect to be accurate in making a selection decision in the future. To determine whether this is an improvement, we use the following formula:

Points in quadrants I and II ÷ Total points in all quadrants

If the percentage from the first formula is higher than that from the second, our proposed test should increase selection accuracy. If not, it is probably better to stick with the selection method currently used.

As an example, look again at Figure 6.1. There are 5 data points in quadrant I, 10 in quadrant II, 4 in quadrant III, and 11 in quadrant IV. The percentage of time we expect to be accurate in the future would be:

$$\frac{II + IV}{I + II + IV} = \frac{10 + 11}{5 + 10 + 4 + 11} = \frac{21}{30} = .70$$

To compare this figure with the test we were previously using to select employees, we compute the satisfactory performance baseline:

$$\frac{I + II}{I + II + III + IV} = \frac{5 + 10}{5 + 10 + 4 + 11} = \frac{15}{30} = .50$$

Using the new test would result in a 40% increase in selection accuracy [.70 − .50 = .20 ÷ .50] over the selection method previously used.

Lawshe Tables

Lawshe tables Tables that use the base rate, test validity, and applicant percentile on a test to determine the probability of future success for that applicant.

The Taylor-Russell tables were designed to determine the overall impact of a testing procedure. But we often need to know the probability that a *particular applicant* will be successful. The **Lawshe tables** (Lawshe, Bolda, Brune, & Auclair, 1958) were created to do just that. To use these tables, three pieces of information are needed. The validity coefficient and the base rate are found in the same way as for the Taylor-Russell tables. The third piece of information needed is the applicant's test score. More specifically, did the person score in the top 20%, the next 20%, the middle 20%, the next lowest 20%, or the bottom 20%?

Once we have all three pieces of information, the Lawshe tables, as shown in Table 6.5, are examined. For our example, we have a base rate of .50, a validity of .40, and an applicant who scored third highest out of 10. First, we locate the table with the base rate of .50. Then we locate the appropriate category at the top of the chart. Our applicant scored third highest out of 10 applicants, so she would be in the second category, the next highest one fifth, or 20%. Using the validity of .40, we locate the intersection of the validity row and the test score column and find 59. This means that the applicant has a 59% chance of being a successful employee.

Brogden-Cronbach-Gleser Utility Formula

Utility formula Method of ascertaining the extent to which an organization will benefit from the use of a particular selection system.

Another way to determine the value of a test in a given situation is by computing the amount of money an organization would save if it used the test to select employees. Fortunately, I/O psychologists have devised a fairly simple **utility formula** to estimate

Table 6.5 Lawshe Individual Prediction Tables

Percentage of Current Employees Considered Satisfactory	r	Applicant Scores on Selection Test				
		Top 20%	Next 20%	Middle 20%	Next 20%	Bottom 20%
30%	.20	40	34	29	26	21
	.30	46	35	29	24	16
	.40	51	37	28	21	12
	.50	58	38	27	18	09
	.60	64	40	26	15	05
40%	.20	51	45	40	35	30
	.30	57	46	40	33	24
	.40	63	48	39	31	19
	.50	69	50	39	28	14
	.60	75	53	38	24	10
50%	.20	61	55	50	45	39
	.30	67	57	50	43	33
	.40	73	59	50	41	28
	.50	78	62	50	38	22
	.60	84	65	50	35	16
60%	.20	71	63	60	56	48
	.30	76	66	61	54	44
	.40	81	69	61	52	37
	.50	86	72	62	47	25
	.60	90	76	62	47	25
70%	.20	79	75	70	67	59
	.30	84	78	71	65	54
	.40	88	79	72	63	49
	.50	91	82	73	62	42
	.60	95	85	74	60	36

Note: Percentages indicate probability that applicant with a particular score will be a successful employee.

Source: "Expectancy charts II: Their theoretical development," C. H. Lawshe and R. A. Brune, 1958, *Personnel Psychology*, 11, 545–599.

the monetary savings to an organization. To use this formula, five items of information must be known.

1. Number of employees hired per year (n). This number is easy to determine: It is simply the number of employees who are hired for a given position in a year.
2. Average tenure (t). This is the average amount of time that employees in the position tend to stay with the company. The number is computed by using information from company records to identify the time that each employee in that position stayed with the company. The number of years of **tenure** for each employee is then summed and divided by the total number of employees.

Tenure The length of time an employee has been with an organization.

3. Test validity (*r*). This figure is the criterion validity coefficient that was obtained through either a validity study or validity generalization.
4. Standard deviation of performance in dollars (SD_y). For many years, this number was difficult to compute. Research has shown, however, that for jobs in which performance is normally distributed, a good estimate of the difference in performance between an average and a good worker (one standard deviation away in performance) is 40% of the employee's annual salary (Hunter & Schmidt, 1982). The 40% rule yields results similar to more complicated methods and is preferred by managers (Hazer & Highhouse, 1997). To obtain this, the total salaries of current employees in the position in question should be averaged.
5. Mean standardized predictor score of selected applicants (*m*). This number is obtained in one of two ways. The first method is to obtain the average score on the selection test for both the applicants who are hired and the applicants who are not hired. The average test score of the nonhired applicants is subtracted from the average test score of the hired applicants. This difference is divided by the standard deviation of all the test scores.

For example, we administer a test of mental ability to a group of 100 applicants and hire the 10 with the highest scores. The average score of the 10 hired applicants was 34.6, the average test score of the other 90 applicants was 28.4, and the standard deviation of all test scores was 8.3. The desired figure would be

$$\frac{34.6 - 28.4}{8.3} = \frac{6.2}{8.3} = .747$$

The second way to find *m* is to compute the proportion of applicants who are hired and then use a conversion table such as that in Table 6.6 to convert the

Table 6.6 Selection-Ratio Conversion Table for Utility Formula

Selection Ratio	*m*
1.00	0.00
.90	0.20
.80	0.35
.70	0.50
.60	0.64
.50	0.80
.40	0.97
.30	1.17
.20	1.40
.10	1.76
.05	2.08

proportion into a standard score. This second method is used when an organization plans to use a test and knows the probable selection ratio based on previous hirings, but does not know the average test scores because the organization has never used the test. Using the previous example, the proportion of applicants hired would be

$$\frac{\text{number of applicants hired}}{\text{total number of applicants}} = \frac{10}{100} = .10$$

From Table 6.6, we see that the standard score associated with a selection ratio of .10 is 1.76. To determine the savings to the company, we use the following formula:

$$\text{Savings } (n) \ (t) \ (r) \ (\text{SD}_y) \ (m) - \text{cost of testing}$$

$$(\text{\# of applicants} \times \text{the cost per applicant})$$

As an example, suppose we hire ten auditors per year, the average person in this position stays two years, the validity coefficient is .30, and the average annual salary for the position is \$30,000, and we have 50 applicants for 10 openings. Thus,

$n = 10$

$t = 2$

$r = .30$

$\text{SD}_y = \$30,000 \times .40 = \$12,000$

$m = 10/50 = .20 = 1.40$ (.20 is converted to 1.40 by using Table 6.6)

cost of testing $= (50 \text{ applicants} \times \$10)$

Using the above formula, we would have

$$(10) \ (2) \ (.30) \ (12,000) \ (1.40) - (50) \ (10) = 100,300$$

This means that after accounting for the cost of testing, using this particular test instead of selecting employees by chance will save a company \$100,300 over the two years that auditors typically stay with the organization. Because a company seldom selects employees by chance, the same formula should be used with the validity of the test (interview, psychological test, references, and so on) that the company currently uses. The result of this computation should then be subtracted from the first.

This final figure, of course, is just an estimate based on the assumption that the highest-scoring applicants accept the job offer. To be most accurate, it must be adjusted by such factors as variable costs, discounting, corporate tax rates, and changes in strategic goals (Boudreau, 1983; Russell, Colella, & Bobko, 1993). Because utility estimates are often in the millions of dollars, there has been concern that managers may not believe the estimates. However, research indicates that managers positively view utility estimates, and thus these estimates can be used to support the usefulness of testing (Carson, Becker, & Henderson, 1998; Hoff, Macan & Foster, 2004). When one considers the costs of constant poor performance, the size of these estimates should not be surprising. The high estimated savings are even more believable when one considers the cost of one employee's mistake. For example:

■ An employee of Oxford Organics Inc. mislabeled an artificial vanilla flavoring sent to General Mills, resulting in \$150,000 in damaged cake frosting.
■ A U.S. Navy mechanic left a 5-inch wrench inside the wheel compartment of a jet, causing the \$33 million plane to crash.

- A typo in a letter by a car dealer told customers to call a 900 number instead of an 800 number. The 900 number turned out to be a sex line, and the dealership had to send out an additional 1,000 letters to apologize and correct the mistake.

Thus, the cost of daily poor performance, combined with the cost of occasional mistakes such as these, provides support for the validity of high utility estimates.

Though utility formulas are useful means for decision making, it should be noted that not all managers trust the results of utility formulas and thus other means for demonstrating validity might be needed. Such methods include benchmarking studies to show that what your organization is doing is a "best practice"; studies looking at applicant and employee reactions to demonstrate that your "clients" feel comfortable with your testing practices (face validity); data indicating that your new hires are successful (e.g., performance ratings, tenure, supervisor comments); data indicating that the results of hiring decisions are consistent with the organization's affirmative action and diversity goals; and data indicating that the hiring process is meeting the organization's goals for filling positions in a timely manner with competent employees. To help you understand the utility tables and formulas, complete Exercises 6.2 and 6.3 in your workbook.

Determining the Fairness of a Test

Measurement bias Group differences in test scores that are unrelated to the construct being measured.

Adverse impact An employment practice that results in members of a protected class being negatively affected at a higher rate than members of the majority class. Adverse impact is usually determined by the four-fifths rule.

Predictive bias A situation in which the predicted level of job success falsely favors one group over another.

Single-group validity The characteristic of a test that significantly predicts a criterion for one class of people but not for another.

Once a test has been determined to be reliable and valid and to have utility for an organization, the next step is to ensure that the test is fair and unbiased. Although there is disagreement among I/O psychologists regarding the definition of test fairness, most professionals agree that one must consider potential race, gender, disability, and other cultural differences in both the content of the test (measurement bias) and the way in which scores from the test predict job performance (predictive bias; Meade & Tonidandel, 2010). **Measurement bias** refers to technical aspects of a test. A test is considered to have measurement bias if there are group differences (e.g., sex, race, or age) in test scores that are unrelated to the construct being measured. For example, if race differences on a test of logic are due to vocabulary words found more often in the White than the African American culture, but these same words are not important to the performance of the job in question, the test might be considered to have measurement bias and thus not be fair in that particular situation. The statistical methods for determining measurement bias can be very complicated and are certainly beyond the scope of this text. However, from a legal perspective, if differences in test scores result in one group (e.g., men) being selected at a significantly higher rate than another (e.g., women), **adverse impact** is said to have occurred and the burden is on the organization using the test to prove that the test is valid (refer back to Chapter 3 if you need a refresher on adverse impact).

Predictive bias refers to situations in which the predicted level of job success falsely favors one group (e.g., men) over another (e.g., women). That is, a test would have predictive bias if men scored higher on the test than women but the job performance of women was equal to or better than that of men.

One form of predictive bias is **single-group validity**, meaning that the test will significantly predict performance for one group and not others. For example, a test of reading ability might predict performance of White clerks but not of African American clerks.

To test for single-group validity, separate correlations are computed between the test and the criterion for each group. If both correlations are significant, the test does not exhibit single-group validity and it passes this fairness hurdle. If, however, only one of the correlations is significant, the test is considered fair for only that one group.

Single-group validity is very rare (O'Connor, Wexley, & Alexander, 1975) and is usually the result of small sample sizes and other methodological problems (Schmidt, 1988; Schmidt & Hunter, 1978). Where it occurs, an organization has two choices. It can disregard single-group validity because research indicates that it probably occurred by chance or it can stop using the test. Disregarding single-group validity probably is the most appropriate choice, given that most I/O psychologists believe that single-group validity occurs only by chance. As evidence of this, think of a logical reason a test would predict differently for African Americans than for Whites or differently for males than for females. That is, why would a test of intelligence predict performance for males but not for females? Or why would a personality inventory predict performance for African Americans but not for Whites? There may be many cultural reasons why two groups *score* differently on a test (e.g., educational opportunities, socioeconomic status), but finding a logical reason that the test would *predict* differently for two groups is difficult.

A second form of predictive bias is **differential validity**. With differential validity, a test is valid for two groups but more valid for one than for the other. Single-group validity and differential validity are easily confused, but there is a big difference between the two. Remember, with single-group validity, the test is valid only for one group. With differential validity, the test is valid for both groups, but it is more valid for one than for the other.

Like single-group validity, differential validity is rare (Katzell & Dyer, 1977; Schmidt & Hunter, 1981). When it does occur, it is usually in occupations dominated by a single sex, tests are most valid for the dominant sex, and the tests overpredict minority performance (Rothstein & McDaniel, 1992; Saad & Sackett, 2002). If differential-group validity occurs, the organization has two choices. The first is not to use the test. Usually, however, this is not a good option. Finding a test that is valid is difficult; throwing away a good test would be a shame.

The second option is to use the test with separate regression equations for each group. Because applicants do not realize that the test is scored differently, there are not the public relations problems that occur with use of separate tests. However, the 1991 Civil Rights Act prohibits score adjustments based on race or gender. As a result, using separate equations may be statistically acceptable but would not be legally defensible.

Another important aspect of test fairness is the *perception* of fairness held by the applicants taking the test. That is, a test may not have measurement or predictive bias, but applicants might perceive the test itself or the way in which the test is administered as not being fair. Factors that might affect applicants' perceptions of fairness include the difficulty of the test, the amount of time allowed to complete the test, the face validity of the test items, the manner in which hiring decisions are made from the test scores (this will be discussed in detail in the next section), policies about retaking the test, and the way in which requests for testing accommodations for disabilities were handled.

Differential validity The characteristic of a test that significantly predicts a criterion for two groups, such as both minorities and nonminorities, but predicts significantly better for one of the two groups.

I have over 20 years of professional school system human resources (HR) experience. My first job out of graduate school was as a personnel examiner for the Los Angeles Unified School District, the second largest school district in the nation. While working there, I thoroughly learned public professional HR management and practices while progressing through the ranks of senior personnel examiner; principal personnel examiner; and assistant personnel director, selection.

After being in recruitment and selection for many years, I decided to expand my HR horizon by joining a small district, Bassett Unified School District, as its assistant superintendent, Human Resources Development.

As the assistant superintendent, Human Resources Development, I worked closely with the Personnel Commission, the Board of Education, and the district superintendent. My major duties and responsibilities included overseeing the administration of a comprehensive merit system and HR development program for certificated and classified employees. More specifically, I developed and recommended short- and long-term HR strategies, policies, goals, and objectives; served as the Personnel Commission's secretary; identified appropriate procedures to ensure fair and equal employment opportunity and investigated or assisted in the investigation of complaints concerning violations of state or federal law involving fair employment practice; negotiated and administered collective bargaining agreements with both the teachers' union and the classified employees' union;

Courtesy of T. R. Lin, Ph.D

T. R. Lin, Ph.D.
Director, Classified Personnel
La Mesa–Spring Valley School District

selected, assigned, trained, supervised, and evaluated the performance of HR staff; served as the expert adviser to the Personnel Commission and Board of Education and was a member of the superintendent's cabinet; and directed the recruitment, selection, assignment, and compensation activities for both certificate and classified HR programs.

Currently, I am the director of Classified Personnel Services at La Mesa–Spring Valley School District in southern California. This job allows me to consolidate almost all the duties mentioned above, but on the non-teaching, HR side.

As you can see, my two most recent jobs include all the HR topics covered in a typical I/O psychology textbook. I remember as a graduate student at the School of Industrial and Labor Relations at Cornell University that I was never able to get a real-life internship experience outside of the campus because my foreign student visa limitation prohibited me from obtaining real work. Therefore, I could get only on-campus research assistantships. Although these made my research and data analysis skills quite solid, I missed valuable opportunities to put my classroom lessons to work in the real world. When I was in the Los Angeles Unified School District, I hired, supervised, and mentored at least 50 interns we recruited through I/O graduate programs locally and globally. Many of them ended up with successful careers in public HR systems. Therefore, my advice to you is to do an internship during your college career whenever you can.

Making the Hiring Decision

After valid and fair selection tests have been administered to a group of applicants, a final decision must be made as to which applicant or applicants to hire. At first, this may seem to be an easy decision—hire the applicants with the highest test scores. But the decision becomes more complicated as both the number and variety of tests increase.

Multiple regression A statistical procedure in which the scores from more than one criterion-valid test are weighted according to how well each test score predicts the criterion.

If more than one criterion-valid test is used, the scores on the tests must be combined. Usually, this is done by a statistical procedure known as **multiple regression**, with each test score weighted according to how well it predicts the criterion. Linear approaches to hiring usually take one of four forms: unadjusted top-down selection, rules of three, passing scores, or banding.

Unadjusted Top-Down Selection

Top-down selection
Selecting applicants in straight rank order of their test scores.

With **top-down selection**, applicants are rank-ordered on the basis of their test scores. Selection is then made by starting with the highest score and moving down until all openings have been filled. For example, for the data in Table 6.7, if we had

Table 6.7 Hypothetical Testing Information

Applicant	Sex	Test Score
Ferguson	M	99
Letterman	M	98
Fallon	M	91
Kimmel	M	90
Winfrey	F	88
Lopez	M	87
Leno	M	72
Hasselbeck	F	70 Passing Score
Banks	F	68
Stewart	M	62
Colbert	M	60
Gifford	F	57
Jones	F	54
O'Brien	M	49
Maher	M	31

four openings, we would hire the top four scorers, who, in this case, would be Ferguson, Letterman, Fallon, and Kimmel. Notice that all four are males. If, for affirmative action purposes, we wanted to hire two females, top-down selection would not allow us to do so.

The advantage to top-down selection is that by hiring the top scorers on a valid test, an organization will gain the most utility (Schmidt, 1991). The disadvantages are that this approach can result in high levels of adverse impact and it reduces an organization's flexibility to use nontest factors such as references or organizational fit.

In a **compensatory approach** to top-down selection, the assumption is that if multiple test scores are used, the relationship between a low score on one test can be compensated for by a high score on another. For example, a student applying to graduate school might have a low GRE score but have a high undergraduate grade point average (GPA). If the GPA is high enough, it would compensate for the low GRE score. To determine whether a score on one test can compensate for a score on another, multiple regression is used in which each test score is weighted according to how well it predicts the criterion. When considering the use of a compensatory approach, it is essential that a high score on one test would actually compensate for a low score on another. For example, in a recent audit, the OFCCP argued that the organization being audited should let a high score on a personality inventory compensate for a low score on a physical ability exam. OFCCP's reasoning was that because men and women scored similarly on the personality inventory, adverse impact would be reduced. However, the argument doesn't make sense as personality will not compensate for the inability to be able to lift a heavy package.

Compensatory approach

A method of making selection decisions in which a high score on one test can compensate for a low score on another test. For example, a high GPA might compensate for a low GRE score.

Rule of Three

Rule of 3 A variation on top-down selection in which the names of the top three applicants are given to a hiring authority who can then select any of the three.

A technique often used in the public sector is the **rule of three** (or rule of five), in which the names of the top three scorers are given to the person making the hiring decision (e.g., police chief, HR director). This person can then choose any of the three based on the immediate needs of the employer. This method ensures that the person hired will be well qualified but provides more choice than does top-down selection.

Passing Scores

Passing score The minimum test score that an applicant must achieve to be considered for hire.

Passing scores are a means for reducing adverse impact and increasing flexibility. With this system, an organization determines the lowest score on a test that is associated with acceptable performance on the job. For example, we know that a student scoring 1,300 on the SAT will probably have better grades in college than a student scoring 800. But, what is the lowest score on the SAT that we can accept and still be confident that the student will be able to pass classes and eventually graduate?

Notice the distinct difference between top-down selection and passing scores. With top-down selection, the question is, "Who will perform the *best* in the future?" With passing scores, the question becomes, "Who will be able to perform at an *acceptable level* in the future?"

As you can imagine, passing scores provide an organization with much flexibility. Again using Table 6.7 as an example, suppose we determine that any applicant scoring 70 or above will be able to perform adequately the duties of the job in question. If we set 70 as the passing score, we can fill our four openings with any of the eight applicants scoring 70 or better. Because, for affirmative action reasons, we would like two of the four openings to be filled by females, we are free to hire Winfrey and Hasselbeck. Use of passing scores allows us to reach our affirmative action goals, which would not have been met with top-down selection. By hiring applicants with lower scores, however, the performance of our future employees will be lower than if we used top-down selection (Schmidt, 1991).

Though the use of passing scores appears to be a reasonable step toward reaching affirmative action goals, determining the actual passing score can be a complicated process full of legal pitfalls (Biddle, 1993). The most common methods for determining passing scores (e.g., the Angoff and Nedelsky methods) require job experts to read each item on a test and provide an estimation about the percentage of minimally qualified employees that could answer the item correctly. The passing score then becomes the average of the estimations for each question. Legal problems can occur when unsuccessful applicants challenge the validity of the passing score.

Multiple-cutoff approach A selection strategy in which applicants must meet or exceed the passing score on more than one selection test.

If there is more than one test for which we have passing scores, a decision must be made regarding the use of a **multiple-cutoff** or a multiple-hurdle approach. Both approaches are used when one score can't compensate for another or when the relationship between the selection test and performance is not linear. With a multiple-cutoff approach, the applicants would be administered all of the tests at one time. If they failed any of the tests (fell below the passing score), they would not be considered further for employment.

For example, suppose that our job analysis finds that a good police officer is intelligent, has a college degree, is confident, can lift 50 pounds, and does not have a criminal record. Our validity study indicates that the relationships of both intelligence and confidence with job performance are linear: The smarter and more confident the officer, the better he or she performs. Because the relationships between strength, not having a criminal record, and having a college degree are not linear, we would use a multiple-cutoff approach in which applicants would need to pass the background check, have a college degree, and be able to lift 50 pounds. If they meet all three requirements, their confidence levels and cognitive ability test scores are used to determine who will be hired.

One problem with a multiple-cutoff approach is the cost. If an applicant passes only three out of four tests, he will not be hired, but the organization has paid for the applicant to take all four tests.

To reduce the costs associated with applicants failing one or more tests, **multiple-hurdle approaches** are often used. With a multiple-hurdle approach, the applicant is administered one test at a time, usually beginning with the least expensive. Applicants who fail a test are eliminated from further consideration and take no more tests. Applicants who pass all of the tests are then administered the linearly related tests; the applicants with the top scores on these tests are hired.

To clarify the difference between a multiple-cutoff and a multiple-hurdle approach, let us look at the following example. Suppose we will use four pass/fail tests to select employees. The tests have the following costs and failure rates:

Test	Test Cost	Failure Rate
Background check	$25	10%
Psychological screen	$50	10%
Medical exam	$100	10%
Physical ability test	$5	10%
Total per applicant	$180	

If the tests cost $180 per applicant and 100 applicants apply for a position, a multiple-cutoff approach would cost our organization $18,000 (100 applicants × $180 each) to administer the tests to all applicants. But with a multiple-hurdle approach, we can administer the cheapest test (the strength test) to all 100 applicants. Because 10% of the applicants will fail this test, we can then administer the next cheapest test to the remaining 90. This process continues until all tests have been administered. A savings of $3,900 will result, based on the following calculations:

Test	Test Cost	Applicants	Total Cost
Physical ability test	$5	100	$500
Background check	$25	90	$2,250
Psychological screen	$50	81	$4,050
Medical exam	$100	73	$7,300
Total cost			$14,100

If a multiple-hurdle approach is usually less expensive, why is it not *always* used instead of a multiple-cutoff approach? First, many of the tests cited above take time to conduct or score. For example, it might take a few weeks to run a background check or a few days to interpret a psychological screening. Therefore, the tests usually must be administered on several occasions, and an applicant would have to miss several days of work to apply for a particular job. Because people often cannot or will not take more than one day off from one job to apply for another, many potentially excellent applicants are lost before testing begins.

Second, research has shown that in general the longer the time between submission of a job application and the hiring decision, the smaller the number of African American applicants who will remain in the applicant pool (Arvey, Gordon, Massengill, & Mussio, 1975). African American populations have higher unemployment rates than Whites, and people who are unemployed are more hurried to obtain employment than people with jobs. Thus, because the multiple-hurdle approach takes longer than multiple-cutoff, it may bring an unintended adverse impact, and affirmative action goals may not be met.

Banding

As mentioned previously, a problem with top-down hiring is that the process results in the highest levels of adverse impact. On the other hand, use of passing scores decreases adverse impact but reduces utility. As a compromise between top-down hiring and passing scores, **banding** attempts to hire the top test scorers while still allowing some flexibility for affirmative action (Campion et al., 2001).

Banding takes into consideration the degree of error associated with any test score. Thus, even though one applicant might score two points higher than another, the two-point difference might be the result of chance (error) rather than actual differences in ability. The question then becomes, "How many points apart do two applicants have to be before we say their test scores are significantly different?"

We can answer this question using a statistic called the **standard error (SE)**. To compute this statistic, we obtain the reliability and standard deviation (SD) of a particular test from the test catalog (or we can compute it ourselves if we have nothing better to do on a weekend!). This information is then plugged into the following formula:

$$SE = SD\sqrt{1 - \text{reliability}}$$

For example, suppose we have a test with a reliability of .90 and a standard deviation of 13.60. The calculation of the standard error would be

$$SE = 13.60\sqrt{1 - .90}$$
$$SE = 13.60\sqrt{.10}$$
$$SE = 13.60 \times .316$$
$$SE = 4.30$$

Bands are typically—but do not have to be—determined by multiplying the standard error by 1.96 (the standard score associated with a 95% level of confidence). Because the standard error of our test is 4.30, test scores within 8.4 points (4.3 × 1.96) of one another would be considered statistically the same. If we take this concept a bit further, we can establish a hiring bandwidth of 8.4. For example, using our standard error of 4.3 and our bandwidth of 8.4 (8), look at the applicants depicted in Table 6.7. Suppose that we have four openings and would like to hire at least two women if possible. Because the highest scoring woman in our example is Winfrey at 88, a top-down approach would not result in any women being hired. With a nonsliding band, we are free to hire anyone whose scores fall between the top score

(Ferguson at 99) and 91 (99 − 8.4). As with top-down selection, use of a nonsliding band in this example would not result in any women being hired. With a sliding band, however, we start with the highest score (Ferguson at 99) and subtract from it the bandwidth (8.4). In this case, 99 − 8.4 = 90.6, meaning that all applicants scoring between 91 and 99 are considered statistically to have the same score. Because no female falls within this band, we hire Ferguson and then consider the next score of Letterman at 98. Our next band of 98 through 90 (98 − 8.4) still does not contain a female, so we hire Letterman and then consider the next score of Fallon at 91. Our new band of 94 to 86 contains four applicants, one of whom is a woman. Because we are free to hire anyone within a band, we would probably hire Winfrey to meet our affirmative action goals. We would then hire Fallon as our fourth person. With banding, one more woman was hired than would have occurred under a top-down system. Note, however, that our goal to hire two women was not reached, as it was when we used passing scores. To practice how to construct a band, complete Exercise 6.4 in your workbook.

Though the concept of banding has been approved in several court cases (*Bridgeport Guardians v. City of Bridgeport*, 1991; *Chicago Firefighters Union Local No. 2 v. City of Chicago*, 1999; *Officers for Justice v. Civil Service Commission*, 1992), only selecting minorities in a band would be illegal. Instead, affirmative action goals must be considered as only one factor in selecting applicants from a band. For example, by allowing some flexibility in hiring, the use of banding might allow a police chief to hire a lower-scoring Spanish-speaking applicant or an applicant with computer skills over a higher-scoring applicant without these desired, but not required, skills.

Though banding seems to be a good compromise between top-down hiring and passing scores (Zedeck, Cascio, Goldstein, & Outtz, 1996), it is not without its critics (Campion et al., 2001). Research indicates that banding can result in lower utility than top-down hiring (Schmidt, 1991), that it may not actually reduce adverse impact in any significant way (Gutman & Christiansen, 1997), and that its usefulness in achieving affirmative action goals is affected by such factors as the selection ratio and the percentage of minority applicants (Sackett & Roth, 1991).

ON THE JOB   Applied Case Study

Thomas A. Edison's Employment Test

In Chapter 1, we mentioned that in 1920, inventor Thomas Edison created a 163-item test that he used to hire managers and scientists. All applicants were given two hours to answer a basic set of questions covering geography, science, history, and literature, and then, depending on the position applied for, some questions specific to their field. Edison created the test because he wanted to hire the best employees and he didn't trust college graduates. This distrust can be seen in his quote, "Men who have gone to college I find to be amazingly ignorant. They don't seem to know anything."

To pass the test, an applicant had to get 90% of the questions correct, a score thought to be comparable to an IQ of 180 (although there is no proof of this). According to Edison, of the first 718 male college graduates who took the test (there were no female applicants), only 57 (7.9%) had a grade of at least 70% (a passing score in college) and only 32 (4.5%) scored above 90%, Edison's passing score to be considered "Class A" men.

What were some of the questions?

■ What countries bound France?

■ Where is the finest cotton grown?

- What city in the United States leads in making laundry machines?
- What has the greater area, Greenland or Australia?

As you can imagine, the test was not popular with applicants. Edison scored the test himself and, not only did he not share the test scores with the applicants, he had a rule that forbade applicants from communicating the questions to others. At least two applicants leaked the test results to the media, and on May 11, 1929, the *New York Times* published 141 of the questions that one of the unsuccessful applicants, Charles Hansen, could remember (you have to be pretty bright to remember 141 questions verbatim!). The media challenged Edison by giving him pop quizzes similar to the one he created. He averaged 95% on these pop quizzes! Interestingly, Edison's son, Theodore, didn't pass the test, although he had a bachelor's degree in physics from the Massachusetts Institute of Technology.

Due to the criticism that his test placed too much emphasis on rote memory of trivial details, Edison defended his test in the October 23, 1921, issue of the *New York Times* with the following quotes:

- "If a man cannot remember things well in general, he cannot remember where to turn for them and how to look them up quickly and effectively. The man who tries to substitute a research method for a memory cannot act decisively and safely in an emergency."

- "It costs too much to learn whether a man is a good executive by trying him out on the job."

- "When I call upon any of my men for a decision, I want it right away. When his department calls on him for a decision, it wants it right away. It's all very well to say that you have got to look up the data on which the decision will be based, that you know just where to look. But I want the decision now, and the department wants the decision now. It isn't convenient for me to wait."

- You can take Edison's test at http://www.nps.gov/archive/edis/edifun/quiz/quizhome.htm

- What do you think of Edison's test?

- Do you agree with his reasoning about the importance of memory?

- How would you have set the passing score for the test?

- If the test were used today, would it be considered legal? Biased? Fair?

FOCUS ON ETHICS   Diversity Efforts

In this chapter, you learned that employment tests must be valid and fair to pass legal scrutiny. You also learned that such methods as passing scores, rules of three, and banding can provide some flexibility in who gets hired—flexibility that often is used to reduce adverse impact. Almost every topic in this chapter has potential ethical issues associated with it. From an ethical perspective, should an employer care about issues such as adverse impact? How far should an organization go to increase diversity? Over the years I have had many discussions with colleagues who thought that their organization either wasn't doing enough to ensure fairness in its testing process or was going so far to the extreme that minorities and women were being favored.

What Do You Think?

- To increase diversity, it is often legal to consider race or gender as *a* factor in selecting employees. Although legal, do you think it is ethical that race or gender be a factor in making an employment decision? How much of a role should it play?

- Is it ethical to hire a person with a lower test score because he or she seems to be a better personality fit for an organization?

- If an I/O psychologist is employed by a company that appears to be discriminating against Hispanics, is it ethical for her to stay with the company? What ethical obligations does she have?

Chapter Summary

In this chapter you learned:

- Test length, item homogeneity, and scorer accuracy can affect the reliability of a test.
- There are three ways to measure reliability: (a) the test-retest method, which measures temporal stability; (b) the alternate-forms method, which measures forms stability; and (c) the internal consistency method (split-half, K-R 20, and coefficient alpha), which measures item homogeneity.
- Tests can be validated using five approaches: content, criterion, construct, known-group, and face.
- Information about tests can be obtained from such sources as the *Mental Measurements Yearbook*.
- The utility of a test can be determined using the Taylor-Russell tables, the Lawshe tables, proportion of correct decisions, and utility formulas.
- The fairness of a test can be determined by testing for adverse impact, single-group validity, and differential validity.
- Selection decisions can be made in four ways: top-down, rule of three, top-down with banding, or passing scores.

Questions for Review

1. What is the difference between reliability and validity?
2. What method of establishing validity is the best?
3. Why is the concept of test utility so important?
4. What is the difference between single-group and differential validity?
5. Why should we use anything other than top-down selection? After all, shouldn't we always hire the applicants with the highest scores?

Media Resources and Learning Tools

- Visit our website. Go to www.cengage.com/psychology/aamodt, where you will find online resources directly linked to your book, including chapter-by-chapter quizzing, flashcards, crossword puzzles, application activities, and more.
- Want more practice applying industrial/organizational psychology? Check out the *I/O Applications Workbook*. This workbook (keyed to your textbook) offers engaging, high-interest activities to help you reinforce the important concepts presented in the text.

Chapter

7

EVALUATING EMPLOYEE PERFORMANCE

© Chris Ryan/OJO Images/Getty Images

Learning Objectives

➡ Know how to create a performance appraisal instrument

➡ Know how to administer a performance appraisal system

➡ Understand the problems associated with performance ratings

➡ Be able to conduct a performance appraisal review

➡ Understand how to legally terminate an unproductive employee

➡ Learn how to monitor the legality of a performance appraisal system

ave you ever received a grade that you did not think was fair? Perhaps you had an 89.6 and the instructor would not "round up" to an A, or the test contained questions that had nothing to do with the class. If so, you were probably upset with the way your professor appraised your performance. In this chapter, we will discuss the process of evaluating and appraising employee performance, which is similar to evaluating a student's performance.

As shown in Figure 7.1, the performance appraisal process can be divided into 10 interrelated steps. Each of these steps will serve as a major section in this chapter.

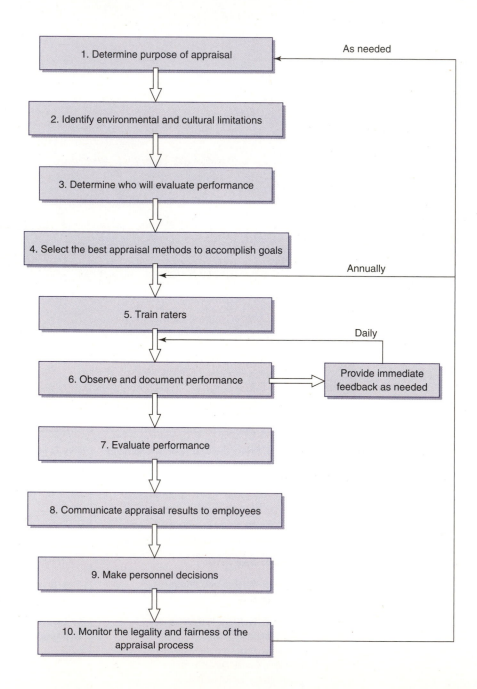

Figure 7.1

The Performance Appraisal Process

Step 1: Determine the Reason for Evaluating Employee Performance

The first step in the performance appraisal process is to determine the reasons your organization wants to evaluate employee performance. That is, does the organization want to use the results to improve performance? Give raises on the basis of performance? This determination is important because the various performance appraisal techniques are appropriate for some purposes but not for others. For example, a performance appraisal method—the **forced-choice rating scale** (see Appendix at the end of the chapter)—is excellent for determining compensation but terrible for training purposes. Likewise, the use of 360-degree feedback is an excellent source for improving employee performance but is not appropriate for determining salary increases. Surprisingly, most organizations do not have specific goals for their performance appraisal systems. As a result, it comes as no surprise that several national surveys found that the vast majority of performance appraisal systems are not successful (Coens & Jenkins, 2002).

Though there are many uses and goals for performance appraisal, the most common include providing employee feedback and training, determining salary increases, making promotion decisions, making termination decisions, and conducting personnel research.

Forced-choice rating scales A method of performance appraisal in which a supervisor is given several behaviors and is forced to choose which of them is most typical of the employee.

Providing Employee Training and Feedback

By far, the most important use of performance evaluation is to improve employee performance by providing feedback about what employees are doing right and wrong. Even though employee training should be an ongoing process (see Chapter 8), the semiannual **performance appraisal review** is an excellent time to meet with employees to discuss their strengths and weaknesses. But more important, it is the time to determine how weaknesses can be corrected. This process is thoroughly discussed later in the chapter.

Performance appraisal review A meeting between a supervisor and a subordinate for the purpose of discussing performance appraisal results.

Determining Salary Increases

As mentioned in Chapter 2, a job's worth is determined by many factors, including the degree of responsibility and level of education required to perform the job. But the difference in compensation between two individuals within the same job is a function of both tenure and job performance. That is, it would not seem fair to pay a poor-performing employee the same amount as an excellently performing one. Thus, one important reason for evaluating employee performance is to provide a fair basis on which to determine an employee's salary increase. If performance appraisal results are to be used to determine salary increases, a numerical rather than narrative format is probably needed.

Making Promotion Decisions

Another reason for evaluating performance is to determine which employees will be promoted. Although it would seem only fair to promote the best employee, this often does not occur. For example, the policy in some organizations is to promote employees with the most seniority. This is especially true of organizations whose employees belong to unions. Even though promoting employees on the basis of

Peter Principle The idea that organizations tend to promote good employees until they reach the level at which they are not competent—in other words, their highest level of incompetence.

performance or tenure seems fair, it may not always be smart. The best employee at one level is not always the best at the next level. Promoting the best or most senior employee often results in the so-called **Peter Principle**—the promotion of employees until they reach their highest level of incompetence. If performance evaluations are used to promote employees, care should be taken to ensure that the employee is evaluated well on the job dimensions that are similar to those of the new position.

For example, the five important job dimensions of a salesperson might be sales, communication skills, accuracy of paperwork, client rapport, and responsibility. The four important job dimensions of sales manager would be communication skills, accuracy of paperwork, motivational ability, and employee rapport. The salesperson with the highest scores on the overlapping dimensions, which in this case are communication skills and accuracy of paperwork, should be the one promoted. Sales volume might not even be used as a factor in this decision.

Another use of performance appraisal data is in training-needs analysis, which will be discussed in greater detail in Chapter 8. If many employees score poorly on a performance appraisal dimension, an increase or change in training is probably necessary for all employees. If only a few employees have low scores, training at an individual level is indicated. Thus, performance appraisal can provide useful information about an organization's strengths and weaknesses.

Making Termination Decisions

Unfortunately, providing feedback, counseling, and training to employees does not always increase performance or reduce discipline problems. When performance management techniques are not successful, the results of a performance review might suggest that the best course of action is to terminate the employee. Methods for doing this and the legal issues that surround such decisions will be discussed in great detail at the end of this chapter.

Conducting Personnel Research

A final reason for evaluating employees is for personnel research. As discussed in previous chapters, employment tests must be validated, and one way this can be done is by correlating test scores with some measure of job performance. To do this, however, an accurate and reliable measure of job performance must be available. The same is true in evaluating the effectiveness of training programs. To determine effectiveness, an accurate measure of performance must be available for use in determining whether performance increases as a result of training.

Although not the most important reason for evaluating employee performance, personnel research is still important, especially in organizations where union contracts forbid the use of performance evaluations in personnel decisions. In those situations, performance evaluations are still needed for effective personnel research.

Step 2: Identify Environmental and Cultural Limitations

The second step in the performance appraisal process is to identify the environmental and cultural factors that could affect the system. For example, if supervisors are highly overworked, an elaborate, time-consuming performance appraisal system will not be successful. In an environment in which there is no money available for merit pay, developing a numerically complex system will become frustrating, and the results of the evaluation may not be taken seriously. In an environment in which employees are very cohesive, the use of peer ratings might reduce the cohesiveness.

Step 3: Determine Who Will Evaluate Performance

360-degree feedback A performance appraisal system in which feedback is obtained from multiple sources such as supervisors, subordinates, and peers.

Multiple-source feedback A performance appraisal strategy in which an employee receives feedback from sources (e.g., clients, subordinates, peers) other than just his/her supervisor.

Traditionally, employee performance has been evaluated solely by supervisors. Recently, however, organizations have realized that supervisors see only certain aspects of an employee's behavior. For example, as shown in Figure 7.2, a branch manager might observe only 30% of a teller's work behavior; the rest is observed by customers, peers, and support staff in other parts of the bank. Furthermore, the teller might behave very differently around her supervisor than around other people. Consequently, to obtain an accurate view of the teller's performance, these other sources can be used to provide feedback. The buzzwords for using multiple sources to appraise performance are **360-degree feedback** and **multiple-source feedback**. About 28% of large U.S. organizations use some form of multiple-source feedback (Mercer Consulting, 2005). A survey by the Society for Human Resource Management (SHRM, 2000) reported that 360-degree feedback was used by 18% of organizations for nonexempt positions, 29% for exempt positions, and 32% for executive-level positions. It is important to note that 360-degree feedback is primarily used as a source of training and employee development and is seldom used in the appraisal process to determine salary increases or to make promotion and termination decisions. Sources of relevant information about employee performance include supervisors, peers, subordinates, customers, and self-appraisal. As shown in Table 7.1, often there is little agreement in the way two supervisors evaluate an employee or a supervisor and a peer might rate an employee. Interestingly, supervisors whose self-ratings agree with

Figure 7.2

Who Observes Employee Performance?

Table 7.1   Correlations Between Raters

Agreement Between	Correlation Coefficient
Two supervisors	.50
Two peers	.37
Two subordinates	.30
Supervisors and peers	.34
Supervisor and subordinates	.22
Supervisor and self	.22
Peers and subordinates	.22
Peers and self	.19

Source: Conway & Huffcutt, 1997.

others' ratings tend to be better performers than supervisors whose ratings are not consistent with those of others (Witt, 1996).

Supervisors

By far the most common type of performance appraisal is the supervisor rating. In fact, Bernardin and Beatty (1984) estimated that more than 90% of all performance appraisals are conducted using supervisors' ratings of performance. Though supervisors may not see every minute of an employee's behavior, they do see the end result. A supervisor may not actually see a teller sign up customers for Visa cards but will review the daily sales totals. Likewise, a professor does not see a student actually research and write a paper but infers the levels of these behaviors by viewing the results—the finished term paper.

Peers

Whereas supervisors see the *results* of an employee's efforts, peers often see the actual *behavior*. Peer ratings usually come from employees who work directly with an employee; a bank teller could be rated by other bank tellers. However, other employees in the organization, those who often come in contact with the employee, can also provide useful information. For example, our teller could be rated by employees from the loan support or Visa card departments.

Research has shown that peer ratings are fairly reliable only when the peers who make the ratings are similar to and well acquainted with the employees being rated (Mumford, 1983). Most important, peer ratings have been successful in predicting the future success of promoted employees, as they correlate highly with supervisor ratings (Cederbloom, 1989).

Research suggests that certain employees are more lenient in their peer ratings than are other employees. Saavedra and Kwun (1993) found that high performers evaluate their peers more strictly than do low performers. This difference in ratings is probably because employees compare others to themselves. Thus, the average employee does not appear impressive to a high performer but may do so to a less productive employee.

Though peers may provide a unique view of performance, employees tend to react worse to negative feedback from peers than from experts (Albright & Levy, 1995). Employees who score high in self-esteem, high in self-monitoring, and low in individualism react most favorably to peer ratings (Long, Long, & Dobbins, 1998).

Subordinates

Subordinate feedback (also called upward feedback) is an important component of 360-degree feedback, as subordinates can provide a very different view about a supervisor's behavior. However, with the exception of students rating teachers, formal methods are neither common nor well regarded by managers (McEvoy, 1988, 1990). Subordinate ratings can be difficult to obtain because employees fear a backlash if they unfavorably rate their supervisor, especially when a supervisor has only one or two subordinates. For example, when the supervisors at one mental health facility gave poor performance ratings to their boss, each was "called on the carpet" for having the audacity to rate the boss poorly. After such a browbeating, what do you think is the probability the subordinates will be honest in the future? Subordinates' feedback can be encouraged if supervisors appear open to employee comments (Baumgartner, 1994); if the ratings are made anonymously (Antonioni, 1994); if the ratings are used for developmental purposes (Avis & Kudisch, 2000); and if the employee feels competent to make the rating, feels there will be no retaliation for making honest ratings, and will somehow benefit by providing honest ratings (Smith & Fortunato, 2008).

Does multisource feedback help improve performance? A meta-analysis (Smither, London, & Reilly, 2005) found that although the effect was small, feedback from direct reports ($d = .24$) resulted in greater performance changes than did feedback from peers ($d = .12$) or supervisors ($d = .14$). Multisource feedback is most effective when the feedback indicates that the employee needs to change his or her behavior, the employee perceives that the changes are feasible, and the employee is open to receiving constructive feedback (Smither et al., 2005). Performance increases can be enhanced when the feedback is provided in a workshop conducted by a feedback facilitator rather than by a direct supervisor (Seifert, Yukl, & McDonald, 2003). Though supervisor performance might increase from upward feedback, such feedback does not appear to improve the overall performance or stock value of an organization (Pfau & Kay, 2002a).

Customers

Although it would be unlikely that an organization would ask customers to fill out a performance appraisal instrument on an employee, organizations do value customer feedback. Informally, customers provide feedback on employee performance by filing complaints or complimenting a manager about one of her employees. Formally, customers provide feedback by completing evaluation cards such as that shown in Figure 7.3.

Organizations also seek customer feedback in the form of *secret shoppers*—current customers who have been enlisted by a company to periodically evaluate the service they receive. In exchange for their ratings, secret shoppers get a few dollars and a free meal. For years, I have been "employed" by a national marketing company to eat at local restaurants and secretly complete a rating of the quality of food and service. The compensation is only $5 per visit plus reimbursement for the meal, but it is a fun experience. I only wish they would have granted my request for sunglasses and a trench coat!

McBurger Queen Restaurants

Dear Customer:

We value your business and strive to make each of your visits a dining pleasure. To help us reach our goal, we would appreciate your completing this card and placing it in our suggestion box on your way out.

1. Was your food cooked properly?   Y N
2. Was your server friendly?   Y N
3. Was your server efficient?   Y N
4. Do you plan to return?   Y N

5. Who was your server? _____

Comments:

_____
_____
_____
_____

Figure 7.3
Customer Evaluation Card

Self-Appraisal

Allowing an employee to evaluate her own behavior and performance is a technique used by only a small percentage of organizations (Atwater, 1998). In Bismarck, North Dakota, self-ratings account for 25% of city employees' evaluations (peer ratings account for 25% and supervisor ratings 50%).

Research on self-appraisal, however, has found what we might expect to find: Employee self-appraisals tend to suffer from leniency (Beehr, Ivanitskaya, Hansen, Erofeev, & Gudanowski, 2001) and correlate only moderately (.29) with actual performance (Mabe & West, 1982) and poorly with subordinate (Conway & Huffcutt, 1997) and management ratings (Beehr et al., 2001). However, when evaluations are made with clear rating standards and social comparison information, agreement is increased between self- and supervisor-ratings (Keeping & Sulsky, 1996; Schrader & Steiner, 1996). When peer ratings are lower than self-ratings, employees react negatively to, and question the accuracy of, negative feedback (Brett & Atwater, 2001).

The leniency found in the self-ratings of U.S. workers may not generalize to other countries. Self-ratings of Japanese, Korean, and Taiwanese workers suffer from modesty rather than leniency, whereas self-ratings from workers in the United States, mainland China, India, Singapore, and Hong Kong are characterized by leniency (Barron & Sackett, 2008). Further research is still needed to investigate potential cultural differences in self-ratings.

Self-appraisals of performance appear to be most accurate when the self-appraisal will not be used for such administrative purposes as raises or promotions (Atwater, 1998). They are also more accurate when employees understand the performance appraisal system (Williams & Levy, 1992) and when employees believe that an objective record of their performance is available with which the supervisor can compare the self-appraisal (Farh & Werbel, 1986). To think more about who should evaluate performance, complete Exercise 7.1 in your workbook.

Step 4: Select the Best Appraisal Methods to Accomplish Your Goals

The next step in the performance appraisal process is to select the performance criteria and appraisal methods that will best accomplish your goals for the system. *Criteria* are ways of describing employee success. For example, it might be decided that attendance, quality of work, and safety are the three most important criteria for a successful employee. Now the methods for measuring the criteria must be chosen and created. That is, how can we measure attendance, quality, and safety?

Prior to developing the actual performance appraisal instrument, two important decisions must be made: the focus of the performance appraisal dimensions and whether to use rankings or ratings.

Decision 1: Focus of the Appraisal Dimensions

As shown in Table 7.2, the appraisal dimensions can focus on traits, competencies, task types, or goals.

Trait-Focused Performance Dimensions

A trait-focused system concentrates on such employee attributes as dependability, honesty, and courtesy. Though commonly used, trait-focused performance appraisal instruments are not a good idea because they provide poor feedback and thus will not result in employee development and growth. For example, think of a

Table 7.2   Four Ways to Focus Performance Dimensions

Competency Focus	Task Focus
Report-writing skills	Crime prevention
Driving skills	Arrest procedures
Public-speaking skills	Court testimony
Knowledge of the law	Use of vehicle
Decision-making skills	Radio procedures
Physical ability skills	Following rules and regulations
Goal Focus	**Trait Focus**
Prevent crimes from occurring	Honesty
Arrest/cite law breakers	Courtesy
Finish shift without personal injury	Responsibility
Have arrests and citations stand up in court	Dependability
Minimize citizen complaints	Assertiveness
Ensure public safety	Cooperation

performance-review meeting in which the supervisor tells an employee that she received low ratings on responsibility and friendliness. Because traits are personal, the employee is likely to become defensive. Furthermore, the employee will want specific examples the supervisor may not have available. The only developmental advice the supervisor can offer would be to "be more responsible and friendly." Such advice is not specific enough for the employee to change her behavior.

Competency-Focused Performance Dimensions

Rather than concentrating on an employee's traits, competency-focused dimensions concentrate on the employee's knowledge, skills, and abilities. For example, competency-focused dimensions might include writing skills, oral presentation skills, and driving skills. The advantage to organizing dimensions by competencies is that it is easy to provide feedback and suggest the steps necessary to correct deficiencies. That is, if an employee is evaluated as having poor writing skills, the obvious corrective measure would be for the employee to take a writing course.

Task-Focused Performance Dimensions

Task-focused dimensions are organized by the similarity of tasks that are performed. For a police officer, such dimensions might include *following radio procedures* or *court testimony*. Note that a task-focused dimension usually includes several competencies. For example, to receive a high rating on the dimension of *court testimony*, the officer would need the competencies of public speaking, organization, and knowledge of the law. The advantage of this approach is that because supervisors are concentrating on tasks that occur together and can thus visualize an employee's performance, it is often easier to evaluate performance than with the other dimensions. The disadvantage is that it is more difficult to offer suggestions for how to correct the deficiency if an employee scores low on a dimension. That is, is the low score on *court testimony* due to a lack of knowledge or to poor public speaking skills?

Goal-Focused Performance Dimensions

The fourth type of performance dimension is to organize the appraisal on the basis of goals to be accomplished by the employee. Sticking with our police officer example, goals might include preventing crimes from occurring, finishing the shift without personal injury, and minimizing the number of citizen complaints. The advantage of a goal-focused approach is that it makes it easier for an employee to understand why certain behaviors are expected. Take, for example, the behavioral expectations of having a police officer wear a seat belt and body armor. If these expectations were listed under the dimension of *Following Department Policy*, the officer might not be too concerned with changing behavior about following "some stupid rule." If, however, these two expectations were listed under the goal of *staying alive*, it would be clearer that they are there for an important purpose.

Contextual Performance

In the above discussion, the four ways to focus performance dimensions all concentrated on the technical aspects of performing a job. In recent years, psychologists have begun to study *contextual performance*, that is, the effort an employee makes to get along with peers, improve the organization, and perform tasks that are needed but are not necessarily an official part of the employee's job description. Many organizations include rating scales addressing the technical aspects of the job as well as the contextual aspects. That is, they want employees who will be not only effective performers but good organizational citizens as well. In academia, it is not uncommon to deny tenure to a faculty member who is technically competent but does not "play well with others."

Contextual performance is important because not only are these prosocial organizational behaviors important to the success of an organization, but they also tend to be similar across jobs, whereas the dimensions involved in task performance differ across jobs (Borman & Motowidlo, 1997). Furthermore, the selection tests that might best predict task performance (e.g., cognitive ability, job knowledge) are not the same tests that might predict contextual performance (e.g., integrity tests, personality inventories). To better understand how to choose the type of dimension, complete Exercise 7.2 in your workbook.

Decision 2: Should Dimensions Be Weighted?

Once the type of dimension has been determined, the next decision is whether the dimensions should be weighted so that some are more important than others. Grading systems in the classes you have taken provide good examples of weighting dimensions. For example, you may have had a class where the final exam was given more weight than other exams or a class in which a particular project carried more weight than others.

Weighting dimensions makes good philosophical sense, as some dimensions might be more important to an organization than others. For example, the dimension of patient care would be more important for a nurse than would be keeping a professional appearance. Though both are important parts of the job, providing poor patient care has more of an impact for the organization than not wearing the proper clothing. Another advantage to differentially weighting dimensions is that it may reduce racial and other biases (McFarland, Wolf, & Nguyen, 2005).

Though differential weighting of dimensions makes sense and has some advantages, many organizations choose to weight all performance dimensions equally because it is administratively easier to compute and to explain to employees.

Decision 3: Use of Employee Comparisons, Objective Measures, or Ratings

Once the types of dimensions have been considered, the next decision is whether to evaluate performance by comparing employees with one another (ranking), using objective measures such as attendance and number of units sold, or having supervisors rate how well the employee has performed on each of the dimensions.

Employee Comparisons

Rank order A method of performance appraisal in which employees are ranked from best to worst.

To reduce leniency, employees can be compared with one another instead of being rated individually on a scale. The easiest and most common of these methods is the **rank order**. In this approach, employees are ranked in order by their judged performance for each relevant dimension. As Table 7.3 shows, the ranks are then averaged across each dimension to yield an overall rank.

Table 7.3   Ranking Method of Evaluating Performance

Employee	Dimension			Total
	Knowledge	Dependability	Quality	
Barrino	1	1	1	1.00
Underwood	2	3	2	2.33
Hicks	3	2	3	2.67
Sparks	4	5	4	4.33
Cook	5	4	5	4.67

Rank orders are easily used when there are only a few employees to rank, but they become difficult to use with larger numbers. Ranking the top few and bottom few employees is relatively easy, but deciding which 2 of 50 employees should be placed at the 30th and 31st ranks is more difficult.

To make this process easier, **paired comparisons** can be used. This method involves comparing each possible pair of employees and choosing which one of each pair is the better employee. An example is shown in Figure 7.4. Practice using the paired-comparisons method by completing Exercise 7.3 in your workbook.

Paired comparison A form of ranking in which a group of employees to be ranked are compared one pair at a time.

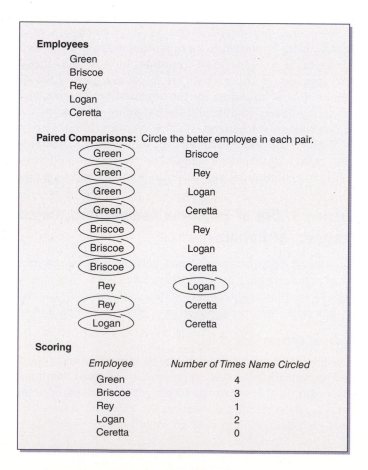

Figure 7.4

Example of Paired-Comparison Method

Even though comparing one pair of employees at a time is easier than simultaneously comparing a large number of employees, it does have its drawbacks. With large numbers of employees, the time necessary to make all of the comparisons becomes prohibitive. For example, to determine how many comparisons must be made, we can use the following formula:

$$\text{number of comparisons} = \frac{n(n-1)}{2},$$

where n = the number of employees. Thus, if we have 10 employees to compare:

$$\text{number of comparisons} = \frac{(10)(10-1)}{2} = \frac{(10)(9)}{2} = \frac{90}{2} = 45.$$

Thus, we would need to make 45 comparisons for each performance dimension. Although this number is not extreme, evaluating 100 employees would result in 4,950 separate comparisons! And with five performance dimensions, some unfortunate supervisor would have to make almost 25,000 separate comparisons! Obviously, the supervisor would not favor such a task.

The final type of employee comparison system is called **forced distribution**. With this method, a predetermined percentage of employees are placed in each of the five categories shown in Table 7.4. Forced distribution systems are used by more than 20% of Fortune 1000 companies (Bates, 2003a). Also called "rank and yank," forced distributions were a favorite method of Jack Welch, the former chief executive officer of General Electric, who required managers to fire the bottom-performing 10% of their employees each year. Though such systems seem harsh, the limited research on the topic suggests that rank-and-yank systems result in increased levels of organizational productivity, especially during the first few years in which the system is in place (Scullen, Bergey, & Aiman-Smith, 2005). Employees, however, consider forced distribution scales to be the least fair method of performance appraisal (Roch, Sternburgh, & Caputo, 2007).

Forced distribution systems are much easier to use than the other two employee comparison methods, but they also have a drawback. To use the method, one must assume that employee performance is normally distributed, that is, that there are certain percentages of employees who are poor, average, and excellent. As will be discussed in more detail in Chapter 8, employee performance probably is not normally distributed because of restriction of range. There probably are few terrible employees because they either were never hired or were quickly fired. Likewise, truly excellent employees probably have been promoted. Thus, employee performance is distributed in a nonnormal fashion.

Forced distribution method A performance appraisal method in which a predetermined percentage of employees are placed into a number of performance categories.

Table 7.4   Forced-Distribution Method of Performance Appraisal

Hudson	Barrymore Streep	Aniston Parker Roberts Jolie	Diaz Witherspoon	Bullock
10%	20%	40%	20%	10%
Terrible	Below average	Average	Good	Excellent

Perhaps another way to look at this concept is by examining the grades given in a class. When students ask an instructor to "curve" a test, technically they are asking her to force their grades into a normal curve—that is, there will be approximately 10% As and 10% Fs. (Of course, what these students are really often asking for is extra points.)

Suppose that you are at the bottom of your class, yet you still have a 75% average on class exams. Do you deserve an F? What if you are the last person in the D category and a student withdraws from the class with two weeks to go? To keep the distribution normal, you are given an F. Do you consider this fair?

Perhaps the greatest problem with all of the employee-comparison methods is that they do not provide information about how well an employee is actually doing. For example, even though every employee at a production plant might be doing an excellent job, someone has to be at the bottom. Thus, it might appear that one worker is doing a poor job (because she is last), when in fact she, and every other employee, is doing well.

Objective Measures

A second way to evaluate performance is to use what are commonly called objective, or hard, criteria. Common types of objective measures include quantity of work, quality of work, attendance, and safety.

Quantity of Work.   Evaluation of a worker's performance in terms of **quantity** is obtained by simply counting the number of relevant job behaviors that take place. For example, we might judge a salesperson's performance by the number of units she sells, an assembly line worker's performance by the number of bumpers she welds, or a police officer's performance by the number of arrests she makes.

Although quantity measures appear to be objective measures of performance, they are often misleading. As shown in Figure 7.5, it is important to realize that many factors determine quantity of work other than an employee's ability and performance. Furthermore, for many people's jobs it might not be practical or possible to measure quantity; computer programmers, doctors, and firefighters are examples.

Quality of Work.   Another method to evaluate performance is by measuring the quality of the work that is done. **Quality** is usually measured in terms of **errors**, which are defined as deviations from a standard. Thus, to obtain a measure of quality, there must be a standard against which to compare an employee's work. For example, a

Quantity A type of objective criterion used to measure job performance by counting the number of relevant job behaviors that occur.

Quality A type of objective criterion used to measure job performance by comparing a job behavior with a standard.

Error Deviation from a standard of quality; also a type of response to communication overload that involves processing all information but processing some of it incorrectly.

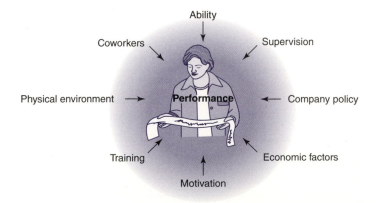

Figure 7.5

Factors Affecting Performance

© Nina Greipel/AP Photo

Quality is a relevant criterion for many jobs.

seamstress's work quality would be judged by how it compares with a "model" shirt; a secretary's work quality would be judged by the number of typos (the standard being correctly spelled words); and a cook's quality might be judged by how her food resembles a standard as measured by size, temperature, and ingredient amounts.

Kentucky Fried Chicken, for example, evaluates the quality of its franchises' food by undercover inspectors. These inspectors purchase food, drive down the road, and after parking, use a thermometer to see whether the food has been served at a standard acceptable temperature and also a scale to determine whether the weight of the mashed potatoes is within the acceptable range.

Note that the definition of an error is *any* deviation from a standard. Thus, errors can even be work quality that is higher than a standard. Why is this an error? Suppose a company manufactures shirts that are sold for $20. To keep down the manufacturing cost of its shirts, the company probably uses cheaper material and has its workers spend less time per shirt than does a company that manufactures $150 shirts. Thus, if an employee sews a shirt with 15 stitches per inch instead of the standard 10, the company will lose money because of higher quality!

When I was working my way through school, I held a summer job at an amusement park. The job involved wearing a pink and purple uniform and cooking prefabricated pizza. The standard for the large pepperoni pizza was 2 handfuls of cheese and 15 pieces of pepperoni. Now all pizza lovers recognize this to be a barren pizza. The cooks thus tried to increase the pizza quality by tripling the number of pepperoni pieces. The management quickly explained to the young "gourmet chefs" that exceeding the standards was considered poor work performance and that employees who did so would be fired.

A similar situation developed at a factory that produced parts for telephones. Most of the employees were older and took great pride in their work quality and in the fact that their parts had the lowest percentage of errors in the company. They were told, however, that their quality was too high and that the parts were lasting so long that the company was not getting much repeat business. Quality errors can occur in many strange ways!

Attendance.   A common method for objectively measuring one aspect of an employee's performance is by looking at attendance (this is discussed in greater detail in Chapter 10). Attendance can be separated into three distinct criteria: absenteeism, tardiness, and tenure. Both absenteeism and tardiness have obvious implications for the performance appraisal process. The weight that each has in the overall evaluation of the employee largely depends on the nature of the job.

Tenure as a criterion, however, is used mostly for research purposes when evaluating the success of selection decisions. For example, in a job such as food preparer at McDonald's, there is probably little difference in the quantity and quality of hamburgers or French fries that are cooked. But an employee might be considered "successful" if she stays with the company for at least four months and "unsuccessful" if she leaves before that time. In fact, the importance of tenure can be demonstrated by noting that several major fast-food restaurants and convenience stores have established bonus systems to reward long-tenure employees—that is, those who have worked for a company at least six months. For each hour the employee works, the company places a specified amount of money into an account that can be used by the employee to pay such education expenses as books and tuition.

Safety.   Another method used to evaluate the success of an employee is safety. Obviously, employees who follow safety rules and who have no occupational accidents do not cost an organization as much money as those who break rules, equipment, and possibly their own bodies. As with tenure, safety is usually used for research purposes, but it can also be used for employment decisions such as promotions and bonuses.

Ratings of Performance

The most commonly used option in evaluating performance is to have supervisors rate how well the employee performed on each dimension. Though there are many variations of how these rating scales can be created, the two most common are the graphic rating scale and the behavioral checklist.

Graphic rating scale A method of performance appraisal that involves rating employee performance on an interval or ratio scale.

Graphic Rating Scale.   The most common rating scale is the **graphic rating scale**. An example is shown in Table 7.5. As you can see, such scales are fairly simple, with 5 to 10 dimensions accompanied by words such as *excellent* and *poor* anchoring the ends of the scale.

The obvious advantage of graphic rating scales is their ease of construction and use, but they have been criticized because of their susceptibility to such rating errors as halo and leniency, which are discussed later in this chapter.

Behavioral Checklists.   As shown in Figure 7.6, behavioral checklists consist of a list of behaviors, expectations, or results for each dimension. This list is used to force the supervisor to concentrate on the relevant behaviors that fall under a dimension.

Table 7.5   Example of a Graphic Rating Scale

Initiative	Poor	1	2	3	4	5	Excellent
Cooperation	Poor	1	2	3	4	5	Excellent
Dependability	Poor	1	2	3	4	5	Excellent
Attendance	Poor	1	2	4	4	5	Excellent

Radio Procedures

Behavioral Elements

_____ Uses proper codes and signals when sending information

_____ Understands codes and signals when receiving information

_____ Voice is clear and easy-to-understand in normal situations

_____ Voice is clear, easy to understand, and does not indicate panic in high stress situations

_____ Follows proper radio procedures

_____ Monitors the proper channels

_____ Knows the location of all district officers

_____ Never communicates improper information over the radio

_____ Keeps dispatch informed of current status

_____ Treats communications officers with respect and courtesy

Dimension Rating

_____ 5 Consistently exceeds requirements, no improvements needed

_____ 4 Exceeds most requirements

_____ 3 Usually meets requirements, acceptable performance

_____ 2 Usually meets most requirements, but needs improvement

_____ 1 Does not meet minimum requirements, needs immediate and extensive improvement

Comments

_____

_____

_____

_____

Figure 7.6

Example of a
Behavioral Checklist

Behavioral checklists are constructed by taking the task statements from a detailed job description (e.g., "Types correspondence") and converting them into behavioral performance statements representing the level at which the behavior is expected to be performed (e.g., "Correspondence is typed accurately and does not contain spelling or grammatical errors").

When creating the statements for each dimension, one should carefully consider whether to write the statements in the form of behaviors or in the form of results. Examples of behavior-based statements for a bank teller might include "Properly greets each customer," "Knows customers' names," and "Thanks customer after each transaction." The obvious advantage to a behavior-focused system is the increased amount of specific feedback that can be given to each employee.

Result-focused statements concentrate on what an employee *accomplished* as a result of what she did. For example, "Distributed at least 25 Visa applications each month," "Teller drawer was not short at the end of the day," and "Completed annual report on time." Result-focused systems are tempting because they evaluate employees on their contribution to the bottom line: Did their behavior on the job result in a tangible outcome for the organization? To practice writing behavioral statements, complete Exercise 7.4 in your workbook.

Contamination The
condition in which a criterion
score is affected by things other
than those under the control of
the employee.

A problem with result-focused statements is that an employee can do everything asked of her by an organization and still not get the desired results due to factors outside of her control. These factors are referred to as **contamination**. In banking, a teller might not be successful in getting customers to sign up for Visa cards because the bank's interest rate is not competitive. In law enforcement, a police officer might not write many traffic citations because she patrols an area in which there are few cars. In retail, a salesperson has poor sales because of her geographic location. For example: Two salespersons work in different locations. Mary Anderson sells an average of 120 air conditioners per month, whereas Tamika Johnson averages 93. Is this criterion free from contamination? Definitely not.

The number of sales is based not only on the skills of the salesperson but also on such factors as the number of stores in the sales territory, the average temperature in the territory, and the relations between the previous salesperson and the store owners. Thus, if we used only the number of sales, Mary Anderson would be considered our top salesperson. But if we take into account that sales are contaminated by the number of stores in the territory, we see that Mary Anderson sold 120 air conditioners in 50 possible stores, whereas Tamika Johnson sold 93 air conditioners in 10 stores. Thus, Mary Anderson sold an average of 2.4 air conditioners per store in an area with an average temperature of 93 degrees; Tamika Johnson sold an average of 9.3 air conditioners per store in an area with an average temperature of 80 degrees. By considering the potential areas of contamination, a different picture emerges of relative performance. As this example clearly shows, factors other than actual performance can affect criteria. Therefore, it is essential to identify as many sources of contamination as possible and to determine ways to adjust performance ratings to account for these contamination sources.

After considering the behaviors in the checklist, a supervisor provides an overall rating of the employee's performance on each dimension. As shown in Figure 7.7, employees can be rated in three ways: how they compared with other employees, the frequency with which they performed certain behaviors, and the extent to which the behaviors met the expectations of the employer.

Comparison with Other Employees. Supervisors can rate performance on a dimension by comparing the employee's level of performance with that of other employees. It is important to note that when such scale anchors as "below average," "average," and "above average" are used, the evaluation involves rating employee performance in comparison with other employees. Though this approach will reduce such problems as overly lenient or overly strict ratings, it potentially forces a supervisor to rate employees who are performing well as being worse than other employees.

Frequency of Desired Behaviors. Behaviors can be rated based on the frequency with which they occur. For example, we expect our production workers to follow safety guidelines. As part of our performance appraisal system, supervisors are asked to decide whether their employees "always," "almost always," "often," "seldom," or "never" follow the rules. As you can imagine, it is often difficult for a supervisor to distinguish between levels such as "almost always" and "often."

Extent to Which Organizational Expectations Are Met. Perhaps the best approach is to rate employees on the extent to which their behavior meets the expectations of the organization. Such an approach allows for high levels of feedback and can be applied to most types of employee behavior. Some behaviors, however, are not suitable for such

Figure 7.7

Examples of Three
Scales to Measure
Behavior

Comparison of Other Employees

Refers to customers by name

_____ Much better than other tellers

_____ Better than other tellers

_____ The same as other tellers

_____ Worse than other tellers

_____ Much worse than other tellers

Frequency

Refers to customers by name

_____ Always

_____ Almost always

_____ Often

_____ Seldom

_____ Never

Extent to Which Organizational Expectations Were Met

Refers to customers by name

_____ Greatly exceeds expectations

_____ Exceeds expectations

_____ Meets expectations

_____ Falls below expectations

_____ Falls well below expectations

a scale. Take, for example, the expectation that a police officer always wear her seat belt. If she wears it all the time, she has *met* expectations (a rating of 3): There is no way to get a higher rating because one cannot wear a seat belt more often than always and thus cannot ever exceed expectations. When such a situation is possible, the scale can be adjusted to be similar to that shown in Figure 7.8.

As shown in Figures 7.9 through 7.11, in addition to graphic rating scales and behavioral checklists, a variety of methods to rate performance are available, including behaviorally anchored rating scales (BARS), mixed-standard scales, and forced-choice scales. Because these scales are not commonly used, but are historically and psychometrically interesting, information about them has been included in the Appendix to this chapter.

Evaluation of Performance Appraisal Methods

In the previous pages and in the chapter Appendix, several methods for evaluating employee performance are offered. Of course, we might now ask, Is any one of these methods the best? Probably not. Research has shown that such complicated techniques as BARS, forced-choice scales, and mixed-standard scales are only occasionally superior to the inexpensive and uncomplicated graphic rating scale (Murphy, 2008).

Although techniques such as behavioral checklists are only slightly more psychometrically sound, they still have some advantages over graphic rating scales. Because employees are directly involved in creating them, they tend to see performance-evaluation results as being more fair. Furthermore, many supervisors who make such ratings prefer many of the behavioral approaches (Dickenson & Zellinger, 1980).

```
┌─────────────────────────────────────────────────────────────────────────────┐
│                      Use of Weapons and Vehicle                               │
│                                                                               │
│  Behaviors that can meet or exceed expectations                               │
│  _____ Effectively handled vehicle in pursuit or emergency situations       │
│  _____ Demonstrated marksmanship above minimum requirements                 │
│  _____ Demonstrated appropriate judgment in determining the use of force    │
│  _____ Demonstrated appropriate judgment in making pursuit decisions        │
│                                                                               │
│  Behaviors that can only meet expectations                                    │
│  _____ Weapons ratings are current and meet minimum requirements            │
│  _____ Weapons were carried in an appropriate manner                        │
│  _____ When weapons were used, reports were filed on time                   │
│  _____ When weapons were used, reports contained accurate information       │
│  _____ When driving, seat belts were always worn                            │
│  _____ Carried only weapons issued and/or authorized by the Department      │
│  _____ Applied force only when use of force was justified                   │
│                                                                               │
│  Dimension Rating                                                             │
│  _____ 5 Consistently exceeds requirements, no improvements needed          │
│  _____ 4 Exceeds most requirements                                          │
│  _____ 3 Usually meets requirements, acceptable performance                 │
│  _____ 2 Usually meets most requirements, but needs improvement             │
│  _____ 1 Does not meet minimum requirements, needs immediate and extensive improvement │
└─────────────────────────────────────────────────────────────────────────────┘
```

Figure 7.8

Rating Behaviors that Can Only Meet Expectations

Finally, feedback from behavior-based methods is easier to give and to use to provide suggestions for improvement.

It is important to understand that although the various performance appraisal methods may yield results that are technically similar, the way in which the performance appraisal system is administered can affect employee trust and satisfaction. Gaby and Woehr (2005) found that the greater the employee perception of the fairness of the performance appraisal system, the greater was their job satisfaction and commitment to the organization.

Though many of the behavioral methods yield similar results, the same is not true when comparing subjective and objective methods. A meta-analysis by Bommer, Johnson, Rich, Podsakoff, and Mackenzie (1995) indicates that objective and subjective results are only slightly correlated ($r = .39$). Interestingly, there was a stronger relationship between objective and subjective ratings of quantity ($r = .38$) than between objective and subjective ratings of quality ($r = .24$).

From a legal perspective, courts are more interested in the due process afforded by a performance appraisal system than in its technical aspects. Reviews of 295 circuit court (Werner & Bolino, 1995) and 145 federal district court cases (Foster, Dunleavy, Campion, & Steubing, 2008) suggest that decisions based on performance appraisal ratings are most likely to survive a legal challenge if they are based on a job analysis, raters received training and written instructions, raters had the opportunity to actually

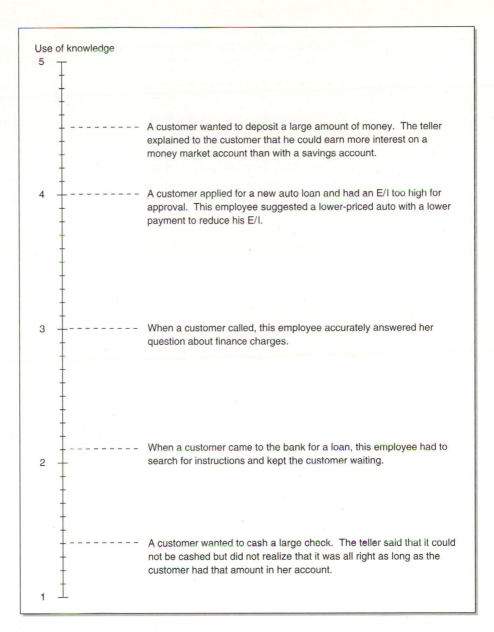

Figure 7.9

Example of a Behaviorally Anchored Rating Scale

Use of knowledge

5

— — — — — — — — A customer wanted to deposit a large amount of money. The teller explained to the customer that he could earn more interest on a money market account than with a savings account.

4 — — — — — — — A customer applied for a new auto loan and had an E/I too high for approval. This employee suggested a lower-priced auto with a lower payment to reduce his E/I.

3 — — — — — — When a customer called, this employee accurately answered her question about finance charges.

— — — — — — — When a customer came to the bank for a loan, this employee had to search for instructions and kept the customer waiting.

2

— — — — — — — A customer wanted to cash a large check. The teller said that it could not be cashed but did not realize that it was all right as long as the customer had that amount in her account.

1

Figure 7.10

Example of a Forced-Choice Rating Scale

Directions: In each of the following items, check the one statement that is *most like* the teller being rated and the one statement that is *least like* the teller being rated.

		Most	Least	
1.	a)	✔		Teller is always on time (neutral).
	b)			Teller is never short at end of day (poor).
	c)		✔	Teller smiles at each customer (excellent).
2.	a)		✔	Teller usually cross-sells (excellent).
	b)	✔		Teller keeps work area neat and orderly (poor).
	c)			Teller is friendly to other employees (neutral).

Figure 7.11

Example of a Mixed-
Standard Scale

Directions: Place a "+" after the statement if the typical behavior of the teller is usually better than that represented in the statement, a "0" if the typical behavior of the teller is about the same as that represented in the statement, and a "–" if the typical behavior of the teller is worse than that represented in the statement.

	Rating
1. Teller constantly argues with other employees (P).	_____
2. Teller smiles at customers (A).	_____
3. Teller asks customers how their families are doing (E).	_____
4. Teller helps other employees when possible (A).	_____
5. Teller is always friendly to and talks with other employees (E).	_____
6. Teller asks customers what they want (P).	_____

Items 1, 4, and 5 are from the Employee Relations Dimension.
Items 2, 3, and 6 are from the Customer Relations Dimension.

observe the performance of the employee, performance standards had been communicated to the employee, employees were allowed to review and comment on the appraisal results, employees were warned of performance problems and given a chance to improve their performance, and ratings from multiple raters are consistent. Interestingly, an analysis of appellate court cases suggests that conservative courts (e.g., Fourth Circuit) are more likely to base their decisions on the validity and accuracy of the performance appraisal instrument, whereas liberal courts (e.g., Ninth Circuit) are more likely to base their decisions on fairness issues (Lee, Havighurst, & Rassel, 2004).

Step 5: Train Raters

Although training supervisors to evaluate performance is essential to a sound and legal performance appraisal system, a 2010 ERC survey found that few organizations spend the time and resources necessary to do this properly. This lack of training is surprising given that research has indicated that training supervisors to become aware of the various rating errors and how to avoid them often increases accuracy and reduces rating errors (Hauenstein, 1998), increases the validity of tests validated against the ratings (Pursell, Dossett, & Latham, 1980), and increases employee satisfaction with the ratings (Ivancevich, 1982). This is especially true when the training technique uses discussion, practice in rating, and feedback about rating accuracy rather than lecture (Smith, 1986). These training effects, however, are short-lived (Noble, 1997) unless additional training and feedback are provided, and they can even reduce the accuracy of ratings by substituting new errors (Bernardin & Pence, 1980).

The effectiveness of rater training also is a function of training format. Raters who receive **frame-of-reference training** make fewer rating errors and recall more information than do untrained raters or raters receiving information about only job-related behaviors (Athey & McIntyre, 1987; Day & Sulsky, 1995; Gorman & Rentsch, 2009; Roch & O'Sulivan, 2003). Frame-of-reference training provides raters with job-related information, practice in rating, and examples of ratings made by experts as well as the rationale behind those expert ratings (Hauenstein & Foti, 1989). The goal of frame-of reference training is to communicate the organization's definition of

Frame-of-reference training A method of training raters in which the rater is provided with job-related information, a chance to practice ratings, examples of ratings made by experts, and the rationale behind the expert ratings.

effective performance and to then get raters to consider only relevant employee behaviors when making performance evaluations (Uggerslev & Sulsky, 2008).

Though training raters is certainly important, it is also important to explain the performance appraisal system to employees. Not surprisingly, the better that employees understand the performance appraisal system, the greater is their satisfaction with the system (Whiting, Kline, & Sulsky, 2008).

Step 6: Observe and Document Performance

Critical incidents A method of performance appraisal in which the supervisor records employee behaviors that were observed on the job and rates the employee on the basis of that record.

The next step in the performance appraisal process is for supervisors to observe employee behavior and document **critical incidents** as they occur. *Critical incidents* are examples of excellent and poor employee performance. Such documentation is usually written in a critical incident log—formal accounts of excellent and poor employee performance that were observed by the supervisor. Critical incidents should be communicated to the employee at the time they occur (details on how to provide feedback will occur later in this chapter as well as in Chapter 9). Documentation is important for four reasons. First, documentation forces a supervisor to focus on employee behaviors rather than traits and provides behavioral examples to use when reviewing performance ratings with employees.

Second, documentation helps supervisors recall behaviors when they are evaluating performance. As shown in Figure 7.12, without documentation, instead of recalling all

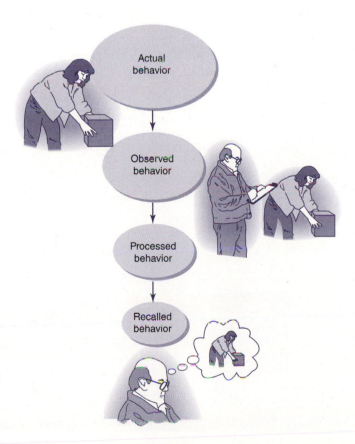

Figure 7.12

Information Loss in the Performance Appraisal System

of an employee's behavior or at least a representative sample of behavior, supervisors tend to recall only a small percentage of an employee's actual behavior. Supervisors tend to remember the following:

■ *First impressions.* Research from many areas of psychology indicates that we remember our first impression of someone (primacy effect) more than we remember later behaviors. Consequently, supervisors recall behaviors that are consistent with their first impression of an employee, even though those first behaviors may not have been representative of the employee's typical performance. Being aware of first impressions is important because performance can be *dynamic*, meaning that a person who is the top performer one year may not be the top performer during another year (Reb & Greguras, 2008).

■ *Recent behaviors.* In addition to first impressions, supervisors tend to recall the most recent behavior that occurred during the evaluation period.

■ *Unusual or extreme behaviors.* Supervisors tend to remember unusual behaviors more than they remember common behaviors. For example, if an average-performing police officer captures an important criminal, the officer's performance evaluations are likely to be inappropriately high. Likewise, a good officer who makes a terrible mistake is likely to receive inappropriately low ratings.

■ *Behavior consistent with the supervisor's opinion.* Once we form an opinion of someone, we tend to look for behaviors that confirm that opinion. If a supervisor likes an employee, she will probably recall only behaviors consistent with that opinion. The opposite would be true for a supervisor who disliked an employee. Once you get on someone's bad side, it is hard to get off of it.

Third, documentation provides examples to use when reviewing performance ratings with employees. Instead of telling an employee that she is constantly getting into

The performance review is the final step in the performance appraisal process.

arguments with customers, a supervisor can use documented critical incidents to show the employee the specific incidents and behaviors that are problematic.

Fourth, documentation helps an organization defend against legal actions taken against it by an employee who was terminated or denied a raise or promotion. As will be discussed later in this chapter, the courts closely examine the accuracy of the performance ratings upon which personnel decisions are based. Judges and juries are not likely to accept a supervisor's rating as proof of poor performance. Instead, they want to see proof of the behaviors that caused the supervisor to rate the employee poorly. Without documentation, employers will seldom win lawsuits filed against them (Foster, 2002). The courts' need for documentation is supported by research indicating that when evaluators must justify their performance ratings, their ratings are more accurate (Mero & Motowidlo, 1995).

To use critical incidents to document performance, a supervisor maintains a log of all the critical behaviors she observes her employees performing. These behaviors are then used during the performance appraisal review process to assign a rating for each employee. The log refreshes the supervisor's memory of her employees' performance and also provides justification for each performance rating. The use of logbooks to record behaviors not only provides an excellent source of documentation but also results in more accurate performance appraisals (Bernardin & Walter, 1977). This is especially true if the logs are organized by employee rather than maintained as only a random collection of incidents observed on the job (DeNisi & Peters, 1996).

Employee Performance Record A standardized use of the critical-incident technique developed at General Motors.

A more formal method for using critical incidents in evaluating performance was developed by Flanagan and Burns (1955) for use by General Motors. Called the **Employee Performance Record**, this method consists of a two-color form similar to that shown in Table 7.6. Half of the sheet is used to record examples of good behaviors, and the other half to record examples of poor behaviors. On each side, there are columns for each of the relevant performance dimensions. Supervisors have a separate record for each employee and at the end of the day can record the observed behaviors.

The advantage of this format is that supervisors are allowed to record only job-relevant behaviors. At the end of the performance appraisal period (every 6 months), the supervisor has a record of job-relevant behaviors recorded in an organized fashion. The Employee Performance Record had several positive effects for General Motors. The number of disciplinary warnings declined, suggestions in the company suggestion box increased, and productivity increased. When the use of critical incidents was first announced, supervisors at General Motors were opposed, thinking it would take too much time. The actual time per day spent on recording the incidents, however, was only five minutes.

Step 7: Evaluate Performance

Obtaining and Reviewing Objective Data

When it is time to appraise an employee's performance, a supervisor should first obtain and review the objective data relevant to the employee's behavior. For example, a police sergeant might review the numbers of tickets an officer wrote, arrests made, and citizen complaints received. A production supervisor might review the number of

Table 7.6 Employee Performance Record

Dimension	Type of Performance	
	Poor	**Excellent**
Knowledge	1/17/11 *Could not answer client's question regarding EEOC policy on adverse impact* 7/28/11 *Used the wrong formula to calculate adverse impact during an audit* 11/06/11 *Could not explain the difference between criterion and content validity to a client*	1/3/11 *Went out of his way to learn about some new changes being made by OFCCP that would affect our work with clients. Ron shared these new changes at our staff meeting*
Teamwork	10/12/11 *Took credit for the work done by all members of his team*	2/4/11 *Another employee was swamped with work and Ron volunteered to help with her workload* 5/7/11 *Praised his work group for their excellent work on an OFCCP audit* 9/2/11 *Stayed late to help another employee finish an analysis that was due the next day*
Customer relations		1/4/11 *Called all his clients to wish them a happy New Year and to see if they were aware of some new changes in OFCCP policy* 3/6/11 *I received a call from one of Ron's clients stating how much they enjoyed working with him and how helpful he had been* 8/12/11 *I received an email from one of Ron's clients praising him for his excellent work ethic and attitude*
Accuracy of work	4/12/11 *Report sent to client had several typos* 6/7/11 *Left out several pages of a report that was sent to a client*	

days an employee was absent, number of units produced, and the tons of material wasted. These data, when combined with critical-incident logs, provide a solid basis on which to rate an employee. As mentioned earlier in the chapter and shown in Figure 7.5, when reviewing objective data, it is essential that potential sources of contamination (e.g., shift, equipment, training, coworkers, geographic area) be considered. Complete Exercise 7.5 in your workbook to get experience dealing with contamination problems.

Reading Critical-Incident Logs

After obtaining objective data, the supervisor should go back and read all of the critical incidents written for an employee. Reading these incidents should reduce errors of primacy, recency, and attention to unusual information.

Completing the Rating Form

Once critical-incident logs have been read and objective data reviewed, the supervisor is ready to assign performance appraisal ratings. While making these ratings, the supervisor must be careful not to make common rating errors involving distribution, halo, proximity, and contrast.

Distribution Errors

A common type of error in evaluating employee performance involves the distribution of ratings on a rating scale; such errors are known as **distribution errors**. Distribution errors are made when a rater uses only one part of a rating scale. For example, on a five-point scale, a supervisor might rate all of her employees a 4 or a 5. One kind of distribution error is called **leniency error**, because certain raters tend to rate every employee at the upper end of the scale regardless of the actual performance of the employee. For example, on our five-point scale, the supervisor rates everyone a 4 or 5. Leniency error can in part be explained by the discomfort felt by supervisors about giving low ratings. That is, supervisors who are uncomfortable about how employees react to a low rating are more likely to be lenient than supervisors who are comfortable with negative employee reactions (Canali et al., 2005). Another partial explanation for leniency is that supervisors don't really know the difference between good and bad performance, so they err on the positive side. Conducting frame of reference training should help reduce leniency in supervisors that don't know the difference between good and bad performance. In addition to fairness consideration, leniency error can pose legal problems if an organization terminates an employee who has a history of high performance ratings.

A related error is **central tendency error**, which results in a supervisor rating every employee in the middle of the scale. For example, in our five-point scale, the supervisor rates everyone a 3. Still another error, **strictness error**, rates every employee at the low end of the scale. For example, on our five-point scale, our supervisor rates everyone a 1 or 2. You have probably encountered such errors in your academic career when you took classes from "easy graders" or "hard graders."

These types of errors pose problems for an organization because two employees doing equal work will receive different ratings if one employee is supervised by a lenient rater and another by a strict rater. This problem can be partially eliminated by having several people rate each employee, although this is not often feasible, especially in small branch offices with only one manager or supervisor. There are times when distribution errors are caused by company policy—whether official or unofficial. In many organizations, there is pressure to not give an employee the highest rating. Such pressure is due either to an attempt to save money on raises or a cultural belief that "no one is perfect."

Halo Errors

A *halo error* occurs when a rater allows either a single attribute or an overall impression of an individual to affect the ratings that she makes on each relevant job dimension. For example, a teacher might think that a student is highly creative. Because of that, the teacher might rate the student as being intelligent and industrious when, in fact, the student's grades are below average. In this case, the instructor has allowed the student's creativity to cloud her judgment of the student's other abilities. Halo effects occur especially when the rater has little knowledge of the job and is less familiar with the person being rated (Kozlowski, Kirsch, & Chao, 1986). Halo error is also

---

Distribution errors Rating errors in which a rater will use only a certain part of a rating scale when evaluating employee performance.

Leniency error A type of rating error in which a rater consistently gives all employees high ratings, regardless of their actual levels of performance.

Central tendency error A type of rating error in which a rater consistently rates all employees in the middle of the scale, regardless of their actual levels of performance.

Strictness error A type of rating error in which a rater consistently gives all employees low ratings, regardless of their actual levels of performance.

When Montgomery County decided its Performance Management Program needed some updating several years ago, I was asked to lead the effort. We began the process by forming a cross-representative team of employees, which spent months studying different types of pay philosophies, including merit pay, pay-for-performance, broad banding, bonus systems, and traditional versus non-traditional models, as well as scored versus nonscored and anniversary date versus "one time of year" appraisals.

Prior to this effort, the county had a one-page evaluation instrument that included a checklist of five criteria: quality of work, quantity of work, relationship with others, work habits, and dependability/reliability. It was viewed more as an instrument to activate a merit increase than as a means for employees to receive any constructive feedback or guidance for future work.

After months of study and work, we elected to develop a phased-in behavioral and competency-based program using a simple rating scale of 0 to 3: *needs improvement, competent, commendable*, and *outstanding/exceptional*, respectively. Phase I implementation involved the setting of six county/core competencies with behavioral statements. The employee team, along with the county's management team, constitutional officers, and agency heads, provided input into developing the competencies, which are customer service, compliance with policies and procedures, teamwork, communication skills, departmental/job knowledge, and training/self-development/continuous improvement.

The team spent considerable time on the numeric elements of the system and geared its design on the positive side, with really only one negative dimension, *needs improvement*. They chose a very simple system that could not be connected with an "average" or a school grading system. To date, it has followed a fairly predictable bell curve with results. Linking pay to it has been considered but has not been implemented as yet.

I facilitated introductory training sessions on the planned program to all evaluators and employees. These sessions included training on conducting performance appraisals, eliminating rater bias, how to write position competencies and behaviors (for Phase II), and documenting performance issues. All supervisors also received 6 hours of basic supervisory skills training on documentation, coaching, time management, and delegation. Phase II involved directors, agency heads, and constitutional officers writing position competencies specific to each of their positions. They vary in number; the smaller the number, the larger the weight they carry, since position competencies represent one-half of the total score. Two positions classified the same

© Karen Edmonds

Karen A. Edmonds, SPHR, IPMA-CP

Director of Human Resources
Montgomery County, Virginia

but crossing departmental lines may have different position competencies based on the particulars in each department/agency.

As part of the original development of the program, plans were included for a career-development component. This has begun to take shape as small groups of employees in career families are planning career paths. These are reviewed for consistency across the board, both internally within departments and agencies and externally across departmental lines within the county. Since local governments do not always have the opportunity for employees to progress upward through the pay system, "lateral" paths are also being developed, whereby individuals may progress within the same pay range. This allows for professional development and growth throughout the county, thereby encouraging retention.

I have found that a dynamic performance management system is crucial to our workplace. It has to fit the culture of our organization and the expectations of our leadership. It is primarily a communications tool through which feedback and opportunity are intertwined. Without the benchmark of performance appraisal, the employee is left adrift, missing the benefit of knowing where he/she stands. Its absence can be a breeding ground for assumptions and often disappointment. I believe that the basics of a good performance appraisal system can be summarized as follows:

1. The fundamental tenets support the mission or goals of the organization;
2. It is consistently applied.
3. It is supported by the leaders of the organization.
4. It is manageable and simple to understand.
5. It provides information to both the employee and the employer.

Although the mechanics of the right system can seem difficult to figure out, in the end it's about people. The performance appraisal process is often viewed as time-consuming, but it is also time well spent. It is an investment in the employee and the organization. It yields the rewards that come with paying attention as we lead very hectic lives in the workplace. The process presents an opportunity to celebrate accomplishments, along with providing for planning and direction. It allows for open dialogue about the challenges and concerns that can be present in the employment relationship. Finally, I believe that it provides an assurance that the employee's successful performance is a priority to the organization. After all, it is in the best interest of both the employer and the employee for that to be so.

more common in peer ratings than in supervisor ratings of subordinates (Viswesvaran, Schmidt, & Ones, 2005).

Usually, halo error is statistically determined by correlating the ratings for each dimension with those for the other dimensions. If they are highly correlated, halo error is often said to have occurred. As one might expect, there are explanations other than halo error for the high correlation among rating dimensions. Some psychologists have argued that consistent ratings across several dimensions might indicate actual consistencies in employee performance across dimensions rather than rating error. Thus a teacher who is rated highly in classroom teaching, ability to work with students, knowledge, and fairness of grading actually may excel in those things. At this time, the best explanation for the consistency across rating dimensions is that some of the consistency is due to actual performance and some to halo and other rating errors (Viswesvaran et al., 2005).

Halo errors may or may not be a serious problem (Balzer & Sulsky, 1992), but they can be reduced by having supervisors rate each trait at separate times. That is, the supervisor might rate the employee on attendance one day and then on dependability the next. Of course, in reality, such a practice is seldom possible. Examples of halo, leniency, central tendency, and strictness errors are shown in Figure 7.13.

Proximity Errors

Proximity errors occur when a rating made on one dimension affects the rating made on the dimension that immediately follows it on the rating scale. For example, a

Figure 7.13
Examples of Rating Errors

supervisor gives an employee a rating of 5 on the first dimension. Because the second dimension is *physically located* on the rating form next to the first, there is a tendency to provide the same rating on both the first and second dimensions. The difference between this error and halo error is in the cause of the error and the number of dimensions affected. With halo error, all dimensions are affected by an overall impression of the employee. With proximity error, only the dimensions physically located nearest a particular dimension on the rating scale are affected; the reason for the effect, in fact, *is* the close physical proximity of the dimension rather than an overall impression.

Contrast Errors

The performance rating one person receives can be influenced by the performance of a previously evaluated person (Bravo & Kravitz, 1996). For example, a bank manager has six employees who are evaluated twice a year—on February 5 and again on August 5. The manager makes the evaluations in alphabetical order, starting with Joan Carr and then going to Donna Chan. Joan Carr is the best employee the bank has ever had, and she receives the highest possible rating on each dimension. After evaluating Carr, the manager then evaluates Chan. When compared with Carr, Chan is not nearly as effective an employee. Thus, Chan receives lower ratings than she might normally receive simply because she has been evaluated immediately after Carr. Her performance has been contrasted to Carr's performance rather than to some objective standard.

Such contrast errors can also occur between separate performance evaluations of the same person. That is, the ratings received on one performance appraisal will affect the ratings made on an appraisal six months later. For example, an employee's performance during the first six months of the year is "excellent," and she receives outstanding performance ratings. For some reason, the employee's actual behavior in the next six months is only "good." What type of performance ratings will she receive? Based on the results of a study by Murphy, Gannett, Herr, and Chen (1986), the answer probably is that her ratings will be less than "good." In contrast to her initial excellent performance, the employee's subsequent performance (which may indeed have been "good") appeared to be lower than it actually was. Contrast effects occur only when the person making the evaluation actually sees the employee perform (Smither, Reilly, & Buda, 1988) and rates the employee (Summer & Knight, 1996) during both rating periods.

If a new supervisor reads that an employee's previous evaluations were excellent but she observes poor performance by the employee, she will probably continue to give excellent ratings—even though the employee's performance deteriorated. Smither and his colleagues call this rating error **assimilation**. To get a better feel for rating errors, complete Exercise 7.6 in your workbook.

Low Reliability Across Raters

As shown back in Table 7.1, two people rating the same employee seldom agree with each other (Conway & Huffcut, 1997; Viswesvaran, Ones, & Schmidt, 1996). There are three major reasons for this lack of reliability. First, raters often commit the rating errors previously discussed (e.g., halo, leniency). Thus, if one rater engages in halo error and another in contrast error, it is not surprising that their ratings of the same employee are different.

Second, raters often have very different standards and ideas about the ideal employee. For example, I recently conducted a performance appraisal workshop for a

Assimilation A type of rating error in which raters base their rating of an employee during one rating period on the ratings the rater gave during a previous period.

police department. After viewing a video clip of an officer handling a disturbance call, one sergeant rated the officer's performance as excellent and another rated the officer's performance as being terrible. When asked about their different ratings, one sergeant indicated that he thought officers should be aggressive and take command of a situation, whereas the other sergeant thought officers should be more citizen oriented. Thus, the same employee behavior elicited two very different ratings because each sergeant had a different "prototype" of the ideal cop.

Third, two different raters may actually see very different behaviors by the same employee. For example, a desk sergeant may see more administrative and paperwork behaviors, whereas a field sergeant may see more law enforcement behaviors. Thus, different ratings by the two sergeants may simply reflect the fact that each has observed the officer perform in very different situations. As mentioned earlier, one way to reduce the number of rating errors and increase reliability is to train the people who will be making the performance evaluations.

Sampling Problems

Recency Effect.   Performance appraisals are typically conducted once or twice a year. The evaluation is designed to cover all of the behaviors that have taken place during the previous 6 months to a year. Research has demonstrated, however, that recent behaviors are given more weight in the performance evaluation than behaviors that occurred during the first few months of the evaluation period. Such an effect penalizes workers who performed well during most of the period but tailed off toward the end, and it rewards workers who saved their best work until just before the evaluation.

In baseball, the Los Angeles Dodgers had several years where they lost many games early in the season, which eliminated them from pennant contention. But several players played well and produced great statistics during the final month of the season; the press called this period the "salary drive," as opposed to the "pennant drive." This suggests that the players may have been aware of the recency effect. They hoped that high performance before contracts were renewed would bring better evaluations and thus higher salaries for the next year. It seems that students are well aware of the recency effect when they argue that the high score on their final exam should carry more weight than the lower scores on previous exams!

Infrequent observation
The idea that supervisors do not see most of an employee's behavior.

Infrequent Observation.   As shown back in Figure 7.2, another problem that affects performance appraisals is that many managers or supervisors do not have the opportunity to observe a representative sample of employee behavior. **Infrequent observation** occurs for two reasons. First, managers are often so busy with their own work that they have no time to "walk the floor" and observe their employees' behavior. Instead, they make inferences based on completed work or employee personality traits (Feldman, 1981). A good example involves a teacher who completes a reference form for a student. Reference forms commonly ask about characteristics such as the applicant's ability to cooperate or to get along with others. The teacher must base her evaluation on the term papers that she has seen and the student's test grades. Rarely does she have the opportunity to watch the student "get along with" or "cooperate with others." Instead, because a group project was turned in on time and received an excellent grade, she surmises that the student must have cooperated and gotten along well with other group members.

Employees often act differently around a supervisor than around other workers, which is the second reason managers usually do not make accurate observations. When the supervisor is absent, an employee may break rules, show up late, or work slowly. But when the boss is around, the employee becomes a model worker. In the eyes of the supervisor, the employee is doing an excellent job; the other workers, however, know better.

As discussed earlier in the chapter, this problem can be alleviated somewhat by having several raters evaluate the employee. Other raters can be other supervisors, fellow workers (peer ratings), and even customers. A meta-analysis by Conway and Huffcutt (1997) indicated that supervisor ratings on the average correlate .34 with peer ratings. Thus, even though the two groups somewhat agree, the agreement is certainly not perfect.

Unfortunately, ratings from these sources are often subject to more errors than the uninformed ratings made by a supervisor. For example, customers may complain about a worker even though she is following policy, and a worker may provide low evaluations of her coworkers so that she will receive a higher raise. Even with these problems, multiple raters remain a good idea.

Cognitive Processing of Observed Behavior

Observation of Behavior.   As shown in Figure 7.14, just because an employee's behavior is observed does not guarantee that it will be properly remembered or recalled during the performance appraisal review. In fact, research indicates that raters recall those behaviors that are consistent with their general impression of an employee (Cooper, 1981a; Feldman, 1981; Martell, Guzzo, & Willis, 1995), and the greater the time interval between the actual behavior and the performance rating, the greater the probability that rating errors will occur (Murphy, Martin, & Garcia, 1982; Nathan & Lord, 1983). Furthermore, raters who are familiar with the job being evaluated recall more judgments about performance but fewer behaviors than do raters who are unfamiliar with the job (Harriman & Kovach, 1987; Hauenstein, 1986). The decrease in memory accuracy over time can be reduced if several raters, rather than one, are used to evaluate performance (Martell & Borg, 1993).

But even though memory-based ratings lead to more distortion, in many circumstances they are more accurate than ratings made immediately after the behaviors occur (Murphy & Balzer, 1986). The reason for these increases in halo and accuracy is not yet clear. Supervisors perhaps realize that it will be a long interval between observation of employee behavior and the formal evaluation of that behavior and that they will not be able (without great effort or the use of logbooks) to remember specific behaviors. Thus, they form an overall impression of the employee and an overall impression of an ideal and a poor employee and evaluate the employee based on comparison with the ideal.

Stress Perceived psychological pressure.

Emotional State.   The amount of **stress** under which a supervisor operates also affects her performance ratings. Srinivas and Motowidlo (1987) found that raters who were placed in a stressful situation produced ratings with more errors than did raters who were not under stress. This finding is important because performance evaluations are often conducted hurriedly, as supervisors evaluate employee performance so they can return to their "real" work. Methods for reducing this problem will be discussed later in this chapter.

Bias.   Raters who like the employees being rated may be more lenient (Lefkowitz, 2000; Varma, DeNisi, & Peters, 1996) and less accurate in their ratings than would raters who neither like nor dislike their employees (Cardy & Dobbins, 1986). But this does not mean that a person who is liked will always receive higher ratings than

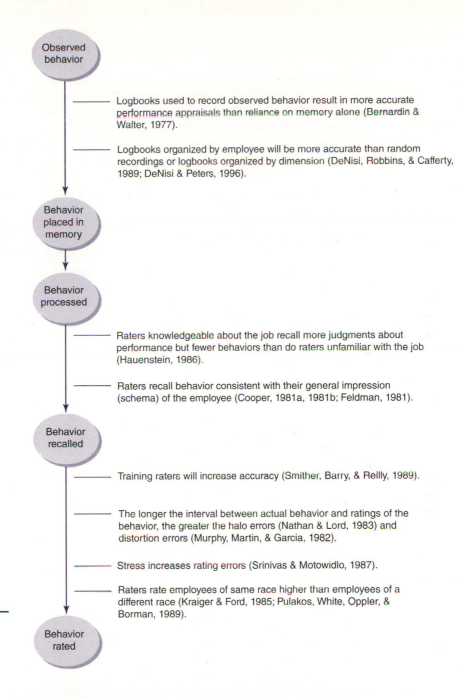

Observed
behavior

Logbooks used to record observed behavior result in more accurate performance appraisals than reliance on memory alone (Bernardin & Walter, 1977).

Logbooks organized by employee will be more accurate than random recordings or logbooks organized by dimension (DeNisi, Robbins, & Cafferty, 1989; DeNisi & Peters, 1996).

Behavior
placed in
memory

Behavior
processed

Raters knowledgeable about the job recall more judgments about performance but fewer behaviors than do raters unfamiliar with the job (Hauenstein, 1986).

Raters recall behavior consistent with their general impression (schema) of the employee (Cooper, 1981a, 1981b; Feldman, 1981).

Behavior
recalled

Training raters will increase accuracy (Smither, Barry, & Reilly, 1989).

The longer the interval between actual behavior and ratings of the behavior, the greater the halo errors (Nathan & Lord, 1983) and distortion errors (Murphy, Martin, & Garcia, 1982).

Stress increases rating errors (Srinivas & Motowidlo, 1987).

Raters rate employees of same race higher than employees of a different race (Kraiger & Ford, 1985; Pulakos, White, Oppler, & Borman, 1989).

Behavior
rated

Figure 7.14
Factors Affecting
Information Loss

Affect Feelings or emotion.

someone who is disliked. The rater may overcompensate in an effort to be "fair." The rater's feelings, or **affect**, toward an employee may interfere with the cognitive processing of actual performance information.

Research on the presence of racial bias in performance evaluations is both controversial and mixed. Two reviews of the literature (Landy, Shankster, & Kohler, 1994; Latham & Wexley, 1994) concluded that racial biases do not play a significant role in performance appraisals. A meta-analysis of 74 studies by Kraiger and Ford (1985) found a racial similarity bias in that White raters gave higher performance ratings to

White employees, and African American raters gave higher ratings to African American employees. Interestingly, this bias occurred only with studies involving real organizations—laboratory research seldom revealed racial bias in performance ratings. Complicating this issue is a study by Stauffer and Buckley (2005) arguing that much of the research in this area is flawed and that when the proper method (repeated measures) is used, evidence of racial bias in performance ratings exists.

A meta-analysis by Bowen, Swim, and Jacobs (2000) and a large data set of 360-degree feedback ratings by Church, Rogelberg, and Waclawski (2000) suggest that gender bias does not seem to be an issue in performance ratings. Meta-analysis results also indicate that age is not related to performance ratings (Ng & Feldman, 2008).

Step 8: Communicate Appraisal Results to Employees

As was stated in the beginning of this chapter, perhaps the most important use of performance-evaluation data is to provide feedback to the employee and assess her strengths and weaknesses so that further training can be implemented. Although this feedback and training should be an ongoing process, the semiannual evaluation might be the best time to formally discuss employee performance. Furthermore, holding a formal review interview places the organization on better legal ground in the event of a lawsuit (Foster et al., 2008; Malos, 1998).

Normally, in most organizations a supervisor spends a few minutes with employees every 6 months to *tell* them about the scores they received during the most recent evaluation period. This process is probably the norm because most managers do not like to judge others; because of this dislike, they try to complete the evaluation process as quickly as possible (Grensing-Pophal, 2001b).

Furthermore, seldom does evaluating employees benefit the supervisor. The best scenario is to hear no complaints, and the worst scenario is a lawsuit. In fact, one study demonstrated that dissatisfaction and a decrease in organizational commitment occurs even when an employee receives an evaluation that is "satisfactory" but not "outstanding" (Pearce & Porter, 1986). Finally, in the "tell and sell" approach to performance appraisal interviews, a supervisor "tells" an employee everything she has done poorly and then "sells" her on ways she can improve. This method, however, accomplishes little.

Research suggests that certain techniques can be used to make the performance appraisal interview more effective: time, scheduling, and preparation.

Prior to the Interview

Allocating Time

Both the supervisor and the employee must have time to prepare for the review interview. Both should be allowed at least an hour to prepare before an interview and at least an hour for the interview itself.

Scheduling the Interview

The interview location should be in a neutral place that ensures privacy and allows the supervisor and the employee to face one another without a desk between them as a communication barrier. Performance appraisal review interviews should be scheduled at least once every 6 months for most employees and more often for new employees. Review interviews are commonly scheduled 6 months after an employee begins working for the organization. If this date comes at a bad time (such as during the holidays, a busy time for retail stores), the interview should be scheduled for a more convenient time. It is important to note that although the *formal* performance appraisal review occurs only once or twice a year, informal "progress checks" should be held throughout the year to provide feedback.

Preparing for the Interview

While preparing for the interview, the supervisor should review the ratings she has assigned to the employee and the reasons for those ratings. This step is important because the quality of feedback given to employees will affect their satisfaction with the entire performance appraisal process (Mount, 1983). Furthermore, employees perceive and react to the amount of time that a supervisor uses to prepare for the interview.

Meanwhile, the employee should rate her own performance using the same format as the supervisor (Roberts, 2003). The employee also should write down specific reasons and examples that support the ratings she gives herself, as well as ideas for personal development.

During the Interview

Because employees and supervisors are often anxious about performance reviews, it is a good idea to begin the interview with some small talk until the jitters go away. Once the employee and supervisor are feeling as comfortable as they are going to get, the supervisor should communicate the following: (1) the role of performance appraisal—that making decisions about salary increases and terminations is not its only purpose; (2) how the performance appraisal was conducted; (3) how the evaluation process was accomplished; (4) the expectation that the appraisal interview will be interactive; and (5) the goal of understanding and improving performance.

The review process is probably best begun with the employee communicating her own ratings and her justification for them (Bacal, 2004). Research indicates that employees who are actively involved in the interview from the start will be more satisfied with the results (Gilliland & Langdon, 1998; Roberts, 2003).

The supervisor then communicates her ratings and the reasons for them. The supervisor should limit this communication to statements about behavior and performance rather than traits that are or are not possessed by the employee. Of course, it would be nice to avoid negative feedback because employees then are more satisfied with their reviews and don't develop negative attitudes toward management (Brett & Atwater, 2001). But few employees are perfect, and some negative feedback is inevitable. Because of this, positive feedback generally should be given first, followed by the negative feedback, and finishing with more positive feedback (Stone, Gueutal, & McIntosh, 1984). This process is often referred to as the "feedback sandwich," in which the negative feedback is sandwiched between positive feedback. Liberal use of positive feedback not only helps employees accept the negative feedback, but also helps supervisors who tend to avoid providing negative feedback in an effort to reduce the chance of interpersonal conflict (Waung & Highhouse, 1997). Any major differences between the employee's self-ratings and those given by the supervisor should be discussed until both understand the differences.

Though it would be nice if we were evaluated solely on how well we do our job, few would argue that performance ratings can be highly subjective and that part of our evaluation is a function of how well we are liked and respected by our supervisors. To help get a positive evaluation, you must ensure that your supervisor knows that you are valuable and are a team player. Alan Schoenberg (1998) provides the following advice on how to score points with your boss:

➡ Remember that "time is money." Don't waste time during work hours. Get to the point when you meet with your boss. When a job is done, move on to the next project.

➡ Dress professionally.

➡ Be prepared when you attend a meeting, arrive early, act interested, and always support your boss (you can always disagree later in private).

➡ Deliver more than you promise.

➡ Be positive. Praise others in public. Don't complain about your current employer and coworkers or about previous employers. Nobody likes a whiner!

➡ Put your customers first and make them rave about you!

➡ Ask questions and learn from your mistakes.

The next step is perhaps the most important. Because few employees receive perfect evaluations, it is essential to discuss the reasons an employee's performance is not considered to be perfect. The employee may lack some knowledge as to how to perform the job properly, may have been assigned too many duties, or may have outside problems that affect her work performance.

The supervisor's acknowledgement that there may be external reasons for an employee's poor performance can increase the employee's satisfaction with the review and enable her to perceive the feedback and evaluation as accurate and helpful. In addition, it will help the employee understand and appreciate the supervisor's perceptions (Bannister, 1986). Feedback should be candid, specific, and behavioral rather than personal. Awareness and acknowledgment of external factors for performance is especially important because we have a tendency, called the *fundamental attribution error*, to attribute others' failure or poor performance to personal rather than situational factors.

Once the problems have been identified, the next and most difficult task is to find solutions. What can the supervisor do to help? What can the organization do? What can the employee do? The idea here is that solutions to the problems result from joint effort. Too often we attribute poor performance solely to the fault of the employee, when, in fact, performance is affected by many factors including ability, motivation, company policy, supervisor ability, coworker attitudes, and the physical environment.

Because communicating appraisal results that will affect an employee's raise and providing feedback for improvement are very different processes and have different implications for an employee, a good practice is to separate the two into two different conversations. By communicating the appraisal results first, and then discussing strategies to improve performance at a later date, the employee can think about her performance ratings and be better able to discuss future options.

At the conclusion of the interview, goals should be mutually set for future performance and behavior, and both supervisor and employee should understand how these goals will be met. Goals and goal setting will be thoroughly discussed in Chapter 9. For now, however, we should keep in mind that goals should be concrete and reasonable and set by both employee and supervisor. The Career Workshop Box gives tips on how employees can help themselves in terms of performance appraisals.

To practice conducting a performance appraisal review interview, complete Exercise 7.7 in your workbook.

Step 9: Terminate Employees

As discussed in the preceding pages, the primary use of performance appraisal results is to provide feedback to employees about their behavior. Performance appraisal results are also used to make positive personnel decisions such as raises and promotions. Unfortunately, there are times when managers have to terminate an employee's employment. Over the next few pages, we will discuss the legal aspects of terminating an employee.

Employment-at-Will Doctrine

Employment-at-will doctrine The opinion of courts in most states that employers have the right to hire and fire an employee at will and without any specific cause.

In the United States, there is a big difference between terminating an employee in the public sector and terminating an employee in the private sector. In the private sector, the **employment-at-will doctrine** in most states allows employers freedom to fire an employee without a reason—at will. In the public sector, an employee can be fired only for cause.

The idea behind employment at will is that because employees are free to quit their jobs at will, so too are organizations free to terminate an employee at will (Delpo, 2009). Though employment-at-will is common in the United States, countries such as France enforce the restriction that no employee can be fired unless it is for cause.

There are some limitations to the employment-at-will doctrine (Falcone, 2002):

- *State law.* States such as California, Montana, and New York have laws that an employee can be fired only for cause—e.g., breaking a rule, demonstrating an inability to perform.
- *Provisions of federal or state law.* Employees cannot be fired for reasons protected by federal or state law. For example, an employer cannot fire an employee because she is female, pregnant, nonwhite, or over the age of 40.
- *Public policy/interest.* Employers cannot terminate an employee for exercising a legal duty such as jury duty or refusing to violate the law or professional ethics. For example, a large savings and loan institution ordered one of its appraisers to appraise homes higher than their actual values so that its customers could qualify to finance property. Citing federal regulations and professional ethics against inflating property values, the employee refused the company order. After being terminated, the employee successfully filed a lawsuit (one of more than 200 filed by employees against this institution) claiming that he had been fired for refusing to violate the law and the ethical standards of his profession.
- *Contracts.* Obviously, if an individual employee has a signed employment contract stipulating a particular period of employment, an organization cannot fire the employee without cause. Likewise, unions enter into collective bargaining agreements (contracts) with employers that also limit or negate employment-at-will.
- *Implied contracts.* Employment-at-will is nullified if an employer implies that an employee "has a job for life" or can be fired only for certain reasons.

For example, if an interviewer tells an applicant, "At this company, all you have to do is keep your nose clean to keep your job," the employer will not be able to terminate the employee for minor rules infractions or for poor performance.

- *Covenants of good faith and fair dealing.* Though employers are generally free to hire and fire at will, the courts have ruled that employers must still act in good faith and deal fairly with an employee. These rulings have been based on an item in the *Uniform Commercial Code* (UCC) stating, "Every contract ... imposes an obligation of good faith in its performance or enforcement," and the fact that courts consider employment decisions to be a form of a contract.

To protect their right to use a policy of employment-at-will, most organizations include **employment-at-will statements**, such as that shown in Figure 7.15, in their job applications and employee handbooks. These statements usually hold up in court.

Employment-at-will statements Statements in employment applications and company manuals reaffirming an organization's right to hire and fire at will.

Legal Reasons for Terminating Employees

In situations not covered by employment-at-will, there are only four reasons that an employee can be legally terminated: probationary period, violation of company rules, inability to perform, and an economically caused reduction in force (layoffs).

Probationary Period

In many jobs, employees are given a probationary period in which to prove that they can perform well. Though most probationary periods last 3 to 6 months, those for police officers are usually a year, and the probationary period for professors is 6 years! Employees can be terminated more easily during the probationary period than at any other time.

Violation of Company Rules

Courts consider five factors in determining the legality of a decision to terminate an employee for violating company rules. The first factor is that a rule against a particular behavior must actually exist. Though this may seem obvious, organizations often have "unwritten" rules governing employee behavior. These unwritten rules, however, will not hold up in court. For example, a manufacturer fired an employee for wearing a gun under his jacket at work. The employee successfully appealed on the grounds that even though "common sense" would say that guns should not be brought to work, the company did not have a written rule against it.

Figure 7.15
Sample Employment-at-Will Statement

I understand that, if employed, I have the right to end my employment with Sordi Industries. Likewise, I understand that my employment with Sordi industries is not for any definite period of time, and Sordi Industries has the right to terminate my employment with or without cause and with or without notice. I understand that no representative of Sordi Industries is authorized to imply any contract for permanent employment.

If a rule exists, a company must prove that the employee knew the rule. Rules can be communicated orally during employee orientation and staff meetings and in writing in handbooks, newsletters, bulletin boards, and paycheck stuffers. Rules communicated in handbooks are the most legally defensible. To prove that an employee knew a rule, organizations require employees to sign statements that they received information about the rule, read the rule, and understand the rule.

The third factor is the ability of the employer to prove that an employee actually violated the rule. Proof is accomplished through such means as witnesses, video recordings, and job samples. Human resources professionals almost have to be detectives because proving rule violations is often not easy. For example, two supervisors saw an employee stagger into work and could clearly smell alcohol on her breath. She was terminated for violating the company rule against drinking. During her appeal of the termination, she claimed that she staggered because she had the flu and what the supervisors smelled was cough syrup rather than alcohol. The employee won the appeal. As a result of this case, the company now has an on-site nurse, and breathalyzer tests are administered to employees suspected of using alcohol at work.

The fourth factor considered by the courts is the extent to which the rule has been equally enforced. That is, if other employees violated the rule but were not terminated, terminating an employee for a particular rule violation may not be legal (*Huske v. Honeywell International*, 2004; *Pineda v. United Parcel Service*, 2003). This factor poses a dilemma for many organizations. Because courts look at consistency, lawyers advise organizations to fire any employee who violates a rule. To not fire a rule breaker sets a precedent, making termination of future rule breakers more difficult. There are many times when a good employee breaks a rule, a situation that normally would result in termination. However, because the employee is highly valued, the organization does not want to fire the employee.

Such a situation occurred at a bank. In violation of a bank rule, a teller did not ask for the ID of a customer who cashed what turned out to be a forged check. The bank was torn as to what it should do. Because the employee was one of their best tellers, the bank did not want to fire her. However, not firing her in this case would increase the chance that they would lose a future lawsuit if they terminated another employee for doing the same thing. The bank's unusual decision was to terminate the employee, but it called a competitor, told it of the situation, and asked if it would hire her—which it did.

The fifth and final factor is the extent to which the punishment fits the crime. Employees in their probationary period (usually their first 6 months) can be immediately fired for a rule infraction. For more tenured employees, however, the organization must make a reasonable attempt to change the person's behavior through **progressive discipline**. The longer an employee has been with an organization, the greater the number of steps that must be taken to correct her behavior. Discipline can begin with something simple such as counseling or an oral warning, move on to a written warning or probation, and end with steps such as reduction in pay, demotion, or termination.

For violations of some rules, progressive discipline is not always necessary. It is probably safe to say that an employer can terminate an employee who steals money or shoots someone at work.

Inability to Perform

Employees can also be terminated for an inability to perform the job. To do so, though, an organization will need to prove that the employee could not perform the

Progressive discipline
Providing employees with punishments of increasing severity, as needed, in order to change behavior.

job and that progressive discipline was taken to give the employee an opportunity to improve. For an employer to survive a court challenge to terminating a poor-performing employee, it must first demonstrate that a reasonable standard of performance was communicated to the employee. The organization must next demonstrate that there was a documented failure to meet the standard. Such documentation can include critical-incident logs and work samples (e.g., poorly typed letters for a secretary, improperly hemmed pants for a tailor).

A properly designed performance appraisal system is the key to legally terminating an employee (Martin, Bartol, & Kehoe, 2000). Legal performance appraisal systems (Smith, 1993)

- are based on a job analysis,
- have concrete, relevant standards that have been communicated to employees,
- involve multiple behavioral measures of performance,
- include several raters, each of whom has received training,
- are standardized and formal, and
- provide the opportunity for an employee to appeal.

Reduction in Force (Layoff)

Employees can be terminated if it is in the best economic interests of an organization to do so. Reductions in force, more commonly called layoffs, have been used by the vast majority of Fortune 500 companies in the past few decades. In cases of large layoffs or plant closings, the Worker Adjustment and Retraining Notification Act (WARN) requires that organizations provide workers with at least 60 days' notice. Though layoffs are designed to save money, research indicates not only that force reductions have a devastating effect on employees (Leana & Feldman, 1992), but that they often do not result in the desired financial savings (Cascio, 2002). Layoffs are extensively discussed in Chapter 14.

The Termination Meeting

Prior to the Meeting

Once a decision has been made to terminate an employee, certain steps should be taken to prepare for the meeting in which the decision will be communicated to the employee. The first step is to ensure that the legal process has been followed. For example, if an organization is about to terminate an employee for a rule violation, it must be sure that a rule actually existed, that the employee knew the rule, that the organization has proof that the rule was violated, that progressive discipline was used, and that the rule was applied equally to all employees. An important responsibility for human resources professionals is to ensure that a termination decision is legally defensible.

The next step is to determine how much help, if any, the organization wants to offer the employee. Forms of help can include references, severance pay, and outplacement assistance. Usually, greater levels of help are given to employees who sign agreements not to sue the organization.

The final step is to schedule an appropriate place and time for the meeting to occur. The meeting should be held in a neutral, private location. To avoid potential damage caused by a hostile reaction to the termination decision, the meeting should not be held in a supervisor's office. Rather than late on Friday afternoon, as is traditional, the meeting should take place on a Monday or Tuesday so that the employee has an opportunity to seek advice and the organization has a chance to talk to its employees (Karl & Hancock, 1999; Papaj, 2004). When a termination is made on a Friday afternoon, the employee is unable to contact sources of help over the weekend. Likewise, the terminated employee has all weekend to get on the phone to tell her side of the story to other employees, while the organization must wait until Monday to refute the gossip.

During the Meeting

During the meeting, the supervisor should get to the point about terminating the employee. The employee usually knows why she has been called in, and there is no reason to prolong the agony. The supervisor should rationally state the reasons for the decision, express gratitude for the employee's efforts (if sincere), and offer whatever assistance the organization intends to provide. Administrative duties such as obtaining copies of keys and completing paperwork are then performed. Finally, the employee is asked to gather personal belongings and is escorted out the door.

I realize that this advice sounds cold. However, terminating an employee is a difficult task, and there is little that can be done to make it pleasant. If you have ever ended a romantic relationship, I think you will understand the feelings that go into terminating an employee. It is an emotional time, and the key is to be brief and professional.

After the Meeting

Once the meeting is over, the natural reaction of the supervisor is to feel guilty. To relieve some of this guilt, a supervisor should review the facts—she gave the employee every chance to improve, but the employee chose not to. A human resources professional for Valleydale Foods tells employees this: "Through your behavior, you fired yourself. I'm just completing the paperwork."

When an employee is fired, other employees will be tense. Consequently, it is important to be honest with the other employees about what happened; at the same time, negative statements about the terminated employee's character must be avoided.

Step 10: Monitor the Legality and Fairness of the Appraisal System

Performance appraisal systems are subject to the same legal standards as are employment tests and other employment decisions. As such, performance ratings should be analyzed each rating period to determine if there are gender, race/ethnicity, or age differences. If there are such differences, the organization should determine whether the differences are justified by factors such as experience or if the differences are due to discrimination. Likewise, the personnel decisions that are based on the performance appraisal ratings should be analyzed to ensure discrimination does not occur in the raises, bonuses, promotions, and terminations that result from the performance ratings. Questions that should be asked by the organization during this monitoring process include the following:

- Has the organization provided training to supervisors regarding how to evaluate performance, communicate appraisal results, mentor underperforming employees, and make decisions on the basis of the appraisal results?
- Are there gender, race, ethnicity, disability, or age differences in performance ratings? If so, are the differences supported by actual differences in performance?
- Do employees with similar performance ratings receive similar outcomes such as raises, promotions, discipline, training, or promotion (*Russell v. Principi*, 2001)?
- Are there gender, race, ethnicity, disability, or age differences in the opportunities given to improve performance (*Johnson v. Kroger*, 2003; *Mayer v. Nextel*, 2003)? That is, if a low-rated Asian employee is provided opportunities for improvement, is a similarly situated Hispanic employee given the same opportunities?
- Are there employees who historically have received high ratings suddenly being given a low rating (*Shackelford v. Deloitte & Touche*, 1999)? If so, is the drop in ratings due to an actual performance decrease or to potential discrimination?

ON THE JOB Applied Case Study

Firing an Employee at Kohl's Department Store

Three employees were fired from the Kohl's Department Store in Mechanicsville, Virginia, for violating the store policy about using coupons. The store sent each employee 11 15%-off coupons as part of a "friends and family" sale: 1 coupon was for the employee and the other 10 were to be given to family and friends. There were a lot of extra coupons, so on a Saturday, 18-year-old Rikki Groves, Rebecca Hagen, and Katie Kombacher gave the coupons to customers who did not have one. They assumed that these coupons were similar to other sale coupons used by the store and that the cashier could scan an already used coupon for a customer who did not have a coupon. According to Groves, who had been with Kohl's for 3 months, none of the managers told employees that these coupons were different from those processed every day. A few days after the incident, the person in charge of store security called Groves into a closed-door meeting a few hours before the end of her shift. He began to interrogate Groves, telling her that he had observed her using the coupons through the store camera and that she would have to pay the store $1,000 to cover the coupons she

gave to customers or the store would call the police and have her arrested for embezzlement. The head of store security then began taking pictures of her and required her to sign a document that barred her from returning to the store for the next year. Groves started making payments toward the $1,000 when the story was published in a local newspaper. After outraged citizens complained and threatened to cut up their Kohl's credit cards and stop patronizing the store, the store returned Groves's money and said she would not have to pay it back. The three women were not offered their jobs back nor were they given an apology. A spokesperson for the local police department indicated that the threat of arrest used by Kohl's was incorrect because what Groves did was not a crime, but a matter of internal policy.

- How could the store have better handled the termination? Should the three employees have been fired?
- What could Kohl's have done to have prevented the situation in the first place?
- What could the employees have done differently?

The Ethics of the At-Will Doctrine

As mentioned in this chapter, the employment-at-will doctrine has been around for a very long time. It is based on English Common law of the eighteenth century, which said that the length of employment was presumed to be for one year when there is work to be done and when there is not. A New York State treatise writer, Horace Gay Wood, in his book *Master and Servant* (1877), expanded on the doctrine, stating that a hiring with no definite ending date is a hiring at will. That is, unless both master and servant agree that service was to extend for a specified time, it should be considered an indefinite hiring, and it us up to the servant, should he be terminated, to prove otherwise. From what was then called "Wood's Rule" came the U.S. interpretation of employment law: an employer is free to discharge individuals at any time for cause or for no cause at all, and the employee is equally free to quit at any time for any reason.

Many debates have arisen over the years as to the fairness or ethics of such a doctrine. Critics have long feared that it gives too much power to businesses over the lives of their employees. To have such a rule that allows a company to fire even good employees whenever and for whatever reason is unfair and unethical. The doctrine provides little protection to employees who work hard and who work well. And there is little job security in an at-will company. Theoretically, employees can be fired just because a supervisor may not like them or because of how they dress or look. An excuse often given to employees who are terminated under "at-will" is, "You just aren't the right fit for this company." Then there was a case where an armored truck driver was fired for leaving his post even though he only did so to save someone's life (*Gardner v. Loomis Armored, Inc.*, April 4, 1996).

Opponents say that from a business perspective, the doctrine provides little incentive for people to work hard, because, if employees can be terminated no matter how hard they work, what's the benefit of putting in the extra effort? Motivation can even suffer if employees are working under "fear" of their jobs. Finally, because at-will employees are treated differently than "for just cause" employees, critics state that it is unfair and unequal treatment under the law, which violates the Fourteenth Amendment. Also, motivation can suffer when employees fear that they can be terminated at any time.

Supporters state that the doctrine provides equal fairness to both the employer and employee when it comes to termination of employment. They say it is only fair that if an employee can terminate employment at any time, then the employer should have that same right. They cite the limitations to the doctrine, outlined in this chapter, provide further protection to employees. Supporters further state that the doctrine is not totally free from lawsuits, as evidenced by the lawsuit filed and won by the defendant in the above *Gardner* case. Additionally, applicants don't have to work for or sign an employment at-will statement at an at-will company if they think the doctrine is unfair. They have the right to seek employment elsewhere.

What Do You Think?

- What are other ethical dilemmas in the at-will doctrine?

- Which argument do you agree with: that of critics of the doctrine or supporters?

- Are there other limitations that should be imposed on the doctrine, other than those outlined in your textbook, that would make the doctrine more ethical, and therefore, fairer?

- Do you agree that having different laws for public and private sector employees (at will versus for just cause) is fair?

Chapter Summary

In this chapter you learned:

- There are ten steps in creating a performance appraisal system: (1) determine the reasons for performance evaluation, (2) identify environmental and cultural limitations that might affect the success of an appraisal system, (3) determine who will evaluate performance, (4) create an instrument to evaluate performance, (5) explain the system to those who will use it, (6) observe and document performance,

(7) evaluate employee performance, (8) review the results of the evaluation with the employee, (9) make personnel decisions such as giving raises or terminating employees, and (10) monitor the system for fairness and legal compliance.

■ Common rating errors such as leniency, central tendency, strictness, halo, proximity, contrast, recency, and infrequent observation of behavior hinder the accuracy of performance appraisal results.

■ Important factors in the success of the performance appraisal review include scheduling the review to eliminate or minimize interruptions, letting the employee discuss her feelings and thoughts, and mutually setting goals for improvements in future performance.

■ In organizations not subject to employment-at-will, employees can be terminated only for violating a company rule or inability to perform or as part of a force reduction.

Questions for Review

1. What do you think is the most important purpose for performance appraisal? Why?
2. What problems might result from using a 360-degree feedback system?
3. The chapter mentioned a variety of ways to measure performance. Which one do you think is the best? Why?
4. What do you think is the best way to communicate performance appraisal results to employees?
5. Is the employment-at-will doctrine a good idea? Why or why not?

Media Resources and Learning Tools

■ Visit our website. Go to www.cengage.com/psychology/aamodt, where you will find online resources directly linked to your book, including chapter-by-chapter quizzing, flashcards, crossword puzzles, application activities, and more.

■ Want more practice applying industrial/organizational psychology? Check out the *I/O Applications Workbook*. This workbook (keyed to your textbook) offers engaging, high-interest activities to help you reinforce the important concepts presented in the text.

Additional Types
of Rating Scales

Behaviorally Anchored Rating Scales

To reduce the rating problems associated with graphic rating scales, Smith and Kendall (1963) developed behaviorally anchored rating scales (BARS). As shown in Figure 7.9, BARS use critical incidents (samples of behavior) to formally provide meaning to the numbers on a rating scale. Although BARS are time-consuming to construct, the process is not overly complicated.

Creating BARS

Generation of Job Dimensions

In the first step in BARS construction, the number and nature of job-related dimensions are determined. If a job analysis has already been conducted, the dimensions can be obtained from the job analysis report. If for some reason a job analysis has not been conducted, a panel of some 20 job experts—the employees—is formed. This panel determines the important dimensions on which an employee's performance should be evaluated. If 15 to 20 employees are not available, several supervisors can meet and develop the job dimensions as a group (Shapira & Shirom, 1980). Usually, 5 to 10 dimensions are generated (Schwab et al., 1975).

Generation of Critical Incidents

Once the relevant job dimensions have been identified, employees are asked to generate examples of good, average, and bad behavior that they have seen for each dimension. Thus, if five dimensions have been identified, each employee is asked to generate 15 critical incidents—a good, an average, and a bad incident for each of the five dimensions. If the organization is fairly small, employees may need to generate more than one example of the three types of behavior for each dimension.

Sorting Incidents

To make sure that the incidents written for each job dimension are actually examples of behavior for that dimension, three job experts independently sort the incidents into each of the job dimensions. The dimension into which each incident has been sorted by each of the three sorters then is examined. If at least two sorters placed an incident in the same dimension, the incident becomes part of that dimension. But if each sorter has placed the incident in a different category, the incident is considered to be ambiguous and thus is discarded.

Three sorters achieve results similar to those for 100 sorters (Chapter 2). Many developers of BARS, however, use as many sorters as possible so that employees have a part in developing the scales. If many employees are involved, a 60% level of sorter agreement should be used to determine whether an incident is part of a dimension.

Rating Incidents

Another group of job experts is given the incidents and asked to rate each one on a scale that can have from five to nine points as to the level of job performance that it represents (Bernardin, LaShells, Smith, & Alveres, 1976). The ratings from each rater for all of the incidents are then used to determine the mean rating and standard deviation for each incident (typically by computer).

Choosing Incidents

The goal of this step is to find one incident to represent each of the points on the scale for each dimension. To do so, the incidents whose mean ratings come closest to each of the scale points and whose standard deviations are small are kept (Maiorca, 1997). This procedure usually results in the retention of less than 50% of the incidents (Green, Sauser, Fagg, & Champion, 1981).

Creating the Scale

The incidents chosen in the previous step are then placed on a vertical scale such as that shown in Figure 7.9. Because the mean for each incident is unlikely to fall exactly on one of the scale points, they are often placed between the points, thus serving as anchors for future raters.

Using BARS

To use the scale when actually rating performance, the supervisor compares the incidents she has recorded for each employee with the incidents on each scale. This can be done in one of two ways. The most accurate (and the most time-consuming) method compares each of the recorded incidents with the anchors and records the value of the incident on the scale that most closely resembles the recorded incident. This is done for each recorded incident. The value for each incident is summed and divided by the total number of incidents recorded for that dimension; this yields an average incident value, which is the employee's rating for that particular job dimension.

In the second method (easier, but probably less accurate) all of the recorded incidents are read to obtain a general impression of each employee. This general impression is compared with the incidents that anchor each scale point. The scale point next to the incident that most closely resembles the general impression gained from the incidents then becomes an employee's score for that dimension.

The third way to use BARS (and the least recommended) is to use the incidents contained in the BARS to arrive at a rating of the employee without recording actual incidents. Instead, the BARS are only used to provide meaning to the 5 scale points.

Forced-Choice Rating Scales

One problem with BARS is that supervisors often do not use the anchors when rating employees. Instead, they choose a point on the scale and then quickly glance to see which anchor is associated with the number. Because of this tendency, BARS do not often reduce leniency in ratings.

To overcome this problem, *forced-choice rating scales* have been developed. These scales use critical incidents and relevant job behaviors, as do BARS, but the scale points are hidden. An example of a forced-choice scale is shown in Figure 7.10.

In using the forced-choice scale to evaluate employee performance, the supervisor chooses the behavior in each item that appears most typical of that performed by a given employee. The supervisor's choices then are scored by a member of the personnel department to yield the employee's rating on each dimension. The scores on each of the dimensions can be summed to form an overall rating.

The development of a forced-choice rating scale is a long and complicated process, which partly explains why it is not commonly used. However, this method of evaluation does have its advantages. For example, because the supervisor must choose behaviors without knowing "the key," common rating errors such as leniency and halo are less likely. Consequently, performance evaluations should be more accurate.

Creating a Forced-Choice Scale

To create a forced-choice scale, the first step is similar to that for BARS: Critical incidents and relevant job behaviors are generated. These incidents, of course, are available only when a job analysis has been conducted.

In the second step, employees rate all of the behaviors on the extent to which excellent employees perform them. After an approximately one-month interval, the employees again rate the items. This time, however, they rate the extent to which bad employees perform the behaviors. Finally, after another month, the employees again rate the behaviors, this time for their desirability.

In the third step, the actual items for the rating scale are created. This is done by computing a value for each behavior by subtracting the average rating given to each behavior that describes the bad employee from the average rating given to each behavior that describes the good employee. Behaviors with high positive values are considered to discriminate good from bad employees, items with high negative values are considered to discriminate bad from good employees, and behaviors with values near zero are considered neutral.

The next step in creating the items is to pick good, bad, and neutral behaviors that have similar desirability ratings. Thus, each rating item has three behaviors: One indicates good performance, one indicates poor performance, and one indicates neither good nor bad performance. Furthermore, all of the behaviors for an item have the same level of desirability. This process is repeated until several items have been constructed for each of the relevant job dimensions.

The disadvantages of the forced-choice scale probably outweigh its advantages. First, evaluations on forced-choice scales can be "faked." A supervisor who wants to give an employee a high rating need only think about a good employee when evaluating the employee in question. Second, supervisors often object to forced-choice scales because the scoring key is kept secret. Not only does this secrecy deprive a supervisor of any control over the rating process, but it can be seen by supervisors as a lack of trust in their abilities to evaluate their employees. Most important, however, because the key must be kept secret, forced-choice scales make feedback almost impossible. Thus they should be used only when the major goal of the performance appraisal system is accurate employee evaluation for purposes such as promotion and salary increases.

Mixed-Standard Scales

To overcome some of the problems of forced-choice scales, Blanz and Ghiselli (1972) developed mixed-standard scales, an example of which is shown in Figure 7.11.

Table 7.7 Original Scoring System for Mixed-Standard Scales

	Statement Type		
Good	**Average**	**Poor**	**Dimension Score**
+	+	+	7
0	+	+	6
−	+	+	5
−	0	+	4
−	−	+	3
−	−	0	2
−	−	−	1

Mixed-standard scales are developed by having employees rate job behaviors and critical incidents on the extent to which they represent various levels of job performance. For each job dimension, a behavior or incident is chosen that represents excellent performance, average performance, and poor performance. These behaviors then are shuffled, and the end results look similar to those shown in Figure 7.11.

To evaluate an employee, a supervisor reads each behavior and places a plus (+) next to it when a particular employee's behavior is usually better than the behavior listed, a zero (0) if the employee's behavior is about the same as the behavior listed, or a minus (−) if the employee's behavior is usually worse than the behavior listed. To arrive at a score for each scale, the supervisor uses a chart like the one shown in Table 7.7. An overall score can be obtained by summing the scores from each of the scales.

Although mixed-standard scales are less complicated than forced-choice scales, they also have their drawbacks. The most important is that supervisors often make what are called "logical rating errors." For example, it would make no sense for a supervisor to rate an employee as better than the example of excellent performance or worse than the example of poor performance. Yet these types of errors are common. Logical rating errors can still be scored by using the revised scoring method developed by Saal (1979) (Table 7.8), but their existence alone casts doubt on the accuracy of the entire performance appraisal.

Behavioral Observation Scales

Behavioral observation scales (BOS), developed by Latham and Wexley (1977), are a more sophisticated method for measuring the frequency of desired behaviors. Even though BOS have no psychometric advantages over BARS (Bernardin & Kane, 1980), they are simpler to construct and easier to use (Latham, Fay, & Saari, 1979). BOS also provide high levels of feedback and are better than simple rating scales at motivating employees to change their behavior (Tziner, Kopelman, & Livnech, 1993).

The development of a BOS is relatively straightforward. The first few steps are the same as with a BARS: Critical incidents and behaviors are obtained from employees, the incidents are placed into categories, and each incident is rated as to the level of job performance it represents.

Table 7.8   Revised Scoring System for Mixed-Standard Scales

	Statement Type		
Good	**Average**	**Poor**	**Dimension Score**
+	+	+	7
0	+	+	6
+	+	0	6
+	0	+	6
−	+	+	5
+	+	−	5
+	0	0	5
+	−	+	5
0	+	0	5
−	+	+	5
−	0	+	4
+	0	−	4
+	−	0	4
0	+	−	4
0	0	0	4
0	−	+	4
−	+	0	4
−	−	+	4
+	−	−	3
0	0	−	3
0	−	0	3
−	+	−	3
−	−	+	3
−	0	0	3
−	−	0	2
0	−	−	2
−	0	−	2
−	−	−	1

Source: Adapted from Saal (1979).

As shown in Table 7.9, the behaviors are then listed. Supervisors read each behavior on the list and use the following scale to find the frequency for an employee performing that specific behavior:

1 = Employee engaged in behavior less than 65% of the time
2 = Employee engaged in behavior 65–74% of the time
3 = Employee engaged in behavior 75–84% of the time
4 = Employee engaged in behavior 85–94% of the time
5 = Employee engaged in behavior 95–100% of the time

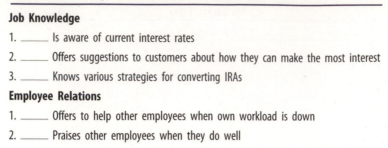

Table 7.9 Example of a Behavioral Observation Scale

Job Knowledge

1. _____ Is aware of current interest rates
2. _____ Offers suggestions to customers about how they can make the most interest
3. _____ Knows various strategies for converting IRAs

Employee Relations

1. _____ Offers to help other employees when own workload is down
2. _____ Praises other employees when they do well

After each employee has been rated on each behavior, the scores from each item in each dimension are summed to give the dimension score. Dimension scores are then summed to yield an overall score. The greatest advantage to BOS is that a supervisor can show employees the *specific behaviors* that they currently do correctly and the specific behaviors that they should do to receive higher performance evaluations.

Because supervisors conduct evaluations only once every 6 months, BOS have been criticized for actually measuring only the *recall* of behaviors rather than measuring the actual *observation* of behaviors (Murphy et al., 1982). The importance of this distinction between recall and actual observation comes from research that has demonstrated that after some period of time, we cannot recall specific behaviors; instead, we "recall" behaviors that are consistent with sets of traits or prototypes we attribute to employees (Feldman, 1981). That is, we assign certain traits or prototypes to employees; 6 months later, we recall behaviors that are consistent with those traits or prototypes. Furthermore, the closer an employee's behavior is to the prototype, the more accurate the performance evaluations (Mount & Thompson, 1987). Thus, as objective and behavioral as BOS appear, they may not be as accurate as initially believed because of cognitive processing distortions.

© Chris Ryan/OJO Images/Getty Images

Learning Objectives

➡ Know how to conduct a training needs analysis

➡ Be aware of the various training methods

➡ Know how to conduct a training program

➡ Understand the psychological theory behind successful training

➡ Be able to evaluate the effectiveness of a training program

E mployee performance can be improved in many ways. In Chapters 4 and 5, you learned that one way to have high employee performance is to select employees with the necessary knowledge and skills. Another way to improve employee performance is to train employees who have the *ability* to perform the job, but might not have the *knowledge, skills*, or *motivation* to perform the job.

Training A planned effort by an organization to facilitate the learning of job-related behavior on the part of its employees.

Training is the "systematic acquisition of skills, rules, concepts, or attitudes that result in improved performance" (Goldstein & Ford, 2002).

Training is essential for an organization because it ensures that employees have the knowledge and skills necessary to perform the job. In some cases, a lack of skill or knowledge is due to an organization having difficulty hiring applicants with the necessary knowledge and skills to perform a job. Thus, training compensates for the inability to select desired applicants. For example, ATK—one of the few manufacturers of missile propellant—finds it almost impossible to find engineers with knowledge and experience in its niche field, so it hires outstanding engineers and then trains them in its specialty area. In other cases, an employee might have the necessary skills and knowledge when hired, but jobs, technology, and laws change. Thus, employees might have the necessary knowledge and skills one year, but have deficiencies by the next.

In proactive organizations, training is used to teach knowledge and skills that, while not currently needed, will be needed in the future. For example, AT&T conducted an analysis of one of its jobs and determined that the field was changing so much that few of its employees had the skill that would be needed to perform the job five years in the future. As a result, it provided training programs for employees to prepare them for the upcoming technology changes.

Collectively, organizations realize the importance of training by spending more than $125 billion on it each year (ASTD, 2010). Major organizations spend an average of 2.14% of their payroll on training—$1,081 per employee (ASTD, 2010). In some organizations, including the Palace Hotel in Inverness, Scotland, training is viewed as so valuable that employee training is mentioned in the hotel's mission statement.

Though most organizations value and provide organization-sponsored training, Netflix is an example of an organization that does not. It believes that employees should be responsible for their own training and professional development and thus leaves it to the employees to develop themselves (Grossman, 2010). One of the reasons Netflix can do this is that rather than hiring new college graduates, it tends to hire experienced employees who have already demonstrated their high-level skills and self-motivation.

Determining Training Needs

Needs analysis The process of determining the training needs of an organization.

Conducting a **needs analysis** is the first step in developing an employee training system (Noe, 2010). The purpose of needs analysis is to determine the types of training, if any, that are needed in an organization, as well as the extent to which training is a practical means of achieving an organization's goals. The importance of needs assessment was demonstrated by a meta-analysis indicating increased training effectiveness when a needs assessment had been done prior to the creation of the training program (Arthur, Bennett, Edens, & Bell, 2003). As shown in Figure 8.1, three types of needs analysis are typically conducted: organizational analysis, task analysis, and person analysis (Goldstein & Ford, 2002).

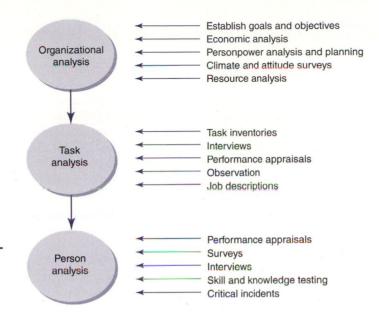

Figure 8.1
The Training Needs Assessment Process

Organizational analysis
- Establish goals and objectives
- Economic analysis
- Personpower analysis and planning
- Climate and attitude surveys
- Resource analysis

Task analysis
- Task inventories
- Interviews
- Performance appraisals
- Observation
- Job descriptions

Person analysis
- Performance appraisals
- Surveys
- Interviews
- Skill and knowledge testing
- Critical incidents

Organizational Analysis

Organizational analysis
The process of determining the organizational factors that will either facilitate or inhibit training effectiveness.

The purpose of **organizational analysis** is to determine those organizational factors that either facilitate or inhibit training effectiveness. For example, an organization may view training as important but may not have the money to fund its training program, may be unable to afford the employee time away from work to be trained, or may not wish to spend money on training because employees leave the organization after a short period of time. A properly conducted organizational analysis will focus on the goals the organization wants to achieve, the extent to which training will help achieve those goals, the organization's ability to conduct training (e.g., finances, physical space, time), and the extent to which employees are willing and able to be trained (e.g., ability, commitment, motivation, stress) (McCabe, 2001).

A good example of the importance of organizational analysis comes from the AT&T business center previously mentioned. Employees at the center needed training due to the addition of new technology and a renewed company interest in customer service. However, because of recent layoffs and an increase in business, managers refused to let employees receive training "on the clock." As a result, an expensive series of newly developed training programs sat on the shelf.

An organizational analysis should include a survey of employee readiness for training. For example, a large organization recently had several rounds of layoffs and had not given its employees salary increases in three years. When the organization introduced a new training program, it was surprised to find that the employees were so angry at the company that they were "not in the mood for training." As you can imagine, the training program was a bust! Thus training will be effective only if the organization is willing to provide a supportive climate for training, it can afford an effective program, employees want to learn, and the goals of a program are consistent with those of the organization (Broadwell, 1993).

Task Analysis

If the results of the organizational analysis indicate that a positive organizational climate for training exists, the next step is to conduct a task analysis. The purpose of a task analysis is to use the job analysis methods discussed in Chapter 2 to identify the tasks performed by each employee, the conditions under which these tasks are performed, and the competencies (knowledge, skills, abilities) needed to perform the tasks under the identified conditions. The most common job analysis methods used for this purpose include interviews, observations, and task inventories. If an organization has detailed and current job descriptions already written, the task analysis process is fairly easy and does not take much time. If such job descriptions are not available, the task analysis process can be expensive and time-consuming.

Once the tasks and competencies for a job have been identified, the next step is to determine how employees learn to perform each task or obtain each competency. For example, due to a rigorous employee selection process, we might expect employees to be able to perform many of the tasks at the time they are hired. Some tasks might be so simple that they can be performed without the need of previous experience or future training. For other tasks, we might have formal training programs to teach employees the necessary competencies needed to perform them.

As shown in Figure 8.2, the task analysis process is usually conducted by listing tasks in one column and how the tasks are learned in a second column. As you can see, the hypothetical bank needs to develop training courses in dealing with difficult customers and in cross-selling, because these are competencies not tapped during the selection process nor learned in current bank training programs.

As another example, let's examine the job of a secretary. Obviously, tasks involving typing will be found throughout the job description. If we take just one of these tasks—typing internal memos—we can see that certain knowledge and skills are involved: typing skills, knowledge of the company's word-processing package, knowledge of the computer used to do the word processing, and knowledge of the memo format used by the organization.

In all probability, the company will require that a newly hired secretary already possess typing skills; thus learning how to type will not be a training need. Knowledge of the word-processing program may or may not be required at the time of hire. If not required, then learning the program will involve extensive training, whereas learning how to use a computer also becomes a training need (this training, however, should take only a short time). Finally, learning the memo format used by the organization is another training need, but one with relatively little time required. With these needs in mind, the supervisor or the training officer must arrange for the new employee to receive needed training. To practice conducting a task analysis, complete Exercise 8.1 in your workbook.

Figure 8.2

Comparing Task Analysis Results with Training Programs

Task	How Task Is Learned
Answer customer questions about rates	Daily rate charts
Process customer transactions	Basic teller training
Calm irate customers	
Check loan applications for accuracy	Loan-processing course
Ask customers to complete Visa applications	
Input customer transactions into computer	Basic teller training
Answer customer questions about services	Basic teller training

Person Analysis

The third and final step in the needs analysis process is determining which employees need training and in which areas. **Person analysis** is based on the recognition that not every employee needs further training for every task performed. For example, trainers at Applebee's restaurants test management trainees on essential on-the-job tasks. When the trainees demonstrate proficiency, the training ends. Thus, some trainees complete the management training program in half the time it takes others. A person analysis should also include an evaluation of an employee's readiness for the training. That is, does the employee have the ability and motivation to successfully complete the training?

To determine the individual training needs for each employee, person analysis uses performance appraisal scores, surveys, interviews, skill and knowledge tests, and/or critical incidents.

Performance Appraisal Scores

Perhaps the easiest method of needs analysis is to use employees' **performance appraisal scores**. Low ratings on a particular dimension for most employees may indicate that additional training in that dimension is needed. Conversely, if most employees score high on a particular dimension, relatively little training time is needed. For example, as can be seen in Table 8.1, the bank employees as a whole need little training in loan processing or data entry, but they do need further training in cross-selling, customer relations, and keeping accurate teller drawers. But even though most employees can accurately process loans, Fernandez needs further training in this area; both Abbott and Harrigan probably can skip the training in teller drawer accuracy.

Although using performance appraisal scores appears fairly easy as a method of needs assessment, three problems can interfere with their use. First, as discussed in the previous chapter, several types of rating errors can reduce the accuracy of performance appraisal scores. The most relevant here are leniency errors and strictness errors. If the performance appraisal scores are consistently high because of leniency error, a human resources professional might incorrectly conclude that employees are proficient in a particular area and thus need no training. Likewise, consistently low scores might be interpreted as a need for training when, in fact, the actual cause of the low scores is rater error.

The second problem is that rarely are there situations in which all employees score either high or low on a dimension. Instead, it is more common for only a few employees to score poorly. In this case, a person examining the average performance

Table 8.1 Using Performance Appraisal Scores for Training Needs Assessment

	Employee					
Performance Dimension	**Abbott**	**Finch**	**Osterman**	**Fernandez**	**Harrigan**	**Average**
Cross-selling	2	1	2	5	1	2.2
Loan processing	5	5	5	1	4	4.0
Data input accuracy	5	5	5	5	5	5.0
Customer relations	2	2	2	2	2	2.0
Teller drawer accuracy	5	3	1	2	5	3.2
Average	3.8	3.2	3.8	3.0	3.4	

appraisal scores might conclude that training in a particular dimension is unnecessary. But that conclusion would be only partially correct. True, not everyone needs training in that dimension, but concluding that training should not be conducted would be incorrect. The correct interpretation is that training should be conducted for the few employees who scored low for that dimension.

Third, the current performance appraisal system may not provide the type of information needed to conduct a training needs analysis. As discussed in Chapter 7, performance appraisal systems must be specific to be useful. To practice using performance appraisal scores to conduct a person analysis, complete Exercise 8.2 in your workbook.

Surveys

Surveys Questionnaires asking employees about the areas in which they feel they need training.

Another common approach to determine training needs is to design and administer a survey that asks employees what knowledge and skills they believe should be included in future training. **Surveys** offer several advantages. First, they eliminate the problems of performance rating errors, which were discussed previously. Second, employees often know their own strengths and weaknesses best. Thus, to determine what employees need, ask them. Finally, training needs can be determined with surveys even when the organization has not previously made an effort to design an effective performance appraisal system or adequate job descriptions. The main disadvantages of surveys are that employees may not be honest and the organization may not be able to afford the training suggested by the employees.

As with any type of survey, training needs surveys can be conducted in many ways. The most common method is a questionnaire that asks employees to list the areas in which they would like further or future training. Perhaps a better method is to provide a *list* of job-related tasks and components of knowledge and have employees rate the need for training on each. The results of these ratings are given to supervisors, who then "validate" the results. This process is used to determine whether the supervisors agree with their employees' perceptions and to prioritize training needs.

Interviews

The third method of needs analysis is the interview, which is usually done with a selected number of employees. Interviews are not used as extensively as surveys, but they can yield even more in-depth answers to questions about training needs (Patton & Pratt, 2002). The main advantage of interviews is that employee feelings and attitudes are revealed more clearly than with the survey approach. The main disadvantage of interviews is that interview data are often difficult to quantify and analyze (Brown, 2002).

Skill and Knowledge Tests

Skill test A test that measures an employee's level of some job-related skill.

Knowledge test A test that measures the level of an employee's knowledge about a job-related topic.

The fourth way to determine training needs is with a **skill test** or a **knowledge test.** Some examples of areas that could be tested to determine training needs include knowledge of lending laws for loan officers, knowledge of company policy for new employees, free-throw shooting for basketball players, and the dreaded midterm exam for this course.

If all employees score poorly on these tests, training across the organization is indicated. If only a few employees score poorly, they are singled out for individual training. The greatest problem with using testing as a method to determine training needs is that relatively few tests are available for this purpose. An organization that wants to use this method will probably have to construct its own tests, and proper test construction is time-consuming and expensive.

Critical Incidents

The fifth method for determining training needs is the critical-incident technique discussed in Chapters 2, 4, and 7. Although not a commonly used method, it will be discussed here because it is relatively easy to use, especially if a proper job analysis is available. To use this technique for needs assessment, the critical incidents are sorted into dimensions and separated into examples of good and poor performance, as discussed in Chapter 2. Dimensions with many examples of poor performance are considered to be areas in which many employees are performing poorly and in which additional training is indicated.

Establishing Goals and Objectives

Once the needs analyses have been conducted, the next step in developing a training program is to establish the goals and objectives for the training. The importance of this process cannot be emphasized enough, as the training goals will determine the resources allocated to the training, the methods used to deliver the training, and the methods used to evaluate the success of the training. In setting goals, it is important to first determine what the organization wants to accomplish given the time and resources that will be allocated to the training. For example, if your organizational analysis indicated that due to financial and time constraints a four-hour training session is all that the organization can afford to teach its supervisors conflict management skills, it would be unreasonable to establish the goal that supervisors be able to mediate conflicts between employees (a skill). Instead, a more reasonable goal might be that by the end of the four-hour training, supervisors will be able to identify the common causes of conflict (a knowledge). When the organization can afford several days of training, the goal of obtaining conflict mediation skills might be more obtainable.

Training goals and objectives should concretely state the following (Mager, 1997):

- What learners are expected to do
- The conditions under which they are expected to do it
- The level at which they are expected to do it

In other words, vague objectives such as "to be a better salesperson" should be replaced with specific objectives such as increasing customer contacts by 10% and increasing new accounts by 5%. Goal statements usually include an action word, an item, a condition, and a standard. For example,

- By the end of this training session, you will be able to answer (action word) customer questions about loan rates (item) without asking others (condition) 90% of the time (standard).
- By the end of this training session, you will be able to balance (action word) the teller drawer (item) without assistance (condition) in 30 minutes with no errors (standard).
- By the end of this training session, you will be able to compute (action word) adverse impact levels (item) using Excel (condition) with no errors (standard).

Choosing the Best Training Method

Once goals and objectives have been established, the next step in developing a training program is to choose the training method—such as those shown in Table 8.2—that will best accomplish those goals and objectives. For example, if the goal is for employees to learn an actual skill, some type of hands-on training will be necessary (e.g., role-plays, simulations). Because most training programs have multiple goals and objectives, the best training programs often use a variety of methods so that employees will understand the reasons for doing a certain task, how it should be done, and in what situations it should be done (Lawson, 2000). In the following pages, several training methods will be discussed.

Using Lectures to Provide Knowledge

Lectures are a good training source if the goal is for employees to obtain knowledge, but unless they are accompanied by such techniques as simulations and role-plays, they are not usually effective at teaching skills.

Putting together a lecture-based training program can take a great deal of time. The trainer must research a topic, develop a training outline, create visuals (e.g., PowerPoint slides), create handouts, and obtain or create supporting materials such

Table 8.2   Examples of Available Training Methods

Classroom Setting

    Lecture

    Case study

    Simulation

    Role-play

    Behavior modeling

    Video/DVD

Distance Learning

    Printed materials

    Video/DVD

    Interactive video

    Podcast

    Webinar

    Webcast

On-the-Job Learning

    Modeling

    Job rotation

    Apprentice training

    Coaching

    Mentoring

    Performance appraisal

as videos and role-play exercises. Though some authors use an estimate of 30 hours of preparation for every hour of training (Zemke, 1997) and others use 50 hours (Diekmann, 2001), I use an estimate of 16 hours of preparation for every hour of training. Of course, the actual time needed to develop a training seminar is a function of the trainer's knowledge of the topic, the amount of talking a trainer expects to do, and the ready availability of videos, exercises, and role-plays related to the topic.

An important part of any training presentation is the handouts to the audience. The purpose of handouts is to provide material that the trainees can take back to their jobs. Providing comprehensive notes is important because people forget about half the training content once they leave the room and then forget another 25% within 48 hours (Nichols & Stevens, 1957). Handouts should include

- a cover sheet with the title of the training program as well as the date and location in which the training took place;
- a list of goals and objectives;
- a schedule for the training (e.g., breaks, ending times);
- a biographical sketch of the trainer;
- the notes themselves in outline form, full text, or copies of the PowerPoint slides;
- activity sheets such as personality inventories, free writes, or group activity information;
- references and suggestions for further reading; and
- a form to evaluate the quality of the training program.

Using Case Studies to Apply Knowledge

Once employees have received the information they need through lecture, it is important that they be able to apply what they have learned. One way to do this is through the **case study**. Case studies are similar to leaderless group discussions and situational interview problems (which were discussed in Chapter 5), and are considered to be good sources for developing analysis, synthesis, and evaluation skills (Noe, 2010). With this method, the members of a small group each read a case, which is either a real or hypothetical situation typical of those encountered on the job. The group then discusses the case, identifies possible solutions, evaluates the advantages and disadvantages of each solution, and arrives at what it thinks is the best solution to the problem.

Case study A training technique in which employees, usually in a group, are presented with a real or hypothetical workplace problem and are asked to propose the best solution.

For case studies to be most successful, the cases should be taken from actual situations. For example, to make their case study more realistic, General Electric employees in New York use actual information about a problem within the company. Trainees not only discussed the problem but interviewed employees to gather more information. This use of a **living case** was found to be superior to the typical case study. Not only was the problem relevant, but also the solution could actually be used, thus providing an incentive for the trainees to take the training program seriously. A drawback to the living case study, however, is that trainees may not be the best individuals to solve the problem.

Living case A case study based on a real situation rather than a hypothetical one.

In addition to being realistic, case studies should be interesting. They are best when they are written in the form of a story, contain dialogue between the characters, use realistic details, are descriptive and easy to follow, contain all information necessary to solve the problem, and are difficult enough to be challenging (Owenby, 1992).

To increase the effectiveness of case studies, trainees should first be taught the principles involved in solving a particular type of problem, helped to use those principles in discussing the case, and then have the principles reinforced after reading the case study. If the key principles are not taught and reinforced, trainees tend to focus too much on the content of a particular case study when trying to solve future problems rather than using the key principles (Allen & Connelly, 2005).

Using Simulation Exercises to Practice New Skills

Whereas case studies are effective in applying knowledge and learning problem-solving skills, **simulation** exercises allow the trainee to practice newly learned skills. Simulations offer the advantage of allowing the trainee to work with equipment under actual working conditions without the consequences of mistakes. For example, using a cash register or taking a customer's order is easy to learn. But it is a much more difficult task with a long line of angry customers or irritable coworkers. Simulation exercises allow the trainee to feel such pressure but without actually affecting the organization's performance.

Like all training methods, simulation exercises come in many different forms. Some, such as airline simulators, are extremely expensive and complex to use, but others, such as a simulated restaurant counter, are relatively inexpensive. For example, each week at the Salamander Restaurant in Cambridge, Massachusetts, servers role-play such situations as medical emergencies and computer breakdowns. Another good example of an inexpensive simulation exercise is that used by nurses to teach patients with diabetes how to administer their insulin shots—the patients practice by injecting water into oranges.

Whatever the method used, a simulation exercise can be effective only if it physically and psychologically simulates actual job conditions. For example, dummy simulators are a standard part of cardiopulmonary resuscitation (CPR) training provided by the American Red Cross. People practice CPR on the dummies, which simulate the human body and also provide feedback on pressure and location of chest compressions. Although the use of these CPR simulators is probably better than lecture alone, there is some concern that the dummies do not adequately simulate the feel of the human chest. Even worse, practicing CPR on a dummy in front of fellow employees does not involve the pressure or environment that is often encountered in an actual emergency.

Although most simulators do not exactly replicate actual physical and psychological job conditions, they are still better than the single alternatives of either lecture or actual practice. That is, training a pilot is cheaper on a simulator than on a passenger jet, and it is safer (for humans) for a medical student to practice on a pig than on a sick patient. Rapid advances in virtual reality technology hold tremendous promise for trainers (Zielinski, 2010). Virtual reality is already being used to train soldiers, surgeons, air traffic controllers, and police officers. The day that we can exactly simulate real working conditions may not be far away.

Practicing Interpersonal Skills Through Role-Play

Whereas simulations are effective for learning how to use new equipment or software programs, **role-play** allows the trainee to perform necessary interpersonal skills by acting out simulated roles. For example, when conducting seminars in conflict mediation, consultant Bobbie Raynes has her audience members participate as actors in predetermined situations. The participants are given a conflict situation and are told to use what they have learned to mediate the conflict. When Medtronic, a manufacturer of heart valves, decided to teach its sales force how to use DVD–based demonstrations, it began with an hour of classroom training and then used role-plays so that the salespeople could practice their new presentation skills.

Role-play is used in many types of training situations, from supervisors practicing performance appraisal reviews to sales clerks taking customer orders. One interesting variation of the role-play exercise has an employee playing the role of "the other person." For example, a supervisor might play the role of an employee, or a sales clerk might play the role of a customer who is frustrated with recently purchased merchandise. In this way, the employee can better understand the reasoning and feelings of the people with whom he works.

Though role-plays allow employees to practice what is being taught, they are not for everyone. Many employees feel uneasy and embarrassed about being required to "act" (Becker, 1998). This reluctance can be reduced to some extent by using warm-up exercises and praising employees after they participate (Swink, 1993).

Farber (1994) thinks that role-play should be replaced by "real play," in which employees practice their skills on actual customers. For example, salespeople can be trained by having the sales staff sit around a conference table and take turns making calls to actual/potential customers. The group then discusses the technique of the person making the call.

Increasing Interpersonal Skills Through Behavior Modeling

Behavior modeling A training technique in which employees observe correct behavior, practice that behavior, and then receive feedback about their performance.

One of the most successful training methods has been **behavior modeling** (Taylor, Russ-Eft, & Chan, 2005). Behavior modeling is similar to role-play except that trainees role-play ideal behavior rather than the behavior they might normally perform. The behavior modeling technique begins with a discussion of a problem, why it occurred, and the employee behaviors necessary to correct the problem. These behaviors are called *learning points* and are essentially rules to follow in solving a problem. Next, trainees view videos of employees correctly and incorrectly solving the problem. The trainees take notes during the tape and are given an opportunity to ask questions.

After viewing the video, trainees mentally rehearse the solution to the problem in the way that the employee solved it on the video. Finally, employees role-play (behaviorally rehearse) situations and receive feedback on their performances. Employees are also given the opportunity to play the role of the "other" person so that they will gain the same insight they would have by role-play training. Employees then discuss ways to apply their new skills on the job. By this procedure, employees will already have had experience dealing with the problem in the proper way when they encounter the same situation on the job. In other words, positive transfer of learning will have occurred.

Of course, for behavior modeling to be successful, the videos must represent commonly encountered problems and situations—thus demonstrating the importance of a thorough job analysis. By observing and interviewing employees and by collecting critical incidents, the necessary problems and situations can be obtained. An important and related issue is whether employees should be trained on specific situational skills or on generic skills that will cover any situation. For example, a specific situational skill would be handling a bank customer who is angry about a bounced check. The related generic skill would be calming *any* angry customer. Obviously, generic skills are more difficult to teach and require the modeling of many different types of behavior in many different situations.

Another issue involves the number and types of models that are viewed in the training video. Russ-Eft and Zucchelli (1987) conducted a study at Zenger-Miller, Inc. (Cupertino, California) in which employees viewed either one or two models. If the employees saw two models, they saw either two models performing correct behaviors or one model performing correctly and the other performing incorrectly. The study results indicated that viewing two models increased training performance more than viewing one but that the addition of a negative model was no more effective in increasing training performance than two positive models. When the proper procedures are followed, the results of a meta-analysis indicate that behavior modeling can significantly increase employee performance (Taylor, Russ-Eft, & Chan, 2005).

Motivating Employees to Attend Training

Once the training program has been developed, the next step is to motivate employees to attend the training. The most obvious way to "motivate" employees to attend training is to *require* them to attend training "on the clock." However, the majority of training opportunities are optional, and 10% of training opportunities take place on the employee's own time (Galvin, 2003). Here are some strategies to motivate employees to attend training:

■ Relate the training to an employee's immediate job. Employees are more likely to attend when the material covered in training will directly affect their immediate job performance. For example, employees would be more motivated to attend a training session on a computer program that the organization will begin using in two weeks than a training session on "Future Trends in Office Automation." Thus, training should be provided "just in time" rather than "just in case."

Can common sense be trained?

- Make the training interesting. Employees are more likely to attend when they know they will have a good time as well as learn something useful.
- Increase employee buy-in. When employees play a role in choosing and planning the types of training offered, they are more likely to attend. Baldwin, Magjuka, and Loher (1991) found that employees given a choice about training programs were more motivated than employees not given a choice. Employees given a choice, but then not given the program they chose, were the least motivated.
- Provide incentives. Common incentives for attending training include certificates, money, promotion opportunities, and college credit. Microsoft increased employee participation in voluntary training by 2,000% when it created a program, "Ready, Set, Go," in which employees who participated in voluntary training received points that could be exchanged for merchandise, travel, and gift certificates (Renk, 2004).
- Provide food. Medeco Security Locks in Salem, Virginia, has optional monthly training sessions in which a topic is presented while the employees eat lunch provided by the company. Consultants Bobbie Raynes and GeGe Beall both have used free pizza as incentives to get employees to attend short training sessions during lunch or dinner.
- Reduce the stress associated with attending. Frequently, employees want to attend training but don't because they can't afford to take time away from their scheduled duties. To encourage employees to attend training, organizations should provide workload reductions or staffing assistance.

Delivering the Training Program

Once the training program has been created, there are three broad methods of delivering the training: in the classroom, through distance learning, and on the job.

Conducting Classroom Training

Initial Decisions

Prior to conducting classroom training, several decisions need to be made by an organization.

Who Will Conduct the Training? Training seminars can be conducted by a variety of sources including in-house trainers who are employees of the organization, outside trainers who contract with the organization, videos, and local universities. In-house trainers are used when a training program will be presented too frequently to justify the cost of an outside trainer or when the training topic is so specific to the organization that finding outside trainers would be difficult.

External trainers are used when the trainers in an organization lack the expertise on a particular topic or when the cost of internally developing a training program exceeds the cost of contracting with an external trainer. For example, an organization needing two days of training in communication skills would be better served contracting with an external trainer at $2,000 a day than spending the $20,000 it would take to develop the training program on its own. However, if the training program were to be offered twice a week for two years, the organization might be better served using in-house trainers.

Tens of thousands of training consultants around the country offer seminars to industry. Needs analysis, however, must be used to determine whether such seminars are actually necessary. Sam Miller, human resources director for Roanoke (Virginia) Electric Steel Company, has commented that he receives an average of two brochures each day advertising various seminars. Even though a seminar may sound interesting, it should be used only if it directly relates to some aspect of the job or to the people doing the job. For example, a seminar on communication skills may sound interesting, but it probably would not improve an electronics assembler's performance, whereas a seminar on electronics might. Likewise, a seminar on personal money management may not relate to the assembler's job, but it may be useful if it solves outside problems that affect his job performance or attendance.

Rather than using actual trainers, many organizations use videos as part of their training programs. Videos have a clear economic advantage over live lecture when the training session is to be repeated many times. A consultant-conducted seminar usually costs between $100 and $500 per hour plus expenses, whereas most videos can be purchased for $200 to $600. Thus a two-hour video will pay for itself if used only two or three times. Developing a seminar in-house takes about 30 hours of preparation ($750) for each seminar hour (Zemke, 1997). Developing a custom video costs between $1,000 and $3,000 per finished minute (Sosnin, 2001b). Thus the development of a custom two-hour training video would cost between $120,000 and $360,000!

Many organizations are beginning to use local colleges and universities to handle their training needs. The advantages of using colleges and universities are lower costs, access to excellent training facilities, access to well-known faculty, and the potential for employees to receive college credit for completing the training (Martyka, 2001). Local universities are typically used for technical (e.g., electronics, computer programming) and leadership training and are most appropriate when only a few employees need training at any given time and the cost of setting up a training lab is prohibitive. A good example of an organization using a variety of training options can be found at an AT&T manufacturing plant: Seminars on problem solving are conducted by the training staff, communication skills seminars are taught by an outside trainer, and classes on the principles of electronics are offered at a local community college.

Where Will the Training Be Held? Training can be offered on-site or at an off-site location such as a hotel, university, or conference center. The obvious advantage of conducting training on-site is that it is less expensive. However, many organizations have neither the space nor the equipment needed for on-site training. Holding training off-site has the advantage of getting the employees away from the work site and allowing them to concentrate on their training. In some cases, off-site training locations in Las Vegas, Miami, or San Diego are chosen as an incentive to get employees to attend training or as a reward for performing well at work.

How Long Should the Training Be? Determining the length of a training session is an interesting dilemma. From a cost-efficiency perspective, it is better to conduct a weeklong training session rather than divide the training into 10 half-day sessions spread over a one-month period. However, from an interest perspective, few employees enjoy attending 40 hours of training in a week.

For the highest level of learning, training material should be presented in small, easily remembered chunks distributed over a period of time (distributed learning) rather than learned all at once (massed learning). As shown in a meta-analysis by Donovan and Radosevich (1999), if too much training occurs at one time, employees will not be able to pay attention to all that is being taught or be able to remember that on which they did concentrate. Consequently, training performance will be lower when training is massed rather than distributed.

Massed practice Concentrating learning into a short period of time.

The best example of the principle of **massed versus distributed practice** is studying for exams. If we *distribute* the reading over several days, the material is relatively easy to learn. But if we wait until the night before the test to read three chapters—that is, *mass* the reading—we will not retain much at all.

Preparing for Classroom Training

Adjusting for the Audience. The characteristics of the audience play an important role in developing a training program. A trainer must consider the size, demographics, and ability of the audience. For example, with a large audience, not only will the trainer need to use a microphone, but it becomes difficult to supplement lecture material with such exercises as role-play, simulation, and group discussion. An audience of women often will react differently to certain examples and types of exercises than will an audience of men. Likewise, examples used for a younger audience might not work on an older audience.

The ability level of the audience members is another important factor. If they are low on experience or ability, the training will need to proceed at a slower pace than if they were more experienced or more skilled. The toughest situation for a trainer is when the audience has mixed levels of ability. If the trainer sets a slow pace to help the lower-ability trainees, the higher-ability trainees become bored. If the trainer caters to the higher-ability trainees, the other trainees fall behind. For these reasons, most trainers present material at a moderate pace. Not surprisingly, the research evidence is clear that employees who perform well in training are bright, believe they can perform well (have high self-efficacy), are motivated, and are goal oriented (Salas & Cannon-Bowers, 2001).

Delivering the Training Program

Introducing the Trainer and the Training Session. Training sessions usually begin with the introduction of the trainer. This can be done by the trainer introducing himself or by another person doing the introduction. The introduction should be short and should establish the credentials of the trainer. The length of the introduction depends on the time allocated for the training and the extent to which the audience already knows the trainer. If necessary, a more complete biography of the trainer can be placed in the training materials so that the audience can see the trainer's credentials without the trainer appearing to be bragging.

After the introduction of the trainer, the objectives of the training seminar, the training schedule (e.g., starting times, break times, meal times, quitting times), and seminar rules (e.g., turning off cell phones, not smoking, not criticizing audience members) are covered. When possible, it is a good idea for the schedule to include a 10-minute break at the end of each hour and one and a half hours for lunch.

The Career Workshop Box gives tips on etiquette for audience members.

I am the president of DCI Consulting, a human resources (HR) consulting and software-development company that specializes in HR risk management. We work with clients in assuring compliance with federal employment laws and help them identify and prevent potential liability in employment discrimination issues. Our practice areas include affirmative action compliance; nondiscrimination in hiring, promotion, termination, and pay; proactive training; salary equity analysis; and a host of other things. It is our job to keep our clients out of trouble as well as to assist them when they are under investigation by the Department of Labor or the Equal Employment Opportunity Commission.

As one of the many hats I wear as president of the firm, I conduct training seminars and speaking sessions on HR risk management. The training seminars range from highly technical and statistical to nontechnical issues that are softer in content. I find training to be one of the most interesting and challenging aspects of my job. Each time I conduct a training program, something new and different comes up based upon the participants and the organization's culture.

One thing I have learned over the years is that not everyone is born to be an effective trainer. There are tips, however, that you can follow that, with practice, can help facilitate your performance as a trainer. With that being said, here is my top 10 list of things that will help make you a good trainer.

There is a difference between technical and nontechnical training.

Soft-skills training and technical training are very different types of training. I find it much more challenging to present technical

Courtesy of David Cohen, MS

David Cohen, M.S.
President, DCI Consulting Group Inc.

material over soft-skills material. Eight hours of statistics training can be quite boring. Use exercises, case studies, and other things to keep people engaged. A joke here and there also goes a long way. Know the technical material of your training and plan accordingly.

Trainers are like wine—they get better over time.

It takes lots of time and experience to be a really good trainer. Be patient. You will have your fair share of times when you don't perform well. For your first training program, start by practicing in front of a mirror, then making the move to present in front of your friends or family, and finally taking the plunge into your first training. It gets easier as you get more experience and practice.

Get to know your audience prior to the training.

It is very important to have a firm understanding of who is going to be in the training session. Prior to your training, find out the knowledge level of the participants, number of participants, their attitude toward attending the seminar, organizational culture, issues within the company that may relate to your training, and so forth. This will help you get an understanding of the company and the participants and will enable you to tailor the training to their needs and skill level.

Know the material.

It is very important that you have a thorough understanding of the material prior to presenting. I have been to training sessions

Using Icebreakers and Energizers. Following the introduction of the trainer, most training programs start with some sort of icebreaker or energizer. Types of icebreakers include the following:

- Introductions such as asking each trainee to introduce the person next to him or her, or having a scavenger hunt in which trainees are given a list of questions (e.g., "Who likes baseball?" "Who has a daughter?") and are asked to mingle with the other trainees to obtain answers to the questions.
- Jokes or stories.
- Activities in which trainees, either individually or in small groups, are given a question or problem to solve.
- Open-ended questions to elicit audience response and encourage discussion.

that have bombed because the trainer sat and read from notes during the entire session. There is nothing worse than attending a seminar like this. Review your material prior to the training until you know it inside out. It is one thing to understand material and another to actually teach/present it. Keep practicing until you can do it in your sleep.

Don't make up answers.

You will quickly lose the credibility of your participants if you provide answers that are not true. If you are unsure about a question that may come up—and you will be—tell the participant that you don't know the answer to that question but will look into it and get back to him or her with an answer. Or, you can always turn the question back to the group to see if anyone in the audience has the answer. Never make up an answer on the spot just to answer the question. This will come back to haunt you!

Use different formats while presenting.

I like to use several formats when presenting. I find that variety keeps the participants interested and engaged during the entire training program. Nobody likes attending a seminar where the person lectures to them for eight hours. Use such things as PowerPoint, group activities, videos, group exercises, roundtable discussions, web demos, and case studies. This not only will make your training program more interesting, but it will help participants learn the materials.

Wear good shoes.

It may sound funny, but it's true. I bought a cheap pair of shoes prior to a training program, and I paid the price: back pain and a sore neck. Remember, when you train you will be standing for a long period of time. A poor pair of shoes will make for an extremely uncomfortable training experience.

Be prepared.

Always check that you have all of your materials and information prior to walking out the door. I like to use a checklist of all the things I need to take with me prior to the training.

Use stories and experiences.

People love to hear different war stories and experiences when you present the material. It helps to present the material and apply it to real-life settings. When I conduct a training program on employment discrimination, I share actual cases I have been involved in and the outcomes. This helps me drive home the importance of the training material.

Humor goes a long way.

I once asked a colleague what made him such a great trainer. He said, "I may not be the brightest person in the world, but people find me funny." His point was well taken. People like to be amused and entertained when they come to a training session. Effective use of humor can be a great way to engage and entertain your audience. This will help break up the monotony of the session.

Oh, yeah, one more piece of good advice. Always supply good snacks and drinks. The caffeine will keep them awake, and the food will keep them happy.

Every training session you conduct will be different. Different audiences lead to different experiences. This is what makes training such fun. Remember, the most effective way to foster an environment of learning is when you entertain and educate participants at the same time. Your audience will remember you for that!

■ Free writes in which audience members are asked to write about the topic. For example, in a training seminar on sexual harassment, trainees were asked to write about a time when they either were harassed or saw another employee being harassed. In a training seminar on dealing with difficult customers, trainees were asked to write about an angry customer they had to deal with and how they handled the situation.

There are three considerations in choosing an icebreaker: the goal of the icebreaker, the length of the training session, and the nature of the audience.

For an icebreaker to be successful, it must accomplish a goal. The most common goals for icebreakers are to get people to know one another, to get them talking, to wake them up, and to get them thinking about the topic. For example, introductions work well when it is important that the audience members know one another, and

Whether you are in class or attending a training workshop, your behavior as an audience member not only impacts the presenter and the other audience members, but also gives others an impression of you as a professional. Here is some advice provided by consultant and trainer Bobbie Raynes:

➡ Get to the workshop on time so as not to disturb other audience members or the workshop presenter. It is a good idea to actually get there early, grab a good seat, and take advantage of the snacks that are often available.

➡ Come prepared. Have a pen and some paper so you can take notes if necessary.

➡ If there are snacks, take only your share. Leave some for the other audience members.

➡ Turn off your cell phone (or at least put it on vibrate). If you must answer a call, do so outside of the training room.

➡ Don't use your laptop to take notes—the sound of the keys is distracting to both the audience and the workshop presenter. If you want to take notes, do it the old-fashioned way—use a pen and paper!

➡ Try not to make unnecessary noises (e.g., cracking gum, rocking back and forth in your chair, constantly clicking a pen on and off). I can't tell you how many times I have had audience members complain about another person making noise!

➡ Stay awake! If you feel you are falling asleep, quietly leave the room.

➡ Let the presenter know you are listening by nodding your head, making eye contact, or asking questions. This provides important feedback to the presenter. Based on the audience reaction, the presenter can change the way he/she is doing something so that it better meets the needs of the audience.

➡ If you have a question, raise your hand and ask. Never feel shy about asking questions, because trainers like to get them, and if you are having trouble following something, you can be sure others are as well.

➡ Be courteous to other audience members and allow them to ask their questions, too. Don't do all the talking!

➡ If you disagree with something the presenter is saying, politely ask the presenter for a further explanation. If you still disagree, talk to the presenter after the workshop.

➡ Listen to other audience members without judging their comments. You can respond to them, but shooting down others' ideas and thoughts is not in good form.

➡ At the end of the workshop, introduce yourself to the presenter. If you enjoyed the workshop, say so.

➡ If the presenter asks you to evaluate the workshop when it is over, do so. This is the only way the presenter will know what to change or do differently. If there is room for comments, briefly explain why you liked or disliked something. The more specific you are, the more helpful the evaluation.

➡ Throw away your coffee cups, soda cans, or any other trash that you may have accumulated during the workshop.

free writes work well when the goal is to get the audience thinking about a topic. Having an icebreaker for the sake of having an icebreaker is not a good idea.

If the training session will last only a few hours, the icebreaker should be short—if one is even used. If the training session will last an entire week, time should be spent on introductions and "group bonding" activities.

Certain types of icebreakers work better with some audiences than they do with others. For example, having a group of trainees introduce themselves by saying their name and a trait starting with the first letter of their name (e.g., Friendly Fred, Timid Temea, Zany Zach) is not likely to go over as well with a group of police officers as it might with a group of social workers.

Delivering the Presentation. Though this is not a public speaking text, here are some tips you might find useful in delivering a training presentation:

■ Make eye contact with the audience.
■ Use gestures effectively. That is, don't wave your hands or use other gestures unless they help make a point.

- Don't read your presentation. Use visuals such as your PowerPoint slides to guide you. If you know your material and have practiced your presentation, all you should need is the occasional reminder that can be provided by glancing at your PowerPoint slides projected on the screen.
- Don't hide behind the podium.
- Use a conversational style. A training presentation is not a speech, lecture, or sermon. Talk *with* your audience, not *at* them.
- Be confident. Avoid the use of fillers, speak at an appropriate volume, and don't brag about yourself. If you know your stuff, the audience will notice—you don't have to tell them how smart you are.
- Speak at a pace that is neither too fast nor too slow.
- Avoid swearing, making off-color or offensive remarks, and demeaning other people, groups, or organizations.
- Try to make the presentation interesting. This can be done by using fun (e.g., humor, stories) or a variety of activities (e.g., lecture, video, discussion, activity), creating energy either through the speaker's pace or through audience activity, and involving the audience by allowing them to share their opinions, stories, and expertise.
- Don't force humor. If you are a naturally funny person, it will show. When using humor, make sure it meets an objective such as demonstrating a point or keeping the audience awake during a dull topic. Otherwise, humor for the sake of humor can be distracting. Humor should never be at the expense of others—the only safe target is yourself (in moderation).
- When answering audience questions, repeat the question if the room is large. If you are unsure of the question, ask the audience member to repeat the question or try to paraphrase the question (e.g., "Is what you are asking …"). After answering the question, ask whether you have answered it sufficiently. If you don't know the answer to a question, don't bluff. You can ask if anyone in the audience knows the answer—nine out of ten times they do.

As with college lectures, many activities can take place within a seminar, including lecture, the use of videos, discussion, and question-and-answer periods. Again, the choice of activities depends on the task or skill to be taught. If the skill is complicated, such as operating a machine or dealing with an angry customer, lecture alone will not be enough. The seminar should also include some type of practice or role-play. If the information is not complicated but involves such visual material as building locations, flowcharts, or diagrams, visual aids should be added to the lecture. If the material covered is not comprehensive or if the feelings of the employees toward the material are important, then discussion should be included. Discussion not only helps further learning but also allows employees to feel that their opinions are important.

Conducting Training Through Distance Learning

One disadvantage of traditional classroom instruction is that all employees must be taught at the same pace and in the same location. This is unfortunate because some employees are brighter or more experienced than others and will be bored if a training seminar moves too slowly. Other employees, however, will become frustrated if the seminar goes too quickly. Thus, to allow employees to learn material at their own pace, at a time and place that is convenient to them, many organizations are using some form of distance learning.

Distance learning technologies can generally be placed into one of two broad categories: **asynchronous** or **synchronous**. With asynchronous technologies, employees can complete the training at their own pace and at a time of their choosing. In contrast, synchronous technologies require employees to complete the training at the same time and at the same pace, although they may be in different physical locations.

Asynchronous Distance Learning

With this method, employees are provided with media materials for learning the content, as well as with a series of exams that measure what they have learned from them. If employees do not pass the test at the end of each unit, they usually must reread the material and retake the test until they pass. In this way, employees study at their own pace, and the exams ensure that employees understand the material. With asynchronous distance learning, information can be provided to the employee in a variety of ways including printed materials, videos, DVDs, and web-based programs. To increase the effectiveness of these programs and make them more interactive, trainees often can have access to an instructor or other trainees through email, chat rooms, and message board forums.

The training program used by Life of Virginia is a good example. One problem encountered by the company was that more than 1,000 sales agents were spread over 140 offices throughout the country. Thus, to conduct a training program that would be both effective and practical, Life of Virginia used sales experts to create seven training modules: marketing and asking for referrals, calling for appointments, interviews, preparing the insurance recommendation, presenting the recommendation, delivering the insurance policy, and periodic review. Each module contained a 5- to 10-page reading assignment, a written exercise on the reading, a video showing models performing the appropriate behaviors, a situational problem, and a series of questions to be answered by each insurance agent. Agents study at their own pace, taking between two and four weeks per module. This training program resulted in a 25% annual increase in sales and a 10% decrease in turnover.

The H. E. Butt Grocery Company decided to use interactive video at its grocery stores because of the difficulty in getting employee schedules coordinated for group training. With **interactive video**, employees see a videotaped situation on a television, computer screen, or iPod. At the end of each situation, employees choose their response to the situation and the computer selects a video that shows what would happen based on the employee's response. Butt's first interactive video training focused on food safety practices and included such features as a virtual notepad, allowing trainees to take notes on the computer, and a bacteria growth simulator (don't you wish you had one of those?).

Captain D's Seafood Kitchen provides another example of a company that successfully used a computer-based training program. Captain D's spent $2 million to develop its training programs and install computers in each of its 350 restaurants. As a result of this training, mystery-shopper ratings increased by 4% (Maurer, 2001).

Similar success was found at FedEx. Because FedEx has more than 700 locations, costs for sending trainers to each location are high. As a solution to this high cost, FedEx placed more than 1,200 interactive video units at its 700 locations. This change from live seminars to interactive video reduced training expenses, reduced customer contact training time from 32 to 8 hours, and resulted in the company's receiving several awards for its innovative program (Wilson, 1994).

In the public sector, many law enforcement agencies are using training programs offered over the Internet. For example, the Federal Law Enforcement Training Center provides more than 1,700 courses through e-learning, and the U.S. Capitol Police provides its officers access to more than 2,100 web-based courses. Two law enforcement agencies in Florida saved $296,000 in travel-related expenses in one year by using e-learning. Because creating an e-learning training program can be expensive, most organizations contract with a learning portal, that is, a website containing a variety of e-courses. For example, TrainSeek.com is a learning portal with more than 2,000 e-courses.

Most asynchronous distance learning training takes advantage of the concept of **programmed instruction**. Programmed instruction is effective because it takes advantage of several important learning principles (Goldstein & Ford, 2002). First, learning is *self-paced*—that is, each trainee proceeds at his own pace. You have probably been in classes in which the lecturer went too quickly and in others in which the lecturer went too slowly. When the presentation speed of the material does not parallel the comprehension speed of the learner, frustration occurs, and the material will not be learned as well as it might.

Second, each trainee is *actively involved* in the learning. This contrasts sharply with the lecture method, where the employee might sit through two hours of lecture without being actively involved. Think of your favorite classes: The instructor probably allowed you to become involved and actually do things. (That is why some of the chapters in the text are so detailed. By making the text inclusive and complete, your instructor can spend class time on projects instead of straight lecture.)

Finally, programmed instruction presents information in *small units* or chunks, because learning smaller amounts of material is easier than learning larger amounts. To demonstrate this point, think of the exam for this class. Would your score on the test be higher if you read and reviewed one chapter each week or if you waited until the night before the test to read five chapters? (The answer is obvious, and hopefully you did not answer the question from experience!) A meta-analysis by Manson (1989) concluded that programmed instruction can lead to improved performance at relatively low cost, and a meta-analysis by Allen, Mabry, Mattrey, Bourhis, Titsworth, and Burrell (2004) found that test scores for students in distance learning classes were no different than those earned by students in traditional courses.

Synchronous Distance Learning

Rather than using printed or prerecorded materials for distance learning, many training programs are conducted live where the trainer communicates to an audience that might be "attending" over the phone, through the Internet, or by satellite TV.

Fast-growing sources of synchronous distance learning are teleconferences, webinars, and webcasts. **Webinars** (short for web-based seminar) and **webcasts** are training programs transmitted over the web. The difference between the two is that a webinar is interactive whereas a webcast involves one-way communication from the trainer. With a teleconference, trainees are sent a PowerPoint presentation that they view on their computer while the trainer conducts the audio portion of the training over the phone. As with webinars, teleconferences can be interactive in nature.

Another fast-growing source of synchronous distance learning is interactive, online communities of learning such as **blogs, wikis,** and **listservs**. With each of these methods, rather than waiting for an annual conference or scheduled training program, employees can ask questions, get immediate answers, post opinions, and share information with others in similar fields.

Meta-analysis results indicate that distance learning techniques are at least as effective as classroom training and their effectiveness increases when learners can

Programmed instruction A training method in which employees learn information at their own pace.

Webinar Short for "web seminar," an interactive training method in which training is transmitted over the Inernet.

Webcast A noninteractive training method in which the trainer transmits training information over the Internet.

Blog A website in which the host regularly posts commentaries on a topic that readers can respond to.

Wiki A collection of web pages in which users can create web pages on a topic and readers can freely edit those pages.

Listserv A program that automatically distributes e-mail messages to a group of people who have a common interest.

control the pace of the learning and when feedback is given regarding the learner's progress (Sitzmann, Kraiger, Stewart, & Wisher, 2006).

Conducting On-the-Job Training

In the previous section, we discussed how employees can be trained in classroom settings and through distance learning. In this section, we will discuss how employees learn through on-the-job training (OJT), an important topic given that some researchers estimate that over 60% of employee training is OJT (DeRouin, Parrish, & Salas, 2005). Though there is some disagreement about what constitutes OJT, a good definition is that OJT is *informal training by experienced peers and supervisors that occurs on the job and during job tasks* (DeRouin et al., 2005). OJT works best for teaching skills that require supervision to learn, are best learned through repetition, and benefit from role modeling (Gallup & Beauchemin, 2000).

Learning by Modeling Others

Modeling Learning through watching and imitating the behavior of others.

Also called *social learning*, **modeling** is a vitally important method of learning for training in organizations. As the name implies, employees learn by watching how other employees perform, or model, a behavior.

Modeling as a learning technique is astoundingly pervasive and is the basis of the behavioral modeling method of training discussed earlier. Think of how you first learned a sport such as baseball. You probably learned your batting stance by watching a favorite player. Why do you dress the way you do? Mostly because you model the way your peers and idols dress. We are most likely to learn through modeling when we are unsure about how to behave. For example, in our first days on a new job, we watch how others act. Do they take only the allotted time on breaks? Do they treat customers politely? Do they pay attention to their work? We learn how to behave at work by watching others so that we will fit in. A theory of job satisfaction that will be discussed in Chapter 10 hypothesizes that we even decide how satisfied we will be in our job by matching our level of job satisfaction with the levels exhibited by other employees.

Modeling is most effective under certain conditions. These conditions mainly involve characteristics of the employee whose behavior is being duplicated and the characteristics of the person attempting to model that performance.

Characteristics of the Model. Of course, we do not model everyone else's behavior. Instead, we tend to model behavior of people who are similar to us, who are successful, and who have status. For example, if we were deciding what new clothes to purchase, whom would we model? If male, would we pick Barbara Walters or Joe Biden? After all, both have status and have been successful. No, instead we would look for someone who was more similar to us in both gender and age.

Likewise, if we are going to model our golf swing after someone, who would it be? Almost certainly, we would choose someone on the professional tour because of his or her status and success. But which player would it be? It would not be one of the worst golfers on the tour. Instead, we probably would choose Tiger Woods, Annika Sörenstam, or another successful golfer. Finally, which successful golfer would it be? It would probably be the successful golfer who was most similar to us in terms of race, sex, hair color, hometown, style, and so on.

This raises an important point about models in industry. We tend to look for a model who is similar to us. For modeling to be effective, the appropriate role models for employees should be similar to them in significant ways. That is why it is essential that a school faculty have both minority and female teachers, that an organization have both minority and female managers, and that television shows portray all types of people in different occupational roles.

Characteristics of the Observer. For an employee to model another's behavior, three conditions are necessary (Bandura, 1977). First, the employee must pay attention to the behavior of other employees. All the role models in the world will be unable to effect a behavior change in an employee if the employee pays no attention to the role model.

Second, the employee must be able to *retain* the information that is being modeled. Have you ever watched a person dance, and then later tried the dance yourself? For most of us it is difficult to do if there are many steps to remember (for some of us it is difficult to do if there are only two steps to remember!). Thus, even though we might have been paying close attention, there were too many behaviors to recall or retain. That is why training techniques that use modeling concentrate on only a few behaviors at a time.

Finally, the employee must have the ability or skill to *reproduce* the behavior that is seen. For example, suppose a new employee observes a veteran employee winding coils. If the new employee does not have the proper dexterity, technique alone will not enable the employee to be as successful as the veteran. Thus, it is important to limit the scope of the behaviors being modeled, so that they are at a skill level that can be reproduced by the observing employee.

Learning Through Job Rotation

Job rotation A system in which employees are given the opportunity to perform several different jobs in an organization.

Another excellent on-the-job training method is **job rotation**, in which an employee performs several different jobs within an organization. Job rotation is especially popular for managerial training because it allows a manager trainee to experience and understand most, if not all, of the jobs within the organization that his subordinates will perform.

Kroger and WalMart train their assistant managers as clerks, stockers, and baggers before promotion to manager. Allstate trains its manager trainees in a similar fashion by having them spend a few months in sales, underwriting, personnel, cash control, and marketing. With job rotation, these organizations believe their managers will perform better by understanding more clearly how each employee performs his job. At Applebee's restaurants, executives exchange positions with restaurant employees so that the executives don't lose touch with routine problems. At Levy Restaurants in Chicago, 20 to 40 selected employees hoping to be managers spend four days at their normal job and one day working in a new area of the restaurant; 75% eventually get promoted. Also, chef trainees at Levy Restaurants spend their first week in the dining room, four weeks in the kitchen, and one week performing administrative tasks.

Job rotation is also commonly used to train nonmanagerial employees. Aside from increasing employee awareness, the main advantage of job rotation is that it allows for both lateral transfers within an organization and greater flexibility in replacing absent workers. For example, if two bank tellers are ill, an employee who normally approves loans is able to temporarily take over the tellers' tasks. Increased use of work teams is making job rotation, or **cross-training**, much more common.

Cross-training Teaching employees how to perform tasks traditionally performed by other employees.

Another advantage, which will be discussed in greater detail in Chapter 10, is that job rotation can improve job satisfaction by reducing the boredom that often comes with a task-repetitive job. Job rotation works best if a corporate trainer is assigned to supervise employees throughout the duration of their rotations (Nadler, 1993). Such a situation provides more stability than would occur if the employee had a different supervisor for each rotation.

An interesting innovation is taking job rotation training outside the organization and encouraging employees to volunteer for worthwhile charities and nonprofit organizations (Caudron, 1994). For example, GATX Capitol employees helped renovate a day-care center, EDS employees helped clean a local beach, and Helene Curtis employees raised funds to battle AIDS. The United Way takes advantage of corporate volunteerism through its "Loaned Executive" program, in which organizations "lend" their executives to the United Way to help raise funds.

Employers report that volunteerism increases morale while also increasing employee communication, time management, and planning skills. Added benefits include increased respect for diversity, self-esteem, and social obligation (Caudron, 1994).

Learning Through Apprentice Training

Apprentice training A training program, usually found in the craft and building trades, in which employees combine formal coursework with formal on-the-job training.

Apprentice training is used by more than 50,000 people annually and is typically found in crafts and trades such as carpentry and plumbing. With apprentice training, an individual usually takes 144 hours of formal class work each year and works with an expert for several (usually four) years to learn a particular trade and perhaps become eligible to join a trade union. Although apprenticeships are usually formal agreements between labor and management and are regulated by the U.S. Department of Labor's Bureau of Apprenticeship and Training, as well as by state agencies, apprenticeships can also be less formal.

For example, an apprentice working with a plumber will initially help the plumber by carrying supplies, picking up parts from suppliers, and holding tools. But with time, the apprentice is taught the necessary knowledge and skills for plumbing. When the apprenticeship is complete, the apprentice can start his own business.

Apprenticeships are good for both the apprentice and the expert. The apprentice learns a valuable trade, and the expert or the organization gets inexpensive labor—usually one half the cost of expert labor. This is why apprenticeships have become more popular over the last few decades. Organizations also use apprenticeships to "grow their own" employees for jobs that are difficult to fill. For example, Moog Components Group in Blacksburg, VA, developed an apprenticeship program to develop machinists. To complete the program, apprentices must complete 8,000 hours of on-the-job training and successfully complete seven classes taught by the local community college. To make the classes more convenient for the 34 apprentices, the community college holds the classes at the Moog facility (Jackson, 2008).

Despite this increased popularity, however, apprenticeship programs have been criticized for two major reasons. First, the emphasis during the apprenticeship often is on the production of work as opposed to teaching new skills to the apprentice. Second, unions use apprenticeships to restrict entry into their trades, which results both in inflated wages caused by high demand and a lower supply of workers, and in unfair minority hiring practices. Employers often shun apprenticeships for fear that the apprentice will become a competitor or join a competing company.

Learning Through Coaching and Mentoring

Coaching. Coaching is another popular method of training new employees and typically takes one of two forms: experienced employees working with new employees and professional coaches who work with all employees.

Experienced Employees as Coaches. In this form of coaching, a new employee is assigned to an experienced employee, who is told to "show the kid the ropes." Coaching can be highly effective, allowing the new employee the chance to learn from a job expert. After all, who knows a job better than a person who has mastered it for several years? Coaching provides just-in-time training, flexible scheduling, customized training, and a smaller financial commitment than many other types of training (Leeds, 1996).

Coaching, however, has its own problems. First, good workers are not necessarily good trainers, and good trainers are not necessarily good workers. Being able to do a job is not the same as explaining it. For example, have you ever asked a great dancer to show you some dance steps, but they were unable to explain how they danced? In sports, the best coaches often have been terrible players. This is not to say, of course, that excellent employees or players will never be good teachers or coaches. For example, in the world of sports we have seen such successful basketball players as Doc Rivers, Larry Bird, and the late John Wooden become excellent coaches. In education, we see successful people leave industry to become fine educators. The key is finding a way to identify those workers who will be good coaches or trainers. One solution has been to establish "train-the-trainer" programs, in which future trainers or coaches are taught the skills they will need to train other employees.

A second problem with coaching is that it diminishes the expert's productivity (Wexley & Latham, 2002). That is, while the expert shows the new employee how to do the job, his own production declines. If he is on a bonus system, he may lose money as his production declines, as will the organization if the experienced employee is an outstanding worker. One solution to this problem is for the organization to reward workers who do well in training new employees.

Many organizations, such as Pitney-Bowes, have also adopted **pass-through programs**, in which experienced workers are temporarily assigned to the training department. These workers are taught training techniques and then spend several months training new employees before resuming their old jobs.

Professional Coaches. To overcome the problems mentioned here, many organizations are using "corporate coaches." Corporate coaches are similar to consultants, yet rather than working with the organization as a whole, they are hired to coach a particular employee—usually a manager. The job of a corporate coach goes beyond traditional training, as they also help employees identify strengths and weaknesses, set goals, and solve problems. Daimler AG is an example of an employer that uses coaches in its call centers. Each call center has a professional coach who works with employees and managers. For example, a manager may be having a problem with an employee who is short with customers. As a result, the manager goes to the coach for help. The coach might begin by listening to some of the employee's calls and then work with the manager on how to provide feedback to the employee. The coach might listen as the manager talks to the employee and provide additional feedback to the manager.

Mentoring. Mentoring is a form of coaching that has recently received much attention. A **mentor** is a veteran in the organization who takes a special interest in a new employee and helps him not only to adjust to the job but also to advance in the organization. Typically, mentors are older and at least one level or position above the employee being mentored. American Cytec agricultural products is a good example of an organization using mentoring. Cytec previously had its sales trainees spend 6 months in the classroom but has reduced classroom training to 3 months and now puts the trainees in the field with 1 of 31 "master reps" who serve as mentors. With time, trainees get greater responsibility until they can finally handle calls on their own. This change to mentoring is credited with a substantial increase in sales.

As with coaching, not all employees make good mentors; thus, both the mentor and the mentor-employee match must be carefully chosen. However, meta-analysis results indicate that, in general, having a mentor is beneficial to an employee's career (Eby, Allen, Evans, Ng, & DuBois, 2008; Kammeyer-Mueller & Judge, 2008). Interestingly, a study of 609 mentoring relationships found that mentoring was more effective when the relationship was informal rather than formal (Ragins & Cotton, 1999).

Performance Appraisal. As discussed in Chapter 7, one of the major uses for employee performance evaluation is training. One excellent method of on-the-job training is to have a supervisor meet with an employee to discuss his strengths and weaknesses on the job. Once the weaknesses have been identified, the supervisor and employee can determine what training methods would best help the employee to improve his job knowledge or skill.

But using performance appraisal for both training and determining raises and promotions can be difficult. As pointed out by Kirkpatrick (1986), three factors account for this difficulty. First, the focus on salary administration is on *past* behavior, whereas the focus for training is on *future* behavior. Second, performance appraisal for salary administration often is subjective and emotional, whereas such appraisal for training is objective and unemotional. Finally, salary administration looks at overall performance, whereas training looks at detailed performance. Because of these differences, Kirkpatrick (1986) suggests the use of two separate performance appraisal systems in an organization—one for salary administration and the other for training. To apply what you have learned about the various training methods, complete the "Designing a Training Program" exercise in your workbook.

Motivating Employees to Learn During Training

Providing Incentives for Learning

Employees motivated to learn perform better in training than their less motivated counterparts (Mathieu, Tannenbaum, & Salas, 1992). This motivation to learn is often related to the perception that there is an incentive (e.g., a pay raise or job advancement) to learning. That is, an electronics assembler who is taking a course in electronics will probably not study and learn unless he can see how that knowledge will improve his performance enough to result in a desirable outcome, such as a salary increase or chance of promotion. Types of incentives that can be used to motivate learning include money, job security, self-improvement, advancement, fun (an interesting training program), and opportunity to enter a new career. The incentives can be made contingent on a variety of factors, including completion of a training course, demonstration of new knowledge, demonstration of a new skill, or an increase in actual job performance.

A common financial incentive method is **skill-based pay**, which is used by 14% of major U.S. organizations (Mercer Consulting, 2009). With skill-based pay, an employee participates in a training program that is designed to increase a particular skill an employee needs either to be promoted or to receive a pay raise. For example,

Skill-based pay Compensating an employee who participates in a training program designed to increase a particular job-related skill.

employees who are currently in the position of Printer II must learn to set their own type before they can be promoted to Printer III. The employees must be able to demonstrate their mastery of the newly taught skill rather than just attend training sessions. Similarly, in situations where promotion is not possible, pay increases alone are given to employees who master new skills. There are four common skill-based pay plans. *Vertical skill plans* pay for skill in a single job, *horizontal skill plans* focus on skills used across multiple jobs, *depth skill plans* reward employees for learning specialized skills, and *basic skill plans* focus on such basic skills as math and English (Recardo & Pricone, 1996).

At FedEx each year, employees are required to watch eight hours of interactive video training on customer contact. Employees must score 90% on exams given on this material to pass. Ten percent of the employees' performance review (salary increase) is then based on their test scores.

Skill-based pay not only provides incentives for employees to successfully complete training but also results in increased savings for an organization. For example, a General Foods plant in Kansas found a 92% decrease in its quality reject rate and a 33% decrease in fixed overhead costs after introducing a skill-based pay program.

Interest

Employees will be more motivated to learn when the training program is interesting. As a result, trainers who are not effective presenters do not last long. Some training topics are naturally interesting and a trainer doesn't need to do much to spice up the material. For example, the topic of detecting deception is intrinsically interesting to most people, but the topic of performance appraisal is not. A topic can be made interesting by making it relevant to the employees' lives, having activities, using a variety of training techniques, using humor, and maximizing audience participation.

Feedback

Feedback Providing employees with specific information about how well they are performing a task or series of tasks.

Another essential aspect of motivating employees to learn is to provide **feedback**. With some tasks, feedback occurs naturally. For example, in baseball, a batter receives feedback on his swing by seeing how hard and far the ball travels. For other tasks, however, judging the correctness of a behavior without feedback is difficult. For example, if you write a term paper for this class and get a C, your next term paper will probably not improve unless you have been provided feedback about what was right and wrong with the previous paper.

The same is true for training in industry. Our electronics assembler needs feedback early in the training process to know if the winding is tight enough, if there is an easier way to wind the coil, or if the winding is equally distributed on the coil. A balance, however, must be maintained between giving too little and too much feedback. As shown in Figure 8.3, the employee will not learn if too little feedback is given. However, too much or overly detailed feedback causes frustration, and the employee will not learn at an optimal level.

Negative feedback Telling employees what they are doing incorrectly in order to improve their performance of a task.

A final consideration for feedback concerns what type of feedback to give. Research and common sense agree that positive feedback should be given when an employee correctly performs a task during training. Praise provides an incentive to continue correct behavior. But if an employee is not performing a task correctly, should he receive **negative feedback**? Probably, even though negative feedback is more complicated than positive feedback. Negative feedback should probably also be accompanied by specific suggestions for how the employee can improve performance.

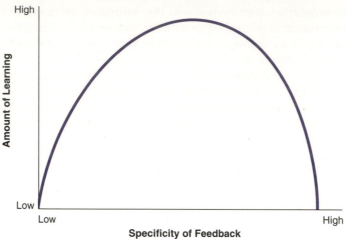

Figure 8.3

Relationship Between Feedback Specificity and Learning

Source: Adapted from Blum and Naylor (1968).

Ensuring Transfer of Training

Transfer of training The extent to which behavior learned in training will be performed on the job.

When an organization spends time and money on training, it expects that the knowledge and skills will be transferred to the job. Unfortunately, this is often not the case (Broad, 2000). There are several strategies for increasing the **transfer of training** to the workplace.

Use Realistic Training Programs

Research in learning has indicated that the more similar the training situation is to the actual job situation, the more effective training will be. This principle is extremely important when a training program is being chosen or designed. For example, if a restaurant is training its employees to wait on tables, the training will be more effective if the employees can practice in an environment that is similar to that encountered when they actually work. This realism might even include "customers" complaining and changing their orders.

An excellent example of making training more realistic comes from the French police. After examining the use of force by officers, Contournet (2004) found that officers most often use their weapons at night, when they are tired after many hours on their shift. Training in use of weapons, however, was conducted in the morning, when cadets first started their day. To ensure better transfer of training, shooting simulations are now being conducted during both the day and the evening hours.

Employees will also be motivated to apply what they learned in training if the training program has a reputation among them as being effective and useful (Switzer, Nagy, & Mullins, 2005). This is not surprising given that employees talk with one another about training, and when they find a training program useful (or not), they certainly pass that information on to other employees.

Have Opportunities to Practice Work-Related Behavior During the Training

Transfer of training is increased by having the trainee practice the desired behavior as much as possible. Such practice is especially important for tasks that will not be performed

Overlearning Practicing a task even after it has been mastered in order to retain learning.

on a daily basis after training has been completed. For example, if a firefighter is learning to perform CPR, he must overlearn the task through constant practice. This **overlearning** is essential because it may be months before the firefighter will practice what he has learned. In contrast, once our electronics assembler learns a task during training, it is time for him to move to another task. Overlearning is not necessary for the coil winder because he will perform the task every hour once training has been completed.

The term *overlearning* does not have the same meaning in training that it has on most college campuses. In training, overlearning means practicing a task even after it has been successfully learned. Many students, however, think of overlearning as the negative consequence of "studying too hard." Although it is commonly believed that one can study too hard and "overlearn" the material, research does not support the conclusion that this type of overlearning occurs or has negative consequences. Therefore, no one will be hurt by studying a little longer. In fact, a meta-analysis by Driskell, Willis, and Copper (1992) indicates that overlearning significantly increases retention of training material.

Finally, to further increase the transfer of training, practice in as many different situations as possible should be provided. For example, we might have our electronics assembler wind coils as fast as possible, wind them slowly, and wind them in various sizes. In this way, the employee will be better able to deal with any changes that occur in the job.

Provide Employees with the Opportunity to Apply Their Training

For information learned in training to transfer to behavior on the job, employees must be given the opportunity and encouraged to apply what they have learned (Broad, 2000; Ford, Quiñones, Sego, & Sorra, 1992; Tracey, Tannenbaum, & Kavanagh, 1995). Employees are more likely to be given opportunities to perform what they learned if their supervisor perceives them to be competent and the organizational climate is supportive (Baldwin & Ford, 1988; Ford et al., 1992). Though this seems obvious, research indicates that many employers are neither supportive nor provide opportunities for employees to apply what is learned—especially if the training was in the form of employees going to school to work on a degree (Posner, Hall, & Munson, 1991). This lack of opportunity can have negative consequences: In a study of over 9,000 employees, Benson, Finegold, and Mohrman (2004) found that employees who were promoted after receiving a graduate degree (given the chance to use their new knowledge) were less likely to turn over than employees who completed their degrees but were not promoted.

One other method for getting employees to apply what they have learned in training is to train all the employees in a work area (team) at the same time. One advantage of doing this is that because all employees have been trained, they can help and encourage each other. That is, if one employee is not properly performing a task, he or she can be coached by another employee. Furthermore, if all employees are applying what they have learned, it sets the proper atmosphere for new employees as well as for employees tempted to go back to the old way of doing things.

Ensure Management Is Supportive of the Training

An important factor in employee motivation to apply training is the atmosphere set by management. That is, employees are most likely to apply their new knowledge and skills if supervisors encourage and reward them to do so.

A good example of the importance of management support can be found at a particular fast-food restaurant. The employees at two restaurants owned by the same company were given customer service training. At one of the restaurants, the training clearly had an effect, as customer complaints were down and secret-shopper scores were up.

At another of the restaurants, there were no changes in complaints or secret-shopper scores. What made the difference? At one restaurant, the supervisor set goals, provided feedback to the employees, actively encouraged them to use their training, and herself modeled the behaviors learned in training. At the other restaurant, the manager hid in the back doing paperwork, a signal to employees that customer service was not important to their boss, regardless of what was emphasized in training.

Have Employees Set Goals

The use of knowledge and skills learned in training can also be encouraged by having employees set goals. For example, tellers at a credit union received two days of training on cross-selling new products. This training included information about new loans and new loan rates, types of retirement accounts, alternative savings plans, and the advantages of using a new "premium" credit card. Each teller might set a goal of daily asking four credit union members if they would like information about one of the new products. Goal setting works best when goals are individually set by each employee, are concrete rather than vague, and are high enough to be challenging but not so difficult as to be impossible. A more comprehensive discussion of goal setting is found in Chapter 9.

Putting It All Together

In this chapter, you have learned many factors that can affect the success of a training program. Before discussing how the success of a training program can be evaluated, let's recap what you have learned. As shown in Figure 8.4, the first issue to consider is whether training is the proper solution to a problem. That is, if employees already possess the necessary skills and knowledge but aren't performing well, the problem is probably one of motivation, communication, or work design rather than a lack of training.

If training is to be the desired intervention, several factors will affect its success:

- Employees must have the skills and abilities to complete the training successfully. For example, if an employee is not bright enough to learn a computer program or doesn't have the dexterity to perform intricate microelectronics assembly, no amount of training will improve his performance.
- There should be minimal outside factors (e.g., work or family problems) that might distract the employee and keep him from concentrating on the training program.
- Employees must be motivated to learn. That is, they must perceive that training is needed, that the training program meets their expectations, that they have the ability to complete the training (self-efficacy), and that there will be some reward (e.g., pay, career advancement) for performing well.
- The training method (e.g., programmed instruction, behavioral modeling, lecture) must be a good match for the employee's learning style, ability, and personality.
- The training method must be a good match for the type of material being learned (e.g., knowledge vs. a physical skill).
- The training program must allow for goal setting, positive feedback, distributed practice, overlearning, and the chance to practice and apply the material learned (transfer of training).
- There must be an opportunity and encouragement to use the newly acquired knowledge at work.

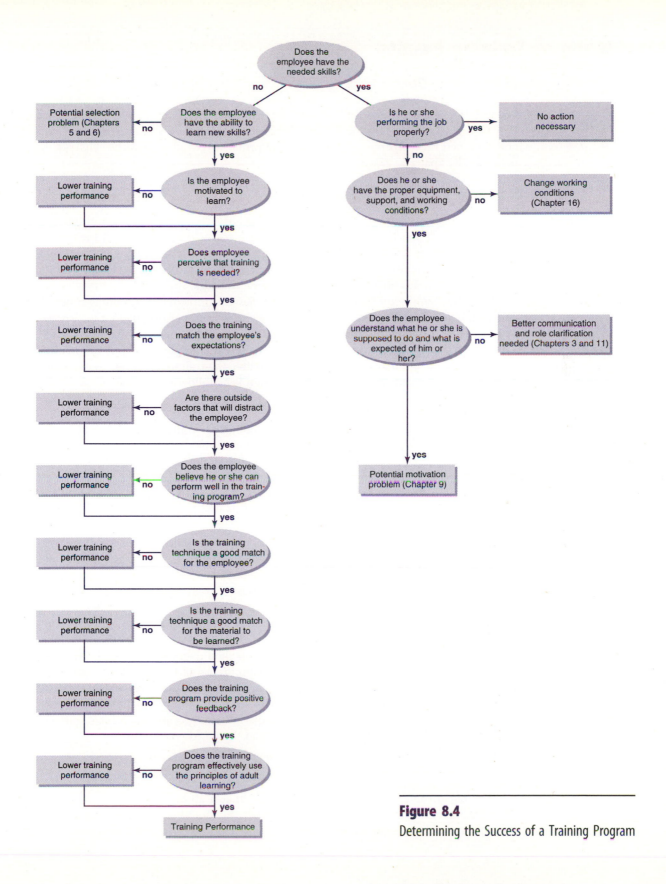

Figure 8.4

Determining the Success of a Training Program

Evaluation of Training Results

As discussed in Chapter 1, one important characteristic of industrial psychology is its reliance on research. Evaluating training results is a good example of this reliance. Because training programs can be costly in both time and money, it is essential that they be evaluated to determine if they can be improved, should continue to be offered, and whether they significantly increase performance or affect positive changes in behavior (Kirkpatrick, 2000).

Research Designs for Evaluation

There are many ways to evaluate the effectiveness of a training program, and two factors differentiate the various methods. The first involves *practicality*, and the second is concerned with *experimental rigor*. Although scientifically rigorous research designs are preferred, their use is not always possible. Yet a practical research design without scientific rigor yields little confidence in research findings.

The most simple and practical of research designs implements a training program and then determines whether significant change is seen in performance of job knowledge. To use this method, performance or job knowledge must be measured twice. The first measurement, a **pretest**, is taken before the implementation of training. The second measurement, a **posttest**, is taken after the training program is complete. A diagram of this simple pretest–posttest design is as follows:

Pretest A measure of job performance or knowledge taken before the implementation of a training program.

Posttest A measure of job performance or knowledge taken after a training program has been completed.

$$\text{Pretest} \rightarrow \text{Training} \rightarrow \text{Posttest}$$

Although this method is fairly simple, its findings are difficult to interpret because there is no control group against which the results can be compared. That is, suppose a significant difference in performance is seen between the pretest and the posttest. If a training program has occurred between the two tests, it would be tempting to credit the training for the increase. The increase, however, may have resulted from other factors, such as changes in machinery, in motivation caused by nontraining factors, or in managerial style or philosophy.

Likewise, suppose no significant increase in performance is observed between pretest and posttest. The natural conclusion might be that the training program did not work. Without a control group, that interpretation is not necessarily correct. The same changes noted above for an increase may have caused a decrease in performance in this second case. Thus, it is possible that the training program actually did increase performance but that other factors reduced it, which resulted in no net gain in performance from training.

To overcome these problems, a control group should be used (Kearns, 2001). For training purposes, a control group consists of employees who will be tested and treated in the same manner as the experimental group, except that they will not receive training. The control group will be subject to the same policy, machinery, and economic conditions as the employees in the experimental group who receive training. The diagram for a pretest/posttest control group design looks like this:

Experimental group: $\text{Pretest} \rightarrow \text{Training} \rightarrow \text{Posttest}$
Control group: $\text{Pretest} \rightarrow \qquad\qquad \text{Posttest}$

The big advantage this second design has is that it allows a researcher to look at the training effect after controlling for outside factors. For example, after going through a training program, employees at R. R. Donnelley & Sons increased their annual commissions by $22,000, and the company increased profits by $34 million. The company was obviously pleased but was worried that the increased performance could have been due to something other than training. So it compared the results with a control group of employees who had not received training. The commissions of the control employees increased by $7,000 over the same period. Thus, the net effect of the training was still sizable—$15,000 per employee—but not as high as the $22,000 originally thought. The control group allowed the company to control for such factors as increased sales agent experience and new company promotions (Montebello & Haga, 1994).

Even though this design is an improvement on the first, it too has its drawbacks. First, except for training manipulation, it is almost impossible to treat a control group the same as the experimental group. Control groups often consist of workers at other plants or on other shifts at the same plant. Such groups are used because there often is no alternative. But the fact that they are in different environments reduces confidence in the research findings.

Even if employees in the same plant on the same shift can be randomly split into control and experimental groups, problems will still exist. The most glaring of these involves the possibility that because the two groups are close to one another, the training effect for the experimental group will spill over to the control group. Employees in the control group also may resent not being chosen for training. This resentment alone may lead to a decrease in performance by employees in the control group. Finally, it is possible that the untrained employees will pressure the newly trained employees to revert to the "old way" of doing things.

With both of the above designs, the pretest itself presents a problem. That is, the mere taking of a test may itself lead to increases in performance. Because of this, a rather complicated method called the **Solomon four-groups design** can be used (Campbell & Stanley, 1963). With this design, one group will undergo training but will not take the pretest, a second group will undergo training but will take the pretest, a third group will not undergo training but will take the pretest, and a fourth group will neither undergo training nor take the pretest. The diagram for this design is as follows:

Group 1		Training → Posttest
Group 2	Pretest →	Training → Posttest
Group 3	Pretest →	Posttest
Group 4		Posttest

This design allows a researcher not only to control for outside effects, but also to control for any pretest effect. This is the most scientifically rigorous of the research designs used to evaluate training, but even this has a serious drawback: It is often not practical. That is, four groups of employees must be used, two of which do not receive training. Thus, to use this design at one organization or plant, ideally a relatively large number of employees must be available and kept from discussing the training with one another.

Evaluation Criteria

In the previous section, we discussed research designs for evaluating training. In each design, a pretest and posttest were included. This section will discuss the types of criteria that can be used for these pretests and posttests. There are six levels at which training effectiveness can be measured: content validity, employee reactions,

Solomon four-groups design An extensive method of evaluating the effectiveness of training with the use of pretests, posttests, and control groups.

employee learning, application of training, business impact, and return on investment (Phillips & Stone, 2002).

Content Validity

At times, the only way that training can be evaluated is by comparing training content with the knowledge, skills, and abilities required to perform a job. In other words, the **content validity** of the training can be examined. For example, if a job analysis indicates that knowledge of electronic circuitry is necessary to perform a job, then a seminar that is designed to teach this knowledge would have content validity. Although content analysis may ensure that a training program is job related, it still does not indicate whether a particular training method is effective. But if a training program is content valid and is conducted by a professional trainer who can *document* previous success with the method in other organizations, it may be a safe assumption that the training program will be successful. Keep in mind, however, that making such an assumption is acceptable only when actually evaluating the effect of training is not possible because there are too few employees for a proper analysis or there are financial or political constraints on conducting a proper evaluation.

Employee Reactions

Employee reactions A method of evaluating training in which employees are asked their opinions of a training program.

The most commonly used method to evaluate training is measuring **employee reactions** to the training (Sitzmann, Brown, Casper, Ely, & Zimmerman, 2008). Employee reactions involve asking employees if they enjoyed the training and learned from the training. These ratings tend to be most influenced by the trainer's style and the degree of interaction in the training program, but are also influenced by the motivation of the trainee prior to training as well as perceptions of organizational support for the training (Sitzmann et al., 2008). Employee reactions are important because employees will not have confidence in the training and will not be motivated to use it if they do not like the training process. However, even though positive employee reactions are necessary for training to be successful, positive employee reactions do not mean that training will lead to changes in knowledge or performance (Pfau & Kay, 2002b).

Because trainee reactions constitute the lowest level of training evaluation, they can often be misleading. For example, most seminars conducted by outside consultants are informative and well presented, so employee reactions are almost always positive, even though the training may not actually affect knowledge or future performance. For example, as shown in Table 8.3, in a meta-analysis by Alliger, Tannenbaum, Bennett, Traver, and Shotland (1997), employee reactions had only a small correlation with learning and application of training.

Employee Learning

Employee learning Evaluating the effectiveness of a training program by measuring how much employees learned from it.

Instead of using employee reactions as the criterion in evaluating training performance, actual **employee learning** can usually be measured. That is, if a training program is designed to increase employee knowledge of communication techniques, then creating a test to determine whether an employee actually learned is possible. This test will be administered before training and then again after the training has been completed. The measurements that will be used for the pretest and posttest, as with selection tests, must be both reliable and valid. Thus, if the purpose of a training program is to increase job knowledge, an appropriate job knowledge test must be constructed or purchased. A trainer can spend a great deal of time creating a training

Table 8.3 Correlations Among Training Evaluation Criteria

	Employee Reactions		Measures of Learning			Application of Training
	E	U	IR	LTR	SD	AT
Employee Reactions						
Enjoyed the training (E)	(.82)	.34	.02		.03	.07
Thought it was useful (U)		(.86)	.26		.03	.18
Measures of Learning						
Immediate retention (IR)			(.77)	.35	.18	.11
Long-term retention (LTR)				(.58)	.14	.08
Skill demonstration (SD)					(.85)	.18
Application of Training (AT)						(.86)

Note: Reliabilities are in parentheses.

Source: Adapted from the meta-analysis by Alliger, Tannenbaum, Bennett, Traver, and Shotland (1997).

program and evaluating its effectiveness, but the whole training effort will be wasted if the measure used to evaluate effectiveness is no good.

The restaurant industry provides many examples of evaluating training effectiveness through employee learning. At Claim Jumper Restaurants, servers must pass a 100-item menu test before they are released from training. At Rock Bottom Restaurants, learning is measured by requiring new employees to obtain written statements from their peers verifying that they have mastered their new duties; 20% do not perform well enough to get the required verification. To make the testing process more fun, Bugaboo Creek Steak Houses hold scavenger hunts to ensure that trainees know where everything is located (Zuber, 1996).

At times, reliable and valid measures of training effectiveness are difficult to obtain. Perhaps a good example of this is seen with the human relations seminars that are common to training programs. Typically, an outside consultant conducts a seminar on a topic such as "better communication skills" or "calming irate customers." A seminar may run from two hours to two days in length. Once completed, however, it is important to measure the effectiveness of the seminar training.

Application of Training

Another criterion for evaluating the effectiveness of training is the degree of **application of training**, or the extent to which employees actually can use the learned material. Learning and memorizing new material is one thing, and applying it is another. For example, if employees learn how to deal with angry customers, their ability to apply this material can be measured by observing how they treat an angry customer while they are actually working. Application of training is often measured though supervisor ratings or through the use of the secret shoppers discussed in Chapter 7.

Business Impact

The fifth criterion that can be used to evaluate a training program's effectiveness is **business impact**. Business impact is determined by evaluating whether the goals for training were met. For example, a restaurant such as Buffalo Wild Wings conducts a

Application of training Measurement of the effectiveness of training by determining the extent to which employees apply the material taught in a training program.

Business impact A method of evaluating the effectiveness of training by determining whether the goals of the training were met.

training program designed to increase sales of top-shelf liquor. A week after the training, if sales of liquors such as Knob Creek bourbon and Absolut vodka increase, and sales of liquors such as Pepe Lopez tequila and Aristocrat vodka decrease, the training would be considered successful because it has had the desired business impact.

Return on Investment

The sixth criterion for evaluating the success of a training program is **return on investment (ROI)**. That is, after accounting for the cost of the training, did the organization actually save money? For example, imagine that a bank trains its tellers to cross-sell Visa cards. The tellers rate the training session as being enjoyable (employee reactions), all of the employees pass a test on sales techniques (knowledge), and sales *attempts* increase by 30% (application). The ROI approach would then ask, "If we spent $5,000 training the tellers, how much more revenue was brought in as a result of the training?" If the answer to the question is more than the amount spent on training, then the program would be considered a success. For example, Parry (2000) demonstrated that training employees how to conduct effective meetings at Southwest Industries cost $15,538 to implement but saved the organization $820,776 in the first year after the training. To apply what you have learned about evaluating training programs, complete Exercises 8.4 and 8.5 in your workbook.

ON THE JOB   **Applied Case Study**

Training at Pal's Sudden Service

Headquartered in Kingsport, Tennessee, Pal's Sudden Service is a quick-service restaurant chain with over 20 locations. Pal's first franchise opened in 1956 with four items: Sauceburgers, Frenchie Fries, milk shakes, and coke. Customers walked up to the outside counter to place and receive their orders. Pal's first drive-through opened in 1985. Although certainly not as large as the McDonald's or Burger King chains, Pal's has a record of excellence including being the first restaurant to receive the prestigious Malcolm Baldrige National Quality Award and the first organization to win the Tennessee Excellence Award more than once. Pal's obsession with high quality might best be demonstrated by their use of the Hoshizaki ice cube shape that causes ice to melt more slowly so that their iced tea will stay cool all day. Pal's takes great pride in quickly getting orders to customers without mistakes. This is a difficult task given the fast pace of the business. Pal's created a unique training program that reduced employee errors from one error every 450 transactions to one mistake for every 3,360 transactions. Furthermore, service time was reduced from 23 seconds to 18 seconds. How did Pal's make such progress? Primarily through training, assessment, and feedback. Each hourly employee goes through 120 hours of training. This extensive training allows employees to be assigned to any of three positions so that they can easily fill in where most needed. The training program includes individual face-to-face training as well as e-learning. Trainees are assessed on their progress and go through additional training if they do not score high enough on the training tests. Training does not stop after the initial training period. Store managers constantly coach employees and every employee gets two or three pop quizzes at the beginning of their shift. The quizzes must be turned in by the end of the shift, and employees are allowed to look up information or ask other employees for answers. If they get less than a perfect score, they go through additional training.

- If you were in charge of training, how would you develop a training program that would reduce the number of transaction errors?

- How would you evaluate the success of your training program?

To see how Pal's handled this case, use the link on your text website. To read more about Pal's unique organizational climate, visit their website at www.palsweb.com.

The Ethics of Using Role-Play in Employee Trainings

As you learned in this chapter, role-plays are good teaching tools when training employees on what is called the "soft skills" of the workplace. "Soft skills" refer to the interpersonal skills, and include skills pertaining to such areas as conflict management, stress management, customer service skills, communication skills, and mediation skills.

The philosophy behind role-plays is that they should serve as a "rehearsal" of actual situations that could occur in the workplace. Trainees are given situations and asked to act them out in front of the other trainees. Sometimes, selected participants act out an example of the "wrong" way to do something, followed by a reenactment of the "right" way to do it. After the situation is done the "wrong" way, participants are usually asked what was wrong and how would they handle the situation differently. Then, the same situation would be acted out, only in the right way.

Sometimes, role-plays consist of trainees acting out a situation based on what they *think* is the right way. For example, when employees are being trained on how to manage conflict, the trainer will spend some time lecturing on the steps to take to manage conflict. Then, trainees are given a scenario to role-play and asked to apply what they have learned to that scenario. After it has been acted out, trainees are then asked to critique how well the role-player did and how that role-player could improve. The idea behind doing role-plays this way is that it gives people an opportunity to practice what they learn in a safe environment, before they have to actually use the skills in a real life situation. Role-plays provide practice and immediate feedback from others that will improve the role-player's performance in actual situations.

The ethical concerns of using role-plays are these: In many training programs, participating in role-plays is mandatory. That is, the trainee cannot say "I don't want to do it." When the training is comprised of just a few participants, usually every participant is asked to act out a scenario in front of the others. Many people do not like to participate in role-plays because it makes them nervous and, at times, terrifies them. So critics would ask: Is it ethical to put people through something with such a negative impact?

Another ethical concern is that role-plays can often be somewhat challenging. For example, a professor at one university, when doing training in his management class, pretends that he is an employee who has a body odor problem. This is a situation that occurs in many organizations! Students are then asked to role-play how, if they were this person's supervisor, they would tell this person of his body odor and the impact it is having at work on other employees. The professor, in an attempt to make it even more real-life, often will yell and even physically push the student in "anger." His thought is that there are many times when employees do get very upset when given this type of evaluation. Many students come out of that role-play upset and even scared! Trainers who use this type of forceful role-play say that in order for people to get comfortable with using their soft skills, they must be faced with scenarios that have actually occurred in organizations and that may occur in one of the organizations in which they may work.

Proponents of role-plays ask how ethical it is NOT to make trainees practice these skills before using them. Merely sitting in a room listening to a trainer and doing exercises is not enough to properly prepare employees for what they might face in real-life situations. For example, just reading or listening how to manage an upset customer does not guarantee that trainees will be able to apply those skills once they leave the training. But, if you make them practice those skills via role-plays, that will better ensure that they will be able to handle the situation.

What Do You Think?

- What are some of the other ethical concerns of using role-plays to teach skills?

- Do you think organizations should implement policies on the type of strategies trainers can use when conducting training?

- Should role-plays be a mandatory part of training?

Chapter Summary

In this chapter you learned:

- The first step in the training process is to conduct a training needs assessment that includes an organizational analysis, task analysis, and person analysis.
- Training methods take many forms. Classroom learning techniques include seminars, audiovisual aids, programmed instruction, case studies, and critical incidents. Sample job performance techniques include simulation, role-play, behavior modeling, and job rotation. Informal training techniques include apprentice training, coaching, and performance appraisal.
- Such psychological principles as modeling, distributed practice, and transfer of training must be considered when conducting a training program.
- It is important to evaluate training success by measuring trainee attitudes, knowledge, ability to apply newly learned material, and improved performance.

Questions for Review

1. In what type of situations is training most useful? Least useful?
2. What motivates employees to learn during training sessions?
3. What would be the best training technique for teaching computer skills? What would be the best technique for customer service skills?
4. Do all new employees model the behavior of more experienced employees? Why or why not?
5. Why would measures of employees' attitudes about a training program and measures of actual learning be different?

Media Resources and Learning Tools

- Visit our website. Go to www.cengage.com/psychology/aamodt, where you will find online resources directly linked to your book, including chapter-by-chapter quizzing, flashcards, crossword puzzles, application activities, and more.
- Want more practice applying industrial/organizational psychology? Check out the *I/O Applications Workbook*. This workbook (keyed to your textbook) offers engaging, high-interest activities to help you reinforce the important concepts presented in the text.

© Chris Ryan/OJO Images/Getty Images

Learning Objectives

➡ Know the types of people who tend to be more motivated than others

➡ Learn how to motivate people through goal setting

➡ Understand the importance of providing feedback

➡ Be able to use operant conditioning principles to motivate employees

➡ Understand the importance of treating employees fairly

➡ Know the types of individual and organizational incentives that best motivate employees

Motivation The force that drives an employee to perform well.

Once an organization has selected and trained its employees, it is important that employees be both motivated by and satisfied with their jobs. Industrial psychologists generally define work **motivation** as the internal force that drives a worker to action as well as the external factors that encourage that action (Locke & Latham, 2002). Ability and skill determine whether a worker *can* do the job, but motivation determines whether the worker *will* do it properly.

As you can imagine, measuring actual levels of motivation can be difficult. As a result, other than *asking* employees about their motivation levels, researchers use behaviors such as those shown in Table 9.1 that *imply* high levels of motivation. There are, of course, problems with using such behaviors as proxies for motivation. For example, an employee might be highly motivated but have a low level of performance because he lacks the ability to do the job. Likewise, an employee might be highly motivated to attend work but suffers an illness that keeps her from attending.

Although actually testing the relationship between motivation and performance is also difficult, psychologists generally agree that increased worker motivation results in increased job performance.

In this chapter, we will explore several theories that seek to explain why workers are motivated by their jobs. None of the theories completely explains motivation, but each is valuable in that it suggests ways to increase employee performance. Thus, even though a theory itself may not be completely supported by research, the resulting suggestions have generally led to increased performance. As you will see in this chapter, the various theories suggest that employees will be highly motivated if

- they have a personality that predisposes them to be motivated;
- their expectations have been met;
- the job and the organization are consistent with their values;

Table 9.1   Work Behaviors that Imply Motivation

High-Performance Level
  Excellent supervisor ratings
  High productivity
  High quality
  Low levels of wasted materials
  Salary
  Number of promotions

Exemplary Attendance
  Not missing work
  Arriving to work early
  Staying late at work

Organizational Citizenship
  Volunteering for extra duties
  Helping coworkers
  Making suggestions for organizational improvement
  Skipping lunch to complete a project

Self-Improvement Efforts
  Attending voluntary training
  Participating during training
  Accepting performance feedback

- the employees have been given achievable goals;
- the employees receive feedback on their goal attainment;
- the organization rewards them for achieving their goals;
- the employees perceive they are being treated fairly; and
- their coworkers demonstrate a high level of motivation.

To get you thinking about motivation in your own life, complete Exercise 9.1 in your workbook.

Is an Employee Predisposed to Being Motivated?

Psychologists have postulated that some employees are more predisposed to being motivated than are others. That is, some employees come to most jobs with a tendency to be motivated, whereas others come with the tendency to be unmotivated. You can probably think of people you know who always appear to be motivated and "gung-ho," and you can probably think of others whom no amount of money would motivate. Researchers have found four individual differences that are most related to work motivation: personality, self-esteem, an intrinsic motivation tendency, and need for achievement.

Personality

If you recall from Chapter 5, most psychologists believe that there are five main personality dimensions: Openness to experience, conscientiousness, extraversion, agreeableness, and stability. As shown in Table 9.2, meta-analyses have found that several of these dimensions are related to behaviors suggesting high levels of motivation. Conscientiousness is the best personality predictor of work performance, **organizational citizenship behavior (OCB)**, and academic performance; stability is most associated with salary and setting high goals; and extraversion is most highly correlated with the number of promotions received.

Self-Esteem

Self-esteem is the extent to which a person views himself as valuable and worthy. In the 1970s, Korman (1970, 1976) theorized that employees high in self-esteem are more motivated and will perform better than employees low in self-esteem. According to Korman's **consistency theory**, there is a positive correlation between self-esteem and performance. That is, employees who feel good about themselves are motivated to perform better at work than employees who do not feel that they are valuable and worthy people. Consistency theory takes the relationship between self-esteem and motivation one step further by stating that employees with high self-esteem actually *desire* to perform at high levels and employees with low self-esteem desire to perform at low levels. In other words, employees try to perform at levels consistent with their self-esteem level. This desire to perform at levels consistent with self-esteem is compounded by the fact that employees with low self-esteem tend to underestimate their actual ability and performance (Lindeman, Sundvik, & Rouhiainen, 1995). Thus, low-self-esteem employees will desire to perform at lower levels than their actual abilities would allow.

Organizational citizenship behaviors (OCBs) Behaviors that are not part of an employee's job but which make the organization a better place to work (e.g., helping others, staying late).

Self-esteem The extent to which a person views him or herself as a valuable and worthy individual.

Consistency theory Korman's theory that employees will be motivated to perform at levels consistent with their levels of self-esteem.

Table 9.2 Relationship Between Big Five Personality Dimensions and Behaviors that Suggest Motivation

| | Potential Indicator of Motivation | | | | | | |
Dimension	Performance	Salary	Promotions	Attendance	OCB	Academic Performance	Goal Setting
Stability	0.15[b]	0.12[d]	0.11[d]	−0.04[c]	.12[e]	.02[f]	.29[a]
Extraversion	0.09[b]	0.10[d]	0.18[d]	−0.08[c]		−.01[f]	.15[a]
Openness	0.06[b]	0.04[d]	0.01[d]	0.00[c]		.12[f]	.18[a]
Agreeableness	0.12[b]	−0.10[d]	−0.05[d]	−0.04[c]	.13[e]	.07[f]	−.29[a]
Conscientiousness	0.24[b]	0.07[d]	0.06[d]	0.06[c]	.18[e]	.22[f]	.28[a]

[a]Judge and Ilies (2002).

[b]Hurtz and Donovan (2003).

[c]Salgado (2002).

[d]Ng, Eby, Sorenson, and Feldman (2005).

[e]Lodi-Smith and Roberts (2007).

[f]Poropat (2009).

Chronic self-esteem The positive or negative way in which a person views himself or herself as a whole.

Situational self-esteem The positive or negative way in which a person views him or herself in a particular situation.

Socially influenced self-esteem The positive or negative way in which a person views him or herself based on the expectations of others.

The theory becomes somewhat complicated in that there are three types of self-esteem. **Chronic self-esteem** is a person's overall feeling about himself. **Situational self-esteem** (also called *self-efficacy*) is a person's feeling about himself in a particular situation such as operating a machine or talking to other people. **Socially influenced self-esteem** is how a person feels about himself on the basis of the expectations of others. All three types of self-esteem are important to job performance. For example, an employee might be low in chronic self-esteem but very high in situational self-esteem. That is, a computer programmer might believe he is a terrible person whom nobody likes (low chronic self-esteem) but feel that he can program a computer better than anyone else (high situational self-esteem).

If consistency theory is true, we should find that employees with high self-esteem are more motivated, perform better, and rate their own performance as being higher than employees with low self-esteem. Research supports these predictions: Ilardi, Leone, Kasser, and Ryan (1993) found significant correlations between self-esteem and motivation, and a meta-analysis by Judge and Bono (2001) found a significant relationship between self-esteem and job performance ($p = .26$).

On the basis of consistency theory, we should be able to improve performance by increasing an employee's self-esteem, and the results of a meta-analysis of 43 studies indicate that interventions designed to increase self-esteem or self-efficacy can greatly increase performance (McNatt, Campbell, & Hirschfeld, 2005). Organizations can theoretically do this in three ways: self-esteem workshops, experience with success, and supervisor behavior.

Self-Esteem Workshops

To increase self-esteem, employees can attend workshops in which they are given insights into their strengths. It is thought that these insights raise self-esteem by showing employees that they have several strengths and are good people. For example, in a self-esteem training program called The Enchanted Self (Holstein, 1997), employees try to increase their self-esteem by learning how to think positively, discovering their positive qualities that may have gone unnoticed, and sharing their positive qualities with others.

Outdoor experiential training is another approach to increasing self-esteem (Clements, Wagner, & Roland, 1995). In training programs such as Outward Bound or the "ropes course," participants learn that they are emotionally and physically strong enough to be successful and to meet challenges.

Experience with Success

With the experience-with-success approach, an employee is given a task so easy that he will almost certainly succeed. It is thought that this success increases self-esteem, which should increase performance, which further increases self-esteem, which further increases performance, and so on. This method is based loosely on the principle of the **self-fulfilling prophecy**, which states that an individual will perform as well or as poorly as he expects to perform. In other words, if an individual believes he is intelligent, he should do well on tests. If he thinks he is dumb, he should do poorly. So if an employee believes he will always fail, the only way to break the vicious cycle is to ensure that he performs well on a task. This relationship between self-expectations and performance is called the **Galatea effect**.

Supervisor Behavior

Another approach to increasing employee self-esteem is to train supervisors to communicate a feeling of confidence in an employee. The idea here is that if an employee feels that a manager has confidence in him, his self-esteem will increase, as will his performance. Such a process is known as the **Pygmalion effect** and has been demonstrated in situations as varied as elementary school classrooms, the workplace, courtrooms, and the military (Rosenthal, 2002). The Pygmalion effect has been portrayed in several motion pictures, such as *My Fair Lady* and *Trading Places*. In contrast, the **Golem effect** occurs when negative expectations of an individual cause a decrease in that individual's actual performance (Babad, Inbar, & Rosenthal, 1982; Davidson & Eden, 2000).

Two meta-analyses have shown that the Pygmalion effect greatly influences performance. The meta-analysis by McNatt (2000) found an overall effect size of 1.13, and the meta-analysis by Kierein and Gold (2001) found an overall effect size of 0.81. If you recall the discussion in Chapter 1, effect sizes of this magnitude are considered to be very large. The Pygmalion and Golem effects can be explained by the idea that our expectations of others' performance lead us to treat them differently (Rosenthal, 1994). That is, if we think someone will do a poor job, we will probably treat that person in ways that bring about that result. If a supervisor thinks an employee is intrinsically motivated, he treats the employee in a less controlling way. The result of this treatment is that the employee actually becomes more intrinsically motivated (Pelletier & Vallerand, 1996). Thus, when an employee becomes aware of others' expectations and matches his own with them, he will perform in a manner that is consistent with those expectations (Oz & Eden, 1994; Tierney, 1998).

Sandler (1986) argued that our expectations are communicated to employees through such nonverbal cues as head tilting or eyebrow raising and through more overt behaviors such as providing low-expectation employees with less feedback, worse facilities, and less praise than high-expectation employees. He also stated that employees are quick to pick up on these cues. Along with Korman (1970) and Rosenthal (1994), Sandler argued that employees then adjust their behaviors to be consistent with our expectations and in a way that is self-sustaining.

Though we know that the Pygmalion effect is true, efforts to teach supervisors to communicate positive expectations have not been successful. On the basis of seven field experiments, Eden (1998) concluded that there was little support for the notion that teaching the "Pygmalion leadership style" would change the way supervisors treated their employees and thus increase employee self-esteem.

Given that consistency theory does have some reasonable research support, the next concern is how it can be used to increase employee performance. If employees do indeed respond to their managers' expectations, then it becomes reasonable to predict that managers who communicate positive and optimistic feelings to their employees will lead employees to perform at higher levels. A good example of such management behavior can be found in a study that increased the self-expectations of a group of auditors employed in four accounting firms (McNatt & Judge, 2004). Half of the new auditors (the experimental group) interviewed with a company representative who told them that they had been selected from a competitive applicant pool, praised them for being highly skilled, and reminded them of their previous accomplishments. The other half of the new auditors (the control group) did not receive this information. The results of the study indicated that the positive interview increased self-efficacy levels, motivation, and job performance, although the effect on performance went away after 3 months. To determine your level of self-esteem, complete Exercise 9.2 in your workbook.

Intrinsic Motivation

Intrinsic motivation Work motivation in the absence of such external factors as pay, promotion, and coworkers.

When people are **intrinsically motivated**, they will seek to perform well because they either enjoy performing the actual tasks or enjoy the challenge of successfully completing the task. When they are extrinsically motivated, they don't particularly enjoy the tasks but are motivated to perform well to receive some type of reward or to avoid negative consequences (Deci & Ryan, 1985). People who are intrinsically motivated don't need external rewards such as pay or praise. In fact, being paid for something they enjoy may reduce their satisfaction and intrinsic motivation (Deci, Koestner, & Ryan, 1999).

An interesting debate has formed between researchers who believe that rewards reduce intrinsic motivation and those who don't. A meta-analysis by Cameron and Pierce (1994) concluded that research does not support the idea that rewards reduce intrinsic motivation. However, the meta-analysis has been criticized by Ryan and Deci (1996) as misrepresenting the data. Thus, it appears that this debate will continue.

Extrinsic motivation Work motivation that arises from such nonpersonal factors as pay, coworkers, and opportunities for advancement.

Work Preference Inventory (WPI) A measure of an individual's orientation toward intrinsic versus extrinsic motivation.

Individual orientations toward intrinsic and **extrinsic motivation** can be measured by the **Work Preference Inventory (WPI)** (Amabile, Hill, Hennessey, & Tighe, 1994). The WPI yields scores on two dimensions of intrinsic motivation (enjoyment, challenge) and two dimensions of extrinsic motivation (compensation, outward orientation). To determine your own level of intrinsic and extrinsic motivation, complete the WPI found in Exercise 9.3 in your workbook.

Needs for Achievement and Power

Need for achievement According to trait theory, the extent to which a person desires to be successful.

Need for affiliation The extent to which a person desires to be around other people.

A theory developed by McClelland (1961) suggests that employees differ in the extent to which they are motivated by the need for achievement, affiliation, and power. Employees who have a strong **need for achievement** are motivated by jobs that are challenging and over which they have some control, whereas employees who have minimal achievement needs are more satisfied when jobs involve little challenge and have a high probability of success. In contrast, employees who have a strong **need for affiliation** are motivated by jobs in which they can work with and help other people.

Finally, employees who have a strong **need for power** are motivated by a desire to influence others rather than simply to be successful.

Have the Employee's Values and Expectations Been Met?

Our work motivation and job satisfaction are determined by the discrepancy between what we *want, value,* and *expect* and what the job actually provides. For example, if you enjoy working with people but your job involves working with data, you are not likely to be motivated by or satisfied with your job. Likewise, if you value helping others, yet your job involves selling things people don't really need, you will probably not be motivated to perform well.

Potential discrepancies between what employees want and what the job gives them affect how motivated and satisfied employees will be with their jobs (Knoop, 1994; Rice, Gentile, & McFarlin, 1991). For example, imagine that Jane most values money and Akeem most values flexibility. Both are in jobs that pay well but have set hours and a standard routine. Though the job and the company are the same, one employee (Jane) will be motivated and the other (Akeem) will not be.

Job Expectations

A discrepancy between what an employee expected a job to be like and the reality of the job can affect motivation and satisfaction. For example, a recruiter tells an applicant how much fun employees have at a particular company and about the "unlimited potential" for advancement. After three months on the job, however, the employee has yet to experience the fun and can't find any signs of potential advancement opportunities. Because these expectations have not been met, the employee will probably feel unmotivated.

Employees compare what the organization promised to do for them (e.g., provide a computer, support continued education) with what the organization actually does. If the organization does less than it promised, employees will be less motivated to perform well and will retaliate by doing less than they promised (Morrison & Robinson, 1997).

As you can guess from these examples, it is important that applicants be given a **realistic job preview (RJP)** (a concept that you no doubt remember from Chapter 4). Though being honest about the negative aspects of a job may reduce the applicant pool, it decreases the chances of hiring a person who will later lose motivation or become dissatisfied.

A good example of this comes from an employee who works for a public mental health agency. Prior to accepting her current job, she had worked in the public sector for ten years in a variety of administrative positions. She was excited about her new opportunity because it was a newly created position with what appeared to be excellent opportunities for personal growth. After a year, however, it became clear that the position was clerical, had no opportunity for advancement, and the most important decision she could make involved whether to order pizza or sandwiches for executive meetings. To make matters worse, this aspiring professional was asked to shop for food to serve at meetings and then serve the food to the managers. As you can imagine, she was deeply disappointed and angry at having been misled. Because her role as a single mother did not allow her to quit her job, she vented her dissatisfaction by buying stale doughnuts for breakfast meetings, letting the coffee get cold, and "forgetting" to bring mayonnaise for her supervisor's sandwich—behaviors that could not get her fired but allowed her in a passive-aggressive manner to maintain some form of control in her work life.

Job Characteristics

Job characteristics theory
The theory proposed by Hackman and Oldham that suggests that certain characteristics of a job will make the job more or less satisfying, depending on the particular needs of the worker.

According to **job characteristics theory**, employees desire jobs that are *meaningful,* provide them with the opportunity to be personally responsible for the outcome of their work (*autonomy*), and provide them with *feedback* of the results of their efforts (Hackman & Oldham, 1976). If there is a discrepancy between the extent to which a job provides these three outcomes and an employee's need for these outcomes, the employee will be less motivated.

According to job characteristics theory, jobs will have *motivation potential* if they allow employees to use a variety of skills (*skill variety*) and to connect their efforts to an outcome (*task identification*) which has meaning, is useful, or is appreciated by coworkers as well as by others in society (*task significance*). Take, for example, a job in which a factory worker stitches the company logo on shirts that were created by other workers and in which the quality of the shirts and the logo stitching are evaluated by employees in the quality control department. Because the job does not involve a variety of skills (lacks skill variety), someone else checks the quality of their work (no feedback, low task identification), putting logos on a shirt is probably not appreciated by society (low task significance), and the employee is closely supervised (low autonomy), the job would be considered to have low motivation potential. As shown in Table 9.3, meta-analysis results demonstrate that jobs with a high motivating potential score result in higher levels of employee satisfaction and performance, and lower levels of absenteeism (Fried & Ferris, 1987).

Needs, Values, and Wants

A discrepancy between an employee's needs, values, and wants and what a job offers can also lead to low levels of motivation and satisfaction (Morris & Campion, 2003). Three theories focus on employees' needs and values: Maslow's needs hierarchy, ERG theory, and two-factor theory.

Table 9.3 Results of the Fried and Ferris (1987) Meta-analysis

Job Characteristic	Satisfaction	Performance	Absenteeism
Skill variety	.45	.09	−.24
Task identity	.26	.13	−.15
Task significance	.35	.14	.14
Autonomy	.48	.18	−.29
Job feedback	.43	.22	−.19
Motivating potential score	.63	.22	−.32

Maslow's Needs Hierarchy

Perhaps the most famous theory of motivation was developed by Abraham Maslow (1954, 1970). Maslow believed that employees would be motivated by and satisfied with their jobs at any given point in time if certain needs were met. As Table 9.4 shows, Maslow believed that there are five major types of needs and that these needs are hierarchical—that is, lower-level needs must be satisfied before an individual will be concerned with the next level of needs. It is helpful to look at a **hierarchy** as if it were a staircase that is climbed one step at a time until the top is reached. The same is true of Maslow's hierarchy. Each level is taken one step at a time, and a higher-level need cannot be reached until a lower-level need is satisfied. Maslow's five major needs are discussed next.

Basic Biological Needs. Maslow thought that an individual first seeks to satisfy **basic biological needs** for food, air, water, and shelter. In our case, an individual who does not have a job, is homeless, and is on the verge of starvation will be satisfied with any job as long as it provides for these basic needs. When asked how well they enjoy their job, people at this level might reply, "I can't complain, it pays the bills."

Safety Needs. After basic biological needs have been met, a job that merely provides food and shelter will no longer be satisfying. Employees then become concerned about meeting their **safety needs**. That is, they may work in an unsafe coal mine to earn enough money to ensure their family's survival, but once their family has food and shelter, they will remain satisfied with their jobs only if the workplace is safe.

Safety needs have been expanded to include psychological as well as physical safety. Psychological safety—often referred to as job security—can certainly affect job motivation. For example, public-sector employees often list job security as a main benefit to their jobs—a benefit so strong that they will stay in lower-paying public-sector jobs rather than take higher-paying, yet less secure, jobs in the private sector.

The importance of safety needs was demonstrated in a 2008 survey asking employees about the work factors that were most important to them. The most important factor was job security, followed by benefits, compensation, and feeling safe in the work environment (SHRM, 2008b). Thus three of the top four needs were related to the safety or security factor.

Social Needs. Once the first two need levels have been met, employees will remain motivated by their jobs only when their social needs have been met. **Social needs** involve working with others, developing friendships, and feeling needed. Organizations attempt to satisfy their employees' social needs in a variety of ways. Company

Hierarchy A system arranged by rank.

Basic biological needs The first step in Maslow's needs hierarchy, concerning survival needs for food, air, water, and the like.

Safety needs The second step in Maslow's hierarchy, concerning the need for security, stability, and physical safety.

Social needs The third step in Maslow's hierarchy, concerning the need to interact with other people.

Table 9.4 Comparison of the Maslow, ERG, and Herzberg Theories

Maslow	ERG	Herzberg
Self-actualization	Growth	Motivators
Ego		
Social	Relatedness	Hygiene factors
Safety	Existence	
Physical		

cafeterias provide workers with a place and an opportunity to socialize and meet other employees, company picnics allow families to meet one another, and company sports programs such as bowling teams and softball games provide opportunities for employees to play together in a neutral environment.

It is important that an organization make a conscious effort to satisfy these social needs when a job itself does not encourage social activity. For example, janitors or night watchmen encounter few other people while working. Thus the chance of making new friends is small.

A good friend of mine worked in a large public agency before becoming a writer and working out of her home. Prior to working at home, she had seldom accepted invitations to attend parties or socialize. In her words, "Once I get home, I don't want to see another person." However, now that her only social contact during the day is a one-sided conversation with a three-legged, neurotic cat, she socializes every chance she gets.

Ego needs The fourth step in Maslow's hierarchy, concerning the individual's need for recognition and success.

Ego Needs. When social needs have been satisfied, employees concentrate next on meeting their **ego needs**. These are needs for recognition and success, and an organization can help to satisfy them through praise, awards, promotions, salary increases, publicity, and many other ways. For example, former *Tonight Show* host Johnny Carson once commented that the most prestigious sign at NBC was not the salary of the television star or producer, but rather whether the person had his or her own parking space. Likewise, many organizations use furniture to help satisfy ego needs. The higher the employee's position, the better her office furniture. Similarly, at one engineering firm in Louisville, Kentucky, engineers are not allowed to mount their diplomas or awards on the wall until they receive their professional certification. At the university where I work, faculty, department chairs, deans, and vice presidents are given furniture that is "commensurate with their status." Perhaps this explains the card table and folding chairs in my office!

Self-actualization needs The fifth step in Maslow's hierarchy, concerning the need to realize one's potential.

Self-Actualization Needs. Even when employees have friends, have earned awards, and are making a relatively high salary, they may not be completely motivated by their jobs because their **self-actualization needs** may not have been satisfied yet. These needs are the fifth and final level of Maslow's needs hierarchy (the top level in Table 9.4). Self-actualization might be best defined by the U.S. Army's recruiting slogan "Be all that you can be." An employee striving for self-actualization wants to reach her potential in every task. Thus, employees who have worked with the same machine for 20 years may become dissatisfied with and less motivated by their jobs. They have accomplished all that can be accomplished with that particular machine and now search for a new challenge. If none is available, they may become dissatisfied and unmotivated.

With some jobs, satisfying self-actualization needs is easy. For example, a college professor always has new research to conduct, new classes to teach, and new clients to consult. Thus, the variety of tasks and the new problems encountered provide a constant challenge that can lead to higher motivation.

Other jobs, however, may not satisfy self-actualization needs. A good example is an employee who welds parts on an assembly line. For eight hours a day, forty hours a week, she performs only one task. Boredom and the realization that the job will never change begin to set in. It is no wonder that the employee becomes dissatisfied and loses motivation.

Evaluation of Maslow's Theory

Needs theory A theory based on the idea that employees will be satisfied with jobs that satisfy their needs.

Although Maslow's **needs theory** makes good intuitive sense and has always been popular with managers and marketing analysts, it lost popularity with academicians in the 1970s before making a resurgence in the new millennium (Latham & Pinder, 2005). The lack of popularity was due to three potential problems with the theory. The first concern was that Maslow's five levels may be too many, and that there are actually only two or three levels (Aldefer, 1972). However, some more recent research (Ronen, 2001) suggests that five might actually be the correct number.

A second problem with the theory is that some people do not progress up the hierarchy as Maslow suggests they do. That is, most people move up from the basic biological needs level to safety needs to social needs and so on. Some people, however, have been known to skip levels. For example, bungee jumpers obviously skip the safety-needs level and go straight to satisfying their ego needs. Thus, when exceptions to the hierarchical structure occur, the theory loses support.

Another problem is that the theory predicts that once the needs at one level are satisfied, the next needs level should become most important. Research, however, has shown that this does not necessarily happen (Salancik & Pfeffer, 1977).

Even though Maslow's theory has not been supported by research, it may still be useful. Some of the theory's specific assertions may not be true, but it still provides guidelines that organizations can follow to increase motivation and satisfaction. Providing recognition, enrichment, and a safe workplace *does* increase employee motivation. The validity of this recommendation is probably why Maslow's theory still is widely used by human resources professionals, even though it is not popular with academicians and researchers who prefer more complicated models.

A situation at a major university provides an example of how Maslow's general principles can be used. After years of increasing enrollment and prestige, a scandal at the university caused a rapid decline in enrollment, financial backing, and staff morale. To fix these problems, a new president was hired. His first acts were to announce a "spirit day" each Friday on which employees could dress casually, an increased emphasis on diversity issues, and his intention to start a new sports team. Employee satisfaction and motivation continued to drop, faculty left in great numbers, and millions of dollars were cut from the budget. What went wrong? Among many things, the president's proposals were aimed at Maslow's level three and above, whereas the employees' needs were at level two—that is, "Will this university survive?" and "Will I still have a job next year?"

ERG Theory

ERG theory Aldefer's needs theory, which describes three levels of satisfaction: *existence*, *relatedness*, and *growth*.

Because of the technical problems with Maslow's hierarchy, Aldefer (1972) developed a needs theory that has only three levels. As shown in Table 9.4, the three levels are existence, relatedness, and growth—hence the name **ERG theory**.

Other than the number of levels, the major difference between Maslow's theory and ERG theory is that Aldefer suggested that a person can skip levels. By allowing for such movement, Aldefer has removed one of the biggest problems with Maslow's theory.

Furthermore, Aldefer's theory explains why a higher-level need sometimes does not become more important once a lower-level need has been satisfied. Aldefer believes that for jobs in many organizations, advancement to the next level is not possible because of such factors as company policy or the nature of the job. Thus the path to the next level is blocked, and the employee becomes frustrated and places more importance on the previous level. Perhaps that is why some unions demand more money and benefits for their members rather than job enrichment. They realize that the jobs will always be tedious and that little can be done to improve them. Thus, the previous needs level becomes more important. This idea has received at least some empirical support (Hall & Nougaim, 1968; Salancik & Pfeffer, 1977).

Two-Factor Theory

As shown in Tables 9.4 and 9.5, Herzberg (1966) believed that job-related factors could be divided into two categories—hygiene factors and motivators—thus the name **two-factor theory**. **Hygiene factors** are those job-related elements that result from but do not involve the job itself. For example, pay and benefits are consequences of work but do not involve the work itself. Similarly, making new friends may result from going to work, but it is also not directly involved with the tasks and duties of the job.

Motivators are job elements that *do* concern actual tasks and duties. Examples of motivators would be the level of responsibility, the amount of job control, and the interest that the work holds for the employee. Herzberg believes that hygiene factors are necessary but not sufficient for job satisfaction and motivation. That is, if a hygiene factor is not present at an adequate level (e.g., the pay is too low), the employee will be dissatisfied and less motivated. But if all hygiene factors are represented adequately, the employee's level of satisfaction and motivation will only be neutral. Only the presence of both motivators and hygiene factors can bring job satisfaction and motivation.

Thus, an employee who is paid a lot of money but has no control or responsibility over her job will probably be neither motivated nor unmotivated. But an employee who is not paid enough *will* be unmotivated, even though he may have tremendous control and responsibility over his job. Finally, an employee who is paid well and has control and responsibility will probably be motivated.

Again, Herzberg's is one of those theories that makes sense but has not received strong research support. In general, researchers have criticized the theory because of the methods used to develop the two factors—the idea that factors such as pay can be both hygiene factors and motivators, and the fact that few independent research studies have replicated the findings obtained by Herzberg and his colleagues (Rynes, Gerhart, & Parks, 2005).

Two-factor theory Herzberg's needs theory, postulating that there are two factors involved in job satisfaction: hygiene factors and motivators.

Hygiene factors In Herzberg's two-factor theory, job-related elements that result from but do not involve the job itself.

Motivators In Herzberg's two-factor theory, elements of a job that concern the actual duties performed by the employee.

Table 9.5 Examples from Herzberg's Two-Factor Theory

Hygiene Factors	Motivators
Pay	Responsibility
Security	Growth
Coworkers	Challenge
Working conditions	Stimulation
Company policy	Independence
Work schedule	Variety
Supervisors	Achievement
	Control
	Interesting work

Do Employees Have Achievable Goals?

Goal setting A method of increasing performance in which employees are given specific performance goals to aim for.

To increase motivation, goal setting should be used. With **goal setting** each employee is given a goal such as increasing attendance, selling more products, or reducing the number of grammar errors in reports. The first goal-setting study that caught the interest of industrial psychologists was conducted by Latham and Blades (1975). Their study was brought about because truck drivers at a logging mill were not completely filling their trucks before making deliveries. Empty space in the trucks obviously cost the company money. To increase each delivery's load, the drivers were given specific weight goals and were told that they would be neither punished nor rewarded for reaching the goal. A significant increase in the average load per delivery resulted. Although this is the most celebrated study, goal setting has been shown to be effective in a wide variety of situations.

For goal setting to be most successful, the goals themselves should possess certain qualities represented by the acronym SMART: specific, measurable, attainable, relevant, and time-bound (Rubin, 2002).

Specific

Properly set goals are concrete and specific (Locke & Latham, 2002). A goal such as "I will produce as many as I can" will not be as effective as "I will print five thousand pages in the next hour." The more specific the goal, the greater the productivity. To underscore this point, we will use an example involving pushups. If a person says he will do as many pushups as he can, does that mean he will do as many as he can until he tires? As many as he can before he begins to sweat? As many as he did the last time? The problem with such a goal is its ambiguity and lack of specific guidelines.

Though setting specific goals makes sense, it is not always easy to do. Microsoft found that nearly 25% of the goals set by employees as part of their performance plans were not specific (Shaw, 2004). The results of focus groups investigating this lack of specificity found that employees believed that with a constantly changing environment, it was difficult to set specific goals because the goals would need constant adjustment.

Measurable

Properly set goals are measurable. That is, if one's goal is to improve performance or increase customer service, can performance or customer service be measured? In the Microsoft study mentioned in the previous paragraph, only 40% of the goals set by employees were measurable (Shaw, 2004).

Difficult but Attainable

Properly set goals are high but attainable (Locke & Latham, 1990). If an employee regularly prints 5,000 pages an hour and sets a goal of 4,000 pages, performance is certainly not going to increase. Conversely, if the goal becomes 20,000 pages, it will also not be effective because the employee will quickly realize that he cannot meet the goal and will quit trying.

A good example of goals set too high comes from the academic retention program at one university. This program is designed to help special students who are having academic trouble and whose grade point averages (GPAs) have fallen below the minimum needed to stay in school. The program involves tutoring, study skills, and goal setting. Although it has generally been a success, many students have failed to improve their academic performance. A brief investigation revealed that the goal-setting process was one of the reasons for these failures. Students were allowed to set their own GPA goals for the semester—and students with GPAs of 1.0 were setting goals of 4.0! Obviously, none of the students was able to reach this goal. The problem typically came when students did poorly on their first test and lost their chance for an A in the class, and thus had no chance of making a 4.0 GPA for the semester. Because their goals could not be attained, the students felt they had failed and quit trying.

Though setting higher goals generally leads to better performance than does setting lower goals, the level of goal difficulty will most affect performance when employees are committed to reaching the goal (Klein, Wesson, Hollenbeck, & Alge, 1999; Locke & Latham, 2002). For example, if a police chief sets a high goal for a police officer to write traffic citations, the officer will not increase the number of citations he writes unless he is committed to the goal. That is, if he believes he can accomplish the goal, agrees that the goal is worthwhile, and will be rewarded for achieving the goal, his commitment to achieve the goal is likely to be high.

Interestingly, setting goals that are too difficult to be accomplished can result not only in decreased performance, but in an increase in unethical behavior as well. When employees feel pressure to reach a goal that they realize can't be met, they at times will engage in unethical behaviors in attempts to reach the goal or to "cook the books" to make it look as if the goals have been met (Schweitzer, Ordóñez, & Douma, 2004).

Not surprisingly, people differ in the extent to which they set high goals. Optimists tend to set higher goals than do pessimists (Ladd, Jagacinski, & Stolzenberg, 1997). In the Big 5 schema, people scoring high in conscientiousness, extraversion, and openness and low in agreeableness and neuroticism also tend to set high goals (Judge & Ilies, 2002).

Relevant

Properly set goals are also relevant. Setting a goal about increasing public speaking skills will not be as motivating to a person working in a landfill as it would be to a police officer who often testifies in court.

Time-Bound

Goals work best when there is a time frame for their completion. For example, a goal to clean one's office would be more motivating if the goal included a date by which the office would be cleaned.

Employee Participation

Until fairly recently, it was generally thought that a goal would lead to the greatest increase in productivity if it was set at least in part by the employee. That is, although performance would increase if the supervisor set the employee's goal, it would increase even more if the employee participated. However, several meta-analyses have indicated that participating in goal setting does not increase performance (Mento, Steel, & Karren, 1987; Tubbs, 1986; Zetik & Stuhlmacher, 2002). However, a

As an organization development (OD) professional, I have been provided the opportunity to implement a variety of broad-based solutions to develop employees, while at the same time work closely with individuals to fine-tune individual performance. I also work with upper management to show them how their behaviors and decisions affect individuals at the lower levels of the organization. It is critical to have strong business relationships at this level in order to obtain acceptance of whatever intervention is necessary to improve performance. These relationships are essential to drive the changes throughout the organization.

Armand Spoto, M.S.

Senior Training Specialist, PointRoll

One of the hottest topics around employee motivation in many organizations today is the concept of employee engagement. More and more organizations are replacing their annual employee satisfaction survey and implementing employee engagement metrics. There are a variety of engagement definitions, but most encompass the degree to which employees commit to something (e.g., job responsibility) or someone (e.g., the manager) in their organization and/or how hard they will work and how long they will stay as a result of their commitment. With more attention being paid to these results, there are more opportunities to apply them within management/leadership development and team effectiveness programs. It also broadens the scope and style of interventions to a much more systemic view of motivation throughout an entire organization.

Throughout my career, I have worked in a variety of companies ranging from Fortune 500 to small start-up organizations. With most small to midsize organizations, middle management is the most ignored population when it comes to employee development opportunities. Unfortunately, they are the most critical group because they are the key link to implementing upper management's strategic plan. When training managers, it is critical to find ways to motivate individuals to use new techniques and skills to improve their performance. Training on any new skill or behavior is a challenge, especially when it provides a major change to the way individuals have performed for long periods of time. Management and leadership development is becoming an even more critical topic as a generation of managers and leaders begin to retire. The next 10 to 15 years will be a critical time to develop the next generation of managers and leaders to replace those who are leaving the workforce. It is absolutely critical for the OD manager to develop and implement strategies which grow and develop young leaders.

When I develop a new training program, I use a variety of concepts to assist the class participants not only in acquiring the new skill, but in actually using the skill in the workplace. I incorporate expectancy theory in training programs by putting myself in the place of the employees and thinking about how this new skill will help them in their jobs. I ask myself questions I think participants would ask. For example:

- How will this help me in my job?
- What makes it better than what I am already doing?
- What activities, or set of activities, will this replace?
- What are the short-term effects compared with the long-term benefits?
- How different is this from what I am currently doing?

This is also referred to as the "What's In It For Me" (WIIFM) factor. When developing any soft- or hard-skills training, you should have a sound rationale for how it will help employees do their jobs better, faster, or cheaper. To motivate participants, it is essential to identify with their needs and how something new can make them more productive.

In my experience, an easy way to initiate behavior change is to incorporate goal setting into the current performance management system. I typically have managers determine their professional and personal goals at the beginning of a project. Once these goals are established, I have each team member evaluate their goals using the SMART methodology you read about in this chapter.

I truly enjoy working in the OD field. It is a smaller niche of what is available to those who pursue a career in industrial/organizational psychology, but it is a rewarding experience. If you are looking to pursue a career in this field, there are two things I recommend as part of your professional development plan. The first is getting as much experience as you can in implementing any change initiatives—in activities like developing and facilitating training programs, management coaching, merger and acquisitions task forces, anything that will provide exposure to the outcomes of change. I believe the best way to design and implement OD interventions is to have a working knowledge of what works in a given organization. The second thing I would recommend is always work on building your relationships. You constantly have to work at achieving buy-in and commitment at all levels of the organization and finding how to connect with as many people as possible. No matter what direction you take in your career, you will have the utmost success when you can work well with others.

meta-analysis indicates that employee participation in goal setting increases the commitment to reaching a goal (Klein et al., 1999). To practice goal setting, complete the Goal Setting Exercise 9.4 in your workbook.

Are Employees Receiving Feedback on Their Goal Progress?

To increase the effectiveness of goal setting, feedback should be provided to employees on their progress in reaching their goals (Locke & Latham, 2002; Stajkovic & Luthans, 2003). Feedback is so important that in a survey of IT (information technology) employees, 80% said that effective feedback would make them less likely to leave their organization (Joinson, 2001). Unfortunately, only 42% of employees report they receive regular feedback on their performance (Bates, 2003b). Feedback can include verbally telling employees how they are doing, placing a chart on a wall, or using nonverbal communication such as smiles, glares, and pats on the back. Feedback best increases performance when it is positive and informational rather than negative and controlling (Zhou, 1998). To encourage employees to ask for feedback, supervisors should indicate their willingness to provide feedback and then reinforce employees who seek it (Williams, Miller, Steelman, & Levy, 1999).

Feedback is constructive when it is given positively with the goal of encouraging and reinforcing positive behavior. For feedback to be effective, it must be given when employees do things properly, not just when they make mistakes. Some tips for providing effective feedback can be found in the Career Workshop Box.

Career Workshop **Providing Feedback**

During your career there will be many times when you need to provide feedback to coworkers, subordinates, and others. Here are some tips for providing effective feedback:

➡ Identify the employee's behavior and focus on it rather than on the employee's personality. For example, if an employee is often late for work, a supervisor might say, "In the past two weeks, you have been late five times" rather than "We are having a problem with your lack of responsibility and commitment to your job."

➡ Explain how the behavior is impacting others. For example, "When you arrive to work ten minutes late, customers become angry because there is no one to help them with their purchases. When other employees cover the register for you, it causes them to get behind on their work, resulting in their missing part of their lunch break or being forced to work overtime."

➡ Ask the employee for suggestions on how the behavior can be changed. If the employee has none to offer, the supervisor

can provide some. A sample conversation might go something like this:

Employee: I know I shouldn't be missing work, but I'm so tired in the morning and often don't hear the alarm.

Supervisor: Can you think of things you can do so that you will not be so tired in the morning?

Employee: I could go to bed earlier, but I love to watch David Letterman and then SportsCenter on ESPN.

Supervisor: Could you try watching the early edition of SportsCenter and tape the David Letterman show so that you can watch it when you get home from work?

Employee: I guess I could give that a try.

➡ After arriving at a solution, the supervisor and the employee should then set a specific goal. For example, they could agree that the employee will be on time every day for the next week.

After an agreed-upon time, the supervisor and the employee should meet to see if the goal has been met and to set new goals.

Self-Regulation Theory

An interesting extension on goal setting and feedback is the concept of **self-regulation**. In the previous section we discussed how it is important to get feedback on goal attainment. Though this feedback often comes from others, the idea behind self-regulation theory is that employees monitor their own progress toward attaining goals and then make the necessary adjustments; that is, they self-regulate.

For example, suppose that an employee has a goal of completing a 100-page report in two weeks. If there are 10 working days in the two-week period, the employee might determine that she should complete 10 pages a day. After two days, the employee counts the number of pages written and compares it with where she thought she should be after two days (20 pages). If she has written only 10 pages, she has some choices to make. Should she change her goal to give herself more time to complete the report, or perhaps change the goal so that the report will be shorter? Should she change her behavior so that she quits working on other projects and concentrates only on the report? Should she work longer hours or get more help so she can complete the report in two weeks?

Though this example describes self-regulation of a specific task (writing a report), employees obviously have many goals, some of which are complex and some that might compete with other goals. For example, an employee might have goals of increasing her job knowledge (learning goal orientation), performing at a high level (performance goal orientation), making a lot of money, advancing within the organization, having a full social life, and spending quality time with the family. If the employee wanted to attend a weeklong seminar to increase her skills, would it come at the expense of her goals to perform at a high level and to spend time with her family? With multiple complex goals, self-regulation becomes more difficult, and employees must make a conscious effort to be aware of their goals, monitor their goal progress, and set priorities so that decisions can be made when encountering competing goals.

Are Employees Rewarded for Achieving Goals?

An essential strategy for motivating employees is to provide an incentive for employees to accomplish the goals set by an organization. As a result, organizations offer incentives for a wide variety of employee behaviors, including working overtime or on weekends, making suggestions, referring applicants, staying with the company (length-of-service awards), coming to work (attendance bonuses), not getting into accidents, and performing at a high level (Henderson, 2006). The basis for these incentive systems are **operant conditioning** principles, which state that employees will engage in behaviors for which they are rewarded and avoid behaviors for which they are punished. Thus, if employees are rewarded for not making errors, they are more likely to produce high-quality work. If employees are rewarded for the amount of work done, they will place less emphasis on quality and try to increase their quantity. Finally, if employees are not rewarded for any behavior, they will search for behaviors that will be rewarded. Unfortunately, these might include absenteeism (which is rewarded by going fishing) or carelessness (which is rewarded by spending more time with friends).

Research and applied literature abound with studies demonstrating the effectiveness of reinforcement. For example:

- Austin, Kessler, Riccobono, and Bailey (1996) provided daily feedback and weekly monetary reinforcement to employees in a roofing crew. This intervention resulted in a 64% labor cost reduction and an 80% improvement in safety.
- Myers, McSween, Medina, Rost, and Alvero (2010) used a combination of employee involvement, feedback, and recognition to reduce injuries in a petroleum refinery by 81%.
- Ply Marts, a building materials supply company in Norcross, Georgia, reduced the number of injuries from 37 per year to 7 by providing daily feedback on injuries and giving employees a bingo number for each day that no employee was injured. Each day, money was added to the pot until an employee got to "bingo" and won the pot (Atkinson, 1999).
- Kortick and O'Brien (1996) devised the "World Series of Quality Control" at a package delivery company in New York. The 104 employees were divided into 13 teams of 8 employees each and competed against one another to have the best shipping accuracy and quantity. Performance information and team standings were posted each week, with the winning team receiving pizzas. At the end of each month, the winning team received individual plaques and dinner at a local restaurant. The intervention resulted in promising increases in shipping accuracy.

Though the research is clear that rewarding employees will often lead to increased motivation and performance, six factors must be considered in determining the effectiveness of incentive programs:

1. Timing of the incentive
2. Contingency of the consequences
3. Type of incentive used
4. Use of individual-based versus group-based incentives
5. Use of positive incentives (rewards) versus negative incentives (punishment)
6. Fairness of the reward system (equity)

Timing of the Incentive

Research indicates that a *reinforcer* or a *punisher* is most effective if it occurs soon after the performance of the behavior. Unfortunately, if the timing of the incentive is too long, the effectiveness of the incentive to improve performance will be hindered. For example, a restaurant employee learning how to wait on tables performs many behaviors in the course of serving a customer. A tip is usually left by the customer after the meal, which provides immediate feedback about the employee's performance. However, if the tip is small, the employee is not sure which particular behavior caused the customer's displeasure. Likewise, if the tip is large, the employee is unsure which particular behavior or behaviors initiated the large tip. Thus the timing of the consequence by itself may not be enough.

Contingency of Consequences

If it is not possible to immediately reward or punish a behavior, it should at least be made clear that the employee understands the behaviors that brought reward or punishment. To return to our example of the waiter, if he is told the reason for the size of his tip, he will be better able to change his behavior. Have you ever given a waiter or waitress a large tip even though the service was terrible? Most of us have. When this happens, however, the waiter or waitress is reinforced for poor performance and has no incentive to improve unless poor performance has its own consequence. In a similar fashion, if the waiter has done an outstanding job but has received a small tip, the probability of his repeating his outstanding performance is reduced. Furthermore, when tips are pooled at restaurants so that each employee gets a share of all tips received, an individual employee's rewards are not as contingent on his own behavior as when tips are not pooled.

The point of these examples is that reward and punishment must be made contingent upon performance, and this contingency of consequence must be clear to employees if we want them to be motivated (Podsakoff, Bommer, Podsakoff, & MacKenzie, 2006). If the reward or punishment cannot be administered immediately, the employee must be told the purpose of the consequence so that the link between behavior and outcome is clear.

Type of Incentive Used

Obviously, it is important to reward employees for productive work behavior. But, as you learned in the discussion of Maslow's hierarchy, different employees have different values, which is why supervisors should have access to and be trained to administer different types of reinforcers. For example, some employees can be rewarded with praise, others with awards, others with interesting work, and still others with money. In fact, a meta-analysis by Stajkovic and Luthans (1997) found that financial, nonfinancial, and social rewards all resulted in increased levels of performance. It is important to conduct periodic employee surveys about what employees want because supervisors and employees often have different ideas about what is rewarding and important (Babcock, 2005).

A good example of the use of a variety of incentives can be found at La Porte Hospital. As part of their award-winning "Caught You Caring" program, La Porte uses public recognition, gift certificates, small gifts, and a variety of other awards to reward employees who engage in excellent patient care. This use of rewards is one of the reasons that La Porte has a turnover rate of only 4% in an industry that has an 18% national turnover rate (Renk, 2004).

The need for variety in rewards is also true of punishment. Threatening an employee with a three-day suspension will be effective only if he needs the money or doesn't like being off work; yelling at an employee will be effective only if the employee does not like being yelled at; and threatening to not promote an employee will be effective only if the employee values promotions and perceives he has a reasonable chance of getting one.

Premack Principle

An interesting method of providing incentives that meet the individual needs of each employee stems from the **Premack Principle** (Premack, 1963), which states that reinforcement is relative and that a supervisor can reinforce an employee with something that on the surface does not appear to be a reinforcer. The best way to explain this principle is to construct a **reinforcement hierarchy** on which an employee lists his preferences for a variety of reinforcers.

Premack Principle The idea that reinforcement is relative both within an individual and between individuals.

Reinforcement hierarchy A rank-ordered list of reinforcers for an individual.

As Figure 9.1 shows, our hypothetical employee most desires money and time off from work and least desires typesetting and cleaning the press. Our employee can enjoy and do a better job of cleaning his press if we give him money for each time he properly completes the task, but such a reward system can become expensive. Thus, according to the Premack Principle, we can get our employee to clean his press properly by allowing him to do one of the activities he likes more than cleaning. From his reinforcement hierarchy, we can see that he ranks throwing out oily rags as more enjoyable because he can take a short break by walking outdoors to the disposal area. Thus all we need for a reward is to let him dispose of the rags.

The Premack Principle may sound silly, but think of the reinforcers you have used to reward yourself for studying. After reading a certain number of pages, you might allow yourself a trip to the water fountain. Certainly, getting a drink of water is hardly anyone's idea of a good time, but it may be more interesting than studying and so can become a reinforcer to increase studying.

When I was in high school, I worked at a printing plant that produced stock reports. All entry-level employees were "collators," whose job was to place 500 copies of a book page on a piece of wood strapped to their necks and then walk around a room placing a piece of paper in each of the 500 slots. This process was repeated about 300 times until a complete book was put together. As you can imagine, the job was extremely boring. To motivate us, our supervisor would "reward" the fastest collators by allowing them to take out the trash, to go pick up lunch (it was kind of cool ordering 100 Whoppers and 100 fries and watching the Burger King employees' expressions), or to move the paper carts from one end of the building to the other. I didn't realize until 10 years later that my boss was using the Premack Principle—rewarding performance of a very boring task by allowing us to perform a less boring task.

As another example, my previous boss (the department chair) was a master at using the Premack Principle. Because salary raises are small in size and never a certainty, it is difficult to motivate faculty to do the "little things" by offering financial rewards. Instead, my boss rewarded good departmental citizenship by giving the best faculty their most desired schedule, their favorite classes, and their favorite committee assignments. From what I have seen, these reinforcers work better than money!

Of course, my boss was successful in using the Premack Principle because he had a good sense of every faculty member's reinforcement hierarchy. For example, I hate serving on committees, whereas a colleague of mine gets her entire self-worth by chairing department and university committees. So my boss reinforced my colleague

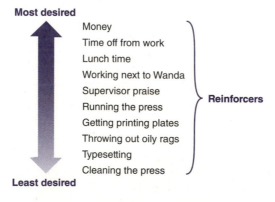

Figure 9.1

Premack Principle

by putting her on committees and reinforced me by giving me some data to play with. Likewise, some faculty love early morning classes, whereas others would rather teach at night.

In an example from the research literature, Welsh, Bernstein, and Luthans (1992) demonstrated the effectiveness of the Premack Principle with employees at a fast-food restaurant. Employees whose errors decreased in a given day were rewarded by being allowed to work at their favorite workstation (e.g., cooking fries versus flipping burgers). This use of the Premack Principle resulted in a decrease in employee errors.

Even though operant conditioning and the Premack Principle have been successful in improving motivation and performance, a note of caution comes from Deci (1972), who believes that for some people and some jobs, work is intrinsically motivating. That is, people are motivated because they enjoy working, not because they are being rewarded. A reasonable body of research, much of it conducted by Deci himself, demonstrates that paying a person for the amount of work done will reduce the degree to which he enjoys performing the task. Thus, when financial incentives are no longer available, the employee will be less motivated to work than before rewards were used. As interesting as this concept sounds, some researchers (e.g., Dickinson, 1989) argue that Deci's conclusion that extrinsic rewards decrease intrinsic motivation are flawed. To apply the Premack Principle to your own life, complete Exercise 9.5 in your workbook.

Financial Rewards

Financial incentives can be used to motivate better worker performance either by making variable pay an integral part of an employee's compensation package or by using financial rewards as a "bonus" for accomplishing certain goals. As shown in Figure 9.2, a compensation plan should include base pay and a benefits package to provide employees with security; salary adjustments to cover such conditions as undesirable shifts and geographic areas with high costs of living; and variable pay to provide an incentive to perform better. Though incentive systems often result in higher levels of performance, when designed poorly they can result in such negative outcomes as increased stress and decreased health and safety (Schleifer & Amick, 1989; Schleifer & Okogbaa, 1990).

Financial incentives in the form of bonuses or prizes are also used to motivate employees. For example, Chick-fil-A and McDonald's have scholarship programs for their employees; Banker Steel in Lynchburg, Virginia provides productivity bonuses; and Abuelo's, the Mexican food restaurant chain, gives "reward pesos" to employees who demonstrate "Xtraordinary" performance. These "pesos" can be exchanged for merchandise from the company store.

Recognition

Rather than providing financial incentives, many organizations reward employee behavior through recognition programs. For example:

- United Airlines holds a special ceremony each year in which employees are given service emblems for each year of service.
- Supermarket chain Dierbergs in St. Louis has initiated a program called Extra Step, which recognizes employees who meet customers' needs. Over a five-year period, the Extra Step program resulted in a decline in turnover from 47% to 25%.

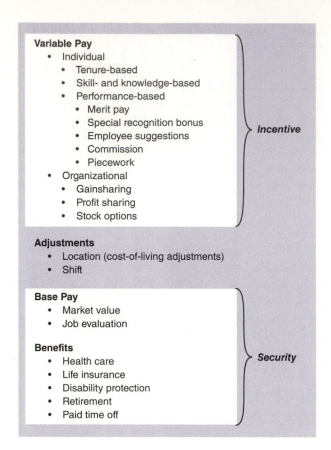

Figure 9.2

Compensation Plan

> Variable Pay
> - Individual
>   - Tenure-based
>   - Skill- and knowledge-based
>   - Performance-based
>   - Merit pay
>   - Special recognition bonus
>   - Employee suggestions
>   - Commission
>   - Piecework
> - Organizational
>   - Gainsharing
>   - Profit sharing
>   - Stock options
>
> } *Incentive*
>
> Adjustments
> - Location (cost-of-living adjustments)
> - Shift
>
> Base Pay
> - Market value
> - Job evaluation
>
> Benefits
> - Health care
> - Life insurance
> - Disability protection
> - Retirement
> - Paid time off
>
> } *Security*

- Most universities award faculty members the titles of associate professor and professor to recognize years of service as well as quality of performance.
- Organizations such as Outback Steakhouse and Saints Medical Center give employees of the month a personal parking space.

In some organizations, recognition awards are given by peers. For example, employees at the Angus Barn Restaurant in Raleigh, North Carolina, choose peers to receive the "People's Choice" award and employees at Oakland Mercy Hospital in Nebraska vote for the Staff Member of the Year.

Informal recognition programs, called **social recognition**, can prove to be tremendous sources of employee motivation. Social recognition consists of personal attention, signs of approval (e.g., smiles, head nods), and expressions of appreciation (Stajkovic & Luthans, 2001).

Social recognition A motivation technique using such methods as personal attention, signs of approval, and expressions of appreciation.

Travel

Many organizations are offering travel awards rather than financial rewards. For example, every executive at McDonald's is allowed to nominate high-performing employees for a chance to spend a week in one of the company's condos in Hawaii, Florida, or Lake Tahoe, Nevada. At Chick-fil-A, sales teams compete for a vacation in Hawaii. At Motorola, managers can nominate employees for travel awards. In an unusual application of using travel as a reward, candy manufacturer Just Born promised its sales force a trip to Hawaii if they increased company sales by 4% and a January trip to Fargo, North Dakota, if they didn't reach their goal.

Providing a reserved parking space for an employee of the month is one of many ways to recognize valued employees

© Lee Raynes

Individual Versus Group Incentives

Incentives can be given for either individual performance or group performance.

Individual Incentive Plans

Individual incentive plans are designed to make high levels of individual performance financially worthwhile, and the research is clear monetary incentives increase performance over the use of a guaranteed hourly salary (Bucklin & Dickinson, 2001). Individual incentives help reduce such group problems as social loafing, which is discussed in Chapter 13. There are three main problems associated with individual incentive plans. The first is the difficulty in measuring individual performance. Not only are objective measures difficult to find, but supervisors are reluctant to evaluate employees, especially when the outcome will determine the amount of money an employee will receive (Schuster & Zingheim, 1992).

The second problem is that individual incentive plans can foster competition among employees. Though competition is not always bad, it is seldom consistent with the recent trend toward a team approach to work. When done right, however, team environments and individual incentive programs can coexist and result in high levels of employee performance (Steers & Porter, 1991). The third problem is that for an incentive plan to effectively motivate employees, it is essential that employees understand the incentive system. Surprisingly, only 40% of employees report that they understand how their pay is determined (Grensing-Pophal, 2003).

The two most common individual incentive plans are **pay for performance** and **merit pay**.

Pay for Performance. Also called *earnings-at-risk* (EAR) plans, pay-for-performance plans pay employees according to how much they individually produce. Simple pay-for-performance systems with which you are probably familiar include commission (being paid for each unit of something sold) and piecework (being paid for each unit of something produced).

The first step in creating more complicated pay-for-performance plans is to determine the average or standard amount of production. For example, the average number of envelopes sorted by mail clerks might be 300 per hour. The next step is to determine the desired average amount of pay. We might decide that on average, our mail clerks should earn $9 an hour. We then compute the piece rate by dividing hourly wage by the number of envelopes sorted (9/300), which is .03. Thus, each correctly sorted envelope is worth 3 cents. If a mail clerk is good and sorts 400 envelopes per hour, he will make $12 per hour. If our clerk is not a good worker and can sort only 200 pieces per hour, he will make $6 per hour. To protect workers from the effects of external factors, minimum-wage laws ensure that even the worst employee will make enough money to survive. As suggested in Figure 9.2, most organizations provide a base salary to ensure that employees will have at least minimal financial security. In fact, research indicates that employees paid a flat hourly rate plus a performance bonus perform at levels equal to employees who are paid on a piece-rate plan (Dickinson & Gillette, 1993).

A good example of such a plan comes from the Superior Court Records Management Center in Phoenix, Arizona (Huish, 1997). After conducting a study that showed a negative correlation between employee salary and productivity ($r = -.49$), the clerk of the court decided to try a pay-for-performance system. Each employee was given a base salary of $7.20 per hour and, on the basis of the quantity and quality of his work, could earn incentive pay. This pay-for-performance intervention resulted in an average increase in employee pay of $2.60 per hour, a reduction in cost per unit (a unit was a court document page transferred to microfilm) from 39 cents to 21 cents, and a decreased need for storage space.

Tharaldson Enterprises in Fargo, North Dakota, changed its compensation system for the housekeepers employed in its 300 hotels. Rather than being paid by the hour, the housekeepers were paid by the number of rooms they cleaned. This change saved the company $2 million per year and resulted in the housekeepers making more money and working fewer hours than under the old hourly rate system (Tulgan, 2001).

Union National Bank in Little Rock, Arkansas, has had tremendous success by paying its workers for the number of customers they serve, the number of new customers gained, the amount of time taken to balance accounts at the end of the day, and so on. The bank's pay-for-performance program has resulted in the average employee making 25% more in take-home pay, and the bank itself has almost doubled its profits.

Nucor in Charlotte, North Carolina, is another company that has used a pay-for-performance plan. By paying its steelworkers for the amount of work they do, Nucor has seen productivity more than double, and its workers make more than $30,000 per year, while the industry average is some $27,000. Though pay-for-performance plans appear to be successful for both the employee and the employer, some research suggests that employees are not satisfied with such plans (Brown & Huber, 1992).

Merit Pay. The major distinction between merit pay and pay for performance is that merit pay systems base their incentives on performance appraisal scores rather than on such objective performance measures as sales and productivity. Thus, merit pay is a potentially good technique for jobs in which productivity is difficult to measure.

The actual link between performance appraisal scores and the amount of merit pay received by an employee varies greatly around the United States. In the State of Virginia's merit pay system, employees' performance appraisal scores at each office are ranked, and the top 30% of employees each receive a $1,000 annual bonus.

In the merit pay system used by one nonprofit mental health agency, each employee's performance appraisal rating is divided by the total number of performance points possible, and this percentage is then multiplied by the maximum 3% merit increase that can be received by an employee. With this system, an employee must receive a perfect rating to receive the full 3% increase. Most employees receive between 2% and 2.5%.

The merit pay system used by a California public transit system is similar to that used by the mental health agency, with the exception that the merit increase becomes part of an employee's base salary for the next pay period. Thus increases are perpetuated each year, unlike the mental health system's one-time reward. In Bismarck, North Dakota, a computer program uses employee self-ratings (25%), peer ratings (25%), and supervisor ratings (50%) to calculate an employee's merit pay. Bismarck does not award cost-of-living or automatic annual increases (also called *step increases*).

Research on merit pay has brought mixed reviews. Some research has shown that employees like the idea of merit pay, but other research has found that it is not popular with all employees and that many do not consider the merit ratings to be fair (Siegall & Worth, 2001). Not surprisingly, employees are most satisfied with merit pay if they help develop the system (Gilchrist & White, 1990).

One of merit pay's biggest problems is that increases are based on subjective performance appraisals. Aware of this, some supervisors will inflate performance appraisal scores to increase their employees' pay and thus increase the positive feelings of employees toward their supervisors. Managers have also been known to inflate performance appraisal ratings when they believe the base salaries for certain positions are too low.

Another problem with merit pay is that its availability or amount often changes with each fiscal year. Thus excellent performance one year might result in a large bonus, but the same performance another year might bring no bonus at all. This is especially true in the public sector. For merit pay to be successful, funding must be consistently available and the amount must be great enough (about 7%) to motivate employees (Bhakta & Nagy, 2005; Heneman & Coyne, 2007).

Group Incentive Plans

The idea behind group-based, or organization-based, incentive plans is to get employees to participate in the success or failure of the organization. Rather than encouraging individual competition, these plans reward employees for reaching group goals. The problems with group incentive plans are that they can encourage social loafing and can get so complicated that they become difficult to explain to employees. In spite of these potential problems, meta-analysis results indicate that team-based incentive programs result in better performance ($d = 1.40$) than do individual-based programs ($d = .55$, Condly, Clark, & Stolovitch, 2003).

Profit Sharing. Profit sharing was developed in the United States by Albert Gallatin way back in 1794 (Henderson, 2006). As its name implies, profit-sharing programs provide employees with a percentage of *profits* above a certain amount. For example, in addition to their base salary, employees might receive 50% of the profits a company makes above 6%. Organizations will usually not share the initial 5% or so of profits, as that money is needed for research and development and as a safety net for unprofitable years. The profits to be shared can be paid directly to employees as a bonus (cash plans) or placed into the employees' retirement fund (deferred plans). Profit sharing will motivate employees only if they understand the link between performance and profits and believe that the company has a reasonable chance of making a profit. Research indicates that profit sharing results in greater employee commitment (Fitzgibbons, 1997; Florkowski & Schuster, 1992).

Gainsharing A group incentive system in which employees are paid a bonus based on improvements in group productivity.

Gainsharing. Used by about 11% of organizations (Mercer Consulting, 2005), **gainsharing** ties groupwide financial incentives to *improvements* (gains) in organizational performance. Though the first gainsharing program was developed back in 1935 by the Nunn-Bush Shoe Company in Milwaukee, gainsharing has become popular only since the 1970s (Gowen, 1990). Gainsharing programs consist of three important elements: a cooperative/participative management philosophy, incentives based on improvement, and a group-based bonus formula (Gomez-Mejia, Welbourne, & Wiseman, 2000; Hanlon & Taylor, 1992).

Baseline The level of productivity before the implementation of a gainsharing plan.

The typical gainsharing program works as follows. First, the company monitors performance measures over some period of time to derive a **baseline**. Then productivity goals above the baseline are set, and the employees are told that they will receive bonuses for each period that the goal is reached. To make goal setting more effective, constant feedback is provided to employees on how current performance is in relation to the goal. At the end of each reporting period, bonuses are paid on the basis of how well the group did.

An excellent example of a successful gainsharing program can be found at the Dana Corporation Spicer Heavy Axle Division facility in Ohio. Employees at the Dana plant receive a financial bonus when productivity surpasses the baseline. The gainsharing program has dramatically increased the number of employee suggestions, product quality, and productivity. Employees' bonuses average 14% above their normal pay each month, with year-end bonuses between 11% and 16%.

As another example, Southern California Edison employees agreed to surrender 5% of their base pay. In return, they were given the opportunity to earn 10% to 15% of their base pay in a gainsharing plan. In 1995 alone, this plan generated $96 million in savings—$40 million of which was passed on to the employees.

In general, gainsharing plans seem to be effective. A review of gainsharing studies indicates improvements in productivity, increased employee and union satisfaction, and declines in absenteeism (Gowen, 1990). As with any incentive plan, gainsharing is most effective when employees are formally involved in the design and operation (Bullock & Tubbs, 1990) and when there is not a long delay between performance and the financial payoff (Mawhinney & Gowen, 1990).

Stock options A group incentive method in which employees are given the option of buying stock in the future at the price of the stock when the options were granted.

Stock Options. Although **stock options** represent the most complicated organizational incentive plan, they are offered to all employees by more than 33% of companies (Mercer Consulting, 2005). With stock options, employees are given the opportunity to purchase stock in the future, typically at the market price on the day the options were granted. Usually stock options vest over a certain period of time and must be exercised within a maximum time frame. The idea is that as a company does well, the value of its stock increases, as does the employee's profit. For example, suppose AT&T stock is selling for $55 per share on June 1, and the company gives employees the option of purchasing the stock for $55 per share anytime in the next 10 years. Ten years later, the stock is worth $75 per share and the employee can purchase the stock for the $55 per share option price—a $20 per share profit. However, if the stock had fallen from $55 to $45, the employee would not exercise his option to purchase the stock at $55 per share.

Stock options allow employees to share in the long-term success of an organization. In fact, such organizations as GTE, United Airlines, Home Depot, and Foldcraft Company report not only that their employees are making good money through their stock ownership but that organizational productivity has improved as well. At times, stock options may not be good motivators because employees have trouble understanding the concept of stock and because the incentive (profit made on the selling of stock) is psychologically well removed from day-to-day performance. However, having partial ownership in a company can increase performance. For example, in a study of hotel managers, Qian (1996) found a significant correlation between the amount of manager ownership and the hotel's profit margin.

Expectancy Theory

Expectancy theory Vroom's theory that motivation is a function of expectancy, instrumentality, and valence.

An influential theory of worker motivation that integrates many of the factors discussed previously in this chapter is **expectancy theory**, which was first proposed by Vroom (1964) and then modified by others, including Porter and Lawler (1968). This theory has three components, the definitions of which vary with each modification of the theory. The following definitions are combinations of those suggested by others and make the theory easier to understand:

- **Expectancy (E):** The perceived relationship between the amount of effort an employee puts in and the resulting outcome.
- **Instrumentality (I):** The extent to which the outcome of a worker's performance, if noticed, results in a particular consequence.
- **Valence (V):** The extent to which an employee values a particular consequence.

To understand or predict an employee's level of motivation, these components are used in the following formula:

$$\text{Motivation} = E(I \times V)$$

Thus, all possible outcomes of a behavior are determined, the valence of each is multiplied by the probability that it occurs at a particular performance level, and then the sum of these products is multiplied by the expectancy of an employee putting in the effort to attain the necessary level of performance. As can be seen from this formula, the higher the score on each component, the greater the employee's motivation. To expound on this, let us examine each component in more detail.

In terms of *expectancy*, if an employee believes that no matter how hard he works he will never reach the necessary level of performance, then his motivation will probably be low. For *instrumentality*, the employee will be motivated only if his behavior results in some specific consequence. That is, if the employee works extra hours, he expects to be rewarded, or if he is inexcusably absent from work, he expects to be punished. For a behavior to have a desired consequence, two events must occur. First, the employee's behavior must be noticed. If the employee believes he is able to attain the necessary level of performance but that his performance will not be noticed, then his level of motivation will be low. Second, noticed behavior must be rewarded. If no rewards are available, then, again, motivation will be low. As discussed earlier in this chapter, if appropriate behavior does not have positive consequences or if inappropriate behavior does not have negative consequences, the probability that a worker will continue undesired behaviors increases, and the probability that an employee will continue desired behaviors decreases.

For *valence*, if an employee is rewarded, the reward must be something he values. If good performance is rewarded by an award, then the employee will be motivated only if he values awards. Likewise, if we punish an employee by suspending him, the punishment will be effective only if the employee needs the money. If he does not particularly like his job and would rather spend a few days at the lake, the suspension will obviously not be effective. In an applied study, Fox, Scott, and Donohue (1993) found that in a pay-for-performance environment, pay served as an incentive only for employees with a high monetary valence. This theory can be used to analyze the situation experienced by one bank in Virginia. Concerned that the bank's tellers were averaging only three new Visa customers each month, management sought to increase the number of Visa applications taken by each teller. Tellers were expected to ask each customer if he or she had a Visa card. If not, the teller was to give the customer an application. A teller would receive $5 extra per month if he or she increased the number of new Visa customers per month to 25.

The program was a flop, much to management's surprise. Applying expectancy theory, however, would have led an industrial/organizational psychologist to predict the program's lack of success. First, let us look at the expectancy component. If the tellers currently averaged only 3 new Visa customers each month, they probably did not believe that even working hard, they would be able to generate 25 new customers. Thus, the expectancy probability for the program was low.

Second, most tellers probably did not place much value on an extra $5 per month, so the valence component also was low. Thus, with two of three components having low values, the program was destined to fail from the start. The bank later reduced the monthly number of new Visa cards to 10 and increased the teller reward to $20. These simple changes brought about the desired increase in new Visa customers.

In addition to predicting employee effort, expectancy theory has been applied successfully to predict speeding by drivers and cheating by students. To demonstrate this last behavior, imagine the typical examination in a typical college class.

First, look at the expectancy component. We might ask what the probability is for catching a cheater. Students who cheat most likely believe that it is very low. To determine the instrumentality component, we might ask what the probability is for some negative consequence if a cheater is caught. In many universities, this probability is low. Not only is it difficult to prove that a student cheated, but if it is the first time a student is caught, punishment usually results in no more than a few days' suspension.

Finally, we examine the valence component. Even if a student *was* caught and suspended, how terrible would that be? For many students, a few days of vacation may not seem so terrible. Thus, when combining the three components, we should not be surprised that cheating often occurs.

Expectancy theory can also be used to suggest ways to change employee motivation. As we saw with the bank, motivation was increased by making the performance standard more reasonable and by increasing the value of the consequence. Similarly, if we wanted to apply the theory to decrease cheating, we would increase the probability of catching cheaters, make convicting a person who has cheated easier, and make the consequences for cheating more severe.

Although expectancy theory is an interesting and useful method of predicting and increasing employee motivation, some researchers have criticized it. The major criticism involves the components equation. As it is now written, all of the components are multiplied. Some researchers have suggested that perhaps the addition of some components would be more appropriate than their multiplication (Schmidt, 1973). This is because when the components are multiplied, a zero in any component results in a prediction of zero motivation, even when ratings in the other components are high.

A second criticism involves the values assigned to each component (Ilgen, Nebeker, & Pritchard, 1981). Research has indicated that even though valence and instrumentality can be reliably measured (Mitchell, 1974), the theory is most predictive when people behave rationally (Stahl & Harrell, 1981), which they often do not, and have an **internal locus of control** (Lied & Pritchard, 1976), which may not always be the case. Despite problems with the equation, however, the theory is still one of the most useful for predicting employee behavior.

Internal locus of control
The extent to which people believe that they are responsible for and in control of their success or failure in life.

Reward Versus Punishment

Rather than rewarding desired behaviors, we can change employee performance by punishing undesired behaviors. That is, instead of rewarding employees who do not miss work, we punish those who do. Instead of providing monetary incentives for high levels of performance, we suspend employees for low levels of performance. Though many psychologists advise against punishment, it is common, and managers generally believe it to be effective (Butterfield, Trevino, & Ball, 1996).

Proponents of using punishment to change employee behavior argue that if applied properly, punishment not only reduces undesired behaviors in a particular employee but also sets an example for other employees. Opponents of punishment argue that punishment changes behavior only in the short run, does not teach an employee proper behaviors, and causes resentment. Furthermore, punishment causes employees to learn new methods to break rules, rather than teaching them not to break rules. A meta-analysis comparing the reward and punishment behaviors of leaders found that although both reward and punishment behaviors affect employee behavior and attitudes, the magnitude of the effect is stronger for rewards (Podsakoff, Bommer, Podsakoff, & MacKenzie, 2006).

For punishment to be effective, an employee must understand why he is being punished and be shown alternative ways of behaving that will result in some type of desired reinforcement. The punishment must also "fit the crime" in that too severe a punishment will cause resentment and too lenient a punishment will not motivate a change in behavior. As one would imagine, punishment should usually be done in private rather than in front of other employees.

Are Rewards and Resources Given Equitably?

Equity theory A theory of job satisfaction stating that employees will be satisfied if their ratio of effort to reward is similar to that of other employees.

Another factor related to motivation and job satisfaction is the extent to which employees perceive that they are being treated fairly. The first theory on this topic was equity theory (Adams, 1965). **Equity theory** is based on the premise that our levels of motivation and job satisfaction are related to how fairly we believe we are treated in comparison with others. If we believe we are treated unfairly, we attempt to change our beliefs or behaviors until the situation appears to be fair. Three components are involved in this perception of fairness: inputs, outputs, and input/output ratio.

Inputs are those personal elements that we put into our jobs. Obvious elements are time, effort, education, and experience. Less obvious elements include money spent on child care and distance driven to work.

Outputs are those elements that we receive from our jobs. A list of obvious outputs includes pay, benefits, challenge, and responsibility. Less obvious outputs are benefits such as friends and office furnishings.

According to the theory, employees subconsciously list all their outputs and inputs and then compute an **input/output ratio** by dividing output value by input value. By itself, this ratio is not especially useful. But employees then compute the input/output ratios for other employees and for previous work experiences and compare them with their own. For example, imagine that Brad is paid $40,000 as a nurse at County General Hospital. He works 40 hours each week, mostly in the evening and on weekends. He is considered to be one of the most skilled nurses at the hospital and, as a result, is often assigned to the most difficult patients. He has 15 years of nursing experience. Tom is also a nurse at County General making $40,000 a year. He works 9:00 a.m. to 5:00 p.m. and has 10 years of nursing experience. When comparing inputs and outputs, Brad would realize that he receives the same outputs as Tom, but has more inputs (worse schedule, more years of experience); thus his ratio would be lower than Tom's. So what will Brad do? According to equity theory, when an employee's ratio is lower than those of others, he will become dissatisfied and be motivated to make the ratios equal in one or more ways.

First, employees can seek greater outputs by such means as asking for a raise or for more responsibility. Second, employees can make the ratio more equal by reducing their inputs. Thus they might not work as hard or might reduce their attendance.

A less practical way of equalizing the ratios would be to change the ratios of other employees. For example, employees might try to get another employee to work harder and thus increase that employee's inputs. Or they might try to reduce the outputs of another employee by withholding friendship or finding a way to reduce the other employee's bonuses. Fortunately, however, strategies to equalize input/output ratios seldom involve reducing others' outputs. Employees can also restore equity by rationalizing the input/output ratio differences, changing the person with whom they are comparing themselves, or leaving the organization.

In general, research has supported the idea that our motivation decreases when our input/output ratios are lower than others' (Feight, Ferguson, Rodriguez, & Simmons, 2006). For example, research on major league baseball players (Hauenstein & Lord, 1989; Lord & Hohenfeld, 1979) found that players who either had their salary cut during their first year of free agency or lost an arbitration case performed at lower levels the following year. Thus players who thought that their *output* (salary) was too low responded by reducing their *inputs* (performance). In a study of professional basketball players, Harder (1992) found that overpaid players responded by being more team oriented (e.g., passing the ball, rebounding), whereas underpaid players responded by being more selfish (e.g., taking shots).

In an interesting study, O'Reilly and Puffer (1989) found that employees' motivation increased when coworkers received appropriate sanctions for their behavior. That is, when a high-performing group member was rewarded or a poor-performing group member was punished, the satisfaction and motivation of the group increased.

The degree of inequity that an employee feels when underpaid appears to be a function of whether the employee chose the actions that resulted in underpayment (Cropanzano & Folger, 1989). That is, if an employee chooses to work harder than

Inputs In equity theory, the elements that employees put into their jobs.

Outputs In equity theory, what employees get from their jobs.

Input/output ratio The ratio of how much employees believe they put into their jobs to how much they believe they get from their jobs.

Table 9.6 Equity Theory Research

When an employee's inputs are greater than his outputs (underpayment), he

- works less hard (Hauenstein & Lord, 1989)
- becomes more selfish (Harder, 1992)
- has lower job satisfaction (Carr, McLoughlin, Hodgson, & MacLachlan, 1996; Griffeth & Gaertner, 2001)

When an employee's outputs are greater than his inputs (overpayment), he

- is less likely to be persuaded by his underpaid peers (Stewart & Moore, 1992)
- does not feel guilty (Lapidus & Pinkerton, 1995)
- works harder (Adams & Rosenbaum, 1962; Pritchard, Dunnette, & Jorgenson, 1972)
- becomes more team oriented (Harder, 1992)

others who are paid the same, he will not feel cheated, but if he is pressured into working harder for the same pay, he will be unhappy.

An interesting prediction from this theory is a situation in which an employee's input/output ratio is *higher* than the ratio of others. Because the theory is based on equity, the prediction would be that the employee would still strive for equal ratios by either increasing his inputs or decreasing his outputs. In other words, he would either work harder or ask to be paid less. In fact, research has indicated that employees often do respond to being "overpaid" by feeling guilty (Lapidus & Pinkerton, 1995) or working harder (Adams & Rosenbaum, 1962; Pritchard, Dunnette, & Jorgenson, 1972). But feelings of inequity caused by being "overpaid" do not last long and probably do not produce long-term changes in behavior (Carrell & Dittrich, 1978).

Though equity theory has some theoretical problems, it was the springboard for modern research in **organizational justice**. Though this topic will be discussed in greater detail in Chapter 10, the idea behind organizational justice is that if employees are treated fairly, they will be more satisfied and motivated. Whereas equity theory was limited to work outcomes such as pay and promotions, organizational justice theory has focused on the fairness of many aspects of work such as the *process* of how decisions are made (procedural justice), the *outcomes* of the decisions (distributive justice), and the way in which decisions and other information are *communicated* to employees (interactional justice). Table 9.6 summarizes the findings of equity theory research. To practice using expectancy and equity theory, complete the Exercise 9.6 in your workbook.

Organizational justice A theory that postulates that if employees perceive they are being treated fairly, they will be more likely to be satisfied with their jobs and motivated to do well.

Are Other Employees Motivated?

Employees observe the levels of motivation and satisfaction of other employees and then model those levels. Thus, if an organization's older employees work hard and talk positively about their jobs and their employer, new employees will model this behavior and be both productive and satisfied. The reverse is also true: If veteran employees work slowly and complain about their jobs, so too will new employees. The importance of this type of modeling was demonstrated in a study of 187 employees that found that employees who observed other employees engage in antisocial behavior began to act in a similar fashion (Robinson & O'Leary-Kelly, 1998).

Integration of Motivation Theories

As shown in Figure 9.3, people come to a job with a predisposition toward motivation. That is, some people, such as those with high self-esteem, are generally more motivated than others. In this chapter, we discussed many theories of work motivation. Let's review what we have learned:

- From the discrepancy and needs theories, we will be motivated in our jobs if the job itself and the organization meet our expectations and values and satisfy our needs.

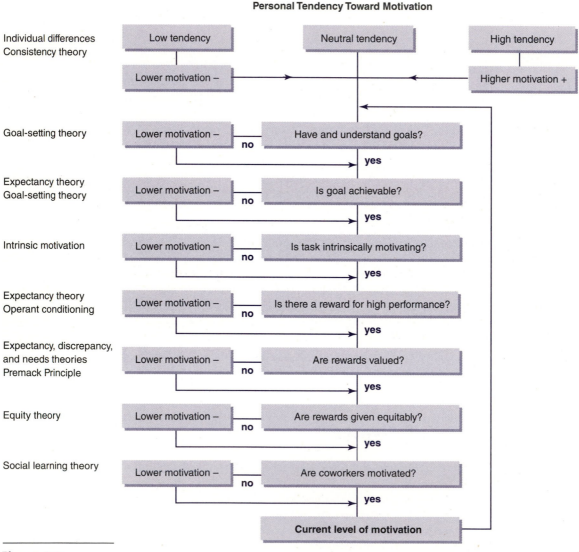

Figure 9.3
Motivation Flowchart

- From goal-setting theory, we find that employees who have, understand, and agree to goals will be more motivated than those without goals or with unclear goals.
- From expectancy theory and goal-setting theory, we know that the goals must be challenging but reasonable.
- From operant learning and expectancy theories, it is clear that extrinsically motivated people will be more motivated if behavior results in a reward.
- From these same two theories plus discrepancy theory, the needs theories, and the Premack Principle, we know that the rewards must have value to the employee to be motivating. Because different people value different rewards, care must be taken to ensure that a variety of rewards are available.
- From equity theory, we know that rewards that are valued will be motivating only if they are given in an equitable way. As discussed previously in the chapter, *perceptions* of equity are as important as the *reality* of equity.
- Social influence theory tells us that if other employees are motivated, there is an increased probability that we will model their behavior and be motivated.

The results of these factors are summed to indicate an employee's current level of motivation. As conditions change, so will the motivation level. To practice what you have learned in this chapter, complete the case study in Exercise 9.7 and develop your own theory in Exercise 9.8.

ON THE JOB   Applied Case Study

Faster Service at Taco Bueno Restaurants

Taco Bueno is a fast-casual Mexican-food restaurant chain. It opened its first restaurant in 1967 in Abilene, Texas, and now has over 185 locations throughout Texas, Oklahoma, Nebraska, Missouri, Louisiana, Kansas, Indiana, New Mexico, and Arkansas. Taco Bueno emphasizes fresh quality food, affordable prices, and fast service times. Rather than bringing in prepared food, items such as salsa, guacamole, and seasoned beef are prepared fresh at each location—a policy that increases the food preparation time but results in higher-quality food. Menu items include burritos, tacos, muchacos, nachos, tostadas, quesadillas, and salads. Customers can order food inside the restaurant or through the drive-thru lane. Both cash and credit cards are accepted.

Five principles constitute the "Bueno Way":

- Integrity: We base our actions and words on the highest level of honesty.
- Customer focus: We strive to deliver 100% guest satisfaction.
- Teamwork: We act as one, encourage communication, and respect diversity.
- Accountability: We see it, own it, and take charge!
- Spirit: We have fun, celebrate victories, and share our success.

The goal of the restaurant is to get the orders to the customers within 60 seconds of their pulling up to the cashier. To meet or better this goal, Taco Bueno wanted to improve the time spent taking and completing orders in the drive-thru lanes at its 185+ restaurant locations. The restaurant's reasoning is that fast delivery speeds not only increase the average number of cars that can be served in an hour, but also reduces the number of people who might not patronize the restaurant if they see long, slow-moving lines.

Taking into consideration what you learned in this chapter on motivation, how would you motivate employees to improve the drive-thru speed at Taco Bueno? To see how Taco Bueno reduced drive-thru service times by more than 14 seconds and experienced record sales, follow the link on your text website.

Ethics of Motivation Strategies

In 2001, a Hooters chain in Panama City Beach, Florida, came up with the idea of having a beer-selling contest to motivate its servers to sell as much beer as possible in the month of April. The top-selling waitress from each Hooters in the area had her name entered into a drawing. The waitress whose name was drawn would win the prize. Based on what the managers at each Hooters told their staff, the competing waitresses thought they would be winning a new Toyota automobile. The competition was a success: Most of the Hooters in the area seemed to have increased their sales of beer.

Jodee Berry was the winning waitress. On the day she was told she was the winner, she was blindfolded and led to the restaurant parking lot. However, instead of receiving a new Toyota car, she was presented with a *Star Wars* toy Yoda doll. Inside the restaurant, the manager and other staff were laughing.

Ms. Berry didn't think it was so funny. She worked hard to win this contest. Her motivation level was high because of the thought of winning a Toyota, not a *toy Yoda*. So, she sued Gulf Coast Wings, Inc., owners of the restaurant, alleging breach of contract and fraudulent misrepresentation. She was seeking as compensation the cost of a new Toyota *car*. The case was settled out of court for an undisclosed amount.

As you read in this chapter, organizations come up with creative ways to try to motivate employees to work harder, work safer, or to cut costs. But the question is: Should there be any limits on the type of motivator that is used? Is it okay to use any motivational strategy just as long as it has the desired results?

Another example of creative motivation is the one employed by a manager of one corporation who bought 10 golden bonsai trees and held a Save a Tree competition. Each month, the 10 lowest users of paper would receive one of the bonsai trees, which could be displayed for the coming month. It did the trick! Employees were motivated to save paper. Apparently, the bonsai tree had a certain appeal to these employees. Everyone wanted one!

In another company, the motivator for working harder was a nice steak dinner at a nice restaurant; the losers of the competition also got to go to the restaurant, but they had to sit at a lousy table and eat beans. After dinner, the winners got to rip the shirts off the back of the losers! This type of motivator, like the Hooters and Save a Tree competitions, was also successful. It did what it set out to do: increase sales for the department.

A professor at a small college motivates his students by promising $100 to the student who makes the highest test grade. If more than one student has the same grade, they split the $100 between them. There are three tests per semester. So, theoretically, a student could end the semester $300 richer! Another professor at a different college offers gift cards to various stores and restaurants to the top classroom performers. The thinking behind these motivators is that it will encourage students to study harder.

Proponents of such motivation techniques say that competition increases motivation, which leads to desired results. Critics say that these types of competition are unethical because they pit employee against employee, encourage cheating or unsafe shortcuts, and can often lead to bullying and the use of fear tactics by some employees against others as a form of intimidating them into losing the competition. They also say that it rewards people for using bad behavior in order to achieve a goal set by the company. It doesn't motivate them to do better at their job. And finally, it treats people differently and unfairly.

What Do You Think?

- Although there were some legal ramifications for what Hooter's did, do you think what they did to the waitress was also unethical?

- Do you think that the waitresses were lied to? If so, do you think lying to employees is unethical?

- What do you think about the motivating strategy of allowing employees to rip off the shirts of other employees? Is humiliating employees ethical?

- Is it ethical to promise money or other monetary compensation to students for studying hard? What if the losing students actually studied harder than the winner, but the winner only did well because he/she just happened to be brighter? Would giving that student the money be fair to the students who studied hard?

- Does the fact that these motivation techniques had the desired result by increasing sales or decreasing the use of paper outweigh any negative consequences of such motivators?

Chapter Summary

In this chapter you learned:

- Employees who have high self-esteem, a high need for achievement, and intrinsic motivation and who are expected to perform well by others are more motivated than their counterparts with low self-esteem and low achievement need who are extrinsically motivated.
- Goals are most effective if they are concrete and specific, are of high but reasonable difficulty, and are set with the input of the employee.
- Providing feedback on goal attainment and performance levels will increase performance.
- Operant conditioning principles can be used to motivate employees.
- It is important to treat employees fairly.
- Common individual incentive plans include pay for performance and merit pay.
- Common organizational incentive plans include profit sharing, gainsharing, and stock options.

Questions for Review

1. Does getting paid for a task that one enjoys performing reduce intrinsic motivation? Why or why not?
2. If the right techniques are used, can everyone be motivated to perform well? Why do you think that?
3. Which of the individual incentive plans is best? Why?
4. Which of the theories in the chapter would be most useful for managers? Why?
5. Is the threat of punishment an effective motivator? Why or why not?

Media Resources and Learning Tools

- Visit our website. Go to www.cengage.com/psychology/aamodt, where you will find online resources directly linked to your book, including chapter-by-chapter quizzing, flashcards, crossword puzzles, application activities, and more.
- Want more practice applying industrial/organizational psychology? Check out the *I/O Applications Workbook*. This workbook (keyed to your textbook) offers engaging, high-interest activities to help you reinforce the important concepts presented in the text.

© Chris Ryan/OJO Images/Getty Images

Learning Objectives

➡ Understand why an employer should even care about job satisfaction and organizational commitment

➡ Be able to identify the individual differences in the predisposition to be satisfied

➡ Learn ways to increase employee satisfaction and commitment

➡ Understand the methods used to measure job satisfaction

➡ Understand why employees are absent from work and what can be done to reduce absenteeism

➡ Understand why employees quit their jobs and what can be done to reduce turnover

Job satisfaction The attitude employees have toward their jobs.

Organizational commitment The extent to which an employee identifies with and is involved with an organization.

I magine the following situations:

- Jean Davis and Maria McDuffie have worked as customer service representatives at Fuller Technologies for the past two years. Jean loves her job and wants to stay with Fuller until she retires in 10 years. Maria hates her job, uses all of her available sick days, and would leave in a heartbeat if she could only find a job that paid as well.
- Rhonda Beall recently met with a career adviser to chart a new course for her life. She hates her current job and has hated every job she has ever had. She is hoping that the career adviser can find "*the* job" for her.
- David Spoto loves his job and can't wait to get to work in the morning. He loves to work, loves his current job, and has loved every job he has ever had.
- Darnell Johnson, human resources (HR) director for Simmons Enterprises, is frustrated because his company has the highest turnover rate in the area. Even more frustrating is that employees stay with Simmons just long enough to gain experience and then leave for lower pay with Raynes Manufacturing, another local employer.

Why does Jean Davis love her job and Maria McDuffie hate the same job? Why do Rhonda Beall and David Spoto have such different attitudes about their jobs and careers? What is Raynes Manufacturing doing better than Simmons Enterprises? This chapter will help you answer these questions about **job satisfaction**—the attitude an employee has toward her job—and **organizational commitment**—the extent to which an employee identifies with and is involved with an organization.

Why Should We Care about Employee Attitudes?

Many job-related attitudes have been studied by psychologists, but the two most commonly studied are job satisfaction and organizational commitment. Though job satisfaction and organizational commitment are different work-related attitudes, they will be discussed together in this chapter because they are highly correlated and result in similar employee behaviors. As shown in Table 10.1, meta-analyses indicate that satisfied employees tend to be committed to an organization (Cooper-Hakim & Viswesvaran, 2005), and employees who are satisfied and committed are more likely to attend work (Hackett, 1989), stay with an organization (Tett & Meyer, 1993), arrive at work on time (Koslowsky, Sagie, Krausz, & Singer, 1997), perform well (Judge, Thoresen, Bono, & Patton, 2001), engage in behaviors helpful to the organization (LePine, Erez, & Johnson, 2002), and engage in ethical behavior (Kish-Gephart, Harrison, & Treviño, 2010) than are employees who are not satisfied or committed.

The relationship between job satisfaction and performance is not consistent across people or jobs. For example, for complex jobs, there is a stronger relationship between job satisfaction and performance than for jobs of low or medium complexity (Judge et al., 2001). For employees who have strong, consistent beliefs about their level of job satisfaction (called *affective-cognitive consistency*), the relationship between job satisfaction and performance is much stronger than it is for employees whose job satisfaction attitudes are not so well developed (Schleicher, Watt, & Greguras, 2004).

Though the relationships between job satisfaction and organizational commitment and attendance, performance, tardiness, and turnover are not as large as one would expect, it is important to note that there are many other factors affecting

Table 10.1 Meta-Analysis Results of the Relationships Among Job Satisfaction, Performance, Turnover, Commitment, and Absenteeism

	Performance	Turnover	Absenteeism Frequency	Absenteeism Duration	Commitment Org.	Commitment Occ.	Intrinsic motivation	Lateness	Job satisfaction	Job involvement	Counterproductive behavior
Job Satisfaction											
Facet											
Pay	.05[s]	-.17[e]	.08[b]	-.07[b]	.34[h]	.23[d]	.29[j]	-.22[j]		.09[m]	
Supervision	.19[a]	-.13[e]	-.13[b]	-.08[b]	.45[h]		.39[j]			.22[m]	
Coworkers	.12[a]	-.13[e]	-.07[b]	-.07[b]		.23[d]		-.16[j]		.17[m]	
Work	.21[a]		-.21[b]	-.14[b]		.53[d]				.42[m]	
Promotion	.15[a]		-.09[b]	-.07[b]						.19[m]	
Type											
Intrinsic	.23[a]		-.25[b]	-.01[b]							
Extrinsic	.18[a]		-.24[b]	-.21[b]							
Overall satisfaction	.30[c]	-.22[e]	-.15[b]	-.23[b]	.59[j]	.44[d]	.59[j]	-.11[j]		.37[m]	-.37[n]
Turnover											
Intent to leave	-.12[r]				-.57			.46[j]		-.10[m]	
Occupation		.45[e]				-.62[d]				-.24[m]	
Organization						-.30[d]					
Actual turnover	-.19[e]				-.23[j]	-.21[d]	-.25[b]	.07[j]	-.22[e]	.04[n]	
Absenteeism	-.29[f]	.21[e]			-.23[g]			.40[j]			
Lateness	-.21[j]				-.29[j]				-.11[j]		
Tardiness		.06[e]									
Performance					.17[h]				.30[c]		
Supervisor ratings			-.32[f]	-.26[f]						.07[m]	
Performance measures			-.22[f]	-.28[f]						.07[m]	
Stress											
Role ambiguity	-.21[p]	-.24[e]							-.34[q]		
Role clarity		.12[e]									
Role overload		.22[e]									
Role conflict	-.07[p]	.16[e]						-.21[j]			
Overall stress										-.01[m]	
Intrinsic motivation					.67[h]						
Job involvement					.42[m]						
Organizational citizenship	.74[t]				.25[o]				.24[k]		-.32[n]
Counterproductive behavior					-.36[n]				-.37[n]		

[a]Iaffaldano and Muchinsky (1985), [b]Hackett (1989), [c]Judge, Thoresen, Bono, and Patton (2001), [d]Lee, Carswell, and Allen (2000), [e]Griffeth, Hom, and Gaertner (2000), [f]Bycio (1992), [g]Farrell and Stamm (1988), [h]Mathieu and Zajac (1990), [i]Oldham, Hackman, and Stepina (1978), [j]Koslowsky, Sagie, Krausz, and Singer (1997), [k]LePine, Erez, & Johnson (2002), [l]Cooper-Hakim and Viswesvaran (2005), [m]Brown (1996), [n]Dalal (2005), [o]Riketta (2002), [p]Tubré & Collins (2000), [q]Abramis (1994), [r]Darnold and Zimmerman (2006), [s]Williams, McDaniel, and Nguyen (2006), [t]Hoffman, Blair, Meriac, and Woehr (2006).

work behavior (Judge et al., 2001). For example, a dissatisfied employee may want to quit her job but not be able to because no other jobs are available. Likewise, a dissatisfied employee may want to miss work but realizes that she will lose pay if she does. Thus we often find that job satisfaction and organizational commitment are related more to a *desire* to quit, miss work, or reduce effort than they are to actual behaviors. To get you thinking about job satisfaction in your life, complete Exercise 10.1 in your workbook.

What Causes Employees to Be Satisfied with and Committed to Their Jobs?

This chapter will explore several theories that seek to explain why workers are satisfied with and committed to their jobs, but none of the theories completely explains these job-related attitudes. Each is valuable, however, because it suggests ways to increase employee satisfaction and commitment. Thus, even though a theory itself may not be completely supported by research, the resulting suggestions have generally led to increased performance or longer tenure.

Before discussing various theories, it is important to note that both of these work-related attitudes are multifaceted. That is, employees may be satisfied with one facet of work (e.g., their pay) but not another (e.g., their coworkers). The most commonly studied facets of job satisfaction are pay, supervision, coworkers, work, and promotion opportunities. Many other facets such as satisfaction with equipment, the work facility, the worksite, and company policy are also important but have not received as much research attention.

Affective commitment The extent to which an employee wants to remain with an organization and cares about the organization.

It is thought that there are three motivational facets to organizational commitment (Meyer & Allen, 1997). **Affective commitment** is the extent to which an employee wants to remain with the organization, cares about the organization, and is willing to exert effort on its behalf. For example, an employee of the Red Cross might like her coworkers and her boss, share the altruistic goals of the organization, and realize that her efforts will result in better organizational performance.

Continuance commitment The extent to which employees believe they must remain with an organization due to the time, expense, and effort they have already put into the organization.

Continuance commitment is the extent to which an employee believes she must remain with the organization due to the time, expense, and effort that she has already put into it or the difficulty she would have in finding another job. Take, for example, a chamber of commerce director who spent 10 years making business contacts, getting funding for a new building, and earning the trust of the local city council. Though she could take a new job with a chamber in a different city, she would need to spend another 10 years with that chamber just to make the gains she has already made. As another example, an employee might hate her job and want to leave, but realizes that no other organization would hire her or give her the salary she desires.

Normative commitment The extent to which employees feel an obligation to remain with an organization.

Normative commitment is the extent to which an employee feels obligated to the organization and, as a result of this obligation, must remain with the organization. A good example of normative commitment would be an employee who was given her first job by an organization, was mentored by her manager, and was trained at great cost to the organization. The employee may feel that she is ethically obligated to remain with the organization because of its extensive investment in her.

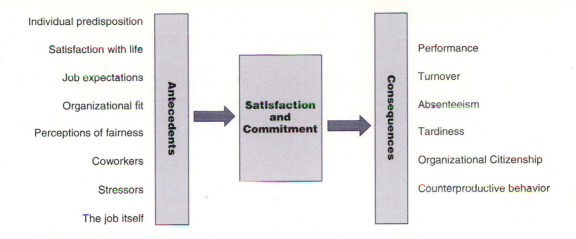

Individual predisposition

Satisfaction with life

Job expectations

Organizational fit

Perceptions of fairness

Coworkers

Stressors

The job itself

Antecedents → **Satisfaction and Commitment** → **Consequences**

Performance

Turnover

Absenteeism

Tardiness

Organizational Citizenship

Counterproductive behavior

Figure 10.1

Antecedents and Consequences of Job Satisfaction and Organizational Commitment

What Individual Differences Affect Job Satisfaction?

As shown in Figure 10.1, one of the factors (called antecedents) that influence levels of job satisfaction and commitment is our personal predisposition to be satisfied. Going back to our examples at the beginning of the chapter, what would explain why David Spoto loves his current job and Rhonda Beall hates hers? According to theories involving individual differences, the key to the answer is the fact that David has been satisfied at every job he has had, whereas Rhonda has never been satisfied with a job. *Individual difference theory* postulates that some variability in job satisfaction is due to an individual's personal tendency across situations to enjoy what she does. Thus, certain types of people will generally be satisfied and motivated regardless of the type of job they hold. This idea also makes intuitive sense. We all know people who constantly complain and whine about every job they have, and we also know people who are motivated and enthusiastic about their every job or task.

For individual-difference theory to be true, it would be essential that job satisfaction be consistent across time and situations. Research seems to support this notion, as meta-analysis results indicate that the average correlation between job satisfaction levels, measured an average of three years apart, is .50 (Dormann & Zapf, 2001).

Complete Exercise 10.2 in your workbook to see how stable your own job satisfaction has been.

Because there seems to be at least some consistency in job satisfaction across time and jobs, the next question concerns the types of people that seem to be consistently satisfied with their jobs. Research in this area has focused on genetic predispositions (Lykken & Tellegen, 1996), core self-evaluations (Judge, Locke, Durham, & Kluger, 1998), and life satisfaction (Tait, Padgett, & Baldwin, 1989).

Genetic Predispositions

An interesting and controversial set of studies (Arvey, Bouchard, Segal, & Abraham, 1989; Arvey, McCall, Bouchard, Taubman, & Cavanaugh, 1994; Keller, Bouchard, Arvey, Segal, & Dawis, 1992) suggests that job satisfaction not only may be fairly stable across jobs but also may be genetically determined. Arvey and his colleagues arrived at this conclusion by comparing the levels of job satisfaction of 34 sets of identical twins who were separated from each other at an early age. If job satisfaction is purely environmental, there should be no significant correlation between levels of job satisfaction for identical twins who were raised in different environments and who are now working at different types of jobs. But if identical twins have similar levels of job satisfaction despite being reared apart and despite working at dissimilar jobs, then a genetic predisposition for job satisfaction is likely.

On the basis of their three studies, Arvey and his colleagues found that approximately 30% of job satisfaction appears to be explainable by genetic factors (Ilies & Judge, 2003). Such a finding does not of course mean that there is a "job satisfaction gene." Instead, inherited personality traits such as negative affectivity (the tendency to have negative emotions such as fear, hostility, and anger) are related to our tendency to be satisfied with jobs (Ilies & Judge, 2003).

What are the implications of these findings? It may be that some people will probably not be satisfied with any job, and supervisors should not lose sleep over the fact that these employees are not happy or motivated. Furthermore, one way to increase the overall level of job satisfaction in an organization would be to hire only those applicants who show high levels of overall job and life satisfaction. Because these findings are controversial and have received some criticism (Cropanzano & James, 1990), more research is needed before firm conclusions can be drawn.

Core Self-Evaluations

Whether the consistency in job satisfaction is due to genetic or environmental factors, a series of personality variables appear to be related to job satisfaction. That is, certain types of personalities are associated with the tendency to be satisfied or dissatisfied with one's job. Judge, Locke, and Durham (1997) have hypothesized that four personality variables are related to people's predisposition to be satisfied with life and with their jobs: emotional stability, self-esteem, self-efficacy (perceived ability to master their environment), and **internal locus of control** (perceived ability to control their environment). That is, people prone to be satisfied with their jobs and with life in general have high self-esteem and a feeling of being competent, are emotionally stable, and believe they have control over their lives, especially their work lives. This view is supported by several meta-analyses and studies:

As shown in Table 10.2, a meta-analysis by Judge and Bono (2001) found these four variables to be related to both job satisfaction and job performance.

- Judge, Locke, Durham, and Kluger (1998) found a significant correlation between a combination of these four variables and job satisfaction ($r = .41$) and life satisfaction ($r = .41$).
- Meta-analyses by Connolly and Viswesvaran (1998), and by Bowling, Hendricks, and Wagner (2008) indicate that overall job satisfaction, as well as different facets of job satisfaction, is related to affectivity. That is, people with a tendency to have positive emotions (positive affectivity) tend to be more satisfied with their jobs than do people with a tendency to have negative emotions (negative affectivity).

Internal locus of control
The extent to which people believe that they are responsible for and in control of their success or failure in life.

Table 10.2 Correlations Between Individual Difference Variables and Satisfaction and Work Behavior

Individual Difference	Satisfaction	Performance	Turnover	Absenteeism	OCB	CWS	Aggression
Affectivity							
Positive	.49[e]	.16[d]	.05[d]		.23[d]		
Negative	−.33[e]	−.13[d]	−.16[d]		−.10[d]	.25[d]	.29[h]
Core Self-Evaluation							
Self-esteem	.26[b]	.26[b]				−.13[j]	
Self-efficacy	.45[b]	.23[b]					
Internal locus of control	.32[b]	.22[b]					
General locus of control	.22[i]						
Work locus of control	.34[i]						
Emotional stability	.24[b]	.19[b]	−.20[g]	.04[f]		−.06[f]	
Personality							
Openness	.02[c]	.06[a]	.10[g]	.00[f]		.14[f]	
Conscientiousness	.26[c]	.24[a]	−.22[g]	−.06[f]		−.26[f]	
Extraversion	.25[c]	.09[a]	−.04[g]	.08[f]		.01[f]	
Agreeableness	.17[c]	.12[a]	−.27[g]	.04[f]		−.20[f]	
Stability	.29[c]	.15[a]	−.20[g]	.04[f]		−.06[f]	

[a]Hurtz & Donovan (2003), [b]Judge & Bono (2001), [c]Judge, Heller, & Mount (2002), [d]Kaplan et al (2008), [e]Connolly & Viswesvaran (2000), [f]Salgado (2002), [g]Zimmerman (2008), [h]Hershcovis et al (2007), [i]Wang, Bowling, & Eschleman (2010), [j]Whelpley & McDaniel (2011).

■ A meta-analysis by Judge, Heller, and Mount (2002) concluded that emotional stability and extraversion were significantly related to job and life satisfaction.

To get an idea of your own predisposition to be satisfied at work, complete Exercise 10.3 in your workbook.

Culture

As shown in Table 10.3, workers in different countries have different levels of job satisfaction. Data from the 2005 International Social Survey Program indicate that of 31 countries surveyed, employees in Mexico were the most satisfied and employees in South Korea the least. U.S. employees ranked 7th in the survey, and employees in Great Britain ranked 14th. In a study of 13,832 employees in 23 countries by FDS International (FDS, 2007), employees in Thailand and The Netherlands had the highest levels of job satisfaction and employees in Korea and Japan the lowest.

Intelligence

In 1997, a police department in New London, Connecticut, created controversy when it announced that applicants who were "too smart" would not be hired (see the Chapter 5 On the Job Box). The police chief's reasoning was that really smart people would be bored and have low job satisfaction. Though there has been little research on the

Table 10.3 International Differences in Job Satisfaction

Job Satisfaction (1–100 scale) 2007 FDS Survey	Job Satisfaction Level (1–7 scale) 2005 ISSP Survey
Thailand (66)	Mexico (5.87)
Netherlands (64)	Switzerland (5.71)
Ireland (59)	Philippines (5.64)
Switzerland (57)	Ireland (5.63)
Portugal (56)	Cyprus (5.52)
UK (56)	Denmark (5.51)
Norway (50)	United States (5.47)
Romania (48)	Germany (5.43)
France (48)	Israel (5.42)
Spain (47)	Dominican Republic (5.37)
Russia (47)	Finland (5.31)
Greece (46)	Canada (5.31)
Sweden (45)	Portugal (5.29)
Australia (45)	Norway (5.28)
United States (44)	UK (5.27)
Canada (44)	Spain (5.24)
Poland (41)	New Zealand (5.24)
Germany (39)	Bulgaria (5.22)
Korea (35)	Australia (5.18)
Japan (26)	South Africa (5.16)
	Hungary (5.16)
	Sweden (5.16)
	Czech Republic (5.09)
	Slovenia (5.07)
	Russia (5.02)
	Taiwan (4.99)
	France (4.97)
	Flanders (4.96)
	Japan (4.95)
	Latvia (4.89)
	South Korea (4.75)

topic, a study by Ganzach (1998) suggests that bright people have slightly lower job satisfaction than do less intelligent employees in jobs that are not complex. In complex jobs, the relationship between intelligence and satisfaction is negligible. A meta-analysis of seven studies by Griffeth, Hom, and Gaertner (2000) found that intelligence and turnover were not significantly related.

Are Employees Satisfied with Other Aspects of Their Lives?

Judge et al. (1998), Judge and Watanabe (1993), and Tait et al. (1989) have theorized not only that job satisfaction is consistent across time but that the extent to which a person is satisfied with all aspects of life (e.g., marriage, friends, job, family, geographic location) is consistent as well. Furthermore, people who are satisfied with their jobs tend to be satisfied with life. These researchers found support for their theory, as their data indicate that job satisfaction is significantly correlated with life satisfaction. Thus people happy in life tend to be happy in their jobs and vice versa.

In an interesting study, Judge and Watanabe (1994) found that for about two-thirds of participants, high levels of life satisfaction are associated with high levels of job satisfaction. In other words, satisfaction with one's job "spills over" into other aspects of life, and satisfaction with other aspects of life spills over into satisfaction with one's job. For the remaining 30% or so of the population, either there is no relationship between life and job satisfaction or there is a negative relationship.

That life satisfaction can influence job satisfaction in the vast majority of people is an important finding. In the twenty-first century, managers are being asked to work miracles in making even the worst of jobs satisfying (think about some of the jobs portrayed on the Discovery Channel's reality TV show, *Dirty Jobs,* which are listed in Table 10.4). Perhaps a more realistic approach is what I refer to as the "John Travolta method." If you will recall from those classic films *Saturday Night Fever* and *Urban Cowboy,* John Travolta had boring jobs (as a paint store employee in *Fever* and as an oil refinery worker in *Urban Cowboy*) but made his life meaningful through his dancing. Now I'm not suggesting that disco and line dancing are the solutions to life's problems (although they are a good start). Instead, I am suggesting that an employee's needs can be met in a variety of nonwork activities such as hobbies and volunteer work. A mistake we have made for years has been to assume that a job must satisfy all of a person's needs. Instead, an organization should work toward fulfilling those needs that it can and should help employees find alternative avenues to meet their other needs.

An interesting study by Judge (1993) demonstrates the importance of individual differences. Judge had more than 200 nurses in a medical clinic complete a questionnaire tapping their propensity to gripe about things in everyday life and also asking them to indicate how satisfied they were with their jobs. Judge then compared the nurses' levels of job satisfaction with whether or not they quit their jobs with the clinic over the next 10 months. The results of this study indicated that for the people who griped about everything in life, there was no significant relationship between satisfaction and turnover ($r = -.05$); however, for the nurses who were not chronic gripers, satisfaction was significantly correlated with turnover ($r = -.39$). In other words, people who are unhappy in life and unhappy on their jobs will not leave their jobs,

Table 10.4   Dirty Jobs: Would You Be Satisfied with Any of These Jobs?

Sewer inspector	Shark-suit tester
Pigeon-poop cleaner-upper	Salmon carcass counter
Baby chicken sexer	Dump-truck cleaner
Sludge recycler	Odor eater
Bug breeder	Owl vomit collector

because they are used to being unhappy. But for people who are normally happy in life, being unhappy at work is seen as a reason to find another job. To get an idea about your own tendency to be satisfied with work and life, complete Exercise 10.4 in your workbook.

Are Employees' Job Expectations Being Met?

As was discussed in Chapter 9, employees come to a job with certain needs, values, and expectations. If there is a discrepancy between these needs, values, and expectations and the reality of the job, employees will become dissatisfied and less motivated. In a test of this *discrepancy theory*, a meta-analysis by Wanous, Poland, Premack, and Davis (1992) concluded that when an employee's expectations are not met, the results are lower job satisfaction ($r = -.39$), decreased organizational commitment ($r = -.39$), and an increased intent to leave the organization ($r = -.29$). These results support the importance of ensuring that applicants have realistic job expectations. Though the meta-analysis results supported the "met expectations" theory, Irving and Meyer (1994) criticized the studies that were included in the meta-analysis. In their own study, Irving and Meyer found that an employee's experiences on the job were most related to job satisfaction and that the *difference* between their expectations and experiences was only minimally related to job satisfaction. More studies using methods similar to Irving and Meyer's are needed to clarify this issue.

In a related meta-analysis, Zhao, Wayne, Glibkowski, and Bravo (2007) investigated the effect of employees perceiving that an organization has not fulfilled its promises and obligations (called psychological contracts) to an employee. When such psychological contract breaches occur, job satisfaction and organizational commitment go down and employee intentions to leave the organization increase. The results of these two meta-analyses support the importance of ensuring not only that applicants have realistic job expectations but that any promises made to employees must be kept.

Is the Employee a Good Fit with the Job and the Organization?

When employees consider how well they "fit" with a job or an organization, they consider the extent to which their values, interests, personality, lifestyle, and skills match those of their *vocation* (e.g., a career such as nursing, law enforcement, or psychology), *job* (its particular tasks), *organization*, *coworkers*, and *supervisor* (Kristof-Brown, Zimmerman, & Johnson, 2005). In addition to these five aspects of fit, Cable and DeRue (2002) believe that needs/supplies fit is also important. Needs/supplies fit is the extent to which the rewards, salary, and benefits received by employees are perceived to be consistent with their efforts and performance.

As shown in Table 10.5, the meta-analysis by Kristof-Brown et al. (2005) clearly demonstrates the importance of fit. Employees who perceive a good fit with their organization, job, coworkers, and supervisor tend to be satisfied with their jobs, identify with the organization, remain with the organization, perform better, and engage in Organizational Citizenship Behaviors (OCBs).

Another "fit" factor that has been shown to be related to job satisfaction and commitment is the extent to which employees' desire for a particular work schedule (e.g., shift, number of hours) matches their actual schedule. As one would expect, the better the fit between an employee's desired schedule and his actual schedule, the greater an employee's job satisfaction, organizational commitment, performance, and likelihood to remain with the organization (Holtom, Lee, & Tidd, 2002).

Table 10.5   Kristof-Brown, Zimmerman, & Johnson (2005) Meta-Analysis Results

Attitude or Behavior	Employee fit with			
	Organization	Group	Supervisor	Job
Job satisfaction	.44	.31	.44	.56
Commitment	.51	.19	.09	.47
Performance	.07	.19	.18	.20
Actual turnover	−.14			−.08
Turnover intentions	−.35			−.46
Absenteeism	−.05			

Branham (2005) believes that there are certain signs to which an organization should pay attention that indicate a job/person mismatch. Some of these signs are that the employee

- does not seem excited when first hired or assigned to a job;
- starts asking for some tasks to be given to other employees;
- applies for other jobs in the organization;
- begins to ask for new projects; and
- appears bored or unchallenged.

Are the Tasks Enjoyable?

Not surprisingly, research is fairly clear that employees who find their work interesting are more satisfied and motivated than employees who do not enjoy their jobs (Gately, 1997). Interestingly, although employees rank interesting work as being the most important factor in a job, supervisors rank salary and bonus as being the most important for employees. This discrepancy is why Glanz (1997) advised employers to take innovative steps to make work more interesting.

Do Employees Enjoy Working with Supervisors and Coworkers?

Research indicates that people who enjoy working with their supervisors and coworkers will be more satisfied with their jobs (Mossholder, Settoon, & Henagan, 2005; Repetti & Cosmas, 1991). Such findings certainly make sense. We all have had coworkers and supervisors who made our jobs unbearable, and we all have had coworkers and supervisors who made our jobs fun to have. In a study of 500 employees at an apparel manufacturing plant, Bishop and Scott (1997) found that satisfaction with supervisors and coworkers was related to organizational and team commitment, which in turn resulted in higher productivity, lower intent to leave the organization, and a greater willingness to help.

Are Coworkers Outwardly Unhappy?

Social information processing theory States that employees model their levels of satisfaction and motivation from other employees.

Social learning theory States that employees model their levels of satisfaction and motivation from other employees.

Social information processing theory, also called **social learning theory**, postulates that employees observe the levels of motivation and satisfaction of other employees and then model those levels (Salancik & Pfeffer, 1977). Thus, if an organization's older employees work hard and talk positively about their jobs and their employer,

One's coworkers can affect job satisfaction.

new employees will model this behavior and be both productive and satisfied. The reverse is also true: If veteran employees work slowly and complain about their jobs, so will new employees.

To test this theory, Weiss and Shaw (1979) had subjects view a training video in which assembly line workers made either positive or negative comments about their jobs. After viewing the videotape, each subject was given an opportunity to perform the job. The study found that those subjects who had seen the positive tape enjoyed the task more than did the subjects who viewed the negative tape. In a similar study conducted by Mirolli, Henderson, and Hills (1998), subjects performed a task with two experimenters pretending to be other subjects (these are called confederates). In one condition, the confederates made positive comments about the task (e.g., "Gee, this is fun"); in a second condition, they made negative comments about the task (e.g., "This sucks"); and in the control condition, they did not make any comments. Consistent with social information processing theory, actual subjects exposed to the confederates' positive comments rated the task as more enjoyable than did the subjects exposed to negative comments.

In general, the research on social information processing theory supports the idea that the social environment does have an effect on employees' attitudes and behaviors (Pollock, Whitbred, & Contractor, 2000; Robinson & O'Leary-Kelly, 1998). As with all of the theories in this chapter, it plays a role in job satisfaction but does not play the only role. One of the appeals of social information processing theory is that it certainly makes intuitive sense. Think of courses you have taken in which one student participated more than anyone else. After a while, the student's level of participation probably decreased to be more in line with the rest of the class. In work as in school, social pressures force individuals to behave in ways that are consistent with the norm, even though the person may privately believe something different (Nail, 1986).

An IT company in Germany, Nutzwerk, believes so strongly in this theory that it makes new employees sign a contract agreeing not to whine and complain. The policy was created after employees started complaining about a woman who kept complaining! So far, two employees have been fired for excessive whining.

Are Rewards and Resources Given Equitably?

Equity theory A theory of job satisfaction stating that employees will be satisfied if their ratio of effort to reward is similar to that of other employees.

One factor related to both job satisfaction and employee motivation is the extent to which employees perceive that they are being treated fairly. As you probably recall from Chapter 9, **equity theory** is based on the premise that our levels of job satisfaction and motivation are related to how fairly we believe we are treated in comparison with others. If we believe we are treated unfairly, we attempt to change our beliefs or behaviors until the situation appears to be fair.

One of the greatest problems with the equity and justice theories is that despite their rational sense, they are difficult to implement. That is, based on equity and justice theories, the best way to keep employees satisfied would be to treat them all fairly, which would entail paying the most to those employees who contributed the most. Although few of us would disagree with this approach, it is difficult to implement for several reasons.

The first is *practicality*. An organization certainly can control such variables as salary, hours worked, and benefits, but it cannot easily control other variables, such as how far an employee lives from work or the number of friends an employee makes on the job.

The second reason that equity is difficult to achieve is that the employee's *perception* of inputs and outputs determines equity, not the *actual* inputs and outputs. For example, two students of equal ability receive the same grade on an exam. One student knows that she studied 10 hours for the exam but never saw the other student in the library. She may feel that the scores are unfair because she studied harder but received the same grade as the student she never saw study. Of course, the other student may have studied 20 hours while at work, but she would not know that. In this case, the student's perception of input level may not match reality.

It is important that employees base their judgments on factual information. Of course, this may be easier said than done. In two national surveys, only 40% of employees stated that they understood how their pay was determined (Grensing-Pophal, 2003). This is an important finding because another survey found that 74% of employees who understood how their pay was determined were satisfied with their jobs compared with only 42% of employees who did not understand the basis for their pay (Grensing-Pophal, 2003). The results of these surveys suggest that to increase perceptions of equity, organizations need to do a better job of explaining their compensation systems.

Another way to increase perceptions of equity would be to allow employees access to the salaries of other employees. In the public sector, employee salaries are available to the public, although most public agencies certainly do not go out of their way to publicize salary information. In the private sector, most organizations keep such information confidential, and some even include statements in their employee manuals that forbid employees from divulging their salaries to one another. Such policies, however, encourage employees to speculate about how much other people make. This speculation usually results in employees thinking the worst and believing that others make more than they do. It is probably in the best interests of an organization to make salary and performance information available to all employees, although each employee's permission must be obtained before such information is released.

Even if an organization were able to maintain complete internal equity, employees would then compare their ratios with those of employees from other organizations.

The problem with such comparisons is that an organization has little or no control over another's policies. Furthermore, perceptions of wages and benefits at other organizations most likely will be more distorted than internal perceptions. Thus, even if equity theory were completely accurate, maintaining a high level of employee satisfaction would still be difficult.

Although equity theory is historically interesting, a more useful approach to fairness issues has been the study of three aspects of **organizational justice**: distributive justice, procedural justice, and interactional justice. **Distributive justice** is the perceived fairness of the actual decisions made in an organization. For example, did one manager get a higher budget than another? Was the higher raise received by one employee justified? Did the right employee get promoted? **Procedural justice** is the perceived fairness of the methods used to arrive at the decision. Take, for example, a situation in which an employee was fired for breaking the rules, but was never given the opportunity to explain what happened. Or, imagine a situation in which an excellent employee was given a promotion, but no other employees were allowed to compete for the promotion. In both situations, an employee might not completely disagree with the *outcome*, but they might be upset with the *process*.

Interactional justice is the perceived fairness of the interpersonal treatment employees receive. That is, a supervisor might spend substantial time talking with, mentoring, and socializing with some employees while completely ignoring others. An interesting example of a problem with interactional justice comes from an organization in which a regional manager took female branch managers to breakfast at McDonald's to discuss sales but took male managers to dinner at a nice restaurant. While the quality of the restaurant is certainly an issue, the 30 minutes spent with the female managers over an Egg McMuffin does not provide the amount or quality of the interaction spent eating steak and having drinks at a strip club (this is actually where the regional manager took the male managers).

As shown in Table 10.6, meta-analysis results indicate that perceived justice is related to several important factors, including job satisfaction, organizational commitment, performance, trust, withdrawal (e.g., turnover, absenteeism), and negative employee reactions (e.g., theft, sabotage). Because the relationships between perceptions of justice and employee attitudes and behavior are so strong, it is essential that employers be open about how decisions are made, take time to develop fair procedures, involve employees in the process of how decisions will be made, provide feedback to employees who might not be happy with decisions that are made, and allow a process for appealing decisions.

Is There a Chance for Growth and Challenge?

For many employees, job satisfaction is affected by opportunities for challenge and growth. As discussed in Chapter 9, Maslow thought that the need for growth and challenge, which he labeled *self-actualization,* is important only after low-level needs (e.g., safety, social) have been met. To help satisfy employee self-actualization needs, organizations can do many things. The easiest and most common are **job rotation, job enlargement**, and **job enrichment**. With job rotation and job enlargement, an employee learns how to use several different machines or conduct several different tasks within an organization. With job rotation, the employee is given the same number of tasks to do at one time, but the tasks change from time to time. With job enlargement, an employee is given more tasks to do at one time.

Organizational justice A theory that postulates that if employees perceive they are being treated fairly, they will be more likely to be satisfied with their jobs and motivated to do well.

Distributive justice The perceived fairness of the decisions made in an organization.

Procedural justice The perceived fairness of the methods used by an organization to make decisions.

Interactional justice The perceived fairness of the interpersonal treatment that employees receive.

Job rotation A system in which employees are given the opportunity to perform several different jobs in an organization.

Job enlargement A system in which employees are given more tasks to perform at the same time.

Job enrichment A system in which employees are given more responsibility over the tasks and decisions related to their job.

Table 10.6   Organizational Justice Meta-Analysis Results

	Organizational Justice Dimension		
	Procedural	**Distributive**	**Interactional**
Job satisfaction	.62[a]	.56[a]	
Commitment			
Organizational	.57[a]	.51[a]	
Affective	.38[c]	.40[c]	.50[c]
Normative	.31[c]	.31[c]	.52[c]
Continuance	−.14[c]	−.06[c]	−.16[c]
Performance	.36[a]	.15[a]	
Absenteeism	−.46[a]	−.50[a]	
Aggression	−.20[b]	−.13[b]	
Counterproductive work behaviors	−.31[a]	−.30[a]	

[a]Colquitt, et al. (2001), [b]Hershcovis et al. (2007), [c]Meyer et al. (2002).

A job can be enlarged in two ways: knowledge used and tasks performed. With knowledge enlargement, employees are allowed to make more complex decisions. With task enlargement, they are given more tasks of the same difficulty level to perform. As one might imagine, satisfaction increases with knowledge enlargement and decreases with task enlargement (Campion & McClelland, 1993).

Job rotation and job enlargement accomplish two main objectives. First, they challenge employees by requiring them to learn to operate several different machines or perform several different tasks. Thus, once employees have mastered one task or machine, they can work toward mastering another.

Second, job rotation helps to alleviate boredom by allowing an employee to change tasks. Thus, if an employee welds parts one day, assembles bumpers on another, and tightens screws on a third, the boredom caused by performing the same task every day should be reduced.

Perhaps an even better way to satisfy self-actualization needs is through job enrichment. The main difference between job rotation and job enrichment is that with job rotation an employee performs different tasks, and with job enrichment the employee assumes more responsibility over the tasks.

In their **job characteristics model** that was discussed in Chapter 9, Hackman and Oldham (1975, 1976) theorized that enriched jobs are the most satisfying. Enriched jobs allow a variety of skills to be used, allow employees to complete an entire task (e.g., process a loan application from start to finish) rather than parts of a task, involve tasks that have meaning or importance, allow employees to make decisions, and provide feedback about performance. Hackman and Oldham developed the **Job Diagnostic Survey (JDS)** to measure the extent to which these characteristics are present in a given job.

If we look again at the job of college professor, job enrichment is clearly an inherent part of the job. That is, the professor decides what she will research and what she will teach in a particular course. This authority to make decisions about one's own work leads to higher job satisfaction.

Job characteristics theory

The theory proposed by Hackman and Oldham that suggests that certain characteristics of a job will make the job more or less satisfying, depending on the particular needs of the worker.

Job Diagnostic Survey (JDS) A measure of the extent to which a job provides opportunities for growth, autonomy, and meaning.

With an assembly line worker, however, responsibility is something that must be added because the employee has minimal control over the way a job is done. After all, bumpers must be assembled in the same way each time and welded to the same place. So what can be done to enrich the typical factory worker's job?

One method is to give workers more responsibility over their jobs. For example, when an employee first begins working for a company, her work is checked by a quality control inspector. After she has been with the company long enough for the first four needs levels to be satisfied, she is given responsibility for checking her own quality. Likewise, more control can be given to the employee about where and when she will eat lunch, when she will take vacation time, or how fast she will accomplish her work. At one Kaiser Aluminum production plant, for example, time clocks were removed so that the workers could assume more responsibility for their performance by keeping track of their own hours.

Even when increased decision-making responsibilities are not possible, job enrichment ideas can still be implemented. For example, many organizations have or work with credit unions whose credit committees and boards of directors consist of company employees. These committees and boards provide excellent opportunities to increase employees' decision-making powers even though the decisions are not directly related to their jobs.

Another method to increase the level of job enrichment is showing employees that their jobs have meaning and that they are meeting some worthwhile goal through their work (Hackman & Oldham, 1975). At some automobile factories, for example, this is accomplished by having employees work in teams to build cars. Instead of an employee performing a single task all day, she does several tasks, as do the other employees in her group. At the end of the day, the employee can see a completed car that she has had a major role in building.

A plant that manufactures transformers provides another example. The training department realized that even though employees spent eight hours a day manufacturing the product, few understood what it did, who used it, and what would happen if it were not manufactured correctly. To correct this problem, the employees participated in a training session in which they were shown how the transformer was used, who used it, and the consequences that resulted from poor manufacturing.

Self-directed teams *See Quality circles.*

Quality circles Employee groups that meet to propose changes that will improve productivity and the quality of work life.

The final method for increasing employees' self-actualization needs that we will discuss here is the use of **self-directed teams**, or **quality circles**. With quality circles, employees meet as a group to discuss and make recommendations about work issues. These issues range from something as trivial as the music played in the work area to something as important as reducing waste or improving productivity. Meta-analysis results indicate that quality circles increase job satisfaction ($d = .25$) and commitment ($d = .22$) for employees in the private sector but not for those in public agencies (Pereira & Osburn, 2007).

In an extensive review of the literature, Wagner (1994) concluded that allowing employees to participate in making decisions results in small but significant increases in performance and job satisfaction. Arthur (1994) found lower turnover in steel mills that allowed employees to make decisions on their own than in steel mills with a more controlling style. In a more recent study, Rentsch and Steel (1998) found that job enrichment resulted in decreased absenteeism.

Though team approaches are popular, there is considerable debate about their effectiveness. Most quality improvement programs using a team approach fail to provide the desired results (Zemke, 1993).

Integration of Theories

In this chapter, we discussed many theories of job satisfaction. The question you must be asking (other than "When does this chapter end?") is, "How, then, do we satisfy employees?" Unfortunately, the answer to this question is complex and depends on a variety of factors. We can, however, use the theories to design an organizational climate that is more conducive to motivation and satisfaction than is the typical climate.

As shown in Figure 10.2, individual-difference theories say that each of us brings to a job an initial tendency to be satisfied with life and its various aspects such as work. A person with a low tendency toward satisfaction might *start* a job with only

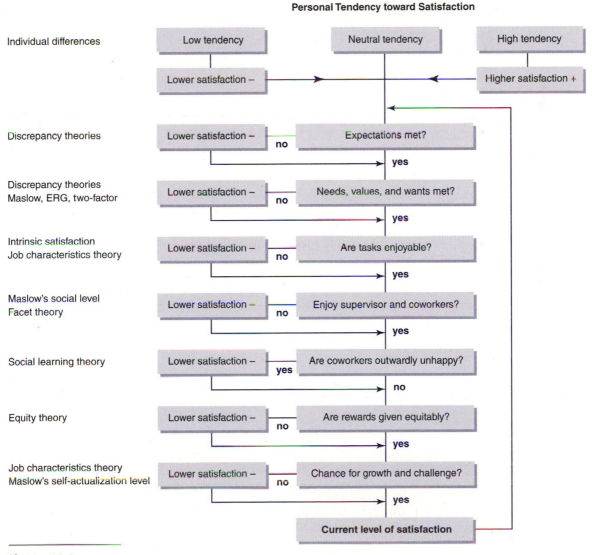

Figure 10.2

Satisfaction Flowchart

6 hypothetical satisfaction points, a person with a neutral tendency might start with 10 hypothetical points, and a person with a high tendency might bring fourteen points.

For example, research indicates that in addition to genetics, such traits as internal locus of control (Stout, Slocum, & Cron, 1987; Surrette & Harlow, 1992), Type A behavior, patience/tolerance (Bluen, Barling, & Burns, 1990), and social trust (Liou, Sylvia, & Brunk, 1990) are related to our tendency to be satisfied with work. Demographically, males and females are equally satisfied with work, Whites are more satisfied than African Americans, and older workers are slightly more satisfied and committed than younger workers (Ng & Feldman, 2010).

Surrette and Harlow (1992) found that people will be most satisfied with a job if they had the *option to choose* that job from other alternatives rather than the job being their only choice. Once people are employed at a job, however, they are most satisfied when they don't have other career alternatives (Pond & Geyer, 1987).

During our years at work, certain events and conditions occur that can add to or decrease our initial level of satisfaction that was due to personal predispositions.

According to discrepancy theories, we will remain satisfied with our job if it meets our various needs, wants, expectations, and values. As discussed previously in the chapter, individuals vary greatly in their needs for such things as achievement, status, safety, and social contact. Thus, not every job can satisfy the needs of every employee during every period of his life. By being aware of employee needs, however, we can select the employees whose needs are consistent with the requirements and characteristics of the job. The Career Workshop Box provides some strategies for those who may be unhappy with their jobs.

According to the intrinsic satisfaction theory and job characteristics theory, we will be more satisfied with our jobs if the tasks themselves are enjoyable to perform. What makes a task enjoyable varies across individuals. For some, working on a computer is fun, whereas for others, nothing could be more boring. Many people enjoy making decisions, solving conflicts, and seeing a project through from start to finish, whereas others don't.

Overall satisfaction can be affected by our satisfaction with individual facets of the job. For example, an incompetent boss, terrible coworkers, low pay, or limited opportunities for advancement can lessen overall job satisfaction. Even trivial things can lessen job satisfaction. I once worked at a job where the vending machines never worked and supplies such as paper and pens were often not available. These factors were irritants for most employees—enough to lessen job satisfaction but certainly not enough to make any of us *dissatisfied* with the job. According to social learning theory, we will be more satisfied if our coworkers are satisfied. If everyone else is whining and complaining, it is difficult to be the only person at work who loves his job.

No matter how much we intrinsically like our work, equity and justice theories predict that we will become dissatisfied if rewards, punishments, and social interactions are not given equitably. If you work harder than a coworker, yet she receives a bigger raise, you are less likely to be satisfied even though money may not be the reason you are working.

On the basis of job characteristics theory and Maslow's level of self-actualization, lack of opportunity for growth, challenge, variety, autonomy, and advancement will decrease satisfaction for many people.

The results of these factors are summed to indicate an employee's current level of satisfaction. As conditions change, so will the level of satisfaction. To apply what you have learned about job satisfaction, complete Exercise 10.5 in your workbook.

Measuring Job Satisfaction and Commitment

This chapter has discussed several theories that seek to explain job satisfaction and commitment. But one important issue that remains is how an employee's level of job satisfaction or commitment is measured. Generally, job satisfaction is measured in one of two ways: standard job satisfaction inventories or custom-designed satisfaction inventories. Commitment is usually measured through standard commitment inventories.

Commonly Used Standard Inventories

Measures of Job Satisfaction

One of the first methods for measuring job satisfaction was developed by Kunin (1955) and is called the **Faces Scale** (a simulation is shown in Figure 10.3). Although the scale is easy to use, it is no longer commonly administered partly because it lacks sufficient detail, lacks construct validity, and because some employees believe it is so simple that it is demeaning.

The most commonly used scale today is the **Job Descriptive Index (JDI)** (Figure 10.4). The JDI was developed by Smith, Kendall, and Hulin (1969) and consists of a series of job-related adjectives and statements that are rated by employees. The scales yield scores on five dimensions of job satisfaction: supervision, pay, promotional opportunities, coworkers, and the work itself.

A similar measure of job satisfaction is the **Minnesota Satisfaction Questionnaire (MSQ)**, which was developed by Weiss, Dawis, England, and Lofquist (1967). The MSQ contains 100 items that yield scores on 20 scales. To get experience taking a satisfaction inventory, complete the short form of the MSQ in Figure 10.5.

The fact that the JDI has five scales and the MSQ 20 underscores the point that job satisfaction is not easy to measure. This is especially true when one considers that employees' responses on the JDI are not highly correlated with their responses on the MSQ (Gillet & Schwab, 1975). Because both the JDI and the MSQ measure specific aspects of job satisfaction, Ironson, Smith, Brannick, Gibson, and Paul (1989) developed the **Job in General (JIG) Scale**. The JIG is useful when an organization wants to measure the overall level of job satisfaction rather than specific aspects.

Nagy (1996) criticized many of the standard measures of job satisfaction because these measures ask only if employees are satisfied with a particular aspect of their job, but not how important that job aspect is to them. Recall from our previous discussion on discrepancy theories that people differ about what is important to them. With this in mind, imagine that both Sally and Temea think their salaries are lower than they should be. Sally is a real social climber and thinks that salary is a measure of one's status in life. Temea, however, has inherited plenty of money and works because she enjoys keeping busy. Although both Sally and Temea think their pay is low, Nagy (1996) argues that only Sally would actually be dissatisfied. To understand these differences, Nagy (1995) created the Nagy Job Satisfaction Scale, which includes two questions per facet: one asking how important the facet is to the employee and the other asking how satisfied the employee is with the facet.

Faces Scale A measure of job satisfaction in which raters place a mark under a facial expression that is most similar to the way they feel about their jobs.

Job Descriptive Index (JDI) A measure of job satisfaction that yields scores on five dimensions.

Minnesota Satisfaction Questionnaire (MSQ) A measure of job satisfaction that yields scores on 20 dimensions.

Job in General (JIG) Scale A measure of the overall level of job satisfaction

Place a check under the face that expresses how you feel about your job in general.

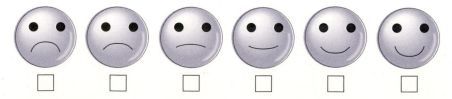

Figure 10.3
Simulation of Faces Scale of Job Satisfaction

Think of your present work. What is it like most of the time? In the blank beside each word given below, write

___Y___ for "Yes" if it describes your work
___N___ for "No" if it does NOT describe It
___?___ if you cannot decide

Think of the pay you get now. How well does each of the following words describe your present pay? In the blank beside each word, put

___Y___ for "Yes" if it describes your pay
___N___ for "No" if it does NOT describe it
___?___ if you cannot decide

Think of the opportunities for promotion that you have now. How well does each of the following words describe these? In the blank beside each word put

___Y___ for "Yes" if it describes your opportunities for promotion
___N___ for "No" if it does NOT describe them
___?___ if you cannot decide

Work on Present Job

____ Routine
____ Satisfying
____ Good
____ On your feet

Present Pay

____ Income adequate for normal expenses
____ Insecure
____ Less than I deserve
____ Highly paid

Opportunities for Promotion

____ Promotion on ability
____ Dead-end job
____ Unfair promotion policy
____ Regular promotions

Think of the kind of supervision that you get on your job. How well does each of the following words describe this supervision? In the blank beside each word below, put

___Y___ if it describes the supervision you get on your job
___N___ if it does NOT describe it
___?___ if you cannot decide

Think of the majority of the people that you work with now or the people you meet in connection with your work. How well does each of the following words describe these people? In the blank beside each word below, put

___Y___ if it describes the people you work with
___N___ if it does NOT describe them
___?___ If you cannot decide

Supervision on Present Job

____ Impolite
____ Praises good work
____ Influential
____ Doesn't supervise enough

People on Your Present Job

____ Boring
____ Responsible
____ Intelligent
____ Talk too much

Source: *The measurement of satisfaction in work and retirement,* by P. C. Smith, L. M. Kendall, and C. L. Hulin (1969), Chicago: Rand McNally. The Job Descriptive Index is copyrighted by Bowling Green State University. The complete forms, scoring key, instructions, and norms can be requested from Dr. Patricia Smith.

Figure 10.4

Sample items from the Job Descriptive Index

Measures of Commitment

Most measures of organizational commitment are relatively short and tap aspects similar to the three types of commitment mentioned previously: affective commitment, continuance commitment, and normative commitment. Perhaps the most commonly

Ask yourself: How **satisfied** am I with this aspect of my job?

Very Sat. means I am very satisfied with this aspect of my job.

Sat. means I am satisfied with this aspect of my job.

N means I can't decide whether I am satisfied or not with this aspect of my job.

Dissat. means I am dissatisfied with this aspect of my job.

Very Dissat. means I am very dissatisfied with this aspect of my job.

On my present job, this is how I feel about...	Very Dissat.	Dissat.	N	Sat.	Very Sat.
1. Being able to keep busy all the time	☐	☐	☐	☐	☐
2. The chance to work alone on the job	☐	☐	☐	☐	☐
3. The chance to do different things from time to time	☐	☐	☐	☐	☐
4. The chance to be "somebody" in the community	☐	☐	☐	☐	☐
5. The way my boss handles employees	☐	☐	☐	☐	☐
6. The competence of my supervisor in making decisions	☐	☐	☐	☐	☐
7. Being able to do things that don't go against my conscience	☐	☐	☐	☐	☐
8. The way my job provides for steady employment	☐	☐	☐	☐	☐
9. The chance to do things for other people	☐	☐	☐	☐	☐
10. The chance to tell people what to do	☐	☐	☐	☐	☐
11. The chance to do something that makes use of my abilities	☐	☐	☐	☐	☐
12. The way company policies are put into practice	☐	☐	☐	☐	☐
13. My pay and the amount of work I do	☐	☐	☐	☐	☐
14. The chances for advancement on this job	☐	☐	☐	☐	☐
15. The freedom to use my own judgment	☐	☐	☐	☐	☐
16. The chance to try my own methods of doing the job	☐	☐	☐	☐	☐
17. The working conditions	☐	☐	☐	☐	☐
18. The way my coworkers get along with each other	☐	☐	☐	☐	☐
19. The praise I get for doing a good job	☐	☐	☐	☐	☐
20. The feeling of accomplishment I get from the job	☐	☐	☐	☐	☐
	Very Dissat.	Dissat.	N	Sat.	Very Sat.

Figure 10.5

Minnesota Satisfaction Questionnaire Short Form

Foster Consulting specializes in all aspects of talent management. We assist organizations in attracting, hiring, engaging, and retaining the talent needed to maximize business results. We offer a range of services including strategy development and execution, organizational research, competency development, assessment centers, employment selection, job analysis, and 360-degree feedback/coaching.

Most of our work involves some type of research using surveys, focus groups, or interviews. These data are used in a variety of ways to solicit input, understand perceptions, improve performance, and gain buy-in. Our research is generally used to help organizations decrease turnover, increase employee engagement or satisfaction, and improve communication or productivity.

We work with our clients to determine which research method, or combination of methods, would best meet their budget, timing, and overall project needs. On some projects we suggest that the client simply conduct an employee survey or focus groups. With others, we recommend they also interview key executives and possibly use ongoing feedback to collect data over a period of time as changes are implemented.

An organization that decides to undergo the full range of employee research may develop an integrated plan for involving key stakeholders. This integrated approach typically starts by engaging the top executives through an interview process. We will partner with the client team, who typically represent areas of the business such as change, communication, human resources, benefits, and compensation, to develop a guide to be used during the interviews. The questions in this guide explore these aspects of executives:

- Perceptions of the business and role that employees play in business success
- Philosophy of the rewards and other human resources programs—what they should be designed to do or not do; for example, should rewards programs be a factor in an employee's decision to join an organization? stay with an organization? become fully engaged in his/her work?
- Assessment of the impact that major changes have had on the organization and its employees
- Views of where the organization's programs should rank against other organizations
- Guidance for the current project team and measures of success

© Heather Foster

Heather King Foster, M.A.
President, Foster Consulting, Inc.

The data gathered from executives are typically used to set the direction for the project, and input gathered from other groups along the way is compared with these data.

Another core group that is often targeted for research efforts is line managers. These leaders are typically closest to employees and have the greatest influence on the communication employees receive. By involving managers early in the process, typically through focus groups, we gain an understanding of their needs and challenges as managers, the role that rewards and other human resources programs play in their ability to attract, retain, and engage employees, and how their views align with those of executives.

Employees often participate in a major change effort through a survey. Input from executive interviews and manager focus groups are combined with data gathered through employee focus groups to develop the survey. The survey is then administered to either the entire employee population or a sample of employees. The more sensitive and impactful the change effort, the more likely the client will want to provide every employee with a chance to participate. We conduct surveys using a variety of methods: web, paper, email, and telephone. Once the survey is administered and data are received, we conduct a number of statistical analyses to understand the data. We look at differences across demographic groups, create indices of items to understand "drivers" of employee perceptions, and look for general trends in the data. Our analyses are then used to write a detailed report of the results, where we pull together all the data that have been gathered thus far on the project. We explain the points of view of executives, managers, and employees, and compare and contrast their perceptions on various issues.

Often, we follow an employee survey with focus groups. These focus groups are used to further explore issues identified in the survey, and can be used to test ideas for change or communication with employees. Another form of gathering additional data from employees is through pulse surveys. These surveys are often administered online to just a sample of employees and are brief in nature. Pulse surveys allow the client to gather quick, "real time" data to gauge employees' perceptions and understanding of changes and communication messages that have been introduced. These results are tracked over time to monitor progress that has been made within the organization as a result of a major change.

The most critical component of any form of research is the client's willingness to use the data. Best-practice organizations ask their employees for feedback on a regular basis, have a good track record for using the data, and constantly keep employees informed of the use of data.

used measure of organizational commitment is that developed by Allen and Meyer (1990). The Allen and Meyer survey has 24 items, 8 each for the 3 factors of affective, continuance, and normative commitment. Examples of questions are as follows:

Affective commitment
- I would be very happy to spend the rest of my career in this organization.
- I really feel as if this organization's problems are my own.

Continuance commitment
- It would be very hard for me to leave my organization right now, even if I wanted to.
- I believe that I have too few options to consider leaving this organization.

Normative commitment
- I would feel guilty if I left my organization now.
- This organization deserves my loyalty.

Other measures include the following:

- **Organizational Commitment Questionnaire (OCQ):** A 15-item questionnaire developed by Mowday, Steers, and Porter (1979) to measure three commitment factors: acceptance of the organization's values and goals, willingness to work to help the organization, and a desire to remain with the organization. Although the questions tap three factors, most people using the scale combine the factors to yield one overall commitment score (Kacmar, Carlson, & Brymer, 1999).
- **Organizational Commitment Scale (OCS):** A nine-item survey developed by Balfour and Wechsler (1996) that measures three aspects of commitment: identification, exchange, and affiliation. Sample questions include, "I felt like a part of the family at this organization" and "What this organization stands for is important to me."

Custom-Designed Inventories

Though most research on job satisfaction is conducted using one or more of the previously mentioned standard inventories, most organizations tap their employees' levels of job satisfaction by using custom-designed inventories. The advantage to custom-designed inventories is that an organization can ask employees questions specific to their organization. For example, a local agency recently restructured many of its jobs and wanted to tap how satisfied its employees were with the changes. To do this, they hired a consultant who designed questions that specifically tapped employees' thoughts and feelings about the changes. Using one of the standard inventories would not have provided the needed information. To learn more about custom surveys, read the employment profile of Heather King.

Consequences of Dissatisfaction and Other Negative Work Attitudes

Absenteeism

As discussed earlier in this chapter and depicted in Figure 10.1, when employees are dissatisfied or not committed to the organization, they are more likely to miss work and leave their jobs than satisfied or committed employees. In the remaining two sections of the chapter, absenteeism and turnover will be discussed and methods to decrease these negative employee behaviors will be presented.

A survey by Kronos, a company specializing in absence control, indicated that in 2010, the average U.S. employee had 5.4 days of unscheduled absence. Although comparable international data are difficult to come by, a survey by the Confederation of British Industry indicated that workers in the United Kingdom missed an average of 6.4 days per year in 2009 and data from Statistics Canada Indicate that the average Canadian employees missed 9.8 days in 2009. Including absences due to holidays, sickness, and parental leave, the average employee in Sweden took 17 weeks off work in 2004 (OECD, 2005)! Comparing U.S. absenteeism rates with those in other countries can be difficult because many countries require employers to provide paid days off for absenteeism whereas the United States has no such laws. In fact, data from the U.S. Department of Labor indicate that 80% of low-paid or part-time employees do not get a single day of paid absence.

Nutreco, an international supplier of food products, provides an excellent example of international differences in absenteeism. In 2000, the overall absenteeism rate for Nutreco was 4.5%, yet the rate varied tremendously across national borders. Absenteeism was lowest for its plants in Canada (1.6%), Ireland (1.9%), and Poland (2.3%) and highest for its plants in the Netherlands (7.8%), Norway (7.2%), and Belgium (6.3%). The absenteeism rates for Chile (2.7%), the UK (3.2%), Spain (3.8%), and France (4.0%) fell in the middle. Organizations throughout the world are concerned with absenteeism, not only because of its high monetary cost, but also because absenteeism is correlated with turnover ($r = .21$) and is thought to be a warning sign of intended turnover (Griffeth et al., 2000).

Because of the high costs of absenteeism and turnover, organizations are expending great effort to reduce the number of unscheduled absences. For these efforts to be effective, it is important that we understand why employees miss work. That is, punishment will reduce absenteeism only if employees make conscious decisions about attending. Likewise, wellness programs will increase attendance only if absenteeism is mostly the result of illness. As can be seen in Table 10.7, in the most recent CCH survey on unscheduled absenteeism, 65% of absences were due to reasons other than

Table 10.7 Trends in absenteeism rates and reasons that people miss work

	Year								
	1999	2000	2001	2002	2003	2004	2005	2006	2007
Absenteeism rate (U.S.)									
CCH survey data	2.70	2.10	2.20	2.10	1.90	2.40	2.30	2.50	2.30
BNA data	1.70	1.70	1.70	1.60	1.60	1.40	1.50		
Annual cost per employee	$602	$610	$755	$789	$645	$610	$660		
Reason for missing work (%)									
Employee illness	21	40	32	33	36	38	35	35	34
Employee stress	19	5	19	12	11	11	12	12	13
Personal needs	20	20	11	21	18	18	18	18	18
Family issues	21	21	21	24	22	23	21	24	22
Sense of entitlement	19	14	9	10	13	10	14	11	13
Other (e.g., bad weather)			8						

Source: CCH Annual Unscheduled Absence Surveys

employee illness. In a 2010 survey of 3,100 employees by CareerBuilder.com, 29% of employees admitted to taking at least one "sick day" off each year even though they weren't sick. The top three reasons for taking the time off were attending to personal errands, catching up on sleep, and relaxing.

Linking Attendance to Consequences

The basis behind rewarding attendance and punishing absenteeism is that employees make a decision each day as to whether they will or will not attend work. Although the decision-making process is not clearly understood, it probably includes weighing the consequences of going to work (or to class) against the consequences of not going. For example, imagine that you have an 8:00 a.m. class and are deciding whether you will attend this morning. By missing class, you can sleep a few hours longer, watch the *Today Show*, and stay out of the rain. By attending class, you will get the notes that you know will be on the test but aren't in the book, get to listen to the instructor's terrific sense of humor, and get to sit next to the great-looking student you think is interested in you. If a good test grade and a chance at a date are most important, you will attend class. If sleep is most important, you will miss class.

If in fact employees make conscious decisions about attending work, attendance can be increased in several ways: rewarding attendance, disciplining absenteeism, and keeping accurate attendance records.

Rewards for Attending

Attendance can be increased through the use of financial incentives, time off, and recognition programs.

Well pay A method of absenteeism control in which employees are paid for their unused sick leave.

Financial Incentives. Financial incentive programs use money to reward employees for achieving certain levels of attendance. One of these programs, **well pay**, involves paying employees for their unused sick leave. For example, Starmark International in Fort Lauderdale, Florida, pays employees $100 for each unused absence. Mercy Medical Center in Baltimore gives employees a $100 bonus for six months of perfect attendance and enters them into a drawing for $3,000 after one year of perfect attendance (Armour, 2003). Some reward the employee by paying the equivalent of her daily salary, whereas others might split the savings by paying the employee an amount equal to half her daily salary for each unused sick day. As shown in Table 10.7, meta-analyses found that well pay programs were the top method for reducing absenteeism.

Financial bonus A method of absenteeism control in which employees who meet an attendance standard are given a cash reward.

A second method provides a **financial bonus** to employees who attain a certain level of attendance. With this method, an employee with perfect attendance over a year might receive a $1,000 bonus, and an employee who misses 10 days might receive nothing.

Games An absenteeism control method in which games such as poker and bingo are used to reward employee attendance.

A third financial incentive method is to use **games** to reward employees who attend work. There are many examples. One company used poker as its game, giving a playing card each day to employees who attended. At the end of the week, employees with five cards compared the value of their hands, and the winning employee would be given a prize such as dinner for two at the best restaurant in town or a gas barbecue grill. Although some studies have reported success in using such games, the meta-analysis by Wagner (1990) found that the mean effect size for games was close to zero.

Paid time off (PTO) An attendance policy in which all paid vacations, sick days, holidays, and so forth are combined.

Time Off. Another approach is the **paid time off program (PTO)**, or paid-leave bank (PLB). With this style of program, vacation, personal, holiday, and sick days are combined into one category—paid time off. For example, in a traditional system, an employee might be given 10 vacation days, 3 personal days, 5 holidays, and 10 sick days, for a total of 28 days. With a PTO program, the employee might be given

Table 10.8 CCH Surveys of Absenteeism Control Policies

Absence Control Policy	Percent Using Method					Effectiveness Rating				
	2000	2004	2005	2006	2007	2000	2004	2005	2006	2007
Disciplinary action	88	91	90	90	89	3.5	3.5	3.4	3.3	3.4
Performance appraisal	58	79	79	82	82	3.2	3.0	3.0	2.9	2.9
Verification of illness		76	76	79	74		3.0	3.2	2.9	3.2
Paid-leave bank	21	63	67	70	60	3.9	3.5	3.5	3.7	3.6
Personal recognition	62	59	66	68	57	3.1	2.6	2.6	2.7	2.6
No-fault systems	31	59	63	67	59	3.7	2.9	3.0	2.8	2.9
Bonus programs	21	49	57	61	51	3.1	3.2	3.3	3.3	3.3
Buy-back programs	17	48	58	59	53	3.4	3.3	3.5	3.4	3.4

CCH = Commerce Clearing House.

26 days in total for the year—companies adopting PTO programs usually offer slightly fewer days off than under their old system (Frase, 2010). An employee who is seldom sick has more days to use for vacation and is protected in case of a long-term illness, and the organization saves money by reducing the total number of unscheduled absences. As shown in Table 10.8, human resources (HR) directors rate buy-back programs, paid-leave banks, and disciplinary action as the most effective absence control methods.

In 37% of PTO programs, an employee can "bank" time off to use at a later date, and 17% of organizations with a PTO program allow employees to donate unused leave to a leave bank for employees who are stricken by a catastrophic illness such as cancer (CCH, 2004). My neighbor provides an excellent example of a PTO in which employees can bank their time off. She works for a hospital and has not missed a day of work in five years. As a consequence, she now has three months' extra vacation time, which she plans to spend with her newborn son.

Recognition Programs. One other way that we can make work attendance more rewarding is through recognition and praise. Formal recognition programs provide employees with perfect-attendance certificates, coffee mugs, plaques, lapel pins, watches, and so forth. As shown in Table 10.8, HR directors do not perceive these programs to be as effective as many of the other programs. Though incentive programs can be an effective means of increasing attendance, many organizations are eliminating perfect-attendance incentives out of a concern that such programs might violate the Family Medical Leave Act (Tyler, 2001).

Discipline for Not Attending

Absenteeism can be reduced by punishing or disciplining employees who miss work. Discipline can range from giving a warning or a less popular work assignment to firing an employee. As shown in Table 10.8 discipline works fairly well, especially when combined with some positive reinforcement for attending.

Clear Policies and Better Record Keeping

Another way to increase the negative consequences of missing work is through policy and record keeping. Most organizations measure absenteeism by counting the number of days missed, or *frequency*. Perhaps a better method would be to record the number

Frequency Method
Patricia Austin
Days missed:

March	4	
April	9	
May	2	
May	30	Days Missed = 8
June	7	Instances = 8
July	2	
Sept	3	
Nov	24	

Instance Method
Christine Evert
Days missed:

April	3	
April	4	
April	5	
July	15	Days Missed = 8
July	16	Instances = 3
Dec	2	
Dec	3	
Dec	4	

Figure 10.6

Frequency and Instance Methods of Measuring Absenteeism

of *instances* of absenteeism rather than the number of days. For example, instead of giving employees 12 days of sick leave, they are given 3 or 4 instances of absenteeism. Missing one day or three consecutive days each counts as one instance of absenteeism.

As shown in Figure 10.6, the number of days missed and the instances of absenteeism often yield different results. By decreasing the number of times that a person can miss work, the odds increase that the employee will use sick leave only for actual illness. These odds can further be increased by requiring a doctor's excuse for missing a certain number of consecutive days.

Absenteeism can be decreased by setting attendance goals and by providing feedback on how well the employees are reaching those goals. An interesting study by Harrison and Shaffer (1994) found that almost 90% of employees think their attendance is above average and estimate the typical absenteeism of their coworkers at a level two times higher than the actual figures. Similar results were found by Johns (1994). Thus, one reason employees miss work is that they incorrectly believe their attendance is at a higher level than their coworkers'. Providing feedback to employees about their absenteeism levels may be one way to reduce absenteeism.

Increasing Attendance by Reducing Employee Stress

Absenteeism can be reduced by removing the negative factors employees associate with going to work. One of the most important of these factors is *stress.* The greater the job stress, the lower the job satisfaction and commitment, and the greater the probability that most people will want to skip work. As will be discussed in great detail in Chapter 15, there are many sources of stress at work including physical danger, boredom, overload, conflict, and bad management practices.

To increase attendance, then, negative factors must be eliminated. The first step in this elimination, of course, is to become aware of the negative factors that bother employees. These can be determined by asking supervisors or by distributing employee questionnaires. Once the problems are known, it is important that management diligently work to eliminate the identified problems from the workplace. As will also be discussed in Chapter 15, employers engage in a variety of programs designed to reduce job-related stress as well as stress from family and personal issues. Meta-analysis results indicate that these programs are successful in reducing employee stress levels, but have only a negligible effect on reducing absenteeism (Richardson & Rothstein, 2008).

To help employees cope with stress and personal problems, 75% of employers offer some form of employee assistance program (EAP) (SHRM, 2011). EAPs use professional counselors to deal with employee problems. An employee with a problem can either choose to see a counselor on her own or be recommended by her supervisor. Some large organizations have their own EAP counselors, but most use private agencies, which are often run through local hospitals.

The motivation for EAPs may be good, but little if any empirical evidence supports their effectiveness. Still, many organizations have used EAPs and have been quite pleased with them. Independently operated EAPs typically claim a three to one return on the dollars invested through increased productivity and reduced absenteeism and turnover.

Increasing Attendance by Reducing Illness

As shown in Table 10.7, about 35% of absenteeism is due to employee illness—a percentage that mirrors that of college students missing class. Kovach, Surrette, and Whitcomb (1988) asked more than 500 general psychology students to anonymously provide the reason for each day of class they missed. Less than 30% of the missed days were the result of illness!

To reduce absenteeism related to illness, organizations are implementing a variety of wellness programs. According to the 2011 SHRM Employee Benefits Survey (SHRM, 2011):

- 75% have some form of wellness program
- 64% provide on-site flu vaccinations
- 42% have on-site health screening (e.g., blood pressure, cholesterol)
- 36% have a smoking cessation program
- 30% subsidize the cost of off-site fitness center dues
- 30% offer a weight-loss program
- 24% have on-site fitness centers
- 12% offer stress reduction programs
- 9% offer on-site medical care

To reduce both absenteeism and health care costs, many employers are rewarding employees whose body mass index, cholesterol levels, and blood pressure levels are within acceptable ranges (Cornwell, 2007). Typically, the reward comes in the form of a reduction in the employee's monthly health care premium. Other organizations take a more punitive approach and increase the premiums of unhealthy employees. For example, beginning in 2009, Clarian Health in Indianapolis, Indiana, began reducing the pay by 10 dollars per paycheck for employees whose body mass index was greater than 29.9.

Two meta-analyses suggest that worksite fitness programs have a small but significant effect on reducing *absenteeism*. The meta-analysis of 11 studies by Parks and Steelman (2008) found an effect size of $-.30$, and the meta-analysis by Wolkove and Layman (2006) found an effect size of $-.37$. Parks and Steelman further found that wellness programs increase job satisfaction ($d = .42$). Results found by Erfurt, Foote, and Heirich (1992) did not support the effectiveness of wellness programs in reducing health problems.

Reducing Absenteeism by Not Hiring "Absence-Prone" Employees

An interesting theory of absenteeism postulates that one reason people miss work is the result of a particular set of personality traits they possess. That is, certain types of people are more likely to miss work than other types. In fact, in one study, only 25% of the employees were responsible for all of the unavoidable absenteeism (Dalton & Mesch, 1991).

Although little research has tested this theory, Kovach et al. (1988) did find that the best predictor of student attendance in general psychology courses was a compulsive, rule-oriented personality. Research by Judge, Martocchio, and Thoresen (1997) supports these findings. Judge and his colleagues found that individuals high in the personality trait of conscientiousness and low in extraversion were least likely to miss work. If more research supports this theory, then a new strategy for increasing employee attendance might be to screen out "absence-prone people" during the selection stage.

Uncontrollable Absenteeism Caused by Unique Events

Many times an individual will miss work because of events or conditions that are beyond management's control. One study estimated that 40% of absenteeism is unavoidable (Dalton & Mesch, 1991). For example, bad weather is one reason absenteeism is higher in the Northeast than in the South. Although an organization can do little to control weather, the accessibility of the plant or office can be considered in the decision of where to locate. In fact, this is one reason many organizations have started in or moved to the so-called Sunbelt in the last two decades. Organizations may also want to offer some type of shuttle service for their employees to avoid not only weather problems but also any resulting mechanical failures of employees' automobiles.

Bad weather can certainly be a legitimate reason for an employee to miss work, but one study found that job satisfaction best predicted attendance on days with poor weather. That is, in good weather, most employees attended, but in inclement weather, only those employees with high job satisfaction attended. Thus, even in bad weather, the degree to which an employee likes her job will help to determine her attendance. As the late industrial psychologist Dan Johnson has asked: "How come we hear about employees not being able to get to work and students not being able to attend class because of bad weather, yet we don't ever hear about an employee or a student who can't get home because of bad weather?" It certainly makes one think!

The Absenteeism Exercise (Exercise 10.6) in your workbook gives you the opportunity to apply theories of absenteeism.

Turnover

Cost of Turnover

As mentioned previously in this chapter and depicted in Table 10.1, employees with low job satisfaction and low organizational commitment are more likely to quit their jobs and change careers than are employees with high job satisfaction and high organizational commitment. Though turnover rates fluctuate from year to year, about 1.4% of an organization's employees leave each month (16.8% per year).

Turnover is a problem because the cost of losing an employee is estimated at 1.5 times the employee's salary (Bliss, 2001). Thus, if an employee's annual salary is $40,000, the cost to replace the employee will be $60,000. Both visible and hidden costs determine this estimate. Visible costs of turnover include advertising charges, employment agency fees, referral bonuses, recruitment travel costs, salaries and benefits associated with the employee time spent processing applications and interviewing candidates, and relocation expenses for the new employee. Hidden costs include the loss of productivity associated with the employee leaving—other employees trying to do extra work, no productivity occurring from the vacant position—and the lower productivity associated with a new employee being trained. Additional hidden costs include overtime of employees covering the duties of the vacant position and training costs once the replacement is hired. The actual cost of turnover for any given position can be more accurately estimated using a formula such as one of those found on the text website.

In terms of turnover in an organization, there are four views on the effect of performance on such factors as safety, productivity, and profitability:

- There is a negative correlation such that higher turnover rates will result in lower organizational performance.
- Because some turnover is healthy for an organization, there is a U-shaped relationship between turnover and performance such that very low or very high levels of turnover will result in lower organizational performance, but a moderate amount of turnover will result in higher performance.
- The negative effect of turnover is strongest when an organization's turnover rate is low, and this effect then diminishes as turnover rates climb.
- The effect of turnover on organizational performance is mediated by the strength of an organization's HR efforts. Turnover will most affect organizations that don't invest in their employees and will least affect organizations that spend time and money to develop their employees.

Though all four theories make good sense, research seems to support the idea that an employee leaving an organization will most affect an organization's performance when the monthly turnover rate for the organization is low and will have a diminishing effect on performance when the turnover rate is high (Shaw, Gupta, & Delery, 2005).

Reducing Turnover

Because of the high cost of turnover, as well as its negative effect on organizational performance (Glebbeek & Bax, 2004), organizations make tremendous efforts to reduce the number of quality employees that quit their jobs. An organization reducing the number of employees leaving by one per month will save $360,000 a year for a $20,000 job and $720,000 a year for a $40,000 job.

The first step in reducing turnover is to find out why your employees are leaving. This is usually done by administering attitude surveys to current employees and conducting exit interviews with employees who are leaving. Salary surveys can also be useful because they allow you to compare your organization's pay and benefit practices with those of other organizations. Surveys are important because there appears to be a real disconnect between the reasons managers think employees leave and the actual reasons: 89% of managers believe employees leave for more money, yet 88% of employees say they left for other reasons (Branham, 2005).

It is important to understand that employee turnover is a *process* of disengagement from the organization that can take days, weeks, or months (Branham, 2005). So, employees don't awaken one day and just decide to leave. Instead, they have been thinking about it for a period of time, which means that better communication between employees and management might prevent the ultimate decision to leave. Employees typically leave their jobs for one of five reasons: unavoidable reasons, advancement, unmet needs, escape, and unmet expectations.

Unavoidable Reasons. Unavoidable turnover includes such reasons as school starting (e.g., quitting a summer job) or ending (e.g., a student quits her job as a part-time receptionist because she has graduated and will be moving), the job transfer of a spouse, employee illness or death, or family issues (e.g., employees staying home to raise their children or take care of their parents). Though employers are taking steps to reduce turnover due to family issues, there is little an organization can do to prevent turnover due to the other reasons.

Advancement. Employees often leave organizations to pursue promotions or better pay. When an organization has few promotion opportunities, there is little it can do to reduce turnover for those employees seeking advancement. A solution used by an increasing number of police departments who have limited promotion opportunities is to allow officers with extensive experience and skills to advance to status positions such as master officer or senior officer. Such positions have no supervisory responsibility but do bring an increase in pay and status.

At times, employers can reduce turnover by offering more pay; however, this will work only if a low compensation or an inadequate benefits package is the prime reason for employees leaving the organization. Furthermore, any increase in pay must be a meaningful amount. That is, if an organization increases pay by $3,000, yet other organizations are paying $6,000 more, the increase in pay most probably will not decrease turnover.

Unmet Needs. Employees whose needs are unmet will become dissatisfied and perhaps leave the organization. For example, if an employee has high social needs and the job involves little contact with people, or if an employee has a need for appreciation and recognition that is not being met by the organization, the employee might leave to find a job in which her social needs can be met. To reduce turnover caused by unmet needs, it is important that an organization consider the **person/organization fit** when selecting employees. That is, if an applicant has a need for structure and close supervision, but the culture of the organization is one of independence, full of "free spirits," the applicant should not be hired because there would be a poor fit between the employee's need and the organization.

Escape. A common reason employees leave an organization is to escape from people, working conditions, and stress. When conflict between an employee and her supervisor, a coworker, or customers becomes unbearable, the employee may see no option other than to leave the organization. Therefore, it is important to effectively deal with conflict when it occurs (this is covered in detail in Chapter 13). Likewise, if working conditions are unsafe, dirty, boring, too strenuous, or too stressful, there is an increased likelihood that the employee will seek employment in an organization with

person/organization fit
The extent to which an employee's personality, values, attitudes, philosophy, and skills match those of the organization.

better working conditions. Providing a mentor to help the employee deal with workplace problems may be a way to reduce turnover (Payne & Huffman, 2005).

Unmet Expectations. Employees come to an organization with certain expectations about a variety of issues, such as pay, working conditions, opportunity for advancement, and organizational culture. When reality does not match these expectations, employees become less satisfied and, as a result, are more likely to leave the organization (Griffeth et al., 2000). As discussed in Chapter 5, turnover due to unmet expectations can be reduced by providing applicants with realistic job previews.

To summarize, organizations can reduce turnover in these ways:

- Conduct realistic job previews during the recruitment stage.
- Select employees who have been referred by a current employee, who have friends and/or family working for the organization, and who did not leave their previous job after only a short tenure (Barrick & Zimmerman, 2005).
- Look for a good person/organization fit during the selection interview.
- Meet employee needs (e.g., safety, social, growth).
- Mediate conflicts between employees and their peers, supervisors, and customers.
- Provide a good work environment.
- Provide a competitive pay and benefits package.
- Provide opportunities to advance and grow.

There are many times when employees remain with an organization even though characteristics of their jobs suggest that they would leave. Lee, Mitchell, Sablynski, Burton, and Holtom (2004) suggest that the extent to which an employee is **embedded** in the organization or the community might explain this lack of turnover. *Embeddedness* is described as the extent to which employees have links to their jobs and community, the importance of these links, and the ease with which these links could be broken and reestablished elsewhere. That is, if an employee has many friends at work or in the community, is actively involved in community organizations, and has a spouse who also has an excellent job, it would be difficult to leave an organization if the only alternative was to relocate to another community. Ramesh and Gelfand (2010) have expanded the concept of embeddedness to include the extent to which an employee fits with the culture of the organization and community, the employee's links to people in the organization and the community, and the sacrifices an employee would make if he left the organization or the community. As expected, Ramesh and Gelfand (2010) found that, in both the U.S. and in India, higher levels of embeddedness resulted in lower levels of employee turnover.

Embeddedness The extent to which employees have links to their jobs and community, the importance of these links, and the ease with which they can be broken and replaced at another job.

Counterproductive Behaviors

As discussed previously, employees who are unhappy with their jobs miss work, are late to work, and quit their jobs at higher rates than employees who are satisfied with their jobs and are committed to the organization. Dissatisfied employees, especially those who are unable to change jobs, also engage in a variety of other counterproductive behaviors in organizations. These counterproductive behaviors can be separated into two types of behaviors: those aimed at individuals and those aimed at the organization (Berry, Ones, & Sackett, 2007). Behaviors aimed at individuals

Dissatisfied employees often act out.

© Dirk Anschutz/Stone/Getty Images

include gossip, playing negative politics, harassment, incivility, workplace violence, harassment, and bullying. Behaviors aimed at the organization include theft and sabotage. Though such behaviors are not limited to unhappy employees, they provide ways for employees to "get back" at the organization or the coworkers they believe are responsible for their lack of happiness.

For example, Cropanzano and Greenberg (1997) found that employees who were unhappy with the way in which they were treated by their supervisors had an increased likelihood of stealing from their employers. The interesting finding of this study was that the employees tended to take things that were of value to the organization but not to them. That is, they didn't steal because they wanted an item, they stole because they wanted to hurt the organization.

Lack of Organizational Citizenship Behaviors

Organizational citizenship behaviors (OCBs) Behaviors that are not part of an employee's job but which make the organization a better place to work (e.g., helping others, staying late).

Employees who engage in **Organizational Citizenship Behaviors (OCBs)** are motivated to help the organization and their coworkers by doing the "little things" that they are not required to do. Examples of OCBs include staying late to get a project done, helping a coworker who is behind in her job, mentoring a new employee, volunteering for committees, and flying in coach when the employee might be entitled to first class.

Not surprisingly, a meta-analysis has demonstrated that job satisfaction is related to OCBs. That is, employees who are satisfied with their jobs and committed to the organization are more likely to "go the extra mile" than are employees who are dissatisfied with their jobs (LePine et al., 2002). Also not surprisingly, meta-analysis results show that there is a negative correlation between OCBs and employee counterproductive behavior (Dalal, 2006).

Applied Case Study

Reducing Turnover at Bubba Gump Shrimp Co.

Following the success of the motion picture *Forrest Gump*, the Bubba Gump Shrimp Company opened its first restaurant in 1996 on Cannery Row in Monterey, California. Today, they have grown to over 30 locations worldwide. The importance of employee relations at the restaurant chain is demonstrated by awards such as the 2005 *Nation's Restaurant News* NRAEF Spirit Award for excellence in hiring, training, retaining, and developing employees; *Chain Leader's* Best Places to Work in 2006, and being named by the *OC Metro Magazine* as the "2006 Best Company to Work for in Orange County." As one would imagine from the name, Bubba Gump specializes in shrimp but also has items such as fish and chips, mahimahi, and ribs. Each restaurant also contains a store in which customers can purchase Forrest Gump souvenirs as well as seafood to prepare at home.

In addition to traditional benefits, the kitchen staff receive a free meal each shift, and all employees receive 50% off meals for themselves and up to three guests when they are not working. Managers receive two weeks of vacation to start, and four weeks after 10 years. They are also part of a bonus program that allows them to earn up to 200% of their potential. The company uses salary surveys to ensure that their pay and bonus package is competitive.

The president of Bubba Gump Shrimp Company believes that one of the secrets to success is to have minimal management turnover. In fact, his focus on turnover has been so successful that he has not had a general manager leave in three years, and he decreased management turnover from 36% to 16% in two years. Before reading about how he did this, answer the questions below.

■ On the basis of what you learned in this chapter, what interventions would you make to reduce management turnover?

■ How would these interventions be different if you were trying to reduce nonmanagerial turnover?

To find out how Bubba Gump Shrimp reduced turnover, use the link found on your text webpage.

Ethics and Organizational Commitment

In a small rural school division in Virginia, a superintendent, with the support of his school board, adopted an attendance reward program for teachers. Teachers with perfect attendance receive a $500 bonus at the end of the school year. Teachers who miss only one day receive $250. The superintendent believes that the program will increase teachers' commitment to the students, parents, and community by rewarding them for not taking days off from work.

This chapter discussed that one of the consequences of low commitment and job dissatisfaction is high absenteeism. In the school mentioned above, absenteeism had significantly risen over the past few years. The superintendent believed the increase was because of a lack of commitment by the teachers. After all, if the teachers were committed, they would try harder not to miss school. "It's human nature," he said, "when you know you might lose your sick days at the end of the year to take those days even when you are not sick. By rewarding good attendance, the school division will increase commitment from these teachers and, consequently, reduce absenteeism." If you talk to the teachers, however, many will say that the school division would rather "buy" their good attendance than determine and fix why teachers choose to be absent in the first place, which is in response to unethical practices by management and the poor treatment of teachers by the administration.

Critics of such incentives say that it is unethical to "buy" commitment. They believe that it is only an excuse for leaders not doing what they should do: change how they treat employees. Many believe that organizational commitment and loyalty comes from how much employees identify with the organization's goals, mission, and leaders. And it comes from variety in work, freedom to make decisions, and freedom to make mistakes without losing their jobs. It is when employees don't believe in what management is doing or when they feel management is mistreating them that their commitment decreases. And, say these critics, you can't get that commitment back simply by "bribing" them with bonuses, incentives, or pay increases. The leaders of today, the critics say, don't want to give more freedom to employees to make decisions; they find it easier to fire employees for mistakes than offering them additional training to perform better, and leaders don't want to take the time to learn better management techniques, because, to them, time away from work means money out of their own pockets.

Supporters of such incentives say that part of organizational commitment is getting better performance out of employees, reducing absenteeism, and reducing turnover. They see nothing wrong in rewarding employees for doing a good job, being at work, and staying at work. Ultimately, these incentives meet the goal they are intended for. So, if such incentives work, why not use them? Proponents counter the argument that management uses incentives instead of finding better ways to treat employees by arguing that incentives are one way of treating employees better.

What Do You Think?

- Do you think that incentives are a form of bribery? If so, do you think it's unethical for companies to do this?

- What would keep you at a company for a longer period? Would incentives such as an Attendance Reward Program or end-of-the-year bonuses make a difference in whether you left a job?

- Do you think that using such incentives is a way for leaders to ignore what they should be doing to make things better for the employees?

- What are some other ethical dilemmas that might occur by offering incentives to increase commitment or job satisfaction?

Chapter Summary

In this chapter you learned:

- Satisfied and committed employees are more likely to have better performance, have lower turnover, miss fewer days of work, be more motivated, engage in organizational citizenship behaviors, and be less likely to engage in counterproductive work behaviors.
- Employees are more likely to be satisfied with their jobs if there is a good fit between their needs and what the job and organization offers, if they are treated fairly, if their coworkers are satisfied, and if the job is not stressful.
- Absenteeism is a problem both in the US and in other countries.
- Absenteeism can be reduced using financial incentives and recognition programs, reducing job-related stress, having clear policies, disciplining employees who miss work, and using wellness programs to reduce illness.
- Employees are likely to leave an organization if they lack advancement opportunities, have needs or expectations that are not met, are not treated fairly, or want to escape from negative working conditions.

Questions for Review

1. Are some employees "destined" to always be dissatisfied with their job? Why or why not?
2. What do most employees value and need in a job?
3. Is it possible to treat all employees equitably? Why or why not?
4. What is the best way to improve employee attendance?
5. Which measure of job satisfaction is best? Why?

Media Resources and Learning Tools

■ Visit our website. Go to www.cengage.com/psychology/aamodt, where you will find online resources directly linked to your book, including chapter-by-chapter quizzing, flashcards, crossword puzzles, application activities, and more.

■ Want more practice applying industrial/organizational psychology? Check out the *I/O Applications Workbook.* This workbook (keyed to your textbook) offers engaging, high-interest activities to help you reinforce the important concepts presented in the text.

Chapter

11

ORGANIZATIONAL COMMUNICATION

© Chris Ryan/OJO Images/Getty Images

Learning Objectives

➡ Know the types of organizational communication

➡ Understand why interpersonal communication often is not effective

➡ Learn how to increase your listening effectiveness

➡ Learn ways to improve your communication skills

Picture the following situations:

- A male employee cannot understand why he was reprimanded for referring to female employees as the "girls in the office."
- A supervisor has tried everything to communicate with her employees, but they still seem lost.
- Customers don't like Sheila because she appears cold and aloof, although she is actually a very caring person.
- A supervisor is frustrated because her employees never read the notices posted on the bulletin board in the break room.

All four situations represent common communication problems. This chapter looks at the ways employees communicate within an organization, problems in the communication process, and the ways communication can be improved. To get you thinking about communication, complete Exercise 11.1 in your workbook.

Types of Organizational Communication

To be an effective employee, manager, client, or consultant, it is essential to communicate effectively with others. Having ideas, knowledge, or opinions is useless unless you can communicate those concepts to others. Most communication in organizations can be classified into four types: upward communication, downward communication, business communication, and informal communication.

Upward Communication

Upward communication
Communication within an organization in which the direction of communication is from employees up to management.

Upward communication is communication of subordinates to superiors or of employees to managers. Of course, in ideal upward communication, employees speak directly to management in an environment with an "open door" policy. In fact, the quality of upward communication is a significant factor in employee job satisfaction (Miles, Patrick, & King, 1996). Such a policy, however, is often not practical for several reasons—perhaps the most important being the potential volume of communication if every employee communicated with a specific manager. Direct upward communication also may not be workable because employees often feel threatened by managers and may not be willing to openly communicate bad news or complaints.

Serial communication
Communication passed consecutively from one person to another.

To minimize the number of different people communicating with the top executive, many organizations use **serial communication**. With serial communication, the message is relayed from an employee to her supervisor, who relays it to her supervisor, who, in turn, relays it to her supervisor, and so on until the message reaches the top. Although this type of upward communication relieves the top executive of excessive demands, it suffers several serious drawbacks.

The first is that the content and tone of the message change as it moves from person to person. As will be discussed later in the chapter, messages are seldom received the way they were sent—especially if the message is being passed orally from person to person.

The second drawback to serial communication is that bad news and complaints are seldom relayed, in part due to the stress associated with delivering bad news (McKee & Ptacek, 2001). Rosen and Tesser (1970) have labeled this reluctance to

MUM (minimize unpleasant messages) effect The idea that people prefer not to pass on unpleasant information, with the result that important information is not always communicated.

Communication channel The medium by which a communication is transmitted.

Proximity Physical distance between people.

relay bad news the **MUM (minimize unpleasant messages) effect**. The MUM effect negatively affects the organization by keeping important information from reaching the upper levels. But for an employee, the MUM effect is an excellent survival strategy—no one wants to be the bearer of bad news. When bad news is passed on to supervisors, employees tend to use politeness to soften the news (Lee, 1993). Interestingly, people have no problem passing on bad news to peers, especially when the organizational climate is generally negative (Heath, 1996).

Serial communication's third drawback, especially with informal **communication channels**, is that it is less effective the farther away two people are from one another. That is, a supervisor is more likely to pass along a message to another supervisor if the two are in close physical **proximity**. It is unlikely, therefore, that an informal message originating with an employee at a plant in Atlanta will reach another employee at the corporate office in Phoenix. The importance of physical proximity cannot be overstated. In fact, a major source of power often comes from being physically near an executive. Seasoned executives have been known to place rising executives in distant offices to reduce their potential power. And going to lunch "with the guys" has long been recognized as a means of obtaining new information and increased power.

As one would imagine, proximity does not play a role when messages are communicated electronically using email (Valacich, Parantia, George, & Nunamaker, 1993). Thus, email may reduce the power of proximity when communication is formal.

Because of these problems with serial communication, organizations use several other methods to facilitate upward communication: attitude surveys, focus groups, suggestion boxes, and third parties.

Attitude Surveys

Attitude survey A form of upward communication in which a survey is conducted to determine employee attitudes about an organization.

Attitude surveys are usually conducted annually by an outside consultant who administers a questionnaire asking employees to rate their opinions on such factors as satisfaction with pay, working conditions, and supervisors. Employees are also given the opportunity to list complaints or suggestions that they want management to read. The consultant then tabulates the responses and reports the findings to management.

For example, Office Depot annually surveys each of its employees. The 48-item survey is administered electronically and is written in the eight languages most commonly spoken by Office Depot employees. Within four weeks after the surveys have been completed, the results are posted on a secure intranet site where managers can see the results that pertain to their area. Managers then use the results to create their action plan for the coming year (Robb, 2004).

Although attitude surveys are commonly used, they are useful only if an organization takes the results seriously. If an organization finds that its employees are unhappy and does nothing to address the problem areas, the survey results will not be beneficial. Furthermore, to increase trust, an organization should share survey results with employees.

If survey results are to be shared, then management must share *all* of them. While proposing a project to a local police department, I encountered a great deal of hostility from many of the senior officers. After a little probing, the officers revealed that several years earlier they had completed an attitude survey for the city. A few months later, the results were made public. The city cited five main complaints by the officers and promised that action would be taken to solve these problems. The officers were happy until they realized that none of their complaints about pay and working conditions were included in the report—the city was ignoring them. The officers became so resentful and mistrustful of consultants and management that they vowed never again to participate in a project.

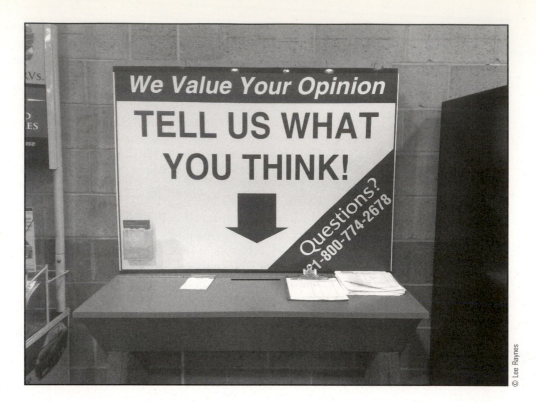

© Lee Raynes

Suggestion boxes are a common source of upward communication.

Focus Groups and Exit Interviews

A second method of upward communication is to hold focus groups, in which an outside consultant meets with groups of current employees to get their opinions and suggestions. This information is then passed on to management. To spur candid responses, the consultant is not told the names of the employees in the focus group, and no direct quotes that could potentially identify a particular employee are passed on. Exit interviews with employees voluntarily leaving an organization also provide an excellent source of information. Although these interviews can be emotionally charged, an organization can learn much by listening to the "real" reason that an employee is leaving the organization (Frase-Blunt, 2004).

Suggestion Boxes

Suggestion box A form of upward communication in which employees are asked to place their suggestions in a box.

Complaint box A form of upward communication in which employees are asked to place their complaints in a box.

A third method for facilitating upward communication is the use of **suggestion** or **complaints boxes**. Theoretically, these two boxes should be the same, but a box asking for suggestions is not as likely to get complaints as a box specifically labeled *complaints* and vice versa. The biggest advantage of these boxes is that they allow employees to immediately communicate their feelings in an anonymous fashion. Suggestion boxes provide a safe voice for subordinates and customers, and essential feedback to the organization as well (Phillips, 2004).

For these boxes to be beneficial, management must respond to the suggestions and complaints in a timely manner. To make the suggestion or complaint box process more efficient, many large organizations use web-based software such as Ideabox, Brightidea, or Imaginatik that allows employees to submit suggestions and complaints, notify management when a comment has been received, and keep the employee informed of the progress and outcome of his suggestion.

Some organizations take suggestions quite seriously and reward employees who provide useful ideas. For example, Texas Industries in Dallas provides bonuses that can reach 20% of an employee's salary, IBM provides a reward equal to 25% of the savings resulting from an idea (up to $150,000), and Ingersoll-Rand gives plaques to employees who submit cost-saving ideas that are ultimately adopted by the company. In a study of organizations encouraging suggestions, the Employee Involvement Association found that over 30% of employees submitted at least one suggestion, approximately 37% of suggestions were adopted, and the value of the typical suggestion was 10 times greater than the cost of rewarding the suggestion (Wells, 2005).

EMPLOYMENT PROFILE

I am the owner and president of Square Peg Consulting, Inc., an organization and training development consulting company. My primary goal is to work with clients to improve the effectiveness of their organizations. I use a whole-systems approach to organization development (OD), focusing on organization alignment as the key to organization effectiveness. A systems approach includes viewing the organization as a living organism, influenced by external and internal elements. There is a cause-and-effect relationship between each element, and organizations are most effective when all the systems within it align. My approach to enabling organizations to better perform is to assess alignment gaps and opportunities and develop interventions that align resources, systems, and processes to better position the organization to achieve business results. Because organizations grow and evolve through their natural organizational life cycle, it is important that they continue to shift and realign themselves to ensure that all their efforts are going in the same direction for maximum efficiency and effectiveness.

One important element of organizational effectiveness is communication. From a diagnostic perspective, one can tell much about an organization's culture from assessing both what and how communication is shared throughout the organization. For example, if an organization claims to have a culture of "empowerment," yet employees are not aware of the organization's goals or vision, there is a potential gap between leadership's intention and the reality in which employees live. As a result, dysfunctional behavior may occur, leading to mistrust and poor performance.

Confusion and dissatisfaction arise when an organization's communication and governance practices are incongruent with the culture it espouses. For instance, a company aspiring to *engage employees in the business* while restricting employee access to information about its financial performance may be viewed cynically by employees. A company proclaiming *to trust and empower employees* while limiting delegation of authority may be perceived as disingenuous.

Amy Podurgal, M.S.
President, Square Peg Consulting, Inc.

© Pat Bartley

Think of the organization's communications strategy as a three-legged stool. One leg is its *external communications* strategy—the messages sent to the outside world about the organization's product or service offerings, including competitive differentiators, market space and positioning, and financial performance. This type of communication helps brand the company in the eyes of current and future customers, shareholders, and job candidates. It includes such things as the company's external website, its marketing materials, and its media relations activities.

The second leg represents the *internal communications* strategy. This communication strategy ensures that employees stay informed about the performance of the company and important changes to policies and practices, and can serve as a vehicle for recognizing employee and team accomplishments. The company newsletter, its intranet site, and its approach to organizing employee meetings are all components of an internal communications strategy.

The third leg is the *organization alignment* strategy, the organized method by which the organization's strategy and tactics are developed and communicated to employees. This helps drive the daily activities of employees and ensures that they are all working in support of the organization's priorities. This usually takes the form of setting objectives and performance management and is where the strategic and operational elements of an organization meet. For organizations to be effective, all three legs of the communications stool must be strategically aligned and working together.

Organizations are living organisms whose systems and structures are set up to accomplish a goal. A publicly traded company's goal may be to grow shareholder value; a sports team's goal may be to win the game; and a symphony orchestra's goal may be to master a piece of music. To create an effective communication strategy, my advice is to take into account the information needs of all constituents in each part of the system.

Third-Party Facilitators

Liaison A person who acts as an intermediary between employees and management, or the type of employee who both sends and receives most grapevine information.

Ombudsperson A person who investigates employees' complaints and solves problems.

Union steward An employee who serves as a liaison between unionized employees and management.

Downward communication Communication within an organization in which the direction of communication is from management to employees.

Bulletin board A method of downward communication in which informal or relatively unimportant written information is posted in a public place.

Policy manual A formal method of downward communication in which an organization's rules and procedures are placed in a manual; legally binding by courts of law.

The use of a third party such as a **liaison** or an **ombudsperson** is another method that can increase upward communication. Both are responsible for taking employee complaints and suggestions and personally working with management to find solutions. The advantage of this system is that the ombudsperson is neutral and works for a solution that is acceptable to both employees and management. Furthermore, the ombudsperson is typically supervised at the vice-presidential level, so she is not concerned about being fired if she steps on a few toes while looking for a solution.

Unfortunately, the ombudsperson method is often not used because organizations do not want the expense of an employee who "does not produce." To overcome this problem, Moore Tool Company in Springdale, Arkansas, started its "Red Shirt" program, in which selected senior employees wear red shirts that identify them as informal ombudspeople. If an employee has a problem, she can seek help from a Red Shirt, who has authority to help find a solution. This system not only opens communication channels but also provides job enrichment for an employee who works at an otherwise boring job.

In organizations that have their employees represented by unions, the job of the ombudsperson is typically handled by the **union steward**. But management/union relationships are often adversarial, so the union steward has a difficult time solving problems because she is not perceived by management or union members as being neutral.

Downward Communication

Downward communication is that of superior to subordinate or management to employees. The downward communication process in organizations has changed greatly over the years (Brandon, 1997). Originally, downward communication involved newsletters designed to bolster employee morale by discussing happy events such as the "three B's"—babies, birthdays, and ball-game scores. Now, however, downward communication is considered a key method not only of keeping employees informed but of communicating vital information needed by employees to perform their jobs. Such communication can be accomplished in many ways, including bulletin boards, policy manuals, newsletters, and intranets.

Bulletin Boards

The **bulletin board** is yet another method of downward communication. The next time you visit an organization, look around for bulletin boards. You will see them everywhere. Their main use, however, is to communicate non-work–related opportunities such as scholarships, optional meetings, and items for sale. Important information is seldom seen because the bulletin board is not the appropriate place to post a change of policy or procedure. Still, bulletin boards have the advantage of low cost and wide exposure to both employees and visitors. This is especially true if the boards are placed in high-traffic areas such as outside restrooms and cafeterias or near time clocks. Electronic bulletin boards, also called *in-house message networks*, allow the display of even more current information.

Policy Manuals

The **policy manual** is the place for posting important changes in policy or procedure. This manual contains all the rules under which employees must operate. Most manuals are written in highly technical language, although they should be written in a less technical style to encourage employees to read them, as well as to make them easier to understand. Furthermore, the contents of these manuals are considered binding contracts by courts, so the manuals must be updated each time a policy changes.

This usually is done by sending updated material to employees so that they can replace older pages with up-to-date ones. To make this process easier, many organizations punch binder holes in the pages to facilitate their replacement. Sosnin (2001b) advises that policy manuals should contain the following six disclaimers:

1. Employment with the organization is at-will (refer to Chapter 7 for a discussion of employment-at-will).
2. The handbook does not create either an expressed or an implied contract.
3. The handbook is a set of guidelines and should not be considered all-inclusive.
4. The material in the present handbook supersedes material in previous handbooks.
5. The handbook can be changed only in writing by the president of the organization, and it can be changed unilaterally at any time.
6. Employees are subject to provisions of any amendments, deletions, and changes in the handbook.

The typical company manual is hundreds of pages long, so it is not surprising that many employees do not want to read it. To reduce length problems, most organizations have two types of company manual. The first, called a *policy manual*, is very specific and lengthy, containing all of the rules and policies under which the organization operates. The second type, usually known as the *employee handbook*, is much shorter and contains only the most essential policies and rules, as well as general summaries of less important rules.

An example that supports the need for two manuals involved security guards at a manufacturing plant. The security guards were paid minimum wage and had an average tenure of about three months before quitting. The company became concerned for two reasons. First, three months was not enough time for the guards to learn all of the policies in the 300-page emergency procedures manual. Second, the manual was written by an engineer, and none of the security guards were able to understand the writing. The organization thus had I/O psychology graduate-student interns develop a short, easy-to-read procedure manual that could be read and understood in a day or two. Tips for effective writing that also apply to manuals are shown in Table 11.1.

Table 11.1   Tips for Effective Writing

Rather Than	Try
Trying to impress someone with your vocabulary	Using a more conversational style
personnel	employees
utilize	use
urban mass-transit vehicle	bus
cognizant	aware
Writing in generalities	Writing what you mean
I wasn't gone long	I was gone for five minutes
A survey said that most of our employees ...	A survey said that 54% of our employees ...
Using an entire phrase	Using a single word
Enclosed please find ...	Enclosed is ...
Motivation is the idea that ...	Motivation is ...
Should it come to pass that you ...	If you ...

Newsletters

As mentioned earlier, **newsletters** are designed to bolster employee morale by discussing happy or innocuous events such as the three Bs (babies, birthdays, and ball-game scores). Newsletters are good sources of information for celebrating employee successes, providing feedback on how well the organization is doing, introducing a new employee, and providing reminders about organizational changes. Though many organizations provide newsletters in print format, the trend is to send them electronically through either email or an intranet. This use of cyber-publications saves printing expenses, allows for faster dissemination of information, and provides greater flexibility for making changes and updates.

Intranets

To replace bulletin boards, newsletters, and company manuals, an increasing number of organizations are turning to **intranets**—organization-wide versions of the Internet (Zeidner, 2005). For example, Fletcher Challenge, a Canadian paper and pulp company, designed FletcherNet to improve employee communication. One of the most useful aspects of this intranet is the speed at which the company can survey employees about new ideas. Other advantages include employee self-service, convenience and 24-hour support, and reduced paper, printing, and postage costs.

Though the potential for intranets has barely been tapped, they are currently common resources for

- online employee handbooks,
- answers to FAQs (frequently asked questions),
- employee activity calendars,
- forms that can be completed online,
- programs to write job descriptions or performance appraisals,
- job postings,
- online benefits information,
- training courses, and
- information about reward and incentive programs (Grensing-Pophal, 2001a).

Business Communication

Business communication is the transmission of business-related information among employees, management, and customers. Business communication methods include memos, telephone calls, and email and voice mail.

Memos

One of the most common methods of business communication is the memorandum, or *memo*. Memos have the advantage of providing detailed information to a large number of people in a short period of time. Although memos used to be received so frequently that most employees didn't read them, their use has been greatly reduced as they have been replaced with email.

Telephone Calls

Another method of business communication is the *telephone call*. In the past, this method was appropriate only when the message was short and when only a few people needed to receive the communication. But with the advent of conference calls, the number of people who can be reached by this method has certainly increased. Furthermore, telephone calls were previously appropriate only for messages that did not involve detail. But the facsimile, or fax, machine now allows detailed sketches or numbers to be sent to people in different locations in a matter of seconds, and these can then be discussed over the telephone.

One limitation of phone calls, of course, is that nonverbal cues are not available. Thus, a major portion of the message is often not communicated. For important calls, however, video-enhanced teleconferencing (videoconferencing) can now be used. In fact, many organizations save interview expenses by having job applicants across the company participate in such teleconferences, which allow both parties to see one another. A second limitation to phone calls is that conversations are not documented. For example, one department recently had a problem with an administrator who continually provided incorrect information over the phone or at meetings, denied that she had done so, and then blamed another department for errors that resulted from the use of the information. To correct this problem, employees quit talking to the administrator over the phone and stuck to email, where every "conversation" was documented. Some advice on proper phone etiquette is provided in the Career Workshop Box.

Email and Voice Mail

Many memos and telephone calls have been replaced with *email* and *voice mail* (sophisticated phone-answering systems). Voice mail and email are used primarily to exchange general and/or *timely* information and ask questions; they are not meant as substitutes for important conversation (Poe, 2001). The advantages to email and voice mail include a reduction in the use and filing of paper and time saved by avoiding "small talk" when communicating a short message by phone.

On the downside, voice mail often results in "phone tag," and both email and voice mail reduce opportunities for personal contact. In fact, Carilion Clinic got rid of its voice mail system because employees and customers were tired of getting answering machines and wanted to talk to "a real person." Well-designed voice mail systems are limited to simple tasks, have short menus, and allow a caller to talk to a real person at any time during the call.

Email has many advantages over voice mail, including the ability to easily document the sending and receiving of email, the opportunity to communicate with many people at one time, and the potential for quick response times, especially when some form of instant messaging is used. The drawbacks to email include misinterpretations due to the absence of paralanguage, the tendency to be too informal, the increased likelihood of expressing negative emotions ("flaming") that might not have been communicated in person, and the tendency to not proofread messages (O'Kane, Palmer, & Hargie, 2007).

Before writing an email message, decide if email is the appropriate communication channel. Email is appropriate for preparing people for meetings, scheduling meetings, communicating common news, distributing memos, and summarizing a conversation (Poe, 2001). Because email eliminates such factors as body language and tone, it is easy to misinterpret the meaning of an email message.

A good rule of thumb is to never put something in an email that you would not want to see published. Examples of material better left unsent include comments about other people, complaints, and offensive jokes. Because of the increased use and misuse of email, many organizations send their employees through email training. Casperson (2002) and Poe (2001) offer the following email etiquette commonly provided in such training:

- Include a greeting (e.g., "Hi, Mark") and a closing (e.g., "Take care").
- Include a detailed subject line.
- Don't write in all caps. It is difficult to read and comes across as if you are screaming.
- If you are going to forward an email message, change the original subject line and delete the long list of previous messages or names of people to whom the email had been previously forwarded.
- Take the same care in writing (e.g., spelling, grammar) that you would take in writing a formal memo.
- Don't spend company time on personal email unless your organization specifically allows you to do so.
- Allow ample time for the receiver to respond; not everyone considers email to require an immediate response.

When leaving a message on someone's voice mail, follow these guidelines:

- Speak slowly.
- Give your name at the beginning of the message and then repeat it at the end of the message.
- Spell your name if the person is not familiar with you or if your name is difficult to spell.
- Leave your phone number, even if you think the person already has it.
- To avoid phone tag, indicate some good times that the person can return your call.
- Don't ramble. Anticipate the possibility of getting voice mail rather than talking to the actual person and have a short message ready.
- Don't include information that you don't want other people to hear.

Business Meetings

As will be discussed in more detail in Chapter 13, a common method of business communication is the dreaded committee meeting. Research indicates that the typical employee spends an average of 4.35 hours attending 3.34 meetings each week (Rogelberg, Leach, Warr, & Burnfield, 2006). Supervisors attended even more meetings (5.0) and spent more time in these meetings (6.6 hours). Though meetings offer several advantages over email, memos, and phone calls, their time demands can result in negative employee attitudes (Rogelberg et al., 2006).

Office Design

To facilitate employee communication, 70% of organizations have adopted what is formally called an "open" or "landscaped" office design, and informally called a "cube farm" (Grossman, 2002). Originally developed by furniture manufacturers in West Germany, the design uses large, open office areas without walls. Individual work units are separated into cubicles by such items as plants, bookcases, desks, and partitions. The idea behind this design is that employees will communicate better with one another and be easier to supervise and help without the physical barriers of walls (Poe, 2000). When it consolidated its many offices into one central location in Minneapolis, Allina Health System was so sold on the idea of an open office environment that even the CEO had a cubicle!

There are three common designs for open or landscaped offices (Martinez, 1990). In a *freestanding design* (also called a *bullpen design*), all desks are placed in a large area that is completely open. With *uniform plans*, desks are placed at uniform distances and are separated by panels into cubicle areas. *Free-form workstations* use a combination of designs so that the different needs of each worker can be accommodated.

Two interesting trends in office design are "boulevards" and portable offices. A boulevard is a wide hallway that runs through several departments. The width of the boulevard allows space for impromptu employee communication, and the path of the boulevard through, rather than around, departments encourages employee interaction. Because landscaped, or open, office environments reduce privacy, many organizations have "portable offices" containing an employee's computer, files, and supplies that can be wheeled into a walled office or cubicle when privacy is needed.

The landscaped office may be appealing, but research has not generally been supportive. Landscaped offices can increase contact and communication and are less expensive than regular offices, but often they can lessen productivity and job satisfaction (Brennan, Chugh, & Kline, 2002). In a study of more than 500 employees in 14 organizations, O'Neill (1994) found that storage space and the ability to adjust or control one's office space were the best predictors of satisfaction with workspace. Variables such as partition type, panel height, and square footage were not related to satisfaction or performance.

Informal Communication

An interesting type of organizational communication is **informal communication**. Often, informal information is transmitted through the **grapevine**, a term that can be traced back to the Civil War, when loosely hung telegraph wires resembled grapevines. The communication across these lines was often distorted. Because unofficial employee communication is also thought to be distorted, the term has become synonymous with an informal communication network (Davis, 1977). Grapevines are common because they provide employees with information, power, and entertainment (Kurland & Pelled, 2000). Not surprisingly, the increased use of email has increased the importance of the grapevine (Smith, 2001).

Davis (1953) studied the grapevine and established the existence of four grapevine patterns: single strand, gossip, probability, and cluster. As Figure 11.1 shows, in the **single-strand grapevine**, Jones passes a message to Smith, who passes the message to Brown, and so on until the message is received by everyone or someone "breaks the chain." This pattern is similar to the children's game of "telephone." In the **gossip grapevine**, Jones passes the message to only a select group of people. Notice that with this pattern only one person passes the message along, and not everyone has a chance to receive, or will receive, it. In the **probability grapevine**, Jones tells the message to a few other employees, and they in turn randomly pass the message along to

Informal communication Communication among employees in an organization that is not directly related to the completion of an organizational task.

Grapevine An unofficial, informal communication network.

Single-strand grapevine A pattern of grapevine communication in which a message is passed in a chainlike fashion from one person to the next until the chain is broken.

Gossip grapevine A pattern of grapevine communication in which a message is passed to only a select group of individuals.

Probability grapevine A pattern of grapevine communication in which a message is passed randomly among all employees.

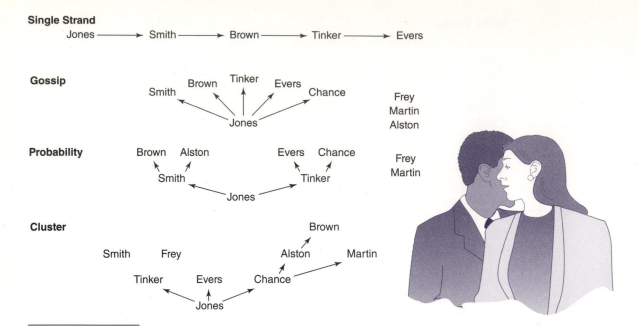

Single Strand

Jones ⟶ Smith ⟶ Brown ⟶ Tinker ⟶ Evers

Gossip

Smith · Brown · Tinker · Evers · Chance
Jones

Frey
Martin
Alston

Probability

Brown · Alston · Evers · Chance
Smith · Tinker
Jones

Frey
Martin

Cluster

Brown
Smith · Frey · Alston · Martin
Tinker · Evers · Chance
Jones

Figure 11.1
Grapevine Patterns

other employees. In the **cluster grapevine**, Jones tells only a few select employees, who in turn tell a few select others.

Research on the grapevine has supported several of Davis's (1953) findings. Sutton and Porter (1968) studied 79 employees in a state tax office and reached several interesting conclusions. They found that employees could be placed into one of three categories. **Isolates** were employees who received less than half of the information, liaisons were employees who both received most of the information and passed it on to others, and **dead-enders** were those who heard most of the information but seldom passed it on to other employees.

Managers tended to be liaisons because they had heard 97% of the grapevine information and most of the time passed it on. Nonmanagerial employees heard 56% of the grapevine information but seldom passed it on. Only 10% of nonmanagerial employees were liaisons; 57% were dead-enders and 33% were isolates.

Although most people consider the grapevine to be inaccurate, research has shown that information in the grapevine often contains a great deal of truth, though it is often incomplete. A review of rumors in organizations indicates that organizational rumors are about 80% accurate (DiFonzo & Bordia, 2006). Such a statistic, however, can be misleading. Consider the following hypothetical example: A message travels through the grapevine that "the personnel director will fire 25 people on Monday morning at nine o'clock." The truth, however, is that the personnel director will *hire* 25 people on Monday morning at nine o'clock. Thus, even though four out of five parts of the message (80%) are correct, the grapevine message paints a picture quite different from reality.

The grapevine contains two types of information: gossip and rumor. While both gossip and rumor contain poorly substantiated information, **gossip** is primarily

3. Find x.

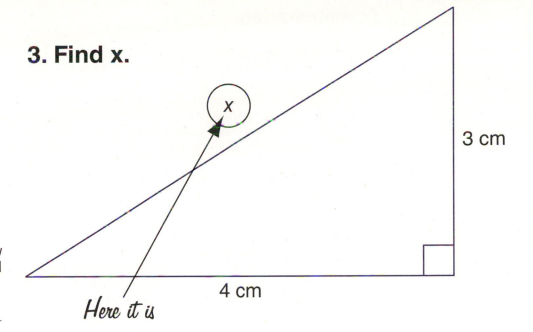

3 cm

Here it is

4 cm

As shown in this answer to a geometry test, directions should be specific to get the desired results

about individuals and the content of the message lacks significance to the people gossiping. **Rumor**, however, contains information that is significant to the lives of those communicating the message, and can be about individuals or other topics (DiFonzo & Bordia, 2006). Usually, rumor will occur when the available information is both interesting and ambiguous. Thus, rumor serves the function of helping to make sense of ambiguous information and of helping manage potential threats, whereas gossip serves to entertain and supply social information (DiFonzo & Bordia, 2007). The most common topics for rumor are personnel changes, job security, and the external reputation of the organization (DiFonzo & Bordia, 2007). Rumor and gossip are often ways in which employees can relieve stress and anxiety, respond to perceived organizational wrongs in a nonaggressive way, maintain a sense of control, and increase their power in an organization (DiFonzo & Bordia, 2006, 2007; Kurland & Pelled, 2000).

Certainly, not all horizontal communication is informal. Employees at the same level often exchange job-related information on such topics as customers and clients, the status of projects, and information necessary to complete a particular task. To increase the amount of job-related horizontal communication, many organizations have adopted the practice of self-managed work groups.

For example, at Columbia Gas Development in Houston, 12-person drilling teams were formed. The team approach greatly increased communication among geologists, engineers, and other staff members who had previously been located in separate departments. As another example, the use of teams at Meridian Insurance in Indianapolis increased communication and efficiency so much that a 29-step process for handling paperwork was reduced to 4 steps.

To apply what you have learned about horizontal communication, complete Exercise 11.2 in your workbook.

Interpersonal Communication

Interpersonal communication involves the exchange of a message across a communication channel from one person to another. As shown in Figure 11.2, the interpersonal communication process begins with a sender encoding and transmitting a message across a communication channel (e.g., by memo, orally, nonverbally) and ends with another person (the receiver) receiving and decoding the message. Although this seems like a simple process, there are three main problem areas where things can go wrong and interfere with the accurate transmission or reception of the message.

Problem Area 1: Intended Message Versus Message Sent

For effective communication, the sender must know what she wants to say and how she wants to say it. Interpersonal communication problems can occur when the message a person sends is not the message she intended. There are three solutions to this problem: thinking about what you want to communicate, practicing what you want to communicate, and learning better communication skills.

Thinking About What You Want to Communicate

Often the reason we don't say what we mean is that we are not really sure what we want to say. For example, think of using the drive-thru window at a fast-food restaurant. As soon as you stop, but before you have a chance to read the menu board, a voice crackles, "Can I take your order?" You intelligently reply something like, "*Uhhhhhhh*, could you hang on a minute?" and then quickly try to place an order as the pressure builds. As you drive off, you realize that you did not really order what you wanted.

Does this scenario sound familiar? If so, you are not alone. Foster and his colleagues (1988) found that many fast-food restaurant customers have so little time to think about their order that they make ordering mistakes. They found that placing a menu sign before the ordering station gave customers more time to think about their

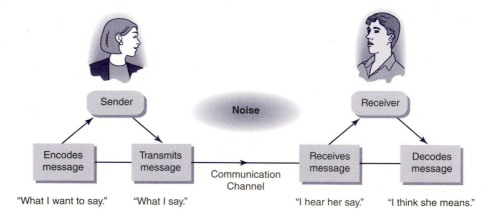

Figure 11.2

The Interpersonal Communication Process

orders and that this decreased average ordering times from 28 seconds to 6 seconds and ordering errors from 29% to 4%.

As another example, think about calling a friend and unexpectedly getting their voice mail recording. Have you ever left a message in which the first few sentences sounded reasonably intelligent? Did the first sentence again begin with *"Uhhhhhhhhh"*? Or have you ever made a call expecting to get the voice mail recording and instead had an actual person answer the phone? These examples show the importance of thinking about what you want to communicate.

Practice What You Want to Communicate

Even though you may know what you want to say, communication errors can occur if you do not actually say what you meant to say. Thus, when communication is important, it should be practiced. Just as consultants practice before giving a training talk and actors rehearse before a performance, you too need to practice what you want to say in important situations. Perhaps you can remember practicing how you were going to ask a person out on a date: changing the tone of your voice, altering your first line, or thinking of topics to discuss so that you would appear spontaneous.

Learn Better Communication Skills

Even if you know what you want to say and how you want to say it, communication errors can still occur if you do not have the proper communication skills. It is essential to take courses in public speaking, writing, and interpersonal communication so that you will be better prepared to communicate effectively. Because of the importance of communication skills, many organizations offer a wide range of communication training programs for their employees.

Problem Area 2: Message Sent Versus Message Received

Even though an individual knows what she wants to say and says it exactly as she planned, as shown in Figure 11.3, many factors affect how that message is received.

The Actual Words Used

A particular word may mean one thing in one situation but something else in another. Take the word *fine* as an example. If I told you that you had *"fine* jewelry," you would probably take the statement as a compliment. If the word were used to describe the weather—"The weather here in California is just *fine*"—it would still have a positive connotation. However, if a spouse asked, "How was the dinner I cooked?" or "How did you like our evening of romance?" an answer of "fine" would probably result in a very lonely evening.

A particular word may also mean one thing to one person and something different to another. For example, an 80-year-old man with a rural background may use the word *girl* as a synonym for *female*. He may not understand why the women at work get upset when he refers to them as the "girls in the office." When I conduct training sessions for police officers, we discuss how such words as *boy, son*, and *pretty little lady* can be emotionally charged and should thus be avoided.

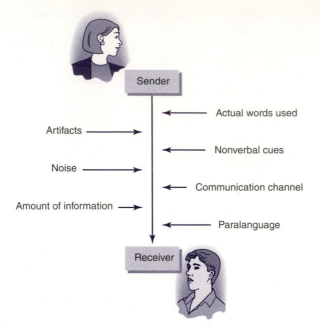

Figure 11.3

Factors Affecting the Message Sent Versus the Message Received

Even within English-speaking countries, a particular word can have different meanings. Take, for example, if someone said, "He was pissed." In the United States, we would interpret that the person was angry, yet people in Ireland would interpret that the person was drunk. If someone in Ireland said, "Where is the crack?" they would be asking the location of a party, not asking about drugs.

Words or phrases that are vague can also cause problems. For example, you need a set of data by the end of the day, so you tell your assistant that you need the data immediately. At the end of the day, however, the data are not there. The next morning, the employee proudly brings you the data that she has compiled in "less than a day" and is confused about why you are angry. In this example, you encoded the message as "I need it by five o'clock," you transmitted the message as "I need it immediately," and the employee decoded it as "She needs it tomorrow."

If someone told you, "I won't be gone long," when would you expect her back? When I ask this question of my classes or seminar audiences, the answers usually range from 10 minutes to 3 hours. Interestingly, at one seminar I conducted, a woman responded that her husband said that very phrase and came back 4 days later.

As the previous examples demonstrate, it is important to be concrete in the words we use. Why, then, are we often vague in the way we communicate? One reason is that we want to avoid confrontations. If a husband tells his spouse that he will be gone for 4 days, he may know that she will object. By being vague, he avoids the initial confrontation and hopes that she will not notice how long he has actually been gone—a common ploy used by us men, but one that never seems to work.

Men		Women	
Talk about major global events		Talk about daily life	
Tell the main point		Provide details	
Are more direct		Are more indirect	
Use "uh-huh" to agree		Use "uh-huh" to listen	
Are comfortable with silence		Are less comfortable with silence	
Concentrate on the words spoken		Concentrate on meta-messages	
Sidetrack unpleasant topics		Focus on unpleasant topics	

Figure 11.4
Gender Differences
in Communication

Source: Adapted from Tannen 1986, 1990.

Another reason for vagueness is that it gives us a chance to "test the water" and see what a person's initial reaction might be before we say what we really want. Asking someone out on a date is a perfect example. Instead of being direct and saying, "Do you want to go out this Friday?" we often say something such as, "So, what are you up to this weekend?" If the response is positive, we become a bit more bold.

Gender is another factor related to the use of words. As shown in Figure 11.4, Deborah Tannen (1995, 2001) believes that men and women speak very different languages and have different communication styles. By understanding these differences, communication in the workplace as well as in the home can be dramatically improved.

Communication can be improved if we choose our words carefully and ask, "How might the other person interpret what I am about to say?" If I use the word *girl*, will anyone be upset? If so, what word could I use that would be better?

Communication Channel

Problems in communication can occur as a result of the communication channel through which the message is transmitted. Information can be communicated in a variety of ways, such as orally, nonverbally, through a second party, or through a written medium such as a letter or memo. The same message can be interpreted in different ways based on the channel used to communicate it. For example, an employee being reprimanded will receive the message very differently if it is communicated in a memo or an email rather than face to face. A miffed employee who gives the cold shoulder to a coworker will receive a different response than if she yelled at the coworker or discussed the anger with her.

Another example of the channel's importance is a supervisor criticizing an employee in front of other employees. The employee might be so embarrassed and angered that she would not hear the content of the message. Again, transmitting a message through an inappropriate channel interferes with the message's meaning and accurate interpretation.

Often, the communication channel is the message itself. For example, if top management sends a "gofer" to deliver a message, it is essentially communicating that either the message or the receiver is not important. A colleague at another university tells about a former boss who always personally delivered good news (e.g., promotions, raises) as well as doughnuts on Friday. But lower-level management always had to communicate the bad news, a practice that was resented by employees.

Perhaps the worst choice of a communication channel occurred in 2006, when Radio Shack *emailed* 400 of its workers in their Fort Worth, Texas, headquarters that they would be losing their jobs. Even worse than the choice of communication channel was the actual wording of the communication, "the work force reduction notification is currently in progress. Unfortunately your position is one that has been eliminated." Employees were given boxes and plastic bags to pack their personal belongings and given 30 minutes to leave. What message do you think this sent to the employees?

Noise

The **noise** surrounding a transmission channel can also affect the way a message is received. *Noise* can be defined as any interference that affects proper reception of a message. An obvious example is actual auditory noise, such as the sound of a subway or elevated train interfering with conversation. Other examples are the appropriateness of the channel, the reputation of the person sending the message, and other information being received at the same time.

Nonverbal Cues

Much of what we communicate is conveyed by nonverbal means. Our words often say one thing, but our actions say another. For example, a supervisor may tell an employee that she is interested in hearing her opinions, while at the same time she is frowning and looking out the window or responding to an email on her BlackBerry. The verbal message from the supervisor may be "I care," but the nonverbal message is "I'm bored." Which message will the employee pay attention to? Most likely, it will be the nonverbal one, even though nonverbal cues often lead to incorrect impressions. Nonverbal cues can be divided into five categories: body language, paralanguage, use of space, use of time, and artifacts.

Body Language. How we move and position our body—our *body language*—communicates much to other people. For example:

- When one's body faces another person, it is often interpreted as a sign of liking, whereas when a person's body is turned away from another, it is often interpreted as a sign of dislike or lack of interest.
- Superiority is communicated by interrupting others, leaning back in a chair, moving closer to someone, or sitting while others stand.
- Making eye contact implies interest. In a casual conversation, increased eye contact is interpreted as a sign of liking, in a bar it may be a sign of flirting, and on a football field it may be interpreted as a sign of aggression. Lack of eye contact can mean many things, including disinterest, discomfort, or embarrassment. A person who makes eye contact while speaking but not while listening is often perceived as being powerful or dominant.
- Raising or lowering the head or the shoulders may indicate superiority or inferiority, respectively.
- Touching someone usually indicates liking, friendship, or nurturance. In fact, a review of several studies indicated that servers who touch their customers will receive a larger tip than those who do not (Azar, 2007). Another study

found that library clerks who briefly touched patrons as they were being handed books were rated by the patrons as being better employees than clerks who did not touch (Fisher, Rytting, & Heslin, 1976). Men initiate contact more often than women (Major, Schmidlin, & Williams, 1990).

■ A meta-analysis by DePaulo etal. (2003) found that when people lie, they are more likely to purse their lips, raise their chin, fidget, and show nervousness than when they are not telling a lie.

As one might expect, gender differences occur in the use of nonverbal cues. For example, Dolin and Booth-Butterfield (1993) found that women use nonverbal cues such as head nodding to show attention more often than do men. In social situations, women touch, smile, and make eye contact more than men do (DePaulo, 1992).

Not surprisingly, there are many cultural differences in nonverbal communication. Here are a few examples:

■ In the United States, a thumbs-up indicates agreement. In Australia, it is considered a rude gesture.
■ In Japan, bowing is preferred to shaking hands.
■ In the United States, people point at objects with their index finger. Germans point with their little finger, and Japanese point with the entire hand. In Japan and the Middle East, pointing with your index finger is considered rude.
■ Showing the soles of one's feet is common in the United States but is considered offensive in Thailand and Saudi Arabia.
■ Sitting with one's legs crossed shows relaxation in the United States but is considered offensive in Ghana and Turkey.
■ Prolonged eye contact is the norm in Arabic cultures, but it shows a lack of respect in many African, Latin American, and Caribbean countries.
■ Touching another person is common in Latin and Middle Eastern countries, but not in northern European or Asian countries.

Research has shown that body language can affect employee behavior. For example, a meta-analysis by Barrick, Shaffer, and DeGrassi (2008) found that the use of appropriate nonverbal communication is highly correlated with interview scores.

Though body language can be a useful source of information, it is important to understand that the same nonverbal cue can mean different things in different situations and cultures. So, be careful and try not to read too much into a particular nonverbal cue.

Use of Space. The ways people make use of space also provides nonverbal cues about their feelings and personality. Dominant people or those who have authority are given more space by others and at the same time take space from others. For example, people stand farther away from such status figures as executives and police officers (and even college professors), and stand in an office doorway rather than directly enter such a person's office. These same status figures, however, often move closer as a show of power. Police officers are taught that moving in close is one method of intimidating a person.

On the other hand, status figures also increase space to establish differences between themselves and the people with whom they are dealing. A common form of this use of distance is for an executive to place a desk between herself and another person. An interesting story is told by a sports agent who was negotiating a player's contract with George Steinbrenner, the late owner of the New York Yankees. When the agent arrived at Steinbrenner's office, he noticed that Steinbrenner sat at one end of a long desk. At the other end was a small chair in which the agent was to sit. Recognizing the spatial arrangement to be a power play, the agent moved his chair next to Steinbrenner's. As the story goes, the Yankee owner was so rattled by this ploy that the agent was able to negotiate an excellent contract for his player client.

Four major spatial distance zones in the United States have been recognized and defined (Hall, 1963): intimacy, personal distance, social distance, and public distance.

The **intimacy zone** extends from physical contact to 18 inches away from a person and is usually reserved for close relationships such as dates, spouses, and family. When this zone is entered by strangers in crowded elevators and the like, we generally feel uncomfortable and nervous. The **personal distance zone** ranges from 18 inches to 4 feet away from a person and is the distance usually reserved for friends and acquaintances. The **social distance zone** is from 4 to 12 feet away and is the distance typically observed when dealing with businesspeople and strangers. Finally, the **public distance zone** ranges from 12 to 25 feet away and is characteristic of such large group interactions as lectures and seminars.

The way an office is furnished also communicates a lot about that person. As mentioned earlier, certain desk placements indicate openness and power; visitors and subordinates prefer not to sit before a desk that serves as a barrier (Davis, 1984). People whose offices are untidy are perceived as being busy, and people whose offices contain plants are perceived as being caring and concerned.

Use of Time. The way people make use of time is another element of nonverbal communication. If an employee is supposed to meet with a supervisor at 1:00 and the supervisor shows up at 1:10, the supervisor is communicating an attitude about the employee, the importance of the meeting, or both. Tardiness is more readily accepted from a higher-status person than from a lower-status person. Dean Smith, the great former basketball coach at the University of North Carolina, suspended any player who was even a minute late for a practice because he believed that tardiness was a sign of arrogance and worked against the team concept.

In a similar fashion, a supervisor sets aside 30 minutes for a meeting and tells others that she is not to be disturbed because she is in conference. A definitive message thus is conveyed, one that is likely to prevent constant interruptions by telephone calls or people stopping by to say hello because they saw an open door.

Care must be taken when considering how others use time, as there are tremendous cultural differences in such things as being late and keeping to time schedules. For example, punctuality is important in the United States, Austria, Canada, and Japan, but not a priority in Brazil, France, Mexico, and Saudi Arabia (Olofsson, 2004).

Paralanguage

Paralanguage involves the way we say things and consists of variables such as tone, tempo, volume, number and duration of pauses, and rate of speech. A message that is spoken quickly will be perceived differently from one that is spoken slowly. In fact, research has shown that people with fast speech rates are perceived as more intelligent, friendly, and enthusiastic (Hecht & LaFrance, 1995) than people with slow rates of speech. People who use many *"uh-hums," "ers,"* and *"ahs"* are also considered less intelligent. Men with high-pitched voices are considered to be weak, but women with high-pitched voices are considered to be petite. People telling lies talk less,

Intimacy zone A distance zone within 18 inches of a person, where only people with a close relationship to the person are allowed to enter.

Personal distance zone A distance zone from 18 inches to 4 feet from a person that is usually reserved for friends and acquaintances.

Social distance zone An interpersonal distance from 4 to 12 feet from a person that is typically used for business and for interacting with strangers.

Public distance zone Distance greater than 12 feet from a person that is typical of the interpersonal space allowed for social interactions such as large group lectures.

Paralanguage Communication inferred from the tone, tempo, volume, and rate of speech.

Inflected Sentences		Meaning
I did not say Bill stole your car.		**Someone else** said Bill stole your car.
I **did not** say Bill stole your car.		I **deny** I said Bill stole your car.
I did not **say** Bill stole your car.		I **implied** that Bill stole your car.
I did not say **Bill** stole your car.		**Someone else** stole your car.
I did not say Bill **stole** your car.		He **borrowed** your car.
I did not say Bill stole **your** car.		Bill stole **someone else's** car.
I did not say Bill stole your **car.**		Bill stole **something else** of yours.

Figure 11.5
Inflection Changes
and Meaning

provide fewer details, repeat words and phrases more often, have more uncertainty and vocal tension in their voice, and speak in a higher pitch than do people telling the truth (DePaulo et al., 2003).

Simple changes in the tone used to communicate a message can change the entire meaning of the message. To demonstrate this point, consider this sentence: "I didn't say Bill stole your car." At first reading, it does not seem unusual, but what does it actually mean? As Figure 11.5 shows, if we emphasize the first word, *I*, the implication is that *someone else* said, "Bill stole your car." But if we emphasize the word *Bill*, the meaning changes to "Someone else stole your car." And so on. Thus, a simple written message can be interpreted in seven different ways. As you can see, many messages are better communicated orally than through memos or email.

Artifacts

Artifacts The things people surround themselves with (clothes, jewelry, office decorations, cars, and so forth) that communicate information about the person.

A final element of nonverbal communication concerns the objects, or **artifacts**, that a person wears or with which she surrounds herself. A person who wears bright and colorful clothes is perceived differently from a person who wears conservative white or gray clothing. Similarly, the manager who places all of her awards on her office wall, the executive with a large and expensive chair, and the student who carries a briefcase rather than a book bag are all making nonverbal statements about themselves.

Research on visitors' perceptions of certain office characteristics has resulted in several interesting but not necessarily surprising findings. One line of research examined the perceptions of visitors to offices that used either open or closed desk arrangements. An **open desk arrangement** faces a desk against a wall so that a visitor can sit next to the person who sits behind the desk. A **closed desk arrangement** places a desk so that a visitor must sit across from the person behind the desk.

Open desk arrangement
An office arranged so that a visitor can sit adjacent to rather than across from the person behind the desk.

Closed desk arrangement
An office arranged so that a visitor must sit across from the person behind the desk.

Visitors to offices that use open rather than closed desk arrangements perceive the offices to be more comfortable, and their occupants as friendlier and more trustworthy, open, interested, and extraverted (Campbell, 1979; McElroy, Morrow, & Wall, 1983; Widgery & Stackpole, 1972). Visitors rate people with messy offices as being active and busy, those with clean offices as being organized and introverted, and those with organized offices (lots of papers placed in stacks) as being active and achievement oriented (McElroy et al., 1983; Morrow & McElroy, 1981). Finally, visitors rate offices with plants and posters as more comfortable, inviting, and hospitable than offices without plants and posters (Campbell, 1979).

Recently, thinking about the placement of desks in an office has gone beyond the simple concept of visitor reactions. Office decorating experts (e.g., Too, 2009) using the concepts of *feng shui*—the Chinese art of placement and design—advise that, to properly use the energy of a room, desks

- should never be placed directly across from a doorway,
- should always face away from a wall, and
- should never be placed in the center of the room.

Research on office design is not only interesting but also important. A supervisor with a messy office and a closed desk arrangement is sending the message that he does not want to be bothered. This may not be his intended message, but it is the one perceived by his subordinates. Thus, if this supervisor wants to be more open and improve communication with his employees, he might start by changing the appearance of his office.

Clearly, people make judgments about others based on their office, and the next logical step is to determine whether people with different types of offices actually have different types of personalities. Limited research, in fact, does seem to show that the appearance of an office provides insight into the personality of the occupant.

McElroy, Morrow, and Ackerman (1983) looked at the personalities of faculty members who had open desk arrangements and those who had closed desk arrangements, and found that those with open desk arrangements were more extraverted and "people oriented" than their closed desk counterparts. Furthermore, faculty members who used open desk arrangements had lower external locus of control and scored higher on the Least-Preferred Coworker (LPC) Scale, which is discussed in Chapter 12.

In another study, Zweigenhaft (1976) compared desk placement using several variables and found that older, higher-status faculty members used closed desk arrangements more than did younger members. Even more interesting was the finding that faculty members who used closed desk arrangements were also evaluated less favorably in the classroom. Thus, desk placement was able to partially predict the effectiveness of a faculty member, providing support for the idea that different types of people arrange their offices in different ways.

In a study of personnel managers, Cochran, Kopitzke, and Miller (1984) compared the office characteristics used by managers with their personalities. They found that dominant, achievement-oriented managers did not decorate their offices with anything other than standard furniture; more outgoing managers had photographs of their vacations to remind them of good times and a clock to let them know when it was quitting time; introverted managers had plants and paintings so that their office would remind them of home; and organized managers had cartoons to show that even though they were neat and compulsive, they also had a sense of humor.

The presence of windows is another factor that seems to affect the way an office is decorated. Heerwagen and Orians (1986) examined the ways people decorated both windowed and windowless offices and found that occupants of windowless offices used twice as many decorative items such as posters, pictures, and paintings. Not surprisingly, the posters in windowless offices contained more landscapes and fewer cityscapes than did offices with windows.

To help you apply your new knowledge of nonverbal communication, complete Exercise 11.3 in your workbook.

Amount of Information

The amount of information contained in a message can affect the accuracy with which it is received. When a message contains more information than we can hold in memory, the information becomes leveled, sharpened, and assimilated. For example, suppose a friend told you the following message over the phone:

John Atoms worked in Detroit for the automobile manufacturer General Floaters Corporation. He came to work on Tuesday morning wearing a brown shirt, plaid pants, white socks, and dark shoes. He leaned forward, barfed all over the floor, and then passed out. He was obviously intoxicated. He had worked for the company for 13 years, so they didn't want to fire him, but they had to do something. The company decided to suspend him for a few days and place him on probation. They were especially sensitive to his problems because he was on his eighth marriage.

What would the story sound like if you passed it on to a friend? When you **level** some of the information, unimportant details are removed. For example, information about the color of the employee's shirt and socks would probably not be passed along to the next person. When you **sharpen** the information, interesting and unusual information is kept. In the example here, the employee's "barfing" and his eight marriages would probably be the story's main focus as it is passed from you to your friend. When you **assimilate** the information, it is modified to fit your existing beliefs and knowledge. Most of us have never heard of the last name Atoms, but we probably have known someone named "Adams." Likewise, "General Floaters" might be passed along as General Motors. You would probably use the word *drunk* rather than *intoxicated*.

Reactions to Communication Overload

With many jobs, communication overload can occur when an employee receives more communication than he can handle. When an employee is overloaded, she can adapt or adjust in one of several ways to reduce the stress: omission, error, queuing, escape, using a gatekeeper, or using multiple channels.

Omission. One way to manage communication overload is **omission**: a conscious decision not to process certain types of information. For example, a busy supervisor may let the phone ring without answering it so that she can finish her paperwork. Although this technique can work if the overload is temporary, it will be ineffective if an employee misses an important communication.

Error. In the **error** type of response, the employee attempts to deal with every message she receives. But in so doing, each processed message includes reception error. The processing errors are not intentional but result from processing more than can be handled.

Perhaps a good example of this would be a student who has two hours in which to study four chapters for a test. A student using the error method would attempt to read and memorize all four chapters in two hours. Obviously, her test score will probably indicate that even though she did all of her reading, much of it was not remembered or not remembered correctly.

The probability of error occurring can be reduced in two ways. First, the message can be made *redundant*. That is, after communicating an important message over the telephone, it is a good idea to write a memo to the other person summarizing the major points of the conversation. Furthermore, after sending an important memo, it is wise to call its recipient to ensure that the memo was not only received but also read.

Second, error can be reduced by having the recipient *verify* the message. Ask the person to repeat the message or to acknowledge that she has read and understood it.

Leveled Describes a message from which unimportant informational details have been removed before the message is passed from one person to another.

Sharpened Describes a message in which interesting and unusual information has been kept in the message when it is passed from one person to another; see Leveled.

Assimilated A description of a message in which the information has been modified to fit the existing beliefs and knowledge of the person sending the message before it is passed on to another person.

Omission A response to communication overload that involves the conscious decision not to process certain types of information.

Error Deviation from a standard of quality; also a type of response to communication overload that involves processing all information but processing some of it incorrectly.

For example, after a customer has placed an order at the drive-thru window of a fast-food restaurant, the employee repeats the order to the customer to make sure she heard it correctly. (Of course, with the poor-quality intercoms used by such places, most people still cannot understand the employee.)

Queuing. Another method of dealing with communication overload is **queuing**—placing the work into a *queue*, or waiting line. The order of the queue can be based on such variables as the message's importance, timeliness, or sender. For example, a memo sent by the company president will probably be placed near or at the beginning of the queue, as will an emergency phone message. On the other hand, a message to return the phone call of a salesperson most likely will go at the end of the queue.

With this method of handling communication overload, all of the work will usually get done. However, queues are effective only if the communication overload is temporary. If the employee is constantly overloaded, she will never reach the messages at the end of the queue.

Escape. If communication overload is prolonged, a common employee response is to **escape**, usually through absenteeism and ultimately through resignation. This response certainly is not beneficial to an organization, but it can be beneficial to an employee if it protects her mental and physical health by relieving stress.

An example of the escape response is often seen with students who withdraw from college courses. A student may enroll in six classes and realize after two months that she does not have enough time to do all of the reading and writing required for six classes. Rather than choosing the error or omission strategy, either of which would result in lower grades, the student withdraws from one of her classes to reduce her overload.

Use of a Gatekeeper. A response to communication overload used by many executives is the use of a **gatekeeper**, a person who screens potential communication and allows only the most important to go through. Receptionists and secretaries are the most obvious examples of gatekeepers.

Use of Multiple Channels. The final coping response to communication overload is the use of **multiple channels**. With this strategy, an organization reduces the amount of communication going to one person by directing some of it to another. For example, in a small restaurant, all of the problems involving customers, employees, finances, and vendors are handled by the owner. But as the business grows, the owner may not be able to handle all of the communication and thus may hire others to deal with finances (a bookkeeper) and vendors (an assistant manager).

Knowing and understanding this list of responses to communication overload is important. When communication overload occurs, employees will react in ways that reduce the increased stress. Some of these strategies (omission, error, escape) result in negative consequences for the organization. Thus, the organization must recognize when overload occurs and aggressively adopt an acceptable strategy to deal with it. To see how you react to communication overload, complete Exercise 11.4 in your workbook.

Problem Area 3: Message Received Versus Message Interpreted

Even though a person knows what she wants to say and says it the way she wants, and even though another individual properly receives the intended message, its meaning can change depending on the way in which the receiver interprets the message. As

Queuing A method of coping with communication overload that involves organizing work into an order in which it will be handled.

Escape A response to communication overload in which the employee leaves the organization to reduce the stress.

Gatekeeper A person who screens potential communication for someone else and allows only the most important information to pass through.

Multiple channels A strategy for coping with communication overload in which an organization reduces the amount of communication going to one person by directing some of it to another person.

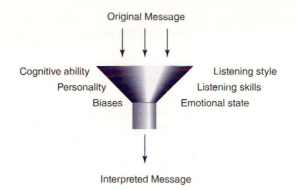

Figure 11.6
Factors Affecting the Message Received Versus the Message Interpreted

shown in Figure 11.6, this interpretation is affected by a variety of factors, such as listening skills, listening style, emotional state, cognitive ability, and personal biases.

Listening Skills

Listening is probably the most important communication skill that a supervisor should master. In a study of managers, Nichols and Stevens (1957) found that 70% of the white-collar workday is spent communicating. Of that, 9% is spent in writing, 16% in reading, 30% in speaking, and 45% in listening. Thus, a manager spends more time listening than doing any other single activity. This is an important point for two reasons.

First, listening is a skill, and our formal education in high school and college does not prepare us for managerial communication (Burley-Allen, 2001). We are required to take English courses to improve our reading and writing and are usually required to take one speech course to improve our oral communication skills, but we spend little, if any, time learning how to listen. Thus, the amount of time spent learning about various types of communication is inversely related to the actual amount of time spent by managers on the job.

Second, listening effectiveness is poor. It has been estimated that immediately after a meeting, we retain only 50% of the material we have heard and only 25% of the material 48 hours later (Nichols & Stevens, 1957). Although much of this loss can be attributed to poor memory practices, some is the result of poor listening habits.

Styles of Listening

What can be done to increase listening effectiveness? Perhaps the most important thing we can do is to recognize that every person has a particular "listening style" that serves as a communication filter. Geier and Downey (1980) have developed a test, the **Attitudinal Listening Profile**, to measure an employee's listening style. Their theory postulates six main styles of listening: leisure, inclusive, stylistic, technical, empathic, and nonconforming (LISTEN).

Leisure listening is practiced by "good-time" people who listen only for words that indicate pleasure. For example, a student who is a leisure listener will pay attention only when the teacher is interesting and tells jokes. As an employee, she is the last one to "hear" that employees are needed to work overtime.

Inclusive listening is the style of the person who listens for the main ideas behind any communication. In an hour-long meeting full of details and facts about a decline in sales, the only information this type of listener will "hear" is the main point

Attitudinal Listening Profile A test developed by Geier and Downey that measures individual listening styles.

Leisure listening The listening style of a person who cares about only interesting information.

Inclusive listening The listening style of a person who cares about only the main points of a communication.

that sales are down and that things had better improve. This listening style can be an advantage when cutting through a jungle of detail, but it can be a disadvantage when detail is important.

Stylistic listening The listening style of a person who pays attention mainly to the way in which words are spoken.

Stylistic listening is practiced by the person who listens to the *way* the communication is presented. Stylistic listeners will not listen unless the speaker's style is appropriate, the speaker "looks the part," or both. For example, when speaking to a stylistic listener, a lecturer on finance will find an attentive ear only if she wears a nice suit. After all, this listener reasons, if the lecturer cannot afford a nice suit, why listen to what she has to say about investing money? Similarly, if the speaker says that an event will be fun, she must *sound* as if she means it. And if an employee calls in sick to a manager who is a stylistic listener, she had better "sound" sick.

Technical listening The listening style of a person who cares about only facts and details.

Technical listening is the style practiced by the "Jack Webbs" of the listening world—those who want "just the facts, ma'am." The technical listener hears and retains large amounts of detail, but she does not hear the *meaning* of those details. In the earlier example of the meeting in which employees are told that sales have decreased, the technical listener will hear and remember that sales last year were 12.3% higher than this year, that profits are down by 21%, and that six employees will probably be laid off—but she will miss the point that unless sales improve, she could be one of those six.

Empathic listening The listening style of a person who cares primarily about the feelings of the speaker.

Empathic listening tunes in to the feelings of the speaker and, of the six listening types, is the most likely to pay attention to nonverbal cues. Thus, an empathic listener will listen to an employee complain about her boss and is the only one of the six types of listeners who will not only pay attention but also understand that the employee's complaints indicate true frustration and unhappiness.

Nonconforming listening The listening style of a person who cares about only information that is consistent with his or her way of thinking.

Nonconforming listening is practiced by the individual who attends only to information that is consistent with her way of thinking. If the nonconforming listener does not agree with a speaker, she will not listen to what the speaker says. Furthermore, the nonconforming listener will pay attention only to those people she considers to be strong or to have authority.

How Listening Styles Affect Communication

The following example will demonstrate the importance of the six listening styles in a work setting. Suppose an employee approaches a supervisor and tells her that she has a temperature of 106 degrees. How would each of the six listeners react?

The leisure listener would pay little attention to the employee because she does not like to hear about unpleasant things, and illness certainly is not pleasant. The inclusive listener would probably tell a story about when she had a high temperature, thinking that the topic of conversation is fever. You may have friends who often say things that are not related to your conversation; as this example points out, they are probably inclusive listeners who mistake the main points of a conversation. In this case, the employee is communicating that she does not feel well; she is not discussing "temperatures I have had."

The stylistic listener would pay attention only if the employee sounded and looked ill. You may have also called a professor or a date and tried to sound ill in order to cancel an appointment or a date. Few people actually sound ill even when they are, but we understand the importance of style in listening and behave accordingly.

The technical listener would hear every word but would not realize their meaning. That is, 10 minutes later, when another employee asked whether Sue is sick, the supervisor would respond, "She didn't say. She has a temperature of 106, but I'm not sure how she is feeling."

The nonconforming listener would pay little attention to the employee. After all, if she actually had a temperature of 106 degrees, she would be dead, and because she is not dead, she must be lying. Of course, the employee exaggerated her temperature because she was emphasizing the point that she is sick. But the nonconforming listener would not "hear" anything once she recognized that an initial statement was incorrect.

In this example, the empathic listener would be the only one who would understand the real point of the communication. The employee is mentioning her temperature because she does not feel well and wants to go home.

Understanding each of the six styles can make communication more effective in two ways. First, becoming aware of your own style allows you to understand the filter you use when listening to others. For example, a student who uses a leisure style may need to recognize that if she listens only to lectures that she finds interesting, she probably will miss a lot of important information. She might want to learn how to concentrate on lectures even when they are boring. Second, understanding the six styles can lead to better communication with others. For example, when speaking to an inclusive listener, we must either write down relevant details that we want her to remember or have her repeat the details. Otherwise, the inclusive listener will remember only the main point: "I know there is a party tonight, but I'm not sure when or where." On the other hand, when we speak to a technical listener, it is important to tell her what the details mean. For example, if you tell a technical listener there will be a party at your house on Thursday at 8:00 p.m., you should also add that she is invited, or she will understand only that there is a party, and not that she has been invited.

Of course, the million-dollar question is, "How can we tell what style of listener is listening to us?" The best way might be to test the listener on the Attitudinal Listening Profile mentioned earlier, but this is hardly practical. The most practical method is to use the person's *speaking* style as an indicator of listening style. If the person usually mentions how she feels about things, she is probably an empathic listener, but if she speaks with a lot of detail, she is probably a technical listener.

Someone speaking to a group, of course, must relate to all styles of listeners. The best communicators will have something for everyone. A good instructor will provide jokes and humorous stories for leisure listeners, use an outline format and provide main points for inclusive listeners, provide specific facts and details for technical listeners, discuss her feelings about the topic for empathic listeners, have good speaking skills and appropriate dress for stylistic listeners, and be confident and accurate for nonconforming listeners. To gauge your own listening style, complete Exercises 11.5 and 11.6 in your workbook.

Tips for Effective Listening

In addition to understanding how your listening style serves as a filter, you can improve your listening effectiveness in many other ways. Below is a summary of tips taken from a variety of sources:

- Stop talking.
- Let the other person finish speaking.
- Focus on what the person is saying rather than on how well they are saying it, what your next response will be, or what you will eat for lunch. Try to understand what the other person is *trying* to say.
- Ask questions to make sure you understand the person's point, but don't ask so many questions that they distract the speaker.

- Be patient and keep an open mind. If you disagree, you can always do so after the person is finished talking.
- Show the speaker you want to listen by using nonverbal cues such as making eye contact and nodding your head.
- Remove or resist distractions that will keep you from listening.
- Be silent for a few seconds after the person has finished speaking. This will encourage the person to continue to talk, you will be sure when they have finished talking, and it will give you time to respond calmly.

To test your own listening skills, complete Exercise 11.7 in your workbook.

Emotional State

The interpretation of a message can certainly be affected by the receiver's emotional state. When we are mad, anxious, depressed, elated, or upset, we do not think as clearly as when our moods are more moderate. Think of the last time you had an argument with someone. How rational and intelligent was your conversation? After the argument was over, did both of you remember what was said in the same way?

Likewise, have you ever attended a class when your mind was somewhere else? My guess is that neither your attention span nor your comprehension of the material was as high as normal.

Cognitive Ability

Cognitive ability is another factor than can affect the way in which a received message is interpreted. That is, a person can receive a message exactly as it was sent, yet not be bright enough to understand it. For example, have you ever attended a class where you had no idea what the professor was talking about? You heard her words and saw her diagrams, but the message still made no sense. Likewise, have you ever told a great pun, only to be disappointed that the person at the receiving end of the joke did not understand it? If so, then you have firsthand experience in understanding how cognitive ability can affect the way in which information is interpreted.

Bias

Our biases obviously affect our ability to interpret information we receive. For example, we can hate a political candidate so much that we can refuse to process any of the positive information we hear about her. We do, however, process every piece of information that is consistent with our opinion.

Improving Employee Communication Skills

Organizations are always looking for employees with excellent communication skills. The difficulty in finding such employees was recently exemplified by the experience of a national insurance company. The company was having difficulty with a position that required employees to respond to customer complaints. The company had hired expensive consultants to teach its employees how to write effective letters, but performance had not improved. The company then constructed sample letters so that an employee could read a customer complaint, find a standard response form, and add a few personal lines. This also did not work. Finally, the company tried using a standardized writing test before hiring its employees. Although the test showed significant prediction for the performance of African American employees, it did not predict the performance of White employees.

© Lee Raynes

Would this be an example of good communication?

This case of single-group validity made the test risky to use. Thus, the question remains: How can an organization increase the communication skills of its employees?

Interpersonal Communication Skills

One of the most common methods used to increase interpersonal communication skills is the training workshop conducted by an outside consultant. Although a large number of consultants lead communication workshops, such workshops often bring only short-term improvement in skills.

An exception to this general failure to produce long-term improvements was reported by Freston and Lease (1987) from their work with Questar Corporation in Salt Lake City. As the personnel manager at Questar, Freston believed that the organization's managers were not properly trained in communication. Questar thus hired Lease as a communications consultant, and together Freston and Lease designed a new training program that included seminars on awareness, nonverbal communication, assertiveness, and listening. In addition to the seminars, Freston and Lease also used role play and group discussion. The revised training program brought more positive attitudes for supervisors and increased performance quality in tasks such as performance appraisal and training.

Written Communication Skills

Attempts to improve the quality of written communication have generally taken two paths. One approach concentrates on improving the writer's skills, and the other concentrates on making material easier to read.

Improving Writing

With increased use of email, effective writing skills are more essential than ever (Tyler, 2003b). It is difficult for an organization to overcome an employee's lack of formal training in writing (or to change bad writing habits). Several consulting firms, however, specialize in the improvement of employee writing by teaching employees the most important concepts of writing. For example, Broadbent (1997) advises that writing can be improved when writers value what they write, set personal standards and goals (e.g., vocabulary usage at a twelfth-grade reading level, no grammar errors, each document proofread twice), and spend considerable time doing their own editing as well as getting others to edit the document. Employees need to analyze their audience: If a written communication is intended for a blue-collar employee, then the readability must be kept simple. If the intended audience is a busy executive, the message must be kept short.

Readability

Written communication can break down when material is too difficult for many employees to read. Here are some examples:

- Federal Aviation Administration regulations and many airline-company pilots' association agreements are too difficult for pilots to read (Blumenfeld, 1985).
- Corporate annual reports are too difficult for most adults to understand (Courtis, 1995).
- The Position Analysis Questionnaire (the job analysis instrument discussed in Chapter 2) is also too difficult for most job incumbents to read (Ash & Edgell, 1975).

Thus, providing employees with important material to read will be an effective communication form only if the employees can understand what is written. In a study of written communication at a restaurant chain, Smith and Christensen (2007) found a wide range of readability levels in written materials given to employees. Though most communication was written at a ninth-grade level, a memo to cooks was written at the fourth-grade level and the sexual harassment policy was written at a level such that an associate's degree (fifteenth grade) would be needed to understand the writing. Given that most of the employees had only a high school education, many probably did not understand the sexual harassment policy.

To solve the problem of complex reading levels in documents written by Washington State employees, in 2004 Governor Chris Gregoire initiated a "plain talk" policy requiring that documents be written at a level that could be understood by the general public.

To ensure that employees will be able to understand written material, several readability indices are available. When using such an index, an organization analyzes the material to be read and then compares its readability level with the typical education of the employees who will read the document. For example, if most employees have high school diplomas but have not been to college, the document should be written at less than a twelfth-grade level.

Each index uses a slightly different formula or method. For example, the **Fry Readability Graph** (Fry, 1977) uses the average number of syllables per word and the average length of sentences to determine readability (Figure 11.7). The **Flesch Index** (Flesch, 1948)—the readability index included in Microsoft Word—uses the

Fry Readability Graph A method of determining the readability level of written material by analyzing sentence length and the average number of syllables per word.

Flesch Index A method of determining the readability level of written material by analyzing average sentence length and the number of syllables per 100 words.

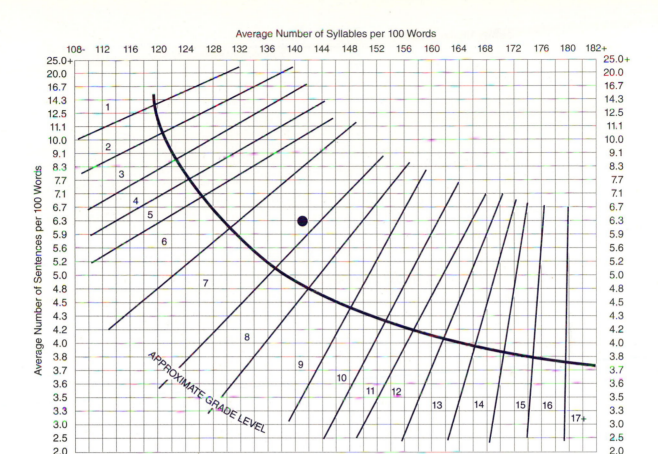

Average Number of Syllables per 100 Words

Expanded Directions for Working Readability Graph

1. Randomly select three sample passages and count out exactly 100 words each, beginning with the beginning of a sentence. Do count proper nouns, initializations, and numerals.
2. Count the number of sentences in the 100 words, estimating length of the fraction of the last sentence to the nearest one-tenth.
3. Count the total number of syllables in the 100-word passage. If you don't have a hand counter available, simply put a mark above every syllable over one in each word. Then when you get to the end of the passage, count the number of marks and add 100. Small calculators can also be used as counters by pushing numeral 1, then pushing the + sign for each word or syllable when counting.
4. Enter graph with *average* sentence length and *average* number of syllables; plot dot where the two lines intersect. Area where dot is plotted will give you the approximate grade level.
5. If a great deal of variability is found in syllable count or sentence count, putting more samples into the average is desirable.
6. A word is defined as a group of symbols with a space on either side; thus *Joe, IRA, 1945,* and *&* are each one word.
7. A syllable is defined as a phonetic syllable. Generally, there are as many syllables as vowel sounds. For example, *stopped* is one syllable and *wanted* is two syllables. When counting syllables for numerals and initializations, count one syllable for each symbol. For example, *1945* is four syllables, *IRA* is three syllables, and *&* is one syllable.

Figure 11.7
Graph for Estimating Readability

Table 11.2 Readability Levels of Selected Publications

Document	Readability Level
FAA regulations	Graduate student
Position Analysis Questionnaire	College graduate
Harvard Law Review	College graduate
Airline Pilot magazine	College student
Study of Values	12th grade
Time magazine	11th grade
Newsweek	11th grade
Otis Employment Test	9th grade
Ladies' Home Journal	8th grade
Reader's Digest	8th grade
Minnesota Multiphasic Personality Inventory–2	8th grade
Most comic books	6th grade

FOG Index A method of determining the readability level of written material by analyzing sentence length and the number of three-syllable words. (The term is interpreted as either the measure of the "fog" a reader may be in or as the acronym FOG, for "frequency of gobbledygook.")

Dale-Chall Index A method of determining the readability level of written material by looking at the number of commonly known words used in the document.

average sentence length and number of syllables per 100 words; the **FOG Index** (Gunning, 1964) uses the number of words per sentence and the number of three-syllable words per 100; and the **Dale-Chall Index** (Dale & Chall, 1948) uses the number of words that are not included in a list of words known by 80% of fourth graders.

All of the readability indices show reasonable reliability and correlate highly with one another (Blumenfeld & Justice, 1975). (The readability levels of selected publications are shown in Table 11.2.) As we can see from these indices, an easily read document has short sentences, uses simple rather than complicated words, and uses common rather than unusual words. To practice how to measure the readability of a document, complete Exercise 11.8 in your workbook.

ON THE JOB   **Applied Case Study**

Reducing Order Errors at Hardee's and McDonald's

As mentioned in this chapter, ordering errors are common at the drive-thru windows of quick-service restaurants such as Hardee's, McDonald's, Burger King, and Wendy's. One of the reasons for these errors is that order takers are distracted and thus don't listen properly. That is, while taking one customer's order, an employee is simultaneously taking money and counting change for another customer, filling drinks, and assembling food orders. Another reason is that some customers may not speak the same language as the person taking the order.

■ From what you learned in this chapter, what could a quick-service restaurant do to increase order accuracy?

■ What are the advantages and disadvantages to your plan?

To find out how some McDonald's and Hardee's franchises reduced ordering errors, use the link found on your text webpage.

Ethical Communication

Transparent communication is when there is open and honest communication between employees and management regarding work-life issues. But how transparent should a company be in situations that may have a negative impact on both the company and employees?

For example, a large insurance company in Maryland is going through some difficult times. The company has not done well financially for about two or three years. As a result, management is considering whether to lay off some employees in the coming year.

When supervisors asked management if they should tell employees of possible layoffs, the supervisors were told not to. The reason was twofold: management is not absolutely sure layoffs would be necessary, and if employees heard such news, it might start a panic. This panic might encourage some employees to look for and take positions in other companies. Management wants to make sure they did not lose any of their good staff. Management also said that not communicating this information would "protect" employees from unnecessary stress caused by worrying about something that may never happen. Management feels it is more ethical not to communicate this news until they are absolutely sure the layoffs would occur.

But not communicating this information could, instead of "protecting" employees, cause problems for some. Employees who are about to make some kind of financial decisions, such as buying a house or a car or spending a large amount of money on a vacation, may make a completely different decision if they know they may be laid off in the near future. Additionally, employees who may have already been offered jobs in another company and are deciding whether to stay or quit may make a different decision if they know about pending layoffs in their current company.

In a 2008 Ethics and Workplace Survey done by Deloitte, LLP, an independent consulting firm, 84% of employees surveyed said that transparent communication leads to a more ethical workplace. These employees may believe that communicating about possible layoffs is more ethical than trying to protect employees from the stress of worrying about something that may never happen.

The other side of transparent communication is the ethical responsibility of *employees* to communicate certain information to their supervisors. For example, there are times when people, while employed in one company, search for other jobs. Usually, those employees will not let their managers know that they are looking for other jobs. The thinking behind not doing that is that if the supervisor finds out, he or she may get upset and retaliate in some way against that employee. If the employee is able to get another position, the usual amount of notice given to the current manager is two weeks.

For some organizations, it may be difficult and/or time-consuming to find someone to replace an employee who has taken a position in another organization. If managers know ahead of time that one of their employees is job searching, the company could start the recruitment process for a replacement. Even if the current employee does not leave after all, the company would at least have names of potential candidates who, in the future, may fill a position should it become vacant. But when a company is not aware that an employee in a hard-to-fill position may leave and is only given two weeks notice that the employee will be quitting, that company could go months before finding a suitable replacement. This could potentially cause financial hardships to the company, as well as increase the workloads of other employees who must take up the slack after a position is vacated.

What Do You Think?

- Do you agree that companies should communicate any and all information that may pertain to employees?

- Would there ever be a time where it would be more ethical to hold back information from employees?

- If you were an employee in the insurance company, what would you consider to be the ethical step to take: inform employees of the possibilities of layoffs or keep that information confidential until the company is absolutely sure layoffs might happen?

- What would be the best, most ethical, channel to use when communicating bad news such as layoffs?

- Do you think it is unethical not to tell your boss that you are looking for another job? What are the situations in which employees have an ethical obligation to provide this information to their managers or supervisors?

Chapter Summary

In this chapter you learned:

- There are three types of organizational communication: upward, downward, and horizontal.
- There are three main problem areas in interpersonal communication: the intended message versus the message actually sent, the message sent versus the message received, and the message received versus the message interpreted.
- Interpersonal communication can be improved with more effective listening skills, understanding the six different styles of listening (leisure, inclusive, stylistic, technical, empathic, and nonconforming), and considering the emotional state, cognitive ability, and personal biases of the sender and the receiver.
- Written communication can be improved by learning better writing skills and by writing organizational documents at a reading level that matches the reading level of most employees.

Questions for Review

1. Why do people hate to communicate bad news?
2. When is email an inappropriate method of communication?
3. What is the best way to stop a rumor?
4. Which is most important: nonverbal cues, paralanguage, or the actual words chosen to communicate? Why?
5. Can people be taught to be effective listeners? Explain your answer.

Media Resources and Learning Tools

- Visit our website. Go to www.cengage.com/psychology/aamodt, where you will find online resources directly linked to your book, including chapter-by-chapter quizzing, flashcards, crossword puzzles, application activities, and more.
- Want more practice applying industrial/organizational psychology? Check out the *I/O Applications Workbook*. This workbook (keyed to your textbook) offers engaging, high-interest activities to help you reinforce the important concepts presented in the text.

© Chris Ryan/OJO Images/Getty Images

Learning Objectives

➡ Learn what types of people become good leaders

➡ Understand the importance of leaders adapting their behavior to each situation

➡ Know what skills are essential for effective leadership

➡ Understand the theories of leadership

➡ Learn how leaders use power and influence

imagine a company with thousands of workers that has seen sales drop in each of the past five years. The president of the company steps down, and a new president is installed. Several years later, the company makes a profit, and everyone hails the new president as the reason for the improvement.

Now imagine a football team with a winning record in each of the last 10 years. The team's coach leaves for another school, and the team loses the majority of its games in the next few years.

In both of these examples, a new leader took over. In the first example, the organization became more successful, whereas in the second example, the team went into decline. How much of the organization's performance can be attributed to the leader? If the leader *was* the major cause of the changes in performance, why was one leader successful and the other a failure? These types of questions will be addressed in this chapter. To get you thinking about leadership, complete Exercise 12.1 in your workbook.

An Introduction to Leadership

Many different theories about leadership have been developed over the last few decades. Although none of the theories "tells the whole story" about leadership, each has received at least some empirical support. Understanding the theories and research behind leadership is important because the theory that company executives believe about leadership will, for the most part, determine how an organization selects or develops its managers.

For example, if we believe that certain people are "born leaders" because of their personal traits, needs, or orientation, then managers could be selected partially on the basis of their scores on certain tests. But if we believe that leadership consists of specific skills or behaviors, then theoretically we should be able to train any employee to become an outstanding leader. If we believe that good leadership is the result of an interaction between certain types of behaviors and particular aspects of the situation, then we might choose certain types of people to be leaders at any given time, or we might teach leaders how to adapt their behavior to meet the situation.

The following pages provide brief explanations of the most popular leadership theories. When reading about each theory, think about what the theory would imply about the selection or development of leaders for an organization. In addition, think of how you manage and the type of leader you wish to be.

Personal Characteristics Associated with Leadership

In the last 100 years, many attempts have been made to identify the personal characteristics associated with leader emergence and leader performance.

Leader emergence A part of trait theory that postulates that certain types of people will become leaders and certain types will not.

Leader Emergence

Leader emergence is the idea that people who *become* leaders possess traits or characteristics different from people who do not become leaders. That is, people who become leaders—such as Presidents George W. Bush and Barack H. Obama and

© Photo Disc/Getty Images

Can leadership be taught?

CEOs Ellen Kullman and Michael Dell—share traits that your neighbor or a food preparer at McDonald's does not. If we use your school as an example, we would predict that the students in your student government would be different from students who do not participate in leadership activities. In fact, research indicates that to some extent, people are "born" with a desire to lead or not lead, as somewhere between 17% (Ilies, Gerhardt, & Le, 2004) and 30% (Arvey, Rotundo, Johnson, Zhang, & McGue, 2006) of leader emergence has a genetic basis.

Does that mean that there is a "leadership gene" that influences leader emergence? Probably not. Instead we inherit certain traits and abilities that might influence our decision to seek leadership. Though early reviews of the literature suggested that the relationship between traits and leader emergence is not very strong, as shown in Table 12.1, more recent reviews suggest that

- people high in openness, conscientiousness, and extraversion and low in neuroticism are more likely to emerge as leaders than their counterparts (Judge, Bono, Ilies, & Gerhardt, 2002);
- high self-monitors (people who adapt their behavior to the social situation) emerge as leaders more often than low self-monitors (Day & Schleicher, 2006; Day, Schleicher, Unckless, & Hiller, 2002);
- more intelligent people are more likely to emerge as leaders than are less intelligent people (Judge, Colbert, & Ilies, 2004); and
- looking at *patterns* of abilities and personality traits is more useful than looking at *single* abilities and traits (Foti & Hauenstein, 2007).

It is especially perplexing that some of the early reviews concluded that specific traits are seldom related to leader emergence because both anecdotal evidence and research suggest that leadership behavior has some stability (Law, 1996). To illustrate this point, think of a friend you consider to be a leader. In all probability, that person is a leader in many situations. That is, he might influence a group of friends about

Table 12.1 Summary of Meta-Analyses of Leader Emergence and Performance

Trait	Leader Emergence		Leader Performance		Meta-analysis
	K	p	K	p	
Personality					
Neuroticism	30	−.24	18	−.22	Judge et al. (2002)
Extraversion	37	.33	23	.24	Judge et al. (2002)
Openness	20	.24	17	.24	Judge et al. (2002)
Agreeableness	23	.05	19	.21	Judge et al. (2002)
Conscientiousness	17	.33	18	.16	Judge et al. (2002)
Self-monitoring	23	.21			Day et al. (2002)
Intelligence	65	.25	151	.27	Judge, Colbert, & Ilies (2004)
Need for achievement			11	.23	Argus & Zajack (2008)

what movie to see, make decisions about what time everyone should meet for dinner, and "take charge" when playing sports. Conversely, you probably have a friend who has never assumed a leadership role in his life. Thus, it appears that some people consistently emerge as leaders in a variety of situations, whereas others never emerge as leaders.

Perhaps one explanation for the lack of agreement on a list of traits consistently related to leader emergence is that the motivation to lead is more complex than originally thought. In a study using a large international sample, Chan and Drasgow (2001) found that the motivation to lead has three aspects (factors): affective identity, noncalculative, and social-normative motivation. People with an **affective identity motivation** become leaders because they enjoy being in charge and leading others. Of the three leadership motivation factors, people scoring high on this one tend to have the most leadership experience and are rated by others as having high leadership potential. Those with a **noncalculative motivation** seek leadership positions when they perceive that such positions will result in personal gain. For example, becoming a leader may result in an increase in status or in pay. People with a **social-normative motivation** become leaders out of a sense of duty. For example, a member of the Kiwanis Club might agree to be the next president because it is "his turn," or a faculty member might agree to chair a committee out of a sense of commitment to the university.

Individuals with high leadership motivation tend to obtain leadership experience and have confidence in their leadership skills (Chan & Drasgow, 2001). Therefore, after researching the extent to which leadership is consistent across life, it makes sense that Bruce (1997) concluded that the best way to select a chief executive officer (CEO) is to look for leadership qualities (e.g., risk taking, innovation, vision) and success early in a person's career. As support for his proposition, Bruce cites the following examples:

- Harry Gray, the former chair and CEO of United Technologies, demonstrated vision, risk taking, and innovation as early as the second job in his career.
- Ray Tower, former president of FMC Corporation, went way beyond his job description as a salesperson in his first job to create a novel sales-training program. Tower continued to push his idea despite upper management's initial lack of interest.

Affective identity motivation The motivation to lead as a result of a desire to be in charge and lead others.

Noncalculative motivation Those who seek leadership positions because they will result in personal gain.

Social-normative motivation The desire to lead out of a sense of duty or responsibility.

- Lee Iacocca, known for his heroics at Ford and Chrysler, pioneered the concept of new car financing. His idea of purchasing a 1956 Ford for monthly payments of $56 ("Buy a '56 for $56") moved his sales division from last in the country to first. What is most interesting about this success is that Iacocca didn't even have the authority to implement his plan—but he did it anyway.

The role of gender in leader emergence is complex. Meta-analyses indicate that men and women emerge as leaders equally often in leaderless group discussions (Benjamin, 1996); men emerge as leaders more often in short-term groups and groups carrying out tasks with low social interaction (Eagly & Karau, 1991); and women emerge as leaders more often in groups involving high social interaction (Eagly & Karau, 1991). Though women often emerge as leaders, historically they have been excluded from the highest levels of leadership and power in politics and business. Thus, it is said that there is a "glass ceiling" for women in leadership and management. This glass ceiling is slowly breaking, as the vast majority of women leaders at the highest levels have achieved their positions since 1990 (Carli & Eagly, 2001).

Leader Performance

In contrast to leader emergence, which deals with the likelihood that a person will *become* a leader, **leader performance** involves the idea that leaders who *perform well* possess certain characteristics that poorly performing leaders do not. For example, an excellent leader might be intelligent, assertive, friendly, and independent, whereas a poor leader might be shy, aloof, and calm. Research on the relationship between personal characteristics and leader performance has concentrated on three areas: traits, needs, and orientation.

Traits

As shown in Table 12.1, a meta-analysis by Judge et al. (2002) found that extraversion, openness, agreeableness, and conscientiousness were positively related to leader performance and that neuroticism was negatively related to leader performance. A meta-analysis by Youngjohn and Woehr (2001) also found that management, decision-making, and oral-communication skills were highly correlated with leadership effectiveness.

As was the case with leader emergence, high self-monitors tend to be better leaders than do low self-monitors (Day & Schleicher, 2006; Day et al., 2002). The concept of **self-monitoring** is especially interesting, as it focuses on what leaders *do* as opposed to what they *are*. For example, a high self-monitoring leader may possess the trait of shyness and not truly want to communicate with other people. She knows, however, that talking to others is an important part of her job, so she says hello to her employees when she arrives at work, and at least once a day stops and talks with each employee. Thus, our leader has the trait of shyness but adapts her outward behavior to appear to be outgoing and confident. To determine your level of self-monitoring, complete Section A in Exercise 12.2 in your workbook.

An interesting extension of the trait theory of leader performance suggests that certain traits are necessary requirements for leadership excellence but that they do not guarantee it (Simonton, 1987). Instead, leadership excellence is a function of the right person being in the right place at the right time. The fact that one person with certain traits becomes an excellent leader while another with the same traits flounders may be no more than the result of timing and chance.

Leader performance A part of trait theory that postulates that certain types of people will be better leaders than will other types of people.

Self-monitoring A personality trait characterized by the tendency to adapt one's behavior to fit a particular social situation.

For example, Lyndon Johnson and Martin Luther King, Jr. were considered successful leaders because of their strong influence on improving civil rights. Other people prior to the 1960s had had the same thoughts, ambitions, and skills as King and Johnson, yet they had not become successful civil rights leaders, perhaps because the time had not been right.

Cognitive Ability

A meta-analysis of 151 studies by Judge et al. (2004) found a moderate but significant corrected correlation ($p = .27$) between cognitive ability and leadership performance. The meta-analysis further discovered that cognitive ability is most important when the leader is not distracted by stressful situations and when the leader uses a more directive leadership style. In studies investigating the performance of U.S. presidents, it was found that the presidents rated by historians as being the most successful were smart and open to experience, had high goals, and interestingly, had the ability to bend the truth (Dingfelder, 2004; Rubenzer & Faschingbauer, 2004). Sternberg (2007) has expanded on the importance of cognitive ability by theorizing that the key to effective leadership is the *synthesis* of three variables: wisdom, intelligence (academic and practical), and creativity.

Needs

A personal characteristic that has received some support pertains to a leader's **need for power**, **need for achievement**, and **need for affiliation**. In fact, as shown in Table 12.1, a meta-analysis by Argus and Zajack (2008) found a significant relationship between need for achievement and leader performance. Research by McClelland and Burnham (1976) and McClelland and Boyatzis (1982) demonstrates that high-performance managers have a **leadership motive pattern**, which is a high need for power and a low need for affiliation. The need is not for personal power but for organizational power.

This pattern of needs is thought to be important because it implies that an effective leader should be concerned more with results than with being liked. Leaders who need to be liked by their subordinates will have a tough time making decisions. A decision to make employees work overtime, for example, may be necessary for the organization's survival, but it will probably be unpopular with employees. Leaders with high affiliation needs may decide that being liked is more important than being successful, causing conflict with their decision.

This theory would also explain why internal promotions often do not work. Consider, for example, a person who worked for six years as a loan officer. He and 10 coworkers often went drinking together after work and went away on weekends. One day he was promoted to manager, and he had to lead the same people with whom he had been friends. The friendships and his need to be liked hindered the new manager when giving orders and disciplining his employees. When he tried to separate himself from his friends, he was quickly thought of as being "too good" for them—a tough situation with no apparent solution, according to this theory.

This does not mean that a leader should not be friendly and care about subordinates. But successful leaders will not place their need to be liked above the goals of the organization. President Richard Nixon was thought to have a high need to be liked. He would often make a tough decision and then apologize for it because he wanted to be liked by both the public and the press.

Needs for power, achievement, and affiliation can be measured through various psychological tests. The most commonly used is the **Thematic Apperception Test (TAT)**.

Need for power According to trait theory, the extent to which a person desires to be in control of other people.

Need for achievement According to trait theory, the extent to which a person desires to be successful.

Need for affiliation The extent to which a person desires to be around other people.

Leadership motive pattern The name for a pattern of needs in which a leader has a high need for power and a low need for affiliation.

Thematic Apperception Test (TAT) A projective personality test in which test-takers are shown pictures and asked to tell stories. It is designed to measure various need levels.

The TAT is a projective test in which a person is shown a series of pictures and asked to tell a story about what is happening in each. A trained psychologist then analyzes the stories, identifying the needs themes contained within them. Obviously, this technique is time-consuming and requires a great deal of training.

Another commonly used measure is the **Job Choice Exercise (JCE)**, developed by Stahl and Harrell (1982). With the JCE, the person reads descriptions of jobs that involve varying degrees of power, achievement, and affiliation needs and rates how desirable he finds each particular job. These ratings are then subjected to a complicated scoring procedure that uses regression analysis to reveal scores on the three needs categories. To find your own need-for-achievement, need-for-power, and need-for-affiliation levels, complete Section D of Exercise 12.2 in your workbook.

Another method to determine leaders' needs is to examine the themes that occur in their writing and speeches. In one interesting use of this method, it was found that Presidents Franklin Roosevelt, Kennedy, and Reagan had high needs for power; Presidents Harding, Truman, and Nixon had high needs for affiliation; and Presidents Wilson, Hoover, and Carter had high needs for achievement (Winter, 1988).

Gender

As with leader emergence, meta-analyses suggest that the role of gender in leader effectiveness is complex. When all studies are combined, men and women appear not to differ in leadership effectiveness (Eagly, Karau, & Makhijani, 1995). However, men were more effective as leaders in situations traditionally defined in masculine terms and in situations in which the majority of subordinates were men. Women were more effective as leaders in situations traditionally defined in less masculine terms. Though men and women appear to be equally effective leaders, a meta-analysis of leadership styles indicated that women were more likely than men to engage in behaviors associated with high-quality leadership (Eagly, Johannesen-Schmidt, & van Engen, 2003).

Task Versus Person Orientation

Over the last 45 years, three major schools of thought—Ohio State Studies (Fleishman, Harris, & Burtt, 1955), Theory X (McGregor, 1960), and **Managerial Grid** (Blake & Mouton, 1984)—have postulated that differences in leader performance can be attributed to differences in the extent to which leaders are task versus person oriented. As shown in Figure 12.1, though the three schools of thought use different terms, they say similar things.

Person-oriented leaders such as country club leaders, Theory Y leaders, and leaders high in consideration act in a warm and supportive manner and show concern for their subordinates. Person-oriented leaders believe that employees are intrinsically motivated, seek responsibility, are self-controlled, and do not necessarily dislike work. Because of these assumptions, person-oriented leaders consult their subordinates before making decisions, praise their work, ask about their families, do not look over their shoulder, and use a more "hands-off" approach to leadership. Under pressure, person-oriented leaders tend to become socially withdrawn (Bond, 1995).

Task-oriented leaders such as **task-centered leaders, Theory X leaders**, and leaders high in **initiating structure** define and structure their own roles and those of their subordinates to attain the group's formal goals. Task-oriented leaders see their employees as lazy, extrinsically motivated, wanting security, undisciplined, and shirking responsibility. Because of these assumptions, task-oriented leaders tend to manage or lead by giving directives, setting goals, and making decisions without consulting

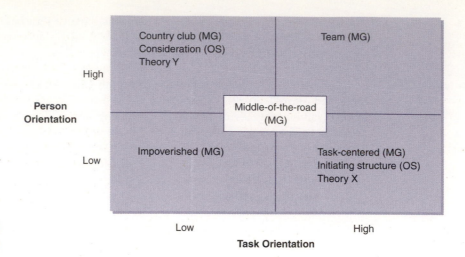

High — Person Orientation

Country club (MG)
Consideration (OS)
Theory Y

Team (MG)

Middle-of-the-road
(MG)

Low

Impoverished (MG)

Task-centered (MG)
Initiating structure (OS)
Theory X

Low   High
Task Orientation

Figure 12.1

Relationship Between Managerial Grid (MG) Theory, Theory X, and Ohio State (OS) Theory

Team leadership A leadership style in which the leader is concerned with both productivity and employee well-being.

Impoverished leadership A style of leadership in which the leader is concerned with neither productivity nor the well-being of employees.

Middle-of-the-road leadership A leadership style reflecting a balanced orientation between people and tasks.

Leadership Opinion Questionnaire (LOQ) A test used to measure a leader's self-perception of his or her leadership style.

Leader Behavior Description Questionnaire (LBDQ) A test used to measure perceptions of a leader's style by his or her subordinates.

their subordinates. Under pressure, they become anxious, defensive, and dominant (Bond, 1995). Interestingly, task-oriented leaders tend to produce humor (e.g., tell jokes and stories), whereas person-oriented leaders tend to appreciate humor (e.g., listen to others' jokes) (Philbrick, 1989). As shown in Figure 12.2, when using the terms from Figure 12.1, the best leaders **(team)** are both task and person oriented, whereas the worst **(impoverished)** are neither task nor person oriented. Some leaders **(middle-of-the-road)** have moderate amounts of both orientations.

A meta-analysis by Judge, Piccolo, and Ilies (2004) found that higher scores on consideration or on initiating structure were associated with such positive leadership criteria as follower satisfaction and group performance. The relationships between person orientation (consideration) and follower satisfaction, follower motivation, and ratings of leadership effectiveness were higher than the relationships between task orientation (initiating structure) and these same three leadership criteria.

A leader's task or person orientation can be measured by several instruments, two of which are the **Leadership Opinion Questionnaire (LOQ)** and the **Leader Behavior Description Questionnaire (LBDQ)**. The LOQ is filled out by supervisors or leaders who want to know their own behavioral style. The LBDQ is completed by subordinates to provide a picture of how they perceive their leader's behavior. A meta-analysis by Eagly and Johnson (1990) indicated that in laboratory studies, women were more likely to have a person orientation and less likely to have a task orientation than were men. They did not find any such difference in studies that were conducted in actual organizations. They did, however, find small gender differences in that women were more likely to use a more participative approach and men more likely to use a more autocratic approach.

As depicted in Figure 12.2, theoretically, person-oriented leaders should have satisfied employees, whereas task-oriented leaders should have productive employees. Leaders scoring high in both (called *team leadership*) should have satisfied and productive employees, whereas leaders scoring low in both (called *impoverished leadership*) should have unhappy and unproductive employees (Fleishman & Harris, 1962; Hutchison, Valentino, & Kirkner, 1998; Korman, 1966; Pool, 1997).

Although these predictions certainly make sense, the meta-analysis by Judge and his colleagues (2004) found that consideration scores (person orientation) were more strongly correlated with follower satisfaction, follower motivation, and ratings of

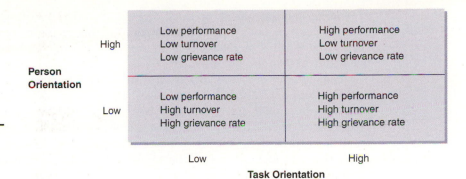

	Low	High
High	Low performance / Low turnover / Low grievance rate	High performance / Low turnover / Low grievance rate
Low	Low performance / High turnover / High grievance rate	High performance / High turnover / High grievance rate

Low   High

Task Orientation

Person Orientation (vertical axis)

Figure 12.2

Consequences of Leader Orientation

leadership effectiveness than were initiating structure scores (task orientation). Correlations with the performance of the work group were similar in magnitude for both consideration and initiating structure.

To complicate matters further, the relationship between person and task orientation is probably more complex than was first thought. Several studies have shown that leader experience and knowledge and such external variables as time pressures and work importance tend to moderate the relationship between person-orientation scores and satisfaction and between task-orientation scores and subordinate performance. To find your own level of task orientation, complete Section C of Exercise 12.2 in your workbook.

Unsuccessful Leaders

The traits and behaviors of unsuccessful leaders are not necessarily the opposite of those of successful leaders (Hackman & Wageman, 2007). In a departure from research to identify characteristics of successful leaders, Hogan (1989) attempted to identify traits of unsuccessful leaders. Hogan was interested in investigating poor leaders because, according to both empirical research and anecdotal accounts, most employees report that one of the greatest sources of stress in their jobs is their supervisors' poor performance, strange behavior, or both. This finding should come as no surprise: You can probably quickly recall many examples of poor performance or strange behavior with current or former supervisors.

Lack of Training. On the basis of years of research, Hogan, Raskin, and Fazzini (1990) concluded that poor leader behavior has three major causes. The first is a *lack of leadership training* given to supervisors. The armed forces are among the few organizations that require supervisors to complete leadership training before taking charge of groups of people. The norm for most organizations, however, is either to promote a current employee or hire a new employee and place him directly into a leadership role. If training is ever provided, it is usually after the promotion and well after the supervisor has begun supervising. The serious consequences of this lack of training can best be understood if we imagine allowing doctors to perform surgery without training or truck drivers to drive on the highways without first learning how to drive.

Cognitive Deficiencies. The second cause of poor leadership stems from *cognitive deficiencies*. Hogan et al. (1990) believes that poor leaders are unable to learn from experience and are unable to think strategically—they consistently make the same mistakes and do not plan ahead. Support for this concept comes from the meta-analysis by Judge et al. (2004), which found a significant relationship between cognitive ability and leader performance.

The manager of a local convenience store that I frequent is an example of a person who does not learn from his mistakes. The manager did not give employees their work schedules until one or two days before they had to work. The employees complained because the hours always changed and they could not schedule their personal, family, and social lives. But the manager continued to do it his way, and most of the employees quit. Eight years later, he still does it his way, and his employees still leave at a high rate.

Personality. The third, and perhaps most important, source of poor leadership behavior involves the *personality* of the leader. Hogan et al. (1990) believed that many unsuccessful leaders are insecure and adopt one of three personality types: the paranoid or passive-aggressive, the high-likability floater, and the narcissist.

The source of insecurity for leaders who are paranoid, passive-aggressive, or both is some incident in their life in which they felt betrayed. This *paranoid/passive-aggressive* leader has deeply rooted, but perhaps unconscious, resentment and anger. On the surface, these leaders are charming, quiet people who often compliment their subordinates and fellow workers. But they resent the successes of others and are likely to act against subordinates in a passive-aggressive manner; that is, on the surface they appear to be supportive, but at the same time they will "stab" another person in the back.

The type of leader who is insecure and seldom rocks the boat or causes trouble is known as a *high-likability floater*. This person goes along with the group, is friendly to everyone, and never challenges anyone's ideas. Thus, he travels through life with many friends and no enemies. The reason he has no enemies is because he never does anything, challenges anyone, or stands up for the rights of his employees. Such leaders will be promoted and never fired because even though they make no great performance advances, they are well liked. Their employees have high morale but show relatively low performance.

Narcissists are leaders who overcome their insecurity by overconfidence. They like to be the center of attention, promote their own accomplishments, and take most, if not all, of the credit for the successes of their group—but they avoid all blame for failure.

Rather than concentrate on *traits*, Rasch, Shen, Davies, and Bono (2008) collected critical incidents of ineffective leader *behavior* and found that such behavior fell under 10 basic dimensions:

- Engaging in illegal and unethical behavior
- Avoiding conflict and people problems
- Demonstrating poor emotional control (e.g., yelling and screaming)
- Overcontrolling (e.g., micromanaging)
- Demonstrating poor task performance
- Poor planning, organization, and communication
- Starting or passing on rumors or sharing confidential information
- Procrastinating and not meeting time commitments
- Failing to accommodate the personal needs of subordinates
- Failing to nurture and manage talent

Interaction Between the Leader and the Situation

As already indicated, a leader's effectiveness often depends not only on the traits she possesses, but also on the particular situation in which the leader finds herself (Hackman & Wageman, 2007). In the past few decades, several theories have emerged that have sought to explain the situational nature of leadership.

Situational Favorability

The best-known and most controversial situational theory was developed by Fred Fiedler in the mid-1960s (Fiedler, 1967). Fiedler believed that an individual's leadership style is the result of a lifetime of experiences and thus is extremely difficult to change. **Fiedler's contingency model** holds that any individual's leadership style is effective only in certain situations. Thus, Fiedler would argue that rather than teaching people to change their leadership styles, leadership training should concentrate on helping people understand their style of leadership and learn how to manipulate a situation so that the two match. To help people understand their leadership style, Fielder developed the **Least-Preferred Coworker (LPC) Scale**.

To complete the LPC Scale, leaders identify the subordinate or employee with whom they would least want to work. Leaders then rate that person on several semantic differential scales that range from *nice* to *nasty* and from *friendly* to *unfriendly*. The higher the leaders rate their least-preferred coworker, the higher the LPC score. This score is then compared with the favorableness of the situation to determine leader effectiveness. Low-scoring LPC leaders tend to be task oriented, whereas high-scoring LPC leaders tend to be more concerned with interpersonal relations (Fiedler, 1978; Rice, 1978). High-LPC leaders would fall in the same quadrant in Figure 12.1 as Theory Y and consideration leaders. Low-LPC leaders would fall in the same quadrant as Theory X and initiating-structure leaders. To find your own LPC score, complete Section B of Exercise 12.2 in your workbook.

The favorableness of a situation is determined by three variables. The first is **task structuredness**. Structured tasks have goals that are clearly stated and known by group members, have only a few correct solutions to a problem, and can be completed in only a few ways. The more structured the task, the more favorable the situation.

The second variable is **leader position power**. That is, the greater the position or legitimate power of the leader, the more favorable the situation. Thus, a group or organizational setting in which there is no assigned leader is not considered to be a favorable leadership situation. The third variable is **leader–member relations**. The more the subordinates like their leader, the more favorable the situation. The leader–member relationship is considered the most important of the three variables.

As shown in Figure 12.3, the relationship between LPC scores and group performance is complex. Basically, low-scoring LPC leaders (those who rate their least-preferred coworker low) function best in situations that are either favorable or unfavorable, whereas high-scoring LPC leaders function best when the situation is only of moderate favorability.

In spite of psychometric problems with the LPC Scale (Kennedy, Houston, Korsgaard, & Gallo, 1987; Stewart & Latham, 1986), research generally has supported Fiedler's theory. Strube and Garcia (1981) conducted a meta-analysis of 145 independent studies that investigated Fiedler's model as well as 33 of Fiedler's own studies and

---

Fiedler's contingency model A theory of leadership that states that leadership effectiveness is dependent on the interaction between the leader and the situation.

Least-Preferred Coworker (LPC) Scale A test used in conjunction with Fiedler's contingency model to reveal leadership style and effectiveness.

Task structuredness The variable in Fiedler's contingency model that refers to the extent to which tasks have clear goals and problems can be solved.

Leader position power The variable in Fiedler's contingency model that refers to the extent to which a leader, by the nature of his or her position, has the power to reward and punish subordinates.

Leader–member relations The variable in Fiedler's contingency model that refers to the extent to which subordinates like a leader.

Figure 12.3
Relationship Between LPC Scores and Group Success

concluded that the ideas were well supported by the research. Schriesheim, Tepper, and Tetrault (1994) found support for the general predictions of leader behavior but not for some of the specific predictions.

Leader Match A training program that teaches leaders how to change situations to match their leadership styles.

Fiedler's training program, called **Leader Match**, has also been supported by research (Strube & Garcia, 1981). This program is based on Fiedler's belief that an individual's leadership style is not easily changed. Thus, to improve their abilities, leaders learn through four-hour workshops how to diagnose situations and then change these situations to fit their particular leadership styles (Csoka & Bons, 1978). Leader Match is probably the only training program in the country concentrating on changing the situation rather than the leader.

Organizational Climate

IMPACT theory A theory of leadership that states that there are six styles of leadership (*in*formational, *m*agnetic, *p*osition, *a*ffiliation, *c*oercive, and *t*actical) and that each style will be effective only in one of six organizational climates.

Another situational theory, known as **IMPACT theory**, was developed by Geier, Downey, and Johnson (1980), who believed that each leader has one of six behavioral styles: *i*nformational, *m*agnetic, *p*osition, *a*ffiliation, *c*oercive, or *t*actical. Each style is effective in only a particular situation, or in what the researchers call an *organizational climate*. As shown in Table 12.2, the six styles are similar to the five bases of power suggested many years ago by French and Raven (1959; Raven, 1965).

Informational Style in a Climate of Ignorance

Informational style A style of leadership in which the leader leads through knowledge and information; most effective in a climate of ignorance.

Ignorance An organizational climate in which important information is not available.

The leader who has an **informational style** provides information in a climate of **ignorance**, where important information is missing from the group. For example, if a car containing four college professors and a mechanic broke down on the side

Table 12.2   Comparison of IMPACT Styles and Bases of Power

IMPACT Style[a]	Base of Power[b]
Informational	Expert
Magnetic	Referent
Position	Legitimate
Affiliation	
Coercive	Coercive/Reward
Tactical	

[a]Geier et al., 1980; [b]French & Raven, 1959.

IMPACT = informational, magnetic, position, affiliation, coercive, or tactical.

of the road, who would become the leader? Almost certainly it would be the mechanic because he would probably be the one who had the most knowledge or information needed to solve the problem.

For many years in the U.S. Senate, John Warner was one of the most powerful and respected congressional leaders. He became powerful because of his expertise in defense matters, an area that was important and that few in Congress knew much about. Thus, Warner used an informational style in a climate of ignorance to become a powerful leader.

Magnetic Style in a Climate of Despair

Magnetic style A style of leadership in which the leader has influence because of his or her charismatic personality; most effective in a climate of despair.

Despair An organizational climate characterized by low morale.

A leader with a **magnetic style** leads through energy and optimism and is effective only in a climate of **despair**, which is characterized by low morale. Ronald Reagan is perhaps the best example of a magnetic leader. As president, he was optimistic and well liked, even by people who may not have agreed with him politically. He was elected at a time when the national mood was depressed because of high inflation, high unemployment, and the Iran hostage situation. The chances of successful leadership increase in a situation of general despair when a magnetic or charismatic individual assumes control (Latham, 1983).

Position Style in a Climate of Instability

Position style A leadership style in which the leaders influence others by virtue of their appointed or elected authority; most effective in a climate of instability.

Instability An organizational climate in which people are not sure what to do.

A person who uses the **position style** leads by virtue of the power inherent in that position. Such a person might lead through statements like "As your captain, I am ordering you to do it" or "Because I am your mother—that's why." Individuals who use a position style will be effective only in climates of **instability**. This style is especially effective during corporate mergers, particularly when people are not sure what actions to take. However, there are often questions about a leader's legitimate scope of power (Yukl, 1994).

Affiliation Style in a Climate of Anxiety

Affiliation style A leadership style in which the individual leads by caring about others and that is most effective in a climate of anxiety.

Anxiety An organizational climate in which worry predominates.

A person with an **affiliation style** leads by liking and caring about others. This style is similar to that of the person-oriented leader discussed previously. A leader using affiliation will be most effective in a climate of **anxiety** or when worry predominates. Former president Jimmy Carter provides an excellent example of the affiliation style. Carter was elected president shortly after the Watergate affair, when many voters were worried that they could not trust politicians or their government. Carter campaigned successfully with statements such as "I care" and "I'm not part of that Washington crowd."

Coercive Style in a Climate of Crisis

Coercive style A leadership style in which the individual leads by controlling reward and punishment; most effective in a climate of crisis.

Crisis A critical time or climate for an organization in which the outcome to a decision has extreme consequences.

A person using the **coercive style** leads by controlling reward and punishment and is most effective in a climate of **crisis**. Such a leader will often use statements such as "Do it or you're fired" or "If you can get the package there on time, I will have a little something for you." This style is typical in war. If soldiers disobey an order, an officer can have them shot. Conversely, if soldiers behave with bravery and distinction, an officer can reward them with a medal or promotion.

Mulder, de Jong, Koppelaar, and Verhage (1986) found support for the situational appropriateness of coercive styles of leadership. They studied the behavior of bankers whose leadership styles had been measured by the Influence Analysis Questionnaire. Mulder and his colleagues found that in crisis situations, bankers tend to use more formal and coercive types of power than they do in noncrisis situations.

The importance of leaders' use of reward and punishment was best demonstrated in a series of studies by Komaki (1998). Komaki and her colleagues observed a wide range of managers/leaders including police sergeants, sailboat skippers, construction supervisors, and investment bankers and concluded that the best managers complimented and rewarded their employees/subordinates who performed well and sanctioned those who did not. Perhaps the most important finding was that the best managers/leaders spend considerable time gathering performance information from their subordinates, sometimes asking simple questions such as, "How is it going?"

Tactical Style in a Climate of Disorganization

Tactical style A leadership style in which a person leads through organization and strategy; most effective in a climate of disorganization.

Disorganization A climate in which the organization has the necessary knowledge and resources but does not know how to efficiently use the knowledge or the resources.

A leader with a **tactical style** leads through the use of strategy and is most effective in a climate of **disorganization**. A good example is a class that breaks into small groups to complete an assignment. Ideally, every student knows the material well enough to complete the assignment, but normally there is a limited amount of time and too much work to do. The person who becomes the leader is the one who is best able to organize the group.

Becoming an Effective Leader According to IMPACT Theory

If IMPACT theory is correct, people can become effective leaders by one of the four methods shown in Table 12.3. The first is by finding a climate that is consistent with their behavioral style. This method, however, involves either a great deal of luck or a lot of patience, as the leader must be in the right place at the right time.

In the second method, leaders change their style to meet a particular climate. That is, if the climate is one of ignorance, individuals change their behavior and use information to lead. On the other hand, if the climate is one of despair, individuals become more outgoing and positive. Thus, people who are willing to adapt their behavior and who have the ability to "play" each of the six leadership styles should be effective leaders.

Although there is continual debate about whether a person can be trained to be a leader, a meta-analysis by Collins and Holton (2004) supports the effectiveness of leadership training. Thus, those who are willing to use different leadership styles can learn the necessary skills and behaviors through training programs.

The third method by which a person can become an effective leader is to change followers' perception of the climate so that the perception matches the leader's behavioral style. This tactic is common in politics, in which each candidate tries to convince the voting public that he or she is the best person for an office.

The fourth method by which a leader can become effective is by actually changing the climate itself rather than simply changing followers' perceptions of the climate. Obviously, this is difficult to do, but it is the strategy advocated in Fiedler's Leader Match training. Such a strategy is difficult but can be successful.

Table 12.3   Four Leadership Strategies

- Find a climate consistent with your leadership style.
- Change your leadership style to better fit the existing climate.
- Change your followers' perception of the climate.
- Change the actual climate.

Subordinate Ability

An important influence on leader effectiveness is the abilities and attitudes of the leader's followers and how these abilities and attitudes interact with the style and characteristics of the leader (Hollander & Offermann, 1990). House (1971) believed a leader's behavior will be accepted by subordinates only to the extent to which the behavior helps the subordinates achieve their goals. Thus, leaders will be successful only if their subordinates perceive them as working with them to meet certain goals and if those goals offer a favorable outcome for the subordinates.

Because the needs of subordinates change with each new situation, supervisors must adjust their behavior to meet the needs of their subordinates. That is, in some situations subordinates need a leader to be directive and to set goals; in others, they already know what to do and need only emotional support. Leaders who adapt their behavior to match the needs of their subordinates will be more effective than leaders who stick to one leadership style (Foster, 1999).

According to House's **path–goal theory**, a leader can adopt one of four behavioral leadership styles to handle each situation: instrumental, supportive, participative, or achievement-oriented.

The **instrumental-style** leader calls for planning, organizing, and controlling the activities of employees. The **supportive-style** leader shows concern for employees, the **participative-style** leader shares information with employees and lets them participate in decision making, and the leader who uses the **achievement-oriented-style** sets challenging goals and rewards increases in performance.

Each style will work only in certain situations and depends on subordinates' abilities and the extent to which the task is structured. In general, the higher the level of subordinate ability, the less directive the leader should be. Likewise, the more unstructured the situation, the more directive the leader should be (Schriesheim & DeNisi, 1981).

House and Mitchell (1974) further advise that to be effective, a leader should

- recognize the needs of subordinates and work to satisfy those needs,
- reward subordinates who reach their goals,
- help subordinates identify the best paths to take in reaching particular goals, and
- clear those paths so that employees can reach their goals.

Path–goal theory is intuitively appealing because it gives a manager direct advice about how to behave in certain situations. Furthermore, because it is behavior based rather than trait based, the theory could be used in training. Unfortunately, a meta-analysis of the research on path–goal theory has not supported its general effectiveness (Wofford & Liska, 1993). If path–goal theory is to have real impact, it will need further revision.

Another theory that focuses on the relationship between leader and follower is the **situational leadership theory** developed by Hersey and Blanchard (1988), who postulated that a leader typically uses one of four behavioral styles: delegating, directing, supporting, or coaching. Hersey and Blanchard termed the most important follower characteristic *follower readiness*, or the ability and willingness to perform a particular task. The degree of follower readiness can be measured by either the manager's rating form or the self-rating form developed by Hersey and Blanchard. Scores from these forms place followers into one of four categories, or readiness (R) levels:

R1: Unable and unwilling or insecure
R2: Unable but willing or confident

Path–goal theory A theory of leadership stating that leaders will be effective if their behavior helps subordinates achieve relevant goals.

Instrumental style In path–goal theory, a leadership style in which the leader plans and organizes the activities of employees.

Supportive style In path–goal theory, a leadership style in which leaders show concern for their employees.

Participative style In path–goal theory, a leadership style in which the leader allows employees to participate in decisions.

Achievement-oriented style In path–goal theory, a leadership style in which the leader sets challenging goals and rewards achievement.

Situational leadership theory A theory of leadership stating that effective leaders must adapt their style of leadership to fit both the situation and the followers.

Figure 12.4

Appropriate
Situational Leadership
Styles Based on
Employee Ability and
Willingness

Employee Ability Level

	Unable	Able
Unwilling	Directing R1	Supporting R3
Willing	Coaching R2	Delegating R4

Employee Willingness Level

R3: Able but unwilling or insecure

R4: Able and willing or confident

As shown in Figure 12.4, for R1 followers, the most effective leader behavior is the *directing approach*. That is, the leader directs the follower by telling him what to do and how to do it. A *coaching approach* should be used with R2 followers because they are willing to do the work but are not sure *how* to do it. Leaders using this approach explain and clarify how work should be done. R3 followers are given plenty of emotional support as well as opportunities for two-way communication. This approach is successful because these followers already know what to do but are not sure whether they *want* to do it. R4 followers are most productive and happy when a delegating leadership style is used. These followers are both willing and able to perform the task. Thus, the only real job for the leader is to delegate specific tasks to subordinates and then let them complete those tasks with minimal supervision or guidance.

Under this theory, effective leaders first diagnose the competency and motivation levels of employees for each goal or series of tasks, and then adapt their leadership style to fit the employees' level. As an employee makes developmental progress, the leader changes styles and becomes less directive. It is important for leaders to discuss this strategy with each employee so that employees will understand why they are being treated a particular way (Blanchard, Zigarmi, & Zigarmi, 1985).

As with many theories of leadership, situational leadership theory has excellent intuitive appeal and has been successful in some organizational applications (Gumpert & Hambleton, 1979) but not others (Goodson, McGee, & Cashman, 1989; Norris & Vecchio, 1992). In general, however, meta-analyses by Shilobod, McMullen, and Raymark (2003) and Day et al. (2002) provide support for situational leadership theory by demonstrating a moderate relationship between leader adaptability and self-monitoring and leadership performance.

Relationships with Subordinates

Leader–member exchange (LMX) theory A leadership theory that focuses on the interaction between leaders and subordinates.

Vertical dyad linkage (VDL) theory A leadership theory that concentrates on the interaction between the leader and his or her subordinates.

Leader–member exchange (LMX) theory was developed by Dansereau, Graen, and Haga (1975) and was originally called **vertical dyad linkage (VDL) theory**. LMX theory is a unique situational theory that makes good intuitive sense. The situational theories discussed earlier concentrate on interactions between leaders and situations, and between leaders and employees with differing levels of ability. LMX theory, however, concentrates on the *interactions* between leaders and subordinates. These interactions are called leader–member exchanges (LMX). The theory originally took its name from the relationship between two people (a *dyad*), the position of the leader above the subordinate (*vertical*), and their interrelated behavior (*linkage*).

LMX theory states that leaders develop different roles and relationships with the people under them and thus act differently with different subordinates. Dansereau and his colleagues believed that subordinates fall into one of two groups—the *in-group*, characterized by a high-quality relationship with the leader, or the *out-group*, characterized by a low-quality relationship with the leader.

In-group subordinates are those who have developed trusting, friendly relationships with the leader. As a result, the leader deals with in-group members by allowing them to participate in decisions and by rarely disciplining them. Out-group subordinates are treated differently from those in the in-group and are more likely to be given direct orders and to have less say about how affairs are conducted (Graen & Uhl-Bien, 1995). As one would imagine, employees with a high-quality LMX are more satisfied with their jobs, are less likely to leave the organization, perform at higher levels, and engage in more organizational citizenship behaviors than do employees with a low-quality LMX (Colella & Varma, 2001; Griffeth, Hom, & Gaertner, 2000; Ilies, Nahrgang, & Morgeson, 2007). To become members of the in-group, employees often engage in such ingratiating behaviors as complimenting their leader. The extent to which these ingratiation attempts work is a function of such factors as the number of employees being supervised (Schriesheim, Castro, & Yammarino, 2000) and whether the employee is disabled (Colella & Varma, 2001).

In general, research on LMX theory has been supportive (Erdogan & Enders, 2007). Though in-group employees often receive higher performance ratings than out-group employees, the relationship between performance and LMX is complicated. Supervisors and employees often have different perceptions of the leader–member exchange, and such factors as the number of employees being supervised and impression-management attempts by employees moderate the relationship between LMX and performance (Schriesheim et al., 2000).

To complicate matters further, supervisors can only help members of the in-group when the supervisors themselves have a good relationship with their bosses. That is, if a supervisor is well liked by her boss and feels supported by the organization, she is better able to help or hurt her subordinates (Erdogan & Enders, 2007; Tangirala, Green, & Ramanujam, 2007).

Specific Leader Skills

Another way to think about leadership is that excellent leaders possess specific *skills* or engage in *behaviors* that poor leaders do not. After observing thousands of leaders in a variety of situations, Yukl (1982), Carter (1952), Hemphill and Coons (1950), and Gibbs (1969) have proposed a behavioral "theory." According to these researchers, leaders do the following:

1. Initiate ideas
2. Informally interact with subordinates
3. Stand up for and support subordinates
4. Take responsibility

5. Develop a group atmosphere
6. Organize and structure work
7. Communicate formally with subordinates
8. Reward and punish subordinates
9. Set goals
10. Make decisions
11. Train and develop employee skills
12. Solve problems
13. Generate enthusiasm

In a job analysis of first-line supervisors at the Maryland Department of Transportation, Cooper, Kaufman, and Hughes (1996) found the following skills to be essential:

- Organizing
- Analysis and decision making
- Planning
- Communication (oral and written)
- Delegation
- Work habits (high-quality work)
- Carefulness
- Interpersonal skill
- Job knowledge
- Organizational knowledge
- Toughness
- Integrity
- Development of others
- Listening

This theory is not particularly exciting and is the least described in textbooks, but it is the way leadership is most often practiced in industry. If this theory is true, then leadership and management are something learned, usually through experience (McCall, 2010). Thus, if the specific behaviors and skills important for effective leadership can be identified, then most people can be trained to become effective leaders, especially if they are given the necessary learning experiences.

In addition to learning leadership skills through experience, many leadership skills can be taught in training programs. The city of San Diego has its own management academy that provides interested employees with the skills necessary to become managers. On weeknights and weekends, employees learn skills such as oral communication, report writing, decision making, conflict management, and performance appraisal. After an employee is trained and tested in each of these important skill areas, he or she receives a certificate of completion. Even though graduates of the management academy are not promised managerial positions, more often than not they are the employees who are promoted.

If you have ever attended a leadership conference, you probably have noticed that the training involves specific leadership skills such as time management, goal setting, persuasion, and communication. Such an agenda typifies the idea that leadership consists of specific and learnable skills and behaviors.

Although it is beyond the scope of this chapter to discuss each of the behaviors and skills listed in Table 12.4, many are covered throughout this text. A discussion of a few additional skills follows.

Table 12.4   Specific Behaviors Taught in Leadership Training Programs

Specific Behavior	Corresponding Chapter in this Text
Communication skills	11
Conflict management	13
Decision-making skills	14
Delegation	
Discipline	7, 10
Motivation	9
Persuasion	
Planning and organizing	
Problem solving	
Providing performance feedback	7
Public speaking, oral communication	8
Reward and punishment	9
Running a meeting	
Soothing and supporting	9
Stress management	15
Team building	13, 14
Time management	15
Training and mentoring	8
Understanding people	
Writing	

Leadership Through Decision Making

Decision making is a specific behavior or skill that is important for a leader to possess. Vroom and Yetton (1973), however, point out that previous research has shown that only in certain situations are decisions best made by the leader; in other situations, decisions are best made with the participation of a leader's subordinates, colleagues, or both. Because of this situational aspect to decision making, Vroom and Yetton believe that leadership performance can be improved by teaching leaders to become better decision makers. To aid this process, Vroom and Yetton developed a decision tree to help leaders decide when decisions should be made alone and when they should be made with the help of others. Of course, developing a chart that would tell a leader what to do in every possible situation is impossible. But the **Vroom-Yetton Model** does provide a flowchart that can tell a leader what *process* to go through to make a decision in a particular situation. This theory will be discussed in further detail in Chapter 14.

Vroom-Yetton Model A theory of leadership that concentrates on helping a leader choose how to make a decision

Leadership Through Contact: Management by Walking Around

Management by walking around (MBWA) is another popular specific behavioral theory. This one holds that leaders and managers are most effective when they are out of

Adapting to the needs of subordinates is an essential component of leadership.

© Keith Brofsky/PhotoDisc/Getty Images

their offices, walking around and meeting with and talking to employees and customers about their needs and progress. Many industry leaders, such as the late Sam Walton of Walmart, have used this approach with great success. MBWA is thought to increase communication, build relationships with employees, and encourage employee participation (Amsbary & Staples, 1991; Miller, 1998).

In an interesting series of studies by Komaki and her associates (Komaki, 1986; Komaki, Zlotnick, & Jensen, 1986), the behavior of bank managers was observed to determine the differences between effective and ineffective managers. The results of the investigations indicated that the main difference between the two was that effective managers spent more time walking around and monitoring the behavior and performance of their employees. Empirical evidence thus seems to support the MBWA concept.

Leadership Through Power

Another strategy leaders often use is management by power. Power is important to a leader because as it increases so does the leader's potential to influence others (Nesler, Aguinis, Quigley, Lee, & Tedeschi, 1999). Leaders who have power are able to obtain more resources, dictate policy, and advance farther in an organization than those who have little or no power.

Earlier in this chapter, French and Raven's bases of power were alluded to in terms of their relationships to Geier et al.'s IMPACT theory. These authors (French & Raven,

Devon Bryan, M.A.
Senior Manager, Human Resources, Avon Products, Inc.

At Avon, we currently view leadership as a competency with four components. The first component is the extent to which leaders understand and successfully manage themselves and their relationships with others. Effective leaders strive for self-awareness and self-regulation. For individuals to successfully demonstrate this competency, they would establish and build productive working relationships with others, take accountability for their own performance and growth, and relate to people in an open, friendly, and accepting manner. They express themselves to individuals and groups in a manner that enhances understanding and understand the existing and potential customers and markets.

The second leadership component is that leaders must have a relentless accountability for results while at the same time being governed by business ethics and embracing change. Leaders must have the courage to make tough calls, to create an environment that continuously raises the bar, and to act decisively using facts and discipline. Effective leaders at Avon drive results and obtain success in spite of obstacles. They make timely and sound decisions and manage resources effectively. They have the ability to influence and interest others in career opportunities, products, programs, and initiatives. To make the best decisions, our leaders are taught to identify and analyze data and options prior to making decisions. To be successful, leaders must develop action plans and schedules to accomplish their goals and objectives.

A third component of leadership competency is the ability to nurture talent. This means putting the right people in the right jobs at the right time. Effective leaders at Avon focus on developing the next generation of leaders by promoting those who deliver results, develop talent, and differentiate performance. Our leaders identify the needs of individuals and provide relevant training and coaching to help them succeed. They identify and engage others to participate in beneficial career opportunities. By earning respect and gaining commitment and cooperation, they inspire others to take action.

The final piece to the leadership puzzle is the ability to break down barriers and to manage matrix relationships. Effective leaders must be strategic thinkers and action-oriented implementers who integrate a diversity of perspectives. They can work across geographical boundaries and work closely with relevant business partners. They have the ability to understand, appreciate, and build on the contributions of those from varied backgrounds and points of view.

Although individuals must possess many core competencies to be effective leaders at Avon, I think leadership is a core competency an organization must develop. Without true leaders, organizations don't innovate. Instead, they copy and are not original.

1959; Raven, 1992) identified five basic types of power: expert, legitimate, reward, coercive, and referent.

Expert Power

Expert power Power that individuals have because they have knowledge.

As mentioned earlier in the chapter, in certain situations, leaders who know something useful—that is, have expert knowledge—will have power. But there are two requirements for **expert power**. First, the knowledge must be something that others in an organization need. In a university's psychology department, a researcher with an excellent grasp of statistics has power over those who do not. Similarly, a soldier who knows how to get around the military bureaucracy has more power than those who know only how to follow established channels and procedures.

Second, others must be aware that the leader knows something. Information is powerful only if other people know that the leader has it or if the leader uses it.

Legitimate Power

Legitimate power The power that individuals have because of their elected or appointed position.

Leaders obtain **legitimate power** on the basis of their positions. For example, a sergeant has power over a corporal, a vice president has power over a supervisor, and a coach has power over players on a football team. Leaders with legitimate power are best able to get employees to comply with their orders (Rahim & Afza, 1993) but have low follower satisfaction (Rahim, 1989).

Reward and Coercive Powers

Leaders also have power to the extent that they can reward and punish others. **Reward power** involves having control over both financial rewards—salary increases, bonuses, or promotions—and nonfinancial rewards—praise or more favorable work assignments (Ward, 2001).

For a leader to have **coercive power**, it is important that others believe she is willing to use her ability to punish; she cannot maintain coercive power if employees believe she is bluffing. Punishment includes such actions as firing or not promoting and the more subtle action of giving someone the cold shoulder.

Referent Power

Another source of power for a leader may lie in the positive feelings that others hold for him. Leaders who are well liked can influence others even in the absence of reward and coercive power. Leaders can obtain such **referent power** by complimenting others, doing favors, and generally being friendly and supportive (Kipnis, Schmidt, & Wilkinson, 1980). Employees of leaders with referent power are most committed to their organizations and satisfied with their jobs (Rahim & Afza, 1993).

Leadership Through Vision: Transformational Leadership

In the past 20 years, it has become popular to separate leadership styles into two types: transactional and transformational. **Transactional leadership** consists of many of the task-oriented behaviors mentioned throughout this chapter—setting goals, monitoring performance, and providing a consequence to success or failure. Transactional leadership is thought to have three dimensions: contingent reward, management by exception–active, and management by exception–passive. The contingent reward dimension refers to leaders who reward followers for engaging in desired activity. *Management by exception–active* refers to leaders who actively monitor performance and take corrective action when needed. *Management by exception–passive* refers to leaders who do not actively monitor follower behavior and who take corrective action only when problems are serious.

Transformational leadership focuses on changing or transforming the goals, values, ethics, standards, and performance of others (Northouse, 2003). Transformational leaders are often labeled as being "visionary," "charismatic," and "inspirational." They lead by developing a vision, changing organizations to fit this vision, and motivating employees to reach the vision or long-term goal. Transformational leaders are confident, have a need to influence others, and hold a strong attitude that their beliefs and ideas are correct (Bryman, 1992). They innovate, challenge the status quo, focus on people, are flexible, look to the future, carefully analyze problems, and trust their intuition (Bass, 1997; Nanus, 1992; Yukl, 1994). Transactional leadership is most related to the personality dimension of extraversion; is positively related to agreeableness, conscientiousness, and openness to experience; and is negatively related to neuroticism (Bono & Judge, 2004).

It is believed that there are three highly related dimensions to transformational leadership: charisma (idealized influence, inspirational motivation), intellectual stimulation, and individual consideration. *Charisma* refers to leaders with high moral and ethical standards who have a strong vision of where they want their followers to go and who use enthusiasm to motivate their followers. *Intellectual stimulation* refers to leaders who encourage change and open thinking, challenge the status quo, and

---

Reward power Leadership power that exists to the extent that the leader has the ability and authority to provide rewards.

Coercive power Leadership power that comes from the leader's capacity to punish others.

Referent power Leadership power that exists when followers can identify with a leader and the leader's goals.

Transactional leadership Leadership style in which the leader focuses on task-oriented behaviors.

Transformational leadership Visionary leadership in which the leader changes the nature and goals of an organization.

appreciate diversity. *Individual consideration* refers to leaders who encourage individual growth and take the time to mentor and coach their followers.

A good example of a transformational leader is Herb Kelleher, cofounder, Chairman Emeritus, and former CEO who turned Southwest Airlines into one of the top airlines in the world. Kelleher is charismatic (on one occasion he settled a dispute by arm wrestling, on another he came to work dressed as Elvis); employee oriented (his employees come first, the customers second); visionary (his concept of a low-cost airline was designed to compete as much with ground transportation as with other airlines); and a great motivator of people.

Interestingly, the meta-analysis by Eagly et al. (2003) found that female leaders engaged in transformational behaviors slightly more often than male leaders. Though male leaders generally engage in more transactional and laissez-faire leadership behaviors than do female leaders, women are more likely to use reward to motivate employees.

Yukl (1994) offered the following guidelines for transformational leadership:

- Develop a clear and appealing vision.
- Develop a strategy for attaining the vision.
- Articulate and promote the vision.
- Act confident and optimistic.
- Express confidence in followers.
- Use early success in small steps to build confidence.
- Celebrate successes.
- Use dramatic, symbolic actions to emphasize key values.
- Lead by example.
- Create, modify, or eliminate such cultural forms as symbols, slogans, and ceremonies.

The research on transformational leadership has yielded positive results. The meta-analysis by Judge, Piccolo, and Ilies (2004) found strong correlations between transformational leadership and several aspects of leader effectiveness, such as follower satisfaction, follower motivation, and group performance. Further research on transformational leadership suggests that it is used on every continent and is best liked by employees (Bass, 1997).

After studying a variety of successful and unsuccessful leaders, Hunt and Laing (1997) concluded that too much effort has been expended in trying to label leaders as "transformational" or "charismatic." Instead, they proposed that excellent leadership should be defined by exemplar—that is, does a leader have characteristics similar to successful leaders and dissimilar to unsuccessful leaders? Support for this notion comes from the meta-analysis by Judge et al. (2004), which, although supporting the effectiveness of transformation leadership, found similar results for transactional leadership.

On the basis of their research, Hunt and Laing (1997) hypothesized that good leaders possess five characteristics not shared by poor leaders: vision, differentiation, values, transmission, and flaws.

Vision

Consistent with the notion of transformational leadership, good leaders have a vision of where they want the organization to go and provide direction toward that end. Hunt and Laing (1997) found that 72% of high-performing leaders were described by their subordinates as being visionary compared with only 34% of the least successful leaders.

Differentiation

Successful leaders are somehow different from their followers. In some cases, the difference might be one of personality; in others, it might be one of charisma, knowledge, or skill. Though successful leaders are somehow different from their followers, they are also similar enough to relate to and empathize with them. A good example of this can be found in presidential elections. Candidates travel the country trying to relate to the people by wearing regional attire (e.g., a cowboy hat in Texas, a John Deere cap in Iowa) but still trying to "look presidential."

Values

Successful leaders have strong values. For example, Walmart founder Sam Walton strongly valued customer service, whereas retired Southwest Airlines CEO Herb Kelleher strongly valued employee relations.

Transmission of Vision and Values

Successful leaders are able to communicate their vision and values to others. In a study of speeches given by U.S. presidents, it was found that presidents who communicated their messages using imagery were considered more charismatic and had higher ratings of "greatness" than presidents who engaged in content-based rhetoric (Emrich, Brower, Feldman, & Garland, 2001).

Flaws

Interestingly, successful leaders typically have a major flaw and they know it. This flaw makes the leader more human and provides a target that followers can focus on when they are upset with the leader. A look at recent presidents shows many with flaws: Jimmy Carter "lusted in his heart," Ronald Reagan tended to ramble and forget, Bill Clinton had his affairs (but didn't inhale), George W. Bush mangled the English language, and Barack Obama smoked cigarettes behind the White House. Our attention to these flaws often kept us from criticizing these presidents on more important problems (e.g., ethics, economy, foreign relations).

Leadership Through Authenticity

Authentic leadership A leadership theory stating that leaders should be honest and open and lead out of a desire to serve others rather than a desire for self-gain.

In 2003, former Medtronic CEO Bill George published a book on leadership that criticized common beliefs about projecting a certain leadership *image* and constantly adapting one's leadership style to fit a given situation. Instead, George (2003) advocated for **authentic leadership**, in which leaders reflect on their own ethics, core beliefs, and values and, rather than leading by copying the leadership style of others, lead by being themselves and acting in accordance with their heartfelt ethics, beliefs, and values to create a positive environment. Rather than leading out of a desire for profit or fame, the authentic leader desires to serve others and leads in a manner that empowers others. Former EEOC chair Cari Dominguez calls this style "leading with your heart" (Dominguez & Sotherlund, 2010).

An important aspect of authentic leadership is self-awareness. For leaders to be successful they need to understand who they are, recognize and accept their weaknesses, and take steps to correct those weaknesses. Authentic leaders have a high self-esteem that gives them the confidence to be courageous and do the right thing as well as the willingness to accept criticism and make personal changes when necessary.

Cultural Differences in Leadership: Project Globe

Over the past few years, an extensive international project involving approximately 150 researchers has been undertaken to study cultural differences in leadership. This endeavor, called Project GLOBE (Global Leadership and Organizational Behavior Effectiveness), has two goals: (1) discover differences and similarities in cultures and (2) determine why these differences exist (House, Javidan, Hanges, & Dorfman, 2002). Project GLOBE researchers have concluded that cultures can differ on these nine dimensions:

- *Uncertainty avoidance*: The extent to which a culture avoids uncertainty by using social norms and rituals.
- *Power distance*: The extent to which power is unequally shared.
- *Social collectivism*: The extent to which a culture encourages collective distribution of resources.
- *In-group collectivism*: The extent to which individuals express pride in their organizations and families.
- *Gender egalitarianism*: The extent to which a culture tries to minimize differences in gender roles and prevent discrimination.
- *Assertiveness*: The extent to which individuals in a culture are assertive and challenging in social relationships.
- *Future orientation*: The extent to which a culture plans for and invests in the future.
- *Performance orientation*: The extent to which a culture encourages and rewards improvement in performance.
- *Humane orientation*: The extent to which a culture encourages and rewards people for being fair, caring, and giving.

A comparison of data from 61 nations revealed that each nation could be placed into 1 of 10 clusters (Gupta, Hanges, & Dorfman, 2002). These clusters are shown in Table 12.5.

Are there cultural differences in leadership?

Table 12.5 Project GLOBE: Cultural Differences in Leadership

	Leadership Style Raw Scores					
	Charisma	Team	Self-protective	Participative	Humane	Autonomous
All Countries						
Mean	5.83	5.76	3.45	5.35	4.77	3.86
Standard deviation	0.33	0.26	0.41	0.41	0.38	0.45
Latin Europe (Israel, Italy, Portugal, Spain, France, French-speaking Switzerland)	5.74	5.83	3.19	5.48	4.24	3.70
Eastern Europe (Hungary, Russia, Greece, Poland, Georgia, Slovenia, Albania, Kazakhstan)	5.73	5.50	3.67	5.09	4.75	4.18
Germanic Europe (Austria, Switzerland, Netherlands, Germany)	5.93	5.62	3.03	5.85	4.71	4.16
Arab Cultures (Qatar, Morocco, Turkey, Egypt, Kuwait)	5.35	5.55	3.79	4.98	4.80	3.69
Anglo Cultures (U.S., England, Australia, Canada, New Zealand, Ireland, South Africa (White sample))	6.04	5.74	3.82	5.72	5.08	3.82
Southern Asia (India, Indonesia, Philippines, Malaysia, Thailand, Iran)	5.97	5.86	3.82	5.06	5.68	3.99
Latin America (Argentina, Bolivia, Brazil, Colombia, Costa Rica, Ecuador, El Salvador, Guatemala, Mexico, Venezuela)	5.91	5.91	3.65	5.25	4.85	3.68
Sub-Sahara Africa (Namibia, Zambia, Zimbabwe, Nigeria, South Africa (Black sample))	5.63	5.57	3.74	5.19	5.22	3.69
Confucian Asia (Taiwan, Singapore, Hong Kong, South Korea, China, Japan)	5.64	5.62	3.73	4.99	5.04	4.03
Nordic Europe (Denmark, Finland, Sweden)	5.88	5.76	2.77	5.64	4.59	3.97

	Leadership Style Standard Scores					
Culture Cluster	Charisma	Team	Self-protective	Participative	Humane	Autonomous
Latin Europe	−0.27	0.27	−0.63	0.32	−1.39	−0.36
Eastern Europe	−0.30	−1.00	0.54	−0.63	−0.05	0.71
Germanic Europe	0.30	−0.54	−1.02	1.22	−0.16	0.67
Arab Cultures	−1.45	−0.81	0.83	−0.90	0.08	−0.38
Anglo Cultures	0.64	−0.08	0.90	0.90	0.82	−0.09
Southern Asia	0.42	0.38	0.90	−0.71	2.39	0.29
Latin America	0.24	0.58	0.49	−0.24	0.21	−0.40
Sub-Sahara Africa	−0.61	−0.73	0.71	−0.39	1.18	−0.38
Confucian Asia	−0.58	−0.54	0.68	−0.88	0.71	0.38
Nordic Europe	0.15	0.00	−1.66	0.71	−0.47	0.24

GLOBE = Global Leadership and Organizational Behavior Effectiveness.

Project GLOBE researchers also determined that six main leadership styles distinguish cultures: charismatic, self-protective, humane, team oriented, participative, and autonomous (Den Hartog, House, Hanges, Ruiz-Quintanilla, & Dorfman, 1999). A *charismatic* style involves vision, inspiration, integrity, and a performance orientation. A *self-protective* style involves following procedure, emphasizing status differences, being self-centered, and saving face. A *humane* style involves being modest and helping others. A *team-oriented* style involves being collaborative, building teams, and being diplomatic. A *participative* style involves getting the opinions and help of others. An *autonomous* style involves being independent and individualistic and making one's own decisions.

Project GLOBE researchers found that the 10 culture clusters differed on the 6 main leadership styles. For example, compared with other clusters, leaders from countries in the Anglo cluster are more self-protective and participative, leaders from countries in the Nordic Europe cluster are more participative and less self-protective, and leaders from the Southern Asia cluster are more humane and less participative.

Leadership: Where Are We Today?

Most of this chapter has described leadership theories. Of course, when several theories address the same topic, the question comes to mind: "Which of the theories is (are) true?" The answer probably is that each is somewhat true and that the best "theory" about leadership is some combination.

As Figure 12.5 shows, if we combine all of the theories discussed in this chapter, leadership emerges as a set of interactions: between a leader's traits and skills,

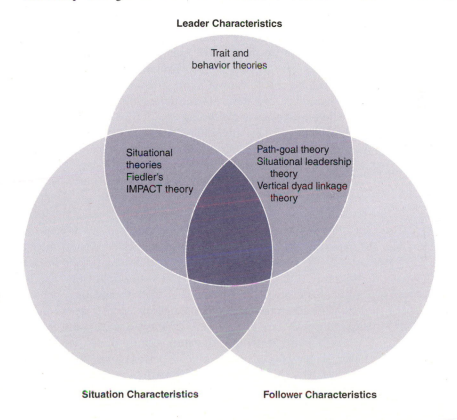

Figure 12.5

Effective Leadership: Interaction of Leader, Situation, and Follower Characteristics

between a situation's demands and characteristics, and between followers' needs and characteristics. If we begin with a leader's traits and skills, a summary of the theories would suggest that individuals would be more likely to be successful leaders if they

- have received leadership training and mastered the skills listed in Table 12.4,
- are high self-monitors,
- are high in both task and person orientations,
- have the leadership motive pattern (high need for power, low need for affiliation),
- are intelligent,
- are emotionally stable (don't possess such problematic personality traits as those of the high-likability floater, the narcissist, or the passive-aggressive person), and
- possess the skills and personality to be a transformational leader

If individuals have these skills and traits, their leadership performance will depend on the characteristics of the situation. Thus, as shown in Table 12.6, certain people will be effective leaders in certain situations when particular types of people are followers. For example, in a structured situation in which the leader has both legitimate and referent power (a highly favorable situation), a low-LPC leader will perform better than a high-LPC leader. If subordinates are unwilling and unable to perform a task, a directive leadership style will work better than a supportive style. If there is a climate of despair and the leader has referent power, a magnetic leadership style will work better than an informational style. Unfortunately, we are not yet at the stage where we can determine the exact matches that result in the best leadership for every situation. But it is probably safe to make the following assumptions.

First, because different situations require different leadership styles and skills, individuals who have a wide variety of relevant skills will be best able to be effective leaders in a larger variety of situations. That is, a person who has only excellent planning skills will be an effective leader only in situations that require planning. But a leader who has excellent skills in planning, persuasion, people, goal setting, and motivation will be able to lead in many different types of situations.

The advice that flows from this assumption is obvious. As Table 12.6 shows, an individual interested in becoming an effective leader should obtain as many leadership skills as possible. By attending leadership conferences, taking college courses, and gaining a variety of experiences, a leader can gain most of these skills. The Career Workshop Box offers such a comprehensive strategy.

Second, because individuals have different needs and personalities, leaders who are able to adapt their interpersonal styles to fit the needs of followers will be better leaders than those who stick to just one behavioral style. It is much easier for a leader to adapt his style to fit the individual needs of his followers than for 30 people with different needs and styles to adapt their behavior to fit their leader's needs and style.

Finally, because a leader must use different skills in different situations and act differently with different followers, it is important that she be able to understand the needs of the situation, the follower, or both and then behave accordingly. Thus, leaders who accurately recognize situational and follower needs will be more effective than those who are unable to distinguish one situation from another.

Why is the study of leadership so important? Research demonstrates that leader performance affects organizational performance. In addition, when employees trust their leaders, the employees perform better, are more satisfied with their jobs, are more committed to the organization, are less likely to quit, and are more likely to engage in organizational citizenship behaviors (Dirks & Ferrin, 2002).

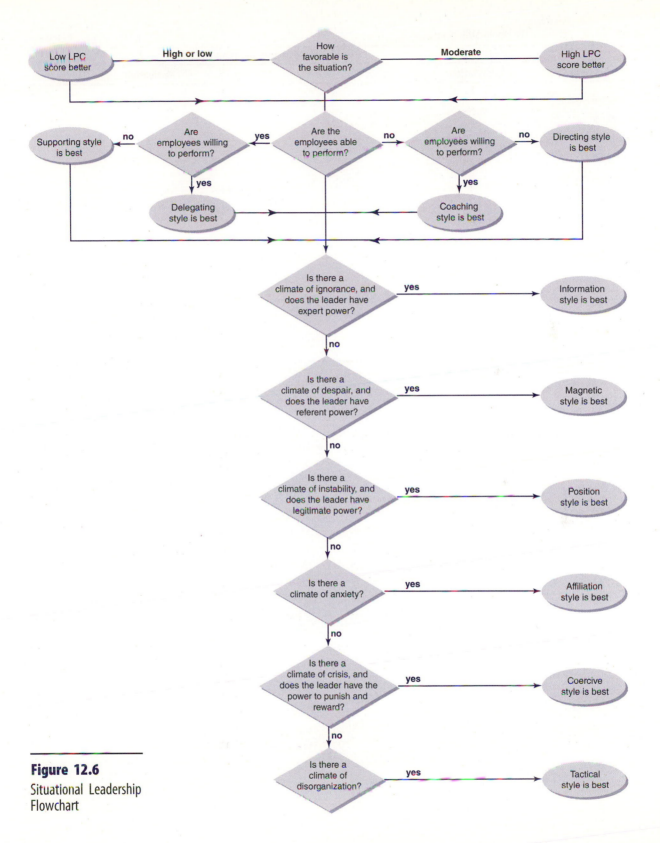

Figure 12.6

Situational Leadership Flowchart

Table 12.6 Effective Leadership Skills

Leadership Skill	Requirements of the Situation/Follower				
	Information	Direction	Empathy/Support	Motivation	Persuasion
Decision making		X			
Goal setting		X			
Persuasion	X	X		X	X
Team building			X	X	
Stress management			X		
Friendliness			X	X	
Empathy			X		
Energy				X	
Time management		X			
Technical knowledge	X				
Intelligence	X	X			

Career Workshop   **Obtaining Leadership Skills**

You will have many opportunities in your life to be a leader: as a parent, coach, supervisor, or president of a civic group. To help you become an effective leader, consider the following tips.

During College

➡ Learn what skills successful leaders need. Reading this chapter is a good start. Seek additional information by surfing the Net, going to the library, and buying self-help books, videos, or DVDs. Then, seek out opportunities where you can practice and build these skills, such as becoming an officer in a club on campus. The more you use a skill, the better you become.

➡ Identify and acknowledge the skills you lack. Successful leaders are willing to acknowledge their weaknesses and then do what it takes to improve. If you aren't sure how strong your skills are, ask someone you trust and who you know will be honest to tell you.

➡ Many colleges provide guest speakers on leadership or provide leadership workshops. Learn when these trainings will be scheduled and make it a point to enroll.

➡ Get a part-time job in an organization such as McDonald's, where you can quickly advance to a supervisory role. Being a lifeguard may be more fun, but getting job-related leadership experience will be much more beneficial.

➡ Enroll in a conflict management course, whether it is offered by the college or by a training program outside of the college. An important skill that a successful leader needs to know is how to successfully manage conflict.

➡ Identify someone on campus or at work who you think is a successful leader. Observe their behavior and the reaction of others to that behavior. Is it a behavior that you want to model? Or is it one that you discover should not be used? Ask the leader questions about how he or she does things and why it's done that way.

➡ If you are strong in a particular subject, volunteer to tutor other college students. This will help build your coaching skills.

After College

➡ When you get your first job, identify someone you think is a successful leader. Do what you did in college: Observe their behavior and ask them questions.

➡ Enroll in leadership development seminars. You may find that your organization will pay for these.

- Join professional organizations and volunteer for committee positions. Eventually you can move into leadership positions such as committee chair or president.

- Volunteer to head committees or teams. You will learn how to better organize people and events, strategic planning, public speaking, dealing with conflict, motivating, and working in teams.

- Volunteer for extra assignments that will provide you with new skills. Others will see that you have initiative and are willing to learn new information and skills.

- Be honest with your coworkers and others at work. One of the biggest factors in successful leadership is the ability to be trusted by others.

ON THE JOB   Applied Case Study

Developing Leaders at Claim Jumper Restaurants

One of the major success factors for any restaurant is the quality of the people managing it. They must enjoy what they do, be technical experts, and have the leadership qualities to manage restaurant employees. Claim Jumper Restaurants, a California-based casual dining chain, developed an interesting program for hiring and developing its restaurant managers.

The first Claim Jumper restaurant opened in Los Angeles in 1977 and there are currently 37 restaurants, most of which are in western states. Each restaurant features Douglas fir logs, natural stone, and natural wood beams to promote a "gold rush" theme. The restaurant is open for lunch and dinner and has a wide menu, including ribs, chicken, steak, seafood, and pasta.

The restaurant chain uses two strategies to hire managers: hiring from the outside and promoting current employees. In 2001, they created a new program to select and develop internal candidates for management positions. Interested employees are first screened to determine if they would make good managers. If

they seem to be a good fit, they are enrolled in the Expeditor Program to learn management skills and gain management experience. If they don't seem like a good fit, they are given feedback on what they can do to increase their readiness for the program.

Employees in the Expeditor Program, now called "Expeditors," work closely with restaurant managers, receive management training and experience, and are provided with feedback on their progress.

- If you were in charge of hiring and developing managers for Claim Jumper Restaurants, what competencies and experiences would you look for?

- On the basis of what you learned in this chapter, how much emphasis would you place on *hiring* the right people as opposed to *developing* current employees into good leaders?

To find out more about the Claim Jumper program, use the link found on your text webpage.

FOCUS ON ETHICS   Ethics and Leadership

Imagine the following four situations:

- A professor with a policy of failing students who miss more than six days of class in one semester decides not to fail one particular student with high absenteeism, even though two other students were failed in the same semester because of their high absenteeism. If the professor fails that third student, the professor knows that the student will be unable to graduate. If the student can't

graduate, she won't be able to enter her master's program in the fall.

- A director of a mental health agency overrepresents the number of clients his agency served for the previous year. The agency gets funds from the state based on how many clients it serves each year. The director knows that if he were to report the correct number of clients, the agency would get significantly less money to use for the next year. A reduction in funds would mean that some staff would have to be laid off, causing the agency to help even fewer clients.

- A supervisor allows her staff to take an hour for lunch even though company policy allows only 30-minute lunch breaks. The supervisor's philosophy is that as long as her employees get their work done, it won't make a difference if they are allowed an hour for lunch instead of 30 minutes.

- A big brother raised in a family who believes that honesty is always the best policy tells his little sister that she looks great in her new dress, even though he thinks she looks terrible.

The examples above involve people in leadership positions. A leader is someone people look up to and are willing to follow; it is a person who is able to get others to reach a goal, who is in a position to guide and influence others' behavior and professional and personal lives; and it is a person of integrity. So based on that definition, any one of us can be, and have been, leaders at one time or another. A professor is a leader in his or her classroom; a director is the leader of an agency; a supervisor is the leader of her department; and an older brother is, or should be, a leader of his younger siblings.

What the leaders in the above examples have in common is that they are bending the rules. Bending the rules means going against policy, regulations, or rules, whether they are set by the leader, as in the professor's classroom policy of failing students with poor attendance, or set by an organization, such as the policy of 30-minute lunch breaks for all employees. There are two thoughts about this concept of "bending the rules": one is that it is unethical and the other is that it is necessary. Those who believe it is necessary to bend the rules will say that all rules are meant to be broken.

Proponents of bending the rules say that it's a moral cop-out when leaders choose not to bend the rules in situations where bending the rules, going against policy, is actually the right and ethical thing to do. For example, in the first situation above, the reason why that one student missed so many days during the semester is because he had cancer and his treatments often made him too sick to come to class. In this case, say the supporters of bending the rules, for the professor to say, "I must abide by my policy," would be a moral cop-out against doing the responsible thing. Sometimes, they say, a leader has to bend the rules for the bigger good.

However, critics of leaders who bend the rules say that a policy is a policy—it's there for a reason and should be followed at all times. If a leader doesn't like the policy or rule, that leader should do what is necessary to change the policy so that he or should won't have to bend it. So, these critics might say in the previous example that the professor, in her policy, should state that allowances should be made for students who miss classes due to a long-term illness. If that wasn't stated in her policy, then it would be unethical for her to break the policy, no matter the reason. Bending the rules breaks trust with others. Critics hold leaders to a higher standard than other employees. Because leaders are, or should be, role models, anything they do is often accepted and copied by others. So, if a leader breaks a policy, what they are saying to others is that it is okay to bend the rules and break policies.

What Do You Think?

- In the first situation, do you think it is unethical for the professor to bend the rules under those circumstances? If you were one of the students failed because of high absenteeism and you found out that the professor didn't fail another student for his high absenteeism, would you think you were being treated unfairly? What would you do?

- Do you think what the leaders did in the other examples was ethical? Why or why not?

- In the example with the brother, is it okay to lie in this situation? Do you consider lying as unethical? Are there ever times when lying is better than telling the truth?

- What are some situations in which bending the rules might be more ethical than following policy?

Chapter Summary

In this chapter you learned:

- Intelligence, interpersonal adjustment, self-monitoring, a leadership motive pattern (high power, low affiliation), and the combination of a task and person orientation are related to high levels of leadership performance.
- Leadership effectiveness is also a function of the interaction between the leader and the situation. Important situational aspects include situational favorability (Fiedler), organizational climate (IMPACT theory), subordinate ability (path-goal theory,

situational leadership theory), and the relationship between leaders and their subordinates (vertical dyad linkage, LMX theory).

- Effective leaders possess specific skills—such as persuasion, motivation, and decision making—that ineffective leaders do not.

Questions for Review

1. Do those who seek leadership roles, those who emerge as leaders, and those who are successful leaders share similar traits?
2. Which of the situational theories seems to provide the best explanation for successful leadership?
3. Hogan identified three main reasons for unsuccessful leadership. Are there others that he did not mention?
4. Can effective leadership actually be taught?
5. How can a leader be more persuasive?

Media Resources and Learning Tools

- Visit our website. Go to www.cengage.com/psychology/aamodt, where you will find online resources directly linked to your book, including chapter-by-chapter quizzing, flashcards, crossword puzzles, application activities, and more.
- Want more practice applying industrial/organizational psychology? Check out the *I/O Applications Workbook*. This workbook (keyed to your textbook) offers engaging, high-interest activities to help you reinforce the important concepts presented in the text.

Chapter 13

GROUP BEHAVIOR, TEAMS, AND CONFLICT

© Chris Ryan/OJO Images/Getty Images

Learning Objectives

➡ Understand what constitutes a group and a team

➡ Learn why people join groups

➡ Know how to increase group performance

➡ Understand how teams operate

➡ Be able to decide when groups perform better than individuals

➡ Know why the team approach is not always the best

➡ Understand the causes of conflict

➡ Know how to reduce conflict

With few exceptions, most employee behavior takes place in groups or teams. Firefighters work together when fighting fires, managers make decisions in committee meetings, and bank tellers work together to deal with customers. Because employees tend to work in groups or teams, it is important for a manager or a leader to understand group dynamics. This understanding is especially important in light of the continuing use of teams by organizations (Lawler, 2001).

To get you thinking about group dynamics, complete Exercise 13.1 in your workbook.

Group Dynamics

Definition of a Group

In reviewing the books written on group dynamics, it quickly becomes clear that there is no agreed-upon definition of a group. Some experts use a general definition that basically defines a group as two or more people who *perceive* themselves as a group and *interact* in some way. Other definitions require that a group must involve some degree of structure and permanency. I prefer the definition used by Gordon (2001), who believes that for a collection of people to be called a group, the following four criteria must be met: (a) The members of the group must see themselves as a unit; (b) the group must provide rewards to its members; (c) anything that happens to one member of the group affects every other member; and (d) the members of the group must share a common goal.

Multiple Members Who Perceive Themselves as a Unit

The first criterion is that the group must have multiple members. Obviously, one person does not constitute a group (even if he is a multiple personality). Therefore, at least two people are necessary to form a group. Usually we refer to 2 people as a *dyad*, to 3 people as a *triad*, and to 4 to 20 people as a *small group* (Forsyth, 2010). To be considered a group, these two or more people must also see themselves as a unit. Thus, three individuals walking down the sidewalk would be considered a group only if they knew one another and were together. Eight separate customers shopping at a store would not be considered a group.

Group Rewards

The second group criterion is that membership must be rewarding for each individual in the group. In the next section, we will discuss the reasons people join groups, but for now it is important to remember that people will join or form a group only if it provides some form of reward.

To demonstrate this point, imagine four students studying for an exam. If the four study in separate rooms and do not share information, they are not a group. Likewise, consider if the same four people sat at one desk in the library. If each person studies the book separately and never communicates with the other three, then the four still will not be a group because none of the individuals is rewarded by being with the others. But if none of the four would have otherwise studied independently, then the four students would be considered a group because being together was rewarding. Even though they did not talk with one another during their time in the library, the fact that they were together provided the structure for each of them to study.

Corresponding Effects

Corresponding effects An event that affects one member of a group will affect the other group members.

The third group criterion is that an event that affects one group member should affect all group members. That is, if something significant happens to one person and does not affect any of the other people gathered with her, then the collection of people cannot be considered a group. This requirement is called **corresponding effects** For example, suppose five bank tellers work side by side, and one teller becomes ill and goes home. If the activities of the other four change as a result of one teller leaving, the five might be considered a group. But if the activities of the other four do not change after one teller leaves, then the tellers cannot be considered a group.

Common Goals

Common goal An aim or purpose shared by members of a group.

The fourth and final criterion is that all members must have a **common goal** In the teller example, if the goal of one of the tellers is to meet only young, single customers and the goal of another teller is to serve as many customers as possible, the tellers are not considered to be a group because they work in different ways and for different reasons.

Why do we care if a collection of people meets the technical definition of a group? The answer lies within your ability to change employee performance. Over the course of this chapter, you will learn many factors affecting group performance. If you apply what you learn, you will be effective in changing performance only if the collection of individuals is actually a *group*.

Reasons for Joining Groups

Assignment

In the workplace, the most common reason for joining groups is that employees are assigned to them. For example, a new employee might be assigned to a department with 5 other employees, 5 employees might be appointed to serve on a committee, and 10 employees are scheduled for the same training class.

Physical Proximity

One especially strong reason that a person might join a particular group, especially if the group is informal, is physical proximity (Forsyth, 2010). That is, people tend to form groups with people who either live or work nearby. For example, think of the intramural teams on your campus. Most teams consist of students who live in the same residence halls or have classes together. At work, employees tend to form groups that consist of those who work in the same general area. And some employees seek close physical proximity to people in power, hoping they will become part of an elite group.

The "bomber wing" provides an interesting example of how physical proximity can create an unlikely group. The bomber wing was a small section of the federal maximum security prison in Florence, Colorado, whose 1999 residents included Ted Kaczynski (the Unabomber), Ramzi Yousef (the World Trade Center bomber), and Timothy McVeigh (the Oklahoma City bomber). Though the three had access to one another for only two hours a week and had to shout across the hall to communicate, they formed quite the social group. Without this proximity, it is unlikely that the three would ever have belonged to the same group (Chua-Eoan, 1999).

Affiliation

Affiliation A leadership style in which the individual leads by caring about others and that is most effective in a climate of anxiety.

Affiliation involves our need to be with other people. Thus, one reason people join groups is to be near and talk to other people. Research has demonstrated that our need for affiliation is very strong. Mayo (1946), for example, found that employees at a textile plant who worked separately from other employees were not as satisfied with their jobs as were employees at the same plant who had the opportunity to work with others. Likewise, McLaughlin and Cheatham (1977) found that "outside" bank tellers who were isolated from their "inside" coworkers had lower job satisfaction.

Perhaps the most interesting demonstrations of the strength of the human affiliation need come from the writings of Schein (1956) and Naughton (1975). These researchers were interested in the reasons American prisoners of war (POWs) in World War II behaved so differently from those in the Korean and Vietnam conflicts. POWs in World War II made more escape attempts, suffered fewer deaths, and provided information less frequently to the enemy than did their counterparts in Korea and Vietnam. Although the American public attributed the differences to a postwar decline in the American character (Hampton, Summer, & Webber, 1978), both Schein and Naughton pointed out the differences from a perspective of group dynamics. In World War II, the POWs were kept in groups that remained together for long periods of time. Thus, these men were able to receive emotional support from one another, they could work together to plan escapes, they were able to hear what each POW said to the enemy, and they knew about and supported a strong group norm about not talking to the enemy. In the two post–World War II Asian conflicts, the situations were entirely different. Rather than living in groups, these POWs were isolated and not allowed to communicate with one another. Naughton (1975) reports that the men were so in need of contact and communication with others that they scraped their cell walls to make noise and establish contact and informal communication with one another. This behavior is similar to that reported by hostages held in Beirut and Syria.

If people are not allowed the opportunity for affiliation, they make attempts to secure at least minimal contact. When even minimal contact is not possible, morale and perhaps even the will to live are lessened. Such is the concern about the new supermaximum prisons being built for inmates who behave violently while incarcerated. In these prisons, inmates spend 23 hours a day alone in concrete stalls without air conditioning. There are no books, magazines, or television and only minimal contact with guards. During the remaining hour each day, inmates are placed alone in an 18-by-20-foot cage where they can pace or toss a basketball at an iron hoop. As one might imagine, prisoners' rights advocates are concerned about the long-term effects of such isolation. Similar concerns were expressed after several suspected al-Qaeda terrorists housed in Guantanamo Bay, Cuba, attempted suicide in February 2003.

Of course, people are not equal in their desire or need to affiliate with others (Ray & Hall, 1995). For example, computer programmers have lower needs and desires to affiliate than do people in many other occupations (Shneiderman, 1980). This point is especially interesting because it is common in the information technology field to place programmers and analysts in groups to debug programs and solve problems (Shneiderman, 1980). Although research is not yet available on the effects of such groupings, putting such strong individualists into groups does not sound like a promising idea. However, people with a high need for affiliation perform better in groups than alone (Klein & Pridemore, 1992). It is especially important to consider the need for affiliation and the negative consequences of isolation given such trends as having employees work from home (telecommuting) and sending employees to work in different countries (expatriates).

Identification

Another reason we join groups is our desire for **identification** with some group or cause. There are many examples of this need to identify with others. In the 1960s and 1970s, young men wore their hair long; although some thought it attractive and comfortable, many others grew long hair because it helped them identify with other males of their generation and separated them from adult males of previous generations. Many of us still know someone who wears his hair long and makes references to the 1960s and 1970s, thus identifying himself with an earlier period. In the 1980s and 1990s, so-called punk and grunge styles of hair and clothes were worn by students in much the same way that long hair and tie-dyed shirts were worn by people in the 1960s. In the current decade, tattoos and body piercing seem to be the mode of expression. For each generation, the purpose of the "odd" self-expression may have been to separate oneself from a previous generation and identify with a new, "better" generation.

Around your school you may notice that many students wear T-shirts with logos or messages. Students wearing "U2," "Los Angeles Lakers," or "Spring Break Cancun 2012" shirts are all identifying with particular groups and thus are making statements about themselves.

In an interesting study of how clothing is used as a means of identification, Cialdini and his colleagues (1976) observed the number of students at several universities who wore school-related clothing such as T-shirts and sweatshirts on the Monday following a school football game. They found that following a football victory, many more students wore school-related clothing than on Mondays following football losses. In a second study, Cialdini et al. also asked students who won the football game. As we might expect, when the football team won, the students answered by saying, "We won." When the team lost, the students answered by saying, "They lost." On the basis of these two studies, Cialdini called this identification process "basking in reflected glory."

Another example of the identification process comes from a major manufacturing plant in Virginia. Several months before union contract talks began, the company gave each employee several nice shirts with the company name printed on the front. The company did this because it had previously noticed that in the months before contract negotiations began, the employees began to wear more union caps and shirts. The company believed that this clothing helped increase the employees' level of identification with the union. To counter this effect, the company hoped that its shirts would influence the negotiation process. Although we cannot determine the exact effect of this strategy, that year was the only one in a decade in which union members did not strike.

Emotional Support

We also join groups to obtain emotional support. Alcoholics Anonymous, Gamblers Anonymous, and Weight Watchers are good examples of groups that provide emotional support for their members. A quick perusal of ads in the local paper or a quick surfing of the Internet will demonstrate the importance of this need, as there are hundreds of different types of support groups.

Assistance or Help

People often join groups to obtain assistance or help. For example, students having problems with an algebra class might form a study group. Or, on the reality show

Survivor, contestants might form alliances to increase the odds of not being voted off the island.

Common Interests

People often join groups because they share a common interest. At school, students joining a geology club share an interest in geology, students joining a fraternity share an interest in socializing, and students joining a service club such as Circle K or Alpha Phi Omega share an interest in helping people.

It is an interesting side note that most campus clubs based on common academic interests, such as a psychology club or a Latin club, are smaller and less active than other campus groups. Apparently, college students have many needs, and common academic interests are usually not as strong as the social needs satisfied by the Greek organizations. For example, a service club on the Radford University campus was having difficulty attracting members, so several advisors suggested that it increase its number of social activities to attract people who had both community service and social needs. This slight change in activities increased membership from 15 to 45.

Genecor, a biotech firm in Palo Alto, California, is a good example of a company that understands the importance of common employee interests. Genecor sponsors a wide variety of employee clubs, including yoga, cooking, and skiing. Although these clubs are voluntary, every employee belongs to at least one. Such activities are part of the reason Genecor was selected by *HR Magazine* in 2005 as the best medium-sized company to work for.

Common Goals

People who join political parties exemplify being in pursuit of a common goal. These people may also share common interests, but their primary purpose is to get a particular person or members of a particular party elected to office.

To apply the material you just learned about why people join groups, complete Exercise 13.2 in your workbook.

Factors Affecting Group Performance

Group Cohesiveness

Group cohesiveness The extent to which members of a group like and trust one another.

Group cohesiveness is the extent to which group members like and trust one another, are committed to accomplishing a team goal, and share a feeling of group pride (Beale, Cohen, Burke, & McLendon, 2003). In general, the more cohesive the group, the greater its

- productivity and efficiency (Beal et al., 2003),
- decision quality (Mullen, Anthony, Salas, & Driskell, 1994),
- member satisfaction (Brawley, Carron, & Widmeyer, 1993; Deluga & Winters, 1991),
- member interaction (Shaw & Shaw, 1962), and
- employee courtesy (Kidwell, Mossholder, & Bennett, 1997).

In its 1989 strike against Pittston Coal Company, the United Mine Workers union realized the importance of cohesiveness and identification needs by adopting a unique strategy. Each union member as well as his or her family members and supportive friends wore camouflage shirts and fatigues as a sign of unity. Every time miners looked around, they saw others dressed alike. The union members thus developed a sense of unity and cohesiveness that helped them last through a lengthy strike. Groups such as the Boy Scouts and the Guardian Angels also wear uniforms to increase group cohesiveness.

But cohesiveness can also lower group performance, especially in a work setting. When employees become too cohesive, they often lose sight of organizational goals. For example, it is common for restaurant employees to put the needs of other employees above those of their customers. Similarly, police departments tend to be highly cohesive—so much so that anyone who is not a police officer is considered an outsider, which can make community relations difficult.

Although the majority of research supports the conclusion that cohesiveness results in better group performance, it is not always necessary for ultimate group success. For example, the Oakland A's in the early 1970s and the Los Angeles Lakers in 2002 were sports teams that won championships despite constant fighting among the players.

Research has also demonstrated that employees in cohesive work groups will conform to a norm of lower production even though they are capable of higher performance (Forsyth, 2010). An excellent example of this conformity to a group norm involved the Hollywood Division of the Los Angeles Police Department in the early 1980s. Many of the division's officers and detectives were extensively involved in property crimes. They would break into various retail stores and radio that they were responding to the ringing burglar alarms. They then placed the stolen goods in their car trunks and proceeded as if they were investigating the break-ins. The officers later met at specific locations to hide and sell the stolen goods. Officers who did not participate in the crimes saw the merchandise and knew what was going on, but they did not report the offenders. Instead, they put their loyalty to their fellow officers above their loyalty to the city or the police department.

Group Homogeneity

Homogeneous groups
Groups whose members share the same characteristics.

Heterogeneous groups
Groups whose members share few similarities.

The homogeneity of a group is the extent to which its members are similar. A **homogeneous group** contains members who are similar in some or most ways, whereas a **heterogeneous group** contains members who are more different than alike. Of course, the difficulty in determining the homogeneity of a group comes from the many ways in which people are different. Group members might be demographically similar (e.g., age, gender, race) but be very different in personality, attitudes, values, and competencies.

An important question for a leader to consider when developing a group is which composition—homogeneous or heterogeneous—will lead to the best group performance. Many research studies have sought to answer this question, but only mixed results have been found, with some studies finding homogeneous groups most effective and others finding heterogeneous groups most effective (Bowers, Pharmer, & Salas, 2000).

Aamodt, Kimbrough, and Alexander (1983) hypothesized that previous research yielded mixed results because the compositions of the best-performing groups were actually somewhere between completely homogeneous and completely heterogeneous. These authors labeled them **slightly heterogeneous groups**. For example, in a five-person group, a group with five men would be considered as homogeneous, one with three men and two women as heterogeneous, and one with four men and one woman as slightly heterogeneous. A meta-analysis by Mascio, Rainey, and Zinda (2008) offered some support for the superiority of slightly heterogeneous groups, as slightly-heterogeneous

Slightly heterogeneous groups Groups in which a few group members have different characteristics from the rest of the group.

groups performed somewhat better than did homogeneous ($d = .17$) and heterogeneous ($d = .12$) groups.

Thus, it appears that the best working groups consist primarily of similar people but have a dissimilar person adding tension and a different vantage point. But it is not yet clear which variable is most important in terms of determining group composition. For example, a group might be homogeneous in terms of race but heterogeneous in gender. Researchers have studied race, gender, personality, intelligence, attitudes, and background, but more research is needed to clarify this issue. Meta-analyses indicate, however, that homogeneous groups result in higher member satisfaction, higher levels of communication and interaction, and lower turnover (Nolan, Lee, & Allen, 1997; Roberson & Colquitt, 2005).

Although group performance is best in slightly heterogeneous groups, the group member who is "different" (e.g., the only female, the only African American, the only introvert) may not have the same level of satisfaction as the rest of the group members. In fact, in a study of more than 255,000 employees at quick-service restaurants, it was found that employees who were the statistical minority in a restaurant in terms of race, sex, or age were more likely to leave the organization than were employees who were in the statistical majority (Sacco & Schmitt, 2005).

Stability of Membership

Stability The extent to which the membership of a group remains consistent over time.

The greater the **stability** of the group, the greater the cohesiveness. Thus, groups in which members remain for long periods of time are more cohesive and perform better than groups that have high turnover (Bell, 2005), and groups whose members have previously worked together perform better than groups whose members are not familiar with one another (Harrison, Mohammed, McGrath, Florey, & Vanerstoep, 2003).

A good example again can be found on a college campus. At most colleges, fraternities and sororities usually are the most active organizations and have high levels of performance; professional clubs and honorary societies such as Psi Chi and Lambda Alpha Beta tend to be the least active. Why is this? Certainly, it cannot be the abilities of the members—honorary societies have members with higher IQs than do most fraternities and sororities. Instead, the answer might be in the stability of the groups. Students tend to join Greek organizations in their freshman or sophomore years, whereas students tend to join professional clubs in their junior year and honorary societies in their senior year, often to help "pad" their résumés. The Greek organizations thus have more stable memberships than the other organizations.

Isolation

Isolation The degree of physical distance of a group from other groups.

Physical **isolation** is another variable that tends to increase a group's cohesiveness. Groups that are isolated or located away from other groups tend to be highly cohesive. A good example is the New River Valley (Virginia) branch of the Truliant Credit Union. The credit union has 15 branches, most located within a few miles of one another and within a few miles of the main branch in Winston-Salem, North Carolina. The New River Valley branch is 100 miles from the next closest branch; physically and psychologically, the branch is isolated from the main part of the organization. The New River Valley branch, however, is the only one to have no turnover in five years, in spite of the low unemployment rate in the area. It is also the branch where the employees are most cohesive.

Outside Pressure

Groups that are pressured by outside forces also tend to become highly cohesive. To some degree, this response to **outside pressure** can be explained by the phenomenon of *psychological reactance* (Brehm, 1966). When we believe that someone is trying to intentionally influence us to take some particular action, we often react by doing the opposite. Consider, for example, a teenaged dating couple. As the boy arrives to pick up his date, the girl's father notices the young man's beard and Harley-Davidson motorcycle and forbids his daughter to go out with him. Before this order, the daughter may not have been especially interested in the boy, but after being told she cannot go on the date, she reacts by liking the boy more.

An interesting example of psychological reactance comes from a study by Ruback and Juieng (1997), who observed drivers leaving their parking spots at a local mall. There were four conditions in the study. In the control condition, the researchers timed how long it took from the moment the driver opened her door to the moment she completely left the parking space when no other cars were present. In the distraction condition, they noted how much time was taken when a car drove past the parking space. In the low-intrusion condition, an experimenter pulled up next to the parking spot, indicating that she was waiting for the spot. In the high-intrusion condition, the waiting driver honked her horn. Consistent with psychological reactance, when a driver honked, it took 42.75 seconds for the parked driver to leave versus 26.47 seconds when there was no driver waiting for the spot (control) and 31.09 seconds when a car drove by (distraction).

On a larger scale, such reactions are commonly seen in labor negotiations. Company managements and unions tend to disagree with and criticize one another. But often such criticism backfires because attacking another group may serve to strengthen that group. In fact, if a company or group wants to increase the cohesiveness of its membership, it can artificially create pressure and attribute it to another group. This tactic involves building a *straw man*—an opponent who does not actually exist but to whom negative statements about the group can be attributed.

Group Size

Groups are most cohesive and perform best when **group size** is small. Studies have shown that large groups have lower productivity (Mullen, Johnson, & Drake, 1987), less coordination, and lower morale (Frank & Anderson, 1971) and are less active (Indik, 1965), less cohesive (Carron, 1990), and more critical (Valacich, Dennis, & Nunamaker, 1992) than smaller groups. In fact, research suggests that groups perform best (Kaplan, 2002; Manners, 1975) and have greatest member satisfaction (Hackman & Vidmar, 1970) when they consist of approximately five members. Thus, a large organization probably works best when it is divided into smaller groups and committees and when work groups contain approximately five people.

This does not mean, however, that small groups are always best. Although small groups usually increase cohesiveness, high performance is seen with only certain types of tasks. **Additive tasks** are those for which the group's performance is equal to the sum of the performances by each group member. Examples of groups performing additive tasks include bowling teams and typing pools. In groups working on additive tasks, each member's contribution is important, and larger groups will probably be better than smaller groups. **Conjunctive tasks** are those for which the group's performance depends on the least effective group member (a chain is only as strong as its weakest link). Examples of conjunctive tasks include an assembly line and friends

Disjunctive tasks Tasks for which the performance of a group is based on the performance of its most talented member.

Social impact theory States that the addition of a group member has the greatest effect on group behavior when the size of the grap is small.

Group status The esteem in which the group is held by people not in the group.

going hiking (you can walk only as fast as the slowest hiker). Because success on a conjunctive task is limited by the least effective member, smaller groups are usually best. **Disjunctive tasks** are those for which the group's performance is based on the most talented group member. Examples of disjunctive tasks include problem solving, brainstorming, and a captain's choice golf tournament (each person plays the best shot of the four golfers). As with additive tasks, larger groups are probably better at disjunctive tasks than are smaller groups.

The addition of more members has its greatest effect when the group is small. Latane (1981) first investigated this idea when he formulated **social impact theory**. Imagine that a four-person committee is studying safety problems at work. If the group is stable and cohesive, adding a fifth person may be disruptive. But in a factory of 3,000 employees, hiring 1 new employee is not likely to change the complexion of the company. That is why sports experts have observed that a single great player can turn around a poor basketball team—as occurred with Bill Walton and the Portland Trailblazers, David Robinson and the San Antonio Spurs, Jason Kidd and the New Jersey Nets, and Steve Nash and the Phoenix Suns—but not a football or baseball team.

Not surprisingly, research indicates that groups working through a computer behave differently from groups working face-to-face. When computers are used, large groups appear to perform best and have the most satisfied members (Dennis, Valacich, & Nunamaker, 1990; Valacich, Dennis, & Connolly, 1994; Valacich et al., 1992). Interestingly, when groups work via a computer, members whose opinion is in the minority are more likely to *express* opinions than when the group meets face-to-face. However, these same minority members are more *persuasive* when the group meets face-to-face (McLeod, Baron, Marti, & Yoon, 1997).

Group Status

The higher the group's status, the greater its cohesiveness. This is an important point: A group can be made more cohesive by increasing **group status**. The group does not actually have to *have* high status, but it is important that its members *believe* they have high status.

Again, look around campus and notice the methods used by various groups to artificially increase their status. On our campus, one fraternity advertises itself as the "Porsche of fraternities," another claims to be the "fraternity of distinction." Of course, there is little difference between the actual status and performance of most organizations, so effective leaders try to increase the cohesiveness of group members by claiming high status—and apparently it works.

One way leaders can increase their group's status is by increasing the perception that the group is difficult to join but that, once in, members will find that the group's activities are special. In most high schools, "two-a-day" practices are typical during the week before football practice begins. During this period, each prospective team member is worked close to exhaustion. Coaches have such "hell weeks" to increase the team's status and thus its cohesion and performance. Obviously, a player cannot get into shape in a week, so the purpose of two-a-day practices is not conditioning—it is to build the status of the group members who survive the week. A similar approach is taken by the Marine Corps. By its tough basic training, the Corps builds the status of its enlistees so that marines and non-marines alike will believe that the Corps consists of just a "few good men."

Fraternities and sororities are also notorious for hazing during their pledge weeks. Aside from the illegality and cruelty of this behavior, hazing serves the purpose of increasing the effort required for a potential member to join, thus increasing the group's cohesiveness and status. Football players, marines, and fraternity or sorority members are not likely to quit a group that they have worked so hard to join.

Group Ability and Confidence

Not surprisingly, groups consisting of high-ability members outperform those with low-ability members (Devine & Phillips, 2001). Furthermore, groups whose members believe that their team can be successful both at a specific task (high team efficacy) and at tasks in general (high team potency) perform better than groups whose members aren't as confident about their probability for success (Gully, Incalcaterra, Joshi, & Beaubien, 2002).

Personality of the Group Members

An important factor affecting group performance is the personality of the group members. Meta-analysis results indicate that in general, groups whose members have task-related experience and score high in the personality dimensions of openness to experience and emotional stability will perform better than groups whose members do not have these characteristics (Bell, 2007). In addition, groups working on intellectual tasks will do better if their group members are bright, and groups working on physical tasks (e.g., sports teams) will do better if their group members score high in the personality dimensions of conscientiousness, extraversion, and agreeableness (Bell, 2005).

A fascinating study reported by Wilson (2007) demonstrates the importance of personality to group performance—in chickens! A company was trying to determine ways to increase the egg production of chickens kept together in small cages and explored two breeding strategies. One was to take the highest producing *individual* chicken in each of the cages and breed them for six generations. The other strategy was to take the highest producing *group* of chickens and let them breed. When the offspring of the nine highest producing individual chickens were placed in a group, they became aggressive and six were killed. It seemed that the reason the individual chickens were so productive is that they did so by lowering the production of the other chickens. The offspring of the best group of chickens, however, were not aggressive and produced at a high rate. Thus, there seems to be a genetic predisposition for being an effective group member.

Communication Structure

Communication structure
The manner in which members of a group communicate with one another.

Another variable that can affect a group's performance is its **communication structure**, or network. For a group to perform successfully, good communication among members is essential. As shown in Figure 13.1, a variety of communication networks can be used by small groups, and even more complex networks are possible with larger groups. Each network has its advantages and disadvantages, but the best networks depend on the situations and goals of their groups. For example, if the goals of fraternities and singles clubs are to encourage members to get to know one another, then a centralized structure will be less conducive than a completely open one. Conversely, if the goal of a group is to solve a problem as quickly as possible, then the centralized network will be the best structure. A good leader carefully chooses the communication network that best facilitates the goals of his group.

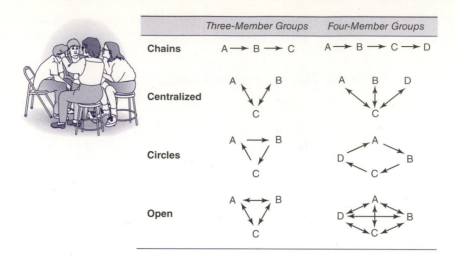

Figure 13.1
Possible Communication Networks for Small Groups

	Three-Member Groups	Four-Member Groups
Chains	A → B → C	A → B → C → D
Centralized		
Circles		
Open		

Group Roles

Another factor that affects the performance of a group is the extent to which its members assume different roles. For a group to be successful, its members' roles must fall into one of two categories: task oriented and social oriented (Stewart, Fulmer, & Barrick, 2005). *Task-oriented roles* involve behaviors such as offering new ideas, coordinating activities, and finding new information. *Social-oriented roles* involve encouraging cohesiveness and participation.

A third category—the *individual role*—includes blocking group activities, calling attention to oneself, and avoiding group interaction. Individual roles seldom result in higher group productivity.

Group members will often naturally assume these roles on the basis of their individual personalities and experiences. For example, people high in conscientiousness tend to fill task-oriented roles, and people high in agreeableness tend to fill social-oriented roles (Stewart et al., 2005). When roles are not naturally filled by group members, leaders must assign roles to certain individuals. For example, if a leader notices that every group member is filling a task-oriented role, she may either recruit a new group member or assign a current member to fill a social role.

Presence of Others: Social Facilitation and Inhibition

At the turn of the nineteenth century, researcher Norman Triplett (1898) noticed that cyclists rode faster when competing against other cyclists than when competing against a clock. Intrigued by this observation, Triplett conducted a study in which children completed a task either alone or while competing against other children. As expected, Triplett found that children who worked against others completed their tasks faster than did children who worked alone.

Since that first study, psychologists have studied what we now call *social facilitation* and *social inhibition*. **Social facilitation** involves the positive effects of the presence of others on an individual's behavior; **social inhibition** involves the negative effects of others' presence. Social facilitation and social inhibition can be further delineated by audience effects and coaction.

Social facilitation The positive effects that occur when a person performs a task in the presence of others.

Social inhibition The negative effects that occur when a person performs a task in the presence of others.

Audience Effects. The phenomenon of **audience effects** takes place when a group of people passively watch an individual. An example would be a sporting event held in an arena.

The strength of the effect of having an audience present is a function of at least three factors (Latane, 1981): an audience's size, its physical proximity to the person or group, and its status. Thus, groups are most likely to be affected by large audiences of experts who are physically close to them. Not surprisingly, meta-analysis results indicate that the presence of others increases performance in people who are extraverts and have high self-esteem and decreases performance in people with low self-esteem and who score high in neuroticism (Uziel, 2007).

Coaction. The effect on behavior when two or more people are performing the same task in the presence of one another is called **coaction**. Examples would be two runners competing against each other without a crowd present, or two mail clerks sorting envelopes in the same room. Shalley (1995) found that coaction decreased creativity and productivity. Three are many studies demonstrating interesting examples of coaction-influenced behavior. For example:

- Rockloff and Dyer (2007) found that gamblers placed larger bets and lost more money when gambling near others than when gambling alone.
- Sommer, Wynes, and Brinkley (1992) found that when people shopped in groups, they spent more time in a store and purchased more goods than when alone.
- de Castro and Brewer (1992) discovered that meals eaten in large groups were 75% larger than those eaten when a person was alone.

Explaining Social Facilitation Effects. More than 200 studies of social facilitation have indicated that performance does not always increase in the presence of others.

Evaluation apprehension can cause performance to drop when trying to learn a new task.

© Lee Raynes

Table 13.1 Tasks Affected by Social Facilitation and Social Inhibition

Skill Level	Facilitation: Increased Performance	Inhibition: Decreased Performance
Well learned	Bicycle racing	
	Pool shooting	
	Simple mathematics	
	Shopping	
	Eating	
	Jogging	
Novice		Pool shooting
		Learning nonsense syllables
		Completing a maze
		Complex mathematics
		New drivers taking a driving test

Performance increases only when the task being performed is easy or well learned; performance decreases when the task is difficult or not well learned (Bond & Titus, 1983; Platania & Moran, 2001). Social facilitation and coaction effects occur not only with humans but also with cockroaches running a maze (Zajonc, Heingartner, & Herman, 1969), chickens eating food (Tolman, 1968), and ants building nests (Chen, 1937). Some research examples are shown in Table 13.1.

Although researchers have not agreed on the exact reason for these findings, four explanations have each received some empirical support. The first explanation holds that the **mere presence** of others naturally produces arousal (Zajonc, 1980). This arousal, or increase in energy, helps an individual perform well-learned tasks but hinders him in performing poorly learned or unpracticed tasks.

The second explanation states that a coacting audience provides a means for **comparison**. If an individual is working on a task with another individual, he can directly compare his performance with the other person's. In some jobs, this comparison effect may increase competition and production quantity, whereas in other jobs, comparison effects may cause employees to slow down to be in line with the working norm.

The third explanation—**evaluation apprehension**—hypothesizes that judgment by others causes the differential effects of social facilitation (Cottrell, 1972). That is, individuals are aware that the presence of others can be rewarding (e.g., when a crowd cheers) or punishing (when a crowd boos). On well-learned tasks, the individual knows that he normally performs well and thus expects a rewarding experience when in the presence of others. When the task is not well learned, however, the individual may believe that she will not perform well and will be embarrassed; thus she performs even worse than if she were alone.

One example of this phenomenon was seen in an experiment by Michaels, Blommel, Brocato, Linkous, and Rowe (1982), who observed students shooting pool and found that good players increased their shot accuracy from 71% to 80% when watched by an audience, whereas poor players' accuracy decreased from 36% to 25% when they were watched. Thombs, Beck, and Mahoney (1993) found that high-intensity drinkers were more likely than low-intensity drinkers to drink in social situations.

Mere presence Theory stating that the very fact that others happen to be present naturally produces arousal and thus may affect performance.

Comparison The effect when an individual working on a task compares his or her performance with that of another person performing the same task.

Evaluation apprehension The idea that a person performing a task becomes aroused because he or she is concerned that others are evaluating his or her performance.

The evaluation-apprehension explanation has special application to industry and training settings. Imagine a waiter who must carry five plates of food to a table. For a new waiter, this is not a well-learned task, and in the presence of others he is likely to be anxious. When the lack of practice in carrying plates is combined with a large restaurant crowd, the chance of an accident increases. So what is the solution? The waiter should practice carrying several plates before the restaurant opens. Evaluation apprehension also occurs when performance is being monitored electronically rather than in person (Davidson & Henderson, 2000). Thus, supervisors who remotely monitor employee performance over a computer must be aware of the potential effects on performance.

Distracting The idea that social inhibition occurs because the presence of others provides a distraction that interferes with concentration.

The fourth explanation proposes that the presence of others is **distracting** to the individual who is trying to perform a task (Sanders, 1981). On well-learned tasks, the individual is able to perform despite the distraction because the behaviors are almost automatic. On a novel or complicated task, however, the distraction caused by other people's presence keeps the individual from concentrating and learning the task. For example, Baxter, Manstead, Stradling, and Campbell (1990) found that drivers with passengers were less likely to signal than were drivers without anyone else in the car, and a meta-analysis by Caird, Willness, Steel, and Scialfa (2008) found that drivers using cell phones had slower reaction times than drivers not using cell phones while driving.

An example that demonstrates the effects emphasized by both the evaluation-apprehension and distraction theories is that of coaching children in sports. In a typical Little League practice, one coach must teach an eight-year-old how to bat while 10 other children stand in the field and wait for a ball to be hit to them. Each time the child at the plate fails to hit the ball, the others tease him. After a while, the children in the field are bored and begin to throw rocks and talk with one another. What is the probability of success in teaching this child to hit under these circumstances? For the coach to be successful, he must teach the child alone and away from other children.

Effects of social facilitation also have been examined in sports by investigating the advantage that a team might have by playing its game at home. In general, having a home crowd behind a team or an individual athlete such as a wrestler increases the probability of winning (Carron, Loughhead, & Bray, 2005; McAndrew, 1993).

Social Loafing. Whereas the social facilitation versus social inhibition theory explains increases and decreases in performance when others are present and either watching the individual or working with her, the **social loafing** theory considers the effect on individual performance when people work together on a task. Social loafing was first investigated by Ringleman (reported in Moede, 1927) in a study in which subjects singly pulled as hard as possible on a rope while he measured their exerted force. Ringleman then had his subjects perform the task in pairs. He expected the force exerted by two subjects to be approximately twice that exerted by a single subject, but to his surprise he found that both subjects exerted less force than when they worked alone.

Social loafing The fact that individuals in a group often exert less individual effort than they would if they were not in a group.

More recent research has supported the theory and has found that social loafing occurs with many tasks (Karau & Williams, 1993). For example, Parrett (2006) found that restaurant customers left a higher tip percentage when they dined alone than when they dined with others. This explains why gratuities often are automatically added to a bill when six or more people dine at a table.

Although it is clear that social loafing occurs, especially in poor performers (Hardy & Crace, 1991), it is not clear *why* it occurs. One theory is that because group members realize that their individual efforts will not be noticed, there is little chance of individual reward. A second theory, called the *free-rider theory* (Kerr & Bruun, 1983), postulates that when things are going well, a group member realizes that his effort is not necessary and thus does not work as hard as he would if he were alone. Support for this theory comes from meta-analysis results showing that people don't socially loaf when their individual inputs are unique and can't be performed by other group members (Karau & Williams, 1993).

The third theory, called the *sucker effect* (Kerr, 1983), hypothesizes that social loafing occurs when a group member notices that other group members are not working hard and thus are "playing him for a sucker." To avoid this situation, the individual lowers his work performance to match those of the other members. This theory, however, does not explain the loafing of other members.

Social loafing is an important variable to keep in mind; having employees work together on a project may not be as productive as having them work individually. Fortunately, social loafing can be reduced by evaluating employees on their individual contributions to the group (Karau & Williams, 1993), explaining the link between individual effort and group performance (Shepperd & Taylor, 1999), and rewarding those who achieve (George, 1995; Shepperd, 1993). Punishing social loafers has unpredictable effects—sometimes it works, sometimes it doesn't (George, 1995; Miles & Greenberg, 1993).

Individual Dominance

Individual dominance When one member of a group dominates the group.

Another variable that can affect group performance is **individual dominance** by a leader or single group member. If the leader or group member has an accurate solution to a problem the group is trying to solve, the group will probably perform at a high level. But if the leader or group member has an inaccurate solution, he will lead the group astray, and it will perform poorly. For example, a study by LePine, Hollenbeck, Ilgen, and Hedlund (1997) found that a group of highly intelligent members perform poorly when its leader is not very intelligent. The same relationship was found for the personality variable of conscientiousness.

Groupthink

Groupthink A state of mind in which a group is so concerned about its own cohesiveness that it ignores important information.

The term **groupthink** was coined by Janis (1972) after studying the disastrous Bay of Pigs invasion of 1961. The Bay of Pigs was the Cuban landing site for 1,400 Cuban exiles who sought to overthrow the government of Fidel Castro. The plan called for the U.S. Navy and Air Force to covertly protect the invasion force and its supply ships. The invaders, however, were met unexpectedly by 20,000 Cuban troops and were quickly killed or captured. The help promised by the U.S. government never appeared. Janis (1972) proposed the concept of groupthink to explain how some of the nation's brightest men could hatch such an ill-conceived plan.

With groupthink, members become so cohesive and like-minded that they make poor decisions despite contrary information that might reasonably lead them to other options. Groupthink most often occurs when the group

- is cohesive;
- is insulated from qualified outsiders;
- has an illusion of invulnerability, infallibility, or both;
- believes that it is morally superior to its adversaries;
- is under great pressure to conform;
- has a leader who promotes a favorite solution; and
- has gatekeepers who keep information from other group members.

Groupthink can be reduced in several ways. First, the group leader should not state his own position or beliefs until late in the decision-making process. Second, the leader should promote open discussion and encourage group members to speak. Third, a group or committee can be separated into subgroups to increase the chance of disagreement. Finally, one group member can be assigned the job of **devil's advocate**—one who questions and disagrees with the group.

Devil's advocate A group member who intentionally provides an opposing opinion to that expressed by the leader or the majority of the group.

As with most things in psychology, the potential for groupthink is complicated. Though cohesive groups with strong leaders often result in groupthink, there are situations in which these two characteristics result in high levels of group performance (Kerr & Tinsdale, 2004).

Individual Versus Group Performance

Nominal group A collection of individuals whose results are pooled but who never interact with one another.

Interacting group A collection of individuals who work together to perform a task

When several people individually work on a problem but do not interact, they are called a **nominal group**. When several individuals interact to solve a problem, they are called an **interacting group**. An important decision a leader must make is when to assign tasks to individuals, nominal groups, or interacting groups. After decades of research investigating group effectiveness, the consensus appears to be that interacting groups will usually outperform one individual, but interacting groups do not outperform nominal groups (Kerr & Tinsdale, 2004).

The importance of the difference between nominal and interacting groups can be found in an interesting study by Liden et al. (1999). Liden and his colleagues had managers, nominal groups of employees, and interacting groups of employees read scenarios about a group member's poor performance and then determine how the

Employees wearing company-provided clothing can increase group identification

© Lee Haynes

employee should be disciplined. The interacting groups and the managers decided on more severe levels of discipline than did the nominal groups.

If the task involves *creating* ideas, individuals should be asked to independently create them and then meet as a group. Although **brainstorming** is a commonly used technique, it is not an effective one. In brainstorming, group members are encouraged to say aloud any and all ideas that come to mind and are not allowed to comment on the ideas until all have been given. When research compares a brainstorming group's creativity with that of a single individual, the brainstorming group will almost always be more creative. However, when comparing the number and quality of ideas created by nominal groups with the quality and number of ideas created by an interacting group in a brainstorming session, the ideas of nominal groups are more creative and of higher quality than ideas of the interacting group (Kerr & Tinsdale, 2004). This difference may partially be due to interacting groups setting lower goals than individuals (Larey & Paulus, 1995).

Due to the increasing cost of travel, it is increasingly common for groups to "meet" electronically (e.g., teleconference) rather than face-to-face. In fact, in my own consulting, it has become rare to fly to a company to participate in a meeting; almost everything is handled through email and teleconferences. The results of a meta-analysis by DeRosa, Smith, and Hantula (2007) suggest that such a practice is not only cost effective, but results in more effective performance than face-to-face group meetings. DeRosa et al. found that electronic brainstorming groups outperform face-to-face interacting groups. The comparison with nominal groups is more complicated. Overall, electronic brainstorming groups and nominal groups appear to perform at equal levels when the groups are small, but electronic groups are superior when the group is large.

The superiority of nominal groups over interacting groups may depend on the type of task. Brophy (1996) found nominal groups to be most effective with a single brainstorming problem and interacting groups to be most effective with complex problems. Similar results were reported by Davis and Harless (1996), who found that with complex problems, interacting groups take better advantage of feedback and learning and thus outperform nominal groups.

An interesting aspect of interacting groups is the tendency for groups to take more extreme positions than the positions of individual members. This tendency, called group polarization, suggests that group members will shift their beliefs to a more extreme version of what they already believe individually, That is, if individual group members are on the risky side, the group will make highly risky decisions. If, however, the individual members are conservative or cautious, the group as a whole will be extremely cautious (Isenberg, 1986).

The tendency to make more risky decisions was demonstrated in a particularly interesting piece of research by Cromwell, Marks, Olson, and Avary (1991) who found that burglars committed more crimes when working as part of a group than when working alone. Another example of increased group riskiness comes from a brokerage firm that was interested in getting its brokers to make riskier but higher-yielding investments. A consulting firm was asked to develop a way to select such brokers. Using its knowledge of group dynamics, the consulting firm told the brokerage company that it could obtain better results by having its brokers make investment decisions in groups rather than individually. Implementing this suggestion, the company later reported that its brokers were indeed making riskier investments.

Although the research seems to conclude that interacting groups offer no performance improvement over nominal groups, Wilson (2007) has criticized this

Brainstorming A technique in which ideas are generated by people in a group setting.

conclusion because it flies in the face of evolutionary research that demonstrates the value of groups in most species. He believes that a problem with previous group research is that the tasks were too easy and that when a task is difficult, interacting groups are superior to nominal groups.

Teams

Now that you have a good understanding of group dynamics, let's focus on a specific type of group behavior that occurs in work teams. The concept of employee work teams has been around for decades (they were often called "quality circles" in the 1970s), but their use greatly increased in the 1990s. Surveys indicate that 72% of Fortune 1000 companies use teams (Lawler, 2001).

Unfortunately, this increase in the use of teams is often the result of "keeping up with the Joneses" rather than a strategically planned method of organization development. As with any type of organizational intervention, teams can improve performance in some, but not all, situations. Teams work best in situations in which (a) the job requires high levels of employee interaction, (b) a team approach will simplify the job, (c) a team can do something an individual cannot, and (d) there is time to create a team and properly train team members (Kriegel & Brandt, 1996).

What Is a Work Team?

According to Devine, Clayton, Philips, Dunford, and Melner (1999), a work team is "a collection of three or more individuals who interact intensively to provide an organizational product, plan, decision, or service" (p. 681). At times, putting employees into teams fails because the team is really a "group" or a "committee" rather than a true team. In fact, according to a survey of practitioners who work with teams, only 48% of work groups would be officially classified as a team (Offermann & Spiros, 2001). Before calling a group of individuals a team, several factors should be considered (Donnellon, 1996).

Identification

Identification is the extent to which group members identify with the team rather than with other groups. For example, suppose a committee was created composed of one representative from each of five different departments (e.g., accounting, engineering, human resources). During the meetings, members use such statements as "Our department won't agree," "This committee just doesn't like those of us in engineering," or "We didn't even want to be on this committee." Notice that the use of *we, our,* and *us* refers to their departments rather than to the committee. According to Donnellon (1996), for the committee to be considered a team, those same words would need to refer to the committee: for example, "How can we convince the accounting department?" or "Our solution is a good one."

Interdependence

In a team, members need and desire the assistance, expertise, and opinions of the other members. If a team member can perform her job without the assistance of others, the team would not meet the definition of a group (see p. 474). For example, some teams, such as a surgical team in a hospital, have very high task

Interdependence The extent to which team members need and rely on other team members.

interdependence in that what one member does greatly influences what another member does. Other teams (most committees) have low task interdependence in that each member completes a task and the separate parts are then compiled. Though each part is important in completing the final product, the completion of each part is not dependent on another group member. The importance of task interdependence was demonstrated by Liden, Wayne, and Bradway (1996), who found that empowerment increased the performance of teams with high task interdependence (e.g., team members had to get information from each other, worked together on projects) but decreased the performance of teams with low task interdependence (e.g., did their work separately, did not have to rely on others).

Power Differentiation

Power differentiation The extent to which team members have the same level of power and respect.

In a team, members try to decrease **power differentiation** by treating others as equals and taking steps to ensure equality. In groups that are not teams, members challenge, correct, and interrupt each other, give orders, and use sarcasm. For example, I worked with one organization that had an "administrative team." What I discovered, however, was that one individual in that team was treated differently, had less authority, and had no voting power. Consequently, rather than being a "team," they were a "committee."

In teams, members apologize for overstepping their roles, ask indirect questions to avoid challenges, and are polite to one another (Donnellon, 1996). For example, in a team, a member might disagree with another member by saying something like, "I don't know your field as well as you do, but what if we tried ..."; whereas, in a nonteam, a member might disagree by saying, "That's so stupid. I'll tell you what will work."

Social Distance

Social distance The extent to which team members treat each other in a friendly, informal manner.

In a team, members try to decrease **social distance** by being casual, using nicknames, and expressing liking, empathy, and common views. Nonteam members use formal language and forms of address, excessive politeness, and impersonal conversations. For example, team members would use such phrases as "Hey, how's it going?" "Thanks, pal," and "I understand your feelings on that." Nonteam members might address another member as "Mr. Jones" rather than "Bob" or agree with someone by saying, "I concur with your opinion" rather than "I'm right with you on that one."

Conflict Management Tactics

Team members respond to conflict by collaborating, whereas nonteam members respond by forcing and accommodating (these terms will be discussed later in the chapter). In nonteams, members react to conflict by threatening, directing, or giving in. In teams, members try to understand the others' views, make attempts to compromise, and use nonthreatening tones (Donnellon, 1996).

Negotiation Process

In teams, members negotiate in a win-win style in which the goal is for every person to come out ahead. In nonteams, members negotiate so that they win and the other members lose.

On the basis of the six factors just discussed, Donnellon (1996) placed teams into one of five categories: collaborative teams, emergent teams, adversarial teams, nominal teams, and doomed teams. Collaborative teams and emergent teams are what I have referred to as true teams, whereas nominal teams and doomed teams are what I have referred to as nonteams. Adversarial teams are somewhere in between a true team and a nonteam.

Though not affecting the extent to which a group is officially a team, teams differ in two other ways. Teams differ as to their **permanency**. That is, some teams are designed to work together permanently, whereas others are formed to solve a particular problem and then are expected to dissolve. For example, I was appointed to a university task force designed to create a new system for students to use to evaluate faculty. Once the system was created, our team disbanded.

Teams can also differ in the **proximity** of their members. Members of surgical teams, baseball teams, and the cast of a Broadway play not only are task interdependent but work physically close to one another. In many instances, however, members of teams may be located across several cities, states, or countries. Because of the expense of bringing such teams to the same location, such companies as IBM, Google, and Intel use **virtual teams**, whose members carry out their team functions through email, teleconferencing, and videoconferencing (Lepsinger & DeRosa, 2010). Though virtual teams can certainly be productive, they tend to struggle with building trust, creating synergy, and overcoming feelings of isolation (Kirkman, Rosen, Gibson, Tesluk, & McPherson, 2002).

Types of Teams

Teams come in many shapes and sizes based on the factors discussed earlier in the chapter. For example, Devine et al. (1999) surveyed organizations and determined that teams differ on two major characteristics: temporal duration (ad hoc versus ongoing) and product type (project versus production). For this chapter, teams will be classified into the four categories determined by Cohen and Bailey (1997): work teams, parallel teams, project teams, and management teams.

Work Teams

Work teams consist of groups of employees who manage themselves, assign jobs, plan and schedule work, make work-related decisions, and solve work-related problems (Kirkman & Shapiro, 2001). They are typically formed to produce goods, provide service, or increase the quality and cost-effectiveness of a product or system. For example, work teams at

- Monarch Marking Systems in Dayton, Ohio, reduced past-due shipments by 70% and doubled productivity;
- GTE Directories in Dallas increased the production of telephone directories by 158%, reduced errors by 48%, and reduced the time to respond to customer complaints from 18.8 days to 2.9 days;
- Xerox in Webster, New York, saved $266,000 by discovering the cause of high failure rates in one of its products.

As shown in Figure 13.2, the traditional method of manufacturing a product is to have employees specialize in performing one particular task. For example, a company might have a supervisor, sorter, assembler, solderer, and quality inspector. The sorter places parts on the assembly line, the assembler puts the parts together, the solderer solders the parts, and the quality control inspector makes sure the part is properly assembled.

In a team approach, there would be no supervisor. Each of the production workers would be called a "team member" and be cross-trained to perform all of the tasks. In this way, if parts were assembled faster than they could be soldered, the sorter might spend some time soldering rather than sorting or waiting. The team would be responsible for checking its own quality, and one of the production workers would

Traditional Approach

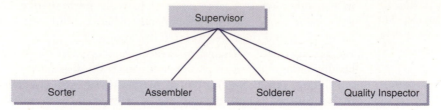

Team Approach

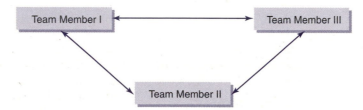

Figure 13.2

Traditional Versus
Team Approaches

probably be appointed as a team leader. The use of production teams saves money by removing management layers and making the team responsible for its own production.

Customer service teams are commonly found in restaurants and retail stores. In the traditional customer service model at a restaurant, each employee is assigned specific tasks (e.g., serving, cooking, busing tables) in specific areas. With the team approach, each employee may still be assigned a primary duty and area but is expected to "do what it takes" to satisfy customers. For example, suppose that Ken is your server at a very busy restaurant. You want another drink (milk, of course), but Ken is at another table. The closest person to you is Barbie, who is busing tables. In the traditional system, a request of more milk from Barbie would result in a response such as "I only bus tables; you'll have to wait for your server." In the team approach, Barbie would have been cross-trained in serving beverages and would be able to comply with your request.

Webber and Klimoski (2004) believe that not all work teams are alike and that an important type of work team is the *crew*. Crews are groups of "expert specialists [who each] have specific role positions, perform brief events that are closely synchronized with each other, and repeat these events across different environmental conditions" (Webber and Klimoski, 2004, p. 265). Examples of crews would include a group of firefighters, a flight crew (pilots, navigators, flight attendants, etc.), and a motion picture production crew (director, cameraman, key grip, etc.). Because crews include highly trained specialists and often rely on technology, they are affected less by changes in membership than are other work teams.

Parallel Teams

Parallel teams, also called **cross-functional teams**, consist of representatives from various departments (functions) within an organization (Keller, 2001). For example, a team formed to reduce the time to ship a product might include members from the sales, shipping, production, and customer service departments. For cross-functional teams to be successful, it is important that they have a clear purpose, receive support from each functional area, and take steps to increase the trust levels of committee members. Building trust in cross-functional teams is especially important, as members

Parallel teams Also called *cross-functional teams,* they consist of representatives from various departments (functions) within an organization.

Cross-functional teams
Teams consisting of representatives from various departments (functions) within an organization.

are often torn between representing the interests of their function and doing what is best for the organization as a whole.

Project Teams

Project teams are formed to produce onetime outputs such as creating a new product, installing a new software system, or hiring a new employee. Once the team's goal has been accomplished, the team is dismantled. The temporary nature of project teams is what distinguishes them from parallel and work teams. The environmental consulting firm of Camp Dresser and McKee provides an excellent example of a project team. The company needed to replace its human resource information system (HRIS), which tracks employment information for its 3,500 employees. Because such a system was used by a wide variety of departments, Camp Dresser and McKee formed a 40-person team to select and implement the new system. Once the system was in place, the team disbanded (Jossi, 2001b).

Management Teams

Management teams coordinate, manage, advise, and direct employees and teams. Whereas work, parallel, and project teams are responsible for directly accomplishing a particular goal, management teams are responsible for providing general direction and assistance to those teams.

How Teams Develop

In an influential theory of team development, Tuckman (1965) proposed that teams typically go through four developmental phases: *forming, storming, norming*, and *performing*. In the **forming stage**, team members get to know each other and decide what roles each member will play. During the early part of this stage, team members are on their best behavior as they try to impress and get along with the other team members. Team members are often excited about the potential to accomplish something but are also anxious about working with others in a team. During the latter part of this stage, the team concentrates on clarifying its mission, determining the goals it wants to accomplish, deciding on the tasks to be done to accomplish their goals, setting rules and procedures, and developing alternative courses of action to reach their goals (Marks, Mathieu, & Zaccaro, 2001). A meta-analysis by Salas, Mullen, Rozell, and Driskell (1997) indicates that formal team building (training on how to be a team) that focuses on role clarification will slightly improve team performance.

During the **storming stage**, the good behavior disappears. On an individual level, team members often become frustrated with their roles, show the stress of balancing their previous duties with their new team responsibilities, and question whether they have the ability to accomplish the goals set in the forming stage. Interpersonally, team members begin to disagree with one another and to challenge each other's ideas. It is from this tension and conflict that the team often gets the energy to perform well in later stages.

During the **norming stage**, the team works toward easing the tension from the storming stage. Team members begin to acknowledge the reality of the team by accepting the team leader and working directly with other team members to solve difficulties. At this point, team members have either accepted their initial roles or made adjustments to roles for which they are better suited.

In the **performing stage**, the team begins to accomplish its goals. Group members make innovative suggestions, challenge one another without defensive responses, and participate at high levels. During this stage, the team continually monitors its progress toward goals, determines additional resources that might be needed, provides assistance and feedback to team members, and makes necessary strategic adjustments (Marks et al., 2001).

Although this theory of team development is commonly used, as one would imagine, there is tremendous variation in how a given team will develop. An alternate theory, called *punctuated equilibrium*, suggests that rather than forming in stages, teams develop direction and strategy in the first meeting, follow this direction for a period of time, and then drastically revise their strategy about halfway through the life of the team (Gersick, 1988).

Why Teams Don't Always Work

Given that the scientific literature suggests that teams are seldom more effective than individuals (Allen & Hecht, 2004), there has been an abundance of advice in the literature about how to create successful teams. In a study investigating this advice, Hyatt and Ruddy (1997) found that customer service teams were most effective when they received the necessary support from management (e.g., information, technology, training), had confidence in their ability to complete their tasks; were customer oriented; exhibited an open, supportive, and professional communication style; had set appropriate goals; and followed an agreed-upon group process. Moran, Musselwhite, and Zenger (1996) identified 12 common problems encountered by teams. Let's look at the six most important ones.

The Team Is Not a Team

Consistent with the previous discussion, teams often aren't successful because they are teams in name only.

Excessive Meeting Requirements

A common problem with teams is that they either meet too infrequently or meet so often that they waste time when they do meet. The key to successful team meetings is to limit the topics to be discussed and to meet only when the entire team is needed to contribute. Furthermore, teams often feel the need to meet for the entire time for which a meeting is scheduled, even though the necessary business could be conducted in much less time. This tendency to "stretch" a meeting can reduce the motivation and enthusiasm of a team.

As an example of the tendency to meet too often, I was placed on one of several teams whose task it was to address specific problems facing the university. Our team leader (committee chair) wanted us to meet every Wednesday at two o'clock until our task was completed. Because of the nature of our task, weeks might pass before we had anything new to bring to the group. Yet we still met every Wednesday. After four weeks, attendance at the meetings dropped to about 50%. When our angry team leader confronted our team members, she was shocked to hear such comments as, "These weekly meetings are a waste of time" and "I always attend the important meetings, just not the worthless ones."

I was on another committee that demonstrated the tendency to stretch meetings. The committee comprised 25 people and met one Friday a month from 3:00 p.m. to 4:30 p.m. When the dean ran the meetings, they always ended at exactly 4:30 p.m. When the dean was out of town, the committee's vice-chair (the second in command, not the person in charge of vice) would start the meetings by saying, "Let's do our business and get out of here." On these occasions, we never stayed past 3:45 p.m.

Lack of Empowerment

Many teams are formed to solve problems but are not given sufficient authority to conduct their business. According to Moran et al. (1996), teams aren't empowered because managers worry that the job won't be done correctly, the teams are moving too fast, and the teams will overstep their boundaries such that other parts of the organization will be affected. This last managerial concern is especially important because as teams work to solve problems, their solutions often involve many different departments. If the teams are not properly empowered, they will lack the authority to overcome the political resistance of each affected department.

Though empowerment is essential for the success of most teams, it is not uncommon for team members to reject their empowered status. After all, with the advantages of empowerment come the risks of making mistakes and getting others angry. To many employees, these risks override the benefits of empowerment.

Lack of Skill

It is assumed that members assigned to a team have the skills necessary to effectively carry out their assignment. Unfortunately, this is often not the case (Yandrick, 2001a). What is most common is for team members to lack either the skills needed to work in a team (e.g., communication, problem solving) or the expertise to solve the problem itself. As an example, universities typically form committees whose membership consists of representatives from various colleges (e.g., arts and sciences, education) and departments (e.g., history, psychology, economics). Such a membership strategy makes sense if the issue is one on which various departments might differ. That is, a committee asked to determine general education requirements or summer school offerings should have representatives from each department. However, a committee formed to develop fund-raising strategies would be better served with a membership of marketing and psychology faculty rather than history and music faculty.

Research on the personal characteristics of team members has revealed some interesting findings. Teams whose members are bright, conscientious, extraverted, and emotionally stable perform better than teams whose members do not possess such characteristics (Barrick, Stewart, Neubert, & Mount, 1998; Devine & Phillips, 2001).

Distrust of the Team Process

Many teams don't succeed because management doesn't trust the concept of teams. A study by the consulting firm Zenger-Miller found that in organizations in which top management was not enthusiastic about the team approach, only 49% of teams made satisfactory progress. However, in teams with supportive management, 84% made satisfactory progress (Moran et al., 1996). Some of this distrust comes from managers being unwilling to give up any authority. Managers, too, need to be trained in the team process if the team concept is going to survive.

Team members must also be receptive to the team process. Research indicates that job satisfaction and organizational commitment are reduced when members are not receptive to the team process (Kirkman & Shapiro, 2001). Another source of team distrust is that not all work is appropriate for teams (Drexler & Forrester, 1998). That is, some tasks (e.g., typing) are better done individually, and others, such as kissing, are performed better with the help of others.

Unclear Objectives

Teams work best when they know why they were formed, what they are expected to accomplish (what the team's "charge" is), and when they are supposed to be finished. Though this would all seem obvious, you would be surprised at how many teams aren't sure what they are supposed to do. As an example, I was on a university committee entitled "Committee on Student Evaluation of Faculty." We spent most of the time during our first few meetings asking, "What are we supposed to do?" "Are we supposed to design a new evaluation instrument?" and "Do we make decisions or do we just make recommendations?" It took almost a month to get clarification, and during that time the committee made no progress, its members became frustrated, and attendance dropped.

To practice what you have learned about teams, complete Exercise 13.3 at the end of this chapter.

Group Conflict

Conflict The psychological and behavioral reaction to a perception that another person is keeping you from reaching a goal, taking away your right to behave in a particular way, or violating the expectancies of a relationship.

When individuals work together in groups or in formal teams, there is always potential for conflict. In fact, in one survey, 85% of employees said that they experience conflict on their jobs and 22% said they have missed work due to the conflict (Tyler, 2010). **Conflict** is the psychological and behavioral reaction to a perception that another person is keeping you from reaching a goal, taking away your right to behave in a particular way, or violating the expectancies of a relationship. For example, Bob might perceive that Lakisha is trying to get the promotion that is "rightfully his" (keeping him from his goal), Andrea might perceive that Jon is trying to pressure her to hire a particular applicant (taking away the right to behave in a particular way), or Carlos might perceive that when Jill goes to lunch with her male colleagues she is violating their agreement not to date other people (violation of a relationship expectation).

It is important to note that one of the key components to conflict is *perception*. For example, two people may share the same goals, but if one person perceives that their goals are different, the possibility of conflict increases. Thus, conflict is often the result of one person's misperception of another's goals, intentions, or behavior. Because conflict can often be attributed to misperceptions, an important part of conflict resolution is for each party to discuss his or her perceptions of a situation.

The level of conflict that occurs is a function of the importance of the goal, behavior, or relationship. That is, one person's behavior may force a change in another's, but if the change in behavior is not important to the individual (e.g., waiting in line for a few minutes), conflict will be less severe than in a situation in which the change is important (e.g., a promotion or a person's reputation).

Dysfunctional conflict Conflict that keeps people from working together, lessens productivity, spreads to other areas, or increases turnover.

Functional conflict Conflict that results in increased performance or better interpersonal relations.

On the basis of a meta-analysis by De Dreu and Weingart (2003), we are pretty safe in saying that most conflict results in lower team performance and lower member satisfaction. This **dysfunctional conflict** keeps people from working together, lessens productivity, spreads to other areas, and increases turnover. Dysfunctional conflict usually occurs when one or both parties feel a loss of control due to the actions of the other party and has its greatest effect on team performance when the task being performed is complex. Though most conflict is dysfunctional, there are times when a moderate degree of conflict can result in better performance. Called **functional conflict**, moderate levels of conflict can stimulate new ideas, increase friendly competition, and increase team effectiveness (Jehn & Mannix, 2001; Jeong, 2008). Furthermore, moderate conflict can reduce the risk of much larger conflicts.

Types of Conflict

Interpersonal Conflict

Interpersonal conflict
Conflict between two people.

Interpersonal conflict occurs between two individuals. In the workplace, interpersonal conflict might occur between two coworkers, a supervisor and a subordinate, an employee and a customer, or an employee and a vendor.

Individual–Group Conflict

Individual–group conflict
Conflict between an individual and the other members of a group.

Conflict can occur between an individual and a group just as easily as between two individuals. **Individual–group conflict** usually occurs when the individual's needs are different from the group's needs, goals, or norms. For example, a marine might want more independence than the Corps will give him, a basketball player might want to shoot when the team needs him to set picks, a faculty member might be more interested in teaching when his university wants him to publish, and a store employee might be more interested in customer relations when the store wants him to concentrate on sales.

Group–Group Conflict

Group–group conflict
Conflict between two or more groups.

The third type of conflict occurs between two or more groups. In academia, such **group–group conflict** occurs annually as departments fight for budget allocations and space. In industry, company divisions often conflict for the same reasons. A good example of group–group conflict occurred between two branches of the same bank located in the same town. The branches competed for customers not only with other banks but with each other. To make matters worse, the two branches were to be consolidated, so their staffs were involved in even more conflict as they tried to establish who would be in charge of the new and unified branch.

Causes of Conflict

Competition for Resources

In the marketplace, when customer demand exceeds product supply, prices increase. Similarly, in groups, when demand for a resource exceeds its supply, conflict occurs. This is often true in organizations, especially when there is not enough money, space, personnel, or equipment to satisfy the needs of every person or every group.

Competition for resources A cause of conflict that occurs when the demand for resources is greater than the resources available.

A good example of this cause of conflict, **competition for resources**, occurs annually when Congress decides on the nation's budget. With only limited tax revenues and many worthy programs, tough choices must be made. But often, instead of working together to solve the country's problems, our representatives come into conflict over whose favorite programs will be funded.

Another example of this competition occurs in colleges and universities across the country. There are probably few universities where parking and office spaces are not a problem. Faculty and students argue about who gets the parking spaces, and once that argument is settled, seniors and juniors argue over what is left.

I once belonged to an organization that initially had no conflict over resources because there were none to fight over. There were no extra offices, no equipment, and no supplies. Organization members even had to supply their own paper! After several years, however, the organization received a large amount of money and a new building with plenty of space. But as expected, conflict increased. All the employees wanted more space, their own printers, and so on. What had once been a very cohesive group was now characterized by conflict because of competition for new resources.

Task Interdependence

Another cause of conflict, **task interdependence**, comes when the performance of some group members depends on the performance of other group members. For example, a group is assigned to present a research report. The person who is assigned to type the report cannot do his job unless he can read what others have written, the person assigned to write the conclusion cannot do so until others have written their sections, and no member of the group is finished until every member has completed the assigned work.

Conflict caused by task interdependence is especially likely when two groups who rely on each other have conflicting goals. For example, the production department in a factory wants to turn out a high volume of goods, whereas the quality control department wants the goods to be of high quality. Neither department can do its job without the help of the other, yet a production department with high quantity goals probably will have lower quality standards than those desired by quality control. By insisting on high quality, the quality control department is forcing the production department to slow down. When this happens, conflict is likely to occur.

Jurisdictional Ambiguity

A third cause of conflict, **jurisdictional ambiguity**, is found when geographical boundaries or lines of authority are unclear. For example, two employees might argue over whose job it is to get the mail, two supervisors might fight over who is in charge when the vice-president is out of town, or two secretaries might disagree about who controls the conference room. When lines of authority are not clear, conflict is most likely to result when new situations and relationships develop. Thus, to some extent, turf wars can be avoided through the use of thorough job descriptions and up-to-date organizational charts.

On an international level, jurisdictional ambiguity is a cause for many wars and conflicts. For example, in 2008, Russia invaded Georgia in part over disputed territory; in the early 1990s Iraq invaded Kuwait under the pretense that Kuwait actually belonged to Iraq; and in the 1980s, England and Argentina fought over who had the right to the Falkland Islands. In cities, jurisdictional ambiguity is often a cause for gang wars.

Communication Barriers

Communication barriers are the fourth cause of conflict. The barriers to interpersonal communication can be *physical*, such as separate locations on different floors or in different buildings; *cultural*, such as different languages or different customs; or *psychological*, such as different styles or personalities. An in-depth discussion of the communication process can be found in Chapter 11.

Beliefs

A fifth cause of conflict is the belief systems of individuals or groups. Conflict is most likely to occur when individuals or groups believe that they

- are superior to other people or groups,
- have been mistreated by others,
- are vulnerable to others and are in harm's way,

- cannot trust others, and/or
- are helpless or powerless (Eidelson & Eidelson, 2003).

Personality

Personality Relatively stable traits possessed by an individual.

A sixth cause of conflict can be found in the **personalities** of the people involved. Conflict is often the result of people with incompatible personalities who must work together. For example, a person who is very quality oriented will probably have conflicts with a person who is very quantity oriented. Likewise, a "big picture" person is likely to have conflicts with a "nuts and bolts" person.

Though it is probably true that most of the conflict attributable to personality is the result of incompatibility, it is also very true that certain people are generally more difficult to work with than others. For example, it has been suggested that people who are dogmatic and authoritarian and have low self-esteem are involved in conflict more often than open-minded people who feel good about themselves (Bramson, 1981; Brinkman & Kirschner, 2006). Little research has gone into investigating "difficult people" who are most likely to cause conflict, but a fair amount has been written about the topic in the popular press. For example, Bernstein and Rozen (1992) describe in great detail three types of "Neanderthals at work"—rebels, believers, and competitors—and how conflict with each can be managed.

The most commonly referred to classification of difficult people was developed by Bramson (1981) and enhanced by Brinkman and Kirschner (2006). The latter postulated that abnormally high needs for control, perfection, approval, or attention form the basis for the difficult personality.

People with high needs for *control* are obsessed with completing a task and take great pride in getting a job done *quickly*. Among such personality types are the *Tank*, who gets things done quickly by giving orders, being pushy, yelling, and at times being too aggressive; the *Sniper*, who controls people by using sarcasm, embarrassment, and humiliation; and the *Know-It-All*, who controls others by dominating conversations, not listening to others' ideas, and rejecting arguments counter to her position.

People with high needs for *perfection* are obsessed with completing a task *correctly*. They seldom seem satisfied with anyone or any idea. These personality types include the *Whiner*, who constantly complains about the situation but never tries to change it; the *No Person*, who believes that nothing will ever work and thus disagrees with every suggestion or idea; and the *Nothing Person*, who responds to difficult situations by doing and saying nothing—she simply gives up or retreats.

People with high needs for *approval* are obsessed with being liked. Their behavior is often centered on gaining approval rather than completing a task correctly or quickly. The *Yes Person* agrees to everything and, as a result, often agrees to do so much that she cannot keep her commitments. The Yes Person seldom provides feedback to others because she is afraid of getting someone mad at her. The *Maybe Person* avoids conflicts by never taking a stand on any issue. She delays making decisions, seldom offers opinions, and seldom commits to any course of action.

People with high needs for *attention* are obsessed with being appreciated. They behave in a manner that will get them noticed. When she doesn't feel appreciated, the *Grenade* throws a tantrum: She yells, swears, rants, and raves. The *Friendly Sniper* gets attention by poking fun at others. Unlike the Sniper, the Friendly Sniper aims to get attention rather than control. The *Think-They-Know-It-All* exaggerates, lies, and gives unwanted advice to gain attention.

Table 13.2 Types of Difficult People

Type	Need	Obsession	Description	Best Way to Handle
Tank	Control	Task completion	Pushes, yells, gives orders, intimidates	Don't counterattack or offer excuses, hold your ground.
Sniper	Control	Task completion	Uses sarcasm, criticizes, humiliates others	Call them on their sarcasm and have them explain what was really behind their comment.
Know-It-All	Control	Task completion	Dominates conversations, doesn't listen	Acknowledge their knowledge, make your statements appear as if they are in agreement.
Whiner	Perfection	Task quality	Constantly complains	Focus their complaints on specifics and solutions.
No Person	Perfection	Task quality	Disagrees with everything	Don't rush them or argue; acknowledge their good intentions.
Nothing Person	Perfection	Task quality	Doesn't do anything	Be patient and ask them open-ended questions.
Yes Person	Approval	Being liked	Agrees to everything	Talk honestly and let the person know it is safe to disagree with you.
Maybe Person	Approval	Being liked	Won't commit or make a decision	Help them learn a decision-making system, and then reassure about the decisions they make.
Grenade	Attention	Being appreciated	Throws tantrums	Don't show anger, acknowledge their complaint, and give them a chance to cool down.
Friendly Sniper	Attention	Being appreciated	Uses jokes to pick on people	Give them attention when they are not making fun of you.
Think-They-Know-It-All	Attention	Being appreciated	Exaggerates, lies, gives advice	Give them attention and ask them for specifics; don't embarrass them.

Do you recognize any of these people? A summary of how to deal with each type of difficult person can be found in Table 13.2. Though early writings on difficult people suggested that their behavior is due to low self-esteem or a high need for control, a study by Raynes (2001) indicated that the cause is much more complicated. For example, Raynes found that *high* self-esteem and confidence were correlated with behaviors associated with the Think-They-Know-It-All and the No Person; the personality variable of extraversion was correlated with gossiping; and a high level of work interest was positively correlated with behaviors associated with the Yes Person and negatively correlated with whining. Advice on how to be a good group member is given in the Career Workshop Box.

To apply what you have learned about the causes of conflict, complete Exercise 13.4 in your workbook.

Conflict Styles

It is generally believed that most people have a particular style they use when faced with conflict. Although a variety of names are assigned to these styles, the consensus among experts is that five are common: avoiding, accommodating, forcing, collaborating, and compromising (Wilmot & Hocker, 2007).

Avoiding Style

Avoiding style The conflict style of a person who reacts to conflict by pretending that it does not exist.

Employees using an **avoiding style** choose to ignore the conflict and hope it will resolve itself. When conflicts are minor and infrequent, this style may be fine, but obviously it is not the best way to handle every type of conflict. When conflict occurs,

Tips for Being a Good Group Member

Whether you are a member of a team or committee, or just part of an office group, the following tips will help you be a better member:

➤ Don't gossip or engage in talk about other people. That is, if another employee comes to you with some gossip or a complaint about another employee, politely tell him or her that you don't feel comfortable talking behind another person's back. Also, suggest that if that person has concerns about someone, it would be best to share them directly with that employee. Being respected is very important to being perceived as a good group or team member. This is one of the best ways to build that respect!

➤ If you or your team is given an assignment or project, be sure that you fully understand the goal of that assignment and what is expected of you. To do this, go to your manager or another colleague to get clarification. Ask about the goal and the expectations. Will you and/or your team be responsible just for gathering and submitting information? Will you serve as an advisory group, giving recommendations or suggestions? Or do you have full authority to carry out all decisions regarding the project or assignment?

➤ Confront conflict as it occurs. Don't wait, thinking that "it will go away." If you have concerns with another person, speak to that person about how you feel. Don't be accusatory. Just explain how you interpreted the events and then ask if you and the other person could discuss how to resolve the situation. Be willing to ask for mediation, if necessary. When two or more members of a group or team are in conflict, everyone suffers, and you get a bad reputation for being a poor group/team member.

➤ Make sure you understand what your role is in the office or the team. This is where a good job description helps! One of the fastest ways to get a bad reputation as a colleague or team member is when others "perceive" that you are stepping into their territory. Again, if you aren't sure what tasks you should be performing, ask someone before you do them, to avoid stepping on toes.

➤ Don't share personal information about yourself. You may find one group or team member willing to listen to issues that are occurring in your personal life, but most employees don't want to hear it. Also, you may run into a problem with information you want kept "secret" getting out to others, which may cause problems for you.

➤ Participate as much as you feel comfortable in group activities. That is, if employees are putting together a birthday party for another employee, offer to help. This will show your desire to be a good group or team member.

➤ Be a good listener. You don't want to participate in office gossip; however, there will be times when someone may just want to "vent." Show them that you can keep confidences and that they can feel safe talking to you. As stated above, if they are venting about another person, suggest that they share those concerns with that individual. Some good listening skills include good eye contact, acknowledgment that you are listening by asking questions or merely by nodding your head, and asking open-ended questions.

➤ In meetings, when everyone is asked for their input, be willing to make suggestions. Don't continually just sit at meetings, refusing to share or discuss ideas. You will quickly get the reputation of being a "difficult team member or difficult employee." On the other hand, don't whine about what's going wrong, don't monopolize the entire meeting with your grievances, and don't brag about how great you are. Give credit where credit is due. Compliment your teammates when they offer a good suggestion or have successfully completed a project.

➤ Recognize when you are in a bad mood or upset. Be sure not to take out on others how you are feeling on any particular day. If there is someone in the group or team that you trust, share your feelings with this person. He or she may help brighten the day.

➤ There are times when you may have to be the leader because of your expertise or knowledge. Or perhaps you are the only person in the office or on a team with the ability to manage conflict. Be willing to step out of your usual role and take on another role as needed. Don't do what many employees and/or team members do and walk away from that new or additional responsibility. If necessary, attend workshops on how to better lead groups/teams, or how to better manage conflict. This will build credibility, trust, and respect.

Withdrawal An approach to handling conflict in which one of the parties removes him/herself from the situation to avoid the conflict.

withdrawal from the situation is one of the easiest ways to handle it. A person can leave a difficult marriage by divorce, an employee can avoid a work conflict by quitting the organization, or a manager can avoid a turf battle by letting another manager win. Common withdrawal behaviors include avoiding the source of conflict, quitting, talking behind the other person's back, and forming alliances with others (Martin & Bergmann, 1996). Even though withdrawal can make one feel better, often it only postpones conflict rather than prevents it.

Triangling An employee discusses a conflict with a third-party such as a friend or supervisor. In doing so, the employee hopes that the third party will talk to the second party and that the conflict will be resolved without the need for the two parties to meet.

An interesting form of avoidance, called **triangling**, occurs when an employee discusses the conflict with a third party, such as a friend or supervisor. In doing so, the employee hopes that the third party will talk to the second party and that the conflict will be resolved without the need for the two parties to meet (Ruzich, 1999). When triangling occurs, supervisors are advised to have the two parties meet to resolve the issue or to use a formal third-party approach such as mediation. (See the Employment Profile Box for advice on how Bobbie Raynes handles third-party mediation.)

Accommodating Style

Accommodating style The conflict style of a person who tends to respond to conflict by giving in to the other person.

When a person is so intent on settling a conflict that he gives in and risks hurting himself, he has adopted the **accommodating style**. People who use this style when the stakes are high are usually viewed as cooperative but weak. I observed an example of this style at a self-serve gas station. Two drivers parked their cars next to the same pump at roughly the same time. Both drivers got out of their cars and simultaneously reached for the only pump. Obviously, one person had to give in to avoid conflict and would have to wait five minutes longer than the other. Yet one driver quickly told the other to "go ahead." Why did this person so quickly accede to the other? Probably because he had an accommodating reaction to potential conflict and because, in this case, the stakes were low.

Forcing Style

Forcing style The conflict style of a person who responds to conflict by always trying to win.

A person with a **forcing style** handles conflict in a win-lose fashion and does what it takes to win, with little regard for the other person. This style is appropriate in emergencies or when there is the potential for a violation on policy, ethical, or legal grounds if the other party does not agree to your proposal. Though this style can be effective in winning, it also can damage relations so badly that other conflicts will result. This strategy of **winning at all costs** occurs especially when a person regards his side as correct and the other person is regarded as the enemy whose side is incorrect. This reaction often occurs when each side needs a victory to gain or retain status. Union/management conflicts provide good examples of this need for status. For a union to survive, its members must perceive it as being useful. Thus, during contract negotiations, union leadership must force management to "give in" or run the risk of losing status with its membership.

Winning at all costs An approach to handling conflict in which one side seeks to win regardless of the damage to the other side.

But the problem with putting status on the line is that it makes backing down to resolve a conflict very difficult. As a conflict escalates, each side "digs in" and becomes less willing to compromise. Unless one side has the resources to clearly win, the win-at-all-costs reaction is likely to prolong conflict. Thus, this strategy is appropriate only if the position holder is actually correct and if winning the conflict is in fact more important than the probable damage to future relationships.

Collaborating Style

Collaborating style The conflict style of a person who wants a conflict resolved in such a way that both sides get what they want.

An individual with a **collaborating style** wants to win but also wants to see the other person win. These people seek win-win solutions—that is, ways in which both sides

In addition to my work as an adjunct instructor and consultant, I conduct workshops on conflict management and do workplace mediations. If conflicts can be acknowledged and addressed quickly, it is much less likely that lawsuits will arise and more likely that employee morale and productivity will remain at an acceptable level. At least 90% of conflict situations that I have handled have been resolved through mediation.

Mediation can work for almost any type of workplace conflict, such as that which occurs between supervisor and employee and between coworkers. However, for mediation to be successful, certain criteria must be met, which include willingness from all parties to try the process, a desire to solve the problem without litigation, and time to mediate (because mediation may take several sessions). The role of a mediator is to be neutral and not judge who is right or wrong. A mediator is merely a facilitator of the communication process between the parties. If the parties get stuck and can't think of a solution to their conflict, the mediator can suggest some ideas the parties may want to try. But ultimately, it should be their agreement, not the mediator's.

A good example of how mediation can be successful in the workplace is a case I handled which involved two coworkers. One coworker was fairly new, eager to try out new ideas, and had an outgoing personality. The other coworker had been at the agency for over 10 years, was quiet, and was very unaccepting of change. Their conflict arose because the older coworker felt that the new coworker was overstepping her boundaries and doing tasks that only the older coworker should have been doing. Also, the new coworker was trying to implement some changes that the other person was resistant to trying, mainly because she had not been allowed to provide her input. During mediation, they reached an agreement about what each person expected of the other. That is, they better defined their job descriptions for each other. They also agreed to hold weekly meetings so that the older coworker could have input on any new ideas that were being proposed.

I often see conflict arise in organizations because of changes being made. Because most of us fear the unknown that change brings, it is

Bobbie Raynes, M.S.
Virginia State Supreme Court Certified Mediator

© Bobbie Raynes

easier not to try anything new. The key is to talk about what fears individuals have and then try to determine whether those fears are real and, if they are, how to overcome them.

Mediation was very successful between the two coworkers in the previous example because they wanted to maintain a good working relationship. It's very stressful to work with someone with whom you don't get along. Mediation provides a safe place for people to discuss their differences and ways to resolve them, often reducing a great deal of this stress. Because parties get to find their own resolution, instead of being told how to handle the problem, it helps them feel more in control over decisions that affect their lives.

Being a mediator is a very challenging, but rewarding, career. Knowing that I have been instrumental in helping people preserve their relationships and resolve their differences has made all the hard work and hours I put into training for this position worthwhile.

If the time comes when you are asked to mediate, here are some tips that can help the session be successful.

- Participate in conflict management training, first!
- Talk separately to each individual involved in the conflict. Make sure the situation is right for mediation.
- Make sure everyone is willing to mediate.
- Assure all parties that you are neutral and will keep the process confidential.
- Use your active listening skills and let them know you "hear" them.
- Let the parties come up with ideas to resolve their conflict.

I have been seeing more and more human resource specialists pursue training in this area so they can better manage their organizations' day-to-day conflicts. If you are interested in this area, many universities offer courses in mediation and other forms of alternative dispute resolution.

get what they want. Though this style is probably the best to use whenever possible, it can be time-consuming and may not be appropriate in emergencies (e.g., determining how best to treat a person having a heart attack).

Compromising Style

Compromising style A style of resolving conflicts in which an individual allows each side to get some of what it wants.

The final strategy is the **compromising style**. The user of this type adopts give-and-take tactics that enable each side to get some of what it wants but not everything

Negotiation and bargaining A method of resolving conflict in which two sides use verbal skill and strategy to reach an agreement.

Least acceptable result (LAR) The lowest settlement that a person is willing to accept in a negotiated agreement.

Maximum supportable position (MSP) The highest possible settlement that a person could reasonably ask for and still maintain credibility in negotiating an agreement.

it wants. Most conflicts are resolved through some form of compromise so that a solution benefits both sides. Compromising usually involves a good deal of **negotiation and bargaining**. The negotiation process begins with each side making an offer that asks for much more than it really wants. For example, union leaders might demand $10 an hour, while management offers $5 an hour. Each side understands what the other is doing, so the union might lower its demand to $9 and management might raise its offer to $6. This process continues until an acceptable compromise has been reached.

An *acceptable compromise* is one that falls within the settlement range for both sides (Acuff, 2008). According to Acuff, a settlement range is between the **least acceptable result (LAR)** and the **maximum supportable position (MSP)** for each side. The LAR is the lowest settlement that a person is willing to accept; it must be realistic and satisfy the person's actual needs. The MSP is the best possible settlement that a person can ask for and still reasonably support with facts and logic. The MSP is usually the negotiator's initial offer. A short-order cook's proposal for $40 an hour would not be reasonably supportable and thus would not be a proper MSP.

As shown in Figure 13.3, negotiations usually begin with each side offering its MSP as an opening bid. The actual negotiating territory is the area between both sides' LARs. Each side then bargains for a settlement closest to its own MSP and the other's LAR. The final settlement will be a function of the skill of each negotiator as well as of time pressures. Such pressures may be exerted by customers who cannot wait for a settlement or by union members who cannot financially afford prolonged negotiations.

An important influence on the outcome of a negotiation is what is called the *best alternative to a negotiated agreement* (BATNA). A BATNA is the best alternative that negotiators have if they can't reach an agreement. For example, if I am buying a car and I already have an offer of $26,500 from one dealer (my BATNA), my least acceptable result when I negotiate with a new dealer will be less than the $26,500. If the dealer won't go lower, I can walk away knowing I already have a better deal. If the dealer is aware of my BATNA, it will reduce his initial offer because he knows that an initial offer greater than my BATNA will not be effective (Buelens & Van Poucke, 2004).

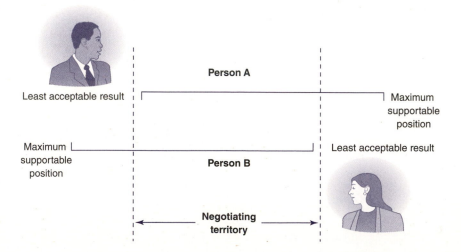

Figure 13.3

Negotiating Territory and Conflict Resolution

Seltz and Modica (1980) have suggested four indicators that tell when negotiations are coming to an end so that each side can prepare its final offer:

1. The number of counterarguments is reduced.
2. The positions of the two sides appear closer together.
3. The other side talks about final arrangements.
4. The other side appears willing to begin putting things in writing.

Although this conflict resolution strategy appears to be the best approach to take, it often is not. Sometimes, compromise results in a bad solution. For example, if Congress wants to include $8 billion in the federal budget to construct a new nuclear power plant and the president wants to budget only $4 billion, then the two are likely to agree on a median figure such as $6 billion. But if the project cannot be completed for less than $8 billion, then the compromise may waste billions of dollars that could be spent elsewhere.

Determining Conflict Styles

A person's method of dealing with conflict at work can be measured by the Rahim Organizational Conflict Inventory II (Rahim & Magner, 1995) or the Cohen Conflict Response Inventory (Cohen, 1997). To determine your own conflict style, complete Exercise 13.5 in your workbook.

Resolving Conflict

Prior to Conflict Occurring

An organization should have a formal policy on how conflict is to be handled. Usually such a policy will state that employees should first try to resolve their own conflicts, and if that is not successful, they can utilize a third-party intervention. Employees should receive training on the causes of conflict, ways to prevent conflict, and strategies for resolving conflict. For example, at the Timken plant in Alta Vista, Virginia, all employees received 12 hours of training on how to resolve conflicts, which included role plays to practice what they learned. Similarly, the City of Plano, Texas, offers employees an optional 40-hour training program in conflict mediation and facilitation.

When Conflict First Occurs

When conflict first occurs between coworkers or between a supervisor and a subordinate, the two parties should be encouraged to use the conflict resolution skills they learned in training to resolve the conflict on their own. These skills include expressing a desire for cooperation, offering compliments, avoiding negative interaction, emphasizing mutual similarities, and pointing out common goals. A key to resolving conflict is to reduce tension and increase trust between the two parties. This can be accomplished by stating an intention to reduce tension, publicly announcing what steps will be taken to reduce tension, inviting the other side also to take action to reduce tension, and making sure that each initiative offered is unambiguous. By taking these steps early on, minor conflict can be resolved quickly, and serious conflict can be resolved through negotiation.

The two parties meet in a private location to address the problem—prior to this meeting, the two parties should not talk to others about the problem. When the two parties actually do sit down together, the employee who arranged the meeting explains his perception of the problem, when it occurred, and the impact that it has had on him (e.g., anxiety, anger, depression, lower productivity). For example, an employee might say, "When you made fun of my accent at lunch last week, it made me feel that you were putting me down and didn't respect me." Or an employee might tell a supervisor, "When the promotion was given to John instead of me, I thought it was because he is a male and I am a female." It is important that the employee address the behavior of the other person rather than such aspects as the person's values, personality, and ability. For example, an employee would not want to say, "You demonstrated what a racist you are by giving the promotion to Henry instead of me." In other words, the focus should not be on who an employee *is* but rather what he has *done*.

The second party then responds to what was said by the first party. If the second party agrees, he might apologize and then agree to stop the behavior. If the second party doesn't agree, she would explain her perception of what happened. The two parties would then exchange views and suggestions until they have reached an agreement on how to resolve the issue. If the two can't agree, the conflict is labeled a **dispute**, and the parties should seek third-party intervention.

An interesting aspect of this idea is called **cooperative problem solving** An example of this approach is when the president of an organization forms a task force or committee with representatives from all of the departments or divisions that will be affected by the solution. Together these representatives work to define the problem, identify possible solutions, and arrive at the best one.

This process doesn't always go smoothly, but it is important that employees try to resolve their own conflicts before seeking help from a third party. Employees who resolve their own conflicts are more likely to buy into a resolution than employees who use a third party. Furthermore, bringing in a supervisor makes it more difficult for employees to admit that they have done something wrong. Of course, employees should not be forced to try to resolve all conflicts on their own. When emotions are high, alcohol or drugs are involved, or one party feels threatened by the other, a third-party intervention is in order.

Third-Party Intervention

If conflict cannot be resolved by the parties involved, it is often a good idea to seek help—that is, to ask for **third-party intervention** This third party usually is provided through mediation, and if that doesn't work, through arbitration.

Mediation. With **mediation**, a neutral third party is asked to help both parties reach a mutually agreeable solution to the conflict. Mediators are not there to make decisions. Instead, their role is to facilitate the communication process by providing the parties with a safe and equitable venue so that they are more willing and able to reach a solution. Mediators can be employees of the organization (e.g., team leader, supervisor, human resource manager) or professional mediators who work with a variety of organizations. Mediators are most successful when two parties do not trust one another (Ross & Wieland, 1996), and they provide the best results when both sides consider the mediator to be competent and trustworthy. For mediation to be successful, both parties must agree that there is a conflict and that a solution can be found by working together.

Mediation has been effective in resolving even the most difficult conflicts. For example, in 2010, 73.4% of the employment discrimination claims that were sent to mediation by the Equal Employment Opportunity Commission were resolved. Furthermore, the mediation process took 100 days—substantially less time than did the typical lawsuit.

Dispute A situation when two parties do not agree.

Cooperative problem solving A method of resolving conflict in which two sides get together to discuss a problem and arrive at a solution.

Third-party intervention When a neutral party is asked to help resolve a conflict.

Mediation A method of resolving conflict in which a neutral third party is asked to help the two parties reach an agreement.

According to Lovenheim and Guerin (2004), mediation is better than filing a lawsuit when

- you need to solve a problem with a person with whom you do not want to end your relationship (e.g., coworker, boss, neighbor);
- you don't want your problems publicized in the newspaper;
- you want to save the costs associated with paying a lawyer; or
- you want to settle your dispute promptly.

Arbitration A method of resolving conflicts in which a neutral third party is asked to choose which side is correct.

Arbitration. With **arbitration**, a neutral third party listens to both sides' arguments and then makes a decision. Within an organization, this neutral party is often the manager of the two employees in conflict. However, if that manager just served as a mediator, then an HR director might be used.

Organizations are increasingly using outside arbitrators to handle discrimination claims by employees. This increase in the use of arbitrators represents organizational attempts to avoid the negative publicity associated with discrimination suits and to reduce the costs that come with lengthy litigation. In 2001, the U.S. Supreme Court ruled that employers can require employees to use arbitration rather than litigation (*Circuit City Stores v. Adams*, 2001). However, arbitration works best when it is provided as an option rather than being a requirement.

Though mandatory arbitration can be effective, arbitration is more expensive than mediation; so much so that mandatory arbitration policies discourage employees from making formal disputes or cause financial hardships if they do (Armour, 2001).

Arbitration decisions can be either *binding* or *nonbinding*. If the decision is binding, the two sides have agreed to abide by the arbitrator's decision regardless of how displeased one or both sides may be with that decision. If the decision is nonbinding, then one or both sides can reject an unfavorable decision. Even though arbitration can end conflicts quickly, usually neither side is as satisfied with the outcome as both would have been if they had settled the conflict themselves or used mediation. Employees are most willing to use arbitration when they perceive that a conflict was the result of intentional behavior by another, resolution of the conflict has important consequences, and the conflicting employees are of equal power (Arnold & Carnevale, 1997).

Some research suggests that performance may drop (Shirreffs & Sommers, 2006; Sommers, 1993) and turnover increase (Bretz & Thomas, 1992) as a result of an arbitrator's decision. As you might imagine, an individual's performance is most likely to drop after losing and most likely to improve after winning an arbitration hearing (Hauenstein & Lord, 1989). To apply what you have learned about reactions to conflict, complete Exercises 13.6 and 13.7 in your workbook.

ON THE JOB | Applied Case Study

Conflict at Work

The director of a nonprofit agency has asked you for help. He has 13 employees and feels that there are a lot of interpersonal issues going on that are causing them to be unhappy and not do a good job of serving the needs of their clients. He senses that there is a lot of tension and has noticed that the employees are reluctant to attend group meetings. When they do attend, there is tension and anger.

- What could be the cause of this problem?
- What would you do to reduce the conflict?

To find out how a certified mediator solved this problem, use the link found on your text webpage.

Group Hazing

A new employee is locked in a meat freezer for 15 minutes before being let out. Dog food is put in a new fireman's dinner without his knowledge. A new employee at a jail is asked to get on the intercom and page Jack Meoff. Are these examples of practical jokes and a form of initiation for new employees? Or is it something else?

One of the best-kept secrets of the workplace is workplace hazing. Critics opposed to stunts like the ones above say that those would fall under hazing. And they say it is unethical because it is intentional humiliation of a person and has no purpose other than to show that employee his or her place in the organization. And it could be dangerous. As evidenced by some of the hazing done in colleges, stunts that start as practical jokes can often be deadly. What if the new employee in the meat locker had been left in it a minute too long? What if there was something in the dog food that the new fireman had been allergic to? Would it still have been considered harmless initiation or would it have been considered hazing?

Supporters of such antics say that it is not a form of hazing but of harmless practical jokes by groups of employees who have been in the organization for a while and who, themselves, have been subjected to the same practical jokes. And, according to these proponents, such a practice does serve a purpose. Anytime a new person enters a group, the group becomes temporarily unstable while the new group member attempts to learn the rules and the existing group members learn to trust the new one. So, these practical jokes can build cohesion between employees who must often work together to get a job done.

In this chapter, you learned that for a group to be effective and perform well, it must be cohesive. Your text lists several ways to build cohesion. Proponents of workplace initiation say that such practical jokes will build cohesion. It is a way for employees to get to know each other better and establish a common bond. Natasha Josefowitz, from San Diego State University, and Herman Gadon, from the University of California-San Diego, explain that it ensures that new employees learn and respect the rules of the group. They further state that membership in a group should be earned and considered a privilege. When employees successfully handle a practical joke, they earn the right to be part of a particular group. Without such initiation practices, it may take longer for employees to be accepted, or they may not become accepted at all. So initiation practices such as those stated above actually have positive benefits for new employees.

Critics believe that the only benefit such jokes have is to those employees carrying out the joke. For those employees, it establishes a hierarchy of who is in charge, who not to cross, and who has the most power. It establishes dominance and fear. And it becomes even more unethical when supervisors or managers know that such practices go on and do nothing about it, such as warn new employees or punish those employees who pull the practical jokes.

What Do You Think?

- Do you think the stunts described above are harmless jokes or a form of hazing? If you consider it to be hazing, are they unethical?

- Are practical jokes ever acceptable in the workplace? Are some less ethical than others?

- Do you think it is ethical for management to support such practical jokes?

- Is it unethical for a manager not to warn new employees that they may be subject to a practical joke as part of an initiation process?

Chapter Summary

In this chapter you learned:

- Groups consist of multiple members who perceive themselves as a unit and share a common goal or goals.
- People join groups due to a need for affiliation, a need to identify with success, a need for emotional support, a need for assistance, common goals, physical proximity, and assignment.

- Factors that influence a group's success include its level of cohesiveness, the composition and stability of its membership, and the group's size, status, and communication structure.
- Teams go through four developmental stages: forming, storming, norming, and performing.
- The team approach is not always the best.
- Conflict usually results from factors such as competition for resources, task interdependence, jurisdictional ambiguity, communication barriers, and personality.
- People react to conflict by ignoring it through withdrawal, trying to win at all costs, trying to persuade the other side to resolve the conflict in their favor, bargaining for an agreement, or asking for third-party help.

Questions for Review

1. How can you use the knowledge of why people join groups to increase group effectiveness?
2. When are interacting groups better than nominal groups or individuals?
3. Why does the presence of others cause increased performance in some situations and decreased performance in others?
4. When can a group be too cohesive?
5. How do we build effective teams?
6. How are mediation and arbitration different?

Media Resources and Learning Tools

- Visit our website. Go to www.cengage.com/psychology/aamodt, where you will find online resources directly linked to your book, including chapter-by-chapter quizzing, flashcards, crossword puzzles, application activities, and more.
- Want more practice applying industrial/organizational psychology? Check out the *I/O Applications Workbook*. This workbook (keyed to your textbook) offers engaging, high-interest activities to help you reinforce the important concepts presented in the text.

Chapter

14

ORGANIZATION DEVELOPMENT

© Chris Ryan/OJO Images/Getty Images

Learning Objectives

- ➡ Know how and why organizations change
- ➡ Understand how to increase employee acceptance of change
- ➡ Understand the importance of organizational culture
- ➡ Know how to handle change
- ➡ Know when empowering employees is a good idea
- ➡ Understand the levels of employee input
- ➡ Understand the types of flexible work schedules
- ➡ Know how to avoid layoffs
- ➡ Know how to properly conduct a layoff
- ➡ Understand the effects of layoffs on victims, survivors, the organization, and the community

You learned about increasing an individual employee's skills through training in Chapter 8. In this chapter, you will learn about organization development—the process of improving organizational performance by making *organization-wide*, rather than *individual*, changes (Burke, 2011). Though there are many aspects to organization development, this chapter will focus on four major issues: managing change, empowering employees, implementing innovative work schedules, and downsizing.

Managing Change

In organizations, change occurs for many reasons and takes on many forms. Some changes are due to such organization development efforts as downsizing, reorganization, or the introduction of teams. Some changes are the result of external mandates like managed care or new government regulations. Still other changes occur due to new leadership or new personnel.

Sacred Cow Hunts

Sacred cow hunt The first step in organizational change, in which employees look for practices and policies that waste time and are counterproductive.

Perhaps the first step toward organizational change is what Kriegel and Brandt (1996) called a **sacred cow hunt** Organizational sacred cows are practices that have been around for a long time and invisibly reduce productivity. A sacred cow hunt, then, is an organization-wide attempt to get rid of practices that serve no useful purpose. Merck Pharmaceutical and Tractor Supply Stores have periodic sacred cow hunts in which cow bells are rung when a sacred cow is found, monthly sacred cow barbecues are held, and employees receive awards and money for finding a sacred cow. In a sacred cow hunt, an organization looks at all of its practices and policies and asks questions like these:

- Why are we doing it? Does it add value, quality, service, or productivity?
- What if it didn't exist?
- Is it already being done by someone else?
- How and when did we start doing this?
- Can it be done better by another person, department, or company?

According to Kriegel and Brandt, common types of sacred cows include the paper cow, the meeting cow, and the speed cow.

The Paper Cow

Paper cows are unnecessary paperwork—usually forms and reports that cost organizations money to prepare, distribute, and read. To determine if something is a paper cow, consider the extent to which the paperwork increases efficiency, productivity, or quality. Ask if anyone actually reads the paperwork. A unique strategy tried by employees at one company was to stop sending a monthly report that had been distributed for years. The employees' thinking was that if the report was actually needed, they would receive complaints. Three months and three missing reports later, no one had complained.

Steve Kerr, an executive at Goldman Sachs, provides an interesting example of how to combat paper cows. The organization issued rubber stamps to managers that said, "Why am I receiving this?" to be used if a manager received a report that he/she did not need. The person sending the report could then get feedback on how many managers were actually using the report. In one situation, every copy of the report was returned with the stamp, *Why am I receiving this?* (Kerr, 2009).

Kerr also recalled a practice in which people generating a report had to indicate the total numbers of hours spent writing the report. When the CEO of a company discovered that 1,015 hours were spent on a trivial report that he requested, he altered his practice of asking for such reports on short notice.

A good annual practice is to review all forms and reports and determine whether they are still needed and, if they are, whether they are needed in their current format. To demonstrate the importance of this practice, review the forms used by your university or organization. How many of them are a third of a page or a quarter of a page? Probably none. There seems to be an unwritten rule that all forms must ask questions until the bottom of the page is reached. I was recently preparing contracts for our graduate assistants and noticed that I was being asked questions about the university from which the students had received their undergraduate degrees, their undergraduate grade point average, and their work histories. Note that these were contracts, not application forms, where this information was already contained. So, in the spirit of a good sacred cow hunt, I called the graduate college to ask why this information was necessary. Their reply? No one knew. Did anyone actually need this information? No. Will you change the form for next year? No. This is an example of a sacred cow hunt—but no sacred cow barbecue. To apply what you have learned about paper cow hunts, complete Exercise 14.1 in your workbook.

The Meeting Cow

Another area ripe for change is the number and length of meetings. Think about meetings you have attended recently. How much meeting time was spent doing business as opposed to socializing? Was the meeting really necessary? To reduce the number and length of meetings, some organizations ask the person calling the meeting to determine the cost of the meeting (e.g., one hour's salary of each attendee, cost of meeting room, cost of refreshments and supplies) and consider whether the cost will exceed the potential benefits. In some of these organizations, the meeting costs are actually posted at the beginning of the meeting! Needless to say, when people are forced to consider the benefits of meetings against their cost, most meetings will not be held.

The Speed Cow

Unnecessary deadlines are another source for potential change. Requiring work to be done "by tomorrow" is sometimes necessary. However, unnecessary deadlines cause employees to work at a faster than optimal pace, resulting in decreased quality, increased stress, and increased health problems.

Kriegel and Brandt (1996) suggest that in addition to sacred cow hunts, effective change can be encouraged by using these strategies:

- Think like a beginner: Ask stupid questions, constantly ask "why" things are being done a certain way, and don't assume that anything makes sense.
- Don't be complacent with something that is working well. Keep looking for ways to improve, new markets to enter, new products to introduce.
- Don't play by everyone else's rules; make your own. Domino's Pizza is a great example of this type of thinking. While all the other pizza chains competed for ways to increase the number of customers entering their restaurants, Domino's decided to change the rules and bring the restaurant to the people rather than bringing the people to the restaurant.
- Rather than penalizing mistakes, reward employees for making the attempt to change or to try something new.

Employee Acceptance of Change

Though change can be beneficial to organizations, employees are often initially reluctant to change. This reluctance is understandable, as employees are comfortable doing things the old way. They may fear that change will result in less favorable working conditions and economic outcomes than they are used to. According to consultant William Bridges (1985), it is common for employees undergoing change to feel out of control and as if they are losing their identity ("Who am I? What am I supposed to do?"), meaning ("How do I fit into the newly changed organization?"), and belonging ("Why do I have to work with a bunch of new people I don't even know?").

Stages

In the past 70 years, there have been many theories regarding the change process. Most of these theories postulate that the change process occurs in between three (Lewin, 1958) and seven (Lippitt, Watson, & Westley, 1958) stages or phases, depending on whether the focus of the theory is the organization (Lewin, 1958), the change agent (Lippitt et al., 1958), or the employee (Carnall, 2008). The difference between a stage and a phase is that stages are distinct time periods, whereas phases can overlap with one another (Burke, 2011).

Many employees work from home in order to balance work and family demands.

© Lee Raynes

Lewin (1958) theorized that *organizations* go through three stages: unfreezing, moving, and refreezing. In the unfreezing stage, the organization must convince employees and other stakeholders (e.g., shareholders, the community) that the current state of affairs is unacceptable and that change is necessary. In the moving stage, the organization takes steps (e.g., training, new work processes) to move the organization to the desired state. In the refreezing stage, the organization develops ways to keep the new changes in place, such as formalizing new policy and rewarding employees for behaving in a manner consistent with the new change.

Carnall (2008) suggests that *employees* typically go through five stages during major organizational changes: denial, defense, discarding, adaptation, and internalization.

Stage 1: Denial. During this initial stage, employees deny that any changes will actually take place, try to convince themselves that the old way is working, and create reasons why the proposed changes will never work (e.g., "We tried that before and it didn't work. Something like that won't work in a company like ours").

Stage 2: Defense. When employees begin to believe that change will actually occur, they become defensive and try to justify their positions and ways of doing things. The idea here is that if an organization is changing the way in which employees perform, there is an inherent criticism that the employees must have previously been doing things wrong.

Stage 3: Discarding. At some point, employees begin to realize not only that the organization is going to change but that the employees are going to have to change as well. That is, change is inevitable, and it is in the best interest of the employee to discard the old ways and start to accept the change as the new reality.

Stage 4: Adaptation. At this stage, employees test the new system, learn how it functions, and begin to make adjustments in the way they perform. Employees spend tremendous energy at this stage and can often become frustrated and angry.

Stage 5: Internalization. In this final stage, employees have become immersed in the new culture and comfortable with the new system and have accepted their new co-workers and work environment.

Important Factors

The extent to which employees readily accept and handle change is dependent on the reason behind the change, the leader making the change, and the personality of the person being changed.

The Type of Change. Organization change expert Warner Burke (2011) distinguishes two types of change: evolutionary and revolutionary. The vast majority of change is *evolutionary*, that is the continual process of upgrading or improving processes; for example, the unpopular change from Windows XP to Vista, a change in the supervisor to whom one reports, or a change in how to submit travel receipts for reimbursement. Burke defines *revolutionary* change as a "real jolt to the system" that drastically changes the way things are done. Examples might include developing a brand-new product line that requires a vastly different skill set, completely changing the organizational structure, or organizational misconduct (e.g., Enron, Adelphia, Arthur

Andersen) that causes an organization to completely change its ethical policies and behavior. Clearly, revolutionary change is more difficult than is evolutionary change.

The Reason Behind the Change. Employee acceptance of change is often a function of the reason behind the change. For example, employees understand (but don't necessarily like) change that is due to financial problems, external mandates, or attempts to improve the organization. Acceptance is lower when employees perceive the change to be in organizational philosophy, a whim on the part of the person making the change ("Hey, let's do teams"), or a change because everyone else is changing ("Everyone else has teams, so we need to create them now before we get left behind"). Employees are least likely to accept change if they don't understand or were not told the reasons behind the change.

The Person Making the Change. Another factor affecting employee acceptance of change is the person making or suggesting the change. Not surprisingly, workers are more positive about change when the source of change is within the work group rather than an external source (Griffin, Rafferty, & Mason, 2004). Changes proposed by leaders who are well liked and respected and who have a history of success are more likely to be accepted than changes proposed by leaders whose motives are suspect (Dirks, 2000; Lam & Schaubroeck, 2000). Let me provide two very different examples.

- In the first example, the head of a small consulting firm decided to change the focus of her business from delivering training seminars to helping companies switch from a traditional organizational approach to a flatter, team-based approach. Though the consultant's employees were apprehensive about the change in focus, they quickly accepted the change because the consultant was well respected for her knowledge, treated her employees as family, and had on a prior occasion changed the company's focus, resulting in a 30% increase in revenue.
- In the second example, due to financial and regulatory reasons, a local mental health agency was forced to move its 120 employees from their current buildings to a new location. A management committee was formed to determine the location for the new building. When the new location was announced, the employees were very upset. The new building was expensive, in a highly congested traffic area, and located far away from most of the agency's clients. The employees' unhappiness was not due to the relocation but to the choice of buildings. It just didn't make sense. That is, it didn't make sense until several of the employees realized that the new building was only five minutes from where each of the deciding committee members lived. I don't think I have to finish the story for you to understand the importance of motive.

The differences in these two stories are clear. In the first, employees quickly accepted change because they trusted the person making the change. In the second, the employees did not accept the change because the decision makers were not well respected and acted in a manner inconsistent with the well-being of the majority of employees.

For organizational change of any type to work, it is essential that employees trust the organization as a whole as well as the specific individuals making the change. Viking Glass in Sioux Falls, South Dakota, realized the importance of trust when it decided to change the organization to foster more employee participation. Viking Glass spent more than a year laying the foundation to increase the extent to which its employees trusted the company. After gaining employees' trust, the company successfully increased the level of employee empowerment.

The Person Being Changed. As one would imagine, there is considerable variability in the way in which people instigate or react to change. **Change agents** are people who enjoy change and often make changes just for the sake of it. A change agent's motto might best be expressed as "If it ain't broke, break it." Though many people like to call themselves change agents, it may not be such a compliment. That is, reasoned change is good, but change for the sake of change is disruptive.

Let me give you an example. When I was about 30, I was president of our local Kiwanis Club. Now before you get too impressed, I was asked to be president because I was the only person in the club who had not yet been president and one of only five or so members who was under the age of 60. My first act as president was to restructure all of the committees and create an impressive-looking matrix to depict these changes. When I presented this matrix at our board meeting, each member just stared at me (some were already asleep), until one person said, "Mike, you can't change committees. It's in the national bylaws." My response was to say "oops" and move on to the next topic. Though this story is not an example of good leadership skills, it is a perfect example of being a change agent. By the way, with some maturity, I hope I have become a change analyst.

Change analysts are not afraid to change or make changes but want to make changes only if the changes will improve the organization. Their motto might be "If it ain't broke, leave it alone; if it's broke, fix it." Change analysts are people who constantly ask such questions as "Why are we doing this?" and "Is there a better way we could be doing this?" But in contrast to the change agent, they are not driven by a need to change constantly.

Receptive changers are people who probably will not instigate change but are willing to change. Their motto is "If it's broke, I'll help fix it." Receptive changers typically have high self-esteem and optimistic personalities and believe they have control over their own lives (Wanberg & Banas, 2000). Receptive changers are essential for any major organizational change to be successful.

Reluctant changers will certainly not instigate or welcome change, but they will change if necessary. Their motto is "Are you sure it's broken?" **Change resisters** hate change, are scared by it, and will do anything they can to keep change from occurring. Their motto is "It may be broken, but it's still better than the unknown."

Implementing Change

Another important factor in employee acceptance of change is the way the change is implemented. That is, how and when will details be communicated? How long will the implementation take? Does the organization have the right personnel for the change? What types of training needs does the organization have?

When organizations are planning change, they intend the change process to be linear in that they begin with Phase 1, move to Phase 2, and so forth until the change is complete. Typically there is an initial timeline for each phase. As you read the following "steps" to implementing change, it is important to understand that the change process seldom (perhaps never) goes as planned and that setbacks will occur, resulting in the need to make revisions to the change process (Burke, 2011).

Change agent A person who enjoys change and makes changes for the sake of it.

Change analyst A person who is not afraid of change but makes changes only when there is a compelling reason to do so.

Receptive changer A person who is willing to change.

Reluctant changer A person who will initially resist change but will eventually go along with it.

Change resister A person who hates change and will do anything to keep change from occurring.

Creating an Atmosphere for Change

According to Denton (1996), one of the first steps in organizational change is to create the proper atmosphere. This process begins by creating dissatisfaction with the current system. Employees should be surveyed to determine how satisfied they are with the current system. If things go as normal, the results of the survey will indicate that many employees are unhappy with the way things are currently done and have suggestions for improvement. By sharing these results with employees, an organization can protect itself from employees reacting to change by remembering the "good old days." Instead, they will focus on the "bad old days" and be more willing to change.

Perhaps a good example of this comes from some friends of mine who had been dating for several years. For the last few months of their relationship, each of the two would privately tell me how stale their relationship had become and say that it was time for a change. Jill made the decision to end the relationship and told Jack of her decision on a Friday night. The following week, Jill was energetic and enthusiastic, talked of dating new people, and even asked if I knew any good-looking single guys. Jack, however, whined all week about how good a relationship he and Jill had had and how he would never be able to find another woman he would love so much. What accounted for the sudden difference in their attitudes? Jill kept the "bad old days" in mind when she made the decision to end the relationship, and Jack remembered only the "good old days" after the relationship ended.

Some of this pining for the good old days seems inevitable. A colleague of mine had been complaining for years about his college president. The president eventually was fired and replaced by a new president who made many strange changes. It didn't take a year before my colleague lamented about how much he missed his former boss. It took only a few reminders of the horror stories he had told me about his previous boss to quiet this lamenting.

After creating dissatisfaction with the status quo, Denton (1996) advises organizations to work hard to reduce the fear of change by providing emotional support, allowing employees to vent and discuss their feelings, and providing employees with a safety net that allows them to make mistakes during the transition period. Fear can also be reduced by having someone in the organization describe the benefits of change.

Communicating Details

Employees are most responsive to change when they are kept well informed (Wanberg & Banas, 2000). Unless there is a need for secrecy (e.g., a merger), employees should be aware of and involved in all aspects of the change, from initial planning to final implementation. If employees are kept in the dark until the very end, they usually suspect that something bad is happening. It seems to be human nature to think the worst when we don't know something. After undergoing a major restructuring, staff at Educational Testing Service (ETS) in Princeton, New Jersey, reported that poor communication was responsible for many of the difficulties encountered in the change process (Wild, Horney, & Koonce, 1996). During their restructuring, ETS learned these important lessons:

1. *Communicating change is hard work.* Early in the change process, ETS thought it had done a good job communicating the reasons for and details of its restructuring. However, a change readiness survey that ETS administered to its employees indicated that many employees didn't understand the change

Though organizational change can be traumatic for employees, it can also be exciting and full of new opportunities. Organizational-change expert Price Pritchett (2008) offered the following advice to employees involved in organizational change. This advice can be communicated by management to other employees throughout the organization.

Speed Up

➡ It is natural for people faced with a new situation to be cautious and want to take things slowly (Kotter & Cohen, 2002). However, Pritchett advises employees to get involved, increase the pace of their work, and not get left behind. This advice is analogous to paddling a canoe: If you move faster than the current, you can control where you are going. If you slow down or remain at the same speed as the current, you will be swept wherever the current takes you.

Take the Initiative

➡ Instead of waiting for instructions and for people to tell you what to do, chart your own course. Show initiative, try to solve problems, make suggestions. Don't be afraid to take risks, and don't be afraid to make mistakes. As hockey star Wayne Gretzky once said, "You miss a hundred percent of the shots you don't take."

Spend Energy on Solutions

➡ Instead of spending energy complaining and resisting change, accept change, and then spend your energy trying to solve problems and make the new system work. Take personal responsibility for fixing what doesn't work and for making suggestions for ways the system can be improved.

To remove the stress associated with change, some psychologists suggest that organizations do innovative things to make work more fun (Brotherton, 1996). Consultant Matt Weinstein offers these suggestions to managers:

➡ Post baby pictures of managers so that employees can laugh at them and realize that the people making the change weren't always in powerful positions.

➡ Create a stress-free zone where employees can go to relax for a few moments. The Brookstar Corporation in Michigan went so far as to put a punching bag in a room so that employees could take out their frustration on the bag rather than on each other.

➡ Give employees a surprise hour off. Store managers at Crate & Barrel tell one employee each week to take an hour and have fun, go shopping, or take a nap.

➡ Other suggestions include holding an ugly tie contest, giving employees stuffed animals, and designing personalized fortune cookies.

Though we certainly have no scientific evidence that any of these techniques will work, the idea is that managers should realize the stress inherent in change and take creative measures to reduce that stress.

---

or were still resisting it. The survey results told ETS that it still had a long way to go in communicating important information to its employees.

2. *Training is needed.* The employees who were given the responsibility for communicating the change had not been properly trained in such areas as dealing with employee hostility and resistance.

3. *Two-way communication is essential.* Employees must have the opportunity to provide feedback to the people making the changes.

4. *Honesty is the best policy.* Be honest with employees and tell them information as it arises rather than waiting until all aspects of the change are completed.

Time Frame

Most successful organizational changes occur in a timely fashion. The longer it takes to change, the greater the opportunity for things to go wrong and the greater the chance that employees will become disillusioned. Many consultants advise that organizations should not remain in a "change mode" for longer than two years.

Training Needs

After an organization has made a major change, it is often necessary to train employees. For example, if an organization changes to a new computer system, all employees working with computers will need to be trained in the use of the new system. Likewise, if an organization is changing to a self-directed team environment, employees will need to be trained in such areas as goal setting, teamwork, presentation skills, and quality analysis.

To apply what you have learned about acceptance of change, complete Exercise 14.2 in your workbook.

Organizational Culture

Organizational culture
The shared values, beliefs, and traditions that exist among individuals in an organization.

Another important consideration in organizational change is organizational culture. Often referred to as *corporate culture* or corporate climate, **organizational culture** comprises the shared values, beliefs, and traditions that exist among individuals in organizations (Schein, 2010; Weber, 1996). It is this culture that establishes workplace norms of appropriate behavior (what's wrong or right) and defines roles and expectations that employees and management have of each other (Nwachukwu & Vitell, 1997; Sackman, 1991). Most cultures have a subculture. For example, the environment in which you were raised is a subculture of a bigger culture, the American culture.

In organizations, each department or office can be a subculture with norms of behaviors that may be different from those of the overall organization. How each department reacts to change is a result of that subculture. Most major changes, such as changing management philosophies, will require a cultural and a subcultural change to support the implementation of new ideas throughout the entire organization. This is discussed in more detail later in this section.

Think of your university as an organization with its own culture and your classroom as a subculture. Your university probably has created a culture of honesty and trust in which each student is expected to adhere to honor codes. To enforce or maintain that culture, it uses sanctions such as taking you before the Judicial Board if you are caught cheating or violating some other rule.

From the first day of class, norms such as good attendance and participation in class have been established, creating a subculture. These norms were probably established by rules that your professor orally communicated or that were written in your class syllabus. If you know that the classroom culture is one where you may be expected to discuss your reading material, you are more likely to read your text each week prior to class. Your professor may use certain rewards (such as giving points for classroom participation) or sanctions (such as taking off points) to maintain the culture. Eventually, this culture, which includes the expectations of the professor, gets communicated to other students, who at that point decide whether or not they want to be members of that culture. In other words, if the class and expectations are too hard, the students will sign up for a different class with a more compatible culture.

Culture and norms also result from observing, or modeling, the behaviors of others. Just like your individual personal cultures, which contained role models such as your parents, clergy, and friends who significantly influenced you over the years, organizational culture also has role models who influence your work behavior and teach you norms (Nwachukwu & Vitell, 1997; Weber, 1996). Going back to the classroom example, if you observe your professor coming in late every class or several of your classmates consistently arriving late or leaving early without negative consequences, this may begin to create a culture of irresponsibility or unaccountability. You may eventually become one of those students with poor attendance because this has become the accepted "norm." To transform that culture into one of accountability and responsibility, the leader (your professor) needs to model appropriate behavior and to use some strategy (such as taking off points for tardiness) to maintain the better culture.

As you can see, organizational culture can aid employees in behaving optimally. However, it can also be a contributing factor in many undesirable behaviors such as unethical decision making. For example, if an organization's top management consistently engages in unethical behaviors and decision making, it is likely that its employees will learn those norms and incorporate them into their own professional value system and behave accordingly (Chen, Sawyers, & Williams, 1997). To change that behavior, the cultural norms that hinder change must be eliminated (e.g., unethical supervisors, positive consequences of unethical behavior such as financial rewards) (Van Slyke, 1996).

As important as it is, organizational culture has traditionally been ignored during restructuring and other changes. This is either because there is a general belief that culture can't be changed or because many organizations do not know how to change their cultures. In fact, in a survey of 500 corporations, 70% stated that they did not have the knowledge to address cultural issues (Sherriton & Stern, 1997). Without such knowledge, changes in the way the company operates, and thus, the way its employees behave, will not be long lasting. Consequently, it is important that an organization knows how to include culture in its change process.

Changing Culture

Making organizational changes doesn't necessarily mean that everything about the existing culture must change. According to one manager, "The change process includes holding on to the successful elements of the present culture and adding new elements that are important" (Laabs, 1996, p. 56). Consequently, the first step in changing culture is assessing the desired culture and comparing it with the existing one to determine what needs to change. Two additional steps are creating dissatisfaction with the current culture to create support for the new one and maintaining the new culture.

Assessing the New Culture

Assessment of the new culture involves a great deal of discussion and analysis and should include the following steps (Sherriton & Stern, 1997).

Step 1: Needs Assessment. Because parts of the existing culture may actually support certain organizational changes, the current culture must be analyzed and compared with the desired culture to determine what might need to change. For example, if an organization wants to move from a traditional hierarchical management philosophy to a more empowering one where employees share more decision-making responsibilities, there will have to be a change in systems, procedures, and policies to fully support the new culture. Areas such as role expectations, job descriptions identifying the new decision-making responsibilities, accountability, rewards, and employee selection systems must be reviewed. Data for an analysis are usually collected through observations, review of existing documentation, and employee interviews and surveys consisting of questions that ask for potential recommendations of changes.

I work at a Virginia Community Services Board. This agency is one of 40 in Virginia whose purpose is to plan and operate community-based services dealing with mental health, mental retardation, and substance abuse. We have a staff of approximately 270, including both full-time and part-time workers. The human resources department was formed in 1988. Since that time, the agency has grown to its current staffing level of about 270. The department has grown to three employees, two human resources assistants, and myself.

Our department is committed to being employee focused. Our mission is to ask ourselves daily: "What can we do to make this a better workplace for the employees of the agency?" This mission is in line with the agency's philosophy of being person centered.

Our department stays quite busy. I conduct both orientations and exit interviews for employees. They see me both coming and going! I am also responsible for developing and administering the fringe benefits, and this involves frequent contact with insurance companies. In addition, I am available to assist and advise the executive director and supervisors on personnel-related matters to ensure compliance with employment law. I also oversee the maintenance of personnel records and files to ensure compliance with licensure requirements.

My most important responsibility is providing a safe place for employees to vent. This has been particularly useful over the last several years. In recent years, our agency has gone through a major reorganization. As with any reorganization, regardless of the magnitude, the stress level of employees increased. I provided empathy and guidance to them to help them through this trying time. Their stress levels increased mainly from the *thought* of the change, as opposed to the change itself. In other words, they feared the unknown. To address the many concerns and questions of employees, we implemented a communications team that provided a positive link for and between employees and a source for answers to rumors and fears.

We involved employees in this reorganization from the beginning. We believed that their insight and input were essential factors for a successful reorganization. Focus groups, involving all levels of employees, were formed a year prior to the implementation of changes. From the

Susan Hurst, SPHR

Human Resources Manager, New River Valley Community Services Board

Courtesy of the author

focus groups, action steps were developed and explained to everyone so that they could see what still needed to be done. The transition to the reorganization was a slow, difficult, but beneficial process. Even after we were "officially" reorganized, there was fine-tuning of the process.

Team development was a core concept for the reorganization. This process began several years ago with the development of facility teams at seven of our locations. Training was provided to all employees involved regarding their roles and responsibilities on their teams. In addition, we reviewed some effective communication and conflict skills they could use.

There continue to be some adjustment issues for both administrators and employees regarding these changes. For example, the employees on the facility teams have new responsibility for specific areas of the operation of the facility to ensure the continuity of not only the quality of services but a clean and safe work environment. These teams are also responsible for a portion of their facility's budget. This level of responsibility and decision making is new, and we have had to help these employees develop skills in this area. For example, we had to teach them not only how to read a budget but how to manage and understand one.

As the agency moves more into the team concept, I will continue to find more creative ways to support the employees and help them make successful changes. I am constantly striving to provide the best services and support to our hardworking, dedicated staff. My goal is to anticipate the changing needs and to be proactive in establishing programs and plans to meet these needs, such as training programs and other methods of employee development.

For those students considering a professional career in human resources, I would offer this advice. You need to be an agent of change. Change is inevitable, but scary. The pulse of the agency is often taken through the human resources department, and if you have successfully created an atmosphere where staff feel comfortable in contacting the department to express concerns, you will be able to, as much as possible, calm their fears and model a positive attitude. Keep smiling; it's all good!

Step 2: Determining Executive Direction. Management must then analyze the needs assessment to determine the decisions or actions that will reinforce the culture and to assess the feasibility of certain changes. Using the previous example, if most of the supervisors and managers in an organization are unwilling to share their decision-making authority, a true "empowering" culture cannot be maintained. Consequently, that may be a change that will not be reinforced by the culture. In fact, according to research, it takes the wholehearted support of top management to implement an empowering philosophy (Schuster et al., 1997). Addressing possible obstacles to culture change during the transformation process can usually minimize unintended consequences (Gilmore, Shea, & Useem, 1997).

Step 3: Implementation Considerations. This area addresses how the new culture will be implemented. Will committees or ad hoc groups be set up to carry out changes or will management execute the changes? If the organization's desired culture includes encouragement of more input by employees, they should be allowed to participate in implementing the empowering organization in order to support the new culture.

Step 4: Training. Culture change means a change of philosophy, and that ultimately means different role expectations. As with any new skill, all organizational members must be trained in a new philosophy for the new culture to thrive and be long lasting. This has often been the biggest barrier in organizations that have declared that their members are now empowered to share in decisions. Employees, both management and lower level, are typically not trained in what that means. As explained later in this chapter, management and employees have different interpretations of what empowerment culture means and how to carry it out. Training can reduce such ambiguity and confusion.

Step 5: Evaluation of the New Culture. As with any changes, an evaluation mechanism must be established to review the new culture. Issues such as whether the change actually has occurred or whether old norms and procedures still exist should be addressed. If change has not occurred, additional strategies must be identified to establish and support the new culture.

Now that the ideal culture has been determined, the next step is implementing it. This is done by creating dissatisfaction with the existing culture (Van Slyke, 1997).

Creating Dissatisfaction with Existing Culture

Just as creating dissatisfaction with the status quo in general is necessary to promote change, for employees to accept a new culture, the existing culture and status quo must be "upset." This might mean communicating to employees the future impact of continuing to "do business as usual." For example, many organizations share data that show technological trends and the financial performance of the company. If employees see this information as negatively affecting either them or the organization as a whole, this can create the necessary displeasure with the status quo and be the catalyst for developing a new business strategy.

Another way to create dissatisfaction is to distribute attitude surveys that ask people how satisfied they are with the organization's goal and to suggest ideas for changes. The results of the survey are distributed throughout the organization so that people can see the dissatisfaction level and will begin to buy into a new culture and other organizational changes.

The key at this point is to seek input from employees in the process. A successful cultural transformation requires commitment from all levels of the organization. When employees have an opportunity to be an actual part of the change, they are more likely to be committed to it (Van Slyke, 1996). Once you have started the process of transformation, it is important that it be maintained.

Maintaining the New Culture

If the new culture is expected to last, developing new reward systems and selection methods should occur. Rewarding current employees for successfully participating and cooperating with the new system is imperative (Kotter & Cohen, 2002). These rewards can include pay for performance in jobs that have increased responsibilities due to the new culture or other changes. But they also go beyond financial rewards, and can include employee recognition and meaningful work.

Selection of Employees

Future employees should be selected on the basis of how well they epitomize the new culture. For example, if the new culture is one of team decision making, new employees should have not only the ability but the willingness and personality to perform in such an environment. As current employees are replaced by new ones, the new culture can become "frozen" into the desired system selected by the leadership (Lewin, 1951). However, continuing to hire employees who prefer a more structured management philosophy and who work better alone will eventually cause the organization to revert to its old culture.

Organizational socialization The process whereby new employees learn the behaviors and attitudes they need to be successful in an organization.

Finally, the socialization process of new employees must reinforce the new culture. **Organizational socialization** is the process whereby new employees learn the behaviors and attitudes they need to be successful in the organization. It also helps any newcomer to the organization define his role and what is expected of him in his position (Morrison, 1993). Both informal and formal strategies can help with this process. Informal strategies of socialization include such things as hearing the same stories repeated by several different employees. For example, you have probably listened to people in the workforce talk about getting the best stories by hanging around the water cooler or the copier. Usually stories about some "bad decision" are discussed. New employees who hear stories consistently repeated will get an understanding of the type of culture the organization has. If the discussions are negative, the new employee will begin to believe that the organization is incompetent, mistreats its employees, or is unethical.

Rituals Procedures in which employees participate to become "one of the gang."

There are also formal ways in which organizations can influence the socialization process. One way is through establishing rituals. **Rituals** are procedures in which employees participate to become "one of the gang." Activities such as annual awards, banquets, or staff picnics are rituals that reinforce the impression of a "caring" organization. Another ritual is requiring all new employees to go through a probationary period before being considered a permanent employee.

Symbols Organizational behaviors or practices that convey messages to employees.

Finally, symbols that represent certain attitudes of the organization can be used. **Symbols** are communication tools that convey certain messages to employees. For example, establishment of an on-site wellness center conveys the organization's interest in health. In addition, communication techniques such as the use of mission and value statements can help acculturate the new person to his environment.

To apply what you have learned about organizational culture, complete Exercise 14.3 in your workbook.

Empowerment

As discussed in Chapter 10, many employees are more satisfied with their jobs if they feel they have some control over what they do. As a result, many organizations are "empowering" employees to participate in and make decisions. As you will see in the following pages, empowering employees can range from asking them for their opinions to giving them complete decision-making control. However, before discussing ways to empower employees—which I will refer to as ways to increase "levels of employee input"—it might be best to first discuss why and when employees should be involved in decision making.

Making the Decision to Empower

Factors in Making the Decision to Empower

Employees need to be involved in decisions in circumstances in which the quality of the decision is important, the decision affects employees, the supervisor doesn't have the knowledge to make the decision, or the employees don't trust the supervisor. As shown in Figure 14.1, Vroom and Yetton (1973) have developed a flowchart to help determine when employees should be involved in making decisions. The flowchart uses the seven factors discussed next.

Importance of Decision Quality. The first factor to be considered in making a decision is whether one decision will be better than another. For example, if a supervisor is trying to decide whether to sign a letter with blue ink or black ink, his decision probably will not make any difference to the organization. Thus, the importance of the decision quality is low, and little time or effort should be spent making it.

Leader Knowledge of the Problem Area. The second factor in decision making involves the extent to which leaders have sufficient information to make the decision alone. If they do, then consultation with others is desired only if leaders want their subordinates to feel involved. If leaders lack sufficient knowledge to make a decision, consultation is essential. For example, it would be difficult for managers to select a benefit package without first asking their employees about the types of benefits they need.

Structure of the Problem. The third factor of concern in decision making is the extent to which a leader knows what information is needed and how it can be obtained—that is, the problem's structure. If the leader does not know how to obtain this information, the decision-making process will require other people, and the decision will take longer to reach.

Importance of Decision Acceptance. The fourth decision-making factor involves the degree to which it is important that the decision be accepted by others. For example, for a supervisor to decide what hours each employee will work, it is important that the employees agree with and have input into the decision-making process. However, if the supervisor is deciding what he wants for lunch, whether others agree with or have input into the decision is not important (unless, of course, the choices involve onions or garlic).

Probability of Decision Acceptance. The fifth decision-making factor is subordinate acceptance. If the leader feels that he can make the decision himself but that acceptance of the decision is important, he must determine whether his subordinates will accept it. If the leader is popular and viewed as being competent, his subordinates will probably accept and follow the decision. But if the leader is not popular, powerful, and competent, he will probably want help from his subordinates and colleagues in making the decision, even though he has the ability to make the decision himself. This is why

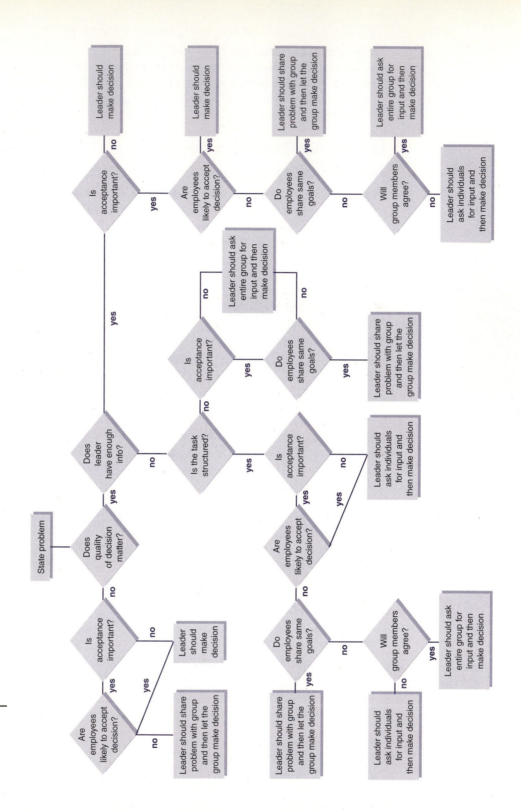

Figure 14.1

The Vroom-Yetton Decision-Making Flowchart

leaders often ask subordinates and colleagues for their opinions. The leader may already know what he will decide, but gaining the support of others by eliciting opinions and comments increases the chances that they will accept his decision when he announces it.

A colleague told me a story that provides an example of the importance of considering the need for subordinate acceptance. At her university, the graduate college changed the way in which it administered and awarded graduate assistantships. The assistant dean was placed in charge of developing and implementing the new system. A week prior to the end of school, the new system was announced, and the graduate faculty went crazy. The awarding of the assistantships came too late to recruit students, the new application forms did not provide the information needed by departments to make decisions, and the deadlines for paperwork were convenient for the graduate college but not for the students or the departments.

What went wrong? If we look at the Vroom-Yetton model, two problems stand out. First, the assistant dean did not have the information necessary to make the decision. She had never taught a class, been a graduate student, or been involved in the financial aid process. In spite of this lack of experience and information, she chose not to consult any of the stakeholders (e.g., faculty, department chairs, graduate students) who would be affected by the decisions. Second, although acceptance of her decision was certainly important, she made no attempt to communicate the reasons for her decisions or to work with the departments to increase acceptance. Furthermore, the staff at the graduate college was viewed by faculty as being incompetent, not trustworthy, and making decisions beneficial to the dean's career but not always in the best interest of the students, faculty, or university as a whole.

Subordinate Trust and Motivation. The sixth factor in the decision-making process is the extent to which subordinates are motivated to achieve the organizational goals and thus can be trusted to make decisions that will help the organization. For example, suppose a marketing survey indicates that a bank will attract more customers if it is open on Saturdays. If the branch manager allows his employees to decide whether the branch should be open on Saturdays, can he trust the employees to make the decision on the basis of what is best for the bank and its customers rather than what is best for the employees? If the answer is no, the branch manager will need to make the unpopular decision after receiving input from his subordinates.

Probability of Subordinate Conflict. The final factor for our consideration in the decision-making process involves the amount of conflict that is likely among the subordinates when various solutions to the problem are considered. If there are many possible solutions and the employees are likely to disagree about which is best, the leader will be best served by gathering information from employees and then, as in the previous situation, making the decision herself.

Decision-Making Strategies Using the Vroom-Yetton Model

Answering the questions in the flowchart shown in Figure 14.1 will lead to one of five possible decision-making strategies: Autocratic I, Autocratic II, Consultative I, Consultative II, or Group I.

With the **Autocratic I strategy** leaders use the available information to make the decision without consulting their subordinates. This is an effective strategy when the leader has the necessary information and when acceptance by the group either is not important or is likely to occur regardless of the decision.

Autocratic II strategy
Leaders obtain necessary information from their subordinates and then make their own decision.

Consultative I strategy
Leaders share the problem on an individual basis with their subordinates and then make a decision that may or may not be consistent with the thinking of the group.

Consultative II strategy
Leaders share the problem with the group as a whole and then make a decision that may or may not be consistent with the thinking of the group.

Group I strategy Leaders share the problem with the group and let the group reach a decision or solution.

With the **Autocratic II strategy**, leaders obtain the necessary information from their subordinates and then make their own decisions. The leader may or may not tell the subordinates about the nature of the problem. The purpose of this strategy is for leaders to obtain information they need to make a decision even though acceptance of the solution by the group is not important.

Leaders using the **Consultative I strategy** share the problem on an individual basis with some or all of their subordinates. After receiving their input, the leader makes a decision that may or may not be consistent with the thinking of the group. This strategy is especially useful in situations in which it is important for the group to accept the decision but in which the group members may not agree regarding the best decision.

Leaders using the **Consultative II strategy** share the problems with their subordinates as a group. After receiving the group's input, the leader makes a decision that may or may not be acceptable to the group. The main difference between this strategy and the Consultative I strategy is that with Consultative II the entire group is involved, whereas in Consultative I only a few employees are asked to provide input. This strategy is used when acceptance of the decision by the group is important and when the individual group members are likely to agree with one another about the best solution.

With the **Group I strategy**, the leader shares the problem with the group and lets the group reach a solution. The role of the leader is merely to assist in the decision-making process. This strategy is effective when group acceptance of the decision is important and when the group can be trusted to arrive at a decision that is consistent with the goals of the organization.

Although relatively little research has been conducted on the Vroom-Yetton model, the results of a few studies have been encouraging. For example, Field and House (1990) and Jago and Vroom (1977) found that managers who used the decision-making strategy recommended by the model made better-quality decisions than managers who used decision-making strategies that the model would not have recommended. Similar results were found by Brown and Finstuen (1993) with military officers and Paul and Ebadi (1989) with sales managers.

To practice using the Vroom-Yetton model, complete Exercise 14.4 in your workbook.

Levels of Employee Input

When employers talk about "empowering" employees, they seldom intend to let employees make all of the decisions affecting an organization. Instead, they most often want to give employees "more say" in day-to-day activities. Unfortunately, when employees are told that they are being "empowered," they often apply a different meaning to the word than that intended by the employer. In fact, one organization that went through a change spent two full meetings with employees to hash out what *empowerment* should and would mean in that organization! Thus, it might be useful to set aside the word *empowerment* and talk instead of levels of employee input and control. Let me provide two examples of why *levels of input* might be a better choice of term than *empowerment*.

Several years ago, I was hired by a large poultry company to help them design a system to empower their employees. In such situations, my first question is always, "Why do you want to empower your employees?" In this case, the response was that they were implementing a total quality management (TQM) system and were at the stage in which they were supposed to empower employees. In other words, the organization was making a change because the managers thought they were "supposed to do it" rather than because something was actually going wrong. When I asked them if they wanted to actually "empower" their employees to make most of the decisions about their jobs, the company responded that it did not. When I asked what they meant by *empower*, their response was that they were not sure. I conducted a training workshop in which I discussed the concept of empowerment and the levels of employee input examined in the following paragraphs. At the end of the workshop, I told them to discuss what they had just learned and make a decision about what level of employee input they wanted their employees to have. It took just a short time for the managers to reach consensus that they wanted their employees at the advisory level, that their employees already had one of the best suggestion/advisory systems in the nation, and that there was no real need to change. In other words, the organization was already "empowering" its employees at the optimal level for that particular industry.

The second example comes from a university setting in which a new president appointed a number of committees to study such issues as summer school and student recruitment, and "empowered" these committees to make changes to improve the current system. The committees worked diligently for several months and then presented their new systems to the president. After a week of consideration, the president thanked the committees and told them that he appreciated their hard work but had decided not to follow any of their recommendations. The committee members were shocked at this response, because, to them, being told they were "empowered" meant that their decisions were final and thus would become the new policy. The president responded by saying that he had empowered them to "study" the issues and make "recommendations." His intent had never been to allow a committee to make a final decision.

As these two examples demonstrate, *empowerment* means many things to many people. As shown in Figure 14.2, there are five main levels of employee input and control.

Following

Employees at the *following* level have no real control over their jobs. They are given instructions about what to do, when to do it, and how it should be done. Furthermore, their work is often checked by other employees (e.g., quality control) or by their supervisor. Employees at this level can be those who are new or inexperienced to the work being performed or those with weak decision-making skills.

Ownership of Own Product

At this level, employees are still told what to do but are solely responsible for the quality of their output. For example, an employee working on an assembly line would follow a set of procedures in assembling a product but would decide whether the quality of the assembled product was good enough. Likewise, a secretary might type a report the way it was submitted by his boss but would be responsible for ensuring that there were no typographical errors.

In essence, this level removes what psychologist Rick Jacobs (1997) calls "redundant systems." With a redundant human system, every person's work is checked by another person. In some organizations, a single piece of work might even be checked by several different people. The logic behind redundant systems is that with more than one person checking quality, there is less chance of a poor-quality product

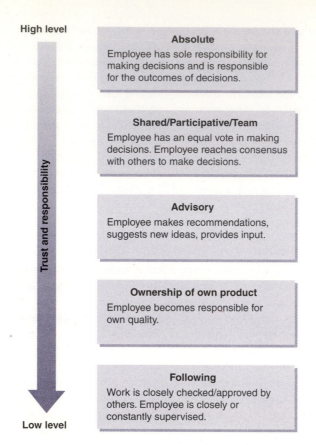

High level

Trust and responsibility

Absolute
Employee has sole responsibility for making decisions and is responsible for the outcomes of decisions.

Shared/Participative/Team
Employee has an equal vote in making decisions. Employee reaches consensus with others to make decisions.

Advisory
Employee makes recommendations, suggests new ideas, provides input.

Ownership of own product
Employee becomes responsible for own quality.

Following
Work is closely checked/approved by others. Employee is closely or constantly supervised.

Low level

Figure 14.2

Levels of Employee Input

reaching a consumer. Furthermore, in many cases, an employee might not have the skill level necessary to check her own work. For example, a secretary might well be an excellent typist but might not have the grammatical skills to know whether her memos contain mistakes. Even if she did have the skills, we have all missed typos because we knew what we wanted to say and thus proofread a sentence the way we meant to say it rather than the way we actually wrote it.

Though redundant systems make sense in many cases, they do have their drawbacks. The most relevant of these to this chapter is that satisfaction, motivation, and performance are often lessened when others check our work. Let me provide you with a prime example. At my university, graduate students must submit a program of studies covering the courses they intend to take during their two years in graduate school. The student completes the program form, signs it, and then gets his advisor to sign it. The advisor must then get his department chair to sign the form, and the department chair must then get the graduate dean to sign the form. Now keep in mind that because 11 of our 12 classes are required and thus standard for all industrial/organizational (I/O) psychology graduate students, theoretically there should be little room for error in choosing courses. However, as an advisor, I often see mistakes made by my students, who then tell me that they didn't bother to read the catalog because they figured that I would catch their mistakes. The problem is that I seldom read the forms because I figure that if there are any mistakes, my department chair will catch them. She never reads the forms because she figures that the dean will catch them. Thus, the very redundant system designed to prevent errors is actually the cause of errors!

As one can imagine, making employees responsible for their own output does a number of things. It motivates employees to check their work more carefully, provides them with a sense of "ownership" in their product, and provides a greater sense of autonomy and independence. In the former Saturn division of General Motors, employees received feedback on problems that drivers encountered with the cars assembled by a particular group of employees. This feedback helped employees gauge their quality control efforts, and it affected the size of their bonus.

Advisory

At the advisory level, employees are asked to provide feedback, suggestions, and input into a variety of organizational concerns. The key at this level is that there is no guarantee that an organization will follow the advice given by the employees; the only guarantee is that the organization will seriously consider the advice.

The idea behind this level is that employees often have the best knowledge about their jobs, so getting their input makes good business sense. As previously discussed, though employees often have the knowledge to make a decision, they are placed at an advisory level because they may not have the "motivation" to make the best decision. In such situations, an organization will ask employees for their opinions and preferences to better understand the employees' positions but will reserve the right to make the actual decision.

Shared/Participative/Team

The fourth level of employee input and control allows an employee to make a decision. However, this decision is made at a group level. For example, an organization might put a team together to find better ways to market its projects or to determine what type of benefits package employees will receive. This level differs from the previous level (advisory) in that only in very rare circumstances will the team's decision *not* be implemented. At this level, employees must not only be well trained in decision making but also be willing to take on the responsibility of making decisions.

Absolute

The final level of employee input and control gives an employee the absolute authority to make a decision on his own—no group consensus, no supervisory approval. It is important to point out, however, that he is also responsible for the consequences of that decision. So if he makes the wrong decision, he may be reprimanded or fired. Because of these potential consequences, many employees are leery about being given absolute power. Thus, it is important in many circumstances to remove the potential for a negative sanction.

For example, Holiday Inn has empowered each of its employees to take any reasonable means necessary to satisfy a customer. This decision was made so that an unhappy guest can have his problem solved immediately rather than passed on to a manager. So if a guest complains to a housekeeper that there were not enough towels in his room, the housekeeper is empowered to deal with the situation. The housekeeper might opt to apologize, or she might opt to take $25 off the night's stay. Let's imagine that a particular housekeeper "comps" ("compensates," or gives for free) a night's lodging for each of 10 people who complained about not having enough towels. The manager thinks that this decision was excessive and fires the housekeeper. What effect will the firing have on future employee decisions?

When employees are empowered to make decisions, they must first receive some training in how to make them. Rather than punishing an employee who makes a bad decision, it is better for the organization to discuss with the employee what might have been a better decision and to explain why the employee's decision was improper. Without such training and coaching, employees are not likely to enthusiastically accept their newly empowered status, especially if their new level of authority is not accompanied by an increase in pay.

Empowerment Charts

Empowerment chart A chart made for each employee that shows what level of input the employee has for each task.

Organizations never have just one level of employee input and control that applies to every employee. Instead, levels will differ by employee as well as by task. For example, a bank teller might be placed at the *absolute* level to decide when she will take her breaks, at the *advisory* level when it comes to hiring new employees, and at the *following* level when it comes to waiving check fees. To reduce confusion, it is a good idea for organizations to develop what I call individual employee **empowerment charts**. An example of such a chart is shown in Figure 14.3.

In the chart, notice that for each task, a range of control/input is allowed. For example, the task of opening new accounts can be performed at the *following, ownership,* or *advisory* level. Our new employee, Jane (J), is at the *following* level, whereas our experienced teller, Emily (E), is at the *advisory* level. In most organizations, a new employee would most likely be placed at the *following* level until she has demonstrated mastery in performing the task. Individual employee empowerment charts reduce confusion and provide a systematic plan for providing employees with more autonomy as their skills and experience increase.

Job Component	Following	Ownership	Advisory	Participative	Absolute
Job-Related Tasks					
Opening new accounts	[----J--E----]				
Approving loans	[----J--E----]				
Waiving check fees	[----J---E----]				
Scheduling Issues					
Taking breaks	[---J-E--------------]				
Taking vacations	[---J-E--------------]				
Scheduling hours	[---J-E----]				
Personnel Issues					
Hiring new staff			[-----E----]		
Innovation Issues					
Changing procedures/methods			[-----E----]		
Developing new products			[-----E----]		

J = Jane, E = Emily

Figure 14.3

Example of an Employee Empowerment Chart

Table 14.1 Consequences to Empowerment

Personal

1. Increased job satisfaction for most

2. Stress

    a. Decreased stress due to greater control

    b. Increased stress due to greater responsibility

Financial

1. Bonuses

2. Pay increases

Career

1. Increased job security

2. Promotions

3. Increased marketability

4. Increased chance of being terminated

Consequences of Empowerment

As shown in Table 14.1, being at a higher level of control/input has many positive aspects. For example, research indicates that increased empowerment typically results in increased job satisfaction for employees in the United States, Mexico, and Poland but not for employees in India (Robert, Probst, Martocchio, Drasgow, & Lawler, 2000). The increased responsibility can result in higher skill levels, which in turn can result in higher pay, increased job security, and increased potential to find other employment. However, empowerment can have its downside. With increased responsibility comes increased stress. With the power to make decisions comes the risk of making bad ones and thus being fired or denied a promotion. Thus, it is not surprising that some employees resist efforts to empower them or their teams (Maynard, Mathieu, Marsh, & Ruddy, 2007).

One of the things that is true throughout life is that people are different, and not everything affects everyone the same way. For example, imagine that we place all of the employees in a fast-food restaurant at the *absolute* level in making decisions such as when to comp drinks or a meal if the service is slow or the food is bad or when to allow customers to make substitutions. For many of these employees, this authority will be welcome, as it reduces the time taken to get permission from a supervisor and provides them with a sense of power. However, for some employees, the increased stress of making acceptable decisions far outweighs any feelings of so-called empowerment.

Flexible Work Arrangements

A popular organization development intervention is to provide employees with flexibility in the hours they work. As shown in Table 14.2, such flexibility might involve the number of hours worked, the times in which the hours are worked, or where the

Table 14.2 Flexible Work Schedules Can Lead to Positive Outcomes Under the Right Conditions

Flexible Work Arrangements		Positive Outcomes		The Employee Wants Flexibility
Flextime				
Compressed Workweeks		Lower Absenteeism		
Reduced Hours		Lower Turnover		Management is supportive
Part-Time work	**Result In**	Higher Productivity	**If**	The job itself allows for flexibility
Peak-Time pay		Higher Job Satisfaction		
Casual Work		Better Work-Life Balance		
Job Sharing		Lower Commuting Costs		
Work from Home				

work itself is performed. Employers who allow flexible work arrangements generally see such positive outcomes as lower absenteeism and turnover, higher productivity, and more highly satisfied employees (Baltes, Briggs, Huff, Wright, & Neuman, 1999; Estes, 1990). In addition, the employees themselves benefit by having a better work-life balance and lower commuting costs.

Interventions involving flexible work arrangements typically follow one of four strategies: Full-time work with the employee selecting the actual work hours, full-time work compressed into fewer than five days, part-time work, and full- or part-time work from home.

Strategy 1: Full-Time Work, Flexible Hours

Flextime A work schedule that allows employees to choose their own work hours.

To accommodate the family lives and personal preferences of employees, 53% of U.S. organizations provide **flextime**, a work schedule in which employees have some flexibility in the hours they work (SHRM, 2011). In the United Kingdom, employees with children under 6 or a disabled child under the age of 18 have the legal right to request flexible work hours and the organization must seriously consider the request. In 2004, 14% of UK employees requested flexible hours and 81% of these requests were granted (Holt & Grainger, 2005). Though family issues typically drive the use of flextime today, flextime actually originated in West Germany as a way to alleviate traffic problems by staggering the hours people worked. The plan then spread to North America, where it was used first in Canada and then in the United States in the mid-1970s.

With flextime, employees are given greater control over the hours they work. It is believed that this increase in control and flexibility has many advantages for employees. First, an employee can take care of personal tasks such as going to the doctor, picking up children from school, and even sleeping in after a rough night. Furthermore, this increased control should enrich the employee's job, thus theoretically resulting in increased job satisfaction (see Chapter 10).

Bandwidth The total number of potential work hours available each day.

Flextime can be arranged in many ways, but all share the same three basic components: *bandwidth, core hours,* and *flexible hours.* As shown in Table 14.3, the **bandwidth** is the total number of potential hours available for work each day. For example, employees can work their eight hours anytime in the 12-hour bandwidth between 6:00 a.m. and 6:00 p.m. PRO Group, a marketing company in Denver, has a

Table 14.3   Diagram of a Bank's Flextime Program

Hours												
Flex					Core			Flex			Core	
6	7	8	9	10	11	12	1	2	3	4	5	6

A.M.   P.M.

12-Hour Bandwidth

Core hours The hours in a flextime schedule during which every employee must work.

Flexible hours The part of a flextime schedule in which employees may choose which hours to work.

Gliding time A flextime schedule in which employees can choose their own hours without any advance notice or scheduling.

Flexitour A flextime schedule in which employees have flexibility in scheduling but must schedule their work hours at least a week in advance.

Modified flexitour A flextime schedule in which employees have flexibility in scheduling but must schedule their work hours a day in advance.

10-hour bandwidth, in which employees can choose to start the day at either 6:30 a.m. or 7:30 a.m. and finish at 3:30 p.m. or 4:30 p.m. These 10-hour bands are the most common (used by 45% of organizations), followed by 12-hour bands (Clark, 2001).

Core hours are those that everyone must work and typically consist of the hours during which an organization is busiest with its outside contacts. For example, a restaurant might have core hours between 11:00 a.m. and 1:00 p.m. to cover its lunchtime business, whereas a bank might have core hours from 12:00 noon to 1:00 p.m. and from 5:00 p.m. to 6:00 p.m. to cover the periods of highest customer volume. In the example from PRO Group given above, the core hours would be between 7:30 a.m. and 3:30 p.m.

Finally, **flexible hours** are those that remain in the bandwidth and in which the employee has a choice of working. For example, if the bandwidth is the 12-hour period from 6:00 a.m. to 6:00 p.m. and the core hours are from 11:00 a.m. to 1:00 a.m., then the employee can schedule the remaining 6 hours (including lunch hour) anywhere from 6:00 a.m. to 10:00 a.m. and from 2:00 p.m. to 6:00 p.m. The actual degree to which these hours are truly flexible depends on the specific flextime program used by the organization.

The most flexible of these schedules is called **gliding time**. With this system, an employee can choose her own hours without advance notice or scheduling. Employees can come and go as they please as long as they work 8 hours each day and 40 hours each week. With gliding time, there are no core hours. For example, at 5W Public Relations in New York, employees can work their hours anytime between 7:00 a.m. and 11:00 p.m. Such a flexible schedule, however, will work only where it is not necessary to always have an employee working, as in typing or accounting. In an organization such as a retail store or a restaurant, such a system would mean that at any given time there might not be *any* employee present—which, of course, is probably not the best way to conduct these types of businesses.

Most flexible working schedules are categorized as **flexitour** or **modified flexitour**, with the employee enjoying greater flexibility in working hours, although the hours must be scheduled in advance. With a flexitour system, the employee must submit a schedule on a weekly, biweekly, or monthly basis, depending on the organization. In a modified flexitour, the employee must schedule her hours in advance but can change these hours on a daily basis with some advance notice.

Flexible working schedules are popular with employees and beneficial to organizations. Many employees opt to start work earlier in the day and come home earlier so that they can beat traffic and spend more time with their children. As mentioned previously, meta-analyses by Estes (1990) and Baltes et al. (1999) found that flextime resulted in less absenteeism, less overtime, higher job satisfaction, less role conflict, and increased productivity.

Interestingly, with employees on flextime often starting work earlier in the day, restaurants such as Burger King and Starbucks have begun opening earlier in the morning to accommodate the early commuters. In urban areas, mass transit systems are also beginning service or seeing peak ridership earlier in the morning (Armour, 2004).

An innovative approach to flextime is the FlexYear option offered by tax firms RSM McGladrey, Inc. and McGladrey & Pullen LLP (Hopke, 2010). Rather than working parts of days, employees approved for FlexYear work certain parts of the year and take the remainder of the year off. Such schedules are common with teachers who often have summers off but are fairly unusual in industry.

Strategy 2: Compressed Workweeks

Compressed workweeks
Work schedules in which 40 hours are worked in less than the traditional 5-day workweek.

Although the vast majority of people still work eight hours a day, five days a week, there is a trend toward working fewer days a week but more hours per day. These deviations from the typical five-day workweek are called **compressed workweeks** and usually involve either 10 hours a day for four days or 12 hours a day for three days.

The first formal use of a compressed workweek was in 1940, when both Mobil Oil and Gulf Oil had their truck drivers work 10 hours a day for four days and then take three days off. The "explosion" in organizations using compressed schedules came in the early 1970s after Riva Poor (1970) published the first book on the topic. In 2011, 35% of organizations surveyed by the Society for Human Resource Management (SHRM) offered compressed workweeks (SHRM, 2011).

The potential advantages of compressed workweeks are obvious from the employees' perspective. They get more vacation days, have more time to spend with their families, have increased opportunities to moonlight, and have reduced commuting costs and times. Furthermore, if parents have different compressed schedules, child-care costs are greatly reduced.

Because it appears obvious that the employee's non-work-related life will improve with a compressed schedule, the important question becomes, "What is the effect of a compressed schedule on an employee's performance at work?" Most people answer that a worker will be more tired, causing more mistakes and accidents.

The research thus far, however, does not support such speculation. Although research generally indicates that workers do feel moderately more fatigued, their work behavior and work attitudes generally *improve* once a compressed weekly work schedule has been adopted. The results of two meta-analyses (Baltes et. al, 1999; Moores, 1990) suggest that compressed schedules generally bring a moderate reduction in absenteeism, a small increase in productivity, a large increase in job satisfaction, and a moderate increase in fatigue. Furthermore, on the basis of data from 3,800 employees in six studies, Moores (1990) concluded that almost 90% of employees who worked compressed schedules were satisfied with them.

Regarding employee health, Williamson, Gower, and Clarke (1994) found that employees who worked 12-hour shifts were healthier than those working 8-hour shifts. There were no differences in productivity or turnover. Duchon, Keran, and Smith (1994) found even more positive results with underground mine workers. Mine workers changing from an 8- to a 12-hour shift reported higher satisfaction, improved sleep, and no negative health or performance changes.

In addition to these empirically verified benefits to employees, an organization that adopts compressed workweeks may realize other advantages. Perhaps the greatest of these is the reduction in start-up and cleanup times associated with many jobs. For example, a printer spends considerable time inking and setting up a press before beginning work. At the end of the day, the printer must also spend time cleaning the press and putting supplies away. If these beginning and ending activities together take an hour, then at least an hour a week can be saved if the printer works four days rather than five. Extended across a year and multiplied by the number of employees in a company, such savings can be substantial.

A word of caution should be made regarding the length of shifts. Though employees seem to suffer few problems with 12-hour shifts, there is probably an upper limit in shift length. For example, Knauth, Keller, Schindele, and Totterdell (1995) found a 14-hour shift for firefighters to be too long.

To help reduce fatigue associated with long working hours, most organizations provide 20 to 40 minutes of paid breaks during the workday. Research suggests that providing four 9-minute breaks is superior to two 15-minute breaks or twelve 3-minute breaks (Dababneh, Swanson, & Shell, 2001). Interestingly, in a 2008 survey by the National Sleep Foundation, 34% of employees said that their employer allows them to take a nap during work breaks and 16% said that their employer actually gave them a place to nap. For example, Google provides "napping pods" that its employees can use, and Arizona-based technology company Jawa allows its employees to use two napping rooms—one with a napping pod and the other with a couch. Such a practice may be a good idea, because in a study of Italian police, Garbarino (2004) found that properly scheduled naps prior to working the night shift resulted in a 28% reduction in automobile accidents.

A study by Barnes and Wagner (2009) provides another good example of the negative effects related to lack of sleep. On Mondays directly following the change to daylight saving time, there were more workplace injuries than other days. Furthermore, workers reported sleeping 40 minutes less that night than on other nights.

Not surprisingly, lack of sleep lowers performance on many cognitive tasks. A meta-analysis by Lim and Dinges (2010) found that short-term sleep deprivation resulted in lower levels of attention, lower cognitive response times, and decreases in memory.

Strategy 3: Reducing Work Hours

A third strategy to increase worker flexibility is to allow employees to work fewer hours. Though part-time work has been a common practice for many years, two programs—peak-time pay and job-sharing—provide examples of the strategic use of part-time work.

Peak-Time Pay

With *peak-time pay*, certain employees are encouraged to work only part time but are paid at a higher hourly rate for those hours than employees who work full time. Thus, an employee will make more per hour than her full-time counterpart, although she will make less money per day.

The concept of peak-time pay came from the banking and fast-food industries, both of which face unique problems. Both types of organizations need to be open during the entire day, yet have only approximately four hours per day that are busy. For example, a McDonald's restaurant might need 20 employees to cover its lunchtime crowd but need only 5 employees from 2:00 p.m. until 5:00 p.m., at which time the dinner crowd begins for another two-hour peak period. Rather than paying 20 employees to sit around for most of the day, it would be better to have 15 employees work for three hours a day during peak time and only 5 employees work the full eight hours.

Unfortunately, few people want to work only three hours a day at $9.00 an hour. And those who would be willing, such as students, are often not available during the most crucial hours. Thus, with peak-time pay, 15 people may be paid $13 or $14 per hour to work only the three peak hours. Thus, the employee makes a reasonable amount of money per day, and the organization still saves money over what it would have spent had its employees worked the entire eight hours.

Casual work A scheduling practice in which employees work on an irregular or as-needed basis.

A practice related to peak-time pay is **casual work**. With casual work, an employee works on an irregular or as-needed basis. For example, a theme park might higher employees for only three months during the summer or a concert hall might hire security guards and janitors only during the nights there is a concert. Organizations also use casual workers to fill-in for absent employees. Take, for example, a hospital that needs two additional registered nurses (RNs) to work on a given Friday night. It communicates the availability of the two shifts to its casual RN pool. The first two members of the pool that respond are assigned to work the shift. Such an arrangement provides tremendous flexibility to employees and ensures that the employer will always be able to fill its staffing needs with experienced workers. As with peak-time work, casual workers usually receive a higher hourly rate of pay than do their full-time counterparts.

Job Sharing

Job sharing A work schedule in which two employees share one job by splitting the work hours.

Job sharing is offered by 13% of organizations (SHRM, 2011) and involves two employees who share their work hours. Rather than one person working 40 hours each week, two employees combine their hours so that they total 40. At first glance, job sharing may seem to be little more than part-time work. There are, however, big psychological, if not administrative, differences.

First, part-time work usually involves lower-level jobs such as those found in the retail and restaurant industries. But job sharing allows people in such complex occupations as teaching and accounting to enjoy the advantages of fewer work hours.

Second, with part-time work, the performance of one employee rarely affects the performance of another. That is, the work completed by two part-time employees results from two separate jobs. But with job sharing, the work may be done by two different employees who share one job title and one position. Poor-quality work by one employee must be corrected by the other.

From a psychological standpoint, the main difference between job sharing and part-time employment is the level of employee commitment, both to the organization and to the other employee. Job-sharing programs are targeted at employees who have family responsibilities. Thus, an organization can attract a highly qualified employee who would not be able to work full time.

Furthermore, it is not uncommon for husbands and wives in similar professions to share the same position. One such situation recently occurred with a high school teaching position: The wife teaches three morning classes while her husband takes care of their two children; the husband then teaches three afternoon classes while his wife cares for their children.

Strategy 4: Working from Home

Some employees set their own work schedules by working at home rather than at the workplace. Although working at home has recently received increased attention, it is certainly not a new concept. For more than a century, women have sewn garments at home and then sold them to factories for piece-rate prices. Today, with the technology advances, other types of work can also be done in the home. Many types of home work are completed with little or no contact with a central office or factory. With **telecommuting** however, an employee uses a computer to electronically interact with a central office. Other terms commonly used for telecommuting are *telework* and *mobile working*. Telecommuting is ideal for such tasks as computer programming, data entry, and telemarketing. Though there are many estimates of the frequency of telecommuting, in the United States, one survey found that 45% of organizations offer some form of telecommuting (SHRM, 2011). This relatively high percentage is not surprising, as a meta-analysis on telecommuting found that telecommuters have less work-family conflict, better relationships with their supervisor, higher job satisfaction, less role stress, lower intention to turnover, and higher performance levels than their nontelecommuting colleagues (Gajendran & Harrison, 2007).

An increasingly popular concept in telecommuting is the neighborhood "telebusiness center." At these centers, employees from a variety of organizations share office space close to their homes but are connected electronically to their respective organizations.

Working at home has many advantages for both the employee and the employer. For the employee, it offers the opportunity to avoid or minimize child-care and commuting costs, while allowing flexibility and comfort in working conditions. For the employer, money is saved on both office space and utilities.

But with the advantages come certain disadvantages, which is why most unions oppose home work (Brennan, 1994). First, it is difficult for a union to organize workers when they are scattered around many locations. Second, it is difficult for the government to enforce safety and fair treatment standards when employees are not in a central location. Third, employees cannot be easily supervised when they work at home. Finally, it becomes difficult to disassociate work from home life. Unfortunately, the actual evaluation of the merits of telecommuting will have to wait until more research has been conducted. Until then, working at home sounds like a promising idea when used with controls and checks to ensure employee safety and fair treatment.

Telecommuting Working at home rather than at the office by communicating with managers and coworkers via phone, computer, fax machine, and other offsite media.

Downsizing

When organizations restructure, the result is often a decrease in the size of their workforce (Figure 14.4). For example, the discontinuation of the space shuttle program in 2011 resulted in 2,600 fewer jobs at United Space Alliance. Such reductions in force are the result of a variety of factors, including economic difficulties, loss of large contracts, pressure by stockholders for quick profits, mergers, new technology replacing humans, and employee empowerment programs resulting in less need for managers. Interestingly, 81% of downsizing organizations were profitable the year prior to downsizing (Cascio, 1995). Thus, economics is not always the major force driving downsizing. For example, the number of layoffs in 2001 and 2002 rose

Figure 14.4

What's in a Word? No Matter What We Call It, Losing One's Job Is Painful

Laid off	Restructured	Fired
Downsized	Dejobbed	Separated
Rightsized	Terminated	Canned
Wrongsized	Axed	Given the boot
Reengineered	Furloughed	RIFfed (Reduction in Force)

tremendously due primarily to the fallout of the September 11, 2001, terrorist attacks and accounting scandals at such organizations as Enron and WorldCom.

Reducing the Impact of Downsizing

Signs of Problems

Short of a catastrophe, organizations usually have some warning that there may be an impending need to downsize. Steps taken at this stage can greatly reduce the need for, or size of, future downsizing (Cascio, 2002).

A strategy taken by many organizations at this stage is to freeze the hiring of new permanent employees and either not fill vacancies caused by employees leaving or retiring or fill vacancies with **temporary employees** (temps). Typically, these temps are hired through temporary employment agencies such as Kelly, Olsten, Bright Services, or Manpower. The advantage to using a temporary agency is that temps are not considered employees of the company and thus have no expectation of a future with the company. If business declines, the company can cancel its contract with the temporary agency. If business remains at a good level, the temp remains with the company.

If temps are going to stay with the organization for a long time, it is essential that they be treated like other employees. That is, they should be given the proper training, receive incentives for excellent performance, be given the supplies they need to do their jobs, and be invited to participate in informal activities such as going to lunch or attending a wedding shower (Vines, 1997).

A related strategy used by more than 80% of organizations is **outsourcing**—using outside vendors to provide services previously performed internally. For example, many organizations have found that it is more cost-efficient and productive to hire an outside vendor to manage their data-processing system than it is to keep five full-time data-processing employees on their payroll. Commonly outsourced functions include employee assistance/wellness programs, benefits and payroll administration, training, data processing, housekeeping, and landscaping.

Another strategy that can be taken at this stage is to encourage employees to change careers and then help these employees learn the skills needed to make the career change. An excellent example of this strategy, called the Alliance for Employee Development and Growth, was developed in the 1980s as a joint venture between AT&T and its union, the CWA (Communication Workers of America). In the 1980s and 1990s, AT&T realized that it would need to lay off many of its employees. To reduce the number of layoffs, the Alliance was created to encourage employees to look at their future, decide whether they would be happier in another career, and then take steps toward changing careers. To help this change, the Alliance provided current employees with $2,250 per year to take classes or receive training in any

Temporary employees Also called "temps"—employees hired through a temporary employment agency.

Outsourcing The process of having certain organizational functions performed by an outside vendor rather than an employee in the organization.

legitimate career area. Thus, an assembly line worker could receive funding to learn to be a cosmetologist, a paralegal, or a computer programmer. Though the Alliance cost AT&T about $15 million per year, the money was easily recovered in decreased downsizing costs when employees left voluntarily, or increased productivity resulting from a better-trained workforce.

A fourth strategy for reducing the need for layoffs is to offer early retirement packages. The idea here is to make it financially worthwhile for an employee to retire earlier than planned. For example, in 2004, Eastman Chemical Company in Kingsport, Tennessee, offered employees two weeks of severance pay for each year of service with the company. Employees taking advantage of the early retirement option also received extended insurance coverage and outplacement assistance. Though early retirement programs are expensive during the first few years, they can save a tremendous amount of money.

A fifth option to layoffs is to ask employees to take pay cuts or defer salary increases (Dyekman & Susseles, 2003). This strategy is based on the idea that most economic recessions last less than a year. If an organization lays off a significant number of its employees, it can take years to get production back to normal when the economy recovers. To get employees to agree to a pay cut, many organizations offer them company stock worth more than the pay cut. When the economy recovers, the employees are financially better off and the company has employees who are more committed to the success of the organization. As you can imagine, employees aren't keen on being asked to take pay cuts. Over the past few years, the airline industry asked employees to take pay cuts so that the airlines could survive. Though employees at most airlines agreed, the mechanics at Northwest Airlines went on strike rather than take lower pay, and some airline employees who accepted the salary reduction took it out on passengers by displaying a surly attitude.

A final strategy involves adjusting work schedules. Many organizations try to avoid layoffs by restricting overtime, implementing job sharing, encouraging employees to work at home, implementing payless holidays or a shortened workweek, and reducing their employees' pay.

Employees can also reduce the effect of downsizing by monitoring their organization's economic health. According to Beyer, Pike, and McGovern (1993), signs of possible trouble include use of any of the workforce reduction strategies previously mentioned, rumors of corporate acquisitions or mergers, loss of a major contract, and increases in the number of "secret" managerial meetings.

Beyer et al. also advised employees to take stock of their personal standing at work to help determine their vulnerability to being laid off. Here are some important questions employees should ask themselves:

- Have I kept up with the latest changes in technology? Have I changed with the times?
- Have I received excellent performance appraisals? Do I actually make a contribution to the organization? Do I have a lot of downtime in which I do nothing?
- Do I hate my job? Does my dissatisfaction show? Does it affect my performance?
- Am I well liked? Do others, especially my manager, include me in both trivial and important decisions? Have I kept a good enough attitude that it would be emotionally difficult for my boss to get rid of me?

Selecting the Employees to Be Laid Off

Should the above measures not be sufficient and a layoff becomes necessary, the next step is to choose which employees will leave the organization. Criteria used to make this decision might include seniority, performance, salary level, and organizational need. To reduce the chances of legal problems, the committee deciding which employees will leave should be diverse in terms of race, sex, and age (Segal, 2001). The committee's decisions should be analyzed to determine potential adverse impact against protected classes (e.g., race, sex) or intentional discrimination against older workers.

The Announcement

The way in which the layoff is announced can affect the success of future programs designed to help employees. Layoff announcements are best done in person. Some organizations opt for a general announcement, whereas others prefer that supervisors notify their employees on a one-to-one basis. At this time, it is essential that employees receive concrete information. A mistake made by many organizations is to announce a downsizing but not to have answers to the hundreds of employee questions and concerns that are bound to follow. Employees need answers to questions like these:

- Why are the layoffs needed?
- Isn't there any alternative?
- When will the layoffs take place?
- Who will be laid off?
- What type of financial assistance will be available?
- Will we get help writing our résumés?
- How will this affect my pension?

When answers to employees' questions are not available, employees become anxious, angry, and resentful and tend to develop their own answers (rumors).

Outplacement Programs

To help layoff victims move on with their lives, many organizations have some type of outplacement program (Weinberg, Sutherland, & Cooper, 2010). These programs typically include emotional counseling, financial counseling, career assessment and guidance, and job search training.

Emotional Counseling. After receiving word of being laid off, employees go through four stages that are similar to the stages of change: denial, anger, fear, and acceptance. In the **denial stage**, employees deny that a layoff will actually occur. They make statements like "I'm sure the company will come to its senses," "There is no way they will actually lay off a person with my seniority," and "This can't be happening." For some employees, this stage will last a few hours; for others, it can last until the minute they are no longer working. When employees are in the denial stage, they will not participate in the efforts to help them (e.g., help with résumé writing or interview skills) because they don't see a need to participate in something that is not going to happen.

In the **anger stage**, employees realize that they will be losing their jobs, and they become angry at the organization, their supervisors, and even their coworkers, especially those who will not be losing their jobs. At this stage it is important that

Denial The first stage in the emotional reaction to change or layoffs, in which an employee denies that an organizational change or layoff will occur.

Anger stage The second stage of emotional reaction to downsizing, in which employees become angry at the organization.

Fear stage The third emotional stage following the announcement of a layoff, in which employees worry about how they will survive financially.

Acceptance stage The fourth and final stage of emotional reaction to downsizing, in which employees accept that layoffs will occur and are ready to take steps to secure their future.

employees be given an appropriate avenue through which to vent their anger and frustration. It is not uncommon to have "support groups" for layoff victims, and the first few meetings of these groups are usually spent venting.

After the anger has subsided, employees move to the **fear stage**. During this third stage, employees start to worry about how they are going to pay bills, feed their families, and find new jobs. At this stage, the emotional counseling moves from a listening stage to one that is more empathic and soothing.

Though layoff victims remain fearful for much of the layoff period, they eventually move to the **acceptance stage**. At this stage, the victims accept that the layoff will occur and are now ready to take steps to secure their future. It is at this last stage that employees are ready for specific offers of assistance.

Financial Counseling. As layoff victims move through the fear stage into the acceptance stage, financial counseling is needed. They are under tremendous stress as they worry about how to make their rent, mortgage, and loan payments and how to pay for utilities, insurance, food, tuition, and medical and dental costs. Most banks and credit unions have certified financial counselors who are well trained in helping people with these concerns. The financial counseling process should include the issues of severance pay, unemployment insurance, medical insurance, and any special programs that might be available to help the layoff victims.

Career Assessment and Guidance. Though many layoff victims will search for jobs similar to the ones that they left, many will need to consider other careers. Psychologists involved in this process will administer a battery of tests that tap an individual's basic abilities (e.g., math, grammar), transferable skills (e.g., woodworking, typing), career interests, and work values (e.g., status, independence, leadership). In discussing potential careers, consideration must be given to such life realities as financial needs, time constraints (e.g., "I can't take four years to earn a degree"), and geographic constraints (e.g., "I want to stay near my family" or "My spouse has a good job and I can't leave the immediate area"). For employees willing and able to relocate or go back to school, finding a new job is not as difficult as it is for employees who are limited to a particular geographic area and are not able or willing to be retrained.

A major issue that arises during this process is the ability of a layoff victim to obtain new training. Jobs in the twenty-first century require higher levels of skill than did their earlier counterparts. So retraining is often necessary to get a new job. However, barriers such as funding and day-care problems, the lack of relevant training sites, and fear of going back to school can keep layoff victims from getting the new training they so desperately need.

To help layoff victims find new employment, workshops are conducted on such topics as understanding the job market, finding potential job openings, writing résumés, performing well in the employment interview, and making decisions about job offers.

Effects of Downsizing

Victims

Victims Employees who lose their jobs due to a layoff.

Research is clear that there are many negative consequences to losing one's job. From a health perspective, **victims** of downsizing report increases in headaches, stomach upsets, sleeping problems, cholesterol levels, physical illness, hospitalization rates, heart trouble, hypertension, ulcers, vision problems, and shortness of breath. Emotionally, victims report high levels of stress, increased drug and alcohol abuse, more marital problems, and feelings of depression, unhappiness, anger, frustration, and dissatisfaction with life. Socially, victims are reluctant to share their feelings with friends, avoid family and friends due to feelings of embarrassment and shame, and avoid social situations and entertainment requiring money.

To reduce the effects of downsizing, Beyer and colleagues (1993) have this advice for layoff victims:

1. Immediately tell families.
2. Evaluate the reasons for the job loss. That is, was the loss inevitable due to problems with the organization, or could better performance, more current skills, or a better attitude have allowed the employee to keep his job?
3. Deal with the emotions that accompany a layoff (e.g., anger, disbelief, guilt, shame) and get help if necessary.
4. Prepare for departure by doing such things as securing references, negotiating a severance package, and taking advantage of outplacement opportunities.
5. Take a vacation or a short rest period to help prepare for the journey ahead.
6. Plan a new course of action and go forward with confidence.

Survivors

Survivors Employees who retain their jobs following a downsizing.

At first, one might think that an organization need not worry about **survivors**—those employees not laid off. After all, these are people who still have their jobs. However, research indicates not only that survivors suffer psychological trauma but that their future productivity is related to the way in which they and their not-so-fortunate counterparts are treated during the downsizing process. Research (Cascio, 2002; Marks, 2003) indicates that survivors

- become afraid of taking risks and are more apprehensive and narrow-minded;
- are more stressed, anxious, secretive, skeptical, cynical, and distrustful;
- have greater role conflict and ambiguity;
- lose confidence in themselves and in management;
- have lower levels of morale and job satisfaction; and
- feel a loss of control.

Survivors will be more productive and feel more secure if they are allowed to participate in decisions and make suggestions, are given a moderate level of job security, are supported by supervisors and the organization, and if the layoff victims were treated well (Kernan & Hanges, 2002; Preston, 2003). It is important that the organization talk positively about the layoff victims, keep an open two-way communication policy with survivors, and communicate the company vision to the survivors. To reduce the negative effects on survivors, organizations must ensure that the procedure used to determine layoffs is fair and clearly communicated to both victims and survivors (Sadri, 1996).

Local Community

Though not often considered, layoffs and plant closings have a tremendous impact on the local community. Local governments suffer as their tax base and revenues are reduced, local charities such as the United Way get fewer donations and often have increased demands for their services, retail stores lose business, banks have greater numbers of loan defaults, crime rates increase, and social problems (e.g., drinking, divorce) increase. On the positive side, layoffs result in an increase in the quality of the available workforce. This increased quality can help other employers and may even result in attracting new industry.

The Organization

Though many organizations continue to downsize, it is not clear that downsizing produces the desired increases in organizational effectiveness. For example:

- Cascio (2002) reports that organizations that downsized between 1982 and 2000 did not improve the financial success of their organizations.
- Henkoff (1990) surveyed almost 1,500 downsized organizations and found that half reported lower productivity.
- A Wyatt Company (1993) survey found that only 46% of downsized organizations reduced expenses, 22% increased productivity, and 9% improved quality.
- De Meuse, Bergmann, Vanderheiden, and Roraff (2004) found that Fortune 100 firms that downsized had lower performance than nondownsizing firms for the first two years following the downsizing. After two years, there were no significant differences between the two groups.

To apply what you have learned about downsizing, complete Exercise 14.5 in your workbook.

ON THE JOB

Applied Case Study

Managing Change at Carlson Restaurants

Carlson Restaurants is an international restaurant chain whose flagship restaurant is TGI Fridays. When Richard Snead took over as CEO, he wanted to focus on diversity issues and make diversity an important part of the culture at Carlson Restaurants. Such a focus was not new to Snead, as he had successfully implemented diversity initiatives at LensCrafters and Burger King prior to coming to Carlson. Snead strongly believed that diversity was essential if an organization was going to have restaurants in different countries and in cities and states with different cultures.

The diversity effort focused on three separate areas: hiring, training, and employee development.

The implementation phase included conducting a needs and culture assessment, creating a high-level diversity team that sought input from employees and managers, and evaluating each location and manager on its diversity efforts and success.

- What factors would you advise the CEO to consider when implementing such a change in organizational culture?
- What should he do to increase employee acceptance of the change?

To find out how Snead managed this change in culture, use the link found on your text webpage.

FOCUS ON ETHICS   Change Management

In today's business world, change is inevitable. Changes in technology occur almost every day (or so it seems). Newer and better companies spring up, forcing other organizations to reevaluate how they do business and to do what's necessary in order to remain competitive or become more so. Fluctuations in the economy also cause change, as companies find ways to deal with lower profit margins. This may mean mergers, downsizing, reorganizations, or even bankruptcies. Whatever the cause for the change, as you read in this chapter, change must be well planned, well managed, and well executed in order to be ethical and successful.

Many companies, when making decisions for change, operate under the philosophy of "the ends will justify the means." The "ends" is the result that the company wants from the change. The "means" is the action taken in order to achieve those results. Critics interpret this philosophy as suggesting that a good result excuses any wrongs committed to attain it. This, they say, is unethical because no excuses are acceptable for committing any wrongs. In the controversial situation of first testing new drugs on animals, critics say that the ends do not justify the means. It is wrong to harm any living being, whether animal or human.

Proponents of animal testing, however, say that whenever implementing any change in an organization, the cost must be weighed against the result. Sometimes a few must be hurt for the good of society. In the example of drug testing on animals, proponents of the philosophy would say that the ends do justify the means because it is done for the good of society: The successful development of important life-saving drugs justifies testing the drugs on animals.

Following are two situations. After reading them, answer the questions under "What do you think?"

Situation A: A small consulting firm was struggling to survive after 9/11. The company got most of its revenue from doing supervisory trainings and other human resources consulting. Almost all organizations within and outside of the United States were financially impacted by 9/11. One of the first places that companies cut back was in their training budget. So, the consulting firm had to make some changes in order to survive or else they would go bankrupt and many people would be out of work. The company operated under the "ends justify the means" philosophy: their goal was to increase revenue, and in order to do that, they had to make changes that negatively impacted on some employees. This is what they did: Employees were no longer reimbursed for

mileage, no matter how far they had to go to provide consulting services. All employees had to pay for their own airfare if they had to travel out of state or the country. All employees had to take one week off without pay, regardless of whether they were salaried or wage employees. The company had a wellness program where they paid for the membership fees for all employees. The company no longer paid the membership. If the employees wanted to continue going, they had to pay the membership themselves.

By taking these steps, the company was able to save a significant amount of money over the next few years. In the past two years, they have been able to give small salary increases to employees.

Situation B: A large manufacturing company, in an effort to reduce turnover and thereby increase productivity and revenue, decided to make a major organizational change: It was going to decentralize its decision making. Decentralizing is when a company allows each department to make decisions on that department's product, service, and budget. When it was centralized, all decisions went through the CEO and her administrators. Departments had to complete a lot of paperwork and often would have to wait weeks to get a decision on something as simple as which applicant to hire for a particular position. This caused a lot of stress and bad feelings, which led to managers and their employees quitting, often without notice. With decentralization, departments could recruit, interview, and select personnel; prepare yearly budgets; make decisions on purchases for the department and staff; and take disciplinary actions—all without checking with the CEO or administrative staff. The thought of the company was that this increased decision-making power would make managers and their employees more willing to stay with the company. This, in turn, would help increase profits.

One manager was excited about this change in management style. She would finally be able to do some things that she thought would help increase the profitability of her department, and subsequently, the entire company. She felt that the more profitable the company was, the better it would be for all employees. So, after being empowered to make more decisions on her own, she decided to fire the department secretary. Although the secretary had been with the company for eight years and had done a good job, it was the manager's opinion that she was not attractive enough. One of the duties of the secretary was to give a sales pitch to potential customers who came in and asked about the company's products. The manager believed the department would get more customers with an attractive secretary waiting on them because the customers would be more willing to listen to a sales pitch from an attractive person rather than an unattractive one.

What Do You Think?

- In situation A, did you see any ethical problems? If so, what were they and why do you say that? What would you do differently, if anything, if you faced this situation as a leader?

- What was the "end" in this case and what was the "means"? That is, what was the change the company wanted to make and what steps did they take to make the change? Did the end justify the means?

- In situation B, were there any ethical problems? If so, what were they and why do you think that?

- What was the "end" in case B and what was the "means?" That is, what was the change the company wanted to make and what steps did they take? Did the ends justify the means? What would you do, as a leader, if you faced this situation?

- What was the change that the department manager wanted to make and how did she do it? Did the end justify the means?

Chapter Summary

In this chapter you learned:

- Employees react to change by going through the stages of denial, defense, discarding, adaptation, and finally, internalization.
- Employees best accept change if the reason behind the change makes sense and the person making the change is trusted and respected.
- Change is best implemented by creating an atmosphere for change, communicating details, making the change over a reasonable period of time, and training employees. Employees can best accept change if they speed up, take initiative, and spend energy on solutions rather than complaining.
- The five levels of employee input are following, ownership of own product, advisory, shared, and absolute.
- Layoffs can be avoided by using temporary employees, outsourcing, offering early retirement programs, and creating alternative work schedules.
- There is a proper way to conduct a layoff.
- Layoffs have negative effects on victims, survivors, the organization, and the community.
- Compressed work schedules and flextime increase job satisfaction and decrease absenteeism.

Questions for Review

1. Why are employees reluctant to change?
2. How important is organizational culture in organization development?
3. When organizations talk about "empowering employees," what do they actually mean?
4. Is downsizing a good idea? Why or why not?
5. What factors determine the effectiveness of flexible work schedules?

Media Resources and Learning Tools

- Visit our website. Go to www.cengage.com/psychology/aamodt, where you will find online resources directly linked to your book, including chapter-by-chapter quizzing, flashcards, crossword puzzles, application activities, and more.
- Want more practice applying industrial/organizational psychology? Check out the *I/O Applications Workbook*. This workbook (keyed to your textbook) offers engaging, high-interest activities to help you reinforce the important concepts presented in the text.

Chapter 15

STRESS MANAGEMENT: DEALING WITH THE DEMANDS OF LIFE AND WORK

© Chris Ryan/OJO Images/Getty Images

Learning Objectives

➡ Learn the definition of stress

➡ Be able to name common stressors

➡ Learn the common consequences of stress (strains)

➡ Understand the effects of stress on behavior

➡ Learn ways to reduce stress

➡ Be familiar with the importance of child-care and elder-care programs

➡ Learn how stress can at times result in workplace violence

A factor that influences your behavior and thus your relations with others at work is stress: Over 70% of workers in the United States consider their jobs to be stressful (Clay, 2011). Not only does stress affect your interpersonal style, it can have serious health implications if ignored and not properly managed. To properly manage stress, you must first identify and understand what causes your stress and then learn ways to handle it. This chapter will identify some of the sources of stress and suggest ways for successfully dealing with it.

Stress Defined

Though psychologists cannot agree on one definition for the word *stress* (Greenberg, 2011; Sulsky & Smith, 2005), it will be defined for the purpose of this chapter as the psychological and physical reaction to certain life events or situations. The stress process begins with life events or situations that cause stress. These life events are called *stressors* and include such things as weddings, job interviews, dentist appointments, basketball games, deadlines, and traffic jams. If we perceive these events as being stressful, our bodies respond in many ways, including elevated blood pressure, increased heart rate, muscle tension, and perspiration. These reactions are called stress reactivity. If these physical reactions occur for periods longer than our body can tolerate, negative physical and psychological consequences can occur (Greenberg, 2011). These consequences are called *strains*.

As you may have already discovered in your life, an event that is a stressor to you may not be stressful to another person. For example, a human resource (HR) director told me a story about an applicant going through what the interview panel had designed to be a stress interview. They grilled the applicant for two hours on such topics as statistical analysis, employment laws, and job analysis. Toward the end of the interview, one panel member asked the applicant, "Are you enjoying this?" To which the applicant replied, "This is fun. We're not through, are we?" The response stunned the panel because previous applicants had reacted to the interview by shaking, crying, and perspiring. This applicant smiled the entire time. What does the story demonstrate? Contrary to popular belief, not all stress is bad.

Eustress Stress that results in positive energy and improvements in performance and health.

Eustress (from the root *eu-*, meaning something that is proper) occurs when stressors result in feelings of challenge or achievement—the feelings of stress get converted into positive energy and actually become motivating. You might say it is a desirable outcome of stress. An example of positive stress is the anxiety you feel before taking a test. If you felt no anxiety at all, you might not have the motivation and energy to spend the necessary time studying for the exam. Thus, some stress in this situation is probably helpful. However, if you are too stressed, your performance will decline. This is what is known as the *optimal level of arousal*, or inverted-U theory. As shown in Figure 15.1, according to the inverted-U theory, having little arousal or too much arousal results in poor performance, whereas a moderate level results in the highest levels of performance (Muse, Harris, & Field, 2003). Of course, the optimal level of arousal is different for each person.

Distress Stress that results in negative energy and decreases in performance and health.

Bad or negative stress, known as **distress**, happens when there is too much stress and when nothing is done to eliminate, reduce, or counteract its effects. Distress usually occurs in situations or at events on which you place great importance (e.g., interviewing for a job), that put great demands on you, and over which you eventually perceive you have little or no control. For example, having to wait in line to drop or

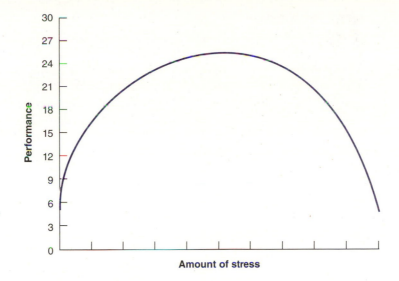

Figure 15.1

The Optimal Level of Arousal

add a class may be irritating, but it's usually not a big enough deal to cause distress. But interviewing for a new job or a new position that you really need for financial reasons can be a big source of stress, particularly if you feel you have little control over whether you get the job. Quite simply, negative stress occurs when we perceive that there is an imbalance between the demands (stressors) placed on us and our ability to meet those demands.

The distinction between eustress and distress is important because when employees report being stressed, their performance will not necessarily diminish. For example, in a study of more than 1,800 U.S. managers, the amount of eustress (called challenge-related stress by the researchers) had no relationship to job satisfaction or attempts to leave the organization. However, managers with high levels of distress (hindrance-related stress) were less satisfied with their jobs, left their jobs more often, and made more attempts to find a new job than did managers with low levels of distress (Cavanaugh, Boswell, Roehling, & Boudreau, 2000). Similar findings were reported in a meta-analysis by Podsakoff, LePine, and LePine (2007).

Predisposition to Stress

There appear to be individual differences in the extent to which people are susceptible to stress or are predisposed to tolerate stressors. For example, rates of coronary heart disease, exacerbated by stress, are higher for divorced persons than married people. Married people report higher satisfaction and less stress than unmarried people, top corporation executives have lower mortality rates than second-level executives, and people who live in suburban environments have more stress-related illness than people who live in rural environments. These individual tolerances can be explained by the following factors.

Stress Personalities

Some personalities are more apt to respond negatively to stressors than are others. These include individuals with Type A personalities and neurotics.

Type A Personalities

Type A personality A stress-prone person who is competitive, impatient, and hurried.

Do you, or does someone you know, talk and walk fast, get impatient easily, and always seem to be in a hurry? Chances are you or the person you know has a **Type A personality**. Type A individuals are characterized mainly by achievement striving, impatience and time urgency, and anger and hostility. They tend to do many things at one time (called *multitasking*). For example, a Type A individual would read the paper while eating lunch, type on the computer while talking to someone on the phone, and eat breakfast while driving to work. Type A's are fast-paced individuals who talk and walk fast, finish other people's sentences, and always seem to be on the go. They are achievement-oriented, competitive individuals who tend to place work before pleasure. These characteristics become exaggerated when the Type A personality experiences stress (Schaubroeck, Ganster, & Kemmerer, 1994). Type A employees under stress are more likely than others to exhibit high blood pressure and high levels of stress-related hormones. In addition, Type A individuals are slower to recover after the stressor is removed (Schaubroeck et al., 1994). To determine if you are a Type A personality, complete Exercise 15.1 in your workbook.

Type B individuals seem to be more laid-back. That is, when a potentially stress-producing event occurs, they are better able to keep it in perspective and use more positive ways to deal with it. They are more relaxed and more agreeable.

Type B personality A non–stress-prone person who is relaxed and agreeable.

Neuroticism

Although research over the years has identified several individual personality traits related to stress (e.g., pessimism, negative affectivity, reduced hardiness, and low self-esteem), research indicates that these individual traits fall under the general trait of **neuroticism**. Neurotics are anxious, often depressed, pessimistic, and lack hopefulness. They are more likely to perceive events as being stressful and more likely to have negative reactions to stressful events than are people who are more emotionally stable (Conard & Matthews, 2008).

Neuroticism A personality trait characterized by a tendency to experience such negative emotions as anxiety, anger, tension, and moodiness.

Gender, Ethnicity, and Race

Much of the research on gender and stress is conflicting. Many studies suggest that women have more stress than men and that depression is twice as common among them. Other studies claim that gender is not a contributor to stress. Presently, perhaps the best interpretation of the research on sex and stress is that women may experience certain stressors more often than men (e.g., sexual harassment, work/family conflict), and men and women may react differently to certain types of stressors (Sulsky & Smith, 2005).

Though there is not much research on the topic, it appears that members of minority groups have higher levels of stress than do nonminorities (Sulsky & Smith, 2005). Furthermore, racial and ethnic differences mostly concern physical reactions to stress. For example, due to a variety of physiological (e.g., vitamin D3 deficiency, type 2 diabetes) and lifestyle factors (e.g., high salt intake, smoking, stress), African Americans experience higher rates of hypertension than other ethnic groups (Walker, 2011).

Stress Sensitization

The amount of stress you have experienced throughout your life seems to affect how you will handle future stress. For instance, if you are exposed to high levels of stress (such as abuse) over a long duration, studies suggest that you are likely to react more quickly and more negatively to situations that are potentially stress producing because, in a sense, you have become "trained" to respond in such a way. That is, if you are used to being jumpy because of the stress you experienced earlier in your life, you are more likely to react that way with future stress. This, of course, has implications for your future health and your stress behaviors. Desensitization can occur through learning new behaviors to handle stress and working through your feelings about past stress.

Sources of Stress

Many events and factors could be considered stressors, and, as previously stated, what is stressful for one person may not be for another. Again, what determines whether something will be a stressor depends a great deal on its importance and the amount of perceived controllability. Stressors can be grouped under two broad categories: personal and occupational. Table 15.1 lists common personal and occupational sources of stress.

Personal Stressors

Personal sources of stress deal with such nonwork issues as family and intimate relationships, marriage, divorce, health issues, financial problems, and raising children. Difficult and angry people are also sources of stress because of the conflict they cause in our personal and work lives. In addition, having to deal with life's changes can be enormously stressful. In fact, many stressors can be considered as our reaction to change, whether the change is moving to a new home, ending or beginning a new relationship, or changing ourselves.

Fear

When we voluntarily or involuntarily leave a stage of our lives that has become comfortable and predictable, we enter another stage in which we don't know what will

Table 15.1 Most Common Causes of Stress

1. Money
2. Work
3. The economy
4. Family responsibilities
5. Relationships
6. Concerns about personal health
7. Housing costs
8. Job stability
9. Concerns about family health
10. Personal Safety

Source: Clay (2011).

happen. The challenge and potential excitement from the change can produce eustress in people who thrive on unpredictability. But to many of us, fear of the unknown produces negative stress. For example, when you were a senior in high school, did you think a lot about what the future would hold? Although eager to move out of the nest and be on their own, many students respond that they are terrified of what could happen. These students don't know if they will be successful in life—they aren't even sure that they can get a job to support themselves. They are certain that they will fail in college, which they feel means failing in life!

Other students respond that they are "psyched" about the thought of moving out and trying a new life! For those of you who are more fearful than challenged by change, you are probably already recognizing that the key to handling "fear of the unknown" is seeing that there aren't the monsters you thought there would be if you made the change. In other words, handling your fears in the future means realizing that most changes do not end up being as bad as you first imagined.

Resistance

Let's face it—some of us just don't want to leave the security and structure of that which is known. We like the predictability in our lives, no matter how boring. We like knowing what is going to happen from day to day, and telling us that we have to change our routine can throw us into a tailspin. Something as minor as having to change brands of toothpaste can be too much for us to handle and send us into a determined stubbornness not to change! A good illustration of resistance to change is holding on to old traditions that are no longer feasible. For example, I met a man at a conference who said that for many years after his divorce he still expected to spend Christmases with his former in-laws! It had been a tradition for him for more than 15 years, and he didn't understand why that tradition should stop just because he was no longer legally part of the family. He continued to call his ex-wife for several Christmases after the divorce, asking to join in the festivities. Of course, he was turned down, and the continued stress from this rejection and his refusal to change eventually led him to seek counseling. He seems to be doing better now and has even begun trying to start his own holiday traditions with the new woman in his life. Resisting change doesn't allow people to cope with inevitable changes that come from living. This resistance leads to stress.

Resentment

Finally, changes that are forced on us, particularly those that we feel we had no control over or input into, can cause resentment. If we don't want the change, don't understand why we have to make the change, and don't like how the change makes us feel (e.g., scared and confused), it raises feelings of resentment. Later in this chapter, we will discuss more about how to deal with life's changes.

Occupational Stressors

Occupational stressors can be grouped under two broad categories: job characteristics and organizational characteristics (Cordes & Dougherty, 1993).

Job Characteristics

Three main job characteristics cause stress: role conflict, role ambiguity, and role overload.

Stress can be a major problem at work.

© Keith Brofsky/PhotoDisc/Getty Images

Role conflict The extent to which an employee's role and expected role are the same.

Role conflict occurs when our work expectations and what we think we should be doing don't match up with the work we actually have to do. For example, a woman who was hired as assistant to the chief executive officer (CEO) of one particular organization was informed upon hire that she would be handling such administrative duties as policy development, participating as an equal partner in management meetings, and serving as a liaison between the CEO and the public. However, after she had been on the job for a while, she heard herself referred to as a "secretary" not only by the CEO but by other department heads too. In fact, the work she ended up doing consisted of mainly taking minutes at various meetings, ensuring that there was food at those meetings, and doing other routine clerical work such as answering the phone and routing interoffice mail. What she expected from the position was incompatible with what she was actually required to do. This role conflict caused her a great deal of stress, and, consistent with research on the effects of role conflict (e.g., Griffeth, Hom, & Gaertner, 2000; Rahim & Psenicka, 1996), she eventually quit her job.

Role conflict can also occur when an employee has competing roles or conflicting roles. For example, an employee's role as manager may require her to work on a Saturday, but her role as a mother requires her to attend her daughter's soccer game on the same day.

Role ambiguity The extent to which an employee's roles and expectations are unclear.

Role ambiguity occurs when an individual's job duties and performance expectations are not clearly defined. In the preceding example, the woman experienced not only role conflict but role ambiguity because what her boss expected her to do was different from what the other staff expected her to do. Although her boss referred to her as a "secretary," a job title that clearly denotes certain duties, he felt that she should have an equal say in certain decisions affecting the organization. The other directors, however, did not consider her their peer and did not feel that she should have the same power or authority that they had. Because the director did not, in the four years she worked there, ever settle that issue, she was never sure just how she was supposed to act at committee meetings. Needless to say, each day brought more and more stress as she struggled to find out, on her own, just what her job responsibilities should be. Consistent with the research of Frone, Russell, and Cooper (1995), the stress of this role ambiguity caused her to become depressed, and consistent with the meta-analysis by Abramis (1994), her job satisfaction decreased.

Role overload The extent to which an employee is able to psychologically handle the number of roles and tasks assigned.

Role overload develops when individuals either feel they lack the skills or workplace resources to complete a task or perceive that the task cannot be done in the required amount of time. Not surprisingly, role overload is highly correlated with stress (Bolino & Turnley, 2005) and negative health outcomes (Shultz, Wang, & Olson, 2010), especially when employees have little control over their jobs (Karasek & Theorell, 1990; Parker & Sprigg, 1999). Furthermore, employees perceiving role overload, role ambiguity, or role conflict are less likely to engage in organizational citizenship behaviors (Eatough, Chang, Miloslavic, & Johnson, 2011).

The key to minimizing the stress that comes from role conflict, ambiguity, and overload is to get clarification about your job duties. Although you are given a job description upon hire, make sure you sit down with your boss to ensure that you know just what he expects from you. In fact, it is wise to discuss the particulars of the job description prior to hire so that you are clear about work expectations. If you have been assigned a project you don't fully understand or feel you can't complete, let your employer know. Further, if possible, suggest that you be allowed to participate in training that can help you complete the project. Finally, it is sometimes beneficial if your boss explains your job responsibilities to other staff. This explanation should reduce any misunderstanding about your role in the organization.

Organizational Stressors

Organizational characteristics that are likely to cause stress include such factors as person-organization fit, organizational rules and policies, supervisory relationships, and organizational change.

Person-Organization Fit

Person/organization fit The extent to which an employee's personality, values, attitudes, philosophy, and skills match those of the organization.

The term **person-organization fit** refers to how well such factors as your skills, knowledge, abilities, expectations, personality, values, and attitudes match those of the organization. At one time, organizations were concerned primarily that applicants had the necessary skills and knowledge to perform certain jobs. Now, organizations, as well as workers, realize that there are other areas in which compatibility is critical for an employee to "fit" into an organization and perform well. For example, a pro-life individual may not work well in an organization such as Planned Parenthood, a non-smoker may not feel comfortable working for Philip Morris, and an environmentally conscious person may be unhappy working for Exxon because the philosophies of the individual and the organization are not the same. As shown in Table 15.2, meta-analysis results indicate that this incompatibility in philosophies and values can cause stress, lower job satisfaction, and increase turnover (Kristof-Brown, Zimmerman, & Johnson, 2005).

Table 15.2 Correlations with Employee Stress

	Corrected Correlation	Meta-analysis
Cause		
Organizational politics	.45	Miller, Rutherford, & Kolodinsky (2008)
Job insecurity	.19	Sverke, Hellgren, & Naswall (2002)
Lack of fit		
Person-Job	.28	Kristof-Brown, Zimmerman, & Johnson (2005)
Person-Organization	.27	Kristof-Brown, Zimmerman, & Johnson (2005)
Lack of support		
Coworkers	.18	Viswesvaran, Sanchez, & Fisher (1999)
Supervisors	.24	Viswesvaran, Sanchez, & Fisher (1999)
Consequence		
Performance	−.13	Podsakoff, LePine, & LePine (2007)
Absenteeism		
Turnover		
Actual	.13	Podsakoff, LePine, & LePine (2007)
Intended	.41	Podsakoff, LePine, & LePine (2007)
Organizational citizenship behaviors	−.16	Chang, Johnson, & Yang (2007)
Satisfaction	−.34	Podsakoff, LePine, & LePine (2007)
Commitment	−.31	Podsakoff, LePine, & LePine (2007)

The management philosophy of an organization may not meet the expectations of some individuals. A person who works best in a very structured environment (e.g., the military) in which everyone must follow a chain of command may not work well in a team-oriented environment in which the workers have the opportunity to make and enforce policy. Incompatibilities between personal and management philosophies can quickly become a stressor (Atkinson, 2000). Other stressors include the relationships between supervisors and employees. If an employee's expectation of that relationship differs from the supervisor's, not only will stress result, but conflict between the parties will inevitably arise.

Change

As discussed in Chapter 14, a major contributor to organizational stress is change, which occurs most often from downsizing and restructuring (Robinson & Griffiths, 2005). Realizing the amount of stress accompanying change, organizations are placing increasing emphasis on workplace wellness by offering programs that teach employees how to cope with change and manage stress.

Relations with Others

Our coworkers and customers can be a major source of workplace stress (see Chapter 13). Though I don't want to rehash material you learned in previous chapters, it is important to understand the stress associated with conflict, working with difficult people, dealing with angry customers, and feeling that you are not being treated fairly. An employee I met at one organization provides a perfect example of this stress. The employee worked at a job she enjoyed, and her personal life was more fulfilling than it had been in years. Despite the positive aspects of her job and life, she had trouble sleeping, lacked energy, and was depressed. What was the source of these strains? A difficult coworker who constantly yelled, used sarcasm, and belittled everyone. Such a story is not unusual and demonstrates the important role that interpersonal relationships can play in causing stress. In fact, a study of more than 15,000 employees over a four-year period found that stress from interpersonal conflict at work resulted in a number of severe psychiatric problems (Romanov, Appelberg, Honkasalo, & Koskenvuo, 1996).

Organizational Politics

Meta-analyses by Chang, Rosen, and Levy (2009) and Miller, Rutherford, and Kolodinsky (2008) found that an important source of employee stress is the perceived use of organizational politics. Organizational politics are self-serving behaviors employees use to increase the probability of obtaining positive outcomes in organizations. *Positive politics* are behaviors designed to influence others with the goal of helping both the organization and the person playing the politics (Holden, 1998). Examples of positive politics include portraying a professional image, publicizing one's accomplishments, volunteering, and complimenting others. *Negative politics* are manipulative behaviors designed to achieve personal gain at the expense of others and the organization (Holden, 1998). Examples of negative politics include backstabbing, withholding important information from others, and spreading rumors. In addition to increasing stress, negative organizational politics results in lower performance, lower levels of job satisfaction, and higher amounts of turnover (Chang et al., 2009; Miller et al., 2008).

Stressors in the Physical Work Environment

Noise

If you have ever been upset when someone played a stereo too loudly while you were studying, then you can understand why psychologists are interested in studying the effects of workplace noise on employee stress. If the "obvious" were true, we could start and end our discussion of noise by stating that high levels of noise increase stress, reduce performance, and make workers unhappy. But as Figure 15.2 shows, the relationship between noise and worker behavior is much more complicated than we might first think.

To understand this relationship, we must first realize that not all noise is the same. Two sounds with the same level of loudness can have different frequencies. For example, the sound of a tugboat whistle is much lower in frequency than a train whistle. Lower frequencies do not affect employee performance as much as higher frequencies.

Furthermore, sounds that have the same frequency, intensity, and loudness can differ in their *pleasantness*. For example, noise levels at rock concerts and nightclubs are certainly loud, yet some of us enjoy the sound enough to pay money to hear it. We would probably not pay money to hear a jet engine producing the same sound levels as a rock concert.

This effect can be seen with an employee who listens to music through head-phones at work. The noise level of the music is often greater than that of the

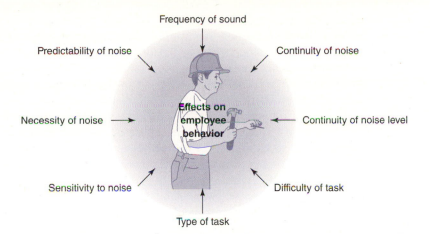

Figure 15.2

Factors Determining Possible Noise Effects

Frequency of sound

Predictability of noise

Continuity of noise

Necessity of noise → Effects on employee behavior ← Continuity of noise level

Sensitivity to noise

Difficulty of task

Type of task

machines in the environment, but it is considered to be more pleasant. Keep in mind, however, that even though the music may be more interesting than the machine noise, the noise level has the same potential effects: Hearing loss can occur just as easily from music as it can from factory noise.

Noises also differ in whether they are continuous or intermittent. Constant noise has less effect on employee behavior, so environments with steady noise levels are not as disrupting as those in which either noise frequency or noise intensity changes.

Another factor that affects the relationship between noise and employee behavior is the *type* and *difficulty of the task*. Noise affects difficult tasks or those that involve cognitive and perceptual skills more than it affects less difficult tasks or those that involve physical performance (Cohen & Weinstein, 1981).

Individual differences in people also determine the degree to which noise will affect performance. Weinstein (1978) examined individual differences in noise sensitivity in college students and found that noise-sensitive students had lower academic performance, were less comfortable in the presence of others, and became more disturbed than their less noise-sensitive peers. Melamed, Harari, and Green (1993) found that Type A personalities' blood pressure and heart rate increased under conditions of high noise but not under conditions of low noise.

The effect of noise also depends on the *necessity* for and *familiarity* of the noise. When certain noises cannot be avoided—for example, the sound of a machine in a manufacturing plant—they are less irritating than unnecessary noises such as an employee talking too loudly or a roommate playing a stereo at full volume (Kjellberg, Landstrom, Tesarz, & Soderberg, 1996).

Likewise, familiar noise is less irritating than unfamiliar noise, probably for two reasons. First, a familiar noise is less distracting or meaningful than the one that we hear for the first time. For example, the regular passing of a train outside an office produces less distracting noise than a suddenly dropped glass. Even though the train is louder, it is expected and familiar and thus not as distracting. Soldiers with war experience have often reported they were able to sleep through artillery explosions but would awaken instantly at the sounds of snapped twigs or close footsteps.

Familiar sounds may also be less distracting because our hearing loses sensitivity to loud sounds. For example, on first entering a factory, the noise levels are often very high and distracting. After a few minutes, however, the noise is less noticeable because we have become temporarily less sensitive to it.

Finally, noise affects certain *types* of employee behaviors in different ways. Noise is more likely to decrease the *quality* of performance rather than its quantity (Hancock, Conway, Szalma, Ross, & Saxton, 2001), to cause people to walk faster and make less eye contact (Korte & Grant, 1980), to decrease job satisfaction (Sundstrom, Town, Rice, Osborn, & Brill, 1994), and to decrease performance on cognitive tasks (Cohen & Weinstein, 1981; Smith & Jones, 1992). But perhaps the greatest effects of noise are not on performance but on employee health and morale.

As Figure 15.3 shows, research indicates that in addition to hearing loss, continued exposure to high levels of noise (measured in decibels [db]) can raise blood pressure of employees in complex jobs (Melamed, Fried, & Froom, 2001), increase worker illness (Cohen, 1972), cause people to be less helpful (Fisher, Bell, & Baum, 1984), and produce more aggression and irritability (Quigley, Leonard, & Collins, 2003). Even low levels of office noise have been found to increase employee stress and reduce task motivation (Evans & Johnson, 2000).

Noise also causes people to narrow their focus of attention so that they concentrate only on the most important stimuli. In one experiment, Korte and Grant (1980) placed unusual objects (e.g., a brightly colored balloon tied to a lamppost) and people (a woman wearing a large pink hat) along the sidewalk of a busy shopping district. Korte and Grant then asked shoppers if they had seen anything unusual and read them a list of the unusual people and things they could have seen. When traffic noise was high, only 35% of the shoppers noticed the items, compared with more than 50% when the noise was low. Although such narrowing of attention may decrease the performance levels of employees for whom it is important to notice many stimuli (e.g., police officers or safety inspectors), it may help the performance of employees who need focus on only a few different stimuli (Broadbent, 1971).

Noise Reduction. Given that noise affects employee morale, health, and perhaps performance, employers have attempted to solve or minimize the problem of noise by several methods. One has been by setting legal time limits on the exposure to noise at

Working in a noisy environment can increase employee stress.

different decibel levels. As you can see from Table 15.3, the legal limits set by the Occupational Safety and Health Administration (OSHA) are not as stringent as those recommended by the National Institute for Occupational Safety and Health (NIOSH).

A second method is to change the environment by using carpeting and acoustically treated ceilings (Sundstrom et al., 1994).

A third method is to reduce the amount of unwanted noise that reaches an employee. Examples have included employees wearing protective ear plugs and muffs or working in soundproof areas away from the sources of noise. In one study, use of hearing protection devices in a noisy factory reduced workers' hostile behaviors (Rabinowitz, Melamed, Feiner, & Weisberg, 1996). Although these methods may limit the effects on employee health, they may also decrease performance in jobs that require detection of or attention to certain types of noise (Mershon & Lin, 1987).

Cause of Noise	Loudness of Noise (in decibels)	Effect of Noise
Rocket launch	180	
	170	
	160	
	150	
Gunshot blast	140	
Jet takeoff	130	Brief exposure can result in permanent deafness (Trahiotis & Robinson, 1979)
	125	
Disco	120	
Riveting machine	115	Maximum legal exposure to noise
Power lawn mower	110	A person cannot speak over a sound at this level
	105	
Textile-weaving plant	100	Blood pressure increases (Burns, 1979)
Food blender	95	Cognitive performance is reduced (Hockey, 1979) Employees report more illness and somatic complaints (Cohen, 1972)
	93	Angry people become more aggressive (Donnerstein & Wilson, 1976) Driving performance decreases (Finkelman, Zeitlin, Filippi, & Friend, 1977)
City traffic	90	Legal acceptable noise limit for 8-hour day (OSHA guidelines)
Computer card verifier	85	Helping behavior decreases (Mathews & Canon, 1975)
Train (100 feet away)	80	Reaction time decreases by 3% (Lahtela, Niemi, Kunsela, & Hypen, 1986)
Car	75	
Noisy restaurant	70	Telephone use is difficult
	68	Reduced detection of grammatical errors during proofreading (Weinstein, 1977)
	65	Hearing loss can occur in sensitive individuals
Normal speech	60	
	50	
Normal noise at home	40	
Soft whisper	30	
	20	
	10	
Breathing	0	

OSHA = U.S. Occupational Safety and Health Administration

Figure 15.3
Effects of Noise at Different Levels

Table 15.3 Maximum Legal Exposure to Noise

Hours of Exposure	Maximum Noise Level (in decibels)	
	OSHA Limits	NIOSH Recommendations
8	90	85
7	91	
6	92	
5	93	
4	95	88
3	97	
2	100	91
1.5	102	
1	105	94
0.5	110	97
0.25	115	100

OSHA = U.S. Occupational Safety and Health Administration; NIOSH = National Institute for Occupational Safety and Health (Centers for Disease Control and Prevention)

Another method used to limit the problem of noise has been through engineering technology—that is, by reducing the actual amount of noise emitted. For example, rubber pads on machines reduce noise by reducing vibration, and belt drives instead of gears reduce the noise made by many types of machines. In one study, using white noise to mask office noise improved performance on a cognitive task. However, the white-noise group still performed worse than the no-noise group (Loewen & Suedfeld, 1992). In offices, airflow from ventilation systems can serve as a source of white noise.

This discussion has concentrated on the potential harmful effects of noise, but noise can also be beneficial in the working environment, especially as a warning method. For example, loud noises alert workers that a forklift is backing up, loud whistles tell workers when it is time to go home, and alarms tell workers when a machine has malfunctioned.

Temperature

Another important issue concerning the working environment is the effect of temperature on employee stress, performance, and health. Many jobs, such as those in the construction and in the steel industry, involve working in intense heat, and others, such as rescue squad work and meatpacking, often involve working in extreme cold.

Perhaps the best place to begin a discussion of the effects of temperature is by describing how the human body tries to maintain an ideal temperature. When body temperature is above normal, we cool down in one of two ways. The first is through **radiation**, with the excess heat radiating away from the body. The second way is by **evaporation**, or by sweating away excess heat.

When body temperature is below normal, blood vessels constrict. Although this process helps protect against cold, it also produces numbness by reducing circulation. That is why our feet and hands are the first parts of the body to feel numb when we are cold. Police officers working a beat can often be seen stomping their feet in cold temperatures to stimulate circulation.

Radiation One way our bodies maintain a normal temperature, by the emission of heat waves.

Evaporation One way our bodies maintain a normal temperature, in which perspiration reduces excess heat.

Effective temperature The combination of air temperature, humidity, airflow, and heat radiation that determines how hot or cold the environment feels.

We must next understand how different factors affect what is called the **effective temperature**, or how hot or cold our environment feels to us. In theory, effective temperature has four components—air temperature, humidity, airflow, and temperature of objects in the environment—but it is usually computed by considering only air temperature and humidity. Note that effective temperature is more than simple air temperature. A 90-degree day in the Nevada desert feels cooler than a 90-degree day in a Georgia swamp. As Table 15.4 shows, the higher the humidity, the warmer the air temperature feels, and thus the higher the effective temperature.

In addition to humidity, airflow is also important. We all can probably recall the feeling of relief from a breeze coming off a lake or the ocean. The air temperature probably did not change, but discomfort decreased along with the effective temperature. Likewise, we might recall a "biting wind" that made a winter day seem so cold.

Finally, the effective temperature is affected by the heat that radiates from other objects in the environment. For example, the field-level temperature of outdoor sports stadiums that use artificial turf is usually much higher than the air temperature in the stands because heat radiates from the artificial turf. Other examples of this radiation effect include how much hotter it feels when sitting with a group of people than when sitting alone or how much hotter it feels when lying on the sand at the beach than when sitting up.

I can remember many summer days in Los Angeles when the air temperature was already more than 100 degrees but was combined with heat radiating from the sidewalk adding 15 degrees more, thus making walking uncomfortable. Similarly, a manager who thinks that her outdoor salespeople will be fine in an 85-degree temperature must also account for the effective temperature caused by radiating heat. An air temperature of 85 degrees above a concrete sidewalk is not the same as 85 degrees above a dirt road.

Both air temperature and humidity interact with the body's ability to cool down through radiation and evaporation. When air temperature is higher than body temperature, we are unable to radiate heat. When humidity is high, it is more difficult to lose body heat through evaporation. Thus, high air temperature and high humidity make the body's "natural cooling system" less effective.

The relevant question here, of course, is what happens when the effective temperature in the working environment is high or low? As shown in Figure 15.4, the answer is that performance usually deteriorates. The degree of deterioration, however, depends on several factors, including the type of task, the workload, and the number and frequency of rest periods that are allowed.

Table 15.4   Effective Temperature as a Function of Air Temperature and Humidity

Humidity (%)	Air Temperature (°F)					
	41	50	59	68	77	86
100	41	52	64	78	96	120
80	41	52	63	75	90	111
60	40	51	62	73	86	102
40	40	51	61	72	83	96
20	39	50	60	70	81	91
0	39	50	59	69	77	86

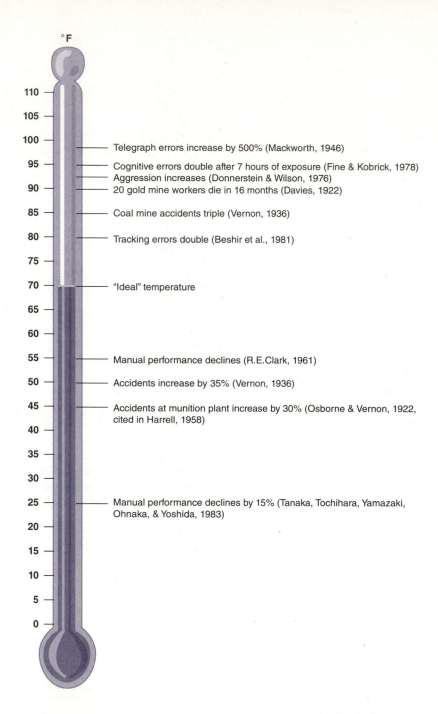

°F

110 —

105 —

100 — ———— Telegraph errors increase by 500% (Mackworth, 1946)

95 — ———— Cognitive errors double after 7 hours of exposure (Fine & Kobrick, 1978)
        ———— Aggression increases (Donnerstein & Wilson, 1976)
90 — ———— 20 gold mine workers die in 16 months (Davies, 1922)

85 — ———— Coal mine accidents triple (Vernon, 1936)

80 — ———— Tracking errors double (Beshir et al., 1981)

75 —

70 — ———— "Ideal" temperature

65 —

60 —

55 — ———— Manual performance declines (R.E.Clark, 1961)

50 — ———— Accidents increase by 35% (Vernon, 1936)

45 — ———— Accidents at munition plant increase by 30% (Osborne & Vernon, 1922,
             cited in Harrell, 1958)
40 —

35 —

30 —

25 — ———— Manual performance declines by 15% (Tanaka, Tochihara, Yamazaki,
             Ohnaka, & Yoshida, 1983)
20 —

15 —

10 —

5 —

0 —

Figure 15.4
Effects of Various
Temperatures on
Employee Behavior

Effects on Tasks. Research indicates that extremely high or low temperatures can affect performance on cognitive, physical, and perceptual tasks. A meta-analysis by Pilcher, Nadler, and Busch (2002) found that performance dropped by 13.9% when temperatures rose above 90 degrees and by 14.9% when temperatures fell below 50 degrees. Hot temperatures had their greatest effect on reaction time and on performance of attentional, perceptual, and mathematical tasks. Cold temperatures had their greatest effect on reasoning, memory, and learning tasks. Interestingly, extreme temperatures seem to have their greatest effect on tasks when only a small amount of time is spent on the task. Thus, it seems that we can eventually adapt to extreme temperatures and perform at close to normal levels.

Though employee comfort and performance is important, heat can also affect the performance of machines and equipment. For example, a California printing and bookbinding company ran into interesting problems involving the airflow in one of its plants. The facility had many different types of printing presses, as well as binders that required the melting of glue chips. As you can imagine, the heat from summer air, binding machines, and employees' bodies combined to make working conditions uncomfortable.

To solve this problem, the managers decided to increase the airflow by opening all of the plant's doors and windows and letting the ocean breezes cool the plant. Unfortunately, the increased airflow not only cooled the plant and made the employees more comfortable but also caused the mechanical collating machines to malfunction. These machines use sensors that warn their operators when too many or too few sheets of paper have been picked up. The breezes ruffled the sheets and thus set off the sensors. The increased airflow may have made the employees more comfortable and productive, but it reduced the equipment's productivity. Because the potential output of the collating machines was much greater than the outputs of the individual employees, the windows were closed. As a result, the employees became irritable but overall productivity increased.

A similar case occurred at a knitting mill whose owners discovered that yarn tended to snap when humidity was low. Therefore, they made no attempt to dehumidify the air. Unfortunately for the millworkers, the high humidity made working conditions uncomfortable. Thus, a decision had to be made as to the ideal humidity level that would keep the employees happy and productive without causing the yarn to snap. So the humidity level was slightly lowered.

A final example of the differential effects of temperature comes from baseball. When temperatures are high, players are uncomfortable, and pitchers tire more quickly than when temperatures are moderate. But the hotter air allows a baseball to travel farther when hit, and there are often more home runs. Thus, the higher temperatures negatively affect pitchers but positively affect batters.

Effects Related to Workload. High temperatures obviously most affect work performance when workloads are heavy. That is, an effective temperature of 95 degrees would quickly affect a person using a sledgehammer but take longer to affect a person pulling weeds. However, exposure to even moderate levels of heat while performing "light" repetitive-motion work can be dangerous. In a study of female laundry workers, Brabant (1992) found increases in discomfort and cardiac strain—results that were not immediately dangerous but had the potential for future health problems.

Rest Periods. Temperature will have the greatest effect on performance when work activity is continuous. With rest breaks, the effects of either heat or cold can be greatly reduced. For example, most people can work for approximately 120 minutes at 90 degrees without impaired performance. At 100 degrees, however, the maximum time for continued performance is approximately 30 minutes; after that time, performance deteriorates (Wing, 1965). Thus, in temperatures of 90 degrees, rest breaks scheduled at a maximum of two hours apart will help keep performance (and the employee) from deteriorating. At 100 degrees, rest breaks must occur at intervals of less than 30 minutes.

An interesting problem developed at a large amusement park when its employees were exposed to summer heat. The park had several employees dress in theme costumes, which we will call "gnomes" to protect the park's reputation. The thick and heavy gnome costumes were worn even during summer when temperatures were almost always in the 90s and 100s. The job of each costumed employee was to walk around the park and greet customers, especially children. Problems, however, began when children punched the gnomes and knocked them over (a rolling gnome was actually a fairly funny sight). Normally, the gnomes kept their sense of humor and laughed, but after an hour in costume in 100-degree temperatures, they sometimes lost their humor and began punching back. And when they were not hitting children, the gnomes were passing out from the heat. Obviously, something had to be done.

To solve the problem, the park's management had the gnomes work four-hour shifts instead of eight. As we might expect from the previous discussion, this solution was ineffective. Why? Because the outside temperature was 100 degrees and the effective temperature inside the costume was at least 20 degrees higher. At such high temperatures, continuous activity brought decreased performance in less than 30 minutes. The solution that worked, of course, was to have the gnomes work for 20 minutes and then take short breaks in an air-conditioned room, thus taking advantage of what we know about exposure limits to heat as well as frequency of breaks.

An interesting adaptation to extreme temperature can be found at ICEHOTEL, located above the Arctic Circle in Sweden. ICEHOTEL is a fascinating structure made completely of ice—the walls, floors, beds, chairs, and even the chandeliers! During the winter, the temperature outside the hotel falls to 30 degrees below zero and the inside temperature stays at a constant 30 degrees. How do the employees and guests handle these temperatures? By wearing snow suits, gloves, and hats while indoors, everyone stays rather toasty. Because the people at the reception desk are exposed to the bitter outside cold each time someone opens the door, the receptionists work 30 minutes at the reception desk and then 30 minutes in a "warmer" part of the hotel before rotating back to the reception desk for another 30 minutes. Thus, through the use of proper clothing and rest periods, ICEHOTEL is able to keep its employees safe and productive (and from what we could see, very happy as well).

Stress Caused by Work Schedules

Shift Work

Even though most people work from 8:00 a.m. or 9:00 a.m. to 5:00 p.m., approximately 25% of all employees work evening or late-night shifts due to economic and safety factors. Police officers and nurses must work around the clock because neither crime nor illness stops at 5:00 p.m.; retail employees must work late hours to accommodate people who are able to shop only late in the day; and factory workers work shifts because one plant can be three times as productive if it operates round the clock.

Because shift work is necessary and affects approximately 25% of all employees, research has attempted to identify its effects as well as ways to reduce any effects that might be negative. A review of the research on shift work (Smith, Folkard, Tucker, & Evans, 2011) clearly indicates that working evening ("swing") and late-night/overnight ("graveyard") shifts has many work and health-related negative effects, including

■ sleep problems,
■ chronic fatigue,

- accidents and injuries,
- gastrointestinal disorders (e.g., constipation, heartburn, gas),
- cardiovascular disorders,
- increased cancer risk,
- increased absenteeism from work (Jamal, 1981)
- lowered low satisfaction (Jamal, 1981)
- lower job performance (Smith, Totterdell, & Folkard, 1995), and
- increased social and family problems (Jamal, 1981; Presser, 2000).

Circadian rhythm The 24-hour cycle of physiological functions maintained by every person.

Many of these negative effects are thought to occur because of disruptions in **circadian rhythms**, the 24-hour cycles of physiological functions maintained by every person. For example, most people sleep at night and eat in the morning, at noon, and in the evening. Although there are individual differences in the exact times for each function (such as eating or sleeping), people generally follow the same pattern. Working evening and late-night shifts disrupts this pattern and often causes digestive, appetite, sleeping, and other health problems (Price, 2011). Unfortunately, we don't "get used to" shift work, and these effects get worse with continued exposure to night shifts (Folkard, 2008). Kaliterna, Vidacek, Prizmic, & Radosevic-Vidacek, 1995). For example, Garbarino (2004) found that Italian police working shifts had more sleep disorders than non-shift workers and that the greater the number of years spent working shifts, the worse the sleep disorders.

Many of the psychological and social effects of shift work are caused by the incompatibility of an employee's schedule with the schedules of other people. That is, a person who works nights and sleeps mornings may be ready to socialize in the afternoon. Unfortunately, fewer people are around. And when the family is active, the employee is sleeping, and thus requires quiet.

As Figure 15.5 shows, many factors influence the degree to which shift work will affect an employee. For example, employees who live with families are affected more than employees who live alone because the former must adjust their sleeping schedules to those of others in the household (Smith & Folkard, 1993). Other important factors are uniqueness of shift, whether a shift is fixed or rotating, frequency of rotation, and individual differences.

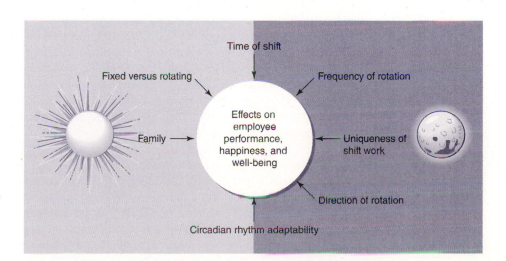

Figure 15.5

Factors Influencing Shift Work Effects

Uniqueness of Shift. The social effects of shift work can be greatly reduced if other organizations in the geographical area also use other shifts. The higher the percentage of organizations with shifts, the greater the number of stores and restaurants that are open during the evening and the greater the number of other people available with whom to socialize.

Fixed Versus Rotating Shifts. Shifts can be either fixed or rotated. With fixed shifts, separate groups of employees permanently work the day shift, swing shift, and night shift. Rotating shifts are those in which an employee rotates through all three shifts, working the day shift for a while, then switching to the swing shift, then working the night shift, and so on. A survey of 623 U.S. and Canadian companies using shifts found that 66% used rotating rather than fixed shifts (Circadian Technologies, 2002).

The rationale for rotating shifts is that the negative effects of working swing and night shifts can be lessened if each employee is allowed to work the day shift part of the time. With fixed shifts, even though two-thirds of all workers will have hours that are not compatible with their circadian rhythms, staying permanently on the same shifts will allow them to physically adjust better than if they change shifts, especially when considering that about two days are needed to adjust to each shift change.

Research on shift rotation has strongly suggested that fixed shifts result in fewer performance, physical, and psychological problems than do rotating shifts (Buddhavarapu, Borys, Hormant, & Baltes, 2002; Frese & Okonek, 1984; Jamal & Jamal, 1982; Verhaegen, Cober, de Smedt, & Dirkx, 1987). For example, Jamal (1981) found that employees on fixed shifts had less absenteeism and tardiness, greater job satisfaction and social participation, and better mental health than did their counterparts working rotating shifts. The results of a meta-analysis (Buddhavarapu et al., 2002) and a traditional review of the literature (Wilkinson, 1992) concluded that fixed shifts were superior to rotating shifts, especially for industrial workers.

Frequency of Rotation. Although fixed shifts are better for individuals than rotating shifts, sometimes shifts must be rotated because employees who feel stuck on swing and night shifts insist on having the opportunity to work days. In such situations, the frequency of the shift rotation must be considered. That is, should the rotation occur daily? Weekly? Monthly? The 2002 Shiftwork Practices Survey (Circadian Technologies, 2002) found that 47% of organizations that rotate shifts do so weekly, 15% rotate every two weeks, and 10% rotate monthly.

Meta-analysis results indicate that fixed shifts result in fewer sleep problems than rotating shifts and that slowly rotating shifts result in fewer sleep problems than do faster rotating shifts (Pilcher, Lambert, & Huffcutt, 2000). If shifts are to be rotated, the rotation should be clockwise (Circadian Technologies, 2002), with later starting times for the morning shift (Barton & Folkard, 1993; Knauth, 1996). Rest periods of at least two days between shift rotations can lessen the negative effects of the rotations (Totterdell, Spelten, Smith, Barton, & Folkard, 1995).

Individual Differences. The final factor concerning the effects of shift work involves individual differences in employees. Obviously, not all employees will react to shift work in the same way because of the differences in their biological time clocks. In fact, we have all probably known people who claimed to be "night people" or to "prefer the morning." These individual differences in time preference are called *chronotypes*.

Several questionnaires have been developed to distinguish so-called morning people from evening people. Perhaps the best of these was developed by Smith, Reilly, and Midkiff (1988), which contains the 13 most reliable and valid questions from three other available scales (Reilly & Smith, 1988). Such a questionnaire can be used to select and place employees in their optimal shifts. Extraverts tend to be evening people more than do introverts (Schröeder, 2010). Males adapt to shift work better than do females, and shift work affects older workers more than younger workers (Oginska, Pokorski, & Oginski, 1993).

Moonlighting

As mentioned previously, one of the concerns with compressed workweeks is the possibility of employee fatigue. The same concern applies to employees working more than one job, or **moonlighting**. For example, an employee might work the day shift as a machine operator for Ford Motor Company and then work the night shift as a store clerk for a 7-Eleven convenience store. People typically moonlight because they want or need to earn extra money. Alboher (2007) distinguishes between moonlighters who work for extra money, and employees whom she refers to as having "slash" careers (e.g., attorney/landscaper). People with slash careers work a second job because they enjoy the second career rather than because they need extra money. According to recent estimates, between 5 and 7 percent of U.S. employees work more than one job (Krell, 2010). Both moonlighting and slash employees raise concerns about the effects of extra work on performance and absenteeism for these employees' primary jobs.

Few studies have investigated the effects of moonlighting. Jamal (1981) and Jamal and Crawford (1984) surveyed more than 400 workers at six organizations and found that moonlighters were no different from non-moonlighters in terms of mental health, quality of life, job performance, and intention to leave their companies. But moonlighters did miss about one day more of work per year than did non-moonlighters.

Arcuri and Lester (1990), Miller and Sniderman (1974), and Mott, Mann, McLoughlin, and Warwick (1965) did not find any negative effects for moonlighting. In fact, Mott and colleagues found that moonlighters were better adjusted and more active in the community than were their non-moonlighting counterparts. Because there seem to be few negative effects to moonlighting, few organizations prohibit it. In fact, in most states it may be illegal to do so. Instead, most organizations have policies that prohibit moonlighting that might be a conflict of interest (e.g., working for a competitor), that uses company equipment in the outside job, or that requires performing outside jobs during company time.

Other Sources of Stress

Minor Frustration

Minor frustration is stress we encounter in our daily lives, and it might include irritations such as waiting in traffic or not being able to get some information from the library. Minor frustrations may try our patience, but in and of themselves they may not be a problem and usually last for only a short duration, such as an hour or a few hours. If we do not have a healthy outlet for our frustrations, they may build up over time until they control us. These short-term frustrations may then carry over to the next day and then the next, until finally they become long-term stressors.

Minor frustrations can be managed through perspective taking. **Perspective taking** means rating the frustration on a scale of 1 to 10, with 10 meaning the situation is worthy of high levels of irritation. A friend of mine rates everything on a scale of life and death. He says that during potential stress-producing situations, he asks himself the

Moonlighting Working more than one job.

Perspective taking Rating a potential stressor by asking how bad it really is compared with all things considered or with a worst-case scenario.

following question: "How bad is this in relation to death?" Because he served in Vietnam, faced death often, and in fact saw many of his buddies killed, most of the situations he confronts get a very low rating. Consequently, he is basically a very peaceful and laid-back individual. Now, most of us can't relate to life's situations on that basis because we have never come close to experiencing death. But we can still ask ourselves: "In the scheme of things, just how important was that incident? Is it important enough for me to have a bad day, increase my chances of a heart attack, or die for?" See how perspective taking works? Making sure you don't make "mountains out of molehills" can keep you from having to deal with the long-term effects of stress.

Forecasting

Forecasting Constant worrying about the future.

The stress from **forecasting** develops from our constantly worrying about the future and wasting time and energy on "what ifs?" This continuous fretting about things over which we may have no control (such as the end of the universe from aliens!) or that may never even happen can become very emotionally and physically draining, not to mention debilitating. Forecasting very quickly becomes long-term stress as we continue to keep our minds and bodies in a fearful and anxious state. Learning how to recognize those areas you can't control and ceasing to worry about them is the key to eliminating stress from forecasting.

Residual Stress

Residual stress Stress that is carried over from previous stressful situations.

Residual stress is stress that is carried over from previous stressful situations that we refuse to "let go." Minor frustrations can become residual stress if we don't handle those daily problems effectively and rehash them over and over again. Many people continue to carry grudges, hurt, or anger from past situations that keep them in a constant state of stress. For example, have you ever been in a relationship that ended unexpectedly? If you didn't want the relationship to end, you may have been very hurt and then become angry. Now, every time you think of that situation, you get angry and hurt all over again. Many people continue to dredge up those bad feelings long after the relationship is over. All this does is recycle the stress process. Residual stress is almost always long term: If not dealt with, it chips away at our physical and emotional well-being until we become prisoners to its effects. This type of stress eventually leads individuals to therapy and counseling to learn positive ways, such as forgiveness, to cope with past negative experiences.

Consequences of Stress

Personal Consequences

How we respond to stress can have devastating consequences. For instance, responding with anger or rage can lead to family members being hurt, the loss of jobs, and perhaps trouble with the law. Responding with the use of alcohol and drugs can lead to addiction, broken relationships, and even death. Financially, the impaired decisions we make while under stress can have negative consequences. In an interesting study, Repetti and Wood (1997) examined the effects of work stress on the relationships between 30 working mothers and their preschool children. The results of the study indicated that on highly stressful workdays, mothers spoke less often to their children and had fewer expressions of affection.

As shown in Figure 15.6, there are numerous physical responses to stress. Some people sweat under extreme stress. For example, many people report that interviewing for a job is very stressful and causes them to sweat. Headaches and body aches are also symptoms of stress. If you are prone to migraines, you may find that your migraines occur more often during stressful situations. Body aches often are the result of tensing up during stressful times. Many people report that when they awake in the morning, their back, neck, shoulders, and legs are very sore, which can be attributed to tensing during sleep. Extreme physical responses to stress include hair loss. Although we are supposed to lose 50 to 100 strands of hair a day, which are replaced by new hair, hair that falls out in clumps is often your body's way of signaling high amounts of stress.

Stress has been labeled the "silent killer" because, as you have already read, it can quietly chip away at your immune system, thereby weakening your body's ability to prevent or fight off illnesses and diseases. It is often the source of escalating blood pressure, heart attacks, strokes, or worse: death. Stress may also increase the symptoms of rheumatoid arthritis because the hormones released in response to stress can cause swelling in the joints (Carpi, 1996). In fact, research suggests that 50% to 70% of all illnesses, such as coronary heart disease, can be attributed to stress. Even minor ailments such as recurring colds can be attributed to recent stressful events.

Stressors	Strains	Behaviors
Personal	**Psychological**	**Health**
Marital problems	Depression	Smoking
Family problems	Anxiety	Drinking
Health problems	Anger	Drug abuse
Financial problems	Sleep problems	
Daily hassles		**Work Related**
Residual stress	**Physical**	Absenteeism
	Illness	Turnover
Occupational	Cardiovascular problems	Lower productivity
Job Characteristics	Headaches	Workplace violence
Role conflict	Joint pain	
Role ambiguity		
Role overload		
Organizational Characteristics		
Person–organization fit		
Work environment		
Change		
Relations with others		
Coworker problems		
Supervisor problems		
Difficult and angry		
customers		
Lack of empowerment		
Personality/Habits		
Type A		
Pessimism		
Tendency to forecast		
Diet		
Exercise		

Figure 15.6
The Stress Process

Depression is another health problem associated with stress. Most of us experience some form of depression from time to time. Usually, a good night's sleep or being with friends and family will lift that depression. Sometimes a few visits to a counselor who can help us sort out our feelings and put things in perspective is helpful. Long-term stress, however, can eventually lead to clinical depression, which often requires medical treatment. In addition, prolonged depression has effects on the body such as stroke-triggering clots, hypertension, and high heart rates (Elias, 1997). Early diagnosis and treatment of depression is the key to managing it. If you feel you are suffering from depression, you may want to consult the counseling center at your college. Or, if your town has a public mental health agency, contact them. Any visit you make to a counselor is confidential.

Organizational Consequences

Job Performance

Studies show that in general, high levels of stress reduce performance on many tasks. However, as mentioned earlier, a curvilinear relationship between stress and job performance may exist in that moderate levels of stress actually improve productivity, increase energy levels, and heighten creativity (Muse, Harris, & Field, 2003).

Burnout

Burnout The psychological state of being overwhelmed with stress.

Burnout, the state of being overwhelmed by stress, is usually experienced by highly motivated professionals faced with high work demands. Initial studies on burnout targeted people in the health-care field as employees most likely to experience burnout. But over the years, the definition has expanded to include other types of workers who become emotionally exhausted and no longer feel they have a positive impact on other people or their job. People who feel burned out lack energy and are filled with frustration and tension. Emotional symptoms of burnout include a loss of interest in work, decreased work performance, feelings of helplessness, and trouble sleeping. As shown in Table 15.5, behavioral signs may include cynicism toward coworkers, clients, and the organization. People who are burned out display detachment toward the people (e.g., clients) with whom they work. Eventually, they may become depressed and respond to burnout through absenteeism, turnover, and lower performance (Parker & Kulik, 1995).

Absenteeism and Turnover

Absenteeism and turnover, resulting in loss of productivity and subsequently revenues, are highest during times of burnout and increased stress as employees struggle

Table 15.5   Signs of Burnout

■ Less energy	■ Apathy
■ Lower productivity	■ Dread of coming to work
■ Consistently late for work	■ Feelings of little impact on coworkers or the organization
■ Complaining and negativity	
■ Decreased concentration	■ Feeling overwhelmed
■ Forgetfulness	■ Tension and frustration

to deal with physical and emotional ailments. About 2.3% of the workforce is absent each day in the United States and 13% of absenteeism is attributed to stress (Commerce Clearing House, 2007). With this in mind, the question then becomes, Is this absenteeism due to illness brought about by stress or does it represent "mental health days," in which employees miss work to take a break from stress? From a study by Heaney and Clemans (1995), it appears that the stress/illness relationship best explains absenteeism. Such absenteeism costs employers billions of dollars a year in lost productivity and is thought to be a warning sign of intended turnover (Mitra, Jenkins, & Gupta, 1992).

Interestingly, even when employees take a "mental health day," the strategy apparently is not highly effective. In a study of hospital nurses, Hackett and Bycio (1996) found that stress was lowered immediately following a day of absence but that taking a day off had no longer-term effects.

Drug and Alcohol Abuse

Unfortunately, as stress levels rise and anger increases, often so does the abuse of drugs and alcohol. Most incidents of domestic and other types of violence occur after an individual has been drinking or using drugs. This doesn't excuse the violator's behavior, but it does indicate the relationship of drugs and alcohol to anger and rage. And there are an increasing number of news reports of violence occurring in the workplace. Of those violent events, many are carried out by employees who have abused drugs and alcohol.

Because of the increasing problems of drug and alcohol abuse in organizations, many companies have set up employment assistance programs (EAPs) to which they refer employees suspected of drug or alcohol abuse, as well as those who are depressed and experiencing other problems. EAPs use professional counselors to deal with employee problems. Some large companies have their own EAP counselors, but most use private agencies, which are often run through local hospitals.

Many organizations also offer stress management programs that help people learn how to cope with stress. Having such organizational programs that can be used as a positive outlet for stress and the problems that come from it can often be beneficial to employees' regaining control over their lives.

Because many of our behavioral responses to stress are learned, the negative ones can be unlearned. Stress management teaches us positive and healthy behavioral responses. The key is to acknowledge the occasions on which you use destructive methods and take measures to correct them. If you don't, you won't like the consequences that result from improperly managed stress.

As organizations recognize the consequences of stress, they are beginning to take better precautions against it. For example, free voluntary counseling is made available by many organizations to all employees exhibiting emotional or discipline problems and particularly to those who have been terminated or laid off.

Health-Care Costs

One other organizational, as well as personal, consequence of stress is an increase in health insurance premiums. Because of the high use of medical facilities and options by others suffering from illnesses caused by stress, organizations that at one time paid the full cost for health insurance benefits are passing the increases on to the employees. This additional financial burden to some employees can be a new source of stress! The answer is to reduce the number of ailments causing stress, thereby decreasing the need to seek medical attention.

Managing Stress

Managing stress, or better yet, changing your behavior to healthfully respond to stress, should occur before, during, and after stress (Tyler, 2003a). Managing stress before it happens means incorporating daily practices (e.g., exercise) that will prepare your mind and body to handle the effects of stress. During stress you should continue with your prestress management techniques (such as reducing caffeine), as well as incorporate some others. Finally, after the stressor is eliminated (if that's even possible!), continue to proactively manage your stress. In addition, there are some other things you should consider. Let's examine some techniques for before, during, and after stress.

Planning for Stress

Some of the techniques that are suggested to proactively reduce stress should also be considered during times you are actually engaged in stress. These are discussed in the following sections.

Exercise

Exercising not only keeps your heart strong and resistant to the effects of stress, but can also help reduce your stress levels during particular stressful moments. It is a good idea to incorporate some kind of exercise program into your life at least three or four times a week for 20 minutes. You can reap great benefits from walking, swimming, running, playing sports, or climbing stairs because these strengthen your cardiovascular system, thereby making you more resistant to the effects of stress. Even such household chores as mowing the lawn, vacuuming, or washing your car can help your cardiovascular system. The good news is that not all exercise has to be strenuous. Certain good prestress relaxation techniques (explained later in this section) can be used during and after stress.

To begin an exercise program, start with "baby steps." For instance, instead of taking the elevator at work or school, walk up the stairs. Or consider this: Stop driving around the mall parking lot 20 times looking for the perfect parking spot! Instead, make a conscious effort to park farther away and walk the distance. From these baby steps, make the transition into a more serious exercise routine. Just remember to pick a program that works for you, which might not be the one your friends use. If you don't like running, don't do it. There is no need to add to your stress by choosing exercises that you absolutely can't tolerate. As a good example, many of my graduate students lift weights to reduce stress. They have repeatedly asked me to join them, but I decline because I know that their plan of "We're going to work on abs for an hour this morning and then shoulders for an hour this evening" involves more time than is practical for my Type A personality. Instead, I stick to the trusty Bullworker I purchased in the 1970s (they actually still make the Bullworker—a piece of isometric exercise equipment).

Organizations realize how important exercise is to managing the effects of stress, as evidenced by the increase in work-site fitness and health programs over the last 15 years. Research shows that exercise can reduce coronary heart disease by reducing blood pressure and lowering cholesterol (Gebhardt & Crump, 1990). In addition, meta-analysis results indicate that employee wellness programs, which often include exercise, result in lower levels of absenteeism and perhaps higher levels of performance (DeGroot & Kiker, 2003).

Exercise is a good way to reduce stress.

© Lee Raynes

A good example of the effectiveness of wellness programs can be found at the Emergency Medical Services (EMS) in Catawba County, North Carolina. Prior to initiation of its wellness program, the EMS was losing an average of two paramedics a year to work-related injuries. To increase wellness, the EMS conducted medical screenings and offered memberships to a local gym. After one year, absenteeism dropped from an average of 78 hours per employee to 57 hours; two employees quit smoking; and 47% of the employees lost body fat (Bradley, 2004).

Laughter

Humor has been shown to buffer stress in several ways (Chubb, 1995; Singer, 2000). First, it can help you put a new perspective on a stressful situation. You have probably heard many jokes about death—many of which are told by police officers, doctors, and morticians! The purpose of such jokes is not to hurt feelings or show callousness but to better deal with an uncomfortable topic that we all must face sooner or later. It is better to laugh at it than to dwell over what we can't control. But be careful when telling such jokes: Not everyone will appreciate the humor, and a little sensitivity and common sense should be exercised before sharing it.

Second, when you are upset and in what seems to be a difficult situation, going to a funny movie, listening to a comedian, or watching a funny television show can help distance you from the situation until you have calmed down enough to begin thinking rationally again.

Physically, laughter can reduce your blood pressure. Studies show that laughing through a funny movie has the same effect on your heart as 10 minutes on a rowing machine (Stanten, 1997). So next time you have the opportunity to go to a funny movie, go! Or, if you have a favorite comedy show that comes on more than once a week, try to watch as many episodes as possible (but don't forget to study for this class).

Though much has been written about the potential stress reduction benefits of humor, a qualitative literature review by Martin (2001) suggests that more research is needed to determine whether humor is as useful as thought to be. Martin's review does not conclude that humor is not useful, but instead concludes that the jury is still out.

Diet

Foods that have been shown to counteract the effects of stress include fresh fruits and vegetables, whole grains, and nonfat yogurt, which contains the B vitamin considered to be lost during high-stress periods of time (Posner & Hlivka, 2009). A daily dose of one or more of these can help you meet stress head on! Also, decrease your intake of fat, because your body has to work overtime to digest fatty foods, adding to your level of stress (Carpi, 1996). To help reduce the effects of stress, many organizations are including healthier items in their vending machines.

Drinking water helps keep your body hydrated and able to cope with daily stressors (maybe all that running to the bathroom is an added bonus to reducing stress and keeping you fit!). Caffeine should be gradually eliminated from your diet altogether. But before your stress level elevates from thinking about going without your daily caffeine boost, notice I said "should be" eliminated. If you can't eliminate caffeine, at least reduce your daily intake. Any change in that area is better than none. Be aware of just how much caffeine you are getting. You may be getting more than you think. It's not just cola and coffee products that contain caffeine; chocolate and many types of medicines and other foods have caffeine as well. If you decide to eliminate caffeine from your diet, do it gradually. Most people who are used to large amounts of daily caffeine experience withdrawal symptoms such as nausea, severe headaches, and fatigue if they go "cold turkey."

Smoking Reduction

Though many smokers say smoking decreases their feelings of stress, research indicates that smoking increases the physiological characteristics associated with stress (Kassel, Stroud, & Paronis, 2003). This is an important finding because research also indicates that smokers increase their smoking when they feel stressed (McCann & Lester, 1996). Thus, smoking and stress become a vicious cycle in which people smoke because they are stressed and then become more stressed because they smoke.

Sleep

There is no one study that says absolutely just how much individuals need to sleep. What studies show is that sleep deprivation or lack of sleep can cause negative behavior such as irritability, fatigue, lack of concentration, and even depression. Alcohol can severely affect your sleep, although it may seem that it helps you go to sleep. Studies show that the sleep of people who have had as little as two drinks before bed is interrupted several times a night. In addition, stay away from caffeine at least six hours before going to bed.

To examine how your own lifestyle prevents or contributes to stress, complete Exercise 15.3 in your workbook.

Support Network

Studies show that people who have someone to talk to, like a family member or a friend, are better able to manage their stress. You may have already experienced this. When you feel you aren't doing well in class, do you talk to someone about your feelings? Do you feel better afterward? Sometimes talking to someone we trust helps put things in perspective. So if you don't have a good support system, seek one out. This may mean joining certain college groups where you can meet people. Attend campus lectures where meeting friends is possible. And for extreme situations, familiarize yourself with the type of professional help that is available on or off campus that can give you the support you need during stressful times.

Self-Empowerment

In Chapter 14 you learned about empowerment. Most of the literature on empowerment is approached from an organizational, managerial perspective. That is, the literature explains how management can empower employees by giving them more control over important decisions that affect their lives. This has become important to organizations because research suggests that not having input into matters that affect us can be a big source of stress.

What most of the literature doesn't discuss is how employees can and need to learn to empower themselves. Ninety percent of workers think employers must act to reduce stress. But because employees cannot control what organizations do, it is more important for them to find their own ways to reduce stress. This is another form of self-empowerment. In addition, instead of complaining about how they don't get to participate in organizational decision making, employees need to take the initiative to volunteer to participate in committees or in group projects; this is one way to take back some control they perceive they have lost.

Individuals can also empower themselves in their personal lives. Instead of playing the victim who believes that life has singled him or her out to play dirty tricks on, individuals must learn to find ways to gain control over those situations they can control. This means taking an active role in finding out why something didn't turn out the way they wanted and making changes to prevent the event from occurring again. Chronic complaining about how everyone mistreats you is, to most people, a behavioral response to what is perceived as lack of control in your life. Most victimization is from learned behavior that we see modeled by family members, friends, coworkers, and even people we don't know, such as those in the news. To break that behavior, attending workshops on assertiveness and decision making can be beneficial. These types of workshops are usually offered through colleges, churches, and community groups. If you are interested in attending such training, check with your university to see what may be available.

To apply the concept of self-empowerment, complete Exercise 15.4 in your workbook.

Coping Skills

Improving your coping skills often means learning how to deal with conflict. It also means learning how to accept what you can't change. I often tell workers who participate in stress management classes that they can't change the fact that their organizations are downsizing or that restructuring is the trend for today's companies. Spending energy and time worrying about it or being angry is a waste of time. The best solution for them is to find areas that they can control to meet organizational change. This includes returning to college or taking technical training to make themselves marketable should they be laid off.

This is good advice for you as a college student as well. Worrying about whether you will graduate with a 4.0 GPA is both emotionally and physically stressful. Though setting a goal of high achievement is admirable, worrying about it for the entire four years you are in college is unproductive. Check out the Career Workshop Box for a summary of relaxation strategies.

Stress Reduction Interventions Related to Life/Work Issues

As shown in Table 15.6, due to the combination of an increasing number of dual-income and single-parent families, a tight job market, and a trend toward longer workdays, many organizations have made efforts to ensure that their employees maintain a balance between work and private life. Such efforts are important, as research suggests that employees with work–family conflicts are several times more likely to suffer from mood, anxiety, and substance-abuse disorders than are employees without such conflicts (Frone, 2000). Though organizational efforts to reduce private life–work conflicts are designed to help employees reduce their stress levels and thus increase their mental and physical health, they are also motivated by the fact that employees with such outside concerns as child and elder care are more prone to miss work and are less productive than employees without such concerns.

Easing the Child-Care Burden

More than 40% of employees in the labor force have children under the age of 18 and thus have a variety of child-care needs (O'Toole & Ferry, 2002). To help employees meet these needs, an increasing number of organizations have become involved with child-care issues. This increase is due in part to research demonstrating that the lack of regular child-care options causes employees with children to miss an additional eight days of work per year and costs an organization with 300 employees an average of $88,000 per year in lost work time (Woodward, 1999). Organizational child-care programs usually fall into one of three categories: on-site care, voucher systems, and referral services. In the first category, organizations such as Aflac Insurance, Discovery Communications, SAS, and Meridian Health built **on-site child-care facilities**. In the United States, less than 1% of organizations have on-site child-care centers, 4% sponsor off-site programs, and 17% offer a child-care referral service (SHRM, 2011). Although less than 1% of US companies have on-site child care centers, more than 25% of the companies in *Money* magazine's Top 100 Companies to Work For had on-site child care centers in 2011.

Some organizations fully fund the cost of child care, whereas others charge the employee the "going rate." There are advantages to both the employee and the organization that pays the full cost of a child enrolled in its facility. For example, the child-care cost can be used as a benefit, meaning that neither the employee nor the organization will have to pay taxes on the amount. Of course, tax laws may eventually change the situation, but until that time, calculating child care as an employee benefit is financially rewarding for both the employee and the organization.

Although the employee response to such on-site programs has been overwhelmingly positive, on-site centers are expensive to start to maintain. Because of such high costs, it is important to determine whether these centers "pay off" by reducing such problems as employee turnover and absenteeism. According to Scarr (1998), secure child care results in reduced levels of absenteeism and tardiness. Positive evidence has been provided from six sources:

- Intermedics, in Freeport, Texas, reported a 23% decrease in turnover and absenteeism.
- Prudential Insurance in Newark, New Jersey, reported $80,000 in annual savings due to their child-care center.

On-site child-care facility A child-care center that is located on the site of the organization employing the parent.

Dealing with Stress

In this chapter you learned that stress can have many negative effects. Following are some tips for dealing with stress.

Use Relaxation Techniques

Abdominal breathing is especially helpful for emotional calming. This requires that you get into a comfortable position, either sitting or lying on your back. Close your eyes and place your left hand on your abdomen and your right hand on your chest. Breathe normally, mentally counting from 1 to 4 as you inhale through your nose. Pause for two counts. Then open your mouth and mentally count from 1 to 6 as you exhale through your mouth. After several minutes of slow, rhythmic breathing, let your hands slowly move to your sides as your abdomen continues to move freely in and out with each breath. When you are finished, open your eyes and sit quietly.

Progressive muscle relaxation is used to relax the body. In a sitting or prone position, close your eyes and tense the following muscle groups: hands and arms, face, neck and shoulders, stomach and abdomen, buttocks and thighs, calves, and feet. Tense each group separately for a few seconds while breathing normally. Slowly release the tension as you focus on the pleasant contrast between tight and relaxed muscles.

Meditation is helpful for quieting a chaotic mind. Sit in a comfortable position and close your eyes. Breathe slowly from the abdomen. Focus your mind on a single word (e.g., *calm*), phrase ("*peace, love, joy*"), or sound ("*ooommm*"). Mentally repeat the chosen sound over and over. Adopt a passive attitude toward the process. When intruding thoughts occur, as they will, slowly and gently redirect your mind back to your repetitive sound. After 15 to 20 minutes, slowly open your eyes.

Your local library or hospital has additional information about relaxation methods. This is a good place to begin if you are interested in finding out more.

Engage in Time Management

Because a general feeling of being out of time can be a big source of stress, using time management techniques before and during stress can be helpful (Jex & Elacqua, 1999). Here is a small sample of the many time-management techniques suggested by Mayer (1990):

➡ Take several hours to clean your desk. I have a ritual in which at the end of the semester, I take almost a full day to clean my desk and office. For the two or three weeks that they stay uncluttered, I feel much more relaxed—as do the visitors to my office.

➡ Place a dollar amount on your time and then determine if any activity is worth the money. For example, if you value your time at $100 per hour and you spend 30 minutes each morning gossiping with a coworker, ask yourself, "Was the conversation worth $50?" If the answer is no, the conversation was a time waster.

➡ Make "to-do" lists, and cross out tasks once they have been accomplished.

➡ Keep a daily time log in which you schedule your appointments, even appointments for yourself. For example, you might schedule 10:00 a.m. to 11:00 a.m. to return phone calls or to read your mail. Treat these self-appointments as you would any other meeting, and don't let people interrupt you.

➡ To avoid waiting in line, do things at times when nobody else is doing them. For example, eat lunch at 11:00 a.m. rather than noon, go to the bank in the middle of the week rather than on Friday, or do your grocery shopping in the evening rather than right after work or on Saturday morning.

Though many of these suggestions seem reasonable, the empirical literature is unclear regarding the actual stress-reduction benefits of such time management techniques as making lists (Adams & Jex, 1999).

- Bristol-Myers Squibb found that users of its on-site child-care center had fewer intentions to leave the company than did other employees.
- Banc One Corporation in Chicago found that users of on-site child-care centers had seven fewer days of absenteeism than nonusers.
- Scott and Markham (1982) reported an average decrease of 19% in absenteeism for organizations that established on-site centers.
- Tioga Sportswear in Fall River, Massachusetts, found a 50% decrease in turnover.

Table 15.6 Percentage of Employers Offering Stress-Reducing Practices

Stress-Reducing Practice	Percent Offering	
	2011 SHRM Survey	2007 CCH Survey
Provide alternative work schedules		54
Flextime	53	
Telecommuting	45	53
Compressed workweek	35	45
Job sharing	13	38
Assist with child care		
Allow employee to bring child to work during emergencies	33	
On-site lactation room	28	
Provide a child-care referral service	17	
Subsidize cost of child care	4	
Assist with elder care		
Provide an elder-care referral service	9	
Provide emergency elder care	2	
Increase employee wellness		
Offer an employee assistance program (EAP)	75	72
Provide wellness information	75	60
Provide health-screening program	42	
Offer a smoking-cessation program	36	
Subsidize fitness-center dues	30	
Offer a weight-loss program	30	
Provide on-site fitness center	24	
Sponsor sports teams	17	
Offer a stress-reduction program	12	
Assist with daily chores		
Legal assistance	20	
Provide dry-cleaning service	10	
Provide take-home meals	3	
Provide concierge services	2	

Source: Society for Human Resource Management (SHRM) 2011 Benefits Survey (SHRM, 2011) and Commerce Clearing House (CCH) 2007 Unscheduled Absence Survey.

As one can imagine, it is difficult to conduct a well-controlled study on the effects of on-site child-care centers, as researchers need measures of absenteeism, turnover, and so on before and after the implementation of the child-care center, as well as a control group with which to compare users of the child care center. Unfortunately, there have been few such studies. Even more unfortunate is that these few studies suggest that on-site child-care centers do not reduce absenteeism or increase performance (e.g., Goff, Mount, & Jamison, 1990; Miller, 1984).

Voucher system Child-care policy in which an organization pays all or some of its employees' child-care costs at private child-care centers by providing the employees with vouchers.

A second avenue that can be taken with child care, one that is especially popular in the UK, is to provide employees with *vouchers* to be used with private day-care centers. From the perspective of the organization, **voucher systems** alleviate both the high start-up costs and the high costs of liability insurance associated with on-site centers. From an employee's perspective, this approach reduces the cost of private child care.

Unfortunately, there are several reasons this approach probably does not reduce employee turnover or absenteeism. First, an employee must still leave work to visit a sick child or to attend parent conferences. Although the Family and Medical Leave Act (FMLA) discussed in Chapter 3 allows an employee to take up to 12 weeks of unpaid leave to care for a sick family member, employees who leave work to care for their families leave a void that organizations may find difficult to fill. Furthermore, because only 25% of organizations provide paid family leave (SHRM, 2011), the financial loss to the employee can create tremendous stress and hardship. A second reason off-site child-care facilities aren't optimal is that most private child-care centers operate from 7:00 a.m. to 6:00 p.m. Thus, employees who work swing or night shifts are not helped. Finally, there is a shortage of quality child care in many areas. Some corporations, such as the Fayetteville, Arkansas, branch of Levi Strauss, donate large sums of money to local child-care centers to expand hours or services. Others, such as Time Warner and SunTrust Bank, contract with outside vendors to provide emergency child-care services for children who are ill. Because it can be difficult to find child-care centers that will take sick children, employers such as the Principal Financial Group in Des Moines, Iowa, have contracted with local health-care agencies to provide in-home care for their employees' sick children. Thirty-three percent of organizations allow their employees to bring their children to work in emergency situations in which child care is not available (SHRM, 2011).

Referral service A system of child care in which an employer maintains a list of certified child-care centers that can be used by its employees.

The final avenue taken by organizations is to provide a **referral service** to quality child-care centers. This approach has been taken by both IBM and Digital Corporation. Although this is certainly a useful service, nothing about it would suggest that it would reduce either absenteeism or turnover.

Hallmark Cards, Inc. is an excellent example of a company with progressive child-care and family benefits. Hallmark allows employees to take six months of unpaid maternity and paternity leave, reimburses employees up to $5,000 for the cost of adopting a child, helps employees locate care for children and aged parents, provides care for mildly ill children, holds parenting seminars, and provides alternative care arrangements for children out of school during holidays, inclement weather, or teacher workdays.

Easing the Elder-Care Burden

In 2009, 16% of the people in the United States were older than 65, a percentage that is projected to increase to 23% by 2034. As the number of elderly increases, so too does the need for elder care. In 2008, more than 44 million employees were providing elder care to a relative (Babcock, 2008); 64% of the people providing elder care also work full- or part-time jobs, and 41% also care for children (O'Toole & Ferry, 2002). According to statistics generated by the National Council on Aging, 50% of employees taking care of an elderly relative were absent from work, arrived at work late, or left work early to care for the relative. Six percent quit working to spend the necessary elder-care time. Given the negative impact on emotional health of working and providing elder care (Lee, Walker, & Shoup, 2001), such statistics are not surprising.

In spite of the great demand for elder care, organizational efforts on this front have lagged behind child-care efforts. According to a survey by the Society for

Human Resource Management (SHRM, 2011), only 9% of organizations provide elder-care referral services, and a less than 1% offer a company-sponsored or on-site elder-care facility. The most common elder-care programs provided by employers include flexible work schedules, resource and referral programs, long-term care insurance, expanded FMLA benefits, flexible spending and dependent care accounts, adult day care, seminars, and support groups. Such companies as AstraZeneca, Freddie Mac, Raytheon, Nike, and Intel offer seminars to employees to teach them how to care for their elderly relatives as well as deal with the stress that goes with such care.

The Federal National Mortgage Association, or "Fannie Mae," is an excellent example of an employer that understands the potential elder-care crisis. After a survey of its employees revealed that 70% expected to take on elder-care responsibilities within five years, Fannie Mae hired a licensed clinical social worker to help employees coordinate elder care. Fannie Mae estimates that it saves $1.50 in absenteeism and turnover costs for every $1.00 it spent on its elder-care program. Most important, 28% of the employees said that they would have quit their jobs had they not had the company-provided help (Wells, 2000).

Easing the Daily-Chore Burden

With work, child-care, and elder-care responsibilities, many employees find it increasingly difficult to complete such basic chores as going to the dentist, getting the car inspected, and picking up dry cleaning. As a result, organizations have implemented a variety of strategies to ease this burden. Popular among these are increasing the use of flexible working hours, increasing the number of paid personal days off, and providing essential services on-site.

By providing essential services on-site, employers assume that employees will work more hours because they will not have to take time away from work to complete common chores. For example, Analytical Graphics of Exton, Pennsylvania, provides its employees with free on-site breakfasts, lunches, and dinners so that employees don't have to leave the building to eat. Not only do employees feel appreciated and save money, but the company gets an additional 30 to 45 minutes of work out of them each day because they can eat while they work.

To ease the daily-chore burden, 2% of organizations provide concierge services for their employees (SHRM, 2011). For a cost between $30 and $1,000 per employee per year, these services will perform such tasks as making restaurant reservations, ordering flowers, having food delivered, scheduling car repairs, picking up dry cleaning, and having a person wait at an employee's home for service calls to repair appliances or conduct other business (Taylor, 2000). Examples of concierge services include Les Concierges, Best Upon Request, Circles, and Time Savers (see the Employment Profile Box).

To make shopping easier for employees, Microsoft, 3M, and Northwest Airlines allow employees to use their computers at work to buy discounted products and services. Thus, employees can purchase a variety of products including groceries and movie tickets without leaving the office. Employees get the benefit of lower prices and ease of shopping, and employers get the benefit of employees working longer hours.

Providing Rest Through Paid Time Off

Working long hours is a major factor in employee stress, as one-third of U.S. employees feel that they are overworked (Clark, 2001). These long hours are compounded by the fact that 14% of employees don't even take time off for lunch and another 56%

engage in other activities during their lunch break (Armour, 2006). Likewise, 60% of employees take laptops, pagers, and cell phones with them on vacation so that they can keep in touch with work (Frase-Blunt, 2001).

To help employees balance life and work, the majority of employers provide paid time off, usually in the form of vacations, holidays, sick days, and rest periods. The amount of paid time off varies across organizations, and some organizations do not provide any paid vacation days for hourly employees. In contrast to the United States, where organizations are not legally mandated to provide paid vacations, many countries do. For example, the legal minimum number of vacation days is 25 in Austria, Sweden, Spain, and France; 20 in Australia, Ireland, Italy, and the UK; and 10 in Canada and Japan.

EMPLOYMENT PROFILE

My entire career has been in human resources; however, a few years ago, I ventured out and created a new corporation called Time Savers, Inc. Time Savers is a concierge/errand service. I made the decision to start this company in response to a growing need to provide people with one of the hottest commodities around: time. I was constantly seeing overworked, stressed employees who never appeared to have time to get everything done, myself included. Many days I dreamed of having a personal assistant who could take care of things like picking up my dry cleaning that had been at the cleaners for weeks, or getting the birthday gift that needed to be shipped out the same day. Now I do these things for others.

According to a recent study by the Families and Work Institute, employees are spending an average of 44 hours per week on the job, and 45% of workers have daily family responsibilities to go home to. Seventy-eight percent of married workers have spouses who are also employed. So what does everyone do on his or her days off? Relax? No, they run errands. Employers also find that many employees are spending company time to complete personal business. With no time for leisure, stress is abundant. Busy people need more time to release tension, and concierge/errand services can help them do just that. We can take away a great many of those to-do items of busy people and give them back some time to do the important things like being with their families, exercising, or just going out to dinner with friends.

The concierge idea has been around for a long time in the hotel industry. Recently, it has begun to emerge in the corporate world and the private sector. I started thinking about the idea of starting this business after visiting a local company that had an in-house concierge service for its employees. I was very impressed with this concept. Companies today are looking for ways to attract and retain good employees. Concierge services are starting to show up on the list of company benefits. I wanted to be a part of this up-and-coming trend.

Lori Hurley, M.S.
President, Time Savers, Inc.

So what did it take for me to get this company off the ground? The first thing I had to do was research. Was this a viable business? Many hours were spent on the Internet, reading books, speaking with others who had existing concierge businesses, talking to my attorney, conferring with my accountant, and asking my friends and acquaintances their thoughts on using concierge services. The results were positive, so I decided to take the chance.

The next several months were spent going through the process of incorporating, developing a business plan, creating a logo, getting my office ready, getting special permits, deciding on a pricing strategy, identifying my target market, and drafting my brochures and advertisements. Finally, I was ready to advertise.

My first customer came within the first month. I was ecstatic. She was a single executive who commuted to another state. I was asked to do a variety of errands, ranging from standing in line at the Division of Motor Vehicles to dropping off dry cleaning, picking up contact lenses, and shopping for personal items. This customer has become a regular client. Other clients followed. I have retrieved mail, shopped for groceries, identified vendors, and taken items for repair, among other services.

The time that I am not spending fulfilling client requests, I am creating marketing materials, making sales contacts, handling the finances, and making plans for the future. I have learned more in the past few months about business than I have in my entire career.

It's very rewarding knowing that I am in some way helping my clients live a more satisfying life. The sky's the limit for my clients, and so are the possibilities for the business. The best advice I can offer is to look for a career in which you can do the things you most enjoy; there are so many opportunities out there that you should never be stuck with a job you don't like.

Table 15.7 Examples of Questions on Self-Reported Stress Questionnaires

- Do you frequently get angry or irritable?
- Do you take on too many responsibilities at work?
- I have trouble sleeping at night (true/false)
- I feel tense and on edge (true/false)
- Are you sad a lot and don't know why?
- Are you more forgetful (missing appointments, losing things)?
- I have to make important snap judgments and decisions (true/false)
- I am not consulted about what happens on my job (true/false)

Measuring Stress

In this chapter we discussed many causes and consequences of stress. A logical question, then, is how do we know when a person is stressed? In research, the most common measures of stress are self-report questionnaires in which people are asked a series of questions about their current level of stress. Commonly used measures of work-related stress and strain include the Occupational Stress Inventory, Job Stress Inventory, Maslach Burnout Inventory, Interpersonal Conflict at Work Scale, Organizational Constraints Scale, Quantitative Workload Inventory, and Physical Symptoms Inventory. Examples of questions found in stress questionnaires can be found in Table 15.7.

The problem with self-reports, of course, is that people may not know they are stressed or may not be truthful in their answers. So, in addition to self-report inventories, physiological and biochemical measures of stress can be used. Physiological measures include blood pressure, perspiration, heart rate, and muscle tension, and biochemical measures include cortisol and catecholamine levels (Sulsky & Smith, 2005).

Workplace Violence

In the past decade, the issue of workplace violence has received considerable interest from psychologists and HR professionals. In part this interest has been spurred by statistics such as these:

- In 2009, 521 employees were murdered at work.
- In 2009, 12% of fatal workplace injuries in the United States were the result of homicide.
- Approximately 572,000 incidents of workplace violence took place in the United States in 2009.
- Fifteen percent of violent crimes were committed while the victim was at work.
- Twenty-five percent of workers in the UK were victims of some form of bullying at work in the past five years.

Though the issue of workplace violence has received increasing interest, the rate of workplace violence has declined steadily since 1993.

Though more than 84% of homicide victims at work in 2009 were men, homicide was only the fourth most common cause of fatal workplace injuries among men (traffic accidents, falls, and being struck by an object are the first three), but was tied with traffic accidents as the most common cause of fatal workplace injuries among women. The gender differences in workplace violence can be explained by the fact that men traditionally work in higher-risk occupations such as mining that have high levels of fatalities caused by such other means as driving and construction accidents.

Though these figures are certainly attention getting, from an HR perspective they can be misleading, as a relatively small portion of the homicides are committed by current or former employees. Incidents of workplace violence can be placed into one of three categories. The first category, representing 70% of job-related homicides, is violence against an employee occurring as a result of a *crime* being committed. The most common examples are employees assaulted during the commission of a robbery. In fact, taxi drivers and convenience store clerks are the two kinds of workers most susceptible to workplace violence (working the graveyard shift at a 7-Eleven store may have more than chronological meaning).

The second category, representing 19% of job-related homicides, is violence against law enforcement officers (e.g., police officers, sheriffs, FBI agents) or security guards while they are in the *line of duty*. Law enforcement officers have a homicide rate of 9.3 per 100,000 employees, and the rate for security guards is 3.6 per 100,000. The average for all workers is 0.7 per 100,000.

The third category, representing 11% of job-related homicides, is violence against an employee or supervisor as an act of *anger or vengeance* by another employee, a customer, or a jilted lover. It is this category of violence that most involves HR professionals and has captured the imagination of the public. Of the homicides in this category, 44% are committed by current employees, 23% are committed by former employees, 21% involve domestic violence, and 12% involve other causes (Grossman, 2002).

Employee violence against other employees is usually the result of interpersonal disagreements. For example, in 2011, an employee of Fast Cuts Barber Shop in Miami, Florida killed a coworker following an argument at work. In another 2011 shooting at a barber shop, a former employee of Belle View Barber Shop in Alexandria, Virginia, killed a former coworker with whom he had been arguing when he was employed.

However, coworkers can be assaulted when employees take out their anger against a supervisor. Thirteen percent of workplace-violence incidents involve employees seeking revenge against a supervisor as a result of being fired, laid off, or subjected to some form of negative personnel action. Here are some examples:

- An employee at the Connecticut State Lottery was upset with his supervisors for "not listening to him," and the employee killed four coworkers before killing himself. Suicide is done by 36% of employees committing workplace violence.
- A Tulsa, Oklahoma, Wendy's employee, angry because his boss asked him to start work early, fired 12 shots from a .380-caliber handgun, wounding his supervisor and five other employees.
- Gregory Gray, a former case manager for Conrad House Community Services in San Francisco, killed a former coworker because he was angry about being fired. Gray brought a handgun, shotgun, and ax to his former place of employment, and had his handgun not jammed, more people would have been killed.
- After receiving notice that he would be fired, Nathaniel Brown, a janitor at Ohio State University killed a supervisor and wounded another before fatally shooting himself.

- Omar Thornton killed 8 employees and then himself after he left a disciplinary hearing in which he was accused of stealing beer from his employer, Hartford Distributors in Connecticut.
- After being suspended from her job at Kraft Foods in Philadelphia, Yvonne Hiller returned to work and killed two employees and wounded another.

Recently, psychologists have expanded their studies of workplace violence to include behaviors referred to as *mobbing* and *bullying*. Mobbing and bullying consist of hostile, alienating, and unethical behavior among employees. Examples of such behavior include intimidating a person, excluding or isolating someone socially, spreading malicious gossip that is not true, yelling at a person, using profanity, and belittling a person's opinions or work. Research suggests that about one in five employees in the United States, United Kingdom, Australia, and Canada report being the victim of bullying. This expanded definition of workplace violence has been adopted by the Canadian Centre for Occupational Health and Safety, whose definition of workplace violence includes the following actions:

- Threatening behavior
- Physical attacks
- Verbal abuse
- Verbal or written threats
- Harassment (any behavior that demeans, embarrasses, humiliates, annoys, alarms, or verbally abuses a person)

Perpetrators of Workplace Violence

Though many types of people commit workplace violence, the typical *employee* who engages in workplace violence (Glotz & Ruotolo, 2006; Turner & Gelles, 2003) has the following profile:

- Is a man (80%) between the ages of 20 and 50 (usually in his 40s). (Yet, the second most deadly workplace shooting in U.S. history was carried out by a woman in southern California in January 2006)
- Has his self-esteem tied to his job and perceives that he has been disrespected or unfairly treated
- Feels that he has no other way of resolving his mistreatment other than violence
- Has demonstrated a recent pattern of problems at work (increased absenteeism, violations of company policy, verbal threats to coworkers, decreased attention to appearance and personal hygiene)
- Has tried to get others to take his dilemma seriously by threatening, harassing, intimidating, yelling, and threatening to file grievances and lawsuits
- Has begun showing signs of paranoid thinking, delusions of persecution, and other bizarre thought patterns
- Has become isolated and withdrawn
- Has ready access to guns

Reducing Workplace Violence

Acts of workplace violence cannot completely be eliminated, but they can be reduced through security measures, employee screening, and management awareness (Epstein, 2003).

Security Measures

Increased security measures can decrease the probability of workplace violence. These measures can include such physical changes as adding surveillance cameras, silent alarms, bright external lighting, bulletproof barriers, sophisticated lock systems, and security guards; making high-risk areas more visible; and using drop safes and posting signs stating that only limited cash is kept on the premises. Staffing changes can include increasing the number of staff on duty; closing during the higher-risk late night and wee hours of the morning; and training employees in how to deal with robberies, conflicts, and angry customers.

Employee Screening

Though the security measures mentioned here are aimed primarily at reducing workplace violence resulting from other crimes such as robbery, they can also aid in reducing violence caused by current and former employees. Another method of reducing violence committed by current and former employees is to use psychological tests, reference checks, and background checks to screen applicants for violence potential.

Background and reference checks can provide information about an applicant's history of violence. These checks are important because employees who engage in workplace violence are chronically disgruntled, have a history of causing trouble, and frequently change jobs. Dietz (1994) provides two interesting examples. An applicant at a California maintenance company was hired in spite of a history of domestic violence and burglary convictions. He later set fire to a bookkeeper who wouldn't give him his paycheck. Another organization was sued because an employee who had killed a coworker was rehired by the same company in an effort to employ ex-cons. After a short period on the job, the employee killed another coworker.

It is important to note that ex-cons cannot categorically be denied employment. An organization must take into account the length of time that has passed since the crime was committed, the seriousness of the crime, and the relevance of the crime to the job in question.

Psychological tests such as the Minnesota Multiphasic Personality Inventory (MMPI-2) and a variety of integrity tests discussed in Chapter 5 can potentially predict violence in people without a history of violence. However, an empirical link between scores on these tests and workplace violence has yet to be made (Tonowski, 1993), in part because the violent event being predicted usually occurs many years after the preemployment testing. Furthermore, incidents of workplace violence are an interaction between a high-risk employee, an organization with poor management for which the employee works, and a stressful event attributed by the employee to the organization (Habeeb & Prencipe, 2001). Thus, a high-risk employee will be violent only under certain circumstances, which constantly change and are difficult to measure. Testing for high-risk employees is made even more difficult because the Americans with Disabilities Act provides limitations to the use of tests designed to determine psychological problems.

Management Awareness

Workplace violence can be greatly reduced by making managers aware of high-risk situations and empowering them to take immediate action. Most experts on workplace violence (e.g., Randazzo, 2008) believe that *berserkers*—employees who "go crazy" and shoot people—give indications that they are going to commit future violence. Such indications include threats, acts of violence, comments about wanting to get even, excessive talk of guns, and comments about famous serial killers and mass murderers. In one survey, 50% of HR practitioners who had incidents of workplace violence in their organizations observed warning signs prior to the incident (Trenn, 1993).

Take, for example, Thomas McIlvane, a fired postal worker who shot eight former coworkers, killing four. Prior to a union hearing appealing his termination, he stated that if he lost his grievance he would make a shooting incident in Oklahoma that took the lives of 14 postal workers "look like a tea party." As another example, prior to being fired and then killing his supervisors, Larry Hansel was reprimanded for excessively talking about a postal worker who killed two coworkers in Escondido, California. Jennifer San Marco, who killed five postal workers in California in January 2006 before taking her own life, had already been placed on medical leave because of her clearly unstable behavior at the postal facility.

Cavanaugh (2001) advises "zero tolerance" for threats and violence. That is, one act and the employee is terminated (fired, not killed). Dietz (1994) suggests that anyone who makes others feel uncomfortable is potential trouble. Turner and Gelles (2003) suggest that employees whose behavior makes others feel scared should be screened for violence potential. This screening includes interviews with coworkers and supervisors as well as meetings with a clinical psychologist. From these interviews and meetings, Turner and his associates place the employee into one of five risk categories:

1. High violence potential, qualifies for arrest/hospitalization
2. High violence potential, does not qualify for arrest/hospitalization
3. Insufficient evidence for violence potential, but sufficient evidence for *intentional* infliction of emotional distress upon coworkers
4. Insufficient evidence for violence potential, but sufficient evidence for *unintentional* infliction of emotional distress upon coworkers
5. Insufficient evidence for violence potential, and insufficient evidence for infliction of emotional distress upon coworkers

The potential for workplace violence can also be reduced through careful handling of terminations and layoffs. Refer to the discussion in Chapter 7 for specific ways to fairly evaluate and terminate employees. In addition to these techniques, free voluntary counseling should be made available to all employees, especially those exhibiting emotional, interpersonal, or discipline problems (Silbergeld & Jan, 2004).

ON THE JOB   **Applied Case Study**

Mira Sermanissian is the human resources director for a manufacturer of airline parts in Montreal. The environment of the company is one of high stress, due in part to the necessity to produce parts with no errors. Because the company operates in a "just-in-time" environment, there is no inventory and the parts not only must be perfect, they must be produced on demand. This need for precision and timeliness has resulted in an environment that some employees compare to that of brain surgery. As a result of this tension, Sermanissian realized that she needed to take steps to ensure that stress would not affect the physical and psychological health of the firm's employees.

- If you were Sermanissian, what would you do to help prevent the effects of stress?

- If stress is not reduced, what are the potential consequences for the employees and for the organization?

To find out how Sermanissian prepared her employees for stress, use the link found on your text webpage.

The Obligation to Reduce Stress

In October of 2007, the American Psychological Association (APA) released a study on stress in the United States. The study reported that one-third of Americans experience extreme stress. Seventy-four percent cite work as their number one stressor. This is up 59% from 2006. Stressors such as reorganizations, constant changes in the way companies do business, having to learn new technology, mergers, layoffs, and being asked to work longer hours can be blamed on workplace stress. And, in answer to the demands placed on workers, 50% of those surveyed in the APA report say that they do not use their allotted vacation time because of too much work. All work and no play, as the saying goes, increases stress and leads to potential health problems.

Negative stress (also called distress), as you learned in this chapter, has significant physiological, physical, and psychological consequences on employees. Distress can raise cholesterol and blood pressure levels, which can lead to heart attacks and strokes. It can make it harder to control diabetes and cause panic attacks. In the APA study, three-fourths of employees surveyed reported severe headaches, fatigue, and upset stomachs. Fifty percent reported that they did not sleep well, which can lead to accidents in the workplace. Forty-three percent report they have bad diets and will overeat and/or drink as a way to make themselves feel better. All of these factors cause dangerous health problems for employees.

In their 2007/2008 Staying@Work report, Watson Wyatt Worldwide, an international consulting firm, reported that 48% of employers surveyed agreed that the stress levels in their companies were high, but only 5% of them said that they were doing anything to help reduce employee stress. Even though stress-related illness costs businesses an estimated $300 billion a year that comes from turnover, layoffs, low productivity, work-related accidents, high insurance premiums, and legal fees, companies don't make the project of reducing workplace stress a top priority.

The question becomes, whose responsibility is it to reduce, or at least better manage workplace stress? Should the employee be held accountable for finding ways to reduce their stress and the negative impact it has on them? Or, ethically, is it the responsibility of companies to find ways to reduce employee stress and keep employees healthy?

Many people would say that, because of the dangerous health issues caused by high stress, businesses should be doing more to help reduce it or to help employees better manage it. In March 2008, the APA recognized five organizations that did believe it was companies' responsibility to promote employee health and well-being. These companies believe that they have an ethical responsibility to reduce the chances of any employee having to suffer the debilitating effects of extreme, long-term stress. They recognize that because of the demands placed on workers by companies and because workers have no control over what is expected of them, companies should do whatever they can to make work less stressful or less unhealthy.

Others say that it is the responsibility of individuals to find ways to decrease or better manage their stress. Employees have options: there are fitness centers they can join, or they can stop smoking, reduce their consumption of alcohol or caffeinated drinks, or read self-help books. They can seek help from counselors or other health professionals. Companies are in the business of making money, not of ensuring that people are healthy. Companies can't make and shouldn't be expected to make people take better care of themselves. And because what is stressful to one person may not be stressful to another, it is impossible to find and offer any one solution that's going to help everyone who is feeling stressed out because of the demands of their jobs. It would be too costly to companies to offer enough stress-reducing alternatives that would address the needs of all employees.

What do you think?

- Do you think companies have an ethical responsibility to offer solutions for employees that will help reduce stress?

- Do you think companies are to blame for the high stress levels in the workplace?

- What are some things that companies can offer or do for their employees?

- Do you think employees have any responsibility for ensuring they stay healthy under stressful conditions? If so, what are some things that employees can do for themselves?

Chapter Summary

In this chapter you learned:

- Stress is a psychological and physical reaction to certain life events or situations.
- Common sources of stress include personal stressors and such occupational stressors as job characteristics (role conflict, role ambiguity, role overload), organizational characteristics, work environment (noise and temperature), change, and relationships with others (e.g., conflict, difficult people, angry customers).
- At a personal level, stress can affect marriages and relationships with others. At a health level, stress results in a number of psychological (e.g., anxiety, depression) and physical disorders (e.g., joint pain, cardiovascular problems). At an organizational level, stress results in burnout, increased drug and alcohol use, lower job satisfaction, increased absenteeism, and increased turnover.
- Type A individuals and pessimists are more prone to stress than Type B individuals and optimists.
- Such techniques as exercise, laughter, a healthy diet, not smoking, getting plenty of sleep, joining support groups, self-empowerment, and time management can reduce stress.
- Workplace violence can result from employee stress.

Questions for Review

1. Why are some people more affected by stress than others?
2. What job characteristics are most likely to result in high levels of stress?
3. Why should organizations be concerned about employee stress?
4. How much attention should organizations pay to noise and temperature?
5. Do stress management techniques actually work? Why or why not?
6. Why does workplace violence occur?

Media Resources and Learning Tools

- Visit our website. Go to www.cengage.com/psychology/aamodt, where you will find online resources directly linked to your book, including chapter-by-chapter quizzing, flashcards, crossword puzzles, application activities, and more.
- Want more practice applying industrial/organizational psychology? Check out the *I/O Applications Workbook*. This workbook (keyed to your textbook) offers engaging, high-interest activities to help you reinforce the important concepts presented in the text.

APPENDIX Working Conditions and Human Factors

Ergonomics and *human factors* are areas of study in which psychologists and engineers try to produce products and systems that are easy to use and safe and will maximize efficiency and minimize physical and psychological strain. Though there are many areas involved in ergonomics and human factors, only four will be highlighted over the next few pages: injury reduction, product design, system efficiency, and transportation.

Preventing Repetitive Stress Injuries

As a result of the amount of precision and computer work performed by employees, hand and wrist injuries commonly occur at work. The most common of these repetitive-stress injuries (RSIs) or cumulative trauma disorders (CTDs) are carpal tunnel syndrome (CTS) and tendonitis. According to the 2010 Liberty Mutual Workplace Safety Index, RSIs are the ninth most common injury affecting U.S. workers and annually cost employers over $1.83 billion in workers' compensation claims.

RSIs are the result of physical stress placed on the tendons and nerves that pass through a tunnel connecting the wrists and hands. The normal stress associated with repeated finger and hand movements is complicated by the awkward angle at which many employees must hold their wrists. Early symptoms of RSI include numbness and tingling in the hands and forearms. Later stages involve pain severe enough to make opening a door or holding a pen difficult if not impossible.

Treatments for carpal tunnel syndrome include taking anti-inflammatory drugs, wearing wrist braces, and undergoing surgery. Many RSIs can be prevented by learning ergonomically proper work techniques, performing warm-up exercises, using wrist rests and special keyboards, taking breaks, and stopping work when numbness or pain begins.

A good example of an intervention to reduce RSIs is provided by Pratt & Whitney in Middletown, Connecticut. After employees complained of the physical stress caused by repetitively using their finger to open plastic bags containing machine parts, the company placed a small letter opener on the top of the carts used to move the parts. The cost for this intervention was only $3 a cart. A more complicated intervention was implemented at a Gold Kist plant in Alabama. To eliminate the need for employees to repetitively push crates of chicken along a series of rollers, the company installed a moving conveyor belt (Grossman, 2000).

Organizations that have trained employees on ways to prevent RSIs have seen excellent results (Smith, 2003b). For example, Mitsubishi reported a 45% decrease in RSIs over a two-year period following training, and 3M reported that its training program resulted in a 50% decrease in workers' compensation claims (Tyler, 1998). The training provided by 3M not only reduced the number of worker's compensation claims by 50%, but also decreased absenteeism by 13% (Tyler, 1998). Due to employer awareness of RSIs, data from the 2010 Liberty Mutual Workplace Safety Index indicate that the number of RSI-related workman's compensation claims has dropped 44% since 1998.

Product Design

Human-factors psychologists are often employed by organizations to improve the user-friendliness of products. Examples might include determining the best layout for a computer keyboard, choosing the optimal size for the finger holes in a pair of scissors, or designing an automobile dashboard to reduce the distance a driver needs to reach to play the car stereo.

A good example of product design comes from a study by Dempsey et al. (1996), who were asked to help design the ideal satchel to be carried by postal workers. To do this, they tested four different satchels to determine which one was most comfortable, worked best in diverse climates, was easiest to use, and provided the best protection against attacking dogs. The results of their study indicated that the most comfortable bag also provided the worst protection against attacking dogs and had some problems with ease of mail retrieval.

A similar study was conducted by Pascoe, Pascoe, Wang, Shim, and Kim (1997) in designing book bags. Pascoe and his colleagues compared the effect that three types of bags—two-strap backpack, one-strap backpack, and one-strap athletic bag—had on the posture and gait of the student wearing the book bag. When compared with no book bag, all three types reduced stride length and increased stride frequency. Furthermore, the one-strap backpack and one-strap athletic bag resulted in uncomfortable changes in posture. However, the two-strap backpack did not result in such changes. Thus, the practical aspects of this study suggest that students should buy a backpack with two straps and, even though it is not as cool as slinging one strap over one shoulder, use both straps.

The search for the ideal work glove provides another example of product design studies. This search took two paths: one that investigated the effects of wearing gloves and another that compared the advantages of certain types of gloves over others. Though gloves clearly increase worker safety, their effect on work performance depends on the type of task performed. For example, researchers have found that wearing gloves increases muscle fatigue (Willms, Wells, & Carnahan, 2009), reduces dexterity (Dianat, Haselgrave, & Stedmon, 2010), and decreases the amount of turning force (the authors of the study called this "maximum volitional torque exertion of supination") that can be exerted by a worker (Shih & Wang, 1997), but it does not affect the ability to discriminate weights (Shih & Wang, 1996).

Acknowledging that gloves reduce the force that can be exerted with the bare hand, Kovacs, Splittstoesser, Maronitis, & Marras (2002) compared nine different types of gloves to determine which type had the least effect on force. Their results indicated that surgical gloves had the least decline in force and leather gloves the greatest decline in force.

An example of a study searching for the optimal glove comes from Nelson and Mital (1995), who investigated the optimal thickness for examination gloves used by physicians (*ouch!*). Their study was conducted because although thicker gloves provide greater protection against needle sticks, they might also reduce the ability of the physician to perform sensitive work. The researchers tested five gloves ranging in thickness from 0.21 mm to 0.83 mm. Nelson and Mital found that the 0.83-mm glove not only resisted routine impacts but provided the same level of dexterity and tactility as a bare hand. Though neither bags nor gloves are particularly exciting topics, these examples show the meticulous human-factors research that goes into the development of good products.

System Efficiency

A major human-factors area, at times referred to as "time and motion studies," is making systems more efficient. These studies usually begin with a job analysis to determine how employees perform their jobs. These job analyses tend to be much more specific than the ones you learned about back in Chapter 2. For example, suppose you were trying to reduce the time it took for a counterperson at a fast-food restaurant to perform his job. As shown in Figure A.1, the employee reached for ketchup packets 150 times, pepper packets 10 times, french-fry containers 140 times, and french fries 140 times. What is wrong with the current layout? As you probably guessed, one of the most frequently retrieved items (ketchup) is farthest away, and the least frequently retrieved item (pepper) is closest. Also note from the correlation table that each time the employee retrieved a french-fry container, he also retrieved french fries, yet the two are located in different areas. To improve efficiency, the

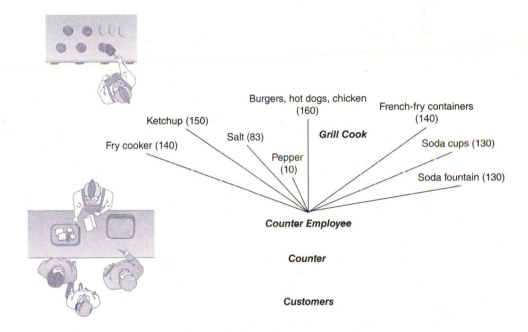

Figure A.1

Layout of a Fast-Food Counter (the numbers indicate the number of times the counterperson walked to get a particular item)

Movement Correlation Chart								
	(F)	(FC)	(K)	(G)	(P)	(S)	(D)	(DC)
Fries (F)	1.00	.86	.70	.10	.30	.63	.63	
Fry containers (FC)			.86	.70	.10	.30	.63	.63
Ketchup (K)				.70	.30	.60	.45	.45
Grilled food (G)					.10	.40	.05	.65
Pepper (P)						.50	.20	.20
Salt (S)							.29	.29
Drinks (D)								1.00
Drink cups (DC)								

most often retrieved items should be moved closer to the employee, and items that are retrieved together would be located near one another.

As another example, due to the high number of musculoskeletal complaints (for example, back pain or sore wrists) by grocery store cashiers, extensive research has gone into designing a checkout stand that is both efficient and comfortable. According to a literature review and new data by Grant and Habes (1995), these are the features of the ideal checkout stand:

- The cashier would face the customer.
- The height of the work surface would be no taller than the cashier's elbows.
- The scanner and keyboard would be in front of the cashier and the cash drawer to his/her side (less than 18 inches away).
- Groceries would be presented to the cashier on a conveyor belt that is narrow (to reduce reach) and that runs from the scanner to the back of the checkout stand.
- Stools, footrests, and antifatigue mats would be present to allow the cashier the choice of sitting or standing.

Transportation

Putting the Brakes on Rear-End Collisions

The goal of human-factors research in the realm of transportation is to make driving safer and easier. For example, human-factors researchers have conducted several studies to reduce rear-end collisions. The first step is to study the driving process and create a process chart that diagrams the events that take place, the order in which they occur, and their duration. Such a process chart might show that the amount of time needed to avoid a collision is a function of (1) the time it takes for the lead driver to scan the environment, determine if there is a reason to brake, make the decision to brake, and then apply the brake and (2) the time it takes for the trailing driver to notice cues (brake lights, turn indicators, slowing of speed), distinguish one cue from another, make a decision to brake, and then apply the brakes. To reduce rear-end collisions, human-factors psychologists look for ways to reduce the processing time at each of the steps shown in the process chart. For example, talking on a cellular phone (Caird, Willness, Steel, & Scialfa, 2008), listening to loud music (Turner, Fernandez, & Nelson, 1996), or talking to a passenger (Young & Stanton, 2007) while driving increases the time it takes to notice such cues as brake lights and traffic signals. Sivak, Flannagan, Sato, and Traube (1994) found that neither neon nor LED brake lights resulted in better reaction times than either standard or enhanced incandescent lights.

Researchers in another study focused on the step of distinguishing one cue from another. They hypothesized that because both your brake lights and your turn indicators are red, a driver following behind you must spend fractions of a second interpreting whether you are braking or using your turn-signal (Luoma, Flannagan, Sivak, Aoki, & Traube, 1997). These fractions of a second could be the difference in avoiding an accident in the case of an immediate stop. Luoma and his research team found that changing the color of the turn signal from red to yellow reduced the time taken to react to a brake signal. This study supports the European and Japanese requirements that turn signals be yellow (in the United States, both red and yellow are allowed). In another study focusing on the ability to discriminate brake lights from other lights, Theeuwes and Alferdinck (1995) found that a brake light mounted in the rear window is more effective if it is located higher on the window rather than toward the bottom of the window.

Another study sought to reduce the time between the lead driver taking his foot off the accelerator and moving it to the brake. To do this, Shinar (1995) developed an advance brake warning (ABW) system in which a sudden release of the accelerator pedal would activate the brake light for one second. If the driver actually hit the brake pedal, the brake light would stay on. If the driver did not brake, the brake light would go off. Though this system provides an early warning system, it could potentially result in false alarms. To study this possibility, Shinar (1995) studied 95,394 times in which six drivers applied their brakes. The ABW was activated during 820 of the 95,394 instances of braking and provided a following driver an average of one-fifth of a second more warning. The false alarm rate was 23% of ABW activations but accounted for only 2% of all brake light activations of less than a second. Thus, the extra warning time did not appear to result in an excessive number of false alarms.

Reducing Speeding

Human-factors experts have also conducted research to determine ways to reduce speeding by changing the driving environment. For example, De Waard, Jessurun, Steyvers, Raggatt, and Brookhuis (1995) hypothesized that drivers would speed less often if speeding were made perceptually uncomfortable (as opposed to traffic citations, making speeding financially uncomfortable). To do this, De Waard et al. removed the white lines on the right side of a single-lane road and replaced them with intermittent chippings that made noise when run over by a speeding car. The idea behind this intervention was that speeding drivers often touch the lines on each side of the lane because they are going too fast to keep their vehicles in the center of the lane. "Penalizing" the speeding driver with a noxious noise reduced average speeds by 3 kilometers per hour—enough of a reduction to increase safety.

In another attempt to reduce speeding, one group of researchers believed that some instances of speeding were the result of drivers being unaware of the speed limit. To reduce this possibility, three researchers at the University of Helsinki in Finland (Lajunen, Hakkarainen, & Summala, 1996) tested three different types of signs telling drivers to slow down as they were entering a "built-up" (densely populated) area, in which the national speed limit was 50 kilometers per hour. The first sign contained the symbol for the built-up area, the second the built-up area symbol plus the symbol for danger, and the third the built-up area symbol plus the number "50" in a circle. As you might expect, drivers reduced their speed most often with the sign that showed the explicit speed limit number and least often with the two signs in which one had to simply know the speed limit in a built-up area. In the United States, these findings might be generalized to replace signs that say "School Zone" with ones that say "School Zone: Speed Limit 25 MPH."

Although this study seems to suggest that signs with text are superior to those with icons and symbols, this is not usually the case. Research indicates that icon/symbol highway signs are easier to read and result in lower reaction times than do text-based highway signs (Long & Kearns, 1996). Why the contradictory findings? It is clear that icon/symbol signs are easier to read than signs containing text. However, seeing a symbol and understanding its meaning are two different things. Look at the

highway signs shown in Figure A.2. All of them are easy to read, yet some of them may not be familiar to you. If you aren't familiar with the meaning, or if you are familiar with the meaning ("slow down" in the figure) but don't know what you are supposed to do (not exceed 25 mph), the benefit of the increased viewing distances of the iconic signs may be nullified by the increased time to interpret them.

Photo courtesy of the author

What lane should you get in to travel to Roanoke?

This use of icons will be effective only if people have knowledge about the meaning of the icons. Let me provide you with a great example of this point. Our interstate highway system is actually very well designed and very well marked in most locations. However, many people can't take full advantage of these well-designed and well-marked highways because they aren't familiar with the codes appearing on the signs. For example, suppose you were driving on I-81 or I-77. That both of these highways end in an odd number tells you that the highway runs north to south; even-numbered highways run east to west. Or suppose you were driving along, wanted to take the highway to Roanoke, and saw the sign in the accompanying photo. What does that sign tell you? Because the arrow is on the left side of the word *Roanoke*, you would need to get in the left lane and take a left turn onto the highway. If the arrow were on the right side or beneath the word *Roanoke*, you would get in the right lane and take a right turn onto the highway. How many people do you think know these rules?

GLOSSARY

360-degree feedback   A performance appraisal system in which feedback is obtained from multiple sources such as supervisors, subordinates, and peers.

Ability   A basic capacity for performing a wide range of different tasks, acquiring knowledge, or developing a skill.

Absolute amount   The actual salary paid for a particular job.

Acceptance stage   The fourth and final stage of emotional reaction to downsizing, in which employees accept that layoffs will occur and are ready to take steps to secure their future.

Accommodating style   The conflict style of a person who tends to respond to conflict by giving in to the other person.

Achievement-oriented style   In path–goal theory, a leadership style in which the leader sets challenging goals and rewards achievement.

Adaptation   The fourth stage of change, in which employees try to adapt to new policies and procedures.

Additive tasks   Tasks for which the group's performance is equal to the sum of the performances of each individual group member.

Adverse impact   An employment practice that results in members of a protected class being negatively affected at a higher rate than members of the majority class. Adverse impact is usually determined by the four-fifths rule.

AET   An ergonomic job analysis method developed in Germany (*Arbeitswissenschaftliches Erhebungsverfahren zur Tätigkeitsanalyse*).

Affect   Feelings or emotion.

Affective commitment   The extent to which an employee wants to remain with an organization and cares about the organization.

Affective identify motivation   The motivation to lead as a result of a desire to be in charge and lead others.

Affiliation style   A leadership style in which the individual leads by caring about others and that is most effective in a climate of anxiety.

Affirmative action   The process of ensuring proportional representation of employees based on variables such as race and sex. Affirmative-action strategies include intentional recruitment of minority applicants, identification and removal of employment practices working against minority applicants and employees, and preferential hiring and promotion of minorities.

Age Discrimination in Employment Act (ADEA)   A federal law that, with its amendments, forbids discrimination against an individual who is over the age of 40.

Alternate-forms reliability   The extent to which two forms of the same test are similar.

Americans with Disabilities Act (ADA)   A federal law, passed in 1990, that forbids discrimination against the physically and mentally disabled.

Ammerman technique   A job analysis method in which a group of job experts identifies the objectives and standards to be met by the ideal worker.

Anger stage   The second stage of emotional reaction to downsizing, in which employees become angry at the organization.

Anxiety   An organizational climate in which worry predominates.

Application of training   Measurement of the effectiveness of training by determining the extent to which employees apply the material taught in a training program.

Apply-in-person ads   Recruitment ads that instruct applicants to apply in person rather than to call or send résumés.

Apprentice training   A training program, usually found in the craft and building trades, in which employees combine formal coursework with formal on-the-job training.

Arbitration   A method of resolving conflicts in which a neutral third party is asked to choose which side is correct.

Archival research   Research that involves the use of previously collected data.

Army Alpha   An intelligence test developed during World War I and used by the army for soldiers who can read.

Army Beta   An intelligence test developed during World War I and used by the army for soldiers who cannot read.

Artifacts   The things people surround themselves with (clothes, jewelry, office decorations, cars, and so forth) that communicate information about the person.

Assessment center   A method of selecting employees in which applicants participate in several job-related activities, at least one of which must be a simulation, and are rated by several trained evaluators.

Assimilated A description of a message in which the information has been modified to fit the existing beliefs and knowledge of the person sending the message before it is passed on to another person.

Assimilation A type of rating error in which raters base their rating of an employee during one rating period on the ratings the rater gave during a previous period.

Asynchronous technologies Distance learning programs in which employees can complete the training at their own pace and at a time of their choosing.

Attitude survey A form of upward communication in which a survey is conducted to determine employee attitudes about an organization.

Attitudinal Listening Profile A test developed by Geier and Downey that measures individual listening styles.

Attractiveness The extent to which a leader is appealing to look at.

Audience effects The effect on behavior when one or more people passively watch the behavior of another person.

Authentic leadership A leadership theory stating that leaders should be honest and open and lead out of a desire to serve others rather than a desire for self-gain.

Autocratic I strategy Leaders use available information to make a decision without consulting their subordinates.

Autocratic II strategy Leaders obtain necessary information from their subordinates and then make their own decision.

Averaging versus adding model A model proposed by Anderson that postulates that our impressions are based more on the average value of each impression than on the sum of the values for each impression.

Avoiding style The conflict style of a person who reacts to conflict by pretending that it does not exist.

Banding A statistical technique based on the standard error of measurement that allows similar test scores to be grouped.

Bandwidth The total number of potential work hours available each day.

Barnum statements Statements, such as those used in astrological forecasts, that are so general that they can be true of almost anyone.

Base rate Percentage of current employees who are considered successful.

Baseline The level of productivity before the implementation of a gainsharing plan.

Basic biological needs The first step in Maslow's needs hierarchy, concerning survival needs for food, air, water, and the like.

Behavior modeling A training technique in which employees observe correct behavior, practice that behavior, and then receive feedback about their performance.

Behavioral observation scales (BOS) A method of performance appraisal in which supervisors rate the frequency of observed behaviors.

Behaviorally anchored rating scales (BARS) A method of performance appraisal involving the placement of benchmark behaviors next to each point on a graphic rating scale.

Benchmark answers Standard answers to interview questions, the quality of which has been agreed on by job experts.

Binding arbitration A method of resolving conflicts in which a neutral third party is asked to choose which side is correct and in which neither party is allowed to appeal the decision.

Biodata A method of selection involving application blanks that contain questions that research has shown will predict job performance.

Blind box ads Recruitment ads that instruct applicants to send their résumé to a box at the newspaper; neither the name nor the address of the company is provided.

Blog A website in which the host regularly posts commentaries on a topic that readers can respond to.

Bona fide occupational qualification (BFOQ) A selection requirement that is necessary for the performance of job-related duties and for which there is no substitute.

Bottom-line measure Evaluation of a training program by determining if the organization actually saved money as a result of the training.

Brainstorming A technique in which ideas are generated by people in a group setting.

Bridge publication A publication with the goal of bridging the gap between the research conducted by academics and the practical needs of practitioners.

Bulletin board A method of downward communication in which informal or relatively unimportant written information is posted in a public place.

Burnout The psychological state of being overwhelmed with stress.

Business communication The transmission of business-related information among employees, management, and customers.

Business game   An exercise, usually found in assessment centers, that is designed to simulate the business and marketing activities that take place in an organization.

Business impact   A method of evaluating the effectiveness of training by determining whether the goals of the training were met.

Case law   The interpretation of a law by a court through a verdict in a trial, setting precedent for subsequent court decisions.

Case study   A training technique in which employees, usually in a group, are presented with a real or hypothetical workplace problem and are asked to propose the best solution.

Casual work   A scheduling practice in which employees work on an irregular or as-needed basis.

Cause-and-effect relationship   The result of a well-controlled experiment about which the researcher can confidently state that the independent variable caused the change in the dependent variable.

Central tendency error   A type of rating error in which a rater consistently rates all employees in the middle of the scale, regardless of their actual levels of performance.

Change agent   A person who enjoys change and makes changes for the sake of it.

Change analyst   A person who is not afraid of change but makes changes only when there is a compelling reason to do so.

Change resister   A person who hates change and will do anything to keep change from occurring.

Chronic self-esteem   The positive or negative way in which a person views himself or herself as a whole.

Chronological résumé   A résumé in which jobs are listed in order from most to least recent.

Circadian rhythm   The 24-hour cycle of physiological functions maintained by every person.

Clarifier   A type of structured interview question that clarifies information on the résumé or application.

Closed desk arrangement   An office arranged so that a visitor must sit across from the person behind the desk.

Cluster grapevine   A pattern of grapevine communication in which a message is passed to a select group of people who each in turn pass the message to a few select others.

Coaching   A method of training in which a new employee receives on-the-job guidance from an experienced employee.

Coaction   The effect on behavior when two or more people are performing the same task in the presence of each other.

Coefficient alpha   A statistic used to determine internal reliability of tests that use interval or ratio scales.

Coercive power   Leadership power that comes from the leader's capacity to punish others.

Coercive style   A leadership style in which the individual leads by controlling reward and punishment; most effective in a climate of crisis.

Cognitive ability   Abilities involving the knowledge and use of information such as math and grammar.

Cognitive ability test   Tests designed to measure the level of intelligence or the amount of knowledge possessed by an applicant.

Collaborating style   The conflict style of a person who wants a conflict resolved in such a way that both sides get what they want.

Common goal   An aim or purpose shared by members of a group.

Communication barriers   Physical, cultural, and psychological obstacles that interfere with successful communication and create a source of conflict.

Communication channel   The medium by which a communication is transmitted.

Communication structure   The manner in which members of a group communicate with one another.

Comparable worth   The idea that jobs requiring the same level of skill and responsibility should be paid the same regardless of supply and demand.

Comparison   The effect when an individual working on a task compares his or her performance with that of another person performing the same task.

Compensable job factors   Factors, such as responsibility and education requirements, that differentiate the relative worth of jobs.

Compensatory approach   A method of making selection decisions in which a high score on one test can compensate for a low score on another test. For example, a high GPA might compensate for a low GRE score.

Competencies   The knowledge, skills, abilities, and other characteristics needed to perform a job.

Competition for resources   A cause of conflict that occurs when the demand for resources is greater than the resources available.

Complaint box   A form of upward communication in which employees are asked to place their complaints in a box.

Composite score   A single score that is the sum of the scores of several items or dimensions.

Compressed workweeks   Work schedules in which 40 hours are worked in less than the traditional 5-day workweek.

Compromising style   A style of resolving conflicts in which an individual allows each side to get some of what it wants.

Computer-adaptive testing (CAT) A type of test taken on a computer in which the computer adapts the difficulty level of questions asked to the test-taker's success in answering previous questions.

Concurrent validity A form of criterion validity that correlates test scores with measures of job performance for employees currently working for an organization.

Conditional reasoning test Tests designed to reduce faking by asking test-takers to select the reason that best explains a statement.

Conflict The psychological and behavioral reaction to a perception that another person is either keeping you from reaching a goal, taking away your right to behave in a particular way, or violating the expectancies of a relationship.

Conjunctive tasks Tasks for which the group's performance is dependent on the performance of the least effective group member.

Consideration The degree to which leaders act in a warm and supportive manner toward their subordinates.

Consistency theory Korman's theory that employees will be motivated to perform at levels consistent with their levels of self-esteem.

Construct validity The extent to which a test actually measures the construct that it purports to measure.

Consultative I strategy Leaders share the problem on an individual basis with their subordinates and then make a decision that may or may not be consistent with the thinking of the group.

Consultative II strategy Leaders share the problem with the group as a whole and then make a decision that may or may not be consistent with the thinking of the group.

Contamination The condition in which a criterion score is affected by things other than those under the control of the employee.

Content validity The extent to which tests or test items sample the content that they are supposed to measure.

Contextual performance The effort employees make to get along with their peers, improve the organization, and "go the extra mile."

Continuance commitment The extent to which employees believe they must remain with an organization due to the time, expense, and effort they have already put into the organization.

Contrast effect When the performance of one applicant affects the perception of the performance of the next applicant.

Contrast error A type of rating error in which the rating of the performance level of one employee affects the ratings given to the next employee being rated.

Control group A group of employees who do not receive a particular type of training so that their performance can be compared with that of employees who do receive training.

Convenience sample A nonrandom research sample that is used because it is easily available.

Cooperation-consideration One of five categories from the trait approach to scoring letters of recommendation.

Cooperative problem solving A method of resolving conflict in which two sides get together to discuss a problem and arrive at a solution.

Core hours The hours in a flextime schedule during which every employee must work.

Corrected validity A term usually found with meta-analysis, referring to a correlation coefficient that has been corrected for predictor and criterion reliability and for range restriction. Corrected validity is sometimes called "true validity."

Correlation A statistical procedure used to measure the relationship between two variables.

Correlation coefficient A statistic, resulting from performing a correlation, that indicates the magnitude and direction of a relationship.

Corresponding effects An event that affects one member of a group will affect the other group members.

Cost per applicant The amount of money spent on a recruitment campaign divided by the number of people that subsequently apply for jobs as a result of the recruitment campaign.

Cost per qualified applicant The amount of money spent on a recruitment campaign divided by the number of qualified people that subsequently apply for jobs as a result of the recruitment campaign.

Counterbalancing A method of controlling for order effects by giving half of a sample Test A first, followed by Test B, and giving the other half of the sample Test B first, followed by Test A.

Country club leadership A style of leadership in which the leader is concerned about the well-being of employees but is not task oriented.

Cover letter A letter that accompanies a résumé or job application.

Crisis A critical time or climate for an organization in which the outcome to a decision has extreme consequences.

Criterion A measure of job performance, such as attendance, productivity, or a supervisor rating.

Criterion group Division of employees into groups based on high and low scores on a particular criterion.

Criterion validity   The extent to which a test score is related to some measure of job performance.

Critical Incident Technique (CIT)   The job analysis method developed by John Flanagan that uses written reports of good and bad employee behavior.

Critical incidents   A method of performance appraisal in which the supervisor records employee behaviors that were observed on the job and rates the employee on the basis of that record.

Critical judge   A person who, when under stress, focuses on his or her negative aspects as well as those of the situation.

Cross-functional teams   Teams consisting of representatives from various departments (functions) within an organization.

Cross-training   Teaching employees how to perform tasks traditionally performed by other employees.

Cutoff approach   A method of hiring in which an applicant must score higher than a particular score to be considered for employment.

Dale-Chall Index   A method of determining the readability level of written material by looking at the number of commonly known words used in the document.

Dead-enders   Employees who receive much grapevine information but who seldom pass it on to others.

Debriefing   Informing the subject in an experiment about the purpose of the study in which he or she was a participant and providing any other relevant information.

Defense   The second stage of change, in which employees accept that change will occur but try to justify the old way of doing things.

Denial   The first stage in the emotional reaction to change or layoffs, in which an employee denies that an organizational change or layoff will occur.

Dependability-reliability   One of five categories from the trait approach to scoring letters of recommendation.

Dependent variable   The measure of behavior that is expected to change as a result of changes in the independent variable.

Derivation sample   A group of employees who were used in creating the initial weights for a biodata instrument.

Desirability   The extent to which a trait or behavior is valued as being good in society.

Despair   An organizational climate characterized by low morale.

Devil's advocate   A group member who intentionally provides an opposing opinion to that expressed by the leader or the majority of the group.

Dictionary of Occupational Titles   The DOT is a directory that was published by the federal government that supplied information for almost 30,000 jobs. It has been replaced by O*NET.

Difference score   A type of effect size used in meta-analysis that is signified by the letter d and indicates how many standard deviations separate the mean score for the experimental group from the control group.

Differential validity   The characteristic of a test that significantly predicts a criterion for two groups, such as both minorities and nonminorities, but predicts significantly better for one of the two groups.

Direct compensation   The amount of money paid to an employee (does not count benefits, time off, and so forth).

Direct mail   A method of recruitment in which an organization sends out mass mailings of information about job openings to potential applicants.

Discarding   The third stage of change, in which employees accept that change will occur and decide to discard their old ways of doing things.

Disjunctive tasks   Tasks for which the performance of a group is based on the performance of its most talented member.

Disorganization   A climate in which the organization has the necessary knowledge and resources but does not know how to efficiently use the knowledge or the resources.

Dispute   A situation when two parties do not agree.

Disqualifier   A type of structured interview question in which a wrong answer will disqualify the applicant from further consideration.

Dissertation   A formal research paper required of most doctoral students in order to graduate.

Distracting   The idea that social inhibition occurs because the presence of others provides a distraction that interferes with concentration.

Distress   Stress that results in negative energy and decreases in performance and health.

Distributed practice   Learning a few things at a time.

Distribution errors   Rating errors in which a rater will use only a certain part of a rating scale when evaluating employee performance.

Distributive justice   The perceived fairness of the decisions made in an organization.

Downward communication   Communication within an organization in which the direction of communication is from management to employees.

Drug-Free Workplace Act   Requires federal contractors to maintain a drug-free workplace.

Drug testing   Tests that indicate whether an applicant has recently used a drug.

Dysfunctional conflict   Conflict that keeps people from working together, lessens productivity, spreads to other areas, or increases turnover.

Effect size   Used in meta-analysis, a statistic that indicates the amount of change caused by an experimental manipulation.

Effective temperature   The combination of air temperature, humidity, airflow, and heat radiation that determines how hot or cold the environment feels.

Ego needs   The fourth step in Maslow's hierarchy, concerning the individual's need for recognition and success.

Embeddedness   The extent to which employees have links to their jobs and community, the importance of these links, and the ease with which they can be broken and replaced at another job.

Empathic listening   The listening style of a person who cares primarily about the feelings of the speaker.

Employee learning   Evaluating the effectiveness of a training program by measuring how much employees learned from it.

Employee Performance Record   A standardized use of the critical-incident technique developed at General Motors.

Employee reactions   A method of evaluating training in which employees are asked their opinions of a training program.

Employee referral   A method of recruitment in which a current employee refers a friend or family member for a job.

Employment agency   An organization that specializes in finding jobs for applicants and finding applicants for organizations looking for employees.

Employment interview   A method of selecting employees in which an interviewer asks questions of an applicant and then makes an employment decision based on the answers to the questions as well as the way in which the questions were answered.

Employment-at-will doctrine   The opinion of courts in most states that employers have the right to hire and fire an employee at will and without any specific cause.

Employment-at-will statements   Statements in employment applications and company manuals reaffirming an organization's right to hire and fire at will.

Empowerment chart   A chart made for each employee that shows what level of input the employee has for each task.

Enzyme multiplied immunoassay technique (EMIT)   A method of drug testing that uses enzymes to detect the presence of drugs in a urine sample.

Equal Employment Opportunity Commission (EEOC)   A branch of the Department of Labor charged with investigating and prosecuting complaints of employment discrimination.

Equity theory   A theory of job satisfaction stating that employees will be satisfied if their ratio of effort to reward is similar to that of other employees.

ERG theory   Aldefer's needs theory, which describes three levels of satisfaction: *existence*, *relatedness*, and *growth*.

Error   Deviation from a standard of quality; also a type of response to communication overload that involves processing all information but processing some of it incorrectly.

Escape   A response to communication overload in which the employee leaves the organization to reduce the stress.

Eustress   Stress that results in positive energy and improvements in performance and health.

Evaluation apprehension   The idea that a person performing a task becomes aroused because he or she is concerned that others are evaluating his or her performance.

Evaporation   One way our bodies maintain a normal temperature, in which perspiration reduces excess heat.

Executive search firms   Employment agencies, often also called headhunters, that specialize in placing applicants in high-paying jobs.

Expectancy   In expectancy theory, the perceived probability that a particular amount of effort will result in a particular level of performance.

Expectancy theory   Vroom's theory that motivation is a function of expectancy, instrumentality, and valence.

Expectation-lowering procedure (ELP)   A form of RJP that lowers an applicant's expectations about the various aspects of the job.

Experiment   A type of research study in which the independent variable is manipulated by the experimenter.

Experimental group   In an experiment, the group of subjects that receives the experimental treatment of interest to the experimenter.

Expert power   Power that individuals have because they have knowledge.

Expertise   The amount of knowledge or skill possessed by a leader.

External equity   The extent to which employees within an organization are paid fairly compared with employees in other organizations.

External locus of control The extent to which people believe that their success and failure is determined by external sources (e.g., luck, other people).

External recruitment Recruiting employees from outside the organization.

External validity The extent to which research results can be expected to hold true outside the specific setting in which they were obtained.

Extrinsic motivation Work motivation that arises from such nonpersonal factors as pay, coworkers, and opportunities for advancement.

Face validity The extent to which a test appears to be valid.

Faces Scale A measure of job satisfaction in which raters place a mark under a facial expression that is most similar to the way they feel about their jobs.

Family and Medical Leave Act (FMLA) Passed in 1993, the FMLA provides 12 weeks of unpaid leave for birth, adoption, or serious illness of a child, parent, spouse, or the employee. All organizations that physically employ 50 or more people within a 70-mile radius of one another are covered by the act.

Fear stage The third emotional stage following the announcement of a layoff, in which employees worry about how they will survive financially.

Feedback Providing employees with specific information about how well they are performing a task or series of tasks.

Feng shui The ancient Chinese practice of arranging objects to maximize positive energy and improve the quality of life.

Fiedler's contingency model A theory of leadership that states that leadership effectiveness is dependent on the interaction between the leader and the situation.

Field research Research conducted in a natural setting as opposed to a laboratory.

Fifth Amendment The amendment to the U.S. Constitution that mandates that the federal government may not deny a person equal protection under the law.

File approach The gathering of biodata from employee files rather than by questionnaire.

Financial bonus A method of absenteeism control in which employees who meet an attendance standard are given a cash reward.

Fixed shift A shift schedule in which employees never change the shifts they work.

Fleishman Job Analysis Survey (F-JAS) A job analysis method in which jobs are rated on the basis of the abilities needed to perform them.

Flesch Index A method of determining the readability level of written material by analyzing average sentence length and the number of syllables per 100 words.

Flexible hours The part of a flextime schedule in which employees may choose which hours to work.

Flexitour A flextime schedule in which employees have flexibility in scheduling but must schedule their work hours at least a week in advance.

Flextime A work schedule that allows employees to choose their own work hours.

FOG Index A method of determining the readability level of written material by analyzing sentence length and the number of three-syllable words. (The term is interpreted as either the measure of the "fog" a reader may be in or as the acronym FOG, for "frequency of gobbledygook.")

Forced distribution method A performance appraisal method in which a predetermined percentage of employees are placed into a number of performance categories.

Forced-choice rating scales A method of performance appraisal in which a supervisor is given several behaviors and is forced to choose which of them is most typical of the employee.

Forcing style The conflict style of a person who responds to conflict by always trying to win.

Forecasting Constant worrying about the future.

Form stability The extent to which the scores on two forms of a test are similar.

Forming stage The first stage of the team process, in which team members "feel out" the team concept and attempt to make a positive impression.

Four-fifths rule When the selection ratio for one group (for example, females) is less than 80% (four fifths) of the selection ratio for another group (for example, males), adverse impact is said to exist.

Fourteenth Amendment The amendment to the U.S. Constitution that mandates that no state may deny a person equal protection under the law.

Fourth Amendment The amendment to the U.S. Constitution that protects against unreasonable search or seizure; the amendment has been ruled to cover such privacy issues as drug testing, locker and office searches, psychological testing, and electronic surveillance.

Frame-of-reference training A method of training raters in which the rater is provided with job-related information, a chance to practice ratings, examples of ratings made by experts, and the rationale behind the expert ratings.

Fry Readability Graph A method of determining the readability level of written material by analyzing sentence length and the average number of syllables per word.

Functional conflict   Conflict that results in increased performance or better interpersonal relations.

Functional Job Analysis (FJA)   A job analysis method developed by Fine that rates the extent to which a job incumbent is involved with functions in the categories of data, people, and things.

Functional résumé   A résumé format in which jobs are grouped by function rather than listed in order by date.

Future-focused question   A type of structured interview question in which applicants are given a situation and asked how they would handle it.

Gainsharing   A group incentive system in which employees are paid a bonus based on improvements in group productivity.

Galatea effect   When high self-expectations result in higher levels of performance.

Games   An absenteeism control method in which games such as poker and bingo are used to reward employee attendance.

Gas chromatography/mass spectrometry analysis   A means of analyzing urine samples for the presence of drugs in which the urine sample is vaporized and then bombarded with electrons.

Gatekeeper   A person who screens potential communication for someone else and allows only the most important information to pass through.

Generalizability   Like external validity, the extent to which research results hold true outside the specific setting in which they were obtained.

Gliding time   A flextime schedule in which employees can choose their own hours without any advance notice or scheduling.

Goal setting   A method of increasing performance in which employees are given specific performance goals to aim for.

Golem effect   When negative expectations of an individual cause a decrease in that individual's performance.

Gossip   Poorly substantiated information and insignificant information that is primarily about individuals.

Gossip grapevine   A pattern of grapevine communication in which a message is passed to only a select group of individuals.

Grade   A cluster of jobs of similar worth.

Graduate Record Exam (GRE)   A standardized admission test required by most psychology graduate schools.

Grapevine   An unofficial, informal communication network.

Graphic rating scale   A method of performance appraisal that involves rating employee performance on an interval or ratio scale.

Graphology   Also called handwriting analysis, a method of measuring personality by looking at the way in which a person writes.

Grievance system   A process in which an employee files a complaint with the organization and a person or committee within the organization makes a decision regarding the complaint.

Group cohesiveness   The extent to which members of a group like and trust one another.

Group I strategy   Leaders share the problem with the group and let the group reach a decision or solution.

Group size   The number of members in a group.

Group status   The esteem in which the group is held by people not in the group.

Group–group conflict   Conflict between two or more groups.

Groupthink   A state of mind in which a group is so concerned about its own cohesiveness that it ignores important information.

Halo error   A type of rating error that occurs when raters allow either a single attribute or an overall impression of an individual to affect the ratings they make on each relevant job dimension.

Hawthorne effect   When employees change their behavior due solely to the fact that they are receiving attention or are being observed.

Hawthorne studies   A series of studies, conducted at the Western Electric plant in Hawthorne, Illinois, that have come to represent any change in behavior when people react to a change in the environment.

Heterogeneous groups   Groups whose members share few similarities.

Hierarchy   A system arranged by rank.

Hold-out sample   A group of employees who are not used in creating the initial weights for a biodata instrument but instead are used to double-check the accuracy of the initial weights.

Homogeneous groups   Groups whose members share the same characteristics.

Hostile environment   A type of harassment characterized by a pattern of unwanted conduct related to gender that interferes with an individual's work performance.

Human factors   A field of study concentrating on the interaction between humans and machines.

Hygiene factors   In Herzberg's two-factor theory, job-related elements that result from but do not involve the job itself.

Hypothesis   An educated prediction about the answer to a research question.

Identification   The need to associate ourselves with the image projected by other people, groups, or objects.

Ignorance   An organizational climate in which important information is not available.

IMPACT theory   A theory of leadership that states that there are six styles of leadership (*i*nformational, *m*agnetic, *p*osition, *a*ffiliation, *c*oercive, and *t*actical) and that each style will be effective only in one of six organizational climates.

Impoverished leadership   A style of leadership in which the leader is concerned with neither productivity nor the well-being of employees.

In-basket technique   An assessment center exercise designed to simulate the types of information that daily come across a manager's or employee's desk in order to observe the applicant's responses to such information.

Inclusive listening   The listening style of a person who cares about only the main points of a communication.

Independent variable   The manipulated variable in an experiment.

Individual dominance   When one member of a group dominates the group.

Individual–group conflict   Conflict between an individual and the other members of a group.

Industrial/organizational (I/O) psychology   A branch of psychology that applies the principles of psychology to the workplace.

Informal communication   Communication among employees in an organization that is not directly related to the completion of an organizational task.

Informational style   A style of leadership in which the leader leads through knowledge and information; most effective in a climate of ignorance.

Informed consent   The formal process by which subjects give permission to be included in a study.

Infrequent observation   The idea that supervisors do not see most of an employee's behavior.

Initiating structure   The extent to which leaders define and structure their roles and the roles of their subordinates.

Inner con artists   A person who procrastinates.

Input/output ratio   The ratio of how much employees believe they put into their jobs to how much they believe they get from their jobs.

Inputs   In equity theory, the elements that employees put into their jobs.

Instability   An organizational climate in which people are not sure what to do.

Institutional review board   A committee designated to ensure the ethical treatment of research subjects.

Instrumental style   In path–goal theory, a leadership style in which the leader plans and organizes the activities of employees.

Instrumentality   In expectancy theory, the perceived probability that a particular level of performance will result in a particular consequence.

Integrity test   Also called an honesty test; a psychological test designed to predict an applicant's tendency to steal.

Interacting group   A collection of individuals who work together to perform a task.

Interactional justice   The perceived fairness of the interpersonal treatment that employees receive.

Interactive video   A training technique in which an employee is presented with a videotaped situation and is asked to respond to the situation and then receives feedback based on the response.

Interdependence   The extent to which team members need and rely on other team members.

Interest inventory   A psychological test designed to identify vocational areas in which an individual might be interested.

Internal locus of control   The extent to which people believe that they are responsible for and in control of their success or failure in life.

Internal pay equity   The extent to which employees within an organization are paid fairly compared with other employees within the same organization.

Internal recruitment   Recruiting employees already employed by the organization.

Internal reliability   The extent to which responses to test items measuring the same construct are consistent.

Internal timekeepers   A type of stress personality who takes on too much work because he or she enjoys doing a variety of things.

Internalization   The fifth and final stage of organizational change, in which employees become comfortable with and productive in the new system.

Internship   A situation in which a student works for an organization, either for pay or as a volunteer, to receive practical work experience.

Interpersonal communication   Communication between two individuals.

Interpersonal conflict   Conflict between two people.

Intervening variable   A third variable that can often explain the relationship between two other variables.

Intimacy zone   A distance zone within 18 inches of a person, where only people with a close relationship to the person are allowed to enter.

Intranet   A computer-based employee communication network used exclusively by one organization.

Intraorganizational communication   Communication within an organization.

Intrinsic motivation   Work motivation in the absence of such external factors as pay, promotion, and coworkers.

Isolate   An employee who receives less than half of all grapevine information.

Isolation   The degree of physical distance of a group from other groups.

Item homogeneity   The extent to which test items measure the same construct.

Item stability   The extent to which responses to the same test items are consistent.

Job Adaptability Inventory (JAI)   A job analysis method that taps the extent to which a job involves eight types of adaptability.

Job analysis   The process of identifying how a job is performed, the conditions under which it is performed, and the personal requirements it takes to perform the job.

Job analysis interview   Obtaining information about a job by talking to a person performing it.

Job analyst   The person conducting the job analysis.

Job characteristics theory   The theory proposed by Hackman and Oldham that suggests that certain characteristics of a job will make the job more or less satisfying, depending on the particular needs of the worker.

Job Choice Exercise (JCE)   An objective test used to measure various need levels.

Job Components Inventory (JCI)   A structured job analysis technique that concentrates on worker requirements for performing a job rather than on specific tasks.

Job Crafting   A process in which employees unofficially change their job duties to better fit their interests and skills.

Job descriptions   A written summary of the tasks performed in a job, the conditions under which the job is performed, and the requirements needed to perform the job.

Job Descriptive Index (JDI)   A measure of job satisfaction that yields scores on five dimensions.

Job Diagnostic Survey (JDS)   A measure of the extent to which a job provides opportunities for growth, autonomy, and meaning.

Job Elements Inventory (JEI)   A structured job analysis technique developed by Cornelius and Hakel that is similar to the Position Analysis Questionnaire (PAQ) but easier to read.

Job enlargement   A system in which employees are given more tasks to perform at the same time.

Job enrichment   A system in which employees are given more responsibility over the tasks and decisions related to their job.

Job evaluation   The process of determining the monetary worth of a job.

Job fair   A recruitment method in which several employers are available at one location so that many applicants can obtain information at one time.

Job in General (JIG) Scale   A measure of the overall level of job satisfaction.

Job knowledge test   A test that measures the amount of job-related knowledge an applicant possesses.

Job participation   A job analysis method in which the job analyst actually performs the job being analyzed.

Job related   The extent to which a test or measure taps a knowledge, skill, ability, behavior, or other characteristic needed to successfully perform a job.

Job rotation   A system in which employees are given the opportunity to perform several different jobs in an organization.

Job satisfaction   The attitude employees have toward their jobs.

Job sharing   A work schedule in which two employees share one job by splitting the work hours.

Job specifications   A relatively dated term that refers to the knowledge, skills, and abilities needed to successfully perform a job. *Competencies* is the more common term used today.

Job Structure Profile (JSP)   A revised version of the Position Analysis Questionnaire (PAQ) designed to be used more by the job analyst than by the job incumbent.

Jobs for Veterans Act   A law passed in 2002 that increased the coverage of VEVRA to include disabled veterans, veterans who have recently left the service, and veterans who participated in a U.S. military operation for which an Armed Forces Service Medal was awarded.

Journal   A written collection of articles describing the methods and results of new research.

Jurisdictional ambiguity   Conflict caused by a disagreement about geographical territory or lines of authority.

Key-issues approach   A method of scoring interview answers that provides points for each part of an answer that matches the scoring key.

Knowledge   A body of information needed to perform a task.

Knowledge test   A test that measures the level of an employee's knowledge about a job-related topic.

Known-group validity A form of validity in which test scores from two contrasting groups "known" to differ on a construct are compared.

KSAOs *K*nowledge, *s*kills, *a*bilities, and *o*ther characteristics required to perform a job.

Kuder-Richardson Formula 20 (K-R 20) A statistic used to determine internal reliability of tests that use items with dichotomous answers (yes/no, true/false).

Laboratory research Research that is conducted in a laboratory setting that can be controlled more easily than research conducted in a field setting.

Lawshe tables Tables that use the base rate, test validity, and applicant percentile on a test to determine the probability of future success for that applicant.

Leader Behavior Description Questionnaire (LBDQ) A test used to measure perceptions of a leader's style by his or her subordinates.

Leader emergence A part of trait theory that postulates that certain types of people will become leaders and certain types will not.

Leader Match A training program that teaches leaders how to change situations to match their leadership styles.

Leader performance A part of trait theory that postulates that certain types of people will be better leaders than will other types of people.

Leader position power The variable in Fiedler's contingency model that refers to the extent to which a leader, by the nature of his or her position, has the power to reward and punish subordinates.

Leaderless group discussion A selection technique, usually found in assessment centers, in which applicants meet in small groups and are given a problem to solve or an issue to discuss.

Leader–member exchange (LMX) theory A leadership theory that focuses on the interaction between leaders and subordinates.

Leader/member relations The variable in Fiedler's contingency model that refers to the extent to which subordinates like a leader.

Leadership motive pattern The name for a pattern of needs in which a leader has a high need for power and a low need for affiliation.

Leadership Opinion Questionnaire (LOQ) A test used to measure a leader's self-perception of his or her leadership style.

Least acceptable result (LAR) The lowest settlement that a person is willing to accept in a negotiated agreement.

Least-Preferred Coworker (LPC) Scale A test used in conjunction with Fiedler's contingency model to reveal leadership style and effectiveness.

Legitimate power The power that individuals have because of their elected or appointed position.

Leisure listening The listening style of a person who cares about only interesting information.

Leniency error A type of rating error in which a rater consistently gives all employees high ratings, regardless of their actual levels of performance.

Letter of recommendation A letter expressing an opinion regarding an applicant's ability, previous performance, work habits, character, or potential for success.

Leveled Describes a message from which unimportant informational details have been removed before the message is passed from one person to another.

Liaison A person who acts as an intermediary between employees and management; or the type of employee who both sends and receives most grapevine information.

Linear A straight-line relationship between the test score and the criterion of measurement.

Listserv A program that automatically distributes e-mail messages to a group of people who have a common interest.

Living case A case study based on a real situation rather than a hypothetical one.

Magazine An unscientific collection of articles about a wide range of topics.

Magnetic style A style of leadership in which the leader has influence because of his or her charismatic personality; most effective in a climate of despair.

Management teams Teams that coordinate, manage, advise, and direct employees and teams.

Managerial Grid A measure of leadership that classifies a leader into one of five leadership styles.

Manipulation The alteration of a variable by an experimenter in expectation that the alteration will result in a change in the dependent variable.

Massed practice Concentrating learning into a short period of time.

Maximum supportable position (MSP) The highest possible settlement that a person could reasonably ask for and still maintain credibility in negotiating an agreement.

Mean effect size Used in meta-analysis, a statistic that is the average of the effect sizes for all studies included in the analysis.

Measurement bias Group differences in test scores that are unrelated to the construct being measured.

Mediation   A method of resolving conflict in which a neutral third party is asked to help the two parties reach an agreement.

Meeting cow   An unnecessary or unnecessarily long meeting scheduled out of force of habit.

Mental agility   One of the intelligence measurement categories developed by Peres and Garcia for analyzing the adjectives used in letters of recommendation.

Mental Measurements Yearbook (MMY)   The name of a book containing information about the reliability and validity of various psychological tests.

Mentor   An experienced employee who advises and looks out for a new employee.

Mere presence   Theory stating that the very fact that others happen to be present naturally produces arousal and thus may affect performance.

Merit pay   An incentive plan in which employees receive pay bonuses based on performance appraisal scores.

Meta-analysis   A statistical method for cumulating research results.

Middle-of-the-road leadership   A leadership style reflecting a balanced orientation between people and tasks.

Minnesota Multiphasic Personality Inventory (MMPI-2)   The most widely used objective test of psychopathology.

Minnesota Satisfaction Questionnaire (MSQ)   A measure of job satisfaction that yields scores on 20 dimensions.

Mixed-standard scale   A method of performance appraisal in which a supervisor reads the description of a specific behavior and then decides whether the behavior of the employee is better than, equal to, or poorer than the behavior described.

Modeling   Learning through watching and imitating the behavior of others.

Modified flexitour   A flextime schedule in which employees have flexibility in scheduling but must schedule their work hours a day in advance.

Moonlighting   Working more than one job.

Motivation   The force that drives an employee to perform well.

Motivators   In Herzberg's two-factor theory, elements of a job that concern the actual duties performed by the employee.

Multiple channels   A strategy for coping with communication overload in which an organization reduces the amount of communication going to one person by directing some of it to another person.

Multiple-cutoff approach   A selection strategy in which applicants must meet or exceed the passing score on more than one selection test.

Multiple-hurdle approach   Selection practice of administering one test at a time so that applicants must pass that test before being allowed to take the next test.

Multiple regression   A statistical procedure in which the scores from more than one criterion-valid test are weighted according to how well each test score predicts the criterion.

Multiple-source feedback   A performance appraisal strategy in which an employee receives feedback from sources (e.g., clients, subordinates, peers) other than just his/her supervisor.

MUM (minimize unpleasant messages) effect   The idea that people prefer not to pass on unpleasant information, with the result that important information is not always communicated.

Need for achievement   According to trait theory, the extent to which a person desires to be successful.

Need for affiliation   The extent to which a person desires to be around other people.

Need for power   According to trait theory, the extent to which a person desires to be in control of other people.

Needs analysis   The process of determining the training needs of an organization.

Needs theory   A theory based on the idea that employees will be satisfied with jobs that satisfy their needs.

Negative feedback   Telling employees what they are doing incorrectly in order to improve their performance of a task.

Negative information bias   The fact that negative information receives more weight in an employment decision than does positive information.

Negligent hiring   An organization's failure to meet its legal duty to protect its employees and customers from potential harm caused by its employees.

Negligent reference   An organization's failure to meet its legal duty to supply relevant information to a prospective employer about a former employee's potential for legal trouble.

Negotiation and bargaining   A method of resolving conflict in which two sides use verbal skill and strategy to reach an agreement.

Neuroticism   A personality trait characterized by a tendency to experience such negative emotions as anxiety, anger, tension, and moodiness.

Newsletters   A method of downward communication typically used to communicate organizational feedback and celebrate employee success.

Noise   Any variable concerning or affecting the channel that interferes with the proper reception of a message.

Nominal group   A collection of individuals whose results are pooled but who never interact with one another.

Nonbinding arbitration   A method of resolving conflicts in which a neutral third party is asked to choose which side is correct but in which either party may appeal the decision.

Noncalculative motivation   Those who seek leadership positions because they will result in personal gain.

Nonconforming listening   The listening style of a person who cares about only information that is consistent with his or her way of thinking.

Nonverbal communication   Factors such as eye contact and posture that are not associated with actual words spoken.

Normative commitment   The extent to which employees feel an obligation to remain with an organization.

Norming   The third stage of the team process, in which teams establish roles and determine policies and procedures.

Objective tests   A type of personality test that is structured to limit the respondent to a few answers that will be scored by standardized keys.

Observation   A job analysis method in which the job analyst watches job incumbents perform their jobs.

Occupational Information Network (O*NET)   The job analysis system used by the federal government that has replaced the Dictionary of Occupational Titles (DOT).

Ombudsperson   A person who investigates employees' complaints and solves problems.

Omission   A response to communication overload that involves the conscious decision not to process certain types of information.

On-site child-care facility   A child-care center that is located on the site of the organization employing the parent.

Open desk arrangement   An office arranged so that a visitor can sit adjacent to rather than across from the person behind the desk.

Operant conditioning   A type of learning based on the idea that humans learn to behave in ways that will result in favorable outcomes and learn not to behave in ways that result in unfavorable outcomes.

Optimal level of arousal   The idea that performance is best with moderate levels of arousal.

Optimist   A person who looks at the positive aspects of every situation.

Organizational analysis   The process of determining the organizational factors that will either facilitate or inhibit training effectiveness.

Organizational citizenship behaviors (OCBs)   Behaviors that are not part of an employee's job but which make the organization a better place to work (e.g., helping others, staying late).

Organizational commitment   The extent to which an employee identifies with and is involved with an organization.

Organizational Commitment Questionnaire (OCQ)   A 15-item questionnaire that taps three organizational commitment dimensions.

Organizational Commitment Scale (OCS)   A 9-item survey that taps three aspects of organizational commitment.

Organizational culture   The shared values, beliefs, and traditions that exist among individuals in an organization.

Organizational fit questions   A type of structured-interview question that taps how well an applicant's personality and values will fit with the organizational culture.

Organizational justice   A theory that postulates that if employees perceive they are being treated fairly, they will be more likely to be satisfied with their jobs and motivated to do well.

Organizational psychology   The field of study that investigates the behavior of employees within the context of an organization.

Organizational socialization   The process whereby new employees learn the behaviors and attitudes they need to be successful in an organization.

Other characteristics   Such personal factors as personality, willingness, and interest that are not knowledge, skills, or abilities.

Outputs   In equity theory, what employees get from their jobs.

Outside pressure   The amount of psychological pressure placed on a group by people who are not members of the group.

Outsourcing   The process of having certain organizational functions performed by an outside vendor rather than an employee in the organization.

Overlearning   Practicing a task even after it has been mastered in order to retain learning.

Overt integrity test   A type of honesty test that asks questions about applicants' attitudes toward theft and their previous theft history.

Paid time off (PTO)   An attendance policy in which all paid vacations, sick days, holidays, and so forth are combined.

Paired comparison   A form of ranking in which a group of employees to be ranked are compared one pair at a time.

Paper cow Unnecessary paperwork generated within organizations out of force of habit.

Paralanguage Communication inferred from the tone, tempo, volume, and rate of speech.

Parallel teams Also called *cross-functional teams,* they consist of representatives from various departments (functions) within an organization.

Participative style In path–goal theory, a leadership style in which the leader allows employees to participate in decisions.

Passing score The minimum test score that an applicant must achieve to be considered for hire.

Pass-through programs A formal method of coaching in which excellent employees spend a period of time in the training department learning training techniques and training employees.

Past-focused question A type of structured-interview question that taps an applicant's experience.

Path–goal theory A theory of leadership stating that leaders will be effective if their behavior helps subordinates achieve relevant goals.

Patterned-behavior description interview (PBDI) A structured interview in which the questions focus on behavior in previous jobs.

Pay for performance A system in which employees are paid on the basis of how much they individually produce.

Peak-time pay A system in which part-time employees who work only during peak hours are paid at a higher hourly rate than all-day, full-time employees.

Perceptual ability Measure of facility with such processes as spatial relations and form perception.

Performance appraisal review A meeting between a supervisor and a subordinate for the purpose of discussing performance appraisal results.

Performance appraisal score A rating representing some aspect of an employee's work performance.

Performing The fourth and final stage of the team process, in which teams work toward accomplishing their goals.

Permanency The extent to which a team will remain together or be disbanded after a task has been accomplished.

Person analysis The process of identifying the employees who need training and determining the areas in which each individual employee needs to be trained.

Personal distance zone A distance zone from 18 inches to 4 feet from a person that is usually reserved for friends and acquaintances.

Personality Relatively stable traits possessed by an individual.

Personality-based integrity test A type of honesty test that measures personality traits thought to be related to antisocial behavior.

Personality inventory A psychological assessment designed to measure various aspects of an applicant's personality.

Personality-Related Position Requirements Form (PPRF) A new job analysis instrument that helps determine the personality requirements for a job.

Personnel psychology The field of study that concentrates on the selection and evaluation of employees.

Person/organization fit The extent to which an employee's personality, values, attitudes, philosophy, and skills match those of the organization.

Perspective taking Rating a potential stressor by asking how bad it really is compared with all things considered or with a worst-case scenario.

Pessimist A person who looks at the negative aspects of every situation.

Peter Principle The idea that organizations tend to promote good employees until they reach the level at which they are not competent—in other words, their highest level of incompetence.

Physical ability tests Tests that measure an applicant's level of physical ability required for a job.

Pleaser A type of person who wants to make everyone happy and is usually cooperative and helpful.

Point method A job evaluation system in which jobs are assigned points across several compensable factors to determine the worth of the job.

Point-of-purchase method A recruitment method in which help-wanted signs are placed so that they can be viewed by people who visit the organization.

Policy manual A formal method of downward communication in which an organization's rules and procedures are placed in a manual; legally binding by courts of law.

Polygraph An electronic test intended to determine honesty by measuring an individual's physiological changes after being asked questions.

Position Analysis Questionnaire (PAQ) A structured job analysis method developed by McCormick.

Position style A leadership style in which the leaders influence others by virtue of their appointed or elected authority; most effective in a climate of instability.

Posttest A measure of job performance or knowledge taken after a training program has been completed.

Power differentiation The extent to which team members have the same level of power and respect.

Practical significance The extent to which the results of a study have actual impact on human behavior.

Practicum   A paid or unpaid position with an organization that gives a student practical work experience.

Predictive bias   A situation in which the predicted level of job success falsely favors one group over another.

Predictive validity   A form of criterion validity in which test scores of applicants are compared at a later date with a measure of job performance.

Pregnancy Discrimination Act   A 1978 federal law protecting the rights of pregnant women.

Premack Principle   The idea that reinforcement is relative both within an individual and between individuals.

Pretest   A measure of job performance or knowledge taken before the implementation of a training program.

Primacy effect   The fact that information presented early in an interview carries more weight than information presented later.

Probability grapevine   A pattern of grapevine communication in which a message is passed randomly among all employees.

Procedural justice   The perceived fairness of the methods used by an organization to make decisions.

Profit sharing   A group incentive method in which employees get a percentage of the profits made by an organization.

Programmed instruction   A training method in which employees learn information at their own pace.

Progressive discipline   Providing employees with punishments of increasing severity, as needed, in order to change behavior.

Project teams   Groups formed to produce onetime outputs such as creating a new product, installing a new software system, or hiring a new employee.

Projective tests   A subjective test in which a subject is asked to perform relatively unstructured tasks, such as drawing pictures, and in which a psychologist analyzes his or her responses.

Proportion of correct decisions   A utility method that compares the percentage of times a selection decision was accurate with the percentage of successful employees.

Protected class   Any group of people for whom protective legislation has been passed.

Prototype   The overall image that a supervisor has of an employee.

Proximity   Physical distance between people.

Proximity error   A type of rating error in which a rating made on one dimension influences the rating made on the dimension that immediately follows it on the rating scale.

Psychological résumé   A résumé style that takes advantage of psychological principles pertaining to memory organization and impression formation.

Psychomotor ability   Measure of facility with such processes as finger dexterity and motor coordination.

Public distance zone   Distance greater than 12 feet from a person that is typical of the interpersonal space allowed for social interactions such as large group lectures.

Public employment agency   An employment service operated by a state or local government, designed to match applicants with job openings.

Pygmalion effect   The idea that if people believe that something is true, they will act in a manner consistent with that belief.

Qualified workforce   The percentage of people in a given geographic area who have the qualifications (skills, education, and so forth) to perform a certain job.

Quality   A type of objective criterion used to measure job performance by comparing a job behavior with a standard.

Quality circles   Employee groups that meet to propose changes that will improve productivity and the quality of work life.

Quantity   A type of objective criterion used to measure job performance by counting the number of relevant job behaviors that occur.

Quasi-experiment   Research method in which the experimenter either does not manipulate the independent variable or in which subjects are not randomly assigned to conditions.

Questionnaire approach   The method of obtaining biodata from questionnaires rather than from employee files.

Queuing   A method of coping with communication overload that involves organizing work into an order in which it will be handled.

Quid pro quo   A type of sexual harassment in which the granting of sexual favors is tied to an employment decision.

Race   According to Congress, the four races are African American, European American, Asian American, and Native American Indian.

Racial bias   The tendency to give members of a particular race lower evaluation ratings than are justified by their actual performance or to give members of one race lower ratings than members of another race.

Radiation   One way our bodies maintain a normal temperature, by the emission of heat waves.

Radioimmunoassay (RIA)   A method of drug testing that uses radioactive tagging to determine the presence of drugs in a urine sample.

Random assignment   The random, unbiased assignment of subjects in a research sample to the various experimental and control conditions.

Random sample   A sample in which every member of the relevant population had an equal chance of being chosen to participate in the study.

Rank order   A method of performance appraisal in which employees are ranked from best to worst.

Realistic job preview (RJP)   A method of recruitment in which job applicants are told both the positive and the negative aspects of a job.

Recency effect   The tendency for supervisors to recall and place more weight on recent behaviors when they evaluate performance.

Receptive changer   A person who is willing to change.

Recruitment   The process of attracting employees to an organization.

Reference   The expression of an opinion, either orally or through a written checklist, regarding an applicant's ability, previous performance, work habits, character, or potential for future success.

Reference check   The process of confirming the accuracy of résumé and job application information.

Referent power   Leadership power that exists when followers can identify with a leader and the leader's goals.

Referral service   A system of child care in which an employer maintains a list of certified child-care centers that can be used by its employees.

Reinforcement hierarchy   A rank-ordered list of reinforcers for an individual.

Rejection letter   A letter from an organization to an applicant informing the applicant that he or she will not receive a job offer.

Reliability   The extent to which a score from a test or from an evaluation is consistent and free from error.

Reluctant changer   A person who will initially resist change but will eventually go along with it.

Residual stress   Stress that is carried over from previous stressful situations.

Respond by calling ads   Recruitment ads in which applicants are instructed to call rather than to apply in person or send résumés.

Restricted range   A narrow range of performance scores that makes it difficult to obtain a significant validity coefficient.

Résumé   A formal summary of an applicant's professional and educational background.

Résumé fraud   The intentional placement of untrue information on a résumé.

Return on investment (ROI)   The amount of money an organization makes after subtracting the cost of training or other interventions.

Reward power   Leadership power that exists to the extent that the leader has the ability and authority to provide rewards.

Right/wrong scoring   A method of scoring interview questions in which the answer is either right or wrong (e.g., What is the legal drinking age in Virginia?)

Rituals   Procedures in which employees participate to become "one of the gang."

Role ambiguity   The extent to which an employee's roles and expectations are unclear.

Role conflict   The extent to which an employee's role and expected role are the same.

Role overload   The extent to which an employee is able to psychologically handle the number of roles and tasks assigned.

Role play   A training technique in which employees act out simulated roles.

Rorschach Ink Blot Test   A projective personality test.

Rotating shift   A shift schedule in which employees periodically change the shifts that they work.

Rule of 3   A variation on top-down selection in which the names of the top three applicants are given to a hiring authority who can then select any of the three.

Rumor   Poorly substantiated information that is passed along the grapevine.

Sabertooth   People who respond to stress with anger.

Sacred cow hunt   The first step in organizational change, in which employees look for practices and policies that waste time and are counterproductive.

Safety needs   The second step in Maslow's hierarchy, concerning the need for security, stability, and physical safety.

Salary survey   A questionnaire sent to other organizations to see how much they are paying their employees in positions similar to those in the organization sending the survey.

Scientist-practitioner model   A teaching model in which students are trained first to be scientists and second to be able to apply the science of their field to find solutions to real-world problems.

Scorer reliability   The extent to which two people scoring a test agree on the test score, or the extent to which a test is scored correctly.

Selection ratio   The percentage of applicants an organization hires.

Self-actualization needs   The fifth step in Maslow's hierarchy, concerning the need to realize one's potential.

Self-directed teams   *See Quality circles.*

Self-esteem   The extent to which a person views him or herself as a valuable and worthy individual.

Self-fulfilling prophecy   The idea that people behave in ways consistent with their self-image.

Self-monitoring   A personality trait characterized by the tendency to adapt one's behavior to fit a particular social situation.

Self-regulation theory   Postulates that employees can be motivated by monitoring their own progress toward the goals they set and adjusting their behavior to reach those goals.

Send-résumé ads   Recruitment ads in which applicants are instructed to send their résumé to the company rather than call or apply in person.

Serial communication   Communication passed consecutively from one person to another.

Sharpened   Describes a message in which interesting and unusual information has been kept in the message when it is passed from one person to another; see Leveled.

Shrinkage   The amount of goods lost by an organization as a result of theft, breakage, or other loss.

Simulation   An exercise designed to place an applicant in a situation that is similar to the one that will be encountered on the job.

Single-group validity   The characteristic of a test that significantly predicts a criterion for one class of people but not for another.

Single-strand grapevine   A pattern of grapevine communication in which a message is passed in a chainlike fashion from one person to the next until the chain is broken.

Situational question   A structured-interview technique in which applicants are presented with a series of situations and asked how they would handle each one.

Situational leadership theory   A theory of leadership stating that effective leaders must adapt their style of leadership to fit both the situation and the followers.

Situational self-esteem   The positive or negative way in which a person views him or herself in a particular situation.

Situation-wanted ads   Newspaper advertisements run by applicants looking for jobs rather than by organizations looking for applicants.

Skill   Proficiency to perform a particular task.

Skill-level determiner   A type of structured-interview question designed to tap an applicant's knowledge or skill.

Skill test   A test that measures an employee's level of some job-related skill.

Skill-based pay   Compensating an employee who participates in a training program designed to increase a particular job-related skill.

Slightly heterogeneous groups   Groups in which a few group members have different characteristics from the rest of the group.

SME conference   A group job analysis interview consisting of subject-matter experts (SMEs).

Social distance   The extent to which team members treat each other in a friendly, informal manner.

Social distance zone   An interpersonal distance from 4 to 12 feet from a person that is typically used for business and for interacting with strangers.

Social facilitation   The positive effects that occur when a person performs a task in the presence of others.

Social information processing theory   States that employees model their levels of satisfaction and motivation from other employees.

Social impact theory   States that the addition of a group member has the greatest effect on group behavior when the size of the group is small.

Social inhibition   The negative effects that occur when a person performs a task in the presence of others.

Social learning theory   States that employees model their levels of satisfaction and motivation from other employees.

Social loafing   The fact that individuals in a group often exert less individual effort than they would if they were not in a group.

Social needs   The third step in Maslow's hierarchy, concerning the need to interact with other people.

Social-normative motivation   The desire to lead out of a sense of duty or responsibility.

Social recognition   A motivation technique using such methods as personal attention, signs of approval, and expressions of appreciation.

Socially influenced self-esteem   The positive or negative way in which a person views him or herself based on the expectations of others.

Solomon four-groups design   An extensive method of evaluating the effectiveness of training with the use of pretests, posttests, and control groups.

Spearman-Brown prophecy formula   Used to correct reliability coefficients resulting from the split-half method.

Speed cow   The tendency for organizations to require employees to work faster and produce work sooner than needed.

Split-half method A form of internal reliability in which the consistency of item responses is determined by comparing scores on half of the items with scores on the other half of the items.

Stability The extent to which the membership of a group remains consistent over time.

Standard deviation (SD) A statistic that indicates the variation of scores in a distribution.

Standard error (SE) The number of points that a test score could be off due to test unreliability.

Stock options A group incentive method in which employees are given the option of buying stock in the future at the price of the stock when the options were granted.

Storming The second stage in group formation in which group members disagree and resist their team roles.

Strain The physical and psychological consequences of stress.

Stress Perceived psychological pressure.

Stressors Events that cause stress.

Strictness error A type of rating error in which a rater consistently gives all employees low ratings, regardless of their actual levels of performance.

Striver An ambitious and competitive person whose source of stress is often self-placed demands.

Strong Interest Inventory (SII) A popular interest inventory used to help people choose careers.

Structured interviews Interviews in which questions are based on a job analysis, every applicant is asked the same questions, and there is a standardized scoring system so that identical answers are given identical scores.

Stylistic listening The listening style of a person who pays attention mainly to the way in which words are spoken.

Subject-matter experts (SMEs) Sources such as supervisors and incumbents who are knowledgeable about a job.

Suggestion box A form of upward communication in which employees are asked to place their suggestions in a box.

Supportive style In path–goal theory, a leadership style in which leaders show concern for their employees.

Surveys Questionnaires asking employees about the areas in which they feel they need training.

Survivors Employees who retain their jobs following a downsizing.

Symbols Organizational behaviors or practices that convey messages to employees.

Synchronous technologies Distance learning programs that require employees to complete the training at the same time and at the same pace, although they may be in different physical locations.

Synthetic validity A form of validity generalization in which validity is inferred on the basis of a match between job components and tests previously found valid for those job components.

Tactical style A leadership style in which a person leads through organization and strategy; most effective in a climate of disorganization.

Task analysis The process of identifying the tasks for which employees need to be trained.

Task-centered leaders Leaders who define and structure their roles as well as the roles of their subordinates.

Task-centered leadership A leadership style in which the leader is more concerned with productivity than with employee well-being.

Task interdependence A potential source of conflict that arises when the completion of a task by one person affects the completion of a task by another person.

Task inventory A questionnaire containing a list of tasks each of which the job incumbent rates on a series of scales such as importance and time spent.

Task structuredness The variable in Fiedler's contingency model that refers to the extent to which tasks have clear goals and problems can be solved.

Taylor-Russell tables A series of tables based on the selection ratio, base rate, and test validity that yield information about the percentage of future employees who will be successful if a particular test is used.

Team leadership A leadership style in which the leader is concerned with both productivity and employee well-being.

Technical listening The listening style of a person who cares about only facts and details.

Telecommuting Working at home rather than at the office by communicating with managers and coworkers via phone, computer, fax machine, and other offsite media.

Temporal stability The consistency of test scores across time.

Temporary employees Also called "temps"—employees hired through a temporary employment agency.

Tenure The length of time an employee has been with an organization.

Terminal master's degree programs Graduate programs that offer a master's degree but not a Ph.D.

Test-retest reliability The extent to which repeated administration of the same test will achieve similar results.

Thematic Apperception Test (TAT) A projective personality test in which test-takers are shown pictures and asked to tell stories. It is designed to measure various need levels.

Theory A systematic set of assumptions regarding the cause and nature of behavior.

Theory X leaders Leaders who believe that employees are extrinsically motivated and thus lead by giving directives and setting goals.

Theory Y leaders Leaders who believe that employees are intrinsically motivated and thus lead with a "hands-off" or a participative approach.

Thin-layer chromatography A method of analyzing urine specimens for drugs that is performed by hand and requires a great deal of analyst skill.

Third-party intervention When a neutral party is asked to help resolve a conflict.

Threshold Traits Analysis (TTA) A 33-item questionnaire developed by Lopez that identifies traits necessary to successfully perform a job.

Top-down selection Selecting applicants in straight rank order of their test scores.

Trade magazine A collection of articles for those "in the biz," about related professional topics, seldom directly reporting the methods and results of new research.

Training A planned effort by an organization to facilitate the learning of job-related behavior on the part of its employees.

Transactional leadership Leadership style in which the leader focuses on task-oriented behaviors.

Transfer of training The extent to which behavior learned in training will be performed on the job.

Transformational leadership Visionary leadership in which the leader changes the nature and goals of an organization.

Triangling An employee discusses a conflict with a third-party such as a friend or supervisor. In doing so, the employee hopes that the third party will talk to the second party and that the conflict will be resolved without the need for the two parties to meet.

Trustworthiness The extent to which a leader is believed and trusted by his or her followers.

Two-factor theory Herzberg's needs theory, postulating that there are two factors involved in job satisfaction: hygiene factors and motivators.

Type A personality A stress-prone person who is competitive, impatient, and hurried.

Type B personality A non–stress-prone person who is relaxed and agreeable.

Typical-answer approach A method of scoring interview answers that compares an applicant's answer with benchmark answers.

Uniform Guidelines Federal guidelines used to guide an employer in establishing fair selection methods.

Union steward An employee who serves as a liaison between unionized employees and management.

Unstructured interview An interview in which applicants are not asked the same questions and in which there is no standard scoring system to score applicant answers.

Upward communication Communication within an organization in which the direction of communication is from employees up to management.

Urbanity A category referring to social skills and refinement; one of the five dimensions in the trait approach to scoring letters of recommendation.

Utility formula Method of ascertaining the extent to which an organization will benefit from the use of a particular selection system.

Valence In expectancy theory, the perceived desirability of a consequence that results from a particular level of performance.

Validity The degree to which inferences from scores on tests or assessments are justified by the evidence.

Validity coefficient The correlation between scores on a selection method (e.g., interview, cognitive ability test) and a measure of job performance (e.g., supervisor rating, absenteeism).

Validity generalization (VG) The extent to which inferences from test scores from one organization can be applied to another organization.

Vertical dyad linkage (VDL) theory A leadership theory that concentrates on the interaction between the leader and his or her subordinates.

Vertical percentage method For scoring biodata in which the percentage of unsuccessful employees responding in a particular way is subtracted from the percentage of successful employees responding in the same way.

Victims Employees who lose their jobs due to a layoff.

Vietnam-Era Veterans Readjustment Act A 1974 federal law that mandates that federal government contractors and subcontractors take affirmative action to employ and promote Vietnam-era veterans.

Vigor A category referring to energy; one of the five dimensions in the trait approach to scoring letters of recommendation.

Virtual job fair   A job fair held on campus in which students can "tour" a company online, ask questions of recruiters, and electronically send résumés.

Virtual teams   Teams that communicate through email rather than face to face.

Vocational counseling   The process of helping an individual choose and prepare for the most suitable career.

Vocational Rehabilitation Act   Federal act passed in 1973 that prohibits federal government contractors or subcontractors from discriminating against the physically or mentally handicapped.

Voice stress analyzer   An electronic test to determine honesty by measuring an individual's voice changes after being asked questions.

Voucher system   Child-care policy in which an organization pays all or some of its employees' child-care costs at private child-care centers by providing the employees with vouchers.

Vroom-Yetton Model   A theory of leadership that concentrates on helping a leader choose how to make a decision.

Wage trend line   A line that represents the ideal relationship between the number of points that a job has been assigned (using the point method of evaluation) and the salary range for that job.

Webcast   A noninteractive training method in which the trainer transmits training information over the Internet.

Webinar   Short for "web seminar," an interactive training method in which training is transmitted over the Inernet.

Well pay   A method of absenteeism control in which employees are paid for their unused sick leave.

Wiki   A collection of web pages in which users can create web pages on a topic and readers can freely edit those pages.

Winning at all costs   An approach to handling conflict in which one side seeks to win regardless of the damage to the other side.

Withdrawal   An approach to handling conflict in which one of the parties removes him/herself from the situation to avoid the conflict.

Wonderlic Personnel Test   The cognitive ability test that is most commonly used in industry.

Work at home   Alternative to having employees come to an organization's building.

Work Preference Inventory (WPI)   A measure of an individual's orientation toward intrinsic versus extrinsic motivation.

Work sample   A method of selecting employees in which an applicant is asked to perform samples of actual job-related tasks.

Work teams   Groups of employees who manage themselves, assign jobs, plan and schedule work, make work-related decisions, and solve work-related problems.

Worrier   A person who always thinks the worst is going to happen.

REFERENCES

Aamodt, M. G. (1986). *Validity of expert advice regarding the employment interview*. Paper presented at the annual meeting of the International Personnel Management Association Assessment Council, San Francisco.

Aamodt, M. G. (2004). *Research in law enforcement selection*. Boca Raton, FL: BrownWalker.

Aamodt, M. G. (2008). Reducing misconceptions and false beliefs in police and criminal psychology. *Criminal Justice and Behavior*, 35(10), 1231–1240.

Aamodt, M. G., & Carr, K. (1988). Relationship between recruitment source and employee behavior. *Proceedings of the 12th Annual Meeting of the International Personnel Management Association Assessment Council*, 143–146.

Aamodt, M. G., Surrette, M. A., & Cohen, D. (2010). *Understanding statistics in I/O psychology and human resource management* (2nd ed.). Belmont, CA: Wadsworth Publishing.

Aamodt, M. G., Kimbrough, W. W., & Alexander, C. J. (1983). A preliminary investigation of the relationship between team racial heterogeneity and team performance in college basketball. *Journal of Sports Sciences*, 1, 131–133.

Aamodt, M. G., Kimbrough, W. W., Keller, R. J., & Crawford, K. (1982). Relationship between sex, race, and job performance level and the generation of critical incidents. *Educational and Psychological Research*, 2, 227–234.

Aamodt, M. G., & Peggans, D. (1988). Tactfully rejecting job applicants. *Personnel Administrator*, 33, 58–60.

Aamodt, M. G., Reardon, C., & Kimbrough, W. W. (1986). The Critical Incident Technique revisited. *Journal of Police and Criminal Psychology*, 2, 48–59.

Aamodt, M. G., & Williams, F. (2005, April). *Reliability, validity, and adverse impact of references and letters of recommendation*. Paper presented at the 20th annual meeting of the Society for Industrial and Organizational Psychology, Los Angeles, CA.

Abramis, D. J. (1994). Work role ambiguity, job satisfaction, and job performance: Meta-analyses and review. *Psychological Reports*, 75(3), 1411–1433.

Acuff, F. (2008). *Negotiate anything with anyone anywhere around the world*. New York: AMACOM.

Adair, B., & Pollen, D. (1985, September 23). No! No! A thousand times no: The declining art of the rejection letter. *The Washington Post*, p. C-5.

Adams, G. A., & Jex, S. M. (1999). Relationships between time management, control, work-family conflict, and strain. *Journal of Occupational Health Psychology*, 4(10), 72–77.

Adams, J. S. (1965). Inequity in social change. In L. Berkowitz (Ed.), *Advances in experimental social psychology* (Vol. 2, pp. 267–299). New York: Academic Press.

Adams, J. S., & Rosenbaum, W. B. (1962). The relationship of worker productivity to cognitive dissonance about wage inequities. *Journal of Applied Psychology*, 46, 161–164.

Alboher, M. (2007). *One person/multiple careers: A new model for work/life success*. New York: Business Plus.

Albright, M. D., & Levy, P. E. (1995). The effects of source credibility and performance rating discrepancy on reactions to multiple raters. *Journal of Applied Social Psychology*, 25(7), 577–600.

Aldefer, C. P. (1972). *Existence, relatedness, and growth: Human needs in organizational settings*. New York: Free Press.

Allard, G., Butler, J., Faust, D., & Shea, T. M. (1995). Errors in hand scoring objective personality tests: The case of the Personality Diagnostic Questionnaire. *Professional Psychology: Research & Practice*, 26(3), 304–308.

Allen, D. G., Mahto, R. V., & Otondo, R. F. (2007). Web-based recruitment: Effects of information, organizational brand, and attitudes toward a web site on applicant attraction. *Journal of Applied Psychology*, 92, 1696–1708.

Allen, M., Mabry, E., Mattrey, M., Bourhis, J., Titsworth, S., & Burrell, N. (2004). Evaluating the effectiveness of distance learning: A comparison using meta-analysis. *Journal of Communication*, 54(3), 402–420.

Allen, M. T., & Connelly, M. S. (2005, April). *Case features and individual attributes in case-based training*. Poster presented at the 20th annual meeting of the Society for Industrial and Organizational Psychology, Los Angeles, CA.

Allen, N. J., & Hecht, T. D. (2004). The "romance of teams": Toward an understanding of its psychological underpinnings and implications. *Journal of Occupational and Organizational Psychology*, 77(4), 439–461.

Allen, T. D., & Meyer, J. P. (1990). The measurement and antecedents of affective, continuance, and normative commitment to the organization. *Journal of Occupational Psychology*, 63(1), 1–18.

Alliger, G. M., Tannenbaum, S. I., Bennett, W., Traver, H., & Shotland, A. (1997). A meta-analysis of the relations among training criteria. *Personnel Psychology*, 50(2), 341–358.

Allport, G. W., & Postman, L. (1947). *The psychology of rumor*. New York: Holt, Rinehart & Winston.

Alm, H., & Nilsson, L. (1995). The effects of a mobile telephone task on driver behaviour in a car following situation. *Accident Analysis and Prevention*, 27(5), 707–715.

AMA (2007). *2007 Workplace monitoring & surveillance*. New York: American Management Association.

Amabile, T. M., Hill, K. G., Hennessey, B. A., & Tighe, E. M. (1994). The Work Preference Inventory: Assessing intrinsic and extrinsic motivational orientations. *Journal of Personality and Social Psychology*, 66(5), 950–967.

Ammerman, H. L. (1965). *A model of junior officer jobs for use in developing task inventories* (HumRRO Tech. Rep. 65–10). Alexandria, VA: Human Resources Research Organization.

Amsbary, J. H., & Staples, P. J. (1991). Improving administrator/nurse communication: A case study of "management by walking around." *Journal of Business Communication, 28*(2), 101–112.

Anderson, N., Salgado, J. F., & Hülsheger, U. R. (2010). Applicant reactions in selection: Comprehensive meta-analysis into reaction generalization versus situational specificity. *International Journal of Selection & Assessment, 18*(3), 291–304.

Anderson, N., & Witvliet, C. (2008). Fairness reactions to personnel selection methods: An international comparison between the Netherlands, the United States, France, Spain, Portugal, and Singapore. *International Journal of Selection & Assessment, 16*(1), 1–13.

Anderson, N. H. (1965). Adding versus averaging as a stimulus combination rule in impression formation. *Journal of Experimental Psychology, 70*, 394–400.

Andersson, B. E., & Nilsson, S. G. (1964). Studies in the reliability and validity of the critical incident technique. *Journal of Applied Psychology, 48*, 398–403.

Andrews, L. W. (2005). Hiring people with intellectual disabilities. *HR Magazine, 50*(7), 72–77.

Anseel, F., Lievens, F., Schollaert, E., & Choragwicka, B. (2010). Response rates in organizational science, 1995–2008: A meta-analytic review and guidelines for survey researchers. *Journal of Business and Psychology, 25*(3), 335–349.

Ansoorian, A. E., & Shultz, K. S. (1997). *The influence of expertise and gender on physical effort ratings*. Poster presented at the 12th annual conference of the Society for Industrial and Organizational Psychology, St. Louis, MO.

Antonioni, D. (1994). The effects of feedback accountability on upward appraisal ratings. *Personnel Psychology, 47*(2), 349–356.

Arbita (2009). *6 must-fund recruitment marketing initiatives for 2010*. Minneapolis, MN: Arbita.

Arcuri, A. E., & Lester, D. (1990). Moonlighting and stress in police officers. *Psychological Reports, 66*, 350.

Argus, K., & Zajack, M. (2008, April). *Need for achievement and leader effectiveness: A meta-analysis*. Poster presented at the 23rd annual conference of the Society for Industrial and Organizational Psychology, San Francisco, CA.

Armour, S. (2001, June 12). Arbitration's rise raises fairness issue. *USA Today*, p. B1-2.

Armour, S. (2003, February 7). Sick days may hurt your bottom line. *USA Today*, p. A1.

Armour, S. (2004, December 6). Working 9-to-5 no longer: More choose flexible hours on the job. *USA Today*, p. B1-2.

Armour, S. (2006, June 12). Lunch break becomes briefer as "hour" shrinks. *USA Today*, p. 3B.

Arnold, J. A., & Carnevale, P. J. (1997). Preferences for dispute resolution procedures as a function of intentionality, consequences, expected future interaction, and power. *Journal of Applied Social Psychology, 27*(5), 371–398.

Arthur, J. B. (1994). Effects of human resource systems on manufacturing performance and turnover. *Academy of Management Journal, 37*(3), 670–687.

Arthur, W., Bennett, W., Edens, P. S., & Bell, S. T. (2003). Effectiveness of training in organizations: A meta-analysis of design and evaluation features. *Journal of Applied Psychology, 88*(2), 234–243.

Arthur, W., Day, E. A., McNelly, T. L., & Edens, P. S. (2003). A meta-analysis of the criterion-related validity of assessment center dimensions. *Personnel Psychology, 56*(1), 125–154.

Arvey, R. D., & Begalla, M. E. (1975). Analyzing the homemaker job using the PAQ. *Journal of Applied Psychology, 60*, 513–517.

Arvey, R. D., Bouchard, T. J., Segal, N. L., & Abraham, L. M. (1989). Job satisfaction: Environmental and genetic components. *Journal of Applied Psychology, 74*, 187–192.

Arvey, R. D., Davis, G. A., McGowen, S. L., & Dipboye, R. L. (1982). Potential sources of bias in job analytic processes. *Academy of Management Journal, 25*, 618–629.

Arvey, R. D., Gordon, M. E., Massengill, D. P., & Mussio, S. J. (1975). Differential report rates of minority and majority job candidates due to time lags between selection procedures. *Personnel Psychology, 28*(2), 175–180.

Arvey, R. D., McCall, B. P., Bouchard, T. J., Taubman, P., & Cavanaugh, M. A. (1994). Genetic influences on job satisfaction and work values. *Personality and Individual Differences, 17*(1), 21–33.

Arvey, R. D., Rotundo, M., Johnson, W., Zhang, Z., & McGue, M. (2006). The determinants of leadership role occupancy: Genetic and personality factors. *Leadership Quarterly, 17*(1), 1–20.

Ash, R. A., & Edgell, S. A. (1975). A note on the readability of the Position Analysis Questionnaire (PAQ). *Journal of Applied Psychology, 60*, 765–766.

Ash, R. A., Levine, E. L., Higbee, R. H., & Sistrunk, F. (1982). *Comparisons of task ratings from subject matter experts versus job incumbents*. Paper presented at the annual meeting of the Southeastern Psychological Association, New Orleans, LA.

ASTD (2010). *State of the Industry: 2010*. Alexandria, VA: American Society for Training and Development.

Athey, T. R., & McIntyre, R. M. (1987). Effect of rater training on rater accuracy: Levels of processing theory and social facilitation perspectives. *Journal of Applied Psychology, 72*, 567–572.

Atkinson, W. (1999). Safety at a price. *HR Magazine, 44*(12), 52–59.

Atkinson, W. (2000). When stress won't go away. *HR Magazine, 45*(12), 104–110.

Atwater, L. E. (1998). The advantages and pitfalls of self-assessment in organizations. In J. W. Smither (Ed.), *Performance appraisal: State of the art in practice*. San Francisco: Jossey-Bass.

Austin, J., Kessler, M. L., Riccobone, J. E., & Bailey, J. S. (1996). Using feedback and reinforcement to improve the performance and safety of a roofing crew. *Journal of Organizational Behavior Management, 16*(2), 49–75.

Avery, D. R. & McKay, P. F. (2006). Target practice: An organizational impression management approach to attracting minority and female job applicants. *Personnel Psychology*, 59, 157–187.

Avis, J., & Kudisch, J. (2000). *Factors influencing subordinates' willingness to participate in an upward feedback system.* Paper presented at the 21st annual Graduate Student Conference in Industrial-Organizational Psychology and Organizational Behavior, Knoxville, TN.

Azar, O. H. (2007). The social norm of tipping: A review. *Journal of Applied Social Psychology*, 37(2), 380–402.

Babad, E. Y., Inbar, J., & Rosenthal, R. (1982). Pygmalion, Galatea, and the Golem: Investigations of biased and unbiased teachers. *Journal of Educational Psychology*, 74, 459–474.

Babcock, L., & Laschever, S. (2008). *Ask for it: How women can use the power of negotiation to get what they really want.* New York: Bantam.

Babcock, P. (2008). Elder care at work. *HR Magazine*, 53(9), 111–118.

Babcock, P. (2005). Find what workers want. *HR Magazine*, 50(4), 51–56.

Bahls, J. E. (1998). Drugs in the workplace. *HR Magazine*, 43(2), 81–87.

Baldridge, D. C., & Veiga, J. F. (2001). Toward a greater understanding of the willingness to request an accommodation: Can requesters' beliefs disable the Americans with Disabilities Act? *Academy of Management Review*, 26(1), 85–99.

Baldwin, T. T., & Ford, J. K. (1988). Transfer of training: A review and directions for future research. *Personnel Psychology*, 41, 63–105.

Baldwin, T. T., Magjuka, R. J., & Loher, B. T. (1991). The perils of participation: Effects of choice of training on trainee motivation and learning. *Personnel Psychology*, 44, 51–65.

Balfour, D. L., & Wechsler, B. (1996). Organizational commitment: Antecedents and outcomes in public organizations. *Public Productivity and Management Review*, 29, 256–277.

Baltes, B. B., Briggs, T. E., Huff, J. W., Wright, J. A., & Neuman, G. A. (1999). Flexible and compressed workweek schedules: A meta-analysis of their effects on work-related criteria. *Journal of Applied Psychology*, 84(4), 496–513.

Balzer, W. K., & Sulsky, L. M. (1992). Halo and performance appraisal research: A critical examination. *Journal of Applied Psychology*, 77(6), 971–986.

Bandura, A. (1977). *Social learning theory*. Englewood Cliffs, NJ: Prentice Hall.

Bangerter, A., König, C. J., Blatti, S., & Salvisberg, A. (2009). How widespread is graphology in personnel selection practice? A case study of a job market myth. *International Journal of Selection and Assessment*, 17(2), 219–230.

Banks, M. H., Jackson, P. R., Stafford, E. M., & Warr, P. B. (1983). The Job Components Inventory and the analysis of jobs requiring limited skill. *Personnel Psychology*, 36, 57–66.

Banks, M. H., & Miller, R. L. (1984). Reliability and convergent validity of the Job Components Inventory. *Journal of Occupational Psychology*, 57, 181–184.

Bannister, B. D. (1986). Performance outcome feedback and attributional feedback: Interactive effects on recipient responses. *Journal of Applied Psychology*, 71, 203–210.

Barnes, C. W., & Wagner, D. T. (2009). Changing to daylight saving time cuts into sleep and increases workplace injuries. *Journal of Applied Psychology*, 94(5), 1305–1317.

Baron, R. A. (1983). Sweet smell of success: The impact of pleasant artificial scents on evaluations of job applicants. *Journal of Applied Psychology*, 68, 709–713.

Barrick, M. R., & Mount, M. K. (1991). The big five personality dimensions and job performance: A meta-analysis. *Personnel Psychology*, 44(1), 1–26.

Barrick, M. R., Mount, M. K., & Gupta, R. (2003). Meta-analysis of the relationship between the five-factor model of personality and Holland's occupational types. *Personnel Psychology*, 56(1), 45–74.

Barrick, M. R., Shaffer, J. A., & DeGrassi, S. W. (2009). What you see may not be what you get: Relationships among self-presentation tactics and ratings of interview and job performance. *Journal of Applied Psychology*, 94, 1394–1411.

Barrick, M. R., Stewart, G. L., Neubert, M. J., & Mount, M. K. (1998). Relating member ability and personality to work-team processes and team effectiveness. *Journal of Applied Psychology*, 83(3), 377–391.

Barrick, M. R., Wider, B. W., & Stewart, G. L. (2010). Initial evaluations in the interview: Relationships with subsequent interview evaluations and employment offers. *Journal of Applied Psychology*, 95(6), 1163–1172.

Barrick, M. R., & Zimmerman, R. D. (2005). Reducing voluntary, avoidable turnover through selection. *Journal of Applied Psychology*, 90(1), 159–166.

Barrier, M. (2003). The mediation disconnect. *HR Magazine*, 48(5), 54–58.

Barron, L. G., & Sackett, P. R. (2008). Asian variability in performance rating modesty and leniency bias. *Human Performance*, 21, 277–290.

Barton, J., & Folkard, S. (1993). Advancing versus delaying shift systems. *Ergonomics*, 36(1), 59–64.

Bass, B. M. (1997). Does the transactional–transformational leadership paradigm transcend organizational and national boundaries? *American Psychologist*, 52(2), 130–139.

Bassett, J. W. (2008). *Solving employee theft.* Charleston, SC: BookSurge Publishing.

Bates, S. (2003a). Forced ranking. *HR Magazine*, 48(6), 62–68.

Bates, S. (2003b). Performance appraisals: Some improvement needed. *HR Magazine*, 48(4), 12.

Baumgartner, J. (1994). Give it to me straight. *Training & Development Journal*, 48(6), 49–51.

Baxter, J. S., Manstead, A. S., Stradling, S. G., & Campbell, K. A. (1990). Social facilitation and driving behavior. *British Journal of Psychology*, 81(3), 351–360.

Beal, D. J., Cohen, R. R., Burke, M. J., & McLendon, C. L. (2003). Cohesion and performance in groups: A meta-analytic clarification of construct relations. *Journal of Applied Psychology*, 88(6), 989–1004.

Beall, G. E. (1991). Validity of the weighted application blank across four job criteria. *Applied H.R.M. Research*, *2*(1), 18–26.

Beatty, A., Sackett, P. R., Kuncel, N. R., Kiger, T., Shen, W., & Rigdon, J. (2011, April). *Estimating the reliability of college grades*. Poster presented at the 26th Annual Conference of the Society for Industrial and Organizational Psychology, Chicago, IL.

Beatty, G. O. (1996). *Job analysis sample size: How small is large enough?* Poster presented at the annual meeting of the Society for Industrial and Organizational Psychology, San Diego, CA.

Becker, R. (1998). Taking the misery out of experiential training. *Training Magazine*, *35*(2), 78–88.

Becker, T. E., & Colquitt, A. L. (1992). Potential versus actual faking of a biodata form: An analysis along several dimensions of item type. *Personnel Psychology*, *45*, 389–406.

Beehr, T. A. (1996). *Basic organizational psychology*. Boston: Allyn & Bacon.

Beehr, T. A., Ivanitskaya, L., Hansen, C. P., Erofeev, D., & Gudanowski, D. M. (2001). Evaluation of 360-degree feedback ratings: Relationships with each other and with performance and selection predictors. *Journal of Organizational Behavior*, *22*, 775–788.

Bell, P. A., Greene, T., Fisher, J., & Baum, A. S. (2006). *Environmental psychology* (5th ed.). New York: Psychology Press.

Bell, S. T. (2007). Deep-level composition variables as predictors of team performance: A meta-analysis. *Journal of Applied Psychology*, *92*(3), 595–615.

Bell, S. T. (2005, April). *The relationship between team composition variables and team performance: A comprehensive meta-analysis*. Paper presented at the 20th annual meeting of the Society for Industrial and Organizational Psychology, Los Angeles, CA.

Benjamin, A. J. (1996). *Evaluation of leader emergence in a leaderless group discussion*. Unpublished master's thesis, University of California, Fullerton.

Ben-Shakhar, G., Bar-Hillel, M., Bilu, Y., Ben-Abba, E., & Flug, A. (1986). Can graphology predict occupational success? Two empirical studies and some methodological ruminations. *Journal of Applied Psychology*, *71*, 645–653.

Benson, G. S., Finegold, D., & Mohrman, S. A. (2004). You paid for the skills, now keep them: Tuition reimbursement and voluntary turnover. *Academy of Management Journal*, *47*(3), 315–331.

Bernardin, H. J., & Beatty, R. W. (1984). *Performance appraisal: Assessing human behavior at work*. Boston: Kent.

Bernardin, H. J., & Buckley, M. R. (1981). Strategies in rater training. *Academy of Management Review*, *6*, 205–212.

Bernardin, H. J., & Kane, J. S. (1980). A second look at behavioral observation scales. *Personnel Psychology*, *33*, 809–814.

Bernardin, H. J., LaShells, M. B., Smith, P. C., & Alvares, K. M. (1976). Behavioral expectation scales: Effects of developmental procedures and formats. *Journal of Applied Psychology*, *61*, 75–79.

Bernardin, H. J., & Pence, E. C. (1980). Effects of rater training: Creating new response sets and decreasing accuracy. *Journal of Applied Psychology*, *65*, 60–66.

Bernardin, H. J., & Walter, C. S. (1977). Effects of rater training and diary-keeping on psychometric error in ratings. *Journal of Applied Psychology*, *62*, 64–69.

Bernstein, A. J., & Rozen, S. C. (1992). *Neanderthals at work*. New York: Ballantine.

Berry, C. M., Ones, D. S., & Sackett, P. R. (2007). Interpersonal deviance, organizational deviance, and their common correlates: A review and meta-analysis. *Journal of Applied Psychology*, *92*(2), 410–424.

Berry, C. M., Sackett, P. R., & Tobares, V. (2010). A meta-analysis of conditional reasoning tests of aggression. *Personnel Psychology*, *63*(2), 361–384.

Berry, L. M. (2003). *Employee selection*. Belmont, CA: Wadsworth.

Beshir, M. Y., El-Sabagh, A. S., & El-Nawawi, M. A. (1981). Time on task effect on tracking performance under heat stress. *Ergonomics*, *24*, 95–102.

Beyer, C., Pike, D., & McGovern, L. (1993). *Surviving unemployment*. New York: Henry Holt.

Bhakta, M., & Nagy, M. S. (2005). Are higher pay increases necessarily better? *Applied H.R.M. Research*, *10*(1), 1–12.

Bianchi, A. B. (1996). The character-revealing handwriting analysis. *Inc.*, *18*(2), 77–79.

Biddle, R. E. (1993). How to set cutoff scores for knowledge tests used in promotion, training, certification, and licensing. *Public Personnel Management*, *22*(1), 63–79.

Bing, M. N., Stewart, S. M., Davison, H. K., Green, P. D., McIntyre, M. D., & James, L. R. (2007). An integrative typology of personality assessment for aggression: Implications for predicting counterproductive workplace behavior. *Journal of Applied Psychology*, *92*(3), 722–744.

Bishop, J. W., & Scott, K. D. (1997). How commitment affects team performance. *HR Magazine*, *42*(2), 107–111.

Blake, R. R., & Mouton, J. S. (1984). *The managerial grid III*. Houston: Gulf.

Blakley, B. R., Quiñones, M. A., Crawford, M. S., & Jago, I. A. (1994). The validity of isometric strength tests. *Personnel Psychology*, *47*(2), 247–274.

Blanchard, K. H., Zigarmi, P., & Zigarmi, D. (1985). *Leadership and the one minute manager*. New York: William Morrow.

Blanz, F., & Ghiselli, E. E. (1972). The mixed standard scale: A new rating system. *Personnel Psychology*, *25*, 185–200.

Bliss, W. G. (2001). Cost of employee turnover can be staggering. *Fairfield County Business Journal*, *40*(19), 20.

Bluen, S. D., Barling, J., & Burns, W. (1990). Predicting sales performance, job satisfaction, and depression using the Achievement Strivings and Impatience-Irritability dimensions of Type A behavior. *Journal of Applied Psychology*, *75*, 212–216.

Blumenfeld, W. S. (1985). Appropriateness of readability of a Federal Aviation Agency regulation, a flight crew manual, and a company pilot labor agreement for an airline's pilots. *Perceptual and Motor Skills*, *61*, 1189–1190.

Blumenfeld, W. S., & Justice, B. M. (1975). Six replicated investigations of the relationship between Flesch and Gunning readability indices. *Perceptual and Motor Skills, 40,* 110.

Bobko, P., Roth, P. L., & Buster, M. A. (2005). Work sample selection tests and expected reduction in adverse impact: A cautionary note. *International Journal of Selection and Assessment, 13*(1), 1–11.

Bobko, P., Roth, P. L., & Potosky, D. (1999). Derivation and implications of a meta-analytic matrix incorporating cognitive ability, alternative predictors, and job performance. *Personnel Psychology, 52*(3), 561–589.

Bocketti, S., Hamilton, M., & Maser, S. (2000). *Comparing the effect of negative information on resumes and interviews.* Paper presented at the 21st annual Graduate Student Conference in Industrial-Organizational Psychology and Organizational Behavior, Knoxville, TN.

Bolino, M. C., & Turnley, W. H. (2005). The personal costs of citizenship behavior: The relationship between individual initiative and role overload, job stress, and work-family conflict. *Journal of Applied Psychology, 90*(4), 740–748.

Bolles, R. N. (2011). *What color is your parachute? 2011: A practical manual for job-hunters and career-changers.* Berkeley, CA: Ten Speed Press.

Bommer, W. H., Johnson, J. L., Rich, G. A., Podsakoff, P. M., & Mackenzie, S. B. (1995). On the interchangeability of objective and subjective measures of employee performance: A meta-analysis. *Personnel Psychology, 48*(3), 587–605.

Bond, C. F., & Titus, L. J. (1983). Social facilitation: A meta-analysis of 241 studies. *Psychological Bulletin, 94,* 265–292.

Bond, G. E. (1995). *Leadership behavior: How personality, stress, and gender affect leader behavior.* Unpublished doctoral dissertation, University of Washington, Seattle, WA.

Bonner, D. (1990). Effectiveness of wellness programs in industry. *Applied H.R.M. Research, 1*(2), 32–37.

Bonner, J. J. (1993). *Measurement of resume content preference.* Unpublished Master's Thesis, Radford University, Radford, VA.

Bono, J. E., & Judge, T. A. (2004). Personality and transformational and transactional leadership: A meta-analysis. *Journal of Applied Psychology, 89*(5), 901–910.

Bordens, K. S., & Abbott, B. B. (2011). *Research design and methods: A process approach* (8th ed.). New York: McGraw-Hill.

Borman, W. C., & Motowidlo, S. J. (1997). Task performance and contextual performance: The meaning for personnel selection research. *Human Performance, 10*(2), 99–109.

Boudreau, J. W. (1983). Economic considerations in estimating the utility of human resource productivity improvement programs. *Personnel Psychology, 36,* 551–576.

Bowen, C. C., Swim, J. K., & Jacobs, R. R. (2000). Evaluating gender biases on actual job performance of real people: A meta-analysis. *Journal of Applied Social Psychology, 30*(10), 2194–2215.

Bowers, C. A., Pharmer, J. A., & Salas, E. (2000). When member homogeneity is needed in work teams. *Small Group Research, 31*(3), 305–327.

Bowling, N. A., Hendricks, E. A., & Wagner, S. H. (2010). Positive and negative affectivity and facet satisfaction: A meta-analysis. *Journal of Business and Psychology, 22,* 115–125 in press.

Brabant, C. (1992). Heat exposure standards and women's work: Equitable or debatable? *Women and Health, 18*(3), 119–130.

Bradley, D. (2004, December). Catawba County, N.C. Emergency Medical Services (EMS) wellness program. *IPMA-HR News,* 6–7.

Bramson, R. (1981). *Coping with difficult people.* New York: Anchor.

Brandon, M. C. (1997). From the three B's to the high C's: The history of employee communication. *Communication World, 14*(5), 18–21.

Branham, L. (2005). *The 7 hidden reasons employees leave.* New York: AMACOM.

Brannick, M. T., Levine, E. L., & Morgeson, F. P. (2007). *Job analysis.* Thousand Oaks, CA: Sage.

Bravo, I. M., & Kravitz, D. A. (1996). Context effects in performance appraisals: Influence of target value, context polarity, and individual differences. *Journal of Applied Social Psychology, 26*(19), 1681–1701.

Brawley, L. R., Carron, A. V., & Widmeyer, W. N. (1993). The influence of the group and its cohesiveness on perceptions of group goal-related variables. *Journal of Sport and Exercise Psychology, 15*(3), 245–260.

Breaugh, J. A. (2008). Employee recruitment: Current knowledge and important areas for future research. *Human Resource Management Review, 18*(3), 103–118.

Breaugh, J. A. (1981). Relationships between recruitment sources and employee performance, absenteeism, and work attitudes. *Academy of Management Journal, 24,* 261–267.

Breaugh, J. A., & Mann, R. B. (1984). Recruiting source effects: A test of two alternative explanations. *Journal of Occupational Psychology, 57,* 261–267.

Brehm, J. W. (1966). *A theory of psychological reactance.* New York: Academic Press.

Brennan, A., Chugh, J. S., & Kline, T. (2002). Traditional versus open office design. *Environment and Behavior, 34*(3), 279–299.

Brennan, J. (1994). New outlaws? *Forbes, 151*(4), 70.

Brett, J. F., & Atwater, L. E. (2001). 360-degree feedback: Accuracy, reactions, and perceptions of usefulness. *Journal of Applied Psychology, 86*(5), 930–942.

Bretz, R. D., & Judge, T. A. (1994). Person-organization fit and the theory of work adjustment: Implications for satisfaction, tenure, and career success. *Journal of Vocational Behavior, 44*(1), 32–54.

Bretz, R. D., & Judge, T. A. (1998). Realistic job previews: A test of the adverse self-selection hypothesis. *Journal of Applied Psychology, 83*(2), 330–337.

Bretz, R. D., & Thomas, S. L. (1992). Perceived equity, motivation, and final offer arbitration. *Journal of Applied Psychology, 77*(3), 280–287.

Brice, T. S., & Waung, M. (1995). Applicant rejection letters: Are businesses sending the wrong message? *Business Horizons, 38*(2), 59–62.

Bridges, W. (1985). How to manage organizational transition. *Training*, 22(9), 28–32.

Brinkman, R., & Kirschner, R. (2006). *Dealing with difficult people*. New York: McGraw-Hill.

Broad, M. (2000). Ensuring transfer of learning to the job. In G. M. Piskurich, P. Beckschi, & B. Hall (Eds.), *The ASTD handbook of training design and delivery*. New York: McGraw Hill.

Broadbent, B. (1997). Writing for the 90's. *Training & Development*, 51(3), 11–12.

Broadbent, D. E. (1971). *Decision and stress*. New York: Academic Press.

Broadbent, D. E., & Little, E. A. (1960). Effect of noise reduction in a work situation. *Occupational Psychology*, 343, 133–140.

Broadwell, M. M. (1993). Seven steps to building better training. *Training*, 30(10), 75–81.

Brophy, D. R. (1996). *Matching individual and group creativity to different types of problems*. Poster presented at the 11th annual conference of the Society for Industrial and Organizational Psychology, San Diego, CA.

Brotherton, P. (1996). The company that plays together. *HR Magazine*, 41(12), 76–82.

Brown, D. L. (1993). Target stores settle out of court in Soroka v. Dayton Hudson. *The Industrial Organizational Psychologist*, 31(2), 88–89.

Brown, J. (2002). Training needs assessment: A must for developing an effective training program. *Public Personnel Management*, 31(4), 569–578.

Brown, K. A., & Huber, V. L. (1992). Lowering floors and raising ceilings: A longitudinal assessment of the effects of an earnings-at-risk plan on pay performance. *Personnel Psychology*, 45(2), 279–311.

Brown, S. H. (1978). Long-term validity of a personal history item scoring procedure. *Journal of Applied Psychology*, 63, 673–676.

Brown, S. P. (1996). A meta-analysis and review of organizational research on job involvement. *Psychological Bulletin*, 120(2), 235–255.

Brown, W. F., & Finstuen, K. (1993). The use of participation in decision making: A consideration of the Vroom-Yetton and Vroom-Jago normative models. *Journal of Behavioral Decision Making*, 6(3), 207–219.

Bruce, H. J. (1997). Looking for a CEO? Look for early career signs of "leadership without portfolio." *Directors & Boards*, 21(2), 20–21.

Bryman, A. (1992). *Charisma & leadership*. Newbury Park, CA: Sage.

Buchanan, L., & Foti, R. J. (1996). *Emergent female leaders: Effects of self-monitoring, priming, and task characteristics*. Poster presented at the 11th annual conference of the Society for Industrial and Organizational Psychology, San Diego, CA.

Buchner, L. M. (1990). Increases in interrater reliability of situational interviews as a function of the number of benchmark answers. *Applied H.R.M. Research*, 1(2), 27–31.

Buckley, M. R., & Eder, R. W. (1989). The first impression. *Personnel Administrator*, 34(5), 72–74.

Buckley, M. R., Jackson, K. A., Bolino, M. C., Veres, J. G., & Feild, H. S. (2007). The influence of relational demography on panel interview ratings: A field experiment. *Personnel Psychology*, 60(3), 627–646.

Buckley, M. R., Mobbs, T. A., Mendoza, J. L., Novicevic, M. M., Carraher, S. M., & Beu, D. S. (2002). Implementing realistic job previews and expectation-lowering procedures: A field experiment. *Journal of Vocational Behavior*, 61, 263–278.

Bucklin, B. R., & Dickinson, A. M. (2001). Individual monetary incentives: A review of different types of arrangements between performance and pay. *Journal of Organizational Behavior Management*, 21(3), 45–137.

Buddhavarapu, S., Borys, J., Homant, M., & Baltes, B. (2002). *The twenty-four hour dilemma: A meta-analytic review of shift work*. Paper presented at the 17th annual conference of the Society for Industrial and Organizational Psychology, Toronto, Canada.

Buelens, M., & Van Poucke, D. (2004). Determinants of a negotiator's initial opening offer. *Journal of Business and Psychology*, 19(1), 23–35.

Bullock, R. J., & Tubbs, M. E. (1990). A case meta-analysis of gainsharing plans as organization development interventions. *Journal of Applied Behavioral Science*, 26(3), 383–404.

Burke, M. E. (2005a). *2004 reference and background checking survey report*. Alexandria, VA: Society for Human Resource Management.

Burke, M. E. (2005b). *2005 reward programs and incentive compensation*. Alexandria, VA: Society for Human Resource Management.

Burke, W. W. (2011). *Organization change: Theory and practice* (3rd ed.). Thousand Oaks, CA: Sage.

Burley-Allen, M. (2001). Listen up. *HR Magazine*, 46(11), 115–120.

Burnett, J. R., & Motowidlo, S. J. (1998). Relations between different sources of information in the structured selection interview. *Personnel Psychology*, 51(4), 963–983.

Burns, W. (1979). Physiological effects of noise. In C. M. Harris (Ed.), *Handbook of noise control*. New York: McGraw-Hill.

Butterfield, K. D., Trevino, L. K., & Ball, G. A. (1996). Punishment from the manager's perspective: A grounded investigation and inductive model. *Academy of Management Journal*, 39(6), 1479–1512.

Bycio, P. (1992). Job performance and absenteeism: A review and meta-analysis. *Human Relations*, 45(2), 193–220.

Cable, D. M., & DeRue, D. S. (2002). Convergent and discriminant validity of subjective fit perceptions. *Journal of Applied Psychology*, 87(5), 875–884.

Cadrain, D. (2006). Drug testing falls out of employers' favor. *HR Magazine*, 51(6), 38–48.

Cadrain, D. (2004). Job detectives dig deep for defamation. *HR Magazine*, 49(10), 34–36.

Cadrain, D. (2003a). Are your employee drug tests accurate? *HR Magazine*, 48(1), 40–45.

Cadrain, D. (2003b). Put success in sight. *HR Magazine*, 48(5), 85–92.

Caird, J. K., Willness, C. R., Steel, P., & Scialfa, C. (2008). A meta-analysis of the effects of cell phones on driver performance. *Accident Analysis and Prevention, 40,* 1282–1293.

Caldwell, C., Thornton, G. C., & Gruys, M. L. (2003). Ten classic assessment center errors: Challenges to selection validity. *Public Personnel Management, 32*(1), 73–88.

Caldwell, D. F., & Burger, J. M. (1998). Personality characteristics of job applicants and success in screening interviews. *Personnel Psychology, 51*(1), 119–136.

Callinan, M., & Robertson, I. V. (2001). Work sample testing. *International Journal of Selection and Assessment, 8*(4), 248–260.

Cameron, J., & Pierce, W. D. (1994). Reinforcement, reward, and intrinsic motivation: A meta-analysis. *Review of Educational Research, 64*(3), 363–423.

Cameron, K. S., Freeman, S. J., & Mishra, A. (1991). Best practices in white-collar downsizings: Managing contradictions. *Academy of Management Executive, 5,* 57–73.

Campbell, D. E. (1979). Interior office design and visitor response. *Journal of Applied Psychology, 64,* 648–653.

Campbell, D. T., & Stanley, J. C. (1963). *Experimental and quasi-experimental designs in research.* Chicago: Rand McNally.

Campion, J. E., Greener, J., & Wernli, S. (1973). Work observation versus recall in developing behavioral examples for rating scales. *Journal of Applied Psychology, 58,* 286–288.

Campion, M. A., Campion, J. E., & Hudson, J. P. (1994). Structured interviewing: A note on incremental validity and alternative question types. *Journal of Applied Psychology, 79*(6), 998–1002.

Campion, M. A., Fink, A. A., Ruggeberg, B. J., Carr, L., Phillips, G. M., & Odman, R. B. (2011). Doing competencies well: Best practices in competency modeling. *Personnel Psychology, 64*(2), 225–262.

Campion, M. A., & McClelland, C. L. (1993). Follow-up and extension of the interdisciplinary costs and benefits of enlarged jobs. *Journal of Applied Psychology, 78*(3), 339–351.

Campion, M. A., Outtz, J. L., Zedeck, S., Schmidt, F. L., Kehoe, J. F., Murphy, K. R., & Guion, R. M. (2001). The controversy over score banding in personnel selection: Answers to 10 key questions. *Personnel Psychology, 54*(1), 149–185.

Campion, M. A., Palmer, D. K., & Campion, J. E. (1997). A review of structure in the selection interview. *Personnel Psychology, 50*(3), 655–702.

Canali, K. G., Alton, S., Perreault, N. E., Rusbasan, D., Reese, A. L., & Barnes-Farrell, J. L. (2005, April). *Understanding performance appraisal leniency: Antecedents and consequences of rating discomfort.* Poster presented at the 20th annual meeting of the Society for Industrial and Organizational Psychology, Los Angeles, CA.

Cardy, R. L., & Dobbins, G. H. (1986). Affect and appraisal accuracy: Liking as an integral dimension in evaluating performance. *Journal of Applied Psychology, 71,* 672–678.

Carli, L. L., & Eagly, A. H. (2001). Gender, hierarchy, and leadership: An introduction. *Journal of Social Issues, 57*(4), 629–636.

Carlson, K. D., Scullen, S. E., Schmidt, F. L., Rothstein, H., & Erwin, F. (1999). Generalizable biographical data validity can be reached without multi-organizational development and keying. *Personnel Psychology, 52*(3), 731–755.

Carnall, C. A. (2008). *Managing change in organizations* (5th ed.). New York: Financial Times Management.

Carpi, J. (1996). Stress: It's worse than you think. *Psychology Today,* Jan/Feb, pp. 34–42.

Carr, S. C., McLoughlin, D., Hodgson, M., & MacLachlan, M. (1996). Effects of unreasonable pay discrepancies for under- and overpayment on double demotivation. *Genetic, Social, and General Psychology Monographs, 122*(4), 475–494.

Carrell, M. R., & Dittrich, J. E. (1978). Equity theory: The recent literature, methodological considerations, and new directions. *Academy of Management Review, 3,* 202–210.

Carroll, S. A. (2008, April). *Detecting faking using a bogus knowledge test: Relationships with impression management, personality, and deviant behavior.* Presented in J. Levashina & M. A. Campion (Co-Chairs), That can't be true! Detecting faking using bogus items. Symposium presented at the 23rd annual meeting of the Society for Industrial-Organizational Psychology, San Francisco, CA.

Carron, A. V. (1990). Group size in sport and physical activity: Social psychological and performance consequences. *International Journal of Sport Psychology, 21*(4), 286–304.

Carron, A. V., Loughhead, T. M., & Bray, S. R. (2005). The home advantage in sport competitions: Courneya and Carron's (1992) conceptual framework a decade later. *Journal of Sports Sciences, 23*(4), 395–407.

Carson, K. P., Becker, J. S., & Henderson, J. A. (1998). Is utility really futile? A failure to replicate and an extension. *Journal of Applied Psychology, 83*(1), 84–96.

Carson, P. P., Lanier, P. A., Carson, K. D., & Guidry, B. N. (2000). Clearing a path through the management fashion jungle: Some preliminary trailblazing. *Academy of Management Journal, 43*(6), 1143–1158.

Carter, J. H. (1952). Military leadership. *Military Review, 32,* 14–18.

Caruso, J. C. (2003). Reliability generalization of the NEO personality scales. In Bruce Thompson (Ed.), *Score reliability: Contemporary thinking on reliability issues.* Thousand Oaks, CA: Sage Publications.

Cascio, W. F. (2002). *Responsible restructuring: Creative and profitable alternatives to layoffs.* San Francisco, CA: Berrett-Koehler.

Cascio, W. F. (1995). Whither industrial and organizational psychology in a changing world of work? *American Psychologist, 50*(11), 928–939.

Cascio, W. F. (2002). Strategies for responsible restructuring. *Academy of Management Executive, 16*(3), 80–91.

Cascio, W. F., Alexander, R. A., & Barrett, G. V. (1988). Setting cutoff scores: Legal, psychometric, and professional issues and guidelines. *Personnel Psychology, 41,* 1–24.

Cascio, W. F., & Phillips, N. F. (1979). Performance testing: A rose among thorns? *Personnel Psychology, 32,* 751–756.

Casperson, D. M. (2002, December). E-mail etiquette: How to make sure your message gets across. *IPMA News,* p. 25.

Caudron, S. (1994). Volunteer efforts offer low cost training options. *Personnel Journal, 73*(6), 38–44.

Cavanaugh, J. (2001, January 15). Death at work: Some killings can be prevented. *People Weekly, 55*(2), 63.

Cavanaugh, M. A., Boswell, W. R., Roehling, M. V., & Boudreau, J. W. (2000). An empirical examination of self-reported work stress among U.S. managers. *Journal of Applied Psychology, 85*(1), 65–74.

Ceci, S. J., & Peters, D. (1984). Letters of reference: A naturalistic study of the effects of confidentiality. *American Psychologist, 39*, 29–31.

Cederbloom, D. (1989). Peer and supervisor evaluations: An underused promotion method used for law enforcement. *Proceedings of the 13th Annual Meeting of the International Personnel Management Association Assessment Council.*

Cellar, D. F., Curtis, J. R., Kohlepp, K., Poczapski, P., & Mohiuddin, S. (1989). The effects of rater training, job analysis format and congruence of training on job evaluation ratings. *Journal of Business and Psychology, 3*(4), 387–401.

Chan, D., & Schmitt, N. (1997). Video-based versus paper-and-pencil method of assessment in situational judgment tests: Subgroup differences in test performance and face validity perceptions. *Journal of Applied Psychology, 82*(1), 143–159.

Chan, D., Schmitt, N., DeShon, R. P., Clause, C. S., & Delbridge, K. (1997). Reactions to cognitive ability tests: The relationship between race, test performance, face validity perceptions, and test-taking motivation. *Journal of Applied Psychology, 82*(2), 300–310.

Chan, K. Y., & Drasgow, F. (2001). Toward a theory of individual differences and leadership: Understanding the motivation to lead. *Journal of Applied Psychology, 86*(3), 481–498.

Chang, C. H., Johnson, R. E., & Yang, L. Q. (2007). Emotional strain and organizational citizenship behaviors: A meta-analysis and review. *Work & Stress, 21*(4), 312–332.

Chang, C. H., Rosen, C. C., & Levy, P. E. (2009). The relationship between perceptions of organizational politics and employee attitudes, strain, and behavior: A meta-analysis. *Academy of Management Journal, 52*(4), 779–801.

Chapman, D. S., & Zweig, D. I. (2005). Developing a nomological network for interview structure: Antecedents and consequences of the structured selection interview. *Personnel Psychology, 58*(3), 673–702.

Chapman, D. S., Uggerslev, K. L., Carroll, S. A., Piasentin, K. A., & Jones, D. A. (2005). Applicant attraction to organizations and job choice: A meta-analytic review of the correlates of recruiting outcomes. *Journal of Applied Psychology, 90*(5), 928–944.

Chen, A. Y., Sawyers, R. B., & Williams, P. F. (1997). Reinforcing ethical decision making through corporate culture. *Journal of Business Ethics, 16*, 855–865.

Chen, S. C. (1937). Social modification of the activity of ants in nest-building. *Physiological Zoology, 10*, 420–436.

Christian, M. S., Edwards, B. D., & Bradley, J. C. (2010). Situational judgment tests: Constructs assessed and a meta-analysis of their criterion-related validities. *Personnel Psychology, 63*(1), 83–117.

Chua-Eoan, H. (1999, March 22). The bomber next door: What are the most dangerous men in America talking about at the Supermax prison in Colorado? *Time, 153*(11), 55.

Chubb, R. (1995). Humor: A valuable laugh skill. *Journal of Child and Youth Care, 10*(3), 61–66.

Church, A. H. (2001). Is there a method to our madness? The impact of data collection methodology on organizational survey results. *Personnel Psychology, 54*(4), 937–969.

Church, A. H., Rogelberg, S. G., & Waclawski, J. (2000). Since when in no news good news? The relationship between performance and response rates in multirater feedback. *Personnel Psychology, 53*(2), 435–451.

Cialdini, R. B. (2009). *Influence: Science and practice* (5th ed.). Boston, MA: Allyn & Bacon.

Cialdini, R. B., Borden, R., Thorne, A., Walker, M., Freeman, S., & Sloane, L. T. (1976). Basking in reflected glory: Three (football) field studies. *Journal of Personality and Social Psychology, 34*, 366–375.

Circadian Technologies (2002). *2002 shiftwork practices survey.* Lexington, MA: Circadian Technologies, Inc.

Clark, M. M. (2001). More companies offering flextime: Are scheduling options flexible enough? *HR News, 20*(6), 1–10.

Clark, R. E. (1961). *The limiting hand skin temperature for unaffected manual performance in the cold.* Natick, MA: Quartermaster Research and Engineering Command, Technical Rep. EP-147.

Clause, C. S., Mullins, M. E., Nee, R., Pulakos, E. D., & Schmitt, N. (1998). Strictly parallel test forms: A development procedure and example. *Personnel Psychology, 51*(1), 193–208.

Clay, R. A. (2011). Is stress getting to you? *Monitor on Psychology, 42*(1), 58–63.

Clements, C., Wagner, R. J., & Roland, C. C. (1995). The ins and outs of experiential training. *Training & Development, 49*(2), 52–56.

Clevenger, J., Pereira, G. M., Wiechmann, D., Schmitt, N., & Harvey, V. S. (2001). Incremental validity of situational judgment tests. *Journal of Applied Psychology, 86*(3), 410–417.

Cochran, A., Kopitzke, K., & Miller, D. (1984). *Relationship between interviewer personality and interior office characteristics.* Paper presented at the 5th annual Graduate Student Conference in Industrial/Organizational Psychology and Organizational Behavior, Norfolk, VA.

Coens, T., & Jenkins, M. (2002). *Abolishing performance appraisals: Why they backfire and what to do instead.* San Francisco: Berrett-Koehler.

Cohen, A. (1972, September). *The role of psychology in improving worker safety and health under the Worker Safety and Health Act.* Paper presented at the annual meeting of the American Psychological Association, Honolulu, HI.

Cohen, D. B. (1997). *Cohen Conflict Response Inventory.* Washington, DC: Author.

Cohen, D. B., Aamodt, M. G., & Dunleavy, E. M. (2010). *Technical advisory committee report on best practices in adverse impact analyses.* Washington, D.C.: Center for Corporate Equality.

Cohen, D. B., & Scott, D. (1996). *Construct validity of a situational interview and patterned behavior description interview.* Paper presented at the 17th annual Graduate Student Conference in Industrial/Organizational Psychology and Organizational Behavior, Toledo, OH.

Cohen, J. (1988). *Statistical power analysis for the behavioral sciences* (2nd ed.). Hillsdale, NJ: Lawrence Erlbaum.

Cohen, P. (1984). College grades and adult achievement. *Research in Higher Education, 20,* 281–293.

Cohen, S. (2002). High-tech tools: Lower barriers for disabled. *HR Magazine, 47*(10), 60–65.

Cohen, S., & Weinstein, N. (1981). Nonauditory effects of noise on behavior and health. *Journal of Personality and Social Psychology, 37,* 36–70.

Cohen, S. G., & Bailey, D. E. (1997). What makes teams work: Group effectiveness research from the shop floor to the executive suite. *Journal of Management, 23*(3), 239–290.

Colella, A., & Varma, A. (2001). The impact of subordinate disability on leader-member exchange relationships. *Academy of Management Journal, 44*(2), 304–315.

Collins, D. B., & Holton, E. F. (2004). The effectiveness of managerial leadership development programs: A meta-analysis of studies from 1982 to 2001. *Human Resource Development Quarterly, 15*(2), 217–248.

Collins, K. (2001). HR must find new ways to battle substance abuse in the workplace. *HR News,* April, 11–16.

Colquitt, J. A., Conlon, D. E., Wesson, M. J., Porter, O. L. H., & Ng, K. Y. (2001). Justice at the millennium: A meta-analytic review of 25 years of organizational justice research. *Journal of Applied Psychology, 86*(3), 425–445.

Commerce Clearing House (2007). *2007 CCH unscheduled absenteeism survey.* Riverwoods, IL: Author.

Conard, M. A., & Ashworth, S. D. (1986). *Recruiting source effectiveness: A meta-analysis and re-examination of two rival hypotheses.* Paper presented at the 1st annual meeting of the Society for Industrial and Organizational Psychology, Chicago, IL.

Conard, M. A., & Matthews, R. A. (2008). Modeling the stress process: Personality trumps stressors in predicting strain. *Personality and Individual Differences, 44*(1), 171–181.

Condly, S. J., Clark, R. E., & Stolovitch, H. D. (2003). The effects of incentives on workplace performance: A meta-analytic review of research studies. *Performance Improvement Quarterly, 16*(3), 46–63.

Connolly, J. J., & Viswesvaran, C. (2000). The role of affectivity in job satisfaction: A meta-analysis. *Personality and Individual Differences, 29*(2), 265–281.

Contournet, G. (2004, October). *Maintenance of order: Legal and psycho-sociological aspects.* Paper presented at the annual meeting of the Society for Police and Criminal Psychology, Rome, Italy.

Converse, J. M., & Presser, S. (1986). *Survey questions: Handcrafting the standardized questionnaire.* Beverly Hills, CA: Sage.

Conway, J. M., & Huffcutt, A. I. (1997). Psychometric properties of multi-source performance ratings: A meta-analysis of subordinate, supervisor, peer, and self-ratings. *Human Performance, 10*(4), 331–360.

Cooper, M., Kaufman, G., & Hughes, W. (1996). Measuring supervisory potential. *IPMA News,* December, pp. 8–9.

Cooper, W. H. (1981a). Conceptual similarity as a source of illusory halo in job performance ratings. *Journal of Applied Psychology, 66,* 302–307.

Cooper, W. H. (1981b). Ubiquitous halo. *Psychological Bulletin, 90,* 218–244.

Cooper-Hakim, A., & Viswesvaran, C. (2005). The construct of work commitment: Testing an integrative framework. *Psychological Bulletin, 131*(2), 241–259.

Cordes, C. L., & Dougherty, T. W. (1993). Review and integration of research on job burnout. *Academy of Management Review, 18*(4), 621–656.

Cornelius, E. T., & Hakel, M. D. (1978). *A study to develop an improved enlisted performance evaluation system for the U.S. Coast Guard.* Washington, DC: Department of Transportation.

Cornelius, E. T., Hakel, M. D., & Sackett, P. R. (1979). A methodological approach to job classification for performance appraisal purposes. *Personnel Psychology, 32,* 283–297.

Cornwell, L. (2007, September 10). Larger employees, smaller paychecks. *Roanoke Times & World News,* pp. A1, A4.

Cortina, J. M., Goldstein, N. B., Payne, S. C., Davison, H. K., & Gilliland, S. W. (2000). The incremental validity of interview scores over and above cognitive ability and conscientiousness scores. *Personnel Psychology, 53*(2), 325–351.

Cottrell, N. B. (1972). Social facilitation. In C. G. McClintock (Ed.), *Experimental social psychology* (pp. 185–236). New York: Holt, Rinehart & Winston.

Courtis, J. K. (1995). Readability of annual reports: Western versus Asian evidence. *Accounting, Auditing and Accountability, 8*(2), 4–17.

Cromwell, P. F., Marks, A., Olson, J. N., & Avary, D. W. (1991). Group effects on decision-making by burglars. *Psychological Reports, 69*(2), 579–588.

Cronbach, L. J. (1951). Coefficient alpha and the internal structure of tests. *Psychometrika, 16,* 297–334.

Cropanzano, R., & Folger, R. (1989). Referent cognitions and task decision autonomy: Beyond equity theory. *Journal of Applied Psychology, 74,* 293–299.

Cropanzano, R., & Greenberg, J. (1997). Progress in organizational justice: Tunneling through the maze. In C. L. Cooper & I. T. Robertson (Eds.), *International review of industrial and organizational psychology* (Vol. 12, pp. 317–372). Chichester: Wiley.

Cropanzano, R., & James, K. (1990). Some methodological considerations for the behavioral genetic analysis of work attitudes. *Journal of Applied Psychology, 75,* 433–439.

Csoka, L. S., & Bons, P. M. (1978). Manipulating the situation to fit the leader's style: Two validation studies of leader match. *Journal of Applied Psychology, 63,* 295–300.

Cucina, J. M., Vasilopoulos, N. L., & Sehgal, K. G. (2005). Personality-based job analysis and the self-serving bias. *Journal of Business and Psychology, 20*(2), 273–290.

Czaja, R., & Blair, J. (2005). *Designing surveys: A guide to decisions and procedures* (2nd ed.). Thousand Oaks, CA: Pine Forge Press.

Daanen, H. A. M., van de Vliert, E., & Huang, X. (2003). Driving performance in cold, warm, and thermoneutral environments. *Applied Ergonomics, 34*(6), 597–602.

Dababneh, A. J., Swanson, N., & Shell, R. L. (2001). Impact of added rest breaks on the productivity and well being of workers. *Ergonomics, 44*(2), 164–174.

Dalal, R. S. (2005). A meta-analysis of the relationship between organizational citizenship behavior and counterproductive work behavior. *Journal of Applied Psychology, 90*(6), 1241–1255.

Dale, E., & Chall, J. S. (1948). A formula for predicting readability. *Educational Research Bulletin, 27*, 37–54.

Daley, A. J., & Parfitt, G. (1996). Good health—is it worth it? Mood states, physical well-being, job satisfaction and absenteeism in members and non-members of a British corporate health and fitness club. *Journal of Occupational and Organizational Psychology, 69*(2), 121–134.

Dalton, D. R., & Mesch, D. J. (1991). On the extent and reduction of avoidable absenteeism: An assessment of absence policy provisions. *Journal of Applied Psychology, 76*(6), 810–817.

Dansereau, F., Graen, G., & Haga, W. J. (1975). *A vertical dyad linkage approach to leadership within the formal organization.* Unpublished report, State University of New York, Buffalo.

Darnold, T. C., & Zimmerman, R. D. (2006, May). *Performance and intent to quit: A meta-analysis and path model.* Poster presented at the annual meeting of the Society for Industrial and Organizational Psychology, Dallas, TX.

Davidson, O. B., & Eden, D. (2000). Remedial self-fulfilling prophecy: Two field experiments to prevent Golem effects among disadvantaged women. *Journal of Applied Psychology, 85*(3), 386–398.

Davidson, R., & Henderson, R. (2000). Electronic performance monitoring: A laboratory investigation of the influence of monitoring and difficulty on task performance, mood state, and self-reported stress levels. *Journal of Applied Social Psychology, 30*(5), 906–920.

Davies, E. (1922). *Transactions of the Institute of Mining Engineering, 63*, 326.

Davis, D. D., & Harless, D. W. (1996). Group v. individual performance in a price-searching experiment. *Organizational Behavior and Human Decision Processes, 66*(2), 215–227.

Davis, K. (1953). Management communication and the grape-vine. *Harvard Business Review, 31*(5), 43–59.

Davis, K. (1977). *Human behavior at work.* New York.: McGraw-Hill

Davis, T. R. (1984). The influence of the physical environment in offices. *Academy of Management Review, 9*, 271–283.

Day, D. V., & Schleicher, D. J. (2006). Self-monitoring at work: A motive-based perspective. *Journal of Personality, 74*(3), 685–714.

Day, D. V., Schleicher, D. J., Unckless, A. L., & Hiller, N. J. (2002). Self-monitoring personality at work: A meta-analytic investigation of construct validity. *Journal of Applied Psychology, 87*(2), 390–401.

Day, D. V., & Sulsky, L. M. (1995). Effects of frame-of-reference training and information configuration on memory organization and rating accuracy. *Journal of Applied Psychology, 80*(1), 158–167.

Dean, M. A., Roth, P. L., & Bobko, P. (2008). Ethnic and gender subgroup differences in assessment center ratings: A meta-analysis. *Journal of Applied Psychology, 93*(3), 685–691.

Deane, C. (1999, January 10). Don't worry, we've got your number. *The Washington Post*, p. C4.

de Castro, J. M., & Brewer, E. M. (1992). The amount eaten in meals by humans is a power function of the number of people present. *Physiology and Behavior, 51*(1), 121–125.

De Meuse, K. P., Bergmann, T. J., Vanderheiden, P. A., & Roraff, C. E. (2004). New evidence regarding organizational downsizing and a firm's financial performance: A long-term analysis. *Journal of Managerial Issues, 16*(2), 155–177.

Deci, E. L. (1972). The effects of contingent and noncontingent rewards and controls on intrinsic motivation. *Organizational Behavior and Human Performance, 8*, 217–229.

Deci, E. L., Koestner, R., & Ryan, R. M. (1999). A meta-analytic review of experiments examining the effects of extrinsic rewards on intrinsic motivation. *Psychological Bulletin, 125*(6), 627–668.

Deci, E. L., & Ryan, R. M. (1985). *Intrinsic motivation and self-determination in human behavior.* New York: Plenum.

DeGroot, T., & Kiker, D. S. (2003). A meta-analysis of the non-monetary effects of employee health management programs. *Human Resource Management, 42*(1), 53–69.

DeGroot, T., & Motowidlo, S. J. (1999). Why visual and vocal interview cues can affect interviewers' judgments and predict job performance. *Journal of Applied Psychology, 84*(6), 986–993.

Delpo, A. (2009). *The performance appraisal handbook: Legal and practical rules for managers* (3rd ed.) Berkeley, CA: Nolo Press.

Deluga, R. J., & Winters, J. J. (1991). Why the aggravation? Reasons students become resident assistants. *Journal of College Student Development, 32*(6), 546–552.

Dempsey, P. G., Ayoub, M. M., Bernard, T. M., Endsley, M. R., Karwowski, W., Lin, C. J. et al. (1996). Ergonomic investigation of letter-carrier satchels: Part I. Field study. *Applied Ergonomics, 27*(5), 303–313.

De Dreu, C. K. W., & Weingart, L. R. (2003). Task versus relationship conflict, team performance, and team member satisfaction: A meta-analysis. *Journal of Applied Psychology, 88*(4), 741–745.

Den Hartog, D. N., House, R. J., Hanges, P. J., Ruiz-Quintanilla, S. A., & Dorfman, P. W. (1999). Culture specific and cross culturally generalizable implicit leadership theories: Are attributes of charismatic/transformational leadership universally endorsed? *Leadership Quarterly, 10*(2), 219–256.

DeNisi, A. S., & Peters, L. H. (1996). Organization of information in memory and the performance appraisal process: Evidence from the field. *Journal of Applied Psychology, 81*(6), 717–737.

DeNisi, A. S., Robbins, T., & Cafferty, T. P. (1989). Organization of information used for performance appraisals: Role of diary-keeping. *Journal of Applied Psychology, 74*, 124–129.

Dennis, A. R., Valacich, J. S., & Nunamaker, J. F. (1990). An experimental investigation of the effects of group size in an electronic meeting environment. *IEEE Transactions on Systems, Man, and Cybernetics, 20*(5), 1049–1057.

Denton, D. K. (1996). 9 ways to create an atmosphere for change. *HR Magazine, 41*(10), 76–81.

DePaulo, B. M. (1992). Nonverbal behavior and self-presentation. *Psychological Bulletin, 111*, 203–243.

DePaulo, B. M., Lindsay, J. J., Malone, B. E., Muhlenbruck, L., Charlton, K., & Cooper, H. (2003). Cues to deception. *Psychological Bulletin, 129*(1), 74–118.

DeRosa, D. M., Smith, C. L., & Hantula, D. A. (2007). The medium matters: Mining the long-promised merit of group interaction in creative idea generation tasks in a meta-analysis of the electronic group brainstorming literature. *Computers in Human Behavior, 23*(3), 1549–1581.

DeRouin, R. E., Parrish, T. J., & Salas, E. (2005). *On-the-job training: A review for researchers and practitioners.* Poster session presented at the 20th annual conference of the Society for Industrial and Organizational Psychology, Los Angeles, CA.

Dessler, G. (2002). *Personnel management.* Upper Saddle River, NJ: Prentice-Hall.

Devine, D. J., Clayton, L. D., Philips, J. L., Dunford, B. B., & Melner, S. B. (1999). Teams in organizations: Prevalence, characteristics, and effectiveness. *Small Group Research, 30*(6), 678–711.

Devine, D. J., & Philips, J. L. (2001). Do smarter teams do better: A meta-analysis of cognitive ability and team performance. *Small Group Research, 32*(5), 507–532.

Dew, A. F., & Steiner, D. D. (1997). *Inappropriate questions in selection interviews: Interviewer knowledge and applicant reactions.* Poster presented at the 12th annual conference of the Society for Industrial and Organizational Psychology, St. Louis, MO.

De Waard, D., Jessurun, M., Steyvers, F. J., Raggatt, P. T., & Brookhuis, K. A. (1995). Effect of road layout and road environment on driving performance, drivers' physiology, and road appreciation. *Ergonomics, 38*(7), 1395–1407.

Dianat, I., Haslegrave, C. M., & Stedmon, A. W. (2010). Short and longer duration effects of protective gloves on hand performance capabilities and subjective assessments in a screwdriving task. *Ergonomics, 53*(12), 1468–1483.

Dickenson, T. L., & Zellinger, P. M. (1980). A comparison of the behaviorally anchored rating and mixed standard scale format. *Journal of Applied Psychology, 65*, 147–154.

Dickinson, A. M. (1989). The detrimental effects of extrinsic reinforcement on intrinsic motivation. *Behavior Analyst, 12*(1), 1–15.

Dickinson, A. M., & Gillette, K. L. (1993). A comparison of the effects of two individual monetary incentive systems on productivity and piece rate pay versus base pay plus incentives. *Journal of Organizational Behavior Management, 14*(1), 63–82.

Dickson, D. H., & Kelly, I. W. (1985). The "Barnum Effect" in personality assessment: A review of the literature. *Psychological Reports, 57*, 367–382.

DiClemente, D. F., & Hantula, D. A. (2000). John Broadus Watson, I-O psychologist. *The Industrial-Organizational Psychologist, 37*(4), 47–55.

Diekmann, F. J. (2001, July 23). Everything you wanted to know about e-learning (But didn't know where to log on to ask). *Credit Union Journal, 5*(30), 6–7.

Dierdorff, E. C., & Rubin, R. S. (2007). Carelessness and discriminability in work role requirement judgments: Influences of role ambiguity and cognitive complexity. *Personnel Psychology, 60*, 597–625.

Dierdorff, E. C., & Wilson, M. A. (2003). A meta-analysis of job analysis reliability. *Journal of Applied Psychology, 88*(4), 635–646.

Dietz, P. E. (1994). *Overview of workplace violence.* Seminar presented to the Society for Human Resource Management, Roanoke, VA.

DiFonzo, N., & Bordia, P. (2006). Rumor in organizational contexts. In R. L. Rosnow & D. A. Hantula (Eds.), *Advances in social and organizational psychology.* Hillsdale, NJ: Lawrence Erlbaum.

DiFonzo, N., & Bordia, P. (2007). *Rumor psychology: Social and organizational approaches.* Washington, DC: American Psychological Association.

Dineen, B. R., Ling, J., Ash, S. R., & DelVecchio, D. (2007). Aesthetic properties and message customization: Navigating the dark side of web recruitment. *Journal of Applied Psychology, 92*(2), 356–372.

Dingfelder, S. F. (2004). A presidential personality. *Monitor on Psychology, 35*(10), 26–28.

Dipboye, R. L. (1977). A critical review of Korman's self-consistency theory of work motivation and occupational choice. *Organizational Behavior and Human Performance, 18*, 108–126.

Dipboye, R. L. (1990). Laboratory vs. field research in industrial and organizational psychology. In C. L. Cooper & I. T. Robertson (Eds.), *International review of industrial and organizational psychology* (pp. 1–34). Chichester, UK: John Wiley.

Dipboye, R. L., Stramler, C. S., & Fontenelle, G. A. (1984). The effects of the application on recall of information from the interview. *Academy of Management Journal, 27*, 561–575.

Dirks, K. T., & Ferrin, D. L. (2002). Trust in leadership: Meta-analytic findings and implications for research and practice. *Journal of Applied Psychology, 87*(4), 611–628.

Dolin, D. J., & Booth-Butterfield, M. (1993). Reach out and touch someone: Analysis of nonverbal comforting responses. *Communication Quarterly, 41*(4), 383–393.

Dominguez, C. M., & Sotherlund, J. (2010). *Leading with your heart: Diversity and ganas for inspired inclusion.* Alexandria, VA: Society for Human Resource Management.

Donnellon, A. (1996). *Team talk: The power of language in team dynamics.* Boston, MA: Harvard Business School Press.

Donnerstein, E., & Wilson, D. W. (1976). Effects of noise and perceived control on ongoing and subsequent aggressive behavior. *Journal of Personality and Social Psychology, 34*, 774–781.

Donovan, J. J., & Radosevich, D. J. (1999). A meta-analytic review of the distribution of practice effect: Now you see it, now you don't. *Journal of Applied Psychology, 84,* 795–805.

Dormann, C., & Zapf, D. (2001). Job satisfaction: A meta-analysis of stabilities. *Journal of Organizational Behavior, 22,* 483–504.

Dougherty, T. W., Turban, D. B., & Callender, J. C. (1994). Confirming first impressions in the employment interview: A field study of interviewer behavior. *Journal of Applied Psychology, 79*(5), 659–665.

Drexler, A. B., & Forrester, R. (1998). Teamwork—not necessarily the answer. *HR Magazine, 43*(1), 55–58.

Driskell, J. E., Willis, R. P., & Copper, C. (1992). Effect of over-learning on retention. *Journal of Applied Psychology, 77*(5), 615–623.

Duchon, J. C., Keran, C. M., & Smith, T. J. (1994). Extended workdays in an underground mine: A work performance analysis. *Human Factors, 36*(2), 258–268.

Dugan, K. M. (2001, October 24). Montgomery, AL fair attracts nearly 1,000 applicants. *Montgomery Advisor.*

Dwight, S. A., & Feigelson, M. E. (2000). A quantitative review of the effect of computerized testing on the measurement of social desirability. *Educational and Psychological Measurement, 60*(3), 340–360.

Dye, D. A., & Reck, M. (1989). College grade point average as a predictor of adult success: A reply. *Public Personnel Management, 18*(2), 239–240.

Dyekman, M., & Susseles, E. (2003, October). Alternatives to layoffs: Other choices offer human resource cost savings. *IPMA-HR News,* 24–25.

Eagly, A. H., Johannesen-Schmidt, M. C., & van Engen, M. L. (2003). Transformational, transactional, and laissez-faire leadership styles: A meta-analysis comparing men and women. *Psychological Bulletin, 129*(4), 569–591.

Eagly, A. H., & Johnson, B. T. (1990). Gender and leadership style: A meta-analysis. *Psychological Bulletin, 108*(2), 233–256.

Eagly, A. H., & Karau, S. J. (1991). Gender and the emergence of leaders: A meta-analysis. *Journal of Personality and Social Psychology, 60*(5), 685–710.

Eagly, A. H., Karau, S. J., & Makhijani, M. G. (1995). Gender and the effectiveness of leaders: A meta-analysis. *Psychological Bulletin, 117*(1), 125–145.

Eatough, E. M., Chang, C.-H., Miloslavic, S. A., & Johnson, R. E. (2011). Relationships of role stressors with organizational citizenship behaviors: A meta-analysis. *Journal of Applied Psychology, 96*(3), 619–632.

Eby, L. T., Allen, T. D., Evans, S. C., Ng, T., & DuBois, D. L. (2008). Does mentoring matter? A multidisciplinary meta-analysis comparing mentored and non-mentored individuals. *Journal of Vocational Behavior, 72*(2), 254–267.

Eden, D. (1998). *Implanting Pygmalion leadership style through training: Seven true field experiments.* Paper presented at the annual meeting of the Society for Industrial and Organizational Psychology, Dallas, TX.

Eidelson, R. J., & Eidelson, J. I. (2003). Dangerous ideas: Five beliefs that propel groups toward conflict. *American Psychologist, 58*(3), 182–192.

Ekeberg, S., Switzer, F., & Siegfried, W. D. (1991). *What do you do with a master's degree in I/O psychology.* Symposium conducted at the sixth annual conference of the Society for Industrial and Organizational Psychology, St. Louis, MO.

Elias, M. (1997). Mood a stroke risk factor: Depression may be prelude. *USA Today,* May, pp. A1.

Emrich, C. G., Brower, H. H., Feldman, J, M., & Garland, H. (2001). Images in words: Presidential rhetoric, charisma, and greatness. *Administrative Science Quarterly, 46*(3), 527–560.

Epstein, D. G. (2003). Safety and security: Preventing workplace violence. *IPMA News,* January, 26–27.

Erdogan, B., & Enders, J. (2007). Support from the top: Supervisors' perceived organizational support as a moderator of leader-member exchange to satisfaction and performance relationships. *Journal of Applied Psychology, 92*(2), 321–330.

Erfurt, J. C., Foote, A., & Heirich, M. A. (1992). The cost-effectiveness of worksite wellness programs for hypertension control, weight loss, smoking cessation, and exercise. *Personnel Psychology, 45*(1), 5–28.

Estes, R. (1990). Effects of flexi-time: A meta-analytic review. *Applied H.R.M. Research, 1*(1), 15–18.

Eurich, T. L., Krause, D. E., Cigularov, K., & Thornton, G. C. (2009). The current use of assessment center programs in the U.S. *Journal of Business and Psychology, 24,* 387–407.

Evans, G. W., Hygge, S., & Bullinger, M. (1995). Chronic noise and psychological stress. *Psychological Science, 6*(6), 333–338.

Evans, G. W., & Johnson, D. (2000). Stress and open-office noise. *Journal of Applied Psychology, 85*(5), 779–783.

Falcone, P. (2002). Fire my assistant now! *HR Magazine, 47*(5), 105–111.

Faragher, E. B., Cass, M., & Cooper, C. L. (2005). The relationship between job satisfaction and health: A meta-analysis. *Occupational and Environmental Medicine, 62,* 105–112.

Farber, B. J. (1994). Sales managers: Get real! Real play, not role play, is the best training you can give your salespeople. *Sales & Marketing Management, 146*(10), 25–26.

Farh, J., Dobbins, G. A., & Cheng, B. S. (1991). Cultural relativity in action: A comparison of self-ratings made by Chinese and U.S. workers. *Personnel Psychology, 44*(1), 129–147.

Farh, J., & Werbel, J. D. (1986). Effects of purpose of the appraisal and expectation of validation on self-appraisal leniency. *Journal of Applied Psychology, 71,* 527–529.

Farr, J. L. (1973). Response requirements and primacy-recency effects in a simulated selection interview. *Journal of Applied Psychology, 57*(3), 228–232.

Farrell, D., & Stamm, C. L. (1988). Meta-analysis of the correlates of employee absence. *Human Relations, 41,* 211–227.

Fay, C. H., & Latham, G. P. (1982). Effects of training and rating scales on rating errors. *Personnel Psychology, 35,* 105–116.

FDS (2007). *What workers want: A worldwide study of attitudes to work and work-life balance.* London: FDS International.

Feight, L., Ferguson, G., Rodriguez, C., & Simons, C. (2006, February). *Can't get no satisfaction: A meta-analysis of equity theory and its effects on satisfaction and motivation.* Paper presented at the annual Graduate Student Conference in

Industrial-Organizational Psychology and Organizational Behavior, Fairfax, VA.

Feinberg, R. A., Meoli-Stanton, J., & Gable, M. (1996). Employment rejection and acceptance letters and their unintended consequences on image, self-concept, and intentions. *Journal of Business and Psychology, 11*(1), 63–71.

Feldman, J. (1981). Beyond attribution theory: Cognitive processes in performance appraisal. *Journal of Applied Psychology, 66,* 127–148.

Ferreter, J. M., Goldstein, H. W., Scherbaum, C. A., Yusko, K. P., & Jun, K. (2008, April). *Examining adverse impact using a nontraditional cognitive ability assessment.* Poster session presented at the 23rd annual meeting of the Society for Industrial-Organizational Psychology, San Francisco, CA.

Fiedler, F. (1967). *A theory of leadership effectiveness.* New York: McGraw-Hill.

Fiedler, F. (1978). Recent developments in research on the contingency model. In L. Berkowitz (Ed.), *Group processes* (pp. 207–223). New York: Academic Press.

Field, R. H., & House, R. J. (1990). A test of the Vroom-Yetton model using manager and subordinate reports. *Journal of Applied Psychology, 75*(3), 362–266.

Fine, B. J., & Kobrick, J. L. (1978). Effects of altitude and heat on complex cognitive tasks. *Human Factors, 20,* 115–122.

Fine, S. A. (1955). What is occupational information? *Personnel and Guidance Journal, 33,* 504–509.

Fine, S. A. (1988). Functional job analysis. In Gael, S. (Ed.), *The job analysis handbook for business, industry, and government (Volume II).* New York: Wiley.

Finkelman, J. M., Zeitlin, L. R., Filippi, J. A., & Friend, M. A. (1977). Noise and driver performance. *Journal of Applied Psychology, 62,* 713–718.

Finkelstein, L. M., Burke, M. J., & Raju, N. S. (1995). Age discrimination in simulated employment contexts: An integrative analysis. *Journal of Applied Psychology, 80,* 652–663.

Fisher, J. D., Rytting, M., & Heslin, R. (1976). Hands touching hands: Affective and evaluative effects of an interpersonal touch. *Sociometry, 39,* 416–421.

Fisher, S. L., & Greenis, J. L. (1996). *The customer in job analysis.* Poster presented at the 11th annual conference of the Society for Industrial and Organizational Psychology, San Diego, CA.

Fitzgibbons, A. (1997). Employees' perceived importance of profit sharing plays a role in profit sharing's organizational impact. *Proceedings of the 18th Annual Graduate Conference in Industrial/Organizational Psychology and Organizational Behavior, 18,* 43–44.

Flanagan, J. C. (1954). The critical incident technique. *Psychological Bulletin, 51,* 327–358.

Flanagan, J. C., & Burns, R. K. (1955). The employee performance record: A new appraisal and development tool. *Harvard Business Review, 33,* 95–102.

Fleishman, E. A., & Harris, E. F. (1962). Patterns of leadership behavior related to grievances and turnover. *Personnel Psychology, 15*(2), 43–56.

Fleishman, E. A., Harris, E. F., & Burtt, H. E. (1955). *Leadership and supervision in industry.* Columbus: Ohio State University Press.

Fleishman, E. A., & Reilly, M. E. (1992a). *Administrator's guide F-JAS.* Palo Alto, CA: Consulting Psychologists Press.

Fleishman, E. A., & Reilly, M. E. (1992b). *Handbook of human abilities.* Palo Alto, CA: Consulting Psychologists Press.

Flesch, R. (1948). A new readability yardstick. *Journal of Applied Psychology, 32,* 221–233.

Fletcher, J., Friedman, L., McCarthy, P., McIntyre, C., O'Leary, B., & Rheinstein, J. (1993). *Sample sizes required to attain stable job analysis inventory profiles.* Poster presented at the 8th annual meeting of the Society for Industrial and Organizational Psychology, San Francisco, CA.

Florkowski, G. W., & Schuster, M. H. (1992). Support for profit sharing and organizational commitment: A path analysis. *Human Relations, 45*(5), 507–523.

Foldes, H. J., Duehr, E. E., & Ones, D. S. (2008). Group differences in personality: Meta-analyses comparing five U.S. racial groups. *Personnel Psychology, 61*(3), 579–616.

Folkard, S. (2008). Do permanent night workers show circadian adjustment? A review based on the endogenous melatonin rhythm. *Chronobiology International, 25,* 183–198.

Forbes, R. J., & Jackson, P. R. (1980). Non-verbal behaviour and the outcome of selection interviews. *Journal of Occupational Psychology, 53,* 65–72.

Ford, D., Truxillo, D. M., Wang, M., & Bauer, T. (2008, April). *Individual differences and the quality of job analysis ratings.* Poster session presented at the 23rd annual meeting of the Society for Industrial-Organizational Psychology, San Francisco, CA.

Ford, J. K., Quiñones, M. A., Sego, D. J., & Sorra, J. S. (1992). Factors affecting the opportunity to perform trained tasks on the job. *Personnel Psychology, 45,* 511–527.

Forsyth, D. R. (2010). *Group dynamics* (5th ed.). Belmont, CA: Wadsworth.

Forsythe, S., Drake, M. F., & Cox, C. E. (1985). Influence of applicant's dress on interviewer's selection decisions. *Journal of Applied Psychology, 70,* 374–378.

Foster, D. A. (1999). *A leader-subordinate fit model of the path-goal theory of leadership.* Unpublished doctoral dissertation, George Washington University, Washington, DC.

Foster, M. (1990). A closer look at the relationship between interviewer-interviewee similarity and ratings in a selection interview. *Applied H.R.M. Research, 1*(1), 23–26.

Foster, N., Dingman, S., Muscolino, J., & Jankowski, M. A. (1996). Gender in mock hiring decisions. *Psychological Reports, 79*(1), 275–278.

Foster, P. (2002). Performance documentation. *Business Communication Quarterly, 65*(2), 108–114.

Foster, R. S., Aamodt, M. G., Bodenmiller, J. A., Rodgers, J. G., Kovach, R. C., & Bryan, D. A. (1988). Effect of menu sign position on customer ordering times and number of food-ordering errors. *Environment and Behavior, 20*(2), 200–210.

Foster, T. C., Dunleavy, E., Campion, J., & Steubing, K. (2008, April). *Understanding performance appraisal litigation: Does justice explain wrongful discharge rulings?* Poster session presented at the 23rd annual meeting of the Society for Industrial and Organizational Psychology, San Francisco, CA.

Foti, R. J., & Hauenstein, N. M. A. (2007). Pattern and variable approaches in leadership emergence and effectiveness. *Journal of Applied Psychology, 92*(2), 347–355.

Fowler-Hermes, J. (2001). The beauty and the beast in the workplace: Appearance-based discrimination claims under EEO laws. *Florida Bar Journal, 75*(4), 32–46.

Fox, J. B., Scott, K. D., & Donohue, J. M. (1993). An investigation into pay valence and performance in a pay-for-performance field setting. *Journal of Organizational Behavior, 14,* 687–693.

Frank, C. L., & Hackman, J. R. (1975). Effects of interviewer-interviewee similarity on interviewer objectivity in college admissions interviews. *Journal of Applied Psychology, 60,* 356–360.

Frank, F., & Anderson, L. R. (1971). Effects of task and group size upon group productivity and member satisfaction. *Sociometry, 34,* 135–149.

Frase, M. (2010). Taking time off to the bank. *HR Magazine, 55*(3), 41–46.

Frase-Blunt, M. (2004). Making exit interviews work. *HR Magazine, 49*(8), 109–113.

Frase-Blunt, M. (2001). Driving home your awards program. *HR Magazine, 46*(2), 109–115.

French, J. R. P., & Raven, B. H. (1959). The bases of social power. In D. Cartwright (Ed.), *Studies in social power* (pp. 150–167). Ann Arbor: University of Michigan Press.

French, M. T., Roebuck, C. M., & Alexandre, P. K. (2004). To test or not to test: Do workplace drug testing programs discourage employee drug use? *Social Science Research, 33*(1), 45–63.

Frese, M., & Okonek, K. (1984). Reasons to leave shiftwork and psychological and psychosomatic complaints of former shiftworkers. *Journal of Applied Psychology, 69,* 509–514.

Freston, N. P., & Lease, J. E. (1987). Communication skills training for selected supervisors. *Training and Development Journal, 41*(7), 67–70.

Fried, Y., & Ferris, G. R. (1987). The validity of the job characteristics model: A review and meta-analysis. *Personnel Psychology, 40,* 287–322.

Frone, M. R. (2000). Work-family conflict and employee psychiatric disorders: The national comorbidity survey. *Journal of Applied Psychology, 85*(6), 888–895.

Frone, M. R., Russell, M., & Cooper, M. L. (1995). Job stressors, job involvement, and employee health: An identity theory. *Journal of Occupational and Organizational Psychology, 68*(1), 1–11.

Fry, E. (1977). Fry's Readability Graph: Clarifications, validity, and extension to level 17. *Journal of Reading, 21,* 243–252.

Gaby, S. H., & Woehr, D. J. (2005, April). *Development and evaluation of a "Climate for Performance Appraisal" measure.* Poster presented at the 20th annual meeting of the Society for Industrial and Organizational Psychology, Los Angeles, CA.

Gael, S. (1988). Subject matter expert conferences. In S. Gael (Ed.), *The job analysis handbook for business, industry, and government* (*Vol. 1,* p. 434). New York: Wiley.

Gajendran, R. S., & Harrison, D. A. (2007). The good, the bad, and the unknown about telecommuting: Meta-analysis of psychological mediators and individual consequences. *Journal of Applied Psychology, 92*(6), 1524–1541.

Gallup, D. A., & Beauchemin, K. V. (2000). On-the-job training. In G. M. Piskurich, P. Beckschi, & B. Hall (Eds.), *The ASTD handbook of training design and delivery.* New York: McGraw Hill.

Galvin, T. (2003). 2003 Industry report. *Training Magazine, 40*(9), 21–45.

Gandy, J. A., & Dye, D. A. (1989). Development and initial validation of a biodata inventory in a merit system context. *Proceedings of 13th Annual Meeting of the International Personnel Management Association Assessment Council,* pp. 138–142.

Gannon, M. J., Norland, D. L., & Robeson, F. E. (1983). Shift work has complex effects on lifestyles and work habits. *Personnel Administrator, 28*(5), 93–97.

Ganzach, Y. (1998). Intelligence and job satisfaction. *Academy of Management Journal, 41*(5), 526–539.

Garbarino, S. (2004). *Shift-work: Sleep disorders, car accidents, and officer performance.* Paper presented at the annual meeting of the Society for Police and Criminal Psychology, Rome, Italy.

Gardner, J. E. (1994). *Determining focus areas for interview preparation research.* Paper presented at the 15th annual Graduate Student Conference in Industrial-Organizational Psychology and Organizational Behavior, Chicago, IL.

Garvey, C. (2000). Getting a grip on titles. *HR Magazine, 45*(12), 112–117.

Garvey, C. (2001). Outsourcing background checks. *HR Magazine, 46*(3), 95–104.

Gately, R. F. (1997, March). Why motivation is free. *IPMA News,* p. 14.

Gaugler, B. B., Rosenthal, D. B., Thornton, G. C., & Bentson, C. (1987). Meta-analysis of assessment center validity. *Journal of Applied Psychology, 72,* 493–511.

Gebhardt, D. L., & Crump, C. E. (1990). Employee fitness and wellness programs in the workplace. *American Psychologist, 45*(2), 262–272.

Geier, J. G., & Downey, D. E. (1980). *Attitudinal listening profile system.* Minneapolis, MN: Performax Systems International.

Geier, J. G., Downey, D. E., & Johnson, J. B. (1980). *Climate impact profile.* Minneapolis, MN: Performax Systems International.

Gelbart, M. (2001, October 30). 425 hopefuls attend Philadelphia job fair for airline workers. *Philadelphia Inquirer.*

George, J. M. (1995). Asymmetrical effects of rewards and punishments: The case of social loafing. *Journal of Occupational and Organizational Psychology, 68*(4), 327–338.

George, W. (2003). *Authentic leadership: Rediscovering the secrets to creating lasting value.* San Francisco: Jossey-Bass.

Gere, D., Scarborough, E. K., & Collison, J. (2002). *SHRM/Recruit Marketplace 2002 recruiter budget/cost survey.* Alexandria, VA: Society for Human Resource Management.

Gersick, C. J. G. (1988). Time and transition in work teams: Toward a new model of group development. *Academy of Management Journal, 31*(1), 9–41.

Gerstner, C. R., & Day, D. V. (1997). Meta-analytic review of leader-member exchange theory: Correlates and construct issues. *Journal of Applied Psychology, 82*(6), 827–844.

Gibbs, C. A. (1969). Leadership. In G. Lindzey & E. Aronson (Eds.), *Handbook of social psychology* (pp. 205–282). Reading, MA: Addison-Wesley.

Giffin, M. E. (1989). Personnel research on testing, selection, and performance appraisal. *Public Personnel Management, 18,* 127–137.

Gilboa, S., Shirom, A., Fried, Y., & Cooper, C. (2008). A meta-analysis of work demand stressors and job performance: Examining main and moderating effects. *Personnel Psychology, 61*(2), 227–271.

Gilchrist, J. A., & White, K. D. (1990). Policy development and satisfaction with merit pay: A field study in a university setting. *College Student Journal, 24*(3), 249–254.

Gillet, B., & Schwab, D. P. (1975). Convergent and discriminant validities of corresponding Job Descriptive Index and Minnesota Satisfaction Questionnaire scales. *Journal of Applied Psychology, 60,* 313–317.

Gilliland, S. W. (1993). The perceived fairness of selection systems: An organizational justice perspective. *Academy of Management Review, 18,* 694–734.

Gilliland, S. W., Groth, M., Baker, R. C., Dew, A. F., Polly, L. M., & Langdon, J. C. (2001). Improving applicants' reactions to rejection letters: An application of fairness theory. *Personnel Psychology, 54*(3), 669–703.

Gilliland, S. W., & Langdon, J. C. (1998). Creating performance management systems that promote perceptions of fairness. In Smither, J. W. (Ed.), *Performance appraisal: State of the art in practice* (pp. 209–243). San Francisco: Jossey-Bass.

Gilliland, S. W., & Steiner, D. D. (1997). *Challenge #6: Interactional and procedural justice.* Paper presented at the 12th annual meeting of the Society for Industrial and Organizational Psychology, St. Louis, MO.

Gilmore, D. C. (1989). Applicant perceptions of simulated behavior description interviews. *Journal of Business and Psychology, 3,* 279–288.

Gilmore, T. N., Shea, G. P., & Useem, M. (1997). Side effects of corporate cultural transformations. *Journal of Applied Behavioral Science, 33*(2), 174–189.

Giluk, T., Stewart, G. L., & Shaffer, J. (2008, April). Interviewer decision making: The role of judgments during rapport building. In M. R. Barrick (Chair), *The role of unstructured information in the employment interview.* Symposium presented at the 23rd annual meeting of the Society for Industrial-Organizational Psychology, San Francisco, CA.

Glanz, B. A. (1997, March). Spread contagious enthusiasm. *IPMA News,* pp. 13–14.

Glebbeek, A. C., & Bax, E. H. (2004). Is high employee turnover really harmful? A empirical test using company records. *Academy of Management Journal, 47*(2), 277–286.

Glotz, B., & Ruotolo, C. (2006, February). *Profiling the workplace killer.* Paper presented at the annual Graduate Conference in Industrial-Organizational Psychology and Organizational Behavior, Fairfax, VA.

Goddard, R., Simons, R., Patton, W., & Sullivan, K. (2004). Psychologist hand-scoring error rates on the Rothwell-Miller Interest Blank: A comparison of three job allocation systems. *Australian Journal of Psychology, 56*(1), 25–32.

Goff, S. J., Mount, M. K., Jamison, R. L. (1990). Employer supported child care, work/family conflict, and absenteeism: A field study. *Personnel Psychology, 43*(4), 793–809.

Goldstein, C. H. (2000). Employee drug testing in the public sector. *IPMA News,* July, 13–16.

Goldstein, I. L., & Ford, J. K. (2002). *Training in organizations* (4th ed.). Belmont, CA: Wadsworth.

Gomez-Mejia, L. R., Welbourne, T. M., & Wiseman, R. M. (2000). The role of risk sharing and risk taking under gainsharing. *Academy of Management Review, 25*(3), 492–507.

Gomm, K. (2005). EU agism law could put an end to "milk round" campus recruitment. *Computer Weekly,* February 1, page 36.

Gonder, M. L., & Walker, D. D. (2000). *Masters-level industrial/organizational psychologist survey results.* Paper presented at the annual meeting of the Society for Industrial-Organizational Psychology, New Orleans, LA.

Goodson, J. R., McGee, G. W., & Cashman, J. F. (1989). Situational leadership theory: A test of leadership prescriptions. *Group and Organization Studies, 14*(4), 446–461.

Gordon, J. R. (2001). *Organizational behavior: A diagnostic approach* (7th ed.) Englewood Cliffs, NJ: Prentice Hall.

Gordon, M. E., Slade, L. A., & Schmitt, H. (1986). The "science of the sophomore" revisited: From conjecture to empiricism. *Academy of Management Review, 11,* 191–207.

Gordon, R. A., & Arvey, R. D. (2004). Age bias in laboratory and field settings: A meta-analytic investigation. *Journal of Applied Social Psychology, 34*(3), 468–492.

Gorman, C. A., & Rentsch, J. R. (2009). Evaluating frame-of-reference rater training effectiveness using performance schema accuracy. *Journal of Applied Psychology, 94*(5), 1336–1344.

Gosling, S. D., Vazire, S., Srivastava, S., & John, O. P. (2004). Should we trust web-based studies? A comparative analysis of six perceptions about internet questions. *American Psychologist, 59*(2), 93–104.

Gowen, C. R. (1990). Gainsharing programs: An overview of history and research. *Journal of Organizational Behavior Management, 11*(2), 77–99.

Graen, G., & Uhl-Bien, M. (1995). Relationship-based approach to leadership: Development of leader-member exchange (LMX) theory of leadership over 25 years: Applying a multi-level multi-domain perspective. *Leadership Quarterly, 6,* 219–247.

Grant, K. A., & Habes, D. J. (1995). An analysis of scanning postures among grocery cashiers and its relationship to checkstand design. *Ergonomics, 38*(10), 2078–2090.

Green, S. B., Sauser, W. I., Fagg, F. N., & Champion, C. H. (1981). Shortcut methods for deriving behaviorally anchored rating scales. *Educational and Psychological Measurement, 41,* 761–775.

Green, S. B., & Stutzman, T. (1986). An evaluation of methods to select respondents to structured job-analysis questionnaires. *Personnel Psychology, 39*, 543–564.

Greenberg, E. R. (1996). Drug-testing now standard practice. *HR Focus, 73*(9), 24.

Greenberg, J. S. (2011). *Comprehensive stress management* (12th ed.). New York: McGraw-Hill.

Greenberg, J. S., & Baron, R. A. (2011). *Behavior in organizations* (10th ed.). Englewood Cliffs, NJ: Prentice Hall.

Grensing-Pophal, L. (2001a). *HR and the corporate intranet: Beyond brochureware.* Alexandria, VA: Society for Human Resource Management.

Grensing-Pophal, L. (2001b). Motivate managers to review performance. *HR Magazine, 46*(3), 45–48.

Grensing-Pophal, L. (2003). Communication pays off. *HR Magazine, 48*(5), 77–82.

Grensing-Pophal, L. (2007). Committing to part-timers. *HR Magazine, 52*(4), 85–88.

Griffeth, R. W., & Gaertner, S. (2001). A role for equity theory in the turnover process: An empirical test. *Journal of Applied Social Psychology, 31*(5), 1017–1037.

Griffeth, R. W., Hom, P. W., & Gaertner, S. (2000). A meta-analysis of antecedents and correlates of employee turnover: Update, moderator tests, and research implications for the next millennium. *Journal of Management, 26*(3), 463–488.

Griffin, M. A., Rafferty, A. E., & Mason, C. M. (2004). Who started this? Investigating different sources of organizational change. *Journal of Business and Psychology, 18*(4), 555–570.

Griffiths, R. F., & McDaniel, Q. P. (1993). Predictors of police assaults. *Journal of Police and Criminal Psychology, 9*(1), 5–9.

Grossman, R. J. (2000). Make ergonomics. *HR Magazine, 45*(4), 36–42.

Grossman, R. J. (2002). Space: Another HR frontier. *HR Magazine, 47*(9), 28–34.

Grossman, R. J. (2010). Tough love at Netflix: The movie rental company minimizes policies but demands high performance. *HR Magazine, 55*(4), 36–41.

Grote, C. L., Robiner, W. N., & Haut, A. (2001). Disclosure of information in letters of recommendation: Writers' intentions and readers' experiences. *Professional Psychology-Research and Practice, 32*(6), 655–661.

Guion, R. M., & Gibson, W. M. (1988). Personnel selection and placement. *Annual Review of Psychology, 39*, 349–374.

Gully, S. M., Incalcaterra, K. A., Joshi, A., & Beaubien, J. M. (2002). A meta-analysis of team-efficacy, potency, and performance: Interdependence and level of analysis as moderators of observed relationships. *Journal of Applied Psychology, 87*(5), 819–832.

Gumpert, R. A., & Hambleton, R. K. (1979). Situational leadership: How Xerox managers fine-tune managerial styles to employee maturity and task needs. *Management Review, 12*, 9.

Gunning, R. (1964). *How to take the FOG out of writing.* Chicago: Dartnell Corp.

Gupta, V., Hanges, P. J., & Dorfman, P. (2002). Cultural clusters: Methodology and findings. *Journal of World Business, 37*, 11–15.

Gurchiek, K. (2006). Lunch hour? More like a half hour. *HR Magazine, 51*(8), 35.

Gutman, A. (2004). Grutter goes to work. The 7th Circuit Court's ruling in Petit v. City of Chicago. *The Industrial-Organizational Psychologist, 41*(1), 71–77.

Gutman, A. (2005). Sexual harassment: Here, there, and everywhere Part 1: English-speaking countries. *The Industrial-Organizational Psychologist, 42*(4), 55–67.

Gutman, A., & Christiansen, N. (1997). Further clarification of the judicial status of banding. *The Industrial-Organizational Psychologist, 35*(1), 75–81.

Guzzo, R. A., Jette, R. D., & Katzell, R. A. (1985). The effects of psychologically based intervention programs on worker productivity: A meta-analysis. *Personnel Psychology, 38*, 275–291.

Habeeb, K., & Prencipe, L. W. (2001, February 5). Avoiding workplace violence. *InfoWorld, 23*(6), 63.

Hackett, R. D. (1989). Work attitudes and employee absenteeism: A synthesis of the literature. *Journal of Occupational Psychology, 62*(3), 235–248.

Hackett, R. D., & Bycio, P. (1996). An evaluation of employee absenteeism as a coping mechanism among hospital nurses. *Journal of Occupational and Organizational Psychology, 69*(4), 327–338.

Hackman, J. R., & Oldham, G. R. (1975). Development of the job diagnostic survey. *Journal of Applied Psychology, 60*, 159–170.

Hackman, J. R., & Oldham, G. R. (1976). Motivation through the design of work: Test of a theory. *Organizational Behavior and Human Performance, 16*, 250–279.

Hackman, J. R., & Wageman, R. (2007). Asking the right questions about leadership: Discussions and conclusions. *American Psychologist, 62*(1), 43–47.

Hackman, R., & Vidmar, N. (1970). Effects of size and task type on group performance and member reactions. *Sociometry, 33*, 37–54.

Hall, D. T., & Nougaim, K. E. (1968). An examination of Maslow's needs hierarchy in an organizational setting. *Organizational Behavior and Human Performance, 3*, 12–35.

Hall, E. T. A. (1963). A system for the notation of promemic behavior. *American Anthropologist, 65*, 1003–1026.

Hampton, D. R., Summer, C. E., & Webber, R. A. (1978). *Organizational behavior and the practice of management.* Glenview, IL: Scott, Foresman.

Hancock, P. A., Conway, G. E., Szalma, J. L., Ross, J. M., & Saxton, B. M. (2001). *A meta-analysis of noise effects on operator performance for IMPRINT.* Orlando, FL: University of Central Florida—Institute of Simulation and Training.

Hanlon, S. C., & Taylor, R. R. (1992). How does gainsharing work? Some preliminary answers following application in a service organization. *Applied H.R.M. Research, 3*(2), 73–91.

Harder, J. W. (1992). Play for pay: Effects of inequity in a pay-for-performance context. *Administrative Science Quarterly, 37*, 321–335.

Hardison, C. M., Kim, D., & Sackett, P. R. (2005, April). *Meta-analysis of Work Sample Criterion Related Validity:*

Revisiting anomalous findings. Paper presented at the 20th annual conference of the Society for Industrial-Organizational Psychology, Los Angeles, CA.

Hardy, C. J., & Crace, R. K. (1991). The effects of task structure and teammate competence on social loafing. *Journal of Sport and Exercise Psychology, 13*(4), 372–381.

Harriman, T. S., & Kovach, R. (1987). The effects of job familiarity on the recall of performance information. *Proceedings of the 8th Annual Graduate Conference in Industrial/Organizational Psychology and Organizational Behavior,* pp. 49–50.

Harris, B. (1979). What ever happened to little Albert? *American Psychologist, 34*(2), 151–160.

Harrison, D. A., Kravitz, D. A., Mayer, D. M., Leslie, L. M., & Lev-Arey., D. (2006). Understanding attitudes toward affirmative action programs in employment: Summary and meta-analysis of 35 years of research. *Journal of Applied Psychology, 91*(5), 1013–1036.

Harrison, D. A., Mohammed, S., McGrath, J. E., Florey, A. T., & Vanerstoep, S. W. (2003). Time matters in team performance: Effects of member familiarity, entrainment, and task discontinuity on speed and quality. *Personnel Psychology, 56*(3), 633–669.

Harrison, D. A., & Shaffer, M. A. (1994). Comparative examinations of self-reports and perceived absenteeism norms: Wading through Lake Wobegon. *Journal of Applied Psychology, 79*(2), 240–256.

Harvey, R. J., Friedman, L., Hakel, M. D., & Cornelius, E. T. (1988). Dimensionality of the Job Element Inventory, a simplified worker-oriented job analysis questionnaire. *Journal of Applied Psychology, 73,* 639–646.

Hasson, J. (2007). Blogging for talent. *HR Magazine, 52*(10), 65–68.

Hattie, J., & Cooksey, R. W. (1984). Procedures for assessing the validities of tests using the "known-groups" method. *Applied Psychological Measurement, 8,* 295–305.

Hauenstein, N. M. A. (1986). *A process approach to ratings: The effects of ability and level of processing on encoding, retrieval, and rating outcomes.* Unpublished doctoral dissertation, University of Akron, Akron, OH.

Hauenstein, N. M. A. (1998). Training raters to increase the accuracy of appraisals and the usefulness of feedback. In J. W. Smither (Ed.), *Performance appraisal: State of the art in practice* (pp. 404–442). San Francisco: Jossey-Bass.

Hauenstein, N. M. A., & Foti, R. J. (1989). From laboratory to practice: Neglected issues in implementing frame-of-reference rater training. *Personnel Psychology, 42,* 359–378.

Hauenstein, N. M. A., & Lord, R. G. (1989). The effects of final-offer arbitration on the performance of major league baseball players: A test of equity theory. *Human Performance, 2*(3), 147–165.

Hausknecht, J. P., Day, D. V., & Thomas, S. C. (2004). Applicant reactions to selection procedures: An updated model and meta-analysis. *Personnel Psychology, 57*(3), 639–683.

Hausknecht, J. P., Halpert, J. A., Di Paolo, N. T., & Moriarty Gerard, M. O. (2007). Retesting in selection: A meta-analysis of coaching and practice effects for tests of cognitive ability. *Journal of Applied Psychology, 92*(2), 373–385.

Hausdorf, P. A., & Duncan, D. E. (2004). Firm size and Internet recruiting in Canada: A preliminary investigation. *Journal of Small Business Management, 42*(13), 325–334.

Hazer, J. T., & Highhouse, S. (1997). Factors influencing managers' reactions to utility analysis: Effects of SDy method, information frame, and focal intervention. *Journal of Applied Psychology, 82*(1), 104–112.

Heaney, C. A., & Clemans, J. (1995). Occupational stress, physician-excused absences, and absences not excused by a physician. *American Journal of Health Promotion, 10*(2), 117–124.

Heath, C. (1996). Do people prefer to pass along good or bad news? Valence and relevance of news as predictors of transmission propensity. *Organizational Behavior and Human Decision Processes, 68*(2), 79–94.

Hecht, M. A., & LaFrance, M. (1995). How (fast) can I help you? Tone of voice and telephone operator efficiency in interactions. *Journal of Applied Social Psychology, 25*(23), 2086–2098.

Heerwagen, J. H., & Orians, G. H. (1986). Adaptations to windowlessness: A study of the use of visual decor in windowed and windowless offices. *Environment & Behavior, 18,* 604–622.

Heilman, M. E., & Alcott, V. B. (2001). What I think of me: Women's reactions to being viewed as beneficiaries of preferential selection. *Journal of Applied Psychology, 86*(4), 574–582.

Heilman, M. E., Block, C. J., & Lucas, J. A. (1992). Presumed incompetent? Stigmatization and affirmative action efforts. *Journal of Applied Psychology, 77*(4), 536–544.

Heilman, M. E., Block, C. J., & Stathatos, P. (1997). The affirmative action stigma of incompetence: Effects of performance information ambiguity. *Academy of Management Journal, 40*(3), 603–625.

Heilman, M. E., Kaplow, S. R., Amato, M. G., & Stathatos, P. (1993). When similarity is a liability: Effects of sex-based preferential selection on reactions to like-sex and different-sex others. *Journal of Applied Psychology, 78*(6), 917–927.

Heilman, M. E., Lucas, J. A., & Kaplow, S. R. (1990). Self-derogating consequences of preferential selection: The moderating role of initial self-confidence. *Organizational Behavior and Human Decision Processes, 46,* 202–216.

Hemphill, J. K., & Coons, A. E. (1950). *Leader behavior description.* Columbus: Personnel Research Board, Ohio State University.

Henderson, N. D., Berry, M. W., & Matic, T. (2007). Field measures of strength and fitness predict firefighters performance on physically demanding tasks. *Personnel Psychology, 60*(2), 431–473.

Henderson, R. I. (2006). *Compensation management in a knowledge-based world* (10th ed.). Englewood Cliffs, NJ: Prentice Hall.

Heneman, R. L., & Coyne, E. E. (2007). *Implementing total rewards strategies.* Alexandria, VA: SHRM Foundation.

Henkoff, R. (1990, June 17). Cost cutting: How to do it right. *Fortune,* p. 73.

Hersey, P., & Blanchard, K. H. (1988). *Management of organizational behavior* (5th ed.). Englewood Cliffs, NJ: Prentice Hall.

Hershcovis, M. S., Turner, N., Barling, J., Arnold, K. A., Dupré, K. E., Inness, M., LeBlanc, M. M., & Sivanathan, N. (2007). Predicting workplace aggression: A meta-analysis. *Journal of Applied Psychology, 92*(1), 228–238.

Herzberg, F. (1966). *Work and the nature of man*. Cleveland: World.

Hills, F. S., Scott, K. D., Markham, S. E., & Vest, M. J. (1987). Merit pay: Just or unjust desserts. *Personnel Administrator, 32*(9), 53–59.

Hockey, G. R. (1970). Signal probability and spatial locations as possible bases for increased selectivity in noise. *Quarterly Journal of Experimental Psychology, 22*, 37–42.

Hoff Macan, T., Avedon, M., & Paese, M. (1994). *The effects of applicants' reactions to cognitive ability tests and an assessment center*. Paper presented at the 9th annual conference of the Society for Industrial and Organizational Psychology, Nashville, TN.

Hoff Macan, T., & Foster, J. (2004). Managers' reactions to utility analysis and perceptions of what influences their decisions. *Journal of Business and Psychology, 19*(2), 241–253.

Hoffman, B. J., Blair, C. A., Meriac, J. P., & Woehr, D. J. (2007). Expanding the criterion domain? A quantitative review of the OCB literature. *Journal of Applied Psychology, 92*, 555–566.

Hoffman, C. C., & Thornton, G. C. (1997). Examining selection utility where competing predictors differ in adverse impact. *Personnel Psychology, 50*(2), 455–470.

Hogan, J., & Quigley, A. (1994). Effects of preparing for physical ability tests. *Public Personnel Management, 23*(1), 85–104.

Hogan, J. B. (1994). Empirical keying of background data measures. In G. S. Stokes, M. D. Mumford, & W. A. Owens, (Eds.), *Biodata handbook* (pp. 69–107). Palo Alto, CA: CPP Books.

Hogan, R., Raskin, R., & Fazzini, D. (1990). The dark side of charisma. In K. E. Clark & M. B. Clark (Eds.), *Measures of leadership* (pp. 343–354). West Orange, NJ: Leadership Library of America.

Hogan, T. P., Benjamin, A., & Brezinski, K. L. (2003). Reliability methods. In Bruce Thompson (Ed.), *Score reliability: Contemporary thinking on reliability issues*. Thousand Oaks, CA: Sage Publications.

Holden, M. (1998). *Positive politics: Overcoming office politics and fast-track your career*. Warriewood, Australia: Business & Professional Publishing.

Hollander, E. P., & Offermann, L. R. (1990). Power and leadership in organizations: Relationships in transition. *American Psychologist, 45*(2), 179–189.

Holstein, B. B. (1997). *The enchanted self*. Amsterdam: Harwood Academic Publishers.

Holt, H., & Grainger, H. (2005). *Results of the second flexible working employee survey*. London: Department of Trade and Industry.

Holtom, B. C., Lee, T. W., & Tidd, S. T. (2002). The relationship between work status congruence and work-related attitudes and behaviors. *Journal of Applied Psychology, 87*(5), 903–915.

Hood, D. (2001). *A meta-analysis of the reliability levels for selection tests used in industry*. Paper presented at the 22nd annual Graduate Conference in Industrial-Organizational Psychology and Organizational Behavior, State College, PA.

Hoover, L. T. (1992). Trends in police physical ability selection testing. *Public Personnel Management, 21*(1), 29–40.

Hopke, T. (2010). Go ahead, take a few months off. *HR Magazine, 55*(9), 71–74.

Hough, L. M., Oswald, F. L., & Ployhart, R. E. (2001). Determinants, detection and amelioration of adverse impact in personnel selection procedures: Issues, evidence, and lessons learned. *International Journal of Selection and Assessment, 9*(1–2), 152–194.

Hosoda, M., Stone-Romero, E. F., & Coats, G. (2003). The effects of physical attractiveness on job-related outcomes: A meta-analysis of experimental studies. *Personnel Psychology, 56*(2), 431–462.

House, R. J. (1971). A path-goal theory of leader effectiveness. *Administrative Science Quarterly, 9*, 321–332.

House, R. J., Javidan, M., Hanges, P., & Dorfman, P. (2002). Understanding cultures and implicit leadership theories across the globe: An introduction to Project GLOBE. *Journal of World Business, 37*, 3–10.

House, R. J., & Mitchell, T. R. (1974, Autumn). Path-goal theory of leadership. *Journal of Contemporary Business, 3*, 81–98.

Howard, J. L., & Ferris, G. R. (1996). The employment interview context: Social and situational influences on interviewer decisions. *Journal of Applied Social Psychology, 26*(2), 112–136.

Huegli, J. M., & Tschirgia, H. D. (1975). Monitoring the employment interview. *Journal of College Placement, 39*, 37–39.

Huffcutt, A. I., & Arthur, W. (1994). Hunter and Hunter (1984) revisited: Interview validity for entry-level jobs. *Journal of Applied Psychology, 79*(2), 184–190.

Huffcutt, A. I., Conway, J. M., Roth, P. L., & Stone, N. J. (2001). Identification and meta-analytic assessment of psychological constructs measured in employment interviews. *Journal of Applied Psychology, 86*(5), 897–913.

Huffcutt, A. I., & Roth, P. L. (1998). Racial group differences in employment interview evaluations. *Journal of Applied Psychology, 83*(2), 179–189.

Huffcutt, A. I., Roth, P. L., Conway, J. M., & Klehe, U. C. (2004). The impact of job complexity and study design on situational and behavior description interview validity. *International Journal of Selection and Assessment, 12*(2), 262–273,

Huffcutt, A. I., Weekley, J. A., Wiesner, W. H., DeGroot, T. G., & Jones, C. (2001). Comparison of situational and behavioral description interview questions for higher-level positions. *Personnel Psychology, 54*(3), 619–644.

Huffcutt, A. I., & Woehr, D. J. (1999). Further analyses of employment interview validity: A quantitative evaluation of interviewer-related structuring methods. *Journal of Organizational Behavior, 20*(4), 549–560.

Hughes, J. F., Dunn, J. F., & Baxter, B. (1956). The validity of selection instruments under operating conditions. *Personnel Psychology, 9*, 321–324.

Huish, G. B. (1997, August). Piece-rate play plan in clerk's office motivates quantum leap in quality productivity. *IPMA News*, pp. 22–27.

Hunt, J. W., & Laing, B. (1997). Leadership: The role of the exemplar. *Business Strategy Review*, 8(1), 31–42.

Hunter, J. E., & Hunter, R. F. (1984). Validity and utility of alternative predictors of job performance. *Psychological Bulletin*, 96(1), 72–98.

Hunter, J. E., & Schmidt, F. L. (1982). Fitting people to jobs: The impact of personnel selection on national productivity. In M. D. Dunnette & E. D. Fleishman (Eds.), *Human performance and productivity: Vol. 1 Human capacity assessment* (pp. 233–284). Hillsdale, NJ: Lawrence Erlbaum.

Hurtz, G. M., & Donovan, J. J. (2000). Personality and job performance: The Big Five revisited. *Journal of Applied Psychology*, 85(6), 869–879.

Hutchison, S., Valentino, K. E., & Kirkner, S. L. (1998). What works for the gander does not work as well for the goose: The effects of leader behavior. *Journal of Applied Social Psychology*, 28(2), 171–182.

Hyatt, D. E., & Ruddy, T. M. (1997). An examination of the relationship between work group characteristics and performance: Once more into the breach. *Personnel Psychology*, 50(3), 533–585.

Iaffaldano, M. T., & Muchinsky, P. M. (1985). Job satisfaction and job performance: A meta-analysis. *Psychological Bulletin*, 97, 251–273.

Ilardi, B. C., Leone, D., Kasser, T., & Ryan, R. M. (1993). Employee and supervisor ratings of motivation: Main effects and discrepancies associated with job satisfaction and adjustment in a factory setting. *Journal of Applied Social Psychology*, 23(21), 1789–1805.

Ilgen, D. R., & Bell, B. S. (2001a). Informed consent and dual purpose research. *American Psychologist*, 56(12), 1177.

Ilgen, D. R., & Bell, B. S. (2001b). Conducting industrial and organizational psychology research: Review of research in work organizations. *Ethics and Behavior*, 11, 395–412.

Ilgen, D. R., Nebeker, D. M., & Pritchard, R. D. (1981). Expectancy theory measures: An empirical comparison in an experimental simulation. *Organizational Behavior and Human Performance*, 28, 189–223.

Ilies, R., Gerhardt, M. W., & Le, H. (2004). Individual differences in leadership emergence: Integrating meta-analytic findings and behavioral genetics estimates. *International Journal of Selection and Assessment*, 12(3), 207–219.

Ilies, R., & Judge, T. A. (2003). On the heritability of job satisfaction: The mediating role of personality. *Journal of Applied Psychology*, 88(4), 750–759.

Ilies, R., Nahrgang, J. D., & Morgeson, F. P. (2007). Leader-member exchange and citizenship behaviors: A meta-analysis. *Journal of Applied Psychology*, 92(1), 269–277.

Imrhan, S. N., Imrhan, V., & Hart, C. (1996). Can self-estimates of body weight and height be used in place of measurements for college students? *Ergonomics*, 39(12), 1445–1453.

Indik, B. P. (1965). Organization size and member participation: Some empirical tests of alternate explanations. *Human Relations*, 15, 339–350.

Ironson, G. H., Smith, P. C., Brannick, M. T., Gibson, W. M., & Paul, K. B. (1989). Construction of a Job in General Scale: A comparison of global, composite, and specific measures. *Journal of Applied Psychology*, 74, 193–200.

Irving, P. G., & Meyer, J. P. (1994). Reexamination of the met-expectations hypothesis: A longitudinal analysis. *Journal of Applied Psychology*, 79(6), 937–949.

Isenberg, D. J. (1986). Group polarization: A critical review and meta-analysis. *Journal of Personality and Social Psychology*, 50(6), 1141–1151.

Ivancevich, J. M. (1982). Subordinates' reactions to performance appraisal interviews: A test of feedback and goal-setting techniques. *Journal of Applied Psychology*, 67, 581–587.

Jackson, D. E., O'Dell, J. W., & Olson, D. (1982). Acceptance of bogus personality interpretations: Face validity reconsidered. *Journal of Clinical Psychology*, 38, 588–592.

Jackson, S. E., & Schuler, R. S. (1985). A meta-analysis and conceptual critique of research on role ambiguity and role conflict in work settings. *Organizational Behavior and Human Decision Processes*, 36(1), 16–78.

Jackson, T. W. (2008). Apprenticeships: Creating new work-forces. *Blue Ridge Business Journal*, 20(12), 18–19.

Jacobs, J. A., & Kearns, C. N. (2001). Responding effectively to a claim of sexual harassment in the workplace. *Association Management*, 53(11), 19–20.

Jacobs, R. (1997). *Organizational effectiveness: Downsizing, one of many alternatives*. Keynote address presented at the 18th annual Graduate Student Conference in Industrial Organizational Psychology and Organizational Behavior, Roanoke, VA.

Jago, A. G., & Vroom, V. H. (1977). Hierarchical level and leadership style. *Organizational Behavior and Human Performance*, 18, 131–145.

Jamal, M. (1981). Shift work related to job attitudes, social participation, and withdrawal behavior: A study of nurses and industrial workers. *Personnel Psychology*, 34, 535–547.

Jamal, M., & Crawford, R. L. (1984). Consequences of extended work hours: A comparison of moonlighters, overtimers, and modal employees. *Human Resource Management*, 4, 18–23.

Jamal, M., & Jamal, S. M. (1982). Work and nonwork experiences of employees on fixed and rotating shifts: An empirical assessment. *Journal of Vocational Behavior*, 20, 282–293.

James, L. R. (1998). Measurement of personality through conditional reasoning. *Organizational Research Methods*, 1, 131–163.

Janis, I. L. (1972). *Victims of groupthink*. New York: Houghton Mifflin.

Janz, T., Hellervik, L., & Gilmore, D. C. (1986). *Behavior description interviewing*. Boston: Allyn & Bacon.

Jehn, K. A., & Mannix, E. A. (2001). The dynamic nature of conflict: A longitudinal study of intragroup conflict and group performance. *Academy of Management Journal*, 44(2), 238–251.

Jeong, H. (2008). *Understanding conflict and conflict analysis*. Thousand Oaks, CA: Sage.

Jex, S. M., & Elacqua, T. C. (1999). Time management as a moderator of relations between stressors and employee strain. *Work & Stress*, 13(2), 182–191.

Johns, G. (1994). Absenteeism estimates by employees and managers: Divergent perspectives and self-serving perceptions. *Journal of Applied Psychology, 79*(2), 229–239.

Joiner, D. (2000). Guidelines and ethical considerations for assessment center operations: International task force on assessment center guidelines. *Public Personnel Management, 29*(3), 315–331.

Joiner, D. (2002). Assessment centers: What's new? *Public Personnel Management, 31*(2), 179–185.

Joinson, C. (1999). Teams at work. *HR Magazine, 44*(5), 30–36.

Joinson, C. (2001). Making sure employees measure up. *HR Magazine, 46*(3), 36–41.

Jones, J. W., & Terris, W. (1989). After the polygraph ban. *Recruitment Today, 2*(2), 24–31.

Jones, M. (2001, September 28). Wisconsin prison hosts first job fair. *Milwaukee Journal Sentinel*, B-1.

Jossi, F. (2001a). Take the road less traveled. *HR Magazine, 46*(7), 46–51.

Jossi, F. (2001b). Teamwork aids HRIS decision process. *HR Magazine, 46*(6), 165–173.

Judge, T. A. (1993). Does affective disposition moderate the relationship between job satisfaction and voluntary turnover? *Journal of Applied Psychology, 78*(3), 395–401.

Judge, T. A., & Bono, J. E. (2000). Five-factor model of personality and transformational leadership. *Journal of Applied Psychology, 85*(5), 751–765.

Judge, T. A., & Bono, J. E. (2001). Relationship of core self-evaluations traits—self-esteem, generalized self-efficacy, locus of control, and emotional stability—with job satisfaction and job performance: A meta-analysis. *Journal of Applied Psychology, 86*(1), 80–92.

Judge, T. A., Bono, J. E., Ilies, R., & Gerhardt, M. W. (2002). Personality and leadership: A qualitative and quantitative review. *Journal of Applied Psychology, 87*(4), 765–780.

Judge, T. A., Colbert, A. E., & Ilies, R. (2004). Intelligence and leadership: A quantitative review and test of theoretical propositions. *Journal of Applied Psychology, 89*(3), 542–552.

Judge, T. A., Heller, D., & Mount, M. K. (2002). Five-factor model of personality and job satisfaction: A meta-analysis. *Journal of Applied Psychology, 87*(3), 530–541.

Judge, T. A., & Ilies, R. (2002). Relationship of personality to performance motivation: A meta-analytic review. *Journal of Applied Psychology, 87*(4), 797–807.

Judge, T. A., Locke, E. A., & Durham, C. C. (1997). The dispositional causes of job satisfaction: A core evaluations approach. *Research in Organizational Behavior, 19*(1), 151–188.

Judge, T. A., Locke, E. A., Durham, C. C., & Kluger, A. N. (1998). Dispositional effects on job and life satisfaction: The role of core evaluations. *Journal of Applied Psychology, 83*(1), 17–34.

Judge, T. A., Martocchio, J. J., & Thoresen, C. J. (1997). Five-factor model of personality and employee absence. *Journal of Applied Psychology, 82*(5), 745–755.

Judge, T. A., Piccolo, R. F., & Ilies, R. (2004). The forgotten ones? The validity of consideration and initiating structure in leadership research. *Journal of Applied Psychology, 89*(1), 36–51.

Judge, T. A., Thoresen, C. J., Bono, J. E., & Patton, G. K. (2001). The job satisfaction-job performance relationship: A qualitative and quantitative review. *Psychological Bulletin, 127*(3), 376–407.

Judge, T. A., & Watanabe, S. (1994). Individual differences in the nature of the relationship between job and life satisfaction. *Journal of Occupational and Organizational Psychology, 67,* 101–107.

Judge, T. A., & Watanabe, S. (1993). Another look at the job satisfaction—life satisfaction relationship. *Journal of Applied Psychology, 78*(6), 939–948.

Juergens, J. (2000). Read all about it. *HR Magazine, 45*(10), 142–150.

Kacmar, K. M., Carlson, D. S., & Brymer, R. A. (1999). Antecedents and consequences of organizational commitment: A comparison of two scales. *Educational and Psychological Measurement, 59*(6), 976–994.

Kammeyer-Mueller, J. D., & Judge, T. A. (2008). A quantitative review of mentoring research: Test of a model. *Journal of Vocational Behavior, 72*(3), 269–283.

Kaplan, A. B., Aamodt, M. A., & Wilk, D. (1991). The relationship between advertising variables and applicant responses to newspaper recruitment advertisements. *Journal of Business and Psychology, 5*(3), 383–395.

Kaplan, I. T. (2002, April). *Effects of group size and problem difficulty on decision accuracy.* Paper presented at the 17th annual meeting of the Society for Industrial and Organizational Psychology, Toronto, Canada.

Kaplan, R. M., & Saccuzzo, D. P. (2009). *Psychological testing* (7th ed.). Belmont, CA: Wadsworth.

Kaplan, S., Bradley, J. C., Luchman, J. N., & Haynes, D. (2009). On the role of positive and negative affectivity in job performance: A meta-analytic investigation. *Journal of Applied Psychology, 94,* 162–176.

Karasek, R., & Theorell, T. (1990). *Healthy work: Stress, productivity and the reconstruction of working life.* New York: Basic Books.

Karau, S., & Williams, K. (1993). Social loafing: A meta-analytic review and theoretical integration. *Journal of Personality and Social Psychology, 65*(4), 681–706.

Karl, K. A., & Hancock, B. W. (1999). Expert advice on employment termination practices: How expert is it? *Public Personnel Management, 28*(1), 51–62.

Kassel, J. D., Stroud, L. R., & Paronis, C. A. (2003). Smoking, stress, and negative affect: Correlation, causation, and context across stages of smoking. *Psychological Bulletin, 129*(2), 270–304.

Katzell, R. A., & Dyer, F. J. (1977). Differential validity revived. *Journal of Applied Psychology, 62,* 137–145.

Kearns, P. (2001). Establish a baseline. *Training, 38*(6), 80.

Keeping, L. M., & Sulsky, L. M. (1996). *Examining the quality of self-ratings of performance.* Poster presented at the 11th annual meeting of the Society for Industrial and Organizational Psychology, San Diego, CA.

Keinan, G. A., & Barak, A. (1984). Reliability and validity of graphological assessment in the selection process of military officers. *Perceptual and Motor Skills, 58,* 811–821.

Keller, L. M., Bouchard, T. J., Arvey, R. D., Segal, N. L., & Dawis, R. V. (1992). Work values: Genetic and environmental influences. *Journal of Applied Psychology, 77*(1), 79–88.

Keller, R. T. (2001). Cross-functional project groups in research and product development: Diversity, communications, job stress, and outcomes. *Academy of Management Journal, 44*(3), 547–555.

Kennedy, J. K., Houston, J. M., Korsgaard, M. A., & Gallo, D. D. (1987). Construct space of the Least Preferred Coworker (LPC) Scale. *Educational and Psychological Measurement, 47*(3), 807–814.

Kernan, M. C., & Hanges, P. J. (2002). Survivor reactions to reorganization: Antecedents and consequences of procedural, interpersonal, and informational justice. *Journal of Applied Psychology, 87*(5), 916–928.

Kerr, N. L. (1983). Motivation loss in small groups: A social dilemma analysis. *Journal of Personality and Social Psychology, 45,* 819–828.

Kerr, N. L., & Bruun, S. E. (1983). Dependability of member effort and group motivation loss: Free-rider effects. *Journal of Personality and Social Psychology, 44,* 78–94.

Kerr, N. L., & Tinsdale, R. S. (2004). Group performance and decisions making. *Annual Review of Psychology, 55,* 623–655.

Kerr, S. (2009). Some random thoughts on the false dichotomies, common coffee spots, and the portability of knowledge. *The Industrial-Organizational Psychologist, 47*(2), 11–24.

Khanna, C., & Medsker, G. J. (2010). 2009 Income and employment survey results for the Society for Industrial and Organizational Psychology. *The Industrial-Organizational Psychologist, 48*(1), 23–38.

Kidwell, R. E., Mossholder, K. W., & Bennett, N. (1997). Cohesiveness and organizational citizenship behavior: A multilevel analysis using work groups and individuals. *Journal of Management, 23*(6), 775–793.

Kierein, N., & Gold, M. A. (2001). *Pygmalion in work organizations: A meta-analysis. Journal of Organizational Behavior, 21,* 913–928.

Kim, B. H. (2008, April). *Truth. Lies and everything in between: Bogus items response processes.* Presented in J. Levashina & M. A. Campion (Co-Chairs), That can't be true! Detecting faking using bogus items. Symposium presented at the 23rd annual meeting of the Society for Industrial-Organizational Psychology, San Francisco, CA.

Kimbrough, A., Durley, J., & Muñoz, C. (2005). TIP-TOPics for students. *The Industrial-Organizational Psychologist, 42*(3), 107–114.

Kingston, N. M. (2009). Comparability of computer- and paper-administered multiple-choice tests for K–12 populations: A synthesis. *Applied Measurement in Education, 22*(1), 22–37.

Kingstrom, P. O., & Bass, A. R. (1981). A critical analysis of studies comparing behaviorally anchored rating scales (BARS) and other rating formats. *Personnel Psychology, 34,* 263–289.

Kipnis, D., Schmidt, S., & Wilkinson, I. (1980). Intraorganizational influence tactics: Exploration in getting one's way. *Journal of Applied Psychology, 65,* 440–452.

Kirkman, B. L., Rosen, B., Gibson, C. B., Tesluk, P. E., & McPherson, S. O. (2002). Five challenges to virtual team success: Lessons from Sabre, Inc. *Academy of Management Executive, 16*(3), 67–79.

Kirkman, B. L., & Shapiro, D. L. (2001). The impact of cultural values on job satisfaction and organizational commitment in self-managing work teams: The mediating role of employee resistance. *Academy of Management Journal, 44*(3), 557–569.

Kirkpatrick, D. L. (1986). Performance appraisal: When two jobs are too many. *Training, 23*(3), 65–68.

Kirkpatrick, D. L. (2000). Evaluating training programs: The four levels. In G. M. Piskurich, P. Beckschi, & B. Hall (Eds.), *The ASTD handbook of training design and delivery* (pp. 133–146). New York: McGraw Hill.

Kirnan, J. P., Farley, J. A., & Geisinger, K. F. (1989). The relationship between recruiting source, applicant quality, and hire performance: An analysis by sex, ethnicity, and age. *Personnel Psychology, 42*(2), 293–308.

Kish-Gephart, J. J., Harrison, D. A., & Trevino, L. K. (2010). Bad apples, bad cases, and bad barrels: Meta-analytic evidence about sources of unethical decisions at work. *Journal of Applied Psychology, 95*(1), 1–31.

Kittleson, M. J. (1995). An assessment of the response rate via the postal service and email. *Health Values: The Journal of Health, Behavior, Education and Promotion, 19*(2), 27–39.

Kjellberg, A., Landstrom, U., Tesarz, M., & Soderberg, L. (1996). The effects of nonphysical noise characteristics, ongoing task and noise sensitivity on annoyance and distraction due to noise at work. *Journal of Environmental Psychology, 16*(2), 123–136.

Kleiman, L. S., & White, C. S. (1991). Reference checking: A field survey of SHRM professionals. *Applied H.R.M. Research, 2*(2), 84–95.

Klein, H. J., Wesson, M. J., Hollenbeck, J. R., & Alge, B. J. (1999). Goal commitment and the goal-setting process: Conceptual clarification and empirical synthesis. *Journal of Applied Psychology, 84*(6), 885–896.

Klein, J. D., & Pridemore, D. R. (1992). Effects of cooperative learning and need for affiliation on performance, time on task, and satisfaction. *Educational Technology Research and Development, 40*(4), 39–47.

Kluger, A. N., & Colella, A. (1993). Beyond the mean bias: The effect of warning against faking on biodata item variances. *Personnel Psychology, 46,* 763–780.

Knauth, P. (1996). Designing better shift systems. *Applied Ergonomics, 27*(1), 39–44.

Knauth, P., Keller, J., Schindele, G., & Totterdell, P. (1995). A 14-hour night-shift in the control room of a fire brigade. *Work and Stress, 9,* 176–186.

Knoop, R. (1994). The relationship between importance and achievement of work values and job satisfaction. *Perceptual and Motor Skills, 79*(1), 595–605.

Knouse, S. B. (1983). The letter of recommendation: Specificity and favorability of information. *Personnel Psychology, 36,* 331–341.

Poster presented at the annual graduate conference for Industrial-Organizational Psychology and Organizational Behavior, Indianapolis, IN.

Vinchur, A. J., & Koppes, L. L. (2007). Early contributors to the science and practice of industrial psychology. In L. L. Koppes (Ed.), *Historical perspectives in industrial and organizational psychology*. Mahwah, NJ: Lawrence Erlbaum.

Vinchur, A. J., Schippmann, J. S., Switzer, F. S., & Roth, P. L. (1998). A meta-analytic review of predictors of job performance for salespeople. *Journal of Applied Psychology, 83*(4), 586–597.

Vincola, A. (1999, April). Back-up child care: An effective solution to a growing need. *IPMA News*, pp. 16–17.

Vines, L. S. (1997). Make long-term temporary workers part of the team. *HR Magazine, 42*(1), 65–70.

Viswesvaran, C., & Ones, D. S. (2003). Measurement error in "big five factors" personality assessment. In B. Thompson (Ed.), *Score reliability: Contemporary thinking on reliability issues*. Newbury Park, CA: Sage Publications.

Viswesvaran, C., Ones, D. S., & Schmidt, F. L. (1996). Comparative analysis of the reliability of job performance ratings. *Journal of Applied Psychology, 81*(5), 557–574.

Viswesvaran, C., Sanchez, J. I., & Fisher, J. (1999). The role of social support in the process of work stress: A meta-analysis. *Journal of Vocational Behavior, 54*, 314–334.

Viswesvaran, C., Schmidt, F. L., & Ones, D. S. (2005). Is there a general factor in ratings of job performance? A meta-analytic framework for disentangling substantive and error influences. *Journal of Applied Psychology, 90*(1), 108–131.

Vroom, V., & Yetton, P. W. (1973). *Leadership and decision making*. Pittsburgh, PA: University of Pittsburgh Press.

Vroom, V. H. (1964). *Work and motivation*. New York: John Wiley.

Waddell, J. R. (1996). You'll never believe what I heard. *Supervision, 57*(8), 18–20.

Wagner, J. A. (1994). Participation effects on performance and satisfaction: A reconsideration of research evidence. *Academy of Management Review, 19*(2), 312–330.

Wagner, R. F. (1950). A study of the critical requirements for dentists. *University of Pittsburgh Bulletin, 46*, 331–339.

Wagner, T. L. (1990). A meta-analytic review of absenteeism control methods. *Applied H.R.M. Research, 1*(1), 23–26.

Wakabayashi, M., & Graen, G. B. (1984). The Japanese career progress study: A seven-year follow-up. *Journal of Applied Psychology, 69*, 603–614.

Walker, H. J., Feild, H. S., Giles, W. F., Armenakis, A. A., & Bernerth, J. B. (2009). Displaying employee testimonials on recruitment web sites: Effects of communication media, employee race, and job seeker race on organizational attraction and information credibility. *Journal of Applied Psychology, 94*(5), 1354–1364.

Walker, R. W. (2011). *African-American healthy: Tapping into the remarkable power of Vitamin D3*. Garden City Park, New York: Square One Publishers.

Wall, H. J. (2000, October). The gender wage gap and wage discrimination: Illusion or reality? *Regional Economist*, pp. 1–5.

Wanberg, C. R., & Banas, J. T. (2000). Predictors and outcomes of openness to changes in a reorganizing workplace. *Journal of Applied Psychology, 85*(1), 132–142.

Wang, Q., Bowling, N. A., & Eschleman, K. J. (2010). Meta-analytic examination of work and general locus of control. *Journal of Applied Psychology, 95*(4), 761–768.

Wanous, J. P. (1980). *Organizational entry: Recruitment, selection, and socialization of newcomers*. Reading, MA: Addison-Wesley.

Wanous, J. P., Poland, T. D., Premack, S. L., & Davis, K. S. (1992). The effects of met expectations on newcomer attitudes and behavior: A review and meta-analysis. *Journal of Applied Psychology, 77*(3), 288–297.

Ward, E. A. (2001). Social power bases of managers: Emergence of a new factor. *The Journal of Social Psychology, 141*(1), 144–147.

Warr, P. (2007). Some historical developments in I-O psychology outside the United States. In L. L. Koppes (Ed)., *Historical perspectives in industrial and organizational psychology*. Mahwah, NJ: Lawrence Erlbaum.

Waung, M., & Brice, T. S. (2000). Communicating negative hire decisions to applicants: Fulfilling psychological contracts. *Journal of Business and Psychology, 15*(2), 247–263.

Waung, M., & Brice, T. S. (2003). *The impact of a rejection communication on rejected job applicants*. Poster presented at the 18th annual meeting of the Society for Industrial and Organizational Psychology, Orlando, Florida.

Waung, M., & Highhouse, S. (1997). *Feedback inflation: Empathic buffering or fear of conflict?* Poster presented at the 12th annual conference of the Society for Industrial and Organizational Psychology, St. Louis, MO.

Webber, S. S., & Klimoski, R. J. (2004). Crews: A distinct type of work team. *Journal of Business and Psychology, 18*(3), 261–279.

Weber, Y. (1996). Corporate cultural fit and performance in mergers and acquisitions. *Human Relations, 49*(9), 1181–1203.

Weinberg, A., Sutherland, V. J., & Cooper, C. (2010). *Organizational stress management: A strategic approach*. New York: Palgrave Macmillan.

Weins, A. N., Jackson, R. H., Manaugh, T. S., & Matarazzo, J. D. (1969). Communication length as an index of communicator attitude: A replication. *Journal of Applied Psychology, 53*, 264–266.

Weinstein, N. D. (1977). Noise and intellectual performance: A confirmation and extension. *Journal of Applied Psychology, 62*, 104–107.

Weinstein, N. D. (1978). A longitudinal study in a college dormitory. *Journal of Applied Psychology, 63*, 458–466.

Weiss, H. M., Dawis, R. V., England, G. W., & Lofquist, L. H. (1967). *Manual for the Minnesota Satisfaction Questionnaire*. Minneapolis: University of Minnesota, Industrial Relations Center.

Weiss, H. M., & Shaw, J. B. (1979). Social influences on judgments about tasks. *Organizational Behavior and Human Performance, 24*, 126–140.

Wells, S. J. (2000). The elder care gap. *HR Magazine, 45*(5), 39–46.

Wells, S. J. (2004). From ideas to results. *HR Magazine, 50*(2), 55–58.

Wells, S. J. (2005). No results, no raise. *HR Magazine, 50*(5), 76–80.

Welsh, D. H., Bernstein, D. J., & Luthans, F. (1992). Application of the Premack Principle of reinforcement to the quality performance of service employees. *Journal of Organizational Behavior Management, 13*(1), 9–32.

Werner, J. M., & Bolino, M. C. (1997). Explaining U.S. Courts of Appeals decisions involving performance appraisal: Accuracy, fairness, and validation. *Personnel Psychology, 50*(1), 1–24.

Wernimont, P. F. (1962). Re-evaluation of a weighted application blank for office personnel. *Journal of Applied Psychology, 46*, 417–419.

Wexley, K. N., & Latham, G. A. (2002). *Developing and training human resources in organizations* (3rd ed.). Upper Saddle River, NJ: Prentice Hall.

Wexley, K. N., Sanders, R. E., & Yukl, G. A. (1973). Training interviewers to eliminate contrast effects in employment interviews. *Journal of Applied Psychology, 57*, 233–236.

Wexley, K. N., Yukl, G. A., Kovacs, S. Z., & Sanders, R. E. (1972). Importance of contrast effects in employment interviews. *Journal of Applied Psychology, 56*, 45–48.

Whelchel, B. D. (1985). Use of performance tests to select craft apprentices. *Personnel Journal, 65*(7), 65–69.

Whelpley, C. E., & McDaniel, M. A. (2011, April). *Self-esteem and counterproductive behaviors: A meta-analytic review.* Poster presented at the annual Meeting of the Society for Industrial-Organizational Psychology, Chicago, IL.

Whetzel, D. L., McDaniel, M. A., & Nguyen, N. T. (2008). Subgroup differences in situational judgment test performance: A meta-analysis. *Human Performance, 21*, 291–309.

Whiting, H. J., Kline, T. J. B., & Sulsky, L. M. (2008). The performance appraisal congruency: An assessment of person-environment fit. *International Journal of Productivity and Performance Management, 57*(3), 223–236.

Widgery, R., & Stackpole, C. (1972). Desk position, interviewee anxiety, and interviewer credibility: An example of cognitive balance in a dyad. *Journal of Counseling Psychology, 19*, 173–177.

Wild, C., Horney, N., & Koonce, R. (1996). Cascading communications creates momentum for change. *HR Magazine, 41*(12), 94–100.

Wilkinson, R. T. (1992). How fast should the night shift rotate? *Ergonomics, 35*(12), 1425–1446.

Williams, J. (2005). *Sell yourself! Master the job interview process.* Arlington, TX: Principle Publications.

Williams, J. R., & Levy, P. E. (1992). The effects of perceived system knowledge on the agreement between self-ratings and supervisor ratings. *Personnel Psychology, 45*, 835–847.

Williams, J. R., Miller, C. E., Steelman, L. A., & Levy, P. E. (1999). Increasing feedback seeking in public contexts: It takes two (or more) to tango. *Journal of Applied Psychology, 84*(6), 969–976.

Williams, M. L., McDaniel, M. A., & Nguyen, N. T. (2006). A meta-analysis of the antecedents and consequences of pay level satisfaction. *Journal of Applied Psychology, 91*(2), 392–413.

Williams, R., & Garris, T. S. (1991). A second look at situation wanted advertisements. *Applied H.R.M. Research, 2*(1), 33–37.

Williamson, A. M., Gower, C. G. I., & Clarke, B. C. (1994). Changing the hours of shift work: A comparison of 8- and 12-hour shift rosters in a group of computer operators. *Ergonomics, 37*(2), 287–298.

Williamson, L. G., Campion, J. E., Malos, S. B., Roehling, M. V., & Campion, M. A. (1997). Employment interview on trial: Linking interview structure with litigation outcomes. *Journal of Applied Psychology, 82*(6), 900–912.

Willihnganz, M. A., & Myers, L. S. (1993). Effects of time of day on interview performance. *Public Personnel Management, 22*(4), 545–550.

Willis, S. C., Miller, T. A., & Huff, G. (1991). Situation-wanted advertisements: A means for obtaining job inquiries and offers. *Applied H.R.M. Research, 2*(1), 27–32.

Willms, K., Wells, R., & Carnahan, H. (2009). Glove attributes and their contribution to force decrement and increased effort in power grip. *Human Factors, 51*(6), 797–812.

Willness, C. R., Steel, P., & Lee, K. (2007). A meta-analysis of the antecedents and consequences of workplace sexual harassment. *Personnel Psychology, 60*(1), 127–162.

Wilmot, W. W., & Hocker, J. L. (2007). *Interpersonal conflict* (7th ed.). New York: McGraw-Hill.

Wilson, D. S. (2007). *Evolution for everyone.* New York: Bantam Dell.

Wilson, M. A., & Harvey, R. J. (1990). The value of relative-time-spent ratings in task-oriented job analysis. *Journal of Business and Psychology, 4*(4), 453–461.

Wilson, W. (1994). Video training and testing supports customer service goals. *Personnel Journal, 30*(10), 47–51.

Wimbush, J. C., & Dalton, D. R. (1997). Base rate for employee theft: Convergence of multiple methods. *Journal of Applied Psychology, 82*(5), 756–763.

Wing, J. F. (1965). Upper tolerance limits for unimpaired mental performance. *Aerospace Medicine, 36*, 960–964.

Winter, D. G. (1988). What makes Jesse run? *Psychology Today, 22*(6), 20–24.

Wisdom, B., & Patzig, D. (1987). Does your organization have the right climate for merit? *Public Personnel Management, 16*, 127–133.

Witt, L. A. (1996). *Listen up! Your upward feedback results are speaking.* Poster presented at the 11th annual conference of the Society for Industrial and Organizational Psychology, San Diego, CA.

Wofford, J. C., & Liska, L. Z. (1993). Path-goal theories of leadership: A meta-analysis. *Journal of Management, 19*(4), 857–876.

Wokoun, W. (1980). *A study of fatigue in industry.* New York: Muzak Board of Scientific Advisors.

Wolkove, M. P., & Layman, J. J. (2006, February). *Methods for controlling absenteeism in an organizational setting: A meta-analysis.* Paper presented at the annual Graduate Student

Conference in Industrial-Organizational Psychology and Organizational Behavior, Fairfax, VA.

Woodward, N. H. (1999). In case of emergency break glass. *HR Magazine*, *44*(8), 83–88.

Wooten, W. (1993). Using knowledge, skill and ability (KSA) data to identify career pathing opportunities: An application of job analysis to internal manpower planning. *Public Personnel Management*, *22*(4), 551–563.

Workplace Visions (1999). Interest in using prison labor is growing. *Workplace Visions*, *4*, 4–6.

Wrzesniewski, A., & Dutton, J. E. (2001). Crafting a job: Revisioning employees as active crafters of their work. *Academy of Management Review*, *26*(2), 179–201.

Wyatt Company. (1993). *Best practices in corporate restructuring.* Washington, DC: Author.

Yandrick, R. M. (2001a). A team effort. *HR Magazine*, *46*(6), 136–141.

Yandrick, R. M. (2001b). Elder care grows up. *HR Magazine*, *46*(11), 72–77.

Young, D. M., & Beier, E. G. (1977). The role of applicant non-verbal communication in the employment interview. *Journal of Employment Counseling*, *14*, 154–165.

Young, M. S., & Stanton, N. A. (2007). Back to the future: Brake reaction times for manual and automated vehicles. *Ergonomics*, *50*(1), 46–58.

Youngjohn, R. M., & Woehr, D. J. (2001, April). *A meta-analytic investigation of the relationship between individual differences and leader effectiveness.* Poster presented at the 16th annual conference of the Society for Industrial and Organizational Psychology, San Diego, CA.

Yukl, G. A. (1982, April). *Innovations in research on leader behavior.* Paper presented at the annual meeting of the Eastern Academy of Management, Baltimore, MD.

Yukl, G. A. (1994). *Leadership in organizations* (3rd ed.). Englewood Cliffs, NJ: Prentice Hall.

Zajonc, R. B. (1980). Compressence. In P. B. Paulus (Ed.), *Psychology of group influence*. Hillsdale, NJ: Lawrence Erlbaum.

Zajonc, R. B., Heingartner, A., & Herman, E. M. (1969). Social enhancement and impairment of performance in the cockroach. *Journal of Personality and Social Psychology*, *13*, 83–92.

Zedeck, S., Cascio, W. F., Goldstein, I., & Outtz, J. (1996). Sliding bands: An alternative to top-down selection. In R. Barrett (Ed.), *Fair employment strategies in human resource management* (pp. 222–234). Westport, CT: Quorum.

Zeidner, R. (2005). Building a better intranet. *HR Magazine*, *50*(11), 99–106.

Zemke, R. (1993). Rethinking the rush to team-up. *Training*, *30*(11), 55–61.

Zemke, R. (1997). How long does it take? *Training*, *34*(5), 69–79.

Zetik, D. C., & Stuhlmacher, A. F. (2002). Goal setting and negotiation performance: A meta-analysis. *Group Processes and Intergroup Relations*, *5*(1), 35–52.

Zhao, H., Wayne, S. J., Glibkowski, B. C., & Bravo, J. (2007). The impact of psychological contract breach on work-related outcomes: A meta-analysis. *Personnel Psychology*, *60*(3), 647–680.

Zhou, J. (1998). Feedback valence, feedback style, task autonomy, and achievement orientation: Interactive effects on creative performance. *Journal of Applied Psychology*, *83*(2), 261–276.

Zickar, M. J., & Highhouse, S. (2001). Measuring prestige of journals in industrial-organizational psychology. *The Industrial-Organizational Psychologist*, *38*(4), 29–36.

Zielinski, D. (2011). Redesigning your careers website. *HR Magazine*, *56*(2), 55–58.

Zielinski, D. (2010). Training games: Simulations teach employees under real-life conditions—without real-world consequences. *HR Magazine*, *55*(3), 64–66.

Zimmerman, R. D. (2008). Understanding the impact of personality traits on individuals' turnover decisions: A meta-analytic path model. *Personnel Psychology*, *61*(2), 309–348.

Zimmerman, R. D., Triana, M. C., & Barrick, M. R. (2010). The criterion-related validity of a structured letter of reference using multiple raters and multiple performance criteria. *Human Performance*, *23*, 361–378.

Zink, D. L. (2002). Chevron U.S.A., Inc. v. Echazabal: Has the Americans with Disabilities Act become a toothless tiger? *The Industrial-Organizational Psychologist*, *40*(2), 70–75.

Zink, D. L., & Gutman, A. (2005, April). *Legal issues in providing and asking for references and letters of recommendation.* Paper presented at the 20th annual meeting of the Society for Industrial and Organizational Psychology, Los Angeles, CA.

Zottoli, M. A., & Wanous, J. P. (2000). Recruitment source research: Current status and future directions. *Human Resource Management Review*, *10*, 435–451.

Zuber, A. (1996). Tapping a human resource: Restaurants fight labor crunch with training programs. *Nation's Restaurant News*, *30*(26), 33–35.

Zweigenhaft, R. L. (1976). Personal space in the faculty office: Desk placement and the student-faculty interaction. *Journal of Applied Psychology*, *61*, 529–532.

Hersey, P., 443
Hershcovis, M.S., 363, 371
Herzberg, F., 332
Heslin, R., 413
Hezlett, S.A., 169
Hicks, L., 127
Higbee, R.H., 46
Highhouse, S., 18, 221, 267
Hill, K.G., 326
Hiller, N.J., 431
Hills, D., 368
Hirschfeld, R.R., 324
Hirsh, H.R., 209
Hlivka, L., 568
Hocker, J.L., 492
Hockey, G.R., 553
Hodgson, M., 351
Hoff Macan, T., 212, 222
Hoffman, B. J., 359
Hoffman, C.C., 23
Hogan, J., 104
Hogan, J.B., 183
Hogan, R., 437, 438
Hogan, T.P., 205
Hohenfeld, J.A., 350
Holden, M., 550
Hollander, E. P., 443
Hollenbeck, J.R., 334, 478
Holstein, B.B., 324
Holt, H., 526
Holtom, B.C., 366, 389
Holton, E. F., 442
Holtz, B.C., 204
Hom, P. W., 359, 364, 445, 547
Honkasalo, M., 550
Hood, D., 203, 204
Hoover, H.C., 435
Hoover, L.T., 173
Hopke, T., 528
Hormant, M., 560
Horney, N., 510
Hornsby, J.S., 40
Hosoda, M., 141
Hough, L.M., 176
House, R.J., 443, 453, 455, 520
Houston, J.M., 439
Howard, J.L., 141, 142
Huber, V.L., 344
Hudson, J.P., 139
Huff, G., 122
Huff, J.W., 526
Huffcutt, A.I., 138, 139, 144, 146, 194, 238, 240, 262, 264, 560
Huffman, A.H., 389
Hughes, J.F., 184
Hughes, W., 446
Huish, G.B., 344
Hulin, C.L., 101, 376
Hull, R., 37

Hülsheger, U.R., 189, 196
Hunt, J.W., 451
Hunter, J.E., 169, 171, 180, 181, 187, 193, 194, 195, 209, 215, 221, 224
Hunter, J.F., 13
Hunter, R.F., 194, 195
Hurley, L., 575
Hurst, S., 514
Hurtz, G.M, 186, 194, 324, 363
Hutchison, S., 436
Hyatt, D.E., 485
Hypen, K., 553

Iacocca, L., 433
Iaffaldano, M.T., 359
Ilardi, B.C., 324
Ilgen, D.R., 20, 349, 478
Ilies, R., 324, 334, 362, 431, 432, 436, 451
Imrhan, S.N., 25
Imrhan, V., 25
Inbar, J., 325
Incalcaterra, K.A., 473
Indik, B.P., 471
Irani, R., 74
Ironson, G.H., 376
Irvine, R., 161
Irving, P.G., 366
Isenberg, D. J, 480
Ivancevich, J.M., 254
Ivanitskaya, L., 240

Jackson, D.E., 212
Jackson, D.N., 186
Jackson, K.A., 59, 139
Jackson, R.H., 167
Jackson, T.W., 306
Jacobs, J.A., 100
Jacobs, R.R., 266, 521
Jagacinski, C., 334
Jago, A.G., 520
Jago, I.A., 176
Jamal, M., 559, 560, 561
Jamal, S.M., 559, 560
James, J., 167
James, K., 362
James, L.R., 189, 190
Jamison, R.L., 572
Jan, G.C., 580
Janis, I.L., 478
Jankowski, M.A., 141
Janz, T., 144
Javidan, M., 453
Jeanneret, P.R., 56
Jehn, K.A., 489
Jenkins, G.D., 565
Jenkins, M., 235
Jensen, J.B., 212
Jensen, M., 448

Jeong, H., 489
Jessurun, M., 587
Jette, R.D., 26
Jex, S.M., 571
Johannesen-Schmidt, M.C., 435
John, O.P., 24
Johns, G., 384
Johnson, B.T, 436
Johnson, D., 552
Johnson, D.A., 471
Johnson, D.E., 358, 359, 390
Johnson, D.L., 45, 195
Johnson, E.C., 366, 367
Johnson, J.B., 440
Johnson, J.L., 252
Johnson, L.B., 434
Johnson, R.E., 548, 549
Johnson, W., 431
Joiner, D., 179
Joinson, C., 336
Jones, C., 144
Jones, D.A., 124
Jones, D.M., 552
Jones, J.W., 188
Jones, M., 161
Jordan, R., 196
Jorgenson, D., 351
Joshi, A., 473
Judge, T.A., 136, 194, 308, 324, 326, 334, 358, 359, 360, 361, 362, 363, 365, 386, 431, 432, 433, 434, 436, 438, 450
Juieng, D., 471
Jun, K., 171
Jung, C., 186
Justice, B.M., 426

Kacmar, K.M., 380
Kaczynski, T., 465
Kaliterna, L., 559
Kammeyer-Mueller, J.D., 308
Kandola, R.S., 169
Kane, J.S., 280
Kaplan, A.B., 120
Kaplan, I.T., 471
Kaplan, R.M., 202
Kaplan, S., 363
Kaplow, S.R., 108
Karasek, R., 548
Karau, S.J., 433, 435, 477
Karl, K.A., 273
Karren, R.J., 334
Kassel, J.D., 568
Kasser, T., 324
Katkowski, D.A., 10
Katz, J.A., 179
Katzell, R.A., 26, 224
Kaufman, G., 446
Kavanaugh, M.J., 311
Kay, I., 239, 316

Kearns, C.N., 100
Kearns, D.F., 587
Kearns, P., 314
Keeping, L.M., 240
Kehoe, P.E., 272
Keinan, G.A., 191
Keith, M.K., 140
Kelleher, H., 451, 452
Keller, J., 529
Keller, L.M., 362
Keller, R.J., 47
Keller, R.T., 484
Kelly, I.W., 212
Kemmerer, B.E., 544
Kemp, C., 204
Kendall, L.M., 277, 376
Kennedy, J.F., 435
Kennedy, J.K., 439
Keran, C.M., 528
Kernan, M.C., 536
Kerr, N.L., 477, 478, 479
Kerr, S., 504
Kerrigan, N., 160, 161
Kesselman, G.A., 63, 64
Kessler, M.L., 338
Khanna, C., 10
Kidd, J., 472
Kidwell, R.E., 468
Kierein, N., 325
Kiker, D.S., 566
Kilgore, E., 87
Kim, B.H., 185
Kim, C.K., 584
Kim, D., 194, 195
Kimbrough, A., 2
Kimbrough, W.W., 46, 47, 62, 469
King, H., 379
King, M.L., 434
King, W. C., 396
Kingston, N.M., 204
Kipnis, D., 450
Kirkman, B.L., 482, 483, 487
Kirkner, S.L., 436
Kirkpatrick, D.L., 308, 314
Kirnan, J.P., 135
Kirsch, M.P., 259
Kirschner, R., 491
Kish-Gephart, J.J., 358
Kjellberg, A., 551
Klehe, U.C., 144
Kleiman, L.S., 165
Klein, H.J., 334, 336
Klein, J.D., 466
Klimoski, R.J., 191, 484
Kline, T., 405
Kline, T.J.B., 255
Kluger, A.N., 185, 361, 362
Knauth, P., 529, 560

Knight, P.A., 262
Knoop, R., 327
Knouse, S.B., 167
Kobrick, J.L., 556
Koestner, R., 326
Kohlepp, K., 45
Kohler, K.N., 265
Kolodinsky, R.W., 549, 550
Komacki, J. L., 442
Komaki, J.L., 448
König, C.J., 191
Koonce, R., 510
Kopelman, R.E., 280
Kopitzke, K., 416
Koppelaar, L., 441
Koppes, L.L., 5, 7
Koprowski, G.J., 196
Korman, A.K., 323, 325, 436
Korsgaard, M.A., 439
Korte, C., 552
Kortick, S.A., 338
Koskenvuo, M., 550
Koslowsky, M., 358, 359
Kotter, J.P., 516
Kovach, R., 264, 385, 386
Kovacs, K., 584
Kovacs, S.Z., 141
Kozlowski, S.W., 259
Kraepelin, E., 7
Kraiger, K., 265, 304
Krain, B.F., 46
Krause, D.E., 179
Krausz, M., 358, 359
Kravitz, D.A., 108, 262
Krell, E., 561
Kremen, M., 127
Kriegel, R., 480, 504, 505
Kriska, S.D., 141
Kristof-Brown, A.L., 366, 367, 548, 549
Kruger, J., 14
Kuder, G.F., 205
Kudisch, J., 239
Kulik, J.A., 564
Kullman, E., 431
Kuncel, N.R., 25, 169
Kunin, T., 376
Kurland, N.B., 405, 407
Kutcher, E.J., 142
Kuusela, V., 553
Kwun, S.K., 238

Laabs, J.J., 513
Lachnit, C., 127
Ladd, D., 334
LaFrance, M., 414
Lahtela, K., 553
Lahy, J. M., 7
Laing, B., 451
Laird, M.D., 40

Lajunen, T., 587
Lam, S.S.K., 508
Lambert, B.J., 560
Landau, K., 59, 60
Landis, R.S., 54
Landstrom, U., 551
Landy, F.L., 46, 47, 141, 265
Langdale, J.A., 141
Langdon, J.C., 195, 267
Lanier, P.A., 8
Lantz, C., 147
Lapidus, R.S., 351
Larey, T.S., 479
Larson, J., 204
Larson, S.L., 191, 192
Laschever, S., 72
Lasek, M., 165
LaShells, M.B., 278
Latane, B., 472, 475
Latham, G.A., 254, 265, 280, 307, 322, 331, 333, 336
Latham, V.M., 441
Law. J.R., 431
Lawler, E.E., 347, 464, 480
Lawler, J.J., 525
Lawshe, C.H., 219
Lawson, K., 290
Layman, J.J., 385
Le, H., 431
Leach, D.J., 404
Leana, C.R., 272
Lease, J.E., 423
LeBreton, J.M., 190
Lee, F., 397
Lee, J.A., 254, 573
Lee, K., 101, 359, 470
Lee, S.J., 448
Lee, T.W., 366, 389
Leeds, D., 307
Lefkowitz, J., 264
Leonard, D.C., 111
Leonard, K.E., 552
Leone, D., 324
LePine, J.A., 358, 359, 390, 478, 543
LePine, M., 543
LePla, L.A., 101
Lepsinger, R., 482
Leslie, L.M., 108
Lester, D., 561, 568
Letvak, S., 89
Lev-Arey, D., 108
Levashina, J., 185
Levine, E., 36, 38, 46, 58, 65, 66
Levine, M., 19
Levine, S.P., 142
Levit, A., 121
Levy, P.E., 239, 240, 336, 550
Lewin, K., 506, 507, 516

Liden, R.C., 479, 481
Lied, T.L., 349
Lievens, F., 24
Lilienfeld, S.O., 187
Lim, J., 529
Lin, L., 553
Lin, T.R., 225
Lindell, M.K., 54
Lindeman, M., 323
Ling, J., 131
Linkous, R.A., 476
Liou, K.T., 374
Lipmann, O., 7
Lippitt, R., 506
Liska, L.Z., 443
Livnech, N., 280
Lloyd, J., 169
Locke, E.A., 312, 322, 333, 336, 361, 362
Lodi-Smith, J., 324
Loewen, L.J., 554
Lofquist, L.H., 376
Loher, B.T., 167, 295
Lonchar, K., 162
London, M., 239
Long, E.J., 239
Long, G.M., 587
Long, W.W., 239
Lopez, F.E., 63, 64
Lopez, F.M., 63, 64
Lord, R.G., 264, 265, 350, 351, 499
Loughhead, T.M., 477
Lounsbury, J.W., 212
Lovenheim, P., 499
Lowenberg, G., 12
Lucas, J.A., 108
Luoma, J., 586
Luthans, F., 336, 339, 341, 342
Lykken, D.T., 361
Lyons, P., 45

Mabe, P.A., 240
Mabry, E., 303
Mackenzie, S.B., 252, 339, 349
Mackworth, N.H., 556
MacLachlan, M., 351
Mager, R.F., 289
Magjuka, R.J., 295
Magner, N.R., 497
Mahoney, C.A., 476
Mahoney, J.J., 191
Mahto, R.V., 130
Mailhot, E.K., 47
Maiorca, J., 278
Major, B., 413
Makihijani, M.J., 435
Malos, S.B., 139, 266
Manaugh, T.S., 167
Mann, F.C., 561

Mann, R.B., 135
Manners, G.E., 471
Manning, R., 19
Mannix, E.A., 489
Manson, T., 303
Manstead, A.S., 476
Markham, S.E., 571
Marks, M.A., 485
Marks, M.L., 536
Maronitis, A., 584
Marras, W.W., 584
Marsh, W.M., 525
Martell, R.F., 264
Marti, M., 472
Martin, C.L., 91, 141, 264, 265
Martin, D.C., 272
Martin, G.E., 494
Martin, J.A., 40
Martin, R.A., 567
Martinez, A.D., 40
Martinez, M.N., 405
Martocchio, J.J., 70, 386, 525
Martyka, J., 296
Mascio, C., 45, 469
Maser, S., 141
Maslow, A.H., 329
Mason, C.M., 508
Massengill, D.P., 229
Mastrangelo, P.M., 192
Matarazzo, J.D., 167
Mathews, K.E., 553
Mathieu, J.E., 308, 359, 485, 525
Matic, T., 176
Matthews, R.A., 544
Mattox, W.R., 25
Mattrey, M., 303
Maurer, S.A., 302
Maurer, T.J., 46, 138, 147
Mawhinney, T.C., 346
Mayer, D.M., 108
Mayer, J.J., 571
Mayer, M., 162
Maynard, M.T., 525
Mayo, E., 465
McAndrew, F.T., 477
McCabe, M.J., 285
McCall, B.P., 362
McCall, M.W., 446
McCann, N., 568
McCarthy, J. M., 139, 147, 167
McCarthy, P.M., 8, 46
McCauley, D.E., 46
McClelland, C.L., 371
McClelland, D.C., 326, 434
McCormick, E.J., 56
McDaniel, M.A., 138, 171, 194, 196, 207, 224, 359, 363
McDaniel, Q.P., 176
McDonald, R.A., 239
McElroy, J.C., 415, 416

McEvoy, G.M., 239

McFarland, L.A., 141, 179, 196, 243

McFarlin, D.B., 327

McGee, G.W., 444

McGovern, L., 533

McGrath, J.E., 470

McGregor, D., 435

McGue, M., 431

McIntosh, B., 267

McIntyre, C., 46

McIntyre, M.D., 190

McIntyre, R.M., 254

McKay, P.F., 133

McKee, T.L., 396

McLaughlin, M.L., 465

McLendon, C.L., 468

McLeod, P.L., 472

McLoughlin, C., 351

McLoughlin, Q., 561

McManus, M.A., 131, 135

McMullen, L.J., 444

McNatt, D.B., 324, 325, 326

McNelly, T.L., 180

McPherson, S.O., 482

McSween, T.E., 338

McVeigh, T., 465

Meade, A.W., 223

Mecham, R.C., 56

Medina, R.E., 338

Medsker, G. J., 10

Meehan, B.T., 161

Mehrabian, A., 167

Meinert, D., 162, 163

Melamed, S., 551, 552, 553

Melner, S.B., 481

Menard, D., 12

Mendoza, J.L., 136

Mento, A.J., 334

Meoli-Stanton, J., 195

Meriac, J.P., 359

Mero, N.P., 257

Mershon, D.H., 553

Mesch, D.J., 386

Meyer, J.P., 358, 359, 360, 366, 371, 380

Meyer, Z., 132

Michaels, J.W., 476

Midkiff, K., 561

Miles, E.W., 396

Miles, J.A., 477

Milkovich, G.T., 40

Miller, B.K., 549, 550

Miller, C.E., 336

Miller, C.W., 448

Miller, D., 416

Miller, D.T., 14

Miller, G.W., 561

Miller, R.L., 59

Miller, S., 296

Miller, T.A., 122

Miller, T.I., 572

Mills, A.E., 180

Miloslavic, S.A., 548

Minton-Eversole, T., 133

Mirolli, K., 368

Mirza, P., 86

Mital, A., 584

Mitchell, T.R., 349, 389, 443

Mitra, A., 565

Mobbs, T.A., 136

Moberg, J.L., 2, 3

Modica, A.J., 497

Moede, W., 7, 477

Mohanned, S., 470

Mohiuddin, S., 45

Mohrman, S.A., 311

Montebello, H.R., 315

Moore, A.K., 58

Moore, B., 6

Moore, J.C., 351

Moore, S., 2, 3

Moores, J., 528

Moran, G.P., 475

Moran, L., 485, 486, 487

Morgan, A., 141

Morgan, J., 191

Morgeson, F.P., 38, 58, 142, 171, 185, 187

Moriarty Gerard, M.O., 203

Morin, R., 25

Morris, M.A., 187, 328

Morrison, E.W., 327, 516

Morrow, P.C., 415, 416

Moscoso, S., 170

Mossholder, K.W., 367, 468

Motowidlo, S.J., 146, 148, 243, 257, 264, 265

Mott, P.E., 561

Mount, M.K., 40, 186, 195, 207, 267, 282, 363, 487, 572

Mouton, J.S., 435

Mouw, T., 128

Mowday, R., 380

Muchinsky, P.M., 359

Mueller, M., 47

Mulder, M., 441

Mullen, B., 20, 468, 471, 485

Mullins, M.E., 204, 310

Mullins, W.C., 30, 46

Mumford, M.D., 238

Muñoz, C., 2

Munson, J.M., 311

Munson, L.J., 101

Munsterberg, H., 5, 6

Murphy, K.R., 251, 262, 264, 265, 282

Murphy, L.L., 213

Murray, H., 186

Muscio, B., 7

Muscolino, J., 141

Muse, L.A., 542, 564

Musselwhite, E., 485

Mussio, S.J., 229

Myers, C., 7

Myers, L.S., 147

Myers, W.V., 338

Nadler, E., 556

Nadler, P., 305

Nagao, D.H., 141

Nagy, M.S., 11, 161, 310, 345, 376

Nail, P.R., 368

Nanus, R., 450

Nash, S., 472

Naswall, K., 549

Nathan, B., 264, 265

Naughton, R.J., 466

Naughton, T.J., 40

Nebeker, D.M., 349

Nee, R., 204

Nelson, J.B., 584

Nelson, K., 586

Nesler, M.S., 448

Neubert, M.J., 487

Neuman, G.A., 526

Neustel, S., 203

Ng, T., 308, 324

Ng, T.W.H., 27, 168, 194, 266, 374

Nguyen, D.H., 99

Nguyen, J.D., 359

Nguyen, N.T., 196, 243

Nichols, R.G., 291, 419

Niebuhr, R.E., 98

Niemi, P., 553

Nilsson, S.G., 47

Nixon, R.M., 434, 435

Noble, S.A., 254

Noe, R., 284, 291

Nolan, J., 470

Normand, J., 191

Normandy, J.L., 192

Norris, W.R., 444

Northouse, P.G., 450

Nougaim, K.E., 332

Novicevic, M.M., 136

Nunamaker, J.F., 397, 471, 472

Nwachukwu, S.L., 512

Nye, C.D., 187

Obama, B.H., 80, 430, 452

O'Brien, R.M., 338

O'Connor, E.J., 224

O'Dell, J.W., 212

Odle-Dusseau, H.N., 140

Oduwole, A., 141

Offermann, L.R., 443, 481

Oginska, H., 561

Oginski, A., 561

Ohnaka, T., 556

O'Kane, P., 404

Okogbaa, O.G., 341

Okonek, K., 560

Oldham, G.R., 328, 359, 371, 372

O'Leary, B.S., 46

O'Leary, G., 162

O'Leary-Kelly, A.M., 351, 368

Olofsson, G., 414

Olson, D., 212

Olson, D.A., 548

Olson, J.N., 480

Olson, R., 8

Olson-Buchanan, J.B., 212

O'Neill, M.J., 405

Ones, D.S., 169, 188, 194, 196, 207, 261, 262, 389

Oppler, S.H., 265

Ordóñez, L., 334

Oreg, S., 121

O'Reilly, C.A., 350

Orians, G.H., 416

Osborn, D.P., 552

Osborne, E.E., 556

Osburn, H.G., 372

O'Sullivan, B.J., 254

Oswald, F.L., 176, 185

Oswald, S.L., 98

Otondo, R.F., 130

O'Toole, R.E., 570, 573

Otting, L.G., 140

Outtz, J., 230

Overman, S., 134

Owenby, P.H., 291

Owens, D., 128

Owens, W.A., 184, 185

Oz, S., 325

Padgett, M.Y., 361

Padgett, V.R., 177

Paese, M., 212

Pajo, K., 167

Palmer, D.K., 139

Palmer, E.M., 120

Palmer, M., 404

Papaj, R., 273

Parantia, D., 397

Parker, P.A., 564

Parker, S.K., 548

Parks, K.M., 385, 386

Parks, L., 332

Paronis, C.A., 568

Paronto, M.E., 47

Parrett, M., 477

Parrish, TJ, 304

Parry, S.B., 318

Pascoe, D.D., 584

Pascoe, D.E., 584
Pass, J.J., 46
Patrick, D., 24
Patrick, J., 58
Patrick, S.L., 396
Patton, G.K., 358, 359
Patton, W.D., 206, 288
Paul, K.B., 376
Paul, R.J., 520
Paulus, P.B., 479
Payne, K., 191
Payne, S.C., 139, 389
Pearce, J.L., 266
Pearlman, K., 209
Pedigo, L.C., 171
Peeters, M.A.G., 27
Peggans, D., 38, 196, 197
Pelled, L.H., 405, 407
Pelletier, L.G., 325
Pence, E.C., 254
Pereira, G.M., 171, 372
Peter, L.J., 37
Peters, D., 164
Peters, L.H., 257, 264
Peterson, N.G., 60
Petrick, J.A., 86
Pfau, B., 239, 316
Pfeffer, A., 331, 332
Pfeffer, J., 367
Pharmer, J.A., 469
Philbrick, K.D., 436
Phillips, A.P., 151
Phillips, F.P., 398
Phillips, J.J., 316
Phillips, J.L., 473, 487
Phillips, J.M., 136
Piasentin, K.A., 124
Piccolo, R.F., 436, 451
Pickren, W., 5
Pierce, W.D., 326
Pike, D., 533
Pilcher, J.J., 556, 560
Pinder, C. C., 331
Pine, D.E., 53
Pingitore, R., 142
Pinkerton, I., 351
Plamondon, K.E., 63, 64
Platania, J., 475
Ployhart, R.E., 176, 204
Poczapski, P., 45
Podsakoff, N.P., 339, 349, 543, 549
Podsakoff, P.M., 252, 339, 349
Podurgal, A., 399
Poe, A.C., 403, 404
Pohley, K., 179
Pokorski, J., 561
Poland, T.D., 366
Pollack, T.G., 368
Pollen, D., 196

Polly, L.M., 195
Pomeroy, A., 119, 125
Pond, S.B., 374
Pool, S.W., 436
Poor, R., 528
Poropat, A.E., 324
Porter, L.W., 266, 343, 347, 380, 406
Posner, B.Z., 311
Posner, R.B., 568
Posthuma, R.A., 142
Potosky, D., 196
Prager, I., 46
Pratt, A.K., 101
Pratt, C., 288
Premack, D., 339
Premack, S.L., 366
Prencipe, L.W., 579
Presser, H.B., 559
Preston, L.A., 536
Prewett-Livingston, A.J., 141
Price, M., 559
Pricone, D., 309
Pridemore, D.R., 466
Prien, E.P., 46, 179
Prien, K.O., 46
Pritchard, R.D., 17, 349, 351
Pritchett, P., 511
Prizimic, Z., 559
Probst, T.M., 525
Psenicka, C., 547
Ptacek, J.T., 396
Puffer, S.M., 350
Pulakos, E.D., 63, 64, 139, 144, 204, 265
Pursell, E.D., 254

Qian, Y.J., 347
Quigley, A., 104
Quigley, B.M., 448, 552
Quinn, J.F., 86
Quiñones, M.A., 176, 179, 181, 194, 311

Rabinowitz, S., 553
Rader, M., 138
Radosevich, D.J., 297
Radosevic-Vidacek, B., 559
Rafaeli, A., 191
Rafferty, A.E., 508
Raggatt, P.T., 587
Ragins, B.R., 308
Ragsdale, K., 28
Rahim, M.A., 449, 450, 497, 547
Rainey, R., 45, 469
Raju, N.S., 89
Ramanujam, R., 445
Ramesh, A., 389
Ramsay, L.J., 185
Randazzo, M.R., 579

Rasch, R.L., 438
Raskin, R., 437
Rassel, G., 254
Rauschenberger, J., 183
Raven, B.H., 440, 448, 449
Ray, J.J., 466
Raymark, P.H., 64, 140, 444
Raymond, M.R., 203
Raynes, B.L., 111, 168, 295, 492, 494, 495
Reade, Q., 162
Reagan, R.W., 435, 441, 452
Ream, M., 6
Reardon, C., 62
Reb, J., 256
Recardo, R.J., 309
Reck, M., 169
Reddon, J.R., 186
Reeve, C.L., 121
Reichard, R.J., 20
Reilly, R.R., 239, 262
Reilly, C., 560
Reilly, M.E., 63, 173, 184
Reilly, R.R., 265
Reiter-Palmon, R., 23
Reitz, J., 194
Renk, K., 295, 339
Rentsch, J.R., 12, 254, 372
Repetti, R.L., 367, 562
Reymen, I.M., 27
Rheinstein, J., 46
Riccobono, J.E., 338
Rice, R.W., 327, 439, 552
Rich, G.A., 252
Richardson, K.M., 385
Richardson, M.W., 205
Richman-Hirsch, W.L., 212
Riddle, D., 12
Rieke, M.L., 210
Riketta, R.S., 359
Robb, D., 397
Robbins, T., 265
Roberson, Q.M., 121, 470
Robert, C., 525
Roberts, B.W., 324
Roberts, G.E., 267
Robertson, D.W., 46
Robertson, I.T., 169
Robertson, I.V., 178
Robin, J., 190
Robiner, W.N., 164
Robinson, D., 472
Robinson, D.D., 51
Robinson, D.E., 553
Robinson, O., 549
Robinson, R.K., 102
Robinson, S.L., 327, 351, 368
Roch, S.G., 19, 27, 245, 254
Rockloff, M.J., 475

Rockmore, B.W., 63
Rodriguez, C., 350
Roebuck, C.M., 192
Roehling, M.V., 139, 543
Rogelberg, S.G., 266, 404
Rohmert, W., 59, 60
Roland, C.C., 325
Romanov, K., 550
Ronen, S., 331
Roosevelt, F.D., 435
Roraff, C.E., 537
Rosen, B., 482
Rosen, C.C., 550
Rosen, S., 396
Rosenbaum, W.B., 351
Rosenthal, D.B., 180
Rosenthal, R., 325
Ross, J.M., 552
Ross, W.R., 498
Rost, K., 338
Roth, L., 230
Roth, P.L., 139, 144, 169, 170, 171, 178, 180, 186, 194, 196
Rothstein, H.R., 184, 224, 385
Rothstein, M., 186
Rotundo, M., 99, 431
Rouhiainen, P., 323
Rouleau, E.J., 46
Rounds, J., 187
Rowe, J.S., 476
Rowe, P.M., 141
Rozell, D., 485
Rozell, E.J., 181
Rozen, S.C., 491
Ruback, R.B., 471
Rubenzer, S.J., 434
Rubin, R. S., 53, 333
Rucci, A. J., 2
Ruddy, T.M., 485, 525
Ruiz-Quintanilla, S.A., 455
Ruotolo, C., 578
Rupert, G., 127, 136
Russ-Eft, D.F., 293, 294
Russell, C.J., 222
Russell, J.T., 214
Russell, M., 548
Rutherford, M.A., 549, 550
Rutte, C.G., 27
Ryan, A.M., 141, 165
Ryan, R.M., 324, 326
Rynes, S.L., 40, 124, 212, 332
Rytting, M., 413

Saad, S., 224
Saal, F.E., 280
Saari, L.M., 280
Saavedra, R., 238
Sablynski, C.J., 389
Sacco, J.M., 141, 470
Saccuzzo, D.P., 202

Swink, D.F., 293

Switzer, F.S., 169, 170, 171, 186

Switzer, K.C., 310

Sylvia, R.D., 374

Szalma, J.L., 552

Tait, M., 361

Tanaka, M., 556

Taniirala, S., 445

Tannen, D., 411

Tannenbaum, R.J., 46

Tannenbaum, S.I., 308, 311, 316, 318

Taubman, P., 362

Taylor, H.C., 214

Taylor, K., 574

Taylor, K.M., 477

Taylor, M.S., 135

Taylor, P.J., 167, 293, 294

Taylor, R.R., 346

Taylor, S., 123, 133

Teachout, M.S., 181

Tedeschi, J.T., 448

Tellegen, A., 361

Tepper, B.J., 440

Terpstra, D.E., 181

Terris, W., 188

Tesarz, , M., 551

Tesluk, P.E., 482

Tesser, A., 396

Tetrault, L.A., 440

Tett, R.P., 186, 194, 358, 359

Theeuwes, J., 587

Theorell, T., 548

Thomas, L. L., 25

Thomas, S.C., 212

Thomas, S.L., 499

Thombs, D.L., 476

Thompson, D.E., 65, 282

Thompson, T.A., 65

Thoresen, C.J., 358, 359, 386

Thornton, G.C., 212

Thornton, G.W., 179, 180

Thorsteinson, T.J., 120

Tidd, S.T., 366

Tierney, P., 325

Tighe, E.M., 326

Tilton, K., 167

Tinsdale, R.S., 142, 478, 479

Titsworth, S., 303

Titus, L.J., 475

Tobares, V., 190

Tochihara, Y., 556

Tolman, C.W., 475

Tomarelli, M., 164

Tonidandel, S., 223

Tonowski, R., 579

Too, L., 415

Toth, C.S., 152, 183

Totterdell, P., 529, 559, 560

Tower, R., 432

Town, J.P., 552

Tracey, J.B., 311

Trahiotis, C., 553

Traube, E.C., 586

Traver, H., 316, 320

Travolta, J., 365

Trenn, K., 580

Treviño, L.K., 349, 358

Triana, M.C., 167

Trice, E., 125

Tross, S., 46

Troxtel, D.D., 147

Truman, H.S., 435

Truxillo, D.M., 47, 192

Tsai, A., 167

Tubbs, M.E., 334, 346

Tubré, T.C., 17, 359

Tucker, P., 558

Tuckman, B., 485

Tulgan, B., 344

Turban, D.B., 140

Turner, J.T., 578, 580

Turner, M.L., 586

Turnley, W.H., 548

Twomey, D.P., 97

Tyler, K., 78, 133, 383, 424, 488, 566, 583

Tyler, P., 170

Tziner, A., 280

Uggerslev, K.L., 124, 255

Uhl-Bien, M., 445

Unckless, A.L., 431

Useem, M., 515

Uziel, L., 475

Valacich, J.S., 397, 471, 472

Valentino, K.E., 436

Vallerand, R.J., 325

Van De Water T.J., 5

van Engen, M.L., 435

Van Iddekinge, C.H., 139, 140

Van Poucke, D., 496

Van Slyke, E.J., 513, 515

Van Tuijl, H.F., 27

Vanderheiden, P.A., 537

Vanerstoep, S.W., 470

Varma, A., 264, 445

Vasey, J., 46, 47

Vasilopoulos, N.L., 47

Vazire, S., 24

Vecchio, R.P., 444

Veiga, J.F., 91

Veres, J.G., 47, 139

Verhaegen, P., 560

Verhage, J., 441

Verley, J., 8

Vernon, H.M., 556

Vidacek, S., 559

Vidmar, N., 471

Vincent, C., 45

Vinchur, A.J., 7, 171, 186

Vines, L.S., 532

Viswesvaran, C., 46, 188, 196, 207, 261, 262, 358, 359, 362, 363, 549

Viteles, M., 6

Vitell, S.J., 512

Vroom, V., 347, 447, 517, 518, 520

Waclawski, J., 266

Wageman, R., 437, 439

Wagner, D.T., 529

Wagner, J.A., 372

Wagner, R.F., 47

Wagner, R.J., 325

Wagner, S.H., 362

Wagner, T., 382

Walker, H. J., 130

Walker, M., 573

Walker, R.W., 544

Wall, H.J., 72

Wall, L.C., 415

Walter, C.S., 257, 265

Walters, A.E., 72

Walton, B., 472

Walton, S., 452

Wanberg, C.R., 509, 510

Wang, M., 548

Wang, M.J., 47, 584

Wang, Q., 363

Wang, Y.T., 584

Wanous, J.P., 135, 366

Ward, E.A., 450

Warner, J., 441

Warr, P., 7

Warr, P.B., 59, 404

Warwick, D.P., 561

Watanabe, S., 365

Watson, J., 5, 506

Watt, J.D., 358

Waung, M., 196, 197, 198, 267

Wayne, S.J., 366, 481

Webber, R.A., 466

Webber, S.S., 484

Weber, C.L., 40

Weber, Y., 512

Webster, E., 7

Weekley, J.A., 144, 204

Weinberg, A., 534

Weingart, L.R., 488

Weins, A.N., 167

Weinstein, N.D., 551, 552, 553

Weiss, H.M., 368, 376

Weitz, J., 141

Welbourne, T.M., 346

Welch, J., 245

Wells, R., 584

Wells, S.J., 399, 574

Welsh, D.H., 341

Werner, J.M., 37, 252

Wernimont, P.F., 184

Wernli, S., 62

Wesley, S., 46

Wesolowski, M., 40

Wesson, M.J., 334

West, S.G., 240

Westley, B., 506

Wexley, K.N., 141, 224, 265, 280, 307

Whelchel, B.D., 179

Whelpley, C.E., 363

Whetzel, D.L., 138, 196

Whitbred, R.C., 368

Whitcomb, A.J., 385

White, C.S., 165

White, K.D., 345

White, L.A., 265

Whiting, H.J., 255

Whitney, D., 139

Widgery, R., 415

Widmeyer, W.N., 468

Wiechmann, D., 171

Wieland, C., 498

Wiesner, W.H., 136, 144

Wild, C., 510

Wilk, D., 120

Wilkinson, I., 450

Wilkinson, R.T., 560

Williams, F., 151, 163, 166, 194

Williams, J., 147

Williams, J.R., 240, 336, 359

Williams, K., 477

Williams, L., 413

Williams, P.F., 513

Williams, R., 122

Williamson, A.M., 528

Williamson, L.G., 139

Willihnganz, M.A., 147

Willis, C.E., 264

Willis, R.P., 311

Willis, S.C., 122

Willms, K., 584

Willness, C.R., 101, 476, 586

Wilmot, W.W., 492

Wilson, A, 46

Wilson, D. S., 473, 480

Wilson, D.W., 556

Wilson, M.A., 54, 65

Wilson, W., 302, 435

Wimbush, J.C., 188

Wing, J.F., 557

Winter, D.G., 435

Winters, J.J., 468

Wirtz, D., 14

SUBJECT INDEX

Merit pay, 344, 345
Meta-analysis, 25–27
Mexico
    family leave, 102
    protected classes, 84
Microsoft, 132, 295, 574
Middle-of-the-road leaders, 436
Miller Brewing Company, 101
Miller v. AT&T, 102
Minnesota Satisfaction Ques-
    tionnaire (MSQ), 376, 378
Minor frustration, 561
Minor's Landscape Services, 128
Mitsubishi, 583
Mixed-standard rating scales,
    279–280
MMPI-2, 185
Modeling and training, 304–305
Modified flexitour, 527
Monarch Marking Systems, 483
Monster.com, 130, 131
Moog Components Group, 306
Moonlighting, 561
Moore Tool Company, 400
Morgan Stanley, 82, 133
Motivating employees
    behaviors implying
        motivation, 322
    equity theory, 349–351
    ERG theory, 331–332
    expectancy theory, 347–349
    feedback, 336
    goal setting, 333–336
    group incentive plans,
        345–346
    intrinsic motivation, 326
    job characteristics, 328
    job expectations, 327–328
    Maslow's need hierarchy,
        329–331
    needs, 326–327
    personality, 323–324
    Premack Principal, 339–340
    punishment, 349
    recognition, 341–342
    rewards, 337–347
    self-esteem, 323–326
    self-regulation theory, 337
    two-factor theory, 332
Motivation potential, 328
Motivators, 332
Multiple channels, 418
Multiple cutoff, 227
Multiple-hurdle approach, 228
Multiple-source feedback, 237
MUM effect, 397
Myspace, 134

Nagy Job Satisfaction Scale, 376
Naps, 529

Narcissists, 438
National origin, 86
National security, 97
*National Treasury Employees v.
    Von Rabb*, 109
Need for achievement
    and leadership, 433
    and motivation, 326
Need for affiliation
    and leadership, 433
    and motivation, 326
Need for power
    and leadership, 433
    and motivation, 327
Needs analysis, 284–289
Negative feedback, 309
Negative-information bias, 141
Negligent hiring, 162
Negligent reference, 165
Negotiation, 496
Negotiation process, 482
Netherlands - absenteeism, 381
Neuroticism, 544
New London, CT, 363
Newsletter, 402
Nextel, 82
Nike, 574
Noise, 550–554
Noise and communication, 412
Nominal group, 479
Nonbinding arbitration, 79
Noncalculative motivation, 432
Nonconforming listener, 420
Nonverbal cues, 412–413
Nonverbal cues and
    interviewing, 142
Norfolk & Southern
    Corporation, 151
Normal personality, 185
Normative commitment, 360,
    380
Norming stage, 485
North Miami, Florida, 97
Northwest Airlines, 533, 574
Norway - absenteeism, 381
Novartis, 82
Nucor, 344
Nunn-Bush Shoe Company, 346
Nutreco, 381
Nuttzwerk, 368

Oakland Mercy Hospital, 342
Objective tests, 187
Occupational Information
    Network (O*NET), 60
Occupational Stress Inventory,
    576
*O'Connor v. Consolidated Coin
    Caterers*, 89
O'Connor v. Ortega, 110

Office and locker searches, 110
Office Depot, 397
Office design, 405
*Officers for Justice v. Civil
    Service Commission*, 230
Ohio State studies, 435
Ombudsperson, 400
Omission, 418
On the job training, 304–308
*Oncale v. Sundowner Offshore
    Services*, 99
One-on-one interviews, 138
On-site child care facilities, 570
Open desk arrangement,
    415–416
Operant conditioning, 337
Optimal level of arousal, 542
Organizational analysis, 285
Organizational citizenship
    behaviors, 323, 390
Organizational citizenship
    correlates, 359, 363
Organizational climate,
    440–442
Organizational commitment
    correlates, 359
    definitions, 358, 360
    measures of, 377, 380
Organizational Commitment
    Questionnaire, 380
Organizational Commitment
    Scale, 380
Organizational Constraints
    Scale, 576
Organizational culture,
    512–516
Organizational fit, 366–367
Organizational fit questions,
    144
Organizational justice, 351, 370
Organizational politics, 550
Organizational psychology, 4
Organizational socialization,
    516
Orthodox Jews, 86
Other characteristics, 55
Outback Steak House, 342
Out-group, 445
Outplacement programs,
    534–535
Outputs, 356
Outside pressure, 471
Outsourcing, 532
Overlearning, 311
Overt integrity tests, 188

Paid time off programs,
    382–383
Paired comparisons, 244–245
Pal's Sudden Service, 318

Panel interviews, 138
Paper cow, 504–505
Paralanguage, 414–415
Parallel teams, 484
Passing scores, 227–229
Passive applicants, 134
Passive-aggressive leaders, 438
Pass-through programs, 307
Past-focused interview
    questions, 144
Path-goal theory, 443
Patterned-Behavior
    Description Interviews
    (PBDI), 144
Pay for performance, 344
Peak-time pay, 529
Peer ratings, 238
Pepperdine University, 13
Perceptual ability, 172
Performance appraisal
    appraisal focus, 241–243
    attendance, 248
    behavioral checklists,
        248–251
    behavioral observation
        scales, 280, 282
    behaviorally anchored rating
        scales, 277–278
    cultural limitations,
        236–237
    employee comparisons,
        243–246
    evaluating performance,
        257–265
    forced-choice rating scales,
        278–279
    forced distribution,
        245–246
    graphic rating scales, 248
    job analysis, 35
    mixed-standard scales,
        279–280, 281
    observing performance,
        255–257
    paired comparisons, 244
    performance review inter-
        view, 266–268
    quality of work, 246–247
    quantity of work, 246
    rank order, 243–244
    rater training, 254–255
    rating errors, 259–263
    reasons for, 235–236
    safety, 248
    terminating employees,
        269–273
    360-degree feedback,
        237–241
Performance appraisal review,
    235, 266–268

Performance appraisal scores - training, 287, 308
Performance correlates, 359, 363
Performing stage, 485
Permanency, 483
Person analysis, 287–289
Personal distance zone, 414
Personality and conflict, 491–492
Personality
    absenteeism, 386
    employee selection, 185–187
    group performance, 473
    job analysis, 47
    job satisfaction, 363
    leadership, 431–432, 433, 438
    motivation, 323
    stress, 543–544
Personality inventories, 185–187
Personality-Related Positions Requirement Form (PPRF), 64
Personality-based integrity tests, 188
Personnel psychology, 4
Person-organization fit, 366–367, 388, 548
Personpower planning, 37
Perspective taking, 561
Peter Principle, 37, 236
Petit v. City of Chicago, 105
Pharakhone v. Nissan, 102
Physical ability tests, 172, 175–176
Physical appearance and discrimination, 93
Physical proximity, 465
Physical Symptoms Inventory, 576
Pineda v. United Parcel Service, 271
Pitney-Bowes, 307
Ply Marts, 338
Poland - absenteeism, 381
Policy manual, 400–401
Political affiliation, 93
Polygraph, 188
Position Analysis Questionnaire (PAQ), 56–58
Position style for climate of instability, 441
Posttest, 314
Power differentiation, 482
POWs, 466
Practical significance, 26
Practicum, 12

Pratt & Whitney, 583
Prayer, 87
Predictive bias, 223
Predictive validity, 208
Pregnancy Discrimination Act, 91–92
Premack Principle, 339–341
Presence of others, 474–478
Pretest, 314
Primacy effect
    interviews, 140
    performance appraisal, 256
    resumes, 152
Priming, 152
Principal Financial Group, 573
Privacy issues, 109–111
Probability grapevine, 405
Probationary period, 270
Procedural justice, 370
Product design, 584
Profit sharing, 346
Programmed instruction, 303
Progressive discipline, 271
Project GLOBE, 453–455
Project teams, 485
Projective tests, 186
Proportion of correct decisions, 218–219
Protected classes, 82–92
Proximity and communication, 397
Proximity errors, 261–262
Proximity of team members, 483
Prudential Insurance, 124, 570
Psychological contracts, 366
Psychological exams, 192
Psychological reactance, 471
Psychological resumes, 152, 155
Psychological tests and privacy, 110–111
Psychology and Industrial Efficiency, 5
Psychomotor ability, 172
Psychopathology tests, 186
PsycINFO, 17
Public distance zone, 414
Public employment agencies, 125
Public policy, 269
Punctuated equilibrium, 486
Punishment, 349
Pygmalion effect, 325

Qualified work force, 107
Quality circles, 372
Quality of work, 246–247
Quantitative Workload Inventory, 576
Quantity of work, 246

Quasi-experiment, 22
Questionnaire approach to biodata, 181
Queuing, 418
Quid pro quo, 98–99

R.R. Donnelley & Sons, 314
Race
    job analysis, 47
    performance appraisal, 265–266
    protected classes, 85
    stress, 544
Racial bias and performance appraisal, 265–266
Radiation, 554
Radio Shack, 412
Radioimmunoassay (RIA), 192
Rahim Organizational Conflict Inventory, 497
Ramadan, 87
Random assignment, 28
Random sample, 28
Rank order, 243–244
Rankin v. Seagate Technologies, 102
Rater reliability, 262–263
Raytheon, 130
Raytheon, 574
Readability, 424–425
Realistic job previews, 136–137, 327
Rear end collisions, 586–587
Recency effect, 263
Receptive changers, 509
Recognition, 341–342
Recognition - absenteeism, 383
Recruitment
    blogging, 131–132
    direct mail, 128
    diversity, 133
    electronic media, 121–122
    employee referrals, 125–128
    employer-based websites, 129–130
    employment agencies, 124–125
    evaluating recruitment effectiveness, 134–136
    executive search firms, 125
    Internet recruiters, 130–132
    Internet, 128–132
    job fairs, 132
    newspaper ads, 119–121, 123
    nontraditional populations, 133
    passive applicants, 134
    point-of-purchase methods, 122–124

public employment agencies, 125
    realistic job previews, 136–137
    recruiters, 124
    situation-wanted ads, 122
Reduction in force, 272
Redundant systems, 521–522
Reference, 160
Reference check, 160
Reference detectives, 165
Referent power, 450
Reinforcement hierarchy, 339
Rejecting applicants, 195–197
Relaxation techniques, 571
Reliability, 202–206
Reliability coefficient chart, 207
Religion, 86–89
Religious attire, 88–89
Reluctant changers, 509
Rene v. MGM Grand Hotel, 99
Rent-a-Center, 83
Repetitive-stress injuries, 583
Resentment, 546
Residual stress, 562
Resistance, 546
Respond by calling ads, 119, 123
Rest periods, 557
Restricted range, 209
Resume fraud, 160–163
Resumes, 151–155
Return interviews, 138
Return on investment, 318
Revolutionary change, 507
Reward power, 450
Rheineck v. Hutchinson Technology, 101
Ridge House and Safe Harbors, 133
Right/wrong approach, 145
Rituals, 516
Roanoke County, Virginia, 70
Roanoke Electric Steel, 296
Rock Bottom Restaurants, 130, 317
Roderick Jackson v. Birmingham Board of Education, 94
Roebuck v. Odie Washington, 101
Role ambiguity, 547–548
Role conflict, 547
Role overload, 548
Role play, 292–293, 319
Rorschach Ink Blot Test, 186
Rotating shifts, 560
Rugged Warehouse, 124
Rule of 3, 227
Rumor, 407
Russell v. Principi, 274

behavioral modeling, 293–294
case studies, 290–291
classroom training, 295–301
coaching and mentoring, 306–308
distance learning, 301–303
evaluating training, 314–318
goals and objectives, 289
job rotation, 305
lecture, 289–290
modeling, 304–305
needs assessment, 284–289
role play, 292–293
simulation exercises, 292
training motivation, 294–295, 308–309
transfer of training, 310–312
Trait-focused performance dimensions, 241
Transaction Information Systems, 126
Transactional leadership, 450
Transfer of training, 310–312
Transformational leadership, 450–452
Travel, 342
Triad, 464
Triangling, 494
Triblo v. Quality Clinical Laboratories, 110
Turnover
correlates of, 359, 363
cost of, 386–387
reducing, 387–389
Twitter, 134
Two-factor theory, 332
Type A personalities, 544

Type B personalities, 544
Typical-answer approach, 145

U.S. v. Phillip Paradise, 105, 106
Ulane v. Eastern Airlines, 86
Unclear policy and poor record keeping, 383–384
Uniform Commercial Code, 270
Uniform Guidelines, 38
Union National Bank, 344
Union Special, 128
Union steward, 400
United Airlines, 341, 347
United Kingdom
absenteeism, 381
vacation days, 575
workplace violence, 576
United Space Alliance, 531
United Way, 306
Unstructured interviews, 138–142
Unsuccessful leaders, 437–438
Unusual behaviors, 256
Unusual information, 152–153
Use of time, 414
Utility formula, 219–221

Valence, 347
Valid testing procedures, 97
Validity, 206–213
Validity of tests, 193–195
Validity coefficient, 163
Validity Generalization (VG), 209
Values, 452
Vega-Rodriguez v. Puerto Rico Telephone, 111
Veritas, 162

Vertical dyad linkage (VDL) theory, 444
Vertical percentage method, 182
Veteran's preference rights, 97
Victims of downsizing, 535–536
Vietnam-Era Veterans Readjustment Act, 92
Viking Glass, 508
Violation of company rules, 270
Virtual job fairs, 124
Virtual teams, 483
Vision, 451
Vocational counseling, 187
Vocational Rehabilitation Act, 89
Voice mail, 403–404
Voice stress analyzer, 188
Voucher systems, 573
Vroom-Yetton Model, 447, 517–520

Wage trend line, 69
Waivers - references, 164
Walker v. Secretary of the Treasury, 85
WalMart, 305, 448
Wards Cove. V. Antonio, 105
Webb v. City of Philadelphia, 89
Webcasts, 303
Webinars, 303
Wegmans Food Markets, 128
Well pay, 382
Wellness programs, 385
Wendy's, 123

Western Electric Company, 8
Western State Paving v. Washington State, 106
White Memorial Medical Center, 126
Whizzinator, 110
Wikis and training, 303
Winning at all costs, 494
Withdrawal, 494
Wonderlic Personnel Test, 170
Work schedules
casual work, 530
compressed workweeks, 528–529
flextime, 526–528
job sharing, 530
moonlighting, 561
peak-time pay, 529–530
shift work, 558–561
working from home, 531
Work at home, 531
Work Preference Inventory (WPI), 326
Work samples, 177
Work teams, 483–484
Worker Adjustment and Retraining Notification Act (WARN), 272
Workplace violence, 576–580
WorldCom, 532
Written interviews, 138

Xerox, 483

YouTube, 134

Zenger-Miller, 294, 487